Lecture Notes in Artificial Intelligence   1079

Subseries of Lecture Notes in Computer Science
Edited by J. G. Carbonell and J. Siekmann

Lecture Notes in Computer Science

Edited by G. Goos, J. Hartmanis and J. van Leeuwen

Zbigniew W. Raś   Maciek Michalewicz (Eds.)

Foundations of
Intelligent Systems

9th International Symposium, ISMIS '96
Zakopane, Poland, June 9-13, 1996
Proceedings

 Springer

Springer
Berlin
Heidelberg
New York
Barcelona
Budapest
Hong Kong
London
Milan
Paris
Santa Clara
Singapore
Tokyo

Series Editors
Jaime G. Carbonell, Carnegie Mellon University, Pittsburgh, PA, USA
Jörg Siekmann, University of Saarland, Saarbrücken, Germany

Volume Editors

Zbigniew W. Raś
Department of Computer Science, University of North Carolina
Charlotte, NC 28223, USA

Maciek Michalewicz
Institute of Computer Science, Polish Academy of Sciences
Ordona 21, 01-237 Warsaw, Poland

Cataloging-in-Publication Data applied for

Die Deutsche Bibliothek - CIP-Einheitsaufnahme

Foundations of intelligent systems : 9th international
symposium ; proceedings / ISMIS '96, Zakopane, Poland, June
9 - 13, 1996. Zbigniew W. Raś ; Maciek Michalewicz (ed.). -
Berlin ; Heidelberg ; New York ; Barcelona ; Budapest ; Hong
Kong ; London ; Milan ; Paris ; Santa Clara ; Singapore ;
Tokyo : Springer, 1996
  (Lecture notes in computer science ; Vol. 1079 : Lecture notes in
  artificial intelligence)
  ISBN 3-540-61286-6
NE: Raś, Zbigniew W. [Hrsg.]; ISMIS <9, 1996, Zakopane>; GT

CR Subject Classification (1991): I.2, F.4.1, H.3.3, F.1, H.3

ISBN 3-540-61286-6 Springer-Verlag Berlin Heidelberg New York

© Springer-Verlag Berlin Heidelberg 1996
Printed in Germany

Typesetting: Camera ready by author
SPIN 10512986   06/3142 – 5 4 3 2 1 0   Printed on acid-free paper

Preface

This volume contains the papers selected for presentation at the Ninth International Symposium on Methodologies for Intelligent Systems - ISMIS'96, held in Zakopane, Poland, June 9-13, 1996. The symposium was hosted by the Polish Academy of Sciences and sponsored by the Oak Ridge National Laboratory, Polish Academy of Sciences, UNC-Charlotte, Warsaw University of Technology, and others.

ISMIS is a conference series that was started in 1986 in Knoxville, Tennessee. Since then it has been held in Charlotte (North Carolina), once in Knoxville, once in Torino (Italy), and once in Trondheim (Norway).

The Program Committee selected the following major areas for ISMIS'96:

- Approximate Reasoning
- Evolutionary Computation
- Intelligent Information Systems
- Knowledge Representation and Integration
- Learning and Knowledge Discovery
- Logic for Artificial Intelligence

The contributed papers were selected from 124 full draft papers by the following Program Committee: Hojjat Adeli, Jacques Calmet, Jaime Carbonell, B. Chandrasekaran, Su-Shing Chen, Wesley Chu, Misbah Deen, Kenneth DeJong, Robert Demolombe, Jon Doyle, Ed Fox, Michael Georgeff, David Hislop, Yves Kodratoff, Jan Komorowski, Robert Kowalski, Catherine Lassez, T.Y. Lin, Michael Lowry, Alberto Martelli, Robert Meersman, Maciek Michalewicz, Ryszard Michalski, Masao Mukaidono, John Mylopoulos, Setsuo Ohsuga, Lin Padgham, Rohit Parikh, Zdzislaw Pawlak, Francois Pin, Luc De Raedt, Zbigniew Ras, Barry Richards, Colette Rolland, Lorenza Saitta, Erik Sandewall, Andrzej Skowron, John Sowa, Jeffrey Ullman, Carlo Zaniolo, Maria Zemankova, and Jan Zytkow. Additionally, we acknowledge the help in reviewing the papers from: James Baker, Francesco Bergadano, Sanjiv Bhatia, Hendrik Blockeel, Jianhua Chen, Antoine Cornuejols, Jim Cunningham, Luc Dehaspe, Bipin Desai, Saso Dzeroski, Laura Giordano, Diana Gordon, Jerzy Grzymala-Busse, Daniele Gunetti, Himanshu Gupta, Tony Hunter, Cezary Janikow, Wim Van Laer, Patrick Lambrix, Georg Meyer, Zbigniew Michalewicz, Mike Minock, Neil Murray, Gilbert Ndjatou, Jan Plaza, Arcot Rajasekar, Ralph Ronnquist, Joachim Schue, Roman Swiniarski, Francesca Toni, Anita Wasilewska, Martyna Weigl, Xiaohong Yang, and Wojtek Ziarko.

The Symposium was organized by the Institute of Computer Science, Polish Academy of Sciences. The Organizing Committee consisted of Maciek Michalewicz (Chair), Ewa Gasiorowska-Wirpszo, Mieczyslaw Klopotek, Urszula Krus, and Slawomir Wierzchon. Piotr Dembinski (Miroslaw Dabrowski, posthumous) was the general chair of the Symposium.

We wish to express our thanks to Thomas Back, Michael Brodie, Augustin Eiben, Attilio Giordana, Matthias Jarke, Zbigniew Michalewicz, Henri Prade, Gregory Piatetsky-Shapiro, and Erik Sandewall who presented the invited talks at the symposium. We would like to express our appreciation to the sponsors of the symposium and to all who submitted papers for presentation and publication in the proceedings. Special thanks are due to Alfred Hofmann of Springer-Verlag for his help and support.

We would like to dedicate this symposium to Miroslaw Dabrowski who unexpectedly died last summer. Without his help and support this symposium would never have taken place in Poland.

February, 1996   Z.W. Ras, M. Michalewicz

Table of Contents

Invited Talks

Communications

Session 1A   Knowledge Representation

Session 1B   Learning and Discovery Systems

Putting Objects to Work on a Massive Scale

Michael L. Brodie

GTE Laboratories Incorporated
40 Sylvan Road, Waltham, MA 02254, USA
Brodie@gte.com

Abstract

Distributed computing and, in particular, object computing, holds remarkable promise for future ISs and for more productive collaboration between our vast legacy IS base world-wide. This claim is not new to those who have read trade, research, or vendor literature over the past five years. GTE has made a significant attempt to benefit from this technology. We have found that it is ultimately considerably more difficult and less beneficial than the literature or its proponents would have had us believe. This chapter outlines challenges that we and others faced in attempting to put objects to work on a massive scale. The challenges were confirmed in a world-wide survey that we conducted of over 100 corporations that are attempting to deploy distributed object computing applications based on technologies such as CORBA, DCE, OLE/COM, distributed DBMSs, IP networks, workflow management systems, and proprietary technologies.

Distributed object computing has offered a vision, significant challenges, some progress toward a computing infrastructure, and some benefits. Whereas distributed computing infrastructure and IIP interoperability is critical, application interoperability is the fundamental challenge to users of distributed computing technology. Large corporations spend on the order of $1 billion IT annually addressing application interoperability. Although application interoperability is claimed to be the objective of distributed computing infrastructures, there has been little progress toward this critical ultimate requirement.

This chapter presents a vision for and some progress toward collaboration from the vantage point of a large organization attempting to benefit from DOC technologies. Requirements are presented in a distributed computing framework which is much more comprehensive than anything offered by the distributed object computing vendors at this point. It has four parts:

- *Next Generation Information Systems*
- *Computing Environment*
- *Computational Model*
- *Domain Orientation*

Relative to this framework, we describe GTE's distributed object requirements, challenges we face and faced, and experience with distributed object computing infrastructure technologies, and in particular with some of these technologies. We conclude with the basic requirement for benefiting from future distributed interoperation: application, IP/IT interoperation based on shared semantics. The fundamental challenge is so stated:

No. Vision: there is no democracy in the information jungle.

The Challenge

Future computing hardware and software will be abundant, inexpensive, powerful, and distributed. This IS/IT computing infrastructure will, on any scale, will be the basis for building enterprise-wide, indeed worldwide, ISs that are distributed across computers that

Putting Objects to Work on a Massive Scale

Michael L. Brodie

GTE Laboratories Incorporated
40 Sylvan Road, Waltham, MA 02254, USA
Brodie@gte.com

Abstract

Distributed computing, and distributed object computing in particular, holds remarkable promise for future ISs and for more productive collaboration between our vast legacy IS base world-wide. This claim is not new to those who have read trade, research, or vendor literature over the past five years. GTE has made a significant attempt to benefit from this technology. We have found that it is currently considerably more difficult and less beneficial than the literature or its proponents would have had us believe. This chapter outlines challenges that we and others faced in attempting to put objects to work on a massive scale. The challenges were confirmed in a world-wide survey that we conducted of over 100 corporations that are attempting to deploy distributed object computing applications based on technologies such as CORBA, DCE, OLE/COM, distributed DBMSs, TP monitors, workflow management systems, and proprietary technologies.

Distributed object computing has offered a vision, significant challenges, some progress toward a computing infrastructure, and some benefits. Whereas distributed computing infrastructure and its interoperability is critical, application interoperability is the fundamental challenge to users of distributed computing technology. Large corporations spend on the order of $1 billion US annually addressing application interoperability. Although application interoperability is claimed to be the objective of distributed computing infrastructures, there has been little progress toward this critical ultimate requirement.

This chapter presents a view of distributed object computing from the vantage point of a large organization attempting to deploy it in the large scale. Requirements are presented in a distributed computing framework which is necessarily more comprehensive than anything offered by the distributed object computing vendors and proponents. It has four parts:

- Next-Generation Information Systems
- Computing Environment
- Computational Model
- Domain Orientation

Relative to this framework, we outline GTE's approach to distributed object computing, challenges we face and faced, why it is so hard, alternative distributed object computing infrastructure technologies, and an estimation of the state of these technologies. We conclude with the basic requirement for industrial-strength, enterprise-wide interoperable "applications." This nontechnical requirement has always been a fundamental challenge for software.

No, Virginia, there is no distributed object computing, yet.

1   The Challenge

Future computing hardware and software will be scaleable, service-oriented, and distributed. That is, computing requirements, on any scale, will be met by combining cooperating computing services that are distributed across computer networks. Distributed object computing (DOC) is a critical component in this long-term view, particularly for distributed and cooperative next-generation Information Systems (ISs). The current challenge is to develop an adequate long-term computing vision and a sensible migration toward that vision.

This chapter presents an evaluation of progress toward the above goals from the point of view of a large "end user" organization which is attempting to deploy DOC applications on the large scale. Each viewpoint has its biases. This chapter does not share the biases of a DOC technology vendor or consortium, an academic, or a consultant. End users, more directly than the others, must pay for and live with the resulting ISs. End users are responsible for the entire life cycle of an IS. Characteristic of DOC technology, end users must compose a significant number of component parts to achieve their requirements.

We are currently at the beginning of a 20-year cycle, at the end of which some variety of DOC will be the technology of choice for ISs. However, from our current status, significant intellectual and behavioral change is required. It may take 5–10 years for the technology to become complete and robust. Methodologies, tools, education, and the shift in the user base to the new technology may extend that period to 20 years. This is similar to the 20-year shift to relational database technology, except that DOC has a comprehensive scope (i.e., all of computing) and is orders of magnitude more complex.

The chief architects of 12 successful large-scale DOC applications all agreed that DOC is considerably more complex than previous approaches. DOC may be so hard because it requires a philosophical shift. Theories in computer science are rational (e.g., inductive) and form the basis of programming languages and IS design. ISs are typically designed top down by means of functional decomposition, from IBM's 360 project. Object-Oriented ISs require the philosophical approach on the other side of the dialectic, namely, empiricism. Next-generation ISs will be composed, bottom up, from existing or newly created components. The rational and empirical approaches are fundamentally different and require different ways of thinking. This age-old dialectic was initiated by René Descartes [DEC], who introduced rationalism in 1637, and by John Locke [LOC], who introduced empiricism in 1690. Immanuel Kant [KAN] attempted to mediate between the two views in 1781. The point is that composing systems from components (e.g., reuse) is a basic premise of next-generation ISs, and computer scientists are simply not used to thinking about ISs empirically. We do not have empirical theories or tools to assist us with this approach. Our lack of familiarity with and tools for such an approach may lie at the heart of the difficulty of the paradigm shift and explain why reuse has been so elusive. But, then, I digress.

DOC technology is in an early and immature phase. This can be seen in terms of the technology adoption life cycle, defined by Geoffrey Moore [MOR]. Early adopters, called innovators and visionaries, are change agents who get rewarded for instituting change to get a jump on the competition through radical changes (improvements). Later adopters, called pragmatists, conservatives, and skeptics, need technology to work well in their existing technology base, which they want to enhance, not overthrow. Between the early adopters and the later adopters is a chasm. The chasm represents the challenges in making the cost/benefits obtained by the early adopters acceptable to the later adopters. The chasm also represents a major change in the customer types due to their radically different motivations.

For a new technology to be successfully adopted, it must broach the chasm, since the marketplace is established by the later and not the early adopters.

The DOC benefits are often discussed. The costs are not. The DOC vision claims to address current business goals, including improvements in time to market of the target product or service; development, deployment, and continuous operations costs; flexibility to accommodate constant changes in business processes, policies, and practices; quality; and lowering risk. It also claims to provide means to overcome problems of previous technologies, including technical (e.g., software crisis), managerial, and administrative. Specific technical objectives include reuse, plug and play, component assembly, workflow-enabled business processes, and service or component orientation. The ultimate technical goal is interoperability at all levels and across the entire life cycle.

DOC technology is in the early adoption stage and is rapidly facing the chasm. DOC technology promoters must now focus on satisfying the requirements of the later adopters. They must address the real state of DOC technology, which our experience and survey suggests is as follows. DOC is inherently hard, and is not understood. The relevant theory and technology is immature and evolving rapidly. There are rare successes that are due to genius chief architects and their staffs. The claimed benefits (e.g., reuse, productivity) are very hard to realize. Most DOC technology does not meet industrial-strength requirements. Hence, it is not ready for prime time. Since there is currently no dominant DOC infrastructure choice (e.g., CORBA, OLE/COM), how do you architect or plan a DOC application? This chapter outlines some of the requirements of the later adopters, based on the experience of an early adopter.

Not surprisingly, there is a pattern here if you replace "DOC" with any "promising advanced computing technology" in the past 20 years. To address the current challenge of developing an adequate long-term computing vision and a sensible migration toward that vision, we must act differently than in the past. What is a reasonable time frame for the transition? What are reasonable increments?

2   Distributed Object Computing Framework

An end user requires a complete distributed computing framework with which to guide an IS through its life cycle. There are at least four parts to such a framework.

- Next-Generation Information Systems
- Computing Environment
- Computational Model
- Domain Orientation

An IS designer must have a conceptual model of *next-generation information systems*. Such a model could consist of a business process that solves a specific business problem. The business process can be expressed in terms of a workflow which, in turn, invokes business services which execute the workflow tasks.

The *computing environment* consists of a distributed computing infrastructure and a complete life cycle support environment. The infrastructure provides the services required to support the execution of workflows, the dynamic invocation of business services, and the distributed object space that supports the software components with which the business services and workflows are implemented.

These are called CORBAservices™ in the terminology of the Object Management Group™ (OMG™). The life cycle support environment provides all the necessary tools to support a comprehensive life cycle for ISs — from inception to cradle to grave. Some of these tools are included in what OMG terms CORBAfacilities™. Ideally, these tools will enforce application or domain-specific standards for services at all levels.

The *computational model* refers to the object model that underlies the computing environment. Rather than being a single object model, it will be a family of interoperable object models, each member of which has a specific role in the computing environment. Due to different computational and programming requirements, there would be different object models for infrastructure services (e.g., persistence service), business services (e.g., telecommunications billing), and applications development (e.g., workflow services, component assembly).

Domain orientation concerns the tailoring of business services with respect to application domain standards to achieve application interoperability. Domain orientation involves not just standards within a domain (e.g., telecommunication billing) but also across domains, since few business processes or value chains exist solely within one domain. For example, a telephone call involves billing, routing, possibly advanced services, maintenance, and testing, to mention a few.

In the DOC context, domain orientation involves terminology, ontology, domain (object) models, object/systems interface specifications, and frameworks. Application interoperability requires that two applications mutually understand the messages that they exchange. At least with respect to those messages, they must share (e.g., map to) a common terminology; ontology — definitions of the essential elements of the shared domain; and business processes model — definitions of the way business is conducted in the domain. These shared models can be defined in terms of domain-specific object models which can be standardized in terms of interface specifications for classes from which the IS is composed. A framework for a given application domain is the life cycle support environment (i.e., tools and computing artifacts such as class libraries and interface definitions) that supports and enforces the relevant domain standards. Frameworks are developed by specializing a computing environment with the standard object models of the domain, as manifested in class libraries and interface specifications.

A basis for application interoperability can be defined across application domains by means of families of interoperable object models and corresponding interoperable domain frameworks. For example, a generic (domain independent) object model may be extended to produce a billing object model which, in turn, could be specialized to produce a telecommunications billing model as well as others (e.g., a healthcare billing model). Interoperability between healthcare applications and telecom applications (e.g., telemedicine) would be eased by the fact that the corresponding object models were interoperable through the underlying billing object model. Returning to the telecom billing model, it could be specialized to deal with the different subdomains of telecom billing (e.g., residential, small business, large business, and interexchange). If these object models were developed by a standards body (e.g., the International Telecommunications Union), individual companies would want to specialize them further to support their unique requirements. This results in an interoperable object model family or hierarchy [MAN].

The above domain standards could be enforced, to a degree, by a computing environment by ensuring that the appropriate domain standards (e.g., object models, classes, interface definitions, business processes) are used within a domain and between specific domains. Corresponding to the supported object model families or hierarchies, there would be hierarchies of domain-specific computing environments.

A DOC technology end user requires a comprehensive DOC framework, as described above. Over the past 20 years, the relational database community has developed such a framework, which has resulted in the greatest progress ever made toward application interoperability. In the relational framework, next-generation ISs were SQL-based and forms-based applications that shared a common schema. The computing environment consisted of a standardized relational DBMS plus a rich suite of database application programming environments, including CASE environments. The relational computational model has been defined and accepted in national and international standards. There has been little domain orientation in relational database technology. However, it has been discussed in that context for approximately 20 years due to the application interoperability challenges that naturally arose when applications could communicate so readily via a schema.

3   GTE's DOC Experience

The decision to use DOC as a fundamental technology of ISs is a complex and expensive one in GTE, due in part to its size. GTE Telephone Operations (Telops) is the largest U.S. local exchange carrier. It is the world's 4th largest public telephone company and the 44th largest public company. It supports 23 million telephone lines, has 90,000 employees, and has annual revenues of $20 billion US. To support this business, GTE's information technology is large scale. The annual information technology expense is $1 billion US. There are approximately 1,700 ISs and over 140 terabytes of data.

In 1993, GTE made a major commitment to re-engineer its business. The goals of business process re-engineering were to permit GTE to respond to rapidly changing business requirements and to the then imminent revolution in the telecommunications business. Other goals included achieving the highest quality telecommunications products and services and increasing shareholder benefits. These goals are included in this chapter not to advertise, but to reflect the changing demands placed on information technology (e.g., DOC) to be responsive to business needs.

It was in the context of re-engineering that GTE's investigation of DOC turned from research to practice. In 1987, GTE began to investigate distributed object computing infrastructures and applications as a way to significantly improve IS support of its business goals. In 1992, GTE's IT organization began a definition of an applications architecture on the assumption that vendors would provide DOC infrastructures. In 1993, Telops began the definition of a Telops computing environment, as defined in Section 2, and to specify the constituent technologies and services. Initially, the computing environment would consist primarily of non-DOC technology, but would be defined in DOC terms. Plans were begun for architecture migration and for corresponding ISs and data servers. Unlike previous technologies, distributed computing encourages resource sharing across applications. Hence, the IT organization and decision-making procedures had to be redefined so that stakeholders across application (e.g., organizational) boundaries could cooperate to achieve a shared technology base. This organizational change was as significant as the technology transition.

The long-term computing environment assumes a model of next-generation ISs, as defined above, driven by business processes defined in terms of workflows and business services. The work of defining the computing environment and specifying the constituent services was challenging. Ideally, there would be a range of vendor products from which to generalize and select. However, this was and is far from the case for DOC technology. Due to the requirement to provide high-quality, robust, reliable products and services, considerable attention was given to a comprehensive life cycle. The minimal services provided in most DOC vendor products focused mostly on the initial 15% of the life cycle, namely analysis, design, and development. As a result, GTE focused on the missing services, including class libraries, repository services, comprehensive methodologies, tool support across the life cycle, run-time services, testing, and continuous operations support (i.e., the part of the life cycle that consumes 85% of the total IS costs).

A challenge, which can be greater than those of DOC technology is that of migrating from the existing computing environment and applications base to the corresponding ones for DOC. The challenges and approaches to their resolution as covered in [BRO] are not addressed here. Considering the scale of the GTE environment, you can see that key requirements, defined in [BRO], include the following: ISs cannot be stopped during the migration; the migration must be incremental; the migration will take many years; the computing environment must be designed to support migration; continuous migration will be a way of life; and sequencing of migration increments for shared data and programs requires complex configuration management, to mention a few.

In 1994, GTE began the Carrier Access Billing System (CABS II) as its first distributed object computing project, as a joint development between GTE and Ameritech. CABS II was begun after an extensive study to ensure that such a system was achievable. For example, the DOC infrastructure (i.e., TCSI's Object Services Package™ (OSP™) — the logical equivalent of an OMG Object Request Broker™ (ORB™) plus object services) — was selected based, in part, on the fact that it had been used in several large-scale DOC applications that had been successfully deployed for several years. In addition to OSP, the technical infrastructure included UNIX servers and clients, PC clients, and SQL relational DBMS.

A domain-specific DOC computational model (i.e., a billing object model) was developed for CABS II as well as a corresponding billing framework. Having a class library of basic billing objects not only assisted in the design and development of CABS II, it also helped to establish a base for application interoperability by being included in a GTE class library. The CABS II chief architect claims that the CABS II billing object model and framework was one of the major advantages of the CABS II project. Using the framework, those developing business solutions work almost entirely with billing objects, not with a general-purpose object model. What is more, all business solutions in CABS II use the same billing objects.

CABS II is a large-scale DOC application, as measured by the statistics in Table 1. These August 1995 numbers have since increased. In Table 1,

"Message" means an object instance service invocation message plus an object instance service response message (if any).

Table 1: CABS II Sizes

Business/domain classes	250
Implementation classes	4,500
Class instances (estimate)	
Data	3×10^{10}
Nonusage data	10^6
Servers	50–75
Clients	1,000s
TP rate	2,200/second
Message rate	6,100/second

4   DOC Deployment Status: A Survey

Although it did not start out to do so, GTE conducted a survey of DOC deployment around the world. Initially, in support of GTE's DOC program, we initiated information exchange between GTE and a few organizations of comparable size with a comparable commitment and investment in DOC. Following the popular notion from Jack Welch, CEO of GE, we tried to identify and possibly adopt the best DOC practices. Much to our surprise, we found few, if any, comparable organizations with comparable experience. Indeed, two such exchanges ended with the other organizations acknowledging that they were possibly years behind. A second motivation was to confirm the experiences and approaches followed in CAB II. A third motivation came from GTE's end user membership in OMG. In OMG meetings, we had heard so little from other end users in terms of technical requirements and challenges. We also experienced acknowledgment but little action or apparent understanding by the vendor-dominated organization toward end user requirements. Specifically, there appeared to be no substantive work in support of application interoperability.[1] This may have been due to the lack of end user experience with large-scale DOC applications. A survey might shed light on this question. Finally, we were very interested from the point of view of GTE's nine-year research effort into these topics [DOC] as to the state of technology vs. the state of research. What are the pragmatic research challenges? The survey was fruitful in each of the above areas.

The survey was informal. We contacted any organization that was an OMG end user or for which there was a rumor or claim that they were attempting to deploy DOC applications (e.g., customers of DOC infrastructure products such as ORBs). A survey form was used which evolved as we learned more about DOC deployment issues. The survey was sent to over 100 end users from whom we received 61 responses on 196 DOC applications in various stages of deployment, as indicated in Table 2.

DOC applications can be built using a wide range of combinations of alternative infrastructure technologies, as indicated in Table 3. These include

---

[1] The first OMG request for proposal in support of application interoperability was issued in January 1996. It is entitled "Common Facilities RFP-4: Common Business Objects and Business Object Facility."

OMG CORBA-compliant ORBs, Microsoft's OLE/COM™, OSF/DCE™ products, a wide range of database management systems (SQL, object-relational, object-oriented, and several flavors of distributed DBMSs), transaction processing monitors, workflow managers, messaging backplanes, and proprietary DOC infrastructures (e.g., TCSI's OSP™, SSA Object Technology's Newi™, and NeXt's Portable Distributed Objects™, NextStep™, and OpenStep™).

Table 2: Survey Results

	CORBA	Proprietary	Total
Large scale			
Deployed 1–3 years		12	12
Deployed, not confirmed	25	5	30
To be deployed 0–3 years	6	59	65
Limited scale/features, deployed	6	13	19
Prototype/evaluation/pilot	17	53	70
TOTAL	54	142	196

Table 3: Major Infrastructure Technology Used

Infrastructure Technology	Applications Surveyed (%)
Proprietary	80
DBMS	50
TP monitor	30
CORBA	20
OLE/COM	10
Workflow managers	10
DCE	0

All successfully deployed large-scale DOC applications that we found ran on proprietary DOC infrastructures. DBMSs are the obvious choice for data management in any infrastructure. However, distributed DBMSs may become the primary DOC infrastructure for some applications. Although distributed DBMS products now meet many distributed computing requirements, they are just beginning to be deployed. TP monitors are in widespread use (e.g., most credit card and ATM transactions). They form the backbone of many distributed computing architectures. During the survey, we found no confirmed large-scale applications deployed on a CORBA-compliant ORB. After the survey, we found one (i.e., The British Immigration Service's Suspect Index System which runs on ICL's DAIS™). The ORB-based applications were of limited scale (the largest involved five servers), of limited features (e.g., distribution not used), or were not deployed. Although OLE/COM is in widespread use on desktops, network OLE, the corresponding DOC infrastructure, was not yet available. We had claims of over 100 large-scale applications deployed on workflow management systems (WFMS), but were able to find only 10, and in those, the WFMS did not seem to be the critical infrastructure element. We found no DCE-based applications.

Following the survey, we found five modest-scale DCE-based deployments and indications that there are likely to be many more. The clear winner was "combination." Table 3 adds up to 200%, indicating that most applications use a combination of infrastructure technologies. After interoperation is possible, this will likely be the dominant infrastructure. Which will be the component infrastructures, and what degree of heterogeneity will be practical?

Building a DOC application from scratch in a DOC environment can be considerably easier than integrating legacy applications with a DOC technology. We found most DOC applications to be pure and most of the rest to be legacy IS integrations (Table 4). The challenges include dealing with the complexities of mapping from a DOC environment to a variety of potentially heterogeneous non-DOC environments. This is generally done with DOC wrappers around the legacy applications. Potentially more significant challenges arise in penetrating the legacy application to provide access to the functions and data. Indeed, Jim Kirkley, III, an engineer with probably the greatest experience and expertise in such wrappers, advises against penetrating the legacy application at all below its existing API. It is likely that the biggest market, world-wide, for DOC technology will be, at least initially, for legacy IS integration. In the long term, the most obvious requirement is for lots of legacy applications interoperating with lots of DOC applications. This is also clearly the hardest type of application type to build. At GTE we start with 100% non-DOC applications. CABS II must interoperate with many legacy ISs. Other guidelines from Jim include the following: keep the shared objects small (e.g., just interface objects); and do not map legacy functions to externally visible objects. Leave the legacy alone and build an interface with proxies that, in turn, invoke legacy functions. Separate, where possible, the logical model from the distribution model (as supported by DEC's ObjectBroker™) so that you can ignore distribution issues when doing the logical design and you can accommodate changes in the physical/distribution layer without having to change the logical level.

Table 4: DOC Application Type

Application Type	Applications Surveyed (%)
Pure DOC application	50
DOC for legacy IS integration	40
DOC applications + legacy IS integration	10

The survey found that CABS II was the largest DOC application, in terms of the statistics listed in Table 5. It was larger than Texas Instruments' TI WORKS™, a suite of applications for running a semiconductor CIM fabrication plant. Based on the information gathered in the survey, TI WORKS was the most successful large-scale DOC application. It does not use an ORB. CABS II was larger in all categories, including the number of classes in object instances, the latter by four orders of magnitude. However, this scale is considerably smaller than current large-scale mainframe-based ISs. The "Other" column in Table 5 refers to the 11 large-scale DOC applications that we found which were smaller again than TI WORKS.

We surveyed the respondents on several issues of significance to GTE's DOC effort. We found that 92% of the successful large-scale DOC applications used asynchronous (e.g., queued) messaging, while 40% of the small-scale ISs and prototypes used synchronous (e.g., RPC) messaging, such as provided in OMG's CORBA.[2] The reasons for asynchronous messaging included robustness (e.g., recoverable queues), performance, scalability, nonblocking behavior, and flexibility (e.g., via queue management). We found only three organizations that were working on an enterprise-wide DOC architecture and three that were working on smaller architectures for divisions or business processes. Four organizations had formal class libraries; four were building ontologies or domain models; and four were developing frameworks, as defined above (including CABS and TI WORKS).

Table 5: Scale

	CABS II	DOC Suite	Other
Domain classes	250	200	100 to 200
Implementation classes	4,500	1,000	1,000 to 3,000
Object instances	10^{10}	10^6	10^4–10^6
Servers	50 to 75	400 to 1,000	10 to 20
Clients	1,000s	400 to 1,000	100 to 300
TP rate/second	2,200		600 to 800

We found only three applications that were built on infrastructures that supported logical-physical object separation. For more than 20 years, DBMS technology has supported a degree of data independence. Programs are insulated from changes in the physical structure, since they deal with logical schema entities which are mapped by the DBMS to the underlying physical representation. Hence, the physical DBMS can be optimized without impacting programs. In all but three DOC applications, logical and physical object representations are identical. This means that changes to objects' logical or physical representation require changes to the entire system. This is practically infeasible at the scale of CABS II.

There were a few obvious conclusions from the survey of DOC deployment. First, for such a rapidly evolving technology, the situation changes constantly. The premise of this chapter is that DOC technology will be the base of future ISs. However, the current state, at the time of the survey, indicates that considerable maturation is required. Second, there are lots of object-oriented applications, but very few true DOC applications. This survey was not about object-oriented applications; it was about DOC applications. Third, almost all successful DOC applications were based on homogeneous, proprietary infrastructures and were not readily interoperable with other applications, the antithesis of the DOC vision. Fourth, DOC is inherently very hard and lacks general solutions and tools (i.e., they must be developed by highly skilled staff). Fifth, there are a few success stories (e.g., TI WORKS), and their success is due largely to the highly skilled staff. Sixth, there may be more significant successful DOC projects that we did not find or which did not respond. For example, the financial community claimed

---

[2] In 1Q96, OMG will consider an asynchronous messaging service, but it may not be a first-class citizen with its RPC-based service.

30 successful large-scale DOC applications, 25 based on CORBA ORBs (see Table 2 "Deployed, not confirmed"). However, they were unwilling to provide the details to substantiate the claims. I did obtain details of one such claimed DOC application and found that it was deployed but was not using distribution (i.e., copies on different machines did not communicate). Finally, claims of success cannot be taken at face value. We followed up on a few public claims of and awards for successes and found them to be either unconvincing, unsubstantiated, or significantly less than claimed. For example, a high level of reuse was claimed for a large-scale deployed DOC application that was built in a partnership between two organizations. We found that one partner, an end user, did not get any reuse. The other partner, a solutions vendor, got considerable reuse since they had sold the system multiple times.

The survey seems to suggest the following lessons. First, the major challenge remains the development of an adequate long-term computing vision and a sensible migration toward that vision. Successful large-scale DOC applications devoted considerable effort to developing a model of next-generation ISs and a computing environment (e.g., architecture beyond the current application), and planned for a long-duration migration to the vision (e.g., one major application at a time). Second, mission-critical production applications should be pursued using DOC only if the requirements clearly demand it, and then with great care. Third, small non-mission-critical pure DOC applications are the easiest, while the obvious near-term win, legacy IS integration, is considerably harder. The conventional requirement will be for a substantial mix of both, and that is the hardest type of application to build. Fourth, DOC infrastructures are being developed as products and standardized (e.g., in OMG and OSF's DCE) apparently without having been tested on real DOC application requirements. Indeed, there are few in existence. Finally, the high risk involved in DOC application development and deployment requires explicit risk management. So, how should you architect and plan that system today for delivery in three to five years?

5   Industrial-Strength DOC Requirements

Based on our experience and on the survey, we identify a number of requirements that DOC technology must satisfy to meet the needs of large-scale industrial applications. The requirements are given with respect to the distributed computing framework introduced above. As OMG is the world-wide focus of DOC technology development, many of the requirements are given with respect to the current state of OMG technology. However, the comments can apply equally to any DOC technology. One could easily say that OMG is at the beginning of a long, complex technology development and cannot be expected to provide a complete solution. That is precisely the point of this chapter. This section looks at some specifics to illustrate the point and, it is hoped, to encourage effort toward fulfilling the end user requirements.

Industrial-strength applications require that all the pieces be in place, from the hardware up to the end user applications and throughout the entire life cycle. A comprehensive framework is missing and so are the constituent industrial-strength tools and technology. End users require such a framework and the relevant components since they must put together all the components to build an application, let alone an enterprise-wide environment of interoperable applications. Considerable effort has been invested in the DOC infrastructure (i.e., OMG CORBA, CORBAservices, and CORBAfacilities) in the absence of a global framework or a model of the target ISs that the infrastructure will support. Work is beginning in OMG's Analysis and Design Task Force to address application development life cycles, object analysis and design methodology metamodels, and relevant technologies. Work is also going on in the Business Object Domain Task Force (BODTF) in the area of business objects and business object facilities. This work is to be commended. The fact that they are just beginning, and the difficulty of placing them in the OMG object management architecture, indicates the current state of DOC technology. How can you build a DOC application before such technology is in place? Our survey found that the answer is "with highly skilled people."

Industrial-strength applications are often built with large project staffs. The computational model that the staff uses must be complete and at a level appropriate to the problems being solved. The OMG computational model could be considered to be the OMG's core object model, augmented by the CORBAservices and some of the CORBAfacilities. Collectively, these provide the capabilities required by staff to develop DOC applications. CORBAservices will be in development for some years. Some services are not yet adopted (e.g., asynchronous messaging), some are underspecified (e.g., concurrency and transaction services), some require getting some bugs out (e.g., event service), while still others have not yet entered the process (e.g., rules). Hence, the computational model is not complete. CORBAservices and the "computational model" is at too low a level for application programming staff. There is no high-level programming model for CORBA-based application development. DOC programming environments such as NextStep, SSA Object Technology's Newi, Forté's Forté™, and TI's Composer™ provide more complete and higher level computational models required for industrial-strength applications. OMG's BODTF work on business objects and business object facilities will begin to address some of these issues over the next two to three years. Finally, the recently created OMG Architecture Board is responsible for ensuring the consistency of OMG technology specifications. Its job will be to ensure that the OMG computational model, as described above, is consistent with respect to a specific and complete OMG core object model. This is a significant challenge. The OMG concept of profile is required to support domain-specific object models but is not yet adequately defined.

Industrial-strength applications require a comprehensive life cycle, from inception to design, development, deployment, evolution, and ultimately termination or replacement. There is no widely accepted life cycle for DOC applications. It is unlikely that an organization would begin an industrial-strength large-scale application without understanding the entire life cycle and without having an adequate computing environment to support it. OMG does not provide such a life cycle nor do the CORBAfacilities provide the support tools. These will, no doubt, be specified over the next few years. Currently, there is considerable focus on the first 15% of the life cycle. Industrial-strength applications incur 85% of their costs in that latter 85% of the life cycle. Even within the first 15%, there are significant gaps. There is little support for distribution design for applications, objects/data, and execution (e.g., parallelization, load balancing), or implementation. There is no DOC repository. There are no models, metrics, or tools to assist in testing. There is almost no support for continuous operations support.

There are other problems with the DOC infrastructure that are related to open research problems and that pose significant challenges for large-scale industrial applications. For example, OMG technology provides several messaging backplanes. There is the ORB, with its basic messaging service. There is the query service for query messages to query processors. Similarly, there is transaction service and a persistence service. For high-volume transactions, should you use the CORBA messaging service to then access a DBMS transaction service, or should you access the DBMS or TP monitor directly, using SQL? Similar engineering questions arise for queries and persistence. Hence, there are between one and four messaging backplane choices for application developers. If you choose anything other than the CORBA messaging service, you must then manage the resulting "messaging architecture." You might also consider whether your "objects" should be represented as objects or in the basic representation of the DBMS. A related problem is that you may wish to have persistence, query, and transaction services over all objects in the CORBA DOC environment. However, these services are provided over those objects that reside in a component that supports the service. This will not likely include components other than DBMSs and TP monitors for some time. This means that providing those services will mean crossing from the CORBA DOC environment and type system to that of the DBMS and TP monitors. This will generally mean translating between object-type and non-object-type systems.

Another computing environment problem concerns one of the great successes of OMG, the OMG IDL™ (interface definition language). OMG IDL is being adopted widely, independently of, or in anticipation of, the success of CORBA. Hence, IDL is becoming the vernacular API, the interface specification language of many, many systems. Since IDL can't be all things to all people, it is seen, specifically in our survey, as very limited. Each systems project wants to extend IDL for its own requirements. Unfortunately, many variants of IDL are now evolving.

Our experience with respect to ORB products was supported by the survey. These products are at an early stage of development and are incomplete, just as CORBAservices and CORBAfacilities specifications are incomplete. Most ORB products do not support the minimal adopted CORBAservices and CORBAfacilities and may not for some time. In addition, by mid-1995, large-scale industrial-strength applications push the limits of all ORB products with which we or the survey respondent had experience. They did not meet requirements for robustness, scale, and reliability. We are aware of no ORB that supports adequate means of testing, quality assurance, appropriate metrics for sizing and tuning, or monitoring and maintenance (e.g., performance tuning — recall the lack of logical-physical separation). As stated earlier, most CORBA products lack an adequate asynchronous queued messaging service as a first class citizen with RPC. Some of these problems are overcome by proprietary products. For example, Forte provides a wonderful function called the "rolling upgrade", which permits client applications to be upgraded from one version to another while the system is running, all from a single point in the distributed system.

Finally, the fundamental requirement of industrial-strength, enterprise-wide interoperable applications is interoperability. Comprehensive interoperability involves interoperability across the entire life cycle. All artifacts produced during the life cycle should be accessible, in principle, by all tools. All tools should be able to interoperate with others, again, in principle. Interoperability is required from the bottom to the top. At the bottom, there is hardware platform interoperability which is "vendor hard." It is entirely within the capabilities of the platform vendors to resolve the problem. At the next level, infrastructure interoperability is "Turing hard." Whoever solves the problems of interoperable object models and distributed object computing services and facilities should be awarded the Turing Award. It is a very significant challenge. However, interoperability at the next level, application interoperability, is "Nobel hard." A solution here should garner a Noble Prize. The next section concludes this chapter by illustrating this challenge, indicating its significance, and emphasizing that it is not a technical issue.

6 Toward Industrial-Strength, Enterprise-Wide Interoperable Applications

In the period 1913–1915, Niels Bohr, the Danish physicist and Nobel laureate, published the papers that defined his new theory of atomic structure, for which he received the Nobel Prize in physics in 1922. The significance of his theory of the erratic changes in energy levels of electrons circling the nucleus was understood almost immediately by physicists world-wide. Within a few years, Niels Bohr's ideas, one man's ideas, had helped to evolve man's understanding of the atom and of elementary matter. This was possible, in part, because physicists world-wide shared a common domain orientation, as defined in Section 2, for elementary particles. There was a common terminology, a shared ontology (i.e., the basic concepts of particle physics), and a number of shared domain models (e.g., Rutherford's nuclear model of the atom). The shared domain models were standardized in mathematical models (analogous to interface specifications of object models), and placed in frameworks (i.e., the larger mathematical models of physics such as quantum mechanics). The shared domain orientation permitted physicists around the world to cooperate (i.e., interoperate). The shared domain orientation in physics was the result of hundreds of years of science, at least back to Sir Isaac Newton (1643–1727). The process that created it was that of science itself. Now, although there are many differences and constant attempts to change and improve the domain orientation of physics, any two physicists can cooperate based on a mutually shared domain orientation.

Following the principles of component orientation motivating DOC technology, consider the creation of a telecommunications billing system from components. The components may be entire subsystems (e.g., a rating system, an account management system, a bill generation system) or one or more class libraries of billing classes (e.g., customer, bill, line item). The use of these components together to produce a single billing system requires application interoperability. Each pair of components must have a shared understanding of the objects (e.g., functions and data) involved in any messages that they exchange. Of course, it is more complex when a communication involves more than two components. Also, a deeper understanding (e.g., of objects that they do not exchange or the business process within which they participate) may be required. However, it is sufficient for this discussion to restrict our consideration to the messages exchanged by two components, the minimal application interoperability requirement.

Mutual understanding of objects in exchanged messages requires a shared domain orientation. The components must share or be able to map to a common terminology. To the degree that it affects their behavior, they must share a common ontology (i.e., definition of the basic concepts, such as customer). They may also require a shared domain model (i.e., the business process of producing a bill). However, this is dependent on the nature of the functions of the two components. It would be helpful, but not necessary, if the shared domain orientation were enforced by interface specifications and a framework.

How can we ensure that the billing system components have a shared domain orientation? Consider the elementary particle domain model shared by physicists world-wide. This was hundreds of years in the making, under assumptions of sharing and cooperation. Is there a comparable context or history for telecommunications billing? The International Telecommunications Union (ITU) is the international standardization body for telecommunications. It attempts to create shared domain orientations in various domains. It has been most successful in the areas of hardware and network management. However, there is no world-wide shared domain orientation for basic telecommunications domains such as billing, provisioning, automation, and repair. Work is under way in these areas, using object-orientation as a tool to define such models. As you can easily see, the challenge is not technical (i.e., how to define a model in object-oriented models). The challenge involves defining mutually agreeable terminologies, ontologies, and domain models. How long will it take to achieve such agreements between thousands of telecommunications companies in countries all over the world, each with different cultures, economic models, levels of sophistication, and business models? The models are not static. For example, the landmark U.S. Telecommunications Bill of 1996 will revolutionize the U.S. telecommunications business and related models. Unlike physical models, which have the physical world as a basis for verification, billing models are pure abstractions, with no such direct means for empirical verification. A billing model can be verified, but with considerable difficulty.

A large number of standards bodies or consortia are attempting to create domain orientations. A brief search of the literature and the World Wide Web uncovered activities in the areas listed in Table 6. Within healthcare alone, there are more than 15 such activities in Europe (Table 7) and many in the USA. The RICHE activity has developed an entire domain orientation, as defined in Section 2. It has defined a terminology, several ontologies, several domain models, interface specifications, and a framework which is produced by a consortium. RICHE has been adopted by more than 15,000 hospitals in Europe.

Most of these activities are intended primarily to provide standardization for the domain and not necessarily for the associated ISs. There is significant value to establishing a shared domain orientation, independently of establishing computing standards. However, many of these activities are attempting to extend the agreements to computing. When the activities have been initiated by the computing community (e.g., Great Britain's Common Basic Specification), they have often encountered resistance from the domain (e.g., the healthcare community). This suggests that domain orientations are almost entirely the business of the domain and not the business of the technologist. Technologists can assist with the formulation of the object-oriented domain models, interface specifications, and computing frameworks, but not with the terminologies, ontologies, or domain models.

Table 6: Areas Pursuing Domain Standardization

Manufacturing	Healthcare	Transportation
Engineering	Mathematics	Bibliographic Data
Medicine	Retail	DoD
Space	Computer	Software Meta Data
Legal Insurance	Art	Petroleum
Spatial and Multimedia Applications		Financial Services
Telecommunications Management Network		
Telecommunications Billing		

Table 7: Healthcare Domain Standardization Activities

Common Basic Specification (GB)	RICHE (Europe)
READ3	HELIOS II
NUCLEUS	CANON
General Architecture for Languages, Encyclopedias and Nomenclatures	
GALEN-IN-USE	CEN TC251
GAMES	DILEMMA
PRESTIGE: SYNAPSES	SNOMED
The Good European Health Record	
Framework for European Services in Telemedicine	
Strategic Health Informatics Networks for Europe	
Computer Based Medical Records Institute	
Patient-Oriented Management Architecture (USA)	

The examples in Tables 6 and 7 illustrate opportunities and challenges. The opportunities are obvious. A shared domain orientation assists all members of the domain, within some limits (e.g., errors and limitations). In addition, the domain orientation could provide a basis for application interoperability of ISs within the domain and a basis for component orientation, class libraries, and other claimed benefits for DOC. The challenges are equally obvious. As with the telecommunications standards, it is a challenging, and apparently never ending, human (not technical) task to achieve a standard. There are all the usual challenges with standards. As illustrated in Table 7, there are multiple standards in any one field. The large number of domains to be standardized only suggests the exponential number of relationships between domains to be standardized. Real-life activities (e.g., value chains and their associated business processes and supporting ISs) cross domains. The needle and the drug being inserted by a nurse into a patient in a hospital had to be manufactured from raw materials, put into inventory, ordered, transported, accounted for, billed for, and paid for. The nurse had to be assigned to the task which is part of a medical procedure. And, of course, let's not forget the patient. How do you establish domain orientations across domains? For example, each domain in the needle example may have its own domain orientation. Each may also have some concepts shared with the others (e.g., customer). To what degree do the domains overlap (i.e., have shared concepts), and how do you achieve agreement on those overlaps, bilaterally or universally? One final challenge could be termed legacy migration. Let's assume that we have an adequate domain orientation and are able to define new interoperable classes, components, and, from them, applications. How do you migrate from the existing heterogeneous "legacy" base of ISs and computing infrastructures to the brave new world? At a minimum, it will be an iterative, evolutionary transition. This requires that the legacy ISs, which are unlikely to conform to the domain orientation, must interoperate with the new ISs that do. We are back to square one, a massive IS environment with one DOC application being added, further contributing to the heterogeneity and application interoperability challenges in hopes of ultimately reducing these problems.

The person who solves the problem of domain orientation, or even application interoperability within a domain, deserves a Noble Prize, perhaps the Nobel Peace Prize, for it will certainly not be a technical achievement, but something far more valuable.

In conclusion, application interoperability is a fundamental requirement for end users of DOC technology. It is not a technical problem. However, DOC technology should be developed to facilitate the definition of the domain models, the interface specifications, and the supporting frameworks. The DOC community should understand the nature and full scope of this challenge, work directly with the domains that they should serve, and focus effort accordingly on the relevant domain models (i.e., interoperable domain model families) and supporting frameworks. No small task!

7   Conclusions

We are at the beginning of a 20-year paradigm shift to distributed object computing. By that time, some variant of DOC will be the dominant computing paradigm and will be effectively and readily deployable. Long before that time, it will have met many of its current claims. Indeed, there are already major successes with large-scale industrial-strength DOC applications.

For the moment, DOC is in its infancy and does not meet industrial-strength requirements or the claims of its proponents. DOC is not yet ready for prime time. Although GTE has experienced one of the DOC successes, it has decided to significantly slow the deployment of DOC technology and applications. Following a significant study of and investment in DOC technologies and methodologies, we have concluded that the benefits do not currently warrant the costs to overcome the challenges described in this chapter. The claims for increased productivity, reuse, and lowered costs cannot be achieved with other than very highly skilled staff who must work with immature technology and methods. We will continue to investigate the area and observe its progress and will be prepared to take full advantage of the technology when DOC is more mature. We look forward to a highly competitive market for the DOC infrastructure and highly competitive products.

Regardless of when DOC technology is deployed, we continue to face on a daily basis the ultimate end user challenge of application interoperability.

Although this challenge is essentially not technical, DOC has the potential to succeed based on its ability to support domain orientation, as described above. The community developing DOC technology should consider establishing application interoperability as its primary goal and defining a comprehensive distributed object computing framework such as outlined above. DOC technology development should be driven by the requirements of industrial-strength applications and specifically to support the requirements domain orientation.

References

[BRO] Brodie, M.L., and M. Stonebraker, *Migrating Legacy Systems: Gateways, Interfaces, and the Incremental Approach*, Morgan Kaufmann Publishers, San Francisco, CA (1995).

[DEC] Descartes, R., *Essais Philosophiques* (Philosophical Essays), *Discours de la méthode* (Discourse on Method) (1637).

[DOC] Manola, F., S. Heiler, D. Georgakopoulos, M. Hornick, and M. Brodie, "Distributed Object Management," *International Journal of Intelligent and Cooperative Information Systems, 1*, 1 (1992).

[KAN] Kant, I., *Critique of Pure Reason* (1781).

[LOC] Locke, J., *Essay Concerning Human Understanding* (1690).

[MAN] Manola, F., and S. Heiler, "A 'RISC' Object Model for Object System Interoperation: Concepts and Applications," TR-0231-08-93-165, GTE Laboratories Incorporated (1993).

[MOR] Moore, G., *Crossing the Chasm*, HarperBusiness, New York (1991).

Trademarks

The following are trademarks of their respective companies: ORB™, CORBA™, CORBAservices™, Object Request Broker™, CORBAfacilities™, OMG™, OMG IDL™, and Object Management Group™ of the Object Management Group; DCE of the Open Software Foundation; OLE™ and COM™ of Microsoft Corporation; Object Services Package™ and OSP™ of TCSI Corporation; Forté of Forté Software, Inc.; DAIS™ of International Computers Limited; Newi™ of SSA Object Technology; Portable Distributed Objects™, PDO™, NextStep™, and OpenStep™ of NeXT Software, Inc.; ObjectBroker™ of Digital Equipment Corporation; WORKS™ and Composer™ of Texas Instruments Incorporated.

Approximate and Commonsense Reasoning:
From Theory to Practice

Didier Dubois and Henri Prade

Institut de Recherche en Informatique de Toulouse (IRIT), Université Paul Sabatier
118 route de Narbonne, 31062 Toulouse Cedex, France
Email: {dubois, prade}@irit.irit.fr

Abstract. This paper provides an overview of present trends in approximate and commonsense reasoning. The different types of reasoning, which can be covered by this generic expression, take place when the available information is either incomplete, or inconsistent, or pervaded with uncertainty, or imprecise and qualitative. The conclusions which are then obtained are usually plausible but uncertain. Yet, approximate or commonsense reasoning is useful in practical problems such as prospect evaluation, diagnosis, forecasting and decision tasks, where better information cannot be got. Classical logic is insufficient for handling these types of reasoning. Different ideas of orderings play a role in these reasoning processes: plausibility orderings between interpretations or situations which are unequally uncertain, similarity orderings with respect to prototypical situations or cases, preference orderings between acts or situations when the problem is a matter of choice. These orderings can be encoded using purely ordinal scales, or scales with a richer structure (when it is meaningful and compatible with the quality of the available information). This general idea of ordering provides a kind of unification between the different reasoning modes and somewhat typifies approximate and commonsense reasoning. Advances in default reasoning, inconsistency handling, data fusion, updating, abductive reasoning, interpolative reasoning, and decision issues in relation with Artificial Intelligence research, are briefly reviewed. Open questions and directions for future research which seem especially important for the development of practical applications are pointed out. The paper is largely based on authors' research experience, and as such, presents a rather personal view, which may not be exempt from some biases.

1 - What is Approximate and Commonsense Reasoning?

Approximate reasoning, inexact reasoning, uncertain reasoning, plausible reasoning, commonsense reasoning are expressions which have been used, with slightly different intended meanings, in the Artificial Intelligence area for about twenty years in relation with the activities of distinct research trends such as nonmonotonic reasoning, reasoning under uncertainty, and fuzzy logic. Up to a few noticeable exceptions, research on these three topics has been developing along separate roads and often with different prospects. Most of their respective results are still currently presented in specialized and well-identified workshops and conferences. Nonmonotonic reasoning focuses on reasoning under incomplete information and commonsense knowledge using symbolic approaches based on logical machineries. Reasoning under uncertainty uses numerical models, especially probability theory and causal Bayesian networks, while the mainstream of fuzzy logic concentrates on the handling of fuzzy rules. Viewed in that way, the concerns of the three schools seem rather different. Moreover, most of the works on nonmonotonic logics are theoretically oriented. Numerical uncertainty research is much interested in computational issues on the probabilistic side, and in the development of other representation frameworks such as belief function theory or possibility theory. Fuzzy logic is especially known for its applications to rule-based control. Apart these three communities, there are still other, more recent, research groups devoted to human-like reasoning issues, like case-based reasoning whose concerns are practically oriented. However all these approaches have more in common than it seems at first glance.

Noticeably, all these schools are interested in formalizing aspects of reasoning which go beyond classical deductive reasoning. In a way or in another, they can be seen as attempts at providing more rigorous basis for different types of problems empirically handled by expert systems, in order to overcome the limitations of these inference systems. Nonmonotonic reasoning aims at offering a proper treatment of rules having implicit exceptions. Uncertainty approaches propose theoretically founded uncertainty calculi based on different representation principles regarding the modelling of partial ignorance, or the use of independence assumptions. Fuzzy logic rather increases the representation capabilities of usual rule-based systems by allowing for the introduction of properties whose satisfaction is a matter of degree, in the condition or conclusion parts of the rules. Moreover the idea of ordering is present in all these approaches. The existence of an ordering between the more or less plausible/ normal states of the world, or equivalently between the more or less exceptional situations which can be encountered, underlies nonmonotonic logics. In numerical approaches, this ordering is explicitly reflected by the measures of uncertainty. Fuzzy set membership degrees encode orderings whose interpretation may differ according to the application, as pointed out in the following.

It seems that there are three main distinct notions which are naturally a matter of degree in approximate or commonsense reasoning: uncertainty, similarity and preference. Approximate reasoning plays an important role in three classes of applications: reasoning under uncertainty, classification and data analysis, and decision-making problems. Interestingly enough, these three directions, that have been investigated by many researchers, actually correspond and/or exploit three semantics which have been proposed for fuzzy set membership grades, respectively in terms of uncertainty, similarity and preference. Indeed, considering the degree of membership $\mu_F(u)$ of an element u in a fuzzy set F, defined on a referential U, one can find in the literature, three interpretations of this degree:

- degree of uncertainty: this interpretation is the one at work in possibility theory (Zadeh, 1978; Dubois and Prade, 1988) where fuzzy sets are used to represent imprecise, uncertain or linguistically expressed pieces of information. $\mu_F(u)$ is then the degree of possibility that a parameter x has value u, given that all that is known about it is that "x is F". F then describes the more or less plausible values of x;

- degree of similarity: $\mu_F(u)$ is the degree of proximity of u from prototype elements of F. Historically, this is the oldest semantics of fuzzy set membership grades (Bellman, Kalaba and Zadeh, 1966). This view is particularly suitable in classification, clustering, regression analysis and the like, where the problem is that of abstraction from a set of data. It is also at work in fuzzy control techniques, where the similarity degrees between the current situation and the prototypical ones described in the condition parts of the rules, are the basis for the interpolation mechanism between the conclusions of the rules. Besides, similarity plays a crucial role in case-based reasoning. It can be also used in decision (see Section 2.6);

- degree of preference: this interpretation is closely connected with decision analysis. Then a fuzzy set F represents a flexible constraint restricting a set of more or less preferred objects (or values of a decision variable x) and $\mu_F(u)$ represents an intensity of preference in favor of object u, or the feasibility of selecting u as a value of x. This view is the one later put forward by Bellman and Zadeh (1970). μ_F may be them thought as a utility function. Approximate reasoning is then concerned with the propagation of preferences when several constraints (which may be fuzzy) relate the variables. Examples of applications are in design and scheduling problems where it is natural to express preferences about characteristics of the object to be realized, or about due dates.

If/then rules often provide a convenient format for expressing pieces of knowledge. However the accurate representation of rules using classical logic is not an obvious matter, especially if the rule may have exceptions, or involve fuzzy terms in its linguistic expression. In fact, the intended use and meaning of rules may be very different according to the cases and should be properly understood when representing rules. Clearly, rules may express preference, uncertainty, or similarity. When they are decision-oriented, rules are of the general form "if <situation i> then <decision i>. Obviously, a graded set of recommended decisions may also appear in the conclusion part of the rule. The idea of similarity may be also at work in the condition part of the rules, which is then of the form, "the more the state of the world corresponds to <situation i>, the more recommended is <decision i>". Rules expressing uncertainty are more oriented towards reasoning tasks. They are of the form "if p_i is true then q_i is true with certainty λ_i" (where the level of certainty is expressed in the framework of some uncertainty calculus), or they involve some probability, or possibility, distribution δ_i in their conclusion part as in the rule "if p_i is true, then the possible values of x are restricted by δ_i". If the condition part involves similarity, it leads to rules of the form "the more x is A_i, the more certain q_i" where A_i is a gradual property whose truth is a matter of degree. There exist also purely gradual rules, which are of the form "the more X is A_i, the more Y is B_i" (or equivalently "the less Y is B_i, the less X is A_i") which provide a qualitative description of relations between variables X and Y in terms of the gradual properties A_i and B_i; such a rule does not involve any uncertainty by itself. Other rules do not express a restriction in their conclusion part on the possible values of a variable, but rather assert that the possibility/feasibility of some values is guaranteed, as in the rules "the more X is A, the more possible Y is B" and "the more X is A, the larger the set of possible values for Y". In these "possibility rules", asserting that the value of Y belongs to a set B do not prevent from having other values out of B possible also, it is why the conclusions of several possibility rules fired by the same situation, have to be combined disjunctively. This contrasts with gradual rules, or rules with conclusions pervaded with uncertainty whose conclusions have to be combined conjunctively. This points out that a proper understanding of the intended meaning of rules is very important in approximate reasoning. All the above-mentioned types of rules can be represented in the framework of fuzzy set or possibility theory; see (Dubois and Prade, 1992).

After this brief survey of different types of approximate or commonsense knowledge, where the notions of preference, uncertainty and similarity[1] are present, an overview of the main types of reasoning is now presented.

2 - The Main Paradigms

2.1 - Default Reasoning

Default reasoning is at the core of the knowledge-based systems enterprise. The problem is the handling of the presence of (possibly hidden) exceptions in the rule-base of an expert system. The kind of plausible reasoning that is involved here can be summarized as follows: how to automatically derive plausible conclusions about an incompletely described situation, on the basis of generic knowledge describing what is the normal course of things. For instance, in a medical expert system, generic knowledge encodes what the physician knows about the relationships between symptoms and diseases, and the situation at hand is a given patient on which some test results are available, and plausible inference is supposed to perform a diagnosis task. More generally, this kind of problem can be cast in the setting of taxonomic reasoning, where generic knowledge describe the links between classes and subclasses, and some factual evidence provides an incomplete description of an instance to be classified. The particularity of the problem is that the generic knowledge encoded as a set of rules is pervaded with uncertainty due to the presence of exceptions. Solving this problem in a satisfactory way presupposes that three requirements be met, as emphasized in (Dubois and Prade, 1994a)

i) *The necessity of a clear distinction between factual evidence and generic knowledge.* This distinction is fundamental and has been explicitly acknowledged in the expert systems literature at the implementation level (facts versus rules). The generic rules encode a background knowledge that is used to jump to conclusions that the only consideration of the available factual evidence would not allow. Clearly, accounting for the arrival of a new piece of evidence does not produce the same effect as the arrival of a new rule or the mofication of a rule. The arrival of a new piece of evidence does not affect the generic knowledge, but modifies the reference class of the case under study. On the contrary the introduction of a new rule causes a revision of the generic knowledge.

ii) *The need for representing partial ignorance in an unbiased way.* There are three extreme epistemic attitudes with regard to a proposition p: on the basis of current evidence and background knowledge one can be sure that p is true, sure that p is false, or the truth-value of p can be unknown. The third situation corresponds to partial ignorance, and its representation should not depend on the count of situations in which p is true, since this count can depend on how these situations are described, i.e., is language-dependent.

iii) *The inference at work cannot be monotonic.* A plausible reasoning system is expected not to be cautious, namely to go beyond the conclusions strictly entailed by the incomplete evidence. This is done by assuming that the particular situation

---

[1] Let us mention the idea of *permission* as a fourth basic notion which may appear in commonsense knowledge. As the three other notions, permission might be a matter of degree.

under study is as normal as possible, so that it is possible to jump to adventurous, but plausible conclusions. The price paid by this kind of deductive efficiency is that such conclusions may be canceled upon the arrival of new evidence, when the latter tells us that the current situation is not so normal. This is in obvious contradiction with the monotonicity property of classical logic that forbids conclusions to be retracted when new axioms come in.

Classical logic can neither provide plausible conclusions when information is incomplete nor leave room for implicit exceptions in rules. Thus classical logic fails to satisfy requirement iii) and representation of generic knowledge by universally quantified formulas does not allow for exceptions. The solutions proposed by the expert systems literature were either based on the propagation of certainty coefficients (like in MYCIN and PROSPECTOR), or based on an explicit handling of the reasons for uncertainty at the control level. However these solutions were partially ad hoc, and exception handling in rule-based systems has motivated further, better founded streams of work, namely Bayesian networks and nonmonotonic reasoning. While the first of these approaches could be safely developed due to the strong probabilistic tradition, the second line of research proved to be more adventurous, but eventually fruitful. Although Bayesian approach provides a debatable representation of partial ignorance (point (ii) above, see Dubois, Prade and Smets (1995) for a detailed discussion), it turns out that many lessons from the Bayesian net literature are worth being learned, in order to solve the exception-tolerant inference problem while remaining in the tradition of logic, especially the handling of contexts by means of conditional probability.

In the last ten years, many works in nonmonotonic reasoning have concentrated on the determination of natural properties for a nonmonotonic consequence relation, likely to achieve a satisfactory treatment of plausible reasoning in the presence of incomplete information (Gabbay, 1985; Kraus et al., 1990; Gärdenfors and Makinson, 1994). Besides, Pearl (1988) has suggested that Adams (1975)' logic of infinitesimal probabilities was a good basis for nonmonotonic reasoning, and indeed the core properties of a nonmonotonic consequence relation are present in this logic. These properties constitute the basis of the inference system P (P for preferential) proposed by Kraus, Lehmann and Magidor (1990), which provides a very cautious inference system. In order to get a less conservative inference, Lehmann (see Lehmann and Magidor, 1992) and Pearl (1990) have proposed to add a property, first suggested by Makinson, called rational monotony, and a particular entailment (named "rational closure entailment" (Lehmann and Magidor, 1992)) has been defined which satisfies rational monotony. Remarkably enough, Adams' logic of infinitesimal probabilities or equivalently, system P, can be expressed in terms of conditional objects (Dubois and Prade, 1994b). A conditional object q|p can be seen as a purely symbolic counterpart of the conditional probability Prob(q|p) (Goodman et al., 1991). Thus it shows that probabilities do not play a crucial role in the modelling of preferential entailment, since no probability degree, infinitesimal or not, are necessary with conditional objects. Only the conditional structure is important. It can be easily handled in terms of a 3-valued semantics much simpler than the preferential semantics (Kraus et al., 1990).

The logic of system P, or equivalently of conditional objects, has also the merit of displaying the difference between two modes of belief revision: evidence focusing and knowledge expansion that can be defined as follows, where K stands for the knowledge base storing generic knowledge and E gathers the factual evidence:

- *Evidence focusing*: a new piece of evidence p arrives and makes the available information on the case at hand more complete. Then E is changed into E ∪ {p} (supposedly consistent). K remains untouched. But the plausible conclusions from K and E ∪ {p}, i.e., r such that K ⊨ r | E ∧ p, may radically differ from those derived from K and E, where we use a conditional object notation (see Dubois and Prade (1994b) for the technical definition of ⊨); it means equivalently that the nonmonotonic consequence relation E ∧ p ⊢ r can be derived from the conditional knowledge in K using the rules of system P (Kraus et al., 1990).

- *Knowledge expansion*: it corresponds to adding new generic rules tainted with possible exceptions. Insofar as the new knowledge base is consistent (see Lehmann and Magidor (1992), and Dubois and Prade (1994) for the definition of the consistency of a conditional knowledge base) it is clear that due to the monotonicity of inference ⊨, all plausible conclusions derived from K can still be derived from K' since if K is a subset of K' and K ⊨ r | E then K' ⊨ r | E. But more conclusions may perhaps be obtained by K'.

- *Knowledge revision*: it encompasses the situation when the result of adding new generic rules to K leads to an inconsistency. In that case some mending of the knowledge base must be carried out in order to recover consistency. Preliminary results along this line are in Boutilier and Goldszmidt (1993).

The distinction between focusing and expansion cannot be made at all in revision theories that represent cognitive states by sets of formulas in propositional logic, such as Gärdenfors (1988) theory.

In possibility theory "p generally entails q" is understood as "p ∧ q is a more plausible situation than p ∧ ¬q". It defines a constraint of the form $\Pi(p \wedge q) > \Pi(p \wedge \neg q)$ that restricts a set of possibility measures Π. Thus, a set K of generic knowledge statements of the form "p_i generally entails q_i", is equivalent to a collection of constraints $\{\Pi(p_i \wedge q_i) > \Pi(p_i \wedge \neg q_i), i = 1,n\}$ which define (if they are consistent) a family of possibility measures. It is shown in (Dubois and Prade, 1995a) that the entailment of a statement "generally q in context p" (i.e., $\Pi(p \wedge q) > \Pi(p \wedge \neg q)$) understood as a consequence of the set constraints modelling K which holds for any possibility measure, is precisely equivalent to the entailment of system P. Rather than working with a family of possibility measures, we can select a particular one which provides a "faithful" representation of K, which can be computed as follows. For each interpretation ω of the language, the maximal possibility degree $\pi(\omega) = \Pi(\{\omega\})$ is computed, that obeys the set of possibilistic contraints representing K. This is done by virtue of the principle of minimal specificity (or commitment) that assumes each situation as a possible one insofar as it has not been ruled out. Then each generic statement is turned into a material implication $\neg p_i \vee q_i$, to which a weight $N(\neg p_i \vee q_i)$ is attached where N is measure of necessity associated with the less specific possibility distribution π. It comes down, as shown in Benferhat et al. (1992) to rank-ordering the generic rules giving priority to the most specific ones, as done in Pearl (1990)'s system Z. It offers a convenient framework for implementing "rational closure" (Lehmann and Magidor, 1992) which is thus captured. Possibilistic logic does not allow for a direct encoding of pieces of generic knowledge such as "birds fly" under the form of a pair of a classical formula and a weight. However, it provides a target language in which plausible inference from generic knowledge can be achieved in the face of incomplete evidence, once the weights are computed as said above.

Generally speaking, a possibilistic knowledge base K is a set of pairs (p,s) where p is a classical logic formula and s is a lower bound of a degree of necessity (N(p) ≥ s). It can be viewed as a stratified deductive data base where the higher s, the safer the piece of knowledge p. Reasoning from K means using the safest part of K to make inference, whenever possible. Denoting $K_\alpha = \{p, (p,s) \in K, s \geq \alpha\}$, the entailment $K \vdash (p,\alpha)$ means that $K_\alpha \vdash p$. K can be inconsistent and its inconsistency degree is $inc(K) = \sup\{\alpha, K \vdash (\bot,\alpha)\}$ where $\bot$ denotes the contradiction. In contrast with classical logic, inference in the presence of inconsistency becomes non-trivial. This is the case when $K \vdash (p,\alpha)$ where $\alpha > inc(K)$. Then it means that p follows from a consistent and safe part of K (at least at level α). This kind of syntactic non-trivial inference is sound and complete with respect to the above defined preferential entailment. Moreover adding p to K and nontrivially entailing q from $K \cup \{p\}$ corresponds to revising K upon learning p, and having q as a consequence of the revised knowledge base. This notion of revision is exactly the one studied by Gärdenfors (1988) at the axiomatic level. See Dubois, Lang & Prade, 1994 for details.

2.2 - Abductive Reasoning

Abductive reasoning is viewed as the task of retrieving plausible explanations of available observations on the basis of causal knowledge. Rules relating causes and manifestations are pervaded with exceptions and uncertainty. Sometimes it is possible to assess, at least qualitatively, the level of certainty with which a cause or a set of causes entail a manifestation. Then a rather simple approach can be proposed (under the hypothesis that there is only one failure at a time in the systems) which takes advantage of the level of certainty for rank-ordering the plausible explanation. See Cayrac et al. (1994) for instance. More generally the idea of parsimonious covering (Peng and Reggia, 1990) which look for explanations involving a minimal set of causes should be used. Lastly let us mention the fuzzy set approach first introduced by Sanchez, which does not deal with uncertainty strictly speaking but rather consider with which intensity a manifestation can be observed when a cause is present.

Assumption-based Truth Maintenance Systems (De Kleer, 1986) cope with incomplete information by explicitly handling assumptions under which conclusions can be derived. To this end some literals in the language are distinguished as being assumptions. Possibilistic logic offers a tool for reasoning with assumptions. It is based on the fact that in possibilistic logic a clause (¬h ∨ q, α) is semantically equivalent to the formula with a symbolic weight (q, min (α, t(h)) where t(h) is the (possibly unknown) truth value of h. The set of environments in which a proposition p is true can thus be calculated by putting all assumptions in the weight slots, carrying out possibilistic inference so as to derive p. The subsets of assumptions under which p is true with more or less certainty can be retrieved from the weight attached to p. This technique can be used to detect minimal inconsistent subsets of a propositional knowledge base and can be applied to diagnosis problems (see Benferhat et al., 1994). Diagnosis problems can be related to nonmonotonic reasoning also in the sense that, an abnormal exceptional state of affairs corresponding to a failure mode is found to be inconsistent with the usual course of things describing the generic behavior of the system to be diagnosed (consistency-based approach). See (Console and Torasso, 1991).

2.3 - Reasoning under Inconsistency

As already said, inconsistency can be encountered in different reasoning tasks, in particular:

- when reasoning with exception-tolerant generic knowledge, where the knowledge base includes default rules and instanciated facts, and later a new information is received that contradicts a plausible conclusion derived from the previous knowledge base;
- in abductive reasoning, for instance in model-based diagnosis, when observations conflict with the normal functioning mode of the system and the hypothesis that the components of the system are working well; this leads to diagnose what component(s) fail(s);
- when several consistent knowledge bases pertaining to the same domain, but coming from n different experts, are available. For instance, each expert is a reliable specialist in some aspect of the concerned domain but less reliable on other aspects. A straightforward way of building a global base Σ is to concatenate the knowledge bases K_i provided by each expert. Even if K_i is consistent, it is rather unlikely that $K_1 \cup K_2 \cup ... \cup K_n$ will be consistent also.

This subsection briefly discusses the treatment of inconsistency caused by the use of multiple sources of information. Reasoning under inconsistent pieces of information, although it requires to go out of the framework of classical logic in order to avoid triviality, has been considered for a long time in the literature by philosophers (e.g., Rescher and Manor, 1970), but is also of interest in combining knowledge bases (e.g., Baral et al., 1992). Then the syntactic appearance of the knowledge base is of primary importance (Nebel, 1991) since it is semantically inconsistent. In such problems, it is interesting to consider that knowledge bases are all stratified, namely that each formula in the knowledge base is associated with its level of certainty corresponding to the layer to which it belongs. The use of priorities among formulas has been shown to be very important to appropriately revise inconsistent knowledge bases (Fagin et al., 1983). In particular, Gärdenfors (1988) has proved that any revision process that satisfies natural requirements is implicitly based on priority ordering. In the context of merging several knowledge bases, the introduction of priorities between pieces of information in Σ can be explained by the two following scenarios:

- Each consistent knowledge base K_i, issued from a source of information, is "flat" (i.e., without any priority between their elements). But we have a total pre-ordering between the sources of information according to their reliability. In this case merging different sources of information lead to a prioritized knowledge base Σ, where the certainty level of each formula reflects the reliability of the source. A particular case is when each piece of information in Σ is supported by a different source.
- All sources of information are equally reliable (and thus have the same level of reliability), but inside each consistent knowledge base K_i there exists a preference

relation between pieces of information given by an expert, who rank-orders them according to their level of certainty. Here again, the combination of the different sources of information gives an uncertain knowledge base, provided that the scales of uncertainty used in each knowledge base K_j are commensurate.

The most elementary form of non-trivial entailment from an inconsistent prioritized knowledge base is possibilistic logic. On the basis of the stratified structure of the knowledge base, many other types of entailment can be proposed; see e.g., (Benferhat et al., 1995; Elvang-Goransson et al., 1993). These entailments are more powerful/adventurous than the possibilistic logic entailment which only consider the consistent part of the bases which is above the level of inconsistency. Several of these entailments are based on the notion of consistent argument (in favor of a conclusion) whose strength depends on the layer of the least certain formulas involved in the argument. An argumentative entailment may then be proposed which allows for the production of consequences for which the strongest argument pro is stronger than the strongest argument against. We may also think of attaching, to each formula in the base, a weight which reflects to what extent there exist arguments that support both the formula and its negation; such "paraconsistency" weight can then be propagated. See Benferhat et al. (1995) for details.

2.4 - Data Fusion

In numerical settings, the problem of combining pieces of evidence issued from several sources of information can be encountered in various fields of application, particularly in i) sensor fusion, i.e., when pieces of information coming from different sensors are to be aggregated, ii) multiple source interrogation systems where each of the sources can provide precise, imprecise or uncertain information about values of interest, iii) expert opinion pooling, when different individual statements have to be synthesized. Our basic claim is that there cannot be a unique mode of combination, which would be satisfactory in any situations, even when the framework for representing information is chosen.

Various combination problems exist, especially, i) preference aggregation versus information aggregation and ii) the combination of information coming from parallel sources versus the revision of already available information. In the preference aggregation problem it makes sense to find the opinion of the "average man" in an homogeneous group of individuals, to look for trade-offs between preferences, while on the contrary, if the information aggregation is a matter of truth and reliability, logical combinations are natural candidates. In this latter case conjunctive combinations apply when all the sources are reliable, while disjunctive combinations deal with the case of unreliable sources hidden in a group of other reliable ones. Obviously weighted logical combinations may be considered in particular when the sources are not equally reliable. Averaging operations in information aggregation can be justified when the set of sources can be viewed as a single random source producing different inputs. In that case, indeed, the set of data to be fused can be interpreted as standard statistics. For instance several successive measurements from a single sensor can be viewed as the result of a random experiment. Then the discrepancies between the sources can be explained in terms of random variability. However in the case of unique measurements issued from distinct sensors, or in the case of expert opinions, it is not clear that averaging combination modes make sense. Besides, the case of merging information from *parallel* sources should be distinguished from the problem of belief revision where sources do not play a symmetrical role. In the first situation, all the sources provide information simultaneously, while in the revision process there is a chronological ordering between the source which represents the present state of belief and the source which issues the new information. In each case the pooling obeys different requirements, for instance belief revision is generally not commutative; see Dubois and Prade (1994c).

2.5 - Interpolative Reasoning

Similarity is the basic tool in at least three cognitive tasks: classification, case-based reasoning and interpolation. In classification tasks, objects are put in the same class insofar as they are indistinguishable with respect to suitable criteria. Similarity is meant to describe indistinguishability, and an important limiting case is obtained using equivalence relations leading to the partitioning of a set of objects. Classification based on equivalence relations is done in the theory of rough sets (Pawlak, 1991). Case-based reasoning (Kolodner, 1993) exploits the similarity between already solved problems and a new problem to be solved in order to build up a solution to this new problem. When this solution to a new problem is obtained by adapting solutions to already solved problems, the reasoning methodology then comes close to a matter of interpolation, whereby the value of a partially unknown function at a given point of a space is estimated by exploiting the proximity of this point to other points for which the value of the function is known. Although interpolative inference is part of usual commonsense reasoning tasks, it has been seldom considered as amenable to logical settings, because it fundamentally relies on a gradual view of proximities that is absent from classical logic. In contrast, uncertain reasoning, which also involves gradual notions, has received a logical treatment. Results in nonmonotonic reasoning show that some form of uncertain reasoning can be captured by equipping the set of interpretations with an ordering structure expressing plausibility (Lehmann and Magidor, 1992; Shoham, 1988). It may be thus tempting to model interpolative reasoning by equipping a set of logical interpretations with a proximity structure.

This kind of investigation has been started by Ruspini (1991) with a view to cast fuzzy patterns of inference such as the generalized modus ponens of Zadeh (1979) into a logical setting. Indeed in the scope of similarity modeling, a basic reasoning pattern can be expressed informally as follows,

p is close to being true; p approximately implies q $\vdash$ q is not far from being true

where "close", "approximately", and "not far" refer to the similarity relation S, while p and q are classical propositions. This pattern expresses an *extrapolative syllogism*, and is in accordance with the generalized modus ponens of Zadeh. An example of situation where this type of inference pattern looks natural is the following. Consider the expert advice in finance: "if you have saved more than 10.000 $ (p) then you should invest 50 % of your capital". Suppose you have 9.500 $ (p'). Using classical logic, p' $\not\vdash$ p, and thus p' $\land$ (p $\rightarrow$ q) $\not\vdash$ q. But in practice people would not wait to reach the 10.000 $ threshold and would start investing some percentage of their savings, all the closer to 50 % as these savings amount to near 10.000 $. In that case the similarity stems from the metric structure equipping the monetary scale.

This type of reasoning is at work in fuzzy control applications, albeit without clear logical foundations. Klawonn and Kruse (1993) have shown that a set of fuzzy rules can be viewed as a set of crisp rules along with a set of similarity relations. Moreover an interpolation-dedicated fuzzy rule 'if is A then Y is B" can be understood as "the more x is A the more Y is B" and the corresponding inference means that if $X = x$ and $\alpha = \mu_A(x)$ then Y lies in the level cut B_α. When two rules are at work, such that $\alpha_1 = \mu_{A_1}(x)$, $\alpha_2 = \mu_{A_2}(x)$, then the conclusion $Y \in (B_1)_{\alpha_1} \cap (B_2)_{\alpha_2}$ lies between the cores of B_1 and B_2, i.e., on ordered universes, an interpolation effect is obtained. It can be proved that Sugeno's fuzzy reasoning method for control can be cast in this framework (Dubois, Grabisch, Prade, 1994). More generally interpolation is clearly a kind of reasoning based on similarity (rather than uncertainty) and it should be related to current research on similarity logics (Dubois et al., 1995). More generally similarity relations and fuzzy interpolation methods should impact on current research in case-based reasoning.

The long term perspective of such a line of research could be to provide logical foundations to some forms of "fuzzy logic", and also case-based reasoning where similarity plays a basic role. The idea would be to start from a set of conditional statements of the form "p is not far from implying q", that forms a conditional similarity-oriented knowledge base given by a domain expert, and to reconstruct an underlying, "least committed", similarity measure, using the characteristic axioms of a similarity-based inference machinery, by analogy to the treatment of conditional knowledge bases in nonmonotonic reasoning.

2.6 - Decision and Artificial Intelligence

Decision theory has been mainly developed in economy and in operations research for a long time. It is only recently that decision under uncertainty is become a topic of interest in Artificial Intelligence, especially among people interested in planning. However we may foresee a richer complementarity between the two fields. In this section, we point out two examples illustrating this view.

Recently, Gilboa and Schmeidler (1992) have advocated a similarity-based approach to decision where a case is described taking inspiration from case-based reasoning, as a triple (situation, act, result) and where a decision-maker's utility function u assigns a numerical value u(r) to a result r. When faced with a new situation s_0, the decision-maker is supposed to choose an act which maximizes a counterpart of classical expected utility used in decision under uncertainty, namely

$$U_{s_0,M}(a) = \Sigma_{(s,a,r) \in M}\, S(s_0,s) \cdot u(r)$$

where S is a non-negative function which estimates the similarity of situations, here the similarity of the current situation s_0 against already encountered ones stored in the repertory set M.

It is worth noticing that this similarity-based utility looks like Sugeno's computation of the command to perform in a fuzzy controller. Indeed both expressions use an interpolation mechanism, but for solving a different problem. A set of rules "if X is $A^{(i)}$ then $Y = b^{(i)}$" i = 1,n à la Sugeno can be equivalently viewed as a set of pairs (situation, result) = $(a^{(i)}, b^{(i)})$ equipped with a similarity relation S, provided that $\forall i$, $A^{(i)} = \{a^{(i)}\} \circ S$. In Sugeno's approach the notion of result and utility of result are not distinguished, or if we prefer all the "results" $b^{(i)}$ have the same utility. What plays the role of an action in the sense of Gilboa and Schmeidler, is here the fact itself of applying the set of fuzzy rules, which explains why there is no maximization in Sugeno's approach. The similarity-based utility is perhaps more akin to the fuzzy vote procedure proposed in Bensana et al. (1988) for selecting a (scheduling) decision b in a situation x from a set of rules "if X is $A^{(i)}$ then $Y = b^{(i)}$ with weight $w^{(i)}$" ($w^{(i)}$ can be viewed as the utility of the result of the rule), by maximizing an index of the form $U(b) = \Sigma_{i:b=b}(i) \mu_{A}(i)(x) * w^{(i)}$.

Another line of research is to design a logical machinery able to compute the best decision in a given situation, according to some normative theoretical framework. Possibility theory offers such a framework where both inference and decision under uncertainty can be captured. Indeed a counterpart to von Neumann and Morgenstern' expected utility theory has been proposed in the framework of possibility theory. The existence of a utility function, representing a preference ordering among possibility distributions (on the consequences of decision-maker's actions) that satisfies a series of axioms pertaining to decision-maker's behavior, has been established (Dubois and Prade, 1995b). The obtained utility is a generalization of Wald's criterion, which is recovered in case of total ignorance; when ignorance is only partial, the utility takes into account the fact that some situations are more plausible than others. Mathematically, the qualitative utility is nothing but the necessity measure of a fuzzy event in the sense of possibility theory (a so-called Sugeno integral). The possibilistic representation of uncertainty, which only requires a linearly ordered scale, is qualitative in nature. Only max, min and order-reversing operations are used on the scale. The axioms express a risk-averse behavior of the decision maker and correspond to a pessimistic view of what may happen. The proposed qualitative utility function is currently used in flexible constraint satisfaction problems under incomplete information.

It can also be used in association with possibilistic logic, which is tailored to reasoning under incomplete states of knowledge. A crucial point in decision theory is to make a clear difference between knowledge about the world and decision maker's preferences. We have seen that default or uncertain conditional knowledge can be represented in the framework of possibilistic logic. Similarly, more or less preferred states associated with different levels of priority can be also represented by possibilistic formulas, since necessity measures capture both the ideas of certainty and priority. Indeed a constraint is less prioritary in as much it is possible to violate it; this idea has been extensively used when extending the Constraint Satisfaction Problem framework to flexible constraints having different levels of priority (Dubois, Fargier and Prade, 1994). Thus we build two possibilistic logic bases, one for the knowledge about the world and one for the preferences. Possible decisions correspond to literals that can be fixed to true or false by the decision-maker. Then, we are looking for the decision(s) which are such that, when added to the knowledge base describing what is known about the world, it entails that the preferred states are satisfied. In possibilistic logic this entailment becomes a matter of degree and corresponds to the pessimistic view, risk-averse point of view captured by the qualitative utility function built in the framework of possibility theory. An optimistic point of view would only require the consistency of the knowledge base to which the decision is added, with the set of formulas expressing the preferences.

2.7 - Updating

One of the most challenging problems in databases and knowledge-based systems is that of modifying a knowledge base under the arrival of a new piece of information. Basically, if the new information contradicts the contents of the knowledge base, there exists several ways of restoring consistency, unless strict guidelines are supplied that lead to a unique solution. An important distinction has been drawn by Katsuno and Mendelzon (1991) between revising a knowledge base and updating it. In revision, the new information is meant to improve our cognitive state regarding a given situation; what was plausibly thought as being true may actually be false. In updating, the new information is meant to inform the knowledge base that something has changed in the actual world; what was thought to be true may no longer be true because things have changed.

In order to discuss the problem of updating a knowledge base describing the behaviour of an evolving system, it would be fruitful to unify three points of view on this problem: the point of view of the system analyst who describes the evolution of a system via a transition graph between states, the point of view of formal philosophers who have laid bare the postulates of rational updating, and the point of view of database research, where the update is achieved at the syntactic level by means of transition constraints (e.g., Cholvy, 1994). Such transition constraints partially determine a transition graph between states of the system. Such a graph can be viewed as a possibilistic Markov chain (Dubois et al., 1995). The same observation can be derived from Katsuno and Mendelzon's postulates, except that the obtained transition graph underlies an inertia property.

3 - Concluding Remarks — Going From Theory to Practice

In this paper, different forms of reasoning which can be considered as approximate or commonsense reasoning have been surveyed. The role played by the ideas of uncertainty, preference and similarity has been emphasized. These notions are naturally a matter of degree. However it seems reasonable to use in practice models which are as qualitative as possible, i.e., to use ordinal scales for graded uncertainty, preference or similarity (except if the available data allows for a less qualitative representation). Possibility theory and fuzzy sets can be used in this spirit.

Although considerable progress have been made in the last twenty years in the modelling of approximate and commonsense reasoning, important issues still need to be investigated before developing applications on a large scale. Some of these directions of research have already been pointed out in the main part of the paper. Let us briefly mention two others.

Concerning reasoning with rules having exceptions: all the considered approaches suffer from the same limitations regarding the blocking of property inheritance problem (a subclass cannot inherit any property of a superclass as soon as the subclass is already exceptional with respect to one property of the superclass). A possible way for overcoming this problem is to add pieces of conditional independence information of the form "in the context α, accepting β has no influence on accepting γ". This kind of information can be represented in the possibility theory framework by adding constraints which are of the same form as the constraints modelling default rules; see (Benferhat et al., 1994), and (Delgrande and Pelletier, 1994) for a related proposal. Expressing independence information may be the right way to get conclusions which are in agreement with intuitions. Another important issue for practical applications is the validation of knowledge bases: this applies for any kind of non-standard knowledge base: default conditional base, fuzzy rules base, etc.

References

Adams E.W. (1975) The logic of conditionals. D. Reidel, Dordrecht.

Baral C., Kraus S., Minker J., Subrahmanian V.S. (1992) Combining knowledge bases consisting in first order theories. Computational Intelligence, 8(1), 45-71.

Bellman R., Kalaba L., Zadeh L.A. (1966) Abstraction and pattern classification. J. Math. Anal. & Appl., 13, 1-7.

Bellman R., Zadeh L.A. (1970) Decision making in a fuzzy environement. Management Science, 17, B141-B164.

Benferhat S., Dubois D., Lang J., Prade H. (1994) Hypothetical reasoning in possibilistic logic: basic notions, applications and implementation issues. In: Between Mind and Computer (P.Z. Wang, K.F. Loe, eds.), World Scientific Publ., 1-29.

Benferhat S., Dubois D., Prade H. (1992) Representing default rules in possibilistic logic. Proc. 3rd Inter. Conf. on Principles of Knowledge Representation and Reasoning (KR'92), Cambridge, MA, Oct. 26-29, 673-684.

Benferhat S., Dubois D., Prade H. (1994) Expressing independence in a possibilistic framework and its application to default reasoning. Proc. ECAI'94, 150-154.

Benferhat S., Dubois D., Prade H. (1995) How to infer from inconsistent beliefs without revising? Proc. IJCAI'95, Montréal, Canada, Aug. 20-25, 1449-1455.

Bensana E., Bel G., Dubois D. (1988) OPAL: A multi-knowledge-based system for industrial job-shop scheduling. Int. J. Prod. Res., 26, 795-819.

Boutilier C., Goldszmidt M. (1993) Revision by conditional beliefs. Proc. AAAI'93, July 11-15, 649-654.

Cayrac D., Dubois D., Haziza M., Prade H. (1994) Possibility theory in "fault mode effect analyses" —A satellite fault diagnosis application—. Proc. of the IEEE World Cong. on Computational Intelligence, Orlando, FL, June 26-July 2, 1176-1181.

Cholvy L. (1994) Database updates and transition constraints. Int. J. Intelligent Systems, 9, 169-180.

Console L., Torasso P. (1991) A spectrum of logical definitions of model-based diagnosis. Computational Intelligence, 7(3), 133-141.

De Kleer J. (1986) 'An assumption-based TMS' and 'Extending the ATMS'. Artificial Intelligence, 28, 127-196.

Delgrande J., Pelletier F.J. (1994) A formal to relevance. Proc. 1994 Fall Symp., New Orleans, Louisiana, Nov. 4-6, 1994, AAAI Press, 40-43.

Dubois D., Dupin de Saint-Cyr F., Prade H. (1995) Updating, transition constraints and possibilistic Markov chains. In: Advances in Intelligent Computing — IPMU'94 (B. Bouchon-Meunier et al., eds.), LNCS, Vol. 945, Springer Verlag, Berlin, 263-272

Dubois D., Esteva F., Garcia P., Godo L., Prade H. (1995) Similarity-based consequence relations. In: Symbolic and Quantitative Approaches to Reasoning and Uncertainty (Proc. ECSQARU'95, 1995) (C. Froidevaux, J. Kohlas, eds.), Springer Verlag, 171-179.

Dubois D., Fargier H., Prade H. (1994) Propagation and satisfaction of flexible constraints. In: Fuzzy Sets, Neural Networks and Soft Computing (R.R. Yager, L.A. Zadeh, eds.), Van Nostrand Reinhold, New York, 166-187.

Dubois D., Grabisch M., Prade H. (1994) Gradual rules and the approximation of control laws. In: Theoretical Aspects of Fuzzy Control (H.T. Nguyen et al., eds.), Wiley, New York, 147-181.

Dubois D., Lang J., Prade H. (1994) Possibilistic logic. In: Handbook of Logic in Artificial Intelligence and Logic Programming, Vol. 3 (D.M. Gabbay et al., eds.), Oxford University Press, 439-513.

Dubois D., Prade H. (1988) Possibility Theory. Plenum Press, New York.

Dubois D., Prade H. (1992) Fuzzy rules in knowledge-based systems. In: An Introduction to Fuzzy Logic Applications in Intelligent Syst. (R.R. Yager, L.A. Zadeh, eds.), 45-68.

Dubois D., Prade H. (1994a) Non-standard theories of uncertainty in knowledge representation and reasoning. Proc. 4th Inter. Conf. on Principles of Knowledge

Representation and Reasoning (J. Doyle et al., eds.), Bonn, 1994, 634-645. Revised version in: The Knowledge Engineering Review, 9, 1994, 399-416.

Dubois D., Prade H. (1994b) Conditional objects as nonmonotonic consequence relationships. IEEE Trans. on Systems, Man and Cybernetics, 24(12), 1724-1740.

Dubois D., Prade H. (1994c) Possibility theory and data fusion in poorly informed environments. Control Engineering Practice, 2(5), 811-823.

Dubois D., Prade H. (1995a) Conditional objects, possibiliy theory and default rules. In: Conditionals : From Philosophy to Computer Sciences (G. Crocco et al., eds.), Oxford University Press, 311-346.

Dubois D., Prade H. (1995b) Possibility theory as a basis for qualitative decision theory. Proc. 14th Inter. Joint Conf. on Artificial Intellig. (IJCAI'95), Montréal, 1924-1930.

Dubois D., Prade H., Smets P. (1995) Representing partial ignorance. IEEE Trans. on Systems, Man and Cybernetics, to appear.

Elvang-Goransson M., Krause P., Fox J. (1993) Dialectic reasoning with inconsistent information. Proc. 9th Conf. on Uncertainty in Artificial Intelligence (D. Heckerman, A. Mamdani, eds.), 114-121.

Fagin R., Ullman J.D., Vardi M.Y. (1983) On the semantics of updates in database. Proc. 2nd ACM SIGACT-SIGMOD Symp. on the Principles of Databases Systems, 352-365.

Gabbay D.M. (1985) Theoretical foundations for non-monotonic reasoning in expert systems. In: Logics and models of Concurrent Systems (K.R. Apt, ed.), 439-457.

Gärdenfors P. (1988) Knowledge in Flux. The MIT Press, Cambridge, MA.

Gärdenfors P., Makinson D. (1994) Nonmonotonic inference based on expectations. Artificial Intelligence, 65, 197-245.

Gilboa I., Schmeidler D. (1992) Case-based decision theory. Discussion Paper No. 994, Northwestern University. Revised, 1993.

Goodman I.R., Nguyen H.T., Walker E.A. (1991) Conditional Inference and Logic For Intelligent Systems. North-Holland, Amsterdam.

Katsuno H., Mendelzon A.O. (1991) On the difference between updating a knowledge base and revising it. Proc. 2nd Conf. on Principles of Knowledge Representation and Reasoning (KR'91) (J. Allen et al., eds.), Cambridge, MA, 387-394.

Klawonn F., Kruse R. (1993) Equality relations as a basis for fuzzy control. Fuzzy Sets and Systems, 54, 147-156.

Kolodner J. (1993) Case-Based Reasoning. Morgan and Kaufmann, San Francisco, CA.

Kraus S., Lehmann D., Magidor M. (1990) Nonmonotonic reasoning, preferential models and cumulative logics. Artificial Intelligence, 44, 167-207.

Lehmann D., Magidor M. (1992) What does a conditional knowledge base entail? Artificial Intelligence, 55(1), 1-60.

Nebel B. (1991) Belief revision and default reasoning: Syntax-based approaches. Proc. 2nd Inter. Conf. on Principles of Knowledge Representation and Reasoning (J. Allen et al., eds.), Cambridge, MA, April 22-25, 114-121.

Pawlak Z. (1991) Rough Sets — Theoretical Aspects of Reasoning about Data. Kluwer Academic Publ., Dordrecht.

Pearl J. (1988) Probabilistic Reasoning in Intelligent Systems. Morgan & Kaufmann.

Pearl J. (1990) System Z: a natural ordering of defaults with tractable applications to default reasoning. Proc. 3rd Conf. on the Theoretical Aspects of Reasonig About Knowledge (TARK'90), Morgan and Kaufmann, San Mateo, CA, 121-135.

Peng Y., Reggia (1990) Abductive Inference Models for Diagnostic Problem-Solving. Springer Verlag, New York.

Rescher N., Manor R. (1970) On inference from inconsistent premises. Theory and Decision, 1, 179-219.

Ruspini E. (1991) On the semantics of fuzzy logic. Int. J. Approx. Reasoning, 5, 45-88.

Sanchez E. (1977) Solutions in conposite fuzzy relations equations — Application to medical diagnosis in Brouwerian logic. In: Fuzzy Automated and Decision Processes (M.M. Gupta et al., eds.) North-Holland, 221-234.

Shoham Y. (1988) Reasoning about Change. The MIT Press, Cambridge, MA.

Zadeh L.A. (1978) Fuzzy sets as a basis for a theory of possibility. Fuzzy Sets & Systems, 1, 3-28.

Zadeh L.A. (1979) A theory of approximate reasoning. In: Machine Intelligence, Vol. 9 (J.E. Hayes, D. Michie, L.I. Mikulich, eds.), Elsevier, New York, 149-194.

Cooperative Information Systems Engineering

Matthias Jarke, Manfred A. Jeusfeld, Peter Peters, Peter Szczurko
Informatik V, RWTH Aachen
Ahornstr. 55, 52056 Aachen, Germany
e-mail: {jarke,jeusfeld,peters,szczurko}@informatik.rwth-aachen.de

Abstract:
Cooperative information systems (CIS) aim at *continued cooperativity* between user groups through componentized networks of information systems. Change management is therefore a definitional part of CIS. We advocate a conceptual modeling strategy for addressing this task, and illustrate it with experiences gained in WibQuS, a project aimed at CIS support for Total Quality Management in manufacturing organizations. These experiences emphasize the role of meta models in focusing the change process. Specific meta models and supporting environments are presented for : cooperative business process modeling in distributed organizations; simulation analysis of short-term and long-term effects of information flow designs; forward and reverse mappings between a distributed (relational) system interoperability layer and the information flow model. Models are not just analyzed at change time, but also support planned and unplanned information flows at runtime.

1 Cooperative Information Systems and the WibQuS Project

Information systems have traditionally been characterized as hardware/software/people *systems* that maintain data about a specific *subject domain* for one or more *users*, sometimes within a formal organization. The database community has dedicated much work to subject domain modeling (e.g. relational, object-oriented and semantic data models) and efficient systems implementation (e.g. query processing, concurrency control, and recovery).

Relatively less attention has been paid to the usage side, both at the system level of user interface research and at the design level of modeling usage by individuals, teams, and formal organizations. Recently, this has begun to change due to massive complaints by user organizations that their central needs are not being adequately addressed by information technology.

One of the responses raising to this challenge is the vision of *cooperative information systems* (CIS [3, 10, 5]) which see information systems as a communications medium among user groups in and across organizations. On one hand, this brings groupware and organizational research into the information systems fields. On the

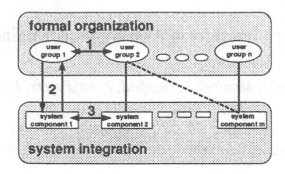

Fig. 1 Static structure of CIS

other, it changes conventional database wisdoms about the required information modeling, system implementation and integration technologies.

A CIS is a layered network of user and system components as sketched in figure 1. At the *system level*, we observe a trend towards componentization of software (including the 'wrapping' of legacy software) into small and easily re-configurable objects. Coordination between these units is no longer hardcoded in applications but dynamically achieved by workflow mechanisms.

At the *usage level*, we observe very similar phenomena. Formal organizations are being decomposed into small autonomous units with market-oriented rather than hierarchical coordination [17]. Each of these units have their own local information systems configuration, either from new or from legacy components. But they may also be customers or suppliers of other units with respect to information services. Thus, in a CIS, we have necessary interactions between user groups, between system components, between user groups and system components, and – most importantly for us – between user groups *through* system components.

Why is all this happening? The answer – at both levels – is *reactiveness to change* [8, 30]. Organizations have to react quickly to ever-changing market requirements. System technology has to react quickly to organizational change as well as technical innovation. Hierarchies have turned out to be too clumsy, therefore the trend towards small largely autonomous units that can react quickly.

Total Quality Management (TQM) is one of several business philosophies that can be associated with this trend. It aims at continuous improvement of all processes in a company by emphasizing customer orientation throughout, relying on local ideas and improvement initiatives, propagated through the organization via cleverly designed feedback cycles. Therefore, TQM appears as a prototypical example of a (not necessarily computerized) CIS.

The question of how to design and implement such CIS was investigated since 1992 by a consortium of five German engineering centers, an organizational science group, and ourselves in a project called WibQuS[1] [13]. Figure 2 shows how the CIS levels are instantiated in TQM [28].

---

1   WibQuS is the German abbreviation "Knowledge-based Systems in Quality Management"

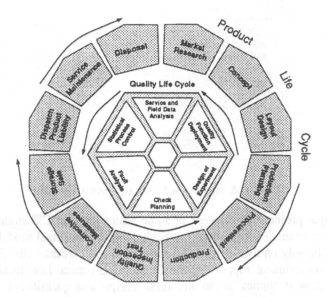

Fig. 2 The quality life cycle as a CIS

The outer circle of product life cycle stages corresponds to the organization part of figure 1. Traditionally, the stages have been associated with different departments or companies, each with their local IT solution. Due to business process orientation, the forward flow of task information is now reasonably under control. However, the feedback loop around the whole cycle takes too much time for companies to stay competitive. The idea of TQM is to introduce smaller feedback cycles that provide selected information about particular quality issues in the backward direction, thus enabling rapid and continuous improvement. This so-called *quality cycle* can be supported by additional local methods and software tools as shown in the inner part of figure 2, which corresponds to the system half of figure 1.

Broadcasting all quality information to everyone will quickly overwhelm and turn off users. The goal of our work in WibQuS was therefore to develop a set of methods and tools which would help companies *analyze possible information flows, estimate the impact of different information flow designs, and provide different degrees of operational information flow support for planned and unplanned information flows wrt. the chosen strategies.* Since quality problems are constantly changing, the interplay of all these tasks must be organized in a way that makes change as easy as possible.

Obviously, this was a tall order. We do not claim that we have solved all of the issues involved. To get anywhere, some hopefully not too unrealistic simplifications were made. Most importantly, the system integration layer was based on distributed relational databases. Thus, system interoperability problems were reduced to making the major RDB products interoperate[2]. Despite such limitations, we hope that some general lessons for CIS can be drawn from this experience.

---

[2]   Subsystems did use SYBASE, ORACLE, and INFORMIX databases which turned out to be enough of a challenge to integrate in the easily reconfigurable way we wanted.

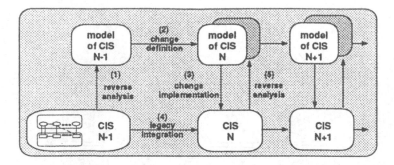

Fig. 3 A model-based change process for CIS

This paper presents an overview of some issues faced in CIS engineering, using WibQuS as an example. In section 2, we advocate a conceptual modeling approach which relies heavily on *user-definable meta models* to coordinate distributed change, and discuss its technical support by the ConceptBase meta data manager. Section 3 describes how it applies in the structural design and quantitative evaluation of organizational information flows while section 4 discusses the mapping to the system level. Section 5 lists some limitations and summarizes ongoing work.

2 Change Management through Conceptual Models

2.1 A Basic Change Process for CIS

Even if the organization is federated, the units must still be coordinated such that they move towards common goals and, more importantly, that adaptation to *changing* goals is always possible. Given that coordination mechanisms should be loose and market-like, how can we create the necessary market infrastructure and force fields that let the organization drift in the direction management and customers want?

Our solution is based on *conceptual modeling* (figure 3). It is a generalization of the task-artefact cycle for user interface design [4] : you (1) reverse-engineer the rationale from the existing man-machine system into a conceptual model, then (2) analyze a proposed change conceptually, finally (3) implement the agreed change, (4) taking into account the existing legacy context. Then the cycle repeats, *ad infinitum*.

There are different ways how to manage the change cycle. One of the commercially most successful is the ARIS/SAP approach [29]. You start with an ARIS reference model for the business process and customize it to your specific situation. Each component of the reference model is linked to a parameterized SAP software component. Your software system is largely configured by parameter tuning.

Where feasible, this approach has been shown to reduce IS development costs by up to 80%. However, the feasibility obviously depends on the coverage of the reference model and, in particular, on the regularity of the business process itself. In more complex cooperative settings which include creative aspects, it either does not cover much of the required information flows, or tends to over-constrain user cooperation.

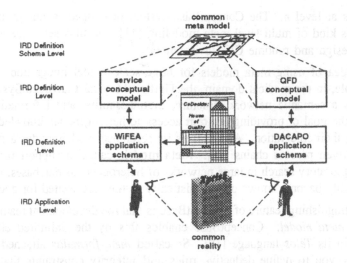

Fig. 4 Integrating different business views with meta models and CoDecide

Structuration theory [23] gives one possible explanation for these observations. According to this theory, organizational structure and organizational change are inextricably linked. If you want a structured operational workflow, a centrally driven reference model adaptation process will work well. If you want a distributed CIS, your design approach also needs to be distributed and cooperative. Moreover, if you want to support organizational change, your models of reality must necessarily reflect the purpose of the change. In figure 3, the reverse-engineering therefore link goes back to a revised version of the model from which the system was initially constructed. In other words, the change cycle actually does *not* start with step (1) but with an initial vision of step (2), the intended change. In previous work, we have expressed this idea by defining requirements engineering as 'the process of establishing a vision in the existing technical, cognitive, and social context' [14].

2.2 Meta Modeling Support in ConceptBase

In WibQuS, *user-defined meta models* serve as the 'compass' which keeps the distributed change process aligned with the vision. To illustrate, figure 4 shows how designers of two WibQuS applications (WiFEA support for service technicians and DACAPO for quality function deployment) are coordinated in defining their viewpoints of the same corporate reality [12] – step (1) in figure 3. They abstract their observations of reality into local application models using their own conceptual notation. These notations are further abstracted into a common meta model which is defined jointly by the owners of the notations and then serves as a basis for communication about the coherence of different models.

To indicate how this can be supported by a repository, the left of the figure relates the picture to the levels of the ISO Information Resource Dictionary Standard [9]. In IRDS, the concepts on level *n+1* (the defining level) constitute a type system for level *n* (the defined level). A sub-repository at level *n+1* can thus coordinate subsystems at level *n*. The ConceptBase system developed in our group supports exactly this kind of multi-level meta modeling [11], and thus serves as an mediator between design and runtime CIS environment.

The idea of using meta models for large-scale model integration is not new. For example, in the medical domain, the Unified Medical Language System UMLS [20] offers a semantic network structure, metathesaurus, and information sources map with the goal of providing uniform access to heterogeneous knowledge sources and aiding their integration. ARIS offers its reference models under a meta model of event-driven process chains [29]. Meta models can also support runtime tasks such as exploratory search in large networks of heterogeneous databases, where node schemata only become known opportunistically as they are visited for querying [24].

A distinguishing feature of ConceptBase is that the development team can define *their own meta model*. ConceptBase enables this by the unlimited classification hierarchy in its *Telos* language [19]. So-called *meta formulas* attached to a meta class allow you to define deductive rules and integrity constraints that specialize automatically to each class which is an instance of this meta class. The thus specialized formulas then apply to the instances of these classes. This makes meta formulas robust with respect to notational variations and is a good means for conflict analysis across heterogeneous representations or worldviews.

The common language defined in the meta model alone is usually not enough to ensure coherence of distributed modeling. It is therefore augmented with additional conflict analysis and negotiation support tools which are defined at the same level as the methods and tools they try to relate. In ConceptBase, they are specialized automatically or configured semi-automatically from two generic instruments defined with the meta model: query classes and matrix-based visualizations.

Query classes are parameterized and possibly materialized views defined by necessary and sufficient membership constraints similar to description logics [2]. They defer the checking of consistency and completeness of the perspectives generated by parallel development to a moment definable by the teams themselves. Usually, a large number of query classes can be associated with a meta model and later applied in the negotiations between the modeling teams whose modeling work is based on this meta model[3].

CoDecide is a visualization toolkit for conflict analysis [12]. A CoDecide shows interrelationships between submodels via one or more matrix representations. The toolkit approach allows modelers to quickly develop specialized visualizations for particular kinds of conflicts. Different synchronization styles, ranging from fully shared editing to asynchronous cooperation with partial visibility of mutual views can be supported. A standard example of a conflict visualization interface based on CoDecide is the so-called 'House of Quality' shown in the middle of figure 4 which offers a comprehensive visualization of the interrelationships within and between two parties, plus some external context such as versions or competing solutions.

---

[3] In a commercial analysis environment based on ConceptBase, about 80 such query classes were identified to uncover analysis errors, differences in opinion, and problems of the business process [21].

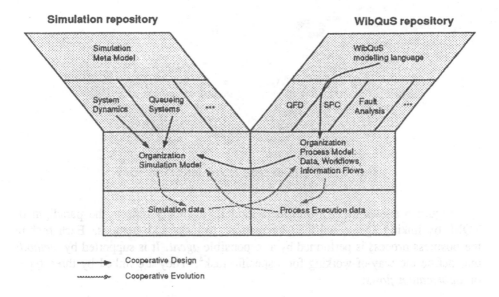

Fig. 5 CIS design and simulation process based on meta modeling

3 Designing and Simulating CIS Information Flows

In this section, we discuss the change management process at the level of organizational information flows. Here, meta models firstly help to link the analysis step (1) in figure 3 with step (2), and secondly to identify suitable design choices by simulation in the transition from step (2) to step (3).

Figure 5 shows the interplay of meta models for these tasks.. On the right branch, starting from the *WibQuS meta model*, organizational quality management process models are coordinated using reference method models at the second level. These process models are mapped to a multi-simulation model (left branch) which is itself based on interoperability between different simulation methods defined through a *simulation meta model*. The interplay of simulation and actual process allows ongoing evolution of the distributed organizational knowledge base: the observation of real processes leads to changes of the simulation model which in turn indicates necessary changes of the organizational process structure. In the remainder of this section, we discuss the two branches in more detail.

3.1 Cooperative Modeling of Information Flows

There is usually a large conceptual and spatial distance among the different groups involved in CIS design and use. This distance needs to be bridged to some degree before a successful modeling process can start. The modeling process does not aim at generic mutual understanding but has a *specific purpose*. Only after some agreement on this purpose has been reached, distributed modeling should start. Much of the purpose can be coded in a *business process meta model* that defines the language in which modelers communicate about models and model interactions.

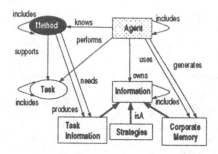

Fig. 6 The WibQuS meta model for CIS in TQM

Figure 6 shows the WibQuS meta model. It clearly reflects the paradigm of TQM, by linking agents and their interactions to tasks and methods. Each *task* in the business process is performed by a responsible *agent*. It is supported by *methods* that define the way-of-working for a specific task[4]. They are linked by three types of *information flows*:

1. *Task information* drives and monitors the operational business processes. It is provided and consumed by the methods along the process chain.
2. *Corporate memory* is important organizational knowledge about products and processes that results from accumulated execution and analysis of business processes. It is generated and used by the agent that performs the task.
3. The goal of a *strategy* is the definition of a common context according to which tasks are organized and information is interpreted. This is reflected in the meta model itself.

The development and application of this meta model in WibQuS comprised three phases. The *first phase* was the joint design of the meta model itself. These negotiations proved a useful investment because they gave the teams a shared ontology for future cooperation. In the *second phase*, the six engineering teams developed models of the different methods by parallel instantiation of the modeling language making use of the client-server architecture of ConceptBase. The *third phase*, partially overlapping with the second one, consisted of negotiations to ensure coherence between the models. In addition to the tools mentioned in section 2.2, a discussion structure based on the IBIS model represented subjective conflicts that could not be expressed in terms of inconsistency or incompleteness of the model itself. At the end, query classes were used to vote on the still unclear concepts.

The end result was a network of almost 600 Telos classes which constituted the first formal model of the quality cycle in manufacturing enterprises. Quantitative analyses of data flow and organizational learning, as well as mappings to the system level, were piggybacked on this conceptual infrastructure.

---

4   Methods and tasks form an AND/OR decomposition structure: a task can be supported by one or several methods while a method consists of a partial order over subtasks.

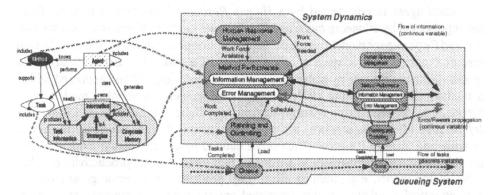

Fig. 7 Mapping of the conceptual to the simulation model

3.2 Analyzing Information Flows By Multi-Simulation

Each of the information flow categories must be analyzed according to different criteria and with different quantitative modeling techniques. The analysis of task information is driven by its transaction costs, its timeliness, and its completeness. The exchange of corporate memory is analyzed to find out its long term effects on quality, flexibility, or personnel qualification.

Task information criteria describe short-term, local effects which relate directly to the business process. The analysis of such criteria is usually performed by Petri-Net or Queuing System simulation [6; 22].

The analysis of *corporate memory* is much harder, because its effects are related to long-term feedback loops within an organization: information has to be accumulated, condensed and then transferred to the organizational units where its effects are supposed to happen. These processes are not just related to the task workflows and cannot be measured by hard business variables like time and money, but by *the way they influence* the variables that produce those time-and-money effects. In his work on software project dynamics, Abdel-Hamid [1] showed that System Dynamics simulation is well-suited for such tasks. We generalized his model to the case of multiple interacting organizational units with explicit information flow management and error propagation models [25].

In addition, information flow planning in CIS requires modeling the *interplay* between the short-term and long-term effects. At the system level, this implies a *heterogeneous simulation* by interoperating discrete (Queueing Systems) and continuous (System Dynamics) simulation techniques. Fishwick recently showed that every quasi-continuous simulation technique can be mapped to a discrete-event technique if the time increment is sufficiently small [7]. Our MultiSim environment generalizes this idea to a graphical simulation definition and execution environment [27].

The kernel of MultiSim is a ConceptBase *repository for simulation techniques*. We developed a definition language for simulation techniques by which simulation languages like SD, Queueing Systems, or Petri-Nets can be modelled and connected. We do not show this meta model directly but rather the mapping between its major submodels and the WibQuS meta model constructs (figure 7).

Each *agent* is represented by a *Human Resource Management* model. *Tasks* are represented by *Planning and Controlling/Queue* models. *Methods* are mapped on *Method Performance* models which describe how manpower made available by human resource management is spent on various parts of a task. The *Error Management* module analyzes the rate by which errors are generated, detected and reworked within a method and the resulting effort in needed manpower. A variable models error propagation between Error Management models along the business process. The *Information Management* model describes the amount of work necessary to access, provide and manage the information flows defined in the conceptual model. It also provides the corporate memory as a resource that influences the productivity of other tasks in the model, e.g. training effort, task productivity, or error generation. A first empirical validation of this integrated environment in a business process re-engineering project for a manufacturing company showed a surprisingly good match between model and reality [27].

4 Operational Support for CIS Information Flows

The cooperative modeling process identifies *possible information flows* while the multi-simulation approach helps the organization evaluate which of these should be *specifically facilitated*. These choices can be *implemented* by linking certain views on the conceptual model to the system level, a federated network of relational databases. This supports the integration of steps (3) and (4) in figure 3. The mappings are maintained in a *Quality Trader* which was implemented by linking ConceptBase to the Sybase OMNI-SQL gateway for distributed execution, and a relational database for maintaining temporary exchange data such as contract status.

Three kinds of mappings are derived from the WibQuS meta model. The 'owns' link in figure 6 is mapped to ownership of database nodes. This partitioning is often given and must simply be recorded as a dependency link in the meta database. Section 4.1 shows how the conceptual structure of task and memory information is related to the underlying database schemata; this allows users to make *unplanned information searches* in a browser-based environment. *Planned information flows* are mapped to stored queries and workflow structures (section 4.2) which are more efficient to use but more difficult to change than the unplanned ones.

4.1 Mappings Between Concept and System Layer

Task information flows were defined in a subset of Telos that is basically an extended Entity-Relationship language. Many techniques exist how to map such models to efficient relational schemas; the reverse mapping, how to extract conceptual models from existing relational databases, has also been studied. Since both questions are equally relevant in the CIS context, we developed a *symmetric approach* where the mapping in both directions is constrained by the same meta model [16]. In figure 8, the organization level of figure 1 is shown to the right, the system level to the left. Steps (1)-(5) sketch how, as an example, reverse-modeling is driven by the lowest common ancestor of the meta classes of which the two concepts that have to be mapped, are

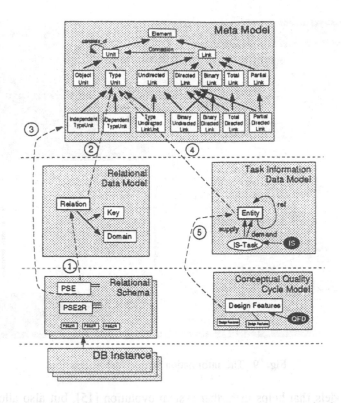

Fig. 8 Meta model constraining the mapping between concepts and relations

instances. Since the expressiveness of both formalisms is not the same, the process is partially interactive (steps 3 and 5) : reverse mapping demands a semantic enrichment whereas forward mapping demands performance-oriented design choices.

CIS engineering uses neither of these directions throughout but demands a sophisticated interleaving. As *organizational model and system implementation co-evolve*, business and system modelers should benefit form each others work. Typically, system designers know more details while business modelers have a broader overview. Once a link between the two models has been established, business modelers can apply reverse engineering to elaborate their conceptual task information models, and forward mapping to inform system designers about the usage context.

The main purpose of schema design in CIS is support for inter-group information flows. To interpret the thus exchanged messages, it turns out to be useful to standardize their contents using a shared meta model of the manufacturing product and process. In WibQuS, this meta model was a relational schema derived from the STEP standard, augmented with quality attributes. This *product and process model* became part of all exchange schemata of the federated databases. Now, the conceptual task information model for each subsystem must be considered a *view* on this standard model which further complicates the reverse and forward engineering task.

A complete methodology for co-engineering organization and system models is still under development. The result is in any case a set of dependencies between

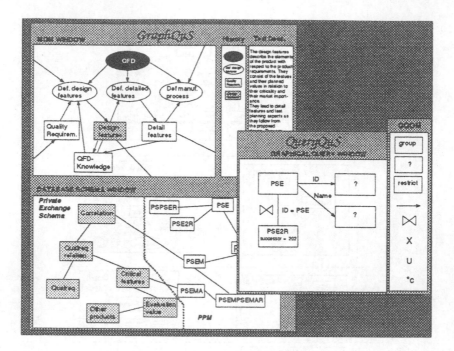

Fig. 9 The information search and access tool

the two models that helps in further system evolution [15], but also allows the end-user to view the distributed relational database through the conceptual model [26] in a two-level filter-browser (figure 9). Agent-oriented, method-oriented, product-oriented, or change-step oriented perspectives serve as filters to prevent 'getting lost in hyperspace'. In the upper window, the filtered conceptual model is shown; an exchangeable palette of graphical types facilitates user understanding. The lower window shows the corresponding part of the relational schema. The user can graphically formulate relational queries which are automatically augmented with the applied filter definitions; location transparency is provided by the quality trader.

4.2 Supporting Planned Information Flows

Units in a market-like organization interact in customer-supplier relationships. Workflows in WibQuS are therefore modeled in *request-commit-perform-evaluate cycles*[18] which map task delegation between agents (figure 6). The quality trader encodes the necessary data structures in a special relational schema, shown as an Entity—Relationship diagram in the middle of figure 10. Active communication tasks record tuples concerning their (order, argument list) and status (negotiation, commitment, error). The task description can be just a specification for humans, it can be an executable program, or it can be a parameterized database query.

Figure 10 illustrates the latter case for an interaction between the WiFEA service support tool and the DACAPO quality planning tool in WibQuS. The service person has used her tool to zoom into the details of a forklift to be serviced, and detected

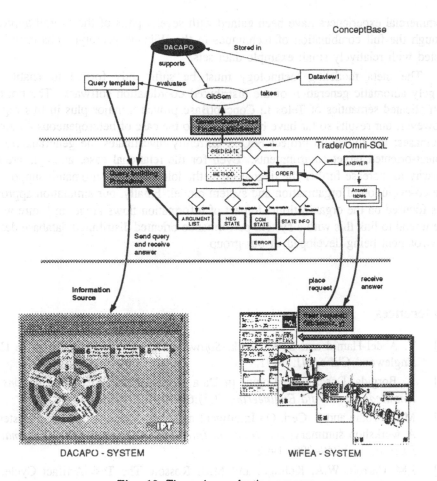

Fig. 10 The order evaluation process

some problem. She now wants to know if this problem is a known bug and therefore invokes the standard task `GibSem` which returns detailed information about a structure element in the product and process model. The task is placed in the `order` relation and abstracted to a ConceptBase query class which was defined in the conceptual model when fixing `GibSem` as a standard information flow. ConceptBase now determines that the owner of this information is the quality planning subsystem. The corresponding SQL query is constructed in Omni-SQL and sent to DACAPO's Oracle database. After negotiation, the query is executed there and the resulting tables are made available to the WiFEA database (implemented using Informix). A monitor window of the Quality Trader allows to control this process from each involved node.

5 Summary and Conclusion

The WibQuS experiences show that many tasks involved in the planning and operation of federated organizations with cooperative information systems can be coordinated by user-definable and repository-supported meta models. Promising first commercial experiences have been gained with several parts of the overall approach though the full combination of techniques in the WibQuS prototype has only been tested with relatively small example data sets.

The meta modeling technology must be sufficiently formal to enable the largely automatic generation of the distributed coordination software. The not-too-complicated semantics of Telos in ConceptBase proved a major plus in this regard. However, our results so far have been limited to the case of heterogeneous relational databases; the follow-up project FoQuS currently investigates the generalization to object-oriented target environments. Even for the relational case, attempts are underway to increase further the degree of methodological and automated support for the co-evolution of organization and system model. Finally, our simulation approach has focused on the organizational impact of information flows alone; in future work, we intend to link this with a system-performance oriented distributed database design environment being developed in our group.

References

[1]   T. Abdel-Hamid and S. Madnick. *Software Project Dynamics*. Prentice Hall, Englewood Cliffs, NJ, 1991.

[2]   A. Borgida. Description Logics in Data Management. *IEEE Transactions on Knowledge and Data Engineering*, 7(5):671 – 682, 1995.

[3]   M.L. Brodie and S. Ceri. On Intelligent and Cooperative Information Systems: A workshop summary. *Int. Jour. on Intelligent and Cooperative Information Systems*, 1(2):249–290, 1992.

[4]   J.M. Carroll, W.A. Kellogg, and M.B. Rosson. The Task-Artifact Cycle. In J.M. Carroll, editor, *Designing Interaction: Psychology at the Human-Computer Interface*. Cambridge, 1991.

[5]   G. De Michelis, E. Dubois, M. Jarke, F. Matthes, J. Mylopoulos, K. Pohl, J. Schmidt, C. Woo, and E. Yu. Cooperative Information Systems: A Manifesto. In *4th Intl. Conf. on Cooperative Information Systems*, Brussels, Belgium, 1996.

[6]   W. Deiters, V. Gruhn, and R. Striemer. The FUNSOFT Approach to Business Process Management. *Wirtschaftsinformatik*, 37(5):459 – 466, 1995.

[7]   P.A. Fishwick. *Simulation Model Design and Execution*. Prentice Hall, Englewood Cliffs, N.J., 1995.

[8]   A. Heinzl and R. Srikanth. Entwicklung der betrieblichen Informationsverarbeitung. *Wirtschaftsinformatik*, 37(1):10 – 17, 1995.

[9]   ISO/IEC. Information Technology – Information Resource Dictionary System (IRDS) - Standard ISO/IEC 10027. Technical report, ISO/IEC International Standard, 1990.

[10] M. Jarke and C.A. Ellis. Distributed Cooperation in Integrated Information Systems. *Int. Jour. of Intelligent and Cooperative Information Systems*, 2(1):85 – 103, 1993.

[11] M. Jarke, R. Gallersdörfer, M.A. Jeusfeld, M. Staudt, and S. Eherer. ConceptBase – A Deductive Object Base for Meta Data Management. *Journal of Intelligent Information Systems*, 4(2), 1995.

[12] M. Jarke, M. Gebhardt, S. Jacobs, and H. Nissen. Conflict Analysis Across Heterogeneous Viewpoints: Formalization and Visualization. In *29th Annual Hawaii Conf. on System Sciences (Vol. 3)*, pages 199 – 208, Wailea, Hawaii, 1996.

[13] M. Jarke, M. Jeusfeld, and P. Szczurko. Three Aspects of Intelligent Cooperation in the Quality Life Cycle. *Int. Jour. of Intelligent and Cooperative Information Systems*, 2(4):355–374, 1993.

[14] M. Jarke and K. Pohl. Establishing Visions in Context: Towards a Model of Requirements Processes. In *14 th Conf. on Information Systems*, Orlando, USA, 1993.

[15] M. Jeusfeld and M. Jarke. Repository Structures for Evolving Federated Database Schemas. In *IFIP Working Conference on Models and Methodologies for Enterprise Integration*, Heron Island, Australia, 1995.

[16] M.A. Jeusfeld and U. Johnen. An Executable Meta Model for Re-Engineering of Database Schemas. *International Journal of Cooperative Information Systems*, 4(2):237 – 258, 1995.

[17] T. Malone, J. Yates, and R.I. Benjamin. Electronic Markets and Electronic Hierarchies. *Communications of the ACM*, 30(6):484 – 497, 1987.

[18] R. Medina-Mora, T. Winograd, R. Flores, and C.F. Flores. The Action Workflow Approach to Workflow Management Technology. In *4th Intl. Conf. on Computer-Supported Cooperative Work*, pages 281 – 288, Toronto, Canada, 1992.

[19] J. Mylopoulos, A. Borgida, M. Jarke, and M. Koubarakis. Telos: a Language for Representing Knowledge about Information Systems. *ACM Transactions on Informations Systems*, 8(4):325–362, 1990.

[20] National Library of Medicine. Unified Medical Language System (5th edition). Technical report, US Department of Health and Human Services, 1994.

[21] H. Nissen, M. Jeusfeld, M. Jarke, G.V. Zemanek, and H. Huber. Managing Multiple Requirements Perspectives with Meta Models. *IEEE Software, March*, 1996.

[22] A. Oberweis, G. Scherrer, and W. Stucky. INCOME/STAR: Methodology and Tools for the Development of Distributed Information Systems. *Information Systems*, 19(8):643 – 660, 1994.

[23] W. Orlikowski and D. Robey. Information Technology and the Structuring of Organizations. *Information Systems Research*, 2:143 – 169, 1991.

[24] M.P. Papazoglou, N. Russell, and D. Edmond. A Semantic-Oriented Translation Protocol for Heterogeneous Federated Database Systems. Technical report, Queensland University of Technology, Australia, 1995.

[25] P. Peters. *Modeling Information Flow in Quality Management (forthcoming)*. PhD thesis, RWTH Aachen, 1996.

[26] P. Peters, U. Löb, and A. Rodriguez Pardo. A Task-Oriented Graphical Interface to Federated Databases. In *Proc. of 3rd Int. Conf. of the Int. Soc. for Decision Support Systems*, pages 223 – 231, Hong Kong, 1995.

[27] P. Peters, M. Mandelbaum, and M. Jarke. Simulation-Based Method Engineering in Federated Organizations. In *submitted for Method Engineering 96*, Atlanta, Georgia, 1996.

[28] T. Pfeifer. *Quality Management (in German)*. Carl Hanser Verlag, Muenchen, 1993.

[29] A.-W. Scheer. *Wirtschaftsinformatik (Reference Models for Industrial Business Processes (in German)*. Springer Verlag, Berlin, Heidelberg,...., 1993.

[30] M.S. Scott-Morton. The 1990s research program: Implications for Management and the Emerging Organization. *Decision Support Systems*, 12(2):251–256, 1994.

Towards a WorldWide Knowledge Base
Extended Abstract

Erik Sandewall

Department of Computer and Information Science
Linköping University
S-58183 Linköping, Sweden
erisa@ida.liu.se

Abstract. The paper proposes that the basic idea of the WWW can be generalized to the domain of data structures or information structures. This means that "packages" of structured information are represented as short text files, stored in web-accessible locations (URL:s), and are loaded as needed by the web-oriented database tool. We suggest that this technique may help to get done what has not been achieved before in the history of A.I. research: a comprehensive, universally usable knowledge base of common knowledge.

1 Questions

Why doesn't there exist, after 35 years of research in artificial intelligence, a comprenhensive knowledge base of common-sense knowledge which everyone can use as a starting-point for her projects? Since "symbolic", "representation-oriented", and "knowledge-based" approaches have dominated throughout the history of A.I., why is it that every research group and every project builds its own knowledge base more or less from scratch, to fit its particular application area? If common-sense knowledge is truly universal and can not be cut into small self-contained pieces, why is it that almost every project that professes to use a knowledge-based approach does exactly that?

And, if we agree that the present situation is unreasonable and that a comprehensive universal knowledge base is a necessity for A.I., what are the possibilities of changing the situation by using the new software technologies that have emerged in recent years, in particular, the World-Wide Web technology?

The present paper attempts to give a brief answer to the first set of questions, and a more extensive answer to the second set.

2 Why don't we have a comprehensive knowledge base today?

The present absence of one or more widely used knowledge bases is of course due to a combination of several factors. I will therefore only identify a few aspects of the relevant background.

Disdain for trivial information bears a great part of the blame. We act as though there were a strict difference between data bases and knowledge bases, where data bases would deal with large volumes of uniformly structured data, so they were trivial from an A.I. point of view. A.I. would deal with Real Knowledge, which is known to have a Very Rich Structure.

The problem with this point of view is that it leads us to only consider Quite Complicated Solutions, in particular, quite complicated ways of structuring information. The view that simple techniques can't be A.I. has two consequences: it gives us structures that are hard to agree upon, because everyone has his own opinion about how to solve the difficult problems. Also, it focusses the attention on the design of how to structure the information and how to build software that operates on it, leaving insufficient room for efforts to actually build the knowledge base.

There are exceptions, of course. What about the CYC project? True, it has attempted to actually build an encyclopaedic knowledge base. However, it has chosen a quite advanced structure, making it difficult for others to embrace it. Also, the decision to make the knowledge base proprietary is a major problem from the point of view of the research community. Where would UNIX be if it had been proprietary from the start?

The KIF effort seems to suffer from a similar problem: it provides a quite expressive language, but it invites dissent about many parts of its technical solution. Efforts to standardize terminological languages may be more promising and we return to them below.

The importance of starting with simple solutions has been demonstrated again and again in the history of software: big and complex products hardly gain acceptance, even if they are so good that they solve all the customer's problems (which of course is unlikely anyway). The best way to win is to begin with something *very simple* that solves *some* of the customer's problems, to gain acceptance for it and to obtain a "customer base", and then to gradually extend the capability of the tool.

In the case of data bases vs knowledge basis, it would help to recognize three levels rather than two. For simplicity I call them "data bases", "information bases", and "knowledge bases", respectively:

- *data bases* deal with uniformly structured data which are strongly typed: the database schema specifies which properties are allowed for which objects, what must be the type of each property, etc.
- *information bases* deal with data which are structured, for example as property-lists (to use the Lisp term), but which are not strongly typed using "declarations" or "schemas". Still, the kinds of information that are represented there are fairly simple, and the data volumes are moderate.
- *knowledge bases* are as we know them from A.I., requiring solutions to the large number of problems for representing e.g. common-sense knowledge.

I submit that knowledge bases are rarely useful unless they are combined with information bases: there is a lot of routine information around which must be present together with the very flexible contents of the knowledge base proper.

The need for the middle level, information bases, has also been observed from time to time in the database community, with proposals for "binary data bases", "object-oriented data bases" (in one sense of the phrase "object-oriented"), and so forth. However, this direction does not seem to ever have established a strong life of its own in that community either.

3 The virtue of simplicity

On the background that has just been described, one obtains at once the following strategy for the future:

- Let us define a simple initial format for expressing information (in the above sense of that word). The format should be so simple and straight-forward that acceptance is easy, and implementation of the basic software support is trivial.
- Build up stores of common-sense information using that format. Examples of such information abound: basic geographical information (countries, cities, languages, etc), basic historical and political information, and so on.
- Obtain maximal availability for these information stores. In particular, organize them in such a way that different contributions can easily be combined.
- Identify a few early, useful application areas for the totality of common-sense information that has been built up, and demonstrate these applications widely.
- Once this has been done, add more facilities to the basic initial format. Preferably, the additions should be done in a modular fashion, so that they can selected or deselected somewhat independently.

From the point of view of practical computing, this strategy is elementary and very obvious, but it differs considerably from the common approaches in A.I.

The first items in the list are not difficult. Basic set-theory notation offers a very natural candidate for the notation: sets, sequences, and mappings provide a well-known, versatile, and yet very simple notation. One should also assume a few distinct types for the elements of sets, sequences, etc, corresponding to the atomic data types in Lisp. Thus one needs numbers, strings, and symbols, and then the composite structures (sets, sequences, mappings) that can be constructed from them. – The now-standardized notation for terminological languages is another likely candidate.

The crucial issues are availability and first applications. This is where the World-Wide Web comes in.

4 Universal availability

Consider the researcher who has built up a store of common-sense information according to the simple principles that have just been described. How does he distribute it to others?

In older days, until a few years ago, he or she would have written a few papers about it, and offered to distribute the software and the data bases by the file transfer methods of the day, typically by ftp. Distribution would be relatively slow; any prospective user would have to import both programs and data, try it out, and then figure out how to interface with his own software or software provided from other sources.

After the advent of WWW, it can be done quite differently. Consider the difference between using a WWW browser and using ftp: in ftp, you have to specify by separate interactive commands each of the file transfers you wish to make. In the browser, you are working *inside* the information, and you get the browser to load additional modules (additional "pages") as it needs them.

Translate this to the database or information-base context. In the old style of working, one would transmit the whole information base from its originator to its prospective user. Now, it is feasible to have an information-base tool which keeps a certain collection of information "packages" in working memory, and which loads additional packages from the net as it needs them. Each information package should be able to contain a certain amount of information (for example, a property-list for a particular object), but packages must also be able to contain links to other packages *located at other hosts*, just like HTML pages do.

In this way, it becomes possible to emerge an information base by the many contributions of users everywhere on the Internet, just as the world-wide web structure has emerged from a very large number of interlinked, individual contributions.

5 First applications

Besides the technical solution, there is also a need for good first applications. Interestingly enough, this aspect is also provided in the context of the world-wide web.

The basic observation is that it is fairly inconvenient to write WWW pages directly in HTML. There are at least two alternative ways of dealing with this problem. One possibility is to build interactive tools which allow the user to drag icons, choose from pull-down menues, etc. The other solution is to maintain a small database or, in our terms, an information base as the primary store of information, and to generate WWW pages from the data base. Both approaches have their pros and cons, but there are a number of specific advantages for the generative approach, just as Emacs/Latex has advantages over WYSIWYG editors. For example, if a particular name, word, or phrase is to be associated with the same home page and the same URL in many different occurrences, then it is convenient to generate automatically the pages where these references occur.

The first applications of such an information base can therefore be to maintain information from which world-wide web pages in HTML are generated.

6 Experimental implementation

The approach which has now been described in outline has also been implemented, and has been described in more detail in other papers which are accessible from

> `http://vir.liu.se/brs/database/`

The following implementation technique has been used. Each information package is represented as a text file under Unix, using a Lisp-based notation. We have implemented an information-base software tool which reads these text files as it needs them, just like a web browser does, but for structured data. The tool has been implemented in Xlisp, and is presently being used for two purposes: for E-mail management, and for maintenance of the WWW pages of the ECSTER electronic colloquium. ECSTER stands for "European Colloquium on Spatial and Temporal Reasoning", and is run within a special interest group of Compulog. To get a feeling for the generated web pages representing the information structure, please refer to

> `http://vir.liu.se/brs/`

and the pages that are referenced from there.

7 A programming-language perspective: the eternal Lisp

The programming language Lisp, which was used for this implementation, has been the workhorse of A.I. research ever since the area started. Its use in the approach being described here is not accidental, nor is it based on conservatism or nostalgia. On the contrary, it is motivated by the most characteristic property of Lisp: *the existence of a convention and corresponding software support for representing data structures as text*. This property of Lisp is the fundamental reason for its persistence, in my opinion, and it has not yet been incorporated into widely used languages such as Pascal or C++. It has also not been incorporated into the favored newcomer today, that is, Hot Java.

However, Hot Java is interesting from another point of view in this context. If the key invention in WWW was to allow small modules of marked-up text, which could be loaded as needed into the browser, the corresponding generalization in Hot Java is to allow procedures or other fragments of programs to be treated in the same way: requested as needed, and loaded into the interpreter. The present proposal extends the same principle to a third dimension: not only marked-up text and program fragments, but also packages of "information" (data without the restrictions of strong typing) can be treated in this dynamic way.

8 From information base to knowledge base

The last question from the impatient A.I. researcher may then be: fine, this will give us a world-wide information base, but when and how will it develop into the world-wide knowledge base that is alluded to in the title of the paper. The answer is simple: *just wait.*

9 References

Please refer to the URL (WWW address) mentioned in section 6 for the full versions of my papers on this topic (including papers that may have appeared after the present article), as well as for references to related work.

Data Mining and Knowledge Discovery in Business Databases

Gregory Piatetsky-Shapiro

GTE Laboratories, MS 45, 40 Sylvan Road, Waltham MA 02154, USA
gps@gte.com

Abstract. The rapid and constant growth of databases in business, government, and science has far outpaced our ability to interpret and make sense of this data avalanche, creating a need for a new generation of tools and techniques for intelligent and automated database analysis. These tools and techniques are the subject of the rapidly emerging field of data mining and knowledge discovery in databases (KDD). This paper surveys the state of the art in this field, with a particular focus on the issues and challenges in applying KDD to business databases.

1 Introduction

In the last decade, we have seen an explosive growth in our capabilities to both generate and collect data. The introduction of bar codes for almost all commercial products, combined with the widespread computerization of many business transactions, along with great advances in scientific data collection (ranging from space satellites to molecular biology), have generated a flood of data. At the same time, advances in data storage technology, such as faster, higher capacity, and cheaper storage devices, terabyte-capable database management systems, and data warehousing methodology, have allowed us to capture this data deluge and transform it "mountains" of stored data.

Presenters at recent Data Warehousing Conference [12] described many applications dealing with tens and hundreds of Gigabytes of data, and even Terabytes (10^{12}) size databases are not uncommon. Huge databases are being constructed in many scientific fields as well. The NASA Earth Observing System (EOS) satellites are projected to generate on the order of 50 Gbytes of data per *hour* [39].

Such volumes of data clearly overwhelm the traditional interactive methods of data analysis such as spreadsheets and ad-hoc queries. Those methods can create informative reports from data, but cannot analyze the contents of those reports to focus on important knowledge. A significant need exists for a new generation of techniques and tools with the ability to *intelligently* and *automatically* assist humans in analyzing the mountains of data for nuggets of useful knowledge. These techniques and tools are the subject of the emerging field of data mining and knowledge discovery in databases (KDD).

This field has been recently receiving significant attention from researchers as evidenced by the growing interest in KDD workshops [30], [14], which culminated in the first international conference on KDD [15].

2 Data Mining vs. Knowledge Discovery

We define Knowledge Discovery in Databases in [17] as the *non-trivial process of identifying valid, novel, potentially useful, and ultimately understandable patterns in data.*

Let us examine these terms in more detail. We want discovery be *non-trivial* meaning that the discovery system should use some non-trivial logic for discovery. We emphasize that discovery is generally a multi-step *process* with many iterations and loops (see section 4). The result of discovery is a set of *patterns* expressed in some language. The discovered patterns should be *valid* in the sense of being supported by data and statistical evidence, and *novel*, at least with respect to system's knowledge. The patterns should be (potentially) *useful*, leading to some useful actions, either directly (via system actions) or indirectly (via user actions). We believe that "usefulness" should be an important part of the pattern evaluation metric [32]. In many applications patterns need to be *understandable*, to allow verification, explanation, and possibly to increase human knowledge.

Historically the notion of finding useful patterns (or nuggets of knowledge) in raw data has been given various names, including data mining, knowledge extraction, information discovery, data archaeology, data pattern processing, and even "information harvesting". The database researchers have used the term "data mining", along with the statisticians, data analysts and the MIS (Management Information Systems) communities. The term *knowledge discovery in databases*, or KDD for short, more popular in AI and machine learning communities, was coined in 1989 to refer to the broad process of finding knowledge in data, and to emphasize the desired goal of "mining", i.e. knowledge.

Here we adopt a view (more fully explained in [17]) that KDD refers to the overall *process* of discovering useful knowledge from data while *data mining* refers to the application of algorithms for extracting patterns from data without the additional steps of the KDD process (such as incorporating appropriate prior knowledge and proper interpretation of the results). These additional steps are essential to ensure that useful information (knowledge) is derived from the data. Blind application of data mining methods (rightly criticised as "fishing" or "dredging" in the statistical literature) without a proper domain knowledge interpretation and statistical validation can lead to discovery of spurious and invalid patterns.

2.1 Knowledge Discovery and Related Fields

KDD is a broad research area which relies upon methods from several related fields, primarily machine learning, statistics, visualization, reasoning with uncertainty, and expert systems for the data analysis part, and database management theory, data warehousing methodology, and high performance computing for the data access part.

KDD and Statistics. While KDD relies on the statistical theory for assessing the significance of the findings, KDD puts more emphasis on the automation of the entire process of data analysis, including the expert statistician's "art" of the hypothesis selection.

KDD and Machine Learning. Some KDD systems involve data description and presentation which would not be considered part of machine learning. The KDD systems that focus on prediction from examples have a broad overlap with the inductive machine learning, but with the emphasis on algorithms and systems that would be able to scale up to large data volumes and deal with messy data typical for business applications.

KDD and Data Warehousing. Data warehousing, which is a very popular MIS trend for collecting and cleaning operational, transactional business data and transforming it into an analysis-oriented data warehouse. Typically this process involves merging related transactions (e.g. combining all phone call logs from a switch to get a record of all subscriber calls), data cleaning, and storing historical data in an easy to access way. While currently the primary motivation for data warehouse construction is better decision support via interactive tools [12], automated data mining is the logical next step. Most vendors of data warehousing tools are already planning to add data mining capabilities.

KDD and OLAP. OLAP (*On-Line Analytical Processing*) is a set of principles recently proposed by Codd [11] which sets standards for making interactive data analysis fast and user-friendly. Many systems have implemented OLAP principles by using a multi-dimensional database systems, which store data as a multi-dimensional cube (hence the name) and presummarize aggregate measures along important dimensions. Such systems are indeed able to deliver fast response to aggregation-type queries, but are not designed for autonomous knowledge discovery or for predictive modeling.

3 Goals, Tasks, and Methods

Knowledge Discovery is an umbrella term that is used to describe a large variety of activities for making sense of data. We will categorize these activities by using the dimensions of Goals, Tasks, and Methods.

The **Goals** are defined by the intentions of the user. The two main KDD goals are

- **Prediction**: use available data to predict unknown or future values of some variables. A typical example may be a database marketing application which predicts which customers are likely to buy a particular product based on their previous buying patterns.
- **Description**: find some interesting (according to user criteria) patterns and present them to the user in an easy to understand way. For example, the KEFIR system [25] finds and describes key changes among various aggregate measures that describe health care costs.

The main distinction between prediction and description is who interprets the discovered knowledge – the system (in case of prediction) or the user (in case of description). The boundaries between these goals are not sharp, since some of the predictive models can be used for description (to the degree that they are understandable), and some of the descriptive models could be used for prediction.

The next dimension, the discovery **tasks** differ in the types of patterns to be discovered. The discovery **methods** are the broad classes of algorithms that can be used to implement a particular tasks. The relationship between goals, tasks, and some methods is shown in figure 1.

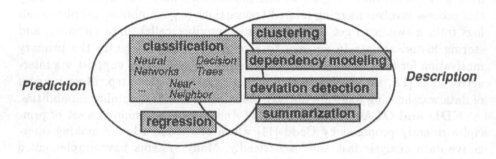

Fig. 1. Goals vs Tasks

The major data mining tasks are:

- **Classification**: given a set of preclassified examples, learn a function that maps an example into one of several discrete classes. Classification, a predictive task, has been one the most studied problems in machine learning and statistics and has many business-oriented applications such as database marketing [5], customer modeling, and fraud detection. The most popular classification methods include decision-trees [9] [35], neural networks [20], and example-based methods [13].
- **Regression:** given a set of examples, learn a function that maps a data item into a real-valued variable. Regression is also a predictive task. There is a tremendous wealth of work on time-series forecasting (e.g. [40]) which is relevant to regression. The most popular methods for regression include non-linear regression [18] and neural networks. Still, there are relatively few data mining applications using regression, perhaps because it is more difficult to predict a real-valued amount (e.g. the amount the customer spends) than a discrete value (whether the customer will buy a product).
- **Clustering:** is a common descriptive task where one seeks to identify a finite set of categories or clusters to describe the data [22], [10]. The categories may be mutually exclusive and exhaustive, or consist of a richer representation such as hierarchical or overlapping categories. A typical applications is a market segmentation into a set of similar customer sub-populations.

- **Dependency Modeling:** is a task of finding significant dependencies between all variables (data fields) (unlike classification where there is only a single target variable). This task can be used both for descriptive and predictive purposes. There are two major classes of algorithms for this task:
  - **Symbolic association:** given a set of examples, find interesting associations between subsets of different features, e.g. (A and B) → C. Several algorithms for finding such associations have been developed by Agrawal, Mannila, and others [1]. A typical application of associations is "market basket analysis" determining which products customer buys together. A related task is the recognition of sequences which are associations of items over time [2], such as A followed by B (with possibly some intervening items) is usually followed by C.
  - **Causal dependencies:** given a set of variables, find a probabilistic dependency network between them. [28] [38]. These networks are finding applications in areas such as of medical expert systems, information retrieval, and modeling of the human genome.
- **Summarization:** involves methods for finding a characteristic description for a subset of data [19]. Summarization techniques are often applied to interactive exploratory data analysis and automated report generation.
- **Change and Deviation Detection:** focuses on discovering the most significant changes in some key measures of data from previous or expected values. Representative applications involve financial analysis [6], and reporting on healthcare data [25].

These data mining tasks are at the center of the knowledge discovery process. However, as we will discuss in the next section, there is a lot more that needs to be done for a real application.

4 Knowledge Discovery Process

The Knowledge Discovery Process is the process of using data mining methods to extract potentially useful knowledge from data. Here we broadly outline the basic steps of this process (see Brachman and Anand [8] for more detail).

- **Feasibility:** Analyze the goals of the user, the application domain, and the feasibility and potential payback of applying KDD. Identify the appropriate data mining goal: prediction or description, and the suitable tasks.
- **Data Warehousing:** Create an analysis-oriented data storage. This involves merging related transactions to bring together data about same entities, cleaning data errors, getting additional relevant data, and storing historical data. Data warehousing is a necessary but very time consuming and expensive step. In the ideal case, the KDD application can piggyback on top of an existing data warehouse constructed for interactive decision support. If data warehouse is not available, then generally this step would be the most costly and time consuming for large-scale data mining.

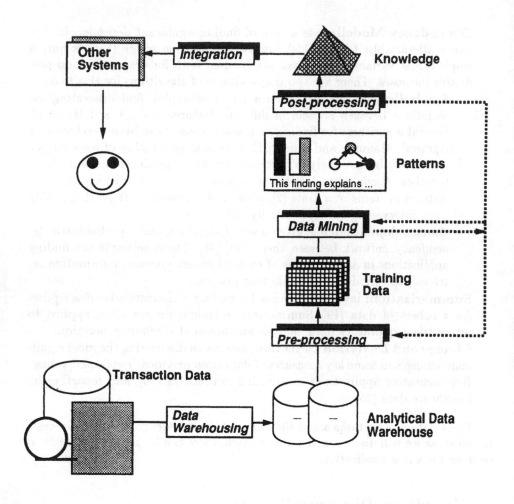

Fig. 2. A Typical Knowledge Discovery Process

- **Pre-processing:** This involves first understanding which business terms map to what data fields and then converting the relevant data to the form suitable for the data mining algorithm(s). For predictive data mining this includes building training and test data samples, stratifying samples if the target class is too rare, data scaling and conversion, removing outliers, selecting a relevant subset of features, merging historical data, and dealing with missing data. For descriptive data mining this step involves defining pattern interestingness, the search space, and other background domain knowledge.

- **Data Mining:** This is the actual selection and application of the data mining algorithm(s) to search for the patterns of interest. A popular method for setting discovery parameters has been to use a wrapper approach [23] where an algorithm is repeatedly run with different settings until the best results are obtained. The result of the data mining step is a set of patterns.

- **Post-processing:** For the predictive algorithms this includes evaluating the discovered models on the original data sets and obtaining various performance statistics. For the descriptive data mining this includes relating and explaining the discovered patterns and presenting them in a human-oriented way.
- **Integration:** Finally, the results of data mining typically need to be integrated with other systems, such as word processors, spreadsheets, financial models, billing systems, or marketing databases.

The KDD process always involves significant iterations and loops among the steps. Although most of the previously published work has focused on the data mining step, in actual practice the majority of effort is typically spent on data warehousing, and pre- and post-processing steps. Automation of these steps is the next frontier for the data mining research.

5 Application Issues

The industries which rely the most on information manipulation have been the early adopters of data mining. These industries include banking, investment, insurance, retail, telecommunications, and healthcare. Here we mention only a few representative examples.

Most of the reported applications have been using the classification task. A majority of US retailers, according to a cover story in Business Week [5] are using or planning to use "Database Marketing", which is a method of analyzing customer databases, looking for patterns among existing customer preferences and using those patterns for more targeted selection of future customers. More effective targeting of customers has been reported to almost double the rate of response to direct mail solicitation [5].

The investment industry has been using a variety of data mining methods [4] for selecting stocks and other financial instruments. However, only a few companies are willing to publish the details.

Another application of the classification task has been for fraud detection. A system for detecting healthcare provider fraud in electronically submitted claims, has been developed at Travelers Insurance [24]. The U. S. Treasury has developed the FAIS system for detecting the money laundering activities [37]. Neural network based tools, such as Nestor FDS [7] have been developed for detecting credit-card fraud and are reportedly watching millions of accounts.

Several successful applications have been developed for analysis and reporting on change in data. These include Spotlight from A.C. Nielsen [3] for supermarket sales data, and KEFIR from GTE, for health care databases [25].

Other recent applications are described in [14], [15], [33], [16].

5.1 Evaluating a Potential KDD Application

The criteria for evaluating the feasibility of potential KDD applications in business can be divided into practical and technical. The practical criteria are similar to those for other applications of advanced technology, while the technical ones are more specific to KDD.

The practical criteria begin with the potential payback of the application, as measured by greater revenue, lower costs, higher quality, or savings in time. The desired solution should not be easily obtainable by simpler means, and the project should have strong organizational support. There should be both a champion for using new technology, and a domain expert who can provide the necessary knowledge to help focus the discovery on what is useful. Finally, for applications which mine the personal data the privacy and legal issues should be considered.

The technical criteria include:

- Prior knowledge: there should be some knowledge about the application, including what are the target variables and relevant fields, the measures for utility, the patterns already known, etc. At the same time the knowledge should be incomplete or else there would not be any need for discovery.
- Sufficient data available: this means having enough relevant examples for building a model. In general, the more fields there are and the more complex are the patterns being sought, the more data is needed.
- Relevant fields: It is critical to have data fields relevant to the discovery task: no amount of data will allow prediction based on attributes that do not capture the required information.
- Data reliability: the level of data errors is an important consideration. High amounts of errors make it hard to identify patterns unless a large number of cases can mitigate random noise and help clarify the aggregate patterns.

5.2 Privacy and Knowledge Discovery

When dealing with databases of personal information, governments and businesses have to be careful to adequately address the legal and ethical issues of invasion of privacy. Ignoring this issue can be dangerous, as Lotus found in 1990, when they were planning to introduce a CD-ROM with data on about 100 million American households. The stormy protest led to the withdrawal of that product [36].

Current discussion centers around guidelines for what constitutes a proper discovery. The Organization for Economic Cooperation and Development guidelines for data privacy [27], which have been adopted by most European Union countries, suggest that data about specific living individuals should not be analyzed without their consent. They also suggest that the data should only be collected for a specific purpose. Use for other purposes is possible only with the consent of the data subject or by authority of the law.

In the U.S. there is ongoing work on draft principles for fair information use related to the National Information Infrastructure (NII), commonly known as the "information superhighway". These principles permit the use of "transactional records", such as phone numbers called, credit card payments, etc., as long as such use is compatible with the original notice. The use of transactional records can be seen to also include discovery of patterns.

In many cases (e.g. medical research, socio-economic studies) the goal is to discover patterns about groups, not individuals. While group pattern discovery appears not to violate the restrictions on personal data retrieval, an ingenious combination of several group patterns, especially in small datasets, may allow identification of specific personal information. Solutions which allow group pattern discovery while avoiding the potential invasion of privacy include removal or replacement of identifying fields, performing queries on random subsets of data, and combining individuals into groups and allowing only queries on groups. These and related issues are further discussed in [34].

5.3 Challenges for Application Development

Here we focus on the challenges standing in the way of successful applications of knowledge discovery.

Too many records: Databases with sizes measured in tens of Gigabytes (and more) are quite commonplace today, yet very few data mining tools can handle these sizes. However, a closer scrutiny typically reveals that a relatively small part of the database is relevant for any particular data mining task. Other solutions include sampling (for predictive tasks), high-performance, parallel hardware, faster algorithms, and better database support for data mining operations.

Too many fields: Many large databases also have hundreds or thousands of fields spread over dozens of tables. While most data mining algorithms run in time of $N \log N$ (or less) in the number of records, they typically are at least N^2 or slower in the number of fields. While ideally we would like to feed all the fields to the data mining method and watch the knowledge come out, in practice it is usually better to have a separate *feature selection* stage, where a subset of relevant features is selected (perhaps repeatedly) before data mining.

Too many patterns: When the algorithm searches for the best parameters for one particular model using a limited set of data, it may overfit the data. For example, if a system tests N models at the 0.001 significance level, then on average, with purely random data, $N/1000$ of these models will be accepted as significant. Such overfitted models, however, do not capture any inherent patterns and will perform poorly on test data. Possible solutions include using separate test sets during modeling, Bonferroni adjustments of significance levels, cross-validation, and other statistical strategies.

Missing and erroneous data: This problem is especially acute in personal information databases. U.S. census data reportedly has error rates of up to 20% in many fields. Important attributes may be missing if the database was not designed with discovery in mind. Possible solutions include using larger samples, which can compensate for noise in aggregate patterns and statistical strategies to identify hidden variables and dependencies [21], [38].

User acceptance: users, who are accustomed to interactive tools like spreadsheets find it hard to use discovery tools which have a different metaphor and usually longer response times. Also, many of the discovery tools are oriented towards data analysts and are not suitable for the real business users who want to see the problems framed in business terms.

Integration with other systems: Last but not least, a stand-alone discovery system is of limited usefulness. Typically, the discovery systems needs to be integrated with DBMS and other legacy data sources on the input side. The output of a discovery system needs to be integrated both with existing user analysis tools (ad-hoc queries, spreadsheets, visualization) and with the operational systems that can use the results.

Although the challenges are many and the difficulties are substantial, the future of data mining applications looks bright. There is a widespread realization of the potential value of data mining and a growing number of researchers and developers are working on the topic. However, data mining by itself is only a part of the overall application and all other components, as described in section 4 need to be addressed for a successful application.

Acknowledgments

I want to thank Brij Masand, Usama Fayyad, Padhraic Smyth, and Sam Uthurusamy for their insights which contributed to this paper.

References

1. Agrawal, R., Mannila, H., Srikant, R., Toivonen, H., Verkamo, A. 1996. Fast Discovery of Association Rules. in AKDDM, Cambridge, MA: AAAI/MIT Press.
2. Agrawal, R. and Psaila, G. 1995. Active Data Mining, in Proceedings of KDD-95: First International Conference on Knowledge Discovery and Data Mining, Menlo Park, CA: The AAAI Press.
3. Anand, T. and Kahn, G. 1992. SPOTLIGHT: A Data Explanation System. In *Proc. Eighth IEEE Conference on Applied AI*, 2–8. Washington, D.C.: IEEE Press.
4. Barr, D. and Mani, G. 1994. Using Neural Nets to Manage Investments. *AI Expert*, 16–21, February.
5. Berry, J. 1994. Database Marketing. *Business Week*, 56–62, Sep 5.
6. Berndt, D. and Clifford, J. 1996. Finding Patterns in Time Series: A Dynamic Programming Approach. In AKDDM, Cambridge, MA: AAAI/MIT Press.
7. Blanchard, D. 1994. News Watch. *AI Expert*, 7, December.
8. Brachman, R., and Anand, T. 1996. The Process of Knowledge Discovery in Databases: A Human-Centered Approach, in AKDDM, Cambridge, MA: AAAI/MIT Press.
9. Breiman, L., Friedman, J. H., Olshen, R. A., Stone, C. J. 1984. *Classification and Regression Trees*. Belmont, CA: Wadsworth.

10. Cheeseman, P. 1990. On Finding the Most Probable Model. In *Computational Models of Scientific Discovery and Theory Formation*, Shrager, J. and Langley P. (eds). Los Gatos, CA: Morgan Kaufmann, 73–95.

11. Codd, E.F. 1993. Providing OLAP (On-line Analytical Processing) to User-Analysts: An IT Mandate. E.F. Codd and Associates.

12. Data Warehousing Conference Proceedings, DCI Consulting, Andover, MA, 1996.

13. Dasarathy, B. V. 1991. *Nearest Neighbor (NN) Norms: NN Pattern Classification Techniques*. Los Alamitos, CA: IEEE Computer Society Press.

14. Fayyad, U. M. and Uthurusamy, R. 1994. Editors, Proceedings of KDD-94: the AAAI-94 workshop on Knowledge Discovery in Databases, AAAI Press report WS-03, Menlo Park, CA: The AAAI Press.

15. Fayyad, U. M. and Uthurusamy, R. 1995. Editors, Proceedings of KDD-95: First International Conference on Knowledge Discovery and Data Mining, Menlo Park, CA: The AAAI Press.

16. Fayyad, U., Piatetsky-Shapiro, G., Smyth, P., and Uthurusamy, 1996. R. Editors, Advances in Knowledge Discovery and Data Mining, Cambridge, MA: AAAI/MIT Press.

17. Fayyad, U., Piatetsky-Shapiro, G., Smyth, P. 1996. From Data Mining to Knowledge Discovery: an Overview, in AKDDM, Cambridge, MA: AAAI/MIT Press, 1-29.

18. Friedman, J. H. 1989. Multivariate Adaptive Regression Splines. *Annals of Statistics*, 19: 1–141.

19. Han, J., Cai, Y. and Cercone, N. 1992. Knowledge Discovery in Databases: An Attribute-Oriented Approach, in Proc. of 1992 Int'l Conf. on Very Large Data Bases (VLDB'92), Vancouver, Canada, pp. 547-559.

20. Haykin, S. 1994. *Neural Networks, a Comprehensive Foundation*. Macmillan, New York, NY.

21. Heckerman, D. 1996. Bayesian Networks for Knowledge Discovery in AKDDM, Cambridge, MA: AAAI/MIT Press.

22. Jain, A. K. and Dubes, R. C. 1988. *Algorithms for Clustering Data*. Englewood Cliffs, NJ: Prentice-Hall.

23. Kohavi, R. 1995, Wrappers for Performance Enhancement and Oblivious Decision Graphs, Ph. D., Stanford University, http://robotics.stanford.edu/ronnyk

24. Major, J. and Riedinger, D. 1992. EFD: A Hybrid Knowledge/Statistical-Based System for the Detection of Fraud. *Int. J. of Intelligent Systems*, 7(7): 687–703.

25. Matheus, C., Piatetsky-Shapiro, G., and McNeill, D. 1996. Selecting and Reporting What is Interesting: The KEFIR Application to Healthcare Data. in AKDDM, Cambridge, MA: AAAI/MIT Press, 495-516.

26. Matheus, C., Chan, P. and Piatetsky-Shapiro, G. 1993. Systems for Knowledge Discovery. *IEEE Trans. on Knowledge and Data Engineering*, 5(6): 903–913.

27. O'Leary, D. 1995. Some Privacy Issues in Knowledge Discovery: OECD Personal Privacy Guidelines. *IEEE Expert*, April 1995.

28. Pearl, J. 1992. *Probabilistic Reasoning in Intelligent Systems* Los Gatos, CA: Morgan Kaufmann.

29. iatetsky-Shapiro, G. and Frawley, W. 1991. Editors, *Knowledge Discovery in Databases*, Cambridge, MA: AAAI/MIT Press.

30. Piatetsky-Shapiro, G. 1993. Editor, *Proceedings of KDD-93: the AAAI-93 workshop on Knowledge Discovery in Databases*. AAAI Press report WS-02, Menlo Park, CA: The AAAI Press.

31. Piatetsky-Shapiro, G., Matheus, C. Smyth, P. and Uthurusamy, R. 1994. KDD-93: Progress and Challenges in Knowledge Discovery in Databases. *AI Magazine*, 15(3): 77–87.

32. Piatetsky-Shapiro, G. and Matheus, C 1994. The Interestingness of Deviations, in *Proceedings of KDD-94: the AAAI-94 workshop on Knowledge Discovery in Databases*. Fayyad, U. M. and Uthurusamy, R., (eds.), AAAI Press report WS-03, 28–44, Menlo Park, CA: The AAAI Press.

33. Piatetsky-Shapiro, G. 1995. Editor, Special issue on Knowledge Discovery in Databases. *J. of Intelligent Information Systems*, 4:1, January.

34. Piatetsky-Shapiro, G. 1995b. Knowledge Discovery in Personal Data vs. Privacy a Mini-symposium. *IEEE Expert*, April 1995.

35. Quinlan, J. 1992. *C4.5: Programs for Machine Learning*. Los Gatos, CA: Morgan Kaufmann.

36. Rosenberg, M. 1992. Protecting Privacy, Inside Risks column. *Communications of ACM*, 35(4): 164.

37. Senator, T. et al, 1995. The Financial Crimes Enforcement Network AI System (FAIS), AI Magazine, Winter 1995, 21-39.

38. Spirtes, P., Glymour, C., and Scheines, R. 1993. *Causation, Prediction, and Search*, New York: Springer-Verlag.

39. Way, J. and Smith, E. A. 1991. The Evolution of Synthetic Aperture Radar Systems and their Progression to the EOS SAR. *IEEE Trans. on Geoscience and Remote Sensing*, 29(6): 962–985.

40. Weigend, A. and Gershenfeld, N. (eds.) 1993. *Predicting the Future and Understanding the Past*. Redwood City, CA: Addison-Wesley.

41. Ziarko, W. 1994. Rough Sets, Fuzzy Sets and Knowledge Discovery, Berlin: Springer Verlag.

Learning Composite Concepts in Description Logics: A First Step

Patrick Lambrix and Jalal Maleki

Department of Computer and Information Science
Linköping University
S-581 83 Linköping, Sweden
email: {patla,jalma}@ida.liu.se

Abstract. This paper proposes the use of description logics as a representational framework for learning composite concepts. Description logics are restricted variants of first-order logic providing a form of logical bias that dates back to semantic networks. Some recent work investigates concept learning in the context of these formalisms. Also, having recognized the importance of part-whole hierarchies in commonsense reasoning, researchers have started to incorporate part-of reasoning into description logics. In our approach we represent composite concepts in such a formalism. On one hand we have a relatively rich representation language with an infinite space of possible concepts. On the other hand we have special constructs for handling part-of relations that can be used in the learning algorithm to reduce the overall search space.

1   Introduction

Description logics are languages tailored for expressing knowledge about concepts and concept hierarchies. They are usually given a Tarski style declarative semantics, which allows them to be seen as sub-languages of predicate logic. One starts with primitive concepts and roles, and can use the language constructs (such as intersection, role quantification etc.) to define new concepts and roles. Concepts can be considered as unary predicates which are interpreted as sets of individuals whereas roles are binary predicates which are interpreted as binary relations between individuals. The basic reasoning tasks are classification and subsumption checking.

Given the fact that first-order logic has been restricted in several ways for its use in the field of machine learning, description logics seem to make another good candidate restriction as a learning framework. However, it is only recently that learning algorithms are being developed within this framework [3, 4, 7].

There is also a growing recognition that part-whole hierarchies are a very general form of representation, widely used by humans in commonsense reasoning. Consequently, description logics are extended to integrate part-of reasoning with classification (e.g. [6, 10, 12]).

---

* The authors would like to thank Nada Lavrač for useful comments on a previous draft. The first author is supported by grant 95-176 from the Swedish Research Council for Engineering Sciences (TFR).

In this paper we propose learning algorithms to learn composite concepts in a particular description logic which is specially tailored to handle part-of reasoning. On one hand we have a highly expressive representation framework with an infinite space of possible concepts. On the other hand, we have special constructs for handling part-of which can be used in the learning algorithms to reduce the overall search space.

2 The Framework

In this work we take as our framework a relatively simple description logic [10] with only unstructured roles and a limited number of constructs, but which was specifically designed to include the part-of relation. The language introduces part names which are similar to roles to represent different part-of relations. Further, the language allows specification of constraints between the parts of a composite concept. In the remainder of this section we briefly describe the *Tbox* language, the necessary notions about part-of and finally the *Abox* language .

2.1 Tbox: Is-a

```
concept          ::=              role            ::= identifier
         ⊤                        atomic-concept  ::= identifier
       | ⊥                        part-name       ::= identifier
       | atomic-concept           number          ::= non-negative-integer
       | (and concept⁺)
       | (all role concept)
       | (atleast number role)
       | (atmost number role)
       | (part part-name atomic-concept)
       | (parts number part-name)
       | (pp-constraint role part-name part-name)
```

The language we use to express terminological knowledge is defined as above [10]. *Terminological axioms* are used to introduce names for concepts, and definitions of those concepts. Let A be a concept name (*identifier*) and C be a concept description, (*concept*), then terminological axioms can be of the form: $A \leq C$ for introducing necessary conditions (primitive concepts), or $A \doteq C$ for introducing necessary and sufficient conditions (defined concepts).

A *terminology (Tbox)* T is a finite set of terminological axioms with the additional restrictions that (i) every concept name used must appear exactly once on the left hand side of a terminological axiom, (ii) all concepts must be defined (appear on the left hand side) before they are used, and (iii) T must not contain cyclic definitions directly or indirectly, via either $\doteq$, $\leq$, a **part** construct or any combination of these.

The terminological axiom *standard-family* $\doteq$ (**and** (**part** *husband man*) (**parts** *1 husband*) (**part** *wife woman*) (**parts** *1 wife*) (**part** *offspring child*) (**parts** *2 offspring*) (**pp-constraint** *married husband wife*) (**pp-constraint** *mother wife* *offspring*) (**pp-constraint** *father husband offspring*)) describes the concept of a *standard-family* which is defined as being composed of a part, *husband*, (that belongs to the concept *man*), a part, *wife*, (that belongs to the concept *woman*), and two *offspring* parts (that belong to the concept *child*) with the constraints that the *husband* is *married* to the *wife*, the *wife* is the *mother* of the *offspring* and the *husband* is the *father* of the *offspring*.

An interpretation of the language consists of a tuple $\langle \mathcal{D}, \varepsilon \rangle$, where $\mathcal{D}$ is the domain of individuals and ε the extension function. Let $\mathcal{P}$ be the set of part name names, $\mathcal{C}$ be the set of atomic concepts, and $\mathcal{R}$ the set of role names. Then, $\varepsilon \colon (\mathcal{P} \rightarrow 2^{\mathcal{D} \times \mathcal{D}}) \cup (\mathcal{R} \rightarrow 2^{\mathcal{D} \times \mathcal{D}}) \cup (\mathcal{C} \rightarrow 2^{\mathcal{D}})$.
The semantics for the different terms in the language are defined as follows [10]. For convenience we write $x \vartriangleleft_n y$ for $\langle x, y \rangle \in \varepsilon[n]$ where $n \in \mathcal{P}$.

$\varepsilon[\top] = \mathcal{D}$
$\varepsilon[\bot] = \emptyset$
$\varepsilon[(\textbf{and } A_1 \ldots A_m)] = \bigcap_{i=1}^{m} \varepsilon[A_i]$
$\varepsilon[(\textbf{all } r\ A)] = \{\ x \in \mathcal{D} \mid \forall y \in \mathcal{D} \colon \langle x,y \rangle \in \varepsilon[r] \rightarrow y \in \varepsilon[A]\}$
$\varepsilon[(\textbf{atleast } m\ r)] = \{\ x \in \mathcal{D} \mid \sharp \{\ y \in \mathcal{D} \mid \langle x,y \rangle \in \varepsilon[r]\ \} \geq m\ \}$
$\varepsilon[(\textbf{atmost } m\ r)] = \{\ x \in \mathcal{D} \mid \sharp \{\ y \in \mathcal{D} \mid \langle x,y \rangle \in \varepsilon[r]\ \} \leq m\ \}$
$\varepsilon[(\textbf{part } n\ A)] = \{\ x \in \mathcal{D} \mid \forall y \in \mathcal{D} \colon y \vartriangleleft_n x \rightarrow y \in \varepsilon[A]\}$
$\varepsilon[(\textbf{parts } m\ n)] = \{\ x \in \mathcal{D} \mid \sharp \{\ y \in \mathcal{D} \mid y \vartriangleleft_n x\ \} = m\ \}$
$\varepsilon[(\textbf{pp-constraint } r\ n_1\ n_2)] = \{\ x \in \mathcal{D} \mid$
$\forall y_1, y_2 \in \mathcal{D} \colon (y_1 \vartriangleleft_{n_1} x \land y_2 \vartriangleleft_{n_2} x) \rightarrow \langle y_1, y_2 \rangle \in \varepsilon[r]\}$

Subsumption (**is-a**) is defined as usual. $C_2 \Rightarrow C_1$ iff $\varepsilon[C_2] \subseteq \varepsilon[C_1]$ for every interpretation $\langle \mathcal{D}, \varepsilon \rangle$. We obtain the semantics that if $B \Rightarrow A$, then B may have additional kinds of parts, or more specialized parts than A, and the constraints between the parts of B may be stronger than those between the parts of A. If A has m_1 n-parts, B has m_2 n-parts and $m_1 \neq m_2$, then there is no subsumption relationship between A and B.

The language is targeted to the case where we know the number of parts for each occurring part name in a concept definition. To obtain this case we require that each concept definition has a **parts** construct for each occurring part name.

2.2 Tbox: Part-of

We use the following notation and definitions. If (after normalization [9]) (**part** $n\ A$) occurs in the definition of B, then A is a *direct n-part* of B. We say that A' is an *n-part* of B (written $A' \vartriangleleft_n B$) iff ($\exists A \colon (A$ is a direct n-part of $B) \land (A' \Rightarrow A))$. A is a *part* of B (written $A \vartriangleleft B$) iff $\exists n \colon A \vartriangleleft_n B$.

In the example above we have that *child* is a direct *offspring*-part of *standard-family*. If we know that *young-child* $\Rightarrow$ *child* then we also know that *young-child* is a *offspring*-part of *standard-family*.

If for a part name n, (**parts** $m\ n$) occurs in the definition of A, then we write that $N(n,A) = m$, otherwise $N(n,A) = 0$. $N(n,A)$ represents the number of n-parts which occur in the definition of A. The total number of defined parts for a concept A, denoted $N(A)$, is $\sum_n N(n,A)$. If (**pp-constraint** r n_1 n_2) occurs in the definition of A, then we write $A_{n_1} r_{n_2}$.

Another basic notion is the notion of *module*. (For the formal definition see [10].) In order for A to be a module for B (written $A \lhd_{\mathbf{mod}} B$) it is required that (i) the number of defined parts in A is strictly less than the number of defined parts in B; (ii) that all part names defined for A are also defined for B, with the number of each such defined part being at least as many for B as for A; (iii) that the domains for part names in A are included in the domains of those part names for B; and finally (iv) that all constraints defined between part names are at least as strong for A as for B. A module is essentially a collection of parts, such that none are redundant and the appropriate pp-constraints required by the composition are fulfilled.

Let *couple* be defined as *couple* $\doteq$ (**and** (**part** *husband man*) (**parts** *1 husband*) (**part** *wife woman*) (**parts** *1 wife*) (**pp-constraint** *married husband wife*)), then *couple* is a module of *standard-family*.

2.3 Abox

The language in which we can state information about individuals is defined as follows.

statement   ::=
   (**concept-filler** *individual concept*)
   | (**role-fillers** *individual role individual*)
   | (**part-fillers** *individual part-name individual*)
individual   ::=   *identifier*

The terms *concept*, *part-name* and *role* are defined as for the *Tbox* syntax. If (**concept-filler** x C) appears in an *Abox*, then this means that $x \in \varepsilon[C]$. Similarly, (**role-fillers** x r y) means that $\langle x, y \rangle \in \varepsilon[r]$ and (**part-fillers** y n x) means that $y \lhd_n x$.

An *Abox* is a finite set of statements in the above language such that there are no cycles of parts. We will assume that within one *Abox* an individual has a unique name.

3 Learning Task

The learning task is defined as follows:
Given:
- *Tbox* language to describe concepts
- background knowledge described in *Tbox* language $\cup$ *Abox* language
- example set described in *Tbox* language $\cup$ *Abox* language. We allow the user to present several kinds of information to the learning system. Assume that the concept to learn is C^*. Then the system handles the following cases (positive and negative examples):

membership and non-membership of individuals:
- $x \in \varepsilon[C^\star]$, i.e. a particular individual belongs to the extension of the concept to learn
- $x \notin \varepsilon[C^\star]$, i.e. a particular individual does not belong to the extension of the concept to learn
and a set of constraints that $C^\star$ should fulfill:
- $C^\star \Rightarrow C$, i.e. a particular concept subsumes the concept to learn
- $C \Rightarrow C^\star$, i.e. a particular concept is subsumed by the concept to learn
- $C \lhd_n C^\star$, i.e. a particular concept is an n-part of the concept to learn
- $C \lhd_{\mathbf{mod}} C^\star$, i.e. a particular concept is a module of the concept to learn

Find:
- a concept description for $C^\star$ that satisfies the conditions in the examples

4 Useful Operations

In the learning algorithms we need generalization and specialization operations. Given two concepts C_1 and C_2 we can generalize to obtain the *least common subsumer* of the two concepts. We give the definition and a computation strategy in this section. As the language contains the **and**-construct, finding a more specific concept for the pair C_1 and C_2 can be defined as (**and** C_1 C_2).

Another useful operation is to associate with an individual a concept. This concept should reflect the properties of the individual as close as possible. We give a possible way of defining this notion.

4.1 LCS

The *least common subsumer* (LCS) of a pair of concepts is the most specific description in the infinite space of possible descriptions that subsumes the pair [2]. As our language includes the **and**-construct this LCS is unique.

We extend the computation of the LCS in [2] to also cope with the constructs related to part-of in figure 1. Figure 2 defines a *standard-family-with-boys* as a *standard-family* where the two *offsprings* are *boys*. A *family-with-2-girls* is also similar to a *standard-family* but the two *offsprings* are *girls* and we do not have the constraint that the *wife* and the *husband* are *married*. The LCS of the two concepts gives us then a family where the *offspring* belong to the concept *child* and we do not have the *married*-constraint. During the computation we make use of the fact that LCS(*boy,girl*) = *child*.

4.2 Specific Concepts

We repeat the definition from [5]. A concept C is a *specific concept* for an individual x with respect to a knowledge base $\langle Tbox, Abox \rangle$ iff (i) $x \in \varepsilon[C]$ and (ii) $\forall D: x \in \varepsilon[D] \rightarrow C \Rightarrow D$ in $Tbox$.

$\text{LCS}((\text{and } C_{11} \,..\, C_{1k}),(\text{and } C_{21} \,..\, C_{2l})) := (\text{and } C_{1121} \,...\, C_{112l} \,...\, C_{1k21} \,...\, C_{1k2l})$
with $C_{1i2j} = \text{LCS}(C_{1i}, C_{2j})$
$\text{LCS}((\text{all } r_1 \ C_1),(\text{all } r_2 \ C_2)) := \text{if } r_1 = r_2 \text{ then } (\text{all } r_1 \ \text{LCS}(C_1, C_2)) \text{ else } \top$
$\text{LCS}((\text{atmost } m_1 \ r_1),(\text{atmost } m_2 \ r_2)) := \text{if } r_1 = r_2 \text{ then } (\text{atmost } \max(m_1, m_2) \ r_1) \text{ else } \top$
$\text{LCS}((\text{atleast } m_1 \ r_1),(\text{atleast } m_2 \ r_2)) := \text{if } r_1 = r_2 \text{ then } (\text{atleast } \min(m_1, m_2) \ r_1) \text{ else } \top$
$\text{LCS}((\text{part } n_1 \ C_1),(\text{part } n_2 \ C_2)) := \text{if } n_1 = n_2 \text{ then } (\text{part } n_1 \ \text{LCS}(C_1, C_2)) \text{ else } \top$
$\text{LCS}((\text{parts } m_1 \ n_1),(\text{parts } m_2 \ n_2)) := \text{if } (n_1 = n_2 \text{ and } m_1 = m_2) \text{ then } (\text{parts } m_1 \ n_1) \text{ else } \top$
$\text{LCS}((\text{pp-constraint } r_1 \ n_{11} \ n_{12}),(\text{pp-constraint } r_2 \ n_{21} \ n_{22})) :=$
if $(n_{11} = n_{21} \text{ and } n_{21} = n_{22} \text{ and } r_1 = r_2)$ then (pp-constraint $r_1 \ n_{11} \ n_{12}$) else $\top$
For primitive concepts C_1 and C_2: $\text{LCS}(C_1, C_2) := \text{if } C_1 = C_2 \text{ then } C_1 \text{ else } \top$
other cases (with different constructors): $\text{LCS}(C_1, C_2) := \top$

Fig. 1. Least Common Subsumer

$boy \doteq (\text{and } male \ child)$
$girl \doteq (\text{and } female \ child)$
$standard\text{-}family\text{-}with\text{-}boys \doteq$
(and (part husband man) (parts 1 husband) (part wife woman) (parts 1 wife)
(part offspring boy) (parts 2 offspring) (pp-constraint married husband wife)
(pp-constraint mother wife offspring) (pp-constraint father husband offspring))
$family\text{-}with\text{-}2\text{-}girls \doteq$ (and (part husband man) (parts 1 husband) (part wife woman)
(parts 1 wife) (part offspring girl) (parts 2 offspring) (pp-constraint mother wife offspring)
(pp-constraint father husband offspring))
$\text{LCS}(standard\text{-}family\text{-}with\text{-}boys, family\text{-}with\text{-}2\text{-}girls) = (family\text{-}with\text{-}2\text{-}children \doteq)$
(and (part husband man) (parts 1 husband) (part wife woman) (parts 1 wife)
(part offspring child) (parts 2 offspring) (pp-constraint mother wife offspring)
(pp-constraint father husband offspring))

Fig. 2. LCS of two kinds of family concepts

Depending on extra language constraints there are several possibilities for computing specific concepts. In general it is not possible to completely fit all the relevant information about an individual into a single concept in the language [11]. As a solution to this problem in [5] extra constructs are defined which are only to be used internally by the system but not by the user. Here we associate with an individual x a concept $\text{SC}(x)$ which can be defined in our language. We give some properties of this concept in figure 3. In the example in figure 4 we assume that we have complete knowledge of the world and that all roles and part names are closed.

5 Learning Concepts

The algorithms we propose are targeted to learn descriptions of composite concepts. We propose to maintain two version spaces[8]: one for the is-a relation

concept-filler	role-filler involving the parts

$$\frac{kb \vdash x \rightarrow C}{SC(x) \Rightarrow C}$$

In the case where the part names n_1 and n_2 are closed:

$$\frac{kb \vdash (\forall y_1 \lhd_{n_1} x, y_2 \lhd_{n_2} x : < y_1, y_2 > \in \varepsilon[r])}{SC(x) \Rightarrow (\textbf{pp} - \textbf{constraint } r\ n_1\ n_2)}$$

role-filler   *part-filler*

$$\frac{kb \vdash < x, y > \in \varepsilon[r]}{\exists C : (y \rightarrow C \wedge SC(x) \Rightarrow (\textbf{all } r\ C))}$$
$$\frac{kb \vdash \#\{y \mid < x,y > \in \varepsilon[r]\} = m}{SC(x) \Rightarrow (\textbf{atleast } m\ r)}$$

$$\frac{kb \vdash y \lhd_n x}{\exists C : (y \rightarrow C \wedge SC(x) \Rightarrow (\textbf{allp } n\ C))}$$
$$\frac{kb \vdash \#\{y \mid y \lhd_n x\} = m}{N(SC(x), n) \geq m}$$

In the case that the role r is closed:
$$\frac{kb \vdash \#\{y \mid < x,y > \in \varepsilon[r]\} = m}{SC(x) \Rightarrow (\textbf{atmost } m\ r)}$$

In the case that the part name n is closed:
$$\frac{kb \vdash \#\{y \mid y \lhd_n x\} = m}{SC(x) \Rightarrow (\textbf{parts } m\ n)}$$

Fig. 3. Specific Concepts.

(**concept-filler** f (**all** *accounts large*))
(**concept-filler** *Mary woman*)
(**concept-filler** *Jane child*)
(**part-fillers** *Mary wife* f)
(**part-fillers** *Jane offspring* f)
(**role-fillers** *John father Marc*)
(**role-fillers** *Mary mother Marc*)
(**concept-filler** *John man*)
(**concept-filler** *Marc child*)
(**part-fillers** *John husband* f)
(**part-fillers** *Marc offspring* f)
(**role-fillers** *John married Mary*)
(**role-fillers** *John father Jane*)
(**role-fillers** *Mary mother Jane*)
$SC(Marc) = child$
$SC(Jane) = child$
$SC(Mary) = $ (**and** *woman* (**atleast** *2 mother*) (**atmost** *2 mother*) (**all** *mother child*))
$SC(John) = $ (**and** *man* (**atleast** *1 married*) (**atmost** *1 married*) (**all** *married* $SC(Mary)$)
(**atleast** *2 father*) (**atmost** *2 father*) (**all** *father child*))
$SC(f) = $ (**and** (**all** *accounts large*) (**part** *husband* $SC(John)$) (**parts** *1 husband*)
(**part** *wife* $SC(Mary)$) (**parts** *1 wife*) (**part** *offspring child*) (**parts** *2 offspring*)
(**pp-constraint** *married husband wife*) (**pp-constraint** *mother wife offspring*)
(**pp-constraint** *father husband offspring*))

Fig. 4. Specific concept: example

(or subsumption) and one for the part-of relation (i.e. parts and modules). The first version space is represented[2] by a set $\mathcal{G}$ of concepts that are more general than the concept to learn $C^\star$, a set $\mathcal{S}$ of concepts that are more specific than $C^\star$ and a set $\mathcal{N}$ of individuals which do not belong to the extension of $C^\star$. The second version space is represented by a set $\mathcal{C}$ of concepts for which $C^\star$ can be used as a building block and a set $\mathcal{B}$ of concepts which $C^\star$ can use as building blocks. Finally, we also keep information about the possibility or necessity of

---

[2] As the **and** of two more general concepts is also a more general concept, and the LCS of two more specific concepts is also a more specific concept, $\mathcal{G}$ and $\mathcal{S}$ actually are singletons or the empty set.

occurrence of part names. $\mathcal{P}^-$ denotes the part names which cannot occur in the definition of $C^\star$. $\mathcal{P}_n$ is a set of tuples $\langle n, min, max, C \rangle$ for the part names which necessarily occur in the definition of $C^\star$ where n is the part name, min and max specify the interval to which the number of n-parts in $C^\star$ belongs, and C is the domain of n for $C^\star$. $\mathcal{P}_p$ is a similar set for part names which possibly occur in $C^\star$. Finally, we also keep information about which constraints between the parts are possible.

In this section we discuss the learning algorithms informally and point out the extra information we obtain by a special handling of part-of[3]. In the examples involving subsumption and individuals we obtain also extra information about part-of. Similarly, the examples involving part-of give information for the is-a hierarchy. Below we assume that the concept to learn $C^\star$ is *standard-family*.

5.1 Learning Using Concepts and Subsumption

In the case where we know that $C^\star \Rightarrow C$ we have immediately a more general concept and the standard updates can be performed. However, we also know the following: (i) the part names which occur in the definition of C also occur in the definition of $C^\star$, (ii) the part names which occur in the definition of C occur in $C^\star$ with the same number, and (iii) the domain for the part name in C subsumes the domain for the corresponding part name in $C^\star$. For instance, if we know that *standard-family* $\Rightarrow$ *family-with-2-children* (figure 2) , then *husband*, *wife* and *offspring* must occur in the definition of *standard-family* with N($husband,C^\star$) = 1, N($wife,C^\star$) = 1 and N($offspring,C^\star$) = 2. We also know that the *husband*-part for *standard-family* is a *man*, the *wife*-part for *standard-family* is a *woman*, and each *offspring*-part for *standard-family* is a *child* (or more specific).

In the case where $C \Rightarrow C^\star$ we have immediately a more specific concept. We use LCS in the updates. We also know that: (i) the part names which occur in the definition of C are the only possible part names for the definition of $C^\star$, (ii) if some part name occurs in both definitions then the numbers are the same, and (iii) if some part name occurs in both definitions then the domain for the part name in $C^\star$ subsumes the domain for the corresponding part name in C. Knowing that *standard-family-with-boys* $\Rightarrow$ *standard-family* would tell us that the only part names occurring in the definition of *standard-family* can be *husband*, *wife* and *offspring*, although not all have to occur. However for the part names which do occur we also know the exact number. Similarly we know that for the occurring part names that the domains are more general than the ones in *standard-family-with-boys*. For instance, an *offspring* in *standard-family* is more general than a *boy*.

---

[3] With the standard updates below we mean the basic updates of the $\mathcal{G}$, $\mathcal{S}$, $\mathcal{C}$ and $\mathcal{B}$ sets. The updates in the data structures originating from the extra information are straightforward and we do not discuss the actual updates.

5.2 Learning Using Individuals

In the case where $x \in \varepsilon[C^\star]$ we know that a specific concept covering x is more specific than $C^\star$. Therefore we can use $SC(x)$ as a learning example. Furthermore, we also know that (i) the definition of $C^\star$ can only contain the part names for which there is a part in x. Having f as in figure 4 as an example for *standard-family* tells us that $SC(f) \Rightarrow$ *standard-family*.

The examples where $x \notin \varepsilon[C^\star]$ are used to find inconsistencies or concepts for which there is no definition in the language.

5.3 Learning Using Concepts and Part-of

In the case where $C \lhd_n C^\star$ we have a building block for $C^\star$ and we have that: (i) if (**part** n A) occurs in the definition of $C^\star$ then $C \Rightarrow A$, and (ii) $N(n,C^\star) \geq 1$. Knowing that *young-child* is an *offspring*-part of *standard-family*, gives us that (**part** *offspring* A) occurs in the definition of *standard-family* and *young-child* $\Rightarrow A$.

In the case where $C \lhd_{\mathbf{mod}} C^\star$ we have a building block for $C^\star$ and we have that: (i) if (**part** n A) occurs in C then (**part** n A') occurs in $C^\star$ such that $A \Rightarrow A'$, (ii) for the part names occurring both in C and $C^\star$ no other **pp-constraint**-terms can occur in the definition of $C^\star$ than the ones which occur in the definition of C, (iii) $N(C^\star) > N(C)$, and (iv) $N(n,C^\star) \geq N(n,C)$. The fact that *couple* $\lhd_{\mathbf{mod}}$ *standard-family* implies that a *standard-family* has at least 1 *husband*-part which is at least as general than a *man* and at least 1 *wife*-part which is at least as general than a *woman*. We also know that the only constraint between *husband* and *wife* can be that they are *married*.

6 Related Work

In [3, 4] concepts are learned in CLASSIC [1]. The language is more expressive than the standard part of the language we use, but there are no constructs to deal with part-of. Examples are concepts. A concept is a positive example if it is subsumed by the concept to learn and negative otherwise. It is shown that C-CLASSIC[4] is PAC-learnable. The algorithm is based on the LCS version in [2]. Learning from individuals is done by generalizing the individuals into concepts. A number of experiments have been performed.

KLUSTER [7] starts from a knowledge base of individuals linked together by roles. The first step in KLUSTER's learning is to build a basic taxonomy which is expressed in a sub-language of BACK [9]. This sub-language is the same as the standard part of our language except for the fact that KLUSTER allows role constructs. The learning problem for KLUSTER is to build discriminating concept definitions starting from the basic taxonomy.

---

[4] C-CLASSIC is a restriction of CLASSIC and has the constructors **and**, **all**, **atleast**, **atmost**, **fills**, **one-of**, **min** and **max**.

7 Future Work

In the case of role fillers and part fillers in the computation of $SC(x)$ for an individual x there is still a certain degree of freedom to find the concept the role or part filler belongs to. A trivial possibility is to assign to this concept the value $\top$. Another possibility is to use the SC of this other individual in the computation and be aware of the possibility of cycles (as we did in figure 4). We will investigate other ways and experiment.

The description logic we use as framework does not allow disjunction. However, [3] shows how disjunctive concepts may be learned in CLASSIC. As far as our algorithms are similar this approach seems to be mappable to our algorithm.

References

1. Borgida, A., Brachman, R.J., McGuinness, D.L., Resnick, 'CLASSIC : A Structural Data Model for Objects', *Proceedings of SIGMOD 89*, pp 59-67, 1989.
2. Cohen, W., Borgida, A., Hirsh, H., 'Computing Least Common Subsumers in Description Logics', *Proceedings of AAAI 92*, pp 754-760, 1992.
3. Cohen, W., Hirsh, H., 'Learning the CLASSIC Description Logic: Theoretical and Experimental Results', *Principles of Knowledge Representation and Reasoning: Proceedings of the Fourth International Conference - KR 94*, pp 121-133, 1994.
4. Cohen, W., Hirsh, H., 'The Learnability of Description Logics with Equality Constraints', *Machine Learning*, Vol 17, pp 169-199, 1994.
5. Donini, F., Era, A., 'Most Specific Concepts Technique for Knowledge Bases with Incomplete Information', *Proceedings of the First International Conference on Information and Knowledge Management*, pp 545-551, 1992.
6. Franconi, E., 'A Treatment of Plurals and Plural Qualifications based on a Theory of Collections', *Minds and Machines*, Vol 3(4), pp 453-474, 1993.
7. Kietz, J.-U., Morik, K., 'A Polynomial Approach to the Constructive Induction of Structural Knowledge', *Machine Learning*, Vol 14, pp 193-217, 1994.
8. Mitchell, T., 'Generalization as Search', *Artificial Intelligence*, Vol 18(2), pp 203-226, 1982.
9. Nebel, B., *Reasoning and Revision in Hybrid Representation Systems*, Lecture Notes in Artificial Intelligence, 422, Springer-Verlag, 1990.
10. Padgham, L., Lambrix, P., 'A Framework for Part-Of Hierarchies in Terminological Logics', *Principles of Knowledge Representation and Reasoning: Proceedings of the Fourth International Conference - KR 94*, pp 485-496, 1994.
11. Schaerf, A., 'Which Semantics for Individuals in the Tbox?', *Proceedings of the International Workshop on Description Logics*, pp 5-8, 1994.
12. Speel, P.-H., Patel-Schneider, P., 'CLASSIC extended with physical whole-part relations', *Proceedings of the International Workshop on Description Logics*, pp 45-50, 1994.

Comparison of Conceptual Graphs for Modelling Knowledge of Multiple Experts

Rose DIENG

INRIA, ACACIA Project, 2004 Route des Lucioles, BP 93,
06902 Sophia-Antipolis Cedex, FRANCE, E-mail: dieng@sophia.inria.fr

Abstract. When modeling expertise from multiple experts, expertise conflicts among the expertise models of the different experts must be tackled, so as to build their common expertise model. The domain level of an expertise model can be represented using Sowa's conceptual graph formalism. This paper presents a method for conflict management during knowledge modeling from multiple experts: this method is based on the comparison and integration of multiple conceptual graphs corresponding to different viewpoints, the integration being guided by different integration strategies.

1 Introduction

Expertise capitalization in a company or development of a knowledge-based system (KBS) may involve several experts stemming from the same or different domains. The knowledge engineers (KEs) must detect and solve expertise conflicts: (a) different terminologies, (b) incompatible terminologies, (c) different compatible reasonings, (d) incompatible reasonings. Few knowledge acquisition (KA) methods take into account expertise conflict management [19] [10] [7] [3]. After the KE elicited rough data from the different experts, he must analyze the elicited data in order to build a model common to all experts, models common only to subgroups of experts, and models specific to an expert and not shared by other experts. The KE can either build such models directly from the rough data, or build each expert's expertise model independently and then compare the obtained expertise models in order to find their common parts and their specific parts. When several KEs are involved, a KE may be responsible for modelling one expert, or for modelling a specific aspect throughout the different experts. In our KA framework, we represent each expert by an artificial agent [5]. Our model of agent indicates *individual features* and *social features* related to the agent interactions with the other agents. Such features must then be instantiated by the KE for the application. A significant individual aspect is the agent expertise model, described using the Kads method [24] with three layers: domain, inference and task (see Figure 1). Moreover, we represent the concepts and relations of the domain layer through knowledge graphs. In [4] [3], we had proposed techniques for comparing knowledge graphs representing multiple experts. In this paper, we will adapt such techniques to Sowa's conceptual graph formalism [20] [21] [22], so as to offer a conflict management mechanism based on the comparison and integration of multiple conceptual graphs (CGs) representing knowledge of multiple experts.

We rely on the model of simple conceptual graphs, as defined in [20][21] [22] [1] [25].

A canon S is a tuple = $(\mathcal{T}c, \mathcal{T}r, \mathcal{B}, \mathcal{M}, \text{conf})$ where $\mathcal{T}c$ is a lattice of concept types, $\mathcal{T}r$ a relation type lattice, $\mathcal{B}$ a set of "star graphs" in bijection with $\mathcal{T}r$, and indicating the signature of each relation type, M a set of individual markers, conf a conformity relation relating type labels to individual markers. A *conceptual graph defined with respect to a canon S* is a connected, bipartite, labelled graph, the labelling respecting some constraints. We denote it $(C, \mathcal{R}, \mathcal{A})$ where C is the set of concept nodes, $\mathcal{R}$ the set of R-vertices, $\mathcal{A}$ the set of the "basic links" denoted $rel(C_1, ..., C_n)$, with $rel \in \mathcal{R}$, and $\forall\ i \in$ [1.. arity(rel)], C_i = neighbour (i, rel) $\in C$. We suppose that $\forall\ rel_1$ and $rel_2 \in \mathcal{T}r \setminus \{Re-lation, Absurd-relation\}$ such that $rel_1 < rel_2$, we have: arity (rel_1) = arity(rel_2) and type (neighbour (i, B (rel_1))) $\leq$ type (neighbour (i, B (rel_2))). To each concept type, the function Names associates a set composed of its main name and of its synonyms.

After presenting our algorithm of comparison of CGs, we will present possible integration strategies that may guide the construction of an integrated graph. In conclusion, after a comparison with related work, we will evoke possible extensions of our work.

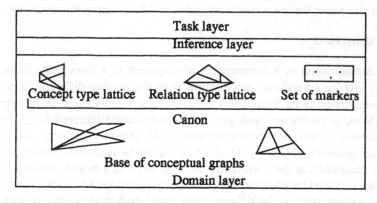

Fig. 1. Expertise model of an agent.

2 Exploitation of Conceptual Graphs for Multi-expertise

2.1 Modelling Domain Models Through Conceptual Graphs

Let us consider several experts whose knowledge was modelled separately. To each expert corresponds an artificial agent, to which a *canon* (i.e. a concept type lattice, a relation type lattice, a set of markers and the conformity relation), and a *base of true canonical CGs* are associated. This base can be partitioned according to such viewpoints stressed in the application: eg. *subpart-viewpoint, electrical-viewpoint, mechanical-viewpoint, influence-viewpoint*. For sake of simplicity, we suppose that in each agent, there is at most one CG corresponding to a given viewpoint.

2.2 Algorithm of Integration of two Expertise Models

The steps of the integration algorithm of the expertise models of two agents are:

1. Compare both canons.
2. Compare both bases of CGs: for each viewpoint, compare the two corresponding graphs, CG_1 and CG_2. It can be decomposed as follows: (a) to each concept type, root

in the common canon, associate the C-vertices of CG_1 and CG_2, compatible with this root; (b) establish the relations between "basic links" of both CG: rel_1 $(C_{11},...,C_{1n})$ and rel_2 $(C_{21},...,C_{2n})$; (c) establish the relations between CG_1 and CG_2.

3. Build the base of integrated CGs, according to the chosen integration strategy: using the relations previously set up, build the integrated CGs for each viewpoint.

2.3   Comparison of two Canons

Searching the common canon associated to several experts of the same domain can be compared to the search of an ontology common to the experts. One can work either at the knowledge level [16], without choosing a representation formalism or at the symbol level, once chosen a representation formalism. Our choice of the CG formalism allows us to propose CG-based algorithms. All the steps cannot be automated as the experts must be involved in conflict resolution. For building the common canon:

1. *Compare the two concept type lattices*: solve the name conflicts, compare the definitions associated to a concept type in both canons and try to join the subtypes of a concept type. If necessary, some new concept types may be added and the names of some concept types may be changed. After that, a "common concept type lattice", corresponding to the integration of both lattices of concept types, is obtained. With each concept type appearing in this integrated lattice, the different names used by the different specialists must be stored. An automated matching of two concept types of two agents is complex. Generally, when the experts stem from the same domain, they often use the same term for the same concept, which is not the case for experts of different domains. A sophisticated matching procedure should be able to compare: two atomic concept types, an atomic concept type and a concept type definition, two concept type definitions, the "neighbouring" of two concept types (i.e. father(s), sons, brothers...), the schemas associated to two concept types. At present, C_1 and C_2 are matched iff cardinal (Names (C_1) $\cap$ Names (C_2) is greater than a given threshold.

2. *Compare the two relation type lattices*: solve the name conflicts, the relation signature conflicts, and try to join the subtypes of a given relation type. Some new types may be added and some type names may be changed. Then, the obtained "common relation type hierarchy" corresponds to the integration of the two hierarchies of relations. The different names adopted by the experts must be stored. Then $\mathcal{B}_{com}$, set of the "star graphs" indicating the signatures of the common relation types is built.

3. *Compare the two sets of markers*. An individual marker appearing in both canons and satisfying both conformity relations represents the same individual. As a generic referent automated matching is complex, we suppose that the experts agree on the names of the generic referents. Then, the common conformity relation $conf_{com}$ is built.

2.4   Comparison of Conceptual Graphs

Once obtained the common canon ($\mathcal{T}_{c\text{-com}}$, $\mathcal{T}_{r\text{-com}}$, $\mathcal{B}_{com}$, $\mathcal{M}_{com}$, $conf_{com}$), the comparison algorithm proceeds as follows:

1. In each CG of an agent, replace the expert's terms by the agreed terms adopted in the common lattices of concept types and of relation types.

2. *For each viewpoint* v *for which both experts have associated CGs, compare the two corresponding CGs,* $CG_1 = CG$ (Agent$_1$,v) *and* $CG_2 = CG$ (Agent$_2$,v):

- For each concept (resp. relation) type, root in the common concept type lattice $\mathcal{T}_{c\text{-com}}$ (resp. the common relation type lattice $\mathcal{T}_{r\text{-com}}$), a preprocessing on CG_1 and CG_2 helps to gather the C-vertices (resp. R-vertices) that belong to this type and that can be compared to each other later: e.g. C-vertices such as [Driver's error], [Excessive-speed : *x] can be associated to the concept type *Driver's-error*.

  For each viewpoint v, for each agent Agent$_i$, let $CG_i = CG$ (Agent$_i$,v) :

  a) for each root ∈ sons (T, $\mathcal{T}_{c\text{-com}}$),
     store-comparable-concepts (CG_i, root) → Lconcepts (CG_i,root)

  b) for each root-rel ∈ sons (T, $\mathcal{T}_{r\text{-com}}$),
     store-comparable-relations(CG_i, root-rel) → Lrelations (CG_i,root-rel).

- Establish relations between "basic links": for each root-rel ∈ sons (T, $\mathcal{T}_{r\text{-com}}$),
  for each rel$_1$ ∈ Lrelations (CG_1, root-rel), for each rel$_2$ ∈ Lrelations (CG_2, root-rel),
  let n be the common arity of rel$_1$, rel$_2$, root-rel,
  if for each i ∈ [1..n] comparable-concepts (neighbour (i, rel$_1$), neighbour (i, rel$_2$))
     then find-basic-links (rel$_1$, CG_1) → Llinks (rel$_1$, CG_1)
          find-basic-links (rel$_2$, CG_2) → Llinks (rel$_2$, CG_2)
          store-relations-on-relations (rel$_1$, rel$_2$) → Lrelations (rel$_1$, rel$_2$).
  Establish relations between CG_1 and CG_2 (cf. Section 2.6, page 5).

3. Build integrated-CG (CG_1, CG_2, strat), the integrated graph according to the chosen integration strategy (cf. Section 2.7, page 6).

2.5 Examples of Relations Among Basic Links

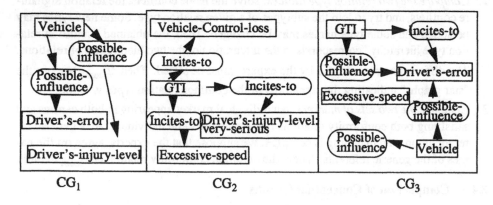

CG$_1$ CG$_2$ CG$_3$

Fig. 2. Conceptual graphs of two experts, on the viewpoint interaction-vehicle-driver

The definitions of possible relations among basic links can be found in [6]. This section gives an example in accidentology (cf. Figure 2).

In CG_1, let us denote $Link_1$ = [Vehicle] → (Possible-influence) → [Driver's-error],
$Link_2$ = [Vehicle] → (Possible-influence) → [Driver's-injury-level].
In CG_2, let us denote: $Link_3$ = [GTI] → (Incites-to) → [Excessive-speed],
$Link_4$ = [GTI] → (Incites-to) → [Vehicle-control-loss],
$Link_5$ = [GTI] → (Incites-to) → [Driver's-injury-level: very-serious],
In CG_3, let us denote: $Link_6$ = [GTI] → (Possible-influence) → [Driver's error],
$Link_7$ = [GTI] → (Incites-to) → [Driver's-error],
$Link_8$ = [Vehicle] → (Possible-influence) → [Excessive-speed],
$Link_9$ = [Vehicle] → (Possible-influence) → [Driver's-error].
We have the following relations among such basic links:
is-relation&concept-total-specialization ($Link_3$, $Link_1$); is-relation&concept-total-specialization ($Link_4$, $Link_1$); is-relation&concept-partial-specialization&partial-instantiation ($Link_5$, $Link_2$); is-concept-partial-specialization ($Link_6$, $Link_1$); is-relation&concept-partial-specialization ($Link_7$, $Link_1$); is-concept-partial-specialization ($Link_8$, $Link_1$) and is-same-link ($Link_9$, $Link_1$).

2.6 Relations among Conceptual Graphs

Definitions. Let CG_1 = (C_1, R_1, A_1) and CG_2 = (C_2, R_2, A_2) two CGs; C_i is the set of C-vertices of CG_i, R_i the set of R-vertices of CG_i and A_i the set of basic links of CG_i.
A *graph morphism* h between CG_1 and CG_2 is a 3-uple of functions: (h_c: $C_1 → C_2$, h_r $R_1 → R_2$, $h_a : A_1 → A_2$) such that:
$\forall rel_1 \in R_1$, $\forall i \in [1..arity(rel_1)]$, h_c (neighbour (i, rel_1)) = neighbour (i, h_r (rel_1))
and $\forall link_1 = rel_1(C_{11}, ... C_{1n}) \in A_1$, $h_a(link_1) = h_r$ (rel_1) (h_c (C_{11}), ... h_c (C_{1n})).

Subgraph and Supergraph: CG_2 is a *subgraph* of CG_1 (i.e. CG_1 is a *supergraph* of CG_2 iff there exists a surjective graph morphism (h_c: $C_1 → C_2$, h_r :$R_1 → R_2$, $h_a : A_1 → A_2$) such that $\forall link_2 = rel_2(C_{21}, ... C_{2n}) \in A_2$, $\exists link_1 = rel_1 (C_{11}, ... C_{1n}) \in A_1$, satisfying $link_2 = h_a(link_1) \wedge$ is-same-link ($link_2$, $link_1$).

Contraction and Expansion: CG_2 is a *contraction* (resp. an *expansion*) of CG_1 iff CG_2 is obtained from CG_1 by a contraction (resp. an *expansion*) of a type definition.
CG_2 is an expansion of CG_1 iff CG_1 is a contraction of CG_2.

Specialization:

- CG_2 is a *"concept total specialization"* of CG_1 iff $\exists$ a graph morphism (h_c: $C_2 → C_1$, h_r :$R_2 → R_1$, $h_a : A_2 → A_1$) from CG_2 to CG_1 such that $\forall link_2 \in A_2$, is-concept-total-specialization ($link_2$, h_a ($link_2$)).

- CG_2 is a *"concept partial specialization"* of CG_1 iff $\exists$ a graph morphism (h_c, h_r, h_a) from CG_2 to CG_1 such that $\forall link_2 \in A_2$, (is-concept-partial-specialization ($link_2$, h_a

(link$_2$)) $\vee$ is-same-link (link$_2$, ha (link2))) and $\exists$ link$_2$ $\in \mathcal{A}_2$ such that: is-concept-partial-specialization (link$_2$, h$_a$ (link$_2$)).

- CG$_2$ is a *"relation total specialization"* of CG$_1$ iff $\exists$ a graph morphism (h$_c$, h$_r$, h$_a$) from CG$_2$ to CG$_1$ such that $\forall$ link$_2$ $\in \mathcal{A}_2$, is-relation-specialization(link$_2$, h$_a$(link$_2$)).

- CG$_2$ is a *"relation partial specialization"* of CG$_1$ iff $\exists$ a graph morphism (h$_c$, h$_r$, h$_a$) from CG$_2$ to CG$_1$ such that $\forall$ link$_2$ $\in \mathcal{A}_2$, (is-relation-specialization (link$_2$, h$_a$ (link$_2$)) $\vee$ is-same-link (link$_2$, h$_a$ (link$_2$))) and $\exists$ link$_2$ $\in \mathcal{A}_2$ such that is-relation-specialization (link$_2$, h$_a$ (link$_2$)).

Likewise, we define a *"relation & concept total specialization"*.

Generalization:

- CG$_2$ is a *"concept total (resp. partial) generalization"* of CG$_1$ iff CG$_1$ is a *"concept total (resp. partial) specialization"* of CG$_2$.

- CG$_2$ is a *"relation total (resp. partial) generalization"* of CG$_1$ iff CG$_1$ is a *"relation total (resp. partial) specialization"* of CG$_2$.

- CG$_2$ is a *"relation & concept total (resp. partial) generalization"* of CG$_1$ iff CG$_1$ is a *"relation & concept total (resp. partial) specialization"* of CG$_2$.

Instantiation:

- CG$_2$ is a *"total instantiation"* of CG$_1$ iff $\exists$ a graph morphism (h$_c$, h$_r$, h$_a$) from CG$_2$ to CG$_1$ such that $\forall$ link$_2$ $\in \mathcal{A}_2$, is-total-instantiation (link$_2$, h$_a$ (link$_2$)).

- CG$_2$ is a *"partial instantiation"* of CG$_1$ iff $\exists$ a graph morphism (h$_c$, h$_r$, h$_a$) from CG$_2$ to CG$_1$ such that $\forall$ link$_2$ $\in \mathcal{A}_2$, is-partial-instantiation (link$_2$, h$_a$ (link$_2$)) $\vee$ is-same-link (link$_2$, h$_a$ (link$_2$)) and $\exists$ link$_2$ $\in \mathcal{A}_2$ satisfying: is-partial-instantiation (link$_2$, h$_a$ (link$_2$)).

Likewise, we define a *"relation specialization & total (resp. partial) instantiation"*.

Conceptualization:

- CG$_2$ is a *"total (resp. partial) conceptualization"* of CG$_1$ iff CG$_1$ is a *"total (resp. partial) instantiation"* of CG$_2$.

- CG$_2$ is a *"relation generalization & total (resp. partial) conceptualization"* of CG$_1$ iff CG$_1$ is a *"relation specialization & total (resp. partial) instantiation"* of CG$_2$.

2.7 Construction of the base of integrated CG

Strategies of Integration. Once obtained the relations between basic links of both graphs, the building of the integrated graph CG$_{com}$ by integration of both CGs must be guided by a *strategy* for solving conflicts: a given strategy can be chosen if its preconditions are satisfied. In case of choice between two related basic links $link_1$ $\in \mathcal{A}_1$, and $link_2 \in \mathcal{A}_2$ among which there exists a relation, the basic link to be stored in CG_{com} depends on the relation between both links and on the chosen strategies.

Strategy of the highest direct generalization: only the following relations between basic links are successively considered: is-relation&concept-total-generalization, is-relation&concept-partial-generalization, is-relation-generalization, is-concept-total-generalization, is-concept-partial-generalization. The KE includes in CG_{com} the "most general" between $link_1$ and $link_2$, (i.e. the result of the function *most-general* ($link_1$, $link_2$)). If the function gives no result, both links $link_1$ and $link_2$ are included in CG_{com}. The *preconditions* are: an expert focuses on particular cases, while the other expert expresses general knowledge, valid in more general cases; the KE prefers to always restrict to what was explicitly expressed by at least one expert: he takes no initiative for generalizing the knowledge expressed by an expert.

Strategy of the highest indirect generalization: the same relations as in the previous case are considered. The KE includes the result of the function *common-generalization* ($link_1$, $link_2$) in CG_{com} (i.e. the "minimal generalization" common to $link_1$ and $link_2$), but the KE may take the initiative to replace type (rel_1) and type (rel_2) by their minimal common supertype and to replace type (neighbour (i,rel_1)) and type (neighbour (i,rel_2)) by their minimal common supertype. The *preconditions* are: the characteristics of the expert are the same as in the previous case; if needs be, guided by an expert's knowledge, the KE can take the initiative for generalizing the other expert's knowledge.

Strategy of the highest direct specialization: the same relations as in the previous case are considered. The KE includes in CG_{com} the "most specialized" between $link_1$ and $link_2$, (i.e. the result of the function *most-specific* ($link_1$, $link_2$)). The KE always respects what was said by at least one expert. The *preconditions* are: an expert is more specialized than the other, on a given aspect and uses more precise expressions; the KE prefers to restrict to what was explicitly expressed by at least one expert: he takes no initiative for specializing the experts' knowledge or for restricting its validity.

Strategy of the highest indirect specialization: the same relations as in the previous case are considered. The KE includes the result of the function *common-specialization* ($link_1$, $link_2$) in CG_{com} (i.e. the "maximal specialization" common to $link_1$ and $link_2$), but the KE can take the initiative to use, instead of type (rel_1) and type (rel_2), their maximal common subtype, or to use, instead of type (neighbour (i,rel_1)) and type (neighbour (i,rel_2)), their maximal common subtype. The preconditions on the experts are the same as in the previous case; in case of need, the KE can use the knowledge expressed by an expert, in order to specialize the other expert's knowledge or to restrict its validity domain.

Strategy of the highest direct conceptualization: only the following relations between basic links are successively considered: is-relation-generalization&total-conceptualization, is-relation-generalization&partial-conceptualization, is-total-conceptualization, is-partial-conceptualization. The KE includes the result of the function *most-generic* (link$_1$, link$_2$) in CG$_{com}$. If it gives no result, both links link$_1$ and link$_2$ are included in CG$_{com}$. The *preconditions* are: an expert focuses on too particular cases and on too specific examples, while the other expert expresses general knowledge, at a better level of abstraction; the KE prefers to always restrict to what was explicitly expressed by at least one expert: he takes no initiative for generalizing the knowledge expressed by an expert.

Strategy of the highest indirect conceptualization: the same relations as in the previous case are considered. The KE includes in CG$_{com}$ the result of the function *common-conceptualization* (link$_1$, link$_2$) (i.e. the "minimal conceptualization" common to link$_1$ and link$_2$), but the KE can take the initiative to replace referent (neighbour (i,rel$_1$)) and referent (neighbour (i,rel$_2$)) by a generic referent. The *preconditions* on the experts are the same as in the previous case; the KE can take the initiative to conceptualize the experts' knowledge.

Strategy of the highest direct instantiation: the relations to consider are the same relations as in the previous case. The KE includes in CG$_{com}$ the "most instantiated" between link$_1$ and link$_2$ (i.e. the result of the function *most-instantiated* (link$_1$, link$_2$)). The KE always respects what was said by at least one expert. The *preconditions* are: an expert gives useful and precise examples; the KE prefers to restrict to what was explicitly expressed by at least one expert: he takes no initiative for instantiating the experts' knowledge.

Strategy of the greatest confidence: the KE includes the basic link of the most competent expert. As a *precondition*, an expert has a higher competence level in a field.

Strategy of experts' consensus: the KE includes only a basic link on which both experts agree. The *preconditions* are: (1) both experts have the same competence level in the field and the KE has no criterion for choosing one rather than the other; (2) or, for "psychological" reasons, it is impossible to make a selection between both experts; (3) or, the future KBS is explicitly aimed at relying only on the experts' intersecting knowledge.

The KE chooses the integration strategy, according to the experts' individual features and to their expertises: their specialities, the way they expressed during the elicitation sessions (level of precision, presence or absence of examples illustrating abstract knowledge, capability to abstract knowledge from particular cases...). The strategy may either be global, and applied throughout the integration algorithm, or, be local and change according to the context. So, throughout a given integration, the previously described strategies may be combined. The strategy choice could be automated, thanks to a decision procedure based on the strategy preconditions: the KE would describe explicitly the features of the involved experts (as in a user model). When several strategies are possible, the KE must choose one with the help of the experts. For example, in traffic accident analysis, if two psychologists are respectively specialists of GTI vehicle drivers and of drivers' errors, the KE can adopt (a) the greatest confidence strategy when comparing parts of the CGs concerning GTI vehicle drivers or drivers' errors, (b) otherwise, the highest direct specialization strategy whenever it can be applied, and (c) the strategy of experts' consensus in the remaining cases.

Building of the Integrated CG. For integrating CG$_1$ and CG$_2$, examine the relations between the two sets of basic links $\mathcal{A}_1$ and $\mathcal{A}_2$. According to the integration strategy, only some relations are useful; there is a priority between the relations. In order to find a matching function *match*: $\mathcal{A}_1 -> \mathcal{A}_2$, (a) if $\forall$ link$_1 \in \mathcal{A}_1$, it remains at most one relation linking link$_2$

$\in \mathcal{A}_2$ with $link_1$, then match $(link_1) = link_2$; (b) in case of multiple such relations, some of them must be eliminated in order to find an actual matching function from $\mathcal{A}_1$ to $\mathcal{A}_2$. At the end, the different parts of the obtained graph CG_{com} must be connected thanks to a maximal join. The resulting CG_{com} could then be reused in other applications on the same domain, even though its construction relies on a specific KE whose integration strategy choice depends on his "subjective" opinion on the involved experts.

2.8 Influence on the Agents

If successful, the algorithm of comparison of the different CGs of the same viewpoint leads to integrated CGs, according to the integration strategy. Then a new agent can be built; its expertise model domain layer represents the knowledge common to both experts is described by the integrated CGs. The remaining parts of each expert constitute his specific knowledge and can be gathered in a new agent specific to this expert. Each of the two compared experts is now represented by a compound agent, made of the common agent and the specific agent.

The algorithm of comparison of two CGs can be refined, so as to take into account several experts. Several approaches seem possible: (1) Compare the experts progressively, by always comparing two agents: first compare two of the experts, chosen according to an adequate strategy, then compare a third one with the common agent obtained after comparison of the first two experts, etc. (2) Compare the experts all together directly. (3) Partition the set of the experts into n subsets, according to an adequate criterion, and then associate to each subset the common agent obtained by the comparison of its agents, and lastly, compare the n common agents obtained. Within a given subset, the agents may again be compared by the three ways.

3 Conclusions

We proposed an algorithm for comparison of CGs representing the viewpoints of several experts. Related research concerns: study of terminology conflicts due to the possibility of disagreement of the experts on some concepts or on the vocabulary [19] [10]; coexistence of multiple perspectives in distributed KA [8]; techniques for comparing several viewpoints and managing conflicts among them [7] or for integrating new knowledge into an existing KBS [9] [15]; integration of vocabularies [14]; building a common ontology from several ones on the same domain [12]; matching and integrating ontologies [23]; techniques for detecting and solving conflicts in cooperative design [13]; graph isomorphism and algorithms for matching CGs [17] [25] [2]; building shared ontologies [11]. As a further work, we will refine and extend the CG comparison algorithm with more complex integration strategies and for more than two experts, and study the influence of the experts' comparison order and the possible convergence towards a "minimal" common knowledge. Last, we will exploit a formalization of relations among CGs [18].

Acknowledgements

We deeply thank the French "Ministère de l'Equipement, des Transports et du Tourisme" (contract 93.0003), the PRC-IA (Grafia Project) and the ModelAge Working Group (contract EP:8319) that funded this research, and the anonymous referees for their judicious suggestions.

References

1. M. Chein, and M. L. Mugnier. Conceptual Graphs: Fundamental Notions. *RIA*, 6(4):365-406, 1992.

2. O. Cogis, and O. Guinaldo. A Linear Descriptor for Conceptual Graphs and a Class for Polynomial Isomorphism Test. In G. Ellis et al, eds, *Conceptual Structures: Applications, Implementation and Theory*, Springer-Verlag, LNAI 954, pp. 263-277, Santa Cruz, CA, Aug. 1995.

3. R. Dieng. Conflict Management in Knowledge Acquisition. In I. Smith (Ed), *AIEDAM, Special Issue on Conflict Management in Design*, 9(4):337-351 September 1995.

4. R. Dieng, O. Corby, and S. Labidi. Expertise Conflicts in Knowledge Acquisition. In B. Gaines, and M. Musen, eds, *Proc. of KAW-94*, pp. 23-1 – 23-20, Banff, Canada, Jan. - Feb. 1994.

5. R. Dieng, O. Corby, and S. Labidi. Agent-Based Knowledge Acquisition. In L. Steels et al, eds *A Future for Knowledge Acquisition: EKAW'94*, Springer-Verlag, LNAI 867, pp. 63-82, Sept. 1994.

6. R. Dieng. *Comparison of Conceptual Graphs for Modelling Knowledge of Multiple Experts*. INRIA Research Report, February 1996.

7. S. Easterbrook. Handling conflict between domain descriptions with computer-supported negotiation. *Knowledge Acquisition*, 3(3):255-289, September 1991.

8. S. M. Easterbrook. Distributed Knowledge Acquisition as a Model for Requirements Elicitation. In *Proc. of EKAW-89*, pp. 530-543, Paris, France, July 1989.

9. J. Eggen, A. M. Lundteigen., and M. Mehus. Integration of Knowledge from Different Knowledge Acquisition Tools. In B. Wielinga et al, eds, *Proc. of EKAW-90*, Amsterdam, Feb. 1990. IOS Press.

10. B. R. Gaines, and M. L. G. Shaw Comparing the Conceptual Systems of Experts. In *Proceedings of the 9th IJCAI (IJCAI-89)*, pp. 633-638, Detroit, 1989.

11. C. Garcia. *Construction coopérative d'ontologies dans un cadre de multi-expertise*. Rapport de stage de DEA Informatique, LIRMM, Montpellier, September 1995.

12. M. M. Kayaalp and J. R. Sullins Multifaceted Ontological Networks: Reorganization and Representation of Knowledge in Natural Sciences. In *Proc. of KAW-94*, pp. 25-1 – 25-19, Banff, Canada, Jan. - Feb. 1994.

13. M. Klein. Detecting and resolving conflicts among cooperating human and machine-based design agents. *Artificial Intelligence in Engineering*, 7:93-104, 1992

14. G. W. Mineau, and M. Allouche. Establishing a Semantic Basis: Toward the Integration of Vocabularies. In Gaines et al eds *Proc. of KAW'95*, pp. 2-1 – 2-16, Banff, Canada, Feb. 1995.

15. K. S. Murray, and B. W. Porter. Developing a tool for knowledge integration: initial results. *International Journal of Man-Machine Studies*, 33:373-383, 1990.

16. A. Newell. The knowledge level. *Artificial Intelligence*, 18:87-127, 1982.

17. J. Poole, and J. A. Campbell. A Novel Algorithm for Matching Conceptual and Related Graphs. In G. Ellis et al eds, *Conceptual Structures: Applications, Implementation and Theory*, pp. 293-307, Santa Cruz, CA, USA, August 1995. Springer-Verlag, LNAI 954.

18. M. Ribière, R. Dieng, M. Fornarino, A.-M. Pinna-Dery. *Intégration d'un formalisme de liens dans le formalisme des graphes conceptuels*. INRIA Research Report, February 1996.

19. M. L. G. Shaw, and B. R. Gaines. A methodology for recognizing conflict, correspondence, consensus and contrast in a knowledge acquisition system. *Knowledge Acqu.*, 1(4):341-363, Dec. 1989.

20. J. F. Sowa. *Conceptual Structures: Information Processing in Mind and Machine*. Reading, Addison-Wesley, 1984.

21. J.F. Sowa. Conceptual Graphs Summary. In T.E. Nagle et al, eds *Conceptual Structures: Current Research and Practice*, England, Ellis Horwood Workshops, 1992.

22. J.F. Sowa. Relating Diagrams to Logic. In *Proc of ICCS'93*, Québec City, Canada, August 1993.

23. G. Wiederhold. Interoperation, Mediation and Ontologies. *Proc. of FGCS'94 Workshop on Heterogeneous Cooperative Knowledge Bases*, Tokyo, Japan, pp. 33-48, Dec. 1994.

24. B. Wielinga, G. Schreiber, and J. Breuker. KADS: a modelling approach to knowledge engineering. *Knowledge Acquisition*, 4:5-53, 1992.

25. M. Willems. Projection and Unification for Conceptual Graphs. In Ellis et al eds, *Conceptual Structures: Applications, Implementation and Theory*, pp. 278-292, Santa Cruz, Aug. 1995. Spring.-Verl., LNAI 954.

Semantical Considerations for Knowledge Base Updates

Yan Zhang

Department of Computing
University of Western Sydney, Nepean
PO Box 10, Kingswood
NSW 2747, Australia
E-mail: yan@st.nepean.uws.edu.au

Abstract. Recent research has shown that under some circumstances, the conventional minimal change methods were inappropriate for updating knowledge bases with disjunctive effects. In this paper we propose a new method for the knowledge base update based on a persistence principle, which provides conservative results for updating knowledge bases with implicit and disjunctive effects. As it will be shown, our approach avoids the difficulty with the minimal change principle. To characterize properties of the persistence-based update method, we investigate the relationship between the minimal change update semantics and persistent update semantics in detail.

1 Introduction

The knowledge base update has been widely studied in AI. It generally addresses the following question: given a knowledge base (i.e., a set of logical formulas as a description of the world), what changes may be caused by an occurrence of new knowledge and how to specify the new knowledge base when the old one has changed?

Consider the following Scenario. Peter is a second year computer science student. When the semester began, he enrolled two computer science courses CS201 and CS301. After two weeks, he decided to drop course CS301. However, the department rule requires that a second year computer science student must enroll at least two computer science courses with level 200 or 300. That means, at least Peter has to enroll another computer science course with level 200 or 300. Suppose that in this semester, there are two 200 level courses CS201 and CS202 available, and two 300 level courses CS301 and CS303 available. Therefore, what Peter can choose is to do late enrollment in course CS202 or CS303. If the department maintains a knowledge base of Peter's course enrollment information, then the general question of updating such a knowledge base is how to specify the resulting knowledge base after something has changed within the old knowledge base (i.e., Peter dropped course CS301 and intends to enroll course CS202 or CS303).

It is well known that the *minimal change principle* was employed in most formalizations of propositional knowledge base updates [6, 1, 5, 4]. In general, the minimal change principle says that during a state transition, the change between states should be *as little as possible*. In the above Peter's course-enrollment example, after dropping course CS301, according to the minimal change principle, Peter would like to enroll one of CS202 or CS303, but not both. This seems reasonable since to satisfy the department law, Peter only needs to enroll one more course with level 200 or 300. In this case, the minimal change gives the right result.

However, recent research has revealed that under some circumstances, such minimal change was inappropriate for representing state change with disjunctive effects. The following example illustrates the difficulty[1]. Suppose a table is painted with one part white and one part black. Therefore, a box on the table implies that it may be entirely within the white region, *or* within the black region, *or* touching the both regions. This constraint can be expressed by a logical formula like:

$$Ontable(Box) \supset Inwhite(Box) \lor Inblack(Box). \tag{1}$$

Suppose initially a box is not on the table, and after a while, the box is put on the table. Using the minimal change principle, however, the fact that the box is put on the table will imply that the box must be only within one of white or black region. Obviously, this solution is not reasonable from our intuition.

In this paper we propose a new method for propositional knowledge base updates based on a *persistence principle*, which provides conservative results for updating knowledge bases with implicit and disjunctive effects generally. As it will be shown, our approach avoids the difficulty with the minimal change principle. To characterize properties of our persistence-based update method, we investigate the relationship between the minimal change update semantics and persistent update semantics in detail.

The paper is organized as follows. The second section proposes a persistent semantics for updates. The third section compares our persistent update semantics with minimality-baed update semantics in detail. Finally, the fourth section concludes the paper with some discussions.

2 A Persistent Semantics for Updates

2.1 The Language

Consider a finitary propositional language $\mathcal{L}$. We represent a *knowledge base* by a propositional formula ψ. A propositional formula ϕ is *complete* if ϕ is consistent and for any propositional formula μ, $\phi \models \mu$ or $\phi \models \neg\mu$. $Models(\psi)$ denotes the set of all models of ψ, i.e., all interpretations of $\mathcal{L}$ in which ψ is true. We also consider *state constraints* about the world. Let C be a satisfiable propositional

---

[1] This example was originally suggested by Ray Reiter. A similar example was also proposed by Zhang and Foo in [7].

formula that represents all state constraints about the world[2]. Thus, for any knowledge base ψ, we require $\psi \models C$. Let I be an interpretation of $\mathcal{L}$. We say that I is a *state* of the world if $I \models C$. A knowledge base ψ can be treated as a *description* of the world, where $Models(\psi)$ is the set of *possible states* of the world with respect to ψ.

Let ψ be the current knowledge base and μ a propositional formula which is regarded as a new knowledge (information) about the world. Then, informally, the general question of updating ψ with μ is how to specify the new knowledge base after combining the new knowledge (information) μ into the current knowledge base ψ. In Peter's course-enrollment example, the constraint that a second year student must enroll at least two CS courses with level 200 or 300 may be expressed by a formula C:

$(Enrolled(CS201) \vee Enrolled(CS202) \vee Enrolled(CS301)) \wedge$
$(Enrolled(CS201) \vee Enrolled(CS202) \vee Enrolled(CS303)) \wedge$
$(Enrolled(CS201) \vee Enrolled(CS301) \vee Enrolled(CS303)) \wedge$
$(Enrolled(CS202) \vee Enrolled(CS301) \vee Enrolled(CS303))$.

then the initial knowledge base of Peter's course-enrollment can be represented by formula $\psi \equiv Enrolled(CS201) \wedge Enrolled(CS301) \wedge C$, and the new knowledge is $\mu \equiv \neg Enrolled(CS301) \wedge (Enrolled(CS202) \vee Enrolled(CS303))$. So, the question is: what is the new knowledge base of Peter's course-enrollment after updating ψ with μ.

2.2 Updating States

In order to deal with propositional knowledge base updates properly, we first consider state updates. As it will be shown next, in our formalism, updating knowledge base ψ with μ is defined by updating all possible states of ψ with μ, and this is achieved by the *persistence principle*. Informally, the persistence principle says that *a fact persists during a state transition if it is logically irrelevant to those facts that must change or are subject to change during this state transition*. Note that the persistence principle provides a general principle for modeling state change. We have shown that this principle can be effectively applied in reasoning about action and temporal reasoning [7, 8]. As we will show in this paper, the persistence principle can be also used to formalize propositional knowledge base updates.

Before we present the following formal definitions, we first introduce some useful concepts. Let Σ be a set of formulas and f a propositional literal (positive or negative propositional letter). We say that Σ is a *minimal support set* of f if (i) $\Sigma \models f$; (ii) $f \notin \Sigma$; and (iii) there does not exist a proper subset Σ' of Σ such that $\Sigma' \models f$. Let f_1 and f_2 be two propositional literals. We say that disjunction $f_1 \vee f_2$ is *non-trivially entailed* by Σ if (i) $\Sigma \models f_1 \vee f_2$; (ii) $\Sigma \not\models f_1$

---

[2] Usually, we use a set of formulas to represent state constraints. In this case, C can be viewed as a conjunction of all such formulas.

and $\Sigma \not\models f_2$. In this case, we also call that disjunction $f_1 \vee f_2$ is *non-trivial* with respect to Σ[3].

Definition 1. Let I be a state of the world, i.e., $I \models C$, μ a propositional formula and consistent with C. We define the *persistent set* of I with respect to μ, denoted as $\Delta(I, \mu)$, as follows:

1. $\Delta_0 = I - \{f \mid f \in I \text{ and } \{\mu\} \cup C \models \neg f\}$,
2. $\Delta_1 = \Delta_0 - \{f_1, \cdots, f_k \mid \{\mu\} \cup C \models \bigvee_{i=1}^{k} [\neg] f_i \text{ where } \{f_1, \cdots, f_k\} \subseteq I,$
   $$C \not\models \bigvee_{i=1}^{k} [\neg] f_i \text{ and for any proper subset } M \text{ of }$$
   $$N = \{1, \cdots, k\} \; \{\mu\} \cup C \not\models \bigvee_{j \in M} [\neg] f_j\},$$
3. $\Delta_i = \Delta_{i-1} - \{f \mid f \in I, \{\mu\} \cup C \not\models f, \text{ and for } every \text{ minimal support set } F$
   of f in I, there exists at least one element of F, f', which
   is in $I - \Delta_{i-1}\}$,
4. $\Delta = \bigcap_{i=0}^{\infty} \Delta_i$.

The *persistent set* $\Delta(I, \mu)$ of I is defined as
$$\Delta(I, \mu) = \{f \mid f \in I \text{ and } \Delta \cup C \models f\}.$$
The notation $[\neg]$ means that the negation sign $\neg$ may or may not appear. $\square$

We now explain this definition in detail. Consider a state of the world I and a formula μ where μ is consistent with C. Obviously, after updating I with μ, a fact f in I *must change* if f is inconsistent with μ with respect to C, i.e., $\{\mu\} \cup C \models \neg f$. We call such a fact *non-persistent* with respect to μ (i.e., condition 1 in the above definition). On the other hand, suppose there exists some fact f where f or its negation $\neg f$ appears in a non-trivial disjunction with respect to $\{\mu\} \cup C$, we say that f is *indefinitely affected* by μ. The intuitive meaning of an indefinite effect is that after updating I with μ, the satisfaction of μ (together with C) in the resulting state may or may not cause a change of the truth value of f, but we do not know which is the case (i.e., condition 2). Moreover, for a fact f, if for *every* minimal support set F in I of f, there exists some fact in F which is non-persistent or indefinitely affected by μ, then we say that f is *implicitly affected* by μ. Because after updating I with μ, f may lose its support. In this case, it is incautious to assume that f persists. Furthermore, this rule is used recursively: a fact f is *implicitly affected* by μ if for *every* minimal support set F in I of f, there exists some fact in F which is implicitly affected by μ (i.e., condition 3). We call those facts that are indefinitely or implicitly affected by μ *mutable*. Thus, a fact in I *must* persist if it is neither non-persistent nor mutable. We take all such facts to form the persistent set, as presented in the above definition (condition 4).

So far, the possible state resulting from updating I with μ is defined as follows.

Definition 2. Let I be a state of the world, i.e., $I \models C$, and μ a propositional formula that is consistent with C. An interpretation I' of $\mathcal{L}$ is a *possible state* of the world resulting from updating I with μ, iff

---

[3] This definition can be easily extended to any disjunction with more than two propositional literals.

1. $I' \models C$,
2. $I' \models \mu$, and
3. $\Delta(I, \mu) \subseteq I'$.

Denote the set of all possible states of the world resulting from updating I with μ as $Update(I, \mu)$. □

2.3 Updating Knowledge Bases

Based on definitions of state updates, we can define the persistence-based update operator $\diamond_{psa}$ (*persistent set approach*) as follows.

Definition 3. Let ψ be a knowledge base, μ a propositional formula. $\psi \diamond_{psa} \mu$ denotes the *persistent update* of ψ with μ^4, where

1. If ψ implies μ or ψ is inconsistent then $\psi \diamond_{psa} \mu \equiv \psi$, otherwise
2. $Models(\psi \diamond_{psa} \mu) = \bigcup_{I \in Models(\psi)} Update(I, \mu)$. □

In the above definition, condition 1 says that if ψ implies μ, then nothing is changed since the knowledge μ has been represented by knowledge base ψ; or if ψ is inconsistent, then any update can not change it into a consistent knowledge base. Condition 2 says that if ψ is consistent and does not imply μ, then ψ should be changed, and this change follows the persistence principle as defined previously. The following example illustrates how our approach represents knowledge base update.

Example 1. Continue considering Peter's course-enrollment example presented previously. Suppose that there are two constraints in the course-enrollment domain: someone enrolled course CS202 implies that she/he is preparing to study course CS303; and someone enrolled course CS204 also implies that she/he is preparing to study course CS303. Thus, the constraints C is the conjunction of the following two formulas:

$$Enrolled(CS202) \supset Prestudy(CS303), \tag{2}$$

$$Enrolled(CS204) \supset Prestudy(CS303). \tag{3}$$

We also assume that there is one more course CS204 available in the semester. Currently, Peter enrolled courses CS201 and CS202, but did not enroll course CS204. So, the knowledge base of Peter's course-enrollment is

$$\psi \equiv Enrolled(CS201) \wedge Enrolled(CS202) \wedge \neg Enrolled(CS204) \wedge C.$$

Clearly, $\psi \models Prestudy(CS303)$. Now, Peter decides to drop course CS202. So, the department administrative assistant needs to update ψ with $\neg Enrolled(CS202)$. The question is: does Peter still prepare to study course CS303?

Of course, updating ψ with $\neg Enrolled(CS202)$ has an implicit effect on propositional letter $Prestudy(CS303)$ because of constraint (2). It seems that if

---

[4] Here we only consider the *well-defined* update, that is, μ is consistent with C.

there is no more information, we cannot predict the truth value of $Prestudy(CS303)$ in the resulting knowledge base definitely. If we predict that $Prestudy(CS303)$ is still true after updating ψ with $\neg Enrolled(CS202)$ (as the policy of the minimal change principle), it means that dropping course CS202 does not affect Peter's intention of studying CS303. This seems unreasonable if the reason of dropping CS202 is indeed that Peter does not want to study CS303. If we predict that $Prestudy(CS303)$ is false after updating ψ with $\neg Enrolled(CS202)$ (as in foundational theory, eg. TMS [2]), on the other hand, it seems that dropping CS202 certainly implies that Peter does not want to study CS303. However, constraint (2) does not imply such information.

From our persistence principle, since there is no further information, we can only state that the truth value of $Prestudy(CS303)$ is *mutable* after updating ψ with $\neg Enrolled(CS202)$. Thus, using the persistent update approach, we have the following result:

$$\psi \diamond_{psa} \neg Enrolled(CS202) \equiv$$
$$Enrolled(CS201) \wedge \neg Enrolled(CS202) \wedge \neg Enrolled(CS204) \wedge C. \; \square$$

3 Persistent Update and Minimal Change

In this section, we will compare the persistent update approach with some well known minimality-based approaches in detail.

3.1 Winslett's PMA

We first briefly review Winslett's possible models approach (PMA) [6][5]. Similarly, in the PMA, a description of the world (knowledge base) is represented by a set of propositional formulas (or take the conjunction of the set of formulas), denoted as ψ. Domain constraints about the world is represented by a subset C of ψ. All models of ψ are called *possible states* of ψ. Then updating ψ with a formula μ is achieved by updating every possible state of ψ with μ, but with a minimal change principle on models.

Formally, let I_1 and I_2 are two interpretations, we say that I_1 and I_2 *differ* on propositional letter f if f appears in exactly one of I_1 and I_2. $Diff(I_1, I_2)$ denotes the set of all different propositional letters between I_1 and I_2. Then updating a model I of ψ with μ by the PMA generates a set of interpretations, $Incorporate(I, \mu)$, such that for each $I' \in Incorporate(I, \mu)$,

1. μ and each formula in C are true in I';
2. for any I'' satisfying 1, $Diff(I, I'') \subseteq Diff(I, I')$ implies $I'' = I'$.

Finally, updating ψ with μ, denoted as $\psi \diamond_{pma} \mu$, is defined as

$$Models(\psi \diamond_{pma} \mu) = \bigcup_{I \in Models(\psi)} Incorporate(I, \mu).$$

---

[5] Here we simplify the PMA to the propositional case in order to compare it with our approach consistently.

Example 2. Recall the box example presented in section 1, the initial knowledge base (the box is not on the table) can be represented by the formula $\psi \equiv \neg Ontable(Box) \wedge \neg Inwhite(Box) \wedge \neg Inblack(Box) \wedge (1)$. Now the box is dropped on the table. Consider updating ψ with $\mu \equiv Ontable(Box)$ by using the PMA. From the above definition, we have the following result:

$\psi \diamond_{pma} \mu \equiv Ontable(Box) \wedge (1) \wedge$
$((Inwhite(Box) \wedge \neg Inblack(Box)) \vee (\neg Inwhite(Box) \wedge Inblack(Box)))$,

which says that the box can only be entirely within the white region or black region, but not both. Using our method presented in section 2, we have a more plausible result:

$\psi \diamond_{psa} \mu \equiv Ontable(Box) \wedge (1) \wedge (Inwhite(Box) \vee Inblack(Box))$,

which says that the box can be entirely in the white or black region, or touching both regions. $\square$

From the above discussion, we can see that the PMA and our our persistence-based method are quite different. But it should be noted that both of them are state-based, i.e., updating a knowledge base is achieved by updating every possible state of the world. Hence, we can compare these two approaches by examining their differences in updates on states. We first consider *mutable sets* obtained from these two methods respectively.

Let I be a possible state of ψ, C the set of state constraints about the world, μ a propositional formula, and $\Delta(I, A)$ the persistent set of I with respect to μ obtained by Definition 1. Obviously, the *non-persistent set* (i.e., facts that *must change*) of I with respect to μ obtained by both the PSA and PMA is as follows

$$\Gamma(I, \mu) = \{f \mid f \in I \text{ and } \{\mu\} \cup C \models \neg f\}.$$

The mutable set obtained from the PSA is

$$\delta_{PSA}(I, \mu) = I - \Delta(I, \mu) - \Gamma(I, \mu).$$

Since in the PMA, $\bigcap Incorporate(I, \mu)$ is the set of all facts that are true in every possible model. Therefore, the mutable set obtained from the PMA is

$$\delta_{PMA}(I, \mu) = I - \bigcap Incorporate(I, \mu) - \Gamma(I, \mu).$$

Definition 4. Let I be a possible state of ψ, C the set of state constraints about the world, $F \subseteq I$ and $f \in I$. We say that F *influences* f, if there exists a minimal support set Σ of f with respect to C in I, such that $F \subseteq \Sigma$. $\square$

Directly from the above definition, we know that if F influences f, then for any non-empty subset F' of F, F' influences f. We say that F *uniquely influences* f if there exists a *unique* minimal support set Σ of f with respect to C in I such that $F \subseteq \Sigma$. Suppose δ and F be two subsets of I, we say that δ *is influenced* by F if for every $f \in \delta$, f is influenced by F.

Theorem 5. *The following results hold.*

1. *If* $\delta_{\mathrm{PSA}}(I,\mu) - \delta_{\mathrm{PMA}}(I,\mu) \neq \emptyset$, *then for any fact* $f \in \delta_{\mathrm{PSA}}(I,\mu) - \delta_{\mathrm{PMA}}(I,\mu)$, f *is influenced by some subset of* $\Gamma(I,\mu)$ *or indefinitely (implicitly) affected by* μ;
2. *If* $\delta_{\mathrm{PMA}}(I,\mu) - \delta_{\mathrm{PSA}}(I,\mu) \neq \emptyset$, *then for any fact* $f \in \delta_{\mathrm{PMA}}(I,\mu) - \delta_{\mathrm{PSA}}(I,\mu)$, f *is neither uniquely influenced by any subset of* $\Gamma(I,\mu)$ *nor indefinitely (implicitly) affected by* μ. $\square$

The above theorem simply says that each *mutable* fact obtained by the PSA is influenced by some non-persistent facts, or indefinitely (implicitly) affected by μ. In other words, during a knowledge base update, by the PSA, every fact that may change must have some logical relation(s) to those facts that may or must change, while by the PMA there may be some facts which have to change without any logical reasons.

3.2   Katsuno and Mendelzon's Update Semantics

The motivation of Katsuno and Mendelzon's proposal for update is an observation on the difference between revision and update, as they discussed in [5, 4]. let ψ be a knowledge base and μ a formula. Then Katsuno and Mendelzon presented the following eight postulates that, as they argued, should be satisfied by any update operator $\diamond$.

(U1) $\psi \diamond \mu$ implies μ.
(U2)   If ψ implies μ then $\psi \diamond \mu \equiv \psi$.
(U3)   If both ψ and μ are satisfiable then $\psi \diamond \mu$ is also satisfiable.
(U4)   If $\psi_1 \equiv \psi_2$ and $\mu_1 \equiv \mu_2$ then $\psi_1 \diamond \mu_1 \equiv \psi_2 \diamond \mu_2$.
(U5) $(\psi \diamond \mu) \wedge \phi$ implies $\psi \diamond (\mu \wedge \phi)$.
(U6)   If $\psi \diamond \mu_1$ implies μ_2 and $\psi \diamond \mu_2$ implies μ_1 then $\psi \diamond \mu_1 \equiv \psi \diamond \mu_2$.
(U7)   If ψ is complete then $(\psi \diamond \mu_1) \wedge (\psi \diamond \mu_2)$ implies $\psi \diamond (\mu_1 \vee \mu_2)$.
(U8) $(\psi_1 \vee \psi_2) \diamond \mu \equiv (\psi_1 \diamond \mu) \vee (\psi_2 \diamond \mu)$.

In fact, Katsuno-Mendelzon's update postulates characterize the update semantics for a class of update operators that are based on the principle of minimal change in knowledge base updates. For instance, the PMA update operator $\diamond_{pma}$ satisfies all postulates (U1) – (U8). Here, we will examine the relations between our persistent update semantics and Katsuno-Mendelzon's update semantics by investigating the satisfiability of Katsuno-Mendelzon's update postulates under our persistent update semantics. We first give the following result.

Theorem 6. *The persistence-based update operator* $\diamond_{psa}$ *satisfies Katsuno-Mendelzon's postulates (U1) – (U4), (U6) and (U8).* $\square$

Generally, (U5) and (U7) are not satisfied under the persistent semantics because the intuitive meaning of (U5) and (U7) is to represent a minimal change for update while the persistent update does not follow this principle generally.

Although the persistent update operator does not satisfy the postulates (U5) and (U7) in the general case, we have the following theorem, which says that under some restrictions, (U5) and (U7) can be satisfied by the persistent update operator.

Theorem 7. *The following results hold.*

(U5') If $\psi \diamond_{psa} \mu \models [\neg]\phi$ but $\psi \not\models \phi$, then $(\psi \diamond_{psa} \mu) \wedge \phi$ implies $\psi \diamond_{psa} (\mu \wedge \phi)$.

(U7') If $\psi \diamond_{psa} \mu_1 \models [\neg]\mu_2$ (or $\psi \diamond_{psa} \mu_2 \models [\neg]\mu_1$), then $(\psi \diamond_{psa} \mu_1) \wedge (\psi \diamond_{psa} \mu_2)$ implies $\psi \diamond_{psa} (\mu_1 \vee \mu_2)$. □

3.3 The AGM Revision

Katsuno and Mendelzon proved that the AGM revision postulates [3] are equivalent to the following postulates [5]:

(R1) $\psi \circ \mu$ implies μ.
(R2) If $\psi \wedge \mu$ is satisfiable then $\psi \circ \mu \equiv \psi \wedge \mu$.
(R3) If μ is satisfiable then $\psi \circ \mu$ is also satisfiable.
(R4) If $\psi_1 \equiv \psi_2$ and $\mu_1 \equiv \mu_2$ then $\psi_1 \circ \mu_1 \equiv \psi_2 \circ \mu_2$.
(R5) $(\psi \circ \mu) \wedge \phi$ implies $\psi \circ (\mu \wedge \phi)$.
(R6) If $(\psi \circ \mu) \wedge \phi$ is satisfiable then $\psi \circ (\mu \wedge \phi)$ implies $(\psi \circ \mu) \wedge \phi$.

We can characterize the difference between our persistent update and the AGM revision by verifying the satisfaction of (R1) — (R6) under the persistent update semantics, as we did for Katsuno and Mendelzon's update semantics previously. The following summarizes the difference.

Theorem 8. $\diamond_{psa}$ *satisfies the AGM revision postulates (R1) and (R4), but violates (R2), (R3), (R5) and (R6). □*

4 Conclusion

In this paper, we have proposed a propositional knowledge base update method based on the persistence principle. We showed that under many situations, our approach provides plausible results for representing implicit and disjunctive effects of updates. We also compared the semantical difference between our approach and and well known minimality-based update theories.

A limitation of our approach is that sometimes the persistence principle may give too conservative solutions in updates. Consider a domain with the following constraint:

$$Walking(Fred) \supset Alive(Fred), \tag{4}$$

which means that if Fred is walking, then Fred is alive. Suppose the current knowledge base is:

$$\psi \equiv Walking(Fred) \wedge (4).$$

Obviously, we have $\psi \models Alive(Fred)$. Now if Fred stops walking, what is the result of updating ψ with $\neg Walking(Fred)$? According the PSA, we have the following result:

$$\psi \diamond_{psa} \neg Walking(Fred) \equiv \neg Walking(Fred) \wedge (4).$$

Note that from $\psi \diamond_{psa} \neg Walking(Fred)$, we can not derive if Fred is alive or not. But intuitively, Fred stopping walking will not affect the fact of Fred being alive. In this sense, our approach is too conservative.

An effective way to deal with this problem is to distinguish *general constraints* and *causal constraints* explicitly in the formalism. More details will be addressed in a forthcoming paper. In particular, a general constraint represents a normal logical relation among literals, while a causal constraint represents some causal relation among literals. Then the minimal change principle will be applied to general constraints, and the persistence principle is only applied to causal constraints. Some ideas of this issue has been addressed in [9].

Acknowledgements

This research is supported in part by a grant from the Australian Research Council. I thank Norman Y. Foo for many valuable discussions on this subject.

References

1. Dalal, M.: Investigations into a theory of knowledge base revision: Preliminary report. In *Proceedings of Seventh National Conference on Artificial Intelligence (AAAI'88)*. Morgan Kaufmann Publisher, Inc. (1988) 475–479
2. Doyle, J.: A truth maintenance system. *Artificial Intelligence* 12 (1979) 231–272
3. Gardenfors, P.: *Knowledge in Flux*. MIT Press. (1988)
4. Katsuno, H., Mendelzon, A.O.: On the difference between updating a knowledge database and revising it. In *Proceedings of Second International Conference on Principles of Knowledge Representation and Reasoning (KR'91)*. Morgan Kaufmann, Inc. (1991) 387–394
5. Katsuno, H., Mendelzon, A.O.: Propositional knowledge base revision and minimal change. *Artificial Intelligence* 52 (1991) 263–294
6. Winslett, M.: Reasoning about action using a possible models approach. In *Proceedings of the Seventh National Conference on Artificial Intelligence (AAAI'88)*. Morgan Kaufmann Publisher, Inc. (1988) 89–93
7. Zhang, Y., Foo, N.Y.: Reasoning about persistence: a theory of actions. In *Proceedings of Thirteenth International Joint Conference on Artificial Intelligence (IJCAI'93)*. Morgan Kaufmann Publishers, Inc. (1993) 718–723
8. Zhang, Y., Foo, N.Y.: Applying the persistent set approach in temporal reasoning. *Annals of Mathematics and Artificial Intelligence* 14 (1995) 75-98
9. Zhang, Y.: Compiling causality into action theories. In *Proceedings of The Third Symposium on Logical Formalizations of Commonsense Reasoning (CommonSense'96)*, Stanford (1996) 263-270

Partial Evaluation in
Constraint Logic Programming

Agata Wrzos-Kamińska

Department of Computer Systems and Telematics,
Norwegian University of Science and Technology, N-7034 Trondheim
email: agata@idt.unit.no

Abstract. Partial evaluation is an optimization technique which aims at specializing general programs in order to improve their efficiency. Within the field of Logic Programming the technique is known as partial deduction. In this paper we generalize the concept of partial deduction so that it applies to the framework of Constraint Logic Programming (CLP). We also lift the main theoretical results on partial evaluation in Logic Programming to the CLP case, thus providing a formal foundation for partial evaluation of constraint logic programs.

1 Introduction

Partial evaluation is an optimization technique which aims at specializing general programs in order to improve their performance. The use of partial evaluation can result in substantial gains of efficiency. Generally, the idea can be explained as follows [10]. If some of the input data are known beforehand, a program can be specialized, and this can be achieved in an automated way. Specialization is done by performing those computations of the program that depend only on the given input arguments, and by generating code for remaining computations which depend on the as yet unavailable data. The resulting specialized version may be not as simple and elegant as the general program, but it will be more efficient.

Partial evaluation allows an advanced and very convenient programming methodology. Namely, one may well write highly parameterized and modularized programs, each of them solving a whole class of similar problems. Such general programs may be inefficient; but with the use of a partial evaluator they may be automatically specialized to any interesting setting of parameters, yielding as many customized, more efficient versions (*residual programs*) as desired. The approach is excellent for documentation, modification and human usage; it can ease the programming and maintenance effort.

One of the domains where partial evaluation has been successfully applied is *Logic Programming* (LP). Within the field, applications of the technique include meta-programming, program optimization, explanation-based learning and software engineering.

A great advantage of LP is its declarativeness. However, the paradigm has also its limitations, probably the major of them being the syntactic nature of the domain of computation. This drawback is overcome in *Constraint Logic Programming* (CLP), a generalization of LP where other kinds of objects besides terms are considered, and where other kinds of relations over objects than equations may be evaluated. In CLP, Logic Programming has been combined with another declarative paradigm, that of *constraint solving*. An important property of constraints is that they allow to define objects implicitly, by specifying their properties. As indicated in [7], a fundamental weakness of conventional LP programs comes from the fact that they compute results in a form of substitutions, that is strictly of the explicit type. In CLP, implicit representations were introduced via constraints, significantly increasing the expressive power of the language.

In this paper, we generalize the concept of partial deduction as defined for LP [11], [13] so that it applies to the framework of Constraint Logic Programming. We also lift the main theoretical results on partial evaluation in Logic Programming to the CLP case, thus providing a formal foundation for partial evaluation of constraint logic programs. This should allow to enjoy the virtues of partial evaluation in the powerful paradigm of Constraint Logic Programming, at the same time guaranteeing correctness of transformations.

The reader is assumed familiar with basic concepts of Logic Programming [12]. The rest of the paper is organized as follows. In the next section, we give an introduction on main ideas underlying CLP, its semantics, and the concept of partial deduction. In section 3, we define the concept of partial evaluation for CLP. In section 4, formal results for the declarative and operational semantics of CLP are presented. Finally, in section 5 we summarize the results and discuss some directions for future work.

2 Preliminaries

2.1 Constraint Logic Programming

In this section, we introduce main ideas that underlie the paradigm of CLP [6], [4, 5]. We do it by comparison to conventional LP. The presentation is partially based on [7] and [8].

The key extension of CLP with respect to LP consists in allowing a user's domain of computation besides the Herbrand universe, admitting constraints other than equalities, and replacing unification by constraint solving [6].

In conventional LP, the domain of computation is the Herbrand universe, i.e. the set of ground terms of some first-order language. Note that we can view unification, which is a part of the resolution, as an implicit representation of equations over terms. CLP generalizes this framework, by incorporating constraints and constraint solving methods. The domain of computation is no longer limited to the Herbrand universe. CLP systems were developed that compute over numerous other domains, like sets, various types of graphs, Boolean expressions, integers, rationals, real numbers, or lambda expressions. Usually these are well understood and formalized domains, for which there exist natural algebraic operators (such as intersection/multiplication, union, disjunction, etc.) and basic predicates, typically including equality/isomorphism and different forms of inequalities ($\subset, \leq, \neq$, etc). These special predicates are examples of (primitive) *constraints*. Their meaning is assumed known and fixed, as opposed to the "ordinary" LP predicates which are defined via program clauses.

Just like a conventional definite LP program, a CLP program consists of a finite set of Horn clauses, written in the form: $h \leftarrow B$. The atom h is still called the *head* of the clause, and B stands for what is called the *body*. In particular, a *goal* (or *query*) is a clause of the form: $\leftarrow B$. The difference is that in CLP constraint atoms (or simply: constraints) may be used in the bodies of clauses in addition to the "usual" atoms (or simply: atoms). We will usually represent CLP clauses as
$$h \leftarrow A, C$$
where A is the finite collection of atoms and C is the finite collection (conjunction) of constraints in the body of the clause.

For a single atom a and a finite collection of constraints C, a *fact* in CLP is a clause of the form $a \leftarrow C$ (also called a *conditional atom*). In addition, we will use the notion of *constrained atom* to denote a conjunction of the form $a \wedge C$ (or: a, C). The operators of conjunction ($\wedge$ or ,) and set union ($\cup$) will often be used interchangeably.

In CLP, ordinary atoms control the resolution procedure, as it is the case in conventional LP. Constraint atoms are accumulated, possibly in a simplified/normalized form, in the so called *constraint store*.

In order to deal with the more general form of program clauses, a CLP interpreter contains a domain-specific constraint solving engine in addition to a standard resolution module. The job of the constraint engine is to maintain the constraint store in a standard form and to decide, upon request from the resolution engine, whether a collection of constraints is consistent (satisfiable).

2.2 Declarative Semantics for CLP

CLP Scheme [6] is a unified framework defining a whole class of CLP languages along with their semantics. The description is parameterized by a choice of domain of computation and constraints. The parameter, which determines the particular instance of the scheme, involves four elements [14, 8]: Σ – a signature which declares the predefined predicate and function symbols; $\mathcal{D}$ – the structure over which computation is performed (the *domain of computation*); $\mathcal{L}$ – the class of constraints that can be expressed; and $\mathcal{T}$ – an axiomatization of (some) properties of $\mathcal{D}$. The pair $(\mathcal{D}, \mathcal{L})$ is called a *constraint domain*.

It is required that $\mathcal{D}$ and $\mathcal{T}$ *correspond* on $\mathcal{L}$, i.e. that (a) $\mathcal{D}$ is a model of $\mathcal{T}$, and (b) for every constraint $c \in \mathcal{L}$, $\mathcal{D} \models \bar{\exists} c$ iff $\mathcal{T} \models \bar{\exists} c$ (where $\bar{\exists}.$ denotes the existential closure of the formula). Usually it is also assumed that $\mathcal{T}$ is *satisfaction complete* with respect to $\mathcal{L}$, i.e. that for every constraint $c \in \mathcal{L}$, either $\mathcal{T} \models \bar{\exists} c$ or $\mathcal{T} \models \neg\bar{\exists} c$. The two conditions ensure that the theory $\mathcal{T}$ sufficiently reflects the domain $\mathcal{D}$: the former condition guarantees that $\mathcal{D}$ and $\mathcal{T}$ agree on satisfiability of constraints; the latter requires that every unsatisfiability in $\mathcal{D}$ is also detected by $\mathcal{T}$.

A $\mathcal{D}$-*model* of a theory T is a model of T that extends $\mathcal{D}$. $T, \mathcal{D} \models \phi$ reads: the formula ϕ is valid in all $\mathcal{D}$-models of T. For more formal details see [8] or [14].

There are two common logical semantics of CLP programs. One simply interprets program clauses as logic formulas, universally quantified over all free variables in the clause. With such interpretation, the semantics of a program P is defined by the set of $\mathcal{D}$-models of P. In particular, the least $\mathcal{D}$-model of P is denoted $lm(P, \mathcal{D})$.

The other semantics is based on the *Clark's completion* (IFF-definition) of a program P, denoted P^* [3]. The semantics is given by the models of $P^*, \mathcal{T}$.

2.3 Top-Down Operational Semantics for CLP

A majority of CLP systems were implemented based on top-down execution. It is also this computation mode which has its direct analogy in SLD-resolution used for evaluation of definite LP programs. [8] presents a general framework in which the operational semantics of many CLP systems can be described; we recount it below.

The top-down operational semantics is defined as a transition system of states. One of the transition rules is resolution; three new rules are introduced to accommodate for constraints.

A *state* in a CLP system is given by the triple $\langle Q, Sa, Sp \rangle$. Q is a multiset of atoms and constraints, representing the goal that remains for processing. Sa and Sp are multisets of constraints; together they encode the constraint store acted upon by a constraint solver. Intuitively, Sa represents the set of *active* constraints and Sp is the set of *passive* constraints (a distinction dependent on a particular system). Active constraints are those which were simplified enough to be used for consistency check, thus having a direct influence on program execution. The rest of the constraints that were encountered so far are merely accumulated as passive ones. An initial goal $G = \leftarrow Q$ for execution is represented as the state $\langle Q, \emptyset, \emptyset \rangle$. There is also one other, distinguished state, denoted by *fail*.

There are a few parameters to the transition system, dependent on a particular CLP system. One is a *computation rule* which, for a given state, selects a transition type and an appropriate element of Q. The other two parameters, which give rise to two of the transition rules, are a predicate *consistent* and a function *infer*.

The four transition rules are:

$\mapsto_r$ **resolution:** the rule works analogously as in LP.

If an atom a is selected by the computation rule, and there is a clause $h \leftarrow B$ in the program s.t. a and h have the same predicate symbol, then

$$\langle Q \cup a, Sa, Sp \rangle \mapsto_r \langle Q \cup B, Sa, Sp \cup (a=h) \rangle$$

where the variables in a and h have been renamed apart, and where $a=h$ abbreviates the conjunction of equations between the corresponding arguments of a and h. We say that a is *rewritten* in this transition.

If an atom a is selected by the computation rule, and for every clause $h \leftarrow B$ in the program a and h have different predicate symbols, then

$$\langle Q \cup a, Sa, Sp \rangle \mapsto_r \textit{fail}$$

$\mapsto_c$ **constraint introduction:** introduces new constraints into the constraint solver[1].
If a constraint c is selected by the computation rule then

$$\langle Q \cup c, Sa, Sp \rangle \mapsto_c \langle Q, Sa, Sp \cup c \rangle$$

$\mapsto_i$ **constraint inference:** infers more active constraints from the constraint store.
For $(Sa', Sp') = infer(Sa, Sp)$, $\quad \langle Q, Sa, Sp \rangle \mapsto_i \langle Q, Sa', Sp' \rangle$
A new set of active constraints Sa' is computed from the current constraint store $Sa \cup Sp$; at the same time Sp is simplified to Sp'.[2] It is required that $\mathcal{D} \models (Sa \wedge Sp) \leftrightarrow (Sa' \wedge Sp')$, so that information is neither lost nor "guessed" by *infer*.
The transition is typically performed whenever Sp has been modified by either of the first two rules. Augmenting Sa with new information extracted from Sp enables further pruning of the computation tree by the following rule.

$\mapsto_s$ **consistency check:** tests active constraints for consistency.
If $consistent(Sa)$ then $\quad \langle Q, Sa, Sp \rangle \mapsto_s \langle Q, Sa, Sp \rangle$
and if $\neg consistent(Sa)$ then $\quad \langle Q, Sa, Sp \rangle \mapsto_s \textit{fail}$
The transition is typically performed right after constraint inference: early detection of inconsistencies allows to avoid unnecessary resolution steps and costly backtracking.

A *derivation* is a sequence of transitions $\langle Q_1, Sa_1, Sp_1 \rangle \mapsto \ldots \mapsto \langle Q_i, Sa_i, Sp_i \rangle \mapsto \ldots$ (where $\mapsto$ denotes a transition of an arbitrary type). A state which cannot be rewritten further is called a *final state*. A derivation is *successful* if it is finite and its final state has the form $\langle \emptyset, Sa, Sp \rangle$; if a successful derivation was initiated by a goal G with free variables $\bar{x}$ then $\exists_{-\bar{x}} (Sa \wedge Sp)$ is the *answer constraint* of the derivation for this goal[3] (here, and further on, $\exists_{-\bar{x}}.$ is used to denote the existential closure of the formula except for the variables $\bar{x}$ which remain unquantified). A derivation is *failed* if it is finite and its final state is *fail*. A derivation is *fair* if it is failed or, for every i and every atom $a \in Q_i$, a is rewritten in a later transition. A computation rule is *fair* if it only gives rise to fair derivations. A goal G is *finitely failed* if all the derivations from G for any fair computation rule are failed. A derivation *flounders* if it is finite and its final state has the form $\langle Q, Sa, Sp \rangle$ where $Q \neq \emptyset$.

The *computation tree* of a goal $G = \leftarrow Q$ for a program P in a CLP system is a tree with nodes labeled by states and edges labeled by $\mapsto_r$, $\mapsto_c$, $\mapsto_i$ or $\mapsto_s$, such that: the root is labeled by $\langle Q, \emptyset, \emptyset \rangle$; edges of one type only can go out from a single node; if a node labeled by a state S has an outgoing edge labeled by $\mapsto_c$, $\mapsto_i$ or $\mapsto_s$ then the node has a single child, labeled by a state that can be obtained from S via a respective transition; if a node labeled by a state S has an outgoing edge labeled by $\mapsto_r$ then the node has a child for each matching clause in P, and each child is labeled by a state obtained from S via $\mapsto_r$ transition for that clause; for each $\mapsto_r$ and $\mapsto_c$ edge, the corresponding transition rule uses the atom or the constraint selected by the computation rule.

Every branch in a computation tree is a derivation. Given a computation rule, every derivation following that rule is a branch in the corresponding computation tree.

---

[1] possibly, after transforming them to some standard form
[2] This step may also involve some syntactic transformations of the constraint store, e.g. maintaining the constraints in a normalized form or elimination of auxiliary variables introduced in the course of computation.
[3] For output, the answer constraint is simplified, and presented in a form restricted, as far as possible, to the variables in the original goal.

2.4 Partial Evaluation in Logic Programming

Partial evaluation was introduced into Logic Programming by Komorowski in [11]. Within the field, the technique is known as *partial deduction*. In LP terms, it can be described as follows [13]. Given a program P and a goal G, partial evaluation produces a new program P', which is P specialized to the goal G. The intention is that G should have the same answers with P and P', but it should run more efficiently for P' than for P. The basic way for obtaining P' is to construct "partial" resolution trees for P and to extract P' from the data associated with the leaves of these trees.

Lloyd and Shepherdson [13] provide a formal account of partial evaluation in LP. The aim of our research is to extend the results onto the CLP case. This will allow to bring together the advantages of CLP and partial evaluation.

3 Partial Evaluation in CLP

It has already been noted in [7, 9] that answer constraints may be viewed as partial evaluations of the program. The following standard CLP($\mathcal{R}$) program can serve as an example. The program relates key parameters in a mortgage (the principal; life of the mortgage, in months; annual interest rate, in %, compound monthly; monthly payment; and the outstanding balance):

```
mortgage(P, 0, _IntRate, _MP, P).
mortgage(P, Time, IntRate, MP, B) :-
    Time >= 1,
    Int = P * IntRate/1200,
    mortgage(P+Int-MP, Time-1, IntRate, MP, B).
```

For the goal

```
?- mortgage(P, 120, 12, MP, B).
```

the answer returned by the system is a *relationship* between the three parameters in the goal (the principal, monthly payment and balance), in this case:

```
B = 0.302995*P - 69.7005*MP.
```

The equation may be viewed as a new, simple program, obtained as a result of partially evaluating the original program with respect to the given values Time=120 and IntRate=12.

What the above example shows is, so to say, a case of "full" partial evaluation of the program for the given goal. However, the possibility of partial evaluation of CLP programs should not, and does not need to be limited to the situation where we arrive as far as to the final answer constraint. It is often preferable to "freeze" the evaluation at some earlier stage, performing only part of the computations initiated by the given goal. We shall extend the idea of partial evaluation in CLP to the case where computation can be suspended at an arbitrary stage of derivation. The generalization is important: it allows control of how deep partial evaluation of a program should proceed. For instance, it makes possible to suspend evaluation of procedures external to the program, instead of interpreting lack of these as a failure.

Another extension of the limited concept of partial evaluation as illustrated above allows specialization of more than one single predicate at a time. Our definitions below are generalizations of the ones given in [13]. Since the distinction between active and passive constraints has no importance for our considerations, we will simplify the notation for a state in a CLP system to a pair $\langle Q, S \rangle$, where S denotes $(Sa \cup Sp)$ i.e. the whole of the constraint store.[4]

---

[4] This notation should not be identified with that of [14], where only atoms are collected at the first element of the pair, and where some specific assumptions on transitions are made. The formulation therein corresponds to a very restricted class of systems, called *ideal* in [8].

Definition 3.1 (Resultant)

Let P be a CLP program and G a goal $\leftarrow A, C$; let $A \cup C = Q_0$; and let $\langle Q_0, \emptyset \rangle \mapsto \langle Q_1, S_1 \rangle \mapsto \ldots \mapsto \langle Q_n, S_n \rangle$ be a derivation of $P \cup \{G\}$, where $Q_n = A_n \cup C_n$. Then we say the derivation has the *resultant* $A \leftarrow A_n, C_n \cup S_n$.

In particular, for $n=0$ (a "derivation" with no steps) the resultant is $A \leftarrow A, C$. On the other hand, for a successful derivation $Q_n = \emptyset$ and the resultant is $A \leftarrow S_n$ i.e. it consists of the answer constraint, indeed.

In practice, we shall assume that the set of constraints $C_n \cup S_n$, before it is included in the resultant, is subject to the same simplification (projection) as an answer constraint to be output.

Note that a resultant, as defined above, is not a clause in general: A on the left-hand side may consist of a set (conjunction) of atoms. But for our purposes we shall only be interested in the situation where, besides constraints, there is only one atom a in the goal (the goal consists of a *constrained atom*). In this particular case the resultant does form a clause: $a \leftarrow A_n, C_n \cup S_n$, and this single clause subsumes the whole derivation. Namely, the original derivation from the goal $\leftarrow a, C$ is equivalent to a single resolution step $\mapsto_r$ with the new clause: the resultant of the latter is $a \leftarrow A_n, C \cup C_n \cup S_n$, and it can be proven that $\mathcal{D} \models (C \cup C_n \cup S_n) \leftrightarrow (C_n \cup S_n)$, provided the restriction placed on *infer*.

After the notion of resultant has been defined for CLP, the following definition of partial evaluation carries over from the LP case [13] with only a few adjustments:

Definition 3.2 (Partial Evaluation)

  i) Let P be a program, $Q = a \wedge C$ a constrained atom, and Tr a computation tree for $P \cup \{\leftarrow Q\}$. Let $S_1, \ldots, S_k$ be some non-root states in Tr chosen so that each non-failed branch of Tr contains exactly one of them.

    Let $R_i (i = 1, \ldots, k)$ be the resultant of the derivation from the root $\langle Q, \emptyset \rangle$ down to S_i. Then the set of clauses $R_1, \ldots, R_k$ is called a *partial evaluation of Q in P*.

  ii) If $Q = \{Q_1, \ldots, Q_n\}$ is a finite set of constrained atoms then a *partial evaluation of Q in P* is the union of partial evaluations of $Q_1, \ldots, Q_n$ in P.

  iii) A *partial evaluation of P wrt Q* is a program obtained from P by replacing the set of clauses in P whose head contains one of the predicate symbols appearing in Q (called the *partially evaluated predicates*) by a partial evaluation of Q in P.

Notice that states in the definition (i) of partial evaluation of a goal are chosen so that each of the states "covers" some part of the computation tree for the goal, the subtrees do not overlap, and together they contain all the non-failed branches (potential answers) in the tree.

We now provide a series of examples to illustrate the above definition of partial evaluation in CLP. Consider the following simple CLP($\mathcal{R}$) program:

```
1)    p(X,Y) :- X+2*Y = 3, q(X).
2)    p(X,Y) :- X <= Y, r(X,Y).
3)    q(X) :- 0 <= X, X <= 2.
4)    q(X) :- 3 <= X, X <= 7.
5)    r(X,Y) :- 3*X-Y = 6, 0 <= Y.
```

A partial evaluation of this program wrt $\{p(X, Y) \wedge X=2\}$, where derivations for the predicates q and r were suspended, consists of:

```
      p(X,Y) :- X = 2, Y = 0.5, q(X).
      p(X,Y) :- X = 2, 2 <= Y , r(X,Y).
```

along with the definitions for q and r (clauses 3÷5).

A partial evaluation of the initial program wrt $\{p(X,Y) \wedge X < 4\}$, with derivations for q and r still suspended, is:

```
1')   p(X,Y) :- X < 4, X+2*Y = 3, -0.5 < Y, q(X).
2')   p(X,Y) :- X < 4, X <= Y, r(X,Y).
```

again, with the definitions for q, r included unaltered. This time, the constraint $X+2*Y = 3$ cannot be reduced in the final simplification process, because it is still essential as long as X and Y are not grounded. $-0.5 < Y$ in (1') was inferred from $X+2*Y = 3$ and $X < 4$.

If derivation for q, r is not suspended, partial evaluation of the goal above may proceed further and yield:

```
p(X,Y) :- X+2*Y = 3, -0.5 < Y, 0 <= X, X <= 2.         {1, 3}
p(X,Y) :- X < 4, X+2*Y = 3, -0.5 < Y, 3 <= X.          {1, 4}
p(X,Y) :- X < 4, X <= Y, 3*X-Y = 6, 0 <= Y.            {2, 6}
```

or, with a few more constraint inference steps $\mapsto_i$:

```
p(X,Y) :- X+2*Y = 3, 0 <= X, X <= 2, 0.5 <= Y, Y <= 1.5.
p(X,Y) :- X < 4, X+2*Y = 3, -0.5 < Y, 3 <= X, Y <= 0.
p(X,Y) :- X < 4, X <= Y, 3*X-Y = 6, Y < 6, 3 <= X, 3 <= Y.
```

(Numbers in braces above indicate the clauses used in the resolution steps of the corresponding derivations). Note that the bodies of the three final clauses are in fact answer constraints to the wrt-goal. This will be in general the case whenever derivations in a partial evaluation process are not terminated at any intermediate point.

Recall that partial evaluation has been defined for a *set* of (atomic) goals, not only for a single goal. Thus the definition allows specialization of a number of predicates (program procedures) at a time. In the next section we study conditions which must be satisfied for the goals submitted to partial evaluation so that the transformation does not violate the semantics of the program.

4   Soundness and Completeness Results

In [13] conditions of *closedness* and *independence* were identified which are crucial for soundness and completeness of partial deduction with respect to the procedural and declarative semantics of LP. The independence condition is only important for programs with negation, where negated atoms are admitted in clause bodies and where negation-as-failure rule is used to evaluate them. This is not the case in our considerations here. The closedness condition, though, turns out relevant for partial evaluation of CLP programs. The condition is very natural: it requires that partially evaluated predicates are only used to compute for goals they were specialized to, or their *instances*. This concerns queries to the program as well as calls in the bodies of program clauses. It seems clear that a procedure which was specialized to some particular case may only be considered reliable for this case or its sub-cases. In fact, the condition is not only necessary but at the same time sufficient to guarantee the correctness of partial evaluation transformation.

In order to formulate the condition in the CLP context, we first need to define the concept of *instance*. In LP, the notion is defined based on existence of an appropriate substitution. For CLP, a definition must be stated in a more general way, in terms of constraints rather then substitutions. [14] shows how various notions and results of LP can be lifted to the CLP case. In particular, a concept of instance for conditional atoms is formulated there. Below, a similar definition is given for constrained atoms. In what follows, $\bar{x}$ is used to denote a sequence of distinct variables $x^1, \ldots, x^n$, for an appropriate arity n (and, recall, $\exists_{-\bar{x}}$. is used to denote the existential closure of the formula except for the variables $\bar{x}$ which remain unquantified).

Definition 4.1 (Instance)
A constrained atom $p(\bar{x}) \wedge C_1$ is an *instance* of $p(\bar{x}) \wedge C_2$ iff $\mathcal{D} \models \exists_{-\bar{x}} C_1 \rightarrow \exists_{-\bar{x}} C_2$.

Observe that for two constrained atoms to be compared based on the above definition, they must be in a specific form. Namely, they may only have variables as their arguments, all of them distinct and identical for both atoms. This is not any serious limitation, though, since any two constrained atoms $p(\bar{t}_1) \wedge C_1$ and $p(\bar{t}_2) \wedge C_2$, where $\bar{t}_i = t_i^1, \ldots, t_i^n$ $(i=1,2)$ is an arbitrary sequence of terms, can be easily transformed to the required form. Namely, for $\bar{x}$ chosen to be a sequence of variables, all of them distinct and different from the variables that appear in t_1, t_2, each of the $p(\bar{t}_i) \wedge C_i$ corresponds to $p(\bar{x}) \wedge (x^1=t_i^1 \wedge \ldots \wedge x^n=t_i^n) \wedge C_i$ (that is, the arguments are renamed and the corresponding substitutions are included as additional constraints).

With the notion of instance, the condition of closedness can be defined. In our definition below and in the results that follow, a particular type of formulas will be of special importance:
$$A_1 \leftarrow A_2 \wedge C \qquad (*)$$
where *both* A_1 and A_2 are finite conjunctions of atoms. In particular, this class of formulas includes program clauses and goals, as well as formulas of the form $A \leftarrow C_1$ which are program's answers to the goals $\leftarrow A, C_2$ (where C_1 is an answer constraint for the goal). For formulas of this type, the closedness condition can be formulated relatively easy:

Definition 4.2 (Closedness)
Let T be a set of formulas of the form $(*)$ and $\mathcal{Q}$ a finite set of constrained atoms. We say that T is $\mathcal{Q}$-*closed* if for each clause $A_1 \leftarrow A_2, C$ in T and for any atom $a \in A_i$ $(i=1,2)$ with a predicate symbol that occurs in one of the constrained atoms in $\mathcal{Q}$, $a \wedge C$ is an instance of some constrained atom in $\mathcal{Q}$.

Below, we state some important theorems. They shall guarantee that conclusions/answers obtained from a partially evaluated CLP program are equivalent to conclusions and answers from the original version of the program.

Theorem 4.1
Let P be a CLP program, W a closed first order formula, and $\mathcal{Q}$ a finite set of constrained atoms over a constraint domain $(\mathcal{D}, \mathcal{L})$ with corresponding theory T; let P' be a partial evaluation of P wrt $\mathcal{Q}$. Then the following hold:

(1a) If $P', T \models W$ then $P, T \models W$.

(1b) Let W be of the form $(*)$ and let $P' \cup \{W\}$ be $\mathcal{Q}$-closed. If $P, T \models W$ then $P', T \models W$.

(2) Suppose T is satisfaction complete wrt $\mathcal{L}$.
If W is of the form $(*)$ and if $P' \cup \{W\}$ is $\mathcal{Q}$-closed then: $P'^*, T \models W$ iff $P^*, T \models W$.

The theorem states that *(1a)* partial evaluation transformation is sound for the semantics given by the (usual) logical meaning of the program; *(1b)* provided that the closedness condition is satisfied, partial evaluation is also complete for this semantics; and *(2)* under the closedness condition, partial evaluation is both sound and complete for the semantics given by program completion.

These results for the declarative semantics are much stronger than the corresponding results for partial evaluation in LP given in [13]. This is mainly due to the fact that in the CLP case we only deal with positive atoms in program clauses, so the incompleteness problems for negation are avoided.

The next theorem states that partial evaluation is sound, and under the closedness condition also complete, for the operational semantics of CLP programs.

Theorem 4.2

Let P be a CLP program, $\leftarrow Q$ a goal, and Q a finite set of constrained atoms over a constraint domain $(\mathcal{D}, \mathcal{L})$ with corresponding theory T; let P' be a partial evaluation of P wrt Q. Then the following hold:

(1a) If $P' \cup \{\leftarrow Q\}$ has a successful derivation with answer constraint c' then
$P \cup \{\leftarrow Q\}$ has a successful derivation with answer constraint c s.t. $T \models c' \to c$.

(1b) Let $P' \cup \{\leftarrow Q\}$ be Q-closed. If $P \cup \{\leftarrow Q\}$ has a successful derivation with answer constraint c then $P' \cup \{\leftarrow Q\}$ has a successful derivation with answer constraint c' s.t. $T \models c' \leftrightarrow c$.

(2a) If $P \cup \{\leftarrow Q\}$ finitely fails then so does $P' \cup \{\leftarrow Q\}$.

(2b) Suppose T is satisfaction complete wrt $\mathcal{L}$, and let $P' \cup \{\leftarrow Q\}$ be Q-closed. If $P' \cup \{\leftarrow Q\}$ finitely fails then $P^*, T \models \neg Q$.

Notice that the results *(1a)* and *(1b)* for positive answers are symmetrical, up to the closedness proviso in *(1b)*. There is no such exact symmetry between *(2a)* and *(2b)*. In the case of negative answers, partial evaluation is complete for the operational semantics, as given in *(2a)*. However, the soundness result in *(2b)* is stated with respect to the *declarative* semantics of the original program. In fact, unless we put appropriate restrictions on the computation rule, the converse of *(2a)* does not hold, with or without closedness. Namely, as a very particular case it may happen that the computation tree for $P \cup \{\leftarrow Q\}$ contains some infinite or floundering branches yet all of them are pruned off when derivations for partial evaluation are constructed. In CLP systems employing an incomplete test for consistency it may also happen that an (inconsistent) answer *is* returned for $P \cup \{\leftarrow Q\}$ even though $P^*, T \models \neg Q$. In this sense, a partially evaluated program may turn out more accurate than its original version.

As for the results in *(1a,b)*, note that no reference is made to the computation rule(s) used in derivations for: partial evaluation, $P \cup \{\leftarrow Q\}$, and $P' \cup \{\leftarrow Q\}$. The results are true for any computation rule used to obtain the partial evaluation P' of P. As far as the query is concerned, however, there is no guarantee that the two programs will yield corresponding answer constraints under the same fixed computation rule. In general, it may be necessary to use different computation rules for evaluation with P and P' in order to have the results *(1a,b)* hold. Again, this is due to the potential presence of floundering or infinite derivations.

With some additional conditions on the computation rules, much stronger results can be obtained. We will call a computation rule *safe* if it never gives rise to floundering derivations nor to infinite sequences of transitions only consisting of $\mapsto_i$ and $\mapsto_s$. The class of systems with computation rules that are safe in our sense is slightly more restricted than the class of *progressive* systems as defined in [8]; it comprises all major implemented CLP systems.

The successful derivations and answer constraints referred to in *(1a,b)* of the theorem above will exist for *any* safe computation rule. The stronger versions of the results are as follows:

(1'a) If $P' \cup \{\leftarrow Q\}$ has a successful derivation with answer constraint c' then for any safe computation rule $P \cup \{\leftarrow Q\}$ has a successful derivation with answer constraint c s.t. $T \models c' \to c$.

(1'b) Let $P' \cup \{\leftarrow Q\}$ be Q-closed. If $P \cup \{\leftarrow Q\}$ has a successful derivation with answer constraint c then for any safe computation rule $P' \cup \{\leftarrow Q\}$ has a successful derivation with answer constraint c' s.t. $T \models c' \leftrightarrow c$.

These results allow, for instance, a reliable use of the same (safe) computation rule for evaluation of goals with P and with P'.

Under the condition of closedness for the partially evaluated program and the goal, the converse of *(2a)* will additionally hold for the class of (somewhat unrealistic) CLP systems that were treated in [14] and were called *ideal* in [8].

5 Summary and Future Work

In the paper, a notion of partial evaluation for CLP programs was defined as a direct generalization of the concept given in [13] for the LP case. We also identified a CLP counterpart of the closedness condition presented therein. The condition plays an important role for the correctness of transformation by partial evaluation. Our results show that partial evaluation, as we defined it, is a sound transformation for the declarative semantics given by the logical meaning of the program, as well as for the top-down operational semantics. Under the closedness condition, it is also complete for these two semantics, and it is both sound and complete for the declarative semantics given by program completion. The program completion semantics is one which models the *no* answers from a program in addition to the positive answers. In view of all those results, partial evaluation can safely be used for specializing CLP programs.

Some problems still remain to be studied. It is clear that gains from partial evaluation may vary largely, dependent on how much information is provided in the wrt-goal and how this information relates to the structure of the program. In many cases partial evaluation can result in substantial pruning of the computation tree and considerable optimization of the initial program. In some other cases, however, if the information "pumped" into the program via the wrt-set is not sufficient to let the constraints interact, one may achieve nothing but expansion (unfolding) of predicate definitions. It would be very useful to identify conditions under which one can expect some actual gains from partial evaluation.

It might also be advisable to study the issue of termination and loop detection for partial evaluation in CLP, like it has been done in the case of LP programs [1], [2].

Acknowledgements. I want to thank Prof. Jan Komorowski for inspiring me to do this research. Many thanks to Danilo Montesi for his comments on a draft version of this paper.

References

[1] R.N. Bol. Loop checking in partial deduction. *J. Logic Programming*, 16(1&2):25–46, 1993.

[2] M. Bruynooghe, D. De Shreye, and B. Martens. A general criterion for avoiding infinite unfolding during partial deduction of logic programs. *New Generation Computing*, 11(1):47–79, 1992.

[3] K.L. Clark. Negation as failure. In H. Gallaire and J. Minker, editors, *Logic and Data Bases*, pages 293–322. Plenum Press, 1978.

[4] A. Colmerauer. Equations and inequations on finite and infinite trees. In *Proc. 2nd Int. Conf. on Fifth Generation Computer Systems*, pages 85–99, 1984.

[5] A. Colmerauer. Opening the Prolog III universe. *Byte magazine*, 12(9), August 1987.

[6] J. Jaffar and J.-L. Lassez. Constraint Logic Programming. In *Proc. 14th ACM Symp. on Principles of Programming Languages*, pages 111–119. ACM Press, 1987.

[7] J. Jaffar and J.-L. Lassez. From unification to constraints. In *Proc. Conf. Logic Programming '87*, LNCS 315, pages 1–18. Springer-Verlag, 1988.

[8] J. Jaffar and M.J. Maher. Constraint Logic Programming: a survey. *J. Logic Programming*, 19/20:503–581, 1994.

[9] J. Jaffar, S. Michaylov, P.J. Stuckey, and R.H.C. Yap. The CLP($\mathcal{R}$) language and system. *ACM Transactions on Programming Languages and Systems*, 14(3):339–395, 1992.

[10] N.D. Jones, C.K. Gomard, and P. Sestoft. *Partial Evaluation and Automatic Program Generation*. Prentice Hall, 1993.

[11] H.J. Komorowski. *A Specification of an Abstract Prolog Machine and its Application to Partial Evaluation*. PhD thesis, Linköping University, Sweden, 1981. LSST Dissertations 69.

[12] J.W. Lloyd. *Foundations of Logic Programming*. Springer-Verlag, 2nd edition, 1987.

[13] J.W. Lloyd and J.C Sheperdson. Partial evaluation in logic programming. *J. Logic Programming*, 11(3&4):217–242, 1991.

[14] M.J. Maher. A logic programming view of CLP. In *Proc. 10th Int. Conf. on Logic Programming*, pages 737–753. MIT Press, 1993.

The AQ17-DCI System for Data-Driven Constructive Induction and Its Application to the Analysis of World Economics

Eric Bloedorn and Ryszard S. Michalski[1]

Machine Learning and Inference Laboratory, George Mason University, Fairfax VA

[1]Also with GMU Departments of Computer Science and Systems Engineering, and the Institute of Computer Science at the Polish Academy of Sciences, Warsaw, Poland

Abstract. Constructive induction divides the problem of learning an inductive hypothesis into two intertwined searches: one—for the "best" representation space, and two—for the "best" hypothesis in that space. In *data-driven* constructive induction (DCI), a learning system searches for a better representation space by analyzing the input examples (data). The presented data-driven constructive induction method combines an AQ-type learning algorithm with two classes of representation space improvement operators: *constructors*, and *destructors*. The implemented system, AQ17-DCI, has been experimentally applied to a GNP prediction problem using a World Bank database. The results show that decision rules learned by AQ17-DCI outperformed the rules learned in the original representation space both in predictive accuracy and rule simplicity.

1 Introduction

The basic premise of research on *constructive induction* (CI) is that results of a learning process directly depend on the quality of the representation space in which is occurs. If the representation space is well designed, then learning results will tend to be satisfactory with almost any method (assuming an adequate representation language); otherwise, they may be poor regardless of the method. Constructive induction is oriented toward learning problems in which the representation space, as defined by attributes in the training examples, is of low quality or there is a mismatch between the representation language used and the target concept. A low quality representation space means that the space is spanned over attributes that are weakly relevant or irrelevant for the given learning task. To cope with such problems, constructive induction splits a learning process to two intertwined searches — one for the "best" representation space, and the second for the "best" hypothesis in the found space. Using another terminology that is also used in machine learning, constructive induction includes the problem of automatically determining the best "representation space bias" as a part of the induction process.

The idea of constructive induction is not new [23]. Initial research on this topic concentrated solely on constructing new attributes beyond those provided in the input data [21] [36] [16] [32]. Michalski [23] presented a set of *constructive generalization rules* that describe various ways in which new attributes can be generated. More recent work has viewed constructive induction more generally, namely, as a double-search process, in which one search is for an improved representation space and the second for "best" hypothesis in this space [2] [3] [38]. The improvement of a representation space is done in several ways—by generating new attributes, by removing less relevant or irrelevant attributes, and/or by abstracting values of given attributes (grouping values to larger units).

The search for an improved representation space can be guided by information from three sources [38]: training data (as in data-driven constructive induction—DCI), initial hypotheses learned from the data (as in hypothesis-driven constructive induction—HCI), or expert knowledge provided by the user to the system (as in knowledge-driven constructive induction—KCI). These sources can also be combined into a multistrategy constructive induction method. This paper describes a data-driven method of constructive induction and its application to a problem of learning economic relationships.

2. An Illustration of the Importance of the Representation Space

The concept representation space is defined as a space in which inductive hypotheses are generated. In conventional machine learning methods this space is identical to the space in which training examples are represented. As mentioned earlier, the choice of the representation space has a profound effect on the quality of the generated hypotheses. This effect is well illustrated by the second Monk's problem [34]. The original representation space with the training examples denoted by + and - is shown in Figure 1(a) using DIAV [39]. The shaded area represents the target concept.

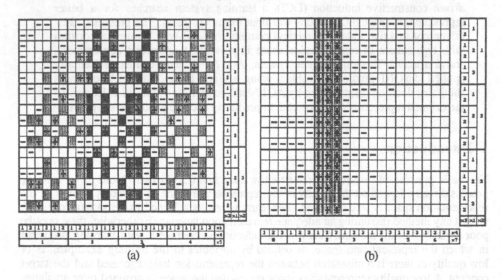

(a)   (b)

Figure 1. Diagrammatic visualization of the Monk 2 representation spaces: (a) the initial space; and (b) improved space due to the data-driven constructive induction.

In this original representation space, the learning problem is difficult because the target concept is highly irregular. An improved representation space, as found by the AQ17-DCI system described in this paper, is shown in Fig. 1,b. In the improved representation space the target concept is highly regular and therefore easy to learn. In this case, the new representation was found by applying a space modification operator that generates the so-called *counting attribute*: #Attr(S, P), which counts the number of attributes in the set S with a property P. The system found that the counting attribute in which S contains all original attributes {x1, x2, x3, ..., x6}, and P is the first value of attribute in its domain is highly relevant for the task at hand. The learned concept was: : #Attr({x1,...x6}, Firstvalue) = 2, that is, *an example belongs to the concept, if exactly two of six attributes take their first value*. This rule exactly represents the intended target concept, and thus has a predictive accuracy of 100%.

3. Relation to Other Research

Research on constructive induction has produced a number of working programs. The first program that was explicitly dedicated to exhibit constructive induction capabilities was INDUCE [22]. INDUCE generates new attributes or new predicates by applying various constructive generalization rules. BACON.3 [14] and ABACUS [9] search for mathematical relationships or laws that summarize numerical (or numerical and symbolic) data. Lenat's AM and Eurisko programs [15] can be viewed as performing a form of knowledge-based constructive induction, as they generate new concepts according to certain heuristics.

Schlimmer's STAGGER [33] is a constructive induction program that uses three cooperating learning modules: weight adjustment, Boolean feature construction, and attribute value aggregation. Muggleton's Duce [25] is an oracle-based approach (knowledge-driven). Pagallo and Haussler's FRINGE, GREEDY3 and GROVE [26] base the construction of new attributes on patterns found in learned decision trees. Another decision tree-based method is CITRE [16], which constructs new terms by repeatedly applying Boolean operators to nodes on the positively labeled branches. A hypothesis-driven approach based on decision rules is AQ17-HCI [38]. In this system patterns prevalent in strong rules are used for constructing new attributes. An approach which uses disjunctive or arithmetic combinations of the original attributes to extend the initial attribute set was developed by Utgoff in STABB [35].

As mentioned earlier, constructive induction is a process in which the original representation space is improved during learning. This can be done by generating new attributes and/or removing less relevant or redundant ones. The latter process has been investigated in the rough set approach (e.g., [27], [41] [28], and [10]). The AQ17-DCI system presented in this paper executes a complementary process of selecting the most relevant attributes. This is done by applying some measure of attribute relevance, for example, PROMISE [1] or information gain ratio [30]. The rough set approach also applies an attribute-value abstraction operator, which removes values that are not needed for describing data. In contrast to this, AQ17-DCI combines less relevant values with adjacent values into larger units, that is, performs an abstraction of the attribute domain.

In summary, AQ17-DCI has the following characteristics which together distinguish it from all other constructive induction methods: 1) the search for a better representation space is based on patterns found in the training data, and is thus not tied to a specific knowledge representation language (as is the case of hypothesis-driven induction); 2) it applies three classes of operators: attribute construction, attribute reduction, and attribute value abstraction 3) it uses both domain-independent or domain-dependent constructive generalization rules; 4) it supports binary as well as multi-argument attribute construction operators.

4. The AQ17-DCI System for Data-Driven Constructive Induction

4.1 Overview

The AQ17-DCI system consists of two components. One component performs a data-driven search for an improved representation space (hence DCI—data-driven constructive induction). The second component employs the AQ15c program for searching for the "best" hypothesis within the current representation space (the name AQ17-DCI means that this is the 17th program in the family of AQ algorithm based induction programs). The AQ algorithm generates an optimal or near-optimal set of rules characterizing training examples, according to a given criterion of optimality (originally described in [18], and [19]). The criterion of optimality may take into consideration such factors as the number of rules, the number of conditions, the cost of attributes in the rules, and others. These factors can be combined into a multicriterion measure of optimality that best reflects the needs of the learning problem at hand.

4.2 Search for an Improved Representation Space

The search for an improved representation space employs three types of representation space modification operators: 1) space expansion through attribute construction (GENERATE), 2) space contraction through selecting only the most relevant attributes from the original space (SELECT), and 3) space contraction through attribute-value abstraction (QUANT). Experiments have shown that representation space expansion is very useful when the attribute construction operators are well-matched with the problem at hand. Representation space contraction, however, must be performed with great care, as it may lead to a removal of information that is crucial for learning a correct hypothesis [5]. For this reason, default thresholds on the space contraction operators are set conservatively. The following sections describe these operators in more detail.

4.2.1 Space Expansion: Attribute Construction By GENERATE

The GENERATE method for constructing new attributes employs both mathematical and logical operators to construct new attributes. In selecting attributes for applying mathematical operators, the system takes into consideration the attribute types. The operation to be performed on the selected attributes is done according to predefined rules (defined by the user). With the attributes and operation selected, the values for the new attribute are calculated. The usefulness of new attributes is evaluated using an attribute quality measure. If the quality measure is above a user-defined threshold, the attribute is added to the available attribute set. If it is below the threshold or the attribute is too complex, the new attribute is discarded. The algorithm applies a variety of relational or arithmetic operators to numeric attributes. A summary of representation space expansion operators is presented in Table 1.

Operator	Arguments	Notation	Interpretation
Equivalence	Attributes x,y	$x = y$	If $x = y$ then 1, otherwise 0
Greater Than	Attributes x,y	$x > y$	If $x = y$ then 1, otherwise 0
Greater Than or Equal	Attributes x,y	$x >= y$	If $x \geq y$ then 1, otherwise 0
Addition	Attributes x,y	$x + y$	Sum of x and y
Subtraction	Attributes x,y	$x - y$	Difference between x and y
Difference	Attributes x,y	$\lvert x - y \rvert$	Absolute difference between x and y
Multiplication	Attributes x,y	$x * y$	Product of x and y
Division	Attributes x,y	x/y	Quotient of x divided by y
Maximum	Attribute set S	$Max\{S\}$	Maximum value in S
Minimum	Attribute set S	$Min\{S\}$	Minimum value in S
Average	Attribute set S	$Ave\{S\}$	Average of values in S
Counting	Attribute set S,P	$\#Attr(S,P)$	No of attributes in S with property P

Table 1. A summary of representation space expansion operators in AQ17-DCI.

4.2.2 Representation Space Contraction

AQ17-DCI contracts the representation space by abstracting attribute-values using QUANT, or by selecting most relevant attributes using SELECT. Table 2 summarizes the representation space contraction operators used in AQ17-DCI. The next two subsections provide details.

Operator	Arguments	Notation	Interpretation
Quantization	An attribute x, and a method M	QUANT(x, M)	Quantization of x using method M Methods available: Chi-merge, Equal-interval and Equal frequency
Selection	Set of attributes S	SELECT(S)	Select subset S' of S by method M Methods: Promise, Information gain

Table 2. A summary of representation space contraction operators in AQ17-DCI.

4.2.2.1 Attribute-value Abstraction Using QUANT

Research on attribute-value abstraction is usually performed under the name attribute-value discretization [7], [8]. We view this process as a form of abstraction because the result of it is a decrease of information about an object [24]. By replacing original attribute values by more abstract ones the representation space is reduced, thus this process represents a representation space contraction transformation. QUANT abstracts attribute values using the ChiMerge method described by Kerber [13]. This abstraction, a.k.a. scaling, is performed for continuous attributes and for discrete attributes with large domains. Because it reduces the size of the representation space, abstraction can significantly speed up the search for hypothesis. It can also improve the quality of hypothesis due to a simplification of the generated descriptions.

The ChiMerge algorithm is a bottom-up process in which initially all values are stored in separate intervals which are then merged until a termination condition is met. The interval merging process consists of continuously repeating two steps: 1) compute χ^2 values (correlations between the value of the class attribute and the value of an attribute), and 2) merge the pair of adjacent intervals with the lowest χ^2 value. Intervals are merged until all pairs of intervals have χ^2 values exceeding the user defined chi-threshold. The chi-threshold is a function of the desired significance level and the number of degrees of freedom (1 fewer than the number of classes), and can be determined from a table. The χ^2 value measures the probability that the attribute interval and class value are dependent. If the interval has a χ^2 value greater than threshold then class and interval are correlated and are retained. High χ^2 threshold settings cause more intervals to be merged which results in fewer intervals, or abstracted attribute values.

4.2.2.2 Attribute Selection Using SELECT

This operation is conventionally described in the literature as *feature selection*. Here, we view this process more generally as a form of reduction of the representation space. SELECT uses a measure of attribute relevance, such as well-known information gain ratio [30], or PROMISE [1] for the purpose of determining which attributes should be used for defining the representation space in which search for the inductive hypothesis will occur. The attributes that score on the attribute relevance measure above a certain threshold are selected as dimensions of the transformed representation space.

5. An Experimental Application to World Economics

This section describes an application of the AQ17-DCI system to a problem of determining the economic and demographic patterns in the countries of the world. The data were obtained from a World Bank database [6]. This database contains economic and demographic records for the countries of the world from 1965 to 1990 [12]. The goal of the experiment presented here was to determine a set of rules characterizing the dependence of GNP (Gross National Product) in various countries during the period from 1986 to 1990 on the available economic and demographic characteristics.

In the experiment we considered 41 countries. Changes of GNP were quantified into four equal-intervals: low (0 to 0.5625), medium (0.5626 to 1.125), high (1.126 to 1.6875) and very high (over 1.6875). The countries were described by 11 attributes, each sampled over a period of 5 years. Thus, each country was described by 55 attributes. AQ17-DCI was applied to determine rules that characterize GNP changes in terms of the given attributes (or their relevant subset). The quality of the generated rules was evaluated by the 10-fold cross-validation method [37]. The learning process involved the following steps:

1. Remove less relevant attributes. AQ17-DCI removed 24 attributes using the SELECT method described in Section 4.2.2.2 with a information threshold set to 0.6.

2. Abstract away unnecessary detail. The domain size of the attributes were reduced from an average of 15.4 values per attribute to 4.3, using the QUANT described in section 4.2.2.1.

3. Construct new problem-relevant attributes. On the average, AQ17-DCI constructed ten new attributes in each run, using the DCI GENERATE method. Examples of these new attributes are shown in Table 3.

Name	Operator used	Description
ChgeEnergyCons86-88	Minus	Change in energy consumption of a country between 1986 and 1988
Birth89ByEnergyCons90	Division	Ratio of Crude Birth Rate in 1989 to Energy Consumption in 1990
AveEnergyCons86-90	Average	Average Energy Consumption of a country between 1986 and 1990

Table 3: Examples of new relevant attributes constructed by AQ17-DCI

The transformations generated by AQ17-DCI resulted in an approximately 80% increase in predictive accuracy. Rules learned in the original representation were only 41.7% accurate, while rules learned in the improved representation space were 76.3% accurate on the testing data. While this improvement is significant, it is not entirely satisfactory. The problem may have been caused by the presence of misclassification errors (incorrectly classified training examples or to the lack in the original data of important relevant attributes (e.g., the type of government, presence of natural disasters, or war). Further research is being done to try to understand how predictive accuracy can be improved.

Constructive induction helped not only to increase the predictive accuracy, but also generated a number of meaningful new attributes. A significant advantage of this method is that rules generated can be easily interpreted by a data analyst, as they are in the form that is directly interpretable in natural language. Here is an example of such a rule:

Countries with very high increase in GNP are characterized by:

[DeathRate is low] &
[AVG(%PopulationAgeBracketB) is very high] &
[AVG(PopulationGrowthRate) is low]
(Total: 13, Unique 9)
         OR
[AVG(UrbanPopulationGrowth) is very low] &
[AVG(UrbanVsRuralGrowthDifference) is very low]
(Total: 7, Unique 3)

where

--"very high increase" is defined as *GNP per capita (in US$) 1990 / GNP 1986 > 1.7*,

--low death rate (per thousand) is defined as 5% to 6%,

--*AVG(%PopulationAgeBracketB)* stands for the average % of population in the age bracket B (ages 15..64); very high means 57%-69%

--*AVG(PopulationGrowthRate)* stands for the average of population growth rate; low means less than 3%

--very low average urban population growth rate means lower than 1%

--very low average difference between the urban and rural growth means less than 2%

--*Total* denotes the total number of countries in the study that are covered by the rule

--*Unique* denotes the number of countries in the study that were covered by this rule and not by any other rule.

Comments:
All averages were computed for the period 1986 to 1990.
Attributes in italics were constructed by the program from the initial attributes.

Rule Interpretation
Countries with a very high increase in GNP are characterized by low death rate, the average percentage of the population age 15 to 64 year olds is very high, and the overall population growth rate is low OR
the average urban population growth is very low, and the average difference between urban and rural population growth rate is very low.

Another useful aspect of the AQ17-DCI system is that it can generate rules that optimize criteria set by the user to best reflect the needs of the task at hand. The user is able to select the type of operators to be used, as well as the information threshold above which new attributes must score in order to be retained. This gives a data analyst a way to generate data descriptions that are most suitable for a given task, and may also help to get insights into the problem that were not possible in the original representation space. The program has default values so that the user does not have to set all of these parameters before making use of these capabilities.

6. Summary

This paper described a method and for data-driven constructive induction, which combines AQ-type rule learning with operators for representation space improvement. These operators can expand the space through attribute construction, and/or contract the space through attribute removal and attribute-value abstraction. The system implementing the method, AQ17-DCI, was tested by applying it to a problem in the area of world economics. In the experiments, AQ17-DCI produced decision rules that had higher predictive accuracy than rules learned in the original representation space, and generated new attributes that provided additional insights into the data. In the GNP prediction problem the space obtained by applying all three types of operators (attribute generation, attribute removal and value abstraction) produced the rules with the highest predictive accuracy. Future research will focus on implementing other operators for attribute construction and the development of a control strategy for guiding the selection of individual operators.

Acknowledgments

The authors thank members of the INLEN group for discussions and criticism. This research was conducted in the Machine Learning and Inference Laboratory at George Mason University. The Laboratory's research is supported in part by the National Science Foundation under grants IRI-9510644 and DMI-9496192, in part by the Office of Naval Research under grant N00014-91-J-1351, in part by the Advanced Research Projects Agency under grant No. N00014-91-J-1854 administered by the Office of Naval Research, in part by the Advanced Research Projects Agency under grants F49620-92-J-0549 and F49620-95-1-0462 administered by the Air Force Office of Scientific Research.

References

1. Baim, P.W., "The PROMISE Method for Selecting the Most Relevant Attributes for Inductive Learning Systems", Rep. No. UIUCDCS-F-82-898, Dept. of Computer Science, University of Illinois-Urbana Champaign, IL, 1982.

2. Bloedorn, E. and Michalski, R.S. "Data-Driven Constructive Induction in AQ17-PRE: A Method and Experiments", *Proceedings of the Third International Conference on Tools for AI*, November 1991a.

3. Bloedorn, E. and Michalski, R.S., "Constructive Induction from Data in AQ17-DCI: Further Experiments," *Reports of the Machine Learning and Inference Laboratory*, MLI 91-12, School of Information Technology and Engineering, George Mason University, Fairfax, VA, December 1991b.

4. Bloedorn, E., Michalski, R., and Wnek, J., "Multistrategy Constructive Induction," *Proceedings of the Second International Workshop on Multistrategy Learning*," Harpers Ferry, WV, May 26-29, 1993.

5. Bloedorn, E., Michalski, R.S., and Wnek, J., "Matching Methods with Problems: A Comparative Analysis of Constructive Induction Approaches", *Reports of the Machine Learning and Inference Laboratory*, MLI 94-2, George Mason University, Fairfax, VA, 1994.

6. Bloedorn, E. and Kaufman, K, "Data-Driven Constructive Induction in INLEN", *Reports of the Machine Learning and Inference Laboratory*, George Mason University, Fairfax, VA, 1996 (to appear).

7. Dougherty, J., Kohavi, R., and Sahami, M., "Supervised and Unsupervised Discretization of Continuous Features", *Proceedings of the Twelfth International Conference on Machine Learning*, pp. 194-201, June 1995.

8. Fulton, T., Kasif, S., and Salzberg S., "Efficient Algorithms for Finding Multi-way Splits for Decision Trees", *Proceedings of the Twelfth International Conference on Machine Learning*, pp. 244-251., June 1995.

9. Greene, G.H., "Quantitative Discovery: Using Dependencies to Discover Non-Linear Terms", *M.S. Thesis*, University of Illinois at Urbana-Champaign, 1988.

10. Gryzmala-Busse, J.W., "LERS - A System for Learning from Examples based on Rough Sets" in Slowinski, R., Ed. Intelligent Decision Support Handbook of Applications and Advances of the Rough Sets Theory, Kluwer Academic Publishers, pp. 3-18. 1992.

11. Jensen, G., "SYM-1: A Program that Detects Symmetry of Variable-Valued Logic Functions", *Report UIUCDCS-R-75-729*, Department of Computer Science, University of Illinois at Urbana-Champaign, 1975.

12. Kaufman, K., "Comparing International Development Patterns Using Multi-Operator Learning and Discovery Tools", *Proceedings of the AAAI-94 Workshop on Knowledge Discovery in Databases*, Seattle, WA, pp. 431-440. 1994.

13. Kerber, R., "ChiMerge: Discretization of Numeric Attributes", *Proceedings of the Tenth National Conference on Artificial Intelligence*, pp. 123-128, San Jose, CA, 1992.

14. Langley, P., "Rediscovering Physics with Bacon 3," *Fifth International Joint Conference on Artificial Intelligence*, pp. 505-507, Cambridge, MA: , 1977.

15. Lenat, Douglas, "Learning from Observation and Discovery", in *Machine Learning: An Artificial Intelligence Approach, Vol. I*, R.S. Michalski, J.G. Carbonell and T.M. Mitchell (Eds.), Palo Alto, CA: Morgan Kaufmann (reprint), 1983

16. Matheus, C. J. and Rendell, L.A., "Constructive Induction on Decision Trees", In *Proceedings of the Eleventh International Joint Conference on Artificial Intelligence*, pp. 645-650, 1989.

17. Michalski, R.S., "Recognition of Total or Partial Symmetry in a Completely or Incompletely Specified Switching Function," Proceedings of the IV Congress of the International Federation on Automatic Control (IFAC), Vol. 27 (Finite Automata and Switching Systems), pp. 109-129, Warsaw, June 16-21, 1969.

18. Michalski, R.S., "On the Quasi-Minimal Solution of the Covering Problem" *Proceedings of the V International Symposium on Information Processing* (FCIP 69), Vol. A3 (Switching Circuits), Bled, Yugoslavia, pp. 125-128, 1969.

19. Michalski, R.S. and McCormick, B.H., "Interval Generalization of Switching Theory." Report No. 442, Dept. of Computer Science, University of Illinois, Urbana. 1971.

20. Michalski, R.S., "Variable-Valued Logic: System VL_1, *Proceedings of the 1974 International Symposium on Multiple-Valued Logic*, pp. 323-346. West Virginia University, Morgantown, 1974.

21. Michalski, R.S. and Larson, J.B., "Selection of Most Representative Training Examples and Incremental Generation of VL_1 Hypotheses: the underlying methodology and the description of programs ESEL and AQ11, " *Report No. 867*, Dept. of Computer Science, University of Illinois, Urbana, 1978.

22. Michalski, R.S., "Pattern Recognition as Rule-Guided Inductive Inference," *IEEE Transactions on Pattern Analysis and Machine Intelligence (PAMI)*, Vol. 2, No. 4, pp. 349-361, 1980.

23. Michalski, R.S., "A Theory and Methodology of Inductive Learning: Developing Foundations for Multistrategy Learning," in *Machine Learning: An Artificial Intelligence Approach, Vol. I*, R.S. Michalski, J.G. Carbonell and T.M. Mitchell (Eds.), Palo Alto, CA: Morgan Kaufmann (reprint), 1983.

24. Michalski, R.S., "Inferential Theory of Learning," in *Machine Learning: An Multistrategy Approach, Vol. IV*, R.S. Michalski, and G. Tecuci (Eds.), Palo Alto, CA: Morgan Kaufmann, 1994.

25. Muggleton, S., "Duce, an Oracle-Based Approach to Constructive Induction", *Proceedings of IJCAI-87*, pp. 287-292, Morgan Kaufman, Milan, Italy, 1987.

26. Pagallo, G., and Haussler, D., "Boolean Feature Discovery in Empirical Learning", *Machine Learning*, vol. 5, pp. 71-99, 1990.

27. Pawlak, Z. "Rough Sets and their Applications", Workshop on Mathematics and AI, Schloss Reisburg, W. Germany. Vol II. pp. 543-572. 1988.

28. Pawlak, Z. "Rough Sets: Theoretical Aspects of Reasoning about Data", Kluwer Academic Publishers, AA Dordrecht, The Netherlands, 1991.

29. Quinlan, J. R., "Learning Efficient Classification Procedures," *Machine Learning: An Artificial Intelligence Approach*, Michalski, R.S., Carbonell, J.G, and Mitchell, T.M. (Eds.), Morgan Kaufmann 1983, pp. 463-482.

30. Quinlan, J.R., "C4.5: Programs for Machine Learning", Morgan Kaufmann, San Mateo, CA, 1993.

31. Reinke, R.E., "Knowledge Acquisition and Refinement Tools for the ADVISE Meta-expert System," *Master's Thesis*, University of Illinois, 1984.

32. Rendell, L., and Seshu, R., "Learning Hard Concepts Through Constructive Induction: Framework and Rationale," *Computer Intelligence*, Vol. 6, pp. 247-270, 1990.

33. Schlimmer, J., "Concept Acquisition Through Representational Adjustment," *Machine Learning*, Vol. 1, pp. 81-106, 1986.

34. Thrun, S.B., Bala, J., Bloedorn, E., Bratko, I., Cestnik, B., Cheng, J., De Jong, K., Dzerowski, S., Fahlman, S.E., Hamann, R., Kaufman, K., Keller, S., Kononenko, I., Kreuziger, J., Michalski, R.S., Mitchell, T., Pachowicz, P., Vafaie, H., Van de Velde, W., Wenzel, W., Wnek, J., and Zhang, J., "The MONK'S Problems: A Performance Comparison of Different Learning Algorithms," *(revised version)*, Carnegie Mellon University, Pittsburgh, PA, CMU-CS-91-197, 1991.

35. Utgoff, P., "Shift of Bias for Inductive Learning,", in *Machine Learning: An Artificial Intelligence Approach*, Vol. II, R. Michalski, J. Carbonell, and T. Mitchell (eds.), Morgan Kaufman, Los Altos, CA, pp. 107-148, 1986.

36. Watanabe, L., and Elio, R., "Guiding Constructive Induction for Incremental Learning from Examples," *Proceedings of IJCAI-87*, pp. 293-296, Milan, Italy: , 1987.

37. Weiss, S. M., and Kulikowski, C. A., *Computer Systems that Learn*, Morgan Kaufmann, San Mateo, CA. 1991.

38. Wnek, J. and Michalski, R., "Hypothesis-driven Constructive Induction in AQ17-HCI: A Method and Experiments," *Machine Learning*, Vol. 14, No. 2, pp. 139-168.1993.

39. Wnek, J. "DIAV 2.0 User Manual: Specification and Guide through the Diagrammatic Visualization System," *Reports of the Machine Learning and Inference Laboratory*, MLI95-5, George Mason University, Fairfax, VA 1995.

40. Wnek, J., Kaufman, K., Bloedorn, E., and Michalski, R.S., "Selective Induction Learning System AQ15c: The Method and User's Guide", *Reports of the Machine Learning and Inference Laboratory*, MLI 95-4.

41. Ziarko, W. "On Reduction of Knowledge Representation", *Proceedings of the 2nd International Symposium on Methodologies for Intelligent Systems*, Charlotte, NC. North Holland, pp. 99-113.

Induction of Classification Rules from Imperfect Data

Ning Shan   Howard J. Hamilton   Nick Cercone

Department of Computer Science, University of Regina
Regina, Saskatchewan, Canada S4S 0A2

Abstract. We present a method for inducing classification rules from imperfect data using an extended version of the rough set model. The salient feature of our method is that it makes use of the statistical information inherent in the information system. Our framework describes the overall induction task in terms of two key subtasks: approximate classification and rule generation.

1 Introduction

Machine Learning is recognized as a means of overcoming the knowledge acquisition bottleneck when building knowledge based systems. Many machine learning algorithms classify examples described by vectors in a multi-dimensional space of features. Inductive learning techniques can automatically discover and refine classification rules from such examples [2,3,5,6].

In real-world applications, learning systems often face *imperfect data*, i.e., examples that are erroneous, incomplete, imprecise, or inconsistent. An *erroneous example* is a misrecorded description of a real-world object, as commonly results from errors during data entry. An *incomplete example* lacks values for one or more attributes. In an *imprecise example*, a value for an attribute is not recorded with sufficient accuracy for the purpose at hand. Two examples are *inconsistent* if for the same values of the condition attributes, they have different values for the decision attributes. Here we will focus on inconsistent examples, but some inconsistencies are due to erroneous, incomplete, and imprecise examples. If an incomplete example is handled by replacing the missing value with each of a set of values, inconsistent examples result. As well, when numerical attribute values are discretized, imprecise examples are created and these examples may be inconsistent. Exact decision rules cannot be derived from inconsistent examples by standard methods [2,3,5]. Classification rules learned from imperfect data may be inexact, i.e., there may be exceptions to rules and examples not covered by any rule.

In this paper, we suggest the β-approximation Decision Matrix (BDM) method for generating inexact but useful classification rules from imperfect data. The BDM method is based on an extension to the rough set model [12]. Statistical information is used to define approximate positive and negative regions of a concept. Each classification rule generated by our learning system is characterized by a *certainty factor*, which is the observed probability that an object matching the condition part of the rule belongs to the concept. We describe the overall induction task in terms of two key subtasks: *approximate classification* and *rule generation*.

To solve a concept learning problem, we must generate a discriminating description of a target concept based on a set of condition attributes. The theory of rough sets recognizes that, given limited information about objects of a universe of discourse, only classes of objects rather than individuals can be distinguished. To produce an *approximate classification table*, we combine equivalence classes as long as the combination process leaves the same equivalence classes in the positive region of the concept.

Rule generation generates a set of probabilistic decision rules from an approximate classification table. As mentioned, each rule is characterized by an *certainty factor*. Decision rules could be obtained directly from the approximate classification table. However, to obtain a minimal set of decision rules with the minimum number of condition attributes, we first apply a decision matrix technique adapted from [8]. To accelerate this technique we have introduced a similarity measurement to rank the equivalence classes before beginning rule generation.

The remainder of this paper is organized as follows. In Section 2, a formal description is given of an information system. Approximate classification based on rough set theory is introduced in Section 3. Rule generation is described in Section 4. Experimental results are given in Section 5 and conclusions are presented in Section 6.

2 Knowledge Representation

We assume that knowledge about the world is given as a set of training examples, which are represented as an *information system* [3]. Formally, an information system S is a quadruple $<U, A, V, f>$, where $U = \{x_1, x_2, ..., x_N\}$ is a finite set of objects; A is a finite set of attributes; the attributes in A are further classified into two disjoint subsets, *condition* attributes C and *decision* attributes D such that $A = C \cup D$ and $C \cap D = \emptyset$; $V = \bigcup_{a \in A} V_a$ is a set of attribute values and V_a is the *domain* of attribute a (the set of values of attribute a); $f : U \times A \to V$ is an information function which assigns particular values from domains of attributes to objects such that $f(x_i, a) \in V_a$, for all $x_i \in U$ and $a \in A$.

An information system only provides partial information about the universe. Objects are indistinguishable from one another when they have the same values for all attributes. Let B be a subset of A, and let x_i, x_j be members of U. A binary relation $R(B)$, called an *indiscernibility relation*, is defined as $R(B) = \{(x_i, x_j) \in U^2 \mid \forall a \in B, f(x_i, a) = f(x_j, a)\}$. We say that x_i and x_j are *indiscernible* by the set of attributes B in S if $f(x_i, a) = f(x_j, a)$ for every $a \in B$. Clearly, $R(B)$ is an equivalence relation on U for every $B \subseteq A$. If several objects are indiscernible by the set of all attributes (A), then they can be represented by a single description plus a count of the instances.

Table 1 shows an example information system. The universe U consists of 16 equivalence classes of objects: $U = \{obj_1, obj_2, ..., obj_{16}\}$. Each equivalence class is described by the set of condition attributes $C = \{attr_1, attr_2, attr_3\}$. These equivalence classes are classified by the set of decision attributes $D = \{class\}$. Two concepts can be defined: $class = 0$ and $class = 1$. The #cases column gives the number of objects in each equivalence class.

We can also define two natural equivalence relations $R(C)$ and $R(D)$ on U. A *concept* Y is an equivalence class of the relation $R(D)$. Without loss of generality, we may consider D as a singleton set. Our objective is to construct decision rules for each concept. Given a concept Y, the partition of U with respect to this concept is defined as $R^*(D) = \{Y, U - Y\} = \{Y, \neg Y\}$.

Based on the set of condition attributes C, any object x_i specifies

U	$attr_1$	$attr_2$	$attr_3$	$class$	$\#cases$
obj_1	0	0	0	0	3
obj_2	0	0	1	0	4
obj_3	0	1	0	0	8
obj_4	0	1	1	0	10
obj_5	1	0	0	0	7
obj_6	1	0	1	0	9
obj_7	1	1	0	0	7
obj_8	1	1	1	0	3
obj_9	0	0	0	1	7
obj_{10}	0	0	1	1	8
obj_{11}	0	1	0	1	7
obj_{12}	0	1	1	1	8
obj_{13}	1	0	0	1	3
obj_{14}	1	0	1	1	5
obj_{15}	1	1	0	1	8
obj_{16}	1	1	1	1	10

Table 1. An example of an information system

an equivalence class $[x_i]_R$ of the relation $R(C)$:

$$[x_i]_R = \{x_j \in U \mid \forall a \in C, \ f(x_j, a) = f(x_i, a)\}$$

We define conditional probabilities as $P(Y|[x_i]_R) = \frac{P(Y \cap [x_i]_R)}{P([x_i]_R)} = \frac{|Y \cap [x_i]_R|}{|[x_i]_R|}$, where $P(Y|[x_i]_R)$ is the probability of occurrence of event Y conditioned on event $[x_i]_R$. That is, $P(Y|[x_i]_R) = 1$, iff $[x_i]_R \subseteq Y$; $P(Y|[x_i]_R) > 0$, iff $[x_i]_R \cap Y \neq \emptyset$; and $P(Y|[x_i]_R) = 0$, iff $[x_i]_R \cap Y = \emptyset$.

3 β-Approximate Classification

Given an information system $S = \{U, A, V, f\}$ and an equivalence relation $R(C)$ on U, an ordered pair $AS = <U, R(C)>$ is called an *approximation space* [3] based on the condition attributes C. Let $Y \subseteq U$ be a subset of objects representing a concept, and $R^*(C) = \{X_1, X_2, ..., X_n\} = \{ [x_1]_R, [x_2]_R, ..., [x_n]_R\}$ be the collection of equivalence classes induced by the relation $R(C)$. In the rough set model, the *lower* and *upper* approximations of a set Y are respectively defined by

$$\underline{R(C)}(Y) = \bigcup_{P(Y|X_i)=1} \{X_i \in R^*(C)\} \quad \text{and}$$

$$\overline{R(C)}(Y) = \bigcup_{P(Y|X_i)>0} \{X_i \in R^*(C)\}.$$

The above definitions do not make use of the statistical information in the boundary region $\overline{R(C)}(Y) - \underline{R(C)}(Y)$. For this reason, a number of extensions to the original rough set model have been proposed [1,4,7,9,12]. In our approach we attempt to rectify this limitation by introducing a β-approximation space.

A β-approximation space AS_P is a triple $< U, R(C), P >$, where P is a probability measure as described in Section 2 and β is a real number in the range $(0.5, 1]$. The β-approximation space AS_P can be divided into the following regions:

1. β-positive region of the set Y:

$$POS_C(Y) = \bigcup_{P(Y|X_i)\geq\beta} \{X_i \in R^*(C)\}.$$

2. β-negative region of the set Y:

$$NEG_C(Y) = \bigcup_{P(Y|X_i)\leq 1-\beta} \{X_i \in R^*(C)\}.$$

The β-positive region of set Y corresponds to all equivalence classes in U with probability $P(Y|X_i)$ greater than or equal to the parameter β. Using our approximate classification table, we will decide whether x_i is in concept Y by looking at $POS_C(Y)$ and $NEG_C(Y)$ rather than by looking at Y itself.

Example 3.1: Given the information system shown in Table 1, the set of condition attributes $C = \{attr_1, attr_2, attr_3\}$ generates the relation $R(C)$ that partitions U into the equivalence classes $R^*(C)$ $= \{X_1, X_2, X_3, X_4, X_5, X_6, X_7, X_8\}$, where $X_1 = \{obj_1, obj_9\}$, $X_2 = \{obj_2, obj_{10}\}$, ..., $X_8 = \{obj_8, obj_{16}\}$. If $Y = \{obj_9, ..., obj_{16}\}$ is the target concept, we calculate the conditional probability for each equivalence class $X_i \in R^*(C)$:

$$P(Y|X_1) = 7/10 = 0.70; \qquad P(Y|X_2) = 8/12 = 0.67;$$
$$P(Y|X_3) = 7/15 = 0.47; \qquad P(Y|X_4) = 8/18 = 0.44;$$
$$P(Y|X_5) = 3/10 = 0.30; \qquad P(Y|X_6) = 5/14 = 0.36;$$
$$P(Y|X_7) = 8/15 = 0.53; \qquad P(Y|X_8) = 10/13 = 0.77;$$

If $\beta = 0.51$, the β-positive region is $POS_C(Y) = \{X_1, X_2, X_7, X_8\}$ and the β-negative region is $NEG_C(Y) = \{X_3, X_4, X_5, X_6\}$. □

Using these regions, we may remove condition attributes from C as long as the positive region $POS_C(Y)$ does not change. The procedure for finding a reduced table is straightforward. We consider each condition attribute $a \in C$ in turn. If the β-positive region $POS_{C-\{a\}}(Y)$ is the same as $POS_C(Y)$, then attribute a is removed from C. The reduced set of condition attributes is called RED.

Continuing from Example 3.1, we try to remove each of $C = \{attr_1, attr_2, attr_3\}$. Since $POS_{C-\{attr_1\}}(Y) = \{X_2, X_4, X_6, X_8\}$, $POS_{C-\{attr_2\}}(Y) = \{X_1, X_2, X_3, X_4, X_6, X_8\}$, and $POS_{C-\{attr_3\}}(Y) = \{X_1, X_2, X_7, X_8\}$, only $attr_3$ can be removed, giving $RED = \{attr_1, attr_2\}$.

4 Generation of Decision Rules

Rule generation is a crucial task in any learning system. For each $X_i \in R^*(RED)$, with description $Des(X_i)$, the decision rule is one of:

(1) $Des(X_i) \to^{c_i} Des(Y)$,   if $P(Y|X_i) \geq \beta$,

(2) $Des(X_i) \to^{c_i} Des(\neg Y)$,   if $P(Y|X_i) \leq 1 - \beta$,

where c_i is the certainty factor [4]:

$$c_i = max(P(Y|X_i), 1 - P(Y|X_i)).$$

Rules may contain attributes whose values are irrelevant in determining the target concept. Furthermore, the rules can be further generalized by removing conditions if no inconsistency results. A decision rule obtained by dropping the maximum possible number of conditions is called a *maximally general rule*. By construction, the maximally general rules contain a minimum number of conditions. The *decision matrix* technique [11] is used here to find all maximally general rules.

Let X_i^+, $i = (1, 2, ... \gamma)$, denote the equivalence classes of the relation $R^*(RED)$ such that $X_i^+ \subseteq POS_{RED}(Y)$, and let X_j^-, $j = (1, 2, ... \rho)$, denote the equivalence classes of the relation $R^*(RED)$

such that $X_j^- \subseteq NEG_{RED}(Y)$. A decision matrix $M = (M_{ij})_{\gamma \times \rho}$ is defined by:

$$M_{ij} = \{(a, f(X_i^+, a)) : a \in RED, f(X_i^+, a) \neq f(X_j^-, a)\}$$

where a is a condition attribute belonging to RED. That is, the entry M_{ij} contains all attribute-value pairs whose values are not the same between the equivalence class X_i^+ and the equivalence class X_j^-.

The set of decision rules computed for a given equivalence class X_i^+ is obtained by treating each element of M_{ij} as a Boolean expression and constructing the following Boolean function, namely:

$$B_i = \bigwedge_j (\bigvee M_{ij}),$$

where $\bigwedge$ and $\bigvee$ are the usual conjunction and disjunction operators.

In the worst case, the time complexity of finding one decision function B_i is estimated in [8] as $O(m^{min(2^m, \gamma)})$, where m is the number of condition attributes and γ is the number of the negative classes $X_j^- \in NEG_{RED}(Y)$. Therefore, we use a similarity measurement to rank the equivalence classes before the rule generation. As in the instance-base learning method [10], instead of treating equivalence classes of the target concept as equally important, we characterize them by their degree of typicality in the representing the concept.

The similarity $SIM(X_i, X_j)$ between two equivalence classes X_i and X_j is the opposite of the Euclidean distance between them:

$$SIM(X_i, X_j) = 1 - \sqrt{\frac{1}{M} \sum_{k=1}^{M} (\frac{X_i^k - X_j^k}{N_k})^2}$$

where X_i^k (X_j^k) is the value of the kth attribute on the equivalence class X_i (X_j). M is the number of condition attributes, and N_k is the number of distinct values in the kth attribute.

$$X_i^k - X_j^k = \begin{cases} 0 & X_i^k \text{ and } X_j^k \text{ have the same symbolic value} \\ 1 & X_i^k \text{ and } X_j^k \text{ have the different symbolic value} \end{cases}$$

The S-similarity of an equivalence class is defined as its average similarity to other equivalence classes belonging to the same region:

$$SIM_S(X_i) = \frac{1}{m-1} \sum_{k=1, k \neq i}^{m} SIM(X_i, X_k)$$

where X_i and X_k belong to the same region and m is the number of equivalence classes in that region. The D-similarity of an equivalence class is defined as its average similarity to all of equivalence classes belonging to the opposite region:

$$SIM_D(X_i) = \frac{1}{m} \sum_{k=1}^{m} SIM(X_i, X_k)$$

where X_i and X_k belong to different regions and m is the number of equivalence classes in the opposite region.

The typicality of an equivalence class X_i is defined as the ratio of its S-similarity to its D-similarity

$$TYP(X_i) = \frac{SIM_S(X_i)}{SIM_D(X_i)}.$$

Higher typicality values indicate better characterization of the target concept. Equivalence classes with higher typicality values are selected first when generating decision rules. For the class X_i with the highest typicality value, we generate all possible decision rules using the decision matrix method. Then we remove the equivalence classes covered by the generated rules. This procedure is repeated until no equivalence classes are left.

X	$attr_1$	$attr_2$	$attr_3$	$class$
X_1	0	0	1	0
X_2	1	0	0	0
X_3	0	0	0	0
X_4	0	1	0	0
X_5	0	1	1	1
X_6	1	0	1	1
X_7	1	1	1	1

Table 2. An example of a partitioned information system

Example 4.1: Table 2 shows a partitioned information system. To generate the decision rules for the concept $class = 0$, we calculate SIM_S, SIM_D and TYP for each equivalence class in the positive region $POS(Y) = \{X_1, X_2, X_3, X_4\}$:

$$SIM_S(X_1) = 0.63;\ SIM_D(X_1) = 0.67;\ \ TYP(X_1) = 0.94;$$
$$SIM_S(X_2) = 0.63;\ SIM_D(X_2) = 0.60;\ \ TYP(X_2) = 1.05;$$
$$SIM_S(X_3) = 0.71;\ SIM_D(X_3) = 0.56;\ \ TYP(X_3) = 1.27;$$
$$SIM_S(X_4) = 0.63;\ SIM_D(X_4) = 0.60;\ \ TYP(X_4) = 1.05;$$

Since $TYP(X_3)$ is highest, we use X_3 to generate decision rules. After applying the decision matrix method, we obtain the rules:

$$r_1 : \quad (attr_1 = 0)\ \&\ (attr_2 = 0) \rightarrow (class = 0)$$
$$r_2 : \qquad\qquad\qquad (attr_3 = 0) \rightarrow (class = 0)$$

No other equivalence classes remain after we remove the equivalence classes covered by these decision rules. Thus, in this example, we need to generate for only one equivalence class instead of for all.

5 Experimental Results

We empirically compared the BDM method to the DM method [8] on 5 artificial domains, each with a different number of Boolean attributes. We generated 10 random concepts for each domain and applied both methods to each. As a measure of efficiency, we measured the number of equivalence classes examined during rule generation. The average results for the 10 runs for BDM and DM are presented in Table 3. For each domain, BDM gives fewer equivalence classes on average.

6 Conclusion

We have proposed a new method for generating decision rules from imperfect data. The salient feature of the proposed method is that it makes use of the statistical information inherent in the information system. Statistical information is used to guide attribute selection and to define the positive and negative regions of a concept. Thus, our method is capable of deriving decision rules from imperfect data. During rule generation, we used a similarity measure for ranking the equivalence classes. Our procedure is appropriate for real-world databases, which seldom provide complete and consistent data.

#attr	Size	BDM	DM
5	32	15.7	32
6	64	25.5	64
7	128	39.8	128
8	256	77.6	256
9	512	135.0	512

Table 3. Performance Comparison

References

1. Katzberg, J. and Ziarko, W., "Variable Precision Rough Sets with Asymmetric Bounds," in Ziarko, W. (ed.), *Rough Sets, Fuzzy Sets and Knowledge Discovery*, Springer-Verlag, 1994, pp. 167-177.
2. Michalski, R.S., Carbonell J.G., and Mitchell, T.M. (eds.), *Machine Learning: An Artificial Intelligence Approach*, vols 1-2. Morgan Kaufmann, San Mateo, California, 1983 and 1986.
3. Pawlak, Z., *Rough Sets: Theoretical Aspects of Reasoning About Data.* Kluwer Academic, 1991.
4. Pawlak Z., and Wong, S.K.M., and Ziarko, W., "Rough Sets: Probabilistic Versus Deterministic Approaches," *International Journal of Man-Machine Studies,* **29**(1): 81-95, 1988.
5. Quinlan, J. R., "Induction of Decision Trees", *Machine Learning,* 1(1):81-106, 1986.
6. Quinlan, J. R., *C4.5 Programs for Machine Learning,* Morgan Kaufmann, San Mateo, California, 1992.
7. Shan, N., Hu, X., Ziarko, W., and Cercone, N., "A Generalized Rough Sets Model," *Proc. of the 3rd Pacific Rim International Conference on Artificial Intelligence,* Beijing, China. 1994, pp. 437-443.
8. Shan, N., *Rule Discovery From Data Using Decision Matrices,* M.Sc. Thesis, Dept. of Computer Science, University of Regina, 1995.
9. Wong, S.K.M. and Ziarko, W., *A Probabilistic Model of Approximate Classification in Inductive Learning,* University of Regina, Technical Report CS-88-01, 1988.
10. Zhang, J., "Selecting Typical Instances in Instance-Based Learning," *Proc. of the 9th International Workshop on Machine Learning,* pp. 474–479, 1992.
11. Ziarko, W. and Shan, N., "A method for computing all maximally general rules in attribute-value systems," *Computational Intelligence,* in press.
12. Ziarko, W., "Variable Precision Rough Set Model," *Journal of Computer and System Sciences,* **46**(1):39-59, 1993.

Induction of Expert System Rules from Databases Based on Rough Set Theory and Resampling Methods

Shusaku Tsumoto and Hiroshi Tanaka

Department of Information Medicine,
Medical Research Institute, Tokyo Medical and Dental University
1-5-45 Yushima, Bunkyo-ku Tokyo 113 Japan
E-mail: tsumoto@cmn.tmd.ac.jp, tanaka@cim.tmd.ac.jp

Abstract. *Automated knowledge acquisition is an important research issue to solve the bottleneck problem in developing expert systems. There have been proposed several methods of inductive learning, such as induction of decision trees, AQ method, and neural networks for this purpose. However, most of the approaches focus on inducing some rules which classify cases correctly. On the contrary, medical experts also learn other information which is important for medical diagnostic procedures from databases. In this paper, a rule-induction system, called PRIMEROSE-REX (Probabilistic Rule Induction Method based on Rough Sets and Resampling methods for Expert systems), is introduced. This program extracts not only classification rules for differential diagnosis, but also other medical knowledge needed for other diagnostic procedures, based on a diagnosing model of a medical expert system RHINOS (Rule-based Headache and facial pain INformation Orgranizing System). This system is evaluated by using training samples of RHINOS domain, and the induced results are compared with rules acquired from medical experts. The results show that our proposed method correctly induces RHINOS rules and estimate the statistical measures of rules.*

1 Introduction

One of the most important problems in developing expert systems is knowledge acquisition from experts [2]. While there have been developed many knowledge acquisition tools to simplify this process, it is still difficult to automate this process. In order to resolve this problem, many methods of inductive learning, such as induction of decision trees [1, 3, 13], rule induction methods [4, 7, 10, 11] and rough set theory [12, 17], are introduced in order to discover knowledge from large databases.

However, most of the approaches focus on inducing some rules, which classifies cases correctly, and extract only information on classification. On the contrary, medical experts also learn other kinds of knowledge, which are important for medical diagnostic procedures, from clinical cases. Focusing on these learning procedures, Matsumura, et al. [8] analyze classificatory and non-classificatory information of medical experts, and propose a diagnosing model, which is composed of the following three reasoning processes: exclusive reasoning, inclusive reasoning, and reasoning about complications. Then, applying this model to headache and facial pain, they have developed a system, RHINOS (Rule-based Headache and facial pain INformation Orgranizing System), which can classify more than 90 percent of clinical cases[8].

Since these processes are found to be based on the concepts of set theory, as shown in [8], it is expected that set-theoretic approaches can describe the diagnosing model and the procedures of knowledge acquisition. In order to characterize these procedures, the concepts of rough set theory are introduced, which describes how to classify a certain set (denoted as a "class") by intersection or union of sets which satisfies one equivalence relation [12]. Based on this theory, a rule-induction system, called PRIMEROSE-REX (Probabilistic Rule Induction Method based on Rough Sets and Resampling methods for Expert systems) is introduced, which extracts rules for an expert system from clinical databases and which estimates statistical measures for classification rules by using resampling methods.

For evaluation, this system is applied to the domain of diagnosis of headache and facial pain. The results show that the derived rules perform a little worse than those of the medical experts, which suggests that we need many training samples and should include more domain knowledge to gain the performance of induced results. However, resampling methods estimate the accuracy of these rules and certainty factors. Therefore combination of rule induction method with resampling methods is effective to estimate the performance of induced results.

The paper is organized as follows: Section 2 discusses diagnosing model of RHINOS and its algorithm for knowledge acquisition. Section 3 illustrates rough set theory and the set-theoretic formulation of RHINOS rules. Section 4 presents our new method, PRIMEROSE for induction of RHINOS-type rules. Section 5 gives experimental results. Section 6 discusses the problems of our work, and finally, Section 7 concludes this paper.

2 RHINOS

RHINOS is an expert system which diagnoses the causes of headache or facial pain from manifestations [8]. In this system, a diagnosing model proposed by Matsumura is applied, which is composed of the following three kinds of reasoning processes: exclusive reasoning, inclusive reasoning, and reasoning about complications.

First, exclusive reasoning is the one that when a patient does not have a symptom which always appears in a disease in the candidates, such a disease can be excluded from them. Second, inclusive reasoning is the one that when a patient has symptoms specific to a disease, the disease can be suspected. Finally, reasoning about complications is that when some symptoms which cannot be explained by that disease, complications of other diseases can be suspected.

Based on the diagnosing model, we consider three kinds of rules corresponding to each process and develop the following algorithms for acquiring these rules from medical experts.

Exclusive Rule. This rule corresponds to exclusive reasoning. In other words, the premise of this rule is equivalent to the necessity condition of the diagnostic conclusion. From the discussion with medical experts, we select the following six basic attributes which are minimally indispensable to defining the necessity condition: *1. Age, 2. Pain location, 3. Nature of the pain, 4. Severity of the pain, 5. History since onset, 6. Existence of jolt headache.*

For example, the exclusive rule of common migraine is the following:

```
To suspect common migraine, the following symptoms are required:
pain location: not eyes and nature: throbbing or persistent or
radiating and history: paroxysmal or sudden and
jolt headache: positive.
```

One of the reason why we select the six attributes is to solve the interface problem of expert systems: if the whole attributes are considered, we also have to input all the symptoms which are not needed for diagnosis. To make exclusive reasoning compact, the only minimal requirements are chosen. It is notable that this kind of selection can be viewed as the ordering of given attributes, and it is expected that such ordering can be induced from databases. Therefore, in PRIMEROSE-REX, an algorithm for induction of exclusive rules scans the whole given attributes. It is because the minimal requirements for describing exclusive rules can be computed after all the exclusive rules are induced. Furthermore, this ordering can be viewed as a "rough" check of induced results and applicability of our diagnosing model. This issue is discussed later in Section 6.

Inclusive Rule. This rule consists of a set of positive rules, the premises of which are composed of a set of manifestations specific to a disease to be included. If a patient satisfies one set, we suspect this disease with some probability. This rule is derived from medical experts by using the following algorithm for each disease: *1. Take a set of manifestations by which we strongly suspect a disease. 2. Set the probability that a patient has the disease with this set of manifestations:SI(Satisfactory Index) 3. Set the ratio of the patients who satisfy the set to all the patients of this disease:CI(Covering Index) 4. If sum of the derived CI(tCI) is equal to 1.0 then end. If not, goto 5. 5. For the patients of this disease who do not satisfy all the collected set of manifestations, goto 1.* Therefore a positive rule is described by a set of manifestations, its satisfactory index (SI), which corresponds to *accuracy measure*, and its covering index (CI), which corresponds to *total positive rate*. Note that SI and CI are given empirically by medical experts.

Formally, each positive rule is represented as a quadruple: $\langle d, R_i, SI_i, CI_i \rangle$, where d denotes its conclusion, and R_i denotes its premise. Thus, each inclusive

rule is described as:
$\langle\{\langle d, R_1, SI_1(, CI_1)\rangle, \cdots, \langle d, R_k, SI_k(, CI_k)\rangle\}, tCI\rangle$, where total CI(tCI) is defined as the CI of a total rule, composed of a disjunctive formula of all rules, $R_1 \lor R_2 \lor \cdots \lor R_k$.

Let us show one of three rules in the inclusive rule of common migraine, whose total CI is equal to 0.9 (tCI=0.9) as an example:

```
If history: paroxysmal, jolt headache: positive,
nature: throbbing or persistent,
prodrome: no, intermittent symptom: no,
persistent time: more than 6 hours, and pain location: not eye,
then common migraine is suspected with accuracy 0.9 (SI=0.9)
and this rule covers 60 percent of the total cases (CI=0.6).
```

In the above inclusive rule, tCI shows that the disjunctive form of above three rules covers 90 percent of total cases of common migraine[1], which also means that 10 percent of common migraine cannot be diagnosed by the above rules.

Disease Image. This rule is used to detect complications of multiple diseases, acquired by all the possible manifestations of a disease. Using this rule, we search for the manifestations which cannot be explained by the diagnosed disease. Those symptoms suggest complications of other diseases. For example, the disease image of common migraine is shown as follows:

```
The following symptoms can be explained by common migraine:
pain location: any or tendency of depression : negative or
jolt headache: positive or ........
```

Therefore, when a patient who suffers from common migraine is depressing, it is suspected that he or she may also have other disease, because this symptom cannot be explained by common migraine.

As shown above, the algorithms for acquisition of these rules are straightforward, and are based on set-theoretic framework[8]. So we introduce rough set theory in order to install these algorithms on computers.

3 Rough Set Theory and RHINOS Rules

Rough Set Theory. Rough set theory clarifies set-theoretic characteristics of the classes over combinatorial patterns of the attributes, which are precisely discussed by Pawlak [12, 18]. This theory can be used to acquire some sets of attributes for classification and can also evaluate how precisely the attributes are able to classify data.

Let us illustrate the main concepts of rough sets which are needed for our formulation. Table 2 is a small example of database which collects the patients who

---

[1] Since tCI is based on total coverage by the disjunctive form of rules, it is not equal to total sum of CI values of all rules.

Table 1. An Example of Database

No.	age	location	nature	severity	history	jolt	prod	nau	M1	M2	class
1	50-59	occular	persistent	weak	persistent	yes	yes	yes	no	no	m.c.h.
2	40-49	whole	persistent	strong	persistent	yes	yes	yes	no	no	m.c.h.
3	40-49	lateral	throbbing	strong	per	no	no	no	yes	yes	migraine
4	40-49	whole	throbbing	weak	paroxysmal	no	no	no	yes	yes	migraine
5	40-49	whole	radiating	strong	acute	yes	yes	yes	no	no	m.c.h.
6	50-59	whole	persistent	weak	subacute	yes	yes	no	no	yes	m.c.h.

NOTATIONS. jolt: jolt headache, M1/M2: tenderness of M1/M2,
m.c.h.: muscle contraction headache.

complained of headache. First, let us consider how an attribute "location" classify the headache patients' set of the table. The set whose value of the attribute "location" is equal to "whole" is {2,4,5,6}, which shows that the 2nd, 4th, 5th, and 6th case (In the following, the numbers in a set are used to represent each record number). This set means that we cannot classify {2,4,5,6} further solely by using the constraint $R = [location = whole]$. This set is defined as the indiscernible set over the relation R and described as follows: $[x]_R = \{2, 4, 5, 6\}$. In this set, {2,5,6} suffer from muscle contraction headache("m.c.h."), and {4} suffers from classical migraine("migraine"), so other additional attributes is needed to dis criminate between "migraine" and "m.c.h."

Using this concept, we can evaluate the classification power of each attribute and define the characteristics of classification in the set-theoretic framework. For example, accuracy and coverage can be defined as:

$$\alpha_R(D) = \frac{|[x]_R \cap D|}{|[x]_R|}, \text{ and } \kappa_R(D) = \frac{|[x]_R \cap D|}{|D|},$$

where $|A|$ denotes the cardinality of a set A, and where $\alpha_R(D)$ and $\kappa_R(D)$ denotes an accuracy of R as to classification of D, $SI(R, D)$ and a true positive rate of R to D, $CI(R, D)$, respectively. In the subsequent sections, the above notations are used to describe RHINOS rules and their induction algorithm. For further information on rough set theory, readers could refer to [12, 17, 18].

RHINOS rules. Using these notations, the above three kinds of rules are described as follows in terms of rough set theory.

Exclusive rules: $R \xrightarrow{\alpha, \kappa} d$ *s.t.* $R = \wedge_i R_i = \wedge \vee_j [a_j = v_k]$, *and* $\kappa_{R_i}(D) = 1.0$.

In the above example, the relation R for "migraine" is described as:
$[age = 40 - 49] \wedge ([location = lateral] \vee [location = whole]) \wedge [nature = throbbing] \wedge ([history = paroxysmal] \vee [history = persistent]) \wedge [jolt = yes] \wedge [prod = yes] \wedge [nau = yes] \wedge [M1 = no] \wedge [M2 = no]$.

Inclusive rules: $R \overset{\alpha,\kappa}{\to} d$ *s.t.* $R = \vee_i R_i = \vee_i(\wedge_j \vee_k [a_j = v_k])$, $\alpha_{R_i}(D) > \delta_\alpha$, *and* $\kappa_{R_i}(D) > \delta_\alpha$.

In the above example, the simplest relation R for "classic", is described as: $[nature = throbbing] \vee [history = paroxysmal] \vee [jolt = yes] \vee [M1 = yes]$. However, induction of inclusive rules gives us two problems. First, SI and CI are overfitted to the training samples. Second, the above rule is only one of many rules which are induced from the above training samples. Therefore some of them should be selected from primary induced rules under some preference criterion. These problems will be discussed in the next section.

Disease Image: $R \overset{\alpha,\kappa}{\to} d$ *s.t.* $R = \vee R_i \vee [a_i = v_j]$, *and* $\alpha_{R_i}(D) > 0$.

In the above example, the relation R for "classic" is described as: $[age = 40-49] \vee [location = lateral] \vee [location = whole] \vee [nature = throbbing] \vee [severity = strong] \vee [severity = weak] \vee [history = paroxysmal] \vee [nausea = yes] \vee [jolt = yes] \vee [M1 = no] \vee [M2 = no]$.

It is notable that each rule is a kind of probabilistic proposition with two statistical measures, which is one kind of an extension of Ziarko's variable precision model(VPRS) [18].

4 Induction of RHINOS rules

An induction algorithm for RHINOS rules consists of two procedures. One is an exhaustive search through all the attribute-value pairs (*selectors* in the AQ terminology [10]), and the other is a heuristic search for inclusive rules through the combinations of all the attribute-value pairs (*complexes* in the AQ terminology).

4.1 Exhaustive Search

Let D and δ_α denote training samples of the target class d (*positive examples*) and a threshold to select attributes for inclusive rules. Then, this search procedure is defined as follows.

1. Repeat the following procedures for all the attribute-value pairs in a list L.
2. Select an attribute-value pair $[a_i = v_j]$ and check whether $[x]_{[a_i=v_j]} \cap D \neq \phi$ ($\alpha_{[a_i=v_j]}(D) > 0$). If so, then goto (3). Otherwise, remove the pair from L, and goto (2) again.
3. The pair is included in the disease image of d, and check again whether $\alpha_{[a_i=v_j]}(D) > \delta_\alpha$. If so, then goto (4). Otherwise, remove the pair from L and goto (2).
4. This pair is registered as an inclusive rule of d. Finally, check again whether $D \subseteq [x]_{[a_i=v_j]}$ ($\kappa_{[a_i=v_j]}(D) = 1$). If so, then this pair is also included in the exclusive rule of d. Remove the pair from L and goto (2).

The above procedure is repeated for all the attribute-value pairs, and computes exclusive rules, disease images, and candidates of inclusive rules. These candidates are input into the heuristic search procedure, discussed in the next subsection.

In the above example in Table 1, let d be "classic", and $[age = 40 - 49]$ be selected as $[a_i = v_j]$. Since $[x]_{[age=40-49]} \cap D(= \{3,4\}) \neq \phi$, this pair is included in the disease image. However, when δ is set to 0.5, this pair is not included in the inclusive rule, because $\alpha_{[age=40-49]}(D) = 0.5$. The problem about the threshold is discussed later in Section 6.

Finally, since $D \subset [x]_{[age=40-49]}(= \{2,3,4,5\})$, this pair is also included in the exclusive rule.

Next, $[age = 50 - 59]$ is selected. However, this pair will be abandoned since the intersection of $[x]_{[age=50-59]}$ and D is empty, or $[x]_{[age=50-59]} \cap D = \phi$.

4.2 Heuristic Search

Since the definition of inclusive rules is a little weak, many inclusive rules can be obtained. For the above example, a relation $[nausea = 1]$ satisfies $D \cap [x]_{[nausea=1]} \neq \phi$, so it is also one of the inclusive rules of "m.c.h.", although accuracy(SI) of that rule is equal to 1/3. In order to suppress induction of such rules, which have low classificatory power, only equivalence relations whose SI is larger than δ_α are selected. For example, when δ_α is set to $1/2(=0.5)$, the above relation $[age = 40 - 49]$ is eliminated from the candidates of inclusive rules, because SI of this relation is less than the precision, Furthermore, PRIMEROSE-REX minimizes the number of attributes not to include the attributes which do not gain the classificatory power, called *dependent* variables. This procedure can be described as follows:

1. Order all the attribute-value pairs included in the above candidates C with respect to the value of CI (coverage).
2. Select the pair which covers training samples of d maximally (R_i s.t. max $\kappa_{R_i}(D)$)) from C.
3. Choose an attribute-value pair $[a_k = v_l]$ which maximally removes the negative examples in $[x]_{R_i}$ (that is, remove $[x]_{R_i} - ([x]_{R_i} \cap D)$).
4. If $\alpha_{R_i \wedge [a_k=v_l]} = 1.0$, or if all the possible attributes are used, then goto (5). Otherwise, goto (3).
5. Remove R_i from the candidates C and goto (2).

For the above example in Table 1, the coverage of $[M1 = yes]$ for "m.c.h" is maximum. Furthermore, since $\alpha_{[M1=yes]}(D) = 1.0$, it is included in inclusive rules of "m.c.h". The next maximum one is $[M2 = yes]$, whose coverage is equal to 3/4. Since this accuracy is also equal to 1.0, it is also included in inclusive rules. At this point, we have two inclusive rules as follows: $[M1 = yes] \xrightarrow{\alpha=1.0, \kappa=1.0}$ "m.c.h." and $[M2 = yes] \xrightarrow{\alpha=1.0, \kappa=0.75}$ "m.c.h." Repeating these procedures, all the inclusive rules are acquired.

4.3 Estimation of Accuracy and Coverage

The above definition of accuracy and coverage shows that only small training samples causes the overestimate. For the above example, both of statistical measures of the simplest rule are equal to 1.0. This means that this rule correctly diagnoses and covers all the cases of the disease "classic". However, in general, these meanings holds only in the world of the small training samples. In this sense, apparent accuracy and coverage are biased. Thus, these biases should be corrected by introducing other estimating methods, since the biases cannot be detected by the original induced method.

Note that this problem is similar to that of error rates of discriminant function in multivariate analysis [6], the field in which resampling methods are reported to be useful for the estimation.

Hence the following two resampling methods are applied to estimation of accuracy and coverage: cross-validation and the bootstrap method, whose characteristics are precisely discussed by Efron[5, 6]. According to the Efron's results, cross-validation estimators are used as the lower bound of accuracy and coverage, and the bootstrap methods as the upper bound of both measures, in PRIMEROSE-REX, as the previously introduced system PRIMEROSE2[15].

Furthermore, in order to reduce the high variance of estimators by cross-validation, we introduce repeated cross-validation method,which is firstly introduced by Walker [16]. In this method, cross-validation methods are executed repeatedly(safely, 100 times), and estimates are averaged over all the trials. In summary, since our strategy is to avoid the overestimation and the high variabilities, combination of repeated 2-fold cross-validation and the Bootstrap method is adopted in this paper.

5 Experimental Results

We apply PRIMEROSE-REX to headache(RHINOS domain), whose training samples consist of 1477 samples, 10 classes, and 20 attributes. The experiments are performed by the following three procedures. First, these samples are randomly split into pseudo-training samples and pseudo-test samples. Second, by using the pseudo-training samples, PRIMEROSE-REX induces rules and the statistical measures[2]. Third, the induced results are tested by the pseudo-test samples. These procedures are repeated for 100 times and average each accuracy and the estimators for accuracy of diagnosis over 100 trials. Experimental results are shown in Table 2. The first column, exclusive rule accuracy denotes how many training samples that do not belong to a class are excluded correctly from the candidates. The second column is equivalent to the averaged classification accuracy. Finally, the third column shows how many symptoms, which cannot be explained by diagnostic conclusions, are detected by the disease image. The first row is the result of PRIMROSE-REX, and the second one is that of medical experts. And, for comparison, we compare the classification accuracy of inclusive rules with that of CART [1], C4.5 [14], CN2 [4] and AQ-15 [11], which is shown in the third to sixth row. Finally, in the seventh and eighth row, the results of estimation are derived by using repeated cross-validation method (R-CV) and the bootstrap method (BS). These results are summarized to the following

---

[2] The threshold δ_α and δ_κ is set to 0.5 in these experiments.

Table 2. Experimental Results (Averaged)

Method	Exclusive Rule Accuracy	Inclusive Rule Accuracy	Disease Image Accuracy
PRIMEROSE-REX	95.0%	88.3%	93.2%
RHINOS	98.0%	95.0%	97.4%
CART	–	85.8%	–
C4.5	–	84.0%	–
CN2	–	87.0%	–
AQ15	–	86.2%	–
R-CV	72.9%	78.7%	83.8%
BS	98.4%	91.6%	95.6%

three points. First, while the induced inclusive rules perform worse than those of medical experts, exclusive rules and disease images gain the same performance, compared with experts' rules. Second, our method performs a little better than four classical empirical learning methods, although the differences are not statistically significant. Finally, third, R-CV estimator and BS estimator can be regarded as the lower boundary and the upper boundary each rule accuracy. Therefore the interval of these two estimators can be used as the estimator of performance of each rule.

6 Discussion

As discussed in Section 2, we intend to formulate induction of exclusive rules by using the whole given attributes, although the original exclusive rules are described by the six basic questions. Therefore induced exclusive rules have the maximum number of attributes whose conjunction R also satisfies $\kappa_R(D) = 1.0$. If this maximum combination includes the six basic attributes as a subset, then this selection of basic attributes is one of good choices of attributes, although redundant. Otherwise, the given six attributes may be redundant or the induced results may be insufficient. For the above example shown in Table 1, the maximum combination of attributes is {age, loc, nat, his, jolt, prod, nau, M1, M2 } [3]. Since this set does not include an attribute "sever", the six given attributes or the induced results are insufficient in this small database. In this case, however, the sixth attributes are acquired by medical experts through a large number of experienced cases. Thus, the induced attributes will be revised by additional samples in the near future.

On the contrary, in the database for the above experiments, the maximum combination is 13 attributes, derived as follows: Age, Pain location, Nature of the pain, Severity of the pain, History since onset, Existence of jolt headache,

---

[3] Severity cannot be a member, since $[sever = wea] \vee [sever = str]$ is included in both exclusive rules.

Tendency of depression, and Tenderness of M1 to M6, which is a superset of the six basic attributes. Thus, this selection can be a good choice.

In this way, the induction of maximum combination can be also used as a "rough" check of induced results or our diagnosing model on exclusive rules, which can be formulated as below [4].

Let A and E denote a set of the induced attributes for exclusive rules and a set of attributes acquired from domain experts. Thus, the following four relations can be considered. First, if $A \subset E$, then A is insufficient or E is redundant. Second, if $A = E$, then both sets are sufficient to represent diagnosing model in an applied domain. Third, if $A \supset E$, then A is redundant or E is insufficient. Finally, fourth, if intersection of A and E is not empty ($A \cap E \neq \phi$), then either or both sets are insufficient.

Reader may say that the above relations are weak and indeterminate. However, the above indefinite parts should be constrained by information on domain knowledge. For example, let us consider the case when $A \subset E$. When E is validated by experts, A is insufficient in the first relation. However, in general, E can be viewed as A obtained by large samples, and $A \supset E$ should hold, which shows that a given database is problematic. Moreover, the constraint on exclusive rules, $\kappa_R(D) = 1.0$, suggests that there exist a class which does not appear in the database, because the already given classes cannot support $\kappa_R(D) = 1.0$, that is, $[x]_R \cap D \neq D$ will hold in the future.

On the other hand, when E is not well given by experts and A is induced from sufficiently large samples, E will be redundant, which means that the proposed model for E does not fit to this database or this domain.

This kind of knowledge is important, because we sometimes need to know whether samples are enough to induce knowledge and whether an applied inducing model is useful to analyze databases.

Thus, the above four relations give simple examinations to check the characteristics of samples and the applicability of a given diagnosing model. It is our future work to develop more precise checking methodology for automated knowledge acquisition.

7 Conclusion

In this paper, we introduce a system, called PRIMEROSE-REX which extracts not only classification rules for differential diagnosis, but also other medical knowledge which is needed for diagnosis, based on a diagnosing model of a medical expert system RHINOS. We evaluate this system by using training samples of RHINOS domain, and compared the induced results with rules acquired from medical experts. The results show that our proposed method correctly induces RHINOS rules and estimates the statistical measures of rules.

---

[4] This discussion assumes that the whole attributes are sufficient to classify the present and the future cases into given classes.

References

1. Breiman, L., Freidman, J., Olshen, R., and Stone, C. (1984). *Classification And Regression Trees*. Belmont, CA: Wadsworth International Group.
2. Buchnan, B. G. and Shortliffe, E. H.(eds.) (1984). *Rule-Based Expert Systems*, Addison-Wesley.
3. Cestnik, B., Kononenko, I., Bratko, I. (1987). Assistant 86: A knowledge elicitation tool for sophisticated users. *Proceedings of the Second European Working Session on Learning*, pp.31-45, Sigma Press.
4. Clark, P., Niblett, T. (1989). The CN2 Induction Algorithm. *Machine Learning*, 3,261-283.
5. Efron, B. (1982). *The Jackknife, the Bootstrap and Other Resampling Plans*. Society for Industrial and Applied Mathematics, Pennsylvania.
6. Efron, B. (1983). Estimating the error rate of a prediction rule: improvement on cross validation. *Journal of American Statistics Association*, **78**, 316-331.
7. Indurkhya, N. and Weiss, S. (1991). Iterative Rule Induction Methods, *Applied Intelligence*, **1**, 43-54.
8. Matsumura, Y., et al. (1986). Consultation system for diagnoses of headache and facial pain: RHINOS. *Medical Informatics*, **11**, 145-157.
9. Mclachlan, G. J. (1992). *Discriminant Analysis and Statistical Pattern Recognition*. John Wiley and Sons, New York.
10. Michalski, R. S. (1983). A Theory and Methodology of Machine Learning. Michalski, R.S., Carbonell, J.G. and Mitchell, T.M., *Machine Learning - An Artificial Intelligence Approach*. Morgan Kaufmann, Palo Alto, CA.
11. Michalski, R. S., Mozetic, I., Hong, J., and Lavrac, N. (1986). The Multi-Purpose Incremental Learning System AQ15 and its Testing Application to Three Medical Domains. *Proceedings of the fifth National Conference on Artificial Intelligence*, 1041-1045, AAAI Press, Palo Alto, CA.
12. Pawlak, Z. (1991). *Rough Sets*. Kluwer Academic Publishers, Dordrecht.
13. Quinlan, J. R. (1986). Induction of decision trees. *Machine Learning*, **1**, 81-106.
14. Quinlan, J.R. (1993). *C4.5 - Programs for Machine Learning*, Morgan Kaufmann, CA.
15. Tsumoto, S. and Tanaka, H. Induction of Medical Expert System Rules based on Rough Sets and Resampling Methods *Proceedings of the Eighteenth Annual Symposium on Computer Applications in Medical Care*, (*Journal of the AMIA* **1**, supplement), pp.1066-1070, 1994.
16. Walker, M. G. and Olshen, R. A. (1992). Probability Estimation for Biomedical Classification Problems. *Proceedings of the sixteenth Symposium on Computer Applications on Medical Care*, McGrawHill, New York.
17. Ziarko, W. (1991). The Discovery, Analysis, and Representation of Data Dependencies in Databases, in: Shapiro, G. P. and Frawley, W. J.(eds), *Knowledge Discovery in Databases*, AAAI press, Palo Alto, CA, pp.195-209.
18. Ziarko, W. (1993). Variable Precision Rough Set Model. *Journal of Computer and System Sciences*, **46**, 39-59.

Mining Patterns at Each Scale in Massive Data

Jan M. Żytkow† & Robert Zembowicz

Computer Science Department, Wichita State University, Wichita, KS 67260–0083
† also Institute of Computer Science, Polish Academy of Sciences, Warsaw
{zytkow, robert}@lore.cs.twsu.edu

Abstract. An important but neglected aspect of data analysis is discovering phenomena at different scale in the same data. Scale plays the role analogous to error. It can be used to focus data exploration on differences that exceed the given scale (error) and to disregard those smaller. We introduce a discovery mechanism that applies to bi-variate patterns, in particular to time series. It combines search for maxima and minima with search for regularities in the form of equations. If it cannot find a regularity for all data, it uses other discovered patterns to divide data into subsets, and explores recursively each subset. Detected patterns are subtracted from data and the search continues in the residuals. Our mechanism does not skip patterns at any scale. Applied at many scales and to many data sets, it seems explosive, but it terminates surprisingly fast because of data reduction and the requirements of pattern stability and significance. We show application of our method on a time series of a half million datapoints. Our example shows that even simple data can reveal many surprising phenomena, and our method leads to fine conclusions about the environment in which they have been gathered.

1 The role of error and scale in data analysis

Consider bi-variate numerical data, for instance a time series. Regularities at different scale (also called tolerance) are common in such data, when large amounts of datapoints are available. For instance, the overall linear growth may be altered with a short cycle periodic pattern. Both patterns may be caused by different phenomena. Real data contain information about many phenomena as a rule, not as an exception. This leads to a challenging vision for automated knowledge discovery: develop a mechanism that discovers as many independent patterns as possible, not overlooking strong patterns at any scale but not accepting spurious regularities which can occur by chance in any data confronted with very large hypotheses spaces. That mechanism should be able to detect patterns of different types, such as equations, maxima and minima, and search for patterns in data subsets if the search fails to detect patterns satisfied by all data.

In this paper we present a data mining mechanism that works efficiently for large amounts of data and makes progress on each of these requirements. We report an application of our methods on a large set of bi-variate data, leading to a surprising interpretation. Despite the danger of a large combinatorial complexity, our methods can be applied efficiently even on very large datasets. We use the notion of pattern stability applied by Witkin (1983).

1.1 The role of error in pattern discovery

If known, error or noise in data plays a very important role in pattern detection. Consider the data in the form $D = \{(x_i, y_i, e_i) : i = 1, ..., N\}$ and the search for equations of the form $y = f(x)$ that fit data (x_i, y_i) within the accuracy of error e_i. For the same $\{(x_i, y_i) : i = 1, ..., N\}$, the smaller is the error $e_i, i = 1, ..., N$, the closer fit is required between data and equations. Even a constant pattern $y = C$ can fit any data, if error is very large, but the smaller is the error, the more complex equations may be needed.

Knowledge of error is important for many reasons during the search for equations (Zembowicz & Żytkow, 1992):

1. When the error varies for different data, the weighted χ^2 value $[(y_i - f(x_i))/0.5e_i]^2$ should be used to compute the best fit parameters for any model. This enforces better fit to the more precise data.

2. The error should be used in the evaluation of each equation $y = f(x)$. For each datum, $0.5e_i = \sigma_i$ can be interpreted as the standard deviation of the normal distribution $N(y(x_i), \sigma_i)$ of y's for x_i. Knowledge of that distribution permits to compute the probability that the data have been generated as a sum of the value $y(x_i)$ and the value drawn randomly from the normal distribution $N(0, \sigma_i)$, for all $i = 1, ..., N$.

3. Error should be propagated to the parameter values of $f(x)$. When patterns are sought for those parameters (e.g., in BACON-like recursive search for multidimensional regularities), the parameter error shall be used as data error.

4. If the parameter error is larger than the value of that parameter, we can assume that the parameter value is zero. Zeroing the parameter at the highest degree polynomial term in $f(x)$ eliminates $f(x)$ even if it fits the data.

5. Many equation finding systems generate new variables by transforming the initial variables x and y. Error values must be propagated to new terms and used in search for equations that apply those terms.

The same conclusions about error apply to other patterns, too. Let us consider maxima and minima. For the same data (x_i, y_i), when the error is large, many differences between the values of y are treated as random fluctuations within error. In consequence, few maxima and minima are detected. When the error is small, however, the same differences may become significant. The smaller is the error, the larger number of maxima and minima shall be detected.

1.2 Phenomena at different scale

It is common that a large data set captures phenomena at different scale. They may belong to the investigated physical process, but may be also due to data collection, instruments behavior, and influences from the environment. They can be characterized independently by their scales in both variables. For instance, in a time series (x is time) one phenomenon may occur in a daily cycle, the cycle for another can be few hours, while still another may follow a monotonous dependence between x and y. Each phenomenon may produce influence of different scale on the value of y. Periodic phenomena, for instance, can have different amplitudes of change in y.

Each datum combines the effects of all phenomena. When phenomena are additive, the measured value of y for each x is the total of values contributed by each phenomenon. Given the resultant data, we want to separate the phenomena by detecting patterns that describe individually each phenomenon. The basic question of this paper is how can it be done by an automated system.

Suppose that a particular search method has captured a pattern P in data D. Subtracting P from D produces residua which hold the remaining patterns. Repeated application of pattern detection and subtraction can gradually recover patterns that account for several phenomena. One has to be cautious, however, of artifacts generated by spurious patterns and their residua.

It is a good idea to start from large scale phenomena, by using a large value of scale in pattern finding. The phenomena captured at the large values of error follow simple patterns. The fit does not have to be exact when it is evaluated by the least square weighted by large error. Many smaller scale patterns may be hidden within error. They can be discovered later, in the residua obtained after subtracting the larger scale patterns.

1.3 The roles for maxima and minima

In this paper we concentrate on two types of patterns: maxima/minima and equations. We explore the ways in which the results in one category can feedback the search for patterns of the other type.

A simple algorithm can detect maxima and minima at a given scale δ:

__Algorithm:__ **Find Maxima (X_{max}, Y_{max}) and Minima (X_{min}, Y_{min})**
given ordered sequence of points (x_i, y_i), $i = 1 \ldots N$, and scale δ
    task $\leftarrow$ unknown, $X_{max} \leftarrow x_1$, $X_{min} \leftarrow x_1$, $Y_{max} \leftarrow y_1$, $Y_{min} \leftarrow y_1$
    for i from 2 to N do
        if task $\neq$ max **and** $y_i > Y_{min} + \delta$ **then**
            store minimum (X_{min}, Y_{min})
            task $\leftarrow$ max, $X_{max} \leftarrow x_i$, $Y_{max} \leftarrow y_i$
        else if task $\neq$ min **and** $y_i < Y_{max} - \delta$ **then**
            store maximum (X_{max}, Y_{max})
            task $\leftarrow$ min, $X_{min} \leftarrow x_i$, $Y_{min} \leftarrow y_i$
        else if $y_i > Y_{max}$ **then** $X_{max} \leftarrow x_i$, $Y_{max} \leftarrow y_i$
        else if $y_i < Y_{min}$ **then** $X_{min} \leftarrow x_i$, $Y_{min} \leftarrow y_i$
    if $Y_{max} - Y_{min} > \delta$ **then** ; handle the last extremum, if any
        if task = min **then** store minimum (X_{min}, Y_{min})
        else if task = max **then** store maximum (X_{max}, Y_{max})

Our discovery mechanism uses the knowledge of maxima and minima in several ways. First, if the number of extrema is N, then the minimum polynomial degree tried by our Equation Finder (EF, Zembowicz & Żytkow, 1992) is $N+1$. A degree higher than N may be needed, because the inflection points also increase the degree of the polynomial. As high degree polynomials are difficult to interpret and generalize, if the number of extrema is larger than 3, only the periodic functions are tried.

Another application is search for regularities on different properties of maxima and minima, such as the location, height, and width. Those regularities can be instrumental in understanding the nature of a periodic phenomenon. A regularity on the locations of the subsequent maxima and minima estimates the cycle length. A regularity on the extrema heights estimates the amplitude function of a periodic pattern. Jointly, they can guide the search for periodic equations.

Still another application is data partitioning. Data between the adjacent extrema detected at scale δ are monotonous at that scale, so that the equation finding search similar to BACON1 (Langley et al., 1987) applies in each partition. We use EF, limiting the search to linear equations and term transformations to monotonous (e.g., $x' = \log x, x' = \exp x$). Since all the data in each partition fit a constant at the tolerance level $1/2 \times \delta$, EF is applied with the standard deviation set at $1/6 \times \delta$.

1.4 Data reduction

The search for extrema at each scale starts at the minimum positive distance in y between adjacent datapoints, or the error of y if it is known. The search also uses the same minimum value as the increment. The search terminates at the first scale at which no extrema have been found. Since an extremum at a larger scale must be also an extremum at each lower scale, when the search proceeds from the low end of scale the extrema detected at a given scale become the input data for the search at the next higher scale. This way the number of data is reduced very fast and the search at all levels can be very efficient. The whole search for extrema at each scale typically takes less than double the time spent at the initial scale.

Algorithm: Detect extrema at all tolerance levels
Given an ordered sequence of points (x_i, y_i), $i = 1 \ldots N$,
$\quad \delta_{min} \leftarrow |\min(y_i - y_{i+1})|$, for all $y_i \neq y_{i+1}$, $i = 1 \ldots N$
$\quad \delta \leftarrow \delta_{min}$, DATA $\leftarrow (x_i, y_i)$, $i = 1 \ldots N$
$\quad$ **while** DATA includes more than two points **do**
$\qquad$ Find all extrema $(X_{min/max}, Y_{min/max})$ in DATA at scale δ
$\qquad$ Store δ , store list-of-all-extrema $(X_{min/max}, Y_{min/max})$
$\qquad \delta \leftarrow \delta + \delta_{min}$, DATA $\leftarrow$ list-of-all-extrema $(X_{min/max}, Y_{min/max})$

The search for equations may benefit from another type of data reduction. A number of adjacent data, at a small distance between their x values, can be binned together and represented by their mean value and standard deviation. The size of the bin depends on the tolerance level in the x dimension. The results of binning are visualized in Figures 1 and 2. Each pixel in the x dimension summarizes about 500 data. About 0.5 mln data have been reduced to about 1000.

1.5 Pattern stability

No scale is apriori more important than another, as patterns can occur at any scale. When the search for patterns is successful at scale δ, the same pattern can often be detected at other scales close to δ, too. Patterns that hold at many levels are called stable (Witkin, 1983). Consider the stability of extrema. Each extremum that occurs at a given level must also occur at all lower levels. Stability applies to extrema pairs and is measured by the range of tolerance levels over which a given maximum is adjacent to a given minimum. Expanding the definition to the set of all extrema at a given scale, we measure stability as the range of tolerance levels over which the set of extrema does not change.

Stability is important for several reasons. As discussed earlier, when a number of extrema are detected at a given scale, regularities can be sought on their location, height, and width. It is wasteful to detect the same regularities many times at different scales and then realize that they are identical. A better idea is to recognize that the set of extrema is the same at several scale levels, and search for regularities only once.

A stable pattern is a likely manifestation of a real phenomenon, while an unstable set of extrema S may be an artifact. Some extrema may be a part of S by chance. The slight variation in the tolerance level removes them from S. The search for regularities in such a set S may fail or lead to weak, spurious regularities. It would be a waste of time to seek their interpretation and generalization. Eventually S can be dismissed but it is a good idea not to consider it in the first place.

Since regularities for extrema may lead to important conclusions about the underlying phenomena, our system pays attention to sets of extrema which are stable across many tolerance levels. It searches the sets of extrema and picks the first stable set at the high end of scale.

Algorithm: Detect stable set of extrema at the high end of scale
Given a sequence of extrema sets EXTREMA$_i$, ordered by δ_i, $\delta_{min} \leq \delta_i \leq \delta_{max}$
    for δ from δ_{min} to δ_{max} do
        Compute the number E_i of extrema in EXTREMA$_i$
        for each different E_i do
            Compute the number N_i of occurrences of E_i ;; The higher is N_i,
        ;; the greater is the stability of the corresponding extrema set EXTREMA$_i$
        Let N_a, N_b two highest numbers among N_i
        return EXTREMA$_i$ for the minimum(E_a, E_b)
        ;; That among two most stable sets which is of higher scale
        and return δ_{stable} = average(δ) for EXTREMA$_i$

1.6 Residual data

Our mechanism treats phenomena as additive. It subtracts the detected patterns from data and seek further patterns in the residua. We will now present the details of subtraction and discuss termination of the search for further patterns.

Both equations and extrema are functional relationships between x and y: $y = f(x)$. Some extrema can be described by equations that cover also many data that extend far beyond the extrema. For instance, a second degree polynomial that captures the data may at the same time fit one extremum. Equations are not available, however, for many extrema. Those we represent point by point. In the first case, when $y = f(x)$ is the best and acceptable equation, the residua are computed as $r_i = y_i - f(x_i)$, and they oscillate around $y = 0$. In the second case we remove from the data all datapoints that represent the extremum.

In the first case the data are decomposed into pattern $y = f(x)$ and residua $(x_i, r_i), i = 1, \ldots, N$, so that $y_i = f(x_i) + r_i$ for $i = 1, \ldots, N$. In the second case, the data are decomposed into pattern $s(x) \to y = f(x)$ and residua (x_i, y_i) for each x_i such that $\neg s(x_i)$, where $s(x)$ describes the scope of the extremum.

If the residua (x_i, r_i) deviate from the normal distribution, the search for patterns applies recursively. Verification of the hypothesis that residua are Gaussian is a complex task. The run test uses all segments of consecutive residua such that the residua in each segment are systematically negative or systematically positive. The statistics of the segment lengths can reveal systematic patterns in residua. We do not use other tests, but many would be needed to verify different features of normal distribution.

Eventually no more patterns can be found in residua. This may happen because regularities in the residua are not within the scope of search or because the residua represent Gaussian noise. In the latter case, the final data model is $y = f(x) + \varepsilon(x)$, where $\varepsilon(x)$ is Gaussian, while $f(x)$ represents all the detected patterns. Since the variability of residua is much smaller than that of the original data, the subtraction of patterns typically takes only a few iterations.

Algorithm: Detect Patterns

$D \leftarrow$ the initial data

until data D are random

    seek stable pattern(s) P in D at the highest tolerance levels

    $D \leftarrow$ subtract pattern(s) P from D

2 Data

As an example we will consider a large number of data collected in a simple experiment. Since we wanted to find the theory of measurement error for an electronic balance, we automatically collected the mass readings of an empty beaker placed on the balance. The beaker weighted about 249.130mg. Since the nominal accuracy of the balance is 0.001g=1mg, we expected a constant reading that would occasionally diverge by a few milligrams from the average value. But the results were very surprising. The measurements have been continued for several days, approximately one datapoint per second. Altogether we got 482,450 readings. Fig. 1 illustrates the data. All datapoints have been plotted, but many adjacent data have been plotted at the same value of x.

We can see a periodic pattern consisting of several large maxima with a slower ascent and a more rapid descent. The heights of the maxima seem constant or slightly growing, and they seem to follow a constant cycle. Superimposed on this constant pattern are smaller maxima of different height. Several levels of even smaller minima and maxima are not visible in Figure 1, because the time dimension has been compresses, but they are clearly visible in the original data.

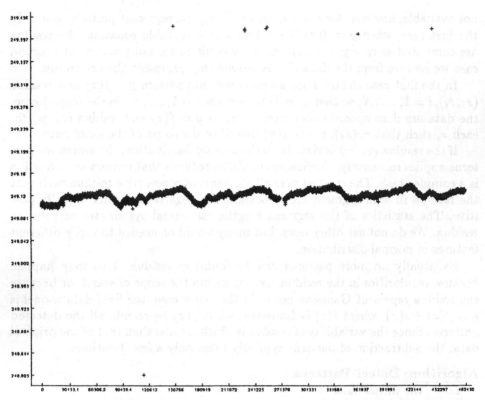

Fig. 1. The raw results of mass measurements on an electronic balance over the period of five days (482450 readings).

Upon closer examination, one can notice seven data points at the values about 249.430g, that is 0.3g above the average result, a huge distance in comparison to the accuracy of the balance. They can be seen as small plus signs in the upper part of Figure 1. There is one point about 0.3g below the average data. Those data must have been caused by the same phenomenon because they are very special and very similar: they are momentary peaks of one-second duration.

Apparently, several phenomena must have contributed to those data. Can all these patterns be detected in automated way by a general purpose mechanism, or are our eyes smarter than our computer programs? Can our mechanism find enough clues about those patterns to discover the underlying phenomena?

3   Results of search for patterns at many scales

We will now illustrate the application of our multi-scale search mechanism on the dataset described in the previous section.

Detect extrema at all tolerance levels: The search for extrema at all levels of tolerance started from 482,450 data and iterated through some 300 scale levels. Since the number of extrema decreased rapidly between the low scale levels, the majority of time has been spent on the first pass through the data. The number of extrema at the initial scale of 1mg has been 29,000, so the data have been reduced to 6%. The number of extrema has been under 50 for $\delta > 9mg$.

Find the first stable set of extrema: The algorithm that finds the first stable set has been applied to all 300 sets of extrema. It detected a stable set at the tolerance levels between 30 and 300. The number of extrema has been 17, including 8 maxima and 9 minima. Eight of those are the outliers discussed in Section 2, while the complementary extrema lie within the main body of data. The stable extrema became the focus of the next step. We will focus on the maxima, where the search has been successful.

Use the stable extrema set: A simple mechanism for identification of similar patterns (Żytkow, 1996) excluded one maximum, which has been a very significant outlier for both the height and width (to limit the size of this paper, we do not discuss the extrema widths). That maximum is an artifact accompanying the minimum located 300mg under the bulk of the data. When applied to the remaining maxima, the equation finder discovered two strong regularities: (1) maxima heights are constant, (2) the maxima widths are constant (equal one second). No equation has been found for their location. These maxima are 1-second deviations from the far more stable readings of mass. Even if they only occurred seven times in nearly half million data, the pattern they follow may help us sometime to identify their cause.

Subtract patterns from data: Since the seven maxima have the width of 1 datapoint each, according to section 1.6 they have been removed from the original data. 482,442 data remained for further analysis (one single-point minimum has been removed, too).

Detect patterns in the residua: The search for patterns continued recursively on the residual data. Now the extrema have been found at the much more limited range of tolerance levels, between 1 and 43. The numbers of maxima at each scale have been depicted in Table 1 in the rows labeled N_{max}. The stability analysis determined a set of five maxima and the corresponding minima, which have been stable at the scale between 23 and 30. No regularity has been found for extrema locations and amplitudes, but interesting regularities have been found for heights and locations of the maxima, from the data listed in Table 2.

Scale	1	2	3	4	5	6	7	8	9	10	11	12	13	14	15	16	17	18	19	20	21	22
N_{max}	14337	3114	2308	808	617	267	204	78	46	26	22	16	15	12	12	11	7	7	7	7	6	6

Scale	23	24	25	26	27	28	29	30	31	32	33	34	35	36	37	38	39	40	41	42	43
N_{max}	5	5	5	5	5	5	5	5	4	3	2	2	2	1	1	1	1	1	1	1	1

Table 1. The number of maxima (N_{max}) found for different scale values.

For those five maxima, stable equations have been found for location and height as functions of the maxima number, N: $location = 86855N - 18261$ and $height = 0.0026N + 249.144$.

The successful regularities have been also found for minima locations and

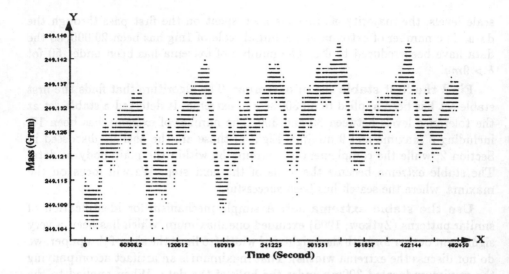

Fig. 2. Mass measurements on electronic balance after the outlier extrema have been subtracted.

Maximum number	1	2	3	4	5
Height	249.137	249.144	249.143	249.148	249.148
Location	69944	155970	239367	328073	418167

Table 2. The first stable group of maxima, at the scale 23–30 in Table 1.

heights. But no equation has been found for all data at the tolerance level $1/6 \times 30mg = 5mg$.

Partition the data: Since no trigonometric equation has been found (cf. section 1.3), the data have been partitioned at the extrema, and search for monotonous equations has been tried and succeeded in each partition. For instance, in two segments of data: down-1 (in Figure 2, data for X from about 70,000 to about 90,000) and down-2 (X from 160,000 to 180,000), the equations are linear:

$$\text{(down-1)} \qquad y = -1.61 \times 10^{-6} \times x + 249.249$$
$$\text{(down-2)} \qquad y = -1.46 \times 10^{-6} \times x + 249.371$$

By subtracting these regularities from the data, two sets of residua have been generated, labeled down-1 and down-2. Further search, applied to residua in each partition, revealed extrema at lower tolerance levels. The patterns for the stable maxima locations as a function of maxima number N, for instance, have been:

$$\text{(down-1)} \qquad \text{location} = 1220 \times N + 70{,}425$$
$$\text{(down-2)} \qquad \text{location} = 1297 \times N + 154{,}716$$

The slope in both equations indicates the average cycle measured in seconds between the adjacent maxima. That cycle is about 21 minutes (1260 seconds).

4 Physical interpretation of the results

How can we interpret the patterns discovered in the data? Keep in mind that the readings should be constant or fluctuate minimally, as the beaker placed on the balance has not changed its mass.

We do not know what caused the one-second extrema at the highest scale. Perhaps some errors in analog-to-digital conversion. But we can interpret many patterns at the lower levels. Consider the linear relation found for maxima locations, $location = 86855N - 18261$. It indicates a constant cycle of 86,855 seconds. When compared to 24 hours (86,400 seconds), it leads to an interesting interpretation: the cycle is just slightly longer than 24 hours. The measurements have been made in May, when each day is few minutes longer then the previous one. These facts make us see a close match between the cycle of day and night and the maxima and minima in the data. The mass is the highest at the end of day. It goes sharply down through the night, which is much shorter than the day in May. Then the mass goes slowly up during the day, until the next sunset.

Why would the balance reflect the time of the day with such a precision? Among many possible explanations we can consider temperature, which changes in a daily cycle. The actual changes in temperature at the balance did not exceed one centigrade and have been hardly noticeable, but if this hypothesis is right, it should apply to other patterns discovered in the same data. The balance has been located in a room with the windows facing east and the morning sun raising temperature from early morning. What about the short term cycles of about 20 minutes? The air conditioning seems the culprit. It turns on and off about every 15–25 minutes, in shorter intervals during the day, in longer intervals at night. The regularities in maxima locations in different data partitions reveal that pattern. The room has been under the influence of both the air-conditioning and the outside temperature, which explains both the daily cycle and the short term cycle. Unfortunately, we could not confirm these conclusions by direct measurements of mass and temperature. Few weeks later our discovery lab has been moved to another building. The balance has been broken and then repaired. In the new location we could not detect a straightforward relationship between readings of the balance and thermometer.

Acknowledgment: special thanks to Jieming Zhu for his numerous contributions to the research reported in this paper.

References

Langley, P., Simon, H., Bradshaw, G. & Zytkow, J. 1987. *Scientific Discovery: Computational Explorations of the Creative Processes.* MIT Press.

Witkin, A.P. 1983. Scale-Space Filtering, in *Proc. of Intl. Joint Conf. on Artificial Intelligence (IJCAI-83)*, AAAI Press, p.1019–1022.

Zembowicz, R., & Żytkow, J.M. 1992. Discovery of Equations: Experimental Evaluation of Convergence, in *Proc. of AAAI-92*, AAAI Press, p.70–75.

Żytkow, J.M. 1996. Automated Discovery of Empirical Laws, to appear in *Fundamenta Informaticae.*

On Evolving Intelligence

Kenneth A. De Jong

George Mason University
Department of Computer Science
Fairfax, VA 22030 USA
kdejong@gmu.edu

Abstract. The field of AI is now more than 30 years old and has produced a variety of impressive intelligent systems as well as some striking failures. As we continue to raise our goals and expectations, it becomes increasingly clear that simple, single methodology approaches are inadequate. However, the design and implementation of complex, multifaceted systems is quite difficult in general, and there are signs that we are reaching the limits of our ability to hand-construct such AI systems. In this paper I argue that evolutionary algorithms have considerable potential for the design of such systems and that we need to seriously consider the notion of evolving intelligence.

1 Introduction

I think that most everyone will agree that we are not much closer today that we were 30 years ago in formulating a precise definition of intelligence. Rather, the AI community (and others) have evolved various "operational" definitions of intelligence which cover a fairly broad range of intelligent behavior, such as:

- The ability to perform intellectual tasks such as prove theorems, play chess, and solve puzzles. The emphasis here is on the ability to build and effectively use mental abstractions.

- The ability to perform intellectually challenging "real world" tasks such as medical diagnosis, tax advising, and financial investing. In addition to mental abstractions, there is a requirement here for more interaction with the world, introducing I/O requirements, the need to deal with uncertainty, and so on.

- The ability to survive, adapt, function in a constantly changing world. These are properties that autonomous agents must have. In addition to raising even more difficult I/O issues such as vision, locomotion, and manipulation, these problems introduce issues of self-assessment, learning, curiosity, and innovation.

In addition to adopting a variety of operational definitions of intelligence, the AI community itself represents a diverse set of activities with different goals, including:

- Modeling human intelligence.
- Building intelligent artifacts.
- Discovering the underlying principles of intelligence.

The symbolic approach to AI takes the position that such goals are best met by viewing intelligence in terms of building abstract internal symbolic models of world, with rules and constraints defining allowable transformations of these symbolic models, and intelligent behavior represented as goal-directed transformations of symbolic models.

This view has certainly been a dominate one in the short history of AI, and has led to significant developments in knowledge representation and problem solving paradigms, and wide-spread success in building knowledge-based applications.

Critics of this approach see considerable difficulty in effectively representing intelligent behavior in a complex, time-varying, uncertain world using static, hand-crafted symbolic models. They have supported such claims with equally impressive systems based on probabilistic models of decision making, fuzzy logic, and artificial neural networks.

It should be clear from the discussion above regarding the wide range of intelligent behavior under study as well as the variety of goals that, if we insist on a single viewpoint, we are caught in the same trap as arguing about whether Lisp or Prolog is the better language for "doing AI". When applied to the entire range of AI activities, any particular approach will have clearly identifiable strengths and weaknesses.

A much more realistic and healthy viewpoint is that we are likely to need a complex combination of approaches to achieve our goals. However, multi-faceted AI systems which embody multiple forms of knowledge representation, reasoning, and learning are considerably more difficult to design and implement that single methodology approaches. What is needed are a new generation of tools and techniques for building more robust hybrid systems. In the remainder of this paper, I would like to share with you my enthusiasm for one such approach which adopts this broader perspective, namely, the notion of evolving intelligence.

2 The Essence of an Evolutionary System

In order to explore the notion of evolving intelligence, we need to discuss briefly the essential features of a (Darwinian) evolutionary system. A generally agreed upon minimal set consists of:

- a population of individuals competing for scarce resources.
- a mechanism for evaluating the fitness of an individual.
- the use of fitness to determine survival and reproductive rates.
- a mechanism of heritability: offspring resemble their parents.

One can then imagine a wide variety of systems (models) which embody these basic properties in different forms and varying degrees of detail. Even the simplest forms of these evolutionary systems have the property that, because of the non-linear interactions among the various components, they can produce quite complex adaptive behavior over time. Hence, a good deal of time and interest has been invested in what I call the "simulation view" of evolutionary systems: studying the emergent properties of evolutionary systems, and understanding better the effects than changes in system components has on overall behavior. To illustrate this, consider the following pseudo-code:

```
EA Procedure:
    Generate an initial population of N individuals.
    Do Forever:
        Select a member of the current population to be a parent
            using fitness as a bias.
        Use the selected parent to produce an offspring which is
            similar to but generally not a precise copy of the parent.
        Select a member of the population to die using fitness
            as a bias.
    End Do
    End EA
```

This evolutionary procedure is certainly not task-oriented in the sense of being designed to solve any particular problem such as sorting or tree traversal. Rather, it is most naturally viewed as a high level simulation of a Darwinian view of how biological populations evolve over time.

However, as we understand such systems better, a second viewpoint emerges: how we might harness the power of evolution to build better problem solving systems. As an example, consider the following slightly modified version of the EA pseudo-code:

```
EA Procedure:
    Generate an initial population of N individuals.
    Do until some stopping criteria is met:
        Select a member of the current population to be a parent
            using fitness as a bias.
        Use the selected parent to produce an offspring which is
            similar to but generally not a precise copy of the parent.
        Select a member of the population to die using fitness
            as a bias.
    End Do
    Return the individual with the highest fitness.
    End EA
```

The effect of these simple changes is to immediately shift one's perception of the EA procedure as being task oriented, namely, a procedure for finding useful points (e.g., extrema) in complex search spaces. From this viewpoint, the interesting evolutionary questions now relate to the properties of the task. In this particular case we would want to know whether EA-based search procedures are more effective than more traditional ones, whether they can be guaranteed to find the correct answer, what changes to the EA search procedure would improve its performance, etc.

In the remainder of the paper we explore these issues with respect to the possibilities of evolving intelligence.

3 Subspecies of Evolutionary Algorithms

The example EA procedures in the previous section were deliberately simplified and underspecified in a number of important ways including how individuals are represented, how fitness is used as a bias, and how offspring are actually produced. Historically, the instantiation of these ideas took quite different forms resulting in several identifiable "subspecies" today.

Genetic algorithms were developed initially by Holland [15] and his students. The goal was to use genetic algorithms as a key element in the design of flexible and robust adaptive systems. There was a strong initial emphasis on the virtues of a universal encoding scheme (genetic-like string representations) and the role of recombination (mating) as an important search operator. Genetic algorithms are the most familiar form of evolutionary algorithms today with many books [11, 23, 16], conferences [7], and articles [4] on the subject.

However, there are two other species of evolutionary algorithms which have developed in parallel with GAs and which offer interesting alternative perspectives. Evolution strategies were developed initially by Rechenberg [26], Schwefel [28], and others to solve a very specific class of problems: difficult parameter optimization problems. As a consequence, they chose a very specific representation for vectors of real numbers, and developed sophisticated self-adapting mutation operators for producing offspring. Today, these evolutionary algorithms represent some of the most efficient techniques for finding the global optima of complex surfaces [29].

A third form, called Evolutionary Programming was developed by Fogel [9] and others expressly for the purpose of evolving intelligent agents. These agents were initially represented as finite state machines, and mutation operators were the primary mechanism for making new and interesting machines from existing (parent) machines. Today these ideas have been extended well beyond the early studies and have been successfully applied to a wide range of problems [8].

The initial focus of genetic algorithms on binary string representations, and the design of evolution strategies for real-valued parameter optimization has resulted in these approaches being frequently classified as non-symbolic methods. I hope to convince you in the remaining sections that evolutionary techniques have a much broader potential for evolving intelligence in whatever form it may take.

4 Examples of Existing Applications

A good place to start is to briefly summarize some of the existing applications of evolutionary algorithms to AI-related problems.

The simplest and most well developed class of applications is that of parameter tuning. The typical situation is one in which a large system has been designed which contains a number of discrete and/or continuous parameters which affect the behavior of the system, and appropriate values of these parameters must be determined experimentally by trying various combinations of values. In all but the simplest systems, various parameters interact in unknown and non-linear ways resulting in a complex, irregular response surface.

Under such circumstances finding optimal parameter combinations presents a difficult search problem not effectively addressed by some form of systematic search or hill climbing technique. Such problems are easily captured in an evolutionary search procedure in which an individual is represented as a chromosome with genes representing parameter values, and the value of the response surface representing the fitness of a particular combination of parameter values (see [2] for an excellent survey).

If you pick up almost any evolutionary or AI conference proceedings, you will find examples of problems of this type in which an evolutionary algorithm is used to determine the parameters of an AI system component such as a heuristic evaluation function, the weights and thresholds of artificial neural networks, the parameters of fuzzy logic membership functions, the parameters of inductive learning algorithms, and so on. This approach appears to have considerable merit when response surfaces are complex, multimodal, and involve noise.

However, there are many AI problems for which the parameter tuning approach is inappropriate in that more complex structural changes are required. Standard examples include finding optimal neural net structures (as well as the weights), building appropriate decision trees, and adapting agendas to changing conditions. If we view such problems as searching data structure spaces for optimal structures, it is fairly obvious that they present difficult search problems for which strong heuristics are required.

One approach to applying evolutionary techniques to such problems is to develop a clever linear representation of the space so that individual data structures have a chromosome-like representation. The advantage to this approach is that most of the code developed for parameter optimization problems is easily adapted to that of evolving data structures. However, there is a hidden difficulty here in that the standard operators used to produce variability in the offspring (e.g., mutation and crossover) invariably produce illegal data structures.

A standard way of handling this problem is to embed domain-specific knowledge into the operators so that viable and interesting offspring are produced. Another approach is to not force a linear representation of the space, but rather to use its natural representation (see, for example, [23]). Individuals are represented directly as graphs, trees, etc., and appropriate operators are designed to make changes to the structures.

This has lead to an interesting (and unresolved) genotype vs. phenotype debate which is beyond the scope of this paper. For now let me just note that both approaches have produced rather striking results in evolving complex neural network structures [12], finite state machines [8], VLSI layout problems [22], and job shop scheduling problems [19] to mention a few.

Even more challenging in general than evolving data structures is the problem of evolving executable code. It seems like an impossible task if we think in terms of programs written in C or Pascal. However, rule-based languages, Prolog, Lisp, or even recurrent neural networks are programming languages with more regularity and simpler semantics, raising the possibility of "automatic programming" in this context.

As we saw earlier, in order to use an evolutionary approach, one needs to design an effective representation of the space (of all programs, in this case), and effective operators for producing viable and interesting new programs from old ones. Early examples of this were Holland's classifier system [17] and Smith's LS system [30]. More recent examples are Grefenstette's Samuel system [13] and Koza's genetic programming paradigm [20, 21]. The specific case of using evolutionary algorithms for symbolic rule induction has also been well studied [5, 18, 10].

5 Current Activities

One of the purposes of the brief survey in the previous section was to provide some evidence regard the broad range of applications of evolutionary techniques as tools for designing and implementing AI systems. Difficult symbolic, non-symbolic, and hybrid systems have been and continue to be successfully developed using evolutionary algorithms.

At the same time, as evolutionary techniques are applied to new and more complex problems, we continue to test the limits of what we can achieve with existing evolutionary paradigms. This has lead to a number of new and important developments in the field which are already improving our understanding of and the power of evolutionary algorithms. In this section, we briefly note a few of these.

One of the most important recent developments is with respect to the theoretical analysis of evolutionary algorithms. Although analysis of the early forms of evolutionary algorithms was available from the start, that theory has not kept pace with the many changes that have been made to the early algorithms and the many new forms which have appeared. Recently, however, that has begun to change with a variety of excellent theoretical work involving Markov models [32, 6], global convergence results [1, 3], PAC analysis [27], and global search theory [24] to mention a few.

The traditional evolutionary algorithms represented a fairly high level model of evolution, abstracting away may details and features found in biological systems. This was done intentionally in order to keep the early studies intellectually and computationally manageable. With these early systems now fairly well understood, there is considerable current work on exploring the usefulness of some of these missing features.

Examples of this include the idea of speciation (mating with similar individuals) [31], morphogenesis (new offspring are not instant adults, but have to go through a growth and development phase) [12], and coevolution (more than one population of evolving individuals) [14, 25]. The cited examples illustrate just a few of a growing number of examples of using these ideas to obtain significant improvements in problem solving capabilities.

An interesting thing to note is that most of the AI problems that have been discussed so far in this paper are static in the sense that there is an implicit assumption that the important features of the world are not changing significantly while problem solving is occurring. However, as we apply our AI techniques to ever more challenging real world problems, this assumption becomes much more difficult to maintain. If we expect to build systems which persist in the world for extended periods, they have to be much more robust and flexible than they are today.

This view of "adaptation" rather than "optimization" was a motivation of much of the early development of these evolutionary algorithms, and is well suited for this next generation of difficult AI problems. It is already appearing in the form of "anytime learning" and "evolutionary robotics".

6 Summary and Conclusions

We began this paper by noting that to achieve our goals we need to build complex, multi-faceted AI systems which embody integrated forms of knowledge representation, reasoning, and learning.

I argued that we need to focus on the development of tools and techniques which can help us build these hybrid systems, and presented evolutionary algorithms as a promising example of such an approach. It is likely, of course, that we will continue to make progress in building AI systems with humans involved in the design, implementation, and maintenance to these systems. However, my sense is that we are reaching the point that we are likely to be the bottleneck to progress if we are too tightly in the loop. An alternative approach which appears to have significant potential involves complementary roles for the human designer laying out the basic system architecture and an evolutionary algorithm tuning, modifying, and adapting the system over time as a function of its operating environment.

References

1. T. Bäck. Order statistics for convergence velocity analysis of simplified evolutionary algorithms. In L.D. Whitley and M.D. Vose, editors, *Proceedings of the Third Workshop on Foundations of Genetic Algorithms*, pages 91–102. Morgan Kaufmann, 1994.
2. T. Bäck and H.-P. Schwefel. An overview of evolutionary algorithms for parameter optimization. *Evolutionary Computation*, 1(1):1–23, 1993.
3. H.G. Beyer. Toward a theory of evolution strategies. *Evolutionary Computation*, 2(4):381–407, 1994.
4. K.A. De Jong. Learning with genetic algorithms: An overview. *Machine Learning*, 3(3):121–138, 1988.

5. K.A. De Jong, W.M. Spears, and D.F. Gordon. Using genetic algorithms for concept learning. *Machine Learning*, 13(3):161–188, 1993.

6. K.A. De Jong, W.M. Spears, and D.F. Gordon. Using markov chains to analyze gafos. In L.D. Whitley and M.D. Vose, editors, *Proceedings of the Third Workshop on Foundations of Genetic Algorithms*, pages 115–138. Morgan Kaufmann, 1994.

7. L.J. Eshelman, editor. *Proceedings of the Sixth International Conference on Genetic Algorithms*. Morgan Kaufmann, 1995.

8. D.B. Fogel. *Evolutionary Computation: Toward a New Philosophy of Machine Intelligence*. IEEE Press, Piscataway, NJ, 1995.

9. L.J. Fogel, A.J. Owens, and M.J. Walsh. *Artificial Intelligence through Simulated Evolution*. John Wiley & Sons, New York, 1966.

10. A. Giordana, L. Saitta, and F. Zini. Learning disjunctive concepts by means of genetic algorithms. In W. Cohen and H. Hirsh, editors, *Proceedings of the Eleventh International Conference on Machine Learning*, pages 96–104. Morgan Kaufmann, 1994.

11. D.E. Goldberg. *Genetic Algorithms in Search, Optimization, and Machine Learning*. Addison-Wesley, New York, 1989.

12. F. Grau. Genetic synthesis of modular neural networks. In S. Forrest, editor, *Proceedings of the Fifth International Conference on Genetic Algorithms*, pages 318–325. Morgan Kaufmann, 1993.

13. J.J. Grefenstette. A system for learning control strategies with genetic algorithms. In J.D. Schaffer, editor, *Proceedings of the Third International Conference on Genetic Algorithms*, pages 183–190. Morgan Kaufmann, 1989.

14. D.W. Hillis. Co-evolving parasites improve simulated evolution as an optimization procedure. In C.G. Langton, C. Taylor, J.D. Farmer, and S. Rasmussen, editors, *Artificial Life II*, pages 313–324. Addison-Wesley, 1990.

15. J.H. Holland. *Adaptation in Natural and Artificial Systems*. University of Michigan Press, Ann Arbor, MI, 1975.

16. J.H. Holland. *Adaptation in Natural and Artificial Systems, 2nd Edition*. MIT Press, Cambridge, MA, 1993.

17. J.H. Holland and J.S. Reitman. Cognitive systems based on adaptive algorithms. In D.A. Waterman and F. Hayes-Roth, editors, *Pattern-Directed Inference Systems*. Academic Press, 1978.

18. C.Z. Janikow. A knowledge intensive genetic algorithm for supervised learning. *Machine Learning*, 13(3):198–228, 1993.

19. S. Kobayashi, I. Ono, and M. Yamamura. An efficient genetic algorithm for job shop scheduling problems. In L.J. Eshelman, editor, *Proceedings of the Sixth International Conference on Genetic Algorithms*, pages 506–511. Morgan Kaufmann, 1995.

20. J.R. Koza. *Genetic Programming*. MIT Press, Cambridge, MA, 1992.

21. J.R. Koza. *Genetic Programming II*. MIT Press, Cambridge, MA, 1994.

22. J. Lienig and K. Thulasiraman. A genetic algorithm for channel routing in vlsi circuits. *Evolutionary Computation*, 1(4):293–312, 1993.

23. Z. Michalewicz. *Genetic Algorithms + Data Structures = Evolution Programs*. Springer-Verlag, New York, 1994.

24. C.C. Peck and A.P. Dhawan. Genetic algorithms as global random search methods. *Evolutionary Computation*, 3(1):39–80, 1995.

25. M.A. Potter and K.A. De Jong. A cooperative coevolutionary approach to function optimization. In Y. Davidor and Schwefel H.-P., editors, *Proceedings of the Third*

Conference on Parallel Problem Solving from Nature, pages 249–257. Springer-Verlag, 1994.

26. I. Rechenberg. Cybernetic solution path of an experimental problem. In *Library Translation 1122*. Royal Aircraft Establishment, Farnborough, 1965.

27. J.P. Ros. Learning boolean functions with genetic algorithms: A pac analysis. In L.D. Whitley, editor, *Proceedings of the Second Workshop on Foundations of Genetic Algorithms*, pages 257–276. Morgan Kaufmann, 1992.

28. H.P. Schwefel. *Numerical Optimization of Computer Models*. John Wiley & Sons, New York, 1981.

29. H.P. Schwefel. *Evolution and Optimum Seeking*. John Wiley & Sons, New York, 1995.

30. S.F. Smith. Flexible learning of problem solving heuristics through adaptive search. In A. Bundy, editor, *Proceedings of the Eighth International Joint Conference on Artificial Intelligence*, pages 422–425. William Kaufmann, 1983.

31. W.M. Spears. Simple subpopulation schemes. In A.V. Sebald and D.B. Fogel, editors, *Proceedings of the Third Conference on Evolutionary Programming*, pages 297–307. World Scientific Publ., 1994.

32. M.D. Vose. Modeling simple genetic algorithms. In L.D. Whitley, editor, *Proceedings of the Second Workshop on Foundations of Genetic Algorithms*, pages 63–74. Morgan Kaufmann, 1992.

Intelligent Mutation Rate Control
in Canonical Genetic Algorithms

Thomas Bäck[1] and Martin Schütz[2]

[1] Informatik Centrum Dortmund, Center for Applied Systems Analysis (CASA),
Joseph-von-Fraunhofer-Str. 20, D–44227 Dortmund
[2] Universität Dortmund, Fachbereich Informatik, LS XI, D-44221 Dortmund

Abstract. The role of the mutation rate in canonical genetic algorithms is investigated by comparing a constant setting, a deterministically varying, time-dependent mutation rate schedule, and a self-adaptation mechanism for individual mutation rates following the principle of self-adaptation as used in evolution strategies. The power of the self-adaptation mechanism is illustrated by a time-varying optimization problem, where mutation rates have to adapt continuously in order to follow the optimum. The strengths of the proposed deterministic schedule and the self-adaptation method are demonstrated by a comparison of their performance on difficult combinatorial optimization problems (multiple knapsack, maximum cut and maximum independent set in graphs). Both methods are shown to perform significantly better than the canonical genetic algorithm, and the deterministic schedule yields the best results of all control mechanisms compared.

1 Introduction

Genetic Algorithms [11, 14] are the best known representative of a class of direct random search methods called *evolutionary algorithms* [6], which are widely used with great success to solve complex optimization and adaptation problems. Representing individuals as binary vectors $\mathbf{x} = (x_1, x_2, \ldots, x_n) \in \{0, 1\}^n$ of fixed length n, the *canonical genetic algorithm* is particularly well suited for combinatorial optimization problems $f : \{0, 1\}^n \to \mathbb{R}$. Based on the fitness values $f(\mathbf{x})$ of the individuals in a population, the classical probabilistic proportional selection operator uses the relative fitness $p(\mathbf{x}_i) = f(\mathbf{x}_i)/\sum_{j=1}^{\mu} f(\mathbf{x}_j)$ to serve as selection probabilities (μ denotes the population size). The crossover operator (applied with crossover probability p_c) exchanges information between different individuals according to a number of crossover points which are randomly chosen on the individual. A choice of two crossover points is recommended e.g. in [7].

This paper focuses on the mutation operator, which introduces innovation into the population by inverting bits with a probability p_m per bit. This operator is typically assessed as a secondary one which is of little importance in comparison to crossover (e.g., [14], p. 111), such that most canonical genetic algorithms work with small, constant settings of $p_m \in [0.001, 0.01]$ (see e.g. [11, 12, 15, 21]).

In contrast to these findings, however, practical applications of genetic algorithms often favor larger or non-constant settings of the mutation rate. Some recently developed theory regarding the optimal mutation rate schedule for a simple objective function provides a good confirmation of the usefulness of larger, varying mutation rates [1, 19]. The theoretical result is used in section 2 to derive a general deterministic mutation rate control schedule for canonical genetic algorithms. An alternative mechanism for controlling the mutation rate consists in the on-line learning or *self-adaptation* of this parameter, which works with great success in evolution strategies and evolutionary programming [6]. In section 3, we present a self-adaptation mechanism for individual mutation rates in genetic algorithms. Finally, section 4 presents experimental results regarding the performance of the mutation rate control mechanisms on some difficult combinatorial optimization problems.

2 Deterministic Mutation Rate Schedules

Independently of each other, Mühlenbein [19] and Bäck [1] investigated the optimal mutation rate for a simple (1+1)-algorithm (a single parent generates an offspring by means of mutation and the better of both survives for the next generation) and the objective function $f(\mathbf{x}) = \sum_{i=1}^{n} x_i$ ("counting ones"). Using an approximation of the probability for improving the objective function value by mutation, Mühlenbein arrived at an optimal mutation rate $p = 1/n$.

This setting yields surprisingly good results for a variety of NP-hard combinatorial optimization problems such as the multiple knapsack problem [18], the minimum vertex cover problem [16], the maximum independent set problem [4], and others [17].

An exact analytical expression for the improvement probability (for the counting ones function) as presented in [1], however, clarifies that the optimal mutation probability depends strongly on the objective function value $f(\mathbf{x})$ and follows a hyperbolic law of the form

$$p = (2 \cdot (f(\mathbf{x}) + 1) - n)^{-1} \qquad (1)$$

(see [3], chapter 6). Notice that the resulting mutation probability decreases from a value of $1/2$ to $1/n$ for $f(\mathbf{x}) \in \{n/2, \ldots, n-1\}$, i.e., the optimal mutation rate control deviates strongly from the general assumption that genetic algorithms need a very small mutation rate.

Though the gain achieved by control schedule (1) regarding the time to absorption is small for the counting ones problem (see [3], chapter 6), we consider it interesting to test an analogue of equation (1) on more complex objective functions. In order to model the hyperbolic shape of (1), independently of the objective function, we use a time-dependent mutation rate p_t (where $t \in \{0, 1, \ldots, T-1\}$ denotes the generation counter, and T is a given maximum number of generations). From the conditions $p_0 = 1/2$ and $p_{T-1} = 1/n$, the hyperbolic formulation $p_t = (a + b \cdot t)^{-1}$ easily yields

$$p_t = \left(2 + \frac{n-2}{T-1} \cdot t\right)^{-1} \qquad . \qquad (2)$$

Of course it is not clear whether this substitution of the distance to the optimum (hidden in equation (1)) by the generation number is useful, but it is certainly possible that equation (2) serves better as a general parameter setting rule than $p = 1/n$ does. It would probably be more desirable, however, if the algorithm could adapt its mutation rate according to the topology of the objective function, using the principle of strategy parameter self-adaptation as developed by Schwefel for evolution strategies [6].

3 Two-Level Learning in Genetic Algorithms

A fascinating alternative to the typical exogenous prescription of strategy parameters consists in the principle of strategy parameter *self-adaptation* or on-line learning as first implemented by Schwefel in the context of multimembered evolution strategies [23, 24, 25]. Independently of this, Fogel et al. [9] developed an almost identical procedure for evolutionary programming (see also [8]). The self-adaptation principle incorporates certain strategy parameters (such as variances and covariances of a generalized, n-dimensional normal distribution in case of evolution strategies) into the representation of each individual. The strategy parameter set of an individual provides a parameter setting for mutation when applied to this particular individual, and strategy parameters evolve by means of mutation (and recombination) just as the object variables do. More specifically, given a continuous parameter optimization problem $f : \mathbb{R}^n \to \mathbb{R}$, the simplest variant of self-adaptation works in evolution strategies with individuals of the form $(x_1, \ldots, x_n, \sigma) \in \mathbb{R}^n \times \mathbb{R}_+$, where σ denotes a single standard deviation for normally distributed mutations. Offspring are created from such an individual according to $\sigma' = \sigma \cdot \exp(\tau \cdot N(0, 1))$ and $x_i' = x_i + \sigma' \cdot N_i(0, 1)$, where $N(0, 1)$ is a normally distributed random number with expectation zero and standard deviation one. Notice that the standard deviation is also subject to mutation (using a logarithmic normal distribution), and the mutated σ is used as the standard deviation for a modification of the x_i. More general variants of this mechanism are described e.g. in [6].

The self-adaptation principle exploits the indirect link between favorable strategy parameters and objective function values and facilitates an adaptation on the level of the strategy parameters almost completely without exogenous control. Consequently, self-adapting strategies are able to adapt their parameters implicitly, according to the topology of the objective function.

The parameter τ in the equation for modifying σ controls the speed of self-adaptation and is a robust exogenous parameter of the algorithm. A setting of $\tau \propto 1/\sqrt{n}$ is generally recommended, but the optimal setting of τ depends on the objective function.

The great success of self-adapting strategy parameters in case of continuous optimization problems suggests a transfer of the general principle to genetic algorithms and discrete optimization problems. Early efforts include the self-adaptation of a binary representation of the crossover operator [22] and a binary representation of the mutation probability for each individual [2], but both were of limited success. In the first case, the limited success is due to the weak impact of a particular crossover operator on the fitness of an individual, such that no particular operator is clearly preferred (with the exception of specially designed objective functions which strongly favor a particular kind of crossover operator; see [20]). In the second case, the binary representation of mutation rates hampered their efficient fine-tuning by self-adaptation. Recently, Fogel et al. transferred the method from evolutionary programming to finite state machines by using an additive normally distributed modification of mutation rates [10], but this mechanism suffers from the difficulty to guarantee that mutation rates have to stay in the interval $]0, 1[$.

To overcome the disadvantages of these proposed mechanisms, we postulate a self-adaptation mechanism of a single mutation rate per individual such that the following requirements are fulfilled:

- The expected change of p by repeatedly mutating it should equal zero, because selection should be the only force bringing a direction into the evolution process.
- Mutation of the mutation rate $p \in]0, 1[$ yields a mutation rate $p' \in]0, 1[$.
- Small changes are more likely than large ones.
- A modification by a factor c occurs with the same probability as a modification by $1/c$.

Based on these requirements, a logistic transformation of the form

$$p' = \left(1 + \frac{1-p}{p} \cdot \exp(-\gamma \cdot N(0, 1))\right)^{-1} \tag{3}$$

can be derived [5, 20], such that p' is distributed according to a logistic normal distribution with probability density function

$$f_{p'}(x) = \frac{1}{\sqrt{2\pi}\gamma x(1-x)} \exp\left(\frac{-\left(\ln\frac{x}{1-x} - \zeta\right)^2}{2\gamma^2}\right), \tag{4}$$

where $\zeta = \ln\frac{p}{1-p}$.

The learning rate γ in equation (3) allows for a control of the adaptation speed as in case of the evolution strategy, but empirical results provide some evidence that γ is independent of n. Presently, we use a value of $\gamma = 0.22$ in the experiments reported here.

For an algorithmic realization of the adaptation scheme defined by equation (3), we consider the additional constraint that mutation rates below a minimum value of $1/n$ do not make any sense: Self-adaptation works by means of the selective advantage or disadvantage of mutation rates, expressed by their impact on the objective function value, such that the mechanism can only work effectively, if at least one bit is mutated on average. For this reason, we simply reset $p' = 1/n$, if equation (3) yields a value smaller than $1/n$.

The genotype of an individual $\mathbf{a} = (x_1, \ldots, x_n, p) \in \{0, 1\}^n \times]0, 1[$ of the self-adaptive genetic algorithm consists of a bitstring of length n and an individual mutation rate p that controls the bitwise mutation of $(x_1, \ldots, x_n)$ according to the mutated mutation rate p', yielding a new individual $\mathbf{a}' = (x'_1, \ldots, x'_n, p')$, where $x_i' = 1 - x_i$ if $U([0,1]) < p'$ (otherwise, $x_i' = x_i$), and $U([0,1])$ denotes a uniform random number sampled from the interval $[0,1]$. Crossover is presently applied only to the binary vector and has no impact on the mutation rate, but it is certainly worthwhile to investigate the effect of intermediary recombination on mutation rates [6].

For evolution strategies, Schwefel has demonstrated that a relatively strong selective pressure as e.g. provided by (μ,λ)-selection (μ parent individuals create $\lambda > \mu$ offspring individuals by recombination and mutation, and the best μ offspring individuals are selected as parents of the next generation) is mandatory for the self-adaptation principle to work [23, 24]. Consequently, we also incorporate (μ,λ)-selection into the self-adaptive genetic algorithm as an alternative to proportional selection.

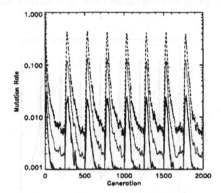 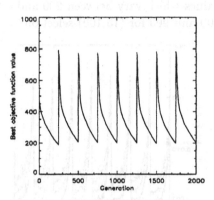

Fig. 1.: The self-adaptation mechanism is shown here for the counting ones function with $n = 1000$ and a genetic algorithm with proportional selection, without crossover. The left plot shows the minimum, average, and maximum mutation rates that occur within the population. The right plot shows the corresponding best objective function value in the population. The optimum location is inverted every 250 generations.

In order to test the feasibility of the new mechanism, an experiment from evolution strategies (with a time-varying version of the sphere model; see [13]) is transferred to the self-adaptive genetic algorithm as follows: The counting ones problem $f(\mathbf{x}) = \sum_{i=1}^{n} x_i \rightarrow \min$ is modified by switching between f and $f'(\mathbf{x}) = n - f(\mathbf{x}) \rightarrow \min$ every g generations. Under optimal circumstances, this problem requires an oscillating behavior of the mutation rate, if the self-adaptation principle works well.

The experiment was performed for $n = 1000$ and $g = 250$ with a self-adaptive genetic algorithm using proportional selection (with a population size of 100) and (15,100)-selection, but without crossover. The results are shown in figure 1 for proportional selection (with linear dynamic scaling and a scaling window of 5 generations; see [12]) and figure 2 for (15,100)-selection. The two plots in both figures show the behavior of the minimum, average, and maximum mutation rate within the population (left plot in the figures) and the best objective function value in the population over 2000 generations (right plot in the figures), averaged over ten independent runs of the genetic algorithm.

Both figures give a clear confirmation that the self-adaptation mechanism works well with both selection schemes. During one cycle of the optimization, the mutation rates decrease drastically from values close to 0.1 to the lower bound of $1/n$. The improvement of the objective function value is very fast and reflects the capability of the self-adaptation method to adapt the mutation rate in an optimal sense with respect to the convergence velocity. It is impressive to see that the mutation rate increases within few generations to a value of 0.1 when the optimum is changed, thus reflecting the high adaptation speed provided by the method and the learning rate $\gamma = 0.22$. The only difference between proportional and (μ,λ)-selection consists in the fact that smaller selective pressure of proportional selection allows for a larger diversity of the mutation rates and implies a slightly slower convergence velocity (reflected by the objective function values which vary between 200 and 800 for proportional selection in contrast to 100 and 900 for (15,100)-selection).

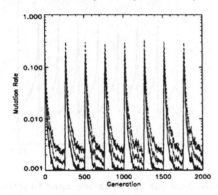 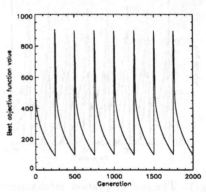

Fig. 2.: The self-adaptation mechanism for a (15,100)-genetic algorithm. See caption of figure 1 for an explanation of these plots.

In the next section, we will present some experimental results comparing the different mutation rate control mechanisms discussed so far for proportional selection and (μ,λ)-selection on some representative combinatorial optimization problems.

4   An Experimental Assessment

Self-adaptation works by exploiting the implicit link between strategy parameters and the objective function value, such that the convergence velocity is optimized and the stochastic local optimization qualities of the algorithm are emphasized by this mechanism. On the contrary, it is not clear whether the performance can also be improved with respect to the global convergence properties on multimodal problems.

To test the global convergence behavior, we take three instances of combinatorial optimization problems that have been shown in previos work to be difficult for canonical genetic algorithms: A multiple 0/1 knapsack problem ($n = 105$) [18], a maximum cut problem for weighted graphs ($n = 100$) [17], and a maximum independent set problem for graphs ($n = 100$) [4]. The knapsack problem (called "weing7-105") stems from Weingartner and Ness [26], the graph for the maximum cut problem is a regular, scalable graph as described in [17], and the graph for the maximum independent set problem is a random graph with small edge density (0.1), obtained by a method described in [4].

It is relatively straightforward to represent potential solutions to these problems by binary strings. Constraints are taken into account for the knapsack problem and the maximum independent set problem by incorporating a graded penalty term into the objective function, such that the farther away from feasibility a solution is, the larger its penalty term becomes. All problems are maximization problems. For further details regarding the problem definitions and the objective functions, the reader is referred to [4, 17, 18].

A genetic algorithm with proportional selection (population size 100) and (15,100)-selection was applied to these three problems, using a constant mutation rate of $1/n$, the self-adaptation of mutation rates (with $\gamma = 0.22$) as presented in section 3, and the deterministic schedule proposed in section 2. For each of the eighteen resulting combinations of selection, mutation rate control mechanism, and problem a total of $N = 100$ independent runs was performed, each running for 2000 (knapsack), 1000 (maximum cut), and 400 generations (maximum independent set), respectively. These values reflect our previos experience with these problems and are sufficiently large to be sure that the runs have converged in local optima.

The results of these experiments are collected in table 1, where each of the eighteen experimental setups is characterized by giving the objective function value of the best known optimum and the ten other best local optima found by the algorithm, together with the number N of runs in which the corresponding solution quality was achieved. Notice that the N-columns not necessarily sum up to a total of 100, because worse results than the 11th best are not shown. Each column ends with the average final best objective function value over all 100 runs. The results confirm our expectation that the constant mutation rate $p = 1/n$ in fact yields the worst performance of the three mutation rate control mechanisms, with slightly better results for proportional selection than for (15,100)-selection. The self-adaptive mutation rate control improves these results on average, but it does not favor the discovery of the best optimum in comparison with the constant mutation rate setting. The deterministic control schedule is the clear winner of this comparison, both regarding the average final objective function value and the number of runs that yield the best optimum. Moreover, the (15,100)-selection in combination with the deterministic schedule clearly outperforms proportional selection and is the only strategy that finds the global optimum of the knapsack problem at all.

5 Conclusions and Further Work

The results reported in this paper are encouraging with respect to the self-adaptation and the deterministic mutation rate control mechanisms and confirm that mutation is a more powerful operator than usually assumed.

Concerning the self-adaptation method, the impact of the learning rate γ is of large importance and has to be investigated in further work. Presently, we assume a large (small) value of γ causes a high (low) speed of adaptation and therefore a low (high) convergence reliability and high (low) convergence velocity. The success of the deterministic schedule is likely to be caused by the fact that it decreases the mutation rate much slower for the large generation numbers used in the experiments than self-adaptation does for the value of γ chosen here. It is certainly possible to choose a value of γ such that the adaptation speed becomes sufficiently small to compare well with the deterministic schedule, and an interesting topic of further research to investigate the relationship between both mechanisms.

As further demonstrated by the time-varying counting ones problem, self-adaptation is a powerful technique in case of dynamic optimization problems where the optimum might vary abruptly over time. For such problems, it is also of interest to look at the relation between the learning rate γ and the dynamics of the optimization problem. Finally, it is also interesting to check whether γ is really independent of the problem dimension n.

Acknowledgement: The first author gratefully acknowledges support by the German BMBF within the project EVOALG, grant 01 IB 403 A.

References

1. Th. Bäck. The interaction of mutation rate, selection, and self-adaptation within a genetic algorithm. In R. Männer and B. Manderick, editors, *Parallel Problem Solving from Nature, 2*, pages 85–94. Elsevier, Amsterdam, 1992.
2. Th. Bäck. Self-Adaptation in Genetic Algorithms. In F. J. Varela and P. Bourgine, editors, *Proceedings of the First European Conference on Artificial Life*, pages 263–271. The MIT Press, Cambridge, MA, 1992.
3. Th. Bäck. *Evolutionary Algorithms in Theory and Practice*. Oxford University Press, New York, 1996.
4. Th. Bäck and S. Khuri. An evolutionary heuristic for the maximum independent set problem. In *Proceedings of the First IEEE Conference on Evolutionary Computation*, pages 531–535. IEEE Press, 1994.
5. Th. Bäck and M. Schütz. Evolution strategies for mixed-integer optimization of optical multilayer systems. In J. R. McDonnell, R. G. Reynolds, and D. B. Fogel, editors, *Evolutionary Programming IV: Proceedings of the Fourth Annual Conference on Evolutionary Programming*, pages 33–51. MIT Press, Cambridge, MA, 1995.
6. Th. Bäck and H.-P. Schwefel. An overview of evolutionary algorithms for parameter optimization. *Evolutionary Computation*, 1(1):1–23, 1993.
7. L. J. Eshelman, R. A. Caruna, and J. D. Schaffer. Biases in the crossover landscape. In J. D. Schaffer, editor, *Proceedings of the 3rd International Conference on Genetic Algorithms*, pages 10–19. Morgan Kaufmann Publishers, San Mateo, CA, 1989.
8. D. B. Fogel. *Evolutionary Computation: Toward a New Philosophy of Machine Intelligence*. IEEE Press, Piscataway, NJ, 1995.
9. D. B. Fogel, L. J. Fogel, and W. Atmar. Meta-evolutionary programming. In R. R. Chen, editor, *Proc. 25th Asilomar Conference on Signals, Systems and Computers*, pages 540–545. Pacific Grove, CA, 1991.

10. L. Fogel, D. B. Fogel, and P. J. Angeline. A preliminary investigation on extending evolutionary programming to include self-adaptation on finite state machines. *Informatica*, 18:387–398, 1994.

11. D. E. Goldberg. *Genetic algorithms in search, optimization and machine learning.* Addison Wesley, Reading, MA, 1989.

12. J. J. Grefenstette. Optimization of control parameters for genetic algorithms. *IEEE Transactions on Systems, Man and Cybernetics*, SMC–16(1):122–128, 1986.

13. F. Hoffmeister and Th. Bäck. Genetic self–learning. In F. J. Varela and P. Bourgine, editors, *Proceedings of the 1st European Conference on Artificial Life*, pages 227–235. The MIT Press, Cambridge, MA, 1992.

14. J. H. Holland. *Adaptation in natural and artificial systems.* The University of Michigan Press, Ann Arbor, MI, 1975.

15. K. A. De Jong. *An analysis of the behaviour of a class of genetic adaptive systems.* PhD thesis, University of Michigan, 1975.

16. S. Khuri and Th. Bäck. An evolutionary heuristic for the minimum vertex cover problem. In J. Kunze and H. Stoyan, editors, *KI-94 Workshops (Extended Abstracts)*, pages 83–84. Gesellschaft für Informatik e. V., Bonn, 1994.

17. S. Khuri, Th. Bäck, and J. Heitkötter. An evolutionary approach to combinatorial optimization problems. In D. Cizmar, editor, *Proceedings of the 22nd Annual ACM Computer Science Conference*, pages 66–73. ACM Press, New York, 1994.

18. S. Khuri, Th. Bäck, and J. Heitkötter. The zero/one multiple knapsack problem and genetic algorithms. In E. Deaton, D. Oppenheim, J. Urban, and H. Berghel, editors, *Proceedings of the 1994 ACM Symposium on Applied Computing*, pages 188–193. ACM Press, New York, 1994.

19. H. Mühlenbein. How genetic algorithms really work: I. mutation and hillclimbing. In R. Männer and B. Manderick, editors, *Parallel Problem Solving from Nature 2*, pages 15–25. Elsevier, Amsterdam, 1992.

20. J. Obalek. Rekombinationsoperatoren für Evolutionsstrategien. Diplomarbeit, Universität Dortmund, Fachbereich Informatik, 1994.

21. J. D. Schaffer, R. A. Caruana, L. J. Eshelman, and R. Das. A study of control parameters affecting online performance of genetic algorithms for function optimization. In J. D. Schaffer, editor, *Proceedings of the 3rd International Conference on Genetic Algorithms*, pages 51–60. Morgan Kaufmann Publishers, San Mateo, CA, 1989.

22. J. D. Schaffer and A. Morishima. An adaptive crossover distribution mechanism for genetic algorithms. In J. J. Grefenstette, editor, *Proceedings of the 2nd International Conference on Genetic Algorithms and Their Applications*, pages 36–40. Lawrence Erlbaum Associates, Hillsdale, NJ, 1987.

23. H.-P. Schwefel. Collective intelligence in evolving systems. In W. Wolff, C.-J. Soeder, and F. R. Drepper, editors, *Ecodynamics, Contributions to Theoretical Ecology*, pages 95–100. Springer, Berlin, 1987.

24. H.-P. Schwefel. Imitating evolution: Collective, two-level learning processes. In U. Witt, editor, *Explaining Process and Change — Approaches to Evolutionary Economics*, pages 49–63. The University of Michigan Press, Ann Arbor, MI, 1992.

25. H.-P. Schwefel. *Evolution and Optimum Seeking.* Sixth-Generation Computer Technology Series. Wiley, New York, 1995.

26. H. M. Weingartner and D. N. Ness. Methods for the solution of the multidimensional 0/1 knapsack problem. *Operations Research*, 15:83–103, 1967.

| Constant mutation rate $p = 1/n$ ||||||||||||
| weing7-105 |||| maxcut |||| misp100-01 ||||
$f_{(15,100)}(\mathbf{x})$	N	$f_{prop}(\mathbf{x})$	N	$f_{(15,100)}(\mathbf{x})$	N	$f_{prop}(\mathbf{x})$	N	$f_{(15,100)}(\mathbf{x})$	N	$f_{prop}(\mathbf{x})$	N
1095445	—	1095445	—	1077	1	1077	7	47	2	47	1
1095382	1	1095382	9	1055	22	1055	19	46	1	46	1
1095206	1	1095266	2	1033	28	1033	33	45	6	45	2
1095137	1	1095264	12	1011	31	1011	17	44	6	44	3
1095035	2	1095206	5	989	16	1007	1	43	11	43	6
1094371	2	1095157	1	967	1	989	23	42	7	42	4
1094356	1	1095137	1	945	1			41	4	41	9
1094262	1	1095112	3					40	9	40	6
1093987	1	1095065	3					39	10	39	8
1093912	1	1095035	2					38	4	38	11
1093860	1	1094931	1					37	6	37	4
$\bar{f} = 1091268$		$\bar{f} = 1093924$		$\bar{f} = 1022.9$		$\bar{f} = 1026.1$		$\bar{f} = 38.6$		$\bar{f} = 37.18$	
Self-adaptive schedule											
1095445	—	1095445	—	1077	—	1077	3	47	8	47	4
1095382	5	1095382	9	1055	11	1055	16	46	3	46	5
1095266	1	1095357	2	1033	38	1033	22	45	13	45	4
1095264	5	1095266	1	1011	26	1011	23	44	9	44	6
1095206	4	1095264	15	989	19	989	22	43	15	43	12
1095141	1	1095206	5	967	5	967	9	42	7	42	11
1095112	1	1095141	2	923	1	961	1	41	8	41	10
1095065	1	1095137	3			946	1	40	6	40	8
1094917	4	1095112	1			945	1	39	7	39	6
1094736	3	1095065	3			923	1	38	8	38	12
1094642	1	1095039	2			901	1	37	5	37	7
$\bar{f} = 1092743$		$\bar{f} = 1094311$		$\bar{f} = 1016.9$		$\bar{f} = 1012.3$		$\bar{f} = 41.49$		$\bar{f} = 40.37$	
Deterministic schedule											
1095445	3	1095445	—	1077	13	1077	12	47	33	47	14
1095382	14	1095382	6	1055	31	1055	32	46	20	46	13
1095357	5	1095266	1	1033	36	1033	36	45	10	45	19
1095264	8	1095264	18	1011	17	1011	17	44	10	44	10
1095232	1	1095207	1	989	3	989	2	43	8	43	11
1095206	5	1095206	7			967	1	42	4	42	8
1095141	5	1095141	1					41	7	41	6
1095112	3	1095081	1					40	1	40	9
1095065	2	1095065	2					39	4	39	3
1095035	6	1095039	1					37	1	38	2
1094987	1	1095035	9					35	1	37	2
$\bar{f} = 1094711$		$\bar{f} = 1094479$		$\bar{f} = 1040.5$		$\bar{f} = 1040.0$		$\bar{f} = 44.61$		$\bar{f} = 43.39$	

Table 1.: Experimental results for the combinatorial optimization problems (multiple knapsack "weing7-105", maximum cut "maxcut", and maximum independent set "misp100-01") obtained by the constant mutation rate, the deterministic schedule and the self-adaptive schedule.

A Fine-Grained Parallel Evolutionary Program for Concept Induction

A. Giordana, F. Neri and L. Saitta

Dipartimento di Informatica, Universitá di Torino,
C.so Svizzera 185, 10149 Torino, Italy.
e-mail: {attilio,neri,saitta}@di.unito.it

Abstract. This paper presents a highly parallel genetic algorithm, called G-NET, designed for concept induction in propositional and first order logics. As well as other systems oriented to the same task, G-NET exploits niches and species for learning multimodal concepts; on the other hand it deeply differs from other systems because of the distributed architecture, which totally eliminates the concept of common memory. A simulator of the system, designed in order to check the possibility of exploiting parallel processing, is evaluated on a standard benchmark. The experimental results show that a multi-processor implemented with standard technology could reach speed-up of thousands of times.

1 Introduction

In the recent literature Genetic Algorithms emerged as a powerful tool for concept induction [7, 16, 8, 2, 3, 9]. In particular, they look attractive because of their exploration capacity, which goes far beyond the one of the traditional search methods, and because of their ability to exploit massive parallelism.

This paper contributes to this aspect and describes a new fine-grained distributed genetic algorithm, called G-NET, designed for supervised concept learning. The new algorithm is compared with other systems based on a more traditional approach.

A recent approach, which proved to be very effective in learning disjunctive concept definitions, is based on the theory of niches and species formation. At a very abstract level, a disjunctive concept definition consists of a set of conjunctive logical formulas, each one capturing a different modality of the concept. As niches and species formation is a way for facing multi-modal search problem, disjunctive concept induction naturally fits this framework.

Several recent algorithms, such as COGIN [8], REGAL [2, 3, 9] and JoinGA [12] can be considered as based on this approach even if they adopt very different methods for promoting species formation. According to the published results, the three systems seem to be effective in solving the task they are designed for and, in the light of the available data, it is difficult to say if one is really better than the others. Nevertheless, no one of them is capable of taking advantage of massive parallel processors.

The new algorithm G-NET shares with REGAL the basic principles, but adopts a different approach with respect to the mating and the replacement strategies which lead to new architectural solutions suitable to exploit massive parallelism on a loosely coupled multi-processor or on a network of workstations interconnected by a high bandwidth channel. We will show that the performances of the new algorithm with respect to the quality of the produced solution remains similar to the one of REGAL or JoinGA, while the explicit parallelism is limited only by the size of the learning set.

The paper is organized as in the following. The next section discusses the problems arising when a genetic algorithm that promotes niches and species formation is distributed on a network of homogeneous computational nodes. Section 3 describes the architecture of the G-NET algorithm into details and Section 4 compares the results obtained by G-NET to the ones obtained by REGAL and Join-GA. Finally, some conclusions are taken in Section 5.

2 Distributing a Multi-Modal GA

A simple distributed architecture proposed in the literature and widely applied is the network (or island) architecture as described in Goldberg's book [5]. The basic scheme is reported in Figure 1. The genetic population is homogeneously subdivided into subpopulations (islands) which evolve in parallel on different computational nodes and periodically interact by exchanging individuals. This model has been theoretically investigated by Pettey and Lauze [4] which proved that it still behaves according to the *schema theorem* [10] and so does not loose the properties of a sequential GA. Moreover, this distributed computational model is attractive because simple and easy to implement on many different computer architectures, ranging from massive parallel computers, such as the CM2 and the CM5, to workstation clusters connected through a commercial LAN.

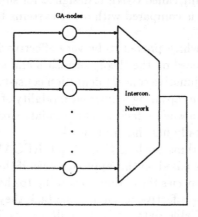

Fig. 1. Network Architecture for a a distributed genetic algorithm

However, the network architecture, in this original formulation, becomes inadequate moving from unimodal GAs, designed for searching for a single maximum, to multi-modal GAs designed for discovering many maxima at the same time. As mentioned above, multi-modal GAs work developing different species, each one settled around a local maximum located in a different region (niche) of the fitness domain. The classical methods for allowing species formations are crowding [1] and sharing functions [6]. New methods have been proposed recently [8, 15, 9, 12] useful for machine learning applications. Finally, a recently proposed method is based on the restricted tournament [11].

Even if different with respect to their principle, all the mentioned methods promote species formation by limiting the genetic pressure among species living in different niches. As small niches tend to host small species, a large population can be required in order to allow the simultaneous formation of all species required for solving a multi-modal problem. This can be intuitively understood by considering that a species can permanently live in a population only when the average number of its individuals is significantly greater than the size of the statistical fluctuations due to the behavior of the GA. Therefore, homogeneously distributing a population according to the network model has the effect of reducing the algorithm speciation capability because the size of the local populations drops proportionally to the node number. On the other hand, the migration rate is not enough to balance this effect. This problem has been investigated in [3].

For this reason, the pure network model is not used with multi-modal GAs and variant and extensions have been proposed where the population is no more distributed homogeneously but different niches and species are assigned to computational nodes in order to reduce the genetic pressure. The REGAL system [9], for instance, adopts a kind of co-evolutionary strategy, which dynamically moves niches and species on different nodes as long as they appear during the evolutionary process. To this aim, the network model has been extended by including a supervisor node (see Figure 2), whose task consists in identifying emerging species and consequently reassigning the populations to the computational nodes. The drawback of Regal's strategy is that explicit parallelism depends on the number of niches the algorithm is capable of discovering. Then, it is not immediate to exploit massively parallel processor without deeply modifying the basic algorithm.

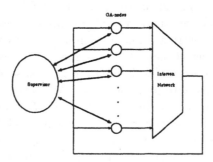

Fig. 2. Regal architecture

3 G-NET Architecture

G-NET is a algorithm designed for concept induction from examples. Given, a learning set $E = E^+ \cup E^-$ consisting of positive and negative examples of a concept h, the task consists in searching for a logical formula Φ, in an assigned language L, which is true of all the positive examples E^+ and is false of all the negative examples E^-. If such a Φ is found, the definition $\Phi \to h$ holds. In general, a concept definition Φ can be a disjunction $\Phi = \phi_1 \vee \phi_2 \vee \ldots \vee \phi_n$ of conjunctive definitions $\phi_1, \phi_2, \ldots, \phi_n$, each one corresponding to a different modality of the concept h. The logical language used by G-NET for describing the conjunctive formulas is a VL_{12} language similar to the one used by Induce [14].

As well as in REGAL [9] and in COGIN [8] multi-modality is faced by promoting the formation of niches and species. The individuals processed by the GA are conjunctive formulas and the positive examples are considered as elementary niches representing life sources for the individuals which cover them[1]. On the contrary, negative examples represent penalties a formula has to pay, so that its fitness is reduced.

Formulas covering a same niche compete among them for survival. Then, the ones which cover many positive examples and no (or few) negative ones tend to outperform the others. However, formulas which do not share niches (or share a small percentage only) tend to coexist without competing among themselves.

The fundamental difference between G-NET and REGAL is in the way the formulas interact and develop the genetic pressure. REGAL still makes use of a global mating pool where all the individual selected by the universal suffrage operator can mate each other. In this way strong formulas put pressure on the other ones trying to enter in the mating pool. To relieve this pressure, REGAL's long term strategy is to isolate the strong disjuncts on different nodes.

G-NET solves the problem eliminating the global mating pool, which is replaced by a set of local mating pools, one for each positive example $e \in E^+$, where a high chance of entering is given to the formulas covering e and a very little chance is given to all the other ones.

As described in Figure 3, G-net consists of a set of $|E^+|$ processors, called PEs, interconnected by a distribution network realizing a full cross-bar switch. Every PE is assigned to a single learning event $e \in E^+$, is provided with a local population and plays a local genetic algorithm aimed at developing a conjunctive concept description ϕ covering e and maximizing an assigned fitness function $f(\phi)$. When a processing element PE, assigned to an example e, discovers a formula ϕ covering also examples different from e, it sends a copy of ϕ to the corresponding processors with probability p_{cv}. Moreover, a non-null probability p_{un} of receiving a copy of ϕ is given also to the PEs associated to events not covered by ϕ in order to preserve the generalization possibility due to the mating of strongly heterogeneous disjuncts. Setting $p_{cv} > p_{un}$, it is possible to limit the genetic pressure among formulas covering disjoint sets of examples.

---

[1] We say that an individual ϕ covers an event $e \in E$ if it is true of e.

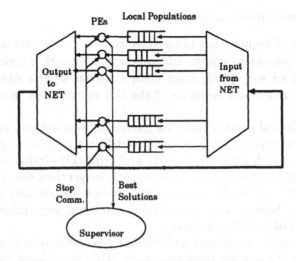

Fig. 3. G-NET Architecture

Owing to this strategy, G-NET tends to develop niches slightly overlapping, dominated by a species corresponding to a concept modality. A complete and (possibly) consistent disjunctive concept definition can be obtained by collecting the best representatives of the different species. This task is accomplished by a supervisor.

Each PE repeats the following procedure, until stopped by the supervisor:

PE Genetic Algorithm

1. Select two individuals from the local population with probability proportional to their fitness.
2. Generate two new individuals ϕ_1 and ϕ_2 by applying the genetic operators
3. Send copies of ϕ_1 and ϕ_2 with probability p_{cv} to the PEs covered by them and with probability p_{un} to the ones not covered.
4. **While** the network is ready **do**

   (a) Receive an individual ψ from the network.

   (b) Replace ψ in the local population using the tournament method.
5. Go to step (1)

In the local genetic algorithm, the replacement is accomplished using the tournament method: for each individual entering from the network an opponent is randomly selected and the victory is assigned with probability proportional to respective fitness. An elitist strategy is used so that in each PE the currently best solution cannot be replaced by a worse individual. This is obtained avoiding to choose the best solution as opponent in a tournament. Every time a new best individual is found by a PE, a copy is sent to the supervisor.

3.1 The interconnection network

The architecture of Figure 3 has to be considered as an abstract one, where the PEs are *virtual processors* and the interconnection network is a *virtual network*. In the following we will specify some computational aspects which are necessary in order to render the behavior of the GA independent from the specific implementation.

From the technical point of view, the interconnection network can be realized in many different ways, which could lead to different behaviors of the GA. For instance, if the network works sequentially and delivers the individuals one at the time, with a delay in between that is significantly longer than the processing time of a single PE, the whole algorithm tends to behave sequentially in some order randomly chosen. Simulating such a working condition, very different behaviors have been observed in different runs.

However, we need an abstract architecture whose behavior can be made independent from the specific implementation. This is achieved by introducing a synchronization between the processing elements PEs and the network. In particular, the network is supposed to have a storage of capacity N, where the individuals coming from the PEs are stored in the network when they arrive. When the storage is full, all the messages are made available at the same time to the different processors and the replacement phase takes place everywhere. In this way, the composition of the local populations tends to be independent from the order the messages entered the network.

This mechanism can be easily implemented ontop of whatever kind of network, by using buffers on the outputs.

3.2 The Supervisor

In this model, the supervisor continuously collects the best individuals sent by the PEs and elaborates a disjunctive concept description eliminating the redundant disjuncts. This concept description is considered the current solution to the induction problem. When the current solution does not improve for an assigned time T_{stop}, the supervisor stops the PEs. As a matter of fact, the algorithm used for this task is very similar to the one used by REGAL (see [9]).

3.3 The Genetic Operators

G-NET algorithm encodes conjunctive formulas (in propositional or First Order Logics) as fixed length bitstrings, where every bit represents a logical condition. Mapping logical formulas on bitstrings is immediate if proper constraints are posed on the logical language L, as it is done in REGAL (see [9] for a detailed description).

Using bitstrings as chromosomes, the classical genetic operators can be exploited. In particular, G-NET uses mutation, the two-points and the uniform crossover, plus two task specific operators: the dropping condition and the adding condition operators as defined in [7]. More specifically, the dropping condition operator eliminates from a chromosome a logical constraint chosen at random. The adding condition operator does the opposite.

As it is done in classical GAs, two individuals selected for mating are processed by a genetic operator with probability p_c or are duplicated and forwarded to the network with probability $1 - p_c$. Suppose the decision of applying a genetic operator has been taken, then the specific operator is selected as in the following. If the two selected individuals ϕ_1 and ϕ_2 are genetically different, the uniform crossover is applied with probability p_{uc}, while the two-points crossover is selected with probability $1 - p_{uc}$. Otherwise, if the two individuals are equals, they are mutated by selecting between dropping condition and adding condition operators. If the individuals are consistent, i.e. do not cover negative examples, the dropping condition is chosen aiming at obtaining more general individuals covering more examples than the parents do. Otherwise, the adding condition operator is applied in the hope of adding the condition necessary to make consistent the formula.

The nice aspect of this strategy is that it automatically adapts to the composition of the population. At the beginning, when the population is very heterogeneous, the crossover is applied with high probability speeding up the convergency towards regions of the landscape which look promising. Afterwards, when the population tends to become homogeneous and the crossover becomes ineffective, the other two operators are applied. In other words, at the beginning a genetic search is dominant whereas at the end, the algorithm shifts towards a stochastic hill climbing strategy.

3.4 The fitness

The fitness function evaluates how a formula ϕ is a good representative for a specific concept instance. This is done by accounting for two parameters measured on the formula: the syntactic simplicity and the consistency. Let $z = 1 - \frac{N_{ac}}{N_{mc}}$ be the simplicity measure, being N_{ac} the number of constraints asserted in a formula and N_{mc} the maximum number of constraints which could be asserted according to the concept description language L. Let, moreover, w be the number of negative examples covered by ϕ. The fitness function is defined by the following expression:

$$f(\phi) = (1 + Az)e^{Bw} \qquad (1)$$

where A and B are user tunable constants. The fitness definition (1) is also the one currently used by the REGAL system.

4 Experimental Evaluation

A prototype of G-NET, where the parallelism is simulated by multiplexing the cpu among different virtual processors by a random scheduler, has been evaluated on a dataset used in the past as a benchmark for REGAL [9] and Join-GA [12]. In this way a direct comparison with these systems can be obtained.

The dataset is the one proposed by Schlimmer [13] and the task consists in discriminating between *edible* and *poisonous* mushrooms. It consists of 8124 instances, 1208 of edible mushrooms and 3196 of poisonous ones. Each instance is described by a vector of 22 discrete, multi-valued attributes. By defining a constraint for each one of the attribute values, a global set of 126 constraints is obtained, which leads to bistrings of 126 bits for encoding the individuals. Randomly selected sets of 4000 instances (2000 edible + 2000 poisonous) have been used as learning sets, while the remaining 4124 instances have been used for testing. With such a large learning set, G-NET can always found a perfect definition for both classes, covering all the examples and no counterexamples on the test set, as also REGAL, Join-GA and other induction algorithms can do.

However, another parameter, which has been used by the previous Genetic Algorithms to evaluate the quality of the found solution, has been the complexity of the final disjunctive solution, measured as the total number of constraints present in there. In the machine learning literature, simple solutions are considered preferable, provided that they are consistent with the test set.

In the following, we report a comparison among REGAL, Join-GA and G-NET made with respect to the task of finding a definition for the concept of *poisonous mushroom*. This concept has been chosen for the evaluation because it turned out to be more difficult for REGAL, and then it is considered more meaningful than the concept of *edible mushroom*.

The best values of complexity found by the three systems are summarized in Table 1. We notice that G-NET can reach results as good as REGAL and Join-GA. On the other hand a direct comparison with respect to the computational complexity is not easy to obtain. Nevertheless, considering the elapsed time required for a sequential run on a Sparc 20 workstation, reported comparable times for REGAL and for G-NET.

System	G-NET	REGAL	Join-GA
Complexity	11	13	12

Table 1. Final complexity of the solution obtained by G-NET, REGAL and Join-GA.

An interesting aspect of G-NET is its capability of exploiting parallel processing. The current prototype allows measures in this sense to obtained by simulating the parallel computing time in dependence of a virtual computing cycle assigned to the parallel elements and to the network. Assuming that the network is faster in delivering the messages than a PE in evaluating and individual on 4000 examples, we have a linear speed up in dependence of the number of processors. The question is how realistic is this assumption. We will use the following relation to correlate the parallelism degree to the network bandwidth:

$$P = \frac{B}{N_{PE} \; Out_{PE}} \tag{2}$$

where B denotes the network bandwidth (measured in bits/second), N_{PE} denotes the number of PE processing in parallel and Out_{PE} denotes the flow of information from a single PE (measured in bits/second).

Considering that the average time required for evaluating a solution on a learning set of 4000 examples is of about 0.25 seconds on a Sparc 20 and assuming that the at each cycle a PE evaluates two elements of 126 bits which are sent to all 2000 PEs (this is a strong maximization), we can conclude that every active PE produces less than 400 bits of information every 0.5 second including the information about the fitness and overhead control bits. Using a broadcast network, such as Ethernet or Broadband networks, broadcasting a message to 2000 processors requires 2000 bits of address in broadcast mode. In conclusion, the bit rate of each PE could be maximized to 5000 bits every 0.5 second, i.e 10000 bits every second.

Using a bandwidth B = 10 Mbits/second, as many commercial LANs have, we obtain that it is possible to feed about 1000 PEs working in parallel.

5 Conclusion

A new distributed model for a Genetic Algorithm designed for concept induction from examples has been presented. The novelty of the algorithm is represented by the fine-grained distributed mating pool, which eliminates every notion of common memory in the system so that a massive parallelism can be easely exploited.

The new architecture has been evaluated on non trivial induction tasks where excellent results have been found. Moreover, we have also shown that, considering a parallel computer based on commercial Cpus (such as Sparc or others) and commercial interconnection networks, it is possible to have a linear speed up until reaching several thousands of processors in parallel.

Therefore, the new architecture seems to be a promising one for facing crucial problems such as concept induction and set covering, and, then, it is worth further exploration.

References

1. De Jong K. A. *Analysis of the Behaviour of a Class of Genetic Adaptive Systems*. PhD thesis, University of Michigan, Ann Arbor, MI, 1975.
2. Giordana A. and Saitta L. Regal: An integrated system for learning relations using genetic algorithms. In *2nd International Workshop on Multistrategy Learning*, pages pp. 234–249, Harpers Ferry, WV, 1993. Center for Artificial Intelligence George Mason University.
3. Giordana A. and Saitta L. Learning disjunctive concepts by means of genetic algorithms". In *Int. Conf. on Machine Learning*, pages 96–104, New Brunswick, NJ, 1994. Morgan Kaufmann.
4. Pettey C.C. and Leuze M.R. A theoretical investigation of a parallel genetic algorithm. In *Int. Conf. on Genetic Algorithms*, pages 398–405, Fairfax, VA, 1989. Morgan Kaufmann.

5. Goldberg D.E. *Genetic Algorithms*. Addison-Wesley, Reading, MA, 1989.
6. Goldberg D.E. and Richardson J. Genetic algorithms with sharing for multimodal function optimization. In *Int. Conf. on Genetic Algorithms*, pages 41–49, Cambridge, MA, 1987. Morgan Kaufmann.
7. Spears W. M. De Jong, K. A. and Gordon F. D. Using genetic algorithms for concept learning. pages 161–188, 1993.
8. Greene D.P. and Smith S.F. Competition-based induction of decision models from examples. pages 229–258, 1993.
9. Neri F. and Giordana A. A distributed genetic algorithm for concept learning. In *Int. Conf. on Genetic Algorithms*, pages 436–443, Pittsburgh, PA, 1995. Morgan Kaufmann.
10. Holland J. H. *Adaptation in Natural and Artificial Systems*. PhD thesis, University of Michigan, Ann Arbor, MI, 1975.
11. Georges R. Harik. Finding multimodal solutions using restricted tournament selection. In *Int. Conf. on Genetic Algorithms*, pages 24–31, Pittsburgh, PA, 1995. Morgan Kaufmann.
12. Hekanaho J. Symbiosis in multimodal concept learning. In *12th International Conference on Machine Learning*, pages 278–285, Lake Tahoe, CA, 1995. Morgan Kaufmann.
13. Schlimmer J.S. Concept acquisition through representational adjustment. Technical Report TR 87-19, Dpt. of Information and Computer Science, Univ. of California, Irvine, CA, 1987.
14. Michalski R. A theory and methodology of inductive learning. In J. Carbonell R. Michalski and T. Mitchell, editors, *Machine Learning: An AI Approach*, pages 83–134, Los Altos, CA, 1983. Morgan Kaufmann.
15. Sears W. A simple subpopulations scheme. In *In Proc. of the Evolutionary Programming Conference*, pages 296–397, San Diego, CA.
16. Janikow C. Z. A knowledge intensive genetic algorithm for supervised learning. pages 198–228, 1993.

Evolutionary Exploration of Search Spaces

A.E. Eiben

gusz@wi.leidenuniv.nl
Leiden University, Department of Computer Science

Abstract. Exploration and exploitation are the two cornerstones of problem solving by search. Evolutionary Algorithms (EAs) are search algorithms that explore the search space by the genetic search operators, while exploitation is done by selection. During the history of EAs different operators have emerged, mimicking asexual and sexual reproduction in Nature. Here we give an overview of the variety of these operators, review results discussing the (dis)advantages of asexual and sexual mechanisms and touch on a new phenomenon: multi-parent reproduction.

1 Introduction

Generate-and-test search algorithms obtain their power from two sources: exploration and exploitation. Exploration means the discovery of new regions in the search space, exploitation amounts to using collected information in order to direct further search to promising regions. Evolutionary Algorithms (EAs) are stochastic generate-and-test search algorithms having a number of particular properties. The standard pseudo-code for an EA is given in Figure 1, after [18]. There are different types of EAs, the most common classification distinguishes Genetic Algorithms (GA), Evolution Strategies (ES) and Evolutionary Programming (EP), [3]. Genetic Programming (GP) has grown out of GAs and can be seen as a sub-class of them. Besides the different historical roots and philosophy there are also technical differences between the three main streams in evolutionary computation. These differences concern the applied representation and the corresponding genetic search operators, the selection mechanism and the role of self-adaptation. Here we will concentrate on the question of operators.

2 Evolutionary search operators

Search operators can be roughly classified by their arity and their type, the latter actually meaning the data type or representation they are defined for. In traditional GAs binary representation is used, that is candidate solutions (individuals or chromosomes) are bit-strings with a fixed length L. The study of sequencing problems, such as routing and scheduling, has yielded order-based representation, where each individual is a permutation, [16, 32]. Parameter optimization problems with variables over continous domains has led to real-valued, or floating point, representation. Genetic Programming uses individuals that are

```
EVOLUTIONARY ALGORITHM
  T := 0
    // start with an initial time
  INITPOPULATION P(T)
    // initialize a usually random population of individuals
  EVALUATE P(T)
    // evaluate fitness of all initial individuals in population
  WHILE NOT DONE DO
    // test for termination criterion (time, fitness, etc.)
    T := T + 1
      // increase the time counter
    P'(T) := SELECTPARENTS P(T)
      // select sub-population for offspring production
    RECOMBINE P'(T)
      // recombine the "genes" of selected parents
    MUTATE P'(T)
      // perturb the mated population stochastically
    EVALUATE P'(T)
      // evaluate it's new fitness
    P := SURVIVE P,P'(T)
      // select the survivors based on actual fitness
  OD
END EVOLUTIONARY ALGORITHM
```

Fig. 1. Pseudo-code of an Evolutionary Algorithm

tree structures, [24]. Accordingly, the search operators are defined for trees instead of strings. Real valued numerical optimization is the standard application area of Evolution Strategies [29]. Therefore, real-valued representation is the standard in ES. The original Evolutionary Programming scheme was applied to finite state machines, using appropriately defined operators, [13]. More recently, combinatorial and numerical optimization problems have been treated by EP, thus involving real-valued representation in the EP paradigm too.

As far as their arity is concerned, the operators used commonly in EAs are either unary or binary. Unary operators are based on analogies of asexual reproduction mechanisms in nature, while binary operators simulate sexual reproduction. The so-called global recombination in ES and recently introduced multi-parent operators in GAs are n-ary.

2.1 Mutation

The most commonly used unary operator is mutation which is meant to cause a random, unbiased change in an individual, thus resulting in one new individual. In GAs for bit-representation a so-called mutation rate p_m is given as external control parameter. Mutation works by flipping each bit independently with probability p_m in the individual it is applied to. Mutation rate is thus a parameter that is used *during* performing mutation in case of bit representation. The probability that an individual is actually mutated is a derived measure:

$$P[\text{individual is mutated}] = 1 - (1 - p_m)^L$$

In case of order-based representation swapping or shifting randomly selected genes within an individual can cause the random perturbation. In this case the mutation rate $p_m = P[\text{individual is mutated}]$ is used *before* mutating to decide whether or not the mutation operator will be applied. For tree-structured individuals replacing a sub-tree (possibly one single node) by a random tree is appropriate. Mutation rate in GP is interpreted as the frequency of performing mutation, similarily to order-based GAs. It is remarkable that the general advice concerning mutation rate in GP is to set p_m to zero, [24].

For the real-valued representation as used in ES, EP and lately in GAs the basic unit of inheritance, i.e. one gene, is a floating point number x_i, rather than a bit. In ES and EP a separate mutation mechanism is used for each gene, i.e. object variable. Mutating a certain value x_i means perturbing that value with a random number drawn form a Gaussian distribution $N(0, \sigma_i)$ by

$$x_i' = x_i + \sigma_i \cdot N(0, 1).$$

That is, σ_i is the standard deviation, also called the mean step size, concerning x_i. It is essential that the σ_i's are not static external control parameters but are part of the individuals and undergo evolution. In particular, an individual contains not only the object variables x_i, but also the strategy parameters σ_i, resulting in $2 \cdot n$ genes for n object variables. (For this discussion we disregard the incorporation and adaptation of covariances.) In ES the mean step sizes are modified log-normally:

$$\sigma_i' = \sigma_i \cdot exp(\tau' \cdot N(0, 1) + \tau \cdot N_i(0, 1))$$

where $\tau' \cdot N(0, 1)$ and $\tau \cdot N_i(0, 1)$ provide for global, repsectively individual control of step sizes, [3].

In Evolutionary Programming the so-called meta-EP scheme is introduced for adapting mean step sizes. It works by modifying σ's normally:

$$\sigma_i' = \sigma_i + \zeta \cdot \sigma_i \cdot N(0, 1)$$

where ζ is a scaling constant, [13]. Summarizing, the main differences between the GA and ES/EP mutation mechanisms are that

- in a GA every gene (bit) of every individual is mutated by the same mutation rate p_m, while ES/EP mutation is based on a different step size for every individual and every gene (object variable);
- p_m is constant during the evolution in a GA, while the step sizes undergo adaptation in ES/EP.

Let us note that in [12] exponentially decreasing mutation rates were succesfully applied in a GA.

Cross-fertilization of ideas from ES and GAs has led to using individual mutation rates that undergo self-adaptation in a GA with binary representation, [2]. The basic idea is to extend each individual with extra bits that represent the individual's own mutation rate. Mutation, then, happens by first decoding these extra bits to the individual's own mutation rate p, mutating the extra bits by probability p, again decoding the (now mutated) extra bits to obtain the mutation rate p' which is finally applied to the 'normal' bits of this individual.

Recently, floating point representation is gaining recognition in GAs for numerical function optimization. Mutating a gene, then, can happen by uniform mutation, replacing x_i by a number x_i' drawn form its domain by a uniform distribution, or by non-uniform mutation, where

$$x_i' = \begin{cases} x_i + \Delta(t, UB_i - x_i) & \text{if a random digit is 0} \\ x_i - \Delta(t, x_i - LB_i) & \text{if a random digit is 1} \end{cases}$$

UB_i and LB_i being the upper, repectively lower bound of the domain and t the generation number (time counter), [25]. The function $\Delta(t, y)$ returns a value from $[0, y]$ getting closer to 0 as t increases. This mechanism yields a dynamically changing mutation step size. This resembles ES and EP, but differs from them in an important aspect. Namely, while in ES and EP step sizes are adapted by the evolutionary process itself, here the changes follow a previously determined schedule.

An interesting GA using bit representation combined with Gaussian mutation is presented in [20, 21]. The individuals are binary coded and undergo crossover acting on bits as usual. However, mutation is applied on the decoded values of the object variables x_i and not on their binary codes. Before mutation random numbers drawn from a Poisson distribution determine the object variables that are to be mutated. Mutation itself works by decoding that part of the binary code that represents a selected variable x_i to a real value and perturbing it by Gaussian noise from $N(0, \sigma_i)$, where σ_i is 0.1 times the maximum value of that gene. In the self-adapting version of this mechanism an extra gene, coded by a binary sequence, is added to the (front of the) individual. During mutation the extra bits coding the extra gene are decoded to a value, this value σ is perturbed by an $N(0, \tau)$ Gaussian noise (τ is a control parameter), resulting in σ' and finally the object variables are mutated according to an $N(0, \sigma')$ distribution.

2.2 Crossover

As for sexual reproduction, the binary operator in GAs is called crossover, it creates two children from two parents. The crossover rate p_c prescribes the probability that a selected pair of would-be parents will actually mate, i.e. that crossover will be applied to them. It is thus used *before* crossing over. The interpretation of p_m and p_c is therefore different in GAs with bit representation. There are two basic crossover mechanisms: n-point crossover and uniform crossover.

The n-point crossover cuts the two parents of length L into $n + 1$ segments along the randomly chosen crossover points (the same points in both parents) and creates $child_1$ by gluing the odd segments form the father and the even segments from the mother. In $child_2$ odd segments come from the mother and even segments come from the father. In the majority of GA applications 1-point crossover or 2-point crossover are used, higher n's are applied seldomly. Uniform crossover decides per bit whether to insert the bit value from the father or from the mother in $child_1$; $child_2$ is created by taking the opposite decisions. Order-based representation requires that each individual is a permutation. Applying n-point and uniform crossover to permutations may create children containing multiple occurrences of genes, i.e. children of permutations will not necessarily be permutations. This fact has led to the design of special order-based crossovers that do preserve the property of 'being a permutation', [16, 32]. One example is the order crossover OX that resembles 2-point crossover. OX cuts the parents in three segments along two randomly chosen crossover points. $Child_1$ inherits the middle segment from $parent_1$ without modification. The remaining positions are filled with genes from $parent_2$ in the order in which they appear, beginning with the first position after the second crossover point and skipping genes already present in $child_1$. $Child_2$ is created alternatively. Clearly, tree-based representation in GP requires special crossover operators too. The standard GP crossover works by randomly chosing one node in $parent_1$ and in $parent_2$ independently. These nodes define a subtree in each parent, crossover exchanges these subtrees by cutting them from $parent_x$ and inserting it at the crossover node in $parent_y$.

In Evolution Strategies there are different sexual recombination mechanisms all creating one child from a number of parents. The usual form of recombination, [3], produces one new individual $\bar{x}'$ from two parents $\bar{x}$ and $\bar{y}$ by

$$x_i' = \begin{cases} x_i \text{ or } y_i & \text{discrete recombination} \\ x_i + \chi \cdot (y_i - x_i) & \text{intermediate recombination} \end{cases}$$

Discrete recombination is pretty much like uniform crossover creating only one child. Intermediate recombination (where $\chi \in [0, 1]$ is a uniform random variable) makes a child that is the weighted average of the two parents. Just like mutation, recombination is applied to the object variables (x_i's) as well as to the strategy parameters (σ_i's). Empirically, discrete recombination on object variables and intermediate recombination on strategy parameters gives best results.

Similar operators are also introduced for GAs with real valued representation applied to convex search spaces [25]. These operators create two children of two parents. The so-called simple crossover choses a random crossover point k and crosses the parents after the k-th position applying a contraction coefficient a to guarantee that the offspring fall inside the convex search space. In particular, if $\bar{x}$ and $\bar{y}$ are the two parents then $child_1$ is

$$\langle x_1, \ldots, x_k, a \cdot y_{k+1} + (1 - a) \cdot x_{k+1}, \ldots, a \cdot y_n + (1 - a) \cdot x_n \rangle$$

and $child_2$ is obtained by interchanging x and y. Single arithmetic crossover effects only one gene in each parent. The children of $\bar{x}$ and $\bar{y}$ obtained by this mechanism are:

$\langle x_1, \ldots, a \cdot y_k + (1-a) \cdot x_k, \ldots, x_n \rangle$ and $\langle y_1, \ldots, a \cdot x_k + (1-a) \cdot y_k, \ldots, y_n \rangle$

where a is a dynamic parameter, drawn randomly from a domain calculated for each pair of parents in such a way that the children are in the convex space. Whole arithmetical crossover is somewhat similar to intermediate recombination in ES in that it creates the linear combinations

$$a \cdot \bar{x} + (1-a) \cdot \bar{y} \quad \text{and} \quad a \cdot \bar{y} + (1-a) \cdot \bar{x}$$

as children of $\bar{x}$ and $\bar{y}$. Here again, the choice of a has to guarantee that the children are in the convex space.

A very particular feature within the EP paradigm is the total absence of sexual reproduction mechanisms. Mutation is the only search operator, and *'recombination in evolutionary programming is a nonissue beacause each solution is typically viewed as the analog of a species, and there is no sexual communication between species.'*, cf. [13] p. 103. Indeed, this view justifies the omittance of recombination, however, this view is only justified by the human operator's freedom in taking any arbitrary perspective. Nevertheless, the fact that apparently all higher species apply sexual recombination indicates that it does have a competitive advantage in natural evolution. This ought to make one cautious and not rejecting it *a priori*.

3 Sex or no sex: importance of crossover and mutation

The traditional views of EA streams on genetic operators are summarized in Table 1, after [3]. Triggered by the provoking success of EP without recombina-

	ES	EP	GA
mutation	main operator	only operator	background operator
recombination	important for self-adaptation	none	main operator

Table 1. Role of mutation and recombination in different EA paradigms

tion, as well as by 'introspective' motives in GA and ES there is more and more research devoted to the usefulness of mutation and recombination. Although neither GAs nor EP were originally developed as function optimizers, [5, 13], such investigations are usually performed on function optimization problems.

Classical GA investigations tried to obtain a robust parameter setting concerning mutation rate and crossover rate, in combination with the pool size [4, 17, 27]. The generally acknowledged good heuristic values for mutation rate and crossover rate are $1/chromosome.length$, respectively 0.7-0.8. Recent studies, for instance [2, 12, 19, 23] provide theoretical and experimental evidence that decreasing mutation rate along the evolution is optimal. This suggests that mutation is important at the beginning of the search but becomes 'risky' at the end. In the meanwhile, GA's 'public opinion' lately acknowledges that mutation has a more important role than (re)introducting absent or lost genes in the population.

As far as recombination is concerned, the main area of interest is traditionally the crossover's ability for combining and/or disrupting pieces of information, called schemata. Formally, a schema can be seen as a partial instantiation of the variables, i.e. a string based on a ternary alphabet $0, 1, \#$, where $\#$ means undefined or don't care. Investigations in, for instance [6, 10, 30, 31], cumulated substantial knowledge on the disruptiveness of n-point and uniform crossover. The most important observation from [6] concerns the relationship between the disruptiveness and the power to recombine schemata. '... *if one operator is better than another for survival,* [i.e. less disruptive] *it is worse for recombination (and vice versa). This ... suggests very strongly that one cannot increase the recombination power without a corresponding increase in disruption.* Another important feature of crossover operators is their exploration power, that is the variety of different regions in the search space that can be sampled. In other words, the number of different chromosomes that can be created by applying an operator. Clearly, *'exploration in the form of new recombinations comes at the cost of disruption',* [10]. Recent research has thus shown that disruption is not necessarily disadvantageous. Nevertheless, no general conclusions on the relationship between the disruptiveness of genetic operators and the quality of the GA they are applied in could be established so far. Most probably this relation is (to some extent) problem dependent.

Besides comparisons of crossover operators, the relative importance, i.e. search power, of sexual recombination and asexual, unary operators is investigated. The experiments reported in [28] show that mutation and selection are more powerful than previously believed. Nevertheless, it is observed that a GA with highly disruptive crossover outperforms a GA with mutation alone on problems with a low level of interactions between genes. It is also remarked that the power of an operator is strongly related to the selection mechanism. In [11] 'crossover's niche' is sought, i.e. problems where pair-wise mating has competitive advantages. This niche turns out to be non-empty, in the meanwhile the authors suspect that sexual recombination in GAs might be less powerful than generally believed. The usefulness of recombination is investigated on NK landscapes that allow gradual tuning of the ruggedness of the landscape in [22]. The conclusion is that *'recombination is useless on uncorrelated landscapes, but useful when high peaks are near one another and hence carry mutual information about their joint locations in the fitness landscape'.* The view presented in [30] relativizes the mutation-or-crossover battle by noting that both operators serve another purpose. *'Mutation serves to create random diversity in the population, while crossover serves as an accelerator that promotes emergent behavior from components.'* Additionally, crossover is useful for maximizing the accumulated payoff, while it can be harmful if optimality is sought.

Based on a comparison of EP and GA in [14] it is argued that crossover does not have any competitive advantage above mutation. Critiques on this investigation, for instance in [28], initiated more extensive comparisons of GAs and EP on function optimization problems. The results in [15] show a clear advatage of EP and make the authors conclude that *'no consistent advantage accrues from representing real-valued parameters as binary strings and allowing crossover to do within-parameter search.'*

Summarizing, at the moment there is a lot of effort payed to establishing the (dis)advantages of sexual, respectively asexual reproduction in simulated evolution. So far there is no generally valid judgement, and it is possible that preferences for either type of recombination are context and goal dependent.

4 More sex: n-ary operators

N-ary recombination operators were first introduced in ESs. The global form of recombination produces one new individual $\bar{x}'$ by

$$x_i' = \begin{cases} x_i \text{ or } y_i & \text{global discrete recombination} \\ x_i + \chi_i \cdot (y_i - x_i) & \text{global intermediate recombination} \end{cases}$$

where $\bar{x}$ and $\bar{y}$ are two parent individuals selected at random from the whole population **for each** i **anew** and drawing $\chi_i \in [0, 1]$ also happens for every i independently, [3]. Thus, although for each component x_i' only two mating partners are consulted, the resampling mechanism causes that the child may inherit genes from more parents. This results in a higher mixing of the genetic information than the 2-parent versions, [1].

In GAs there are three general multi-parent crosover mechanisms. Scanning crossover and diagonal crossover were introduced in [7], where the performance of scanning was studied. In [9] diagonal crossover was investigated, compared to scanning and the classical 2-parent n-point crossover. An extensive overview of experiments is given in [8]. Scanning crossover generalizes uniform crossover, although creating only one child, by chosing one of the i-th genes of the n parents to be the i-th gene of the child. Formally,

$$x_i' = C(x_i^1, \ldots, x_i^n)$$

where C is a choice mechanism choosing a value $C(u_1, \ldots, u_n)$ from $u_1, \ldots, u_n$. The choice can be random, based on a uniform distribution (uniform scanning), or biased by the fitness of the parents (fitness based scanning). It can be deterministic, based on the number of occurrences of the genes (occurrence based scanning). Diagonal crossover generalizes n-point crossover by selecting $(n-1)$ crossover points and composing n children by taking the resulting n chromosome segments from the parents 'along the diagonals'. Figure 2 illustrates this idea.

The Gene Pool Recombination (GPR) in GAs was introduced in [26]. It was further studied and extended with a fuzzy mechanism in [33]. In GPR first

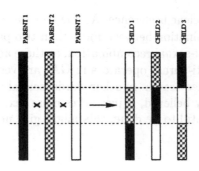

Fig. 2. Diagonal crossover with three parents

a set of parents has to be selected, these form the so-called gene pool. Then the two parent alleles of an offspring are chosen randomly for each position with replacement from the gene pool (as opposed to ES, where they are chosen from the whole population). The offspring's allele is computed using any of the standard recombination schemes that work on two parents. GPR allows for theoretical analysis of GA convergence for infinite populations with binomial fitness distribution.

As for the performance of multi-parent recombination, at the moment there are not many accessible results within ES. In [29] p. 146 the following is stated: *'A crude test yielded only a slight further increase in the rate of progress in changing from the bisexual to the multisexual scheme, whereas appreciable acceleration was achieved by introducing the bisexual in place of the asexual scheme, which allowed no recombination.'* Scanning crossover and diagonal crossover show increased performance when using more parents on several numerical functions [7, 9, 8], and ongoing research proves the same on NK-landscapes. GPR was reported to converge 25 % faster than two parent recombination (TPR) on the ONEMAX problem [26], and the fuzzyfied version of GPR proved to outperform fuzzyfied TPR in speed as well as in realized heritability on the spherical function [33].

5 Conclusions

Evolutionary Algorithms perform search by means of creating genetic diversity by genetic operators and reducing this diversity by selection. There exists a great variety of genetic operators, in this paper we gave an overview. Forced by space constraints this overview was necessarily limited, there are numerous other operatos developed for special purposes. Grouping genetic operators by arity we discussed asexual reproduction (mutation) and sexual recombination between two parents. The importance of sex in Evolution, more technically the relative power of unary and binary operators, is a hot issue in recent EA research. We briefly reviewed some of the related results, noting that at the moment none of them can be given a clear preference. At the end we touched on a new phenomenon: sexual recombination between more than two parents. (This is multiparent, rather than multi-sexual recombination, as there are no genders in EAs.) The first results on multi-parent operators in GAs are very promising, showing that they lead to enhanced search. In other words, sexual recombination is more powerful than previously believed, it just takes more sex, i.e. more parents. Although a lot of work is still to be done, this might give new impetus to the sex or no sex debate.

References

1. T. Bäck F. Hoffmeister and H.-P. Schwefel. A survey of evolution strategies. In *Fourth International Conference on Genetic Algorithms*, pages 2–9. Morgan Kaufmann, 1991.
2. T. Bäck. The interaction of mutation rate, selection, and self-adaptation within a genetic algorithm. In *Parallel Problem Solving from Nature - 2*, pages 85–94. North-Holland, 1992.
3. T. Bäck and H.-P. Schwefel. An overview of evolutionary algorithms for parameter optimization. *Journal of Evolutionary Computation*, 1:1–23, 1993.
4. K.A. De Jong. *An analysis of the behavior of a class of genetic adaptive systems.* Doctoral dissertation, University of Michigan, 1975.
5. K.A. De Jong. Are genetic algorithms function optimizers? In R. Männer and B. Manderick, editors, *Parallel Problem Solving from Nature - 2*, pages 3–13. North-Holland, 1992.
6. K.A. De Jong and W.M. Spears. A formal analysis of the role of multi-point crossover in genetic algorithms. *Annals of Mathematics and Artificial Intelligence*, 5:1–26, 1992.
7. A.E. Eiben, P-E. Raué, and Zs. Ruttkay. Genetic algorithms with multi-parent recombination. In *Parallel Problem Solving from Nature - 3, LNCS 866*, pages 78–87. Springer-Verlag, 1994.
8. A.E. Eiben and C.H.M. van Kemenade. Performance of multi-parent crossover operators on numerical function optimization problems. Technical Report TR-95-33, Leiden University, 1995.
9. A.E. Eiben, C.H.M. van Kemenade, and J.N. Kok. Orgy in the computer: Multiparent reproduction in genetic algorithms. In *Third European Conference on Artificial Life, LNAI 929*, pages 934–945. Springer-Verlag, 1995.
10. L.J. Eshelman and R.A. Caruana andJ.D. Schaffer. Biases in the crossover landscape. In *Third International Conference on Genetic Algorithms*, pages 10–19, 1989.
11. L.J. Eshelman and J.D. Schaffer. Crossover's niche. In *Fifth International Conference on Genetic Algorithms*, pages 9–14, 1993.
12. T. Fogarty. Varying the probability of mutation in the genetic algorithm. In *Third International Conference on Genetic Algorithms*, pages 104–109, 1989.
13. D.B. Fogel. *Evolutionary Computation.* IEEE Press, 1995.
14. D.B. Fogel and J.W. Atmar. Comparing genetic operators with gaussian mutations in simulated evolutionary processes using linear systems. *Biological Cybernetics*, 63:111–114, 1990.

15. D.B. Fogel and L.C. Stayton. On the effectiveness of crossover in simulated evolutionary optimization. *Biosystems*, 32:3:171–182, 1994.

16. B.R. Fox and M.B. McMahon. Genetic operators for sequencing problems. In *Foundations of Genetic Algorithms - 1*, pages 284–300, 1991.

17. D.E. Goldberg. *Genetic Algorithms in Search, Optimization and Machine Learning*. Addison-Wesley, 1989.

18. J. Heitkötter and D. Beasley. *The Hitch-Hiker's Guide to Evolutionary Computation*. FAQ for comp.ai.genetic, 1996.

19. Hesser and Männer. Towards an optimal mutation probability for genetic algorithms. In *Parallel Problem Solving from Nature - 1, LNCS 496*, pages 23–32. Springer-Verlag, 1990.

20. R. Hinterding. Gaussian mutation and self-adaptation for numeric genetic algorithms. In *Second IEEE conference on Evolutionary Computation*, pages 384–389, 1995.

21. R. Hinterding, H. Gielewski, and T.C. Peachey. The nature of mutation in genetic algorithms. In *Sixth International Conference on Genetic Algorithms*, pages 65–72, 1995.

22. W. Hordijk and B. Manderick. The usefulness of recombination. In *Third European Conference on Artificial Life, LNAI 929*, pages 908–919. Springer-Verlag, 1995.

23. B.A. Julstrom. What have you done for me lately? adapting operator probabilities in a steady-state genetic algorithm. In *Sixth International Conference on Genetic Algorithms*, pages 81–87, 1995.

24. J.R. Koza. *Genetic Programming*. MIT Press, 1992.

25. Z. Michalewicz. *Genetic Algorithms + Data structures = Evolution programs*. Springer-Verlag, second edition, 1994.

26. H. Mühlenbein and H.-M. Voigt. Gene pool recombination in genetic algorithms. In *Proc. of the Metaheuristics Conference*. Kluwer Academic Publishers, 1995.

27. J.D. Schaffer R.A. Caruana, L.J. Eshelman and R. Das. A study of control parameters affecting the online performance of genetic algorithms. In *Third International Conference on Genetic Algorithms*, pages 51–60, 1989.

28. J.D. Schaffer and L.J. Eshelman. On crossover as an evolutionary viable strategy. In *Fourth International Conference on Genetic Algorithms*, pages 61–68, 1991.

29. H.-P. Schwefel. *Evolution and Optimum Seeking*. Sixth-Generation Computer Technology Series. Wiley, New York, 1995.

30. W.M. Spears. Crossover or mutation? In *Foundations of Genetic Algorithms - 2*, pages 221–238, 1993.

31. G. Syswerda. Uniform crossover in genetic algorithms. In *Third International Conference on Genetic Algorithms*, pages 2–9, 1989.

32. T. Starkweather, S. McDaniel K. Mathias D. Whitley and C. Whitley. A comparison of genetic sequenceing operators. In *Fourth International Conference on Genetic Algorithms*, pages 69–76, 1991.

33. H.-M. Voigt and H. Mühlenbein. Gene pool recombination and utilization of covariances for the Breeder Genetic Algorithm. In *Second IEEE conference on Evolutionary Computation*, pages 172–177, 1995.

Evolutionary Computation: One Project, Many Directions

Zbigniew Michalewicz,[1,2] Jing Xiao,[1] and Krzysztof Trojanowski[2]

[1] Department of Computer Science, University of North Carolina,
Charlotte, NC 28223, USA
[2] Institute of Computer Science, Polish Academy of Sciences,
ul. Ordona 21, 01-237 Warsaw, Poland

Abstract. The field of evolutionary computation has been growing rapidly over the last few years. Yet, there are still many gaps to be filled, many experiments to be done, many questions to be answered. In this paper we examine a few important directions in which we can expect a lot of activities and significant results; we discuss them from a general perspective and in the context of a particular project: a development of an evolutionary planner/navigator in a mobile robot environment.

1   Introduction

During the last two decades there has been a growing interest in algorithms which are based on the principle of evolution (survival of the fittest). A common term, accepted recently, refers to such techniques as *evolutionary computation* (EC) methods. The best known algorithms in this class include genetic algorithms, evolutionary programming, evolution strategies, and genetic programming. There are also many hybrid systems which incorporate various features of the above paradigms, and consequently are hard to classify; anyway, we refer to them just as EC methods.

The field of evolutionary computation has reached a stage of some maturity. There are several, well established international conferences that attract hundreds of participants (International Conferences on Genetic Algorithms—ICGA [31, 32, 53, 8, 25], Parallel Problem Solving from Nature—PPSN [58, 39, 9], Annual Conferences on Evolutionary Programming—EP [21, 22, 59, 40]); new annual conferences are getting started, e.g., IEEE International Conferences on Evolutionary Computation [48, 49, 50]. Also, there are many workshops, special sessions, and local conferences every year, all around the world. A relatively new journal, *Evolutionary Computation* (MIT Press) [13], is devoted entirely to evolutionary computation techniques; many other journals organized special issues on evolutionary computation (e.g., [18, 43]). Many excellent tutorial papers [6, 7, 63, 19] and technical reports provide more-or-less complete bibliographies of the field [1, 29, 52, 46]. There is also *The Hitch-Hiker's Guide to Evolutionary Computation* prepared initially by Jörg Heitkötter and currently by David Beasley [33], available on comp.ai.genetic interest group (Internet), and a new volume, *Handbook of Evolutionary Computation*, is currently being prepared [5]. There are also a few quite recent (i.e., 1995/96) texts available [4, 20, 42, 57].

Despite of all these developments and activities, there are still many gaps to be filled, many experiments to be done, many questions to be answered. As Ken De Jong observed recently [14] in the context of genetic algorithms:

> "... the field had pushed the application of simple GAs well beyond our initial theories and understanding, creating a need to revisit and extend them."

In this paper we discuss some of the major current trends in this field. The next section provides a short introductory material on evolutionary algorithms. Section 3 discusses briefly one particular project: a development of evolutionary planner/navigator in a mobile robot environment. Section 4 presents some current research direction and discusses them in the context of the project. Section 5 contains a few final remarks.

2 Evolutionary computation

In general, any abstract task to be accomplished can be thought of as solving a problem, which, in turn, can be perceived as a search through a space of potential solutions. Since usually we are after "the best" solution, we can view this task as an optimization process. For small spaces, classical exhaustive methods usually suffice; for larger spaces special artificial intelligence techniques must be employed. The methods of evolutionary computation are among such techniques; they are stochastic algorithms whose search methods model some natural phenomena: genetic inheritance and Darwinian strife for survival. As stated in [12]:

> "... the metaphor underlying genetic algorithms[3] is that of natural evolution. In evolution, the problem each species faces is one of searching for beneficial adaptations to a complicated and changing environment. The 'knowledge' that each species has gained is embodied in the makeup of the chromosomes of its members."

The best known techniques in the class of evolutionary computation methods are genetic algorithms, evolution strategies, evolutionary programming, and genetic programming. There are also many hybrid systems which incorporate various features of the above paradigms; however, the structure of any evolutionary computation algorithm is very much the same; a sample structure is shown in Figure 1.

The evolutionary algorithm maintains a population of individuals, $P(t) = \{x_1^t, \ldots, x_n^t\}$ for iteration t. Each individual represents a potential solution to the problem at hand, and is implemented as some data structure S. Each solution x_i^t is evaluated to give some measure of its "fitness". Then, a new population

---

[3] The best known evolutionary computation techniques are genetic algorithms; very often the terms *evolutionary computation* methods and *GA-based* methods are used interchangeably.

```
procedure evolutionary algorithm
begin
    t ← 0
    initialize  P(t)
    evaluate  P(t)
    while (not termination-condition) do
    begin
        t ← t + 1
        select  P(t) from  P(t − 1)
        alter  P(t)
        evaluate  P(t)
    end
end
```

Fig. 1. The structure of an evolutionary algorithm

(iteration $t + 1$) is formed by selecting the fitter individuals (select step). Some members of the new population undergo transformations (alter step) by means of "genetic" operators to form new solutions. There are unary transformations m_i (mutation type), which create new individuals by a small change in a single individual ($m_i : S \rightarrow S$), and higher order transformations c_j (crossover type), which create new individuals by combining parts from several (two or more) individuals ($c_j : S \times \ldots \times S \rightarrow S$).[4] After some number of generations the algorithm converges—it is hoped that the best individual represents a near-optimum (reasonable) solution.

Despite powerful similarities between various evolutionary computation techniques there are also many differences between them (often hidden at a lower level of abstraction). EC techniques use different data structures S for their chromosomal representations, consequently, the 'genetic' operators are different as well. For example, the original genetic algorithms (GAs), which were devised to model adaptation processes, mainly operated on binary strings and used a recombination operator with mutation as a background operator [34]. On the other hand, evolution strategies (ESs) were developed as a method to solve parameter optimization problems [56]; consequently, a chromosome represents an individual as a pair of float-valued vectors, and Gaussian mutation is the leading operator. The original evolutionary programming (EP) techniques [23] aimed at evolution of artificial intelligence in the sense of developing ability to predict changes in an environment; hence finite state machines were selected as a chromosomal representation of individuals (five mutation operators were proposed in connection with this representation). Another interesting approach was developed relatively recently by Koza [36, 37] who suggested that the desired program should evolve

---

[4] In most cases crossover involves just two parents, however, it need not be the case. In a recent study [15] the authors investigated the merits of 'orgies', where more than two parents are involved in the reproduction process. Also, scatter search techniques [26] proposed the use of multiple parents.

itself during the evolution process. Koza developed a new methodology, named Genetic Programming (GP), which processes tree structured programs.

It is important to note that many researchers modified further evolutionary algorithms by 'adding' a problem specific knowledge to the algorithm. Several researchers have discussed initialization techniques, different representations, decoding techniques (mapping from genetic representations to 'phenotypic' representations), and the use of heuristics for genetic operators. Such hybrid/nonstandard systems enjoy a significant popularity in evolutionary computation community. Very often these systems, extended by the problem-specific knowledge, outperform classical evolutionary methods as well as other standard techniques [41, 42]. However, such systems are quite hard to classify and it is convenient to refer to them just as evolutionary computation techniques. The next section discusses briefly such an evolutionary system: Evolutionary Planner/Navigator for mobile robot environment.

3 The Project: Evolutionary Planner/Navigator

The *motion planning* problem for mobile robots is typically formulated as follows [68]: given a robot and a description of an environment, plan a path of the robot between two specified locations, which is collision-free and satisfies certain optimization criteria. Traditionally there are two approaches to the problem: Off-line planning, which assumes perfectly known and stable environment, and on-line planning, which focuses on dealing with uncertainties when the robot traverses the environment. On-line planning is also referred to by many researchers as the *navigation* problem.

A great deal of research has been done in motion planning and navigation (see [68] and [38] for surveys). However, different existing methods encounter one or many of the following difficulties:

- high computation expenses,
- inflexibility in responding to changes in the environment,
- inflexibility in responding to different optimization goals,
- inflexibility in responding to uncertainties,
- inability to combine advantages of global planning and reactive planning.

In order to address these difficulties, we initiated the study of an Evolutionary Planner/Navigator (EP/N) system; the inspiration to use evolutionary techniques was triggered by the following ideas/observations:

- randomized search can be the most effective in dealing with NP-hard problems and in escaping local minima,
- parallel search actions not only provide great speed but also provide ground for *interactions* among search actions to achieve even greater efficiency in optimization,
- creative application of the evolutionary computation *concept* rather than dogmatic imposition of a standard algorithm proves to be more effective in solving specific types of real problems,

- intelligent behavior is the result of a collection of simple reactions to a complex world,
- a planner can be greatly simplified, much more efficient and flexible, and increase the quality of search, if search is not confined to be within a specific map structure,
- it is more meaningful to equip a planner with the flexibility of changing the optimization goals than the ability of finding the absolutely optimum solution for a single, particular goal.

The EP/N embodies the above ideas by following the evolution program approach, i.e. combining the concept of evolutionary computation with problem-specific chromosome structures and genetic operators. With such an approach, the EP/N is pursuing all the advantages as described above. Less obvious though, is that with the unique design of chromosome structure and genetic operators, the EP/N does not need a discretized map for search, which is usually required by other planners. Instead, the EP/N "searches" the original and continuous environment by generating paths by various evolutionary operators. The objects in the environment can simply be indicated as a collection of straight-line "walls". This representation accommodates both known objects as well as partial information of unknown objects obtained from sensing. Thus, there is little difference between off-line planning and on-line navigation for the EP/N. In fact, the EP/N unifies off-line planning and on-line navigation with the same evolutionary algorithm and chromosome structure.

For more details on the current state of the project, see [66, 67].

4 Evolutionary Computation: Current Directions

As indicated in the Introduction, the field of evolutionary computation has been growing rapidly over the last few years. Yet, there are still many areas in which we can expect a lot of activities and significant results. This section discusses such directions and illustrates some of the points by referring to the EP/N project described in the previous section.

4.1 Function optimization

For many years, most evolutionary techniques have been evaluated and compared to each other in the domain of function optimization. It seems also that the domain of function optimization would remain the primary test-bed for many new comparisons and new features of various algorithms. In this context it is important to investigate properties of evolutionary algorithms on different landscapes, to experiment with various modifications of evolutionary algorithms (e.g., elitist strategy, non random mating, etc.), to explore the role of operators (e.g., mutation versus crossover, different types of operators, etc.), to study the significance of infeasible individuals in the population, etc. In particular, studies on evaluation functions seem to be of great importance; after all the evaluation function serves as the main (sometimes the only) link between evolutionary algorithm and the problem.

The EP/N project falls into the category of 'function optimization': a near-optimal path between the source and destination is being evolved. Clearly, the evaluation function of the EP/N is of utmost importance and accommodates different (often conflicting) optimization goals. Various experiments led us to focus on the short, smooth, and clear (i.e., far from obstacles) paths, thus we faced the interesting and important issue of how to design the evaluation function to accommodate properly all of these requirements. Moreover, during our study on this problem, we discovered an even more interesting issue: how to design the evaluation function to evaluate paths which are not yet collision-free? Such infeasible paths are generated quite often, especially in early generations. If the system generates and discards infeasible individuals, then the evolutionary algorithm will spend most of its time evaluating such infeasible individuals. Moreover, the first feasible path found will likely trigger a premature convergence (i.e., other infeasible individuals will be driven out from the population), and the system will not be able to find better individuals. On the other hand, if we keep these individuals in the population, we have also to address yet another interesting issue: how to compare feasible and infeasible individuals in the population? We experimented with different evaluation functions [44] and analyzed their impacts. Although the EP/N generally worked well even under simple and crude evaluation functions, we found that better designs of the evaluation function greatly improved the quality of results and planning efficiency.

The project provides also with additional aspects of study in the area of evolutionary techniques for function optimization such as (1) behavior of the system in various environments (e.g., with different number and various density of objects, different topology of a feasible part in the search space, etc.), (2) non-stationary environments, where the evaluation function changes with time (due to incomplete information about the environment or the movement of some obstacles), (3) a mixture of evolutionary techniques with memory-based systems (we briefly discuss the issues (2) and (3) in section 4.6), (4) various methods for maintaining diversity in the population, which is essential in the EP/N project: the generation of alternative paths is important in dynamic environments (section 4.3), etc.

4.2 Representation, operators, and other search techniques

Traditionally, GAs work with binary strings, ES—with floating point vectors, and EP—with finite state machines (represented as matrices), whereas GP techniques use trees as a structure for the individuals; each of these techniques has a standard set of operators. However, there is a need for a systematic research on evolutionary algorithms, which

- incorporate the problem-specific knowledge by means of appropriate chromosomal data structures, non-standard operators, and additional local search algorithms,

- represent complex, non-linear objects of varying sizes, and, in particular, represent 'blueprints' of complex objects (e.g., morphogenic evolutionary algorithms [2]), and
- experiment with evolutionary operators for such objects at the genotype level.

These directions can be perceived as important steps towards building complex hybrid evolutionary system.

The EP/N project is very appropriate for such research. For example, there are many possibilities for various path representations: starting from a linked list of coordinates of all knot points of a path (this is the current representation, see [66]), through a set of rules, which provide directions and distances to be traveled, to blueprints of complex rules—e.g., a development of a neural network to control the robot. Various evolutionary operators can be experimented with: e.g., knowledge-based operators, which adopt their actions with respect to the current state of search, Lamarckian operators, which improve an individual during its lifetime—consequently, the improved, "learned" characteristics of such an individual can be passed to the next generation, and multi-parent operators [15]. In addition, incorporation of problem-specific, local search algorithms seems to be worthwhile: such algorithms may enhance fine-grained local search capabilities of an evolutionary algorithm, may help in maintaining diversity of paths, and may be used in the repairing process (i.e., in converting an infeasible path into a feasible one).

The EP/N project also reveals the importance of studying the tradeoff between the amount of problem-specific knowledge being incorporated into an algorithm and the efficiency of an algorithm, which is essential for various on-line systems.

4.3 Non random mating

Most current techniques which incorporate crossover operator use random mating, i.e, mating, where individuals are paired randomly. It seems that with the trend of movement from simple to complex systems, the issue of non random mating would be of growing importance. There are many possibilities to explore; these include introduction of sex or "family" relationships between individuals or establishing some preferences (e.g., seduction [51]). Some simple schemes were already investigated by several researchers (e.g., Eshelman's incest prevention technique [17]), however, the ultimate goal seems to evolve rules for non random mating. A few possibilities (in the context of multimodal optimization) were already explored; these include sharing functions, which permit a formation of stable subpopulations, and tagging, where individuals are assigned labels. However, very little was done in this direction for complex chromosomal structures.

In the EP/N project the aspect of non random mating is quite important. Since the robot's environment is only partially known, it is essential to maintain diversity of paths in the population. Different groups of paths (i.e., subpopulations or species) can explore different areas of the environment; it is important to identify such groups and to maintain their identity. As mentioned earlier, the generation of alternative paths is essential in dynamic and partially-unknown environments: due to unknown obstacles (in the on-line phase) it might be necessary to change the current path.

4.4 Self-adapting systems

Since evolutionary algorithms implement the idea of evolution, it is more than natural to expect a development of some self-adapting characteristics of these techniques. Apart from evolutionary strategies, which incorporate some of its control parameters in the solution vectors, most other techniques use fixed representations, operators, and control parameters. It seems that the most promising research areas are based on inclusion of self adapting mechanisms within the system for:

- Representation of individuals (e.g., adaptive strategies, proposed by Shaefer [60], the Dynamic Parameter Encoding technique [55], and messy genetic algorithms [28]).
- Operators. It is clear that different operators play different roles at different stages of the evolutionary process. The operators should adapt to the current stage of the search and to the current topology of the landscape being searched (e.g., adaptive crossover [54, 61]). This is especially important for time-varying fitness landscapes.
- Control parameters. There were already experiments aimed at these issues: adaptive population sizes [3] or adaptive probabilities of operators [11, 35, 62]. However, much more remains to be done.

It seems that this is one of the most promising directions of research; after all, the power of evolutionary algorithms lies in their adaptiveness.

The adaptiveness is also the key issue in the EP/N project. For example, the current version of the system incorporates 8 operators which play different roles in various environments and at various stages of the evolution process. Recently, a new adaptive procedure was developed [67], which adapts the frequencies of these operators on the basis of their efficiency (i.e., usefulness and the operational cost). Note that different environments require different subset of these operators; the adaptive procedure is responsible for tuning all frequences with respect to the current state of search. Additional work would concentrate on a development of adaptive representations (there is an interesting possibility of changing representation of individuals, e.g., from a linked list into rules and vice versa), additional adaptive operators which change their scope and mechanism on the basis of the current state of search, adaptation of the population size and the population structure (e.g., division of the population into sub-populations).

4.5 Co-evolutionary systems

There is a growing interest in co-evolutionary systems, where more than one evolution process takes place: usually there are different populations (e.g., additional populations of parasites or predators) which interact with each other.

In such systems the evaluation function for one population may depend on the state of the evolution processes in the other population(s). This is an important topic for modeling artificial life, some business applications, etc.

Co-evolutionary systems might also be important for approaching large-scale problems [47]: a (large) problem can be decomposed into smaller subproblems and there can be a separate evolutionary process for each of the subproblem. These evolutionary processes are connected with each other: evaluation of individuals in one population depends also on developments in other populations.

The EP/N project seems ideal for studying some aspects of co-evolutionary systems. First of all, the path planning problem can be decomposed into several sub-problems with different sources and destinations. In complex environments such an approach may lead to increased efficiency of the system. Secondly, the co-evolutionary models would allow us to extend the EP/N project to study some processes of cooperation, where several robots explore an environment and exchange the evolved information. This line of research leads to investigation of intelligent multi-agent scenarios.

4.6 Diploid/polyploid versus haploid structures

Diploidy (or polyploidy) can be viewed as a way to incorporate memory into the individual's structure. Instead of single chromosome (haploid structure) representing a precise information about an individual, a diploid structure is made up of a pair of chromosomes: the choice between two values is made by some dominance function. The diploid (polyploid) structures are of particular significance in non-stationary or partially unknown environments (i.e., for time-varying objective functions) and for modeling complex systems (possibly using co-evolution models). However, there is no theory to support the incorporation of a dominance function into the system; there are also quite limited experimental data in this area.

It might be worthwhile to explore the addition of an "experience-related" behavior to the EP/N system. The current version of the adaptive navigator is memoryless: the population adapts to the current evaluation function which changes over time on the basis of sensed information. However, the system "does not remember" explicitly the past experiences. Consequently, the system does not learn from past experiences. It seems that some sort of "memory" (in addition to the object map of the environment) would enhance further the capabilities of the system.

One possibility would be to develop an adaptive algorithm based on multi-chromosome structures with a dominance function. The EP/N project is very appropriate for studying polyploid structures with a dominance function: the environment is not fully known; besides, some obstacles need not stay in the same place all the time. In such an algorithm, each individual consists of more than one chromosome (each chromosome still represents a single solution, i.e., a path). The dominance function determines one chromosome as the current representative of the individual, which then participates in the evaluation process. The other chromosomes in the structure are "inactive" and play the role of memory: past experiences of the robot. They will, nevertheless, evolve with the currently active chromosome in the same way.

Another possible approach would be based on an additional data structure, where past "footsteps" and other "reasonable" paths discovered earlier during the navigation process are stored. Such a memory would be suitable for a static or a relatively stable environment. As the "short memory" for the current navigation task, it may further enhance the ability of the system to escape from dead-end situations. Since the "memory" of the system stores feasible paths from various points of the environment to the goal, it might be possible for the robot, if trapped, to return to some earlier visited knot point and to continue along different path, thus avoiding dead-end situation.

4.7 Parallel models

Parallelism promises to put within our reach solutions to problems untractable before; clearly, it is one of the most important areas of computer science. Evolutionary algorithms are very suitable for parallel implementations; as Goldberg [27] observed:

> "In a world where serial algorithms are usually made parallel through countless tricks and contortions, it is no small irony that genetic algorithms (highly parallel algorithms) are made serial through equally unnatural tricks and turns."

This is an important direction which will be investigated in connection with the EP/N project. Note that parallel models can provide a natural embedding for other paradigms of evolutionary computation, like non random mating, some aspects of self-adaptation, and co-evolutionary systems. Also, apart from increased efficiency of the system, it would be possible to investigate various paradigms of parallel processing (e.g., island models, massively parallel model, or parallel hybrid GAs [42]) and various migration strategies.

5   Final Remarks

It is worthwhile to note that there are many other approaches to learning, optimization, and problem solving, which are based on other natural metaphors from nature — the best known examples include neural networks and simulated annealing. There is a growing interest in all these areas; the most fruitful and challenging direction seems to be a "recombination" of some ideas at present scattered in different fields.

Moreover, it seems that the whole field of artificial intelligence should lean towards evolutionary techniques; as Lawrence Fogel stated [24] in his plenary talk during the World Congress on Computational Intelligence (Orlando, 27 June – 2 July 1994):

> "If the aim is to generate artificial intelligence, that is, to solve new problems in new ways, then it is inappropriate to use any fixed set of rules. The rules required for solving each problem should simply evolve..."

References

1. Alander, J.T., *An Indexed Bibliography of Genetic Algorithms: Years 1957–1993*, Department of Information Technology and Production Economics, University of Vaasa, Finland, Report Series No.94-1, 1994.
2. Angeline, P.J., *Morphogenic Evolutionary Computation: Introduction, Issues, and Examples*, Proceedings of the 4th Annual Conference on Evolutionary Programming, (eds. J.R. McDonnell, R.G. Reynolds, and D.B. Fogel), MIT Press, Cambridge, MA, pp.387–401, 1995.
3. Arabas, J., Michalewicz, Z., and Mulawka, J., *GAVaPS — a Genetic Algorithm with Varying Population Size*, in [48].
4. Bäck, T., *Evolutionary Algorithms in Theory and Practice*, Oxford University Press, 1995.
5. Bäck, T., Fogel, D., and Michalewicz, Z. (Editors), *Handbook of Evolutionary Computation*, Oxford University Press, New York, 1996.
6. Beasley, D., Bull, D.R., and Martin, R.R., *An Overview of Genetic Algorithms: Part 1, Foundations*, University Computing, Vol.15, No.2, pp.58–69, 1993.
7. Beasley, D., Bull, D.R., and Martin, R.R., *An Overview of Genetic Algorithms: Part 2, Research Topics*, University Computing, Vol.15, No.4, pp.170–181, 1993.
8. Belew, R. and Booker, L. (Editors), Proceedings of the Fourth International Conference on Genetic Algorithms, Morgan Kaufmann Publishers, Los Altos, CA, 1991.
9. Davidor, Y., Schwefel, H.-P., and Männer, R. (Editors), Proceedings of the Third International Conference on Parallel Problem Solving from Nature (PPSN), Springer-Verlag, New York, 1994.
10. Davis, L., (Editor), *Genetic Algorithms and Simulated Annealing*, Morgan Kaufmann Publishers, Los Altos, CA, 1987.
11. Davis, L., *Adapting Operator Probabilities in Genetic Algorithms*, in [53], pp.61–69.
12. Davis, L. and Steenstrup, M., *Genetic Algorithms and Simulated Annealing: An Overview*, in [10], pp.1–11.
13. De Jong, K.A., (Editor), *Evolutionary Computation*, MIT Press, 1993.
14. De Jong, K., *Genetic Algorithms: A 25 Year Perspective*, in [69], pp.125–134.
15. Eiben, A.E., Raue, P.-E., and Ruttkay, Zs., *Genetic Algorithms with Multi-parent Recombination*, in [9], pp.78–87.
16. Eshelman, L.J., (Editor), Proceedings of the Sixth International Conference on Genetic Algorithms, Morgan Kaufmann, San Mateo, CA, 1995.
17. Eshelman, L.J. and Schaffer, J.D., *Preventing Premature Convergence in Genetic Algorithms by Preventing Incest*, in [8], pp.115–122.
18. Fogel, D.B. (Editor), IEEE Transactions on Neural Networks, special issue on Evolutionary Computation, Vol.5, No.1, 1994.
19. Fogel, D.B., *An Introduction to Simulated Evolutionary Optimization*, IEEE Transactions on Neural Networks, special issue on Evolutionary Computation, Vol.5, No.1, 1994.
20. Fogel, D.B., *Evolutionary Computation: Toward a New Philosophy of Machine Intelligence*, IEEE Press, Piscataway, NJ, 1995.
21. Fogel, D.B. and Atmar, W., *Proceedings of the First Annual Conference on Evolutionary Programming*, La Jolla, CA, 1992, Evolutionary Programming Society.
22. Fogel, D.B. and Atmar, W., *Proceedings of the Second Annual Conference on Evolutionary Programming*, La Jolla, CA, 1993, Evolutionary Programming Society.
23. Fogel, L.J., Owens, A.J., and Walsh, M.J., *Artificial Intelligence Through Simulated Evolution*, John Wiley, Chichester, UK, 1966.

24. Fogel, L.J., *Evolutionary Programming in Perspective: The Top-Down View*, in [69], pp.135–146.
25. Forrest, S. (Editor), Proceedings of the Fifth International Conference on Genetic Algorithms, Morgan Kaufmann Publishers, Los Altos, CA, 1993.
26. Glover, F., *Heuristics for Integer Programming Using Surrogate Constraints*, Decision Sciences, Vol.8, No.1, pp.156–166, 1977.
27. Goldberg, D.E., *Genetic Algorithms in Search, Optimization and Machine Learning*, Addison-Wesley, Reading, MA, 1989.
28. Goldberg, D.E., Deb, K., and Korb, B., *Do not Worry, Be Messy*, in [8], pp.24–30.
29. Goldberg, D.E., Milman, K., and Tidd, C., *Genetic Algorithms: A Bibliography*, IlliGAL Technical Report 92008, 1992.
30. Gorges-Schleuter, M., *ASPARAGOS An Asynchronous Parallel Genetic Optimization Strategy*, in [53], pp.422–427.
31. Grefenstette, J.J., (Editor), Proceedings of the First International Conference on Genetic Algorithms, Lawrence Erlbaum Associates, Hillsdale, NJ, 1985.
32. Grefenstette, J.J., (Editor), Proceedings of the Second International Conference on Genetic Algorithms, Lawrence Erlbaum Associates, Hillsdale, NJ, 1987.
33. Heitkötter, J., (Editor), *The Hitch-Hiker's Guide to Evolutionary Computation*, FAQ in comp.ai.genetic, issue 1.10, 20 December 1993.
34. Holland, J.H., *Adaptation in Natural and Artificial Systems*, University of Michigan Press, Ann Arbor, 1975.
35. Julstrom, B.A., *What Have You Done for Me Lately? Adapting Operator Probabilities in a Steady-State Genetic Algorithm*, in [16], pp.81–87.
36. Koza, J.R., *Genetic Programming*, MIT Press, Cambridge, MA, 1992.
37. Koza, J.R., *Genetic Programming – 2*, MIT Press, Cambridge, MA, 1994.
38. Latombe, J.C., *Robot Motion Planning*. Kluwer Academic Publishers, 1991.
39. Männer, R. and Manderick, B. (Editors), Proceedings of the Second International Conference on Parallel Problem Solving from Nature (PPSN), North-Holland, Elsevier Science Publishers, Amsterdam, 1992.
40. McDonnell, J.R., Reynolds, R.G., and Fogel, D.B. (Editors), Proceedings of the Fourth Annual Conference on Evolutionary Programming, The MIT Press, 1995.
41. Michalewicz, Z., *A Hierarchy of Evolution Programs: An Experimental Study*, Evolutionary Computation, Vol.1, No.1, 1993, pp.51–76.
42. Michalewicz, Z., *Genetic Algorithms + Data Structures = Evolution Programs*, Springer-Verlag, 3rd edition, 1996.
43. Michalewicz, Z. (Editor), Statistics & Computing, special issue on evolutionary computation, Vol.4, No.2, 1994.
44. Michalewicz, Z. and Xiao, J., *Evaluation of Paths in Evolutionary Planner/Navigator*, Proceedings of the 1995 International Workshop on Biologically Inspired Evolutionary Systems, Tokyo, Japan, May 30–31, 1995, pp.45–52.
45. Mühlenbein, H., *Parallel Genetic Algorithms, Population Genetics and Combinatorial Optimization*, in [53], pp.416-421.
46. Nissen, V., *Evolutionary Algorithms in Management Science: An Overview and List of References*, European Study Group for Evolutionary Economics, 1993.
47. Potter, M. and De Jong, K., *A Cooperative Coevolutionary Approach to Function Optimization*, George Mason University, 1994.
48. Proceedings of the First IEEE International Conference on Evolutionary Computation, Orlando, 26 June – 2 July, 1994.
49. Proceedings of the Second IEEE International Conference on Evolutionary Computation, Perth, 29 November – 1 December, 1995.

50. Proceedings of the Third IEEE International Conference on Evolutionary Computation, Nagoya, 20 – 22 May, 1996.
51. Ronald, E., *When Selection Meets Seduction*, in [16], pp.167–173.
52. Saravanan, N. and Fogel, D.B., *A Bibliography of Evolutionary Computation & Applications*, Department of Mechanical Engineering, Florida Atlantic University, Technical Report No. FAU-ME-93-100, 1993.
53. Schaffer, J., (Editor), Proceedings of the Third International Conference on Genetic Algorithms, Morgan Kaufmann Publishers, Los Altos, CA, 1989.
54. Schaffer, J.D. and Morishima, A., *An Adaptive Crossover Distribution Mechanism for Genetic Algorithms*, in [32], pp.36–40.
55. Schraudolph, N. and Belew, R., *Dynamic Parameter Encoding for Genetic Algorithms*, CSE Technical Report #CS90-175, University of San Diego, La Jolla, 1990.
56. Schwefel, H.-P., *On the Evolution of Evolutionary Computation*, in [69], pp.116–124.
57. Schwefel, H.-P., *Evolution and Optimum Seeking*, John Wiley, Chichester, UK, 1995.
58. Schwefel, H.-P. and Männer, R. (Editors), Proceedings of the First International Conference on Parallel Problem Solving from Nature (PPSN), Springer-Verlag, Lecture Notes in Computer Science, Vol.496, 1991.
59. Sebald, A.V. and Fogel, L.J., *Proceedings of the Third Annual Conference on Evolutionary Programming*, San Diego, CA, 1994, World Scientific.
60. Shaefer, C.G., *The ARGOT Strategy: Adaptive Representation Genetic Optimizer Technique*, in [32], pp.50–55.
61. Spears, W.M., *Adapting Crossover in Evolutionary Algorithms*, in [40], pp.367–384.
62. Srinivas, M. and Patnaik, L.M., *Adaptive Probabilities of Crossover and Mutation in Genetic Algorithms*, IEEE Transactions on Systems, Man, and Cybernetics, Vol.24, No.4, 1994, pp.17–26.
63. Whitley, D., *Genetic Algorithms: A Tutorial*, in [43], pp.65–85.
64. Whitley, D., *GENITOR II: A Distributed Genetic Algorithm*, Journal of Experimental and Theoretical Artificial Intelligence, Vol.2, pp.189–214.
65. Whitley, D. (Editor), *Foundations of Genetic Algorithms-2*, Second Workshop on the Foundations of Genetic Algorithms and Classifier Systems, Morgan Kaufmann Publishers, San Mateo, CA, 1993.
66. Xiao, J., *Evolutionary Planner/Navigator*, Handbook of Evolutionary Computation, Oxford University Press, 1996.
67. Xiao, J., Michalewicz, Z, and Zhang, L., *Operator Performance of Evolutionary Planner/Navigator*, Proceedings of the 3rd IEEE ICEC, Nagoya, 20–22 May 1996.
68. Yap, C.-K., "Algorithmic Motion Planning", *Advances in Robotics, Vol.1: Algorithmic and Geometric Aspects of Robotics*, J.T. Schwartz and C.-K. Yap Ed., Lawrence Erlbaum Associates, 1987, pp. 95-143.
69. Zurada, J., Marks, R., and Robinson, C. (Editors), *Computational Intelligence: Imitating Life*, IEEE Press, 1994.

Signed Formula Logic Programming: Operational Semantics and Applications (Extended Abstract)

Jacques Calmet[1], James J. Lu[2], Maria Rodriguez[2] and Joachim Schü[1]

[1] Department of Computer Science, Institute for Algorithms and Cognitive Systems,
University of Karlsruhe
{calmet,schue}@ira.uka.de
[2] Department of Computer Science, Bucknell University
{lu,rodriguz}@bucknell.edu

Abstract. Signed formula can be used to reason about a wide variety of multiple-valued logics. The formal theoretical foundation of logic programming based on signed formulas is developed in [14]. In this paper, the operational semantics of signed formula logic programming is investigated through constraint logic programming. Applications to bilattice logic programming and truth-maintenance are considered.

1 Introduction

The logic of signed formulas facilitates the examination of questions regarding multiple-valued logics through classical logic. As such, logic programming based on signed formulas also facilitates the analysis of multiple-valued logic programming systems through classical logic programming. The theoretical foundation and the applications of the logic of signed formulas have been investigated extensively [9, 10, 15, 17]. On the other hand, logic programming based on signed formulas — signed formula logic programming — is recently formalized in [14]. There, the semantical connections between a signed formula logic program and its associated underlying multiple-valued logic program are studied. In addition, the relationships between signed formula logic programming and the class of annotated logic programming [12] are established. It is shown that signed formula logic programming and annotated logic programming together provide a basis for reasoning with "inconsistent" multiple-valued logic programs.

This paper extends the work in [14] by considering first of all, the operational details of signed formula logic programming. It is demonstrated that a signed formula logic program may be formulated as an equivalent constraint logic program. From a practical stand point, this equivalence makes available to signed formula logic programming a wide variety of implementation techniques that have been developed for constraint logic programming. Moreover, the operational behavior of constraint logic programming sheds insights into the search space of signed resolution, which was a procedure proposed in [14] for processing queries with respect to signed formula logic programs. Secondly, in this paper we analyze two independent applications of signed formula logic programming: bilattice logic programming [5] and assumption based truth-maintenance [3]. The application to bilattice logic programming demonstrates how a signed formula logic program may be used to answer questions about an underlying multiple-valued logic program. On the other hand, the application to assumption based truth-maintenance provides a semantical characterization of the popular reasoning system through signed formula logic programming.

The organization of the paper is as follows. Section 2 summarizes the theoretical foundation of signed formula logic programming. Section 3 describes the semantical connection of signed formula logic programming and constraint logic programming. Section 4 investigates the applications of signed formula logic programming to bilattice logic programming (Section 4.1) and assumption based truth maintenance system (Section 4.2).

2 Signed Formula Logic Program

The basic building blocks of signed formulas are a multiple-valued logic Λ and its associated (finite) set of truth values Δ. A *sign* is an expression, which may contain variables, that denotes a non-empty subset of Δ.[3] Suppose S is a sign and $\mathcal{F}$ is a Λ-formula. Then $S : \mathcal{F}$ is a *signed atom*.[4] More complex formulas — *signed formulas* — may be constructed recursively using signed atoms and classical connectives by: $\neg \mathcal{F}$, $\mathcal{F}_1 \mid \mathcal{F}_2$, $\mathcal{F}_1 \& \mathcal{F}_2$, $\mathcal{F}_1 \leftarrow \mathcal{F}_2$, where $\mathcal{F}, \mathcal{F}_1, \mathcal{F}_2$ are signed formulas.[5] If $S : \mathcal{F}$ is a signed atom in which $\mathcal{F}$ contains no occurrences of Λ-connectives, then $S : \mathcal{F}$ is said to be Λ-atomic.

We are interested in signed clauses — signed formulas of the form

$$S_0 : A \leftarrow S_1 : \mathcal{F}_1 \& ... \& S_n : \mathcal{F}_n$$

where $S_0 : A$ is a Λ-atomic signed atom, and each $S_1 : \mathcal{F}_1, ..., S_n : \mathcal{F}_n$ is a signed atom. A finite set of signed clauses is called a *signed formula logic program* (SFLP). In a signed clause, the conjunction appearing on the right hand side of the $\leftarrow$ symbol is called the *body* of the clause, and the single signed atom to the left of the $\leftarrow$ is called the *head* of the clause. Variables that occur in the clause, whether they appear in formulas over Λ or in signs, are assume to stand for all possible ground instantiations, under the restriction that variables appearing in signs are substituted with subsets of Δ, and variables that appear in atoms are substituted with terms in Λ. A bodiless signed clause is sometimes called a *signed fact*, or a *signed unit clause*. A headless signed clause is a *signed query*.

Interpretations over the logic Λ map ground atoms to Δ, and are extended to Λ-formulas according to the meaning of the connectives that appear in the

---

[3] To simplify the presentation, we blur the distinction between the language from which such an expression is constructed, and the objects in Δ over which the symbols of this language is interpreted.

[4] Abstractly, formulas in Λ are constructed from atomic formulas and connectives of various arity. Suppose Θ is an n-ary connective, and $\mathcal{F}_1, ..., \mathcal{F}_n$ are Λ-formulas. Then the the expression $\Theta(\mathcal{F}_1, ..., \mathcal{F}_n)$ is also a Λ-formula.

[5] We use $\mid$ and $\&$ to denote classical or and and respectively. The symbols $\vee$ and $\wedge$ will be used in Section 4.1 to denote connectives in Λ.

formulas. Intuitively, a signed formula $S : \mathcal{F}$ may be thought of as representing the query: "Can $\mathcal{F}$ evaluate to some element in S?" [17].

Definition 1. (Satisfaction) A Λ-interpretation I *satisfies* a variable free signed atom $S{:}\mathcal{F}$ iff $I(\mathcal{F}) \in S$.[6] Satisfaction is extended to arbitrary signed formula in the usual way. A signed clause is satisfied by an interpretation I if each ground instance of the clause is satisfied by I. An SFLP P is satisfied by an interpretation I if each signed clause is satisfied by I; I is said to be a *model* of P. The collection of all models of P is denoted $\mathrm{Mod}(P)$.

An important property of classical logic programming is that a program P possesses an unique minimal model (with respect to an appropriate ordering). In the case of an SFLP, this property does not hold. For instance, using $\Delta = \{0, 0.2, 0.5, 0.8, 1\}$ as our truth values, if we have the program P that contains the single unit signed atom $\{0, 1\} : A \leftarrow$, then P has two models:

$$I_1(A) = 1$$
$$I_2(A) = 0$$

If we regard Δ as ordered according to the usual less than relation, then a reasonable choice for a minimal model is I_2 since $0 \leq 1$. However, as the truth value set Δ need not be equipped with any ordering, consequently if we treat the elements in Δ as being independent of one another, then I_1 and I_2 are incomparable models.

This leaves us with a rather undesirable situation. An SFLP may in general be *disjunctive*, and this complicates computational issues since it may be necessary to answer queries with respect to multiple models — a difficult problem well-known in the research on disjunctive logic programming. Fortunately we may obtain a good approximation to the models $\mathrm{Mod}(P)$ of an SFLP via an extension to the notion of interpretation. Intuitively, extended interpretations can be thought of as functions that measure the "indefiniteness" of each proposition in an SFLP.

Definition 2. (Extended Interpretation) An *extended interpretation* I of Λ is a mapping from ground atoms to subsets of Δ. It extends to arbitrary variable-free Λ-formulas as follows: Suppose Θ is an n-ary connective in Λ, and $\mathcal{F}_1, ..., \mathcal{F}_n$ are variable free Λ-formulas. Then

$$I(\Theta(\mathcal{F}_1, ..., \mathcal{F}_n)) = \{\Theta(\mu_1, ..., \mu_n) \mid \mu_i \in I(\mathcal{F}_i), \forall 1 \leq i \leq n\}$$

Definition 3. (Extended Satisfaction) Suppose I is an extended interpretation and suppose $S : \mathcal{F}$ is a variable free signed atom. I *e-satisfies* $S : \mathcal{F}$ if $I(\mathcal{F}) \subseteq S$. E-satisfaction for arbitrary signed formula is defined in the usual way. The collection of all extended interpretations that e-satisfy $S : \mathcal{F}$ is denoted $\mathrm{EMod}(S : \mathcal{F})$. An extended interpretation that e-satisfies an SFLP P is called an e-model of P, and the collection of all e-models is denoted $\mathrm{EMod}(P)$.

---

[6] This corresponds to the intuitive reading of $S : \mathcal{F}$ since I is a witness to the question "Can $\mathcal{F}$ evaluate to a value in S?"

For a given logic of signed formulas, the class of all extended interpretations forms a complete lattice under the ordering $\sqsubseteq$ given by:

$$I_1 \sqsubseteq I_2 \text{ iff } I_2(A) \subseteq I_1(A) \text{ for any ground atom } A.$$

Care must be taken to observe that the ordering $\sqsubseteq$ "reverses" the ordering $\subseteq$. This does not go against intuition. Since a sign S is interpreted disjunctively, i.e. can a formula evaluate to *one of* the values in S, the ordering $\sqsubseteq$ is, in some sense, modeling definiteness. In other words, an extended interpretation is more definite than another if the first assigns a smaller set of truth values to each formula.

Every SFLP P possesses an unique minimal extended interpretation under the ordering $\sqsubseteq$, denoted $\mathcal{E}_P$. Several equivalent characterizations of $\mathcal{E}_P$ can be given, including the usual fixed point construction of classical logic programming [13]. Details can be found in [14]. The next theorem provides the link between the Λ-models of P and its extended models.

Theorem 4. $\{I(A) \mid I \in Mod(P)\}$ *is an e-model of* P.

In general, an SFLP P may be translated into an equivalent Λ-atomic SFLP.

Theorem 5. *Suppose P is an SFLP. Then there is a Λ-atomic SFLP P' such that $Mod(P) = Mod(P')$.*

Typically, the Λ-atomic SFLP P' will contain many more clauses than P. However, processing queries with respect to Λ-atomic SFLPs are much easier since we may adapt query answering procedures for classical logic programming in a relatively straightforward manner. In the following sections, we restrict attention to Λ-atomic SFLPs.

3 Computing Signed Formula Logic Programs

A query processing procedure for SFLP was examined in [14]. The technique is adapted from signed resolution, as introduced in [1] and extended in [10] and [17]. Although the formalization of this query processing procedure for SFLP is theoretically straightforward, complex implementation issues arise due to the possibility that a signed atom resolved upon may remain in the resolvent. In light of this, we introduce a new method for computing SFLP based on constraint logic programming (CLP) techniques. Due to space limitation, we assume some familiarity with CLP, as described in [11]. Additional details can be found in the full version of this paper, obtainable as a technical report.

To simplify the presentation, we consider below only SFLPs whose Λ-formulas are propositional, but whose signs may still contain variables. This assumption is made for the sake of brevity. All of the ensuing discussion extends to non-ground SFLPs easily.

Definition 6. (Constraint Form) Given a Λ-atomic SFLP P, the *constraint form* of P is the CLP, denoted $CF(P)$, made up of the following three collections of non-ground CLP clauses.

1. $A(V) \leftarrow S \subseteq V \parallel B_1(S_1) \& \ldots \& B_n(S_n)$
   where the signed clause $S : A \leftarrow S_1 : B_1 \& \ldots \& S_n : B_n$ is in P.
2. $A(V) \leftarrow (V_1 \cap V_2) \subseteq V \parallel A(V_1) \& A(V_2)$
   where A is any atom that occurs in P.
3. $A(V) \leftarrow V = \Delta$
   where A is any atom that occurs in P.

The variables V, V_1 and V_2 range over non-empty subsets of Δ. The constraint form of a signed query $Q =\leftarrow S_1 : B_1 \& \ldots \& S_n : B_n$ is obtained as a special case of the first step above. That is, $CF(Q) =\leftarrow B_1(S_1) \& \ldots \& B_n(S_n)$.

The extended interpretations for P and the CLP-interpretations of $CF(P)$ naturally correspond, in the sense of satisfiability, via the following mapping ψ. For any ground atom A and variable free sign S:

$$A(S) \in \psi(I) \text{ iff } I(A) \subseteq S.$$

Hence if we have an SFLP written over the truth values $\Delta = \{0, 0.5, 1\}$, and I is the interpretation that maps A to $\{0.5\}$, then

$$\psi(I) = \{A(\{0.5\}), A(\{0, 0.5\}), A(\{1, 0.5\}), A(\{0, 0.5, I\})\}$$

The next theorem demonstrates that ψ is "meaning preserving".

Theorem 7. *I is an e-model of P iff $\psi(I)$ is a CLP model of $CF(P)$.*

Corollary 8. *$\psi(\mathcal{E}_P)$ coincides with the least CLP model of $CF(P)$.*

Theorem 9. (Soundness and Completeness) *Suppose P is an SFLP and $\leftarrow Q$ is a signed query. Then $P \models Q$ iff there is a CLP-deduction of the empty clause from the program $CF(P)$ beginning with the query $CF(Q)$.*

Two simple prototype interpreters have been implemented in the language C for experimentation. One is based on signed resolution, and the other is based on CLP. We are especially interested in comparing the structure of the search space induced by each of the query processing methods. A more detailed discussion of the relative search space can be found in the long version of the paper.

The idea for applying CLP to SFLP was based in part on the work of Frühwirth [6]. His method generated CLP-queries directly from the original program; the program is not first transformed into a CLP. In addition, only applications to annotated logic programming — a restricted form of SFLP — was considered. The basic idea of transforming a multiple-valued logic program into a constraint logic program was implemented in [2]. Some benchmarking results can be found there. However, the work again applies only to annotated logic programming.

4 Applications

4.1 Bilattice Logic Programming

This section applies SFLP to analyzing finitely valued bilattice logic programs [5]. We are interested in finding, for each bilattice logic program P, an SFLP $SFB(P)$ that can be used to answer questions of the form:

> Given a bilattice logic program P, a sign S and a atom A, can A evaluate to some value in S, under the intended meaning $\|P\|$ of P?

In bilattice logic programming, $\|P\|$ is typically associated with a single interpretation — though several acceptable choices exist. Hence formally, the relationship desired is

$$SFB(P) \models S : \mathcal{F} \text{ iff } \|P\|(\mathcal{F}) \in S.$$

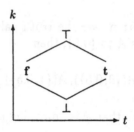

Fig. 1. The Bilattice FOUR.

A logic of bilattice Λ_B is a multiple-valued logic whose set of truth values Δ is a bilattice — a set equipped with two orderings, $\preceq_k$ and $\preceq_t$, each inducing a complete lattice on the elements in Δ. Δ contains four distinguished elements: $\perp$, $\top$, $\mathbf{f}$, and $\mathbf{t}$, which denote respectively the least and the greatest elements with respect to $\preceq_k$, and $\preceq_t$. FOUR shown in Figure 1 is thus the smallest non-trivial bilattice. The least upper bound and greatest lower bound operations with respect to the ordering $\preceq_k$ are denoted $\otimes$ and $\oplus$ respectively, while with respect to the ordering $\preceq_t$, they are denoted $\vee$ and $\wedge$ respectively. The symbol $\neg$ denotes negation, and satisfies the properties $a \preceq_k b \Rightarrow \neg a \preceq_k \neg b$ and $a \preceq_t b \Rightarrow \neg b \preceq_t \neg a$. Furthermore, Δ satisfies the *interlacing* condition, which says that each of the operations $\vee, \wedge$ is monotone with respect to the ordering $\preceq_k$, and similarly, each of the operations $\oplus, \otimes$ is monotone with respect to the ordering $\preceq_t$ [5].

There are a number of constants in the language of Λ_B. A *body formula* is built out of atomic formulas, constants, and the connectives $\neg$, $\vee$, $\wedge$, $\otimes$, and $\oplus$. A Λ_B-clause is an expression of the form $A \leftarrow \mathcal{F}$ where A is an atomic formula, and $\mathcal{F}$ is a body formula. A finite set of Λ_B-clauses is called a bilattice logic program.

A Λ_B-interpretation I assigns a value in Δ to each constant, each ground atom, and are extended to each body formula according to the functions represented by the operators $\neg$, $\vee$, $\wedge$, $\otimes$, and $\oplus$. It is assumed that all interpretations evaluate the constants in the same way, in particular *true* is a constant that evaluates to t, and *false* is a constant that evaluates to f under any Λ_B-interpretation.

As mentioned, several reasonable possibilities exist for the intended meaning of a bilattice logic program P. We focus on the one provided by the operator Φ_P, given by Fitting in [5], which maps from and to Λ_B-interpretations.

Given a Λ_B-interpretation I, $\Phi_P(I)$ is the Λ_B-interpretation that assigns to each atomic formula A, a truth value determined by the following.

$$\Phi_P(I)(A) = \bigvee \{I(\mathcal{F})|A \leftarrow \mathcal{F} \text{ a ground instance in } P\}$$

Φ_P is monotone with respect to $\preceq_k$, and it is monotone with respect to $\preceq_t$ provided that the symbol $\neg$ does not appear in P. In each case, the existence of the least fixed point of Φ_P is guaranteed by the Knaster-Tarski theorem on monotone operators over lattices. We denote $lfp_t(\Phi_P)$ the least fixed point of Φ_P under the $\preceq_t$ ordering.

The fixed point $lfp_t(\Phi_P)$ establishes $\|P\|$. It tells us that for each ground atom A, the truth value of A is *at least* $lfp_t(\Phi_P)(A)$, with respect to the ordering $\preceq_t$. To mimic this semantic using an SFLP, the signs that we choose must allow the iteration of the operator W to reflect $lfp_t(\Phi_P)$. It turns out that the signs of interest are of the form $\uparrow_t \mu = \{\beta \in \Delta | \mu \preceq_t \beta\}$.

Definition 10. *(SFB)* Let P be a bilattice logic program. $SFB(P)$ is the SFLP consisting of the following set of signed clauses.

$\{\uparrow_t t : A \leftarrow \ | A \leftarrow true \in P\} \cup$
$\{\uparrow_t f : A \leftarrow \ | A \leftarrow false \in P\} \cup$
$\{\uparrow_t V : A \leftarrow V : \mathcal{F} \ | A \leftarrow \mathcal{F} \in P \text{ where } \mathcal{F} \text{ is a complex body formula, and}$
$\qquad\qquad V \text{ is a variable that does not occur in the clause}\} \cup$
$\{\uparrow_t t : true \leftarrow, \uparrow_t f : false \leftarrow\}$

The last set in the above union ensures that the constants *true* and *false* are interpreted faithfully in $SFB(P)$.

Theorem 11. *Suppose P is a positive bilattice logic program. Then $lfp_t(\Phi_P)(A)$ evaluates to μ iff $lfp(W_{SFB(P)})$ e-satisfies the signed atom $\uparrow_t \mu : A$.*

$SFB(P)$ can now be used to answer questions about P under the meaning $\|P\|$. Given an atom A and a subset S of Δ, the question of whether A evaluates to S under the intended meaning of P can be expressed as a signed query $\leftarrow S : A$, and an answer may be obtained through procedures such as signed resolution or CLP resolution.

4.2 Assumption-Based Truth Maintenance

A lattice of truth values consisting of subsets of Δ, and whose ordering is the reverse subset ordering can be used to capture the *assumption-based* truth maintenance system described in [3]. The powerset $\mathcal{P}(\mathcal{A})$ of a propositional language $\mathcal{A}$ forms a complete lattice when ordered under the reverse subset ordering, denoted $\preceq$. The basic idea of coding the assumptions under which a proposition hold into its truth values was originally proposed by Ginsberg [8], but his work was carried out in the context of multiple-valued logic theorem proving.

Here, we provide a *semantical characterization* of assumption-based reason maintenance by means of signed formulas. In addition to gaining theoretical insights, since we have revealed that signed formula logic programs can be operationalized by means of constraint logic programs, a possible parallel implementation of an assumption-based reason maintenance system by means of concurrent constraint logic programming languages [18] will therefore be possible.

Informally *assumptions* are primitive data from which all other data can be derived through the use of *justifications*. A justification in the original ATMS is just a propositional Horn-clause without negation. A node consists of a datum, label and justifications. To illustrate the difference between a justification in the ATMS and a clause in the problem solver, consider the following example from DeKleer: the deduction of $Q(a)$ from $P(a)$ and $Q(X) \leftarrow P(X)$ is recorded as a *justification* $\gamma_{P(a)}, \gamma_{Q(X) \leftarrow P(X)} \Rightarrow \gamma_{Q(a)}$ where γ_{datum} refers to a datum in the truth maintenance system. An ATMS determines beliefs based on the justifications so far encountered *not with respect to the logic of the problem solver*. Therefore, the propositional symbols occurring within labels are uninterpreted symbols and justifications are material implications.

In our approach, the underlying logic of the problem solver does the bookkeeping performed by the reason maintenance system. Since the problem solver is a signed logic program, the inferences and data to be recorded by the reason maintenance are restricted. The problem solver datum is either derived, or it is a program clause. An *environment* is a set of given assumptions and a *label* is a set of environments. Formally, a label is a propositional formula in disjunctive normal form, and a datum holds in a given environment if it can be derived from the justifications and the environment. A *Nogood* is a minimal assumption set such that the assumptions contained within cannot be true together with respect to the set of justifications. An ATMS *context* is the set formed by the assumptions of a consistent environment combined with all nodes derivable from those assumptions.

One particular difference between our formulation and the original ATMS is that our semantics does not capture the removal of environments subsumed by Nogoods (labels of atoms with inconsistent truth values). In other words, the semantics of an SFLP is monotonic in contrast to the ATMS where just discovered Nogoods are to be removed. In our case, a Nogood is simply an empty clause with a nonempty sign.

The key idea in redefining assumption-based reason maintenance[7] as signed

---

[7] For historical reasons the term ATMS (assumption based truth maintenance) is sometimes used in this paper.

logic program is to write labels in the form of signs, i.e. define a suitable set of truth values Δ. In this sense our reason maintenance system departs from most other systems as it amalgamates the inference machine of the problem solver and the reason maintenance component. Following the argument of [16], a reason maintenance system itself should be able to detect inconsistencies and to compute automatically the dependencies of new beliefs from older ones instead of just recording them passively. Besides, the amount of time spent for communication between the problem-solver and the reason maintenance system is reduced since the dependency computation takes place without any extra costs during the inference process. As pointed out earlier, we may define Δ as $\mathcal{P}(\mathcal{A})$. Then an appropriate lattice function computing the *minimal label* from the sign of the body literals may be written in the heads of signed clauses. In the next example we show how the fixed point operator W_P computes the label of ground atoms. In this example, the function $f_n : \mathcal{P}(\mathcal{A})^n \mapsto \mathcal{P}(\mathcal{A})$ is defined as

$$f_n(E_1, \ldots, E_n) = \bigcup_{L \in (E_1 \times \ldots \times E_n)} \bigcup_{i=1}^{n} L \downarrow i$$

where $E_i \in \mathcal{P}(\mathcal{A})$ for each $1 \leq i \leq n$, and $L \downarrow i$ denotes the i-th component of L. Let us consider a MVL Λ over $\Delta = \mathcal{P}(\{A, B, C, D, E\})$ and the following SFLP.

$$f_2(V, W) : p \leftarrow V : q, W : r$$
$$\{\{A, B\}, \{B, C, D\}\} : q \leftarrow$$
$$\{\{A, C\}, \{D, E\}\} : r \leftarrow$$

Then, the label of p is computed as follows. The cartesian product $V \times W$ is the following set.

$$V \times W = \{(\{A, B\}, \{A, C\}), (\{A, B\}, \{D, E\}),$$
$$(\{B, C, D\}, \{A, C\}), (\{B, C, D\}, \{D, E\})\}$$

Then the collection of $l_1 \cup l_2$ for each pair (l_1, l_2) in $V \times W$ is the set

$$\{\{A, B, C\}, \{A, B, D, E\}, \{A, B, C, D\}, \{B, C, D, E\}\}$$

This set is the result of $f_2(V, W)$. It is also the truth value assigned to p by $W_P^{\Uparrow \omega}$.

In order to characterize different reason maintenance systems semantically, a similar line of research has been pursued by Fehrer [4] who elaborated independently on a closely related idea. His work focuses on Gabbay's labeled deductive system [7] which is a much more elaborate framework than signed formulas that can be used for general theorem proving in different kinds of logics.

Acknowledgements: Reiner Hähnle's provided numerous useful comments on a preliminary draft of this paper. This material is based upon work supported by the NSF under Grant CCR9225037.

References

1. M. Baaz and C. G. Fermüller. Resolution for many-valued logics. In A. Voronkov, editor, *Proceedings of Conference Logic Programming and Automated Reasoning*, pages 107–118. Springer-Verlag, 1992.

2. D. Debertin. Parallel inference algorithms for distributed knowledge bases (in German). Master's thesis, Institute for Algorithms and Cognitve Systems, University of Karlsruhe, 1994.

3. J. DeKleer. An assumption-based TMS. *Artificial Intelligence*, 28:127–162, 1986.

4. D. Fehrer. A Unifying Framework for Reason Maintenance. In Michael Clarke, Rudolf Kruse, and Serafín Moral, editors, *Symbolic and Quantitative Approaches to Reasoning and Uncertaint y, Proceedings of ECSQARU '93, Granada, Spain, Nov. 1993*, volume 747 of *Lecture Notes in Computer Science*, pages 113–120, Berlin, Heidelberg, 1993. Springer.

5. M. Fitting. Bilattices and the semantics of logic programming. *Journal of Logic Programming*, 11:91–116, 1991.

6. T. Frühwirth. Annotated constraint logic programming applied to temporal reasoning. In *Proceedings of the Symposium on Programming Language Implementation and Logic Programming*, pages 230–243. Springer-Verlag, 1994.

7. Dov M. Gabbay. LDS- labelled deductive systems. Preprint, Dept. of Computing, Imperial College, London, September 1989.

8. M.L. Ginsberg. Multivalued logics: A uniform approach to inference in artificial intelligence. *Computational Intelligence*, 4(3):265–316, 1988.

9. R. Hähnle. Uniform notation of tableau rules for multiple-valued logics. In *Proceedings of the International Symposium on Multiple-Valued Logic*, pages 26–29. Computer Society Press, 1991.

10. R. Hähnle. Short normal forms for arbitrary finitely-valued logics. In *Proceedings of International Symposium on Methodologies for Intelligent Systems*, pages 49–58. Springer-Verlag, 1993.

11. J. Jaffar and J-L. Lassez. Constraint logic programming. In *Proceedings of the 14th ACM Symposium on Principles of Programming Languages*, pages 111–119. ACM Press, 1987.

12. M. Kifer and V.S. Subrahmanian. Theory of generalized annotated logic programming and its applications. *Journal of Logic Programming*, 12:335–367, 1992.

13. J.W. Lloyd. *Foundations of Logic Programming*. Springer-Verlag, 2 edition, 1988.

14. J.J. Lu. Logic Programming with Signs and Annotations. *Journal of Logic and Computation*. to appear.

15. J.J. Lu, N.V. Murray, and E. Rosenthal. Signed formulas and fuzzy operator logics. In *Proceedings of the International Symposium on Methodologies for Intelligent Systems*. Springer-Verlag, 1994.

16. J.P. Martins and S.C. Shapiro. A model for belief revision. *Artificial Intelligence*, 35:25–79, 1988.

17. N.V. Murray and E. Rosenthal. Adapting classical inference techniques to multiple-valued logics using signed formulas. *Fundamenta Informatica*, 21:237–253, 1994.

18. V. Saraswat. *Concurrent Constraint Programming*. PhD thesis, Carnegie-Mellon, 1991.

Automating Proofs of Integrity Constraints in Situation Calculus

Leopoldo Bertossi, Javier Pinto, Pablo Saez[1],
Deepak Kapur and Mahadevan Subramaniam[2]

Abstract. Automated support for proving integrity constraints (ICs) on deductive database update specifications is developed using an induction theorem prover, *Rewrite Rule Laboratory* (*RRL*) [6]. The approach proposed by Reiter [9, 11, 10] for solving the frame problem for such applications in a language of the situation calculus is used as a basic framework. Integrity constraints are propositions that are expected to be true in every accessible state of a database, and they should be provable from the specification of the evolution of the database. Accessible states are defined by induction [12] as those reachable from the initial state by update actions whose execution is possible. Induction theorem provers can only reason about quantifier-free formulas (i.e., universally quantified formulas) whereas in order to express integrity constraints, quantifiers may be used. It is shown that by making use of the fact that in relational data base applications, domain of objects under consideration is finite, such ICs expressed using quantifiers can be mechanically translated into quantifier-free formulas by introducing new predicates and by explicitly building domains of objects involved in updates. Bridge lemmas connecting the semantics of the new predicates to the fluents used to express integrity constraints can be mechanically generated and automatically proved in *RRL*. An interesting feature of the proposed approach is that mechanically generated proofs of integrity constraints have a structure similar to manually-generated proofs.

1 Introduction

In [9], Reiter proposed a solution to the frame problem in theories of action and change written in the situation calculus [7]. In [11], he applied this solution to specifications of deductive databases. In [12], he discussed an application of this approach for proving integrity constraints in deductive data bases. The importance of doing proofs by mathematical induction is clearly evident in these papers. In this paper, we show how such proofs can be mechanized using an induction theorem prover. We report our experience in using *Rewrite Rule Laboratory* (*RRL*), a theorem prover based on rewrite techniques [6].

Specification of theories of action include sentences expressing changes introduced when actions are performed. In most cases, it is desirable to omit the sentences that describe the properties of the world that remain unchanged if an action gets executed. From a logical viewpoint, non-change must be derivable from the logical specification. The problem of inferring non-change from a logical specification of theories of action is referred to as the *frame problem* and has received a great deal of attention in the knowledge representation community.

[1] Pontificia Universidad Católica de Chile, Departamento de Ciencia de la Computación, Santiago 22, Chile. E-mail: {bertossi, jpinto, pdsaez}@ing.puc.cl.
[2] Department of Computer Science, State University of New York at Albany, Albany, NY 12222. E-mail: {kapur, subu}@cs.albany.edu.

Reiter's partial solution to the frame problem (only deterministic actions and no explicit ramifications) [9] transforms preliminary specifications about evolving worlds into monotonic specifications. Roughly speaking, one starts from a preliminary specification that includes a description of the world (from the viewpoint of the database) along with a description of the possible transactions that can be performed. Preliminary specifications embody implicit common-sense assumptions about the possible explanations for changes in truth values of *fluents*, properties that may change as the result of actions performed. The specification of the transactions/actions includes details regarding their preconditions and their effects on the world. The transformed, final, specification contains everything included in the preliminary specification, except for the effect axioms that are replaced by successor state axioms for each fluent. An effect axiom fully specifies when the fluent is true in a successor state obtained by executing an arbitrary possible action. The final specification includes unique name axioms for actions and states.

In addition to the specification, a set of *integrity constraints*, (ICs), are given. They describe certain conditions that the database must always satisfy. An important goal is to ensure that starting from an initial state, and after a sequence of transactions possible on a data base, the integrity constraints are satisfied by the resulting state of the data base. In [12], Reiter showed how such proofs could be manually done using his proposal to solve the frame problem.

Traditional database management systems do not provide facilities for proving that the integrity of the database cannot be violated as a result of performing transactions. Rather, these systems provide facilities for testing the integrity of the database whenever a transaction takes place. There is no guarantee that integrity constraints can never be violated. Testing of only very primitive ICs is supported.

This work forms part of a research being conducted at the Catholic University in Chile, where an automated system called *SCDBR* to reason from and about database specifications is being built [1].

2   A Library Example

In this section we present partial aspects of an example of a library database. The example is very simplified in order to keep the paper succinct. The logical specification of the initial database, the transactions and their effects is given in a situation calculus language, with an additional second-order axiom that inductively defines an *accessibility relation* between situations. This specification is given in the form proposed by Reiter [11].

Fluents are used to model the dynamic properties of a domain. In this example, we consider a single fluent *classified*. Every book in the database is classified with its *ISBN* number and a unique *id*. Two books with the same *ISBN* denote copies of the same book and should have different *id* numbers. The fluent is modeled by a ternary predicate *classified* that takes an isbn, an id and a situation as arguments. $classified(Isbn, Id, S)$ is true if in situation S, the book with id Id is classified with isbn $Isbn$. In a realistic example a number of other fluents such as $Stock$, $LostBook$, $SoldOut$ etc., could be included to model properties of the domain. In addition to fluents, a situation calculus theory may also include static properties, i.e., properties that don't have a situation argument (e.g., the authorship of a book). Our example does not include such properties.

To specify transactions, we need to state: 1) when they are possible, and 2) what changes they provoke. The first is done with *action preconditions* while the second is specified with *successor state axioms*.

Action Preconditions. Action preconditions are formulas that specify the conditions on the state of a data base that have to be met for actions to be executable. For the example, we only consider the actions *classifybook* and *deleteBook*.

We consider that the transaction *deleteBook* is always possible and that the transaction *classifyBook* is possible if no book is classified with the same id:

$$poss(deleteBook(id), s) \equiv true, \tag{1}$$

$$poss(classifyBook(isbn, id), s) \equiv \neg \, \exists isbn' \; classified(isbn', id, s). \tag{2}$$

Successor State Axioms. Successor state axioms provide necessary and sufficient conditions for a fluent to hold after performing an action. For these conditions to be valid, the action's preconditions must be satisfied. In general, these axioms take the form $poss(a, s) \supset f(do(a, s)) \equiv \phi_f^+(a, s) \vee (f(s) \wedge \neg\phi_f^-(a, s))$. Thus, a fluent f holds after performing a possible action a if it held before the action was performed and the action did not falsify f $(\neg\phi_f^-)$ or the fluent was made true by a (ϕ_f^+) [10, 11, 12]. There will be one such axiom per fluent predicate. For instance, for *classified* we have:

$$poss(a, s) \supset classified(isbn, id, do(a, s)) \equiv (a = classifyBook(isbn, id) \vee$$
$$(classified(isbn, id, s) \wedge a \neq deleteBook(id))).$$

Integrity Constraints: Aside from the specifications given above, in general a set of integrity constraints is included in a database specification. These constraints specify conditions that must be met in all valid states of the database. In the example, we use the constraint below, which states that for any situation s, any two books with same identification number have identical ISBN numbers.

$$classified(isbn1, id, s) \wedge classified(isbn2, id, s) \supset isbn1 = isbn2. \tag{3}$$

ICs are specified to hold for the initial state of the database. Then, they must be shown to hold in all states of the database that are accessible from the initial state by means of a finite sequence of actions.

2.1 A Typical Hand Proof of an Integrity Constraint

The initial state of the database is identified with the situation constant S_0. The actions *classifyBook* and *deleteBook* – which classify and delete books, respectively – permit one to reach new states starting from other states. It is assumed that a *deleteBook* action is always possible (1). A *classifyBook* action with an identification number id and an ISBN number $isbn$ is possible in a state s only if there does not exist any classified book in the database with which id is associated (2). We briefly review a proof of the integrity constraint stating that the fluent *classified* is functional (3).

1. It seems quite natural to attempt a proof by induction on states. The basis case is obtained by directly replacing s with S_0 in (3). The resulting sentence would typically follow from the definition of predicate *classified* in S_0, ensuring that IC holds in the initial state S_0.

2. The induction step case involves exhibiting that if IC holds in a state s, then it also holds in $do(a, s)$ obtained by performing any action a that is possible in s. The conclusion is (4) and the inductive hypothesis is (5):
$$classified(isbn1, id, do(a, s)) \wedge classified(isbn2, id, do(a, s))) \supset (isbn1 = isbn2). \tag{4}$$
$$classified(isbn1, id, s) \wedge classified(isbn2, id, s)) \supset (isbn1 = isbn2). \tag{5}$$

3. This can be shown by case analysis on the different types of actions (which is induction on a finite domain). Let us consider the case $a = classifyBook(isbn', id')$. By the successor state axiom of the fluent *classified*, $classified(isbn1, id, do(a, s))$ is equivalent to

$(a = classifyBook(isbn1, id)) \lor (classified(isbn1, id, s) \land a \neq deleteBook(id))$.

For the case when $a = classifyBook(isbn', id')$, this simplifies to:
$$(isbn' = isbn1 \land id' = id) \lor classified(isbn1, id, s),$$
since *classifyBook* is a free constructor. Similarly, *classified(isbn2, id, do(a, s))* is equivalent to
$$(isbn' = isbn2 \land id' = id) \lor classified(isbn2, id, s).$$
Each of the four possible combinations of the above literals leads to $isbn1 = isbn2$: *a)* if $isbn' = isbn1 \land isbn' = isbn2$, then $isbn1 = isbn2$, *b)* if $classified(isbn1, id, s)$ and $classified(isbn2, id, s)$ are true, then $isbn1 = isbn2$ by induction hypothesis. *c)* the remaining two combinations lead to contradictory assumptions and $isbn1 = isbn2$ is vacuously true.

4. The induction step corresponding to the case $a = deleteBook(id')$ can be established in a similar manner.

3 Formalizing Situation Calculus in *RRL*

A main concept in situation calculus is that of *situations* or *states* of the evolving world. Starting with an initial state, actions possible in a current state are executed to get new states. This can be modeled as a data type, which we call `state`. It has two constructor functions: (i) the constant constructor `s0` (corresponding to the initial state `s0` of the situation calculus), and (ii) a constructor `do` which given an action and a state, gives the resulting state after the action assuming that its execution is possible. The constructor `do` is a function from `act` and `state` to `state`, where `act` is a data type modeling actions.

`do` is a partial constructor; its value is undefined if a particular action is not possible in a given state. Such partial constructors cannot be modeled directly[3]. Instead, this is done in two parts: (i) define `do` as a total constructor, and then (ii) define a predicate `reach` to identify the subset of states *reachable* by executing actions possible in other reachable states. The predicate `reach` on states is recursively defined: the initial state `s0` is reachable; `do(a,s)` is reachable if `s` is reachable and action `a` is possible in `s`, i.e., `poss(a,s)` holds.

Reiter assumed that in the situation calculus, different actions executed in a particular state lead to different states, and that if two actions lead to the same state, then the actions must be the same; also, no action can lead to the initial state. This can be specified by declaring the constructors `s0` and `do` as *free*, much like the `successor` for natural numbers and `cons` for lists.

In Reiter's specifications, the definition of the `reach` predicate needs an induction axiom. Such use of induction is implicit in the specification of `state` when it is stated that `state` has `s0` and `do` as its free constructors.

The data type `act` is specified by introducing a constructor for each action type. For example, the action type `classifyBook` is specified as a constructor with `isbn` and `id` as arguments, and produces a value, which is the action corresponding to that `isbn` and `id` numbers. Other actions are similarly specified. The constructors of `act` are free since actions are assumed to be distinct.

In order to specify the preconditions on actions, the predicate `poss` is specified; it takes an action and a state as arguments and decides whether the action can be executed in the state. See below how the preconditions for `deleteBook` and `classifyBook` action types are expressed.

---

[3] See [5] for a method to extend algebraic axiomatizations to specify partial constructors.

Fluents are specified as predicates. For example, the fluent `classified` is recursively defined below by specifying the effect of actions on it. In the initial state, the table for the fluent `classified` is given as a boolean expression. In this example, for simplicity, we have used a very short table for `classified`, which is specified to be true only if the isbn number is i1 in which case ids can be i2 or i3, or if the isbn number is i4 with the id to be i5. How an action affects `classified` is expressed in the second conditional equation given below. Effects of actions on other fluents can be defined in a similar way. A part of the equational specification of the library example as input into *RRL* is given below.

```
reach(s0)                            := true,
reach(do(xa, xs))                    := reach(xs) and poss(xa, xs).
poss(deletebook(xid), xs)            := true,
poss(classifyBook(xisbn, xid), xs)   := ball(xid, xs, dom(xs)).
classified(xisbn, xid, s0)           := cond(xisbn = i1 and xid = i2,
  true, cond(xisbn = i1 and xid = i3, true, xisbn = i4 and xid = i5)),
classified(xisbn, xid, do(xa, xs))   := cond(xa = classifyBook(xisbn, xid),
  true, cond(xa = deleteBook(id), false, classified(xisbn, xid, xs)))
```

It should be evident to the reader that except for the equation for the possibility axiom for `classifyBook`, it is quite straight-forward to generate the above quantifier-free equational axiomatization from Reiter-style specification. Such possibility axioms involving quantifiers are discussed in the next subsection. The translation of the successor state axiom for the fluent `classified` turned out to be straightforward because it is quantifier-free. For certain fluents, the action specifications in the successor state axiom may involve quantifiers. In such cases, translating successor state axioms directly as shown above can lead to equations with extra variables on their right-hand sides. These equations cannot be oriented into rewrite rules by *RRL*. This can be avoided by explicitly instantiating the action a in the left side of successor state axiom of the fluent with every action type and then performing the translation.

Bounded quantification Preconditions for the actions as well as successor state axioms for fluents could be arbitrary first-order formulas. For instance, in the library example, the precondition for $classifyBook$ is equivalent to:

$$poss(classifyBook(xisbn, xid), xs) \equiv (\forall\ xisbn1)\ \neg classified(xisbn1, xid, xs).$$

For automation, it becomes necessary to eliminate such quantifiers so that explicit instantiation of quantified variables can be done automatically.

In relational database applications, there are usually a finite number of objects that satisfy a fluent. Further, an action can only introduce finitely many objects. The domain of objects associated with a given state is finite. Using this observation, it is possible to replace arbitrary quantification by *bounded* quantification. A new function called `dom` is introduced on states; `dom(s)` stands for the finite set of objects possibly existing in the state s. Quantification in state s is then reduced to that over `dom(s)`, and fluents are evaluated relative to `dom(s)`. We thus replace quantifiers by bounded quantifiers and introduce range of the variables to be `dom(s)`. The domain `dom(s)` is constructed by collecting the objects in the initial state and those *mentioned* in any sequence of actions leading to the state s from the initial state s0. This view of databases was proposed by Reiter in [8].

For the library example, the domain construction can be expressed as:

$$\mathrm{dom(s0)} := c(a(i1), c(b(i2), c(b(i3), c(a(i4), c(b(i5), nothing)))))$$

$$\mathrm{dom(do(classifybook(xisbn, xid), xs))} := c(a(xisbn), c(b(xid), dom(xs)))$$

$$\mathrm{dom(do(deletebook(xid), xs))} := c(b(xid), dom(xs)).$$

For every action, the domain constructor is used to introduce into the domain, the arguments passed to the action. The set nothing stands for the empty domain. A constructor c is used to add a new object to a domain. The function symbols a and b coerce isbn and id types to uniformly typed objects in the list.

Bounded quantifiers are simulated using new predicates defined in terms of fluents. A bounded quantifier predicate must be introduced for each formula on which the bounded quantifier acts. For a bounded universal (for all) quantifier on a formula f, we introduce a new predicate ball_f (ball_f stands for bounded for all over f); similarly, for a bounded existential (there exists) quantifier on f, a new predicate bexists_f is introduced. Since bexists_f can be expressed as ¬ ball_f ¬, we discuss how a bounded universal quantifier can be eliminated. The new predicate ball_f is of arity k if f has k free variables, say $x_1, \cdots x_k$ (we are assuming that the current state variable appears free in f; if not, then the arity of ball_f is $k+1$ to include a state variable also). The predicate ball_f$(x_1, \cdots, x_k,$ dom(xs)) will not have the quantified variable as its argument; instead, dom(xs), the domain of the current state variable xs, is an argument to ball_f.

Given a formula with quantifiers, say $\forall x$ f, we define ball_f. If f is quantifier-free, then ball_f is expressed using f; otherwise if f is a formula with a quantifier, say $\exists y$ g, this procedure is recursively applied by introducing a predicate bexists_g, and so on. This translation can be mechanically done.

The definition of new predicates can be mechanically generated by induction on the domain. For the empty domain nothing, ball_f is true (bexists_f will be false on nothing domain). For each type of object possibly introduced by an action, simulated by the application of the domain constructor c on a given domain xdom, ball_f on the extended domain is the same as ball_f on the given domain if the quantification is not on that type of variable; otherwise, it is the conjunction of ball_f on the given domain and f applied on the object introduced by c (in the case of bexists_f, it will be a disjunction).

To translate the possibility axiom for classifyBook, the new predicate introduced is ball_classified, abbreviated as just ball. Its arguments are xid, xs, dom(xs) since xid, xs are the free variables of the possibility axiom of classifyBook; the quantified variable xisbn is replaced by dom(xs). The equation (4) is thus replaced by poss(classifyBook(xisbn, xid), xs) := ball(xid, xs, dom(xs)). The definition of ball is:

$$\mathrm{ball(xid, xs, c(a(xisbn), xdom))} := ball(xid, xs, xdom) \wedge \neg classified(xisbn, xid, xs),$$

$$\mathrm{ball(xid, xs, c(b(xid1), xdom))} := ball(xid, xs, xdom),$$

$$\mathrm{ball(xid, xs, nothing)} := true.$$

It can be easily verified that the above equations ensure that for each *isbn* in the domain corresponding to a state s, the book with identification number xid is not *classified* in the state s.

In order to connect the semantics of the new predicates to the fluents, some intermediate lemmas (which we call *bridge lemmas*) must be proved. For a bounded universal predicate ball_f, a typical lemma needed is: $f(x_1, \cdots x_k) = true \ if \ ball\_f(x_1, \cdots, x_k, dom(xs)).$

Recall that the predicate ball_f is of arity k and the quantified variable is not one of its arguments. The bridge lemmas for a bounded existential predicate bexists_f is similarly constructed. Bridge lemma for the predicate ball is,

classified(xisbn, xid, xs) = false if ball(xid, xs, dom(xs)).

In general, a lemma for each new predicate may be needed. It is possible to reduce the number of new predicates to be introduced by considering blocks of universal quantifiers (as well as blocks of existential quantifiers) together.

In [4], Boyer and Moore developed a logic of bounded quantifiers. The above method for handling bounded quantifiers is closely related to their work.

4 Proving Integrity Constraints in *RRL*

Reasoning about integrity constraints typically involves proving properties by induction over the set of reachable states and the set of possible actions as illustrated in section 2.1. Induction is mechanized in *RRL* using the the *cover set* method proposed in [15] (see [6] for further details).

For doing proofs by induction, *RRL* orients definitions and lemmas into terminating rewrite rules using the algorithms implemented in *RRL* for orienting equations into terminating rewrite rules. The main inference method is that of *contextual rewriting* an equation or a conditional equation by terminating rewrite rules under assumptions, called *context*. Decision procedures for equality on ground terms, propositional calculus and linear arithmetic (quantifier-free theory of natural numbers) are automatically invoked while performing contextual rewriting. In addition, case analysis is performed.

In the cover set method, given a complete definition of a function symbol f on a data structure as a finite set of terminating rewrite rules, in which the left-hand side of each rule is of the form $f(t_1, \ldots, t_k)$, the definition is used to generate an induction scheme on the data structure. The left-hand sides of the defining rules are used to generate all the subgoals of a conjecture to be proved, and the recursive calls to f on the right-hand sides of the rules are used to generate induction hypotheses.

4.1 An Automatically Generated Proof in *RRL*

The integrity constraint *IC* stating that the fluent *classified* is functional can be formulated in *RRL* as:

    (xisbn1 = xisbn2) if classified(xisbn1, xid, xs) and
        classified(xisbn2, xid, xs) and reach(xs).

The above formula was attempted in *RRL* by induction. There are three possible candidate induction schemes corresponding to the subterms classified(xisbn1, xid, xs), classified(xisbn2, xid, xs) and reach(xs) in the conjecture, based on the cover sets generated from the definitions of the predicates *classified* and *reach*, respectively. The schemes suggested by the first two of these terms are identical since the only argument being recursed in both cases is xs. These schemes *subsume* the scheme obtained from the subterm reach(xs) since the induction cases of the latter scheme are refined by those of the former. The most appropriate induction scheme is therefore the scheme suggested by either of the *classified* predicates in the above formula.

These analyses and heuristics are built into *RRL* and are performed automatically without any user guidance. Here is a part of the *RRL* transcript.

```
Let P(XS): XISBN1 == XISBN2 if REACH(XS) and CLASSIFIED(XISBN1,XID,XS)
   and CLASSIFIED(XISBN2,XID,XS)
```

Induction will be done on XS in CLASSIFIED(XISBN1, XID, XS), by scheme:
[1] P(SO)   [2] P(DO(CLASSIFYBOOK(XISBN1, XID1), XS)) if {P(XS)}
[3] P(DO(DELETEBOOK(XID1), XS)) if {P(XS)}

Subgoal [1] corresponds to the base case and follows trivially by case analysis using the definition of the fluent *classified*. Subgoal [2] corresponds to an induction step and establishes that the *IC* holds in a successor state obtained by a *classifybook* action if the *IC* holds in the previous state.

The induction conclusion and the hypothesis are both clauses of four literals each. The combination of the conclusion with each of the literals of the hypothesis leads to four subgoals. Two of these subgoals trivially reduce to true because of contradictory assumptions.

The remaining two subgoals are more complex and use the following intermediate lemma for proofs:

L1 : classified(xisbn, xid, xs) == false if ball(xid, xs, dom(xs)).

The reader may recall that the above is a bridge lemma, connecting the meaning of the new predicate ball introduced to eliminate the universal quantifier in the possibility axiom of classifyBook. This lemma can be used as a rewrite rule to eliminate the occurrence of ball and replace it by classified. In the first subgoal, the assumption classified(xisbn11, xid, do(classifybook(xisbn1, xid1), xs)) along with the assumption (not(classified(xisbn11, xid, xs))) by the definition of classified implies that xisbn1 = xisbn11 and xid = xid1.

Similarly, the assumption classified(xisbn2, xid, do(classifybook(xisbn1, xid1), xs)) leads to two cases on simplification using the definition of classified. In the first case, xisbn2 = xisbn1 and therefore, xisbn11 = xisbn2 as desired. Otherwise, the literal classified(xisbn2, xid, xs) is true. This is contradictory to the assumption reach(do(classifybook(xisbn1, xid1), xs)) that simplifies by the definition of the *reach* and *poss* to ball(xid1, xs, doms(xs)) which by the lemma L1 implies that not(classified(xisbn2, xid, xs)) since xid1 = xid.

The second subgoal is symmetric to the first subgoal, and is established in a similar fashion.

The subgoal [3], corresponds to an induction step that establishes the *IC* in a successor state obtained by a *deletebook* action from the *IC* in the previous state. The proof generated in *RRL* is similar to that of the subgoal [2] leading to four intermediate subgoals.

Comparing hand proof with an automatically generated proof : The reader would recall that the hand proof of the integrity constraint *IC* given in subsection 2.1 proceeds by induction on states. The basis case (step 1 of the hand proof) establishes the *IC* over the initial state S_0. For the induction step case (step 2 of the hand proof), case analysis on the actions is performed leading to two subgoals (steps 3 and 4 of the hand proof).

In the automated proof, the cover set method chooses the induction scheme based on the definition of classified as the most appropriate scheme. This scheme combines the two inductions (induction over reachable states and case analysis over possible actions performed one after another in the hand proof) into a single induction since the definition of the fluent classified is generated from its successor state axiom. The subgoal [1] in the automated proof corresponds to the step 1 of the hand proof, and the subgoals [2] and [3] correspond to the steps 3 and 4 of the hand proof respectively. The machine proof generated by *RRL* thus has the same top-level structure as the hand proof.

The subgoal [1] is established in *RRL* by case analysis on the definition of the fluent *classified* which ensures that *IC* holds at the initial state S_0 as assumed in the step 1 of the hand proof. The four intermediate subgoals generated from the subgoal [2] are essentially the same as the four cases described in the steps $3(a)$-(c) of the hand proof.

In step $3(c)$ of the hand proof, the combinations imply that $\neg \exists$ *isbn' classified(isbn', id, s)*, and *classified(isbn2, id, s)*, a contradiction. In the automated proof, this contradiction is obtained in the subgoals by using the bridge lemma *L*1 that relates the *ball* and the *classified* predicates.

Proving the intermediate lemma: Bridge lemma *L*1 is crucial in the proof of the *IC* above. Recall that *ball(xid, xs, dom(xs))* represents $\forall$ *xisbn* $\neg$ *classified(xisbn, xid, xs)*. This lemma is similar to the logical axiom for universal quantifiers in Hilbert style deductive systems for first order logic: $(\forall x)\phi(x) \supset \phi(y)$. As stated earlier, such bridge lemmas can be easily generated from the definitions of new predicates introduced to eliminate bounded quantifiers. So a user does not have to explicitly specify them. The proof of *L*1 is done by induction in *RRL*. The subterm classified(xisbn, xid, xs) suggests an induction scheme based on the cover set from classified. Here is a part of the *RRL* transcript.

```
Let P(XS): CLASSIFIED(XISBN, XID, XS) == FALSE if BALL(XID, XS, DOM(XS))
Induction will be done on XS in DOM(XS), by scheme:
[1] P(S0)                [2] P(DO(CLASSIFYBOOK(XISBN,XID),XS)) if {P(XS)}
[3] P(DO(DELETEBOOK(XID), XS)) if {P(XS)}
```

The basis case [1] trivially follows from case-analysis on definition of classified. The subgoal [2] is split by *RRL* into two subgoals based on the combination of the clauses as described earlier. One of these subgoals follows by simplification from the definitions of classified, ball and dom. The other subgoal,

```
[2.1] not(CLASSIFIED(XISBN1, XID1, DO(CLASSIFYBOOK(XISBN, XID), XS))) if
BALL(XID1, DO(CLASSIFYBOOK(XISBN, XID), XS),
DOM(DO(CLASSIFYBOOK(XISBN, XID), XS))) and (not(BALL(XID1, XS, DOM(XS))))
```

is established with the help of the following intermediate lemma,

```
L2: ball(xid, do(classifybook(xisbn, xid1), xs), dom(xs)) ==
    ball(xid, xs, dom(xs)) if not(xid = xid1).
```

One of the assumptions ball(xid1, do(classifybook(xisbn, xid), xs), dom(do(classifybook(xisbn, xid), xs))) is simplified by the definitions of dom and ball to ball(xid1, do(classifybook(xisbn, xid), xs), dom(xs)). And, this contradicts the assumption (not(ball(xid1, xs, dom(xs)))) by lemma *L*2.

The subgoal [3] is similarly split into two intermediate subgoals which follow from the following intermediate lemma *L*3 and the definitions.

```
L3: ball(xid, do(deletebook(xid1), xs), dom(xs)) ==
    ball(xid, xs, dom(xs)) if not(xid = xid1).
```

Generalization heuristic : The automated proofs of the intermediate lemmas *L*2 and *L*3 illustrate yet another interesting feature of our theorem prover *RRL* viz. *generalization*. It is well known that in many cases, it is much easier to prove a stronger version of a given property by induction than the property itself. Stronger versions of lemmas are automatically generated by *RRL* using the generalization heuristic. A non-variable subterm appearing in both sides of an equation (or condition in case of a conditional equation) is generalized to a new variable; conditions on variables appearing in the subterm are dropped.

Given lemma $L3$, RRL does not attempt an inductive proof of $L3$, but the generalization heuristic instead generates:

`ball(xid,do(deletebook(xid1,xs),xdom) == ball(xid,xs,xdom) if not(xid = xid1),`

by abstracting the subterm $dom(xs)$ in $L3$ to be an arbitrary domain variable $xdom$. If the more general lemma can be proved, then the proof of $L3$ follows by rewriting. The lemma $L2$ is similarly established in RRL by inductively proving its generalized version (obtained by abstracting $dom(xs)$ by a domain variable $xdom$) using the cover set based on the definition of $ball$.

5 Concluding Remarks

It is shown how Reiter's method for proving integrity constraints of deductive data bases can be mechanized using RRL, an automated theorem prover for induction. Using this methodology, we have been able to prove many simple integrity constraints. Mechanical proofs generated by RRL closely resemble manual proofs resulting from Reiter's approach. In this sense, the proposed methodology implements Reiter's approach using an automated induction theorem prover.

We have discussed how Reiter's approach can be formalized equationally using abstract data types in a quantifier-free calculus, and Reiter-style specifications using quantifiers can be mechanically translated into an equational quantifier-free calculus by introducing new bounded quantifier predicates. For these new predicates, bridge lemmas connecting their semantics to the fluents and related predicates in the original specification are needed. These bridge lemmas can be automatically synthesized and proved in RRL.

We believe that other reasoning capabilities of RRL such as a decision procedure for Presburger arithmetic to reason about numbers would be useful in proving general database integrity constraints involving numbers and arithmetic operations such as $+, -$ and relations such as $>, \geq, <, \leq$.

Our methodology has been applied in the proofs of some ICs, taking only a couple of minutes for each of them. It must be noticed that the proof of the integrity constraints is done only once in the lifetime of the database. Therefore, it is not a big problem for the system to take a few minutes in the proof of an integrity constraint, because once the proof is done, the user knows that his specification is correct and nothing has to be done afterwards in real time situations.

Sheard and Stemple [13] developed an approach for showing the safety of transactions with respect to a given set of integrity constraints, i.e., none of the transactions violate any of the integrity constraints. They proposed a database specification language and described a system based on Boyer and Moore's theorem prover for specifying and reasoning about safety of transactions. Bounded quantification over finite sets and tables in terms of primitives for-some and for-all was used to check if some (or all) objects in a table or a set satisfy a given property. However, their approach supports only a restricted set of transactions. It does not support Reiter's successor state axioms.

In contrast, we prove a much stronger claim for ensuring data base integrity, particularly that the database can never evolve into a state in which the integrity constraints are violated if the initial state satisfies the integrity constraints and the preconditions for the transactions are met. The safety of the individual transactions is a consequence of such a proof. Further, using our approach, we can reason about any action whose successor state axiom could be specified in terms of the general template given in section 2.

References

1. L. Bertossi and J. Ferretti. SCDBR: A Reasoner for Specifications in the Situation Calculus of Database Updates. In *Temporal Logic. Proc. First Intl. Conf. ICTL '94, Bonn, Germany, July 1994, LNAI 827*, 543–545, Springer.

2. L. Bertossi, J. Pinto, P. Saez, D. Kapur, and M. Subramaniam. Automated Proofs of Integrity Constraints in Situation Calculus. Technical Report, Computer Science Dept., SUNY, Albany, Nov. 1995.

3. R.S. Boyer and J S. Moore. *A Computational Logic Handbook*. AP, 1988.

4. R.S. Boyer and J S. Moore. The Addition of Bounded Quantification and Partial Functions to A Computational Logic and Its Theorem Prover. *Journal of Automated Reasoning*, 4:117–172, 1988.

5. D. Kapur. *Constructors can be Partial too*. Dept. of Computer Science, State University of New York at Albany, 1994.

6. D. Kapur and H. Zhang. An Overview of Rewrite Rule Laboratory (RRL). *J. of Computer and Mathematics with Applications*, 1995.

7. J. McCarthy and P. Hayes. Some Philosophical Problems from the Standpoint of Artificial Intelligence. In B. Meltzer and D. Michie, eds, *Machine Intelligence*, vol. 4, 463–502, Edinburgh, Scotland, 1969. Edinburgh University Press.

8. R. Reiter. Towards a Logical Reconstruction of Relational Databases Theory. In J. Mylopoulos and J. Schmidt, eds, *On Conceptual Modeling: Perspectives from AI, Databases and Programming Languages*, 191–233. Springer-Verlag, 1984.

9. R. Reiter. The Frame Problem in the Situation Calculus: a Simple Solution (sometimes) and a Completeness Result for Goal Regression. In V. Lifschitz, ed, *Artificial Intelligence and Mathematical Theory of Computation: Papers in Honor of John McCarthy*, 359–380. Academic Press, 1991.

10. R. Reiter. Formalizing Database Evolution in the Situation Calculus. In *Proceedings of the Fifth Generation Computer Systems*, Tokyo, Japan, June 1992.

11. R. Reiter. On Specifying Database Updates. Technical Report KRR-TR-92-3, University of Toronto, Department of Computer Science, Toronto, Canada, 1992.

12. R. Reiter. Proving Properties of States in the Situation Calculus. *Artificial Intelligence*, 64(2):337–351, 1993.

13. T. Sheard and D. Stemple. Automatic Verification of Database Transaction Safety. TR 88-29, Dept. Computer and Information Science, U. Mass., Amherst, MA, 1988.

14. H. Zhang and D. Kapur. First-Order Theorem Proving using Conditional Rewrite Rules. In Lusk and Overbeek, eds., *Proc. 9th Intl. Conf. on Automated Deduction (CADE-9), LNCS 310*, 1–20. Springer, 1988.

15. H. Zhang, D. Kapur, and M.S. Krishnamoorthy. A Mechanizable Induction Principle for Equational Specifications. In Lusk and Overbeek, eds, *Proc. 9th Intl. Conf. on Automated Deduction (CADE-9), LNCS 310*, 162–181. Springer, 1988.

Towards Programming in Default Logic

Paweł Cholewiński

Department of Computer Science, University of Kentucky, Lexington, KY 40506

Abstract. In this paper we describe a fragment of default logic suitable for encoding problems from other domains. We investigate a subclass of first order open default theories, which we call extensional default theories. This class of default theories allows easy and compact encodings of problems for experimenting with default reasoning systems. Because most existing systems for default reasoning assume that all input defaults are closed or propositional we show how to transform an extensional default theory to a closed first order default theory or a propositional default theory with same extensions.

1 Introduction

In this paper we develop a simple first order nonmonotonic reasoning formalism for describing combinatorial problems. Our framework is based on default logic of Reiter [18]. Default logic offers concise descriptions of various knowledge domains and commonsense reasoning situations. This formalism can be regarded as a proof system obtained from first order logic by adding nonstandard rules called *defaults*. Possible sets of conclusions from a default theory are called *extensions*.

The theory of non-monotonic reasoning is well understood [14]. However, to obtain a full-blown knowledge representation tool from any non-monotonic formalism, reasoning systems must be implemented and methods of programming in these formalisms must be developed. For years, despite tremendous advances in our understanding of nonmonotonic logics, implementation efforts and experimentation with nonmonotonic reasoning have been lagging behind. There are only few reported examples of such work [17, 11, 9, 8, 3].

Recently, several algorithms to compute extensions were proposed [14, 1, 15, 13]. In addition, several systems for default reasoning were implemented and are publicly available (DeReS [6], smodels [16], FROST [10]). However, one of the main problems in the efforts to develop reasoning systems based on non-monotonic logic is the lack of adequate experimentation testbed. This issue was discussed and several encodings which can serve as benchmark problems were presented in [7]. Also, a software system, TheoryBase, to automatically generate logic programs and default theories was developed and is publicly available [7]. TheoryBase is an extension of the Stanford GraphBase [12]. For any graph from the Stanford GraphBase it can generate encodings for such problems as coloring, hamiltonicity or existence of kernels. DeReS and TheoryBase are available by anonymous ftp to al.cs.engr.uky.edu, subdirectory cs/software. However, TheoryBase supports only a fixed amount of propositional encodings. In this paper we propose an extension of TheoryBase to a system which takes as input a user-defined extensional default theory and a graph from Stanford GraphBase and combines them into one first order or propositional default theory.

This paper is organized as follows. In Section 2, we recall basic definitions of default theories and extensions [18]. In Section 3, we introduce extensional default theories. Section 4 presents examples of extensional default theories and Section 5 contains the concluding remarks. Due to the space limitation the proofs are omitted.

2 Basic concepts

Let $\mathcal{L}$ be a first order language over an alphabet $\mathcal{A}$. By $Const(\mathcal{L})$, $Pred(\mathcal{L})$ and $Func(\mathcal{L})$ we denote, respectively, the sets of all constants, predicate symbols and function symbols in $\mathcal{L}$. Similarly, for any formula $\varphi \in \mathcal{L}$ by $Const(\varphi)$, $Pred(\varphi)$ and $Func(\varphi)$ we denote the sets of all constants, predicate symbols and function symbols which occur in φ. A formula is *closed* if it contains no free variables.

By a default, we mean an expression of the form: $\frac{\alpha : \lambda\beta}{\gamma}$, where α and γ are formulas and $\lambda\beta$ is a finite list of formulas, that is, $\lambda\beta = \beta_1, \ldots, \beta_m$ for some formulas $\beta_1, \ldots, \beta_m$. The formula α is called a *prerequisite*, formulas $\beta_1, \ldots, \beta_m$ are called *justifications* and γ is the *conclusion*. A default is *closed* if none of the formulas $\alpha, \beta_1, \ldots, \beta_m, \gamma$ contains a free variable. A default of this form will be also denoted as $\alpha : \lambda\beta \to \gamma$.

In this paper, by a default theory we mean a pair (D, W) where D is a set of defaults and W is a set of formulas. A default theory (D, W) is *closed* if all formulas in W and all defaults in D are closed. We adopt the standard notion of extensions introduced by Reiter [18]. First, we define extensions for closed default theories.

Definition 1. [18] Let (D, W) be a closed default theory and E be a first order theory. For a theory I, by $\mathcal{B}_E(D, I)$ we mean the set

$$\mathcal{B}_E(D, I) = \{\gamma : \alpha : \beta_1, \ldots, \beta_m, \to \gamma \in D \text{ and } I \vdash \alpha \text{ and } \neg\beta_1, \ldots, \neg\beta_m \notin E\}.$$

E is an extension for (D, W) if $E = \bigcup_{i=0}^{\infty} E_i$, where $E_0 = W$ and for $i \geq 0$, $E_{i+1} = Cn(E_i) \cup \mathcal{B}_E(D, E_i)$. $\triangle$

For a default theory (D, W) and a set $U \subseteq D$ by $c(U)$ we denote the set of all conclusions of defaults from U. It is known that if a theory E is an extension for a closed default theory, then E is of the form $Cn(W \cup c(U))$ for some $U \subseteq D$ [18]. For an extension $E = \bigcup_{i=0}^{\infty} E_i$, let U contain exactly those defaults $\alpha : \beta_1, \ldots, \beta_m \to \gamma$ from D for which there is $i \geq 0$ such that $\alpha \in E_i$ and $\neg\beta_1, \ldots, \neg\beta_m \notin E$. This U is called a *generating defaults set* for E and satisfies $E = Cn(W \cup c(U))$. Therefore, to find an extension it is enough to find its generating defaults set. Hence, in the case of finite default theories there is a finite number of candidate theories to be tested to find all extensions.

To define extensions for arbitrary default theories we assume that all formulas in W and all conclusions in D are in *Skolemized form* (see [19] for details).

For a set of function letters $\mathcal{F}$ by $H(\mathcal{F})$ we denote the set of all terms constructible using constant symbols of $\mathcal{L}$ and function symbols from $\mathcal{F}$. By $ground(H(\mathcal{F}))$ we mean the set of all ground terms in $H(\mathcal{F})$. Let (D, W) be a default theory over language $\mathcal{L}$, and S be the set of all Skolem functions in D and W. We define a set of *closed defaults generated by* D (denoted as $\overline{D}$):

$$\overline{D} = \{d(a) : d(x) \in D \text{ and } a \text{ is a tuple of terms of } ground(H(Func(\mathcal{L}) \cup S))\}.$$

Now, we are in a position to define extensions for arbitrary default theories.

Definition 2. [18] E is an *extension* for a default theory (D, W) if and only if E is an extension for the closed default theory $(\overline{D}, W)$. $\triangle$

We will illustrate our results on programming in default logic using problems from graph theory. Here, we give basic notation and definitions which will be used throughout this paper. Let $G = (V, A)$ be a directed graph with the set of vertices $V = \{v_1, \ldots, v_n\}$ and the set of arcs A. We treat names of vertices as constant symbols in language $\mathcal{L}$. By $W(G)$ we denote the following theory consistings of ground atoms:

$$W(G) = \{vertex(v) : v \in V\} \cup \{edge(v, u) : (v, u) \in A\}.$$

To simplify notation, we treat undirected graphs as directed graphs with every edge $\{v, u\}$ represented as a pair of directed edges (v, u) and (u, v).

We conclude this section by recalling definitions of graph coloring and graph kernel. Then we show encodings of 3-coloring problem and kernel detection problem as default theories.

Definition 3. Given an undirected graph $G = (V, A)$ and a set C, a function $f : V \to C$ is a *coloring* of G if for every edge $(u, v) \in A$, $f(u) \neq f(v)$. Function f is a *k-coloring* of G if f is a coloring $f : V \to C$ and $|C| = k$. Finally, graph G is *k-colorable* if there is a k-coloring of G. $\triangle$

Definition 4. Given a directed graph $G = (V, A)$, a set $K \subseteq V$ is called a *kernel* if for every edge $(u, v) \in A$, $u \in V \setminus K$ or $v \in V \setminus K$, and for every vertex $w \in V \setminus K$, there exists a vertex $v \in K$ such that $(w, v) \in A$. $\triangle$

Example 1. Let G be an undirected graph. Figure 1 shows a definition of a default theory $chrom_3(G)$. Our presentations of default theories consist of optional initialization of W and D and a list of additional formulas and defaults.

Default theory $chrom_3(G)$ is a generalized version of propositional encoding Δ^3_{col} from [7]. Its extensions correspond to all proper 3-colorings of graph G. Formally, every extension E contains exactly one atom from the list $red(v)$, $blue(v)$, $green(v)$ for every vertex $v \in V$. Hence, we can construct 3-coloring $f : V \to \{red, blue, green\}$ by assigning to v the color p such that $p(v) \in E$. Graph G is 3-colorable if and only if $chrom_3(G)$ has an extension. The straightforward application of Definition 2 results in generation of a large set of defaults $\overline{D}$. This is due to the fact that we must substitute open variables with all possible

---

W := W(G);
$vertex(X) : \neg green(X), \neg blue(X) \rightarrow red(X);$
$vertex(X) : \neg blue(X), \neg red(X) \rightarrow green(X);$
$vertex(X) : \neg red(X), \neg green(X) \rightarrow blue(X);$
$edge(X,Y) \wedge red(X) \wedge red(Y) : \neg Fred(X,Y) \rightarrow Fred(X,Y);$
$edge(X,Y) \wedge green(X) \wedge green(Y) : \neg Fgreen(X,Y) \rightarrow Fgreen(X,Y);$
$edge(X,Y) \wedge blue(X) \wedge blue(Y) : \neg Fblue(X,Y) \rightarrow Fblue(X,Y);$

Fig. 1. Default theory $chrom_3(G)$.

tuples of constants in $\mathcal{L}$. In the case of $chrom_3(G)$ the number of defaults in $\overline{D}$ is $3(n + n^2)$, where n is the number of vertices of G. The goal of this paper is to describe how to eliminate from $\overline{D}$ defaults which can never be used. Similarly, we will eliminate justifications which are consistent for any context and there is no need to verify them. Our motivation is to find a smaller set of defaults which produce exactly same extensions as the original theory. $\triangle$

To simplify notation, we use the symbol $\Diamond$ to denote lists of formulas. Precisely, for a finite set of ground terms $T = \{t_1, \ldots, t_m\}$ and a formula $\beta(X)$ (where X is a free variable in $\beta(X)$) we assume that

$$\Diamond_{X \in T}\beta(X) = \beta(t_1), \ldots, \beta(t_m).$$

Also, if the set T is not specified then we assume that $T = Const(\mathcal{L})$.

Example 2. Let G be a directed graph. Default theory $kernelS(G)$, given in Figure 2, is a first order version of propositional encoding Δ_{ker}^3 from [7]. Extensions of $kernelS(G)$ correspond precisely to kernels in G in the following sense. For an extension E of $kernelS(G)$ we define a kernel $K \subseteq V$ as $K = \{v : \neg out(v) \in E\}$ (see [7] for details). For a graph with n vertices $\overline{D}$ contains $2(n + n^2)$ defaults. n of these defaults have length $O(n^2)$. The total length of this encoding is $O(n^3)$. In Section 3, we will show that this number can be reduced to $O(n + m)$ by a simple preprocessing procedure. $\triangle$

W := W(G);
$vertex(X) : out(X) \rightarrow out(X);$
$vertex(X) : \neg out(X) \rightarrow \neg out(X);$
$edge(X,Y) \wedge \neg out(X) \wedge \neg out(Y) : \neg Findependent(X,Y) \rightarrow Findependent(X,Y);$
$out(X) : \Diamond_Y(edge(X,Y) \Rightarrow out(Y)), \neg Fdominates(X) \rightarrow Fdominates(X);$

Fig. 2. Default theory $kernelS(G)$.

In this section we recalled the definition of default logic and presented two encodings of graph problems. Although the original encodings were compact in size, their groundings were very large. In the next section we show that this disadvantage of default logic encodings can be easily eliminated in the case of many combinatorial problems.

3 Extensional default theories

In this section we introduce a class of default theories which we call *extensional default theories*. The idea is simple and is similar to concepts used in the design of intensional-extensional databases. Our intention is that members of *Const* are the all individuals of a default theory and free variables in defaults range over exactly these individuals. If we assume that $\mathcal{L}$ contains no function symbols then constants of $\mathcal{L}$ are the only terms constructible in $\mathcal{L}$. However, in general, there can be implicitly defined individuals which are introduced via existential quantifiers. That is, even if $\mathcal{L}$ contains no function symbols, function symbols may appear as the effect of skolemization. Hence, in order to enforce that no new individuals are introduced we will require that (D, W) is in Skolemized form and contains no function symbols. This way we also avoid known problems with grounding open defaults.

Definition 5. A default theory (D, W) is *extensional* if it is in Skolemized form and contains no function symbols. $\triangle$

In the sense of Definition 5 both default theories presented in examples in Section 2 are extensional. To simplify processing of default theories we distinguish a set of predicate symbols which are never redefined by conclusions of defaults. The motivation is to simplify reasoning by early detection of nonapplicable defaults. Given an extensional default theory (D, W) over language $\mathcal{L}$, a predicate symbol $p \in Pred(\mathcal{L})$ is called *intensional* if p occurs in a conclusion of a default from D. By $Pred_I$ we denote the set of all intensional predicates in $\mathcal{L}$. We define a set of predicates P as $P = \bigcup_{i=0}^{\infty} P_i$, where $P_0 = Pred_I$ and

$$P_{i+1} = P_i \cup \{p \in Pred(\mathcal{L}) : \text{ there is } \varphi \in W \text{ such that } p \in Pred(\varphi) \text{ and } Pred(\varphi) \cap P_i \neq \emptyset\}.$$

Let $Pred_R = P \setminus Pred_I$, The predicates from $Pred_R$ are called *intervening*. All other predicates are called *extensional* and by $Pred_E$ we denote the set of all extensional predicates in $\mathcal{L}$. Hence, we have partitioned the set of all predicates in $\mathcal{L}$ into three parts

$$Pred(\mathcal{L}) = P \cup Pred_E = Pred_I \cup Pred_R \cup Pred_E.$$

We say that a formula is extensional (resp. intensional) if it contains only extensional (resp. intensional) predicates. Given a theory T by T_E (resp. T_I) we denote the set of all extensional (resp. intensional) formulas in T.

With each type of predicate we associate the following intuitive meaning. Intensional predicates are the predicates about which we want to draw conclusions. Intervening predicates are the predicates that occur only in W but they can be affected indirectly by firing defaults. The key property of extensional formulas is that their provability can be established regardless of any consistent context $c(U)$, $U \subseteq D$. This allows to prune the input default theory before starting the actual search for extensions. To make these concepts precise, we start with the following lemma implied by elementary properties of first order logic.

Lemma 6. *Let (D, W) be an extensional default theory and T be an arbitrary consistent first order theory. If φ is an extensional formula with respect to (D, W) then $T \vdash \varphi$ if and only if $T_E \vdash \varphi$, and if φ is an intensional formula then $T \vdash \varphi$ if and only if $T_I \vdash \varphi$.* △

Lemma 6 allows for early detection of defaults which never can be used and justifications which are never violated. To use this technique efficiently we introduce the following representation for extensional default theories.

Definition 7. Let (D, W) be an extensional default theory. A default theory (D', W') is an *extensional-intentional* representation of (D, W) if:

1. for any formula φ, $W \vdash \varphi$ if and only if $W' \vdash \varphi$,
2. there is a $1-1$ mapping emb from D to D' such that, for every default $d \in D$

$$d = \alpha : \beta_1, \ldots, \beta_m \to \gamma \in D$$

$d' = emb(d)$ is of the form

$$d' = \alpha_E \wedge \alpha' : (\beta_{E,1} \Rightarrow \beta'_1), \ldots, (\beta_{E,m} \Rightarrow \beta'_m) \to \gamma$$

and satisfies the following conditions:
   (a) α_E is an extensional formula and $\alpha \Leftrightarrow (\alpha_E \wedge \alpha')$ is a tautology,
   (b) for every $i, 1 \leq i \leq m$, $\beta_{E,i}$ is an extensional formula and $\beta_i \Leftrightarrow (\beta_{E,i} \Rightarrow \beta'_i)$ is a tautology.

Moreover, if all formulas in W are either extensional or intensional, W_E is consistent and all of the formulas $\alpha', \beta'_1, \ldots, \beta'_m$ of all defaults in D' are intentional then (D', W') is a *strong* extensional-intentional representation of (D, W). △

Observe that every extensional default theory has an extensional-intentional representation. Indeed, we can always take: $W = W'$, $\alpha_E = \top$, $\alpha' = \alpha$, and for all $i, 1 \leq i \leq m$, $\beta_{E,i} = \top$ and $\beta'_i = \beta$. Hence, without loss of generality we can assume that extensional default theories are always given in some extensional-intentional representation. Now, we define a group of defaults which can never be used in a consistent context.

Definition 8. Given an extensional default theory (D, W), a default $d \in \overline{D}$ of the form

$$d = \alpha_E \wedge \alpha' : (\beta_{E,1} \Rightarrow \beta'_1), \ldots, (\beta_{E,m} \Rightarrow \beta'_m) \to \gamma$$

is called *irrelevant* if d has at least one justification and $W_E \not\vdash \alpha_E$. △

Definition 9. Let (D, W) be an extensional default theory. For any default $d \in \overline{D}$ the *intensional reduct* of d, denoted as d^*, is a default obtained by:

1. Removing from d each justification $\beta_E \Rightarrow \beta'$ for which $W_E \not\vdash \beta_E$. If d has at least one justification and all of its justifications are removed then add the formula $\top$ as a justification.
2. Replacing each remaining justification $\beta_E \Rightarrow \beta'$ by β'.

For any set of defaults $U \subseteq \overline{D}$, the *intensional reduct* of U, denoted by U^*, is obtained from U by:

1. Removing all irrelevant defaults.
2. Replacing each remaining default d by d^*.

The *intensional reduct* of (D, W) is the default theory (D^*, W) where D^* is the intensional reduct of $\overline{D}$. △

Our goal in computing the intensional reduct is to simplify the theory $(\overline{D}, W)$ and preserve its original extensions. Consider the default theory with $W = \{ob(a)\}$ and $D = \{ob(X) : v(X) \Rightarrow in(X) \to in(X), ob(X) : v(X) \Rightarrow \neg in(X) \to \neg in(X)\}$. If we eliminate all justifications $\beta_E \Rightarrow \beta'$ in d because $W_E \not\vdash \beta_E$, and we do not add any additional formulas then the extensions are not preserved. This explains why we avoid creating new justification-free defaults in step (1) of definition of d^*. Definition 9 guarrantees that extensions for an extensional default theory are the same as the extensions of its intensional reduct. Formally, we have the following results.

Theorem 10. *Let (D, W) be an extensional default theory. A theory E is an extension for (D, W) if and only if E is an extension for (D^*, W).* □

We can simplify an extensional default theory (D, W) more if this theory is in strong extensional-intentional representation. In such a case $W = W_I \cup W_E$, W_E is consistent and the extensional predicates do not occur in D^*. Hence, the formulas from W_E have no effect on provability of extensional formulas (Lemma 6). Since all prerequisites, justifications and conclusions in D^* are intensional we can disregard W_E when we decide which defaults are applicable that is, when we compute $\bigcup_{i=0}^{\infty} E_i$. Formally, we state the following proposition as a direct corollary to Lemma 6 and Theorem 10.

Theorem 11. *If a default theory (D, W) is in strong extensional-intentional representation then a theory E is an extension for (D, W) if and only if E_I is an extension for (D^*, W_I). Also, in this case $E = Cn(W_E \cup E_I)$.* △

Example 3. Let G be an undirected graph. Consider the theory $chrom_3(G) = (D, W)$ from Example 1. This theory is in strong extensional-intentional representation. The intensional reduct (D^*, W_I) is a ground default theory. By treating each ground atom as a propositional variable we can look at (D^*, W_I) as at a propositional default theory. This (D^*, W_I) was presented in [7] and it was proven there that its extensions correspond to all 3-colorings of G. From Theorem 11 it follows that extensions of $chrom_3(G)$ encode all 3-colorings of G. The relation between extensions and 3-colorings was given in Example 1. △

Example 4. Let now $(D, W) = kernelS(G)$ from Example 2. The default theory (D^*, W_I) matches the encoding Δ^3_{ker} from [7]. It was also proven in [7] that extensions of Δ^3_{ker} are of the form $E = Cn(\{\neg out(v) : v \in K\} \cup \{out(v) : v \notin K\})$ where K is a kernel of G. Hence, from Theorem 11 we have that extensions of $kernelS(G)$ correspond to kernels in G in the same way. △

Finaly, we discuss two other basic tasks of default reasoning.

Corollary 12. *Let (D, W) be a default theory in strong extensional-intentional representation and φ be an intensional formula. φ is in some extensions of (D, W) if and only if φ is in some extensions of (D^*, W_I). φ belongs to all extensions of (D, W) if and only if φ belongs to all extensions of (D^*, W_I).* △

4 Programming graph problems in default theories

In this section we present a brief overview of techniques suitable for writing default specifications of combinatorial problems. We start with encodings of simple objects such as subsets of a given set or functions between two sets.

Let V be a finite set of objects $\{v_1, \ldots, v_n\}$ and $W_{set}(V)$ be the set of ground atoms defined as $W_{set}(V) = \{vertex(v) : v \in V\}$. We can encode all subsets of V using two defaults: $: out(X) \to out(X)$ and $\neg out(X) \to \neg out(X)$. This technique was used in Example 2. All functions from a V to a finite set $C = \{c_1, \ldots, c_k\}$ can be encoded using k defaults

$$col_i(X) = vertex(X) : \neg c_1(X), \ldots, \neg c_{i-1}(X), \neg c_{i+1}(X), \ldots, \neg c_k(X) \to c_i(X).$$

This method was used in Example 1. Same effect can be achieved by treating $c_1, \ldots, c_k$ as constant names of the language $\mathcal{L}$, adding the set $\{color(c_i) : 0 \le i \le k\}$ to W and using the following single default rule $mapping(X, Q)$:

$$mapping(X, Q) = vertex(X) \wedge color(Q) :$$
$$\Diamond_P(color(P) \wedge P \neq Q \Rightarrow \neg map(X, P)) \to map(X, Q).$$

Many combinatorial problems can be formulated in terms of finding subsets or functions which satisfy some additional conditions (see Examples 1 and 2). Let φ be any formula. Suppose that we are interested only in these extensions of (D, W) in which φ is true. One way to do it is to add to D a new default:

$$d_\varphi =: \neg \varphi, \neg aux \to aux,$$

where aux is an arbitrary new ground atom. In this case, the set $\mathcal{E}' = \{E \in \mathcal{E} : \varphi \in E\}$ is the set of all extensions for $(D \cup \{d_\varphi\}, W)$. This result follows directly

W := $W(G) \cup \{visited(v)\}$;
$edge(X,Y) \wedge visited(X) : \Diamond_Z(edge(X,Z) \wedge Z \neq Y \Rightarrow \neg uses(X,Z))$
$\quad \rightarrow uses(X,Y) \wedge visited(Y)$;
$vertex(X) : \Diamond_X(edge(X,v) \Rightarrow \neg uses(X,v)), \neg notcycle(v) \rightarrow notcycle(v)$;
$vertex(X) : \neg visited(X), \neg unknown(X) \rightarrow unknown(X)$;

Fig. 3. Default theory $hamilton_1(G,v)$.

from [4]. Similarly, if we are interested in such extensions E of (D,W) which do not contain φ, we can add to D the following default:

$$d'_\varphi = \varphi : \neg aux \rightarrow aux.$$

The theory $(D \cup \{d'_\varphi\}, W)$ has as its extensions exactly those extensions for (D,W) which do not contain formula φ.

This technique can be used to write encodings of, for example: maximal independent sets, achromatic colorings, monochromatic triangles, cycles, hamiltonian cycles, maximal and perfect matchings. In particular, all (propositional) benchmark encodings proposed in [7] and [16] can be translated this way into extensional default theories. In Figure 3 we present an encoding for directed hamiltonian cycles in G.

5 Conclusions

In this paper we described a non-monotonic formalism – extensional default theories – which is suitable for encoding combinatorial problems. This formalism is entirely based on standard default logic. We developed a method of eliminating unnecessary defaults and justifications before starting the actual search for solutions. This reduces the search space for extensions. In this paper, we did not discuss the issue of tractability of resulting default theories. Nevertheless, it is worth to mention that, in many cases, extensional default theories can be stratified and reasoning can be perforrmed in a reasonable time [6]. For detailed description of default stratification see [5] and [4].

We presented examples of encodings of problems in graph theory. The approach of using graph based problems as benchmark problems for experimenting with non-monotonic reasoning systems was proposed and widely discussed in [7]. One of the outcomes of this paper is a large testbed for experimentation with default reasoning systems and systems for computing stable models of logic programs.

There are interesting areas for future research. The pruning method of this paper requires initial computation of all grounded instances of open defaults. That can lead to huge closed default theories. This implies that the development of on-line substitution of open defaults and, in general, reasoning in a goal-directed way is important.

References

1. G. Antoniou, E. Langetepe, and V. Sperschneider. New proofs in default logic theory. *Annals of Mathematics and Artificial Intelligence*, 12:215–230, 1994.
2. R. Ben-Eliyahu and L. Palopoli. Reasoning with minimal models: Efficient algorithms and applications. In *Proceedings of KR'94*, San Francisco, CA, 1994. Morgan Kaufmann.
3. C. Bell, A. Nerode, R. Ng, W. Pugh, and V.S. Subrahmanian. Implementing stable semantics by linear programming. In A. Nerode and L. Pereira, editors, *Logic programming and non-monotonic reasoning*. MIT Press, 1993.
4. P. Cholewiński. Reasoning with stratified default theories. In *Proceedings of LP-NMR'95*. Berlin: Springer-Verlag, 1995. Lecture Notes in Computer Science 928.
5. P. Cholewiński. Stratified default theories. In *Proceedings of CSL'94*. Berlin: Springer-Verlag, 1995. Lecture Notes in Computer Science 933.
6. P. Cholewiński, W. Marek, A. Mikitiuk, and M. Truszczyński. Default reasoning system — an implementation of default reasoning. *In preparation.*, 1995.
7. P. Cholewiński, W. Marek, A. Mikitiuk, and M. Truszczyński. Experimenting with nonmonotonic reasoning. In *Proceedings of the 12th International Conference on Logic Programming*, Cambridge, MA, 1995. MIT Press.
8. W. Chen, T. Swift, and D.S. Warren. Efficient top-down computation of queries under the well-founded semantics. *Journal of Logic Programming*, 1994.
9. M. Dixon and J. de Kleer. Massively parallel assumption-based truth maintenance. In *Non-monotonic reasoning*, pages 131–142. Berlin: Springer-Verlag, 1989. Lecture Notes in Artificial Intelligence, 346.
10. S.P. Engelson, R. Feldman, M. Koppel, A. Nerode, and J.B. Remmel. Frost: A forward chaining rule ordering system for reasoning with nonmonotonic rule systems. In *Proceedings of the IJCAI-95 Workshop on Applications and Implementations of Nonmonotomic Reasonigs Systems*, 1995.
11. M.L. Ginsberg. A circumscriptive theorem prover. In *Non-monotonic reasoning*, pages 100–114. Berlin: Springer-Verlag, 1989. Lecture Notes in Artificial Intelligence 346.
12. D. E. Knuth. *The Stanford GraphBase: a platform for combinatorial computing.* Addison-Wesley, 1993.
13. W. Marek, A. Nerode, and J. B. Remmel. Rule systems, well-orderings and forward chaining. *Submitted for publication.*, 1995.
14. W. Marek and M. Truszczyński. *Nonmonotonic logics; context-dependent reasoning.* Berlin: Springer-Verlag, 1993.
15. I. Niemelä. Towards efficient default reasoning. In *Proceedings of IJCAI-95*, pages 312–318. Morgan Kaufmann, 1995.
16. I. Niemelä and P. Simmons. Evaluating an algorithm for default reasoning. In *Proceedings of the IJCAI-95 Workshop on Applications and Implementations of Nonmonotomic Reasonigs Systems*, 1995.
17. D. Poole. A logical framework for default reasoning. *Artificial Intelligence*, 36:27–47, 1988.
18. R. Reiter. A logic for default reasoning. *Artificial Intelligence*, 13:81–132, 1980.
19. J.A. Robinson. Machine-oriented logic based on resolution principle. *Journal of the ACM*, 12:23 – 41, 1965.

A Sound and Complete Fuzzy Logic System Using Zadeh's Implication Operator

Jianhua Chen[†] and *Sukhamay Kundu*
Computer Science Department, Louisiana State University
Baton Rouge, LA 70803-4020
{jianhua, kundu} @bit.csc.lsu.edu

Abstract. We present a formalization of fuzzy logic based on Zadeh's implication operator $a \rightarrow b = \max\{1-a, b\}$. Our logical system allows the specification of both lower and upper bounds of the truth value of a formula. We present a specific system of axioms and inference rules which are both *sound and complete*. We also provide a generalization of the classical resolution method which acts as a decision procedure in a finite fuzzy theory.

Keywords: fuzzy logic, inference rules, resolution method.

1. INTRODUCTION

We consider fuzzy propositional logic with truth values in the interval [0, 1]. This work is motivated by Pavelka's formalization [10] of fuzzy logic based on Lukasiewicz's implication. In [10], the logical system allows one to infer the lower-bound for the truth value of a formula. In [5], a formalization of fuzzy logic using Zadeh's implication was presented, which allows one to infer the upper-bound of a formula. Although several sound inference rules were identified here, they were not complete in that they may not always allow us to infer the best possible upper-bound. In this paper, we combine the ideas in [5] and [10] to define the notions of both the lower and the upper bounds for semantic truth of a formula from a given fuzzy theory. We then propose a particular axiom system and inference rules based on Zadeh's implication, and prove the soundness and completeness of the inference rules. We also present a fuzzy-resolution proof procedure which terminates for any finite fuzzy theory. Our axiom system is simpler than the one in [10], due to the fact that the formulas that we consider are simpler. For instance, in our case a formula like $(A \leq 0.3)$ has truth value 0 or 1, whereas in [10] the truth value of $(A \leq 0.3)$ can be any number in [0, 1]. Using Lukasiewicz's implication, the formula $[0.6 \rightarrow (A \rightarrow 0.3)]$ models the fact that the truth value of $(A \leq 0.3)$ is at least 0.6.

The formulas in our logic are more general than those considered by Lee [7]. For example, the formula $\phi_1: (A \leq 0.4) \rightarrow (B \geq 0.7)$ can be considered in our logic, but not in [7]. In [7], one can consider only formulas of the form $(\psi \leq \alpha)$, where ψ is a boolean formula and $\alpha \in [0, 1]$; one may also use any of $\{\geq, <, >\}$ in place of "$\leq$". An example of such a formula is ϕ_2: $(A \rightarrow B) \geq 0.7$, which can be rewritten as $(A \leq 0.3) \rightarrow (B \geq 0.7)$. Note the relationship $0.3 = 1 - 0.7$ between the constants 0.3 and 0.7 above, whereas in ϕ_1 the constants 0.4 and 0.7 maybe any numbers in [0, 1]. Formula in our logic are arbitrary boolean combinations of those considered in [7]. See [8] for some other related results.

2. THE AXIOMATIZATION

Our logical language has two parts or levels. At the *objective level*, the language consists of ordinary propositions, the logical constant $\perp$ (= false), and the logical connectives $\{\wedge, \vee, \neg, \rightarrow\}$. Let $\mathbf{P} = \{P_1, P_2, \cdots, P_m\}$ be a finite set of propositions at the objective level. These

† Work supported in part by NSF Grant IRI-9409370 and LEQSF Grant LEQSF(RF/1995-97)-RD-A-37.

propositions and their negations are called the objective *literals*. The set of well-formed *objec-tive-formulas* over **P** is denoted by **F**.

At the *meta-level*, the language consists of the uncountably many meta-level proposi-tions of the form $(A \leq \alpha)$ and $(A \geq \alpha)$, for $A \in \mathbf{F}$ and $\alpha \in [0, 1]$, the logical constant $\bot$, and the logical connectives $\{\wedge, \vee, \neg, \rightarrow\}$. The set of well-formed *meta-formulas* are defined in the usual way by starting from the meta-propositions. Note that $(A \rightarrow \alpha)$ and $[(A \leq \alpha) \geq \beta]$ are not (well-formed) formulas in either the objective level or the meta-level. We use $(A < \alpha)$ as a short form for $\neg(A \geq \alpha)$ and similarly for $(A > \alpha)$; likewise, $(A = \alpha)$ is a short form for $(A \leq \alpha)$ $\wedge (A \geq \alpha)$. The meta-propositions and their negations are called meta-literals, or simply literals, when no confusion is likely. A simplest meta-literal is $(P_i \leq \alpha)$ and a more complex meta-literal is $[(P_i \rightarrow P_j) > \alpha]$. A meta-literal of the form $(P_i \leq \alpha)$, $(P_i > \alpha)$, etc. is called an *elemen-tary* meta-literal. The literal $(P_i \leq \alpha)$ is *non-trivial* if $\alpha < 1$, and similarly for $(P_i \geq \alpha)$. The lit-eral $(P_i \leq 0)$ corresponds to the classical literal $\neg P_i$ and $(P_i \geq 1)$ to P_i. Thus, our meta-language contains the classical case.

2.1. Semantic Interpretation

An interpretation I is a mapping from **P** to $[0, 1]$. We extend I to **F** via $\tau(A \wedge B) = \min\{\tau(A), \tau(B)\}$, $\tau(A \vee B) = \max\{\tau(A), \tau(B)\}$, $\tau(\neg A) = 1 - \tau(A)$, $\tau(A \rightarrow B) = \max\{1 - \tau(A), \tau(B)\}$ (Zadeh's implication operator), and $\tau(\bot) = 0$. At the objective level, an interpretation assigns a truth value for each formula in **F** in the interval $[0, 1]$. Given an interpretation I, we can assign a boolean truth value in $\{0, 1\}$ to each meta-proposition $(A \leq \alpha)$ in the obvious way, namely, $\tau(A \leq \alpha) = 1$ if $\tau(A) \leq \alpha$ and similarly for $(A \geq \alpha)$. (Note than neither the relation "$\geq$" nor the number 0.3 here is fuzzy.) Finally, we assign a boolean truth value to each meta-formula like $(A \leq \alpha) \rightarrow (B > \beta)$ using the classical method of combining boolean truth values. We say I *sat-isfies* a meta-formula e if $\tau(e) = 1$; in that case, we say I is a *model* of e.

A *meta-theory* is a finite set of meta-formulas. A model of a meta-theory X is an inter-pretation which is a model of each meta-formula $e \in X$. If X has a model, then we say X is *satisfiable*. We say a theory X entails a meta-formula e if every model of X satisfies e; this is denoted by $X \models e$. A meta-formula e is said to be *valid* if it is entailed by the empty theory, i.e., $\varnothing \models e$, or equivalently, every interpretation is a model of e. An example of a valid meta-formula is $(A \wedge \neg A \leq 0.5)$. Two objective-formulas A and B are said to be *equivalent* if $\tau(A) = \tau(B)$ for each interpretation; for example, $\neg(A \vee B)$ is equivalent to $(\neg A) \wedge (\neg B)$. The equivalence of two meta-formulas e and e' is defined in the same way.

We often identify the interval $[0, \alpha]$ with the literal $(P_i \leq \alpha)$ and the interval $[0, \alpha)$ with the literal $(P_i < \alpha)$; similarly for $(P_i \geq \alpha)$ and $(P_i > \alpha)$. For $P_i \neq P_j$, there is no connection between the interval for a P_i-literal and that for a P_j-literal. Two meta-literals $(P_i \leq \alpha)$ and $(P_i \geq \alpha')$, which involve the same proposition P_i, are said to be *complementary* if $\alpha < \alpha'$; the same is true if strict inequality holds in one or both of the literals (in each case, we may even have $\alpha = \alpha'$). The intervals associated with two complementary meta-literals are disjoint and no inter-pretation satisfies both the literals; Note that unlike the classical case, where the clause $(A \vee \neg A \vee B)$ containing two complementary literals becomes trivial, i.e., equals $\neg \bot$, this is not the case for a meta-clause (defined below) like $[(P_1 \leq 0.2) \vee (P_1 > 0.7) \vee (P_1 < 0.3)]$, which is equiva-lent to $[(P_1 < 0.3) \vee (P_1 > 0.7)]$.

For any objective formulas A, B, and C and any interpretation I, it is easy to see that $\tau(\neg[A \wedge B]) = \tau(\neg A \vee \neg B)$, $\tau([A \wedge (B \vee C)]) = \tau([A \wedge B] \vee [A \wedge C])$, and $\tau(\neg \neg A) = \tau(A)$. However, we do not have $\tau(A \wedge \neg A) = \tau(\bot) = 0$; in general, we can only say $\tau(A \wedge \neg A) \leq 0.5$ and similarly $\tau(A \vee \neg A) \geq 0.5$. For meta-formulas, we have $[(e \wedge e') \leq \alpha]$ is equivalent to $[(e \leq \alpha) \vee (e' \leq \alpha)]$, $[(e \vee e') \leq \alpha]$ is equivalent to $[(e \leq \alpha) \wedge (e' \leq \alpha)]$, $(\neg e \leq \alpha)$ is equivalent to $(e \geq 1 - \alpha)$, $[\neg \neg (e \leq$

$\alpha)]$ is equivalent to $(e \leq \alpha)$, and likewise for the cases $\geq$, $<$, and $>$. We also have $[(e \leq \alpha) \wedge \neg(e \leq \alpha)]$ equivalent to $\perp$. This suggests the definition of a *meta-clause* to be a disjunction elementary of meta-literals.

Lemma 1. Each meta-formula e is semantically equivalent to a conjunction of meta-clauses $e = C_1 \wedge C_2 \wedge \cdots \wedge C_n$, where each C_i is a disjunction of non-trivial elementary meta-literals and no C_i contains more than two P_j-literals for any j.

Proof. Among all P_j literals of the type $(P_j \leq \alpha)$ or $(P_j < \alpha)$ in a clause, we need to keep only the one with the largest associated α. Similarly for P_j-literals of the type $(P_j \geq \alpha)$ and $(P_j > \alpha)$. ♠

2.1.1. Simplification of A Meta-Clause

One can perform some obvious simplifications to reduce the literals in a meta-clause. To be precise, we can eliminate a P_i-literal L_1 from a clause if it *subsumes* (instead of being subsumed by) another P_i-literal L_2 in the clause, where Table 1 shows the conditions for subsumption. This is comparable to the classical case where we eliminate repeated occurrences of P_i or $\neg P_i$ in a clause. If the clause contains the literal $(P_i \geq 0)$ or the literal $(P_i \leq 1)$, then we can eliminate the whole clause. A slightly more general case is where it contains a P_i-literal which is subsumed by the complement of another P_i-literal. For example, the clause $(P_i < 0.6) \vee (P_i \geq 0.3) \vee \cdots$ can be eliminated, since $(P_i \geq 0.3)$ is subsumed by $(P_i \geq 0.6) = \neg(P_i < 0.6)$.

TABLE 1. L_1 subsumes L_2 (similarly for '$\geq$' and '$>$').

L_1	L_2	L_1	L_2
$P_i \leq \alpha$	$P_i \leq \beta$ and $\alpha \leq \beta$ $P_i < \beta$ and $\alpha < \beta$	$P_i < \alpha$	$P_i \leq \beta$ and $\alpha \leq \beta$ $P_i < \beta$ and $\alpha \leq \beta$

2.1.2. Subsumption of Clauses.

If C_1 and C_2 are two clauses, then we say C_1 *subsumes* if C_2 if each literal in C_1 subsumes a literal in C_2. This definition generalizes the notion of subsumption of clauses in the classical case. It is easy to see that C_1 subsumes C_2 if and only if every model of C_1 is also a model of C_2. If $C_1 = C_2$, each subsumes the other; the converse is also true provided each clause itself is assumed to be in reduced form.

Example 1. The meta-formula $\phi = [P_1 \rightarrow (P_2 \wedge P_3)] \leq \alpha$ has 2 clauses $C_1 = (P_1 \geq 1 - \alpha)$ and $C_2 = (P_2 \leq \alpha) \vee (P_3 \leq \alpha)$. If we rewrite the objective part $P_1 \rightarrow (P_2 \wedge P_3)$ as the If we eliminate the second and the third clause by subsumption, then we get back the same clauses as before. In general, one may get different sets of clauses by using different simplifications.

$$
\begin{aligned}
\phi &= [(\neg P_1 \vee P_2) \leq \alpha] \vee [(\neg P_1 \vee P_3) \leq \alpha] \\
&= [(\neg P_1 \leq \alpha) \wedge (P_2 \leq \alpha)] \vee [(\neg P_1 \leq \alpha) \wedge (P_3 \leq \alpha)] \\
&= (P_1 \geq 1 - \alpha) \wedge [(P_2 \leq \alpha) \vee (P_1 \geq 1 - \alpha)] \wedge [(P_1 \geq 1 - \alpha) \vee (P_3 \leq \alpha)] \wedge \\
&\quad [(P_2 \leq \alpha) \vee (P_3 \leq \alpha)]
\end{aligned}
$$

2.2. Semantic Truth Value Bounds

Let X be a meta-theory. We say α is a semantic *upper-bound* for the meta-formula A if $(A \leq \alpha)$ or $(A < \alpha)$ is entailed by X. The notion of semantic *lower-bound* is defined in a similarly way. We are interested in the smallest such upper-bounds and the largest such lower-bounds for various A's. The axiom system given below allows us to derive these bounds by a syntactic (inference) method.

2.3. Syntactic Truth Value Bounds

For our purpose, an axiom system is a pair $\langle A, R \rangle$, where the axioms in A are meta-formulas and the inference rules in R allow us to derive new meta-formulas from other meta-formulas. Given an arbitrary axiom system $\langle A, R \rangle$, a proof or a derivation from a meta-theory X is a finite sequence of meta-formulas

$$\omega = \langle e_1, e_2, \cdots, e_n \rangle,$$

where each e_j is either in $A \cup X$ or is obtained by applying an inference rule in R to one or more previous formulas e_i, $i < j$. We say that ω is a *proof* of e_n, and we write $X \vdash e_n$. An axiom $e \in A$ is called *sound* if it is satisfied by every interpretation I; similarly, a rule r which infers a meta-formula e from meta-formulas $\{e_1, e_2, \cdots, e_n\}$ is called sound if $\{e_1, e_2, \cdots, e_n\} \models e$. An axiom system $\langle A, R \rangle$ is called sound if each of its axioms and rules is sound. In that case, $X \models e$ holds whenever we have $X \vdash e$.

Definition (Syntactical truth value bounds). Let X be a meta-theory. We say α is a syntactic *upper-bound* in X for the meta-formula A if $(A \leq \alpha)$ or $(A < \alpha)$ can be derived from X. The notion of syntactic *lower-bound* is defined in a similar way. ♣

2.4. The Proposed Axiom System

The proposed axioms (1)-(4) given below are rather simple and straightforward. The only inference rule in R is Modus-ponens rule: $\dfrac{e_1,\ e_1 \to e_2}{e_2}$, where e_1, e_2 are any meta-formulas. We do not need Syllogism-rule explicitly since $(e_1 \to e_2) \to [(e_2 \to e_3) \to (e_1 \to e_3)]$ is included as one of our axioms in (1). We can derive $(e_1 \to e_3)$ by two applications of Modus-ponens from $(e_1 \to e_2)$, $(e_2 \to e_3)$, and $(e_1 \to e_2) \to [(e_2 \to e_3) \to (e_1 \to e_3)]$. Since α and β in (2)-(4) can be any real number in $[0, 1]$, there are uncountably many axioms in our system.

(1)   All meta-language instances of tautologies in ordinary propositional logic.

(2)   These axioms state that each meta-formula has a truth value, and they define the short form $(A < \alpha)$ for $\neg(A \geq \alpha)$, and $(A > \alpha)$ for $\neg(A \leq \alpha)$. They also allow us to derive $(A \leq \alpha)$ from $(A < \alpha)$, and $(A \geq \alpha)$ from $(A > \alpha)$ with the help of (1).

$$(A \leq \alpha) \vee (A \geq \alpha) \quad (A < \alpha) \leftrightarrow \neg(A \geq \alpha) \quad (A > \alpha) \leftrightarrow \neg(A \leq \alpha)$$

(3)   This axiom states that each meta-formula has at most one truth value. (By combining this axiom with those in (2), one can derive $(A \leq \beta)$ from $(A \leq \alpha)$, with or without strict inequality in either or both parts, for $\alpha < \beta$.)

$$\neg(A \leq \alpha) \vee \neg(A \geq \beta), \text{ where } \alpha < \beta \text{ in } [0, 1]$$

(4)   These axioms support replacing a meta-formula by its clause form. (Here, "$e \leftrightarrow e'$" is an abbreviation for $(e \to e') \wedge (e' \to e)$. We do not need to include similar axioms for the strict inequalities "$<$" and "$>$" since they are only abbreviations.)

$$([A \wedge B] \leq \alpha) \leftrightarrow [(A \leq \alpha) \vee (B \leq \alpha)] \qquad ([A \wedge B] \geq \alpha) \leftrightarrow [(A \geq \alpha) \wedge (B \geq \alpha)]$$
$$([A \vee B] \leq \alpha) \leftrightarrow [(A \leq \alpha) \wedge (B \leq \alpha)] \qquad ([A \vee B] \geq \alpha) \leftrightarrow [(A \geq \alpha) \vee (B \geq \alpha)]$$
$$([A \to B] \leq \alpha) \leftrightarrow ([\neg A \vee B] \leq \alpha) \qquad ([A \to B] \geq \alpha) \leftrightarrow ([\neg A \vee B] \geq \alpha)$$
$$(A \leq \alpha) \leftrightarrow (\neg A \geq 1-\alpha) \qquad (A \geq \alpha) \leftrightarrow (\neg A \leq 1-\alpha)$$

Since each of our axioms is a valid meta-formula and Modus-ponens inference rule is sound, the following lemma is immediate.

Lemma 2. The proposed axiom system $\langle A, R \rangle$ is sound with respect to the fuzzy logic semantics using Zadeh's implication. ♣

The following results are direct analogues of the results in propositional logic, and they are proved in the same manner. We omit most of the details. We say a meta-theory X is (syntactically) *inconsistent* if for some meta-formula e, we have both $X \vdash e$ and $X \vdash \neg e$. Otherwise, X is said to be *consistent*.

Lemma 3. Let X be a meta-theory and e a meta-formula. Then, $X \vdash e$ if and only if there is a finite subset $\{e_1, \cdots, e_n\} \subseteq X$ such that $\varnothing \vdash [\bigwedge_{i=1}^{n} e_i] \to e$.

Proof. Assume that $\varnothing \vdash [\bigwedge_{i=1}^{n} e_i] \to e$. Then, $X \vdash [\bigwedge_{i=1}^{n} e_i] \to e$, and thus by applying Modus-ponens repeatedly, we get $X \vdash e$. On the other hand, if $X \vdash e$, then by induction on the length of a proof of e from X, we get $\varnothing \vdash [\bigwedge_{i=1}^{n} e_i] \to e$. ♣

Corollary 1. Let X be a meta-theory and e a meta-formula. Then, $X \cup \{\neg e\}$ is inconsistent if and only if $X \vdash e$. ♣

In the next section, we give a generalized resolution method for verifying unsatisfiability of a finite set of meta-clauses. To be precise, a set of clauses S will be unsatisfiable only if one can derive the empty clause □ (which has no literals).

We point out that the "compactness" property of propositional logic is not longer true for our logic. That is, we may have an infinite theory X (involving only a finite number of propositions) which has no model although every finite subset of X has a model. Let $X = \{(P_1 > 0.5)\} \cup \{(P_1 \leq 0.5 + \frac{1}{n}): n \geq 2\}$. Clearly, each finite subset of X is satisfiable and X is not satisfiable. (If these formulas involved only finitely many real numbers, then the compactness property would hold.)

3. RESOLUTION PROOF METHOD

3.1. Resolvent of Two Clauses

Definition (generalized resolvent). Two meta-clauses C_1 and C_2 as shown below, where each L_{ij} is an elementary meta-literal, are said to be P_i-*resolvable* (or simply resolvable) if they contain complementary P_i-literals, say, L_{11} in C_1 and L_{21} in C_2. In that case, we define the P_i-*resolvent* (or simply the resolvent) of C_1 and C_2, denoted by res(C_1, C_2), as indicated below; P_i is said to be the resolving proposition.

$$C_1 = L_{11} \vee L_{12} \vee \cdots \vee L_{1p}$$
$$C_2 = L_{21} \vee L_{22} \vee \cdots \vee L_{2q}, \text{ where } L_{11} \text{ and } L_{21} \text{ are complementary literals.}$$
$$\text{res}(C_1, C_2) = L_{12} \vee L_{13} \vee \cdots \vee L_{1p} \vee L_{22} \vee L_{23} \vee \cdots \vee L_{2q}.$$

Our main goal is to obtain the empty clause □ by repeatedly forming resolvents of pairs of clauses $\{C_1, C_2\}$ by starting from a set of unsatisfiable clauses S. We cannot hope that both C_1 and C_2 have only one P_i-literal. For example, if $S = \{(P_1 < 0.2) \vee (P_1 > 0.7), (P_1 \leq 0.5), (P_1 \geq 0.4)\}$, which is clearly unsatisfiable, there is no such $\{C_1, C_2\}$. However, we can obtain □ by resolving the first two clauses in S and resolving the result with the third clause. One can show that the formation of P_i-resolvents can be restricted to clause-pairs $\{C_1, C_2\}$ where at least one of the two clauses contains only one P_i-literal. In this way, the choices for the clause-pairs becomes more "directed".

Note that if both C_1 and C_2 contain other complementary pairs of literals, then res(C_1, C_2) will contain a complementary pair of literals. However, as noted earlier, such a clause is not in general equivalent to the trivial clause ($= \neg\perp$). The following lemma, which is easily proved, is a direct generalization of the case of boolean logic, and is critical in proving the completeness of our resolution method.

Lemma 4. If C_1 and C_2 are two meta-clauses which are P_i-resolvable, then each model of $\{C_1, C_2\}$ is also a model of their P_i-resolvent $C = \text{res}(C_1, C_2)$. ♣

We now state the refutation algorithm, which always terminates, using the above generalized notion of resolvent.

Algorithm FUZZY-REFUTATION (for inferring ψ from ϕ).

1. Let S be the set of all clauses obtained from each of ϕ and $\neg\psi$. (Any clausal form of ϕ and of $\neg\psi$ suffice.)

2. Choose a pair of clauses C_1 and C_2 in S which are resolvable and which have not been resolved previously. Add the resolvent $C = \text{res}(C_1, C_2)$ to S, if it is not subsumed by any other clause in S. (Mark the pair $\{C_1, C_2\}$ to prevent future attempts to resolve them again.)

3. If $C = \text{res}(C_1, C_2)$ is added to S in Step (2), then reduce S by eliminating all clauses which are subsumed by C. (If $C = \square$, the empty clause, then S reduces to $\{\square\}$.)

4. Repeat Steps (2)-(3) until $S = \{\square\}$ or there is no other resolvable clause-pair in S.

5. In the first case, the answer is "yes" (that is, $\phi \models \psi$) and in the second case the answer is "no". Stop. ♣

3.2. Relationship with Syllogism and Modus-ponens Rules

Consider the meta-clauses $S = \{(P_1 \geq 0.3), (P_2 \leq 0.7), (P_2 \geq 0.4), (P_3 \leq 0.6)\}$ which are obtained from $\phi = [(P_1 \rightarrow P_2) \leq 0.7]$ and $\psi = [(P_2 \rightarrow P_3) \leq 0.6]$. The following Syllogism rule in [5] applied to ϕ and ψ gives $(P_1 \rightarrow P_3 \leq 0.7) = (P_1 \geq 0.3) \wedge (P_3 \leq 0.7)$, which is much weaker than the $\wedge$-combination of clauses in S.

$$\tau(A \rightarrow C) \leq \max\{\tau(A \rightarrow B), \tau(B' \rightarrow C)\}, \text{ for any } B \text{ and } B'$$

The same situation arises if we interchange the values 0.6 and 0.7 in ϕ and ψ. This is very much unlike the classical case, where $P_1 \rightarrow P_2$ and $P_2 \rightarrow P_3$ give the resolvable clauses $\neg P_1 \vee P_2$ and $\neg P_2 \vee P_3$, whose resolvent $\neg P_1 \vee P_3$ is identical with the result $P_1 \rightarrow P_3$ obtained by the application of the classical Syllogism. In the present case, we cannot form a resolvent unless we lower the value 0.7 in ϕ to less than $1 - 0.6 = 0.4$ or lower the value 0.6 in ψ less than $1 - 0.7 = 0.3$; in either case, we can obtain the empty clause $\square$ as the resolvent and there is no model of $\{\phi, \psi\}$ now. The Syllogism rule above once again gives the weaker result, $[(P_1 \rightarrow P_3) \leq 0.6]$ or $[(P_1 \rightarrow P_3) \leq 0.7]$, as the case may be.

A similar situation arises with the following Modus-ponens rule in [5]. From $(P_1 \leq 0.7)$ and $[(P_1 \rightarrow P_2) \leq 0.6]$, we get the clauses $S = \{(P_1 \leq 0.7), (P_1 \geq 0.4), (P_2 \leq 0.6)\}$ and no two of these clauses can be resolved; the result $(P_2 \leq 0.6)$ obtained by the Modus-ponens rule in [5] is weaker than the $\wedge$-combination of clauses in S. When we lower the value 0.7 or the value 0.6, remarks similar to those for Syllogism rule above hold. These observations explain the weakness of the inference rules in [5] although they appear to be the "best" immediate analogues of the corresponding rules in the classical logic.

$$\tau(B) \leq \tau(A \rightarrow B), \text{ for any } A$$

3.3. S-equivalence of Interpretations

The correctness proof of the algorithm FUZZY-REFUTATION follows a similar line as in the classical case, except that we have to consider an infinite number of possible interpretations. Since there are only finitely many propositions $P = \{P_1, P_2, \cdots, P_m\}$ to consider and S is a finite set of clauses, we can reduce the problem to a finite form by defining an equivalence relation on the interpretations as follows. Given an elementary meta-literal $L = (P_i \leq \alpha)$, we say two interpretations I_1 and I_2 are L-equivalent if they give rise to the same truth value (T or F) to L; we write these equivalence classes as $[L] = \{I: \tau(P_i) \leq \alpha \text{ in } I\}$ and and $[L'] = \{I: \tau(P_i) > \alpha \text{ in } I\}$; similarly for other types of P_i-literals. Given a set of clauses S, we say I_1 and I_2 are *S-equivalent* if for every elementary meta-literal L_j appearing in S they assign the same truth value to L_j. If $L_1, L_2, \cdots, L_n$ are the distinct literals appearing in S, then each S-equivalence class can be written as

$$[Q_1]\cap[Q_2]\cap\cdots\cap[Q_n], \text{ where each } Q_j = L_j \text{ or } L'_j. \tag{3}$$

Each equivalence class corresponds to a hypercube in $[0, 1]^m$, where m is the number of propositions in P (m may be much smaller than n). It is possible that one or more terms $[Q_i]$ in (3) is redundant in that they can be eliminated without changing the intersection. It follows that the number of distinct S-equivalence classes is at most 2^n.

3.4. Semantic Tree

We organize the non-empty S-equivalence classes of interpretations in the form of a binary tree as follows. Consider a complete binary tree of level n (the level of the root node is 1), where the left-branch at each level j node corresponds to $[L_j]$ and the right-branch corresponds to $[L'_j]$. We further assume that all P_1-literals are considered first, then all P_2-literals, and so on. Each terminal node is then associated with a unique equivalence class as per (3), except when the intersection is empty. If i is the smallest index in (3) such that the intersection $[Q_1]\cap[Q_2]\cap\cdots\cap[Q_i] = \emptyset$, then clearly $[Q_1]\cap[Q_2]\cap\cdots\cap[Q_{i-1}] \subseteq [Q'_i]$. In this case, we eliminate the subtree at the node associated with $[Q_1]\cap [Q_2]\cap\cdots\cap[Q_i]$ (each terminal node in that subtree also correspond to the empty equivalence class) and we elevate the subtree at the brother node corresponding to $[Q_1]\cap [Q_2]\cap\cdots\cap[Q'_i]$ one level up to its parent node. This reduction process is carried out throughout the tree in a top down fashion. Each non-terminal node in the resulting tree now has a left- and a right-child node. We call this the *semantic-tree* for the set of clauses S, denoted by $T(S)$, for the ordering of literals L_j, $j = 1, 2, \cdots, n$. Each intermediate node of $T(S)$ represents the union of the equivalence classes for terminal nodes that are below that node. (The union itself is a hypercube of $[0, 1]^m$.)

Example 2. Consider the clauses $S = \{C_1, C_2, C_3\}$, where $C_1 = (P_1 < 0.2) \vee (P_1 > 0.7)$, $C_2 = (P_1 \leq 0.5)$, and $C_3 = (P_1 \geq 0.4)\}$. Fig. 2 shows the semantic tree for S and the equivalence class at each terminal node in the form (3). The terminal nodes represent a disjoint partition of the unit P_1-interval $[0,1] = [0, 0.2) \cup [0.2, 0.4) \cup [0.4, 0.5] \cup (0.5, 0.7] \cup (0.7, 1.0]$, caused by the intervals corresponding to the literals appearing in S. In the extreme case, one may have a degenerate interval of the form $[0.4, 0.4]$. If there are k distinct P_i-literals, then there are exactly $(k + 1)$ intervals in the decomposition of $[0, 1]$ for P_i. ♦

We first establish a few preliminary lemmas about the properties of the semantic-tree, which are direct generalizations of the corresponding results for the classical case. We say a clause *C fails* at a node of $T(S)$ if C is falsified by each interpretation represented by that node. If the set of clauses S is unsatisfiable, then we can reduce $T(S)$ further as follows. First, for

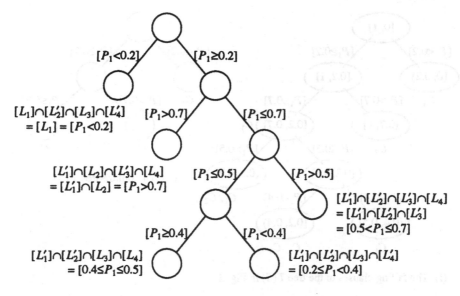

Figure 2. The semantic tree using $L_1 = (P_1 < 0.2)$, $L_2 = (P_1 > 0.7)$, $L_3 = (P_1 \leq 0.5)$, and $L_4 = (P_1 \geq 0.4)$.

each terminal node, there is at least one clause $C_i \in S$ which fails at that node; otherwise the interpretations corresponding to that node would be models of S. It is possible that a clause C_i fails at an intermediate node as well, which happens if and only if C_i fails at each terminal node below that intermediate node. There can also be several clauses which fail at a given node. See Fig. 3(i), where we also show the P_1-interval associated with each node. In the general case, associated with each node of $T(S)$, we will have one interval for each P_i. Next to each node in Fig. 3(i), we also show the clauses which fail at that node. We denote by $F(S)$ the reduced tree obtained from $T(S)$ by deleting all nodes whose parent node has one or more clauses failing at it; we call this reduced tree the *failure-tree* of S. See Fig. 3 (ii).

Lemma 5. If S is an unsatisfiable set of clauses and $S \neq \{\square\}$, then there are two clauses in S which are resolvable.

Proof. Consider the failure-tree $F(S)$ of S and an intermediate node t which is farthest from the root. Let L_j be the P_n-literal associated with the left-branch at t and leading to the left-child t_1; the complementary P_n-literal L'_j leads to the right-child, say, t_2. If we write K, K_1, and K_2 for the P_n-intervals associated with the nodes t, t_1, and t_2, respectively, then $K = K_1 \cup K_2$ (disjoint union); K may equal $[0, 1]$. If C_1 is any clause failing at t_1, then C_1 must contain a P_n-literal L_{11} because otherwise it would fail at t itself. Moreover, the P_n-interval for L_{11} must be disjoint from K_1 and also must intersect K and hence intersect K_2. Similarly, every clause C_2 failing at t_2 has a P_n-literal, L_{21} whose P_n-interval is disjoint from K_2 and intersects K_1. See Fig. 4, where we assume that K_1 is to the left of K_2; here, L_{12} represent another possible P_n-literal in C_1, and similarly L_{22} another possible P_n-literal in C_2. The various intervals K, K_1, and K_2 may be closed or open on one or both ends, except that if K_1 is open at right end then K_2 must be closed at the left end, etc. For t = the parent of the two right-most terminal nodes in Fig. 3(ii), $K = [0.2, 1]$ from Fig. 3(i), $L_j = (P_1 > 0.7)$, $K_1 = [0.2, 0.7]$ and $K_2 = (0.2, 1]$. Since the P_n-interval for L_{11} extends to the right to 1 and that for L_{21} extends to 0 to the left, they are complementary literals and hence $\{C_1, C_2\}$ are P_n-resolvable.

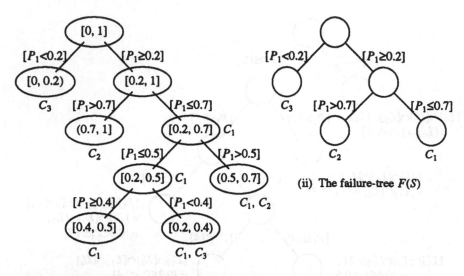

(i) The failing clauses in the tree $T(S)$ in Fig. 2

(ii) The failure-tree $F(S)$

Figure 3. The failure-tree $F(S)$ for the unsatisfiable set of clauses $S = \{C_1, C_2, C_3\}$, where $C_1 = (P_1 < 0.2) \vee (P_1 > 0.7)$, $C_2 = (P_1 \leq 0.5)$, and $C_3 = (P_1 \geq 0.4)$.

Moreover, as seen from Fig. 4, the P_n-resolvent $\text{res}(C_1, C_2)$ will fail at t, and possibly at a higher (closer to the root) node. In particular, the addition of the P_n-resolvent $\text{res}(C_1, C_2)$ to S will reduce the failure-tree by at least two nodes. ♣

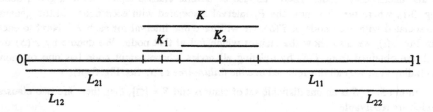

Figure 4. Illustration of the proof of Lemma 5.

Theorem 1 (Soundness and Completeness of FUZZY-REFUTATION). A set of clauses S is unsatisfiable if and only if the successive formation of resolvents by starting with the clauses S lead to the empty clause.

Proof. By Lemma 4, if $C_1, C_2 \in S$ are resolvable and we add $\text{res}(C_1, C_2)$ to S, then the satisfiability of S is not altered. Thus, if we can obtain the empty clause □ via resolvents, then S is unsatisfiable. We now prove the converse. By Lemma 5, we know there is at least one pair of clauses $\{C_1, C_2\} \subseteq S$ which can be resolved, and we can choose these clauses so that the failure tree for $S \cup \{\text{res}(C_1, C_2)\}$ has at least two fewer nodes than $F(S)$. It follows that by repeating the process we shall arrive at the case where the failure-tree consists of just the root-node. But the only clause that can fail at the root node is the empty clause. ♣

Theorem 2 (Completeness of Our Axiom System). Let X be a finite meta-theory and e a meta-formula. Then, we have $X \vdash e$ whenever $X \models e$.

Proof. Clearly, $X \models e$ if and only if $X \cup \{\neg e\}$ is unsatisfiable. By Theorem 1, we have there is a sequence of resolvents leading to $\square = \bot$. Since each resolvent can be viewed as an application of Syllogism rule in our axiom system, this constitutes a proof of $\bot$. The theorem follows from Coro. 1. ♣

Example 3. Consider the meta-theory $X = \{[(A \rightarrow B) \geq 0.4] \vee [(A \vee B) \leq 0.2], (B \leq 0.3)\}$ and suppose we wish to infer $\psi = (A \leq 0.6)$. We get the clauses $\{C_1, C_2, C_3\}$ from X as shown below, of which C_2 is subsumed by C_1 and is eliminated; $\neg \psi$ gives the clause C_4. We get $\text{res}(C_1, C_4) = (B \geq 0.4)$, which can be resolved with C_3 to obtain the empty clause $\square$. It follows that $X \vdash \psi$. To obtain the best upper-bound α for $\tau(A)$, we resolve the clauses of X to obtain A-literals, and they give us the best such bound. In the present case, $\text{res}(C_1, C_3) = (A \leq 0.6)$ gives $\alpha = 0.6$. ♣

$$C_1 = (A \leq 0.6) \vee (B \geq 0.4) \vee (A \leq 0.2) = (A \leq 0.6) \vee (B \geq 0.4) \qquad C_3 = (B \leq 0.3)$$
$$C_2 = (A \leq 0.6) \vee (B \geq 0.4) \vee (B \leq 0.2) \qquad\qquad\qquad\qquad C_4 = (A > 0.6)$$

The above method generalizes directly for inferring the best lower and upper bounds for an objective formula A from a finite meta-theory X. We point out in passing that the generalized resolution method in Section 3.1 can be viewed as a hyper-resolution of ordinary propsitions (one for each disjoint interval of the partition of $[0, 1]$ for each P_i).

4. REFERENCES

[1] Ackermann, R., *An Introduction to many-valued logics*, Dover Pub. Inc., New York, 1967.

[2] Dubois, D., Lang, J., and Prade, H., Fuzzy sets in approximate reasoning (Part 1: inference with possibility, and Part 2: logical approaches) distributions, *Fuzzy Sets and Systems*, 40(1991), pp. 141-202, 203-244.

[3] Goguen, J.A., The logic of inexact concepts, *Synthese*, 19(1968), pp. 325-373.

[4] Gottwald, S., Fuzzy propositional logics, *Fuzzy Sets and Systems*, 3(1980), pp. 181-192.

[5] Kundu, S. An improved method for fuzzy-inferencing using Zadeh's implication operator, *Proceedings of IJCAL Workshop on Fuzzy Logic in AI*, Aug. 1995, Montreal, Canada.

[6] Kundu, S. and Chen, J., Fuzzy logic or Lukasiewicz's logic: a clarification, *Proc. 8th Intern. Symp. for Methodologies for Intelligent Systems*, ISMIS-94, Charlotte, NC. (Oct. 16-19, 1994), pp. 56-64.

[7] Lee, R.C.T., Fuzzy logic and the resolution principle, *J. Assoc. of Computing Mach.*, 19(1), 1972, pp. 109-119.

[8] Lu, J.J., Murray, N.V., and Rosenthal, E., Signed formulas and fuzzy operator logics, *Proc. 8th Intern. Symp. for Methodologies for Intelligent Systems*, ISMIS-94, Charlotte, NC. (Oct. 16-19, 1994), pp. 75-84.

[9] Novak, V., On the syntactico-semantical completeness of first-order fuzzy logic. Part 1, 2, *Kybernetika*, 26(1) (1990) 47-66; (2) (1990) 134-154.

[10] Pavelka, J., On fuzzy logic I, II, III, *Zeitsch. Math. Logik*, 25(1979), pp. 45-52, 119-134, 447-464.

Meeting the Deadline:
On the Formal Specification of Temporal Deontic Constraints

F.Dignum[1], H. Weigand and E. Verharen[2]

[1] Fac. of Maths. & Comp. Sc., Eindhoven University of Technology, The Netherlands
[2] Infolab, Tilburg University, The Netherlands

Abstract. In this paper, we describe a temporal deontic logic that facilitates reasoning about obligations and deadlines. The logic is an extension of deontic dynamic logic, in which only immediate obligations can be specified. In our extension, we can also specify that an obligation starts at a certain time or event, that it must be done immediately, as soon as possible, before a deadline, or periodically. A practical application area are intelligent agents that must be able to reason about their agendas.

1 Introduction

It is not very difficult to develop a program that checks whether deadlines are met. The main idea is to wait until the deadline has passed, which usely can be checked easily, and then check whether a certain action has taken place. However, many difficulties arise when one tries to transform this procedural account of deadlines into a formal one. In an intelligent system (or agent) one would like to be able to reason about this type of constraints in order to check whether they can be fulfilled at all. This holds especially for combinations of different deadlines. Constraints can also be used to influence the behaviour of the agent. The combination of deadlines can be used to plan the actions of an agent. Of course this is only possible if the system has some formal description (besides a procedural one) of the deadlines.

A related issue is the occasion that a certain deadline is not met. What should be the consequences of the failure to meet a deadline? If one sees the failure to meet a deadline as a constraint violation, in some systems this would mean that the system reaches an inconsistent state. In these systems (most database systems currently in use) the constraints have to be fulfilled at any moment in time. Of course this can easily be enforced for static constraints. Any update of the system that violates a constraint is rejected. However, deadlines are constraints with a fundamental different nature. Whether a deadline is met depends on an action that must have taken place. In case this action only depends on the system itself one might force the system to perform the action before the deadline is reached. In this case the deadline would be used as part of the planning system of the intelligent system. The deadlines would not have to be checked afterwards because they would be met by default (if possible of course).

Several problems can arise using this method. First of all it is not clear at what time the action should be planned. As soon as possible or just before the deadline? This problem can be aggrevated by deadlines of which it is not known beforehand when they will be reached. E.g. place an order before the stock falls below a certain level. It is not known at what point in time the stock falls below that level. We argue that the enforcement of the deadline and the planning problem are two separate issues and the enforcement of deadlines should not be implemented by a planning procedure. Of course we do acknowledge that the deadlines influence the planning of the actions of the intelligent system.

A second problem that arises with the enforcement of deadlines is that the system is not always capable of enforcing the performance of a certain action. E.g. upon delivery of the product the customer has to pay the bill within 30 days. The system can base its plans on the fact that the customer has paid within 30 days, but it has no way to enforce this payment (directly). This shows that deadlines cannot always be enforced. Therefore a system should not reach a state of inconsistency whenever a deadline is not met. Rather it should arrive at a state in which it is clear that a deadline has passed, but other (corrective) actions are still possible. (In case of the customer the system could send a reminder or a court order for payment).

A last problem that we like to mention is the case where no specific deadline has been set. A certain action should take place "as soon as possible". E.g. after an accident has been reported the ambulance has to go to the place of the accident as soon as possible. However, it might be that the ambulance first has to deliver another patient at the hospital or that the accident is not very serious and the ambulance does not switch on its siren. In these cases there is not a definite point in time where one can check whether the action has been performed or not.

In this paper we aim at formally describing deadlines such that it is possible to reason about them. One important requirement is that it must be possible to violate the deadline without the system entering an inconsistent state. In order to fulfill this requirement we use a form of dynamic deontic logic. In this logic it is possible to state that a certain action should take place without getting an inconsistency when the action does not take place.

We will show that the following types of deadlines can be described in the logical formalism in a natural and concise form.

1. Deadlines concerning a specific time relative to the current moment.

2. Deadlines that depend on a certain state that may be established by an external action. (e.g. order before the stock is to low).

3. Flexible deadlines, i.e. obligations that should be fulfilled "as soon as possible"

4. Periodic deadlines. I.e. payment of employees each month.

The rest of this paper is organized as follows. First we will introduce the dynamic deontic logic that is used to describe the deadlines. In section 3 we will describe the types of deadlines given above in the dynamic deontic logic (using some concrete examples). Section 4 contains some conclusions and directions for further research.

2 A logic of actions and norms

We now proceed with the definition of a set of *formulas* with which we can describe the behaviour of (interpreted) (trans)actions. This language is a variant of *dynamic logic* ([10]), and was first used for this purpose in [12]. In the present paper we add a few "new" formulas to this language. They are the ones defined in points (5), (6) and (7) below. The formulas defined in (5) involve a variant on the standard dynamic logic definition of the consequence of (trans)actions. The formulas defined in (6) all involve some type of temporal operations on actions. Allthough more approaches exist that combine temporal and deontic logics (e.g. [13, 11, 9]) these approaches tend to express the deontic concepts in terms of the temporal operators. In this paper we take a different approach. We actually "add" the temporal operators to the deontic logic that is used as a basis. The formulas defined in (7) define the "classical" deontic formulas as introduced by v.Wright in [14, 1]. Finally, the formulas defined in (8) introduce a preference relation between actions. They state which action is preferred to be performed at a certain time.

We assume a fixed set *Prop* of atomic propositions and sets *Act* and *Tract* of action expressions and transaction expressions respectively (see below). The set *Form* of formulas with typical elements ϕ and ψ is given by the following BNF:

$$\phi :: - p|\phi \wedge \psi|\neg\phi|[\beta]\phi| \ll \beta \gg \phi|$$
$$PAST(\alpha, i)|PREV(\alpha)|O(\phi)|PREFER(\alpha, \alpha')$$

with p a proposition, α, α' actions and β a transaction (defined below).
Note: Other propositional connectives such as $\vee$ and $\rightarrow$ are assumed to be introduced as the usual abbreviations. Also the special proposition *false* is introduced as the abbreviation of $p \wedge \neg p$ for some $p \in Prop$. The informal meaning of $[\beta]\phi$ is "doing β necessarily leads to a state where ϕ holds". $\ll \beta \gg \phi$ means that after performing the transaction denoted by β the formula ϕ holds and it does not hold before β is completely performed. The meaning of $PAST(\alpha, i)$ is that α has actually been performed i steps ago. The meaning of $PREV(\alpha)$ is "the present state is actually reached by performing α". Note that we make a difference between the possible ways that the state can be reached and the way it actually *is* reached. The informal meaning of $O(\phi)$ is that ϕ should be the case in the present state. The last type of formulas defined above indicate that a certain action α is preferred to performing α'.

The semantics of the formulas in *Form* is given in two stages. First we will give the syntax and intuitive semantics of the transaction expressions, which we will subsequently use in section 2.2 to define the semantics of the formulas.

2.1 Transaction expressions

We start out by giving a definition of *transaction expressions*, which we shall typically denote α, possibly with subscripts. To this end we assume a set At of *atomic action expressions* that are typically denoted by $\underline{a}, \underline{b}, \ldots$. Furthermore, we assume special action expressions **any** and **fail** denoting "don't care what happens" and "failure", respectively.

Definition 2.1 The set Act of action expressions is given by the following BNF:

$$\alpha :: -\underline{a}|\textbf{any}|\textbf{fail}|\alpha_1 + \alpha_2|\alpha_1 \& \alpha_2|\overline{\alpha}$$

The set *Tract* of transaction expressions is given by the following BNF:

$$\beta :: -\underline{a}|\textbf{any}|\textbf{fail}|\beta_1 + \beta_2|\beta_1 \& \beta_2|\overline{\beta}|\beta_1 ; \beta_2$$

Note that the definition of Act is almost the same as for *Tract* except that we do not allow for sequences of actions. To keep the logic as simple as possible the temporal operators only reach over action expressions and not over transaction expressions.

The semantics of (trans)action expressions has two components. The first component is an algebra of uninterpreted actions (called a *uniform* semantics elsewhere [3]), which allows us to interpret equalities between action expressions without taking their effect into account. In the algebraic semantics, each action expression will be interpreted as a choice over possible steps. Due to a lack of space we refer to [7] for a formal account of this part. Most important is that we have a formal semantics for the negation of (trans)actions as well. Informally the semantics of a (trans)action α ($[\![\alpha]\!]$) is given as a set of *traces*.

Definition 2.2 A trace is a finite or infinite sequence $S_1 S_2 \ldots S_n \ldots$ of steps. ϵ stands for the empty trace.

The second component of the semantics is a state-transition semantics of action expressions where we define the effect of steps on the state of the world. Most notable here is that the effect of any action can always be a set of new states. (One for each trace in its semantics)

We define the duration of action expressions as follows.

Definition 2.3 The **duration** of α is defined as $dur(\alpha) = dur([\![\alpha]\!])$.

2.2 Semantics of formulas

Having defined the action expressions within the formulas, we can now give the semantics of formulas in *Form* by means of the notion of a Kripke structure $\mathcal{M} = (\mathcal{A}, \Sigma, \pi, R_{\mathcal{A}}, \leq, R_O)$.
Σ is a set of states (worlds).
$\mathcal{A}$ is a finite set of events.
π is a truth assignment function to the atomic propositions relative to a state:

π is a function $\Sigma \to (Prop \to \{tt, ff\})$, where tt and ff denote truth and falsehood, respectively. Thus, for $p \in Prop$, $\pi(\sigma)(p) = tt$ means that the atomic proposition p is true in state σ.

The accessibility relation $R_{\mathcal{A}}$ specifies how transactions can change states. The relation $R_{\mathcal{A}}$ is defined as follows: $R_{\mathcal{A}} = \{R_t | t \ a \ trace\}$, reflecting that R_t is the relevant entity.

$\leq$ is a function $(\Sigma \times A^*) \times (\Sigma \times A^*) \to \{tt, ff\}$. The function indicates for two state/history pairs which of the two is preferred.

In this paper we only use the preference relation to indicate a preference relation between actions. We do not give a logic for the preference relation itself. However, one might intuitively think that an action α is preferred over an action β if it leads to states in which less constraints are violated or the violations are considered less harmfull(i.e. which are more ideal in a deontic sense). For a thorough treatment of this type of logic we refer to [4]. Here we take the preference relation to be primitive.

R_O is the deontic relation that with respect to a state σ reached by trace γ indicates the ideal situation consisting of state σ' and trace γ'. R_O resembles the classical deontic relation in modal interpretations, except that we do not consider only states, but pairs of states and traces. We assume the relation R_O to be serial. I.e. for every world σ and trace γ there exists at least one pair (σ', γ') such that $R_O((\sigma, \gamma)(\sigma', \gamma'))$ holds.

We now give the interpretation of formulas in *Form* in Kripke structures. We interpret formulas with respect to a structure $\mathcal{M}$ and a pair (σ, γ)

Definition 2.4 Given $\mathcal{M} = (\mathcal{A}, \Sigma, \pi, R_{\mathcal{A}}, R_O, I)$ as above and (σ, γ), we define:

1. $(\mathcal{M}, (\sigma, \gamma)) \models p \Longleftrightarrow \pi(\sigma)(p) = tt$ (for $p \in Prop$)

2. $(\mathcal{M}, (\sigma, \gamma)) \models \phi_1 \wedge \phi_2 \Longleftrightarrow (\mathcal{M}, (\sigma, \gamma)) \models \phi_1$ and $(\mathcal{M}, (\sigma, \gamma)) \models \phi_2$

3. $(\mathcal{M}, (\sigma, \gamma)) \models \neg\phi \Longleftrightarrow$ not $(\mathcal{M}, (\sigma, \gamma)) \models \phi$

4. $(\mathcal{M}, (\sigma, \gamma)) \models [\alpha]\phi \Longleftrightarrow \forall t \in [\![\alpha]\!]\forall\sigma' \in \Sigma[R_t(\sigma, \sigma') \Rightarrow (\mathcal{M}, (\sigma', \gamma \circ S)) \models \phi]$

5. $(\mathcal{M}, (\sigma, \gamma)) \models \ll \alpha \gg \phi \Longleftrightarrow \exists(\sigma', \gamma') : \gamma' = \gamma \circ t \wedge t \in [\![\alpha]\!] \wedge (\mathcal{M}, (\sigma', \gamma')) \models$
   $\phi \wedge \neg \exists\alpha_1\exists\alpha_2 : (\alpha_1; \alpha_2 =_{\mathcal{D}} \alpha) \wedge \exists(\sigma'\gamma') : \gamma' = \gamma \circ t \wedge t \in [\![\alpha_1]\!] \wedge (\mathcal{M}, (\sigma', \gamma')) \models \phi$

6. $(\mathcal{M}, (\sigma, \gamma)) \models O(\phi) \Longleftrightarrow \forall(\sigma', \gamma')[R_O((\sigma, \gamma), (\sigma', \gamma')) \Rightarrow (\mathcal{M}, (\sigma', \gamma')) \models \phi]$

7. $(\mathcal{M}, (\sigma, \gamma)) \models PREV(\alpha) \Longleftrightarrow \exists S \in [\![\alpha]\!], \gamma'[\gamma = \gamma' \circ S]$

8. $(\mathcal{M}, (\sigma, \gamma)) \models PAST(\alpha, i) \Longleftrightarrow \exists\sigma' \in \Sigma\exists\gamma', \gamma''[\gamma = \gamma' \circ \gamma'' \wedge$
   $dur(\gamma'') = i \wedge (\mathcal{M}, (\sigma', \gamma')) \models PREV(\alpha)]$

9. $(\mathcal{M}, (\sigma, \gamma)) \models PREFER(\alpha_1, \alpha_2) \Longleftrightarrow \forall t \in [\![\alpha_2]\!](R_t(\sigma, \sigma_2) \longrightarrow$
   $(\exists t' \in [\![\alpha_1]\!](R_{t'}(\sigma, \sigma_1) \wedge (\sigma_1, \gamma \circ t') \leq (\sigma_2, \gamma \circ t))))$

10. ϕ is *valid* w.r.t. model $\mathcal{M} = (\mathcal{A}, \Sigma, \pi, R_{\mathcal{A}}, R_O, I)$, notation $\mathcal{M} \models \phi$, if $(\mathcal{M}, (\sigma, \gamma)) \models \phi$ for all $\sigma \in \Sigma$ and γ.

11. ϕ is *valid*, notation $\models \phi$, if ϕ is valid w.r.t. all models $\mathcal{M}$ of the form considered above.

The first four definitions are quite standard and we will not explain them any further here. In (5) we define the fact that the condition ϕ becomes true for the first time after performing the (complete) transaction denoted by α.
The definition of the static obligation involves both the state and the trace (and *not* just the state). In this way, we can express that the circumstances described by $PREV(\alpha)$, for example, are obligatory. For example, it might be obligatory to have just done the action indicated by α. This means that the history (i.e. the trace) of an ideal world might differ from the history of the present world. We will use this feature to define obligations on actions shortly.
It should be noted that using the semantic definition of $[\mathbf{any}]\phi$ we can express the usual temporal operators over static formulas as given in e.g. [8]. Points (7) and (8) define extra temporal operators reaching over action expressions! Point (9) defines what it means that one action is preferred over another action.

Before we give a definition of the deontic operators in the next section, we will introduce a helpful operator. This operator indicates that a formula ϕ is true as soon as a formula ψ becomes true. It is defined formally as follows:

Definition 2.5

$$\phi \text{ when } \psi \equiv \ll \gamma \gg \psi \longrightarrow [\gamma](\psi \rightarrow \phi)$$

2.3 Obligations and deadlines

Using the above definitions we can now introduce the deontic operators over actions. We will introduce one general type of obligations: the obligation with deadlines. Using this general type, we will then define some special types of obligations that are often used to describe all types of deadlines.

Definition 2.6 $O(\phi < \alpha < \psi) \equiv O(\alpha < \psi) \text{ when } \phi$
with $O(\alpha < \psi) \equiv \ll \gamma \gg \psi \wedge dur(\gamma) = n \longrightarrow [\gamma](\psi \rightarrow O(\exists i : 0 \leq i < n : PAST(\alpha, i)))$

The most general form $O(\phi < \alpha < \psi)$ stands for the fact that α should be performed after ϕ has become true and before ψ has become true. Intuitively $O(\alpha < \psi)$ stands for the fact that α should be performed before ψ holds true. I.e. if ψ becomes true (sometimes) for the first time after γ then it is obliged that α has been performed in the course of γ (in the last n steps).

The first specialisation of the general obligation is made with respect to the begin and end conditions of the period in which the action should be performed. The definition in the general case is somewhat complicated because whether these conditions hold true might depend on the type of (trans)action that is performed. In the case that we take the conditions to be purely temporal they do not depend on the transaction performed anymore. We distinguish between relative and absolute time conditions. For the absolute time conditions we can introduce a special variable *time*. We assume all actions to take equal time and the length of an action defines the basic unit of time. Using this axiom we define the general obligation with pure temporal deadlines as follows:

Definition 2.7 $O(now + temp_1 < \alpha < now + temp_1 + temp_2) \equiv (time = now \wedge [\mathbf{any}^n]time = now + temp_1) \wedge [\mathbf{any}^n][\mathbf{any}^m]time = now + temp_1 + temp_2) \longrightarrow [\mathbf{any}^{n+m}]O(\exists 0 \leq i < m : PAST(\alpha, i))$
and $O(\alpha < now + temp_2) \equiv (time = now \wedge [\mathbf{any}^m]time = now + temp_2) \longrightarrow [\mathbf{any}^m]O(\exists 0 \leq i < m : PAST(\alpha, i))$

The next specialisation of the general case is in fact the type of dynamic obligation as it is used in most dynamic deontic logics. It is the "immediate" obligation, which means that the action should be performed as the next action. The immediate obligation is defined as follows:

Definition 2.8 $O!(\alpha) \equiv O(\alpha < now + 1)$

From the definitions the following equivalence can easily be proven:

Proposition 2.9 $O!(\alpha) \equiv [\mathbf{any}]O(PREV(\alpha))$

So, α is obligated if, whatever I do now, it will be true immediately afterwards that I was just previously obligated to do α. This means that if I do $\overline{\alpha}$, I reach a state where a violation occurs.

With the general type of obligation with deadlines it is also possible to describe an obligation that has to be fulfilled as soon as possible. This obligation is interpreted as meaning that the action should be performed as soon as no other actions with a higher "preference" are performed. The definition is as follows:

Definition 2.10 $O?(\alpha) \equiv O(true < \alpha < PREV(\beta) \wedge PREFER(\alpha, \beta))$

This obligation can be used when no strict deadline is given, but we want the action to be performed at some time. It resembles the "liveness" property as described in [9], except that the obligated action cannot be postponed indefinite. It has to be performed before an action with lesser importance is performed.

The last type of obligation that we will describe is the periodic obligation. This obligation returns every time a certain condition holds true and should be fulfilled before another condition holds true. E.g. an order should be placed after the stock of computers has fallen below 15 and before the level dropped below 5. Although this seems the same as the general obligation described above it is a bit different. The condition that the stock falls below a certain level will be true periodically (one hopes) and every time this happens an order for replenishment should be made. The periodic obligation is described as follows:

Definition 2.11
$PO(\phi < \alpha < \psi) \equiv \forall n : dur(\gamma) = n \longrightarrow [\gamma](O(\alpha < \psi) \vee justdone(\alpha))$
with
$justdone(\alpha) \equiv (\exists 0 \leq i < n - k : PAST(\alpha, i)) \wedge \gamma = \beta_1; \beta_2 \wedge dur(\beta_1) = k \wedge [\beta_1]\phi \wedge (\forall \beta' : \beta' = \beta_1; \beta_3 \wedge dur(\beta') < n \rightarrow \neg[\beta']\phi))$

justdone(α) states that α has been done after the last time that ϕ became true. The definition of $PO(\phi < \alpha < \psi)$ states that (from now on) it is always obligated to do α before ψ holds true except when α has been "justdone".

3   Modelling deadlines

In this section we will model the types of deadlines given in the introduction within the logical framework developed in the previous section using some concrete example for each type of deadline.

> When a CS student is enrolled in the university then he has to pass the exam in "introduction to programming" within the first year.

This example is modeled as follows:

$$\forall p: \; PREV(Enroll(p, CS) \rightarrow O(Pass(p, IP) < now + year)$$

I.e. if $Enroll(p, CS)$ has just been done then there is an obligation to perform the action $Pass(p, IP)$ between "now" and a year time. We assume that *year* stands for an integer that indicates how many times an action should be performed to advance the absolute time with one year. Although parameterized actions were not explicitly introduced in this paper, we use them in the examples in order to get a more realistic representation. The formal introduction of parameterized actions can be found in [6].

The second example shows some combinations of different types of deadlines.

> After the stock of computers has fallen below 10 an order should be made before the stock is less than 6. If an order has been made the delivery should follow within 5 days. If the delivery is not made in time a reminder should be sent. After the receipt of the goods payment should be affectuated within 30 days.

This example is modelled by the following formulas:

(1) $O(PREV(fall - stock(Computers < 10)) < Order < stock(Computers) < 6)$
(2) $PREV(Order) \rightarrow O(Delivery < now + 5 * day)$
(3) $(PREV(Order) \wedge [\mathbf{any}^{5*day}](\neg \exists_{0 \leq i < 5*day} PAST(Delivery, i))) \longrightarrow$
$$[\mathbf{any}^{5*day}]O!(Send(reminder))$$
(4) $PREV(Receipt) \rightarrow O(Pay < now + 30 * day)$

The third formula is a typical example of how the violation of an obligation triggers another obligation. This is very natural, because the violation of an obligation should lead to some rectifying action, which is usually an obligation as well.

The next example illustrates an obligation that should be fulfilled "as soon as possible".

After a customer has phoned to register a failing central heating system (during the winter) a mechanic should try to repair it as soon as possible, but at least within 24 hours. (From a contract between a service company and a client).

This is an example of having an obligation to perform an action as soon as possible. In this case it might be that the service company is very busy and got several calls at the same time. In that case it is not possible to go to all clients at the same time. However, if the mechanic goes to all the clients one after the other we would say he fulfilled the obligation of the service company. The above example can be modeled as follows:

$$PREV(Report(ch)) \longrightarrow (O?(Try - repair(mechanic, ch)) \wedge$$
$$O(Try - repair(mechanic, ch) < now + 24 * hour))$$

The last example illustrates the use of periodic obligations.

The employees of the company have to be paid their salaries between the 25th and 30th day of each month.

The above example can be modelled very simple as follows:

$$PO(monthday(time) = 25 < Pay(salary, emp) < monthday(time) = 30)$$

where *monthday* is a function that returns the day of the month given an absolute point in time.

4   Conclusions

We have shown in this paper how deadlines can be modelled using a type of dynamic deontic logic. Deadlines play an important role in flexible transactions. In situations where several systems have to cooperate deadlines are a means to specify expectations of the behaviour of the other parties. E.g. if a company delivers a product it expects a payment of the customer within a certain time.

Actions and transactions are necessary ingredients in the specification of deadlines. First of all deadlines are always specified on actions. I.e. every deadline indicates that a certain *action* is expected to take place. Secondly the deadline may be dependent on the (trans)actions that are performed. E.g. You have to pay the rent before you buy a new car. These considerations indicate that a formal specification of deadlines should involve a formal specification of actions. We have chosen a form of dynamic logic to incorporate the actions into the specification language.

A second important property of deadlines is that they are not always kept. In the case that keeping a deadline depends on an action from another system (or person) it is not possible to enforce the deadline. Therefore we should use a formalism that allows the violation of the deadline without getting in an inconsistent state. This requirement is fulfilled by the incorporation of deontic logic into the specification language.

The use of a logic as specification language enables the system to reason about the deadlines. Deadlines can be combined and inconsistent deadlines (deadlines that cannot be kept jointly) can be detected.

The present work also opens some areas for further research. In particular the temporal aspects of the language are rather primitive. We assume that all actions take the same amount of time, which, of course, is not very realistic. A second area for further research is the influence of the deadlines on the (planning of) actions of the system.

Acknowledgements We would like to thank the anonymous referees for giving some very usefull remarks that put this research into a wider context.

References

1. L. Åqvist. Deontic logic. In D.M. Gabbay and F. Guenthner, editors, *Handbook of Philosophical Logic II*, pages 605–714. Reidel, 1984.
2. J.C.M. Baeten and W.P. Weijland. Process Algebra. Cambridge University Press, 1990.
3. J.W. de Bakker, J.N Kok, J.-J.Ch. Meyer, E.-R. Olderog, and J.I. Zucker. Contrasting themes in the semantics of imperative concurrency. In J.W. de Bakker, W.P. de Roever, and G. Rozenberg, editors, *Current Trends in Concurrency: Overviews and Tutorials*, pages 51–121. LNCS 224 Springer, Berlin, 1986.
4. C. Boutilier Toward a Logic for Qualitative Decision Theory. In JonDoyle, Erik Sandewall and Pietro Torasso (eds.), *Principles of Knowledge Representation and Reasoning, proceedings of the fourth international conference*, pages 75–86, 1994, Morgan Kaufmann Publishers, San Francisco, California.
5. M. Broy. A theory for nondeterminism, parallelism, communication and concurrency. In *Theoretical Computer Science*, vol.45, pages 1–62, 1986.
6. F. Dignum and J.-J.Ch. Meyer. Negations of transactions and their use in the specification of dynamic and deontic integrity constraints. In M. Kwiatkowska, M.W. Shields, and R.M. Thomas, editors, *Semantics for Concurrency, Leicester 1990*, pages 61–80, Springer, Berlin, 1990.
7. Contextual permission. a solution to the free choice paradox. In A. Jones and M. Sergot, editors, *Second International Workshop on Deontic Logic in Computer Science*, pages 107–135, Oslo, 1994. Tano A.S.
8. E.A. Emerson. Temporal and Modal Logic. In J. van Leeuwen, editor, *Handbook of Theoretical Computer Science*, pages 995–1072, North-Holland, Amsterdam, 1989.
9. J. Fiadeiro and T. Maibaum. Temporal Reasoning over Deontic Specification. In *Journal of Logic and Computation*, 1 (3), 1991.
10. D. Harel. First Order Dynamic Logic. LNCS 68 Springer, 1979.
11. J.F. Horty. Combining Agency and Obligation. In M. Brown and J. Carmo (eds.), *Deontic Logic, Agency and Normative Systems*, pages 98-122, Springer-Verlag, Berlin, 1996.
12. J.-J.Ch. Meyer. A different approach to deontic logic: Deontic logic viewed as a variant of dynamic logic. In *Notre Dame*, vol.29, pages 109–136, 1988.
13. R. Thomason. Deontic Logic as founded on tense logic. In R. Hilpinen, editor, *New Studies in Deontic Logic*, pages 165-176, D.Reidel Publishing Company, 1981.
14. G.H. von Wright. Deontic logic. In *Mind*, vol.60, pages 1–15, 1951.

Validity Queries and Completeness Queries

Robert Demolombe

CERT/ONERA, 2 Avenue E. Belin BP 4025, 31055 Toulouse, France

Abstract. The concepts of validity and completeness are defined in terms of relationship between a correct representation of the real world and the representation of the real world which is stored in a database. Here a database is understood as a Relational database, that is, a set of atomic facts. It is assumed that some users can guarantee that some parts of the database are valid, and other parts are complete. From this information, for a given standard query, are characterized a subset of the answer to the standard query which is valid, and a superset of the answer which is complete. It is guaranteed that the correct answer is bounded up and down by these two sets.

We give a formal definition of these notions in the semantics. Then we present a sound axiomatics that can be used to define a Prolog program which computes answers to validity queries and completeness queries. The axiomatics is not complete because the definition of the non standard answers involves the notion of inclusion on Relational algebra formulas. If some strong restrictions on the completeness of the axiomatics are imposed the program always terminates.

Keywords: Intelligent Information Systems, Uncertainty, Epistemic Logic.

1 Introduction

In most cases it is not possible to guarantee that the overall information stored in a database is a correct representation of the real world. However there are many application where it can be guaranteed that some parts of the database are **valid**, in the sense that the information represented by these parts is true of the world, or are **complete**, in the sense that the overall information, corresponding to these parts, which is true of the world is represented in the database.

These concepts of validity and completeness can be used to enforce database integrity as Demolombe and Jones have shown in [3] . They can also be used to inform users about the validity and completeness of some parts of an answer to a given query, as it has been shown by Motro in [5, 6]. This latter information can be considered as answers to validity queries and to completeness queries, in the sense that, for a given standard query, a validity query asks what parts of the answer to the standard query are valid, and a completeness query asks what

---

* I am quite grateful to Laurence Cholvy whose valuable comments helped me to improve the quality of this paper. This work has been partially suported by the CEC, in the context of the Basic Research Action MEDLAR 2.

parts are complete. The purpose of this paper is to propose a practical method to compute answers to these queries.

Let us take an example where a database contains information about flights which is represented by the relation schema: F(#Flight,Departure-city, Arrival-city, Company,Day). Assume that the information about validity is: *all the tuples in the relation F corresponding to flights whose departure city or arrival city is Paris, represent true facts of the world*, and the information about completeness is *all the true facts of the world corresponding to flights whose company is Air France are represented by a tuple in the relation F*. Now, if one asks the standard query: *what are the flights from Paris to London ?*, the answer to the corresponding validity query is: *all the tuples in the answer are valid*, and the answer to the completeness query is *the answer is complete for all the tuples where the company is Air France*.

Validity queries and completeness queries raise two problems. The first one is: *how to formally represent information about the valid parts and the complete parts of the database?*, and the second one is: *how to compute answers to validity queries and to completeness queries?*.

In [4] Demolombe and Jones have proposed solutions, based on the theory of signaling acts, for validity queries. [2] In this approach it is assumed that validity of data stored in the database depends on the type of data and on the reliability of users who have inserted these data. That is, some users are assumed to be safe in regard to insertions of some particular data. The formalism that is used to represent this information is a combination of an epistemic logic and of a logic of actions. The context is more general than Relational databases. Indeed, a database is supposed to be any set of propositional sentences. The method to compute answers to validity queries should be based on automated deduction techniques [2], and it is well known that their efficiency is worst than Relational algebra techniques.

In [6] Motro has proposed solutions, in the context of Relational databases, where information about validity and completeness only depends on the type of data, and it is represented by tuples in meta relations [3] associated with each standard relation. For instance for a given relation r the presence of a tuple $< a, x >$ in the associated meta relation v.r about validity means that all the tuples in the relation r of the form $< a, x >$ are guaranteed to be true, and a tuple $< y, b >$ in the meta relation c.p about the completeness of relation p means that all the tuples of the form $< y, b >$ which satisfy p in the world are present in the representation of p in the database. Motro has defined an algebra on the v.relations and on the c.relations to compute the tuples that characterize, for a given standard query, the answer to the validity query and the answer to the completeness query. This algebra is very close to Relational algebra. The only significant difference is for the treatment of variables that appear in tuples, and it can easily and efficiently be implemented using existing techniques. However,

---

[2] In the referenced paper validity queries are called safety queries.

[3] As a matter of homogeneity with this paper, we have slightly changed the terminology used by Motro.

there is a strong limitation on the form of queries. Indeed, queries can only involve selections, projections and joins. No union and no difference is allowed. That means, in logical terms, no disjunction and no negation.

The main contribution of this paper is to give a general formal definition of the concepts of validity and completeness, when these concepts are applied to a database content, or to an answer to a query. In particular we show how these two concepts are related to each other. This is presented in sections 2 and 3.1.

Another contribution is to present an effective method to compute answers to validity queries and to completeness queries. The basic idea is to make use of the definitions of the valid views and of the complete views of the data base to transform standard queries into sets of queries whose answers are the answers to validity queries or to completeness queries. The presented transformation always terminates, but it does not always provides the complete set of transformed queries. This computation method is presented in section 3.

2 Representation of Information About Validity and Completeness

In this section is presented a semantic definition, in terms of extensions, of validity queries and completeness queries.

Definition 1. Relation schema. A relation schema rs of arity n is a relation name r and a tuple of definition domains $< D_{i_1}, \ldots, D_{i_n} >$. That is rs $=< r, < D_{i_1}, \ldots, D_{i_n} >>$.

Definition 2. Relation schema extension. Let rs be the relation schema $< r, < D_{i_1}, \ldots, D_{i_n} >>$, an extension of rs is a subset ρ of $D_{i_1} \times \ldots \times D_{i_n}$.

Definition 3. Database schema. A database schema s is a tuple $< rs_1, \ldots, rs_p >$ of relation schemas. That is s $=< rs_1, \ldots, rs_p >$.

Definition 4. Database schema extension. Let s be the database schema $< rs_1, \ldots, rs_p >$, an extension se of s is a tuple of relation schema extensions se $=< \rho_1, \ldots, \rho_p >$ such that for every i in [1,p] ρ_i is an extension of the relation schema rs_i.

Definition 5. Database state. Let s be a database schema, a database state db corresponding to s is an extension of s. That is db $=< \rho_1, \ldots, \rho_p >$.

Definition 6. World state. Let s be a database schema, a world state w corresponding to s is an extension of s. That is w $=< \rho'_1, \ldots, \rho'_p >$.

Definition 7. Possible states. Let s be a database schema, a set of possible states ST is a set of pairs $< db, w >$, such that db is a database state associated with s, and w is a world state associated with s.

Definition 8. Relational Algebra language. Let s be a database schema, the corresponding Relational Algebra language RA is defined by the following rules.

- If r is a relation name in the database schema s then r ∈ RA.
- If f ∈ RA and g ∈ RA then (f × g) ∈ RA, (f ∪ g) ∈ RA, (f ∩ g) ∈ RA and (f − g) ∈ RA. [4]
- If f ∈ RA and arity of f is n, then $s_c(f)$ ∈ RA, where c is a boolean expression whose atoms are of the form iθj or iθa, where θ is a comparison operator, i and j are in [1,n], and a is in D_i.
- If f ∈ RA and arity of f is n and p =< $i_1, \ldots, i_m$ >, where $\{i_1, \ldots, i_m\}$ is a subset of $\{1, \ldots, n\}$, then $\pi_p(f)$ ∈ RA.

Definition 9. Relational Algebra language evaluation. Let s be a database schema, se be an extension of s, and RA be a corresponding Relational Algebra language. The interpretation of a formula h of RA in se is denoted by h(se). [5]

Definition 10. Inclusion of a formula in another formula. Let f and f' be two formulas of a Relational Algebra language RA corresponding to a database schema s. It is said that f' is included in f iff for every extension se of s we have f'(se) ⊆ f(se). That is f' ⊆ f holds iff ∀se f'(se) ⊆ f(se) holds.

Definition 11. Valid view. Let s be a database schema and ST an associated set of possible states. Let f be a formula of a Relational Algebra language RA corresponding to s. The formula f is a valid view, and this fact is denoted by V(f), iff for every possible state < db, w > in ST we have f(db) ⊆ f(w).
That is V(f) $\stackrel{\text{def}}{=}$ ∀db ∀w (< db, w >∈ ST ⇒ f(db) ⊆ f(w)).

Definition 12. Complete view. Let s be a database schema and ST an associated set of possible states. Let f be a formula of a Relational Algebra language RA corresponding to s. The formula f is a complete view, and this fact is denoted by C(f), iff for every possible state < db, w > in ST we have f(w) ⊆ f(db).
That is C(f) $\stackrel{\text{def}}{=}$ ∀db ∀w (< db, w >∈ ST ⇒ f(w) ⊆ f(db)).

Definition 13. Valid subset and valid superset of a formula. Let f and f' be two formulas of the same Relational Algebra language. It is said that f' characterizes a valid subset of f, and this fact is denoted by $v_{inf}(f, f')$, iff we have V(f') and f' ⊆ f. It is said that f' characterizes a valid superset of f, and this fact is denoted by $v_{sup}(f, f')$, iff we have V(f') and f ⊆ f'.
That is, $v_{inf}(f, f') \stackrel{\text{def}}{=}$ V(f') ∧ f' ⊆ f, and $v_{sup}(f, f') \stackrel{\text{def}}{=}$ V(f') ∧ f ⊆ f'.

Definition 14. Complete subset and complete superset of a formula. Let f and f' be two formulas of the same Relational Algebra language. It is said that f' characterizes a complete subset of f, and this fact is denoted by $c_{inf}(f, f')$, iff we

---

[4] Additional constraints about domains of f and g are omitted for simplicty. They can be found in [7].

[5] A detailed definition of relational algebra expression evaluation can be found in [7].

have $C(f')$ and $f' \subseteq f$. It is said that f' characterizes a complete superset of f, and this fact is denoted by $c_{sup}(f, f')$, iff we have $C(f')$ and $f \subseteq f'$.

That is, $c_{inf}(f, f') \stackrel{def}{=} C(f') \wedge f' \subseteq f$, and $c_{sup}(f, f') \stackrel{def}{=} C(f') \wedge f \subseteq f'$.

Definition 15. Answer to a standard query. Let q be a formula of a Relational Algebra language corresponding to a database schema s. Let db be a database state corresponding to s. The answer to the query represented by the formula q is $q(db)$.

Definition 16. Meta database. Let s be a database schema. A meta database mdb associated with s is a set of valid views and complete views. That is mdb is of the form: $\{V(f_1), \ldots, V(f_n), C(g_1), \ldots, C(g_m)\}$.

Definition 17. Validity query. Answer to a validity query. Let q be a standard query and let mdb be a meta database associated with a database schema s. The validity query associated with q is $v_{inf}(q, x)$. An answer to the validity query $v_{inf}(q, x)$ is a formula q', of the same language as q, such that mdb implies $v_{inf}(q, q')$ and, for every q'' such that mdb implies $v_{inf}(q, q'')$ we have $q'' \subseteq q'$. That is: $(mdb \Rightarrow v_{inf}(q, q')) \wedge \forall q''((mdb \Rightarrow v_{inf}(q, q'')) \Rightarrow q'' \subseteq q')$.

Definition 18. Completeness query. Answer to a completeness query. Let q be a standard query and let mdb be a meta database associated with a database schema s. The completeness query associated with q is $c_{sup}(q, x)$. An answer to the completeness query $c_{sup}(q, x)$ is a formula q', of the same language as q, such that mdb implies $c_{sup}(q, q')$ and, for every q'' such that mdb implies $c_{sup}(q, q'')$ we have $q' \subseteq q''$. That is: $(mdb \Rightarrow c_{sup}(q, q')) \wedge \forall q''((mdb \Rightarrow c_{sup}(q, q'')) \Rightarrow q' \subseteq q'')$.

An intuitive justification for the definition of an answer q' to a validity query $v_{inf}(q, x)$ is that its evaluation $q'(db)$ on the database gives the largest subset of the answer $q(db)$ to the standard query for which we can guarantee that the tuples in this subset satisfy q in the world. That is, such that we have $q'(db) \subseteq q(db)$ and $q'(db) \subseteq q(w)$.

The answer to the validity query can be interpreted as the greatest lower bound of all the formulas q'', ordered by $\subseteq$, such that mdb implies $v_{inf}(q, q'')$. Indeed, if $\{q_1'', \ldots, q_n''\}$ is the non empty set of non equivalent formulas such that mdb implies $v_{inf}(q, q_i'')$, then we have $q' = q_1'' \cup \ldots \cup q_n''$. For this reason sometimes in the following this answer will be denoted by q_{glb}.

An intuitive justification for the definition of an answer q' to a completeness query $c_{sup}(q, x)$ is that its evaluation $q'(db)$ on the database gives the smallest superset of the answer $q(db)$ to the standard query for which we can guarantee that the tuples which satisfy q in the world are in this superset. That is, such that we have $q(db) \subseteq q'(db)$ and $q(w) \subseteq q'(db)$.

The answer to the completeness query can be interpreted as the lowest upper bound of all the formulas q'', ordered by $\subseteq$, such that mdb implies $c_{sup}(q, q'')$. Indeed, if $\{q_1'', \ldots, q_m''\}$ is the non empty set of non equivalent formulas such that mdb implies $c_{sup}(q, q_i'')$, then we have $q' = q_1'' \cap \ldots \cap q_m''$. For this reason sometimes in the following this answer will be denoted by q_{lub}.

Another view of q_{lub} is that we are guaranteed that **all the tuples not in q_{lub} do not satisfy q in the world.** In other terms we have: $t \notin q_{lub}(db) \Rightarrow t \notin q(w)$.

Also, another interpretation is that the correct answer $q(w)$ to the standard query is bounded up and down by $q_{lub}(db)$ and $q_{glb}(db)$. That is, we have: $q_{glb}(db) \subseteq q(w) \subseteq q_{lub}(db)$. This property shows the **practical interest of q_{glb} and q_{lub}**.

3 Computation of Answers to Validity Queries and Completeness Queries

In this section is presented first an axiomatics that allows to infer answers to validity and completeness queries. This axiomatic is intended to support the validity of an associated Prolog program which computes these answers. However the axiomatics is not complete.

The intuitive reason is that the computation of answers envolves testing expressions of the form $f' \subseteq f$, and this is an undecidable problem because it is equivalent to testing whether $F' \rightarrow F$ is a theorem, where F and F' are formulas of first order predicate calculus respectively equivalent to f and f'. Moreover, we want that this program always terminates in a finite time. Therefore, if we impose termination, we have to abandon completeness. Nevertheless, in section 3.1 the proposition 19 gives a set of sufficient conditions that guarantee that $f \subseteq g$ and that covers most of the current cases.

3.1 Axiomatic Definition

Proposition 19. *Let f, f', g and g' be formulas of the same Relational Algebra language. We have the following propositions.*

(i1) $\quad f \subseteq f$

(i2) $\quad f \subseteq f \cup g$

(i3) $\quad g \subseteq f \cup g$

(i4) $\quad f \cap g \subseteq f$

(i5) $\quad f \cap g \subseteq g$

(i6) $\quad s_c f \subseteq f$

(i7) $\quad s_c f \subseteq s_{c \vee c'} f$

(i8) $\quad s_{c'} f \subseteq s_{c \vee c'} f$

(i9) $\quad s_{c \wedge c'} f \subseteq s_c f$

(i10) $\quad s_{c \wedge c'} f \subseteq s_{c'} f$

(i11) $\quad (f' \subseteq f) \wedge (g' \subseteq g) \rightarrow (f' \cup g' \subseteq f \cup g)$

(i12) $\quad (f' \subseteq f) \wedge (g' \subseteq g) \rightarrow (f' \cap g' \subseteq f \cap g)$

(i13) $\quad (f' \subseteq f) \wedge (g' \subseteq g) \rightarrow (f' \times g' \subseteq f \times g)$

(i14) $\quad (f' \subseteq f) \wedge (g \subseteq g') \rightarrow (f' - g' \subseteq f - g)$

$$(i15) \quad (f' \subseteq f) \rightarrow (s_c f' \subseteq s_c f)$$
$$(i16) \quad (f' \subseteq f) \rightarrow (\pi_p f' \subseteq \pi_p f)$$
$$(i17) \quad (f \subseteq g) \wedge (g \subseteq h) \rightarrow (f \subseteq h)$$

Proof. The proofs of propositions (i1) to (i10) are rather trivial. We only give the proof of proposition (i14), others are very similar. From the hypothesis $f' \subseteq f$ we have: for very database extension se, if a tuple t is in f'(se) then t is in f(se), or in formal terms: $t \in f'(se) \Rightarrow t \in f(se)$. In the same way from $g \subseteq g'$ we have $t \in g(se) \Rightarrow t \in g'(se)$. Then, by contraposition, we have $\neg(t \in g'(se)) \Rightarrow \neg(t \in g(se))$. From these two consequences we infer $t \in f'(se) \wedge \neg(t \in g'(se)) \Rightarrow t \in f(se) \wedge \neg(t \in g(se))$, that is, $t \in f' - g'(se) \Rightarrow t \in f - g(se)$, and, from the definition of formulas inclusion, we have $f' - g' \subseteq f - g$. □

Proposition 20. *Let f and g be two formulas of the same Relational Algebra language. We have the following propositions.*

$$(a1) \quad V(f) \wedge V(g) \rightarrow V(f \cup g)$$
$$(a2) \quad V(f) \wedge V(g) \rightarrow V(f \cap g)$$
$$(a3) \quad V(f) \wedge V(g) \rightarrow V(f \times g)$$
$$(a4) \quad V(f) \wedge C(g) \rightarrow V(f - g)$$
$$(a5) \quad V(f) \rightarrow V(s_c f)$$
$$(a6) \quad V(f) \rightarrow V(\pi_p f)$$

$$(b1) \quad C(f) \wedge C(g) \rightarrow C(f \cup g)$$
$$(b2) \quad C(f) \wedge C(g) \rightarrow C(f \cap g)$$
$$(b3) \quad C(f) \wedge C(g) \rightarrow C(f \times g)$$
$$(b4) \quad C(f) \wedge V(g) \rightarrow C(f - g)$$
$$(b5) \quad C(f) \rightarrow C(s_c f)$$
$$(b6) \quad C(f) \rightarrow C(\pi_p f)$$

Proof. Let us consider the proof of proposition (a1). From the hypothesis V(f), for any database state db and world state w we have: if t is a tuple in f(db) then t is in f(w). That is $t \in f(db) \Rightarrow t \in f(w)$. In a similar way from the hypothesis V(g) we have $t \in g(db) \Rightarrow t \in g(w)$. From this two consequences we can infer $t \in f(db) \vee t \in g(db) \Rightarrow t \in f(w) \vee t \in g(w)$, and this is equivalent to $t \in f \cup g(db) \Rightarrow t \in f \cup g(w)$, and by definition of V we have $V(f \cup g)$.

Proofs of propositions (a2), (a3), (a5), (a6), (b1), (b2), (b3), (b5), and (b6) are very similar.

The proof of proposition (a4) is a bit different. From V(f) we have $t \in f(db) \Rightarrow t \in f(w)$, and from C(g) we have $t \in g(w) \Rightarrow t \in g(db)$, which, by contraposition, gives $\neg(t \in g(db)) \Rightarrow \neg(t \in g(w))$. Then we have $t \in f(db) \wedge \neg(t \in g(db)) \Rightarrow t \in f(w) \wedge \neg(t \in g(w))$. Therefore we have $t \in f - g(db) \Rightarrow t \in f - g(w)$. That is $V(f - g)$. The proof of proposition (b4) is very similar. The proof of proposition (b4) is of the same style. □

Proposition 21. *Let f, f', g and g' be formulas of the same Relational Algebra language. We have the following propositions.*

(a7) $V(f) \wedge f' \subseteq f \not\to V(f')$

(a8) $V(f) \not\to V(f \cap g)$

(a9) $V(f \cup g) \not\to V(f)$

(b7) $C(f) \wedge f' \subseteq f \not\to C(f')$

(b8) $C(f) \not\to C(f \cap g)$

(b9) $C(f \cup g) \not\to C(f)$

Proof. The proofs are very similar for each proposition, we just give the proof of proposition (a8). For this, we consider the following example where $V(f)$ holds and $V(f \cap g)$ does not hold: $t \in f(db)$, $t \in g(db)$, $t \in f(w)$ and $t \notin g(w)$. The reason why in this example we do not have $V(f \cap g)$ is that we have $t \in f \cap g(db)$ and $t \notin f \cap g(w)$. $\qquad\qquad\square$

Proposition 22. *Let f, f', g and g' be formulas of the same Relational Algebra language. The following rules hold.*

(r1) $V(f') \wedge (f' \subseteq f) \to v_{\inf}(f, f')$

(r2) $V(f') \wedge (f \subseteq f') \to v_{\sup}(f, f')$

(r3) $C(f') \wedge (f' \subseteq f) \to c_{\inf}(f, f')$

(r4) $C(f') \wedge (f \subseteq f') \to c_{\sup}(f, f')$

(r5) $v_{\inf}(f, f') \wedge v_{\inf}(g, g') \to v_{\inf}(f \cup g, f' \cup g')$

(r6) $v_{\sup}(f, f') \wedge v_{\sup}(g, g') \to v_{\sup}(f \cup g, f' \cup g')$

(r7) $c_{\inf}(f, f') \wedge c_{\inf}(g, g') \to c_{\inf}(f \cup g, f' \cup g')$

(r8) $c_{\sup}(f, f') \wedge c_{\sup}(g, g') \to c_{\sup}(f \cup g, f' \cup g')$

For the operators $\cap$ and $\times$ we have the same rules as for $\cup$

(r9) $v_{\inf}(f, f') \wedge c_{\sup}(g, g') \to v_{\inf}(f - g, f' - g')$

(r10) $v_{\sup}(f, f') \wedge c_{\inf}(g, g') \to v_{\sup}(f - g, f' - g')$

(r11) $c_{\inf}(f, f') \wedge v_{\sup}(g, g') \to c_{\inf}(f - g, f' - g')$

(r12) $c_{\sup}(f, f') \wedge v_{\inf}(g, g') \to c_{\sup}(f - g, f' - g')$

(r13) $v_{\inf}(f, f') \to v_{\inf}(s_c f, s_c f')$

(r14) $v_{\sup}(f, f') \to v_{\sup}(s_c f, s_c f')$

(r15) $c_{\inf}(f, f') \to c_{\inf}(s_c f, s_c f')$

(r16) $c_{\sup}(f, f') \to c_{\sup}(s_c f, s_c f')$

For the operator π_p we have the same rules as for the operator s_c

Proof. The proofs of all the propositions are very similar. We just present the proof of (r9). From the hypothesis $v_{\inf}(f, f')$ we have $V(f')$, and from $c_{\sup}(g, g')$

we have $C(g')$. Then, from (a4) we have $C(f' - g')$. From $v_{inf}(f, f')$ we have $f' \subseteq f$, and from $c_{sup}(g, g')$ we have $g \subseteq g'$. Then from (i14) we have $f' - g' \subseteq f - g$. This consequence and the fact $C(f' - g')$ allow to infer $v_{inf}(f - g, f' - g')$.

3.2 Computational Definition

From the rules presented in proposition 22 we can easily define a Prolog program that computes for a given set of valid views and complete views, and for a given answer to a standard query q, the answers to associated validity queries and completeness queries. These answers are respectively obtained by running the program with the queries $v_{inf}(q, x)$, and $c_{sup}(q, x)$.

In the program are defined the predicates $v_{inf}(x, y)$, $v_{sup}(x, y)$, $c_{inf}(x, y)$, $c_{sup}(x, y)$, $V(x)$, $C(x)$ and $\subseteq (x, y)$. The predicate $\subseteq (x, y)$ denotes $x \subseteq y$, and the function symbols $\cup(x, y)$, $\cap(x, y)$, $\times(x, y)$, $-(x, y)$, $s(x, y)$, $\pi(x, y)$, $\vee(x, y)$, $\wedge(x, y)$ and $\neg(x)$ respectively denote $x \cup y$, $x \cap y$, $x \times y$, $s_x y$, $\pi_x y$, $x \vee y$, $x \wedge y$ and $\neg x$.

The Prolog clauses defining the predicates $v_{inf}(x, y)$, $v_{sup}(x, y)$, $c_{inf}(x, y)$, $c_{sup}(x, y)$, $V(x)$, $C(x)$ and $\subseteq (x, y)$ are trivial reformulations of their corresponding rules in the propositions 19, 20 and 22. For instance, we give these clauses for the predicate $v_{inf}(x, y)$.

$$v_{inf}(x, y) : - V(y), \subseteq (y, x)$$
$$v_{inf}(\cup(x, y), \cup(x', y')) : - v_{inf}(x, x'), v_{inf}(y, y')$$
$$v_{inf}(\cap(x, y), \cap(x', y')) : - v_{inf}(x, x'), v_{inf}(y, y')$$
$$v_{inf}(\times(x, y), \times(x', y')) : - v_{inf}(x, x'), v_{inf}(y, y')$$
$$v_{inf}(-(x, y), -(x', y')) : - v_{inf}(x, x'), c_{sup}(y, y')$$
$$v_{inf}(s(x, y), s(x, y')) : - v_{inf}(y, y')$$
$$v_{inf}(\pi(x, y), \pi(x, y')) : - v_{inf}(y, y')$$

Assumptions about valid views and complete views are represented as data of the program. For instance if it is assumed that $V(r \cup p)$ and $C(s_{1=a}, r)$ hold, we have in the program:

$$V(\cup(r, p)) : -$$
$$C(s(1 = a, r)) : -$$

If we have, for example the query $s_{1=a \vee 1=b} r$ the answer to the corresponding validity query is obtained by running the program with the query:
$v_{inf}(s(\vee(1 = a, 1 = b), r), x)$.

The predicate $\subseteq (x, y)$ is defined by a set of clauses which is a direct reformulation of propositions (i1) to (i16). For instance (i14) and (i15) are reformulated into:

$$\subseteq (-(x', y'), -(x, y)) : - \subseteq (x', x), \subseteq (y, y')$$
$$\subseteq (s(x, y'), s(x, y)) : - \subseteq (y', y)$$

Notice that for program evaluations corresponding to queries of the form $v_{inf}(q,y)$ and $c_{sup}(q,y)$, in clauses like $v_{inf}(x,y) : - V(y), \subseteq (x,y)$, the goal $\subseteq (x,y)$ is called for x and y being instantiated by ground terms. In that case the evaluation of $\subseteq (x,y)$ terminates if the rule (i17) is removed, because the complexity of terms x' and y' are respectively lower than the complexity of terms x and y in the recursive calls to $\subseteq (x,y)$. However if the rule (i17) is envolved, termination is not guaranteed. The global program terminates if the evaluation of $\subseteq (x,y)$ terminates. Indeed, for example, a call of the form $v_{inf}(\cup(f,g),x)$ generates calls to $v_{inf}(f,x')$ and $v_{inf}(g,y')$.

We see that termination can be reached by imposing strong limitations to the completeness of the program. For example, by removing the rule (i17). The definition of a good compromise between termination and completeness has to be investigated, but this is not the main topic of this paper.

4 Comparison with Other Works

Coming back to Motro's work, we have mentioned in the introduction that his method does not work for Relational Algebra formulas that contain either union or difference operators. We can see how we can compute answers to validity queries and to completeness queries, with the presented method, for two queries that contain a union and a difference.

Let, for instance, the meta database be $mdb = \{V(s_{1=a}r), V(s_{2=b}p), C(r),$ $C(s_{1=a \lor 2=b}p)\}$.

Let us consider first the standard query: $q = r \cup p$. From mdb we can infer $V((s_{1=a}r) \cup (s_{2=b}p))$, and from proposition 19 we can infer: $(s_{1=a}r) \cup (s_{2=b}p) \subseteq r \cup p$. Then, we have $q_{glb} = (s_{1=a}r) \cup (s_{2=b}p)$.

Let us consider now the standard query: $q = r - s_{2=b}p$. From mdb we can infer $V(s_{1=a}r)$ and $C(s_{1=a \lor 2=b}p)$, and from proposition 19 we have: $(s_{1=a}r) - (s_{1=a \lor 2=b}p) \subseteq r - s_{2=b}p$. Then, we have $q_{glb} = (s_{1=a}r) - (s_{1=a \lor 2=b}p)$. From mdb we also have $C(r)$ and $V(s_{2=b}p)$. Then, we have $c_{sup}(r,r)$ and $v_{inf}(s_{2=b}p, s_{2=b}p)$, and therefore we have $q_{lub} = r - s_{2=b}p$.

As it has been mentionned in the introduction the notion of validity has already been investigated in a logical framework in [4]. We would like to give some guidelines for a logical reconstruction of the notions of validity an completeness as they are defined in this paper.

Databases, meta databases and queries can be represented in a first order modal language with a fixed domain. In this language we have a doxastic modality B and an epistemic modality K. The intended meaning of $B\varphi$ is "the database believes φ" and the intended meaning of $K\varphi$ is "one knows φ". The axiomatics of the doxastic logic is (KD) (see [1]) plus axiom schemas: (D') $\neg B\varphi \to B(\neg\varphi)$, and (C) $B(\varphi \lor \psi) \to B\varphi \lor B\psi$, which reflect the closed world assumption.

In this logical framework the notions of valid views and complete views might be defined as follows: $V(F) \stackrel{\text{def}}{=} \forall t \, K(B(F(t)) \to F(t))$, and $C(F) \stackrel{\text{def}}{=} \forall t \, K(F(t) \to B(F(t)))$, where $F(t)$ is a formula of classical first order logic, and t is the tuple of free variables in this formula.

5 Conclusion

We have presented a formal representation of information about validity and completeness of parts of a database in terms of valid views and complete views. We have also presented formal definitions of validity queries and completeness queries associated with standard queries, and we have shown that the correct answer to a standard query is bounded up and down by the answers to the completeness query and to the validity query.

For the computation of answers to validity queries and completeness queries we have presented a set of axioms that allows to infer the answers. These answers are formulas of the Relational algebra, and they can be evaluated by standard techniques. We have shown how the axiomatics can be transformed into a Prolog program that computes the answers. The axiomatics is sound but it is not complete. The lack of completeness is not a so dramatic issue as it is for answers to standard queries. Its practical consequence is that correct answers are bounded by larger intervals than it would be possible to compute with a complete axiomatics.

In comparison to the approach by Motro (M) and to the approach by Demolombe and Jones (DJ), the presented approach is more general than M, since there is no restriction on the form of queries, and less general than DJ, since data are restricted to facts. From efficiency point of view, it can be implemented by combining Prolog deduction techniques and algebraic techniques. Then, it is less efficient than M which can be implemented with an extended version of Relational algebra, and it is more efficient than DJ which requires automated deduction techniques for full propositional calculus.

References

1. B. F. Chellas. Modal Logic: An introduction. Cambridge University Press, 1988.
2. L. Cholvy, R. Demolombe, and A.J. Jones. Reasoning about the safety of information: from logical formalization to operational definition. In *Proc. of 8th International Symposium on Methodologies for Intelligent Systems*, 1994.
3. R. Demolombe and A. Jones. Integrity Constraints Revisited. In A. Olive, editor, *4th International Workshop on the Deductive Approach to Information Systems and Databases*. Universitat Politecnica de Barcelona, 1993.
4. R. Demolombe and A. Jones. Deriving answers to safety queries. In R. Demolombe and T. Imielinski, editors, *Nonstandard queries and answers*. Oxford University Press, 1994.
5. A. Motro. Completeness information and its application to query processing. In *Proc. of 12th International Conference on Very Large Data Bases*, 1986.
6. A. Motro. Integrity = validity + completeness. *ACM TODS*, 14(4), 1989.
7. J. D. Ullman. *Principles of Database Systems. Vol1 and Vol2*. Computer Science Press, 1988.

Explanation for Cooperative Information Systems

Michael J. Minock   **Wesley W. Chu**
minock@cs.ucla.edu   wwc@cs.ucla.edu
Computer Science Department, University of California at Los Angeles

Abstract: Cooperative Information Systems provide approximate answers when exact answers are unavailable and provide summary answers when answer sets are too large. Yet without an explanation of how and why such answers were derived, it is hard to estimate their usefulness. Further, the timing and level of detail of such explanations should be user and context dependent. In this paper, we present the architecture, representation, and process of an explanation system which provides such explanations of approximate answers. This explanation system has been implemented and integrated into the Cooperative Information System CoBase (UCLA) for a transportation planning and an electronic warfare domain. Our experience reveals that explanation generation is efficient and receives positive feedback from users.

Keywords: Intelligent Information Systems, Cooperative Information Systems, Explanation, Approximate Answers, Dialogue Management, Knowledge Integration, CoBase.

1.0 Introduction

Traditionally database systems require a user to understand the database schema and return only the exact answers to a user's query. Cooperative Information Systems seek to enrich this conventional query-answer dialogue with the cooperative behaviors observed between humans[7]. Such systems allow a user to pose high-level or imprecise queries and to receive approximations when answer sets do not exist and summaries when answer sets are large. Yet such systems should also be able to explain how they interpreted a user's query and derived answers. In addition, a user should be able to interrogate the system to obtain a precise description of the actions it took in arriving at answers. Through this, a user may critique the techniques used by the system, so that the system is more cooperative in the future.

This paper addresses the use of explanation technology in the CoBase system. CoBase [1][3] is a cooperative information system, providing approximate and associated answers to a user's relational and object-oriented queries. This paper focuses on approximate query answering through query relaxation. Relaxation is 'cooperative' when a user is interested in approximate answers, which is often the case when exact answers are few or do not exist. CoBase uses the Type Abstraction Hierarchy (TAH) knowledge structure to guide query relaxation. High level nodes in the TAH represent general knowledge of a domain, while lower level nodes represent more specific knowledge. Terms and relations in the query are located in the TAH, are generalized, specialized, and then used to reformulate the query. TAHs can be generated automatically from the domain database through conceptual clustering algorithms [9][2]. CoBase emphasizes the scalability and maintainability of the TAH and the portability of the CoBase engine to different domains. CoBase's explanation system inherits these requirements.

The most common and rudimentary method to provide explanation is the placement of print commands within a source code or rulebase. Yet such approaches tie the generation of explanation too closely to the actual steps taken to solve the problem. As a result they explain things only as they happen, enabling only limited summarization of the systems actions. To uncouple system action and explanation, it is necessary to form a trace of the system's actions so that the explanation system has access to all that has occurred and may summarize actions and results. However in the absence of interpretation, these traces may not contain enough information to produce meaningful explanations. Execution traces only record what has occurred, not why. The Explainable Expert Systems (EES) framework[14] bases explanation on knowledge structures that capture the rationale behind system actions. This is achieved by integrating explanation at the expert system specification and design phase, insuring that rationale knowledge is compiled into the expert system. Additional advances in explanation technology have resulted from improvements in how the actual explanation is generated. Initial template based approaches[13] produced one-shot explanations with which a user could not interact to obtain clarification or further description. Current methods tend to rely on a planned approach to generation [12], enabling interaction on portions of explanations.

Section 2 gives an example explanation for CoBase query relaxation. Section 3 presents an overall architecture of the explanation system. Section 4 focuses of how information to be explained is represented, section 5 discusses the explanation generation process, and section 6 compares our approach with previous work.

2.0 Example

Suppose the user poses the query:

Q: *Is there an airport in Gafsa, Tunisia with a runway length greater than 8500' ?'*

It happens that there is no such airport, so CoBase relaxes the location name attribute to find nearby airports with runway lengths greater than 8500'. The following explanation is presented.

There is no airport where
   location is Gafsa and runway length is greater than 8500 feet.

In fact, there is no airport where
   region is South West Tunisia and runway length is greater than 8500 feet.

Through the relaxation of Gafsa to South Tunisia an airport where
   location name is gabes and runway length equal to 9126 feet has been found.

The whole region of Tunisia could still be searched for an airport where
   runway length is greater than 8500 feet.

The user may select text fragments to obtain further explanation. Sensitive text fragments are stacked hierarchically, letting the user interact with a single word, phrase, sentence, or paragraph. For example, when the user "clicks" the text *'Through the relaxation of Gafsa to South Tunisia'* the following options are presented.

   1.) Show map of South Tunisia including Gafsa and Gabes
   2.) Give more detailed description of relaxation action
   3.) Accept feedback to refine relaxation strategy

If the first option is clicked then a map appears, and if the second option is clicked then a more specific description of exactly how the query was relaxed is provided. If the third option is clicked then the user is given the option of providing positive or negative feedback on CoBase's strategy to relax location name over runway length for the current user and context. Such feedback is then absorbed into CoBase's relaxation control knowledge.

Based on the user and context, explanations should occur at appropriate times during processing. One extreme is the system running automatically, only summarizing its work once it has completed. This is the case in the above example. Another extreme is the system explaining each of its actions as they occur, giving the user the ability to monitor progress. Explanations should also be tailored to a user's understanding of the system.

3.0 Architecture

CoBase's explanation system is *capable* of providing interactive, user-sensitive and context-dependent explanations and descriptions of CoBase operations. To provide such explanations, the system requires access to CoBase queries, execution traces, Type Abstraction Hierarchies (TAHs), and answers. The components of CoBase's explanation system (see figure 3.1) are 1.) a set of *generation rules* which produce explanations, 2.) a *query processing model*, by which CoBase queries, TAHs, execution traces and answers are interpreted (classified) , 3.) a *user model* and 4.) a *context model*. The user and context models affect which generation rules are used to produce an explanation. Calls to the explanation system either *provide information* or *produce explanations*.

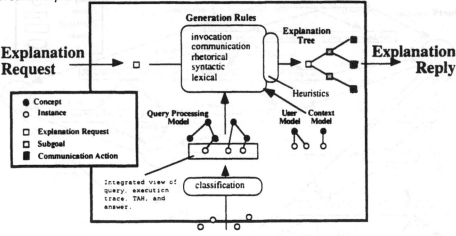

Information Access

Figure 3.1 The architecture of CoBase's explanation system.

As CoBase executes, query, execution trace, and finally answer information is provided to the explanation system. Each piece of information is asserted as an instance of a concept in the query processing model. *Classification rules* may interpret instances as members of more specific concepts. The final result of these assertions and classifications is an integrated view of the query, execution trace, answer, and, by reference, TAH information.

To produce an explanation, the explanation system receives an *explanation request* on an instance in the integrated view (e.g. describe(query-01), explain(process-query-01, answers), etc.) and produces an *explanation reply* consisting of natural language and recommended visualizations. The explanation system solves explanation requests by applying generation rules to produce an *explanation tree*. Generation rules are applied top-down to the explanation request and resulting subgoals, producing the explanation tree in which the explanation request is the root and primitive communication actions are the leaves. Generation rules access information in the integrated view and are often predicated upon the current user and context. Explanation trees are converted into a proper form (C++ objects, HTML, KQML, etc.) and are returned as explanation replies. These replies are presented on a GUI and a simple protocol enables interaction with the presented explanation, causing the explanation system to generate further explanation.

The explanation system has been implemented (in C++ and CLIPS) and integrates into the CoBase system. There are approximately 30 concepts and 20 classification rules in the query processing model. There are approximately 80 general generation rules and 40 domain specific rules for an electronic warfare domain and 30 generation rules for a transportation planning domain. The explanation system can usually produce explanations in under a second on a Sun Sparc 10 workstation.

4.0 Representation of Information for Explanation

Figure 4.1 shows an integrated view of the query, execution trace, TAH, and answer for the example above.

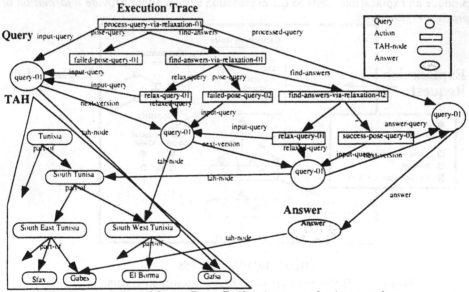

Figure 4.1 Integrated view of Query, Trace, TAH and answers for the example.

Classification rules in the query processing model interpret this information as it added. For example, the instance[1] "process-query-via-multiple-relaxations-01" in figure 4.1 was initially instantiated as a member of the concept "process-query-01". Later, after two relaxation actions, "process-query-01" was reclassified.

---

[1] Instance names reflect the most specific concept they are a member of. For example, "process-query-via-multiple-relaxations-01" is a member of concept, "process-query-via-multiple-relaxations".

4.1 Basic Graph View

The information in figure 4.1 is presented at a conceptual level. Figure 4.2 shows how the explanation system actually represents this information. For reasons of space, figure 4.2 is limited to only a portion of the query and execution trace in figure 4.1.

At its most basic level, information is viewed as a simple directed graph G. Assume the following sets: V a set of vertices, E a set of directed edges, and Σ a set of values. The graph is G=(V,E). There is a partial function Λ that maps the set of vertices to the set of values: $\Lambda(V) \rightarrow \Sigma$ (e.g. in Figure 4.2 $\Lambda(v_1)$ = "condition-1"). This has the effect of naming each vertex. There are four types of vertices: concept V_c, instance V_i, value V_v, and link V_l. Each Concept and Instance vertex has a unique identifier: i.e. for $\Lambda(V_c \cup V_i) \rightarrow \Sigma$, Λ is complete and one to one. For convenience we define the partial identification function I which maps identifier values to their corresponding concept or instance vertices: $I(\Sigma) \rightarrow V_c \cup V_i$ where $I(\sigma) = \Lambda^{-1}(\sigma)$ for $\sigma \in \Sigma$. There are two classes of edges: subsumption E_s and composition E_c. Subsumption edges represent *is-a* type relationships. Composition edges connect instance vertices to label vertices or connect label vertices to instance or value vertices. Such edges represent *property* or *part-of* type relationships.

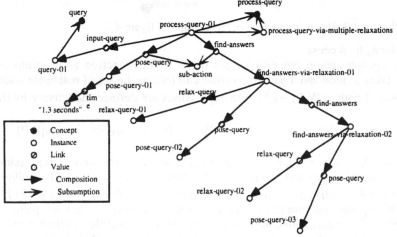

Figure 4.2 Graph portion of execution trace and query in figure 4.1.

4.2 Neighbor Access

The mechanism to access information in the graph consists of two functions: A single step neighbor access function S and a full graph access function T (discussed in section 4.4). For S, given a node in a graph, it is necessary to retrieve the set of neighboring nodes reachable by a given link value. The single step accessor function S takes a concept or instance vertex and a link value as arguments and returns the set of neighboring nodes reachable by the given link: $S(V_c \cup V_i, \Sigma) \rightarrow 2^V$. On the graph in figure 4.2, S(I(process-query-01),input-query) = {I(query-01)}. S also may access neighboring nodes through abstract labels: S(I(process-query-01),sub-action) = {I(pose-query-01),I(find-answers-via-relaxation-01)}.

4.3 Hyper-Graph View

For convenience, the basic graph may be viewed as a directed hyper-graph. In such a view edges may be of arbitrary degree (normal graphs only have edges of degree 2). The hyper-graph is constructed from the basic graph by retaining all concept, instance, and value vertices and introducing hyper-edges with label σ from v to V' where S(v,σ) = V'. To help distinguish between the basic or hyper-graph view, description of hyper-graphs will be in terms of nodes and relationships rather than vertices and edges. Figure 4.3 shows the hyper-graph view of the basic graph in figure 4.2.

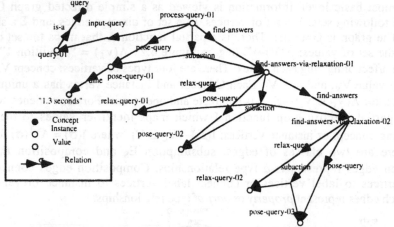

Figure 4.3 Hyper-graph view of basic graph in figure 4.2.

4.4 Full Graph Access

The full graph access function T uses the S access function as its primitive operator. T takes a node and a path expression and returns the set of reachable nodes via the provided path: $T(V,P) \to 2^V$. Path expressions are defined inductively by the grammar

$$P \to e \mid \sigma \mid P \cdot P \mid P^* \mid P^+ \mid P^\wedge \mid P^n \mid or[P\ P] \mid and[P\ P]$$

where $\sigma \in \Sigma$ is a single label, n is an integer and e is the empty expression. Intuitively • composes two path expressions, * allows for any number of P, + allows for one or more P, ^ indicates the maximal number of P, P^n allows for n or fewer P's, *or* follows both paths, and *and* finds those node only reachable by both sub-paths. Ψ is a variant of T which nondeterministically returns a single reachable node: $\Psi(V,P) \to V$. We have developed a formal definition of T and Ψ. For the graph in figure 4.3, T(I(process-query-01),input-query)={I(query-01)}, T(I(process-query-01),find-answer$^+$•pose-query)= {I(pose-query-02),I(pose-query-03)}.

4.5 Graph Synthesis

Either information must be asserted directly into the explanation system or the explanation system must have access to information. Typically smaller, unstructured pieces of information (e.g. Queries, execution traces, and answers, etc.) will be asserted directly while larger, structured pieces of information (e.g. Databases, Type Abstraction Hierarchies, etc.) will be accessed.

Graphs are materialized through a sequence of basic operations which create or destroy vertices and edges in the simple graph view, effecting the value(Λ) and identification(I) functions accordingly. Such operations have been grouped to form a higher level assertion language consisting of five basic operations defined on the hyper-graph: define(concept), is-a (node, concept), instantiate(instance, concept), fill-slot(node, node, slot) and add-value(node, value, slot). This assertion language is complemented by a retraction language that offers reverses of these operations.

To maintain a trace, access to current as well as prior versions of nodes must be maintained. To achieve this the operations new-shallow (node), and new-deep (node) are added to the assertion language. These operation are issued on a node just prior to recording changes to the node. The operation new-shallow creates a new copy of the node and attaches the new and old copy with the slots "next-version" and "prior-version". The operation new-deep performs the same operations as new-shallow, but in addition, the slots from the older node are copied to the new node and updated. By using these operations, a full history of instance and concept nodes is maintained. We have developed a formal definition of these operations.

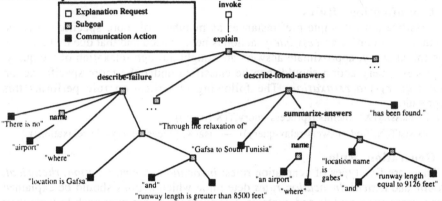

Figure 5.1 Explanation tree for the example

5.0 Explanation Generation Process

With the method for representing, accessing, and asserting information established, we now turn to the process of generating actual explanations. The explanation system accepts an explanation request on information in the graph and generates an explanation tree containing the explanation reply. Explanation requests are ground goal predicates (i.e. all arguments are bound) with arguments being keyword values or nodes (or sets of nodes) in the graph. An explanation tree is created via the depth-first application of generation rules toward solving an explanation request. The explanation request is at the root of the explanation tree, while the text and recommended visualizations are leaves in the tree. Intermediate nodes are the subgoals that are carried out to achieve the root explanation request. We have defined this process formally [10]. Figure 5.1 shows the explanation tree for the example.

This same mechanism is used to interpret information in the graph. The analog to an explanation request is a classification request which is issued on a node (or set of nodes) in the graph. A set of classification rules produce a tree similar to an explanation tree. However classification rules perform assertions or retractions on the graph as their primitive actions. The explanation system does not return these trees as replies, but rather performs them itself, reflecting an interpretation in the graph. Such interpretation is important to provide meaningful, specific explanations. By performing such classifications inside the explanation system, the query, execution trace, and answer information may be asserted directly and efficiently.

All generation and classification rules are of the form as shown in figure 5.2. Goal predicates represent the purpose of the rule. Constraint predicates access information in the graph. If all the constraints are satisfied then the rule's actions may, based on heuristics, be performed. These actions may either be subgoals or primitive communication actions (e.g. text or a visualization call), or, within classification rules, assertions or retractions on the graph.

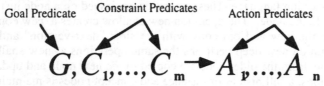

Figure 5.2 The form of classification and generation rules

5.1 Classification Rules

Classification rules interpret instances as members of more specific concepts. For example, assume a *process-query* action is being traced and that due to the failure of the initial query, approximate answers are sought through relaxation of the query. The process-query action should then be classified under the more specific action *process-query-via-relaxation*. The following classification rule performs this interpretation:

(r12 classify(X). member(process-query,T(X,[isa]*)),

exists(T(X, find-answers•relax-query)) → isa(X, process-query-via-relaxation))

5.2 Generation Rules

There are five types of generation rules: *invocation, communication, rhetorical, syntactic* and *lexical. Invocation rules* determine which actions should be explained under various user models and contexts. For example a user may wish to have their query described in English prior to CoBase's attempt to solve the query. In other cases a user may not wish for such a description. CoBase always issues the explanation request *invoke* on the *form-query* action after the query has been formed by the user. The following is an example of a general invocation rule that states that "If an action is of interest to the current user, then describe the action."

(r34 invoke(X),member(Ψ(X,[isa]),T(USER,[isa]⁺•interested)) → describe(X))

Communication rules determine what information will be expressed about a topic in a description or explanation. *Rhetorical rules* capture how that information will be presented. For example, if an explanation of the entire *process-query* action is required, and if the process-query action required relaxations, then describe the failure of the original query and then describe found answers

(r23 describe(X), member(process-query-via-relaxation, T(X,[isa]+))→

describe(Ψ(X,pose-query),failure),describe(Ψ(X,find-answers^)),found-answers))

Syntactic rules constrain text to valid English. For example syntactic rules insure that subjects and verbs agree in number, or that items in a list are properly separated by ,s and *and*s. Finally lexical rules determine the words used to name CoBase actions and objects. For example the following are general lexical rules.

(r19 name(X) → text(Λ(X)))

(r20 name(X), exists(T(X,[name])) → text(Λ(Ψ(X,[name]))))

5.3 User and Context Dependence

Different users require different types of explanation under different contexts. This is accounted for by the fact that more than one generation rule may match to expand a node in the explanation tree. Alternate generation rules vary in which aspects of

CoBase's process or results are expressed and to what depth. Heuristic knowledge controls which generation rule among the matching rules will fire to expand a goal. Through feedback and interaction users refine explanations by altering the heuristic knowledge that determines which rules are selected.

Because user and context models will not be completely accurate, users may interact with an initial explanation to obtain further explanation. These further explanations are generated by issuing explanation requests on nodes in the explanation trees. The solution of explanation requests on explanation tree nodes results in a new explanation tree containing the further explanation. In turn this explanation may be interacted with.

6.0 Comparison to Previous Work

Few Cooperative Information Systems[5] have included an explanation facility. McCoy [8] generated explanations to clear up a user's misconceptions of a database schema. The CARMIN [6] system includes an integrated explanation and answer presentation system. In this system explanations are based on the proof path of a PROLOG meta-interpreter. Aspects of what to include and how to coordinate these explanations were also investigated. In contrast to these approaches, the work here is focused on explanation of approximate answers. In addition our explanation system is interactive, giving the users the capability to fully inspect and critique the query relaxation process.

Similar to EES, information is interpreted prior to generation of explanation. However a model of query processing is built specifically to interpret CoBase operations and trace-generating operations are added to existing CoBase routines. Though this implies that the CoBase engine and the query processing model are maintained separately, this modularizes the explanation system and reduces its impact on the design and implementation of other CoBase components.

We have developed a representation, classification and generation formalism that describes the complete explanation generation task. The particular representation enables the direct expression of one-to-many, many-to-one, and many-to-many relationships and allows for abstraction on the relations between nodes (instances, values, or concepts), enabling specific to generic access of the graph. Abstraction enables very general rules to access the graph thought abstracts labels. The generation formalism provides a structured approach to explanation, thus easing maintenance, integration, and in the future the acquisition, interactive refinement and extension of explanations.

7.0 Conclusion

The completeness, correctness, and precision of explanations depend on access to queries, traces, knowledge, and answers, and depend on the effort expended in populating and refining the explanation rulebase. Elapsed times depend primarily on the cost of synthesizing the explanation tree, particularly the cost of matching explanation rules to expand nodes. A RETE[4] pattern-matcher performs these matches.

As CoBase extends it coverage of cooperative operations, the explanation system will be responsible for explaining more actions. This will include explanation of associated answers to a user's query and explanation of summary (intensional) answers. Efforts will also focus on methods to enable users to interactively refine the explanations they receive [11]. In addition, since explanations are based on the domain-independent CoBase engine, we seek a method that enables system administrators to interactively extend explanations into domain specific forms [11]. Through these experiments, we seek to further explore the benefits of explanation generation for cooperative information system technology.

References

[1] Chu, Wesley W. and Chen, Q. Neighborhood and Associative Query Answering. *Journal of Intelligent Information Systems*, 1(3/4), 1992.

[2] Chu, Wesley W. and Chiang, Kourong. Abstraction of High Level Concepts from Numerical Values in Databases. *Proceedings of the AAAI workshop on Knowledge Discovery in Databases*, July 1994.

[3] Chu, W., Yang, H., Chiang K., Minock, M., Chow, G. and Larson, C. CoBase: A Scalable and Extensible Cooperative Information System. To appear in *Journal of Intelligent Information Systems*, 1996.

[4] Forgy, C.L. RETE: A Fast Algorithm for the Many Pattern/Many Object Pattern Match Problem, *Artificial Intelligence* 19, 1982, 17-38.

[5] Gaassterland, T., Godfrey, P. , and Minker, J. An Overview of Cooperative Answering. *Journal of Intelligent Information Systems*, 1(2):127-157, 1992.

[6] Godfrey, P., Minker, J., Novik, L. An Architecture for a Cooperative Database Systems. *International Conference on Applications of Databases,* June 1994.

[7] Grice, H. Logic and Conversation. In P. Cole and J. Morgan, editors, *Syntax and Semantics*. Academic Press, 1975.

[8] McCoy. *Generating Natural Language Text in Response to Questions About Database Queries*. PhD thesis, University of Pennsylvania, 1982.

[9] Merzbacher, Matthew and Chu, Wesley W. Pattern-based clustering for database attribute values, *Proceedings of the AAAI workshop on Knowledge Discovery in Databases*, 1993.

[10] Minock, Michael J. and Chu, Wesley W. Interactive Explanation for Cooperative Information Systems. *UCLA Computer Science Department Technical Report*, SD950036, 1995.

[11] Minock, Michael J. and Chu, Wesley W. Generation, Refinement, and Extension of Explanations for Cooperative Information Systems. In *Proceedings of CIKM Workshop on New Paradigms in Information Visualization and Manipulation,* December 1995.

[12] Moore, Johanna D. and Paris, Cecile L. 1989. Planning Text for Advisory Dialogue. *In Proceeding of the Twenty-Seventh Annual Meeting of the Association for Computational Linguistics*, Vancouver, British Columbia.

[13] Shortliffe, Edward H. *Computer Based Medical Consultations: MYCIN*. Elsevier North Holland Inc., 1976.

[14] Swartout, William R., Paris, Cecile L., and Moore, Johanna D. Design For Explainable Expert Systems. *IEEE Expert,* Volume 6, Number 3, pages 58-64.

Toward Intelligent Representation of Database Content

Joseph D. Oldham and Victor W. Marek

Department of Computer Science, University of Kentucky, Lexington, KY 40506,
{oldham,marek}@cs.engr.uky.edu

Abstract

We address the problem of automating the display of database records in an intelligent way. By this we mean the synthesis of complete multimedia documents from database records. We propose an architecture for mapping diverse data stored in a database to markup language (SGML) programs. These programs are ready for final presentation. The mapping is based on a computational extension of the linguistic concept of *register*. The resulting presentation represents data as information in an intelligent way. General conditions for such a system are discussed. Our own treatment of registers as *rule based* computational structures is offered with some early results on the behavior of rule based registers.

1 Introduction

We address the problem of automating the display of database records in an intelligent way. By this we mean the synthesis of complete multimedia documents from databases which are not otherwise document databases.

Our databases may be object oriented databses with multimedia data. Because our interest is in *populations* of users a suitable database should hold data that is to be used by at least one community of users with strong communication conventions. For example a suitable database might consist of: *medical records* (communities might include physicians, nurses, financial officers of various sorts), *accident reports* (police, insurance adjustors and claimants, courts), *student records* (advisors, deans, admissions officers in other programs, potential employers, students).

"Intelligent display" means a generated display document must satisfy the document conventions of a user community approximately as well as a document built by hand from the same data and for the same purpose. Our only restriction is that the purpose does not include any but very shallow analysis. Making the database system "speak the communal language" facilitates the ability of any member of the community to make sense of the data. So "intelligent" means the ability to "speak the vernacular" of a community of users. [PR87] refers to a text generation system which can do this as a *tailoring* system.

1.1 Approach

For our approach we take advantage of the existence of markup languages, which become the target languages of the kind of systems we describe. The hard problem is to move from data itself, facts and objects, to complete document content embedded in a markup language program. For this we turn to the language of *register theory*, from descriptive linguistics [GC78]. The control of various registers marks the sophistication of a language user [GC78]. Our "language" is explicitly multimedia. Although registers have been discussed in the literature of natural language processing [BP89] we review the concept briefly: A *register* is a triple ⟨ *field, mode, tenor* ⟩, where:

Field is the domain of discourse. Field understanding provides context for the synthesis of the document. This implies representing the common knowledge of the domain.

Mode is the means of communication, e.g. written vs. spoken, spontaneous vs. planned, or even, *this* plan for written discourse vs. *that* plan for written discourse. Mode is taken here as describing a document *form*.

Tenor describes the purpose of the communication, e.g. to inform, persuade, etc. Tenor informs choice of rhetorical device used within the framework of the mode to represent content.

We claim that this concept of register can be formalized in a way suitable for intelligent display of multimedia database information. In this paper we offer the beginnings of our formalization of registers: *generalized rule defined registers*. Our register is a computational structure which will accept as input a database record and transform that record through a series of steps into a completed document in a target markup language. From now on we assume SGML [HR90] as a target language. Others are possible. The marked up document may be presented to the user via an SGML processor.

Control of registers is a marker of sophistication in language use. Endowing a database with control of a register should increase the user's ability to receive information from the database by making the form of the data intuitive. If the system presentation of data lacks some of the informational coherence of a human presentation then *information* is lost in the human - system interaction. Registers are a way of trying to restore a subtle form of information loss by making the data more readily or better understood by a user, who will be better able to make necessary and correct inferences in less time. We do not believe the problem of intelligent presentation of data from a database as information tailored to a user has been adequately addressed.

1.2 Some Related Work

We begin with some work in text generation. The problem of determining the content of a text document has been studied by McKeown [MC85]. Paris [PR87] introduced the term "tailoring" to represent the process of making text documents user appropriate. Paris and Bateman [BP89] phrase text tailoring in terms of register theory [GC78]. This body of work tells us that with respect to textual components of documents syntactic structure, vocabulary and word order are key to audience appropriate data presentation. We do not yet know what the multimedia correlates are. In fact we are particularly interested in how the availability of multimedia objects alters text content. In terms borrowed from Devlin [DV91] what is the effect on a document when analog information is included? IVORY [CW93] is a tool developed at Stanford University to assist the physician in writing progress notes. It takes a relatively naive approach to tackle the problem of text document generation in one domain. The impact of global discourse structure on the discourse at sentence level is studied in [RV95] with an eye toward text generation as an application.

It may be tempting to look at document generation from data as an extension to very dynamic views. [CBR94, DE94] provide examples of how efforts to extend views to Object-Oriented database management systems (OODBMS) are concerned by other issues such as relating the model (or scheme) used by an application to the scheme of a database. Fundamentally a document is more than a view. It is worth noting that if a tailoring system required a data scheme different from that of the DBMS then using a view mechanism to create an intermediate data representation would avoid attempts to alter the DB scheme directly. Such an approach would allow a presentation module to be built on top of an existing database, with no alteration to the underlying data model required. We term such an approach *noninvasive*.

[CACS94] considers the problem of mapping structured (SGML [HR90]) document data type definitions (DTDs) to an OODB schema (in particular the O_2 [BB88] system.) Instances of a DTD (a document) are then mapped to objects and values under the scheme found by the mapping from the DTD. Structured document management and retrieval is facilitated. They explicitly do not consider going the other way which is our problem. Several points are worth remarking: (1) When a class of documents can be generated from stored facts management and retrieval of those documents is no longer different from any other database operation. (2) Even in storing whole documents and taking advantage of their structure one must confront the issue of order. Order matters in structured documents, but not in database schema. This results in an invasive approach with respect to the O_2 data model in [CACS94]. (3) Under our scheme an inverse mapping from document instance to database record does not in general exist. This is compatible with the results in [CACS94] as the database there is a document database while ours is not. In our approach specific facts stored may lead to linguistic or other media expression in the document, i.e. facts may be "forgotten" or blurred. Once blurred only a class of facts is, in general, recoverable. However it is common and often necessary to store "facts" rather than documents.

[EG95a, EG95b] describe *the writer's problem*. If W is a writer with some background knowledge and some facts and W wants to convey with some particular sense the circumstances associated with the facts by creating a document using some *mode* (in our case a multimedia mode), and if W can assume the reader has certain background knowledge, then how does W proceed? [EG95a, EG95b] focuses on the complementary *reader's* problem. It is worth remarking that since the writer's and reader's problems are complementary, any document created by one system should be understandable by another system. This holds even if a precise inverse mapping to data does not exist.

2 Examples

For the first example we assume the following (non 1-NF) toy scheme and assume HTML rather than SGML:

⟨ NAME, SEX, AGE, PIC, ADDR, DATE, VS, SYMPS ⟩

Example 1. ⟨ Marek,Victor, M, 25, /PtPhoto/VMarek.gif,123/Main/Atown/KY/40512, 8/24/95, 132/84, 92, 99.O, 16, (cough/dry,painful/1/D/nil))

Our register system will deliver a document represented like this:

```
<H1> Patient Victor Marek </H1>
Photo of Mr Marek: <IMG SRC=""/PtPhoto/VMarek.gif", ALT="Mr. Marek">
<H2> Personal Data: </H2>
     Male, 25 years old. <P>
<H3> Mailing Address</H3>
     123 Main St. Anytown, KY 40512<P>
<H2> Presentation of Thursday 8/24/95 </H2>
VS: Within Normal Limits
<P>
Mr. Marek presented with a c/o dry, painful cough. He was afebrile.
The cough began 1 day prior and remained unchanged. No other symptoms
noted.
```

Here is another tuple:

< Oldham/Joseph, M, 82, nil, 217/Cross/Btown/OH/50582, 8/24/95, 100/62, 102, 99.2, 22, (cough/productive, nocturnal/3/D/(dry, constant/2/W)) >

From this we might see:

```
<H1> Patient Joseph Oldham </H1>
<H2> Personal Data: </H2>
     Male, 82 years old. <P>
     <H3> Mailing Address</H3>
     217 Cross St. Sometown, OH 50582<P>
<H2> Presentation of Thursday 8/24/95 </H2>
VS: 100/62, 102, 99.2, 22
<P>
Mr. Oldham presented with mild tachycardia and a temperature of 99.2.
His complaint was 3 days of productive night-time cough. Previously
he had had 2 weeks of dry, constant cough. No other symptoms noted.
```

Finally, we might see either patient presented through a different register, e.g. as:

<H1> Mr Joseph Oldham, age 82</H1>
Mr.Oldham had c/o cough, was tachycardic (102) and febrile (99.2).Had approximately 17 days of cough. Over the prior 3 days cough became productive and restricted to night time.

Example 2. Here we do not show the raw data, which describes a basketball game between two teams, but we do show intermediate representations following application of field, mode and tenor rules in turn.
Step 1:
A set of *Field Rules* is evaluated on the statistics for the game and all participating entities represented in the scheme. We receive something of the following, which we call: the *field representation*:

(University of Arkansas Lost)
(Thurman Top Scorer For Loser)
(Williamson Below Avg Points and Rebounds For Loser)
(University of Arkansas Without Beck)
(Series Tied)
(University of Kentucky Won)
(Mashburn, Delk Top Scorers For Winner)
(Pricket Above Avg Rebound For Winner)
(Rhodes, Ford Injured For Winner)

This set of facts is our first *intermediate representation*. These facts are isolated but represented appropriately to the field and goal of the intended presentation. In general at this stage the facts are unordered. Note there may have been a rule such as:

If ...
and W plays > X Minutes on average for Y
and W does not play against Z
...
then ... (Y without W) ...

This set of rules has most to do with *content selection* for the final document.
Step 2:
We now apply *Mode Instantiation Rules* which decide on the structure of the presentation, within a given set of constraints. (For example two injuries to one team may cause injuries to be mentioned in the lead paragraph.) In this case we may see:

(Rhodes, Ford injured for University of Kentucky)
(University of Kentucky Won Over University of Arkansas)
(University of Arkansas Without Beck)
(Series Tied)

*
(Pricket Above Avg Rebound For University of Kentucky)
(Mashburn, Delk Top Scorers For University of Kentucky)
(Thurman Top Scorer For University of Arkansas)
(Williamson Below Avg Points and Rebounds For University of Arkansas)
*
(Box Score)
(Scoring Graph)

Step 3:
The final processing by the register may now occur, resulting in a marked up document, our final *source representation*. *Tenor rules* are applied to give a pleasant surface representation to the selected and ordered facts.

```
<H1> UK Defeats UA </H1>
--Lead Paragraph
Rodrick Rhodes and Travis Ford were injured last night when the
University of Kentucky won over the University of Arkansas by the
score of .... Arkansas played without Corey Beck. The series
is now tied at ....
<P>
Kentucky was aided by a strong rebounding performance by Jared Prickett
and paced in scoring by Mashburn and Delk. Thurman led Arkansas in
points, but it was a quiet night for Corliss Williamson who was
held below his average in both  rebounding and points.
<IMG SRC="BoxScore">
<IMG SRC="ScoringGraphic">
<IMG SRC="~/Kentucky/Photos/mashburn.gif">
```

3 Some formal definitions

We are now ready to look at our approach to computational registers in some detail. Information is represented in *databases*. Databases are defined by means of *schemes*. We expect object-oriented databases see [Ul88, BM93]. The actual content of database is its *instance*. Instance consists of *records*. In Section 2 we have seen that our databases may consist of objects. Notice that in example 1, the attribute SYMPTOMS was a list of strings. Similarly the attribute NAME was a pair of strings. We will assume (and this always can be enforced) that the domains of attributes are disjoint. The information stored in the database may be text, numerical information or multimedia information (binary large objects, or BLOB fields). In this case the information stored in the field is interpreted as a pointer to the actual location where the information is stored. In our example, the field PIC contained the pointer to the file vmarek.gif with the actual BLOB information. Similar arrangements for aural information, video etc. can be made.

The scheme of the database is a vector of strings called names of attributes. The scheme is supplemented by another vector, of the same length, of *types* of attributes. These could be types such as string, float, BLOB/filename, pairs of strings, lists of strings, etc. We do not define types here.

In addition to instances (composed of objects called *records* to stress their database provenance) we deal with two more types of entities. These are *source representations* and *final presentations.* Although in the abstract setting the set I of source representations can be arbitrary, we think about it as a set of SGML programs (see Section 2). In contrast, the set of final presentations is the collection of interpreted SGML documents on display. Text formatting provides an analogy: source representations are .dvi files, final presentations are text documents [KN84]. We picture our situation as follows:

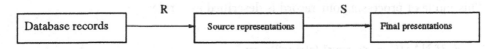

Fig. 1. Transforming the database information into texts

Figure 1 describes the overall approach as exemplified in Example 1. Database records are transformed via the register mapping into finished SGML source representations of documents ready to be processed by an SGML system into a final presentation document.

We will concentrate on the mapping R from database records to source representations. Such mapping, following linguistic terminology, is called a (generalized) *register.*

In the setting of example 2 we see that R is a composition of mappings. Steps 1 through 3 in 2 correspond here to rule based mappings F, M, T, essentially capturing the notions of *field, mode,* and *tenor* in registers. F selects, based on field knowledge, certain facts for translation into expressions appropriate for the field. This is a database mapping. M takes these expression, and using knowledge common to the field and a description of the mode, or form, of the document *orders* these expressions appropriately for intelligent presentation. Again, this is a mapping from one database scheme to another. This captures the "deep" structure of the presentation Finally T delivers a final source representation ready for an SGML or similar system to translate into a polished, reasonably arranged document – a presentation document. We are no longer interested in how the source representation becomes a final presentation as this is a matter for an SGML interpreter, and we have delivered an SGML document. In this setting our figure takes this form:

In principle, a register can be any mapping from records to source representations. We are interested, however, in registers defined by means of *rules.* That is rules describe the way in which database information is transformed into the source representation. For instance, in our Example 1 the first field, NAME is a pair of strings (string1/string2). The information contained in that field is

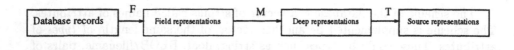

$$R(t) = T(M(F(t)))$$

$$Presentation(t) = S(R(t))$$

Fig. 2. Transformation with register

interpreted as a line of the resulting SGML program:

<H1> Patient string 2 string1 </H1>

This mode of processing our record is described as a rule:

> d: **If** NAME = <string1/string2> **and** ...
> **Then** i.firstline = <H1> Patient string2 string 1 </H1> **and** ...

(Rules can be quite complex, and we displayed a fragment of a rule to see some of its salient features).

Let us look carefully at our rule. Among other things this rule tells us that when we process this record and produce the written progress note for a physician, the field NAME is represented as patient information, with the first string represented as surname, and the second string as a given name. Thus the pair of strings *Doe/John* is interpreted as a line "Patient John Doe". The additional word "Patient" comes from the context – we talk about patients, and not (for instance) participants in an automobile accident. Notice the fact that the NAME field is primary information is additionally highlighted by the choice of the display information (<H1>). Both features presented above are related to the fact that our source representation assign *meaning* to database information.

Formally, we define a rule as an entity of the form:

> d: **If** $p_1(At_1)$ **and** ... $p_k(At_k)$
> **Then** i

Here, $p_1, \ldots, p_k$ are some formulas describing properties of attribute values. For instance, such a property may be that the temperature is between 98.0 and 99.2 (i.e. normal).

Definition 1. A (generalized) register R is rule-based if R is defined by a collection of rules of the form:

> d: **If** $At_1 \in X_1$ and ... $At_k \in X_k$
> **Then** i

Here $i \in I$ and $X_1 \subseteq Dom(At_1), \ldots, X_k \subseteq Dom(At_k)$ Further, X_j is called the jth condition in the rule d and a record t matches rule d if for all j, $1 \leq j \leq k$, $t(j) \in X_j$.

Notice that if the rule d does not explicitly impose conditions on attribute At_j then $X_j = Dom(At_j)$. The condition of the form $At_j = x$ is equivalent to one of the form $At_j \in \{x\}$ More generally, if $\varphi(\cdot)$ is any formula, then the condition of the form $\varphi(At_j)$ is equivalent to one of the form $At_j \in X_j$ where $X_j = \{x : \varphi(x)\}$. For instance, if one of our attributes is called *Temp* and the condition on the attribute *Temp* is: $100.0 \leq Temp \leq 100.5$ (and the step is .1) then our condition is equivalent to $Temp \in \{100.0, 100.1, \ldots, 101.5\}$.

Once the register is defined by use of rules, the order in which the rules are processed usually matters. Thus registers based on rules are, in general, nondeterministic.

We define now some classes of registers.

Definition 2. (a) A rule-based register R is consistent if for every record t and for every pair of rules d_1, d_2 in R if t matches both rules d_1 and d_2 then d_1, d_2 have the same conclusion.

(b) A register R is *complete* if every record matches at least one rule in R.

(c) A register that is both consistent and complete is called *functional*.

(d) A register R is called *partitional* if for every two rules d_1, d_2 in R and for every attribute At_j, the jth conditions X_j^1 and X_j^2 in d_1 and d_2 respectively satisfy the property:

$$X_j^1 = X_j^2 \quad \text{or} \quad X_j^1 \cap X_j^2 = \emptyset$$

(e) Two registers R_0, R_1 are called *equivalent* if for $j = 0, 1$, whenever a record t matches a rule d in R_j then there is a rule d' in R_{1-j} such that t matches d' and the conclusion of d' is the same as that of d.

4 Properties of registers defined by rules

In this section we report on some technical results obtained while working on the properties of registers. These technical results allow us to understand better how registers behave.

Proposition 3. *(a) For every register R there is an equivalent partitional register R'*
(b) When R is functional then so is R'.

We will characterize now registers in which a record can match only one rule.

Definition 4. A functional register R is called decompositional if for every $i \in I$, $R^{-1}(i)$ is empty or there exist nonempty sets $Z_1 \subseteq Dom(At_1), \ldots, Z_k \subseteq Dom(At_k)$ such that

$$R^{-1}(i) = Z_1 \times \ldots \times Z_k$$

Since for $i_1 \neq i_2$, $R^{-1}(i_1) \cap R^{-1}(i_2) = \emptyset$, decomposability means that that for each i, $R^{-1}(i)$ is a "hyperrectangle", and that those hyperrectangles cover the entire universal instance $Dom(At_1) \times \ldots \times Dom(At_k)$.

We have this characterization of decompositional registers.

Proposition 5. *A functional register R is decompositional if and only if there exists register R' such that R' is equivalent to R, and for every i ∈ I, i is the conclusion of at most one rule in R'.*

We will characterize now registers that are both decompositional and partitional. These are particularly simple registers which are generated by very simple rule sets. We start with a definition.

Definition 6. 1. A register R is called *simple* if R is both decompositional and partitional.

2. Let $D = (At_1, \ldots, At_k)$ and $D' = (At'_1, \ldots, At'_k)$ be database schemes. Let $U = \bigcup \{Dom(At_j) : 1 \leq j \leq k\}$ and $U' = \bigcup \{Dom(At'_j) : 1 \leq j \leq k\}$. A mapping $f : U \to U'$ is a database map if for every $x \in U$, and every j, $1 \leq j \leq k$, $x \in Dom(A_j)$ implies that $f(x) \in Dom(At'_j)$.

3. A register R is called *invertible* if all its rules have different conclusions and each rule is matched by exactly one record.

It turns out that database maps can be composed with rules.

Definition 7. Let $D = (At_1, \ldots, At_k)$ and $D' = (At'_1, \ldots, At'_k)$ be database schemes and let $f : U \to U'$ be a database map as above. Let R' be a register over D'. The composition of register R' and database map f is a register R consisting of rules over D (but with the same set of source representations I) :

> d: **If** $At_1 \in f^{-1}(X_1)$ **and** ... $At_k \in f^{-1}(X_k)$
> **Then** i

such that the rule

> d': **If** $At'_1 \in X_1$ **and** ... $At'_k \in X_k$
> **Then** i

belongs to R'. This composition is denoted $f \circ R'$.

Proposition 8. *A register R over a database scheme D is simple if and only if there exists a database scheme D' and a database map $f : U \to U'$ and an invertible register R' over D' such that $R = f \circ R'$.*

Proposition 9. *For every register R there is a database map f and a register R' such that:*
(a) R is equivalent to $f \circ R'$, and
(b) All rules in R' are matched by precisely one record.

Acknowledgments

The second author gratefully acknowledges a partial support by NSF grant IRI-9400568.

References

[BB88] F. Banchilon, G. Barbedette, V. Benzaken, C. Delobel, S. Gamerman, C. Lecluse, P. Pfeffer, P. Richard and R. Velez. The Design and Implementation of O_2, an Object–Oriented Database System, Proceedings of the OODBS II Workshop, Bad Munster, FRG, September 1988.

[BP89] J. A. Bateman and C. L. Paris. Phrasing a Text in Terms the User Can Understand, Proceedings of IJCAI 89.

[BM93] E. Bertino and L. Martino. *Object-Oriented Database Systems: Concepts and Architectures*. Addison-Wesley Reading, MA, 1993.

[CACS94] V. Christophides, S. Abiteboul, S. Cluet and M. Scholl. From Structured Documents to Novel Query Facilities, Proceedings of SIGMOD 94, ACM, 1994.

[CBR94] A. B. Cremers, O. T. Balovnev and W. Reddig. Views in Object–Oriented Databases, Proceedings of ADBIS'94, 1994.

[DE94] M. Dobrovnik and J. Eder. Adding View Support to ODMG–93, Proceedings of ADBIS'94, 1994.

[DV91] K. Devlin. *Logic and Information*. Cambridge University Press, 1991.

[EG95a] D. Estival and F. Gayral. A Study of the Context(s) in a Specific Type of Texts: Car Accident Reports, Computation and Language EPrint Archive, paper 9502032, 1995.

[EG95b] D. Estival and F. Gayral. An NLP Approach to a Specific Type of Texts: Car Accident reports, Proceedings of Workshop on "Context in Natural Language Processing", IJCAI 95.

[GC78] M. Gregory and S. Carroll. *Language and Situation: Language Varieties and Their Social Contexts*. Routledge and Kegan Paul Ltd., 1978.

[HR90] E. van Herwijen. *Practical SGML*. Kluwer Academic Publishers, 1990.

[CW93] K.E. Campbell, K. Wickert, L.M. Fagan and M.A. Musen. A Computer-based tool for generation of pregress notes, Proceedings of the Sixteenth Annual Symposium on Computer Applications in Medical Care, Washington, DC, November, 1993, pp. 284-284.

[KN84] D.E. Knuth. *The* Tex *Book*. Addison Wesley, Reading, MA, 1984.

[MC85] K. R. McKeown. *Text Generation*. Cambridge University Press, 1985.

[PR87] C. L. Paris. *The Use of Explicit User Models in Text Generation: Tailoring to a User's Level of Expertise*. Ph.D. Thesis, Columbia University, 1987, also Technical report CUCS-309-87, Columbia University.

[PA83] Z. Pawlak. Rough Sets, *International Journal of Information and Computer Sciences* 11:145-172, 1982.

[RV95] W. Ramm and C. Villiger. Global Text organization and Sentence-Grammatical Realization: Discourse Level Constraints on Theme Selection, Proceedings RANLP 95, to appear.

[Si64] R. Sikorski. *Boolean Algebras*. Springer Verlag, Heidelberg, 1964.

[Ul88] J.D. Ullman. *Principles of Database and Knowledge-Base Systems*. Computer Science Press, Rockville, MD, 1988.

Reducing Information Systems with Uncertain Attributes*

Marzena Kryszkiewicz and Henryk Rybiński
Institute of Computer Science
Warsaw University of Technology
Nowowiejska 15/19, 00-665 Warsaw, Poland
e-mails: mkr@ii.pw.edu.pl, rybinski@mimuw.edu.pl

Abstract. We present Rough Set approach to reasoning in information systems with uncertain attributes. A similarity relation between objects is introduced. The relation is a tolerance relation. A reduction of knowledge we propose eliminates only information, which is not essential from the point of view of classification. Our approach is general in the sense it does not assume anything about the semantics of null values and uncertain multivalued attributes. We show how to find decision rules, which have minimal number of conditions and do not increase the degree of non-determinism of the original decision table.

Key words. Approximate Reasoning, Knowledge Discovery, Rough Sets, Uncertain Information System, Knowledge Representation Reduction

1 Introduction

In Knowledge Representation Systems it is convenient in some cases to describe objects by assigning sets of values to some attributes instead of single values. We call such attributes *multivalued*. For example, to describe specialization of a student it is useful to provide all the courses he/she attends. The multivalued attributes may be also used in the case where we would like to express uncertainty. Such a situation arises e.g. in federated database systems. The logical consistency of local systems does not guarantee the consistency of the entire federation. This is usually caused by lack of global consistency control mechansim etc. We frequently obtain variant values such that at least one of the variants is definitely true but we do not have enough information to sort out which one it is. If no information is available for given attribute it would be convenient to mark such attribute by null value.

Rough set theory [1] has been conceived as a tool to conceptualize, organize and analyze various types of data, in particular, to deal with inexact, uncertain or vague knowledge in applications related to Artificial Intelligence. In this paper we present Rough Set approach to reasoning in information systems with uncertain attributes. Uncertainty will be expressed below by assigning sets of values or null values to the attributes.

In the context of Rough Set approach different ways in which uncertain values may be handled have been investigated [2-3]. Our approach is substantially different from

---

* This work has been supported by grant: No 8 T11C 038 08 from the State Committee for Scientific Research

those mentioned above, as it does not assume anything about the nature of null and set values and still is capable of reducing dispensable knowledge efficiently. The presented approach is a generalization of the model presented in [4], where the uncertainty was presented only by null values. We define a similarity relation between objects which is reflexive and symmetric, though in general it is not transitive. Such a relation is called a *tolerance relation* [5]. We propose reduction of knowledge that eliminates only that information, which is not essential from the point of view of classification or decision making. This type of knowledge reduction for the case of classical information systems was discussed thoroughly in [5-8].

We also show how to find decision rules, which have minimal number of conditions and do not increase the degree of non-determinism of the original decision table.

2 Uncertain Information Systems

Information system (*IS*) is a pair $S = (O, AT)$, where O - is a non-empty finite set of *objects* and AT is a non-empty finite set of *attributes*, such that $a: O \rightarrow V_a$ for any $a \in AT$, where V_a is called the *domain* of a. Each subset of attributes $A \subseteq AT$ determines a binary *indiscernibility relation* $IND(A)$, as follows:

$$IND(A) = \{(x,y) \in O \times O | \forall a \in A, a(x) = a(y)\}.$$

The relation $IND(A)$, $A \subseteq AT$, constitutes a partition of O, which we will denote by $O / IND(A)$.

In order to express uncertainty we will change the definitions above. Namely, we allow attributes such that $a: O \rightarrow \mathcal{P}(V_a) \cup \{*\}$, where $*$ denotes *null value*. If $a(x) = Q$, $x \in O$, it means that the real value of the attribute a is a non-empty subset of Q, although we do not know which one. If $a(x) = *$ it means that nothing is known about the attribute value for the given object.

If for at least one attribute $a \in AT$ there is an object such that $a(x) = *$ or $card(a(x)) > 1$, then S is called an *uncertain information system*.

Let $SIM(A)$, $A \subseteq AT$, denote binary *similarity relation* between objects that are possibly indiscernible in terms of values of attributes A (i.e. we cannot say with certainty that these objects are different).

Let us define similarity relation more precisely:

$$SIM(A) = \{(x,y) \in O \times O | \forall a \in A, a(x) \cap a(y) \neq \varnothing \text{ or } a(x) = * \text{ or } a(y) = *\}.$$

Property 2.1

$$SIM(A) \text{ is a tolerance relation}; \quad SIM(A) = \bigcap_{a \in A} SIM(\{a\}).$$

Let $I_A(x)$ denote the object set $\{y \in O | (x,y) \in SIM(A)\}$. $I_A(x)$ is the maximal set of objects which are possibly indiscernible by A with x. $I_A(x)$ will be called the *tolerance class* for x with regard to A.

Let $O/SIM(A)$ denote classification, which is the family set $\{I_A(x)|x \in O\}$. The tolerance classes in $O/SIM(A)$ do not constitute a partition of O in general. They may be subsets/supersets of each other or may overlap. Of course, $\bigcup O/SIM(A) = O$.

Example 2.1

Given descriptions of several cars as in Table 2.1 let us try to classify them according to the chosen subsets of attributes.

Car	Price	Mileage	Size	Accident
1	{high}	{high}	{full}	{doors,engine}
2	{low}	*	{full,compact}	{engine}
3	*	*	{compact}	{doors}
4	{high}	*	{full}	{doors}
5	*	*	{full}	{doors}
6	{low}	{high}	{full}	*

Table 2.1.

From Table 2.1 we have: $O = \{1,2,3,4,5,6\}$, $AT = \{P,M,S,A\}$ where P, M, S, A stand for *Price, Mileage, Size, Accident*.

Let us note that $O/SIM(AT) = \{I_{AT}(1), I_{AT}(2), I_{AT}(3), I_{AT}(5), I_{AT}(6)\}$, where $I_{AT}(1) = I_{AT}(4) = \{1,4,5\}$, $I_{AT}(2) = \{2,6\}$, $I_{AT}(3) = \{3\}$, $I_{AT}(5) = \{1,4,5,6\}$, $I_{AT}(6) = \{2,5,6\}$.

It can be also observed easily that $O/SIM(\{P,S,A\}) = O/SIM(AT)$ whereas $O/SIM(\{S,A\}) \neq O/SIM(AT)$ (namely, $O/SIM(\{S,A\}) = \{I_B(1), I_B(2), I_B(3), I_B(4)\}$, where $B = \{S,A\}$ and $I_B(1) = I_B(6) = \{1,2,4,5,6\}$, $I_B(2) = \{1,2,6\}$, $I_B(3) = \{3\}$, $I_B(4) = I_B(5) = \{1,4,5,6\}$).

$\square$

In Example 2.1 car classification by AT is the same as that by $\{P,S,A\}$ and is different from car classification by $\{S,A\}$. Usually, we are interested in minimal subsets of AT, so called *reducts*, that classify in the same way as AT.

Formally, a set $A \subseteq AT$ is a *reduct* of *IS* iff

$$SIM(A) = SIM(AT) \quad \text{and} \quad \forall B \subset A, SIM(B) \neq SIM(AT).$$

For the information system from Example 2.1 we can find out that $\{P,S,A\}$ is its reduct. On the other hand, knowing that e.g. the values of attributes *Price* and *Accident* of an object x are equal to *low* and *engine* respectively is sufficient to classify x to the tolerance class $I_{AT}(2)$. This observation encourages us to define a notion of a *reduct for an object* that should allow to classify objects with less number of required attributes then the number of attributes in a reduct of *IS*.

A set $A \subseteq AT$ is a *reduct* of *IS* for x, $x \in O$, iff

$$I_A(x) = I_{AT}(x) \quad \text{and} \quad \forall B \subset A, I_B(x) \neq I_{AT}(x).$$

3 Set Approximations

Let $X \subseteq \mathcal{O}$ and $A \subseteq AT$. $\underline{A}X$ is *lower approximation* of X, iff:

$$\underline{A}X = \bigcup \{x \in \mathcal{O} | I_A(x) \subseteq X\}.$$

Let $X \subseteq \mathcal{O}$ and $A \subseteq AT$. $\overline{A}X$ is *upper approximation* of X, iff:

$$\overline{A}X = \bigcup \{x \in \mathcal{O} | I_A(x) \cap X \neq \varnothing\} = \{I_A(x) | x \in X\}.$$

Like in classical *IS*, $\underline{A}X$ is a set of objects that belong to X with certainty, while $\overline{A}X$ is a set of objects that possibly belong to X.

Property 3.1

$$\forall A \subseteq AT, \forall X \subseteq \mathcal{O}, (\underline{A}X \subseteq X \subseteq \overline{A}X);$$

$$\forall A, B \subseteq AT, \forall X \subseteq \mathcal{O}, (A \subset B \Rightarrow \underline{A}X \subseteq \underline{B}X);$$

$$\forall A, B \subseteq AT, \forall X \subseteq \mathcal{O}, (A \subset B \Rightarrow \overline{A}X \supseteq \overline{B}X).$$

4 Decision Tables, Decision Rules, Knowledge Reduction

(*Uncertain*) *decision table* (*DT*) is an (uncertain) information system $DT = (\mathcal{O}, AT \cup \{d\})$, where d is a distinguished attribute called *decision* such that $d \notin AT$ and for any $x \in \mathcal{O}$ the decision value is certain $(d(x) \neq *$ and $card(d(x)) = 1)$; the elements of AT are called *conditions*.

Let us define a function $\partial_A : \mathcal{O} \to \mathcal{P}(V_d)$, $A \subseteq AT$, as follows:

$$\partial_A(x) = \{i | i = d(y) \text{ and } y \in I_A(x)\}.$$

∂_A will be called *generalized decision* in *DT*.

If $card(d(x)) = 1$ for any $x \in \mathcal{O}$ then *DT* is *consistent* (*deterministic, definite*), otherwise it is *inconsistent* (*non-deterministic, non-definite*).

Remark: The equation below:

$$X \in \mathcal{O} / IND(\partial_A) \Rightarrow \underline{A}X = X = \overline{A}X$$

does not necessarily hold for an uncertain *DT* (though it holds for classical *DT*).

In the sequel, an attribute-value pair (a, v) will mean that v is the value of an attribute a.

Any *DT* may be regarded as a set of (*generalized*) *decision rules* of the form:

$$\bigwedge_{c \in C} \bigvee_{v \in V_c'} (c, v) \Rightarrow \bigvee_{w \in V_d'} (d, w), \text{ where } C \subseteq AT, V_c' \subseteq V_c \cup \{*\}, V_d' \subseteq V_d.$$

The left-hand side $\bigwedge\limits_{c\in C} \bigvee\limits_{v\in V_c'}(c,v)$ and right-hand side $\bigvee\limits_{w\in V_d'}(d,w)$ will be called *condition* and *decision parts* of the rule respectively.

Let X be a set of objects of property $\bigwedge\limits_{c\in C} \bigvee\limits_{v\in V_c'}(c,v)$ $(C\subseteq AT, V_c'\subseteq V_c\cup\{*\})$ and let Y be a set of objects of property $\bigvee\limits_{w\in V_d'}(d,w)$ $(V_d'\subseteq V_d)$.

A decision rule $\bigwedge\limits_{c\in C} \bigvee\limits_{v\in V_c'}(c,v)\Rightarrow\bigvee\limits_{w\in V_d'}(d,w)$ is *true* in DT iff $\overline{C}X\subseteq Y$.

A decision rule r: $\bigwedge\limits_{c\in C} \bigvee\limits_{v\in V_c'}(c,v)\Rightarrow\bigvee\limits_{w\in V_d'}(d,w)$ $(C\subseteq AT, V_c'\subseteq V_c\cup\{*\}, V_d'\subseteq V_d)$ is *optimal* for an object x in DT (*x-optimal*), iff it is true and the values associated with conditional attributes in r belong to the value set assigned to the corresponding attributes of x in DT, and no other rule, which is constructed from a proper subset of the set of all value-pairs occurring in r, is true.

Let C_i, C_j be the sets of attributes occurring in the condition parts of the rules r_i, r_j, respectively. Let $\omega_c(r)$, be the set of all values occurring in all attribute-value pairs in condition part of rule r for an attribute c, $c\in AT$.

We say that r_i *subsumes* r_j, iff $C_i=C_j$ and the set of decision values is the same in both rules and $\forall c\in C_i, \omega_c(r_i)\supseteq\omega_c(r_j)$.

A decision rule is *optimal* in DT, iff there is an object x for which it is x-optimal and no other y-optimal rule subsumes it, $y\neq x$.

Example 4.1

Let us consider decision table Table 4.1, which extends Table 2.1 by decision attribute d (e.g. *Worth-to-buy*). Determine the family of decision classes $O/IND(d)$ and the family of generalized decision classes $O/IND(\partial_{AT})$. For each decision class compute its lower and upper approximations and write down true decision rules.

Car	Price	Mileage	Size	Accident	d
1	{high}	{high}	{full}	{doors,engine}	good
2	{low}	*	{full,compact}	{engine}	good
3	*	*	{compact}	{doors}	poor
4	{high}	*	{full}	{doors}	good
5	*	*	{full}	{doors}	excel.
6	{low}	{high}	{full}	*	good

Table 4.1.

Solution: From Table 4.1 we have:

$$\mathcal{O}\,/\,IND(d) = \{X_{good}, X_{poor}, X_{excel.}\}, \text{ where } X_{good} = \{1,2,4,6\},\ X_{poor} = \{3\},\ X_{excel.} = \{5\}.$$

So,
$$\underline{ATX}_{good} = \{2\}; \qquad \underline{ATX}_{poor} = \{3\}; \quad \underline{ATX}_{excel.} = \varnothing;$$
$$\overline{ATX}_{good} = \{1,2,4,5,6\}; \qquad \overline{ATX}_{poor} = \{3\}; \quad \overline{ATX}_{excel.} = \{1,4,5,6\}.$$

In Table 4.2 we place the values of generalized decisions.

Car	∂_{AT}
1	$\{good, excel.\}$
2	$\{good\}$
3	$\{poor\}$
4	$\{good, excel.\}$
5	$\{good, excel.\}$
6	$\{good, excel.\}$

Table 4.2.

$$\mathcal{O}\,/\,IND(\partial_{AT}) = \{X_{(good)}, X_{(poor)}, X_{(good,excel.)}\}, \quad \text{where} \quad X_{(good)} = \{2\}, \quad X_{(poor)} = \{3\},$$
$$X_{(good,excel.)} = \{1,4,5,6\}.$$

Hence,
$$\underline{ATX}_{(good)} = \varnothing; \qquad \underline{ATX}_{(poor)} = 3; \quad \underline{ATX}_{(good,excel.)} = \{1,4,5\};$$
$$\overline{ATX}_{(good)} = \{2,6\}; \qquad \overline{ATX}_{(poor)} = \{3\}; \quad \overline{ATX}_{(good,excel.)} = \{1,2,4,5,6\}.$$

Below we list true decision rules for DT:

r_1: $(P,high) \wedge (M,high) \wedge (S,full) \wedge ((A,doors) \vee (A,engine)) \Rightarrow$
$\quad (d,good) \vee (d,excel.)$;

r_2: $(P,low) \wedge (M,*) \wedge ((S,full) \vee (S,compact)) \wedge (A,engine) \Rightarrow (d,good)$;

r_3: $(P,*) \wedge (M,*) \wedge (S,compact) \wedge (A,doors) \Rightarrow (d,poor)$;

r_4: $(P,high) \wedge (M,*) \wedge (S,full) \wedge (A,doors) \Rightarrow (d,good) \vee (d,excel.)$;

r_5: $(P,*) \wedge (M,*) \wedge (S,full) \wedge (A,doors) \Rightarrow (d,good) \vee (d,excel.)$;

r_6: $(P,low) \wedge (M,high) \wedge (S,full) \wedge (A,*) \Rightarrow (d,good) \vee (d,excel.)$.

□

It follows from the definition of generalized decision and the definitions of true and optimal decision rules that the decision part of an optimal rule for x, $x \in \mathcal{O}$, is equal to $(d,w_1) \vee (d,w_2) \vee ... \vee (d,w_n)$, where $\{w_1, w_2, ..., w_n\} = \partial_{AT}(x)$. Thus the problem of finding optimal rules for objects consists in reduction of condition attributes. Reduction of knowledge that preserves generalized decisions for all objects in DT is lossless from decision making standpoint.

Formally, a set $A \subseteq AT$ is a *reduct* of DT (*relative reduct*), iff

$$\partial_A = \partial_{AT} \quad \text{and} \quad \forall B \subset A, \partial_B \neq \partial_{AT}.$$

In order to determine decision rules with minimal number of conditions we may employ the notion of *reduct* for an object in *DT*.

A set $A \subseteq AT$ is a *reduct* of *DT* for *x* (*relative reduct for x*), $x \in \mathcal{O}$, in *DT*, iff

$$\partial_A(x) = \partial_{AT}(x) \quad \text{and} \quad \forall B \subset A, \partial_B(x) \neq \partial_{AT}(x).$$

Remark: Let *A* be a relative reduct. The below equations:

$$X \in \mathcal{O} / IND(\partial_{AT}) \Rightarrow \underline{A}X = \underline{AT}X; \quad X \in \mathcal{O} / IND(\partial_{AT}) \Rightarrow \overline{A}X = \overline{AT}X$$

do not necessarily hold for uncertain *DT*.

Example 4.2

Let us illustrate the remark above for a relative reduct of *DT* from Table 4.1. We can easily check that *B*={*Size,Accident*} is a reduct of *DT*. Below we present lower and upper approximations of classes from the family $X \in \mathcal{O} / IND(\partial_{AT})$ with regard to the set of attributes *B*:

$\underline{B}X_{(good)} = \varnothing;$ $\qquad \underline{B}X_{(poor)} = 3;$ $\qquad \underline{B}X_{(good,excel.)} = \{4,5\};$

$\overline{B}X_{(good)} = \{1,2,6\};$ $\qquad \overline{B}X_{(poor)} = \{3\};$ $\qquad \overline{B}X_{(good,excel.)} = \{1,2,4,5,6\}.$

where $X_{(good)}$, $X_{(poor)}$ and $X_{(good,excel.)}$ have the same meaning as in Example 4.1.

Comparing the above set approximations with the set approximations computed in Example 4.1, we can notice for instance that:

$$\overline{B}X_{(good)} \subset \overline{AT}X_{(good)}; \qquad \underline{B}X_{(good,excel.)} \supset \underline{AT}X_{(good,excel.)}.$$

$\square$

It can be also easily shown that {*Size*} is a reduct for the objects 1, 4, 5, 6 from Table 4.1, {*Price, Accident*} is a reduct for the object 2 and {*Size, Accident*} is a reduct for the object 3. These reducts allow us to obtain the following three *x*-optimal decision rules from Table 4.1:

r_1': $(P,low) \wedge (A,engine) \Rightarrow (d,good);$ /* for the object 2*/
r_2': $(S,compact) \wedge (A,doors) \Rightarrow (d,poor);$ /* for the object 3 */
r_3': $(S,full) \Rightarrow (d,good) \vee (d,excel.).$ /* for the objects 1,4,5,6 */

Let us note that the above decision rules will remain true for the case when all or some null values in *DT* will be replaced by arbitrary values or any set value of multivalued attribute will be substituted by its non-empty subset.

Below we illustrate the case where some of the *x*-optimal rules are not optimal in *DT*.

Example 4.3

In Table 4.3 we store the information on researchers, their possible talents and grades obtained from universities (shortly *T*, *G*, *U* respectively). We put there an evaluation of suitability for a leadership in a computer science grant (*d*) as well.

Researcher	Talent	Grade	University	d
1	{maths,comp.sc.}	{B.,M.Sc.,Ph.D.}	{MIT,NC}	good
2	{comp.sc.}	{Ph.D.}	{NC}	excel.
3	{maths}	{M.Sc.}	{MIT,WUT}	good
4	{maths,philosophy}	*	*	good

Table 4.3.

For the table above we may find out the following generalized decisions which shall result from the similarity of objects (in terms of *SIM*):

$I_{AT}(1) = \{1,2,3,4\}$, $I_{AT}(2) = \{1,2\}$, $I_{AT}(3) = \{1,3,4\}$, $I_{AT}(3) = \{1,3,4\}$.

Hence, $\delta_{AT}(1) = \delta_{AT}(2) = \{good,excel.\}$ and $\delta_{AT}(3) = \delta_{AT}(4) = \{good\}$.

One can easily check that {*Talent*} is a reduct of *DT*.
The simplified decision rules received from the reducts for each object are as follows:

r_1: $\Rightarrow (d,good) \vee (d,excel.)$;   /* for the objects 1,2 */
r_2: $(T,maths) \Rightarrow (d,good)$;   /* for the object 3 */
r_3: $((T,maths) \vee (T,philosophy)) \Rightarrow (d,good)$.   /* for the object 4 */

Hence the optimal rules for the decision table take the form:

r_1': $\Rightarrow (d,good) \vee (d,excel.)$;   /* for the objects 1,2 */
r_2': $((T,maths) \vee (T,philosophy)) \Rightarrow (d,good)$.   /* for the objects 3,4 */

The final set of rules contains only the rules which are not subsumed by others. One can also drop a rule with empty condition part since such a rule is trivial, as its decision part is an alternative of all possible decision values.

□

5 Discernibility Function and Computation of Reducts

In order to compute reducts of uncertain *IS* and uncertain *DT* we will exploit the idea of so called *discernibility functions* [5,6,8,9]. Their main properties are that they are monotonic Boolean functions and their prime implicants uniquely determine reducts.

Let $\alpha_A(x,y)$ be a set of attributes such that $(x,y) \notin SIM(\{a\})$ (i.e. $a(x) \cap a(y) = \emptyset$ and $a(x) \neq *$ and $a(y) \neq *$). Hence, if $(x,y) \in SIM(A)$ then $\alpha_A(x,y) = \emptyset$.

Let $\sum \alpha_A(x,y)$ be a Boolean expression which is equal to 1, if $\alpha_A(x,y) = \emptyset$. Otherwise, let $\sum \alpha_A(x,y)$ be a disjunction of variables corresponding to attributes contained in $\alpha_A(x,y)$.

$$\Delta \text{ is a } \textit{discernibility function for IS, iff } \Delta = \prod_{(x,y)\in O\times O} \sum \alpha_{AT}(x,y).$$

$$\Delta(x) \text{ is a } \textit{discernibility function for object x in IS, iff } \Delta(x) = \prod_{y\in O} \sum \alpha_{AT}(x,y).$$

$$\Delta^* \text{ is a } \textit{discernibility function for DT, iff } \Delta^* = \prod_{(x,y)\in O\times(x\in O \wedge d(x)\notin \delta_{AT}(x))} \sum \alpha_{AT}(x,y).$$

$\Delta^*(x)$ is a *discernibility function* for *object* x in DT, iff $\Delta^*(x) = \displaystyle\prod_{y \in \{z \in \mathcal{O} | d(z) \notin \partial_{AT}(x)\}} \sum_{\delta_{AT}(x)} \alpha_{AT}(x,y).$

Example 5.1

Determine all reducts for *IS* presented in Table 2.1 by computing prime implicants of discernibility functions Δ.

Solution: To construct a discernibility function we will use Table 5.1, in which we place values of $\alpha_A(x,y)$ for any pair (x,y) of objects from $\mathcal{O}$.

x\y	1	2	3	4	5	6
1		P	S			P
2	P		A	PA	A	
3	S	A		S	S	S
4	PA	S				P
5		A	S			
6	P		S	P		

Table 5.1

Hence we have, $\Delta = PSA(P \vee A) = PSA$;

$\Delta(1) = PS$; $\Delta(2) = PA$; $\Delta(3) = SA$; $\Delta(4) = (P \vee A)SP = PS$; $\Delta(5) = SA$; $\Delta(6) = PS$.
Thus, {*Price,Size,Accident*} is a reduct for *IS*, {*Price,Size*} is a relative reduct for the objects 1, 4 and 6 etc.

□

Example 5.2

Determine all reducts for *DT* presented in Table 4.1 by computing prime implicants of discernibility functions Δ^*.

Solution: To construct a discernibility function we build Table 5.2, in which we place values of $\alpha_A(x,y)$ for any pair (x,y) of objects, such that $x \in \mathcal{O}$ and $y \in \{z \in \mathcal{O} | d(z) \notin \partial_{AT}(x)\}$.

x\y	1	2	3	4	5	6
1		S				
2	P		A	PA	A	
3	S	A		S	S	S
4			S			
5			S			
6			S			

Table 5.2.

Hence we have, $\Delta^* = SPA(P \vee A) = SPA$;

$\Delta^*(1) = S$; $\Delta^*(2) = PA(P \vee A) = PA$; $\Delta^*(3) = SA$; $\Delta^*(4) = S$; $\Delta^*(5) = S$; $\Delta^*(6) = S$.

Thus, *{Price,Size,Accident}* is a reduct for *DT*, *{Size}* is a relative reduct for the objects 1, 4, 5, 6 etc.

□

Conclusions

In the paper we have defined uncertain information systems and have shown how they can be used for reasoning in the context of Rough Set approach. The introduced definitions of reducts allow to reduce knowledge representation in the way it does not diminish the original system's abilities to classify objects or to make decisions. Both, reduction of dispensable knowledge and searching for optimal decision rules are transformable to the problem of computing prime implicants of discernibility functions. We have shown that discernibility functions for uncertain information systems may be constructed in a conjunctive normal form. This is a particular feature of uncertain information systems, since in general, the formula defining the discernibility function of a tolerance information system is much more complex [8]. The decision rules that can be derived have the property that they remain true when all or some null values in *DT* are replaced by arbitrary values or any set value of multivalued attribute is substituted by its non-empty subset.

References

[1]   Pawlak Z., *Rough Sets: Theoretical Aspects of Reasoning about Data*, Kluwer Academic Publishers, Vol. 9, 1991.

[2]   Słowiński R., Stefanowski J., Rough Classification in Incomplete Information Systems, *Mathematical and Comput. Modelling*, Vol. 12, No. 10-11, 1989, pp. 1347-1357.

[3]   Słowiński R., Stefanowski J., Handling Various Types of Uncertainty in The Rough Set Approach, in *Rough Sets, Fuzzy Sets and Knowledge Discovery (RSKD '93)*, W. Ziarko (ed.), Springer-Verlag, 1994.

[4]   Kryszkiewicz M., Rough Set Approach to Incomplete Information Systems, in *Proceedings of Second Annual Joint Conference on Information Sciences*, North Carolina, USA, 28 September - 1 October, 1995, pp. 194-197

[5]   Skowron A., Stepaniuk J., Generalized Approximation Spaces, Proceedings of the Third International Workshop on Rough Sets and Knowledge Discovery RSSC '94, San Jose, USA, 1994, pp. 156-163.

[6]   Kryszkiewicz M., *Knowledge Reduction in Information Systems*, Ph.D. Thesis, Warsaw University of Technology, 1994.

[7]   Pawlak Z., Skowron A., A Rough Set Approach to Decision Rules Generation, ICS Research Report 23/93, Warsaw University of Technology, 1993.

[8]   Skowron A., Management of Uncertainty in AI: A Rough Set Approach, ICS Research Report 46/93, Warsaw University of Technology, December 1993.

[9]   Skowron A., Rauszer C., The Discernibility Matrices and Functions in Information Systems, in *Intelligent Decision Support: Handbook of Applications and Advances of Rough Sets Theory*, Slowinski R. (ed.), 1992, Kluwer Academic Publisher, pp. 331-362.

Object and Dependency Oriented Programming in FLO

Anne-Marie Dery and Stéphane Ducasse and Mireille Fornarino

{pinna,ducasse,blay}@essi.fr
Université de Nice Sophia-Antipolis - CNRS URA 1376
650 route des colles - B.P. 145, 06903 Sophia Antipolis CEDEX - FRANCE

Abstract. The FLO language integrates management of inter-object dependencies into the object oriented paradigms. In this paper, we focus on the use of reactive dependencies (*links*) in object-oriented knowledge representation. In particular, we present different *meta-links* (*links* between *links*) and show how the FLO links allow one to design some composition relationships.

1 Introduction

Although the importance of inter-object relationships (also named dependencies or interactions) is well accepted [BC89, BELR92], there is only limited object-oriented language support for their specification and implementation. Confronted with this lack of expressiveness in object models, the programmer has to use traditional object features, such as attributes, to store the references to linked objects, accessors, or daemons, in order to manage constraints and interactions among objects. However, such designs of behavioral relationships [HHG90] lead to several drawbacks. The dependency semantics is not clearly expressed, and dependencies are often hard-wired into object functionalities. This goes against modularity. It is then difficult to modify, specify, or maintain objects and dependencies. Reuse capabilities also decrease.

In response to this lack of expressiveness of object models, the FLO[1][DBFP95] language is an extension of the object-oriented paradigms integrating dependency management. In FLO, the user defines dependencies specifying which methods have to be controlled. Next, he/she can declare the objects involved in the dependencies, without altering object classes. FLO then automatically maintains the consistency of the graph of declared dependencies, by controlling the messages sent to the related objects. The language is currently used for knowledge representation [DFP91] and in the domain of User Interface Management. Moreover, FLO is designed as an extensible language by means of computational reflection [Mae87]. Thus, its expressiveness and the dependency management mechanism may be adapted according to the application's needs.

---

[1] FLO, standing for First class Links between Objects, is a scheme-based object-oriented language.

This paper is organized in three parts. Firstly, we present other work on dependency expression. Secondly, we give an intuitive view of the definition and maintenance of dependencies in FLO. Finally, we describe some examples of use and adaptations of the language for knowledge representation. In particular, we present different meta-links (dependencies between dependencies) and a new operator to design some composition relationships.

2 Motivations

"... no object is an island. All objects stand in relationship to others, on whom they relay for services and control." [BC89] The necessity of dependency definition and management has been known for a long time [Woo75, HK85, EWH85]. Nowadays, different methods of modeling and design [BELR92, NECH92] outline the existence of relationships. Many applications in several domains (graphical interfaces, knowledge representation and acquisition [DT88], hypertext, ...) require the expression of interactions between objects. However, in traditional object-oriented languages there is no way to declare the behavioral dependencies, so the user has to implement them using built-in mechanisms such as inheritance, attributes, method combination, active values, or daemons [SBK86]. Thus, some languages, such as Smalltalk-80, introduce tools for managing inter-object dependencies. Constraint languages also answer to this lack of expressiveness in object-oriented languages. Let us examine these different approaches in the following sections.

Traditional Object-Oriented Solutions. In order to illustrate the traditional implementations of inter-object dependencies, we chose the following example. Let us suppose that a user has created two independent objects: a stack object s1 and a memory object m1. The class stack defines four methods: pop, push, empty?, and empty. The class memory defines the methods store, unstore and notfull?. We want to express a dependency between two instances of these classes, such that all the popped values of the stack instance must be stored within the memory instance associated with the stack . Such a dependency between a stack and a memory is consistent if the memory stores all the popped values of the stack.

A simple implementation consists of creating a subclass of stack to represent stack-with-memory, in adding a slot memory to this class and in specializing the pop method so that its execution implies automatically sending a store message to the memory associated with the stack. Daemons, accessors, references to linked objects, or active values [SBK86] are other similar ways to manage dependency consistency. Such implementations give a poor dependency expressiveness. The dependency semantics is not clearly expressed, and dependencies are hard-wired into object functionalities. Consequently, object structures and functionalities are polluted by non-intrinsic information. Programming and maintaining applications involving inter-object dependencies are then difficult.

The MVC Model. The MVC[2] model [KP88] uses the Smalltalk *dependencies*, which are based upon message propagation between objects: when a model

---
[2] Model View Controller

changes (**changed** method), a notification message (**update:** method) is broadcasted to its dependents. At first glance, the philosophy of the MVC model, which was the clear independence of the different agents, is respected. However, the use of the Smalltalk *dependencies* has several drawbacks. The programmer must know *a priori* which objects are susceptible to being linked. The programmer must manage all the state modifications of the model and the reaction of its dependents: he/she must program the change notifications in all the necessary methods of the linked objects (by adding the **self changed** message and programming the **update:** methods). Furthermore, a class of dependent objects is specific to a class of model objects: contrary to the initial MVC philosophy, these classes are strongly linked. Moreover, from a specification point of view, the Smalltalk dependencies are spread across all the classes: protocols are sometimes difficult to understand because one has to browse the whole class library to track the message flow. The advantage of this approach is that the model does not explicitly know or refer to its dependents.

The ALV Paradigm. The Abstraction-Link-View paradigm [Hil92] emphasizes a clean separation of user interfaces from applications. ALV *links* are objects whose sole responsibility is to facilitate communication between abstraction objects (application) and the view objects (user interfaces). ALV *links* are bundles of constraints that maintain consistency between views and abstraction. No communication support is coded into the view or abstraction objects: they ignore each other. There are many similarities between ALV paradigm and FLO. However, as we will show FLO allows one to control any method, whereas RENDEZVOUS limits link definition to instance variable accesses.

Constraint Languages. In constraint-based languages, dependencies are expressed in terms of constraints between instance variables. When the value of such a constrained variable is modified, a propagation algorithm tries to satisfy the constraints, modifying the linked variables ([FBB92, MGZ92, San93, Ber93, Kum92]). Constraints are not expressed in terms of object interactions, so some inter-object dependencies are difficult to express as constraints between instance variables. In the proposed example, it is clear that the use of constraints is not natural. The user only wants to express interactions between messages of its objects and not mathematical constraints between values of their instance variables. Moreover, some limitations on types of components are imposed by the constraint solvers. And constraint expressions violate encapsulation. However, constraints are a powerful formalism to manage some particular inter-object dependencies between objects. As the constraints are not at the same level of expression as our links, constraints are complementary to our approach.

Contracts. In order to express cooperation between objects, Helm *et al.* in [HHG90] propose *contracts*. *Contracts* are specified through type obligations, which define variables and external interfaces to be supported, and causal obligations, which define a sequence of messages to be sent and an invariant to be maintained. With a contract, classes of linked objects are structured by and around dependencies. To quote the authors, *"the specification of a class becomes*

*spread over a number of contracts and conformance declarations, and is not loc-
alized to one class definition"* [HHG90]. Our approach differs significantly from
that of contracts, because we believe in the equal importance of dependencies
and of the objects they relate.

3 Dependencies in FLO

We claim that the existence of inter-object dependencies changes the behaviors of
linked objects. Thus, in this section, we describe the FLO language via a simple
example, i.e. the nature of our dependencies (named links), the way they are
defined, and the process of link maintenance.

Link Declarations. Let us recall the previous example concerning two independent objects: a stack object s1 and a memory object m1. To express the
previous dependency as a link instance between s1 and m1, the user defines a
link, named *memorized-by*. This link is only expressed by referring to stack and
memory methods, so that all popped values of the stack are stored in the linked
memory, until the memory is full. After that, he/she instantiates this link with
s1 and m1 (line 6).

```
1 ( deflink  memorized-by (:stack :memory)
2    ((( pop :stack) →  ( store :memory :result))
                        ;; the popped value is stored in the memory
3    (( pop :stack) |  ( not-full? :memory))))
                        ;; stack can pop an element only if memory is not full
4 (define s1 (new stack))        ;; we create a stack and a memory
5 (define m1 (new memory))        ;; and an instance of link between these instances
6 (define s1-)m1 (new  memorized-by :stack s1   :memory m1))
```

Definition 1: the link *memorized-by*.

Line 2 of definition 1 shows that, when pop is called for the object denoted by
the *:stack* variable, store must be sent to the object designated by the *:memory*
variable[3], with the result (denoted by the predefined *:result* variable) of the pop
call as argument. The *implies* operator (→) associates a *compensating message*
to a method so that, after applying a specified method, the system automatically performs the associated *compensating message*. Likewise, in line 3, pop
will only be performed on *:stack*, if *:memory* is not full. Thus, the semantics
of the *permitted-if* operator (|) is such that the method can be applied only if
the expression following such a | operator is true. We call such an expression
a *guard*. The link *memorized-by* can be used for linking any instance of stack
with any instance of memory. The instances s1 and m1 become dependent when
an instance of the *memorized-by* link is created between them (see line 6). The
system associates them respectively with the two variables *:stack* and *:memory*
of this instance of *memorized-by* link. After that, FLO automatically ensures the

---

[3] These variables look like Lisp keywords because we want the user to keep in mind
that such variables refer to objects which are associated with such initarg keywords
at creation time.

consistency of this instance of *memorized-by* link, controlling the messages sent to those instances in accordance with the link definitions.

The link definitions are independent even if such links concern the same objects. Suppose that the user wants to have a graphic representation of a stack. On the one hand, he/she has defined the stack object s1, on the other hand, he/she has defined a possible graphic representation gr-s1 with appropriate methods. To link these objects s1 and gr-s1, he/she defines a new link, called *graphically-represented-by* (see definition 2), such that pop method calls imply the removal of the corresponding graphic value, push calls lead to the addition of a new graphic value, and empty calls reset the representation. This definition is independent of the *memorized-by* definition. Thus, the stack instance s1 can be linked at the same time to the memory instance m1 and to the graphic representation gr-s1.

```
( deflink   graphically-represented-by (:stack :graphic)
  ((( pop :stack) → ( remove-top :graphic))
  (( push :stack val) → ( add :graphic ( conv val))))
  (( empty :stack) → ( reset :graphic)))

(define gr-s1 (new single-descriptor))   ;; one graphic object is created
(define s1-graph1 (new  graphically-represented-by :stack s1 :graphic gr-s1))
```

Definition 2: the link *graphically-represented-by*.

An Example of Link Definition Inheritance. Another kind of reuse is necessary: the link reuse. Flo offers a special inheritance mechanism to specialize link definitions.

Let us suppose that we define a new link, called *reactive-gr*, subclass of the link *graphically-represented-by*, such that some messages on the representation now imply modifications of the stack object: if we click on the top value of the graphic object, the stack is popped (line 3). To increase the expressiveness, we have introduced the possibility of renaming the inherited link variables within the new link (line 2 of the definition of *reactive-gr*).

Moreover, new participant objects can be added to a link (see the link *complete-gr* line 4 in the definition 3). For example, the previous representation of the stack can be completed with a button *stop-bt*. When this button is selected, no value may now be pushed or popped in the stack, and the representation of the stack may no longer be selected (lines 6, 7, 8).

```
1 ( deflink  reactive-gr (:stack :react-grap)
2      :inherit (( graphically-represented-by (:graphic  rename-as :react-grap)))
3  ((( click-top :react-grap) → ( pop :stack))))

4 ( deflink  complete-gr (:stack :react-grap :stop-bt) :inherit ( reactive-gr)
6  ((( select :stop-bt x)  → (if (eq x t)
                                      ( inhibit :react-grap)
                                      ( reactive :react-grap)))
7    (( push :stack v) | ( if-not-selected :stop-bt))
8    (( pop :stack) | ( if-not-selected :stop-bt))))
```

Definition 3: an example of link inheritance.

4 Links for Knowledge Representation

In this section, we highlight the power of expressiveness of FLO for object-oriented knowledge representation.

4.1 Meta-Knowledge: Links between Links

Links are themselves objects. Thus as simply as other links, we can express links between links, called "Meta-links[4]". Meta-links are not specific to a particular application, and must be considered as powerfull FLO expressive tools. We first present a simple definition of the link *inverse*, and use it to define dependencies between dependencies as defined in Merise [NECH92].

The Inverse Link. If l^{-1} is the inverse of the link l, then x linked to y by l^{-1} implies that y is linked to x by l (see definition 4). In particular, we can specify the reflective aspect of the inverse link: the inverse of the inverse is the inverse (line 4 of the definition 4). Consequently, defining l^{-1} as the inverse of l is sufficient to define l as the inverse of l^{-1} (line 5).

```
1 ( deflink  inverse (:masterlink :slavelink)
2      :inherit ( binary-link)
3      ((( create :masterlink obj1 obj2) → ( create :slavelink obj2 obj1))
4      (( create :slavelink obj2 obj1) | ( if-not-exist :slavelink obj2 obj1))))

5 (create  inverse  inverse  inverse)
6 (create  inverse father-of son-of)
   ;; the link inverse between son-of and father-of is automatically created
7 (create  father-of Caesar  Brutus)
   ;; the link son-of between Brutus and Caesar is automatically created
8 (create  son-of Jesus God)
   ;; And the link father-of between God and Jesus is automatically created
```

Definition 4: the link *inverse*.

Other Meta-Links. OMT [BELR92] or Merise [NECH92] methodologies characterize different constraints on relationships. The following definitions present some meta-links as defined in Merise. The main idea of this kind of meta-links is to control the link instance creation. We can notice the use of the *inverse* link for the definition of the links *exclusion* and *simultaneity*, and the use of inheritance to define the *simultaneity* link as a specialization of the *inclusion* link, as shown in the definition 5. The sole difference between the *inclusion* and *simultaneity* links is that the last one is the inverse of itself.

---

[4] This possibility follows the same philosophy as the Meta-Constraints of [Ber93].

(deflink   *exclusion* (:masterlink :slavelink) :inherit (*binary-link*)
  (((create :masterlink obj1 obj2) | (if-not-exist :slavelink obj1))))

(create *inverse exclusion exclusion*)
(create *exclusion father-of son-of*)   *;; X can not be both the father-of and the son-of Y*

(deflink   *inclusion* (:masterlink :slavelink) :inherit (*binary-link*)
  (((create :masterlink obj1 obj2)→ (if (if-not-exist :slavelink obj1)
                                       (ask-for-creation :slavelink obj1)))))

(deflink   *simultaneity* (:masterlink :slavelink)   :inherit (*inclusion*))
(create   *inverse simultaneity simultaneity*)
(create   *simultaneity father-of husband-of*)

Definition 5: some Merise links.

Meta-links facilitate the definition of links, outline some properties of links and increase reuse of link definitions. For the sake of understanding, we have just presented binary meta-links, but other links such as the composition of links can be defined.

4.2   Language Extension and Use

In the previous sections, we have presented the standard aspects of FLO. However FLO has been designed to be an extensible language [DBFP95] and we present an additional interesting feature of FLO and its use for composing objects.

A New Operator in FLO for Propagating Messages. As shown in the above examples, the behavior of a linked object is guarded or modified by the links. However, according to some applications, we noticed that linked objects may also acquire new behaviors, which are due only to the link existence. Therefore, the idea is to allow an object to answer some new messages as soon as these messages are defined by links concerning this object. So we propose a new operator, *corresponds* (≫). This operator allows the declaration that a message received by one object of the link has to be re-sent to another object of this link. In this sense - (method1 :object1 arg1) ≫ (method2 :object2 (fct arg1)) - means that when a message corresponding to the method1 is not defined, another (or the same) message is sent, using (or not) calling arguments, to another object (or to itself).

The user of the first example wants to ask the stack *s1* which object is its representation. However, it is clear that only s1 is related to a graphic object, therefore this property is not a class property but a property of the s1 instance. Thus, the programmer defines the link *reactive-gr-new* as a specialization of the link *reactive-gr* and he/she indicates the message corresponding[5] to the representation-of call (line 2 of definition 6).

---

[5] Some FLO primitives allow one to find the same information, but in our sense, in a less natural way.

```
1 ( deflink reactive-gr-new (:stack :react-grap) :inherit-from ( reactive-gr)
2       ((( representation-of :stack) ≫ :react-grap)))
  ;; when linked, the stack knows its representation
3 (define s1 ( new stack))   ;; we create a stack and a graphic object
4 (define gr2 ( new graphical-object))
5 ( representation-of s1) — — — — — >    error no-applicable-method
6  (define s1−)gr2 (new reactive-gr-new :stack s1 :memory gr2))
  ;; Once an instance of link s1−)gr2 is created the stack. s1 knows its representation.
7  ( representation-of s1)    — — — — — >   gr2
```

Definition 6: an example of corresponding messages

Composition and Collection. *"Aggregation is ignored by the popular object-oriented programming" [LSR87].* Some research attempts to address this lack of object-oriented programming by introducing specific dependencies between a part and a whole object (*whole/part association* WPA [Civ93], *is-part-of dependency* [WBWW90], *part dependency* [LSR87], *aggregation* [BELR92]). We do not discuss these different approaches in this paper. However, in this section, we highlight the features of the links for composing objects. Through links, the user can specify the semantics of his/her WPA. In particular, the operator ≫ can be used to manage the composition problem between whole-part entities, exposed by Blake:*"The whole protocol which a part understands ... will have to be re-implemented as the protocol of the whole. The net result is that the part hierarchy is replaced by a single monolithic whole as far as the external world is concerned"* [BC87]. If we link a car (the whole) to the coachwork (a part), when we ask the car for its color, this message has to be re-sent to the part which is able to respond to this message. With the operator ≫, *"the whole protocol which a part understands"* must not be re-implemented, the *corresponding messages* are introduced in links. In our example, we also chose to destroy the coachwork if the car is destroyed.

```
( deflink car-composition (:car :coachwork :wheels)
   ((( color-of :car) ≫ ( color :coachwork))
   ( ....)
   (( destroy :car) → ( destroy :wheels) ( destroy:coachwork))))
(define carcmp ( new car-composition :car a-car  :coachwork  a-coachwork
                        :wheels '(a-wheel wheel a-wheel a-wheel)))
```

Definition 7: an example of composition.

The originality of our approach is that the classes of the part objects need not to be changed when they are involved in a whole-part association. Moreover, as classes are first class objects in FLO, we can also define links on classes. Thus, automatic creation of parts and of links can be declared as links between classes of the whole, of the parts, and of the links.

The concept of group or collection is integrated in the FLO language, by declaring the linked objects as a list. The language offers methods to add (resp.

retract) objects to (resp. from) a collection. In definition 8, a drawing is a collection of shapes. If a drawing is moved all the shapes are moved. A shape can be moved only within the limits of its drawing. To express this dependency, we define the link *together*, by using some built-in primitives of the language.

```
( deflink  together (:master :slaves)
 ((( move :master delta ) → (for-each (x) ( move x delta) :slaves)
  (( move (x in :slaves) delta)) | ( if-in-limits x delta :master)))))

(define adraw (new  drawing))
(define l (new together :master adraw :slaves '(s1 s2)))
( add l :slaves s3)          ;; add a shape to the drawing adraw.
( retract l :slaves s1)      ;; retract the shape s1 from the drawing adraw.
```

Definition 8: an example of group.

5 Conclusion

Current object-oriented languages are not expressive enough to represent the richness in semantic properties and roles of inter-object dependencies. In the traditional object-oriented languages, the implementation of these dependencies is buried into the object code. To respond to this problem, FLO is an object-oriented language integrating the concept of inter-object dependencies in a declarative way [DBFP95]. The user can define links and instantiate links between objects; the language automatically manages their consistency. Through links, the behavior of linked objects is changed (methods are controlled), and it is possible to associate new behaviors to linked objects. FLO allows one to clearly specify the changed object behaviors. This specification does not occur at the class level as in Smalltalk, nor in the object definition. Links are defined in an independent way from the linked objects, enforcing the principle of encapsulation. As links are expressed in terms of the object interfaces, and as they may be dynamically added or removed without interfering with the object implementation, modularity is strengthened. The code of linked objects is kept pure: no relational information is spread across the classes of the linked objects. The classes define the intrinsic knowledge of the objects and the links the relational knowledge. Moreover, knowledge about dependencies can be expressed in particular links between links. The use of these "meta-links" increases the robustness of the applications.

References

[BC87]   Edwin Blake and Steve Cook. On Including Part Hierarchies in Object-Oriented Languages. In *ECOOP'87*, LNCS 276, pages 41–50, 1987.

[BC89]   K. Beck and W. Cunningham. A laboratory for teaching object-oriented thinking. In *OOPSLA'89*, pages 1–6, 1989.

[BELR92]   M. Blaha, W. Permerlani F. Eddy, W. Lorensen, and J. Rumbaugh. *Object-Oriented Modeling and Design*. Prentice-Hall, 1992.

[Ber93]   Pierre Berlandier. The use and interpretation of meta level constraints. LNAI 727, pages 271–280, 1993.

[Civ93]   F. Civello. Roles for composite objects in object-oriented analysis and design. In *OOPSLA'93*, pages 376–393, 1993.

[DBFP95]   S. Ducasse, M. Blay-Fornarino, and A.M. Pinna. A Reflective Model for First Class Dependencies. In *OOPSLA'95*, pages 265–280, 1995.

[DFP91]   AM. Dubois, M. Fornarino, and AM. Pinna. A tool for modelling and reasoning. In *13th IMACS World Congress on Computation and Applied Mathematics*, 1991.

[DT88]   R. Dieng and B. Trousse. 3DKAT, a dependency Driven Dynamic Knowledge Acquisition Tool. In *3rd ISKE*, 1988.

[EWH85]   R. Elmasri, J. Weeldreyer, and A. Hevner. The category concept : An extension to the entity-relationship model. In *Data and Knowledge Engineering*, pages 75–116, 1985.

[FBB92]   B. Freeman-Benson and A. Borning. Integrating constraints with an object-oriented language. In *ECOOP'92*, LNCS 615, pages 268–286, 1992.

[HHG90]   R. Helm, I. Holland, and D. Gangopadhyay. Contracts: Specifying compositions in object-oriented systems. In *OOPSLA'90*, pages 169–180, 1990.

[Hil92]   Ralph D. Hill. The abstraction-link paradigm: Using contraints to connect user interfaces to applications. In *CHI'92*, pages 335–342, 1992.

[HK85]   P. Harmon and D. King. *Expert Systems. Artificial Intelligence in Business*. Judy V. Wilson, re-edited 1985. Re-edited by Wiley Press Book.

[KP88]   G.E. Krasner and S. T. Pope. A cookbook for using the Model-View-Controller user interface paradigm in Smalltalk-80. *JOOP*, August 1988.

[Kum92]   V. Kumar. Algorithms for constraint satisfaction problems: a survey. In *AI Magazine*, volume 13, pages 32–44, 1992.

[LSR87]   M. E. S. Loomis, A. V. Shah, and J. E. Rumbaugh. An Object Modelling Technique for Conceptual Design. In *ECOOP'87*, LNCS 276, pages 192–202, 1987.

[Mae87]   Pattie Maes. Concepts and experiments in computational reflection. In *OOPSLA'87*, pages 147–155, 1987.

[MGZ92]   B.A. Myers, D.A. Guise, and B. Vander Zanden. Declarative programming in a prototype-instance system: object-oriented programming without writing methods. In *OOPSLA'92*, pages 185–199, 1992.

[NECH92]   D. Nanci, B. Espinasse, B. Cohen, and H. Heckenroth. *Ingenierie des systemes d'information avec Merise*. Sybex, 1992.

[San93]   M. Sannella. The skyblue constraint solver. Technical report, Dept of Computer Science and Engineering, University of Washington, 1993.

[SBK86]   M. Stefik, D.G. Bobrow, and K. Kahn. Integrating Access-Oriented Programming into a Multiparadigm Environment. *IEEE Software (USA)*, 3(1):10–18, 1986.

[WBWW90]   R. Wirfs-Brock, B. Wilkerson, and L. Wiener. *Designing Object-Oriented Software*. Prentice Hall, 1990.

[Woo75]   W.A. Woods. What's in a link: Foundations for semantic networks. In Academic Press, editor, *Representation and Understanding: Studies in Cognitive Science*. 1975.

Knowledge Simplification

John Debenham
Key Centre for Advanced Computing Sciences, University of Technology, Sydney,
PO Box 123, NSW 2007, Australia
debenham@socs.uts.edu.au

Abstract

Knowledge simplification is a process which removes unnecessary duplication from raw knowledge. The presence of unnecessary duplication can make knowledge hard to understand and hard to maintain. If two items of raw knowledge share an unstated sub-rule then any changes to that sub-rule will require that those two knowledge items should both be modified; knowledge simplification prevents this duplicate representation of sub-rules. Knowledge simplification is based on an integrated approach to knowledge representation which represents all things in an application using a single schema. A single rule for knowledge simplification is expressed in terms of this representation schema. The conventional normal forms for database are a special case of this single simplification rule.

1. Introduction

Knowledge simplification is a process which is applied during part of a complete design methodology for knowledge-based systems. If a representation of a knowledge-based system contains duplicate representations of things then it will be unnecessarily hard to understand and to maintain. Knowledge simplification is a process which removes such duplications; this is achieved by the application of a single rule. This single rule applies equally to the knowledge (ie "rules") and to the information (ie "relations") in a knowledge-based system. In particular, all of the 'classical' normal forms for relational database may be derived from this single rule as well as some non-classical normal forms. The *classical normal forms* for the relational data model are those normal forms referred to as first, second, third, fourth, fifth and Boyce-Codd normal forms [1]. This single simplification rule is expressed in terms of 'items'; items are a formalism which can represent the traditional database construct the 'relation' (or 'information') as well as the essential knowledge-based construct the 'rule' (or 'knowledge'). Thus the single simplification rule applies equally to information and to knowledge. Knowledge constraints [2] may also be used to protect a knowledge base against the introduction of update anomalies. We will not discuss maintenance here [3], [4], [5]. Our approach promotes the "engineering" of knowledge as a process for making systems easier to maintain [6], [7].

The majority of systems design methodologies treat the "rule base" component separately from the "database" component [9]; this enables well established design methodologies to be employed, but the use of two separate methodologies means that the interrelationship between the things in these two components cannot be represented, integrated and manipulated naturally in the resulting models. Our approach treats the knowledge and the information in a uniform way [10].

[part/sale-price, part/cost-price, mark-up]					
part/sale-price		part/cost-price		mark-up	
part-number	dollar-amount	part-number	dollar-amount	factor	
1234	1.48	1234	1.23	1.2	
2468	2.81	2468	2.34	1.2	
3579	4.14	3579	3.45	1.2	
8642	5.47	8642	4.56	1.2	
7531	6.80	7531	5.67	1.2	
1470	8.14	1470	6.78	1.2	

Figure 1 Value set of the item *[part/sale-price, part/cost-price, mark-up]*

In §2 we describe "items" as a knowledge representation formalism. In §3 a 'join operator' for items is presented. A taxonomy of simplification forms, expressed in terms of the join operator, is given in §4. Examples to illustrate the simplification forms are presented in §5.

2. Items

Items are a formalism for describing the things in an application. They have two important properties: items have a uniform format no matter whether they represent data, information or knowledge things; items incorporate two powerful classes of constraints. The key to this unified representation is the way in which the "meaning" of an item, called its *semantics*, is specified. Items may be viewed either formally as λ-calculus expressions or informally as schema. The λ-calculus view provides a sound theoretical basis for the work; it is *not* intended for practical use. The schema view enables the approach to be employed as a practical modelling tool. Thus the work has both theoretical and practical significance.

Items have a *name* which by convention is written in italics. The semantics of an item is a function which *recognises* the members of the "value set" of that item. The value set of an item will change in time τ, but the item's semantics should remain constant. The value set of a data item at a certain time τ is the set of labels which are associated with a population that implements that item at that time. The value set of an information item at a certain time τ is the set of tuples which are associated with a relational implementation of that item at that time. Knowledge items have value sets too. Consider the rule "the sale price of parts is the cost price marked up by a universal mark-up factor"; suppose that this rule is represented by the item named *[part/sale-price, part/cost-price, mark-up]*, then this item could have the value set as shown in Figure 1. This idea of defining the semantics of items as recognising functions for the members of their value set extends to complex, recursive knowledge items too.

Informally, items are named triples; they consist of the item's semantics, value constraints and set constraints. A value constraint is an expression which must be satisfied by any member of the item's value set. Set constraints are structural constraints on the item's value set; for example, a constraint on the size of the value set. Some items have "components". Items which do not have components are called "basis items"; basis items represent simple data things. Formally, given a value set D_A, a *basis item A* will have the form:

$$A[\ \lambda x \bullet [J_A(x)] \bullet,\ \lambda x \bullet [K_A(x)] \bullet,\ (L)_A\ ]$$

where $J_A(x) = \text{is-a}[x:D_A]$, K_A is an expression which is satisfied by the members of the value set and L is a set constraint on the value set such as the cardinality constraint "< 100" meaning that the value set has less than 100 members. A non-basis item A is defined as follows. Given a set of n items $\{A_1,..., A_n\}$ the *components* of A, given an n-tuple $(m_1, m_2,..., m_n)$, $M = \sum_{i=1}^{n} m_i$, if:

- S_A is an M-argument expression of the form:

$$\lambda y_1^1...y_{m_1}^1...y_{m_n}^n \bullet [S_{A_1}(y_1^1,...,y_{m_1}^1) \wedge\ ......\ \wedge\ S_{A_n}(y_1^n,...,y_{m_n}^n) \wedge J_A(y_1^1,...,y_{m_1}^1,...,y_{m_n}^n)] \bullet$$

- V_A is an M-argument expression of the form:

$$\lambda y_1^1...y_{m_1}^1...y_{m_n}^n \bullet [V_{A_1}(y_1^1,...,y_{m_1}^1) \wedge\ ......\ \wedge\ V_{A_n}(y_1^n,...,y_{m_n}^n) \wedge K_A(y_1^1,...,y_{m_1}^1,...,y_{m_n}^n)] \bullet$$

- C_A is an expression of the form:

$$C_{A_1} \wedge C_{A_2} \wedge...\wedge C_{A_n} \wedge (L)_A$$

where L is a logical combination of:
- a *cardinality constraint*;
- "$\forall_A$" for some i, $1 \le i \le n$, a *universal constraint* which means that "all members of the value set of item A_i must be in this association", and
- "$A_i \Leftarrow X$" for some i, $1 \le i \le n$, where X is a non-empty subset of $\{A_1,..., A_n\} - \{A_i\}$, a *candidate constraint* which means that "the value set of the set of items X functionally determines the value set of item A_i,"

then the named triple $A[\ S_A,\ V_A,\ C_A]$ is an n-adic *item* with *item name* A, S_A is called the *semantics* of A, V_A is called the *value constraints* of A and C_A is called the *set constraints* of A. In practice we represent items in the i-schema notation shown in Figure 2. In the i-schema notation the candidate constraint $A_i \Leftarrow X$ is shown by a line beneath each component in the set X and a 'o' beneath the component A_i.

For example, an application may contain the data item part whose value set is 'part-number'. Suppose that part numbers lie in the interval (1000, 3000) and that there are more that 500 part numbers. The i-schema for the *part* item is shown in Figure 2. Further suppose that there is an association whereby each *part* is associated with a *cost-price*. This association could be subject to the "value constraint" that parts whose part-number is less that 1,999 will be associated with a cost price of no more than $300. This association could also be subject to the "set constraints" that every part must be in this association, and that each part is associated with a unique cost-price. This association could be represented by the information item named *part/cost-price*; the i-schema for this item is shown in Figure 2. Rules, or knowledge, can also be defined as items. Suppose that 'tax' is 5% of 'cost-price'; the item *[cost-price, tax]* is shown in Figure 3. The i-schema for the knowledge item *[part/sale-price, part/cost-price, mark-up]* is shown in Figure 3; this i-schema has four set constraints.

3. Simplification of Items

We now define an operation called "item join" for items. This operation provides the basis of our approach to knowledge simplification. The formal definition of item join is fairly elaborate and may be expressed in terms of λ-calculus expressions. Here we give an informal description of item join which is sufficiently precise to demonstrate the relationship between the knowledge simplification forms.

Given two items $A[\,S_A,\,V_A,\,C_A\,]$ and $B[\,S_B,\,V_B,\,C_B\,]$. Some of the components of A and B may be identical. Let E be the set of identical components of A and B; note that E may be empty. Without loss of generality we assume that E is the 'right hand' components in A and is the 'left hand' components in B. Then the item with name $A \otimes_E B$ is called the *join* of A and B on E and is defined to be the item:

$$(A \otimes_E B)[\lambda xyz \cdot [S_A(x,y) \wedge S_B(y,z)] \cdot,$$

$$\lambda xyz \cdot [V_A(x,y) \wedge V_B(y,z)] \cdot,\ C_{A \otimes_E B}]$$

where $C_{A \otimes_E B}$ is defined as follows. Suppose that C_A is an expression of the form $c_A \wedge G$ where c is that part of C_A which carries the subscript 'A' and G is that part of C_A which carries subscripts other than 'A'. Likewise suppose that C_B is an

A	
A_1	A_2
x	y
J_A	
K_A	
L_A	

part
$\emptyset$
x
is-a[x:part-no.]
1000<x<3000
> 500

part/cost-price	
part	cost-price
x	y
costs(x,y)	
x<1999 → y≤300	
$\forall$	
--------	o

Figure 2 i-schema format, the items *'part'* and *'part/cost-price'*

[cost-price, tax]			[part/sale-price, part/cost-price, mark-up]		
cost-price	tax		part/sale-price	part/cost-price	mark-up
x	y		(x, w)	(x, y)	z
y = 0.05 × x			→ (w = z × y)		
x > y			→ w > y		
$\forall$			$\forall$	$\forall$	
--------	o		--------		o
				o	
			--------		
				o	

Figure 3 i-schema for *[cost-price, tax]* and *[part/sale-price, part/cost-price, mark-up]*

expression of the form $d_B \wedge H$. Then:

$$C_{A \otimes_E B} = (c \wedge d)_{A \otimes_E B} \wedge (G \wedge H)$$

Note that the set E is *a* set of identical pairs of components of A and B. In practice E is frequently the set of *all* identical pairs of components of A and B in which case $A \otimes_E B$ is simply written as $A \otimes B$.

Using the rule of composition $\otimes$, knowledge items, information items and data items may be joined with one another regardless of type. For example, the knowledge item *[cost-price, tax]* can be joined with the information item *part/cost-price* on the set {*cost-price*} to give the information item *part/cost-price/tax*.

$$[cost\text{-}price, tax] \otimes_{\{cost\text{-}price\}} part/cost\text{-}price = part/cost\text{-}price/tax$$

In this way items may be joined together to form more complex items. Alternatively, the $\otimes$ operator may form the basis of a theory of decomposition in which each item may be replaced by a set of simpler items. An item I is *decomposable* into the set of items $D = \{I_1, I_2,..., I_n\}$ if:

- I_i has non-trivial semantics for all i,
- $I = I_1 \otimes I_2 \otimes ... \otimes I_n$, where
- each join is *monotonic*; that is, each term in this composition contributes at least one component to I.

If item I is decomposable then it will not necessarily have a unique decomposition. Our single rule of simplification is to discard decomposable items. Using the above notation, our rule requires that we should discard:

$$(A \otimes_E B)[\lambda xyz \cdot [S_A(x,y) \wedge S_B(y,z)] \cdot,$$
$$\lambda xyz \cdot [V_A(x,y) \wedge V_B(y,z)] \cdot, \ C_{A \otimes_E B}]$$

in favour of both:

$$A[S_A, V_A, C_A] \text{ and } B[S_B, V_B, C_B]$$

provided that the composition is monotonic and that items A and B have non-trivial semantics. For example, our rule requires that we discard the item *part/cost-price/tax* in favour of the items *[cost-price, tax]* and *part/cost-price*.

4. Simplification Forms

In this section we analyse the single rule for knowledge simplification. First we explore the application of the rule to items containing three components and second we consider items containing four components.

4.1 Three Component Items

In this section we explore the application of the single rule for knowledge simplification to items of three components. We use the notation $C_I[H_1, H_2,..., H_k]$ where each H_i is a term of the form $Y \Leftarrow X$ to mean that the set $\{H_1, H_2,..., H_k\}$ contains *all* of the valid candidate constraints on item A.

Given an item if it has two component sets such that one of these component sets is in a candidate constraint for the other component set then we say that that item contains a *functional dependency*. For example in item I if the component sets D and E are candidates for component F, ie if the set constraints of I contains the expression

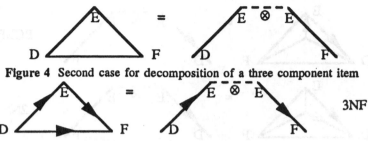

Figure 4 Second case for decomposition of a three component item

3NF

Figure 5 Classical third normal form

Can$(F, D \cup E)$ then item I contains a functional dependency between its components; this is denoted by $C_I[F \Leftarrow (D, E)]$.

Suppose that item I has the three component sets D, E and F; we denote this by $I(D, E, F)$. Consider the different ways in which the item $I = I(D, E, F)$ can be decomposed into two sub-items I_1 and I_2 by:

$$I(D, E, F) = I_2(D, E) \otimes_E I_1(E, F).$$

When two items are joined on the component set which consists of *all* of their identical components we omit the subscript of the join operator. The different ways in which item I can be decomposed are categorised by the different ways in which candidate constraints are present in the set constraints of I; we identify three different cases:

- there are no functional dependencies in I;
- the functional dependencies in I are only between pairs of D, E and F, and
- there is at least one functional dependency in I of the form $Z \Leftarrow (X, Y)$.

Consider the first case, if there are no functional dependencies in I at all then:

$$C_I[\,\varnothing\,], \quad C_{I_1}[\,\varnothing\,], \quad C_{I_2}[\,\varnothing\,]$$

and the decomposition:

$$I(D, E, F) = I_2(D, E) \otimes I_1(E, F) \tag{3.4}$$

is a generalisation of classical fourth normal form.

Now consider the second case when the functional dependencies in I are only between pairs of D, E and F. The specification of functional dependencies between pairs of D, E and F may be represented by entering arrows on the arcs shown in Figure 4. Removing unnecessary duplications, this may occur in five different ways:

$$C_I[\,E \Leftarrow D\,], \quad C_{I_1}[\,E \Leftarrow D\,], \quad C_{I_2}[\,\varnothing\,]$$

$$C_I[\,D \Leftarrow E\,], \quad C_{I_1}[\,D \Leftarrow E\,], \quad C_{I_2}[\,\varnothing\,]$$

$$C_I[\,E \Leftarrow F, E \Leftarrow D\,], \quad C_{I_1}[\,E \Leftarrow D\,], \quad C_{I_2}[\,E \Leftarrow F\,]$$

$$C_I[\,F \Leftarrow D, F \Leftarrow E, E \Leftarrow D\,], \quad C_{I_1}[\,E \Leftarrow D\,], \quad C_{I_2}[\,F \Leftarrow E\,] \tag{3.3}$$

$$C_I[\,F \Leftarrow E, D \Leftarrow E\,], \quad C_{I_1}[\,D \Leftarrow E\,], \quad C_{I_2}[\,F \Leftarrow E\,]$$

These five different ways each represents a valid decomposition but only the fourth is non-trivial; it is a generalisation of classical third normal form and is illustrated in Figure 5.

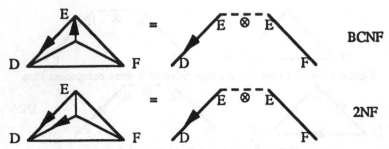

Figure 6 Classical Boyce-Codd and second normal forms

Now consider the third case in which there is at least one functional dependency in I of the form $Z \Leftarrow (X, Y)$. Removing unnecessary duplications, this may occur in three different ways:

$$C_I[\, E \Leftarrow (F, D), \quad D \Leftarrow E \,], \quad C_{I_1}[\, D \Leftarrow E \,], \quad C_{I_2}[\, \emptyset \,] \qquad [3.1]$$

$$C_I[\, F \Leftarrow (D, E), \quad D \Leftarrow E \,], \quad C_{I_1}[\, D \Leftarrow E \,], \quad C_{I_2}[\, \emptyset \,]$$

$$C_I[\, D \Leftarrow (E, F), \quad D \Leftarrow E \,], \quad C_{I_1}[\, D \Leftarrow E \,], \quad C_{I_2}[\, \emptyset \,] \qquad [3.2]$$

These three different ways each represents a valid decomposition but only the first and the third are non-trivial. [3.1] is a generalisation of classical *Boyce-Codd normal form*. [3.2] is a generalisation of the classical *second normal form*. [3.1] and [3.2] are illustrated in Figure 6.

The only other way in which an item of three component sets can be decomposed is by:

$$I(D, E, F) = I_3(F, D) \otimes I_2(D, E) \otimes I_1(E, F).$$

If there are no functional dependencies present in I then this decomposition becomes:

$$C_I[\, \emptyset \,], \quad C_{I_1}[\, \emptyset \,], \quad C_{I_2}[\, \emptyset \,], \quad C_{I_3}[\, \emptyset \,] \qquad [3.5]$$

which is a generalisation of the classical *fifth normal form*. Further if there are functional dependencies present in I then it may be shown that this decomposition reduces to one of the above. Thus we see that the classical normal forms provide a complete characterisation of the ways in which an item of three component sets may be decomposed.

4.2 Four Component Items

In the previous section we analysed the decomposition of items with three component sets. In this section we apply the single rule for knowledge simplification to items of four components. In this way we can derive new, "non-classical" normal forms for items [11].

Suppose that item I has the four component sets A, B, C and D. We now consider the different ways in which this item $I(A, B, C, D)$ can be decomposed which do not reduce to the classical normal forms. The decomposition of I into two sub-items may be achieved in a number of ways; in particular it may be achieved by:

$$I(A, B, C, D) = I_1(A, B, C) \otimes I_2(B, C, D).$$

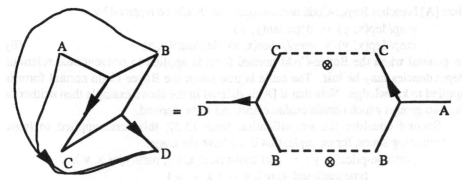

Figure 7 Decomposition of a four component set item

The different ways in which this rule of decomposition can be employed may be categorised by the different ways in which functional dependencies are present in I. We identify three different cases:

- there are no functional dependencies in I;
- the functional dependencies in I are only between pairs of A, B, C and D, and
- there is at least one functional dependency in I of the form $Z \Leftarrow (X, Y)$.

The first and second of these cases reduce to classical normal forms. However in the third case when the functional dependency $D \Leftarrow (C, A)$ is present in I. One way in which functional dependencies may be present in I_1 and I_2 is:

$$C_I[D \Leftarrow (B, A), \ D \Leftarrow (C, B), \ C \Leftarrow (B, A)]$$
$$C_{I_1}[C \Leftarrow (B, A)]$$
$$C_{I_2}[D \Leftarrow (C, B)] \tag{4.1}$$

This rule of decomposition is not equivalent to any of the classical forms introduced above; it is illustrated in Figure 7.

5. Applications

We now apply the simplification forms derived in the previous section to some examples. Our general rule of simplification may be applied to any item. Thus it may be applied to the normalisation of knowledge. We now illustrate the application of simplification forms [3.1], [3.3], [3.4] and [4.1] using logic programming. The use of logic programming has the advantage of being concise, but has the disadvantage of oversimplifying the significance of the forms for three reasons. First, it does not show how the forms apply to whole items including constraints. Second, it does not show how the forms apply to mixed type items. Third, items are capable of representing associations of greater generality than can be represented by a single logic program.

First consider the simplification form [3.1]. In terms of a logic program, if:

    emp/super(x, y) ← pers/job(x, 'W'), emp/dep(x, z), dep/man(z, y)
    emp/super(x, y) ← pers/job(x, 'DM'), pers/job(y, 'GM')   [A]

and:

    pers/job(x, 'GM') ← emp/super(y, x), emp/super(z, y)
    pers/job(x, 'DM') ← emp/super(y, x), emp/super(y, z)
    pers/job(x, 'W') ← emp/super(x, y), emp/super(y, z)

then [A] breaches Boyce-Codd normal form and should be replaced by:

$$emp/dep(x, y) \leftarrow dep/man(y, x)$$
$$emp/dep(x, y) \leftarrow emp/super(x, z), dep/man(y, z) \qquad [B]$$

In general when the Boyce-Codd normal form is applied to conventional relations dependencies may be lost. The same is true when the Boyce-Codd normal form is applied to knowledge. Note that if [A] is deleted in the above example then neither of the two groups which remain enable emp/super to be derived.

Second consider the simplification form [3.3]; this form applied to logic programming states, for example, that if we have the clause:

$$part/sale\text{-}price(\ x, y\ ) \leftarrow part/cost\text{-}price(\ x, z\ ), part/type(\ x, v\ ),$$
$$type/mark\text{-}up(\ v, w\ ), y = (\ z \times w\ )$$

Suppose that buried within this clause is the sub-rule that "the mark-up factor for a spare part is the mark-up factor associated with that spare part's type". This sub-rule could be represented as:

$$part/mark\text{-}up(\ x, y\ ) \leftarrow part/type(\ x, z\ ), type/mark\text{-}up(\ z, y\ )$$

which reveals that the first clause breaches the [3.3] form and should be replaced by the second clause and the following third clause:

$$part/sale\text{-}price(\ x, y\ ) \leftarrow part/cost\text{-}price(\ x, z\ ), part/mark\text{-}up(\ x, w\ ),$$
$$y = (\ z \times w\ )$$

Note that the first of these three clauses can be re-generated from the second and the third by resolution.

Third consider the simplification form [3.4]; this form is applied to logic programming. Suppose that:

$P(x,y,z)$ means "$2^x = y = z + 10$"

$Q(x,y)$ means "$y = 2^x$"

$R(y,z)$ means "$y = z + 10$"

then the logical equivalence:

$$P(\ x, y, z\ ) \leftrightarrow Q(\ x, y\ ), R(\ y, z\ )$$

holds and to comply with [3.4] the predicate P should be discarded in favour of the predicates Q and R.

Fourth consider the simplification form [4.1]. Applied to logic programming form [4.1], illustrated in Figure 7, advises us that the clause:

$$part/profit(\ x, y\ ) \leftarrow part/cost\text{-}price(\ x, w\ ),$$
$$part/mark\text{-}up\text{-}factor(\ x, u\ ), y = w \times (u - 1) \qquad [C]$$

has buried within it the sub-rule that "the sale price of a part is the cost price of that part multiplied by the mark-up-factor associated with that part". This sub-rule could be represented as the clause:

$$part/sale\text{-}price(\ x, y\ ) \leftarrow part/cost\text{-}price(\ x, z\ ),$$
$$part/mark\text{-}up\text{-}factor(\ x, w\ ), y = (\ z \times w\ ) \qquad [D]$$

Further clause [C] also has buried within it the sub-rule that "the profit of a part is the difference of the sale price of that part and the cost price of that part". This sub-rule could be represented as the clause:

$$part/profit(\ x, y\ ) \leftarrow part/sale\text{-}price(\ x, z\ ),$$
$$part/cost\text{-}price(\ x, w\ ), y = z - w \qquad [E]$$

In other words, simplification form [4.1] requires that clause [C] should be replaced by clauses [D] and [E].

6. Conclusion

The goal of knowledge simplification is to transform raw knowledge into a form in which it is easier to understand and easier to maintain. Knowledge simplification is based on an integrated approach to knowledge representation which represents all things in an application using a single schema. A single rule for knowledge simplification has been expressed in terms of this single representation schema. It has been shown that the conventional normal forms for database are a special case of this single rule.

References

1. C.J. Date, *"An Introduction to Database Systems"* (4th edition) Addison-Wesley, 1986.
2. J.K. Debenham, "Knowledge Constraints", in proceedings Eighth International Conference on Industrial and Engineering Applications of Artificial Intelligence and Expert Systems IEA/AIE'95, Melbourne, June 1995, pp553-562.
3. P. Compton, A. Srinivasan, G. Edwards, R. Malor & L. Lazarus, "Knowledge Base Maintenance without a Knowledge Engineer", in proceedings Expert Systems World Congress, J. Liebowitz (Ed), Pergamon Press 1991.
4. F. Coenen and T. Bench-Capon, "Building Knowledge Based Systems for Maintainability", in proceedings Third International Conference on Database and Expert Systems Applications DEXA'92, Valencia, Spain, September, 1992, pp415-420.
5. F. Lehner, H.F. Hofman, R. Setzer, and R. Maier, "Maintenance of Knowledge Bases", in proceedings Fourth International Conference DEXA93, Prague, September 1993, pp436-447.
6. J.K. Debenham, "Managing Knowledge Base Integrity", in proceedings ES'94, Cambridge UK, Cambridge University Press.
7. J.K. Debenham, "Understanding Expert Systems Maintenance", in proceedings Sixth International Conference on Database and Expert Systems Applications DEXA'95, London, September 1995.
8. J.K. Debenham, "Knowledge Systems Design", Prentice Hall, 1989.
9. H. Katsuno and A.O. Mendelzon, "On the Difference between Updating a Knowledge Base and Revising It", in proceedings Second International Conference on Principles of Knowledge Representation and Reasoning, KR'91, Morgan Kaufmann, 1991.
10. J.K. Debenham, "A Unified Approach to Requirements Specification and System Analysis in the Design of Knowledge-Based Systems", in proceedings Seventh International Conference on Software Engineering and Knowledge Engineering SEKE'95, Washington DC, June 1995, pp144-146.
11. J.K. Debenham, "Decomposition of Four Component Items", in proceedings Fourth International Conference DEXA93, Prague, September 1993, pp457-460.

A Model-Based Approach to Consistency-Checking

Stefan Brüning[1] and Torsten Schaub[2]

[1] ZB Informationssysteme, Deutsche Bahn AG, Kölner Straße 26, D-60327 Frankfurt
[2] UFR Sciences, Université d'Angers, 2 Boulevard Lavoisier, F-49045 Angers 01

Abstract: We propose a model-based approach to incremental consistency checking in default theorem proving. We show that the crucial task of consistency checking can benefit from keeping models in order to restrict the attention to ultimately necessary consistency checks. This is supported by the concept of default lemmata that allow for an additional avoidance of redundancy.

1 Introduction

Default reasoning aims at formalizing reasoning from incomplete information. A wide variety of approaches addresses this by appeal to the notion of *consistency*. In most formalisms, a logical formalization of a consistency-driven procedure is then added to a standard logic. In this way, default reasoning is mapped onto *deduction* and *consistency checking*. A prime representative of these approaches is *default logic* [8]; it augments classical logic by *default rules* that differ from standard inference rules in sanctioning inferences that rely upon given as well as absent information. Knowledge is represented in default logics by *default theories* (D, W) consisting of a consistent[3] set of formulas W and a set of default rules D. A default rule $\frac{\alpha : \beta}{\gamma}$ has two types of antecedents: A *prerequisite* α which is established if α is derivable and a *justification* β which is established if β is consistent in a certain way. If both conditions hold, the *consequent* γ is concluded by default. A set of such conclusions (sanctioned by a given set of default rules and by classical logic) is called an *extension* of an initial set of facts: Given a set of facts W and a set of default rules D, any such extension E is a deductively closed set of formulas containing W such that, for any $\frac{\alpha : \beta}{\gamma} \in D$, if $\alpha \in E$ and $\neg\beta \notin E$ then $\gamma \in E$.

We are interested in query-answering in default logics and hence we elaborate on proof procedures that allow for determining whether a formula is in some extension of a given default theory. This question was first addressed in [8]. A common difficulty encountered in this context is the integration of deduction and consistency checking. For instance, [8] puts forward a generate and test approach via a belated consistency check, while [12] computes entire sets of "consistent default rules". Clearly, the former may lead to the generation of numerous proofs before consistency is confirmed or even denied. The latter approach has the advantage that consistency conflicts are eliminated in a preprocessing step, while it risks facing an exponential number of such "consistent default theories". A third alternative is investigated in [11], where a consistency check is envisaged each time a default rule is taken into account. Such a consistency-driven search for a default proof has the advantage that "inconsistent" applications of default rules are pruned right away. On the other hand, such successive checks can be very expensive. Experiments showed however that the search for default proofs primarily guided by the automated theorem prover is not that frequently corrected by consistency checks.

The interesting question is then whether we can find a way to full-fledged pruning of "inconsistent subproofs" while restricting our attention to ultimately necessary consistency checks. For this, we observe that a formula is consistent (or satisfiable) iff it has a

---

[3] The restriction to consistent set of facts is not really necessary, but it simplifies matters.

model. In fact, checking whether a model satisfies a formula can be done in linear time in propositional logic. This leads us to the following approach to incremental consistency checking: We start with a model of the initial set of facts. Each time, we apply a default rule, we check whether the actual model satisfies the underlying default assumptions. If this is the case, we continue proving. If not, we try to generate a new model of the initial set of facts satisfying the current as well as all default assumptions underlying the partial default proof at hand. If we succeed, we simply continue proving under the new model. Otherwise, we know that the considered default assumption cannot be assumed in a consistent way. The second interesting question is then whether a simultaneous treatment of theorem proving and satisfiability checking allows for synergistic procedures by means of structure and information sharing. The idea is to communicate information from the theorem prover to a model generator. This communication is accomplished by lemma handling. We will see that this allows for a drastic reduction of the search space in case a new model has to be generated.

The overall approach is developed by extending an existing approach to query-answering [11] based on the connection method [1]. The choice of the connection method is motivated by its structure-sensitive nature that allows for an elegant characterization of proofs in default logic.

2 Query-answering in default logics

As advocated in [8], query-answering in default logics is only feasible in the presence of *semi-monotonicity*: If $D' \subseteq D$ for two sets of default rules, then if E' is an extension of (D', W), there is an extension E of (D, W) such that $E' \subseteq E$. Given this property, it is sufficient to consider a relevant subset of default rules while answering a query, since applying other default rules would only enlarge or preserve the partial extension at hand. In Reiter's default logic, semi-monotonicity is enjoyed by so-called *normal* default theories. Such theories only contain so-called *normal default rules* whose justification is equivalent to the consequent. Moreover, almost all variants of default logic (cf. [5, 2, 3]) coincide on this fragment. This is why we have chosen normal default theories as an exemplar for our approach. In fact, semi-monotonicity implies that extensions are constructible in a truly iterative way by applying one applicable default rule after another. This results in an incremental and so rather local notion of consistency:[4,5]

Definition 2.1 *Let* (D, W) *be a normal default theory and let* E *be a set of formulas. Then,* E *is an extension of* (D, W) *iff there is some maximal* $D' \subseteq D$ *that has an enumeration* $\langle \delta_i \rangle_{i \in I}$ *such that for* $i \in I$ *the following conditions hold.*

$$E = Th(W \cup Conseq(D')) \tag{1}$$

$$W \cup Conseq(\{\delta_0, \ldots, \delta_{i-1}\}) \vdash Prereq(\delta_i) \tag{2}$$

$$W \cup Conseq(\{\delta_0, \ldots, \delta_{i-1}\}) \not\vdash \neg Conseq(\delta_i) \tag{3}$$

Condition (2) spells out that D' is grounded in W: A set of default rules D is *grounded* in a set of facts W iff there exists an enumeration $\langle \delta_i \rangle_{i \in I}$ of D satisfying (2). Condition (3) expresses an incremental notion of *consistency*. The "consistent" application of a default

---

[4] This type of characterization was first given in [12].
[5] In what follows we denote the prerequisite of a default rule δ by $Prereq(\delta)$ and its consequent by $Conseq(\delta)$. These projections extend to sets of default rules in the obvious way.

rule is checked at each step, whereas this must by done wrt to the *final* extension in any default logic lacking semi-monotonicity.

A *default proof* D_φ for a formula φ from a default theory (D, W) is a finite sequence of default rules $\langle \delta_i \rangle_{i \in I}$ such that $W \cup \{Conseq(\delta_i) \mid i \in I\} \vdash \varphi$ and Condition (2) and (3) are satisfied for all $i \in I$. One can show that $\varphi \in E$ for some extension E of (D, W) iff φ has a default proof D_φ from (D, W). For illustration, consider the statements dealing with Tim and his allergy: "Usually, Tim is lively", "Normally, Tim is stressed if he is lively and must stay at home", and "Normally, Tim is unhappy if he is stressed and scratches". Also, we know that Tim is at home and that he had sugar or milk. Milk causes an allergic reaction, as does sugar under stress. His allergy makes him scratch. This can be represented via the following default theory:

$$D = \left\{ \frac{:lively}{lively}, \frac{lively \wedge home : stress}{stress}, \frac{stress \wedge scratch : unhappy}{unhappy} \right\}$$

$$W = \{home, sugar \vee milk, milk \rightarrow allergy, stress \wedge sugar \rightarrow allergy, allergy \rightarrow scratch\}$$

For instance, we can show that Tim is stressed by means of default proof

$$\left\langle \frac{:lively}{lively}, \frac{lively \wedge home : stress}{stress} \right\rangle. \tag{4}$$

Similarly, we can show that he is unhappy via

$$\left\langle \frac{:lively}{lively}, \frac{lively \wedge home : stress}{stress}, \frac{stress \wedge scratch : unhappy}{unhappy} \right\rangle. \tag{5}$$

We consider for simplicity only propositional normal default theories in atomic format: A default theory (D, W) is in *atomic format* if all formulas occuring in the defaults in D are atomic. A general way for transforming default theories into their atomic format can be found in [11]. For example, the atomic format of the example default theory (D, W) used above is (D', W'), where

$$D' = \left\{ \frac{:lively}{lively}, \frac{R : stress}{stress}, \frac{Q : unhappy}{unhappy} \right\}, \text{ and} \tag{6}$$

$$W' = W \cup \{lively \wedge home \rightarrow R, stress \wedge scratch \rightarrow Q\}. \tag{7}$$

3 A calculus for query-answering

The approach for query-answering in (semi-monotonic) default logics proposed in [11] is based on the connection method [1], which allows for testing the unsatisfiability of formulas in conjunctive normal form (CNF): Formulas in CNF are displayed two-dimensionally in the form of *matrices*, as in (8). A matrix is a set of sets of literals (literal occurrences, to be precise).[6] Each column of a matrix represents a *clause* of the CNF of a formula. For showing that a sentence φ is entailed by a sentence W, we prove that $W \wedge \neg \varphi$ is unsatisfiable. In the connection method this is accomplished by path checking: A *path* through a matrix is a set of literals, one from each clause. A *connection* is a binary set of literals identical except for the negation sign (and possible indices). A *mating* is a set of connections. A mating *spans* a matrix if each path through the matrix contains a connection from the mating. Finally, a formula, like $W \wedge \neg \varphi$, is unsatisfiable iff there is a spanning mating for its matrix.

The approach of [11] relies on the idea that a default rule $\frac{\alpha : \beta}{\gamma}$ can be decomposed into a *classical implication* $\alpha \rightarrow \gamma$ along with two proof-theoretic conditions on the usage of the resulting clauses: *admissibility* (accounting for groundedness) and *compatibility* (enforcing consistency). In order to find out whether a formula φ is in some extension

---

[6] We simply say literal instead of literal occurrences; the latter allow for distinguishing between identical literals in different clauses.

of a default theory (D, W), we proceed as follows: First, we transform all defaults in D into a set of indexed implications: $W_D = \{\alpha_\delta \to \gamma_\delta \mid \delta = \frac{\alpha:\beta}{\gamma} \in D\}$. Second, we transform W and W_D into their clausal forms, C_W and C_D. The clauses in C_D, like $\{\neg\alpha_\delta, \gamma_\delta\}$, are called δ-clauses; all others are called as ω-clauses. Finally, a query φ is derivable from (D, W) iff there is a spanning mating for the matrix $C_W \cup C_D \cup \{\neg\varphi\}$ agreeing with the concepts of admissibility and compatibility.[7]

Let us verify that Tim has stress according to the recipe given above. By abbreviating literals by their first two letters, the defaults in (6) yield: $W_{D'} = \{LI_{\delta_1}, R_{\delta_2} \to ST_{\delta_2}, Q_{\delta_3} \to UN_{\delta_3}\}$. The indexes denote the defaults in (6) from left to right. Next, we transform the facts W' in (7) and $W_{D'}$ into CNF. The resulting clauses are the first ten columns of matrix (8). The full matrix, obtained by adding the clause containing the negated query $\neg ST$, has spanning mating $\{\{HO, \neg HO\}, \{\neg LI, LI_{\delta_1}\}, \{R, \neg R_{\delta_2}\}, \{ST_{\delta_2}, \neg ST\}\}$, whose connections are indicated as arcs linking the respective literals:

$$
\begin{bmatrix}
HO & MI & \neg MI & \neg ST & \neg AL & \neg LI & \neg ST & LI_{\delta_1} & \neg R_{\delta_2} & \neg Q_{\delta_3} & \neg ST \\
 & SU & AL & \neg SU & SC & \neg HO & \neg SC & & ST_{\delta_2} & UN_{\delta_3} & \\
 & & AL & & & R & Q & & & &
\end{bmatrix} \quad (8)
$$

As it stands, this is a classical proof of ST from $W' \cup W_{D'}$. In fact, we will see next that this proof constitutes a default proof (namely the one in (4)) since it is admissible and compatible. For showing this, we use the concept of the *core* of a matrix M wrt a mating Π, $\kappa(M, \Pi)$, which allows for isolating the clauses relevant to the underlying proof:[8] $\kappa(M, \Pi) = \{c \in M \mid \exists \pi \in \Pi \,.\, c \cap \pi \neq \emptyset\}$. The core of (8) wrt the drawn mating is given by all clauses connected by arcs. Then, the proof-theoretic counterpart of groundedness as expressed in Condition (2) can be captured as follows [11]:

Definition 3.1 *Let C_W be a set of ω-clauses and C_D be a set of δ-clauses and let Π be a mating for $C_W \cup C_D$. Then, $(C_W \cup C_D, \Pi)$ is admissible iff there is an enumeration $\langle\{\neg\alpha_{\delta_i}, \gamma_{\delta_i}\}\rangle_{i \in I}$ of $\kappa(C_D, \Pi)$ such that for $i \in I$, Π is a spanning mating for $C_W \cup (\bigcup_{j=0}^{i-1}\{\{\neg\alpha_{\delta_j}, \gamma_{\delta_j}\}\}) \cup \{\{\neg\alpha_{\delta_i}\}\}$.*

Our proof in (8) yields the enumeration: $\langle\{LI_{\delta_1}\}, \{\neg R_{\delta_2}, ST_{\delta_2}\}\rangle$. For admissibility, we must then consider submatrices[9] $C_{W'} \cup \{\emptyset\}$ and $C_{W'} \cup \{LI_{\delta_1}\} \cup \{\neg R_{\delta_2}\}$ of (8). The first (sub)matrix is trivially complementary[10] while the second is complementary due to the complementarity of the following submatrix of (8):

$$
\begin{bmatrix}
HO & MI & \neg MI & \neg ST & \neg AL & \neg LI & \neg ST & LI_{\delta_1} & \neg R_{\delta_2} \\
 & SU & AL & \neg SU & SC & \neg HO & \neg SC & & \\
 & & AL & & & R & Q & &
\end{bmatrix} \quad (9)
$$

So, the original matrix and its mating given in (8) constitute an admissible proof.

Condition (3) motivates the following definition of compatibility verifying consistency of each δ-clause in turn [11]:

---

[7] We consider atomic queries only, since any query can be transformed into atomic format.

[8] Recall that we deal with literal occurrences.

[9] A matrix M is a *submatrix* of another matrix M' if M emerges from M' by removing literals and/or entire clauses.

[10] Because there is no path through an empty clause, each path through the entire matrix is complementary.

Definition 3.2 *Let C_W be a set of ω-clauses and C_D be a set of δ-clauses and let Π be a mating for $C_W \cup C_D$. Let $\langle\{\neg\alpha_{\delta_i}, \gamma_{\delta_i}\}\rangle_{i \in I}$ be an enumeration of $\kappa(C_D, \Pi)$. Then, $(C_W \cup C_D, \Pi)$ is incrementally compatible wrt I iff for all $i \in I$, there is no spanning mating for*

$$C_W \cup (\bigcup_{j=0}^{i-1}\{\{\gamma_{\delta_j}\}\}) \cup \{\{\gamma_{\delta_i}\}\}. \tag{10}$$

For compatibility, we must show that submatrices $C_{W'} \cup \{LI_{\delta_1}\}$ and $C_{W'} \cup \{LI_{\delta_1}\} \cup \{ST_{\delta_2}\}$ of (8) have no spanning mating. That is, we have to show that both contain a non-complementary path. Clearly, the existence of such a path for the latter matrix implies the same for the former matrix, so that we can focus on the latter one: [11]

$$\begin{bmatrix} HO & MI & \neg MI & \neg ST & \neg AL & \neg LI & \neg ST & LI_{\delta_1} & ST_{\delta_2} \\ SU & AL & \neg SU & SC & \neg HO & \neg SC \\ & AL & & R & Q \end{bmatrix} \tag{11}$$

This matrix contains non-complementary path $\{HO, MI, AL, SC, R, Q, LI_{\delta_1}, ST_{\delta_2}\}$ establishing compatibility for the proof in (8). Notably any such path represents a (partial) model of the considered formula. In this way, the actual task can be mapped onto the generation of propositional models. We elaborate on this in Section 4.

The overall method is shown to be sound and complete in [11]. Moreover, [11] develops a corresponding proof procedure: It is carried out by means of inference operations known from the connection method [1] and model elimination [4], called *extension* and *reduction* step. An extension step amounts to Prolog's use of input resolution: A subgoal is resolved with an input clause if the subgoal is complementary to one of the literals in the input clause. Consider matrix (9): We can resolve goal $\neg R_{\delta_2}$ with clause $\{\neg LI, \neg HO, R\}$ (indicated by the respective connection). This results in two new subgoals, $\neg LI$ and $\neg HO$, both of which can be resolved by two further extension steps with unit-clauses yielding no further subgoals. The reduction step renders the inference system complete for (full) propositional clause logic: If a subgoal is complementary to one of its ancestor subgoals, then it is solved. In the connection method the ancestor goals are accumulated in a path corresponding intuitively to a path through a CNF. In (9), the path after the first extension step equals thus $\{\neg R_{\delta_2}\}$. For incorporating default reasoning into this calculus, the extension step has to be adapted: Whenever a δ-clause $\{\neg\alpha_\delta, \gamma_\delta\}$ is used as input clause, one has to guarantee (i) that only γ_δ is resolved upon, and (ii) that after such an "extension step" the ancestor goals of the resulting subgoal $\neg\alpha_\delta$ must not be used for later reduction steps. In [11] it was shown that this simple adaption is sufficient for generating admissible matings. The more crucial task is the verification of compatibility, which the next section deals with.

4 An integrated approach to query-answering

This section is devoted to the implementation of incremental consistency checking.[12] We presuppose an inference procedure for verifying complementarity and admissibility along with a mechanism for finding models of formulas in CNF.

For reducing computational efforts one clearly should avoid exhaustive general purpose mechanisms for consistency checking. Our goal is rather to furnish an approach that

---

[11] This makes sense due to our current purely declarative point of view.

[12] In what follows, we use the terms compatibility and consistency interchangeably.

allows for full-fledged pruning of "inconsistent subproofs" while restricting our attention to ultimately necessary consistency checks. We address this problem by means of a *model-based approach*: We use a model as a compact representation of the compatibility of a default proof at hand. The aim is then to reuse such a model for as many subsequent compatibility checks as possible. Of course, this reusability depends strongly on the chosen model. Hence, we sometimes encounter situations in which we have to look for a "better" model. We support this search by a synergistic treatment of theorem proving and model handling: This treatment is based on so-called *model matrices* which represent in a compact way all models of the initial set of facts that satisfy the justifications of the applied default rules.

First of all, let us make precise how we treat consistency checks via model handling: For a set of formulas W and a sequence of default rules $\langle \delta_j \rangle_{j < i}$ let m be a model for $W \cup Conseq(\{\delta_0, \ldots, \delta_{i-1}\})$. Function ∇ checks whether $W \cup Conseq(\{\delta_0, \ldots, \delta_{i-1}\}) \not\vdash \neg Conseq(\delta_i)$, as stipulated in Condition (3):

$$
\nabla(\delta_i, \langle m, W, \langle \delta_j \rangle_{j<i} \rangle) = \begin{cases} \langle m, W, \langle \delta_j \rangle_{j \leq i} \rangle & \text{if } m \models Conseq(\delta_i) \\ \langle m', W, \langle \delta_j \rangle_{j \leq i} \rangle & \text{if } m \not\models Conseq(\delta_i) \text{ and for some } m' \neq m \\ & \qquad m' \models W \cup \{Conseq(\delta_j) \mid j \leq i\} \\ \bot & \text{if there is no } m'' \text{ such that} \\ & \qquad m'' \models W \cup \{Conseq(\delta_j) \mid j \leq i\} \end{cases}
$$

Function ∇ gives a general description of our approach while making precise the intuition given in Section 1. We refine this specification in the sequel.

At the start of a derivation, m is set to an arbitrary model of C_W[13], as provided by an open path through the matrix of C_W. Note that such models are actually partial models that only fix the truth-values of certain literals; hence, they are refineable along their degrees of freedom. In fact, whenever a δ-clause $\{\neg \alpha_\delta, \gamma_\delta\}$ is selected as input clause, we check whether γ_δ is satisfied by m; that is, due to the nature of m, we check whether $\neg \gamma_\delta \notin m$. If this is the case, γ_δ is added to the partial model m. In this way, we enforce that $m \cup \{\gamma_\delta\}$ is a model for

$$
C_W \cup \{\{\gamma_{\delta_1}\}, \ldots, \{\gamma_{\delta_i}\}\} \cup \{\{\gamma_\delta\}\}, \tag{12}
$$

where $\gamma_{\delta_1}, \ldots, \gamma_{\delta_i}$ stand for the consequents of the previously used defaults. This amounts to the criterion given in Definition 3.2, since matrix (12) equals the one in (10). Otherwise, a new model for (12) has to be generated for carrying on with the current derivation (by searching another open path through matrix (12)). If no such model can be found, δ-clause $\{\neg \alpha_\delta, \gamma_\delta\}$ cannot be used in the current situation.

For reducing computational efforts of searching new models, we consider so-called *model matrices* $M^\star$ that are simplified yet equivalent variants of (12). At the start of a derivation this model matrix equals C_W; during a proof it is extended by the justifications of the used defaults and by certain lemmata provided by the theorem prover. The key idea is then to *simplify* $M^\star$ after each such addition; hence, in case a new model has to be generated, one does not have to start with the full matrix in (10) but rather a matrix which is already simplified as much as possible.[14,15] Each such simplification, has to be

---

[13] Such a model exists since we assume W to be consistent.

[14] In fact, such simplification are doable in an anytime manner.

[15] Note, however, that in case derivation steps have to be withdrawn, the corresponding modifications of the respective model matrices have to be withdrawn, too.

model-preserving, ie. a simplified matrix has to have the same *open paths* as the original one. To this end, simplifications reduce the search space by eliminating closed paths. In this paper, we restrict ourselves to UNIT-reductions and subsumptions. In the former case, we replace a clause $\{L\} \cup c$ by c in the presence of the unit-clause $\{\neg L\}$, while in the latter, we delete a clause c in the presence of one of its proper subsets (cf. [1]).

Let us illustrate our approach by proving that Tim is unhappy, UN, from theory (D', W') in (6/7). For this, we check whether there is a spanning mating Π for

$$M = C_{W'} \cup C_{D'} \cup \{\{\neg UN\}\} \tag{13}$$

such that (M, Π) is admissible and compatible. As initial model of $C_{W'}$, we take $m_0 = \{HO, SU, AL, SC, \neg LI, Q\}$. This is given by the first matrix on the right in Figure 1. Now, we apply the proof procedure described in Section 3. We start the derivation with the query clause $\{\neg UN\}$. Correspondingly, we get one initial goal $\neg UN$, as shown in the first matrix on the left hand side (LHS) of Figure 1. There and in all following matrices, yet unaddressed (sub)goals are marked by dashed boxes.

The second matrix on the LHS shows the first four extension steps, indicated by the depicted connections. Since the first extension step uses δ-clause $\{\neg Q_{\delta_3}, UN_{\delta_3}\}$ (δ-clauses are marked by oval boxes), model matrix $M_1^\star$ (the second matrix on the right hand side (RHS)) contains clause $\{UN_{\delta_3}\}$.[16] Since m_0 satisfies UN_{δ_3}, or in other terms, $\nabla(\delta_3, \langle m_0, W, \langle \rangle \rangle)$ equals $\langle m_0, W, \langle \delta_3 \rangle \rangle$, we extend m_0 to $m_0' = m_0 \cup \{UN_{\delta_3}\}$ and continue with m_0'.

The next extension step, which is applied to subgoal $\neg ST$ (see the third matrix on the LHS), uses δ-clause $\{ST_{\delta_2}, \neg R_{\delta_2}\}$. Since m_0' satisfies ST_{δ_2}, we extend m_0' to $m_0'' = m_0' \cup \{ST_{\delta_2}\}$. Furthermore, we add clause $\{ST_{\delta_2}\}$ to $M_1^\star$ and apply UNIT which gives us model matrix $M_2^\star$, the third matrix on the RHS.

The following three extension steps are applied to subgoals $\neg R_{\delta_2}$, $\neg LI$, and $\neg HO$ (see the fourth matrix on the left). The second one is resolved with δ-clause $\{LI_{\delta_1}\}$. Notably, m_0'' does not satisfy LI_{δ_1}. Therefore, we have to search for a new model m_1 of model matrix $M_3^\star$, which emerges from $M_2^\star \cup \{\{LI_{\delta_1}\}\}$ after the application of UNIT. Note that due to the rigorous application of UNIT-reductions, $M_3^\star$ comprises merely $2^5 = 32$ potential models, as opposed to $2^3 \times 3^3 = 216$ in the case of $C_{W'}$. Formally, we get

$$\nabla(\delta_1, \langle m_0'', W, \langle \delta_3, \delta_2 \rangle \rangle) = \langle m_1, W, \langle \delta_3, \delta_2, \delta_1 \rangle \rangle,$$

with $m_1 = \{HO, SU, AL, SC, R, Q, UN_{\delta_3}, ST_{\delta_2}, LI_{\delta_1}\}$.

Now, the derivation has reached a point where three subgoals, namely $\neg LI$, $\neg HO$, and $\neg R_{\delta_2}$, are proven. This is indicated within matrices by solid boxes. In other words, we have shown that each path through

$$C_{W'} \cup \{\{LI_{\delta_1}\}, \{\neg R_{\delta_2}, ST_{\delta_2}\}, \{\neg Q_{\delta_3}, UN_{\delta_3}\}\} \tag{14}$$

containing one of the proven subgoals is complementary. It is important to realize that this information can be exploited for reducing even more the number of potential models in a model matrix. For instance, each path through $M_3^\star$ is a path through (14).[17] Therefore, if we know that a path through (14) is complementary, this path cannot be a model satisfying the model matrix $M_3^\star$.

---

[16] Note, that clause $\{\neg HO, \neg LI, R\}$ was reduced to $\{\neg LI, R\}$ by UNIT.

[17] This is because (i) each model matrix contains $C_{W'}$ (in a simplified form), and (ii) whenever a δ-clause is used in a derivation, a subset of it is added to the respective model matrix.

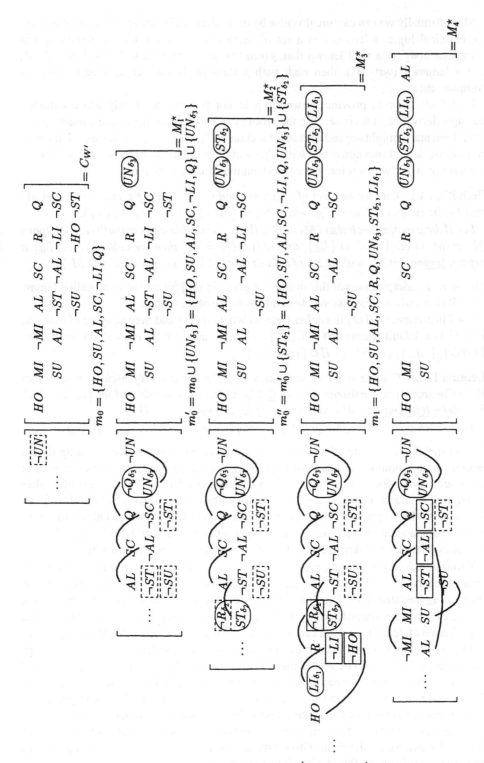

Fig. 1. The derivation of *UN*.

More formally we can capture this idea by the concept of lemmata. In theorem provers for classical logic, a lemma l is a set of literals such that each path containing l is complementary. It is well known that, given two matrices M and M' with $M' \subseteq M$, and a lemma l (wrt M'), then each path p through M containing l as a subset is complementary.

In default theorem proving, however, it is not possible to simply use a lemma l during a derivation. This is because the proof of l (ie. the proof that a path containing l is complementary) might depend on a set of δ-clauses C_{DS}. The use of l during a derivation employing defaults not consistent with C_{DS} would be incorrect. In the context of default theorem proving, we therefore have to extend the concept of lemmata:

Definition 4.1 *Let C_W be a set of ω-clauses and C_D be a set of δ-clauses and let M_1 and M_2 be subsets of $C_W \cup C_D$, where $M_2 = \{c_1 \cup \{L_1\}, \ldots, c_n \cup \{L_n\}\}$.*

Let Π be a mating such that $(M_1 \cup M_2, \Pi)$ is admissible and compatible. If Π spans $M' = M_1 \cup \{L_1\} \cup \ldots \cup \{L_n\}$, and $\kappa(\Pi, M') = M'$ then we call $\{L_1, \ldots, L_n\}$ a <u>default lemma</u> *wrt M_1 and the set of default rules $\{\delta \mid \{\neg\alpha_\delta, \gamma_\delta\} \in (C_D \cap M_1)\}$.*

The formal underpinnings of this notion are given in [10] by means of so-called lemma default rules, whose discussion is beyond the scope of this paper.

For illustration, $\{\neg HO\}$ is a default lemma wrt $\{\{HO\}\}$ and the empty set of defaults, $\{\neg LI\}$ is a default lemma wrt $\{\{LI_{\delta_1}\}\}$ and $\{\delta_1\}$, and $\{\neg R_{\delta_2}\}$ is a default lemma wrt $\{\{HO\}, \{LI_{\delta_1}\}, \{R, \neg LI, \neg HO\}\}$ and $\{\delta_1\}$.

Lemma 1. *Let C_W be a set of ω-clauses and C_D be a set of δ-clauses such that $W \cup Conseq(D)$ is consistent. Let $M' \subseteq C_W \cup C_D$ be a matrix and let $\{L_1, \ldots, L_n\}$ be a* <u>default lemma</u> *wrt M' and some set of default rules $D' \subseteq D$.*

Then, each path p through $C_W \cup C_D$ is complementary if $\{L_1, \ldots, L_n\} \subseteq p$.

Due to the above considerations, a default lemma cannot only be used to simplify the search for an spanning (and admissible) mating but can furthermore be used to restrict the search space for new models in the respective model matrix. In particular, after generating a default lemma of the form $\{L\}$ (a so-called *unit-lemma*), clause $\{\neg L\}$ can be added to the respective model matrix and used for simplification. Other (non-unit) default lemmata can be used as a kind of constraints: While searching for a model in a model matrix, one can skip every path containing a default lemma as a subset.

Turning back to our running example, we could now take advantage of the generated default lemmata $\{\neg LI\}$, $\{\neg HO\}$, and $\{\neg R\}$. However, $M_3^\star$ already contains the corresponding (negated) unit-clauses and therefore these particular default lemmata cannot be used for further simplifcations of $M_3^\star$. Nevertheless, there are situations where the exploitation of default lemmata can be useful. Such a situation is given after the following three inference steps illustrated in the fifth matrix on the left (note that these steps do not use a δ-clause). The reader may verify that now the subgoals $\neg ST$, $\neg AL$, and $\neg SC$ are proven; hence we can add the corresponding negated unit-clauses to $M_3^\star$ (note that we do not have to extend m_1 since m_1 satisfies ST, AL, and SC). In particular, $\neg AL$ turns out to be a useful default lemma since the added unit-clause AL allows for two subsequent UNIT- and two subsumption reductions. The resulting model matrix $M_4^\star$ is the fifth matrix on the right. Obviously, a new model (which is not needed in our example) could now be found with almost no efforts.

Finally, the sole remaining subgoal which has not been treated so far, viz $\neg ST$ in clause $\{Q, \neg SC, \neg ST\}$, can be proven via the previously generated default lemma $\neg ST$. Hence, we have shown on the one hand that (13) has a spanning (and admissible) mating Π. On the other hand, we generated a model, namely m_1, satisfying $C_{W'}$ and the justifications of all applied defaults. Following [11] we therefore can conclude that UN holds in some extension of (D', W').

5 Conclusion

We proposed a promising avenue for replacing incremental consistency checking by model checking. We have demonstrated, on the one hand, that the crucial task of consistency checking can benefit from keeping models to restrict the attention to ultimately necessary consistency checks. In our running example, we have seen that even though three different defaults were used, a new model had to be generated only once. On the other hand, we have shown that the use of model matrices together with a rigorous application of reductions, results in a significant reduction of the underlying search space. Moreover, we have shown that the concept of default lemmata allows for additional avoidance of redundancy in model matrices. In this way, we achieved a synergistic and potentially parallel treatment of theorem proving and satisfiability checking.

Our current experiments on "meaningful" and artificial examples show that a model has to be changed quite rarely in the course of the proof search. That is, on many examples, we observed that the resulting default proofs contained only few occasions for distracting the theorem prover by choosing incompatible δ-clauses. This is an argument in favor of integrating a compatibility check that allows for using information gathered on compatibility checks in the subproofs. As it stands, the approach applies also to Theorist [7] and it is straightforwardly applicable to all default logics employing a so-called joint-consistency check, such as [2, 3]. For other semi-monotonic default logics, like that of [5], employing a separated consistency check for each justification, the model matrix is almost the same, however, one has to keep multiple models.

References

1. W. Bibel. *Automated Theorem Proving*. Vieweg Verlag, Braunschweig, 1987.
2. G. Brewka. Cumulative default logic: In defense of nonmonotonic inference rules. *Artificial Intelligence*, 50(2):183–205, 1991.
3. J. Delgrande, T. Schaub, and W. Jackson. Alternative approaches to default logic. *Artificial Intelligence*, 70(1–2):167–237, 1994.
4. D. Loveland. *Automated Theorem Proving: A Logical Basis*. North-Holland, 1978.
5. W. Łukaszewicz. Considerations on default logic — an alternative approach. *Computational Intelligence*, 4:1–16, 1988.
6. A. Mikitiuk and M. Truszczyński. Rational default logic and disjunctive logic programming. In A. Nerode and L. Pereira, eds, *Second Workshop on Logic Programming and Non-monotonic Reasoning.*, pages 283–299. MIT Press, 1993.
7. D. Poole. A logical framework for default reasoning. *Artificial Intelligence*, 36:27–47, 1988.
8. R. Reiter. A logic for default reasoning. *Artificial Intelligence*, 13(1–2):81–132, 1980.
9. A. Rothschild. Algorithmische Untersuchungen zu Defaultlogiken. Diplomarbeit, FB Informatik, TH Darmstadt, Germany, 1993.
10. T. Schaub. On constrained default theories. In B. Neumann, editor, *Proceedings of the European Conference on Artificial Intelligence*, pages 304–308. John Wiley & sons, 1992.
11. T. Schaub. A new methodology for query-answering in default logics via structure-oriented theorem proving. *Journal of Automated Reasoning*, 15(1):95–165, 1995.
12. C. Schwind. A tableaux–based theorem prover for a decidable subset of default logic. In M. Stickel, editor, *Proceedings of the Conference on Automated Deduction*. Springer, 1990.

Resource-Based vs. Task-Based Approaches for Scheduling Problems

V. Brusoni[1], L. Console[1], E. Lamma[2], P. Mello[3], M. Milano[2], P. Terenziani[1]

[1] Dip. Informatica, Univ. Torino, Corso Svizzera 185, 10149 Torino, Italy
email: {brusoni,lconsole,terenz}@di.unito.it
[2] DEIS, Univ. Bologna, Viale Risorgimento 2, 40136 Bologna, Italy
email: {mmilano, elamma}@deis.unibo.it
[3] Dip. Ingegneria, Univ. Ferrara, Via Saragat, 41100 Ferrara, Italy
email pmello@deis.unibo.it

Abstract. Scheduling deals with the allocation of resources to activities over time, and can be interpreted as a Constraint Satisfaction Problem. Two main types of approaches, both based on constraint satisfaction, can be adopted to formulate a scheduling problem. The first type is resource-based: resources are associated with temporal domains of feasibility which describe and maintain the evolution of their state; the second type is task-based: the assignments of resources to activities are considered as temporally constrained events. This paper shows the use of the two approaches to a case study, the "Train Scheduling Problem". The two approaches are then compared.

1 Introduction

Scheduling can be characterized as the problem of assigning resources to a given set of tasks in such a way that some constraints are satisfied and some goals are achieved. The constraints may regard both the tasks and the resources; the goals may concern the optimal use of the resources or the optimal accomplishment of the tasks.

Scheduling is important in several applications like manufacturing, transportation, computer processing, production planning and so on. In the field of Artificial Intelligence different approaches to scheduling have been investigated [13, 24]. In most of them, constraint processing [14, 17] plays a central role. In fact, a convenient formulation of scheduling problems is that based on Constraint Satisfaction Problems (CSPs) or Constraint Optimization Problems (COPs).

The goal of this paper is to discuss and compare two different approaches by using a case study: the "Train Scheduling Problem", whose precise definition is given in Sect. 3. Both solutions are based on constraint satisfaction, but one is centered on *resources* while the other is centered on *tasks*. In the *resource-based* approach variables represent resources each one associated with a temporal domain representing the intervals in which the resource is available, while in the *task-based* approach, variables represent events like the starting and ending point of an activity.

The two solutions are based on a two-module architecture consisting of: (i) *a planner*, whose goal is that of assigning resources to tasks and (ii) a *constraint manager* for dealing with the temporal constraints involved in the problem. The two modules operate in an interleaved way: not only does the planner ask the constraint manager about the consistency of the proposed (partial or complete) solution, but it can also query the constraint manager to get pieces of information useful for making a decision. The two solutions share the same planner (Sect. 4) but adopt different approaches to constraint solving.

Our resource-based approach (Sect. 5) makes use of a temporal constraint manager tailored to the specific goal, and developed on top of Constraint Logic Programming [25]. Our task-based approach (Sect. 6) makes use of LaTeR [6], a general purpose temporal reasoner. Sect. 7 compares the two approaches, generalizing from the application.

2 Constraint-Based Approaches

A variety of constraint-based approaches have been defined in AI (see [5, 20, 21, 23]) and a common organization has emerged. This is based on two components: a decision-making component (the planner) and a constraint manager. The decision maker is responsible for proposing candidate solutions, i.e., assignments of resources to tasks and is usually based on domain and problem specific knowledge and on heuristics. The role of the constraint manager is to check that the assignments proposed by the planner are consistent. If inconsistencies are detected, the decision-maker backtracks over one or more previous decisions or relaxes one or more problem constraints.

The interaction between the decision maker and the constraint solver can be a simple *generate and test*. A more efficient approach, based on the use of constraints *a-priori* is the *constraint and generate* approach. The planner queries the constraint manager by asking questions on the choices that it is going to make. For example, it asks whether a partial assignment is consistent or which are the intervals of time during which a given resources is available. The constraint manager answers by propagating constraints (*constraint* step), and the planner makes its decisions accordingly (*generate* step). In such a way, a solution is built through a series of interactions between the two modules.

In Sect. 3 we present our case study. We then analyze two possible solutions: a *resource-based* approach (Sect. 5) where variables represent resources and an *event-based* approach (Sect. 6) where variables represent tasks. Both the solutions share the same planner (Sect. 4) and the interaction follows the *constraint and generate* approach.

3 The Case Study

The problem concerns the allocations of resources to trains over time, respecting temporal relations between activities and the capacity limitations of a set of shared resources[4]. According to the classification in [13], the problem is characterized by multiple alternative resources, interfering activities linked by precedence relations and non-uniform duration of activities.

In a station, the resources involved are entrance and departure points, tracks and routes. A route connects a point and a track. There are incompatible resources that cannot be assigned to different trains in overlapping time intervals. Incompatibilities arise because of a common initial point, a common track-segment, or a crossing point along the routes.

For each train we identify the following activities (tasks): occupation of an entrance point; covering of an entrance route; stopping on a track; covering of a departure route. While the entrance and the departure routes are covered in a fixed time, the duration of the stopping on the entrance point and on the track may vary but has a minimal duration which has to be respected.

Resources (i.e., entrance points and routes, tracks, departure routes) have to be assigned to trains according to some principles:

- Safety of service: this principle concerns the incompatibility constraints on the use of resources.

- Minimization of train delays: a train can be delayed on an entrance point or on a track. One of the goals is to minimize, for each train, the total delay.

- Respect of the timetable information (such as arrival and departure times, connections, train priorities, the optimal track on which each train should stop). However, there may be unexpected situations to be managed and which may lead to some changes. In these cases, a cost is assigned to each alternative solution, so that the goal of the scheduler is to minimize these costs.

  - Track: A train can stop on alternative tracks; such tracks can be ordered, for each train, by the increasing degree of inconvenience for travellers.

  - Precedence: Precedence constraints impose that two trains travelling on the same railway branch must enter the station in the order they arrive. Moreover, the timetable may contain precedence relations between pairs of trains (e.g., a slower train should wait for a faster one and give it precedence for the next branch). Such precedence may be ignored if the faster train is late. More generally, respecting or ignoring a precedence has a cost, which is part of the overall cost to be minimized.

  - Waiting for a Connection: the timetable also contains connections between pairs of trains. Also in this case, one is not forced to respect the connection if the delay of the train to be waited for is greater than a given threshold. Thus also this choice contribute to the cost to be minimized.

- Respecting priorities among trains: trains can be characterized by the different priorities (e.g., passenger trains have priority over goods ones, EuroCity express trains have priority over regional trains).

Some of such constraints must be enforced necessarily (e.g., those on incompatibilities), others (e.g., involving precedence) can be relaxed if there is no solution

---

[4] See [10] for a more detailed description of this problem

that satisfies them all. Indeed, partial orders between the constraints can be specified in the domain and this provide heuristics on the order in which constraints can be relaxed. However, when relaxation of some constraints is performed, the "goodness" of the solution decreases, and instead of aiming at reaching an optimal schedule, one has to balance objectives and preferences.

4 The Planner

The planner we designed operates as a heuristic decision maker. It has to assign resources of the station to a next incoming train on the basis of the time-table and of some heuristic knowledge on the problem. The planner performs the following tasks.

When a train Tr is going to enter the station, the planner computes its arrival time At_{real}. It then creates a temporal window starting from At_{real}. and it collects all the trains whose expected arrival time is within the temporal window, in order to avoid interferences.

Such trains are sorted by using an accurate heuristic function, which takes care of the dynamic priority (the priority is dynamic since it may change according to the delay of the train), their distance from the station and their entrance point.

Then the planner assigns an arrival point and route, a track and a departure route to each train, analyzing the trains in the order provided by the above-mentioned sort function. During this step, the planner uses heuristics and interacts with the constraint solver in order to acquire some information about the status of the resources or about when a task could possibly start (end), consistently with the other tasks. In case of inconsistencies, some of the constraints considered by the planner may be relaxed or some assignments retracted.

To perform these steps, several trade-offs have to be evaluated by the planner, in co-operation with the constraint manager. For example, when two trains in a given temporal window are involved in a precedence, the planner must decide either to maintain it or not to respect it, if the delay imposed by the precedence on the waiting train is not convenient. Railway traffic rules impose a delay threshold after which the precedence can be ignored. Therefore, the planner must compute the cost associated with the respect of the precedence (by querying the constraint solver) and the cost associated with the lack of the precedence, and then choose the best solution.

When the system reaches an assignment for every train, no interference among trains occurs. Finally, the planner performs an assignment of resources to the first incoming train as a result of the whole analysis. No commitment is made for the other trains considered in the analysis because the situation may change before the other trains will actually reach the station.

5 A Solution Based on CLP

Constraint Logic Programming (CLP) [15, 16] is a class of programming languages combining the advantages of Logic Programming (LP) and the efficiency of constraint solving. CLP exploits intelligent search techniques (see [25]) which are based on the *a-priori pruning* of the search space by propagating constraints.

The resource-based approach to the train scheduling problem uses a CLP solver on finite domains, since, in this approach, we assume a discrete structure for time. Every resource R_i of the station is associated with a variable whose domain DT_i represents the set of time intervals during which R_i is available. The propagation of temporal and incompatibility constraints on these variables allows the exploitation of efficient searching techniques.

At start-up, every resource is supposed to be always available and has an associated "infinite length" time interval $DT_i = \{[0, +\infty]\}$ – where 0 represents midnight of the current day (we are working on finite domains, so $+\infty$ is represented by a large number).

The assignment of the resource R_i to a train Tr during the time interval $[t_1, t_2] \in DT_i$ causes the deletion of the interval itself from DT_i, so that $[t_1, t_2] \in \overline{DT_i}$ (the complement of DT_i, i.e., the set of intervals in which a resource is not available).

In addition, incompatibility constraints impose that two incompatible resources R_1 and R_2 cannot be assigned to different trains in overlapping time intervals. Thus, if DT_1 and DT_2 are the domains of R_1 and R_2, then $[t_1, t_2]$ is removed from both DT_1 and DT_2, when R_1 (R_2) is assigned to a train: $[t_1, t_2] \in \overline{DT_1} \wedge [t_1, t_2] \in \overline{DT_2}$. In general, when a resource is assigned to a train, the temporal reasoner also deletes the interval from the domains of all the incompatible resources. Thus, the temporal knowledge about the availability of the resources is always up to date and consistent during the computation.

When trying to assign a resource R_i to a train Tr, it may happen that R_i is not available during the entire interval $[t_1, t_2]$ for which it is required. In such a case, the planner queries the temporal reasoner about an interval $[t_3, t_4]$ after $[t_1, t_2]$ and whose length is greater than (or equal to) the length of $[t_1, t_2]$. If the assignment of R_i to Tr during $[t_3, t_4]$ causes a delay $t_3 - t_1$ greater than a given threshold, the planner rejects the solution.

By using CLP with finite domains we obtain a direct implementation of the mechanisms described above. The forward propagation of constraints reduces a priori the temporal domain of incompatible resources according to an assignment of a resource to a train in a particular time interval and this allows us maintain an up to date state for all the resources. We implemented this temporal manager on top of the finite domain library of ECL^{i}PS^e [12].

Some experimental results can be found in [10]. We can summarize them in the following: the computational time ranges from 0.13 sec. in order to analyse one train to 5-6 seconds for considering interferences with 31 following trains. Our system greatly increases the average performances of a human expert involved in this task. An interesting result concerns the fact that the failure/call ratio of logic predicates is always very low (under 20%). These results have been achieved thanks to the very efficient CLP search techniques based on the propagation of constraints.

6 A Solution Based on LATER

LATER is a domain independent manager of temporal information that can be loosely coupled with different applications (see [6]). In LATER, a temporal knowledge base can be described using a high-level language and it is formed by a set of assertions, each one concerning either a piece of quantitative information (e.g., the precise or imprecise location or duration of an event) or a piece of qualitative information (the relative ordering between two events such as in Allen's interval algebra [1]).

We imposed some restrictions on the expressive power of the high-level language in order to have tractable complete reasoning (some types of disjunctive information are excluded); however, the language is expressive enough for most applications. Given these restrictions, the consistency of a knowledge base can be checked in a time cubic in the number of temporal entities.

LATER provides an expressive language for updating and querying a temporal knowledge base and performs such tasks very efficiently: we proved that the complexity of answering queries and of analyzing the consequences of an assertion of new constraints on a part of the knowledge base is cubic in the number of entities involved in the query (assertion) and is independent of the dimension of the knowledge base (see [7]). In particular, LATER can deal with queries interleaved with assertions treating them as hypothetical queries, so that the effects of assertions on the temporal knowledge base can be easily retracted (with no computational effort) when needed.

In order to formalize the temporal constraints in the scheduling problem, we associate a set of events with each train. In particular, given a train Tr, we introduce five events:

- $entrance\_point(Tr, P)$: arrival of Tr at the entrance point P;
- $entering(Tr, R)$: Tr is entering the station using the route R;
- $stopped(Tr, P)$: Tr is stopped on the track P;
- $exiting(Tr, R)$: Tr is exiting the station using the route R;
- $exit\_point(Tr, P)$: arrival of Tr at the exit point P.

All the constraints discussed in Sect. 3 can be expressed as temporal constraints involving such events. For example ($start(I)$ and $end(I)$ denote the start and end point of a time interval I):

- *Constraints on the timetable.* For example, if c is the scheduled time departure of a train Tr, we have: $end(stopped(Tr, P)) \geq c$
- *Constraints between connecting trains.* If $Tr1$ must wait for $Tr2$, we have:
  $$end(stopped(Tr1, P_1)) \ AtLeast \ c \geq \ start(stopped(Tr2, B_2))$$
  where c is a minimum connecting time.
- *Compatibility constraints.* If two trains $Tr1$ and $Tr2$ are assigned two incompatible entering routes R_1 and R_2, the following constraint must be enforced:

$$entering(Tr1, R_1) \ Before \ OR \ After \ entering(Tr2, R_2)$$

Given such a representation, the scheduling problem is solved as follows: the initial temporal knowledge-base for LATER is formed by the constraints that must be necessarily satisfied. The planner starts to build an assignment of routes. In doing that it uses the heuristics sketched in Sect. 3 and can query the temporal constraints maintained by LATER. The process is iterative, in the sense that assignments are built incrementally; at each step in such a construction new constraints are imposed: the consistency of such constraints is checked immediately using LATER and the constraints are added to LATER knowledge base. This phase takes benefit of the ability of LATER of checking consistency efficiently and of performing updates in a local way (see the discussion above). Moreover, the query language of LATER allows the planner to get information about the temporal location of events and about the status and availability of resources.

All the constraints discussed above, except from those concerning compatibility (which involve a form of disjunction not considered in LATER) can be directly managed by LATER. In order to deal with the disjunction that has to be imposed every time two incompatible resources are assigned, we use a simple heuristic: since we know (or we can infer from LATER) the order of arrival of the trains, only one of the disjunctive constraints is imposed. For example, if we know that $Tr1$ will arrive before $Tr2$, we impose only the constraint

$$entering(Tr1, R_1) \ Before \ entering(Tr2, R_2)$$

which can be managed by LATER. Notice that the constraints are imposed only when we actually need to do that and in this sense the approach we use is a sort of least-commitment one [26].

We tested the approach on a set of simple cases. For example, given a station with five tracks and given a set of 8 trains arriving in the same temporal window and mutually constrained by precedence and connections, the average time needed to manage the incremental assertions made by the planner and the queries asked by the planner is around 4 seconds.

7 Comparisons and Discussion

The approach in Sect. 5 is resource-centered, i.e., it maintains information on the availability of resources, while information on the tasks (trains) using the resources can be inferred. The approach in Sect. 6 is centered on tasks (events), i.e., it maintains information on when a task is performed, while information on the availability of resources can be inferred. In the specific problem, both types of information are important; however, there are applications where one of the two approaches is preferable. It usually depends on the kind of constraints involved on the problem. Constraints on tasks like precedence relations, interfering activities and due date constraints privilege the task-based solution, while constraints on resources like capacity or incompatibility constraints privilege the resource-based approach. In fact, in the task based approach precedence constraints and constraints concerning interfering activities constraints can be easily represented as discussed in section 6; due date constraints, which link a task T_i to be finished before its due date D can be expressed as: $end(T_i)$ $before$ D. On the other hand, the resource-based approach represents in a very simple way constrains on resources, such as, e.g., capacity constraints. If a resource has capacity n, a capacity constraint must be introduced to impose that such a resource cannot be engaged by more than n tasks at the same time. This constraint can be easily expressed by associating to a resource n domain variables whose domain represents temporal feasibility intervals. These domain variables are all compatible to each other. In this way, we can assign at least n activities to a resource, corresponding to its capacity. The incompatibility constraints are treated in the way discussed in Sect. 5. When a resource is assigned to a task in the interval $[t_1, t_2]$, this interval is deleted not only from the domain of the resource physically engaged, but from all the resource's domain incompatible with the one assigned.

Therefore, each approach deals naturally with some class of constraints. There are some applications, however, which require both constraints on resources and on tasks. In these cases an integration is needed. In fact, the two approaches (resource and task-based) can be integrated [22]; in particular, each approach can be extended to deal with the aspects considered by the other.

In the resource-based approach one should consider also the intervals in which a resource is allocated to some task. This corresponds to a gap in the domain of the resource (using the notation in Sect. 5). In such a way, we can keep track of the events and activities performed during gaps. Information on gaps could be maintained by another domain called *activity domain*. In fact, while the temporal domain decreases (trains are assigned), the activity domain would increase, keeping track of the assigned activities. If the domain associated with a resource R is: $D_R = \{[0, 7.30], [7.37, 8.00], [8.06, +\infty]\}$ it means that the resource is engaged during the temporal intervals $[7.31, 7.36]$ and $[8.01, 8.05]$. Associated with these "gaps", an activity domain: $Act_{D_R} = \{T_i, T_j\}$ represents the fact that T_i uses the resource R in the interval $[7.31, 7.36]$, while T_j uses the resource R in the interval $[8.01, 8.05]$. In addition, we can add in the activity domain the start and the duration of each task. This is redundant knowledge which can help to retrieve information quickly.

On the other hand, the event-based approach could be extended to cope with resource allocation by associating events with the resources and thus modeling explicitly the intervals in which resources are available or allocated (instead of inferring such information).

As regards temporal reasoning, the resource-based approach in 5 uses a discrete notion of time while the task-based approach uses a continuous structure for time. A continuous structure of time has to be assumed when dealing with qualitative temporal information and mixed qualitative and quantitative information (which is very common in many applications), since the traditional approaches to temporal reasoning would provide incorrect answers in case of discrete time. Thus, the approach in Sect. 5 cannot deal correctly with qualitative information and cannot be extended in a straightforward way to the case of continuous time. On the other hand, the approach in Sect. 6 cannot deal with discrete time, which is also a common and useful way to represent time [2], unless the possibility of reasoning with qualitative information is disregarded.

Moreover, while the resource-based approach uses a constraint manager specifically tailored to the train scheduling management, the task-based approach uses a general purpose temporal manager (thus, a crude comparison of the computation time spent by the two managers is not very significant).

As regards the computational complexity of the problem, it is well-known that scheduling problems belong to the NP-complete class of problems. However, our planner adopted a heuristic function (see Sect. 4) that drastically reduces the complexity of the problem. In fact, if n is the number of alternative resources for a train, m is the number of delay thresholds and t the number of trains analyzed in the temporal window, the number of attempts performed by the system is, in the worst case, equal to $m * n * t$. Of course, on average, the number of performed attempts is lower. This happens for two reasons: first, because the resource required by the train can be free or will be free within a few minutes and a solution can be found after one or few attempts. This happens when the traffic situation is normal. The second reason concerns the propagation of constraints that reduces the number of attempts performed.

The resource-based approach has been extended in order to manage the railway traffic on a whole railway line. It has lead to a distributed approach presented in [10].

The event-based approach takes advantages of the features of LATER as regards query processing and updating. Given the initial temporal knowledge base, constraint propagation is performed before starting the planning phase. In such a phase, the planner asks queries to the temporal manager and performs updates of the temporal knowledge base by adding the constraints associated with the partial solution being built. LATER can deal efficiently with queries and with sequences of interleaved assertions and queries; in particular, the complexity of such tasks depends only on the dimension of queries/assertions and is independent of the dimension of the temporal knowledge base (see the discussion in [7]). This means that the phases of checking the consistency of asserting new constraints and asking queries after such assertions are tasks that do not influence significantly the computational effort for computing the solution and that effort mainly depends on the efficiency of the planner.

References

1. J. Allen, "Maintaining Knowledge About Temporal Intervals", in *Communications of the ACM*, vol. 26, 1983, pp. 832–843.
2. J.F.Allen, J.A.Koomen, "Planning using a Temporal World Model", in *Proc. of IJCAI83*, 1983, pp. 741–747.
3. P.Baptiste, B.Legeard, M.A.Manier, C.Varnier, "A Scheduling Problem Optimization Solved with Constraint Logic Programming", in *Proc. Practical Applications of Prolog PAP94*, pp. 47–66, London (UK), 1994.
4. S.Breitinger, H.C.R.Lock, "Modelling and Scheduling in CLP(FD)", in *Proc. Practical Applications of Prolog PAP94*, pp. 95–110, London (UK), 1994.

5. Y.Caseau, F.Laburthe, "Improved CLP Scheduling with Task Intervals" in *ICLP94*, pp 369–383, S.Margherita (IT), 1994.

6. V. Brusoni, L. Console, B. Pernici, P. Terenziani, "LATER: an efficient general purpose manager of temporal information", to appear in *IEEE Expert*, 1996.

7. V. Brusoni, L. Console, P. Terenziani, "On the computational complexity of querying bounds on differences constraints", in *Artificial Intelligence*, vol. 74, 1995, pp. 367–379.

8. N.Christodoulou, E.Stefanitsis, E.Kaltsas, V.Assimakopoulos, "A Constraint Logic Programming Approach to the Vehicle-Fleet Scheduling Problem", in *Proc. Practical Applications of Prolog PAP94*, pp. 137–148, London (UK), 1994.

9. W.J.Cullyer, W.Wise, "Application of Formal Methods to Railway Signalling", in *Proc. of the Safety and Reliability Society Symposium*, pp. 11–28, Bath (UK), 1989.

10. A.Dalfiume, E.Lamma, P.Mello, M.Milano, "A Constraint Logic Programming Application to a Distributed Train Scheduling Problem", in *Proc. Practical Applications of Prolog PAP95*, Paris (FR),1995.

11. R.Dechter, I.Meiri, J.Pearl, "Temporal Constraint Networks", in *Artificial Intelligence*, vol. 49, 1991, pp. 61–95.

12. ECL^{i}PS^e User Manual Release 3.3, ECRC 1992.

13. M.S.Fox, N.Sadeh, "Why is Scheduling Difficult? A CSP Perspective", in *Proc. of ECAI 90*, pp.754-67, 1990.

14. E.C. Freuder, A.K. Mackworth, "Special Issue on Constraint Based Reasoning", *Artificial Intelligence*, vol. 58, 1992.

15. J.Jaffar , J.L.Lassez, "Constraint Logic Programming", in *Proc. of the Conference on Principle of Programming Languages*, Munich 1987.

16. J.Jaffar, M.J.Maher, "Constraint Logic Programming: a Survey", in *Journal of Logic Programming on 10 years of Logic Programming*, 1994.

17. V. Kumar, "Algorithms for Constraint-Satisfaction Problems: A Survey", in *The AI Magazine*, vol. 13, 1992, pp. 32–44.

18. E.Lamma, P.Mello, M.Milano, "A Meta Constraint Logic Programming Architecture for Qualitative and Quantitative Temporal Reasoning", Technical Report DEIS-LIA-95-001, 1995.

19. A.Mascis, A.Sassano, "Job-Shop, No-Wait in process with Blocking Models for the Ordering of Trains within Big Railway Stations", (in Italian), 1st Nat. Conf. C.N.R. "Progetto Finalizzato Trasporti II", Vol. 4, pp. 2075–2094, Rome 1993.

20. C.Meng, M.Sullivan, "LOGOS: A Constraint-Directed Reasoning Shell for Operations Management", *IEEE Expert* 6, 1, pp.20–28, 1991.

21. J.F.Rit, "Propagating Temporal Constraint for Scheduling", in *Proc. AAAI86*, Philadelphia (PA), pp.383–388, August 1986.

22. S.F.Smith, P.S.Ow, "The Use of Multiple Problem Decomposition in Time Constrained Planning Tasks", in *Proc. of IJCAI85*, pp.1013–1015.

23. S.F.Smith, "A Constraint-Based Framework for Reactive Management of Factory Schedules" in Intelligent Manufacturing, M.D.Oliff, Ed., Benjamin Cummins Publisher, 1987.

24. S.F.Smith, "Knowledge-based Production Management: Approaches, Results and Prospects", in Production Planning and Control Journal, 1992.

25. P.Van Hentenryck, "*Constraint Satisfaction in Logic Programming*", MIT Press, 1989.

26. D.S. Weld, "An Introduction to Least Commitment Planning", in *AI Magazine*, vol. 15, 1994, pp. 27–61.

A Fuzzy Behaviorist Approach to Sensor-Based Robot Control

François G. Pin
Robotics and Process Systems Division
Oak Ridge National Laboratory
P.O. Box 2008
Oak Ridge, TN 37831-6305
Telephone: (423)574-6130, Fax: (423)574-4624, E-mail: pin@ornl.gov

ABSTRACT

Sensor-based operation of autonomous robots in unstructured and/or outdoor environments has revealed to be an extremely challenging problem, mainly because of the difficulties encountered when attempting to represent the many uncertainties which are always present in the real world. These uncertainties are primarily due to sensor imprecisions and unpredictability of the environment, i.e., lack of full knowledge of the environment characteristics and dynamics. An approach, which we have named the "Fuzzy Behaviorist Approach" (FBA) is proposed in an attempt to remedy some of these difficulties. This approach is based on the representation of the system's uncertainties using Fuzzy Set Theory-based approximations and on the representation of the reasoning and control schemes as sets of elemental behaviors. Using the FBA, a formalism for rule base development and an automated generator of fuzzy rules have been developed. This automated system can automatically construct the set of membership functions corresponding to fuzzy behaviors, once these have been expressed in qualitative terms by the user. The system also checks for completeness of the rule base and for non-redundancy of the rules (which has traditionally been a major hurdle in rule base development). Two major conceptual features, the suppression and inhibition mechanisms which allow to express a dominance between behaviors are discussed in detail. Some experimental results obtained with the automated fuzzy rule generator applied to the domain of sensor-based navigation in *a priori* unknown environments, using one of our autonomous test-bed robots as well as a real car in outdoor environments, are then reviewed and discussed to illustrate the feasibility of large-scale automatic fuzzy rule generation using the "Fuzzy Behaviorist" concepts.

1. INTRODUCTION

A significant research activity has taken place over the past two decades in the area of autonomous mobile robot navigation. The paramount complexity of the sensor-based navigation problem in unstructured environments arises mainly from the uncertainties which exist and become pervasive in the overall system (which includes the robot and its surrounding domain). In addition to the typical sensor inaccuracies (there are no such things as "perfect" sensors), the dynamics and unpredictability of the environment generate very large uncertainties in the perception and reasoning systems, i.e., it becomes impossible to generate complete or exact models of the system (robot and environment) and/or of its behavior. These uncertainties, in turn, typically propagate through the control systems and lead to further inaccuracies or errors (e.g., in the robot position, in the sensor orientation) which compound the problem by increasing the uncertainties on the perception. In these conditions, the overall cost (time, computational needs, computing resources, etc.) of achieving the type of precision which was common in structured and static environments jumps by orders of magnitude, either from a requirement for much more refined sensors and perception data, or from the need for very time- and computation-expensive methods such as uncertainty analysis and propagation techniques. The impact of this cost increase is particularly important for real-time systems (where real-time is defined as the guarantee of producing a response within a prescribed amount of time), which become much more difficult to design, if not impractical to implement in realistic situations.

Humans on the other hand, seem to handle/cope very well with uncertain and unpredictable environments, often relying on approximate or qualitative data and reasoning to make decisions and to successfully accomplish their objectives. Several approximate reasoning theories and associated mathematical algebra have been developed over the past two decades (e.g., see methods and references in [1]), the most commonly used today for applications to control systems being Zadeh's Theory of Fuzzy Sets [2]–[4]. This theory is at the basis of very successful implementations varying from control of subway cars, elevators, cement kilns, washing machines, cameras and camcorders, inverted pendulums, to painting processes and color image reconstruction, to even Ping-Pong playing robots (e.g. see [1], [5], [6]). One of the important factors which have prevented the wide-spread utilization of approximate reasoning methodologies in real-time systems has been the lack of computer hardware allowing processing and inferencing directly in terms of approximate or linguistic, or "fuzzy" variables (e.g., far, fast, slow, left, faster) and approximate rules (e.g., if obstacle is close, then go slower; if temperature is high and pressure is increasing, then decrease power a lot). Prospective implementations thus had to rely on simulations of the approximate reasoning schemes on conventional computers based on "crisp" processing. The result was a significant penalty in speed of operation, typically prohibiting applications in most "hard real-time" systems. Over the last half decade, however, several innovations have allowed some bridging of this gap; in particular, unique computer boards have recently been developed which use custom-designed VLSI Fuzzy Inferencing chips (e.g., see [7], [8], and [9]) on VME-bus compatible boards. These systems can be directly programmed in terms of qualitative variables and rules and, when incorporated in a control system, can directly communicate and interface with robotic hardware (e.g., with motors, actuators). Such computer hardware developments have proven extremely useful in supporting the developments needed in the area of approximate reasoning for real-time "intelligent" machines, and have been a strong basis [9],[10] for the activities reported here.

2. FUZZY BEHAVIORIST APPROACH AND RULE GENERATION FOR SENSOR-BASED CONTROL

The problem of autonomous mobile robots navigating in *a priori* unknown and unpredictable environments was selected as a paradigm for research on qualitative reasoning and control systems because its characteristics rank very high on the list of criteria that typically indicate suitability of a reasoning problem for representation using qualitative logic and resolution using trade-offs.

• The input to the control system, particularly when provided by sonar range finders and odometric wheel encoders, is inaccurate, sparse, uncertain and/or unreliable.

• No complete mathematical representation exists of the process termed "navigation" although, as demonstrated by humans, a logic for this process exists which can typically be represented and successfully processed in terms of linguistic variables.

- The approximations involved in the numerical representation of the system and its environment (e.g., geometric representations, map discretization in grid) are significant.
- By its given nature the behavior of an outdoor environment is unpredictable, leading to large uncertainties in its representation and frequent need for trade-off of speed vs. precision.

Several research groups have studied approximate reasoning techniques, in particular fuzzy logic, to mimic human reasoning capabilities in navigation tasks (e.g., see Refs. 10 to 13). In all these applications, the sensor-based decision-making process has been implemented as a set of fuzzy rules which, together, express the desired navigation decisions of the robot for various combinations of the input data. Very successful results have been achieved when the number and complexity of the rules were small. When these increased, however, and/or the perception system grew more sophisticated (i.e., more sensory input data is provided), the typical difficulties encountered with large rule base systems emerged: the lack of established formalism for the development of rule bases — in particular with respect to completeness, interaction, and redundancy of the rules — made the actual coding of the fuzzy rules an iterative empirical process, requiring lengthy trial-and-error experiments.

2.1. Fuzzy Behaviorist Approach

In an attempt to alleviate this general shortcoming of rule-base system development, we recently proposed a "Fuzzy Behaviorist Approach" (FBA) which provides a formalism for the development of fuzzy rule systems for control of autonomous robots. The basic premises underlying our proposed FBA are as follows:

- Each action of the robot results from the concatenation of elemental behaviors.
- Each elemental behavior is a direct mapping from a single stimulus mode to a single output control.
- Each behavior is represented by one or a set of fuzzy rules which are defined by the membership functions of the rule's antecedent (stimuli) and consequence (output controls).
- Each mode of stimulus corresponds to a single dimension of the input space and is independent, in a *possibilistic* framework, of other stimulus modes.
- For behaviors effecting *the same output control dimension*, the possible conflicts between behaviors with stimuli that overlap in the multidimensional input space must be resolved through the expression of the respective dominance between the various behaviors.
- Each type of input data provided by the sensors is fuzzified with a membership function expressing, as a *possibility* distribution, the uncertainty associated with the specific measurement or calculation (see [10] or [14] for a detailed discussion of this process). The inferencing laws of the Fuzzy Sets Theory are then used to embody the rule-based reasoning.

Cast in the framework of Fuzzy Set Theory, these principles can be expressed as follows: the inferencing, I, of the (robot) reasoning system provides the relationship between the input universe of discourse U and the output universe of discourse V. The input universe of discourse U is multidimensional, with each dimension representing a type of input data on which the inferencing can act (e.g., distance to obstacle to the right of route, direction to the goal, distance to the goal), i.e., each input dimension is a mode of stimulus, s_i, that can excite the inferencing. Similarly, the output universe of discourse V, is multidimensional, with each dimension representing a type of output data, i.e., a type of control, c_j, (e.g., turn control, motor #1 speed) that can be implemented. Thus we have:

$$I : U(s_1, s_2, ..., s_i, ..., s_n) \rightarrow V(c_1, c_2, ..., c_j, ..., c_m) . \tag{1}$$

The total numbers of possible stimulus modes, n, and of control modes, m, are of course dependent on the sensory and actuation capabilities implemented on the robot. Each dimension s_i or c_j is a one-dimensional space on which fuzzy sets can be defined using membership functions in the conventional manner (e.g., see references [2], [3], [4], and [5]). An elemental behavior, B_{ij}, is thus defined as a direct mapping from s_i to c_j:

$$B_{ij} : s_i \rightarrow c_j, \tag{2}$$

which is represented by one or several fuzzy rules relating fuzzy subsets of s_i to fuzzy subsets of c_j. As an example, assume s_3 represents the "direction to the goal" input dimension and c_2 represents the "turn control" output dimension, then the behavior B_{32}, "turn control as a function of the goal direction," would include fuzzy rules of the type: IF (direction to the goal is *left*) THEN (turn value is *positive*), where *left* and *positive* are fuzzy subsets defined by their membership functions on s_3 and c_2, respectively.

Note that the fourth requirement of the approach specifies that the input space be designed such that the stimulus modes (input dimensions), s_i, are independent of each other, i.e., such that the possibility for the ith input to be any fuzzy subset in s_i is completely independent of the possibility for any other input to be any fuzzy subset on their stimulus mode. In other words, the possibilities for any and all stimuli to occur are unrelated and independent of each other. This allows a behavior B_{ij} to be extended to a mapping B_{ij}^* from U to V as

$$B_{ij}^* : U(\#, \#, \#, ..., s_i, \#, ..., \#) \rightarrow V(\phi, \phi, ... c_j, \phi, ..., \phi) , \tag{3}$$

where the # and ϕ signs represent "non-significant" input and output dimensions, respectively. By definition, s_i and c_j are the "significant" input and output dimensions of behavior B_{ij}^*. For example, the behavior B_{32} discussed above has 3 (for input) and 2 (for output) as significant dimensions and would be extended to a behavior B_{32}^* on the multidimensional input and output spaces with fuzzy rules now expressed as:

IF (input 1 is *anything* and input 2 is *anything* and direction to the goal is *left* and input 4 is *anything* and ...) THEN (output 1 is *do nothing* and turn value is *positive* and output 3 is *do nothing* and ...)

and the fuzzy subsets *anything* and *do nothing* have membership functions uniformly equal to 1 and to 0 over the entire range of their respective input and output dimensions.

With these features, rule bases embodying sets of elemental fuzzy behaviors can be very easily generated (e.g., see [9] and [10]). They can also be readily augmented with additional behaviors, either to handle situations of increasing complexity (e.g., see [10] and [14]) or if additional perception or control capabilities are added to the system, requiring larger dimensions of the input or output spaces. In these cases, however, a very important aspect of the formalism which needs to be emphasized here is the requirement for independence and non-conflict of the stimuli of the behaviors effecting the *same output controls*. This requirement simply expresses that only one action command can be sent to a single output control for any given stimulus (a single point in the input space). This leads to newly added (or acquired) behaviors having to "dominate," or "be dominated by," some of the existing behaviors in one or more regions of the input space. This concept of dominance between behaviors, which exhibits itself in almost every action of our everyday life, has been illustrated in previous papers [10], [14], with the major point that an indication of what behavior dominates the other in what region of their overlapping areas in the input space, *must be specified into the system if two "seemingly conflicting" behaviors are to produce a reasonable advanced behavior.* In the automated system, this is accomplished through the "suppression" mechanism, in which the output membership function of the dominant behavior is modified, so that its weight will appropriately overpower that of the other behavior in the c.g. calculation. If due to previous dominances and/or suppression requirements with respect to other behaviors, the membership function can not be made adequately overpowering, then the system uses the concept of "inhibition" to express the behavior's dominance. Applying inhibition within the overlapping region of input space consists in partially truncating the input membership function of the "weaker" behavior so that the dominant behavior always triggers with a greater strength. Although both suppression and inhibition mechanisms result in expressing the desired dominance, their concepts are quite different: one basically operates on the relative weight of the behaviors in the output space while the other modifies the triggering conditions of the behaviors in the input space. Figure 1 schematically shows these very intuitive suppression and inhibition mechanisms on a simple example in which two rules, each with two input and one output, act on the speed control of a robot. The first rule, which may be part of a behavior for speed control as a function of frontal obstacle proximity, states that if the obstacle is very close, then the speed should be very small. The second rule states that if the goal is straight ahead then the speed is fast. The membership functions uniformly equal to 1 over their entire range represent the non-significant input dimensions of each behavior.

2.2. Automated System

Just like different people may use different strategies, different rules, and different qualitative variables to express their navigation process, and still navigate efficiently "in their own way," several strategies may be used to embody a particular process in a rule base, i.e., there is not a single or unique rule base representation of a given process. In the automated system, the user inputs the strategy for the rules in a "qualitative" form using the format shown in Fig. 2.

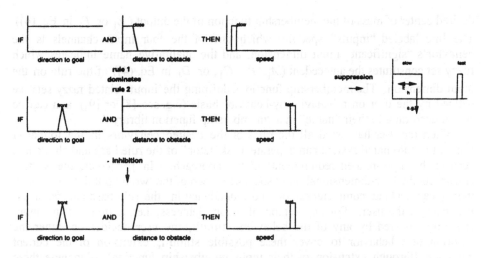

Fig. 1. Schematic of the suppression and inhibition mechanisms.

```
name  :  RN                                     name  :  LF
suppressing list  :  G? LF                      M        :  0.3
E                 :  50          or             Outputs  :  - 10
Outputs           :  20 -                       Inputs   :  - - Far -
Inputs            :  - Near - -
```

Fig. 2. Input format for the automated rule generation system.

The five-line format in Fig. 2 describes one rule, with the first line giving the "reference name" of the rule, the second line listing the names of the rules or behaviors which are suppressed (or inhibited) by this rule, the third line giving the suppression parameter E (which will be described in the following paragraphs), and the last two lines specifying what the desired input and output of the rule on the "significant" (see Section 2.1) input and output dimensions of the behavior are. In the current version of the automated system, each rule is assumed to be of the form

IF (A is A_1 and B is B_1 and C is C_1 and D is D_1) THEN (E is E_1 and F is F_1),   (4)

therefore operating on four input and two output channels. Although extension to any number of input and output channels is possible, this configuration was chosen in the initial version of the automated system because it corresponds to what is available on the custom-designed VLSI fuzzy inferencing chips and boards (see [7], [8], and [9]) which we utilize in our experimental work. Use of the character "?" in the suppression list of line 2, such as "G?" in the example of Fig. 2, indicates that the rule suppresses all other rules whose name includes the other character, in this case all rules whose name begins with the letter "G." If the subject rule does not suppress other rules, then the first character of line 2 is the letter M followed by a number expressing the desired weight m of the output (explained in the following paragraphs), and the line giving the suppression parameter E is omitted. The line labeled "outputs" in Fig. 2 indicates which of the two outputs is effected by the behavior, with the number, expressed in percent of the scaled output range, specifying the desired center of mass of the membership function of the output (E_1 or F_1 in Eq. (4)). The line labeled "inputs" specifies which one of the four input channels is the behavior's "significant" input dimension, and the qualitative name indicates which fuzzy set constitutes the antecedent (A_1, B_1, C_1, or D_1 in Eq. (4)) of the rule on the input dimension. The membership functions defining the input related fuzzy sets are defined by the user on a behavior-by-behavior basis (e.g. see [8] or [9]), and can be stored according to their "name" in a "membership function library."

When the user has listed all the rules of the desired behaviors in the format of Fig. 2, the automated system can generate a "skeleton" of the rule base and check if it verifies the input-related requirements of the approach. In particular, the system constructs the four-dimensional input spaces for each of the two output dimensions, so that it can evaluate completeness of, and redundancy in, the rule base and report all instances to the user. For any region of incompleteness, i.e., regions of the input space not covered by any of the behaviors stimuli, the user decides on either the addition of a behavior to cover these possible stimuli, extension of the current behaviors (through extension of their input membership function) to include these input regions, or no modification if input data within these uncovered regions or "blind spots" are never expected to occur (for example if these regions correspond to values outside the operating range of the sensors). For the regions of redundancy, i.e., areas where stimuli from two or more behaviors are overlapping, the system reports every rule for which a dominance has not been specified but may be required because of the input overlapping. The user can then interactively add to or modify the dominance specifications in lines 2 and 3 of each rule, until all requirements of the approach are verified and all desired dominances are expressed in the rule base. The actual generation of the rule base, including the suppression and/or inhibition mechanism, can then proceed as follows: initially, all rules are given a "standard" output membership function equal to 1 over a width of one bit, centered at the bit value expressed in line 4 of the "qualitative" expression of the rule (see Fig. 2). The system checks the sets of rules that are effecting the *same* output dimension. If no suppression mechanism has been expressed between the rules because dominance is not necessary, then the output membership functions are unconstrained and they remain at their "standard" value. If a dominance has been expressed between two or more rules, then the dominant rule is the one that is modified if suppression is possible, otherwise the dominated rules are modified using inhibition. The automated process and the corresponding equations have been described in detail in [15].

3. SAMPLE EXPERIMENTAL RESULTS

Using the automated fuzzy rule generation system, a variety of rule bases were generated (e.g., see [10], [14]) for the sensor-based navigation of mobile robots in *a priori* unknown environments. The experiments involved both indoor and outdoor environments, and progressed from simple goal tracking navigation in laboratory-type situations to sensor-based driving of a car in parking lot conditions, and from platforms with omnidirectional capabilities to robots with complex car-like kinematics including non-holonomic constraints. In what follows, sample results from some of these experiments are reviewed to illustrate the automatic rule generation process including the suppression and inhibition mechanisms. As discussed in detail in Refs. [13] and [14], the four sensory input to the fuzzy inferencing system are the goal direction (or target direction), which is updated at loop rate using the odometry system; and the minimum distances to obstacles obtained using groups of acoustic range finders in three 75° wide sectors at the left, center, and right of the robot's travel direction. The two output of the inferencing system are the commands for turn increments and speed of the robot. Thus, navigation behaviors with these data can involve Goal Orientation (GO) and "front," "left," or "right" Obstacle Proximity (OP) as input, and Turn Control (TC) and Speed Control (SC) as output.

3.1. Example of Basic Navigation Behaviors

As mentioned previously, several rule bases, representing various "strategies," may be developed to solve a complex problem or to embody a complex behavioral process. Figure 3 shows plots of actual runs made with one of our small omnidirectional robots [16] to illustrate the overall reactive navigation obtained with the automatic generation of fuzzy rules. These plots are also given here to provide an example of the effect on the navigation behaviors which a dominance mechanism (suppression or inhibition) can produce. In the figures, the shaded areas represent the obstacles which were placed in the room, while the path of the robot is illustrated using the succession of circles showing the position of the robot every 20 loop rates. In Fig. 3-a, the rules of a basic rule base described in detail in [10] and [14] were used, which embody a very strong dominance of the obstacle avoidance rules over the goal tracking rules. Consequently, due to the almost constant proximity of the corridor walls, the suppression mechanism is quite effective in the early part of the run and the robot wanders around for quite a long time, guided principally by obstacle avoidance. It eventually gets positioned ideally to enter the corridor and then turns right, in a direction closest to the goal direction. It follows the corridor, and when reaching the end of the wall, turns left toward the goal. Clearly, the dominance of the obstacle avoidance rules over the "move to the goal" behavior may be too strong in this environment. For the sample run shown in Fig. 3-b, this dominance has been decreased, through an increase of the suppression parameter (see Figs. 1 and 2, and [15]), and a corresponding rule base has been generated using the automated system. The robot is now seen to negotiate the entrance of the corridor much more rapidly because of the greater effect of the goal tracking behavior, resulting in a much shorter run to the goal. From an overall behavioral point-of-view, the simple change of the dominance of the "obstacle avoidance" over "move to the goal" behaviors in the rule base, has transformed the "shy" robot, driven mainly by obstacle avoidance in Fig. 3-a, into a "much braver" robot proceeding more rapidly toward its goal in Fig. 3-b. Note that this "transformation" has been accomplished without direct modification of the logic embodied in the elemental behaviors.

3.2. Extension to Robots with Car-Like Kinematics

One of the expected strengths of our proposed Fuzzy Behaviorist Approach using elemental "human-like" behaviors is that the *linguistic logic* embodied in the behaviors should be invariant across systems of similar characteristics. In other words, for robots with similar perceptive abilities and motion capabilities, the linguistic expression of given behaviors, and therefore their representation in the fuzzy framework, should be the same for compatible input and output. For example, a "goal tracking" behavior connecting the perceived goal direction to a rate of turn [e.g., IF (goal is to the right) THEN (apply increment of turn to the right)] should be invariant for any robot which has a means to perceive the goal direction and to perform the required turn.

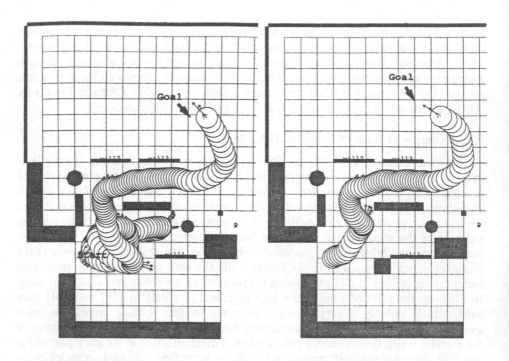

Fig. 3. Actual runs of the robot using automatically generated fuzzy rule bases with a) a strong behavioral dominance of obstacle avoidance over goal tracking, b) a lesser behavioral dominance of obstacle avoidance over goal tracking.

As a demonstration of this transportability of invariant behaviors from one system to another, the same behaviors and the same fuzzy rules that were utilized for the omnidirectional platform were used to implement the autonomous control of a car on the basis of the same three 75° "wide and blurry sonar eyes" and goal direction input. To complete the navigation rule base for the driving of the car, a behavior had to be included to handle situations where "very near" obstacles are detected and the car does not have enough space to complete a turn away from obstacles because of its limited steering angle, therefore requiring some maneuvers using reverse gear. Another strength of our proposed Fuzzy Behaviorist Approach is its capability for superposition of elemental behaviors, allowing for progressive addition of behaviors to the system to resolve situations of increasing complexity

Both simulation and outdoor experiments were performed with the maneuvering behavior-augmented rule base and results can be found in Refs. [10] and [14]. Because of the unavailability of a car with automated actuation, no autonomous navigation tests were performed outdoors. However, the system was investigated for use as a "driver's aid" using one of the company cars. In the driver's aid mode, the same rule base, sensors, and inferencing system as in the previous experiments are used, however the commands produced by the rule base are displayed to the driver to guide him/her in driving the car. The driver conventionally uses the gas and brake pedals and steering wheel to implement the commands that are displayed on a portable computer screen located next to him/her in the cabin. From the system's development point of view, this inclusion of the human in the control chain effectively consisted in including a source of unpredictable noise and delays in the actuation system of the autonomous operation mode. The successful operation of the rule base in this mode of driving (see [19]) thus provided a stringent robustness test of the qualitative inferencing scheme and navigation system.

4. CONCLUDING REMARKS

An automated system to generate fuzzy rules from the qualitative description of a reasoning process has been developed. The automated system is built on the basis of the Fuzzy Behaviorist Approach which we proposed for the development of fuzzy rule bases embodying "human-like" behaviors in sensor-based decision-making systems. The concepts of suppression and inhibition of behaviors and the inclusion of corresponding mechanisms in the automated system have been described. Examples of the use of the automated system to generate fuzzy rule bases for the sensor-based navigation of autonomous robots have been discussed. Sample runs of the robots have been presented to illustrate the navigation behaviors obtained with the automatically generated fuzzy rule bases as well as the effect of a change in the inter-behavior dominance expressed through the suppression and/or inhibition mechanism. Experiments with a real car have also been discussed to illustrate the capability of readily adding behaviors to the fuzzy rule base to resolve situations of increasing complexity and, as shown in the driver's aid feasibility study, the straightforward "linguistic" interfacing capability of the fuzzy behavior-based system. A variety of lessons and observations can be drawn from these experiments. Several of these, relevant to the topics dealt with here, are listed and/or discussed below.

- The entire navigation code or scheme consists of less than 20 fuzzy rules. Compared to the 30,000+ lines of "crisp" coding which were previously utilized to accomplish the same task, the efficiency and gain in code development time, code and data storage space, etc., of the approach seems to be indisputable.
- Our observations showed the approximate reasoning scheme to be much more robust and reliable than the previously used "crisp" codes when faced with sensor inaccuracies and environmental uncertainties. This seems to clearly support the claim that, for situations where precision is not the primary goal, robotic tasks can be very efficiently accomplished using an approximate reasoning scheme, but also can be made more robust with respect to uncertainties through an implicit "folding" of these uncertainties within approximate variables and reasoning schemes.
- As illustrated through the various experiments involving small omnidirectional and indoor robots and/or an outdoor car, approximate reasoning schemes can be built to embody very generic functions, i.e., they do not need to be system-specific. In other words, they can embody a reasoning *strategy* rather than a specific instantiation of the strategy. Furthermore, this genericness of the approximate reasoning schemes provides straight-forward transportability of codes among various systems with *similar* perception and motion *means*.
- A significant consequence of this genericness of approximate reasoning schemes is of course their scale up capability. As shown in the experiments, basic navigation schemes could be augmented and/or enhanced with additional behaviors *without* rewriting the previously tested behaviors. The gain in development time resulting from this property of approximate reasoning schemes is expected to be substantial.

REFERENCES

[1] *Uncertainty in Artificial Intelligence*, eds. L. N. Kanal and J. F. Lemmer, North-Holland (1988).

[2] Zadeh, L. A., "Fuzzy Set," *Information and Control* **8**, 1965, pp. 338–353.

[3] Zadeh, L. A., "Outline of a New Approach to the Analysis of Complex Systems and Decision Processes," *IEEE Transactions on Systems, Man, and Cybernetics* **SMC-3**(1), 1973, pp. 28–45.

[4] Zadeh, L. A., "Fuzzy Logic," *IEEE Computer* **21**(4), April 1988, pp. 83–93.

[5] *Fuzzy Sets and Their Applications to Cognitive and Decision Processes*, eds. L. A. Zadeh, K. S. Fu, K. Tanaka, and M. Shinamura, Academic Press, Inc., New York (1975).

[6] *Industrial Applications of Fuzzy Control*, ed. M. Sugeno, North-Holland (1985).

[7] Watanabe, H., W. Dettloff, and E. Yount, "A VLSI Fuzzy Logic Inference Engine for Real-Time Process Control," *IEEE Journal of Solid State Circuits* **25**(2), 1990, pp. 376–382.

[8] Symon, J. R. and H. Watanabe, "Single Board System for Fuzzy Inference," in *Proceedings of the Workshop on Software Tools for Distributed Intelligent Control Systems*, September 1990, pp. 253–261.

[9] Pin, F. G., H. Watanabe, J. R. Symon, and R. S. Pattay, "Autonomous Navigation of a Mobile Robot Using Custom-Designed Qualitative Reasoning VLSI Chips and Boards," in *Proceedings of the 1992 IEEE International Conference on Robotics and Automation*, Nice, France, May 10–15, 1992, pp. 123–128.

[10] Pin, F. G. and Y. Watanabe, "Navigation of Mobile Robots Using a Fuzzy Behaviorist Approach and Custom-Designed Fuzzy Inferencing Boards," *Robotica* **12**(6), 1994, pp. 491–503.

[11] Yen, J. and N. Pfluger, "A Fuzzy Logic Based Robot Navigation System," in *Proceedings of the AAAI Symposium on Applications of Artificial Intelligence to Real-World Autonomous Mobile Robots*, Cambridge, Massachusetts, October 23–25, 1992, pp. 195–199.

[12] Takeuchi, T. et al., "Fuzzy Control of a Mobile Robot for Obstacle Avoidance," *Information Science* **45**, 1988, pp. 231–239.

[13] Sugeno, M. et al., "Fuzzy Algorithmic Control of Model Car by Oral Instructions," *Fuzzy Sets and Systems* **32**, 1989, pp. 207–219.

[14] Pin, F. G. and Y. Watanabe, "Steps Toward Sensor-Based Vehicle Navigation in Outdoor Environments Using a Fuzzy Behaviorist Approach," *International Journal of Intelligent and Fuzzy Systems* **1**(2), 1993, pp. 95–107.

[15] Pin, F. G. and Y. Watanabe, "Automatic Generation of Fuzzy Rules Using the Fuzzy Behaviorist Approach: The Case of Sensor-Based Robot Navigation," *Intelligent Automation and Soft Computing* **1**(2), 1995, pp. 161–178.

[16] F. G. Pin and S. M. Killough, "A New Family of Omnidirectional and Holonomic Wheeled Platforms for Mobile Robots,," *IEEE Transactions on Robotics and Automation* **10**(4), 1994, pp. 480–489.

Knowledge-Based Fuzzy Neural Networks

LES M. SZTANDERA
Computer Science Department
Philadelphia College of Textiles and Science
Philadelphia, PA 19144, USA
les@larry.texsci.edu; http://larry.texsci.edu/les2.html

Knowledge-based neural networks are concerned with the use of numerical information, which forms the domain knowledge, obtained from sensor measurements to determine the initial structure of a neural network. Research on combining symbolic inductive learning with neural networks, as well as research on combining fuzzy logic with neural networks, is proceeding on several fronts. Fuzzy decision trees and their various algorithmic implementations are one of the most popular choices in applications to learning and reasoning from feature-based examples. Such constructions have drawn increasing attention recently due to comprehensibility of the generated knowledge structure, and wide availability of data in the form of feature descriptions. However, the inability of coping with missing data, imprecise or vague information, and measurements errors create a lot of problems for symbolic artificial intelligence. These problems might be overcome by employing fuzzy methodology. In this paper we present an approach based on fuzzy neural trees for determining the structure of a neural network. An analysis of digital thallium-201 myocardial scintigraphs is presented to corroborate the theory and demonstrate the utility of the approach.

Keywords: Learning and Knowledge Discovery, Knowledge-Based Neural Networks, Neural Heuristics

1 INTRODUCTION

Knowledge-based neural networks are concerned with the use of domain knowledge to determine the initial structure of a neural network. One of the most important questions in determining a feedforward neural network architecture is how to specify the size (number of nodes) in a hidden layer. Lippmann [1] argued that a four layered network with two hidden layers could solve an arbitrary classification problem. Irie and Miyake [2] proved that a three layered back propagation network with an infinite number of nodes in the hidden layer could also solve arbitrary mapping problems. Lippmann [1] also argued that the nodes in a hidden layer corresponded to separate decision regions into which training examples were mapped. Kung and Hwang [3] used the algebraic projection approach to specify how each node should be created. These approaches, however, are based on knowing the properties of the training data, such as decision regions or pattern properties, which may be hard to satisfy in real life applications. Practical approaches for dynamic neural network architecture generation have been sought by Sirat and Nadal [4], and Bichsel and Seitz [5]. In those architectures, at the end of a training process, all training examples are recognized and a neural network architecture is generated. In particular, the "tiling" algorithm of Sirat and Nadal [4] generates a feedforward network in a sequential manner by adding nodes and layers without the need to guess its architecture. However, the algorithm does not specify in what exact sequence a node should be added to give the maximum effect in classifying training examples. A similar algorithm of Bichsel and Seitz [5] uses information entropy to determine generation of nodes and hidden layers. Other algorithm of a special interest, the ID3 algorithm of Quinlan [6] dynamically generates a decision tree using information entropy functions. Studies by Dietterich et. al. [7] and Fisher and Mckusick [8] revealed strong evidence that information entropy could be used as a criterium for determining the number of hidden layers in a neural network. However, issues of overfitting and oversearching have to be thoroughly investigated then. Other authors, Cios and Liu [9], and Fahlman and Labiere [10] also addressed the problem of a dynamic generation of neural network architectures. In recent years, an increased number of scientists have become involved in the subject of hybrid neuro-fuzzy models in the hope of combining the strengths of fuzzy systems and artificial neural networks. One of such hybrid algorithms was proposed recently by Sztandera [11]. The algorithm generates nodes and hidden layers from data until a learning task is accomplished. It operates on numerical data and equates a decision tree with a hidden layer of a neural network. A learning strategy used in this approach is based on faithful ranking of fuzzy sets. This is translated into adding new nodes to a network until specified ranking values are achieved. When this is the case then all training examples are regarded as correctly recognized.

Fuzzy sets were introduced in 1965 by Zadeh [12] as a means for representing, manipulating, and utilizing data and information that possess non-statistical uncertainty. A neural network (NN) is well known for its ability to represent functions. The basis of every fuzzy model is the membership function. So, a natural application of (NN) in fuzzy models is to provide good approximations to the membership functions that are essential to the success of any fuzzy approach. We are going to show the use of this approach for the analysis of digital thallium-201 myocardial scintigraphs [13]. Hovewer, other hybrid approaches are also mentioned to provide a comprehensive view for the readers.

1. 1 A NEED FOR FUZZY SET THEORY APPROACHES IN NEURAL NETWORK STRUCTURES

Artificial neural networks are able to process numerical information and exhibit learning capabilities. Fuzzy systems can process linguistic information encoded by fuzzy sets. Thus, it is not surprising that the fusion of these two technologies is the current research trend. The aim is to be able to create algorithms, and then in hardware implementation, machines with more intelligent behavior.

Research on combining fuzzy logic with neural networks is proceeding on several fronts. Gupta and Qi [14] proposed three models for fuzzy neurons. Ishibuchi et. al. proposed incorporating possibility and necessity measures into a backpropagation neural network algorithm (Ishibuchi et. al. [15]), and a neural network architecture that learns from fuzzy if-then rules (Ishibuchi et. al. [16]). Backpropagation neural networks for fuzzy logic were also investigated by Keller and Tahani [17], and by Keller at al. [18]. The design and computations of fuzzy logic neural networks were analyzed by Hirota and Pedrycz [19], and by Hayashi et. al. [20]. Most of those approaches can be incorporated into Gupta and Qi models for fuzzy neurons. Foundational to their models is the idea that fuzzy sets are inputs to a neuron. The neuron combines its inputs to produce an output, which is also a fuzzy set, not by summation, as in many conventional paradigms, but by aggregation operations. In Gupta and Qi's first model the aggregation operation is an *if-then* rule. In their second model, the fuzzy inputs are degrees of membership that correspond to a pattern of nonfuzzy values and the aggregation can be any process that operates on degrees of membership. In the third model, the neuron's inputs are modified values of fuzzy sets, usually by quantifiers, and aggregation operations are as in the second model.

In addition to overlaying fuzziness on the neurons, researchers have also fuzzified the methods that networks use to learn associations. Fuzzy neural net designers have fuzzified Hebbian learning by characterizing neurons as members of fuzzy sets, postulating interconnections between the members of two fuzzy sets, and setting the interconnection weight as the minimum degree of membership of two connected neurons. Kosko [21] used fuzzy Hebbian learning to set up the Fuzzy Associative Memory (FAM), a system which encodes fuzzy if-then rules.

There also exists an interesting fuzzy approach for generating fuzzy rules from numerical data where interference of human experts is possible (Wang and Mendel [22]).

Our approach is different from the above mentioned ones. We use neural networks to produce membership functions for fuzzy sets as our data are numerical. Moreover, we take advantage of the learning capability of neural networks to manipulate those membership functions, say for classification and pattern recognition processes, prediction, and for ranking in multi-criteria decision making. In the opposite direction, we use fuzzy reasoning architecture, like fuzzy trees, to construct neural networks.

The success of neural networks is explained by the universal approximation property via Stone-Weierstrass theorem [23, 24]. However, there is no standard method for determining the number of neural units in hidden layers. Mathematically speaking, while the graphical form of neural networks indicates that such input-output maps can approximate continuous functions to any degree of accuracy, one still faces the practical problem: which specific network structure will actually do the job?

We address this problem by utilizing numerical information collected in a nuclear cardiology domain [13]. The information, which forms our domain knowledge, was obtained from sensor measurements, and will be used to determine the structure of a neural network.

2 FORMATION OF KNOWLEDGE DOMAIN

Stress Tl-201 scintigraphs were obtained from patients with arteriographically proven single-vessel coronary artery obstructions, and from patients with arteriographically proven normal coronary arteries and normal ventricular function. Tl-201 scintigraphs were collected after maximal exercise from the 78 kV photopeak with a 20% window, using a portable gamma camera equipped with a 1/4 inch crystal and high-resolution collimator. Three views of the left ventricle - anterior (ANT), left lateral (LAT) and left anterior oblique (LAO) required approximatelly 10 minutes each with minimum of 300,000 scintillation counts collected in each view [13]. The goal of the stress is to direct a greater portion of the blood supply to the myocardial region, so as to obtain a greater contrast between those regions of the heart that are ischemic (having a local lack of blood supply) and those regions that are normal. The ischemic areas are known as perfusion defects. The major cause of such perfusion defects is known to be stenosis of the coronary arteries defined by us as reduction of cross-sectional area of an artery's lumen by at least 70%. In order to partially overcome the problem of the wide variations in the anatomy of a heart, yet still be able to make meaningful relative comparisons of different hearts, a normalized planar view of the heart from each of the three different camera angles: anterior, left lateral, and left anterior oblique was proposed [13].

Pixels containing count ratios that fell more than 2.5 standard deviation below normal are considered to be underperfused. Each of the three views was divided into 10 anatomic regions called segments. However, for computer analysis, the regions of all three views were numbered consecutively. Segments 1 through 10 of the anterior view are referred to as regions 1 through 10, segments 1 through 10 of the left lateral view are referred to as regions 11 through 20, and segments 1 through 10 of the left anterior oblique view are referred to as regions 21 through 30. The percentage of underperfused (as compared with normally perfused) pixels in each region represents the magnitude of the perfusion defect for that region. Thus, 30 numbers ranging in size from 0 to 100, each representing the size of the perfusion defect in that region, were generated from each patient scintigraph. Those 30-dimensional vectors collected from 91 patients, who underwent thallium-201 myocardial scintigraphy, were used as inputs for the neuro-fuzzy algorithm [11]. The use of fuzzy decision making is necessitated in order to capture the uncertainties in a digital image. Numerous previous attempts were utilized to attack the problem, however the results were not satisfactory. The fuzzy set theory approach seems to be appropriate in tackling the problem, as it provides a suitable means for analyzing complex systems and decision making processes when the pattern indeterminacy is caused by the inherent variability and fuzziness rather than randomness. Thus, the fuzzy methodology is utilized to increase the amount of information available in decision making. In the proposed approach the fuzzy membership functions are learned by a neural network from the data. In our case, sixty four scans were chosen at random for training and the remaining twenty seven scans were used for testing. The major coronary arteries are classified as the left anterior descending artery (LAD), right coronary artery (RCA), circumflex artery (CCX), and the posterior descending artery. For the data analysis, however, patients having a significant stenosis upstream from the posterior descending artery were classified as having right coronary artery obstruction, regardless of whether this artery arises from the right coronary or circumflex artery. Thus, the training file consists of 64 thirty dimentional vectors which are assigned to the following classes (75% of the population in each class): 8 vectors representing patients with CCX, 22 with LAD, 16 with RCA, and 18 normal patients. These data sets were used as our knowledge domain. The techniques are outlined in the next section.

3 KNOWLEDGE EXTRACTION

The proposed algorithm generates a feed forward network architecture for the Tl-201 scintigraph problem, and after having generated fuzzy subsets at each node of the network, it switches to fuzzy decision making on those subsets. The nodes and hidden layers are added until a learning task is accomplished. The algorithm operates on numerical data and equates a decision tree with a hidden layer of a neural network [11]. A learning strategy used in this approach is based on achieving the optimal *goodness function*. This process of optimization of the goodness function translates into adding new nodes to the network until the desired values are achieved. When this is the case then all training examples are regarded as correctly recognized. The incorporation of fuzzy sets into the algorithm seems to result in a drastic reduction of the number of nodes in the network, and in decrease of the convergence time. Connections between the nodes have a "cost" function being equal to the weights of a neural network. The directional vector of a hyperplane, which divides decision regions, is taken as the weight vector of a node.

Let us repeat here the basic notation after [11]. There are N training examples, N^+ examples belonging to class "+", and N^- examples belonging to class "-". A hyperplane divides the examples into two groups: those lying on the positive (1) and negative (0) sides of it. Thus, we have four possible outcomes:
N_1^+ - number of examples from class "+" on the side 1,

N_0^+- number of examples from class " + " on the side 0, $\qquad$ (1)
N_1^- - number of examples from class "-" on the side 1,
N_0^- - number of examples from class "-" on the side 0.
Let us assume that at a certain level of a decision tree N_r examples are divided
by a node r into N_r^+ belonging to class "+", and N_r^- belonging to class "-". It is
assumed that $N_{0r}^+ = N_r - N_{1r}^+$ and $N_{0r}^- = N_r - N_{1r}^-$. The values N_{1r}^+ and
N_{1r}^- are calculated as follows:

$$N_{1r}^+ = \sum_{i=1}^{N_r} D_i \, out_i \qquad (2)$$

$$N_{1r}^- = \sum_{i=1}^{N_r} (1 - D_i) \, out_i \qquad (3)$$

where D_i stands for the desired output, and out_i is a sigmoid function. Thus, we
have (4):

$$N_{1r}^+ + N_{1r}^- = out_1 + ... + out_{N_r} = \sum_{i=1}^{N_r} out_i = \sum_{i=1}^{N_r} [1 + \exp(-\sum_j w_{ij} x_j)]^{-1}$$

The change in the number of examples, on both positive and negative sides of a
hyperplane, with respect to weights is given by [11]:

$$\Delta N_{1r}^+ = \sum_{i=1}^{N_r} D_i \, out_i \, (1 - out_i) \sum_j x_j \, \Delta w_{ij} \qquad (5)$$

$$\Delta N_{1r}^- = \sum_{i=1}^{N_r} (1 - D_i) \, out_i \, (1 - out_i) \sum_j x_j \, \Delta w_{ij} \qquad (6)$$

The learning rule to minimize the fuzzy entropy f(F) [11] is:

$$\Delta w_{ij} = -\rho \frac{\partial f(F)}{\partial w_{ij}} \qquad (7)$$

where ρ is a learning rate, and f(F) is a fuzzy entropy function. The grades of
membership for fuzzy sets F and F^C to be used in calculation of f(F) are defined
as follows :

$$F = \left\{ \frac{N_{0r}^-}{N_{0r}}, \frac{N_{0r}^+}{N_{0r}}, \frac{N_{1r}^-}{N_{1r}}, \frac{N_{1r}^+}{N_{1r}} \right\} \qquad (8)$$

$$F^C = 1 - F. \qquad (9)$$

If we use the mutual dependence of positive and negative examples on both
sides of a hyperplane then, taking into account that $N_{1r} = N_{1r}^+ + N_{1r}^-$ and N_{0r}
$= N_{0r}^+ + N_{0r}^-$, the resulting fuzzy set F and its complement F^C are defined as:

$$F = \left\{ \frac{N_r^- - N_{1r}^-}{N_r - N_{1r}^+ - N_{1r}^-}, \frac{N_r^+ - N_{1r}^+}{N_r - N_{1r}^+ - N_{1r}^-}, \frac{N_{1r}^-}{N_{1r}}, \frac{N_{1r}^+}{N_{1r}} \right\} \qquad (10)$$

$$F^C = \left\{ \frac{N_r^+ - N_{1r}^+}{N_r - N_{1r}^+ - N_{1r}^-}, \frac{N_r - N_{1r}^- - N_r^+}{N_r - N_{1r}^+ - N_{1r}^-}, \frac{N_{1r} - N_{1r}^-}{N_{1r}}, \frac{N_{1r} - N_{1r}^+}{N_{1r}} \right\} \qquad (11)$$

The four grades of membership (equations (10) and (11)) are used in Dombi's
operations [25] specified by equations (12) and (13) below (with F^C = H):

Fuzzy union

$$\mu_{F \cup H}(x) = \cfrac{1}{1 + [\,(\frac{1}{\mu_F(x)} - 1)^{-\lambda} + (\frac{1}{\mu_H(x)} - 1)^{-\lambda}\,]^{-\frac{1}{\lambda}}} \tag{12}$$

Fuzzy intersection

$$\mu_{F \cap H}(x) = \cfrac{1}{1 + [\,(\frac{1}{\mu_F(x)} - 1)^{\lambda} + (\frac{1}{\mu_H(x)} - 1)^{\lambda}\,]^{\frac{1}{\lambda}}} \tag{13}$$

where λ is a parameter by which different unions/intersections are distinguished, $\lambda \in (0, \infty)$. It is also assumed here, after [25], that Dombi's union equals one if the grades of membership $\mu_F(x)$ and $\mu_H(x)$ are both one, and Dombi's intersection equals zero if they are both zero. The parameter λ has to be estimated for a particular application. Then the fuzzy entropy measure is calculated according to the formula

$$f(F) = \frac{\sum \text{count}\,(F \cap F^C)}{\sum \text{count}\,(F \cup F^C)} \tag{14}$$

where $\sum$ count (sigma-count) is the cardinality of a fuzzy set.

Obtained fuzzy entropy is used to calculate the weights using the learning rule (7). In order to increase the chance of finding the global minimum the learning rule is also combined with Cauchy training [26] in the same manner as suggested in [11]:

$$W_{k+1} = W_k (1 - \zeta) \Delta W + \zeta \Delta W_{\text{random}} \tag{15}$$

where ζ is a control parameter.

The algorithm generates fuzzy subsets A and B at each node. The grades of membership for the fuzzy subsets A and B are initially defined for only two points "m_1" and "m_2" from which we construct the two fuzzy subsets. The points "m_1" and "m_2" are chosen experimentally from a range of *goodness measures*.

The grades of membership for fuzzy sets A and B at points "m_1" and "m_2" are defined as follows (16):

$$\mu_A(m_1) = \frac{N_{0r}^-}{N_{0r}}, \mu_A(m_2) = \frac{N_{0r}^+}{N_{0r}} \quad \text{and} \quad \mu_B(m_1) = \frac{N_{1r}^-}{N_{1r}}, \mu_B(m_2) = \frac{N_{1r}^+}{N_{1r}}$$

Taking into account that $N_{1r} = N_{1r}^+ + N_{1r}^-$ and $N_{0r} = N_{0r}^+ + N_{0r}^-$ results in the following expressions:

$$\mu_A(m_1) = \frac{N_{0r}^-}{N_{0r}^+ + N_{0r}^-} = \frac{N_r^+ - N_{1r}^+}{N_r - N_{1r}^+ - N_{1r}^-}$$

$$\mu_A(m_2) = \frac{N_{0r}^+}{N_{0r}^+ + N_{0r}^-} = \frac{N_r^- - N_{1r}^-}{N_r - N_{1r}^+ - N_{1r}^-} \tag{17}$$

$$\mu_B(m_1) = \frac{N_{\overline{1r}}}{N_{\overline{1r}}^+ + N_{\overline{1r}}}, \qquad \mu_B(m_2) = \frac{N_{\overline{1r}}^+}{N_{\overline{1r}}^+ + N_{\overline{1r}}}$$

Now, we define membership grades for the fuzzy sets A and B from the following functions (18):

$$\mu_A(x) = \begin{cases} \dfrac{x\,\mu_A(m_1)}{m_1} & \text{for } x \leq m_1 \\[2mm] \dfrac{\mu_A(m_2)\,(x - m_1) + \mu_A(m_1)(m_2 - x)}{m_2 - m_1} & \text{for } m_1 \leq x \leq m_2 \\[2mm] 0 & \text{for } x > m_2 \end{cases}$$

$$\mu_B(x) = \begin{cases} 0 & \text{for } x < m_1 \\[2mm] \dfrac{\mu_B(m_2)\,(x - m_1) + \mu_B(m_1)(m_2 - x)}{m_2 - m_1} & \text{for } m_1 \leq x \leq m_2 \\[2mm] \dfrac{\mu_B(m_2)\,((m_1 + m_2) - x)}{m_1} & \text{for } m_2 \leq x \leq m_1 + m_2 \\[2mm] 0 & \text{for } x > m_1 + m_2 \end{cases}$$

If at a certain level we have more than one subset A, and more than one subset B then we perform max operation to get the resulting grades of membership for just one A and one B. These sets are then used in the fuzzy decion making process - ranking of fuzzy sets.
The algorithm uses the following fuzzy decision making criteria.

Fuzzy Decision Making Criteria
For fuzzy subsets A and B, specified at some node of a network, the classification is based on the following definition (Definition 1) [11].

Definition 1. The ranking of fuzzy subsets is faithful, that is, the data samples are fully separated if the following *goodness values* for the ranking indices are established:

$$x_A = \frac{1}{3}(m_1 + m_2), \qquad x_B = \frac{2}{3}(m_1 + m_2) \tag{19}$$

using either the Yager's F1 [27] index or the centroidal method [28]. These indices (19) correspond to fuzzy entropy equal zero. More information about the above ranking indices can be found in [29].

Multicategory Classifier
   We will now consider recognition of C classes, where $C > 2$. The concepts introduced before will be used, however, the final nodes of the tree corresponding to the neural network will be associated now with two of the C classes (instead of one of two classes). We propose a new strategy based on adequate dichotomization of the classes.
   Our approach is to use the algorithm which now runs $(C - 1)$ ranking subroutines, each trying to achieve ranking indices specified by Definition 1, thus separating patterns of class c from all other patterns, and then repeating the

procedure until c equals C - 1. The fuzzy sets are formed and ranked for class c (the first fuzzy set) and for all (c - 1) classes combined together (the second fuzzy set).

The outline of the whole approach follows. The algorithm has five steps. Step 1 divides the input space into several subspaces; Step 2 counts the number of samples in those subspaces; Step 3 generates membership functions for fuzzy subsets out of those numbers; Step 4 executes ranking of formed fuzzy subsets; Step 5 determines separation of categories based on faithful ranking.

Step 1 - Divide the Input Space into Several Subspaces

First, we make use of the learning rule (7) and search for a hyperplane that minimizes the entropy function:

$$\min_{W_i} f(F) = \sum_{r=1}^{R} \frac{N_r}{N} \text{ entropy}(L,r)$$

where: L - is a level of a decision tree, R - total number of nodes in a layer, r - number of nodes, f (F) - entropy function.

Step 2 - Count the number of samples in resulting subspaces

Use here the notation specified in (1). The first class consists of patterns belonging to class c, and the other class consists of all other patterns. Start with random initial vector W_0.

Step 3 - Generate Membership Functions for Fuzzy Subsets

Generate membership functions, using Definition 1, for fuzzy subsets while creating nodes in hidden layers.

Step 4 - Execute Ranking of the Formed Fuzzy Subsets

The ranking is executed according to Yager F1 index [27] with g (u) = u or Murakami et al. [28] centroidal method for x_0 (20):

$$F1(A_i) = \frac{\int_0^1 g(u)\,\mu_{A_i}(u)\,du}{\int_0^1 \mu_{A_i}(u)\,du}, \quad \text{or} \quad x_0 = \frac{\int_0^1 u\,\mu_{A_i}(u)\,du}{\int_0^1 \mu_{A_i}(u)\,du}.$$

Step 5 - Determine Separation of Categories Based on Faithful Ranking

The ranking of fuzzy subsets is faithful, that is, the data samples are fully separated if the goodness measure values for the ranking indices (19) are established. If this is the case then increment c by 1 and return to step 1. Continue until c = C - 1. If the ranking is unfaithful, add a new node into the current layer and go t o Step 1.

To justify the validity of the approach, the method has been applied to a range of neural network benchmark data sets: spiral data, parity data (of dimension 2 through 8), and IRIS multidimensional data set [11], as well as twoclass data, Ishibushi data, and nonlinear function approximation problem [30]. However, as the proof of any theory ultimately lies in its utility for solving real life problems, the method was tested on the Tl-201 scintigraph data.

4 THE RESULTING ARCHITECTURE

Using the proposed algorithm, and 75% of the data for training, the feedforward neural network architecture, with two hidden layers with five nodes in each layer, was generated. The obtained neural network was used then to test the remaining patients from the 25% testing pool. The testing file consisted of 27 thirty dimentional vectors which were assigned to the following classes: 3 vectors representing patients with CCX, 10 representing patients with obstructions in LAD, 7 with obstructions in RCA, and 7 normal patients. All the obstructions have been classified correctly. An alternative method for diagnosing artery coronary obstructions, based on combining fuzzy generalized operators with decision rules generated by machine learning algorithms, is discussed in [31]. However, it did not produce perfect results.

5 CONCLUSIONS

The concept of utilizing fuzzy set theory with neural networks seems to provide a way for the design of knowledge based neural networks. The approach presented here is simple and straightforward in a sense that it is a quick-pass build-up procedure that does not require time consuming training. Hence, it has the same advantage as the fuzzy approach has over the neural approach, namely, it is simple and quick to construct. It also provides us with a whole neural network architecture, with nodes and connection weights between them, based on numerical data obtained from sensor measurements. The alternative trial-and-error approach in determining the structure of a neural network might be too difficult and time consuming.

ACKNOWLEDGMENT

The author would like to thank Lucy M. Goodenday, M.D., Department of Nuclear Cardiology, Medical College of Ohio, for having provided the stress thallium-201 myocardial scintigraph data used in this research.

REFERENCES

[1] P. Lippmann, An Introduction to Computing with Neural Nets, IEEE Acoustics, Speech, and Signal Processing 44 (1987) 4-22.
[2] B. Irie and S. Miyake, Capabilities of Three-Layered Perceptrons, in: Proc. of IEEE Inter. Conf. on Neural Networks, (1988) 641-648.
[3] S. Y. Kung and J. N. Hwang, An Algebraic Projection Analysis for Optimal Hidden Units Size and Learning Rates in Back-Propagation Learning, in: Proc. of IEEE Int. Conf. on Neural Networks, (1988) 363-370.
[4] J. A. Sirat and J. P. Nadal, Neural Trees: a New Tool For Classification, Network 1 (1990) 423-438.
[5] M. Bichsel and P. Seitz, Minimum Class Entropy: A Maximum Information Approach To Layered Networks, Neural Networks 2 (1989) 133-141.
[6] J. R. Quinlan, Induction of Decision Trees, Machine Learning 1 (1986) 81-106.
[7] T. G. Dietterich, H. Hild, and G. Bakiri, A Comparative Study of ID3 and Back-Propagation for English Text-to-Speech Mapping, in: Proc. of the 7th Int. Conference on Machine Learning, Texas (1990).
[8] D. H. Fisher and K. B. Mckusick, An Empirical Comparison of ID3 and Back-Propagation, in: Proc. of the 11th Int. Conf. on AI, (1989) 788-793.
[9] K. J. Cios and N. Liu, A Machine Learning Method for Generation of a Neural Network Architecture: A Continuous ID3 Algorithm, IEEE Neural Networks 2 (1992) 280-291.

[10]   S. E. Fahlman and C. Labiere, The Cascade-Correlation Learning Architecture, in Advances in Neural Information Processing Systems 2, D. S. Touretzky, Ed., (Morgan Kaufmann Publishers, Los Altos, 1990) 524-532.

[11] L. M. Sztandera, Dynamically Generated Neural Network Architectures, J. of Artificial Neural Systems 1 (1994) 41-66.

[12] L. A. Zadeh, Fuzzy Sets, Information and Control 8, (1965) 338-353.

[13] A. D. Nelson, R. F. Leighton, L. T. Andrews, L. S. Goodenday, L. Yonovitz, and D. Thekdi, A Comparison of Methods for the Analysis of Stress Thallium-201 Scintigraphs, in: Proc. of the Comp. in Cardiology Conference, (1979) 315-318.

[14] M. M. Gupta and J. Qi, On Fuzzy Neuron Models, in: Fuzzy Logic for the Management of Uncertainty, L. A. Zadeh and J. Kacprzyk, Eds., (John Wiley & Sons, Inc., New York, 1992) 479-491.

[15] H. Ishibuchi, R. Fujioka, and H. Tanaka, Possibility and Necessity Pattern Classification Using Neural Networks, Fuzzy Sets and Systems 48, (1992) 331-340.

[16] H. Ishibuchi, R. Fujioka, and H. Tanaka, Neural Networks that Learn from Fuzzy If-Then Rules, IEEE Fuzzy Systems 1 (2), (1993) 85-97.

[17] J. M. Keller and H. Tahani, Backpropagation Neural Networks for Fuzzy Logic, Information Sciences 62, (1992) 205-221.

[18] J. M. Keller, R. R. Yager, and H. Tahani, Neural Network Implementation of Fuzzy Logic, Fuzzy Sets and Systems 45, (1992) 1-12.

[19] K. Hirota and W. Pedrycz, Fuzzy Logic Neural Networks: Design and Computations, in: Proc. of the IJCNN'91 (2), Singapore, (1991) 1588-1593.

[20] Y. Hayashi, E. Czogala, and J. J. Buckley, Fuzzy Neural Controller, in: Proc. of 1st Int. Conference on Fuzzy and Neural Systems, San Diego, (1992) 197-202.

[21] B. Kosko, Neural Networks and Fuzzy Systems, (Prentice Hall, Englewood Cliffs, 1992).

[22] L. X. Wang and J. M. Mendel, Generating Fuzzy Rules by Learning from Examples, IEEE Systems, Man, and Cybernetics 22 (6), (1992) 1414-1427.

[23] K. Hornik, Approximation Capabilities of Multilayer Feedforward Networks, Neural Networks 4, (1991) 251-257.

[24] L. X. Wang, Fuzzy Systems are Universal Approximators, in: Proc. of 1st Int. Conference on Fuzzy and Neural Systems, San Diego, (1992) 1163- 1169.

[25] J. Dombi, A General Class of Fuzzy Operators, the De Morgan Class of Fuzzy Operators and Fuzziness Measures, Fuzzy Sets and Systems 8, (1982) 149-163.

[26] H. Szu and R. Hartley, Fast Simulated Annealing, Phys. Lett. A 122 (8) (1987) 157-162.

[27]   R. R.Yager, On Choosing Between Fuzzy Subsets, Kybernetes 9, (1980) 151-154.

[28] S. Murakami, H. Maeda and S. Immamura, Fuzzy Decision Analysis on the Development of Centralized Regional Energy Control System, in: Preprints of IFAC Conference on Fuzzy Information, Knowledge Representation and Decision Analysis, (1983) 353-358.

[29] L. M. Sztandera, A Comparative Study of Ranking Fuzzy Sets Defined by a Neural Network Algorithm - Justification for a Centroidal Method, Archives of Control Sciences 4 (1/2), (1995) 89-111.

[30]. L. M. Sztandera, Fuzzy Neural Trees, Information Sciences 90 (1/4), (1996) 155-177.

[31] K. J. Cios, L.S. Goodenday, and L. M. Sztandera, Hybrid Intelligence Systems for Diagnosing Coronary Stenosis - Combining Fuzzy Generalized Operators with Decision Rules Generated by Machine Learning Algorithms, IEEE Engineering in Medicine and Biology 13 (5), (1994) 723-729.

Coevolutionary Game Theoretic Multi-Agent Systems

Franciszek Seredynski

Institute of Computer Science, Polish Academy of Sciences
Ordona 21, 01-237 Warsaw, Poland
sered@ipipan.waw.pl

Abstract. Multi-agent systems based on N-person games with limited interaction are considered. We are interested in the global behavior of the team of players, measured by the average payoff received by a player. To evolve a global behavior in the system, we propose a coevolutionary algorithm, where only local fitness functions are evaluated while the global criterion is optimised. The multi-agent system is applied to develop a distributed algorithm of dynamic mapping tasks in parallel computers.

1 Introduction

Growing complexity of real life systems, such as e.g. parallel and distributed computers needs new paradigms to control them efficiently. Considering such systems as a collection of individuals acting selfishly and interacting to fulfil their own goals may serve as a useful metaphor for a distributed control in such systems. The consequence of this assumption is conflict between individuals, and therefore game theory modelling conflict has been accepted as a useful tool to study the behavior of complex systems.

A game-theoretic model which has received much attention of late is the prisoner's dilemma (PD) [1]. This game has been explored to yield insight into the conditions of cooperating and defecting between players. The distinctive features of PD is a focus on a player's individual goal. Cooperation in this model is desired and observed, but it is not the ultimate aim of a player. In the area of Distributed Artificial Intelligence (DAI), game-theoretic models are also the subject of current research [5]. In many DAI applications, a global collective behavior of the multi-agent system is expected, rather than simply a fulfilment of players' individual goals. Competing players should act in such systems as a decision group choosing their actions to realise a global goal.

In this paper we present an evolutionary model of N-person games which can be considered as a variant of PD model. The model provides a framework to study rules of global collective behavior in multi-agent systems.

The paper is organized as follows. The following section presents the model of noncooperative N-person games with limited interaction. In Section 3, we propose a coevolutionary distributed genetic algorithm-based scheme to implement the model of iterated N-person games. Section 4 presents an application of the model to a problem of dynamic mapping tasks of a parallel program in parallel computers. The last section contains conclusions.

2 Games with Limited Interaction

A game is given by a set $N = \{0, 1, \ldots, N - 1\}$ of N players, set S_k of actions for each player $k \in N$, and a payoff function u_k which depends only on its own action s_k and the actions of its n_k neighbors in the game. Such a model, termed a game with limited interaction, have been considered from positions of collective behavior of learning automata [12, 13, 9].

The game can be represented by an oriented graph $G = < V, E >$ called an interaction graph. V is the set of nodes corresponding to the set of players while set E represents the pattern of interaction between players: arcs incoming to the k-th node define players whose actions influence the payoff of player k.

In the paper we consider a class of games with limited interaction characterized by a regular interaction graph ($n_k = r$, where r is the degree of the interaction graph) and called homogeneous games. In such games, the payoff function is the same for all players.

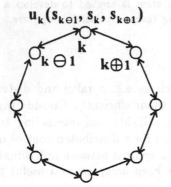

$$u_k(s_{k\ominus 1}, s_k, s_{k\oplus 1})$$

Fig. 1. Interaction graph of a game

Table 1

$s_{k\ominus 1}$	s_k	$s_{k\oplus 1}$	$u_k^1(s_{k\ominus 1}, s_k, s_{k\oplus 1})$
0	D	D	D	10
1	D	D	C	0
2	D	C	D	0
3	D	C	C	0
4	C	D	D	0
5	C	D	C	50
6	C	C	D	0
7	C	C	C	30

The simplest homogeneous game with limited interaction is a game on a ring (Fig. 1). For the game on a ring we can simplify notation of the payoff function to read $u_k(s_k, s_{k1}, s_{k2}, \ldots, s_{kn_k}) = u_k(s_{k\ominus 1}, s_k, s_{k\oplus 1})$, where $\ominus$ and $\oplus$ denotes subtraction and addition modulo N. The payoff function of any player in the game on the ring depends on his actions and on the actions of his two neighbors $k \ominus 1$ and $k \oplus 1$. Assuming that the set S_k of actions for each player is limited to two alternative actions C-cooperate, and D-defect, the payoff function has 8 entries and Table 1 shows an example of a payoff functions u_k^1 used in our study.

It is assumed that each player acts in the game independently and selects his action to maximise his payoff. If players play the game defined by the payoff function u_k^1 and player k and his neighbors $k \ominus 1$ and $k \oplus 1$ all select action **D** in a trial, his payoff will be defined by a sequence of actions (**D,D,D**) and is equal to 10 (entry 0 of Table 1). If player k selects action **C** while both his neighbors select action **D**, player k will receive the payoff equal to 0.

The most widely used solution concept for noncooperative games is a Nash equilibrium point. A Nash point is an N-tuple of actions, one for each player, such that anyone who deviates from it unilaterally cannot possibly improve his expected payoff. If s_k denotes an action of the k-th player, then a Nash equilibrium point is an N-tuple $(s_0^*, s_1^*, \ldots, s_k^*, \ldots, s_{N-1}^*)$ such that $u_k(s_0^*, s_1^*, \ldots, s_k^*, \ldots, s_{N-1}^*)$ $\geq u_k(s_0^*, s_1^*, \ldots, s_k, \ldots, s_{N-1}^*)$ for $s_k \neq s_k^*$ and $k = 0, 1, \ldots, N - 1$.

A Nash equilibrium point will define payoffs of all the players in the game. However, we are not interested in the payoff of a given player, but in some global measure of the payoff received by players. This measure can be e.g. the average payoff $\overline{u}(s)$ received by a player as a result of combined actions' $s = (s_0, s_1, \ldots, s_{N-1})$, i.e.

$$\overline{u}(s) = \left(\sum_{k=0}^{N-1} u_k(s) \right) /N, \qquad (1)$$

and it will be our global criterion to evaluate the behavior of the players in the game. The question which arises immediately concerns the value of the function (1) in a Nash point. Unfortunately, this value can be very low.

Analysing all possible actions' combinations in the game and evaluating their prices, i.e. a value $\overline{u}(s)$, we can find actions' combinations characterized by a maximal price and we can call them maximal price points. Maximal price points are actions' combinations which maximise the global criterion (1), but they can be reached by players only if they are Nash points. A maximal price point usually is not a Nash point and the question which must be solved is how to convert a maximal price point into a Nash point. The solution of this problem for homogeneous games is the concept of a conjugated exchange process [14]

For the game on a ring from Fig. 1, the conjugated exchange process transforms the payoff u_k of the player k into a new payoff w_k in the following way:

$$u_k \longrightarrow w_k = (u_{k \ominus 1} + u_k + u_{k \oplus 1})/3. \qquad (2)$$

3 Coevolutionary Systems

The need of an extension of the traditional GAs [4, 6, 3] into the direction of coevolutionary systems has been lately recognized. While a *cooperative coevolutionary approach* to function optimization has been proposed [8], *loosely coupled GAs (LCGAs)* have been proposed [11] to support the above described game-theoretic model of computation, suitable for distributed decision-making.

The modyfied algorithm of LCGAs implementing the game on a ring is shown in Fig. 2. The algorithm can be specified in the following way:

#1: for each player create an initial subpopulation of his actions
- create randomly for each player an initial subpopulation of size n of player actions taking values from the set S_k of his actions; Fig. 2 shows the initial subpopulations of the size $n = 4$ of actions for players $k \ominus 1$, k and $k \oplus 1$ respectively; the value of n defines a game horison for a player; actions predefined in a subpopulation of a given player will be used in subsequent n games (see, Fig. 3)

#2: play a single game

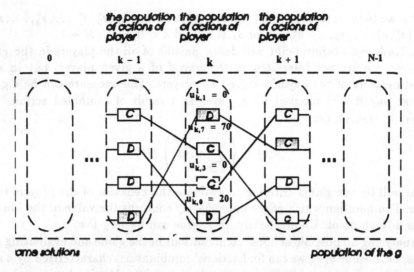

Fig. 2. Loosely coupled GA-based system

- in a discrete moment of time each player selects randomly one action from the set of actions predefined in his subpopulation and not used until now, and presents it to his neighbours in the game; shadowed actions in Fig. 2 shows possible situation after the first trial: players $k \ominus 1$, k and $k \oplus 1$ have selected respectively actions **D**, **D** and **C**; the chain of selected actions can be interpreted as a possible solution of the game.
- calculate the output of the game: each player evaluates his local payoff u_k in the game; in the game with the function u_k^1 player k obtains for action **D** (Fig. 2, shadowed box) the payoff $u_{k,1}(\mathbf{D}, \mathbf{D}, \mathbf{C}) = 0$
- if the game with the conjugate exchange process is played, each player informs his neighbours in the game about his current payoff, and calculates his modified payoff w_k.

#3: repeat step #2 until n games are played
#4: for each player create a new subpopulation of his actions (see, Fig. 3)

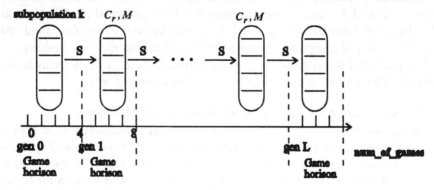

Fig. 3. Evolving a subpopulation k in LCGAs from Fig. 2

- after playing n games each player knows the value of his payoff received for a given action from his subpopulation (see, Fig. 3); chains of actions present actually found solutions of the game

- the values of the payoff are considered as values of a local fitness function defined during a given generation (initially, gen 0) of GA; standard GAs operators of selection (S), crossover (C_r) and mutation (M) are applied locally to subpopulations of actions; these actions will be used by players in games played in the next game horizon

#5: return to step #2 until the termination condition is satisfied

- if a given subpopulation evolved during $l+1$ generations then the number of played games num_of_games can be defined as $num\_of\_games = n * (l + 1)$.

Let us analyse payoff functions u_k^1 from Table 1 for the game on the ring. The game with the payoff function u_k^1 has the maximal price point $s_{mp} = $ (C,C,C,C,C,C,C,C). Each player taking part in the game defined by the vector of actions s_{mp} obtains a payoff equal to $u_{k,7}^1(C,C,C) = 30$. The average payoff $\overline{u}_k^1$ received by the team of players achieves the maximal value equal to 30. However, the actions' combination s_{mp} is not a Nash point because it is reasonable for each player to change his action $C \rightarrow D$ and obtain a higher payoff equal to $u_{k,5}^1(C,D,C) = 50$. The game has a Nash point $s_N = (D,D,D,D,D,D,D,D)$. One can see that in this Nash point there is no reason for any player to change his action $D \rightarrow C$ and obtain instead of the payoff $u_{k,0}^1(D,D,D) = 10$, a lower payoff equal to $u_{k,2}^1(D,C,D) = 0$. We can therefore expect that in such a game players will not achieve the maximal price point but will rather play this Nash game. It is easy to see that introducing into the game a local cooperation defined by the conjugate exchange process (2) converts the maximal price point into the Nash point. We can expect that in this game players will find and play the game corresponding to the maximal price point.

Below we present the results of experiments with the game on the ring with the number of players $N = 16$. In such a game, the number of possible game solutions (actions' combinations) is equal to 2^{16}. Figs 4 and 5 show the average payoff $\overline{U}(s) = (\sum_{i=1}^{l+1}\sum_{j=1}^{n}\sum_{k=0}^{N-1} u_k(s))/(n*(l+1)*N)$ of a player, obtained in the game. Each point of the curves represents the mean of 30 runs of the game.

Fig. 4 presents the results of an experimental study of the game without a local cooperation defined by the conjugated exchange process. One can see that for the observed range of mutation probabilities, the average payoff received by a player depends little on p_m under constant n, but it depends on the size n of a population of player actions. With increasing n, the average payoff received by a player in the game becomes closer to the value 10 defined by the Nash point, and is far from the value defined by a maximal price point.

Results of an experimental study of the game with cooperation according to the conjugated exchange process are shown in Fig. 5. One can see that similarly as in the previous experiment, the average payoff received by a player depends little on p_m under a constant n, but it depends largely on n. The qualitative change of the players' behavior in the game with the conjugated exchange process is of note, if compared with their behavior in the same game without the conjugated exchange process. The players discover and play the maximal price point when n is large enough. They now show the ability of the global behavior

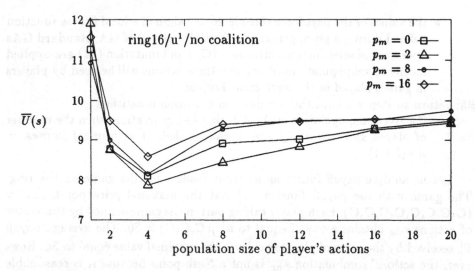

Fig. 4. The average payoff received by a player during 250 generations

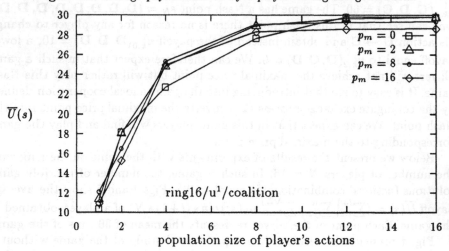

Fig. 5. The average payoff received by a player during 250 generations

which is realized is in a fully distributed manner, without any knowledge about either the global optimization criterion or a number of players participating in the game.

4 Application: Dynamic Mapping Problem

Mapping [7] and scheduling [2] parallel programs in parallel and distributed computers are one of the central questions to be solved to efficiently use their computational power. One of the possible solutions of e.g. the mapping problem is a coordinated migration of program modules in a parallel and distributed system [9, 10]

Current results concerning mapping communicating processes of a parallel program into parallel architectures show that applying static mapping algorithms raises the efficiency of using parallel computers, when characteristics of programs do not change during their execution. However, if characteristics of the programs change in time, static policies can not be efficiently applied.

We propose an approach to dynamic mapping based on a multi-agent interpretation of a parallel program migrating in a parallel system environment to search an optimal allocation of program modules in a topology of a parallel system. To find multi-agent system strategies of migration in the system graph we use LCGAs presented in the previous section.

Models of parallel programs and parallel computers presented below are oriented on MIMD machine environment and are formulated as follows. A parallel program is represented by a weighted undirected graph $G_p =< V_p, E_p >$ with a set V_p of N_p nodes and a set E_p of edges. The nodes of the program graph represent processes and the edges represent a fixed communication pattern between processes. Node weights b_k characterize computation costs of the processes and edge weights a_{kl} characterize a communication cost between a given pair of processes located in neighbouring system nodes. A parallel computer is represented by an undirected graph $G_s =< V_s, E_s >$ called a system graph, with a set V_s representing nodes of the system and a set E_s representing an interconnection pattern of the system .

Let θ be a mapping function from the vertex set of the program graph to the vertex set of the system graph and Θ the set of all mapping functions, i.e. $\Theta = \{\theta : V_p \rightarrow V_s\}$. We suppose that a local cost function $C(k, \theta)$ is defined for kth program node mapped to the system graph. This function is defined as [9, 10]

$$C(k, \theta) = 0.5 \sum_{l=1}^{r_k} a_{kl} * d_{min}(\theta(k), \theta(l)) + \sum_{n=1}^{n_i} b_n, \qquad (3)$$

and it describes a cost of communications of the kth program node with its neighbour program nodes, and the computational load of a system node to which the kth program node was mapped, where r_k is the number of neighbour program nodes of the kth node; $d_{min}(\theta(k), \theta(l))$ is a minimal number of hops between system nodes $\theta(k)$ and $\theta(l)$ where are located neighbour program nodes k and l respectively, and n_i is a number of program nodes located in the system node $\theta(k)$.

The problem of static mapping can be formulated as the problem of seeking a mapping function $\theta \in \Theta$ that minimises the total cost function $C(\theta)$ defined as a sum of the local cost functions (3), i.e.

$$\min_{\theta \in \Theta} (C(\theta) = \sum_{k \in V_p} C(k, \theta)). \qquad (4)$$

The dynamic mapping formulation of the problem can now be easily obtained due to locally defined cost functions and a multi-agent interpretation of the mapping problem.

We assume that a collection of agents is assigned to nodes of the program graph in a such way that one agent is assigned to one program node. Each agent has some number of actions which influence a local cost function of a program node attached to the agent. If nodes of the program graph together with agents attached to them are placed in some way, e.g. randomly into the system graph, the agents' actions can be interpreted in terms of possible moves of the agents in the system graph.

The dynamic mapping algorithm can be specified in the following way:

– agents assigned to the processes and located in some system nodes are considered as players taking part in a game with limited interaction; each agent-player has $r + 1$ actions interpreted as follows: do not migrate or migrate to one of r nearest neighbour system nodes, where r is the degree of the system graph. Taking an action by a player corresponds to the player simulating the action, not a physical move
– each player has a local cost function (3) describing the communications and computational costs
– the objective of each player is to minimise its local cost function
– the objective of the game is to find the optimal (in the sense of the global criterion (4)) directions of the migration of the program graph in the system graph while each player can move at the distance of one hop only
– after a predefined number of games a migration of the program nodes (together with the agent-players) is performed; the game starts again.

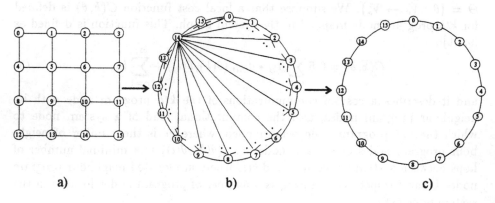

Fig. 6. Behavior of a dynamically changing program represented by a sequence of three program graphs respectively a), b) and c)

The coevolutionary multi-agent system with LCGAs implementation was used to solve the dynamic mapping problem. In the experiment described below it is supposed that a parallel program dynamically changes in time during its execution (see, Fig. 6) and a target parallel machine is a torus 4×4. Fig. 6 shows behavior of the parallel program represented by a sequence of three graphs describing changing in time the communication pattern and a computation load of the program. Fig. 7 shows performance of the dynamic mapping algorithm implemented with use of LCGAs. The program represented initially by a grid

4×4 from Fig. 6a (with parameters $a_{kl} = 10$, $b_k = 2$) is randomly mapped into the target system, what results in the initial physical allocation of the program with the cost $C(\theta) = 450$ (see, Fig. 7). It is assumed that the execution of the program begins, but at the same time the mapping algorithm starts its work monitoring the system, and searching optimal migration strategies for program modules. One can see, that during the first 50 generations of LCGAs, the system is able to find directions of program modules migration in a fully distributed way, providing decrease in the the cost allocation. After 50 generations, a physical migration of the program modules is performed, which results in a new, better allocation, and the dynamic mapping algorithm continues to work. After three migrations of the program graph a near optimal mapping is found.

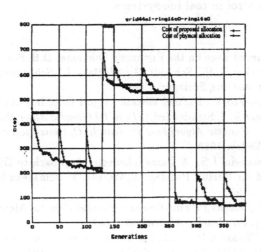

Fig. 7. Performance of a distributed dynamic mapping algorithm

It is assumed that after 130 generations the parallel program changes its communication pattern of activity and computation load, which is modelled by a complete graph shown in Fig. 6b ($a_{kl} = 2$, $b_k = 10$). It is clear that the previously found allocation of the program is not optimal now, and the value of the cost function $C(\theta)$ is now near to 800 (see, Fig. 7). The distributed dynamic mapping algorithm starts immediately to search for a new optimal allocation, without the need of any central synchronization (which would be necessary in the case of standard GAs).

After 260 generations the parallel program changes its communication activity again, as modelled by the graph from Fig. 6c ($a_{kl} = 2$, $b_k = 10$). The behavior of the distributed dynamic mapping algorithm is similar to that described above. The algorithm is able to catch the changes of the program graph parameters without any central synchronization and continues in a fully distributed way searching for an optimal mapping.

5 Conclusions

We have considered the model of games with limited interaction. We addressed the problem of a global behavior of the team of players in the game. To evolve a global behavior in the system, we proposed a coevolutionary algorithm with an evaluation of the local fitness functions of players. Conducted experiments have shown that the system is capable of evolving a global behavior, if rules of local cooperation between players are preserved. Behavior of the system is similar to that predicted by game theory with its concept of a Nash equilibrium. We have applied the developed coevolutionary multi-agent system to solve the dynamic mapping problem. We believe that presented results give rise to think that the developed model can serve as a useful metaphor for distributed decision-making and distributed control in real life systems.

References

1. *BioSystems*, Special issue on the Prisoner's Dilemma, D.B. Fogel (ed.), 37:1-2, 1996
2. Błażewicz J., Ecker K.H., Schmidt G., Węglarz J., *Scheduling in Computer and Manufacturing Systems*, Springer, 1994
3. Dorigo M., Maniezzo V., Parallel Genetic Algorithms: Introduction and Overview of Current Research. J. Stender (ed.), *Parallel Genetic Algorithms*, IOS Press, 1993
4. Goldberg D.E., *Genetic Algorithms in Search, Optimization and Machine Learning*, Addison-Wesley, 1989
5. Levy R., Rosenschein J.S., A Game Theoretic Approach to Distributed Artificial Intelligence and the Pursuit Problem. E. Werner, Y. Demazeau (eds.), *Decentralized A.I.-3*, Elsevier, 1992
6. Manderick B., Spiessens P., Fine-Grained Parallel Genetic Algorithms, *Proc. of the Third Int. Conf. on Genetic Algorithms*, 1989
7. Norman M.G., Thanish P., Models of Machines and Computation for Mapping in Multicomputers, *ACM Computing Surveys*, v. 25, N3, 1993
8. Potter M.A., De Jong K.A., A Cooperative Coevolutionary Approach to Function Optimization, *Parallel Problem Solving from Nature - PPSN III*, Y. Davidor, H. -P. Schwefel and R. Männer (eds.), LNCS 866, Springer, 1994
9. Seredynski F., Task Allocation by a Team of Learning Automata, *Proc. of the 6th Int. Symp. on Methodologies for Intelligent Systems*, K.S. Harber (ed.), Charlotte, USA, 1991
10. Seredynski F., Frejlak P., Genetic Algorithms Implementation of Process Migration Strategies, *Parallel Computing: Trends and Applications*, G.R. Joubert, D. Trystram, P.J. Peters and D.J. Evans (eds.), Elsevier, 1994
11. Seredynski F., Loosely Coupled Distributed Genetic Algorithms, *Parallel Problem Solving from Nature - PPSN III*, Y. Davidor, H. -P. Schwefel and R. Männer (eds.), LNCS 866, Springer, 1994
12. Tsetlin M.L., *Automaton Theory and Modelling of Biological Systems*, Academic Press. N.Y., 1973
13. Varshavsky V.I., Some Effects in the Collective Behaviour of Automata, *Machine Intelligence* 7, Edinburgh University Press, 1972
14. Varshavsky V.I., Zabolotnyj A.M., Seredynski F., Homogeneous Games with an Associated Exchange Process, *Engineering Cybernetics*, v.15, N6, 1977

Searching for Features Defined by Hyperplanes

Nguyen Hung Son, Nguyen Sinh Hoa, Andrzej Skowron

Institute of Mathematics, Warsaw University
Banacha 2, Warsaw Poland.
email: skowron/son/hoa@mimuw.edu.pl

Abstract. We consider decision tables with real value conditional attributes and we present a method for extraction of features defined by hyperplanes in a multi-dimensional affine space. These new features are often more relevant for object classification than the features defined by hyperplanes parallel to axes. The method generalizes an approach presented in [18] in case of hyperplanes not necessarily parallel to the axes. We propose genetic strategies searching for hyperplanes discerning between objects from different decision classes.

1 Introduction

Several approaches have been proposed [6], [7], [8], [11], [12], [15], [16] to find effective methods for real value attributes quantization (discretization). In [18] we have presented a method based on the rough set and Boolean reasoning approaches. The new attributes are defined by cuts i.e. hyperplanes parallel to axes. In this paper we apply genetic strategies to define new attributes by hyperplanes not necessarily parallel to axes. Our approach allows for more flexible change of hyperplane positions than those proposed in [7], [12] and in the consequence we obtain, for some benchmarks, better quality of new object classification than the reported in [7], [12]. The quality of any hyperplane can be measured in different ways (see e.g. [7], [12]). We apply as a basic measure a function counting the number of object pairs from different decision classes discerned by the hyperplane. We suggest also to take into account, as a kind of penalty measure, the number of objects pairs from the same decision class discerned by the hyperplane. Any hyperplane is represented by a set of some vectors parallel to two-dimensional hyperplanes and a point on a fixed axis. This allows to represent enough large set of hyperplanes and to keep the representation compact. We use genetic strategies [9], [13] in searching for hyperplanes with a sub-optimal quality.

Our approach can be also treated as an application of Boolean reasoning for extraction from the set of features defined by hyperplanes (not necessarily parallel to axes) those which define relevant features. Nevertheless the problem is more complex than the discussed in [18] (where only hyperplanes parallel to axes are considered) because the search space of features is larger. This is the reason that we use genetic algorithms to obtain efficient searching heuristics.

Our approach to quantization (discretization) of real value attributes can also be treated as an attempt to find new features more relevant for unseen object classification. In this case the quality of quantization is evaluated from the point of view of classification quality of unseen so far objects.

The paper is structured as follows. In Section 1 we introduce some basic definitions and notation. The quality measures of hyperplanes are defined in Section 2. The hyperplane representation is discussed in Section 3. We present our learning algorithm using a genetic strategy in Section 4. The complexity of our algorithm is discussed in Section 5. The results of experiments are reported in Section 6. We conclude with some remarks related to further research problems.

2 Rough Set Preliminaries

Information system is a pair $\mathbf{A} = (U, A)$ where U is a non-empty, finite set called the universe and A is a non-empty, finite set of *attributes*, i.e. $a : U \to V_a$ for $a \in A$, where V_a is called the *value set* of attribute a. Elements of U are called *objects*.

Every information system $\mathbf{A} = (U, A)$ and a non-empty set $B \subseteq A$ define a *B-information function* by $Inf_B(x) = \{(a, a(x)) : a \in B\}$ for $x \in U$. The set $\{Inf_A(x) : x \in U\}$ is called the *A-information set* and it is denoted by $INF(\mathbf{A})$.

We consider a special case of information systems called decision tables. A *decision table* is any information system of the form $\mathbf{A} = (U, A \cup \{d\})$, where $d \notin A$ is a distinguished attribute called *decision*. The elements of A are called *conditions*.

We assume that the set V_d of values of the decision d is equal to $\{1, \ldots, r(d)\}$ for some positive integer called *the range of d*. The decision d determines the partition $\{C_1, \ldots, C_{r(d)}\}$ of the universe U, where $C_k = \{u \in U : d(u) = k\}$ for $1 \le k \le r(d)$. The set C_k is called the *k-th decision class* of $\mathbf{A}$.

Let $\mathbf{A} = (U, A)$ be an information system. With any subset of attributes $B \subseteq A$, an equivalence relation, denoted by $IND_A(B)$ (or $IND(B)$, in short) called the *B-indiscernibility relation*, is associated and defined by:

$$IND(B) = \{(u, u') \in U \times U : a(u) = a(u') \text{ for any } a \in B\}.$$

Objects u, u' satisfying relation $IND(B)$ are indiscernible by attributes from B.

A minimal subset B of $\mathbf{A}$ such that $IND(A) = IND(B)$ is called a *reduct* of $\mathbf{A}$.

If $\mathbf{A} = (U, A \cup \{d\})$ is a decision table and $B \subseteq A$ then we define a function $\partial_B : U \to 2^{\{1, \ldots, r(d)\}}$, called the *generalized decision* in $\mathbf{A}$, by

$$\partial_B(u) = \{i : \exists_{u' \in U} [(u' \, IND(B) \, u) \wedge (d(u') = i)]\}.$$

A decision table $\mathbf{A}$ is called *consistent (deterministic)* if $card(\partial_A(u)) = 1$ for any $u \in U$, otherwise $\mathbf{A}$ is *inconsistent (non-deterministic)*.

A subset B of the set A of attributes of decision table $\mathbf{A} = (U, A \cup \{d\})$ is a relative reduct of $\mathbf{A}$ iff B is a minimal set with respect to the following property: $\partial_B = \partial_A$. The set of all relative reducts of $\mathbf{A}$ is denoted by $RED(\mathbf{A}, d)$.

A *decision rule* of a decision table $\mathbf{A} = (U, A \cup \{d\})$ is any expression of the form $\tau \Rightarrow d = i$ where $i \in V_d$ and τ is a Boolean combination of descriptors i.e. expressions $a = v$ where $a \in A$ and $v \in V_a$. If τ is a Boolean combination of descriptors then by $\tau_\mathbf{A}$ we denoted the meaning of τ in the decision table $\mathbf{A}$, i.e. the set of all objects in U with the property τ, defined inductively as follows:

i. if τ has the form $(a = v)$ then $\tau_\mathbf{A} = \{u \in U : a(u) = v\}$;

ii. $(\tau \wedge \tau')_\mathbf{A} = \tau_\mathbf{A} \cap \tau'_\mathbf{A}$; $(\tau \vee \tau')_\mathbf{A} = \tau_\mathbf{A} \cup \tau'_\mathbf{A}$.

The decision rule $\tau \Rightarrow d = i$ for $\mathbf{A}$ is *true* in $\mathbf{A}$ iff $\tau_\mathbf{A} \subseteq (d = i)_\mathbf{A}$; if $\tau_\mathbf{A} = (d = i)_\mathbf{A}$ we say that the rule is $\mathbf{A}$-*exact*.

3 Hyperplane quality

Let $\mathbf{A} = (U, A \cup \{d\})$ be a decision table [14] where $U = \{u_1, \ldots, u_n\}$ is a finite set of objects called the *universe* and let $A = \{f_1, \ldots, f_k\}$ be a *set of real value features (attributes)* determined on objects i.e. $f_i : U \to \Re$ is a real function from universe U for any $i \in \{1, \ldots, k\}$ and $d : U \to \{1, \ldots, r\}$ is a *decision*.

Assuming that objects u_i are discernible by conditional attributes we can characterize them as points:

$$P_i = (f_1(u_i), f_2(u_i), ..., f_k(u_i)) \text{ for } i \in \{1, 2, \ldots, n\}$$

in k-dimensional affine space $\Re^k$.

Any of these points belongs to one of the decision classes $C_1, C_2, ..., C_r$ defined by the decision d i.e.

$$C_i = \{u \in U : d(u) = i\} \text{ for } i \in \{1, \ldots, r\}.$$

Any hyperplane in $\Re^k$:

$$H = \{(x_1, x_2, ..., x_k) \in \Re^k : a_1 x_1 + a_2 x_2 + \cdots + a_k x_k + a = 0\}$$
$$\text{for some } a, a_1, a_2, \ldots, a_k \in \Re$$

splits C_i into two subclasses defined by:

$$C_i^{U,H} = \{u \in C_i : a_1 f_1(u) + a_2 f_2(u) + \cdots + a_k f_k(u) + a \geq 0\};$$

$$C_i^{L,H} = \{u \in C_i : a_1 f_1(u) + a_2 f_2(u) + ... + a_k f_k(u) + a < 0\}.$$

In the paper we will apply some measures estimating the quality of hyperplanes with respect to the decision classes $C_1, C_2, ..., C_r$.

In [18] we have applied the following measure to estimate the quality of hyperplanes parallel to axes:

$$award(H) = \sum_{i \neq j} card\left(C_i^{U,H}\right) \cdot card\left(C_j^{L,H}\right)$$

If $award(H) > award(H')$ then the number of discernible pairs of objects from different decision classes by the hyperplane H is greater than the corresponding number defined by the hyperplane H'.

Let $u_i = card(C_i^{U,H})$ and $l_i = card(C_i^{L,H})$ for $i = 1,\ldots,r$ and let $u = u_1 + \cdots + u_r$; $l = l_1 + \cdots + l_r$. Then we have the following equality:

$$award(H) = \sum_{i \neq j} u_i l_j = u \cdot l - \sum_{i=1}^{r} u_i l_i$$

We can also define the function $penalty(H)$ as follows:

$$penalty(H) = \sum_{i=1}^{r} card\left(C_i^{U,H}\right) \cdot card\left(C_i^{L,H}\right) = \sum_{i=1}^{r} u_i l_i$$

We apply here the function $award$ to measure the quality of hyperplanes not necessarily parallel to axes i.e.

$$power_1(H) = award(H).$$

One cam also use the more advanced functions like:

$$power_2(H) = \frac{award(H)}{penalty(H) + c};$$

$$power_3(H) = w_1 \cdot award(H) - w_2 \cdot award(H).$$

Applications of these functions will be discussed in our next paper. Here we report the results of experiments with $award(H)$ only. We would like to point out that the application of the penalty function can be an effective tool in searching for relevant features not only defined by hyperplanes.

4 Hyperplane representation

Our goal is to present a searching algorithm for the best hyperplanes with respect to a fixed quality measure of hyperplanes. It is obvious that the hyperplane representation should be efficient i.e. it should allow to represent as many hyperplanes by as small as possible number of bits. Moreover, because we will apply genetic algorithms the complexity of the fitness function should be taken into account. Hence we use the following representation.

Let us fix an axis (e.g. the x_1) and a positive integer l. In any two-dimensional plane $L(x_1, x_i)$ we choose vectors $v_1^i, v_2^i, ..., v_{2^l}^i$ (which are not parallel to x_1) defined by:

$$v_j^i = \left[\alpha_j^i, 0, \ldots, 0, \overset{i\text{-th position}}{1}, 0, \ldots, 0\right] \text{ for } i = 2, .., k \text{ and } j = 1, .., 2^l$$

These vectors can be chosen e.g. by applying one of the following steps:

1. Random choice of 2^l values: $\alpha_1^i, \alpha_2^i, \ldots, \alpha_{2^l}^i$.
2. The values $\alpha_1^i, \alpha_2^i, \ldots, \alpha_{2^l}^i$ are chosen in such a way that all angles between successive vectors are equal i.e. $\alpha_j^i = ctg\left(j\frac{\pi}{1+2^l}\right)$
3. The sequence $\alpha_1^i, \alpha_2^i, \ldots, \alpha_{2^l}^i$ is an arithmetical progression (e.g. $\alpha_j^i = j - 2^{l-1}$).

Let us observe that any vector from the list $v_1^i, v_2^i, \ldots, v_{2^l}^i$ can be represented by l bits, namely the vector v_j^i is encoded by the l-bit string $binary(j)$ being the binary representation of integer j.

It is easy to observe that any set of vectors of the form $\left\{v_{j_2}^2, v_{j_3}^3, \ldots, v_{j_k}^k\right\}$ is linearly independent since they are of the following form:

$$v_{j_2}^2 = \left[\alpha_{j_2}^2, 1, 0, 0, \ldots, 0\right]$$
$$v_{j_3}^3 = \left[\alpha_{j_3}^3, 0, 1, 0, \ldots, 0\right]$$
$$\cdots\cdots\cdots$$
$$v_{j_k}^k = \left[\alpha_{j_k}^k, 0, 0, 0, \ldots, 1\right]$$

Let $\mathbf{L} = Lin(v_{j_2}^2, v_{j_3}^3, \ldots, v_{j_k}^k)$ be a linear subspace generated by vectors $v_{j_2}^2$, $v_{j_3}^3, \ldots, v_{j_k}^k$ Hence $rank(\mathbf{L}) = k - 1$. To define a hyperplane spanned over these vectors it is necessary to fix a point on $\Re^k$. Since vectors of the form $v_{j_i}^i$ are not parallel to the axis x_1 one can choose this point on axis x_1 i.e. a point of the form $\mathbf{P}_0 = (p, 0, 0, \ldots, 0)$.

Now we define a hyperplane defined by $\left(\mathbf{P}_0, v_{j_2}^2, v_{j_3}^3, \ldots, v_{j_k}^k\right)$ as follows:

$$H = \mathbf{P}_0 \oplus \mathbf{L} = \left\{\mathbf{P} \in \Re^k : \overrightarrow{\mathbf{P}_0\mathbf{P}} \in \mathbf{L}\right\}$$
$$= \left\{(x_1, x_2, \ldots, x_k) \in \Re^k : [x_1 - p, x_2, \ldots, x_k] = b_2 v_{j_2}^2 + b_3 v_{j_3}^3 + \cdots + b_k v_{j_k}^k\right\}$$
$$\text{for some } b_2, \ldots, b_k \in \Re$$
$$= \left\{(x_1, x_2, \ldots, x_k) \in \Re^k : x_1 - p = \alpha_{j_2}^2 x_2 + \alpha_{j_3}^3 x_3 + \cdots + \alpha_{j_k}^k x_k\right\}$$
$$= \left\{(x_1, x_2, \ldots, x_k) \in \Re^k : x_1 - \alpha_{j_2}^2 x_2 - \alpha_{j_3}^3 x_3 - \cdots - \alpha_{j_k}^k x_k - p = 0\right\}$$

Having the hyperplane H defined by $\left(\mathbf{P}_0, v_{j_2}^2, v_{j_3}^3, \ldots, v_{j_k}^k\right)$ one can check in time $O(k)$ on which side of the hyperlane H a given object $u \in U$ is (Figure 1). This function is called $Test_H : U \to \{0, 1\}$ and is defined by

```
Function Test(P₀, v²ⱼ₂, v³ⱼ₃, ..., vᵏⱼₖ, u) : {0,1}
    If (f₁(u) − α²ⱼ₂f₂(u) − α³ⱼ₃f₃(u) − ··· − αᵏⱼₖfₖ(u) ≥ p) then
    Test := 1
    Else Test := 0;
```

where $u = (f_1(u), \ldots, f_k(u))$.

Assuming the vectors $v_{j_2}^2, v_{j_3}^3, \ldots, v_{j_k}^k$ are given one can find the projection on x_1 parallel to $\mathbf{L} = Lin(v_{j_2}^2, v_{j_3}^3, \ldots, v_{j_k}^k)$ of any object $u \in U$ in time $O(k)$.

```
Function Projection(v²ⱼ₂, v³ⱼ₃, ..., vᵏⱼₖ, u) : Real;
    Projection := f₁(u) − α²ⱼ₂f₂(u) − α³ⱼ₃f₃(u) − ··· − αᵏⱼₖfₖ(u);
```

5 Learning algorithm

In this section we describe our learning algorithm. This is an algorithm searching for hyperplanes which should discern between all pairs of objects discernible by the generalized decision in a given decision table. In the case of consistent decision table the algorithm will be continued until the hyperplanes cut the space $\Re^k$ into regions containing objects from one decision class only. In the general case this condition is replaced by the equation $\partial_{\mathbf{B}} = \partial_{\mathbf{A}}$, where $\mathbf{B} = (U, B \cup \{d\})$ is a decision table defined by replacing the set A of atributes of a given decision table $\mathbf{A} = (U, A \cup \{d\})$ by the set B of test functions defined by hyperplanes constructed as follows.

5.1 The general algorithm

Step 1 *Initialize a new table* $\mathbf{B} = (U, B \cup \{d\})$ *such that* $B = \emptyset$;
Step 2 *(Search for the best hyperplane)*
   for $i := 1$ to k do
      Search for the best hyperplane H_i *attached to the axis* x_i *using genetic algorithm;*
   $H := $ *Best hyperplane from the set* $\{H_1, H_2, ..., H_k\}$;
Step 3 $B := B \cup \{Test_H\}$;
Step 4 If $\partial_{\mathbf{B}} = \partial_{\mathbf{A}}$ then *Stop* else goto *Step2*.

5.2 Searching for the best hyperplane attached to x_1

Chromosomes : Any chromosome consists of a bit vector of the length $l(k-1)$ containing the $(k - 1)$ fragments of the length l. The $i - th$ fragment ($i = 1, 2, .., k - 1$) corresponds to one of the vectors of the form v_j^{i+1}. Let us consider two examples of chromosomes (assuming $l = 4$):

$$chr_1 = \underset{1}{0010} \ \underset{2}{1110} \ ... \ \underset{i}{0100} \ ... \ \underset{k-1}{1010}$$

$$chr_2 = \underset{1}{0000} \ \underset{2}{1110} \ ... \ \underset{i}{1000} \ ... \ \underset{k-1}{0101}$$

Operators: The genetic operators are defined as follows:

1. Mutation and Selection are defined in standard way [13]. Mutation of chr_1 is realized in two steps; first one block e.g. $i - th$ is randomly chosen and next the contents of it (in our example "0100") is randomly changed into a new block e.g. "1001". The described example of mutation is changing the chromosome chr_1 into chr_1', where:

$$chr_1' = \underset{1}{0010} \ \underset{2}{1110} \ ... \ \underset{i}{1001} \ ... \ \underset{k-1}{1010} \ .$$

2. Crossover is done by exchange of the whole fragments of chromosome corresponding to one vector. More exactly, the result of crossover of two chromosomes is also realized in two steps; first the block position i is randomly chosen and next the contents of $i-th$ blocks of two chromosomes are exchanged. For example, if crossover is performed on chr_1, chr_2 and $i-th$ block position is randomly chosen then we obtain their offspring:

$$chr'_1 = 0010\ 1110\ ...\ 1000\ ...\ 1010$$
$$1 \quad\ 2 \quad ...\ i \quad ...\ k-1$$

$$chr'_2 = 0000\ 1110\ ...\ 0100\ ...\ 0101$$
$$1 \quad\ 2 \quad ...\ i \quad ...\ k-1$$

Fitness function: The fitness of any chromosome is equal to the number of object pairs from different decision classes discerned by the best hyperplane among hyperplanes parallel to all vectors encoded in the chromosome. It is computed as follows:

In the first step a procedure searching for the best hyperplane is executed and as an output the point of intersection of the hyperplane with a fixed axis is returned. The procedure is searching for projections of all objects on the distinguished axis. The projections are parallel to all vectors defined by the chromosome and they are calculated by the procedure *Projection*. Next the set of projection points is sorted and the hyperplane is located at the best position between these projections. The best position is defined by the best hyperplane containing this point. The hyperplane quality and in the consequence the fitness of the chromosome can be calculated using different measures introduced in Section 2.

5.3 Complexity

The most time consuming step in our algorithm concerns of the computation of the fitness function values. The value of this function for a given chromosome is equal to the number of discerned pairs by the best hyperplane among hyperplanes parallel to all vectors encoded in this chromosome. Searching for this hyperplane is realized in time $O(nk + n\log n)$ where n is the number of objects and k is the number of conditional attributes.

6 Experiments

The presented method has been implemented. We compare here two strategies called simple and genetic. The simple strategy is described in [18], where the hyperplanes parallel to axes are considered only. The genetic strategy is the strategy presented in the paper (in both cases we use the same quality measure of hyperplanes). The results of experiments are showing that the quality of classification (in most cases) is increasing comparing to the quantization method from [18]. It is also interesting to note that the proposed method is gives better results when the training table is small comparing to the size of the testing table. Another advantage of the proposed method comparing to the method presented in [18] is that the number of extracted hyperplanes as well as the number of generated decision rules are decreasing. We pay for that because the time necessary to extract hyperplanes not necessarily parallel to axes is increasing. The results of experiments have been compared to the reported in the literature results on some benchmarks. In the case of IRIS data our algorithm has produced two hyperplanes and only one decision rule for each decision class. Only two cases have been not classified correctly. Some other results of experiments are presented in Table 1. In all cases the probabilities p_m and p_c of mutation and crossover, respectively have been tuned for each experiment separately.

Table name	Nr of Objects	Nr Of Features	Nr Of Classes	Training table	Testing table	Simple Strategy	Genetic Strategy
Iris	150	4	3	60	90	95.6%	97.7%
Heart	270	13	2	120	150	72.66%	80%
Diabetes	768	8	2	300	468	63.79%	71.74%
Australian	690	14	2	300	390	79.49%	80.6%

Table 1. The results of experiments on tables chosen from U.C.Irvine repository

It is possible to improve our method by constructing a hybrid method. This method consists of two steps. In the first step a modification of the presented method is applied i.e. a set of hyperplanes with a "good" discerning quality is generated (instead of the best hyperplane only). In the second step the method based on dynamic reducts [2] is used to choose the best subset of the set of features generated by the hyperpalnes (received as the result of the first step) with respect to the quality of classification of unseen objects.

7 Conclusions

We have presented a method searching for hyperplanes discerning between points from different decision classes. The method is based on Boolean reasoning and is implemented by using a genetic strategy. The results of experiments are promising. In the future we plan to apply our method using some other quality measures like those constructed from penalty measure proposed in Section 2 or those proposed e.g. in [7], [11], [16]. We also plan to extend our method for discretization of attributes with values being vectors of reals as well as to data tables with null values. Another extension which we plan to investigate is related to decision tables with real value (continuous) decision.

References

1. Brown, F.M. (1990). Boolean reasoning, Dordrecht: Kluwer.
2. Bazan, J., Skowron, A., Synak, P. (1994). Dynamic reducts as tool for extracting laws from decision table, Proc. of the Symp. on Methodologies for Intelligent System, Charllotte, NC, October 16-19, 1994, Lecture Notes in Artificial Intelligence 869, Berlin: Springer-Verlag 1994, 346-355.
3. Breiman, L., Friedman, J.H., Olshel, R.A. & Stone, C.J. (1984). Classification and Regression Trees. Wadsworth International Group.
4. Catlett, J. (1991). On changing continuos attributes into ordered discrete attributes. In Y. Kodratoff, (ed.), Machine Learning-EWSL-91, Proc. of the European Working Session on Learning, Porto, Portugal, March 1991, Lecture Notes in Artificial Intelligence, Berlin: Springer-Verlag 1991, 164-178.
5. Chan, C.-C., Bartur, C., & Srinivasasn, A. (1991). Determination of quantization intervals in rule based model for dynamic systems. Proc. of the IEEE Conference on System, Man, and Cybernetics, Charlottesville, VA, October 13-16, 1719-1723.
6. Chmielewski, M. R. & Grzymala-Busse, J. W. (1994). Global Discretization of Attributes as Preprocessing for Machine Learning. Proc. of the III International Workshop on RSSC94, San Jose, CA, November 1994, 294-301.
7. Dougherty, J., Kohavi R. & Sahami, M. (1995). Supervised and Unsupervised Discretization of Continuos Features. Proc. of the Twelfth International Conference on Machine Learning, San Francisco: Morgan Kaufmann.
8. Fayyad, U. M. & Irani, K.B. (1992). On the handling of continuos-valued attributes in decision tree generation. Machine Learning 8, 87-102.
9. Holland, J.H., Adaptation in Natural and Artificial Systems, (1975) University of MIchigan Press, Ann Arbor.
10. Kodratoff, Y. & Michalski, R. (1990). Machine learning: An Artificial Intelligence approach, vol.3, Morgan Kaufmann.
11. Lenarcik, A. & Piasta, Z. (1994). Deterministic Rough Classifiers. Proc. of the III International Workshop on RSSC94, November 1994, San Jose, CA, 434-441.
12. Murthy, S., Kasif, S., Saltzberg, S. & Beigel, R. (1993). OC1: Randomized Induction of Oblique Decision Trees. Proc. of the Eleventh National Conference on AI, July 1993,322-327.
13. Michalewicz, Z. (1992). Genetic Algorithms + Data Structures = Evolution Programs. Berlin: Springer-Verlag.
14. Pawlak Z.(1991). Rough sets: Theoretical aspects of reasoning about data. Dordrecht: Kluwer.
15. Pao, Y.-H. & Bozma, I. (1986). Quantization of numerical sensor data for inductive learning. In J. S. Kowalik (ed.), Coupling Symbolic and Numerical Computing in Expert System. Amsterdam, The Netherlands: Elsevier Science Publ., 69-81.
16. Quinlan, J. R. (1993). C4.5: Programs for Machine Learning. San Mateo: Morgan Kaufmann Publishers.
17. Skowron A., Rauszer C. (1992). The Discernibility Matrices and Functions in Information Systems. In: Intelligent Decision Support - Handbook of Applications and Advances of the Rough Sets Theory, ed. R.Slowiski, Dordrecht: Kluwer 1992, 331-362.
18. Skowron, A. & Nguyen, H.S. (1995). Quantization of real values attributes. In: Proc. of the Second Joint Annual Conference on Information Sciences, Wrightsville Beach, North Carolina, September 28 - October 1 1995, USA.

Appendix

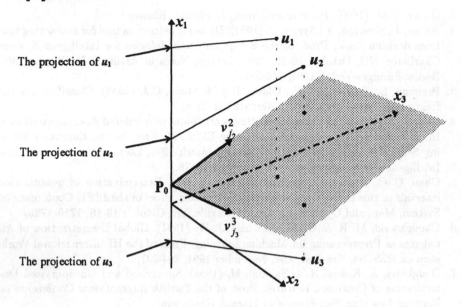

Figure 1: The hyperplane based on vectors $v_{j_2}^2, v_{j_3}^3$ and attached to the point $\mathbf{P_0}$

Inductive Database Design

Hendrik Blockeel and Luc De Raedt

Department of Computer Science, Katholieke Universiteit Leuven
Celestijnenlaan 200A, B-3001 Heverlee, Belgium
email : {Hendrik.Blockeel,Luc.DeRaedt}@cs.kuleuven.ac.be

Abstract. When designing a (deductive) database, the designer has to decide for each predicate (or relation) whether it should be defined extensionally or intensionally, and what the definition should look like. An intelligent system is presented to assist the designer in this task. It starts from an example database in which all predicates are defined extensionally. It then tries to compact the database by transforming extensionally defined predicates into intensionally defined ones. The intelligent system employs techniques from the area of inductive logic programming.

Keywords: Logic for Artificial Intelligence, Learning and Knowledge Discovery, Database Design, Inductive Logic Programming

1 Introduction

When designing databases, the designer has to determine the structure of the database by determining the extensional and intensional predicates, and by providing definitions for each of the intensional predicates. At present, there exists few guidelines to help the designer in this task, which makes designing deductive databases a hard task. Nevertheless, the design ultimately determines the quality of the database.

In this paper, we present a novel approach, called inductive database design, to assist database designers in their task. The key assumption underlying inductive database design, is that it is often easy to give an example state of the database in which all predicates (or relations) are defined extensionally. Given an example state, techniques from the field of inductive logic programming can be used to discover clauses that are valid in the example state. The inductive database design method we propose employs these clauses in order to transform some of the extensional predicates into intensional ones. During this process it is guided by the principle of compaction, which states that the better database is the more compact one, i.e. the one that requires less memory. Though the technique we present can — in principle — be used fully automatically, we believe it is more adequate to view it as an intelligent assistant that gives advice to the database designer, who should be given the opportunity to reject the definitions proposed by the system.

The paper is organised as follows: in Section 2, we review some concepts of deductive databases and logic programming, in Section 3, we review the inductive logic programming system CLAUDIEN [1, 8], which will be adapted for use in our inductive database design tool, in Section 4, we address the problem of finding intensional definitions for predicates, in Section 5, we present an experiment, and finally, in Section 6, we conclude and touch upon related work.

2 Logic Programming Concepts and Datalog

The database framework we will use is based on the Datalog subset of clausal logic. More specifically, we will use the follow notions.

A *clause* is a universally quantified logical formula of the form $A_1, ..., A_m \leftarrow B_1, ..., B_n$ where the A_i and B_j are positive literals (atoms). The above clause can be read as A_1 or ... or A_m if B_1 and ... and B_n. Extending the usual convention for *definite clauses* (where $m = 1$), we call $A_1, ..., A_m$ the *head* and $B_1, ..., B_n$ the *body* of the clause. A *fact* is a definite clause with empty body ($m = 1$, $n = 0$).

Definition 1. A clause is range-restricted iff all variables occurring in the head also occur in the body.

Range-restriction is often imposed in the database literature, it allows to avoid the derivation of non-ground true facts.

Definition 2. An extensional predicate is a predicate defined by a set of functor-free ground facts.

Definition 3. An intensional predicate is a predicate defined by a set of functor-free and range-restricted definite clauses.

Definition 4. An integrity constraint is a range-restricted functor-free clause.

Definition 5. A deductive database is a couple $\langle \mathcal{E}, \mathcal{I} \rangle$, where $\mathcal{E}$ is a set of extensional predicate definitions and $\mathcal{I}$ is a set of intensional predicate definitions.

Definition 6. A clause c is valid in a definite clause theory T iff c is true in the least Herbrand model of T.

To verify whether a clause $A_1, ..., A_m \leftarrow B_1, ..., B_n$ is true in a definite clause theory T, one can run the query $\leftarrow B_1, ..., B_n, \neg A_1, ..., \neg A_m$ on a database containing T. If the query finitely fails, the clause is valid, otherwise it is invalid.

3 Inductive Logic Programming

In this section, we give a brief overview of the inductive logic programming system CLAUDIEN [1, 8, 2, 3].

The CLAUDIEN system starts from a definite clause theory T and a language L (which is a set of well-formed clauses) and finds a set of maximally general clauses that are valid in the given theory.

Definition 7. Clause c_1 is more general than clause c_2 iff there exists a substitution θ such that $c_1\theta \subset c_2$ (where clauses are seen as sets of literals).

We will also say that c_1 θ-subsumes c_2 (cf. Plotkin [6]). As shown by Plotkin, θ-subsumption induces a partial order on the set of all possible clauses, which is exploited by many inductive logic programming systems [5].

We can now illustrate the CLAUDIEN setting. Given the database

$$\{male(maarten), female(soetkin), human(maarten), human(soetkin)\}$$

and as L the set of all constant-free clauses containing maximum 3 literals, CLAUDIEN would discover the following clauses, which are all valid in the database:

$$human(X) \leftarrow male(X)$$

$$human(X) \leftarrow female(X)$$

$$\leftarrow male(X), female(X)$$

$$female(X), male(X) \leftarrow human(X)$$

Roughly speaking, CLAUDIEN works as follows (cf. Figure 1). It keeps track of a list of candidate clauses Q, which is initialised to the maximally general clause (in L). It repeatedly deletes a clause c from Q, and tests whether c is valid in the theory. If it is, c is added to the final hypothesis, otherwise, all maximally general specialisations of c (in L) are computed (using a so-called *refinement operator* ρ) and added back to Q. This process continues until Q is empty and all relevant parts of the search-space have been considered. It should be mentioned that CLAUDIEN employs several techniques to prune and optimize the search, cf. [2].

$Q := \{max(L)\}$
$H := \emptyset$
while $Q \neq \emptyset$ do
    delete c from Q
    if c is valid in T
    then add c to H
    else add $\rho(c)$ to Q

Fig. 1. The CLAUDIEN algorithm (simplified)

To specify the set of clauses to consider, i.e. the language bias, CLAUDIEN employs so-called dlab_templates (cf. [2, 4]). For instance:

```
dlab_template('Q(X,Y) <-- 1-4:[P(X), P(Y), Q(X,Y), Q(Y,X)]').
dlab_var('P', 1-1, [male, female]).
dlab_var('Q', 1-1, [parent, father, mother]).
```

specifies that clauses should have one binary predicate in the head, and one to four predicates in the body. The dlab_variables P and Q are placeholders for real predicates; they can be substituted by the predicates in the corresponding dlab_var declaration. Several occurrences of a dlab_variable can be substituted by different predicates.

For instance, if unary predicates are male and female, and binary predicates are parent, father and mother, then

$$father(X, Y) \leftarrow male(X), parent(X, Y)$$

is part of the specified language.

4 Finding Intensional Definitions

As intensional definitions typically consist of a small set of rules, while extensional definitions consist of a large set of facts, a database will be much more compact if many predicates are defined intensionally. The question is then, how extensional definitions can be turned into intensional ones in such a way that the database becomes as compact as possible.

We will use the following approach. For each predicate, we try to find a set of clauses that intensionally defines the predicate. These clauses should be as simple as possible. They can be found using a modified version of CLAUDIEN. In a second step, we show how multiple predicates can be defined intensionally using the results of the first step.

4.1 Defining One Predicate Intensionally

While the CLAUDIEN system was designed to find all the clauses C in a hypothesis space that are valid in a database, our goal is only to find a small number of clauses which together form a good intensional definition. To this end, CLAUDIEN is run a number of times, and each time one best clause is chosen, "best" meaning that the clause predicts more facts that have not been predicted yet, than any other clause.

Because in each run, we are only interested in the best clause, it is possible to prune the search space much more than when all the solutions have to be found. Instead of only pruning branches that cannot lead to a solution, CLAUDIEN can now prune any branch that cannot lead to a better solution than the best up till now. This causes a great gain in efficiency, compared to the "standard" CLAUDIEN system.

The modified CLAUDIEN algorithm, which we call CLAUDIEN*, is shown in Figure 2.

CLAUDIEN* will only generate clauses within the language bias L that define the predicate p in terms of the predicates in P. The rootclauses $\{max(L)\}$ with which Q is initialized, depend on the language bias that is used.

We define the compaction achieved by a clause c as $comp(c) = C(c) - P(c)$, where $C(c)$ is the complexity of the clause (the number of literals in it) and $P(c)$

Procedure Claudien*(p : predicate, P : set of predicates) returns clause
   $Q := \{\max(L)\}$
   $c_{best} :=$ *none*
   while $Q \neq \emptyset$ **do**
      delete c from Q
      if c is valid in T **then** $c_{best} := c$
      else
         add $\rho(c)$ to Q
         remove from Q every r where $comp(r) \geq comp(c_b)$
   return c_{best}

Fig. 2. CLAUDIEN*, the modified CLAUDIEN algorithm

the number of facts that can be derived using the clause. $P(c)$ is computed as indicated in Figure 3. As a fact consists of one literal, $comp(c)$ is indeed the difference in the number of literals in the database, when the predicted facts are replaced by the clause.

Function $P(c : Clause)$ returns integer
   Let p be the predicate in $head(c)$
   Let DB be the database obtained by deleting all facts for p
   Let H_p be the set of definite clauses already found for p
   $P(c) =| covers(DB \wedge H_p \wedge c) | - | covers(DB \wedge H_p) |$

Fig. 3. Computing the number of new facts covered by a clause

The covers relation employed is intensional coverage, i.e. $covers(DB)$ is the set of all ground facts logically entailed by DB.

It is easy to prove that this search algorithm is admissible, i.e. that the best solution will always be found.

Theorem 8. *Let c and d be clauses and let b be the best clause found so far.*
If $comp(c) > comp(b)$ then for every refinement d of c, $comp(d) > comp(b)$.

Proof. CLAUDIEN* refines clauses only by adding literals of the form $P(\ldots)$ to them, where P is a database predicate. This increases the complexity of the clause. Therefore, as d is a refinement of c, $C(d) > C(c)$. On the other hand, because $body(d) \supseteq body(c)$, the set of facts predicted by d must be a subset of the set of facts predicted by c, hence $P(d) \leq P(c)$.

In our implementation, the heuristic used to order the clauses in Q, is $C(c) + N(c) - P(c)$, where $N(c)$ is the number of facts covered by a clause that should not be covered (so it gives some idea of how much the clause will still have to be refined before becoming valid). Although this heuristic does not influence the solution that will be found, a good heuristic will lead to better clauses being found earlier, and will therefore allow more pruning.

As CLAUDIEN*, only finds one clause (the most compacting one), and this clause is not necessarily complete as an intensional definition (there may still be facts that cannot be derived by it), it has to be run repeatedly until every fact of the predicate can be derived. This leads to the *FID* (Find an Intensional Definition) algorithm, which shown in Figure 4.

When computing the compaction caused by a clause, only facts that are predicted by the clause *and that are not predicted using any already existing rules* should be taken into account. That is why the facts predicted by a clause that is added to the definition are marked.

Function FID(p : predicate, P : set of predicates) **returns**
           intensional definition of p using predicates in P or false
  $D := \emptyset$
  while D is not complete **do**
      run CLAUDIEN*
      if a new clause c has been found
      then add c to D, and mark the facts predicted by c
      else return false
  if D is complete **then return** D

Fig. 4. *FID*: an algorithm for finding an intensional definition

If an intensional definition for a predicate p is found by the above algorithm, it is guaranteed to be *sound and complete*. Soundness means that no facts can be derived using this definition, that were not in the original database. Completeness means that every fact in the extensional definition of the predicate can be derived with the intensional definition. It is easy to see that these properties hold.

Theorem 9. *Any intensional definition found by FID is complete.*

Proof. This follows trivially from the fact that the algorithm only returns an intensional definition for p if all the facts for p are indeed predicted by it.

Theorem 10. *Any intensional definition found by FID is sound.*

Proof. The intensional definition consists of valid rules (as CLAUDIEN* does not induce invalid rules). Now let S be the set of facts that is implied by the original database. For each application of any individual rule in the intensional definition, if before the application of the rule no facts are in the database that are not in

S, the application of the rule itself can only allow the derivation of facts that are in S (because the rule is valid). Repeated application of one or more rules for p will not change this condition.

The completeness and soundness properties of an intensional definition guarantee that by replacing an extensional definition with an intensional one, no information is lost nor gained: the new database is equivalent to the original one.

4.2 Finding Several Definitions

Having an algorithm that finds an intensional definition for one predicate, it may seem a trivial task to define as much predicates as possible intensionally. However, this is not so easy. The fact that two predicates may have an intensional definition does not imply that they can both be defined intensionally at the same time. An intensional definition of one predicate may preclude an intensional definition of another predicate. The following example illustrates this.

Example 1. Suppose we have a tiny database which contains the following extensional definitions:

p(1). p(2). p(3).   q(1). q(2). q(3).

There exists an intensional definition for p, which can replace its extensional definition:

p(X) :- q(X).   % intensional definition for p

and similarly, q can be defined intensionally using the following rule:

q(X) :- p(X).   % intensional definition for q

However, we cannot replace both extensional definitions by their corresponding intensional definition, as that would destroy the original information (the least Herbrand model would be empty).

This shows that not every predicate for which an intensional definition exists, will indeed be defined intensionally.

To compute which predicates to define intensionally, we use the algorithm in Figure 5. This algorithm computes a partition $\mathcal{E}, \mathcal{I}$ of the predicates $\mathcal{P}$. First, it initializes $\mathcal{E}$ to the set of predicates for which *FID* is unable to construct intensional definitions. For every predicate that is not in this initial set $\mathcal{E}$, an intensional definition exists, but whether this definition will be used to define the predicate depends on how the other predicates are defined. It is, however, possible to find a set $\mathcal{I}'$ of predicates that can certainly be defined intensionally, irrespectively of what is done with the other predicates.

Consider the predicates that can be defined using only predicates initially in $\mathcal{E}$. (The term "uses" is only used here with respect to *other* predicates than the

```
P := set of all predicates
for all  p ∈ P do
    let f(p) := FID(p, P)
E := {p ∈ P | f(p) = false}
I' := ∅
repeat
    repeat
        I' := {p ∈ P | f(p) contains only predicates in E ∪ I' ∪ {p}}
    until I' does not change anymore
    if I' has changed in the above loop
    then
        M := (P − I') − E
        for all  p in M:
            if  FID(p, E ∪ I' ∪ {p}) ≠ false
            then f(p) := FID(p, E ∪ I' ∪ {p})
until I' does not change anymore
I := I'
repeat
    let p_b be the predicate in M for which f(p_b) achieves maximal compaction
    add p_b to I and remove p_b from M
    for all  p ∈ M do
        if  f(p) is incorrect given I and E
        then add p to E
until M = ∅
define the predicates p in I intensionally using f(p)
```

Fig. 5. Computing E, I

one being defined; the latter one is always allowed to occur in its own definition, so that direct recursion is allowed.) We call this set of predicates I_1'. We successively define the sets I_n' as the sets of predicates that can be defined using only predicates in

$$\bigcup_{i<n} I_i' \cup E'$$

Finally, I' is defined as

$$I' = \bigcup_{i=1}^{\infty} I_i'$$

I' is computed in the first, inner repeat loop of Algorithm 5.

The set of predicates that are not in E initially nor in I' is called M. In the final database DB all the predicates in I' will belong to I, whereas some of the predicates in M will belong to E and some to I.

Since for each predicate only one definition was returned by the above algorithm, it is possible that some predicates that are now in M in fact should belong to I, i.e. some definition using only predicates initially in E and I' exists but was not returned by FID.

To make the final $\mathcal{I}$ set as large as possible, it is therefore useful to rerun the FID procedure with a reduced search space, now allowing only predicates in $\mathcal{E}$ and those predicates already known to belong to $\mathcal{I}$ in the body of the clauses. This can be done iteratively until no predicates are added to $\mathcal{I}$. This is realized in the outer repeat loop of the algorithm.

Of the predicates that remain in $\mathcal{M}$, the algorithm must then decide which predicates should be defined intensionally, and which extensionally. This is done using a hill-climbing approach (the last loop of Figure 5). In each step, the intensional definition that leads to the greatest compaction is chosen. This may make other intensional definitions invalid, so in the next step a smaller set of intensional definitions will be considered. This is continued until no new predicates can be defined intensionally.

5 An experiment

We have run our system on a small family database. This database contains extensional definitions for the predicates *parent, married, married1* (an asymmetrical relation containing only the couple (X, Y) when *married* contains both (X, Y) and (Y, X)), *grandparent, sibling, sibling-in-law, parent-in-law, grandparent-in-law, aunt-or-uncle* and *niece-or-cousin*. All together, the extensional definitions contain 723 facts.

In the first run, FID returns a definition for every predicate except *parent* and *married1*. Most of these definitions are found in a couple of minutes; the total time for all the predicates is about 40 minutes. As $\mathcal{E} = \{parent, married1\}$, the system first adds $\{grandparent,\ parent-in-law,\ sibling,\ married\}$ and then $\{sibling-in-law,\ aunt-or-uncle,\ grandparent-in-law\}$ to $\mathcal{I}$, so that finally $\mathcal{M} = \emptyset$, and no extra runs of FID are needed.

When the database is redesigned in this way, its size is reduced from 723 literals to 117 (of which 88 for the extensional definitions, and 29 for the intensional definitions). It is clear that the new database must have a close to minimal size, as the information about parenthood and marriage is crucial, and all the other predicates are derived from this using a simple definition.

6 Conclusions

In this paper, we have discussed the problem of designing a deductive database in such a way that it becomes simpler and more structured. We have presented a novel approach to this problem, called inductive database design, in the form of a system that automatically derives rules and builds intensional definitions, using the compaction caused by a rule as a measure for its usefulness in an intensional definition. An experiment shows that this system performs quite well on a small example database.

Although the system can be used in a fully automatic way, it is more appropriate to think of it as an intelligent tool helping the database designer. Many decisions made by the system are based on heuristics, and the system has a high chance of making the right decisions, but some supervision by the user is certainly recommended.

Our current system can still be extended in many directions. Topics for future research include:

- noise handling: at this moment, no exceptions to rules are allowed
- a comparison between several compaction criteria
- interactivity: at this moment the only way the user can influence the outcome of the system is through the language bias. There should be more opportunities to interfere with the design process.
- integrity constraints: we believe that the described techniques can also be used to find semantic integrity constraints for the database

Finally, we want to mention the work of Sommer [7], which is related to ours in the sense that both consider the problem of restructuring a knowledge base. The main difference is that in [7], existing rules are restructured, while our system can start from a purely extensional database.

Acknowledgements

This research is financed with a grant from the Flemish Institute for the Advancement of Scientific-Technological Research in the Industry (IWT), and it is also part of the European Community ESPRIT project no. 20237 (ILP2). Luc De Raedt is supported by the Belgian National Fund for Scientific Research.

References

1. L. De Raedt and M. Bruynooghe. A theory of clausal discovery. In *Proceedings of the 13th International Joint Conference on Artificial Intelligence*, pages 1058–1063. Morgan Kaufmann, 1993.
2. L. De Raedt and L. Dehaspe. Clausal discovery. Submitted.
3. L. De Raedt and S. Džeroski. First order *jk*-clausal theories are PAC-learnable. *Artificial Intelligence*, 70:375–392, 1994.
4. L. Dehaspe and L. De Raedt. DLAB: a declarative language bias formalism. This volume.
5. S. Muggleton and L. De Raedt. Inductive logic programming : Theory and methods. *Journal of Logic Programming*, 19,20:629–679, 1994.
6. G. Plotkin. A note on inductive generalization. In *Machine Intelligence*, volume 5, pages 153–163. Edinburgh University Press, 1970.
7. E. Sommer. Rulebase stratification: an approach to theory restructuring. In S. Wrobel, editor, *Proceedings of the 4th International Workshop on Inductive Logic Programming*, volume 237 of *GMD-Studien*, pages 377–390, Sankt Augustin, Germany, 1994. Gesellschaft für Mathematik und Datenverarbeitung MBH.
8. W. Van Laer, L. Dehaspe, and L. De Raedt. Applications of a logical discovery engine. In *Proceedings of the AAAI Workshop on Knowledge Discovery in Databases*, pages 263–274, 1994.

Enhancing Query Processing of Information Systems

Grace S Loo[1], Tharam Dillon[2], John Zeleznikow[2] And Kok-Huat Lee[3]

[1] The University of Auckland, New Zealand. g.loo@auckland.ac.nz
[2] La Trobe University, Melbourne, Australia.
tharam@latcs1.lat.oz.au; johnz@latcs1.lat.oz.au
[3] through 1.

Abstract. Current database and information systems only provide for inflexible query processing. In this paper we have developed techniques for supporting the answering of inadequate queries to information systems introducing certain level of intelligence and flexibility. Our approach uses the notion of α-cut in fuzzy set theory to provide acceptable approximate answers for a given inadequate query. We illustrate the proposed α-cut approach for a variety of different queries which may involve different types of selection conditions. The selection conditions considered may contain fuzzy terms measured on a numeric, nominal or linguistic scale. They may employ one or more linguistic hedges of (very), or of (fairly) for query modification. Fuzzy numbers and fuzzy intervals are introduced as representations of selection conditions of inadequate queries. It is not essential to construct extensive metadata into the existing database to implement the proposed approach. A user friendly system which makes use of the proposed theory has been developed. It can support selection conditions that contain linguistic hedges of (very) and (fairly), comparators (approximately), (more-than) and (less-than), and terms that are numeric, nominal or linguistic. The test results bear positive evidence to the ease of implementation of the proposed approach.

Keywords: Approximate, alpha-cut, fuzzy sets, inadequate queries, intelligent, linguistic, metric, query weakening, relational database.

1   Introduction

A conventional query answering system can only process a query that is crisp where the selection condition is *precisely formulated*. It will provide the query with exact answers, if available, otherwise it will give an empty answer. Users of conventional query system must know exactly the specific information that is to be searched. They must also know the database schema, and the specific query language to access the database. However, the conventional query system does not have the capability of answering a class of *inadequate queries* as defined in [Loo et al.90/94]. For such queries the selection conditions include (a) vague or imprecise expressions, or (b) linguistic terms and expressions. This paper addresses the problem of inadequate queries. Several methods are available in the literature for handling inadequate queries. The best known are the metric and fuzzy-set approaches. The metric approach involves in using a well-defined metric as a measure of semantic proximity among data, and the notion of "neighbourhood" or more generally "acceptance region" for securing approximate answers to a given query, usually with the aid of specially designed comparators such as "near-to" and "similar-to". The metric approach is discussed in [Motro88] and [Loo et al.94]. Loo et al. [1994] propose a generic approach to handle inadequate queries where the queried attribute may be numeric or nominal. The fuzzy-set approach employs the concepts of fuzzy sets introduced by [Zadeh65] to model vagueness and imprecision in natural or artificial language. Much research has been conducted with this approach in various disciplines; see [Bezdek & Pal92], [Chu & Chen92], [Cuppens & Demolombe88], [Marks II94], [Dubois et al.93], [Zadeh78] and [Zimmermann91]. Andreasen & Pivert [1994] apply the notion of fuzzy sets for query weakening to obtain non-empty answers. Their method consists in using, repeatedly if needed, the modifier "rather" on the selection condition that may involve fuzzy or linguistic terms. Loo et al. [1994] employ the notion of an α-cut of fuzzy sets as a flexible way of securing approximate answers for inadequate queries where the queried attribute may be nominal or numeric.

This paper generalises the work of [Loo et al.94] in dealing with inadequate queries. Much effort is directed towards providing a simple, though relatively crude, method of handling selection conditions that involve linguistic hedges (*very*) and (*fairly*). The queried attribute may be numeric, nominal or linguistic.

2 An α-cut of a Fuzzy Number as an Acceptance Region

In this study we shall consider inadequate queries where the selection condition may contain (i) vague or imprecise expressions, (ii) linguistic terms, and (iii) linguistic hedges in combination with (i) and (ii). Expressions such as (salary about $40,000), (integers close to 30), (age approximately between 50 and 65), and (temperature near to 20^0 C) are vague, using imprecise qualifiers such as 'close to', 'about', 'approximately' and 'near to'. Some frequently encountered linguistic terms are: 'young', 'old', 'tall', 'short', 'high', 'low', 'average', 'good' and 'satisfactory'. Some examples of linguistic hedges are: 'very', 'fairly', 'more-or-less', and 'rather'. To answer an inadequate query, we may model the selection condition as a fuzzy set, and employ its α-cut to provide an *acceptance region* of approximate answers for the query.

Concepts and Definitions of Fuzzy sets

A fuzzy set (or subset) A on a universal set U is characterised by a membership function $\mu_A(x)$ such that $\mu_A(x) \in [0, 1]$ for each x in U. An element x with a higher value of $\mu_A(x)$ is perceived to have a higher 'possibility' of being a member in A. The *support* of A is defined by: supp A = $\{x \in U \mid \mu_A(x) > 0\}$. An α-cut of A, denoted by A_α, is defined by: $A_\alpha = \{x \in U \mid \mu_A(x) \geq \alpha\}$ for $\alpha \in [0, 1]$.

The case of a Single-Attribute Query

Consider a simple single-attribute inadequate query of the form:
      Q1: Retrieve cases where *x is close to* y_0
In Q1, the selection condition (close to y_0) is an imprecise target, with y_0 as the reference target. The queried attribute x may be nominal, numeric or linguistic. To process Q1, we need to represent the imprecise target (close to y_0) by a fuzzy set A, and choose an appropriate α-cut thereof as an acceptable interpretation for the selection condition, and hence as an *acceptance region* of approximate answers for the given query. In applying this fuzzy-set approach, one difficulty that arises in practice is the determination of an 'appropriate' grade membership function $\mu_A(x)$ for modelling the imprecise selection condition (close to y_0). Though $\mu_A(x)$ is usually formulated in a subjective manner, it must be constructed so as to reflect adequately the context of the problem under investigation. When the queried attribute is numeric, the desired $\mu_A(x)$ may be represented by a known but appropriate standard function. Some of the well-

known standard functions used in applications include "S" and "Π" functions, triangular functions, and Gaussian functions; see [Bandemer & Nather92, ch 4], [Zadeh65] and [Zimmermann91]. In this section we shall consider a numeric-attribute situation to demonstrate the usefulness of fuzzy numbers and fuzzy intervals as models for representating the imprecise targets (close to y_0) of Q1. As noted in [Loo et al.94], (close to y_0) may be usefully represented by a L-R-type fuzzy number or a L-R-type trapezoidal fuzzy interval defined on the real line R^1. A fuzzy number is defined to have only one element that has a membership grade 1, while a fuzzy interval has two or more elements that have a membership grade 1. In this study, we propose to model (close to y_0) by a unimodal Triangular Fuzzy Number (TFN). See figure 1.

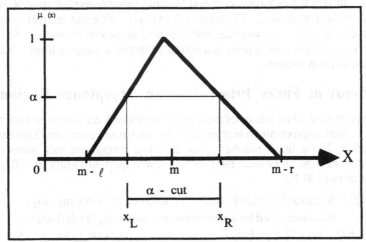

Figure 1. An α-cut of a triangular fuzzy number A = (m, ℓ, r)$_{TFN}$

Definition 1:   A triangular fuzzy number A, denoted by A = (m , ℓ , r)$_{TFN}$, is characterised by a membership function μ_A (x) defined by:
$$\mu_A (x) = [1 + (x - m)/\ell] \text{ for } (m - \ell) \leq x \leq m ; \quad \mu_A (x) = 1 \text{ at } x = m ;$$
$$\mu_A (x) = [1 - (x - m)/r] \text{ for } m \leq x \leq (m + r); \text{ and } \mu_A (x) = 0 \text{ elsewhere.}$$

The fuzzy number A = (m, ℓ, r)$_{TFN}$ is unimodal. It is characterised by three parameters: the central point m, a left spread ℓ and right spread r. The central point m is the only point that has a membership grade equal to 1. When the left and right spreads are equal, say equal to e, we have a symmetric triangular fuzzy number denoted by: A = (m, e, e)$_{TFN}$. The following Result 1 is due to Loo et al. [1994].

Result 1:   An α-cut A_α of A = (m, ℓ, r)$_{TFN}$ is provided by A_α = [x_L , x_R] , where
$$x_L = m - (1 - \alpha) \ell , \text{ and } x_R = m + (1 - \alpha) r$$

If (close to y_0) with a single-valued y_0 is modelled by (m, ℓ, r)$_{TFN}$, an α-cut defined in Result 1 then provides an acceptance region of approximate answers to Q1. In modelling (close to y_0) by (m, ℓ, r)$_{TFN}$, we need to set m equal to the reference target y_0. In so doing, we implicitly assume that there exists an imprecision below y_0 of a maximum size equal to the left spread ℓ , and an imprecision above y_0 of a maximum size equal to the right spread r. To illustrate, suppose an imprecise target (close to 30) is represented by (m = 30, ℓ =8 , r = 8)$_{TFN}$. At a chosen level α, say 0.5, we follow Result 1 to construct the 0.5-cut of (close to 30) as the close interval [26 , 34]. Thus (close to 30) is to be interpreted as equivalent to the interval [26 , 34]. An element x in the universal set U should therefore be accepted as an approximate answer to Q1 if its value lies between 26 and 34, and rejected otherwise.

In general, the width of an α-cut defined in Result 1 is equal to $(1 - \alpha)(\ell + r)$. The size of an α-cut will thus become narrower for a higher α, or a lower ℓ, or a smaller r. A narrower α-cut suggests that a higher degree of proximity of a given element x to y_0 is required if the element is to be accepted as an approximate answer to the query. In practice, if no preferred value of ℓ (or r) is available, we may use a certain (small) proportion of y_0 as an initial value of ℓ (or r); the value ℓ and r need not be equal. The value of ℓ (or r) may however be revised in subsequent trials if required. As for α the choice of $\alpha = 0.5$ provides an initial feasible value to use. It may be revised in subsequent trials if so desired. Different α levels give different interpretations to the same imprecise target. They produce nested sets of approximate answers for the same query. An α-cut of a higher α level is a subset of that of a lower α level . The case of $\alpha = 1$ produces crisp answers.

3   An α-cut of Fuzzy Interval as an Acceptance Region

When two or more distinct values of the queried attribute X are assigned a membership grade 1, it is more appropriate to represent the imprecise selection condition by a fuzzy interval rather than a fuzzy number. The L-R-type fuzzy intervals would provide useful models of representation. They include the important family of **TR**apezoidal **Fuzzy Numbers (TRFN)**.

Definition 2:   A trapezoidal fuzzy number A, denoted by $A = (m_1, m_2, \ell, r)_{TRFN}$, is characterised by a membership function $\mu_A(x)$ defined by:

$\mu_A(x) = [1 + (x - m_1)/\ell]$ for $(m_1 - \ell) \leq x \leq m_1$; $\mu_A(x) = 1$ for $m_1 \leq x \leq m_2$;
$\mu_A(x) = [1 - (x - m_2)/r]$ for $m_2 \leq x \leq (m_2 + r)$; and $\mu_A(x) = 0$ elsewhere.

All values in the interval $[m_1, m_2]$ have a membership grade 1. They form the core of the trapezoidal fuzzy number. Using Result 1, we obtain the following Result 2.

Result 2:   An α-cut of $A = (m_1, m_2, \ell, r)_{TRFN}$ is provided by: $A_\alpha = [x_L, x_R]$, where $x_L = m_1 - (1 - \alpha) \ell$, and $x_R = m_2 + (1 - \alpha) r$.

Result 2 provides a simple practical procedure of constructing an $\alpha - cut$ to secure an acceptance region of approximate answers for the following Q2-type query:

Q2: Retrieve all cases where *age (in years) is "approximately between 55 and 65"*
In Q2, the selection condition (approximately between 55 and 65) is an *imprecise target interval*. It may therefore be represented by a fuzzy interval. The crisp interval [55, 65] is the *reference target interval* that must be retrieved as crisp answers. As an illustration, to process Q2, we may represent the required target interval (approximately between 55 and 65) by $(m_1 = 55, m_2 = 65, \ell = 5, r = 5)_{TRFN}$. Suppose an 0.6-cut is needed. Using Result 2, we obtain, after much simplification, (approximately between 55 and 65)$_{0.6}$ = [53 , 67].

4   Modelling Linguistic Hedges

The selection condition of a query may be intensified (or weakened) by employing one or more linguistic hedges of "very" (or "fairly"). The following sections are devoted to seeking acceptable approximate answers to each of these selection conditions.

4.1 An α-cut for a Selection Condition Involving one "very"

Consider inadequate query Q3: Retrieve all cases where x *is very close to* y_0

In Q3, the required target (very close to y_0) consists of the primary selection condition (close to y_0), and a linguistic hedge "very" which serves to modify the meaning of (close to y_0). The objective here is to obtain an α-cut of a fuzzy set that models (very close to y_0) for answering Q3, using (close to y_0) as a reference fuzzy set. The required (very close to y_0) may be determined, independent of (close to y_0), in a subjective manner as described in section 2 and section 3. If (close to y_0) is known, (very close to y_0) must be constructed as a fuzzy subset of (close to y_0) where

$$\forall\ x \in U \quad \mu_{\text{very (close to } y_0)}(x) \leq \mu_{\text{close to } y_0}(x) \tag{1}$$

with $\mu_{\text{close to } y_0}(x)$ and $\mu_{\text{very (close to } y_0)}(x)$ being respectively the membership function of (close to y_0) and (very close to y_0). More specifically, we propose to define the desired fuzzy set (very close to y_0) to be

$$\forall\ x \in U \quad \mu_{\text{very (close to } y_0)}(x) \leq [\mu_{\text{close to } y_0}(x)]^n \text{ for n} > 1 \tag{2}$$

where the index n is any real number greater than 1. The definition given in (2) is consistent with (1) since $\mu_{\text{close to } y_0}(x)$ is typically not greater than 1 for all x in U.

For n = 2, we have the special case: (very close to y_0) = (close to y_0)^2, which is the concentration CON of (close to y_0) as defined in [Zadeh73].

(Very close to y_0) may be determined by (2), and its α-cut constructed as an acceptance region for answering Q3. However, without having to determine the explicit form of (very close to y_0), we can easily construct its α-cut from that of a well-defined reference fuzzy set (close to y_0). This follows from Theorem 1.

Theorem 1: An α-cut of A^n is the α_0-cut of A, where $\alpha_0 = \alpha^{1/n}$ for any positive number n. That is, $(A^n)_\alpha = (A)_{\alpha^{1/n}}$ for n > 0, and $0 < \alpha \leq 1$.

Proof of Theorem 1. Let the crisp interval $[x_L, x_R]$ be the α-cut of A^n and the α_0-cut of A as well For every element x in $[x_L, x_R]$, we have

$$(\mu_A(x))^n = \mu_{A^n}(x)\ , \quad \text{giving} \quad \mu_A(x) = (\mu_{A^n}(x))^{1/n} \tag{3}$$

Specifically, at $x = x_L$ we have $\mu_{A^n}(x_L) = \alpha$, and $\mu_A(x_L) = \alpha_0$, giving from (3) that: $\alpha_0 = \alpha^{1/n}$. Similarly, it can be shown that at $x = x_R$, $\alpha_0 = \alpha^{1/n}$. QED.

The result of Theorem 1 is true for any n. It provides a simple practical method of securing an α-cut of A^n from that of the reference fuzzy set A. Two special cases are stated in the following corollaries where we set A = (close to y_0).

Corollary 1a: If (very close to y_0) = (close to y_0)^n for n >1 , then an α-cut of (very close to y_0) is the $\alpha^{1/n}$-cut of (close to y_0).

Corollary 1b: If (very close to y_0) = (close to y_0)^n for n >1, and (close to y_0) is (m, e , e)$_{\text{TFN}}$, then

$$\text{(very close to } y_0)_\alpha = [\ y_0 - (1 - \alpha^{1/n})\ e\ ,\ y_0 - (1 + \alpha^{1/n})\ e\ ] \tag{4}$$

The result (4) is obtained be replacing α by $\alpha^{1/n}$ in Result 1.

4.2 An α-cut for a Selection Condition that Involves Multiple Hedges of "very"

Consider Q4: Retrieve all cases where x is (very ... very close to y_0)
where the required selection condition (very ... very close to y_0) employs the modifier
(very) successively k times to modify the reference target (close to y_0) with k being an
integer not less than 1. Our aim here is to obtain an α-cut of the required selection
condition as an acceptance region for Q4. The present (very ... very close to y_0) is a
special case of a more general selection condition denoted by $A_{k \, (very)}$, where k hedges
of (very) are applied successively to modify the meaning a given fuzzy set A; we set:
A = (close to y_0) for Q4. To process $A_{k \, (very)}$, we assume that at *any* stage of query
modification, applying the hedge (very) once on any fuzzy set B produces a fuzzy set
B^p for p > 1. More specifically, we model

$$A_{j \, (very)} = (A_{(j-1) \, (very)})^p \quad \text{for } p > 1, \text{ and for } j = 1, 2, \dots k. \tag{5}$$

where $A_{0 \, (very)}$ = A. The intensifying impact of (very) stated in (5) is assumed 'equal'
at every stage j of modification. Within the framework of (5), we obtain Theorem 2.

Theorem 2: $A_{k \, (very)} = (A)^{p^k}$ for $p > 1$, and for any positive integer k.

Theorem 2 can be easily proved using mathematical induction and condition (5).

Theorem 3: If $A_{k \, (very)} = (A)^{p^k}$ for $p > 1$, then an α-cut of $A_{k \, (very)}$ is equivalent
to the α_k-cut of A, where $\alpha_k = (\alpha)^{p^{-k}}$.

The proof of Theorem 3 follows from Theorem 1. Theorem 3 provides a simple
practical way of obtaining an α-cut of $A_{k \, (very)}$ from that of the reference fuzzy set A.
Three special cases where A = (close to y_0) are given in the following corollaries.

Corollary 3a: If (close to y_0)$_{k \, (very)}$ = (close to y_0)$^{p^k}$, for $p > 1$, then an α-cut of
(close to y_0)$_{k \, (very)}$ is equivalent to the α_k-cut of (close to y_0), where $\alpha_k = (\alpha)^{p^{-k}}$.

Corollary 3b: If (close to y_0)$_{k \, (very)}$ = (close to y_0)$^{2^k}$, then an α-cut of
(close to y_0)$_{k \, (very)}$ is the α_k-cut of (close to y_0), where $\alpha_k = (\alpha)^{2^{-k}}$.

Corollary 3c: In Corollary 3b, if (close to y_0) is modelled by (m, e , e)$_{TFN}$, then
an α-cut of (very close to y_0) is the α_k-cut of (close to y_0) where $\alpha_k = (\alpha)^{2^{-k}}$, giving

$$(\text{close to } y_0)_{k \, (very)}]_\alpha = [y_0 - (1 - \alpha_k) e , y_0 + (1 - \alpha_k) e] \tag{6}$$

The proof of (6) follows from Corollary 3b and Result 1.

4.3 An α-cut for a Selection Condition Involving one "Fairly"

Consider Q5: Retrieve all cases where x is *fairly close to* y_0
In Q5, the required selection condition (fairly close to y_0) is formulated by modifying
(close to y_0) using the linguistic hedge (fairly). Our aim is to obtain an α-cut of
(fairly close to y_0) for answering Q3. The required (fairly close to y_0) may be
determined, independent of (close to y_0), in a subjective manner as described in
sections 2 and 3. If (close to y_0) is known and used as the reference fuzzy set, then
(fairly close to y_0) should be determined such that

$$\forall \ x \in U \ \mu_{\text{fairly (close to } y_0)}(x) \geq \mu_{\text{close to } y_0}(x) \qquad (7)$$

Condition (7) is imposed to ensure that any element x in the universe U must have a higher possibility of being a member in (fairly close to y_0) than in (close to y_0). More specifically, we model: (fairly close to y_0) = (close to y_0)^n, for $n < 1$. That is,

$$\forall \ x \in U \ \mu_{\text{fairly (close to } y_0)}(x) \geq [\mu_{\text{close to } y_0}(x)]^n \ \text{ for } n < 1. \qquad (8)$$

(8) is consistent with (7) since $\mu_{\text{close to } y_0}(x)$ is typically not greater than 1 for all x in U. In particular, with n = 0.5, we get (fairly close to y_0) = (close to y_0)$^{0.5}$, which is the dilation **DIL** of (close to y_0) as defined in [Zadeh73]. We may use formula (7) to obtain an explicit form of the desired (fairly close to y_0) and construct its α-cut. However, without having to determine (fairly close to y_0) explicitly, we can *easily* construct its α-cut from the α-cut of a well-defined reference fuzzy set (close to y_0). This follows from Theorem 4.

Theorem 4: If (fairly close to y_0) = (close to y_0)^n for $n < 1$, then an α-cut of (fairly close to y_0) is the α_0-cut of (close to y_0) where $\alpha_0 = \alpha^{1/n}$.

The proof of Theorem 4 follows from Theorem 1 where we set A = (close to y_0), and define A^n = (fairly close to y_0), for n < 1.

Corollary 4ca If (fairly close to y_0) = (close to y_0)^n for $n < 1$, and (close to y_0) is (m, e , e)$_{\text{TFN}}$, then an α-cut of (fairly close to y_0) is the $\alpha^{1/n}$-cut of (close to y_0), producing

$$(\text{fairly close to } y_0)_\alpha = [\ y_0 - (1 - \alpha^{1/n}) \, e \, , \, y_0 - (1 + \alpha^{1/n}) \, e \ ] \qquad (9)$$

The right-hand-side expression of (9) is obtained by replacing α in Result 1 by $\alpha^{1/n}$. The result of Theorem 4 provides a simple practical method for constructing the needed α-cut of the required selection condition (fairly close to y_0).

4.4 An α-cut for a Selection Condition that Involves Multiple Hedges of "Fairly"

Consider Q6: Retrieve all cases where *x is* $A_{k \text{ (fairly)}}$
where $A_{k \text{ (fairly)}}$ denotes the complex selection condition (fairly ... fairly A) which employs k hedges of (fairly) to modify the reference target A. To process the selection condition $A_{k \text{ (fairly)}}$, we model that for p < 1,

$$A_{j \text{ (fairly)}} = (A_{(j-1) \text{ (fairly)}})^p \ \text{ for } j = 1, 2, \dots k. \qquad (10)$$

Here $A_{0 \text{ (fairly)}}$ = A. The weakening impact of (fairly) stated in (10) is assumed 'equal' at each stage j of modification. With this model setup (10), the selection condition A_k (fairly) may then be represented by a fuzzy set provided by Theorem 5.

Theorem 5: $A_{k \text{ (fairy)}} = (A)^{p^k}$ for $p < 1$, and for any positive integer k.

Theorem 5 can be proved using mathematical induction together with (10).

Theorem 6: If $A_{k \text{ (fairly)}} = (A)^{p^k}$ for $p < 1$, then an α-cut of $A_{k \text{ (fairly)}}$ is the α_k-cut of A, where $\alpha_k = (\alpha)^{p^{-k}}$.

The proof of Theorem 6 follows from Theorem 1.

Corollary 6a: If (close to y_0)$_{k\ (fairly)}$ = (close to y_0)$^{p^k}$, for $p < 1$, then an α-cut of

(close to y_0)$_{k\ (fairly)}$ is equivalent to the α_k-cut of (close to y_0), where $\alpha_k = (\alpha)^{p^{-k}}$.

Corollary 6b If (close to y_0) is modelled by (m, e , e)$_{TFN}$, then an α-cut of

(close to y_0)$_{k\ (fairly)}$ is the α_k-cut of (close to y_0), where $\alpha_k = (\alpha)^{2^k}$, producing

$$[\text{(close to } y_0)_{k\ (fairly)}]_\alpha = [y_0 - (1 - \alpha_k)\, e , y_0 + (1 - \alpha_k)\, e] \tag{11}$$

5 An α-cut for a Selection Condition Involving a Nominal term

Consider Q7: Retrieve all cases where colour is "white"
In Q7, the selection condition "white", a nominal term, is the reference target.
Suppose here we are interested in not only the colour "white" but also other colours
that can be considered acceptably "close to white". Within this premise, the selection
condition "white" is relaxed to mean (close to white) and be modelled as a fuzzy set,
denoted by the same term (white). To answer Q7, each colour available in the queried
database is considered a member of the reference fuzzy set (white), and is assigned a
membership grade which is used as a measure of its *semantic* distance to the specific
reference colour "white". These membership grades should be assigned to reflect a
certain ordering among the various colours considered. As an illustration, suppose the
queried attribute COLOUR has six different colours: W = white, Y = Yellow,
O = orange, R = red, G = green and B = blue. Further, suppose the reference fuzzy set
(white) is modelled by

(white) = 1/W + 0.9/Y + 0.7/O + 0.3/R + 0.5/G + 0.1/B

where the symbol (0.3/R) denotes (colour R with a membership grade 0.3), and other
pairs are similarly defined. In this situation, for instance, an 0.6 cut of (white) yields
the crisp set {W, Y, O}, indicating that any case whose colour is either "W", "Y" or
"O" should be accepted as an approximate answer to Q7. Further, suppose the
operator CON is used to interpret the meaning of the modifier (very) then, from
Corollary 1a, an α-cut of (very white) is identical with the $\sqrt{\alpha}$–cut of (white). Hence,
if $\alpha = 0.5$, then $\sqrt{\alpha} \cong 0.71$, giving: (very white)$_{0.5} \cong$ (white)$_{0.71}$ = {W, Y}. When
the operator DIL is used to interpret the meaning of the modifier (fairly) then, from
Corollary 4a, an α-cut of (fairly white) is the α^2–cut of (white). Hence if $\alpha = 0.7$,
then $\alpha^2 \cong 0.49$, giving: (fairly white)$_{0.7}$ = (white)$_{0.49}$ = {W, Y, O, G}. Other
selection conditions that involve several modifiers of (very), or of (fairly) can be
constructed in the same manner. They can be processed in the same way by the
proposed α-cut approach where we invoke the results of Theorem 3 or Theorem 6 to
obtain the needed approximate answers.

6 An α-cut for a Selection Condition Involving a Linguistic term

Consider Q8: Retrieve all employees where age is *old*
In Q8, the selection condition (old) is a fuzzy linguistic term. It may thus be
modelled by a fuzzy set. Here, (old) is defined over the queried attribute AGE which is
assumed to be numeric with values recorded (say) in years. To process Q8, as an
illustration, we consider any age below 50 as definitively *not old,* and any age not
smaller than 75 as *definitively old*. In this manner, we represent (old) by a 'left-sided'
fuzzy number of the form: (old) = (m = 75, ℓ = 25, r = ∞)$_{TFN}$, using Definition 1,

where the left spread $\ell = 75 - 50 = 25$. Thus, by invoking Result 1, for instance, we obtain a 0.8-cut of (old) as: (old)$_{0.8}$ = [70 , ∞), which provides an acceptance region for Q8. In addition, suppose we use the CON operator to interpret each modifier "very". Then, as an illustration, a 0.7-cut for (very very old) is provided by Corollary 3b to be the α_0-cut of (old) where $\alpha_0 = (0.7)^{2^{-2}} \approx 0.9$. Thus, (very very old)$_{0.7}$ = (old)$_{0.9}$ = [72.5, ∞). Further, suppose we wish to find a 0.89-cut of (fairly old), using the DIL operator to model the modifier "fairly". Here, we may invoke Corollary 4b and obtain (fairly old)$_{0.89}$ ≅ (old)$_{0.8}$ = [72.5 . ∞).

In the above example, a left-sided fuzzy number of the form (m, ℓ, r = ∞)$_{TFN}$ is used to model and process the 'left-sided' linguistic term (old). The same (m, ℓ, r = ∞)$_{TFN}$ may be used to model and process other 'left-sided linguistic terms such as *high, tall, heavy* and *big*. On the other hand, we may use a *'right-sided'* fuzzy number of the form (m, ℓ = ∞ , r)$_{TFN}$ to model and process a *'right-sided' fuzzy term*. Common linguistic terms which are 'right-sided' include *young, low, short, light* and *small*. In general, the proposed α-cut approach can be applied to handle the situations where the linguistic terms are modelled by any well-defined L-R-type fuzzy set.

7   Concluding Remarks

In this paper we have proposed using an α-cut as an acceptance region of approximate answers for a variety of inadequate queries. Triangular fuzzy numbers and trapezoidal fuzzy intervals are singled out for special mentioning as semantic representations of selection conditions. Our main attention is focused on intensifying (or weakening) the selection conditions by employing one or more hedges of "very" (or "fairly"). Our proposed α-cut technique is appealing at implementation level. The theoretical results given in section 4 provide a simple procedure of deriving needed α-cuts for relatively complex selection conditions from that of the reference fuzzy set. No essential extensive meta-databases need to be created in applying the proposed technique. The general results obtained on modelling the modifier (very) and (fairly) provide a powerful tool for query intensification and query weakening. The operator "rather" of [Andreasen & Pivert94] in query weakening is similar to our notion of "fairly". However, with our α-cut approach, we can easily expand the *effective* support (i.e. the α-cut here) of the required fuzzy set for modelling (fairly) by simply choosing a lower α value to use. No re-formulation of the fuzzy set in question for broadening its support is needed. Moreover, through changing the α value, users can easily change their selections of acceptance regions to suit their needs, without incurring any additional systems support. Finally, it is possible to process the modifiers of (very) and (fairly) even on systems which do not offer facilities to process them. Existing relational databases can support the proposed α-cut technique without any structural reorganisation. We need only to specify the α-cut of a given complex selection condition to be equivalent to the α_0-cut of the reference fuzzy set, where α_0 may be user-determined or system-generated according to theorems 1, 3 or 6, as the case may be. Users may refer to table 1 to determine the α_0 value to use for a corresponding pre-set α level. Table 1 is constructed to deal with cases where α-cuts of A^n are considered equivalent to the α_0-cut of the fuzzy set A for selected numbers n. For a given α, the required α_0 may be determined (i) from columns where n < 1 for modelling (fairly), and (ii) from columns where n > 1 for modelling (very).

Table 1. Conversion of α to α_0 where $\alpha_0 = (\alpha)^{1/n}$

	α_0 where n =						
α	0.3	0.5	0.8	1	1.5	2	3
1	1	1	1	1	1	1	1
0.9	0.704	0.81	0.877	0.9	0.932	0.949	0.965
0.894	0.688	0.799	0.869	0.894	0.928	0.946	0.963
0.89	0.678	0.792	0.864	0.89	0.925	0.943	0.962
0.8	0.474	0.64	0.757	0.8	0.862	0.894	0.928
0.7	0.305	0.49	0.64	0.7	0.788	0.837	0.888
0.64	0.226	0.410	0.572	0.64	0.743	0.8	0.862
0.6	0.182	0.36	0.528	0.6	0.711	0.775	0.843
0.5	0.099	0.25	0.420	0.5	0.630	0.707	0.794

Many concepts developed in this paper have been implemented on a prototype IDB-KROOM: *I*ntelligent *D*ata*b*ase: Inadequate Query through *K*nowledge, *R*elationships, and *O*bject-*O*riented *M*odelling. IDB-KROOM is *user friendly*, operating on an existing relational database system. It offers two options: linear and non-linear methods of modelling selection conditions. The linear method employs the triangular fuzzy numbers of the form: $(m, \ell, r)_{TFN}$. The non-linear option employs one other L-R-type fuzzy number which is non-triangular. For the present study, test runs have been conducted to secure α-cuts for answering certain inadequate queries on a small database of 131 records. Attention is focused on processing selection conditions that involve the linguistic hedges (very) and (fairly). The prototype IDB-KROOM system can also support multiple selection conditions that employ the Boolean operators AND and OR. Some selected test results using the *linear* option are given in the appendix. They are conducted to answer three basic selection conditions typified by: (i) "age is *old*", (ii) "age is *very old*", and (iii) "age is *fairly old*". For case (i), we model: (old) = $(m = 50, \ell = 10, r = \infty)_{TFN}$. We classify the range "age equal to 50 or above" as *definitively old*, "age below 40" as *definitively not old*, and "age between 40 and 50" as an *area of imprecision*. Using the linear option of the system, the tests produce a 0.8-cut of (old) as: EMPLOYEE.AGE > 48. That is, $(old)_{0.8} = (48, \infty)$, suggesting that employees aged higher than 48 should be accepted as approximate answers. There are 47 instances satisfying this condition. For case (ii), we model: (very old) = $(old)^{2}$. The tests give a 0.64-cut of (very old) as: EMPLOYEE.AGE > 48, which is identical with the 0.8-cut of (old), returning 47 identical instances. For case (iii), we model: (fairly old) = $\sqrt{(old)}$. A 0.89-cut of (fairly old) is: EMPLOYEE.AGE > 48, which is identical with the 0.8- cut of (old). To sum, we thus have: $(\text{very old})_{0.64} = (\text{old})_{0.8}$, and $(\text{fairly old})_{0.89} = (\text{old})_{0.8}$. These empirical results support our theory developed in section 4. They underscore the ease of implementation of our proposed α-cut approach. For the present illustration, we model (old) to have an area of imprecision defined by "age between 40 and 50". However, our system allows users to specify their own areas of imprecision to suit their needs. For instance, if a user specifies "age between 50 and 100" to be an area of imprecision for (old), and chooses the linear option, the system will automatically use the model: (old) = (m = 100, ℓ = 50, r = ∞)$_{TFN}$.

Acknowledgements

This project has been made possible by the partial financial support provided by The University of Auckland and La Trobe University.

References

Andreasen, T. and Pivert, O. 1994. 'On the weakening of fuzzy relational queries'. In Z. Ras and M Zemankova (eds.) LNCS/LNAI 869 *Proc. Methodologies for Intelligent Systems*, 8th Int. Sym, ISMIS'94, Charlotte, NC, USA, October. Springer-Verlag.

Bandemer, H. and Nather, W. 1992. Fuzzy Data Analysis. Doredrecht, Kluer Academic Publishers.

Bezdek, J. C. and Pal, S. K. 1992. Fuzzy Models for Pattern Recognition. Piscataway, NJ, IEEE Press.

Chu, W. W. and Chen, Q. 1992. 'Neighbourhood and associative query answering'. In *Journal of Intelligent Information System*, 1, pp.355-382.

Cuppens, F. and Demolombe, R. 1988. 'Co-operative answering: a methodology to provide intelligent access to databases'. L. Kerschberg (ed.) *Proc. 2nd Int. Conf. on Expert Database Systems*, Virginia, April, pp.333-353.

Dubois, D., Prade, H. and Yager, R. 1993. Fuzzy Sets for Intelligent Systems. Morgan Kaufmann, California.

Loo, S. L. 1992. ' A taxonomy for an intelligent database'. In B. Srinivasan and J. Zeleznikow, eds. *Research and Practical Issues in Databases, Proc. of the 3rd Australian Database Conf.* Melbourne, Australia, February, World Scientific, pp.344-355.

Loo, S. L., Dillon, T. and Zeleznikow, J. 1990. 'Intelligent accessing of database with inadequate and incomplete queries'. In Proc. Int. Conf. on Systems Management '90 - The Impact of Information Technology on Systems Management, 11 - 18 June 1990, Hong Kong, pp.248 - 253.

Loo, S. L., Dillon, T., Zeleznikow, J. and Lee, K. H. 1994. 'Two approaches for answering inadequate queries - Empirical project IDB-KROOM'. In Proc. Workshop Flexible Query Answering System'94, Copenhagen, November, Roskilde University Press, pp.127-146.

Marks II, R. J. (ed.) 1994. Fuzzy Logic Technology and Applications. The Institute of Electrical and Electronic Engineers, Inc., New York.

Motro, A. 1988. ' VAGUE: A User Interface to Relational Databases that Permits Vague Queries'. *ACM Trans. on Office Information Sys.*, 6(3), July, pp. 187-214.

Zadeh, L. A. 1965. 'Fuzzy sets'. In *Information and Control*, V8.3, June, pp.338-353.

Zadeh, L. A. 1973. 'Outline of a new approach to the analysis of complex systems and decision processes'. In *IEEE Transactions on Systems, Man And Cybernetics*, SMC-3, pp.28-44.

Zadeh, L. A. 1978. 'Fuzzy sets as a basis for the theory of possibility'. In *Fuzzy Sets and Systems*, 1, pp.3-28.

Zimmermann, H. J. 1991. Fuzzy Set Theory - and Its Applications. 2nd revised ed. Boston, Kluwer Academic Publishers.

397

The fuzzy term OLD is tested with alpha = 0.8 using the Linear - 96 method. OLD has a typical value of 50.

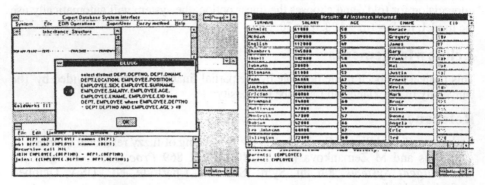

The fuzzy term VERY OLD is tested with alpha = 0.64 using the Linear - 96 method. OLD has a typical value of 50.

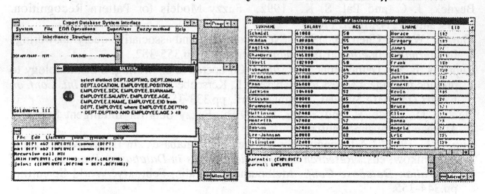

The fuzzy term FAIRLY OLD is tested with alpha = 0.89 using the Linear - 96 method. OLD has a typical value of 50.

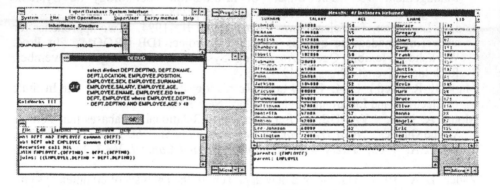

Structuring and Retrieval of the Complex Predicate Arguments Proper to the NKRL Conceptual Language

Gian Piero Zarri   and   Luca Gilardoni

CNRS - CAMS
54, boulevard Raspail
75270 PARIS Cedex 06, France
zarri@cams.msh-paris.fr

QUINARY SpA
via Crivelli, 15/1
20122 MILANO, Italy
lg%quinary@iunet.it

Abstract. Extracting a "reasonable" amount of the information contained in "narrative" documents like, e.g., news agency stories, requires the use of a reasonably rich representation language, which in turn requires a query languages powerful enough to exploit this richness. This paper deals with the conceptual structures used in NKRL (NKRL = Narrative Knowledge Representation Language) to describe the "structured arguments" of the NKRL semantic predicates. We describe here the query language, and the corresponding matching algorithm, which allows us to retrieve correctly the information stored in these arguments.

1 Introduction

NKRL (the "Narrative Knowledge Representation Language") has been created to provide a normalised description of the semantic content (the "meaning") of relatively complex narrative texts. In an industrial context, "narrative texts" may correspond, e.g., to news stories, telex reports, corporate records, normative documents, intelligence messages, etc. NKRL is a fully implemented language; the most recent versions have been realised in the context of two European projects : NOMOS, Esprit P5330, and COBALT, LRE P61011.

In this paper, we will focus, mainly, on the conceptual structures ("AECS sub-language") used to model the structured arguments of the NKRL semantic predicates.

2 The general framework of the NKRL language

2.1 The two "layers", and the "catalogue"

NKRL is a two layers language. The lower layer consists of a set of general tools pertaining to four integrated components.

The "descriptive component" concerns the tools used to produce a formal representation (called "predicative templates") of some general classes of narrative events, like 'moving a generic (concrete or abstract) object', 'having a negative attitude towards someone', 'having the control of some person or social body'. Templates are structured into a hierarchy, H_TEMP(lates), which corresponds, therefore, to a "taxonomy of events".

Templates' instances (called "predicative occurrences"), i.e., the NKRL representations of single, specific events like 'Lucy moves the wardrobe (this particular one)' or 'Mr. Smith has fired Mr. Brown', are in the domain of another NKRL component, the "factual component". Templates and predicative occurrences are both characterised by a general, threefold format, where the central piece is a semantic predicate, like BEHAVE, MOVE, PRODUCE etc., whose arguments (role fillers) are introduced by roles as SUBJ(ect), OBJ(ect), SOURCE, etc., see [5] for more details.

The "definitional component" supplies the formal representation of the defining properties of all the general entities and notions, like *physical_entity*, *human_being_or_social_body*, *control_power*, which can be used in the framework of the two components above. The corresponding NKRL structures are called "concepts" (basically, they can be equated to frames), and are grouped into a hierarchy which, for historical reasons, is called H_CLASS(es) — H_CLASS is, therefore, a hierarchy of concepts, and corresponds well to the usual "ontologies".

The instances of concepts, like lucy_, wardrobe_1, company_x, are called "individuals", and pertain to the "enumerative component". Throughout this paper, we will use the italic type style to represent a "*concept_*", the roman style to represent an "individual_".

The upper layer of NKRL consists mainly of a sort of "catalogue" where we can find a complete description of the formal characteristics and the modalities of use of the well-formed, "basic templates" (like 'moving a generic object' mentioned above) associated with the language. Presently, the basic templates — that bear some similarities to Sowa's conceptual graphs [3] — are about 150 ; by means of simple specialisation operations, it is then possible to obtain from them all the (specific) "derived" templates that could be concretely needed to implement a particular, practical application — e.g., 'move an industrial process' — and the corresponding occurrences. In NKRL, the set of legal, basic templates can be considered, at least in a first approach, as fixed, and it is part of the definition of the language, see also Section 7., "Conclusions".

2.2 An example

Fig. 1 supplies a simple example of NKRL code. It translates a fragment of COBALT news : 'Milan, October 15, 1993. The financial daily Il Sole 24 Ore reported Mediobanca had called a special board meeting concerning plans for capital increase'.

In Fig. 1, c1 and c2 are symbolic labels of occurrences, instances of basic NKRL templates ; MOVE and PRODUCE are predicates ; SUBJ, OBJ, TOPIC ("à propos of...") are roles. With respect now to the arguments (role fillers), sole_24_ore, milan_, mediobanca_ (an Italian merchant bank), summoning_1, etc. are individuals ; *financial_daily*, *special_*, *cardinality_* and *several_* (this last belonging, like *some_*, *all_* etc., to the *logical_quantifier* intensional sub-tree of H_CLASS) are concepts. The SPECIF(ication) operator is used to represent the properties of a concept or individual, see next Section ; *several_* is used within a SPECIF list having *cardinality_* as first element as a standard way of representing the "plural number" mark, see c2.

The arguments, and the templates/occurrences as a whole, may be characterised by the presence of particular codes, the "determiners". For example, the "location determiners" are associated with the arguments by using the "colon", ":", operator, see c1. For the "temporal determiners", "date-1" and "date-2", see [4].

c1) MOVE SUBJ (SPECIF sole_24_ore *financial_daily*): (milan_)
      OBJ #c2
      date-1: 15_october_93
      date-2:

c2) PRODUCE SUBJ mediobanca_
      OBJ (SPECIF summoning_1 (SPECIF
            board_meeting_1 mediobanca_ *special_*))
      TOPIC (SPECIF plan_1 (SPECIF *cardinality_ several_*)
            capital_increase_1)
      date-1: circa_15_october_93
      date-2:

Fig. 1. An example of NKRL coding.

A MOVE construction like that of occurrence c1 ("completive construction") is necessarily used to translate any event concerning the transmission of an information ("The financial daily Il Sole 24 Ore reported ..."). Accordingly, the filler of the OBJ(ect) slot in the occurrences (here, c1) which instantiates the MOVE transmission template is always a symbolic label (here, #c2) which refers to another predicative occurrence, i.e., that bearing the informational content to be spread out ("... Mediobanca had called a meeting ...").

3 The AECS sub-language

In Fig. 1, the arguments made up of a SPECIF(ication) list are examples of NKRL structured arguments (or "expansions").

In NKRL, structured arguments of templates and occurrences are built up in a principled way by making use of a specialised sublanguage, AECS, which includes four binding operators, the "disjunctive operator" (ALTERNative = A), the "distributive operator" (ENUMeration = E), the "collective operator" (COORDination = C), and the "attributive operator" (SPECIFication = S), see, e.g., [1, 5]. Their intuitive meanings are given in Table 1. Accordingly, structured arguments in NKRL are lists of undefined length, which may include both concepts and individuals and which are labelled by making use of the AECS operators.

Because of their recursive nature, the AECS operators could give rise to very complex expressions, difficult to interpret and disentangle (unify). Therefore, to build up well-formed NKRL expansions, the definitions of Table 1 are used in association with the so-called "priority rule", visualised by using the following expression :

(ALTERN (ENUM (COORD (SPECIF)))).

This is to be interpreted as follows : it is forbidden to use inside the scope of a list introduced by the binding operator B, a list labelled in terms of one of the binding operators appearing on the left of B in the priority expression above — e.g., it is impossible to use a list ALTERN inside the scope of a list COORD. A vivid example of the utility of this rule can be found, e.g., in [5].

Operator	Mnemonic Description
ALTERN	The "disjunctive operator". It introduces a set of elements, i.e., concepts, individuals, or lists labelled with other expansion operators. Only one element of the set takes part in the particular relationship with the predicate defined by the role-slot to be filled with the expansion ; however, this element is not known.
COORD	The "collective operator" : all the elements of the set take part (necessarily together) in the relationship with the predicate defined by the role-slot.
ENUM	The "distributive operator ": each element of the set satisfies the relationship, but they do so separately.
SPECIF	The "attributive operator". It is used to link a series of attributes (properties) with the concept or individual that constitutes the first element of the SPECIF list, in order to better characterise this last element. Each attribute appearing inside a SPECIF list can be recursively associated with another SPECIF list.

Table 1. NKRL operators for structured arguments.

4   The syntactic structure of the AECS sub-language

The basic syntactic constructs of the AECS language are the so-called "coord-branches", composed of a single NKRL entity, concept or individual, possibly specialised through the association with a SPECIF list :

<coord-branch>::= <entity> | (SPECIF <entity> {<coord-branch>}+)

An example of coord-branch could be the following :

(SPECIF offer_1 share_1 (SPECIF share_2 (SPECIF *cardinality_ many_*)))

which describes an offer of two different shares. In this example, both 'share_1' and 'share_2' specify the characteristics of the main argument 'offer_1', while the internal SPECIF form expresses more information on one of the attributes, 'share_2', i.e., '*cardinality_ many_*'.

The coord-branches can be represented under tree-format, see Fig. 2. Please note that each coord-branch in the form "(SPECIF <entity> (SPECIF ...))" is subsumed by any other coord-branch obtained by cutting the branch at any level. For example :

(SPECIF offer_1 (SPECIF share_2 (SPECIF *cardinality_ many_*)))

is subsumed by the more general structure :

(SPECIF offer_1 share_2).

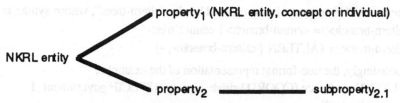

Fig. 2. coord-branch expressed in tree-format.

The "coord-trees" are built upon the coord-branches by associating several of these branches ; the general definition of a coord-tree is, therefore :

<coord-tree>::= (COORD {<coord-branch>}+) .

For example, the AECS expression :

(COORD british_airways (SPECIF government_1 prime_minister))
means, according to the definition of the COORD operator given in the previous Section, that British Airways and the government of the prime minister take part, in a co-ordinated and concomitant manner, in a given event. The representation in tree-format of this expression is given in Fig. 3. Please note that coord-trees subsume each of their coord-branches (i.e., they carry the same information augmented).

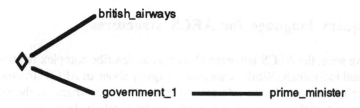

Fig. 3. An example of coord-tree.

According to the priority rule, see the previous Section, the "enum-trees" are built upon the coord-trees ; they subsume their branches, i.e., their coord-trees :

<enum-branch>::= <coord-branch> | <coord-tree>
<enum-tree>::= (ENUM {<enum-branch>}+)

We give now in Fig. 4 the tree-format representation of the example :
(ENUM air-france (COORD british_airways (SPECIF government_1 prime_minister)))

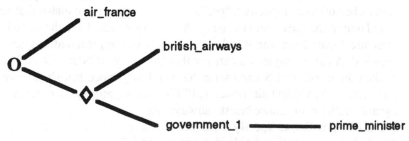

Fig. 4. An example of enum-tree.

The last AECS structure is represented by the "altern-trees", whose syntax is :

\<altern-branch\>::= \<enum-branch\> | \<enum-tree\>

\<altern-tree\>::= (ALTERN {\<altern-branch\>}+)

Accordingly, the tree-format representation of the example :

(ALTERN air-france (COORD british_airways (SPECIF government_1
prime_minister)))

can be represented as in Fig. 5. ALTERN's semantics is quite similar to that of an exclusive OR, stating that one and only one of the arguments take part in the event.

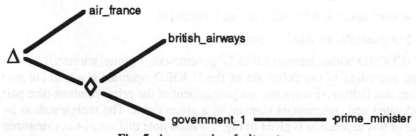

Fig. 5. An example of altern-tree.

5 A query language for AECS structures

As we have seen, the AECS language allows us to describe complex relations among concepts and individuals. While, sometimes, a query about an AECS structure must be able to exploit completely the information carried by this structure, the situation in which only part of this information is really useful is relatively frequent. Please take as an example the AECS expression '(COORD john_ paul_)', that expresses the fact that both John and Paul take part in a particular event in a co-ordinated manner. While sometimes this is exactly the information looked for with a query (i.e., whether they are involved "necessarily together" in the event), it is often the case that the information we want to obtain is simply if John (or Paul) takes part in the event.

Therefore, a query language operating on the AECS structures must be able to express a wide range of query modalities, and to obtain constantly the correct results. Keeping in mind the possibility of expressing the AECS structures in term of trees, we can state here the following basic requirements for this query language :

1) It must be possible to specify a "perfect match", defined as a match that succeeds if and only if the query, and the target AECS expression, have the same identical structure (apart from variables), i.e., if their tree representations are strictly identical. As an example, we can say that the query '(ENUM ?x ?y)' succeeds against the target AECS expression '(ENUM air_france british_airways)', but fails against '(COORD air_france (SPECIF british_airways air_company))' or against '(ENUM air_france british_airways twa_)'.

2) It must be possible to specify a perfect match apart from "cardinality", i.e., a match that succeeds if and only if the query, and the target expression, have the same identical structure — apart from variables and, chiefly, without taking into

account the cardinality of the AECS lists. In this case, '(ENUM *?x ?y*)' succeeds against '(ENUM air_france british_airways)' and against '(ENUM air_france british_airways twa_)', but fails against '(COORD air_france british_airways)'.

3) It must be possible to specify a "subsumed" match, i.e., a match that succeeds if and only if the query, and the target expression, carry an information which is globally congruent from a semantic point of view. For example, we admit here the presence, in the target expression, of additional SPECIF lists (lists of attributes). According to this paradigm, '(COORD *?x ?y*)' succeeds against '(COORD air_france british_airways)', against '(COORD air_france (SPECIF british_airways *air_company*))', and '(COORD air_france british_airways twa_)'.

4) It must be obviously possible to mix the above kind of queries, in such a way that, for example, *perfect match is required for the top level structures of the query and target trees, but not for the underlying parts*, see also the examples of Table 2 below. In this way, e.g., '(ALTERN *?x ?y*)' can match against '(ALTERN twa_ (COORD air_france british_airways))'.

We can now define a query language for AECS structures. In order to make queries clearer, the query language is based on the logical structures of the original AECS sub-language, augmented to allow a) the use of variables, and b) the correct specification of the kind of match required by the query. The AECS query language is therefore defined in the following way. Take AECS as the basis, but allow :

- the use of variables (*?x*), possibly with constraints ;
- the use of the operator STRICT-SUBSUMPTION, taking as argument an NKRL entity (variable, concept or individual), or one of the AECS structures (coord-branches, coord-trees, enum-trees, altern-trees) defined in the previous Section ;
- the use of the operator STRICT-CARDINALITY, taking as argument an NKRL argument, or one of the AECS structures defined in the previous Section.

STRICT-CARDINALITY and STRICT-SUBSUMPTION have the following operational meaning :

- the presence of a STRICT-SUBSUMPTION operator forces the interpretation of the argument according to a "no-subsumption" rule, thus requiring a "perfect match", see point 1 before, on the type (NKRL entity, coord-branch, coord-tree, enum-tree, altern-tree)) of the argument ;
- the presence of a STRICT-CARDINALITY operator forces the interpretation of the argument according to a "fixed-cardinality" rule, thus requiring a perfect match, see point 2 before, on the cardinality of the argument ;
- the absence of any of the two special operators implies the "subsuming" rule, see point 3 before, thus producing a successful match if the semantics of the query construct *is subsumed* by the semantics of the matched construct.

The semantics of the two operators is operationally defined in the next Section. To illustrate what expressed above, we give in Table 2 some examples concerning different modalities of matching the target structure : '(ENUM twa_ (COORD air_france (SPECIF british_airways *air_company*) continental_))'. Additional examples are given in the discussion of the algorithm, next Section. For some examples of use of the above operators within the COBALT's query language, see, e.g., [1].

The query : '(ENUM *?x* (STRICT-SUBSUMPTION (COORD air_france british_airways continental)))' will succeed, binding *x* to 'twa_'. Please note that the STRICT-SUBSUMPTION operator concerns only the general structure of the coord-trees, and not the structure of the single coord-branches.
The query : '(ENUM *?x* (COORD air_france (STRICT-SUBSUMPTION british_airways) continental))' will fail, because of the STRICT-SUBSUMPTION restriction which prevents 'british_airways' from matching a coord-branch.
The query : '(ENUM *?x* (STRICT-CARDINALITY (COORD air_france british_airways)))' will fail, because of the STRICT-CARDINALITY restriction.
The query : '(STRICT-SUBSUMPTION (ENUM *?x* (COORD air_france british_airways)))' succeeds, binding *x* to "twa_". The STRICT-SUBSUMPTION restriction only concerns the top-level structure of the enum-trees.
The query : '(ENUM *?x* air_france)' will succeed, binding *x* to "twa_".
The query : '(STRICT-SUBSUMPTION (ENUM *?x* (STRICT-SUBSUMPTION air_france)))' fails, due to the '(STRICT-SUBSUMPTION air_france)' restriction.
The query : '(STRICT-SUBSUMPTION (COORD air_france british_airways))' fails.
The query : '(COORD air_france british_airways)' will succeed.

Table 2. Examples of AECS unifications.

6 The AECS matching algorithm

The AECS matching algorithm can be defined in a recursive way as following :
1) *A coord-branch query (i.e., a concept or individual, or a variable, or a SPECIF list) matches a target coord-branch iff*
    — *there is a variable substitution on the heads, such that their heads are identical AND*
    — *the tail of the query coord-branch is empty (no SPECIF sub-branch) OR*
    — *there is a permutation of the order of the tail of the target (matched) coord-branch, and of the order of the tail of the query coord-branch, such that each SPECIF sub-branch matches.*

According to this rule, for example :
- *?x* matches against 'twa_' binding *x* to 'twa_' ;
- *?x* matches against '(SPECIF twa_ *air_company*)' binding *x* to 'twa_' ;
- '(SPECIF twa_ *?x*)' does not match against 'twa_' ;
- '(SPECIF twa_ *?x*)' matches against '(SPECIF twa_ *air_company american_*)' binding *x* to both '*air_company*' and '*american_*'.

2) *A "restricted" coord-branch query (i.e., a concept or individual, or a variable, or a SPECIF list restricted by a preceding STRICT-SUBSUMPTION construct) matches a coord-branch iff*
    — *there is a variable substitution on the heads, such that their heads are identical AND*

— *inhere is a permutation of the order of the tail of the target (matched) coord-branch, and of the order of the tail of the query coord-branch, such that each SPECIF sub-branch matches in the restricted sense.*

According to this rule, for example :

- *?x* does not match against '(SPECIF twa_ *air_company*)' ;
- '(SPECIF twa_ *?x*)' does not match against 'twa_' ;
- '(SPECIF twa_ *?x*)' matches against '(SPECIF twa_ *air_company*)' binding *x* to 'air_company'.

3) *Other queries are handled as summarised below. With respect to the queries including a '(STRICT-CARDINALITY arg)' restriction, not explicitly detailed here for simplicity's sake, the rules are the same that would apply in the presence of a bare argument ('arg'), after having checked that the cardinality constraint.*

— *Restricted coord-branch queries, e.g., '(STRICT-SUBSUMPTION ?x)' :*
  when matched against simple coord-branches : match according to the sub-algorithm 2 above ;
  when matched against anything else : fail.

— *Unrestricted coord-branch queries, e.g., ?x :*
  when matched against simple coord-branches : match according to the sub-algorithm 1 above ;
  when matched against coord-trees : match for each unrestricted match against one of the coord-branches in the target ;
  when matched against enum-trees : match for each unrestricted match against one of the enum-branches in the target ;
  when matched against altern-trees : fail.

— *COORD "strict subsumption" queries, e.g., '(STRICT-SUBSUMPTION (COORD ?x ?y))' :*
  when matched against coord trees : match for each permutation of the coord-branches in the query such that each coord-branch in the query matches against the corresponding coord-branch in the target ;
  when matched against anything else : fail.

— *COORD queries, e.g., '(COORD ?x ?y)' :*
  when matched against simple coord-branches : fail ;
  when matched against coord-trees : match for each permutation of the coord-branches in the query such that each coord-branch in the query matches against the corresponding coord-branch in the target ;
  when matched against enum-trees : match for each coord-branch in the target enum-tree such that the query and that branch match ;
  when matched against altern-trees : fail.

— *ENUM "strict subsumption" queries, e.g., '(STRICT-SUBSUMPTION (ENUM ?x ?y))' :*
  when matched against enum-trees : match for each permutation of the enum-branches in the query such that each enum-branch in the query matches against the corresponding enum-branch in the target ;
  when matched against anything else : fail.

— *ENUM queries, e.g., '(ENUM ?x ?y)' :*
  when matched against enum-trees : match for each permutation of the enum-branches in the query such that each enum-branch in the query matches against the corresponding enum-branch in the target ;
  when matched against anything else : fail.

— *ALTERN "strict subsumption" queries, e.g., '(STRICT-SUBSUMPTION (ALTERN ?x ?y))' :*
  when matched against altern-trees : match for each permutation of the
      altern-branches in the query such that each altern-branch.in the query
      matches against the corresponding altern-branch in the target ;
  when matched against anything else : fail.
— *ALTERN queries, e.g., '(ALTERN ?x ?y)' :*
  when matched against altern-trees : match for each permutation of the
      altern-branches in the query such that each altern-branch in the query
      matches against the corresponding altern-branch in the target ;
  when matched against anything else : match iff exactly one of the
      altern-branches matches against the target.

7 Conclusions

In this paper, we have described the conceptual structures proper to a (very limited) subset, the AECS sublanguage, of a complete knowledge representation language, NKRL, used to provide a normalised description of the meaning of complex narrative documents. One of the main characteristics of NKRL resides in the addition of a "taxonomy of events" to the traditional "taxonomy of concepts", see [2]. A second important feature is represented by the fact that the catalogue of "basic templates", see Section 2.1 above, is part and parcel of the definition of the language. This particular approach implies that: i) a system-builder does not have to create himself the structural knowledge needed to describe the events proper to a large class of narrative documents ; ii) it becomes easier to secure the reproduction or the sharing of previous results.

We have then explained how it was possible to set up a query language allowing to retrieve correctly the AECS information of the structured arguments. This can show, among other things, that the "NKRL technology" is not only interested in producing a suitable, conceptual representation of narrative texts, but it is also able to propose flexible tools in order to make use efficiently of this representation.

References

1. Gilardoni, L. (1993) *COBALT Deliverable 2 Addendum : Interface Between Component Parts* (Report COBALT/QUI/14/93). Milano: Quinary SpA.
2. Skuce, D., ed. (1995) *Proceedings of the IJCAI'95 Workshop on Basic Ontological Issues in Knowledge Sharing*. Ottawa: Department of Computer Science of the University of Ottawa.
3. Sowa, J.F. (1984) *Conceptual Structures : Information Processing in Mind and Machine*. Reading (MA): Addison-Wesley.
4. Zarri, G.P. (1992) "Encoding the Temporal Characteristics of the Natural Language Descriptions of (Legal) Situations", in *Expert Systems in Law*, Martino, A., ed. Amsterdam: Elsevier Science Publishers.
5. Zarri, G.P. (1994) "A Glimpse of NKRL, the 'Narrative Knowledge Representation Language'", in *Knowledge Representation for Natural Language Processing in Implemented Systems - Papers from the 1994 Fall Symposium*, Ali, S., ed. Menlo Park (CA): AAAI Press.

On the Handling of Imperfect Data
in Relational Database Systems
- From Null Values to Possibility Distributions -

Patrick BOSC, Olivier PIVERT

IRISA-ENSSAT BP 447 22305 LANNION Cedex FRANCE
e-mail : bosc@enssat.fr, pivert@enssat.fr
tel : (33) 96 46 50 30, fax : (33) 96 37 01 99

Abstract. In this paper, we present a brief survey of some approaches that have been proposed for the treatment of imperfect data in relational database systems and we focus on the possibility theory-based approach which is shown to provide a unifying way of handling uncertain and imprecise data. We are then concerned with the Boolean querying of possibilistic databases. We point out some interesting properties as well as some current research issues relating to the use of the possibilistic approach in a relational database context.

1 Introduction

Up to now, database management systems have been mainly used for business purposes to respond to a certain range of applications where data are perfectly known. However, in real life, information is often imperfect in several ways. Indeed, the attribute value of an item may be completely unknown, partially known (i.e. known as belonging to a proper subset of the attribute domain), or uncertain [24]. Besides, an attribute may be irrelevant for some of the considered items; moreover we may not know whether the value does not exist or is simply unknown.

In this paper, we consider different approaches that have been proposed for the treatment of imperfect data and we focus on the possibility theory, which is shown to provide a unifying way of handling uncertain and imprecise data. We only consider imperfection in atomic data values and not in association between values. In section 2, we present a brief survey of different approaches that have been proposed to deal with imperfect data values. In section 3, we consider the Boolean querying of databases where values may be represented by possibility distributions. We also point out some aspects related to the definition of an extended relational algebra allowing to handle such possibilistic databases.

2 Some Approaches to the Representation of Imperfect Data

Let us recall that in this paper, we only consider imperfection in atomic data values. Hereafter, we present several approaches that have been proposed to handle such imperfect information. Other approaches like maybe tuples and disjunctive databases are not described here since they concern imperfection in associations between data (see for instance [31] for a survey).

2.1 Null Values

Underlying the relational database model is the assumption that the information to be represented fits into relations. As noted in [30], this implies in particular that the data are represented by values of the attributes in the schema. This assumption can thus fail when part of the information is not specified. To tackle this problem, the use of null values in the relational database model has been proposed by several researchers.

For databases under the Closed World Assumption, two notable types of null values have been proposed [2, 7, 8]: i) existential value (denoted ω): the value exists, but it is not known, ii) inexistent value (denoted $\perp$): the value does not exists (in other words, it is not applicable). The first type of relations containing null values are the Codd relations. An example of a Codd relation is:

emp	dept	tel
Smith	Sales	5512
Black	Sales	ω
Victor	Sales	$\perp$

from which we can infer that Black has one phone, but we do not know the number, and Victor does not have a phone. Inapplicable values were studied by various researchers [8, 11, 26, 29]. An aspect of the existential null value was pointed out by Lipski [19, 20] who defined information which surely (alternatively possibly) can be extracted from a database in the presence of unknown values, and proposed a query language containing these modal operators.

Imielinsky and Lipski [16] introduced several unknown values for obtaining a richer modeling power, and they generalized the relational algebra operators. Null values are represented by variables, where two different variables may or may not represent the same constant. An example is:

professor	course	classroom
Marc	Databases	AX210
Pierre	x	H1309
Thomas	Mechanics	y
Thomas	Languages	y

In this example, the course taught by Pierre in classroom H1309 and the rooms in which Thomas teaches his two courses are unknown, but we know that Thomas teaches both his courses in the same classroom.

Different extensions of Codd relations have been proposed [12, 13]. If Codd relations are supplemented with global conditions composed of equalities and/or inequalities (for instance $x \neq y \wedge x \neq$ Mechanics $\wedge y \neq$ H3322), the g-relations are obtained. Conditional relations are obtained by adding to Codd relations or to g-relations a column containing local conditions composed of equalities and inequalities.

2.2 Or-sets and Restricted Cardinality Sets

Or-sets (or disjunctive sets) [15, 18, 19] generalize existential null values. An existential value represents an attribute whose actual value is in a database domain. An or-set represents an attribute whose value is in an explicit, smaller set. An ordinary atomic value can be viewed as a singleton. An existential value corresponds to an or-set containing the entire attribute domain. Or-sets can also contain a special value Ø to represent the possibility of there being no value. An example of a relation containing or-sets is:

professor	course
Marc	Databases
Thomas	{Physics, Chemistry, Biology}
{Susan, Martha, Ø}	Algebra

In this relation, the second tuple represents that Thomas teaches one of the course of the set {Physics, Chemistry, Biology}. The third tuple represents that either Susan teaches Algebra, or that Martha does, or that the course is not taught.

As for the existential values, certain and possible information may be obtained from a database containing or-sets. Algebraic operations on or sets have been defined by several researchers e.g. [14, 20]. Nevertheless, as shown in [15], it is not possible to define algebraic operators over relations having or-sets that satisfy the requirements (preservation of true sets, recursiveness) for a correct generalization of the relational algebra.

Generalized or-sets have been proposed in [22] in order to extend the expressive power of or-sets. They are sets in which the actual value is understood to be some non-empty subset of the stored set. Another kind of sets are defined in [21], the restricted cardinality sets (rc-sets). An rc-set is a pair (S, ρ_S) where S is a set of values from the attribute domain and ρ_S is a pair (p, q) such that $0 \leq p \leq q \leq n$ with n denoting the number of elements in S. An rc-set is interpreted as meaning that the actual value of the attribute is some subset s of the stored set of candidates S such that $p \leq card(s) \leq q$. If $q = 0$ the actual value is the empty set. These sets suffer from the same drawbacks as or-sets as far as associated algebraic operators are concerned.

2.3 The Possibilistic Approach

The possibility theory [28] provides a purely ordinal model for uncertainty where imprecision is represented by means of a preference relation coded by a total order over the possible situations. This constitutes the fundamental difference between this theory and the probability theory which is quantitative. The possibility theory is structurally more qualitative, but is better suited to the representation of imprecise information [9]. In particular, the ability of representing in an absolute way the complete ignorance is a typical aspect of the possibility theory. More generally, the possibility theory allows to model uncertain information which is not of a stochastic but rather of a subjective nature.

The concept of possibility distribution in a universe X was introduced by L.A. Zadeh [28]. It concerns an application π of X to [0, 1] which is interpreted as a restriction of the possible values of a variable taking its values in X. We denote $\pi(a)$ the degree of possibility that the effective value of x should be a.

The possibilitic approach can be applied for representing uncertain values in a relational database in the following way [23, 24, 25]. The available information about the value of a single-valued attribute A for a tuple x is represented by a possibility distribution $\pi_{A(x)}$ on $D \cup \{e\}$ where D denotes the domain of attribute A and e is an extra-element which stands for the case when the attribute does not apply to x. If information is consistent, there should exist a value in $D \cup \{e\}$ for $A(x)$, which leads to the normalization condition $\max_d \pi_{A(x)}(d) = 1$ (i.e., at least one value in $D \cup \{e\}$ is completely possible). For instance, the information "Paul is young" will be represented by: $\pi_{Age(Paul)}(e) = 0$ and $\pi_{Age(Paul)}(d) = \mu_{young}(d)$, $\forall d \in D$. Here, μ_{young} is a membership function which represents the vague predicate "young" in a given context. It is important to notice that the values restricted by a possibility distribution are considered as mutually exclusive. $\pi_{A(x)}(d) = 1$ only means that d is a completely possible value for $A(x)$, but does not mean that it is certain that d is the value of A for x (or in other words that d is necessarily the value of A for x), except if $\forall d' \neq d$, $\pi_{A(x)}(d') = 0$. This approach proposes a unified framework for representing precise values of attributes (singletons), as well as imprecise ones (regular sets) or vague ones (fuzzy sets), and the following null value situations: i) the value of A for x is completely unknown : $\forall d \in D$, $\pi_{A(x)}(d) = 1$, $\pi_{A(x)}(e) = 0$, ii) the attribute A does not apply to x : $\forall d \in D$, $\pi_{A(x)}(d) = 0$, $\pi_{A(x)}(e) = 1$, and iii) we don't know whether we are in situation i or ii : $\forall d \in D$, $\pi_{A(x)}(d) = 1$, and $\pi_{A(x)}(e) = 1$. Multiple-valued attributes can be dealt with in this framework too [25].

It is worth comparing the expressive power of the possibilistic approach with the other models presented above. The possibilistic framework allows to represent unknown values and inapplicable values. On the other hand, it is not a priori possible to represent marked unknown values, unless we introduce the notion of marked possibility distributions. Moreover, the possibility theory-based approach can obviously be seen as a generalization of or-sets (a notion of preference is added).

In this brief survey, we have not considered probabilistic database models (see for instance [1, 17]). Probabilistic databases are a somewhat different case since uncertain data is there of a stochastic nature. The possibilistic representation explicitly handles imprecision (e.g. incomplete knowledge) which the probabilistic representation do not.

3 Boolean Querying of Possibilistic Databases

3.1 Possibility Measure, Necessity Measure and Matching Mechanism

According to the possibilistic view [24], when a condition applies to imperfectly known data, the result of a query evaluation can no longer be a single value. Since the precise values of some attributes for some items are not known, the fact that these items satisfy or not the query (to some degree) may be uncertain. It is why two degrees attached to two points of view are used: the extent to which it is possible that the condition is satisfied and the extent to which it is certain that the condition is satisfied. From the possibility distributions $\pi_{A(x)}$ and a condition P, we can compute the fuzzy set ΠP (resp. NP) of the items whose A-value possibly (resp. necessarily) satisfies the condition P. Three kinds of conditions are to be considered : i) $A \theta v$ where A denotes an attribute, θ is a comparison operator and v is a constant, ii) $A \in S$ where S is a set of constants, iii) $A \theta B$ where A and B denote two attributes. In the following, we consider the case where such conditions are crisp, and we point out some interesting properties concerning in particular the ordering of the answers obtained.

Atomic Conditions Involving One Attribute

In the first two cases (A θ v, A ∈ S), the membership degree of a tuple x to ΠP and NP are respectively given by [24] :

$$\mu_{\Pi P}(x) = \Pi(P; A(x)) = \sup_{d \in D} \min(\mu_P(d), \pi_{A(x)}(d)) \tag{1}$$

$$\mu_{NP}(x) = N(P; A(x)) = \inf_{d \in D \cup \{e\}} \max(\mu_P(d), 1 - \pi_{A(x)}(d)) \tag{2}$$

$\Pi(P; A(x))$ estimates to what extent there is a value restricted by $\pi_{A(x)}$ compatible with P and $N(P; A(x))$ to what extent all the values more or less possible for A(x) are included in P (the condition P being seen here as a crisp set of acceptable values). Since we only consider Boolean querying, function μ_P is such that $\mu_P(d) = 1$ if P(d) is true, 0 otherwise. The condition P corresponds either to a comparison (case i) or to the belonging to a set of values (case ii).

Example. If John's age and the predicate P: "age ∈ [20, 25]" are represented according to the following figure:

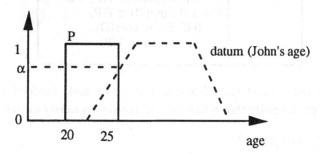

the computation of "John's age ∈ [20, 25]" will be based on the computation of the values:

$\min(\pi_{John's\ age}(d), \mu_P(d))$ for which the supremum (α) will be taken to obtain Π.

and:

$\max(1 - \pi_{John's\ age}(d), \mu_P(d))$ for which the lowest value (0) corresponds to N.

The following table shows some properties of the possibility and necessity degrees depending on the situations for the information available (precise, interval or fuzzy). In this table, D denotes the possibility distribution associated to datum d and T(P) is the set of values x such that P(x) is true. The notions of core and support of a possibility distribution D are defined as:

core(D) = {x ∈ U | $\pi_D(x) = 1$}

supp(D) = {x ∈ U | $\pi_D(x) > 0$}

where U denotes the universe underlying the possibility distribution.

precise (d)	$(\Pi, N) \in \{0, 1\} \times \{0, 1\}$ $\Pi = N = 1$ if $d \in T(P)$, 0 otherwise

interval	$(\Pi, N) \in \{0, 1\} \times \{0, 1\}$
	
	$\Pi = 1$ if $D \cap T(P) \neq \varnothing$,
	    0 otherwise
	
	$N = 1$ if $D \subseteq T(P)$,
	    0 otherwise

fuzzy	$(\Pi, N) \in [0, 1] \times [0, 1]$
	
	$\Pi = 1$ if core(D) $\cap$ T(P) $\neq \varnothing$,
	    0 if supp(D) $\cap$ T(P) $= \varnothing$
	$N = 1$ if supp(D) $\subseteq$ T(P),
	    0 if $\exists\, x \in$ core(D)
	        and $x \notin$ T(P)

In the considered context (i.e., Boolean querying), and provided that $\pi_{A(x)}$ is normalized, it can be easily shown that ΠP and NP always satisfy the relation:

$$\forall x, \mu_{NP}(x) > 0 \Rightarrow \mu_{\Pi P}(x) = 1 \tag{3}.$$

Atomic Conditions Involving Two Attributes

In case of a condition A θ B, if we assume that A and B are non-interactive attributes, the membership degrees of a tuple (x, y) to ΠP and NP are respectively given by [24]:

$$\mu_{\Pi P}(x, y) = \Pi(P; A(x), B(y))$$
$$= \sup_{(d, d') \in D \times D} \min(\mu_\theta(d, d'), \pi_{A(x)}(d), \pi_{B(y)}(d')) \tag{4}$$

$$\mu_{NP}(x, y) = N(P; A(x), B(y))$$
$$= \inf_{(d, d') \in D \cup \{e\} \times D \cup \{e\}} \max(\mu_\theta(d, d'), 1 - \pi_{A(x)}(d), 1 - \pi_{B(y)}(d')) \tag{5}$$

where θ denotes the comparison operator involved in condition P.

Here again, it can be shown that ΠP and NP satisfy relation (3) provided that $\pi_{A(x)}$ and $\pi_{B(y)}$ are normalized.

Compound Conditions

Compound conditions involving disjunction, conjunction or negation of elementary conditions can be handled using the following basic relations of possibility theory, which express decomposability properties of possibility and necessity degrees with respect to conjunctions and disjunctions provided that the attribute values are logically independent (for any value of $A_1(x)$, all values compatible with $\pi_{A_2(x)}$ are allowed and conversely):

$$N(P ; A(x)) = 1 - \Pi(\overline{P}; A(x));$$
$$\Pi(P_1 \times P_2; A_1(x) \times A_2(x)) = \min (\Pi(P_1; A_1(x)), \Pi(P_2; A_2(x)));$$
$$N(P_1 \times P_2; A_1(x) \times A_2(x)) = \min (N(P_1; A_1 x)), N(P_2; A_2(x)));$$
$$\Pi(P_1 + P_2; A_1(x) \times A_2(x)) = \max (\Pi(P_1; A_1(x)), \Pi(P_2; A_2(x)));$$
$$N(P_1 + P_2; A_1(x) \times A_2(x)) = \max (N(P_1; A_1(x)), N(P_2; A_2(x)))$$

where the attribute A_i and the condition P_i ($i = 1, 2$) refer to the same domain, the overbar denotes the set complementation (defined by $\mu_{\overline{P}}(d) = 1 - \mu_P(d)$), $A_1(x) \times A_2(x)$ denotes an extended Cartesian product, expressing a conjunction, defined by:

$$\pi_{A_1(x) \times A_2(x)}(d_1, d_2) = \min (\pi_{A_1(x)}(d_1), \pi_{A_2(x)}(d_2))$$

$P_1 \times P_2$ is similarly defined, $P_1 + P_2 = \overline{\overline{P_1} \times \overline{P_2}}$ expresses a disjunction, namely:

$$\mu_{P_1 + P_2}(d_1, d_2) = \max (\mu_{P_1}(d_1), \mu_{P_2}(d_2)).$$

Note that the above expressions of $N(P_1 + P_2; A_1(x) \times A_2(x))$ and $\Pi(P_1 \times P_2; A_1(x) \times A_2(x))$ require the logical independence of the attribute values respectively restricted by $\pi_{A_1}(x)$ and $\pi_{A_2}(x)$, to be valid.

Obviously, for a compound condition P, ΠP and NP satisfy relation (3) provided that $\pi_{A(x)}$ and $\pi_{B(y)}$ are normalized. Thus, it is possible to compute the set of items which more or less possibly satisfy an elementary condition and to distinguish among them the items which more or less certainly satisfy this condition. In other words, we have a total order on the set of answers. An item with degrees ($\Pi 1$, $N1$) is a better answer than an item with degrees ($\Pi 2$, $N2$) if $\Pi 1 > \Pi 2$ or if $\Pi 1 = \Pi 2$ (= 1) and $N1 > N2$.

3.2 Towards an Extended Relational Algebra ?

Prade and Testemale [24] have defined some extended operators allowing to manipulate relations including values represented by possibility distributions. The selection operation is defined in terms of fuzzy pattern matching, i.e. it delivers a double fuzzy relation corresponding to the tuples that possibly and necessarily satisfy the selection condition (cf formulae (1) and (2)). Of course, when the selection bears only on exactly known values (i.e. not represented by possibility distributions), the result is not a double relation but a single one. The definition of the join operation is based on formulae (4) and (5). This operation also delivers a double fuzzy relation.

The projection operation applies only on these relations to eliminate certain attributes not requested by the user in the answer.

An important point lies in the fact that the extended relational operators defined in this framework do not really form an algebra in the usual sense since they cannot be composed. As soon as a selection (or a join) is performed, the result is no longer a relation but a double one (by nature, the matching procedure produces a pair of degrees for each item returned) and the projection can only remove attributes from it and it keeps the associated degrees. As a consequence, the selection is not permutable and a query will basically consist of operations building a relation onto which a selection followed by a final projection will apply. Thus, some queries are not expressible in this language whose expressive power is more limited than the usual relational algebra. Another problem, which is not pointed out in [24] concerns the definition of set oriented operators in the context of extended relations.

Set oriented operations must be considered carefully in particular because the usual notion of redundancy has to be reconsidered. As usual, two extended relations will be said compatible if their attributes are in one-to-one correspondence such that corresponding attributes are defined on the same domain [7]. The union of two compatible extended relations R and S corresponds to the union defined on the Cartesian product of the set of fuzzy subsets of the respective attribute domains [24]. After performing a union, it is necessary to eliminate the tuples considered as redundant. In ordinary algebra, two tuples are redundant if they are identical. When possibility distributions are involved, the notion of identity has to be revisited. Observe that if two quantities x and y are known to be equal, the possibility distributions π_x and π_y which restrict their possible values in case of incomplete information should be equal, i.e. $x = y \Rightarrow \pi_x = \pi_y$, but the converse is false. Knowing that $\pi_x = \pi_y$, it is only *possible* that $x = y$ (when π_x and π_y are not membership functions of singletons). Thus, in an extended relation resulting from a union, two identical tuples (each of them including at least one possibility distribution) cannot be considered redundant in general. A similar problem is encountered when defining the intersection: a tuple will belong to $R \cap S$ if it is redundant with a tuple of R and a tuple of S.
To give a sound definition of tuple redundancy, we need to make an assumption concerning the extended relations which will constitute the arguments of a set oriented operator. These relations must correspond to the same source of information. In other words, each of these relations must be obtained from a restriction (bearing only on exactly known values since the set oriented operators are defined for single relations and not for double ones) of the same initial extended relation. In this case, tuple redundancy can be defined properly in terms of tuple identity, i.e. two tuples are redundant if they have exactly the same representation as far as both usual (crisp) attribute values and possibility distributions are concerned.

From a practical point of view, the fact that the extended operators defined above do not form an algebra is of course a severe drawback of the possibilistic database model. To deal with this problem, an approach that seems to be promising consists in manipulating so-called twofold extended relations i.e. relations where each tuple is associated with a possibility degree and a necessity degree. In initial relations (i.e. relations that are not issued from a selection) these degree are both equal to 1. We are currently investigating this approach but preliminary results show that most of the usual compositionality properties can be preserved in this framework.

4 Conclusion

This paper is concerned with the handling of imperfect data in relational database systems. Imprecision and uncertainty are almost unavoidable when we want to represent and to store the available information as it is, without losing a significative part of it. The possibility theory offers a technically sound and powerful framework for dealing both with imprecision and uncertainty, and is notably more general than some other approaches (e.g. null values, or-sets). We have shown how the values of an imprecise information could be represented by an appropriate possibility distribution and we have described the principle of selecting this data by means of usual (crisp) conditions. In the general case, each element receives two satisfaction degrees: one expresses the possibility, the other the certainty that the data satisfies the criterion. We have shown that, in the case of Boolean querying, the pair of measures {possibility, necessity} induce a total order on the set of answers. We have also pointed out the fact that the extended operators that have been proposed in this context [24] do not form an algebra. Efficient query evaluation in an uncertain/imprecise context remains an open problem although some works have already been undertaken [3, 6, 27].

Another extension, not dealt with in this paper, concerns the selection of (possibly imprecise) data by means of conditions which may themselves be imprecise or vague. Several works exists concerning the fuzzy set-based interpretation of such queries (see e.g. [9, 10, 24] about fuzzy querying of imprecise data and [4, 5] about fuzzy querying of precise data). The implementations which already exist (especially for fuzzy querying systems) tend to show that, when clearly identified, problems can be solved in a reasonable computational time.

References

[1] Barbara D., Garcia-Molina H., Porter D., The Management of Probabilistic Data, IEEE Transactions on Knowledge and Data Engineering, 4, pp.487-502, 1992.

[2] Biskup J., A formal approach to null values in database relations. In H. Gallaire & J.M. Nicolas eds., Advances in Data Base Theory, vol. 1, Plenum Press, pp. 299-341, 1981.

[3] Bosc P. Galibourg M., Indexing principles for a fuzzy data base, Information Systems, 14, pp. 493-499, 1989.

[4] Bosc P., Pivert O., Some approaches for relational database flexible querying, International Journal of Intelligent Information Systems, 1, pp. 323-354, 1992.

[5] Bosc P., Pivert O., SQLf: A Relational Database Language for Fuzzy Querying, IEEE Transactions on Fuzzy Systems, 3, pp. 1-17, 1995.

[6] Boss B., An Index based on Superimposed Coding for a Fuzzy Object Oriented Database System, Proc. NAFIPS'94, pp. 289-290, 1994.

[7] Codd E.F., Extending the Database Relational Model to Capture More Meaning, ACM Transactions on Database Systems, 4, pp. 397-434, 1979.

[8] Codd E.F., Missing Information (applicable and inapplicable) in relational databases, SIGMOD Record, 15, pp. 53-78, 1986.

[9] Dubois D., Prade H., Possibility Theory: an Approach to Computerized Processing of Uncertainty, Plenum Press, New York, 1988.

[10] Dubois D., Prade H., Testemale C., Weighted fuzzy pattern matching, Fuzzy Sets and Systems, 28, pp. 313-331, 1988.

[11] Gottlob G., Zicari R., Closed World Databases Opened Through Null Values, Proc. 14th VLDB Conference, Los Angeles, USA, pp. 50-61, 1988.

[12] Grahne G., Dependency satisfaction in databases with incomplete information. Proc. 10th VLDB Conference, Singapore, pp. 37-45, 1984.

[13] Grahne G., The Problem of Incomplete Information in Relational Databases, PhD thesis, University of Helsinki, Finland, March 1989.

[14] Grant J., Incomplete information in a relational database, Annales Societatis Mathematicae Polonae, Series IV: Fundamenta Informaticae III, 3, pp. 363-378, 1980.

[15] Imielinski T., Incomplete information in logical databases, IEEE Transactions on Data Engineering, 12, pp. 29-40, 1989.

[16] Imielinski T, Lipski W., Incomplete information in relational databases, Journal of the ACM, 31, pp. 761-791, 1984.

[17] Lee S.K., An Extended Relational Database Model for Uncertain and Imprecise Information, Proc. 18th VLDB Conference, Vanvouver, Canada, pp. 211-220, 1992.

[18] Libkin L., Wong L., Semantic representations and query languages for or-sets, Proc. 12th PODS, pp. 37-48, 1993.

[19] Lipski W., On semantic issues connected with incomplete information databases, ACM Transactions on Database Systems, 4, pp. 262-296, 1979.

[20] Lipski W., On databases with incomplete information, Journal of the ACM, 28, pp. 41-70, 1981.

[21] Michalewicz Z., Groves L.J., Sets and uncertainty in relational databases, in B. Bouchon, L. Saitta and R.R. Yager eds., Uncertainty and Intelligent Systems, IPMU'88, LNCS 313, Springer Verlag, pp. 127-137, 1988.

[22] Michalewicz Z., Yeo A., Sets in relational databases, Proc. of the Canadian Information Processing Society, pp. 237-245, 1987.

[23] Prade H., Lipski's approach to incomplete information data bases restated and generalized in the setting of Zadeh's possibility theory, Information Systems, 9, pp. 27-42, 1984.

[24] Prade H., Testemale C., Generalizing Database Relational Algebra for the Treatment of Incomplete or Uncertain Information and Vague Queries, Information Sciences, 34, pp. 115-143, 1984.

[25] Prade H., Testemale C., Fuzzy relational databases: representational issues and reduction using similarity measures, Journal of the American Society for Information Science, 38, pp. 118-126, 1987.

[26] Vassiliou Y., Null values in database management: a denotational approach, Proc. ACM-SIGMOD International Conference on Management of Data, Boston, USA, pp. 162-169, 1979.

[27] Yang Q., Liu C., Wu J., Yu C., Dao S, Nakajima H., Efficient Processing of Nested Fuzzy SQL Queries, Proc. IEEE International Conference on Data Engineering, Taiwan, 1995.

[28] Zadeh L.A., Fuzzy sets as a basis for a theory of possibility, Fuzzy Sets and Systems, 1, pp. 3-28, 1978.

[29] Zaniolo C., Database relations with null values, Journal of Computer and System Sciences, 28, pp. 142-166, 1984.

[30] Zicari R., Databases and Incomplete Information, in Proc. of the Workshop on Uncertainty Management in Information Systems: From Needs to Solutions, A. Motro & P. Smets eds., Puerto de Andraitx, Mallorca, Spain, pp. 52-63, 1992.

[31] Zimanyi E, Pirotte A., Imperfect knowledge in databases, Proc. of the Workshop on Uncertainty Management in Information Systems: From Needs to Solutions, P. Smets & A. Motro eds., Avalon, Santa Catalina, USA, pp. 136-186, 1993.

Modified Component Valuations in Valuation Based Systems as a Way to Optimize Query Processing

Sławomir T. Wierzchoń, Mieczysław A. Kłopotek

Institute of Computer Science
Polish Academy of Sciences
ul. Ordona 21, 01-237 Warszawa, Poland
e-mail: stw@ipipan.waw.pl and klopotek@ipipan.waw.pl

Abstract. Valuation-Based System can represent knowledge in different domains including probability theory, Dempster-Shafer theory and possibility theory. More recent studies show that the framework of VBS is also appropriate for representing and solving Bayesian decision problems and optimization problems.

In this paper, after introducing the valuation based system (VBS) framework, we present Markov-like properties of VBS and a method for resolving queries to VBS.

Keywords: Approximate Reasoning, Knowledge Representation and Integration, valuation based systems, query processing, graphical representation of domain knowledge

1 Introduction

Though graphical representation of a domain knowledge has quite long history, its full potential has not been recognized until recently. We should mention here pioneering works of J. Pearl, reported in his monography published in 1988 [5]. Further development in this domain has been achieved by Shenoy and Shafer [11] next and by Shenoy [7] who proposed a unified framework for uncertainty representation and reasoning, called Valuation-Based System, VBS for short [7]. It can represent knowledge in different domains including probability theory, Dempster-Shafer theory and possibility theory. More recent studies show that the framework of VBS is also appropriate for representing and solving Bayesian decision problems [9] and optimization problems [8]. The graphical representation is called a *valuation network*, and the method for solving problems is called the *fusion algorithm*. Closely related to VBS is the algorithm of Lauritzen and Spiegelhalter [4] and HUGIN approach developed by Jensen and co-workers [2].

A Bayesian network (as well as its generalization - VBS) can be regarded as a summary of an expert's experience with an implicit population. Detailed documentation of such knowledge with an explicit population is stored in a database. It appears that there exists a strong connection between these two approaches. First of all, databases are used for knowledge acquisition and Bayesian network identification - see [5] or [1] for a deeper discussion. Studies by Wen [14], and

Wong, Xiang and Nie [15] establish a link between knowledge-based systems for probabilistic reasoning and relational databases. Particularly, they show that the belief update in a Bayesian network can be processed as an ordinary query, and the techniques for query optimization are directly applicable to updating beliefs. The same idea we find in Thoma's [12] works, who proposed a scheme for storing Shafer's belief functions which generalizes graphical models.

In this paper after introducing the valuation based system framework (Section 2), we present Markov-like properties of VBS (Section 3) and a method for resolving queries to VBS (Section 4).

2 Valuation Based Systems

The VBS framework was introduced in [7]. In VBS, a domain knowledge is represented by entities called *variables* and *valuations*. Further, two operations called *combination* and *marginalization* are defined on valuations to perform a local computational method for computing marginals of the joint valuation. The basic components of VBS can be characterized as follows.

Valuations

Let $\mathcal{X} = \{x_1, x_2, ...x_n\}$ be a finite set of variables and Θ_i be the domain (called also *frame*), i.e. a discrete set of possible values of i-th variable. If h is a finite non-empty set of variables then $\Theta(h)$ denotes the Cartesian product of Θ_i for x_i in h, i.e. $\Theta(h) = \times\{\Theta_i | x_i \in h\}$. $\mathcal{R}$ stands for a set of non-negative reals. For each subset s of $\mathcal{X}$ there is a set $D(s)$ called the domain of a valuation. For instance in the case of probabilistic systems $D(s)$ equals to $\Theta(s)$, while under the belief function framework $D(s)$ equals to the power set of $\Theta(s)$, i.e. $D(s) = 2^{\Theta(s)}$. Valuations, being primitives in the VBS framework, can be characterized as mappings $\sigma : D(s) \rightarrow \mathcal{R}$. In the sequel valuations will be denoted by lower-case Greek letters, ρ, σ, τ, and so on. Following Shenoy [10] we distinguish three categories of valuations:

- *Proper valuations*, $\mathcal{P}$, represent knowledge that is partially coherent. (Coherent knowledge means knowledge that has well defined semantics.) This notion plays an important role in the theory of belief functions: by proper valuation it is understood an unnormalized commonality function.
- *Normal valuations*, $\mathcal{N}$, represent another kind of partially coherent knowledge. For instance, in probability theory, a normal valuation is a function whose values sum to 1. Particularly, the elements of $\mathcal{P} \cap \mathcal{N}$ are called proper normal valuations.
- *Positive normal valuations*: it is a subset $\mathcal{U}_s$ of $\mathcal{N}_s$ consisting of all valuations that have unique identities in $\mathcal{N}_s$.

Further there are two types of special valuations:

- *Zero valuations* represent knowledge that is internally inconsistent, i.e. knowledge whose truth value is always false; e.g., in probability theory zero valuation is a valuation identically equal zero. It is assumed that for each $s \subseteq \mathcal{X}$ there is at most one valuation $\zeta_s \in \mathcal{V}_s$. The set of all zero valuations is denoted by $\mathcal{Z}$.
- *Identity valuations*, I, represent total ignorance, i.e. lack of knowledge. In probability theory an identity valuation corresponds to the uniform probability distribution. It is assumed that for each $s \subseteq \mathcal{X}$ the commutative semigroup (w.r.t. the binary operation $\otimes$ defined later) $\mathcal{N}_s \cup \{\zeta_s\}$ has an identity $\iota_s \in \mathcal{V}_s$. Commutative semigroup may have at most one identity.

Combination

By combination we understand a mapping $\otimes : \mathcal{V} \times \mathcal{V} \to \mathcal{N} \cup \mathcal{Z}$ that satisfies the following six axioms:

(C1) If $\rho \in \mathcal{V}_r$ and $\sigma \in \mathcal{V}_s$ then $\rho \otimes \sigma \in \mathcal{V}_{r \cup s}$;
(C2) $\rho \otimes (\sigma \otimes \tau) = (\rho \otimes \sigma) \otimes \tau$;
(C3) $\rho \otimes \sigma = \sigma \otimes \rho$;
(C4) If $\rho \in \mathcal{V}_r$ and zero valuation ζ_s exists then $\rho \otimes \zeta_s \in \mathcal{V}_{r \cup s}$.
(C5) For each $s \subseteq \mathcal{X}$ there exists an identity valuation $\iota_s \in \mathcal{N}_s \cup \{\zeta_s\}$ such that for each valuation $\sigma \in \mathcal{N}_s \cup \{\zeta_s\}$, $\sigma \otimes \iota_s = \sigma$.
(C6) It is assumed that the set $\mathcal{N}_\emptyset$ consists of exactly one element denoted $\iota_\emptyset$.

In practice combination of two valuations is implemented as follows. Let $(+)$ be a binary operation on $\mathcal{R}$. Then $(\sigma \otimes \rho)(x) = \sigma(x.s)(+)\rho(x.r)$ where x is an element from $D(s)$ and $x.r$, $x.s$ stand for the projection (relying upon dropping unnecessary variables) of x onto the appropriate domain $D(r)$ or $D(s)$. In probability theory combination corresponds to pointwise multiplication followed by normalization, and in Dempster-Shafer theory to the Dempster rule of combination.

In the field of uncertain reasoning combination corresponds to aggregation of knowledge: when ρ and σ represent our knowledge about variables in subsets r and s of $\mathcal{X}$ then the valuation $\rho \otimes \sigma$ represents the aggregated knowledge about variables in $r \cup s$. Moreover Wen [14], and Wong, Xiang and Nie [15] showed that under probabilistic context combination corresponds to the (generalized) join operation used in the data-based systems. Hence the belief update in a Bayesian network can be processed as an ordinary query, and the techniques for query optimization are directly applicable to updating beliefs. Similar idea we find in Thoma's [12] works, who proposed a scheme for storing Shafer's belief functions.

If $\rho \otimes \sigma$ is a zero valuation, we say that ρ and σ are inconsistent. On the other hand, if $\rho \otimes \sigma$ is a normal valuation, then we say that ρ and σ are consistent.

An implication of axioms **C1** - **C3** is that the set $\mathcal{N}_s \cup \{\zeta_s\}$ together with the combination operator is a commutative semigroup. If zero valuation ζ_s exists then ζ_s is - by **C4** - the zero of this semigroup. Similarly, by **C5**, the identity valuation is the identity of the semigroup $\mathcal{N}_s \cup \{\zeta_s\}$.

Marginalization

While combination results in knowledge expansion, marginalization results in knowledge contraction. Let s be a non-empty subset of $\mathcal{X}$. It is assumed that for each variable X in s there is a mapping $\downarrow (s - \{X\}) : \mathcal{V}_s \rightarrow \mathcal{V}_{s-\{X\}}$, called marginalization to $s - \{X\}$ or deletion of X, that satisfies the next six axioms:

(M1) Suppose $\sigma \in \mathcal{V}_s$ and suppose $X, Y \in s$. Then
$$(\sigma^{\downarrow(s-\{X\})})^{\downarrow(s-\{X,Y\})} = (\sigma^{\downarrow(s-\{Y\})})^{\downarrow(s-\{X,Y\})} \; ;$$
(M2) If zero valuation exists, then $\zeta_s^{\downarrow(s-\{X\})} = \zeta_{s-\{X\}}$;
(M3) $\sigma^{\downarrow(s-X)} \in \mathcal{N}$ if and only if $\sigma \in \mathcal{N}$;
(M4) If $\sigma \in \mathcal{U}$ then $\sigma^{\downarrow(s-X)} \in \mathcal{U}$;
(CM1) Suppose $\rho \in \mathcal{V}_r$ and $\sigma \in \mathcal{V}_s$. Suppose $X \notin r$ and $X \in s$. Then
$$(\rho \otimes \sigma)^{\downarrow((r \cup s)-\{X\})} = \rho \otimes \sigma^{\downarrow(s-\{X\})}$$
(CM2) Suppose $\sigma \in \mathcal{N}_s$. Suppose $r \subseteq s$ and suppose that ι is an identity for $\sigma^{\downarrow r}$. Then
$$\sigma \otimes \iota = \sigma.$$

Axiom **M1** states that if we delete from s, the domain of a valuation $s \in \mathcal{V}_s$, two variables, say X and Y, then the resulting valuation defined over the subset $r = s - \{X, Y\}$ is invariant to the order of these variables deletion. Particularly, deleting all variables from the set s we obtain the valuation whose domain is the empty set (its existence is guaranteed by axiom **C6**); by axiom **M3** this element equals to $\iota_\emptyset$ if and only if σ is a normal valuation.

Axioms **M2** - **M4** state that the marginalization preserves coherence of knowledge. Axiom **CM1** plays an important role in designing the Message Passing Algorithm (MPA, for short) which will be described later, and axiom **CM2** allows to characterize properties of the identity valuations; some of them are given in the Lemma 1 below.

Lemma 1. *(Shenoy, [10]). If axioms* **C1** - **C6**, **M1** - **M4**, **CM1** *and* **CM2** *are satisfied then the following statements hold.*
  1. Let $\sigma \in \mathcal{V}_s$ and $r \subseteq s$. $\sigma \in \mathcal{N}_s \cup \{\zeta_s\}$ if and only if $\sigma \otimes \iota_r = \sigma$.
  2. If $\sigma \in \mathcal{V}_s$ and $r \subseteq s$ then $\sigma \otimes \iota_r = \sigma \otimes \iota_\emptyset$.
  3. $\iota_s \otimes \iota_r = \iota_{s \cup r}$.
  4. If $r \subseteq s$ then $\iota_s^{\downarrow r} = \iota_r$.

Removal

Removal, called also direct difference, is an "inverse" operation to the combination. Formally, it can be defined as a mapping $\circledR : \mathcal{V} \times (\mathcal{N} \cup \mathcal{Z}) \rightarrow \mathcal{N} \cup \mathcal{Z}$, that satisfies the three axioms:

(R1) If $\sigma \in \mathcal{V}_s$ and $\rho \in \mathcal{N}_r \cup \mathcal{Z}_r$ then $\sigma \circledR \rho \in \mathcal{N}_{r \cup s} \cup \mathcal{Z}_{r \cup s}$.

(R2) For each $\rho \in \mathcal{N}_r \cup \mathcal{Z}_r$ and for each $r \subseteq \mathcal{X}$ there exists an identity ι_r such that $\rho \circledR \rho = \iota_r$.

(CR) If $\sigma, \tau \in \mathcal{V}$ and $\rho \in \mathcal{N} \cup \mathcal{Z}$ then $(\sigma \otimes \tau) \circledR \rho = \sigma \otimes (\tau \circledR \rho)$.

Note that we can define the (pseudo)-inverse of a normal valuation by setting $\rho^{-1} = \iota_\emptyset \circledR \rho$. The main properties of removal are summarized in Lemma 2 given below.

Lemma 2. *(Shenoy, [10]) Suppose that $\sigma, \tau \in \mathcal{V}$ and $\rho \in \mathcal{N} \cup \mathcal{Z}$. Then:*

1. $(\sigma \otimes \tau) \circledR \rho = (\sigma \circledR \rho \otimes \tau) \otimes \tau$.
2. *If $\sigma \in \mathcal{V}_s$ and $r \subseteq s$, then $\sigma \circledR \iota_r = \sigma \otimes \iota_\emptyset = \sigma$.*
3. $[(\sigma \otimes \rho) \circledR \rho] \otimes \rho = \sigma \otimes \rho$.
4. $\rho^{-1} \otimes \rho = \rho \otimes \rho^{-1}$.
5. $\sigma \circledR \rho = \sigma \otimes \rho^{-1}$.

The propagation algorithm

With the concepts already introduced we define a VBS as a 5-tuple $(\mathcal{X}, \mathbf{S}, (\sigma_s)_{s \in \mathbf{S}}, \otimes, \downarrow)$, where $\mathbf{S}$ is a family of subsets of the set of variables $\mathcal{X}$. The aim of uncertain reasoning is to find a marginal valuation

$$\rho = (\otimes \sigma_s | s \in \mathbf{S})^{\downarrow r}, r \subseteq s, s \in \mathbf{S}. \tag{1}$$

To apply the method of local computations, called the message-passing algorithm (MPA, for brevity) observe first that $(\mathcal{X}, \mathbf{S})$ is nothing but a hypergraph. With this hypergraph we associate so-called Markov tree $T = (\mathbf{H}, \mathbf{E})$ i.e. a hypertree, or acyclic hypergraph, $(\mathcal{X}, \mathbf{H})$, being a covering of $(\mathcal{X}, \mathbf{S})$ and organized in a tree structure - see (Shafer and Shenoy, [7]) for details. We say that $(\mathcal{X}, \mathbf{H})$ covers $(\mathcal{X}, \mathbf{S})$ if for each s in $\mathbf{S}$ there exists h in $\mathbf{H}$ such that $s \subseteq h$. Now if $(\mathcal{X}, \mathbf{H})$ is a hypertree if it can be reduced to the empty set by recursively: 1) deleting vertices which are only in one edge, and 2) deleting hyperedges which are subsets of other hyperedges. These two steps define so-called Graham's test. The sequence of hyperedge deletion determines a tree construction sequence (i.e. a set of undirected edges $\mathbf{E}$) for a Markov tree T.

Now, the message passing algorithm can be summarized as follows: it tells the nodes of a Markov tree in what sequence to send their messages to propagate the local information throughout the tree. The algorithm is defined by two parts: a fusion rule, which describes how incoming messages are combined to make marginal valuations and outgoing messages for each node; and a propagation algorithm, which describes how messages are passed from node to node so that all of the local information is globally distributed. Just as propagation takes place along the edges of the tree, fusion takes place within the nodes. It is important to notice that in fact the MPA coincides with the two steps determining the tree construction sequence (i.e. Graham's test).

3 Computing marginals in a Markov tree

Assume that we have constructed a Markov $T = (\mathbf{H},\mathbf{E})$ tree representative of a given VBS, and let us assign a unique number $i \in I = \{1, 2, ..., n\}$, $n = \text{Card}(\mathbf{H})$, to each node in the tree. Denote V_i the original valuation stored in the i-th node of the tree, and R_j the resultant valuation computed for j-th node according to the rule (1). Following [7] this R_j is computed due to the rule

$$R_j = V_j \otimes (\otimes\{M_{i \to j} | i \in N(j)\})^{\downarrow j} \tag{2}$$

where $N(j)$ stands for the set of neighbours of the node j in the Markov tree, $\downarrow j$ means marginalization to the set of variables corresponding to the node j, and $M_{i \to j}$ is the message sent by node i to the node j calculated according to the equation (3)

$$M_{i \to j} = (V_i \otimes (\otimes\{M_{k \to i} | k \in (N(i) - \{j\})\}))^{\downarrow j} \tag{3}$$

It is obvious, that to find R_j we place the node j in the root of the Markov tree and we move successively from leaves of the tree to its root. Note that if k is a leaf node and ι is its neighbour, then $M_{k \to i} = (V_k)^{\downarrow i}$, hence (2) and (3) are defined properly.

A disadvantage of this algorithm is such that we can compute marginals for sets contained in the family $\mathbf{H}$, or for subsets of these sets only. To find marginal for a any subset of variables we need a more elaborated approach. This problem was studied firstly by Xu [16]. Below we present its more economical modification.

First of all we need a generalization of a set chain representation, which has the next form under probabilistic context [4]: For a given tree construction sequence $\{h_1, h_2, ..., h_2\}$ by a separator we understand a set s_i such that $s_i = h_i \cap (h_1 \cup h_2 \cup ... \cup h_{i-1})$. Separators are easily identified in a Markov tree, namely if $\{h_i, h_j\} \in \mathbf{E}$ then $s_i = h_i \cap h_j$. Now, with given tree construction sequence the joint probability distribution can be represented as follows

$$P(x_1, x_2, ..., x_n) = R_1 \prod\{(R_i/S_i) | i = 2, ..., n\} \tag{4}$$

where R_i and S_i are the marginal probabilities defined over the set of variables represented by the sets h_i and s_i, respectively. It appears, that for all VBS's this property can be nicely extended, as we can see below. First we prove a lemma on an important property of VBS removal operator [1]

Lemma 3. *In Valuation-Based Systems, the following property of removal operator holds:*

$$(\rho \circledR \rho^{\downarrow r}) \otimes \rho^{\downarrow r} = \rho$$

---

[1] Shenoy [10] assumes implicitly this property but does not prove it.

Proof. From **CM2**: $\rho \otimes \iota_\emptyset = \rho$. From **CR**: $(\rho \otimes \iota_\emptyset) \circledR \rho^{\downarrow r} = \rho \otimes (\iota_\emptyset \circledR \rho^{\downarrow r})$. But by definition: $\iota_\emptyset \circledR \rho^{\downarrow r} = (\rho^{\downarrow r})^{-1}$, hence $(\rho \circledR \rho^{\downarrow r}) \otimes \rho^{\downarrow r} = (\rho \otimes (\rho^{\downarrow r})^{-1}) \otimes \rho^{\downarrow r}$. From **C2** $(\rho \otimes (\rho^{\downarrow r})^{-1}) \otimes \rho^{\downarrow r} = \rho \otimes ((\rho^{\downarrow r})^{-1} \otimes \rho^{\downarrow r})$. But we know that: From **R2** $\rho \circledR \rho = \iota_\rho$. From **CM2** $(\rho \otimes \iota_\emptyset) \circledR \rho = \iota_\rho$. From **CR** $\rho \otimes (\iota_\emptyset \circledR \rho) = \iota_\rho$, hence $\rho \otimes \rho^{-1} = \iota_\rho$. Therefore $\rho \otimes ((\rho^{\downarrow r})^{-1} \otimes \rho^{\downarrow r}) = \rho \otimes \iota_{\rho^{\downarrow r}}$. So we get due to axiom: **CM2** $\rho \otimes \iota_{\rho^{\downarrow r}} = \rho$ which proves our claim.

Now let us try to transform a Markov tree valuation to the form similar to equation (4).

Assume that we have constructed a Markov tree $T = (\mathbf{H}, \mathbf{E})$ representative of a given VBS, and let us assign a unique number $i \in I = \{1, 2, ..., n\}$, $n = \text{Card}(\mathbf{H})$, to each node in the tree. Denote V_i the original valuation stored in the i-th node of the tree. Let us consider the following transformation algorithm: starting with the node $k=n$ down to 1 we run a "valuation move" step such that we will "move" valuation from nodes with smaller number i to ones with higher one so that final valuation stored in the k-th node of the tree will be $R_k \circledR S_k$, where R_k and S_k are the marginal valuations defined over the set of variables represented by the sets h_k and s_k, respectively. Each step is a kind of unidirectional message-passing (towards the actual node k) in that a message is calculated at a node and then (1) removed from the valuation of the node and (2) added to the node closer to k. The valuation of nodes $i = 1, ..., k$ at the beginning of step concerning node k is denoted with $V_{i,k}$. At the end of a step, the valuation is denoted with $V_{i,k-1}$ except for node k which is denoted with $R_k \circledR S_k$.

The Algorithm:
begin

1. for $k := n$ step -1 downto 1 $V_{k,n} := V_k$
2. for k:=n step -1 downto 2 **begin**
   (a) Construct a subtree $\Gamma_k = (\mathbf{H}_k, \mathbf{E}_k)$ of T consisting only of nodes $\mathbf{H}_k = \{1, ..., k\}$.
   (b) Introduce the order $<_k$ compatible with the tree Γ_k, but such that the node k is considered as its root (the smallest element in $<_k$).
   (c) Mark all nodes of the Γ_k inactive
   (d) while the the direct successor of node k in ordering $<_k$ inactive
   if, in ordering $<_k$, all direct successors of node i are active, then: begin
      i. Active node i
      ii. Denote all its direct successors as inactive
      iii. Let j be direct predecessor of i in $<_k$
      iv. Calculate

$$V'_{i,k} := (V_{i,k} \otimes (\otimes \{M_{l \to i} | l \in (N(i)_k - \{j\}\})); \quad M_{i \to j} := V'^{\downarrow j \cap i}_{i,k};$$

If $(i, k) \notin \mathbf{E}_k$ calculate: $V_{i,k-1} := V'_{i,k} \circledR M_{i \to j}$; where $N(i)_k$ stands for the set of neighbours of the node i in the Markov subtree Γ_k,
   end

(e) Let $k+$ denote the direct successor of node k in $<_k$. Calculate $R_k :=$
$V_{k,k} \otimes M_{k+\to k}$; $S_k := R_k^{\downarrow k \cap k+}$; $V_{k+,k-1} := (V'_{k+,k} ⊛ M_{k+\to k}) \otimes S_k$
end

3. Calculate $R_1 := V_{1,1}$

end

Theorem 4. *If R_i and S_i have been calculated by the above algorithm for the Markov tree T, then*

$$R = \otimes\{V_i | i = 1..n\} = R_1 \otimes (\otimes\{(R_i ⊛ S_i) | i = 2..n\})$$

where R stands for the joint valuation defined over $\mathcal{X}$.

Proof. In any subtree Γ_k for any node i with predecessor j in $<_k$ except k and $k+$ we have, due to Lemma 3

$$V_{i,k} \otimes (\otimes\{V'_{l,k} | l \in (N(i)_k - \{j\}\}) =$$
$$= V_{i,k} \otimes (\otimes\{V_{l,k-1} \otimes M_{l\to i} | l \in (N(i)_k - \{j\}\}) =$$
$$= V'_{i,k} \otimes (\otimes\{V_{l,k-1} | l \in (N(i)_k - \{j\}\})$$

hence update on passage of activation does not change the joint valuation. Also we have that

$$V'_{k+,k} \otimes V_{k,k} = (V'_{k+,k} ⊛ M_{k+\to k}) \otimes (V_{k,k} \otimes M_{k+\to k}) =$$
$$= (V'_{k+,k} ⊛ M_{k+\to k}) \otimes R_k = ((V'_{k+,k} ⊛ M_{k+\to k}) \otimes S_k) \otimes (R_k ⊛ S_k) =$$
$$= V_{k+,k-1} \otimes (R_k ⊛ S_k)$$

The theorem is then provable by induction (on k running from n to 1)

Theorem 5. *In the previous theorem, $R_i = R^{\downarrow h_i}$*

Proof. It is easily seen that R_k is always the projection of the joint valuation of the subtree Γ_k (compare the message passing algorithm of Shenoy and Shafer [11]). Hence especially R_n is the projection of R onto node n.
Further, let $R_{\Gamma_k} = V'_{k,k} \times (\otimes\{V_{i,k} | i = 1, 2, ..., k-1\}$ Then, due to **CM1** we have: $R_{\Gamma_{k-1}} = R_{\Gamma_k}^{1 \cup 2 \cup ... \cup k-1}$. This implies, by induction, that R_k is the projection of R onto node k for every $k = 1, 2, ..., n$.

These two theorems 4, 5 may be summarized as follows.

Theorem 6. *Let $T = (H, E)$ be a Markov representative of a VBS $(\mathcal{X}, S, (\sigma_s)_{s \in S}, \otimes, \downarrow)$. Let R_i stands for the valuation marginalized to the set v_i of variables and S_j stands for the marginal potential assigned to the separator of the pair $\{h_i, h_j\}$. Then*

$$R = \otimes\{V_i | i = 1..n\} = R_1 \otimes (\otimes\{(R_i ⊛ S_i) | i = 2..n\})$$

where R stands for the joint valuation defined over $\mathcal{X}$.

Note that this theorem and the subsequent one are generalizations of theorems presented by Wierzchoń, [13], in that the restricting condition that the removal operation has to satisfy the property $(\rho \otimes \sigma)\circledR(\delta \otimes \sigma) = (\rho\circledR\delta)$ for any normal valuations ρ, σ and δ has been dropped. They represent also generalizations of properties of Dempster-Shafer belief functions presented in [3].

With the theorem 6 we can easily compute join valuations for subsets being set theoretical union of members of the family **H**. This fact presents Theorem 7 below.

Theorem 7. *Let $\Gamma = (\mathbf{N}, \mathbf{F})$ be a subtree of a Markov tree $T = (\mathbf{H}, \mathbf{E})$ satisfying assumptions of Theorem 6 Assume that for each node $h_j \in \mathbf{H}$ the marginal valuation, R_j, has been already computed. If h_r stands for the root node in the subtree Γ then*

$$R^{\downarrow\cup\mathbf{N}} = \otimes\{V_i|i \in \mathbf{H}\}^{\downarrow\cup\mathbf{N}} = R_r \otimes (\otimes\{(R_i\circledR S_i)|i \in \mathbf{N} - \{v_r\})\}$$

*where $\cup\mathbf{N}$ stands the set theoretical union of all sets contained in **N**.*

Proof. The result is straight-forward if we recall the axiom **CM1** and the separator property of the Markov tree.

Now, if $h \subseteq \cup\mathbf{N}$ then $R^{\downarrow h}$ is computed as $(R^{\downarrow\cup\mathbf{N}})^{\downarrow h}$. Xu [16] proposed the local computation technique to find such a marginal: it is simple consequence of Theorem 7 above and of Lemma 2.5 in [10].

4   Query processing in VBS

The problem of query processing was formulated by Pearl [5] first. In this approach we modify the original Bayesian belief network by adding new nodes with appropriate edges. Consider for instance the query $q = (x_1 \wedge x_2) \vee x_3$ - see (Pearl, [5], p. 224). Obviously, this q introduces new subset $h = \{x_1, x_2, x_3\}$ to **H**. In Pearl's approach we add two additional nodes joined to the original network by three edges. In our approach we simply must compute $R^{\downarrow h}$, and next we should find valuations over the set of configurations logically equivalent to q.

The only problem is to find the subtree Γ with $h \subseteq \cup\mathbf{N}$. In [13] it was shown that the minimal subtree, in the sense that $\cup\mathbf{N}$ is as small as possible, can be found by applying modified Graham's test. The modification concerns step (1) of this test: a variable is deleted only if it does not belong to the set h. This procedure is much more effective than that one suggested by Xu [16].

We can, however, pose the question, whether or not the optimal subtree of the Markov tree $T = (\mathbf{H}, \mathbf{E})$ with hypertree **H** covering an original hypergraph Swould be "better" for query answering than an optimal hypertree cover $T' = (\mathbf{H}', \mathbf{E}')$ of the result of the above-mentioned modified Graham test run over the original hypergraph **S**. The answer is to this question is a bit ambiguous. One can construct examples where T' would be more optimal than the subtree T in terms e.g. of the maximum number of nodes in an edge. However, we must take into account that for each query not only T' but also the valuation for each node of the tree T' has to be calculated from the entire hypergraph **S**. But we do not need to do that with subtrees of T, because we have to calculate the R_j's for a given tree T once and we do not need to recalculate them when selecting a subtree, and if the subtree is small enough we save much calculation compared with processing of T' (even if T' has a more optimal structure for a given query).

Concluding this paper we want to stress that this approach is implemented in the VBS system designed by our group.

References

1. Cooper, G.F., and Herskovits, E., (1992). A Bayesian method for the induction of probabilistic networks from data. Machine Learning, 9:309-347.
2. Jensen, F.V., Lauritzen, S.L., and Olesen, K.G., (1990). Bayesian updating in causal probabilistic networks by local computations. Computational Statistics Quarterly, 4: 269-282.
3. Kłopotek, M.A., (1994). Beliefs in Markov Trees - From Local Computations to Local Valuation. In: R. Trappl, Ed.: *Cybernetics and Systems Research*, World Scientific Publishers, Vol.1. pp. 351-358.
4. Lauritzen, S.L., and Spiegelhalter, D.J., (1988). Local computation with probabilities on graphical structures and their application to expert systems. J. Roy. Stat. Soc., B50: 157-244.
5. Pearl, J. (1988). Probabilistic Reasoning in Intelligent Systems: Networks of Plausible Inference. Morgan Kaufman.
6. Shafer, G. (1976) A Mathematical Theory of Evidence, Princeton University Press, Princeton, NJ.
7. Shenoy, P.P. (1989) A valuation-based language for expert systems, International Journal of Approximate Reasoning, 3:383-411.
8. Shenoy, P.P. (1991) Valuation-based systems for discrete optimization, Uncertainty in AI 6, (P.P. Bonissone et al., eds), North-Holland, Amsterdam, pp. 385-400.
9. Shenoy, P.P. (1993) A new method for representing and solving Bayesian decision problems, Artificial Intelligence Frontiers in Statistics: AI and Statistics III (D.J. Hand, ed.), Chapman & Hall, London, pp.119-138.
10. Shenoy, P.P. (1994). Conditional independence in valuation-based systems, International Journal of Approximate Reasoning, 10:203-234.
11. Shenoy, P.P., and Shafer, G. (1986). Propagating belief functions using local computations. IEEE Expert, 1(3), 43-52.
12. Thoma, H.M., (1991). Belief function computations, in: I.R. Goodman et al (Eds.), Conditional Logics in Expert Systems, North-Holland, pp. 269-308
13. Wierzchoń, S.T., (1995). Markov-like properties of joint valuations, submitted.
14. Wen, W.X., (1991). From relational databases to belief networks, in: B.D'Ambrosio, Ph. Smets, and P.P. Bonissone (Eds.), Proc. 7-th Conference on Uncertainty in AI, Morgan Kaufmann, pp. 406-413.
15. Wong, S.K., Xiang, Y., and Nie, X., (1993). Representation of Bayesian networks as relational databases, in: D. Heckerman, and A. Mamdani, (Eds.), Proc. 9-th Conference on Uncertainty in AI, Morgan Kaufmann, pp. 159-165.
16. Xu, H., (1995). Computing marginals for arbitrary subsets from marginal representation in Markov trees, Artificial Intelligence, 74, 177-189.

Learning for Decision Making:
The FRD Approach and a Comparative Study

Ibrahim F. Imam and Ryszard S. Michalski[†]

Machine Learning and Inference Laboratory
George Mason University
Fairfax, VA. 22030
[†]Also with the Institute of Computer Science, Polish Academy of Sciences
{iimam, michalski} @aic.gmu.edu

ABSTRACT

This paper concerns the issue of what is the best form for learning, representing and using knowledge for decision making. The proposed answer is that such knowledge should be learned and represented in a declarative form. When needed for decision making, it should be efficiently transferred to a procedural form that is tailored to the specific decision making situation. Such an approach combines advantages of the declarative representation, which facilitates learning and incremental knowledge modification, and the procedural representation, which facilitates the use of knowledge for decision making. This approach also allows one to determine decision structures that may avoid attributes that unavailable or difficult to measure in any given situation. Experimental investigations of the system, FRD-1, have demonstrated that decision structures obtained via the declarative route often have not only higher predictive accuracy but are also are simpler than those learned directly from facts.

1 INTRODUCTION

The main step in the development of intelligent systems or task-oriented agents is the formulation of knowledge that governs the system's decision making process. In many situations, an attractive route for creating such knowledge is to acquire it through learning from the known facts.

A powerful and effective representation for decision-oriented knowledge is a *decision structure*, which is an acyclic graph that specifies an order of the application of certain tests to an object (or a situation) to arrive at a decision about that object. The nodes of the structure are assigned individual tests (e.g., a single attribute, a function, or a relation), the branches are assigned possible test outcomes (or ranges of outcomes), and the leaves are assigned one specific decision or a set of candidate decisions (with corresponding probabilities), or an undetermined decision [6, 7]. A decision structure reduces to a familiar decision tree, when each node is assigned a single attribute and has at most one parent, the branches from each node are assigned single values of that attribute, and leaves are assigned single, definite decisions. Thus, the problem of generating a decision structure is a generalization of the problem of generating a decision tree.

A decision tree/structure is an effective tool for describing a decision process, as long as all the required tests can be measured, and the decision making situations it was designed for do not change much (e.g., all attributes in the structure can be measured and there is no significant change in the frequency distribution of different decisions). Problems arise when these assumptions do not hold. For example, in some situations measuring certain attributes may be difficult or costly. In such situations it is desirable to reformulate the decision structure so that the "expensive" attributes are evaluated only if necessary (are assigned to the nodes far away from the root). If an attribute cannot be measured at all, it is useful to either modify the structure so that it does not contain that attribute, or—when this is impossible—to specify a set of alternative candidate decisions in this situation and their probabilities. A restructuring is also desirable if there is a significant change in the frequency of occurrence of different decisions.

A restructuring of a decision structure (or a tree) in order to suit new requirements is usually quite difficult. This is because a decision structure is a procedural knowledge representation, which imposes an evaluation order on the tests. In contrast, no evaluation order is imposed by a declarative representation, such as decision rules. Tests (conditions) of rules can be evaluated in any order. For a given set of rules, one can usually build a large number of logically equivalent decision structures (trees), which differ in the test ordering. Due to the lack of "order constraints," a declarative representation (rules) is much easier to modify to adapt to different situations than a procedural one (such as a decision structure or a tree). On the other hand, to apply decision rules to make a decision, one needs to decide in which order tests are evaluated, and thus, needs to develop a decision structure. The above indicates that the form in which knowledge can be most easily learned and updated is different than the form in which it is most readily used for decision making.

The paper presents an attractive solution of the above opposite requirements. In the proposed method, knowledge is acquired, modified and stored in a declarative form (of decision rules). Whenever it is needed for decision making, it is efficiently transformed into a task-oriented decision structure. The implemented system, called FRD-2 (from Facts to Rules to Decisions), creates decision structures that are tailored for a given decision making situation. The input for this process are either decision rules or original facts (examples of situation-decision pairs). The decision rules can be obtained be a rule learning program (we used AQ15c and AQ17-DCI) or from a domain expert. The earlier work on the above ideas was presented in several papers (e.g., [6, 11]. This paper presents a description of an extended method used in FRD-2 system and its testing on several problems.

2 RELATED RESEARCH

The method used here for learning decision structures from decision rules is similar to learning decision trees from examples. The problem of learning decision trees from examples is the problem of generating decision trees that classify sets of given examples according to the decision classes they belong to. The essential aspect of any inductive decision tree method is the attribute selection criterion. The attribute selection criterion measures how good the attributes are for discriminating among the given set of decision classes. The best attribute according to the selection criterion is chosen to be assigned to the root of the tree.

The attribute selection criteria can be divided into three categories. These categories are logic-based, information-based, and statistics-based. The logic-based criteria for selecting attributes use logical relationships between the attributes and the decision classes to determine the best attribute to be a node in the decision tree, such as the MAL criterion "Minimizing Added Leaves" [9]. The MAL criterion uses conjunction and disjunction operators. The information-based criteria are based on information theory. These criteria measure the information conveyed by dividing the training examples into subsets. Examples of such criteria include the information gain, an entropy reduction measure [13], the gini index of diversity [3], Gain-ratio measure [14], and others [4, 5]. The statistics-based criteria measure the correlation between the decision classes and the other attributes. Such criteria use statistical distributions in determining whether or not there is a correlation. Examples of statistical criteria include the Chi-square and the G statistics [12].

3 THE FRD-2 METHOD

The proposed methodology separates the function of knowledge acquisition or discovery from the function of applying knowledge to decision making. The first function is performed by an inductive learning program that searches for knowledge relevant to a given class of decisions, and stores the learned knowledge in the declarative form of decision rules. The second function is performed when the need for decision making arises in some particular situation. Such a function involves assigning a value to a decision variable based on values of attributes characterizing the decision making situation. Figure 1 shows an architecture of the system, called FRD (from Facts to Rules to Decisions). The decision rules are learned by either the AQ15 [10] or AQ17-DCI [2] learning systems. They also can be directly edited into the system. The transformation of decision rules to decision structures is accomplished using the AQDT-2 algorithm.

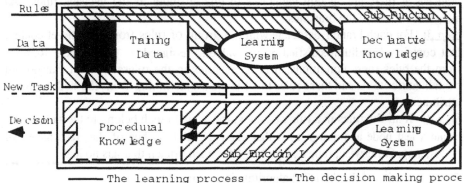

Figure 1: An architecture of the FRD-1 system.

A decision making problem arises when there is a case or a set of cases to which the system has to assign a decision. Each case is defined by a set of attribute values. Some attribute values may be missing or unknown. A decision structure is derived from the rules that suits the given decision making problem. The learned decision structure associates the given set of cases with the corresponding decisions.

The AQDT-2 algorithm works by determining the "best" test (here, an attribute) at each step of the process. The "best" test is determined by analyzing the decision rules. The system aims at producing decision structures with the minimum number of nodes or the minimum cost (where the "cost" is defined as the total cost of classifying examples, given the cost of measuring individual attributes and the expected probability distribution of examples of different decision classes). The best test (attribute) is selected on the basis of its utility, which is a combination of one or more of the following elementary criteria: 1) *cost* , which reflects the cost of measuring an attribute or performing a test (if the cost of tests is unknown or irrelevant, all tests assume the same default cost), 2) *disjointness*, which captures the effectiveness of the test in discriminating among decision rules for different decision classes, 3) *importance*, which determines the importance of a test in the rules, 4) *value distribution*, which characterizes the distribution of the test importance over its of values, and 5) *dominance*, which measures the test presence in the rules. Following is a description of the AQDT-2 algorithm:

The AQDT-2 Algorithm

Given: A set of rules and a decision making situation.

Determined: A decision structure optimized for the given decision making situation.

Step 1: Evaluate each attribute occurring in the ruleset context using the selected attribute ranking criterion. Select the highest ranked attribute, say attribute A.

Step 2: Create a node of the tree (initially, the root; afterwards, a node attached to a branch), and assign to it the attribute A. In standard mode, create as many branches from the node as the number of legal values of the attribute A, and assign these values to the branches. In compact mode (decision structures), create as many branches as there are disjoint value sets of this attribute in the decision rules, and assign these sets to the branches.

Step 3: For each branch, associate with it a group of rules from the ruleset context that contain a condition satisfied by the value(s) assigned to this branch. Remove from the rules these conditions. If there are rules in the ruleset context that do not contain attribute A, add these rules to all branches stemming from the node assigned attribute A.

Step 4: If all the rules in a ruleset context for some branch belong to the same class, create a leaf node and assign to it that class. If all branches of the trees have leaf nodes, stop. Otherwise, repeat steps 1 to 4 for each branch that has no leaf.

The complexity of the AQDT-2 algorithm is estimated by:

$$Cmplx(AQDT) = O(r * m * \log l)$$

where r is the total number of rules, m is the number of attributes, and l is maximum the number of rules and the number of attributes.

4 EMPIRICAL TESTING OF THE FRD-1 SYSTEM

This section presents empirical results from extensive testing of the FRD-1 system on several problems, using different amounts of training examples and applying different settings of the system's parameters. For comparison, it also presents results from applying a well-known decision tree learning system (C4.5) to the same problems. The system was applied to the following problems: EAST-WEST (or TRAINS), MONK-1, MONK-2, MONK-3, Engineering Design, Mushrooms, and Breast Cancer.

The experiments were performed 100 times with different relative sizes of the training data: 10%, 20%, ..., 90%. Specifically, from the set of all available examples for each problem, 100 randomly selected subsets of 10% of data were chosen for rules learning, then 20%, etc. The remaining examples in each case were used for testing the obtained descriptions and determining their prediction accuracy.

4.1 Learning Task-oriented Decision Structures

This subsection briefly illustrates the capabilities of the system for learning task-oriented decision structures. Experiments involved the East-West Challenge problem [8]. The East-Westbound problem is concerned with discriminating between two groups of train-like structures. Each "train" consists of several cars (two to four), each containing various loads of different shapes.

To describe the East-West Challenge problem in the suitable format, a set of eight (8) attributes was generated that can completely describe any car in the train. Each train is described by one rule, which can be of different length. To specify the number (position) of a given car in the train, each of the eight attributes is associated with a two-digit code (i, j); the first identifies the location of the car and the second identifies the attribute itself. For example, the number 3 in the attribute "x32" refers to the third car, and the number 2 refers to the car shape. Thus, attribute x32 describes the shape of the third car. Table 1 shows a summary of these data.

Table 1: The set of attributes used in the experiments

Name	Attribute	Values					
		0	1	2	3	4	5
x_i1	Car_top	open	closed				
x_i2	Car_shape	rectangle	hexagon	bucket	u_shaped	ellipse	
x_i3	Car_length	short	long				
x_i4	Car_frame	not_double	double				
x_i5	Top_shape	none	peaked	flat	arc	jagged	
x_i6	No_of_wheels	two	three				
x_i7	Load_shape	rectangle	hexagon	circle	triangle	utriangle	diamond
x_i8	No_of_loads	no_loads	one	two	three		

i= 1, 2, 3, 4 and stands for the car number.

To demonstrate the capability of the system to learn decision structures under different constrains regarding what attributes can be easily measured, the experiments involved different "admissible" sets of attributes. For example, Figure 3a, shows a decision structure learned using only attributes describing the first car. This decision structure classifies correctly 19 trains (out of 20). Figure 3b shows a decision structure learned using only attributes describing the second car. It classifies correctly 18 trains. Both decision structures have leaves with multiple decisions, which means that there is identical first or second car in the two decision classes (sets of trains). Figure 3c shows a decision structure learned using attributes describing the third car only. It classifies correctly all 20 trains with three cars or more (14). In Figure 3d, attributes x37 and x34 were given lower cost than attribute x31. The last decision structure classifies correctly any train with three or more cars correctly.

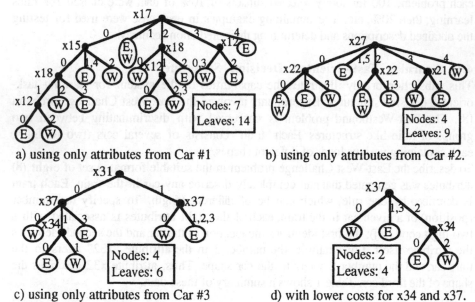

a) using only attributes from Car #1   b) using only attributes from Car #2.

c) using only attributes from Car #3   d) with lower costs for x34 and x37.

Figure 3: Task-oriented decision structures learned by AQDT-2 with different costs.

4.2 Comparing decision trees from FRD-1 and C4.5 s

This subsection presents a comparison between the decision trees obtained by FRD-1 and C4.5, a well-known program for learning decision trees [14]. This The experiments were performed on 6 different data sets. Both systems were set to their default parameters. The experiments were divided into two parts. The first part is concerned with designed problems, the MONKs [15], and the second part was concerned with real-world problems: Wind bracing for tall buildings [1], Mushrooms classification, Breast cancer diagnosis.

All the results reported here are the average of 100 runs. For each data set, we reported the predictive accuracy, the complexity of the learned decision trees, and the time taken for learning. Figure 4 shows the results from comparative study on the three MONKs problems. Figure 5 shows the results obtained when using the wind bracing, mushroom, and the breast cancer problems.

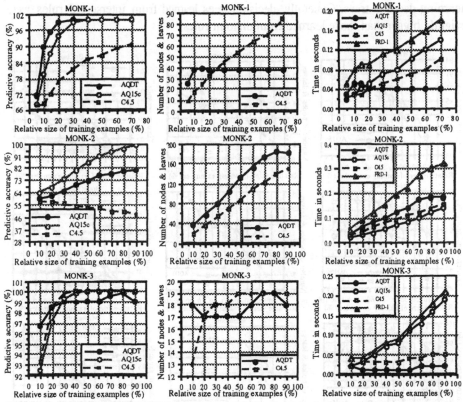

Figure 4: Results from AQDT-2, AQ15c and C4.5 on designed problems (MONKS).

4.3 Analysis of the Results

This section includes an analysis of the results presented in section 4-2. The analysis covers the relationship between different characteristics of the input rules and the performance of the approach. Table 2 shows the best parameter settings for learning decision rules with different databases. The information in this table is based on the predictive accuracy of decision trees learned by AQDT-2 from decision rules learned by AQ15c with different parameter settings. Some heuristics were used in driving these information. One heuristic was: if the difference in predictive accuracy between two widths of the beam search is less than 2%, then the smaller is better. Another one was: if the predictive accuracy of different types of covers is changing (i.e. for one type of covers, it is higher with some widths of beam search or with certain rule's type and lower with other types of covers), the best cover is determined according to the best width of the beam search and the best rule type.

It was clear that AQDT-2 works better with characteristics rules rather than discriminant. In most problems, when changing the width of the beam search of the AQ15c system, the changes in the predictive accuracy of decision trees learned by AQDT-2 were within ±2%. Disjoint rules were better than intersected rules for learning decision trees. Generally, decision trees learned from intersected rules were slightly bigger than those learned from disjoint rules.

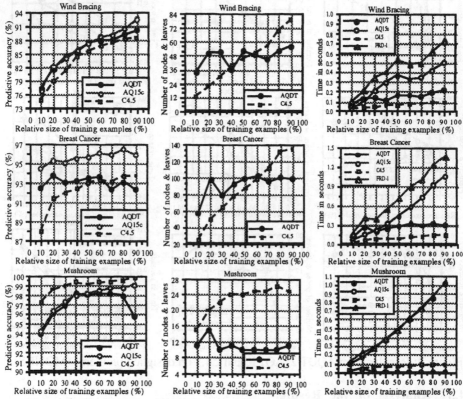

Figure 5: Results from AQDT-2, AQ15c and C4.5 using real world problems.

Table 2: Settings of parameters "cover type" and "description type" in AQ15c that produced the highest prediction accuracy of decision trees

Characteristics of the Data	Cover Type	Description Type
Average Size, Complex, Noise-Free	IC	Characteristic
Small Size, Simple, Noise-Free	DC	Characteristic
Small Size, Complex, Noise-Free	DC	Characteristic
Small Size, Simple, Noisy	DC or IC	Characteristic
Large Size, Complex, Noise-Free	DC	Characteristic
Large Size, Complex, Noisy	IC	Characteristic

where IC indicates Intersecting Cover, and DC indicates Disjoint Covers.

The major functional differences between FRD-1 and other decision tree learning systems (e.g. C4.5) can be summarized as follows: 1. FRD-1 can create decision tree/structure from decision rules or from examples; 2. FRD-1 can create decision structures that are more general than decision trees, and these structures may, therefore, be much simpler than decision trees; 3. If an attribute is difficult or impossible to measure in a given situation, FRD-1 can create a decision structure that avoids using it altogether; 4. FRD-1 can optimize a decision structure/tree according to a multicriterion measure that be tuned to the problem at hand.

5. CONCLUSION

This paper presented a methodology for determining task-oriented decision structures. These decision structures can be obtained in three ways: 1) by first learning decision rules from examples and then deriving from them decision structures (briefly, FRD) 2) by building structures directly from examples (briefly, FD), or 3) by deriving decision structures from user created decision rules (briefly, UD). In the experiments performed, the first way (FRD) usually gave the most accurate and simplest decision structures. The FRD mode of operation, as well as UD, allows the system to adapt the structure to the particular decision making situation.

A criticism against the FRD mode may be that in order to determine a decision structure from examples, it is necessary to go through two levels of processing, while there exist methods that can produce decision trees directly from examples. Putting aside the issue that decision structures are more general than decision trees, one can point out that this methodology can also produce decision trees from examples directly, if one so desires.

An advantage of the FRD-1 system is the ability of the system to create decision structures, which are more general than decision trees, has frequently produced very simple representations of the decision processes. Other important features of this method are that by storing decision knowledge in the declarative form of modular decision rules, the methodology makes it easy to modify decision knowledge to account for new facts or changing conditions. The process of deriving a decision structure from a set of rules is very fast and efficient, because the number of rules per class is usually much smaller than the number of examples per class. The FRD system can also accept decision rules from different sources.

Future research needs to investigate the best areas of applicability of this methodology, confirm these findings on other decision making tasks and to develop the ability of building more complex decision structures that those explored here.

ACKNOWLEDGMENTS

The authors thank the UCI repository of machine learning databases for the data used in most of the presented experiments. They also thank M. Mustafa and T. Arciszewski for providing the wind bracing data.

This research was done in the Machine Learning and Inference Laboratory at George Mason University. The Laboratory's activities are supported in part by the Advanced Research Projects Agency under grant No. N00014-91-J-1854 administered by the Office of Naval Research, in part by the Advanced Research Projects Agency under grants F49620-92-J-0549 and F49620-95-1-0462 administered by the Air Force Office of Scientific Research, in part by the Office of Naval Research under grant N00014-91-J-1351, and in part by the National Science Foundation under grants DMI-9496192 and IRI-9020266.

REFERENCES

[1] Arciszewski, T, Bloedorn, E., Michalski, R., Mustafa, M., and Wnek, J., "Constructive Induction in Structural Design", Reports of Machine Learning and Inference Laboratory, MLI-92-7, George Mason University, 1992.

[2] Bloedorn, E., Wnek, J., Michalski, R.S., and Kaufman, K., "AQ17: A Multistrategy Learning System: The Method and User's Guide", Reports of Machine Learning and Inference Laboratory, MLI-93-12, George Mason University, 1993.

[3] Breiman, L., Friedman, J.H., Olshen, R.A. & Stone, C.J., "Classification and Regression Structures", Belmont, California: Wadsworth Int. Group, 1984.

[4] Clark, P. & Niblett, T., "Induction in Noisy Domains" in I. Bratko and N. Lavrac, (Eds.), Progress in Machine Learning, Sigma Press, Wilmslow, 1987.

[5] Cestnik, B. & Karalic, A., "The Estimation of Probabilities in Attribute Selection Measures for Decision Structure Induction" in Proceeding of the European Summer School on Machine Learning, July 22-31, , Belgium, 1991.

[6] Imam, I.F. and Michalski, R.S., "Learning Decision Structures from Decision Rules: A method and initial results from a comparative study", in Journal of Intelligent Information Systems JIIS, Vol. 2, No. 3, pp. 279-304, Kerschberg, L., Ras, Z., & Zemankova, M. (Eds.), Kluwer Academic Pub., MA, 1993.

[7] Kohavi, R., "Bottom-Up Induction of Oblivious Read-Once Decision-Graphs: Strengths and Limitations", Proceedings of AAAI-94, pp. 613-18, Seattle, 1994.

[8] Michie, D., Muggleton, S., Page, D. and Srinivasan, A., "International East-West Challenge", Oxford University, UK, 1994.

[9] Michalski, R.S, "Designing Extended Entry Decision Tables and Optimal Decision Trees Using Decision Diagrams", *Technical Report No.898*, Urbana: University of Illinois, 1978.

[10] Michalski, R.S., Mozetic, I., Hong, J. and Lavrac, N., "The Multi-Purpose Incremental Learning System AQ15 and Its Testing Application to Three Medical Domains", Proceedings of AAAI-86, (pp. 1041-1045), Philadelphia, PA., 1986.

[11] Michalski, R.S., and Imam, I.F., "Learning Problem-oriented Decision Structures from Decision Rules: The AQDT-2 System", in The Proceedings of the International Symposium on Methodology for Intelligent Systems, ISMIS-94, Charlotte, NC, October, 1994.

[12] Mingers, J., "An Empirical Comparison of selection Measures for Decision-Structure Induction", Machine Learning, Vol. 3, No. 3, (pp. 319-342), Kluwer Academic Publishers, 1989.

[13] Quinlan, J.R., "Learning efficient classification procedures and their application to chess end games" in R.S. Michalski, J.G. Carbonell and T.M. Mitchell, (Eds.), Machine Learning: An Artificial Intelligence Approach. Los Altos: Morgan Kaufmann, 1983.

[14] Quinlan, J. R., "Probabilistic decision structures," in Y. Kodratoff and R.S. Michalski (Eds.), Machine Learning: An Artificial Intelligence Approach, Vol. III, San Mateo, CA, Morgan Kaufmann Publishers, (pp. 63-111), June, 1990.

[15] Thrun, S.B., Mitchell, T. and Cheng, J., (Eds.) "The MONK's Problems: A Performance Comparison of Different Learning Algorithms", Technical Report, Carnegie Mellon University, October, 1991.

The Application of Rough Sets-Based Data Mining Technique to Differential Diagnosis of Meningoenchepahlitis

Shusaku Tsumoto

Department of Information Medicine
Medical Research Institute
Tokyo Medical and Dental University
1-5-45 Yushima, Bukyo-ku Tokyo 113, Japan

Wojciech Ziarko

Department of Computer Science
University of Regina
Regina, Saskatchewan, Canada S4S 0A2

Abstract

The application of rough sets-based data mining tool called KDD-R to the analysis of clinical data is described. The main practical problem tackled with the data mining technique is a differential diagnosis of bacterial versus viral meningoenchephalis. We present the relevant aspects of the variable precision rough sets model underlying the system KDD-R, the basic operational stages of KDD-R, and the results and their clinical interpretation conducted by the domain expert.

1 Introduction

Data mining is considered to be one of the most promising directions spanning database and AI research. The primary objective of data mining methodologies and systems is to help the data analyst to discover potentially significant facts or data patterns hidden in databases in the form of invisible relationships. A comprehensive review of systems and approaches to data mining can be found in (Piatetsky-Shapiro 1991,1993; Fayyad and Uthurusamy 1995).

In this paper, we focus on the application of rough sets-based (see, for example, Pawlak 1991) data mining methodology to the problem of analysis of medical data. The methodology is rooted in the extended Variable Precision Rough Sets model (VPRS) (Ziarko 1993, Katzberg and Ziarko 1994) and is implementd in the experimental data mining system called KDD-R. We apply KDD-R to a clinical database of meningoencephalitis, neurlogical infectious disease, collected at the Matsudo Municipal Hospital in Japan by the first author. One of the most important problems occuring when dealing with meningoenchephalitis is to make a differential diagnosis between bacterial and viral infection as fast as possible, since each therapy is different in each case and the sooner the right therapy is initiated the better are the chances of complete recovery. Bacterial meningoenchepahlitis requires high doses of venous injection of antibiotics, whereas the viral infection requires injection of anti-viral drugs. Both treatments are completely independent, and the bacterial infection treatment is not effective to treat the viral infection. Furthermore, if the treatment is delayed, it is possible that a patient would suffer from the unrecoverable brain damage. Consequently, the rapid emergency action is indispensable to prevent the brain damage. Thus, the immediate selection of the final diagnosis is crucial to start the therapy without any delays, as well as it is important to determine what interactions of factors contribute to the final diagnosis.

In what follows we describe the methodology used in identifying the diagnostic patterns used in differentiating between bacterial and viral infection. We describe the relevant aspects of the KDD-R system and present in detail the medical data analysis problem along with results and their interpretation done by a medical professional. In general, most of the obtained results coincide with the existing medical knowledge about the disease. However, some results are new, and even surprising, and indicative of the need for further research to verify them completely before adapting them into clinical practice.

2   Data Mining: Rough Sets Approach

The object of the data mining in the rough sets approach is a flat table with rows containing information about objects or situations from a certain universe of discourse, expressed in terms of attribute values representing some characteristics of the objects, medical cases in this application. In KDD-R, the permissible attribute values are integers, reals or strings. A partial listing of such a table containing information about patients suffering from either viral or bacterial infection is shown in Table 1. In general, the analysis is focused on the investigation of the relationship between two, user-defined groups of attributes referred to as condition attributes and decision attributes respectively. The collection of decision attributes typically contains only a single attribute, and this will be our assumption throughout this paper. For example, in the medical application described here, the decision attribute reflects different kinds of infections whereas the condition attributes correspond to observed symptoms and medical test results.

In the analysis of the relationship, each value v of the decision attribute is corresponds to a set $|v|$ of table rows matching this value. The collection of objects represented in the table is referred to as the universe. In practice, it is essentially a sample from a larger, possibly infinite set of objects. Our primary problem is to obtain, based on the contents of the table, plausible and strongly supported by available evidence hypotheses about the true nature of

case	AGE	SEX	DIAG	COLD	HEADACHE	...	CSF_{CELL}	CSF_{PRO}
$case_1$	25	M	VIRUS	2	0	...	144	38
$case_2$	42	M	VIRUS	0	3	...	117	37
$case_3$	58	F	VIRUS	0	12	...	660	86
$case_4$	29	F	VIRUS	0	2	...	464	88
$case_5$	40	M	VIRUS	0	5	...	208	348
...	...	...	...	...	...	...	...	...
$case_{92}$	42	M	VIRUS	0	0	...	143	38
$case_{93}$	25	F	VIRUS	0	5	...	114	59
$case_{94}$	59	M	VIRUS	0	10	...	590	86
$case_{95}$	27	F	VIRUS	6	3	...	480	42
$case_{96}$	23	F	VIRUS	4	2	...	149	25

Table 1: An Excerpt of Patient Data

the relationship between the occurrence of combinations of some properties of condition attributes values in objects belonging to the general population and the occurrence of the value v of the decision attribute. When doing that, we construct from the original data table a relatively small "derivative" generalized *classification table* in which the precise numeric values (if any) are replaced with general qualitative categories, such as $PRESSURE = NORMAL$, $TEMPERATURE = HIGH$, or value ranges, such as $CSF_{CELL} > 1000$. The classification table represents the *classification* of objects into categories rather than individual objects. Following that step, we try to form the description of the set $|v|$ in terms of values of the condition attributes by using information contained in the classification table. Because, in general, it is not possible to construct precise description, an approximate description is constructed instead using the ideas of rough sets theory, and in particular the VPRS model. In this approach, the target set Y is described approximately by defining its three approximation regions, that is, lower bound or the positive region, the boundary region and the negative region.

In comparison to the original Pawlak's definition (Pawlak 1991), the VPRS technique provides a degree of flexibility in specifying the lower bound, boundary region and the negative region of a set Y by allowing a controlled degree of overlap of lower bound and negative region with the set Y complement or the set Y, respectively.

More precisely, for given lower and upper limit parameters ℓ and u respectively, such that $0 \leq \ell \leq u \leq 1$, the ℓ-lower approximation (or ℓ-positive region) of the target Y is given by

$$\underline{R}_\ell(Y) = \bigcup \{E \in R^* : c(E,Y) \leq \ell\}$$

where R^* is a collection of the classes of abstraction E of an equivalence relation $R \subset U \times U$. The equivalence relation R represents the classification of objects belonging to the universe U into disjoint categories based on values of condition attributes. The parameter $c(E,Y)$ is a classification factor defined as

$$c(E,Y) = 1 - \frac{card(E \cap Y)}{card(E)}$$

The classification factor is a measure of the relative degree of intersection of a class of abstraction E with the complement of the target set Y. In KDD-R the equivalence relation $R \subset U \times U$ is treating as equivalent any two rows with identical values of condition attributes.

The (ℓ, u)-boundary region of the set Y is given by

$$BNR_{\ell,u}(Y) = \bigcup \{ E \in R^* : \ell < c(E, Y) < u \}$$

and the u-negative region is defined as

$$NEG_u(Y) = \bigcup \{ E \in R^* : c(E, Y) \geq u \}.$$

Intuitively, the ℓ-positive region of the target decision (set) Y is a specification of objects which can be assigned an estimated probability of occurence in the set Y at a level not lower than $1 - l$. The u-negative region, on the other hand, defines objects which can be assigned the probability greater than u of not occuring in the target set Y. In other words, the lower approximation objects are relatively likely to occur in the set Y and the negative region objects are relatively unlikely to to be memebers of set Y. The boundary region objects are kind of in-between as the estimated probabilities of occurence either in the set Y or its complement $-Y$ are not sufficiently biased in either direction. When conducting data mining using these ideas, the analyst specifies first the region of interest and then attempts to find sufficiently supported by evidence data patterns ("rules") included in the selected region. Most typically, l-positive region rules are of interest although in some industrial problems u-negative region rules are also important (Katzberg and Ziarko, 1995). In what follows we elaborate on this aspect of data mining methodology in the context of the KDD-R system used in our experiments.

3 System KDD-R

System KDD-R is a result of almost ten years of research on the application of the methodology of rough sets to data analysis. It follows earlier PC-based systems such as, for example, Dataquest, DataLogic (Reduct, 1991) and RoughDas (Slowinski and Stefanowski, 1992), or UNIX-based system LERS (Grzymala-Busse 1992-1994) also developed within rough sets framework. KDD-R in the current form is UNIX-based and the underlying mathematics is derived from the VPRS model of rough sets. The main objective of the system is identification of strong, repetitive patterns in data, referred to as rules. The rules computed by KDD-R relate the co-occurrences of some specific features of data (attribute-value pairs), with estimated co-occurrence probabilities. For example, the occurrence of the features "$WBC = 8000$" and "$CSF_{CELL} \leq 1000$" relates to the occurrence of the property "Infection is VIRUS" with the estimated probability 0.91. In the practice, knowing such connections among features helps in making more accurate decisions.

The key difference between KDD-R and other systems aimed at identification of rules in databases is its focus on computation of rules strongly supported by data. In other words, only such patterns (rules) are identified by KDD-R which permit for credible estimates of associated probabilities. Weak patterns are not considered since the probability estimates are likely to be incorrect. Consequently, the newest version of KDD-R, in comparison to rule induction algorithms known in machine learning literature , does not compute neither "minimal cover rules" nor all rules, but only the rules satisfying the predefined strength and probability constraints are identified. The rules are presented to the user in a simple matrix form or in the natural language form such as, for example, the rule: **if** $WBC = 8000$ and $CSF_{CELL} \leq 1000$ **then** $VIRUS$ with probability 0.91.

KDD-R identifies all rules satisfying the constraints and enables the user to select the ones of special interest to him/her. The computed rules can also be used collectively for the purpose of prediction by using KDD-R's decision making component. KDD-R can process both numeric and qualitative data with missing values. When processing missing values replacement values are not used in place of missing ones. The other feature of KDD-R is its ability to identify degrees of connectivity among attributes which helps in finding clusters of connected, or interacting attributes which are subsequently used to construct rules.

The main processing stages of KDD-R are:

1. Data quantization, which involves splitting the numeric data into discrete ranges. The ranges are numbered, resulting in a tabular representation in which all attributes are integers drawn from a relatively narrow domain.

2. Selection of the subset of attributes to be used to construct the rules. At this stage either the attribute clustering program is used, or the selection is done according to user's preference.

3. Searching for the rules satisfying the imposed criteria. The details of this procedure are described in (Ziarko 1996).

4. Rule translation to obtain natural language descriptions of the discovered patterns.

Before using KDD-R, when specifying system parameters, user is asked to provide the lower and upper limit parameters, ℓ and u. He or she also needs to indicate whether the data analysis will be focused on the ℓ-lower bound or on the u-upper bound of each value of the decision attribute, where the u-upper bound is simply a union of ℓ-lower bound and (ℓ, u)-boundary region. In the experiments described here the analysis was focused on the ℓ-lower bounds of sets corresponding to values VIRUS and BACTERIA of the decision attribute.

Data preprocessing in KDD-R involves defining a secondary set of features which are functions of original attribute values. The original attribute values are often to detailed to capture repetitive regularities, or patterns occurring in the data. The secondary feature definitions can be either provided by the user based on domain knowledge, or can be produced automatically using, for example, some statistical (Lenarcik and Piasta 1993) or heuristic techniques.

In the application discussed here the definitions were provided by the domain expert.

4 Description of the Clinical Data

The database used in our experiments is described by 26 condition attributes, which include the results of physical and laboratory examinations, and one decision attribute. The excerpt from the database is shown in Table 1. The decision attribute is a diagnosis of a neurologist, which is the recognition either of bacterial or viral meningoenchalitis. The data collection so far consists of 96 cases, composed of 66 viral cases and 30 bacterial ones. The collection is growing continuosly as more and more cases of meningoenchalitis are analyzed and recorded in Matsudo hospital. Out of 26 condition attributes 17 attributes describe the results of physical examinations and 9 attributes describes the results of laboratory examinations. The former attributes include the age of a patient, sex, the onset, and other neurlogical findings. The latter attributes include the results of blood examinations (for instance white blood cell count), examinations of cerebulo spiral fluid (for instance cell count, concentration of protein and glucose), the specification of findings in CT (computer tomography) medical images, and the results of electroencephalographic(EEG) examination. All these information is collected just when a patient is admitted, which means that the data describe the initial condition of a patient before any therapy is initiated.

The decision attribute describes one of the two types of meningoencephalitis, bacterial and viral. The actual diagnosis is made by a neurologist. Bacterial meningoenchephalitis is caused by the invasion of bacteria into the meninges and cerebulospinal fluid via the bloodstream, the ears, or the infected sinuses. The most common bacteria causing meningitis are the following: Streptococcus pneumoniae, Neisseria meningitis, Hemophilus influenzae and Listera monocytogenes.

On the other hand, viral meningoenchalitis is thought to be caused by the invasion of virus via the same route as the bacterial infection. The most common viruses causing meningitis are the following: mumps virus, arboviruses, herpes simplex viruses, Epstein-Barr viruses, enteroviruses, cytomegalovirus, adenovirus, and rabies virus.

The main difference between these two categories is in their prognosis. In the cases of viral meningitis, except for herpes simplex, the prognosis is very good, even if the initial condition is severe. Most of these cases do not need any medication. However, in the cases of bacterial meningitis, the prognosis is not good if we do not start antibacterial therapy as soon as possible, that is, bacterial meningitis is a medical emergency. This also applies to herpes simplex meningoencephalitis. In this type of diseases, a patient often suffers from aphasia, a memory disturbance, which is often not curable and may be fatal if we do not start antiviral therapy soon enough.

Thus, accurate and fast differential diagnosis between these two categories of meningoencephalitis is very crucial to come up with an appropriate and effective treatment plan. The analysis of patient records and identification of data patterns leads to better understanding of relationships or dependencies linking patients general condition with the occurence of particular kind of meningitis, and in this sense has the potential of helping to improve the accuracy of such a diagnosis while reducing the time lag between occcurence of first symptoms and final diagnosis.

5   Results and Interpretation

In the analyzed data approximately 67 percent of subjects suffered from viral infection and the remaining 33 percent suffered from bacterial disease. Consequently, when computing lower bound rules, the lower limit parameter l was set to 0.1 to try to discover rules with decision probability greater or equal to 0.9 for viral infection. For bacterial infection the parameter l was set to 0.5 to attempt to discover rules with decision accuracy of at least 0.5, which represents over 50 percent gain compared to frequency distribution-based decision. In case of viral infection the minimum accuracy gain was 34 percent which is close to the maximum achievable gain of 49 percent.

5.1   General Interpretation of Results

The obtained rules provided us with four interesting general results.
Firstly, CSF_{CELL} (cell count) is the most important attribute, which is consistent with the general medical knowledge about this infection. Secondly , values of the indicators of viral infection, such as BT, CRP, and CSF_{CELL} are much lower than in cases of bacterial infection. Third, interestingly, women do not suffer very often from bacterial infection, as opposed to men. However, such a role of sex has not been discussed in medical literature so far. Thus, this observation may be either a new discovery or may be dependent on data. We also found that most of the above patients suffer from chronic diseases, such as DM, LC, and sinusitis, which are the risk factors of bacterial meningitis. Fourth, age is also an important factor not to suspect viral meningitis, which also matches the fact that most old people suffer from chronic diseases.

Finally, our conclusion is that other conditional attributes, expecially physical examinations, are not useful for differential diagnosis. Especially, among 17 attributes, only BT(body temprature), SEX, AGE have proven to be the most important factors for diagnostic classification in our databases.

5.2   Some Important Discovered Rules

The following discovered rules to identify viral infection are important from the clinical viewpoint. The rules are generally consistent with medical knowledge. Especially, rules including the term "age" are very appealing. The rules are assigned the computed estimates (Rule Probability) of probability of occurence of rule conclusion given satisfaction of rule conditions. The number of cases satisfying each rule's conditions is called rule support and is also listed. Inuitively, the degree of support behind each rule can be used as a measure of "crediblity" of the empirical rule.

1. **IF** $WBC \leq 8000$ AND $CRP \leq 1.2$ AND $CSF_{CELL} \leq 1000$ **THEN** $VIRUS$ (Supported by 44 case(s), Rule Probability: 0.91)

2. **IF** $WBC \leq 8000$ AND $CSF_{CELL} \leq 1000$ **THEN** $VIRUS$ (Supported by 47 case(s), Rule Probability: 0.91)

3. **IF** $AGE \geq 40$ AND $CRP \leq 1.2$ AND $CSF_{CELL} \leq 1000$ **THEN** $VIRUS$ (Supported by 34 case(s), Rule Probability: 0.91)

4. **IF** $AGE \geq 40$ AND $WBC \leq 8000$ AND $CSF_{CELL} \leq 1000$ **THEN** $VIRUS$ (Supported by 19 case(s), Rule Probability: 0.95)

The following results seem to depend on the actual data set used for the analysis. However, these results give us some indication which potential factors should be closely examined. That is, for instance, sex seems to be also an important factor as it is demonstrated in our data. It may be a new discovery. Because the number of samples is a little small, we will look at this factor closely when new training samples are obtained.

5. **IF** $WBC \leq 8000$ AND $SEX = F$ AND $CSF_{CELL} \leq 1000$ **THEN** $VIRUS$ (Supported by 24 case(s), Rule Probability: 1.00)

6. **IF** $WBC \leq 12000$ AND $SEX = F$ AND $CSF_{CELL} \leq 1000$ **THEN** $VIRUS$ (Supported by 36 case(s), Rule Probability: 0.97)

7. **IF** $AGE < 40$ AND $SEX = F$ AND $CSF_{CELL} \leq 1000$ **THEN** $VIRUS$ (Supported by 23 case(s), Rule Probability: 1.00)

Similarly to the above rules to identify viral infection, the following rules to determine bacterial infection are consistent with the general medical knowledge. Especially, rules including the term "age" are most interesting.

8. **IF** $WBC \leq 12000$ AND $CSF_{CELL} > 1000$ **THEN** $BACTERIA$ (Supported by 24 case(s), Rule Probability: 0.67)

9. **IF** $CRP \leq 1.2$ AND $CSF_{CELL} > 1000$ **THEN** $BACTERIA$ (Supported by 19 case(s), Rule Probability: 0.58)

10. **IF** $CSF_{CELL} > 1000$ **THEN** $BACTERIA$ (Supported by 29 case(s), Rule Probability: 0.72)

The rule number 10 is very important. Although it is very simple, its accuracy is high and its support is relatively very high (29 cases or 87.8 percent of all cases with viral infection). Thus, in a case whose cell count is larger than 1000, we should suspect bacterial meningitis.

11. **IF** $AGE \geq 40$ AND $CSF_{CELL} > 1000$ **THEN** $BACTERIA$ (Supported by 15 case(s), Rule Probability: 0.80)

Compared with the rule number 10, this rule shows us that 15 out of 29 patients, or approximately fifty percent of patients whose cell count is larger than 1000, are more than 40 years old and this increases the risk of bacterial meningitis by eight percent.

12. IF $CRP > 1.2$ THEN $BACTERIA$ (Supported by 19 case(s), Rule Probability: 0.74)

13. IF $WBC > 8000$ AND $CRP > 0.6$ THEN $BACTERIA$ (Supported by 16 case(s), Rule Probability: 0.75)

14. IF $AGE \geq 40$ AND $WBC > 8000$ THEN $BACTERIA$ (Supported by 19 case(s), Rule Probability: 0.58)

Compared with the rule number 11, the above rule suggests that the condition $WBC > 8000$ is not as sensitive as $CSF_{CELL} > 1000$.

The following results for bacterial infection seem to be dependent on our data. As in viral infection, sex seems to be also an important factor affecting the occurence of bacterial meningitis.

15. IF $WBC > 8000$ AND $SEX = M$ THEN $BACTERIA$ (Supported by 19 case(s), Rule Probability: 0.68)

16. IF $SEX = M$ AND $CSF_{CELL} > 1000$ THEN $BACTERIA$ (Supported by 24 case(s), Rule Probability: 0.67)

6 Closing Remarks

The analysis of the results of rules discovery as presented in this paper revealed that comparison between discovered rules could also be very interesting. Especially, in the case of bacterial meningitis, rules comparison could potentialy lead to a deeper insight into the interactions of factors affecting the disease. For example, consider a case when A implies B with high accuracy and this relationship has strong support in data. If A jointly with some condition C also implies B, and if A and another condition D imply B with strong support in data, then, we may want to know the relation between C and D under the occurence of the condition "A", especially the set-theoretic relation between C and D. If C covers D, or vice versa, then we can deduce "D implies C" under the condition "A", or vice versa. If D and C have no semantic correlation, this may be also an interesting observation. In our case, C corresponds to $AGE > 40$, and D corresponds to $SEX = M$. If C implies D, then $SEX = M$ seems to be more important than $AGE > 40$, and the ratio of $AGE > 40$ to $SEX = M$ will be of interest. Otherwise, looking at the relation between C and D from the statistical viewpoint is also interesting.

In summary, the Bacterial Meningits creates an analytical context to investigate the relations between attributes. However, this analysis requires more comprehensive tools, including relational query languages and statistical analysis routines which are beyond the scope of KDD-R system in its current form.

7   Acknowledgment

The research reported in this paper was supported in part by an operating grant from the Natural Sciences and Engineering Research Council of Canada.

References

Katzberg , J. and Ziarko, W. 1994. *Variable Precision Rough Sets with Asymmetric Bounds*, In Ziarko, W. (ed.) Rough Sets, Fuzzy Sets and Knowledge Discovery, Springer-Verlag, pp.167-177.

Pawlak , Z. 1991. *Rough Sets: Theoretical Aspects of Reasoning About Data.* Kluwer Academic Publishers.

Piatetsky-Shapiro , G. (ed.) 1993. *Proc. of AAAI-93 Workshop on Knowledge Discovery in Datbases*, Washington D.C.

Piatetsky-Shapiro , G. and Frawley, W. J. (eds.) 1991. *Knowledge Discovery in Databases*, AAAI/MIT Press.

Ziarko , W. 1993. *Variable Precision Rough Set Model.* Journal of Computer and System Sciences, Vol. 46, No. 1, pp.39-59.

Fayyad , U. and Uthurusamy, R. (eds.) 1995. *Proceedings of the First International Conference on Knowledge Discovery and Data Mining*, Montreal, Canada 1995.

A Rough Set Framework for
Data Mining of Propositional Default Rules

Torulf Mollestad
Dept. of Computer Systems and Telematics
Institute of Computer Science
The Norwegian University of Science and Technology
7034 Trondheim, Norway
torulf@idt.unit.no

Andrzej Skowron
Institute of Mathematics
University of Warsaw
02-097 Warsaw
Banacha 2, Poland
skowron@mimuw.edu.pl

Abstract

As the amount of information in the world is steadily increasing, there is a growing demand for tools for analysing the information. In this paper we investigate the problem of *data mining*, that is, constructing decision rules from a set of primitive input data. The main contention of the present work is that there is a need to be able to reason also in presence of inconsistencies, and that more general, possibly unsafe rules should be made available through the data mining process. Such rules are typically simpler in structure, and allow the user to reason in absence of information. A framework is suggested for the generation of propositional *default* rules that reflect normal intradependencies in the data.

1 Introduction

As the amount of information in the world is steadily increasing, there is a growing demand for tools for analysing the information, finding patterns in terms of implicit dependencies in data. Realising that much of the collected data will not be handled or even seen by human beings, systems that are able to generate pragmatic summaries from large quantities of information will be of increasing importance in the future. Although simple statistical techniques for data analysis were developed long ago, advanced techniques for intelligent data analysis are not yet mature. As a result, there is a growing gap between data generation and data understanding. At the same time, there is a growing realisation and expectation that data, intelligently analysed and presented, will be a valuable resource to be used for a competitive advantage.

Recently, the concept of *knowledge discovery* [PSF91] has been brought to the attention of the business community. One main reason for this is that there is a general recognition that there is untapped value in larger data bases. Knowledge discovery (KD) is the nontrivial extraction of implicit, previously unknown, and potentially useful information from data. Knowledge discovery is thus a form of machine learning which discovers interesting knowledge and represents the information in a high-level language. If the underlying source of information is a database, the term *data mining* is used to denominate the process of automatic extraction of information. The information is then represented in terms of rules reflecting the intra-dependencies in the data. Applications of such rules include customer behaviour analysis in a supermarket or banking environment, and telecommunications alarm diagnosis and prediction. Typically, such rules would emulate an expert's reasoning process when *classifying* objects.

A great deal of work done in data mining has concentrated on the generation of rules that cover the situation where the training data is entirely consistent, i.e. all objects that are indiscernible are classified equally. In these cases, *definite* rules may be generated, that map all objects into the same decision class. There is however in many cases a clear need to be able to reason also in presence of inconsistencies. Different experts may disagree on the classification of one particular object, in which case it is desirable to assign different *trust* to the respective conclusions. Also, if objects are classified inconsistently, we want still to be able to generate rules that reflect the *normal* situation. Such normalcy rules typically sanction a particular conclusion given some information, whereas additional knowledge may invalidate previous conclusions.

In this work we look at the problems related to incompleteness and uncertainty/inconsistency in information systems, we wish to be able to generate rules that are able to handle these common phenomena. More specifically, we investigate how Rough Sets [Paw82, Paw91] can be applied to the problem of generating *default rules* [Rei80, Poo88, PGA86] from a set of primitive sample data, these rules enable us to express *common* relationships. The conclusions that are drawn from a default theory rely on the soundness of a set of assumptions, that themselves may be disproved when new knowledge is made available. This generalises the notion of decision rules, and provides a framework under which more, potentially interesting, statistical information may be extracted. Much of this information would be lost if the knowledge extraction process is restricted to generating definite rules only.

The input to the knowledge extraction process is a set of *example objects* and information about their properties. To learn rules from a set of examples, we assume the existence of an *oracle* that has complete knowledge of the domain – the world or universe. The oracle is able to classify the elements of the universe in the sense that he can make decisions with respect to some restricted set of *decision properties*. In doing this, he identifies a set of concepts – the classes of the classification. The task of the *learner* is to learn the oracle's knowledge, by trying to find the characteristic features of each concept, finding description of the oracle's concepts in terms of attributes that are available to the learner. The task of learning is thus the problem of expressing the oracle's basic concept in terms of the learner's basic concepts. In this paper we establish a framework for learning under uncertainty. The chosen representation of default rules is inspired by David Poole's Theorist [Poo88, Poo89, PGA86], which provides a simple setting for default reasoning, effectively implementing Reiter's Default Logic [Rei80, PGA86]. Poole's system operates with two sets of first order formulae, *facts* and *defaults*, that may be used as premises in a logical argument. The facts are closed formulae that are taken to be true in the domain, whereas the defaults may be seen as possible hypotheses that *may* be used in a theory to explain a proposition, provided that consistency is maintained (see also [MS96, Mol95] and [Mol96]).

The Rough Set approach [Paw82, Paw91, SGB91] was designed as a tool to deal with uncertain or vague knowledge in AI applications, and has shown to provide a theoretical basis for the solution of many problems within knowledge discovery. The notion of classification is central to the approach; the ability to distinguish between objects, and consequently reason about partitions of the universe. In Rough Sets, objects are perceived only through the information that is available about them – that is, through their values for a predetermined set of attributes. In the case of inexact information, one has to be able to give and reason about *rough* classifications of objects.

Due to space restrictions we have been able only to give brief summaries of the two fields that serve as the major motivation and basis for the work, namely Non–monotonic reasoning and Rough Sets theory. In the following we assume that the basic concepts of RS theory are known to the reader. Further information, including definitions, may be found in the full version of this paper [MS96].

2 Extraction of Knowledge from Information Systems

In this section we present a simple example that will help clarify the concepts and also serve as an illustration throughout the rest of the paper. The information system $\mathcal{A} = (U, A)$, displayed in Table 1, resulted from having observed a total of one hundred objects (the universe U) that were classified according to condition attributes $C = \{a, b, c\}$. Furthermore, the oracle's classification is represented as a set of decision attributes $D = \{d\}$ $(A = C \cup D)$.

	a	b	c	d	
E_1	1	2	3	1	(50×)
E_2	1	2	1	2	(5×)
E_3	2	2	3	2	(30×)
E_4	2	3	3	2	(10×)
$E_{5,1}$	3	5	1	3	(4×)
$E_{5,2}$	3	5	1	4	(1×)

Table 1: The example information system

The partition of the universe induced by the condition attributes contains $n = 5$ classes, namely E_1 through E_5. The objects that have the same values for the attributes $C = \{a, b, c\}$ (indiscernible objects) are represented by their equivalence classes $E_1, ..., E_5$ in the partition $U/\text{IND}(C)$. For instance, the class E_1 contains 50 objects, that are all characterised by their attribute-value vector $a_1 \wedge b_2 \wedge c_3$. The class E_5 is shown split into two disjoint sets of objects; $E_5 = E_{5,1} \cup E_{5,2}$, reflecting the two different decisions; $d = 3$ (for $E_{5,1}$) and $d = 4$ ($E_{5,2}$). Hence, the system is indeterministic with respect to the objects in class E_5.

The discernibility matrix $M_D(C) = \{m_D(i, j)\}_{n \times n}$ (over the condition attributes $C = \{a, b, c\}$) for the decision system is given in table 2. Note that, for pragmatic reasons, we do not have to distinguish between classes that are mapped into the same decision X_j. Hence, the items in the discernibility matrix that record the differences between these classes are not considered.

In the right side of the table we have shown the relative discernibility functions, i.e. the sets of attributes that are needed to discern one particular class E_i from all other classes. For instance, in order to be able to separate the objects in class E_1 from any object class that maps into another decision, we need to make use of both attributes a and c.

	E_1	E_2	E_3	E_4	E_5	
E_1	×	c	a	ab	abc	ac
E_2	c	×	×	×	ab	$c(a \vee b)$
E_3	a	×	×	×	abc	a
E_4	ab	×	×	×	abc	$a \vee b$
E_5	abc	ab	abc	abc	×	$a \vee b$

Table 2: Discernibility Matrix for the Decision System

The discernibility function for the entire system is $ca(a \vee b)(a \vee b \vee c) = ca$, hence, only two of the three attributes are needed to distinguish the classes *when the decision mapping is taken into account*.

Several authors have worked on applying the Rough Set approach to the problem of decision rules generation, designing algorithms to extract information from a set of primitive data by building propositional rules that cover the available input knowledge [Yas91, GB88, GB92, Sko93, SGB91, PS93, HCH93]. In the example given above, a typical learning task would be to define the oracle's knowledge (the classification of objects wrt. the decision attribute set D) in terms of the properties available to the learner; i.e. the attributes contained in the set $C \subseteq A$. In the following we will use the following shorthand notation; the expression $E_{a1_{v1}...ai_{vi}...an_{vn}}$ denotes the class over U that is defined by the corresponding values for attributes $a1...an$. For example, referring to the example given in table 1, the class $E_{a_2 c_3}$ is equal to $E_3 \cup E_4$.

By using the lower approximations of the sets $X_j \in U/\text{IND}(D)$, decision rules may be generated for the cases where objects can be classified with full certainty into some decision class. As mentioned above, the rules are defined as a mapping between an object/class description over the set of condition attributes into a description over the decision attribute(s). Definite rules are generated according to the below schema if all objects of E_i with full certainty have the decision j, in other words, if E_i is fully contained in X_j.

$$\text{Des}(E_i, C) \rightarrow \text{Des}(X_j, D), \text{ where } E_i \subseteq X_j$$

where the *Class Description* $\text{Des}(E, B)$ of an object class E, attributes $B \subseteq A$, is a value trace over the set of attributes B, i.e. a set of attribute–value pairs over B that characterise E.

In defining the rules, the *minimal* class description of each class is used, which is exactly the values for the attributes in a relative reduct for the class. See the discernibility matrix given in table 2, the minimal set of attributes needed to distinguish E_1 from all other classes is ac. Hence, one rule is generated for this class, mapping the value trace over the reduct $(a_1 c_3)$ into the decision class d_1. There are two minimal class descriptions of the E_2 class; namely $a_1 c_1$ and $b_2 c_1$, corresponding to each of the two disjuncts of the relative discernibility function for the class. From the table we find that the objects contained in classes E_1 through E_4 all may be mapped deterministically into one of the decision classes. Each of these classes is contained in the lower approximation $\underline{C}X_j$ for some decision class $X_j, j \in \{1, 2\}$. The following five (definite) rules are generated, applying the minimal class descriptions:

$$
\begin{aligned}
E_1: & \quad a_1 c_3 \rightarrow d_1 \\
E_2: & \quad a_1 c_1 \rightarrow d_2 \\
 & \quad b_2 c_1 \rightarrow d_2 \\
E_3, E_4: & \quad a_2 \rightarrow d_2 \\
E_4: & \quad b_3 \rightarrow d_2
\end{aligned}
$$

However, for the class E_5, the ambiguity with respect to the decision d means that no definite rule can be generated. All objects in the class are contained in the boundary region of both classes X_3 and X_4.

3 Default Rule Generation

The procedure described above was able to generate rules that cover the deterministic situation, i.e. where all objects of a particular class $E_i \in U/\text{IND}(C)$ are mapped into the same decision class. The example given in the last section does however demonstrate the fact that it is not always possible to obtain a set of deterministic rules that completely covers the entire training set. More importantly, in general we do not even want to generate such a set of overly specific rules. Even if they do cover all the objects in the training information system, such rules may prove completely insufficient when used on other input data.

It is very often important to be able to handle inconsistencies in the data. From such data we may still be able to extract a lot of interesting information, specifically knowledge that reflects the *most common* or *normal* situation. A strict requirement on the absolute correctness of the rules has proven insufficient in many real world applications. Computer systems – as well as people – are often under pressure to make a decision under strict time constraints, and the ability to reason in absence of knowledge is a great advantage. To reason in this way, we may choose to believe in some rule provided that the evidence supporting it is strong enough. Furthermore, results have been shown [Qui86] that suggest that simplified, "uncertain" rules in general prove better than the original ones when applied to new cases.

Finding such simple and natural expressions for regularities in databases is useful in various analysis or prediction tasks. Hence, we do want to obtain a set of rules that model the *general characteristics* of the data, and that are less susceptible to noise. In the following we define a framework for the generation of propositional *default* rules. We will also show how default reasoning may be used as a framework to represent and reason about indeterministic information systems.

Ultimately, the reason that indeterminacy arises in information systems is the lack of ability to represent – in the particular information system – some attributes that differentiate the objects in the "real" world. If an expert classifies two objects with the same information vector in the system differently, this is because he is able to distinguish them according to some attribute(s) that are not represented in the system. These attributes may however be significant only in very special situations, and the data collected may suggest that one particular decision effectively covers a great majority of the cases.

Default rules that account for some *normal* dependency between objects and their properties may be accepted if there exists a decision that dominates to a certain extent the set of objects characterised by the rule. Consider the general rule schema $\mathrm{Des}(E_i, C) \to \mathrm{Des}(X_j, D)$. To find whether the rule can be accepted as a default relation between classes $E_i \in U/\mathrm{IND}(C)$ and $X_j \in U/\mathrm{IND}(D)$, we test the value for the membership degree function versus a threshold μ_{tr} by testing that

$$\mu_C(E_i, X_j) = \frac{|E_i \cap X_j|}{|E_i|} \geq \mu_{tr}$$

In other words, we accept the default rule for the condition class E_i provided that the value $\mu_C(E_i, X_j)$ exceeds a predetermined *threshold* value μ_{tr} for some dominating decision class X_j. Note that, in the deterministic situation, $\mu_C(E_i, X_j) = 1$, since the class E_i is in its entirety contained in X_j.

Again referring to the example given in section 1, we aim at characterising the data represented in the class E_5 (non–deterministic). The computation yields $\mu_C(E_5, X_3) = 4/5$, and provided that this value is greater than the preset threshold, two default rules are generated for the class (for each of the two minimal class descriptions), namely $a_3 \to d_3$ and $b_5 \to d_3$.

Which rules will be generated in the process depends upon the setting of μ_{tr}. The threshold value may be a preset constant, or be parametrised by the classes in $U/\mathrm{IND}(C)$ [Mol96].

In the above, we have suggested generating definite rules from the deterministic subpart of the information system, as well as default- or "common pattern" rules for the nondeterministic part. The default rules are generated in the cases where $1 > \mu \geq \mu_{tr}$. From any (deterministic or nondeterministic) information system, we are however often interested in finding more general patterns in the data. We propose to do this by a framework that is able to generate and reason about classes for which no unique decision can be made. In fact, sets may be constructed that cover more objects (and hence have a simpler description), by forming unions of the classes induced by the condition attributes C. Rules are generated that map these composed classes into the decision that dominates the set. The rules that result generally have at least two great advantages as compared to deterministic rules: they are always *simpler* in structure, and though not entirely correct wrt. the training data, they will in many cases prove to be better when handling yet unseen cases, being less susceptible to noise. The ability of the system to classify future events will in general greatly depend on the system's ability to *generalise* over its knowledge.

In the core of the approach is the idea of *creating* indeterminacy in information systems, generating rules that cover the majority of the cases. There are in principle three ways of *creating* an indeterminacy in an information system [Mol96], here we consider generation of indeterminacy through selecting *projections* over the condition attributes, allowing certain attributes to be excluded from consideration. In doing this, we effectively join equivalence classes over the condition attributes, classes which may be mapped into different decisions.

Classes in the equivalence relation defined by the condition attributes C are "glued" together by selecting suitable projections C_{Pr} of C, while ensuring that, for the resulting object class, one particular decision remains the dominating one. This simple idea is fundamental to the approach. In this paper, we suggest a framework for extracting such "normal" dependencies from the information system. The basic steps are the following:

1. Selection of projections $C_{Pr} = C - C_{Cut}$ over the attributes. The projections are selected such that *new indeterminacies* result.

2. By each such projection, classes are glued together into more compound object classes $E_{(k,C_{Pr})} \in U,'\text{IND}(C_{Pr})$, $k = 1.. \mid U/\text{IND}(C_{Pr}) \mid$.

3. Default rules are generated, ensuring that one particular decision X_j remains the dominating one by checking that

$$\mu_{C_{Pr}}(E_{(k,C_{Pr})}, X_j) = \frac{\mid E_{(k,C_{Pr})} \cap X_j \mid}{\mid E_{(k,C_{Pr})} \mid} \geq \mu_{tr}$$

4. Facts are constructed that may potentially block the application of a default. Such blocks are generated for those classes E_i which are now contained in the compound class, but which deterministically map into another decision than the dominating one, in other words that $E_i \cap X_j = \emptyset$.

Each new class $E_{k,C_{Pr}} \in U/\text{IND}(C_{Pr})$, where k ranges over the new equivalence classes generated, may be constructed as a union of those $E_i, E_j \in U/\text{IND}(C)$ that originally were discernible only by attributes that were removed in the projection, i.e. $m_D(i,j) \subseteq C_{Cut}$. In other words:

$$E_{k,C_{Pr}} = \bigcup \{E_i \cup E_j \mid E_i, E_j \in U/\text{IND}(C), m_D(i,j) \subseteq C_{Cut}\}$$

The selection of projections that will potentially lead to interesting rules is in other words dictated by the content of the discernibility matrix. Any two object classes E_i and E_k may be glued together by making a projection which excludes all the attributes represented by the discernibility matrix element $m_D(i,k) = \{a \in C \mid a(E_i) \neq a(E_k)\}$. Furthermore, the consequence of removing a set of attributes may be studied simply by syntactically removing all the corresponding boolean variables from the discernibility matrix. The cells in the matrix that become empty signify exactly the classes that are glued together by performing the projection.

The only immediate way of creating indeterminacies in the system is to remove the information (in terms of attributes) that distinguishes classes that are mapped into different decisions. These minimal distinguishing attribute sets are represented by the factors in the discernibility function. Hence, indeterminacy is introduced by removing each of the attributes that are represented by corresponding boolean variables in each respective factor. For instance, for a system having discernibility function, say, $a(b \lor c)$, there are two immediate ways of creating an indeterminacy; either removing a or removing both attributes b and c.

There are exactly as many different projections as there are conjuncts in the discernibility function. Each projection results in a "new" indeterministic information system, defined over the condition attributes $C_{Pr} \subseteq C$. From each of these systems, a recursive call is made to the rule generation procedure, which will eventually generate still more simplified rules. The projection operation is defined over subsets of the condition attributes C. Hence, the recursive process is defined on the lattice over the powerset 2^C. Using the properties of the discernibility function, described above, we may reduce the search in the lattice significantly. For instance, in the example IS, having discernibility function ac, we find that two immediately interesting projections are $C - \{a\} = \{b, c\}$ and $C - \{c\} = \{a, b\}$. Each of these projections are made, respective rules are generated, and recursive calls are made initiating further search from each of the subsystems. The search for the example system is illustrated in figure 1.

As mentioned above, rules are generated provided that the objects contained in the class $E_{k,C_{Pr}}$ in a given, high fraction of the cases still are classified correctly into the decision j. The number of objects *from the training set* that are wrongly classified (into the decision class X_l, $l \neq j$) by rules generated in this way is equal to $(1 - \mu(E_{k,C_{Pr}}, X_j)) \mid E_{k,C_{Pr}} \mid$.

The new object classes may be characterised by their minimal description/information vectors $\alpha_{C_{Pr}} = \mathrm{Des}(E_{C_{Pr}}, MinDes)$, where $MinDes$ is a prime implicant of the relative discernibility function $f(E_{C_{Pr}}, C_{Pr})$. Recall that $\mathrm{Des}(E, C)$ computes the value trace of the class E over the attributes C. Since there may exist several such minimal descriptions of a given class, the schema gives rise to potentially several rules. Default rules (Δ) and facts $(\mathcal{F})$ are constructed according to the following schema:

$$\Delta: \quad \mathrm{Des}(E_{k,C_{Pr}}, C_{Pr}) \rightarrow \mathrm{Des}(X_j, D)$$
$$\mathcal{F}: \quad \mathrm{Des}(E_i, C_{Cut}) \rightarrow \neg\mathrm{Des}(X_j, D) \text{, where}$$

$$E_i \in U/\mathrm{IND}(C), \ E_i \subseteq E_{k,C_{Pr}} \text{ and } E_i \cap X_j = \emptyset.$$

Note that in addition to the default rules, some *facts* are generated that may potentially block the defaults. These rules are generated for the "minority" classes, the antecedents of the counterexample rules are expressions over the set of attributes that were removed in the projection. The counterexamples, then, are exactly those sets E_i that are distinguishable from the other $E_{i'} \subseteq E_{k,C_{Pr}}$ by the attributes in C_{Cut}.

Let us now consider the method at work with an example. As shown in section 2, we are, from the given information system, able to generate five definite rules that cover the available "certain" knowledge.

The algorithm is initially called with argument $C - \emptyset$, i.e. not removing any attributes. At this (top) level in the lattice, the definite rules are generated $(\mu = 1)$, and default rules that cover the indeterministic part of the IS $(\mu < 1)$. The total set of definite rules generated for the example are found in section 2. The only class which is indeterministic wrt. the decision is E_5. The degree of membership $\mu_C(E_5, X_3) = 4/5$, whereas $\mu_C(E_5, X_4) = 1/5$. Class E_5 has relative discernibility function $a \vee b$. Hence, the following rules may be extracted (each rule is shown with its corresponding μ value):

$$\Delta(C - \emptyset): \quad \begin{array}{ll} a_3 \rightarrow d_3|_{4/5} & a_3 \rightarrow d_4|_{1/5} \\ b_5 \rightarrow d_3|_{4/5} & b_5 \rightarrow d_4|_{1/5} \end{array}$$

As argued above, the value for the discernibility function for the system will at each point suggest which paths may allow new and interesting rules to be obtained. In this example, additions may only be obtained through the deletion of either one of attributes a or c. Deleting the attribute b from the condition attributes would not create any new indeterminacy, and hence, no new rules could be generated. Making the two interesting projections yields two new systems over $C - \{a\}$ and $C - \{c\}$, that have discernibility matrices $M_D(C - \{a\})$ and $M_D(C - \{c\})$, respectively.

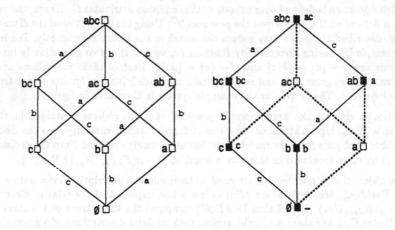

Figure 1: The search in the lattice

The search in the lattice is shown in figure 1, where rules are generated at nodes abc, ab, bc, c, b and $\emptyset$. Note again that the paths traversed are directed by the value for the discernibility function of the nodes at different levels, shown on the right hand side of each node in the lattice. For the projections $C - \{a\}$ and $C - \{c\}$, respectively, the following new sets of (default) rules are generated:

$$\Delta(C - \{a\}): \quad \begin{array}{ll} b_2c_3 \rightarrow d_1|_{50/80} \\ b_2c_3 \rightarrow d_2|_{30/80} \end{array} \qquad \Delta(C - \{c\}): \quad \begin{array}{ll} a_1 \rightarrow d_1|_{50/55} \\ a_1 \rightarrow d_2|_{5/55} \end{array}$$

Continuing to remove attributes from the two systems obtained will imply that new defaults may be generated. The system over $C - \{a\}$ has discernibility function bc. Further removal of attributes b or c yields two new sets:

$$\Delta(C - \{ab\}): \quad \begin{array}{ll} c_3 \rightarrow d_1|_{50/90} \\ c_3 \rightarrow d_2|_{40/90} \\ c_1 \rightarrow d_2|_{5/10} \\ c_1 \rightarrow d_3|_{4/10} \\ c_1 \rightarrow d_4|_{1/10} \end{array} \qquad \Delta(C - \{ac\}): \quad \begin{array}{ll} b_2 \rightarrow d_1|_{50/85} \\ b_2 \rightarrow d_2|_{35/85} \end{array}$$

If, starting from the system over $C - \{ab\}$, the attribute c is removed, there is obviously nothing that enables us to distinguish the different classes any more. The rules generated at the bottom level of the lattice reflect simply the distribution of values for the decision attribute d, i.e the fraction of the objects that are classified into the respective decisions.

In practice one would not want to generate rules that do not have a particular coverage above the threshold. The threshold value may be set at any level ($\mu_{tr} \leq 1$), thereby effectively discarding the rules with insufficient confidence. Sorting the generated rules by their respective values of the degree of membership μ, having set the threshold value $\mu_{tr} = 0.55$, we obtain the table given below:

$$\mathcal{F}: \quad a_1 c_3 \rightarrow d_1 \qquad\qquad \Delta: \quad a_1 \rightarrow d_1|_{50/55=0.91}$$
$$a_1 c_1 \rightarrow d_2 \qquad\qquad\qquad a_3 \rightarrow d_3|_{4/5=0.80}$$
$$b_2 c_1 \rightarrow d_2 \qquad\qquad\qquad b_5 \rightarrow d_3|_{4/5=0.80}$$
$$a_2 \rightarrow d_2 \qquad\qquad\qquad b_2 c_3 \rightarrow d_1|_{50/80=0.62}$$
$$b_3 \rightarrow d_2 \qquad\qquad\qquad b_2 \rightarrow d_1|_{50/85=0.59}$$
$$c_3 \rightarrow d_1|_{50/90=0.56}$$

Assume now that a new object is observed, for which the value of the a attribute is found to be 1, whereas the values for all the other attributes for the object are unknown. The definite rules do not sanction any conclusion in this case, we may however apply the first default rule to conclude (by assumption) that the decision in this case should be 1. If, later, further knowledge is made available, the assumption (and therefore the conclusion) may have to be retracted. The framework described here allows the counterexamples (blocks) to defaults to be recorded explicitly. For instance, consider again the first (highest priority) default rule (having given it a unique name);

$$\mathrm{def}_{a_1 d_1}: a_1 \rightarrow d_1$$

The rule was output at level $C - \{c\}$ in the lattice, and the counterexample is produced in terms of the attributes that were cut out, that is c in this case. Hence, we record the value of this attribute for all those object classes that are contained in $E_{a_1} = E_1 \cup E_2$ and that map into any decision other than d_1. In the example, this concerns the objects in the class E_2, for which the value for c is 1. A fact is generated that blocks the default in this case. Notice that other objects may well exist in the information system that have $c = 1$ and that still map into decision $d = 1$. Hence, the knowledge that $c = 1$ should be used to *block* the application of the default, instead of the conclusion itself. A rule is generated that may block $\mathrm{def}_{a_1 d_1}$:

$$c_1 \rightarrow \neg\mathrm{def}_{a_1 d_1}$$

4 Summary and Related Work

In this paper we contend that default rules provide a powerful tool for representing common characteristics of a set of data. We suggest that Rough Set theory may be applied to solve the problem of generation of default decision rules from such primitive (sample) data. The framework and its properties is extensively described in [Mol96]. Related work [Yas91, GB88, HCH93, Sko93] is summarised in [MS96]. An algorithm has been developed which is in the process of being implemented and tested. Apart from the specific issue tackled, we foresee several interesting topics and questions for future investigation [MS96], including a generalisation to handling first-order clauses or default rules, arranging the rules into different priority strata ([Bre89]) and the problem of updating the rule base when new data becomes available. This study shows that Rough Sets will prove beneficial to the research in these areas.

References

[Bre89]   G. Brewka. Proc. of IJCAI-89. In *Preferred subtheories: An Extended Logical Framework for Default Reasoning*, pages 1043–1048, 1989.

[GB88]   J.W. Grzymala-Busse. Knowledge Acquisition under Uncertainty – A Rough Set Approach. *Journal of Intelligent and Robotic Systems*, 1:3–16, 1988.

[GB92]   J.W. Grzymala-Busse. LERS – A System for Learning from Examples based on Rough Sets. In R. Slowinski, editor, *Handbook of Applications and Advances of the Rough Sets Theory*, pages 3–1?. 1992.

[HCH93]   X. Hu, N. Cercone, and J. Han. An Attribute–Oriented Rough Set approach for Knowledge Discovery in Databases. In W. P. Ziarko, editor, *Rough Sets, Fuzzy Sets and Knowledge Discovery*, pages 90–99. Springer Verlag, 1993.

[Mol95]   T. Mollestad. Learning Propositional Default Rules using the Rough Set Approach. In A. Aamodt and J. Komorowski, editors, *Scandinavian Conference on Artificial Intelligence*, pages 208–219, Trondheim, Norway, May 1995. IOS Press.

[Mol96]   T. Mollestad. *A Rough Set Approach to Default Rules Data Mining*. PhD thesis, The Norwegian Institute of Technology, Trondheim, Norway, September 1996. To appear.

[MS96]   T. Mollestad and A. Skowron. A Rough Set Framework for Data Mining of Propositional Default Rules (*Full Version*). Available at http://www.idt.unit.no/IDT/grupper/KS-grp/report_technical/tech_papers.html, 1996.

[Paw82]   Z. Pawlak. Rough Sets. *International Journal of Information and Computer Science*, 11(5):341–356, 1982.

[Paw91]   Z. Pawlak. *Rough Sets – Theoretical Aspects of Reasoning about Data*. Kluwer Academic Publishers, 1991.

[PGA86]   D. Poole, R. Goebel, and R. Aleliunas. Theorist: A Logical Reasoning System for Defaults and Diagnosis. In N.J. Cercone and G. McCalla, editors, *The Knowledge Frontier: Essays in the Representation of Knowledge*, pages 331–352. Springer–Verlag, New York, 1986.

[Poo88]   D. Poole. A Logical Framework for Default Reasoning. *Artificial Intelligence*, 36:27–47, 1988.

[Poo89]   D. Poole. Explanation and Prediction: An Architecture for Default and Abductive Reasoning. *Computational Intelligence*, 5(2):97–110, 1989.

[PS93]   Z. Pawlak and A. Skowron. A Rough Set Approach to Decision Rules Generation. Technical report, University of Warsaw, 1993.

[PSF91]   G. Piatetsky-Shapiro and W.J. Frawley, editors. *Knowledge Discovery in Databases*. AAAI/MIT, 1991.

[Qui86]   J.R. Quinlan. Induction of Decision Trees. *Machine learning*, 1:81–106, 1986.

[Rei80]   R. Reiter. A Logic for Default Reasoning. *Computational Intelligence*, 13:81–132, 1980.

[SGB91]   A. Skowron and J. Grzymala-Busse. From Rough Set Theory to Evidence Theory. Technical report, Warsaw University of Technology, 1991.

[Sko93]   A. Skowron. Boolean Reasoning for Decision Rules generation. In J. Komorowski and Z.W. Ras, editors, *7th International Symposium for Methodologies for Intelligent Systems, ISMIS '93*, pages 295–305, Trondheim, Norway, June 1993. Springer Verlag.

[Yas91]   R. Yasdi. Learning Classification Rules from Databases in the Context of Knowledge-Acquisition and -Representation. *IEEE Transactions on Knowledge and Data Engineering*, 3:293–306, September 1991.

An Empirical Study on the Incompetence of Attribute Selection Criteria

Ibrahim F. Imam

Machine Learning and Inference Laboratory
George Mason University
4400 University Dr., Fairfax, VA 22030
iimam@aic.gmu.edu

ABSTRACT

One of the main tasks in most supervised learning systems is the evaluation of the attributional relevancy in the given databases. Such relevancy is mainly concerned with the relationship between the available attributes and the decision classes. Attributes relevant to the decision classes are used to represent the learned knowledge, while irrelevant attributes are removed or ignored during the learning process. This paper investigates the relationship between attributional relevancy to decision classes and to learning systems. The experimental results from different databases show that some attributes relevant to decision classes may be irrelevant to the learning system. Experiments are performed on eight different databases using the C4.5 system for learning decision trees from examples.
Key words: relevancy, machine learning, decision trees.

1. Introduction

Machine learning systems are effective tools for discovering hidden, previously unknown knowledge from data. Memory optimization, complexity reduction, and noise filtering are major problems to be handled by such systems. One of the common approaches to overcome these problems is to remove irrelevant attributes and noisy examples from the data before applying the discovery system [4, 10, 16]. Relevancy is usually measured, between the decision classes and one or more attributes, using a utility function or a statistical test. Attributes relevant to the decision classes are used to form a concept description of patterns existing in the data. Irrelevant attributes are either ignored or removed from the data. This usually improves the predictive accuracy of the obtained concept. However, the improvement in many cases does not reach the global maximum but is instead trapped in local maximum [7].

This paper investigates the relationship between attributional relevancy to decision classes and to a decision tree learning system. To analyze this issue, attributional relevancy to the decision classes is measured by two utility functions, the Gain or the Chi-square criteria [9, 13]. Attributional relevancy to the learning system is measured by the change in the error rate of knowledge learned before and after removing one attribute from the given data. Experiments performed on different databases show that for some attributes classified as relevant by both utility functions, knowledge obtained from data after removing any of those attributes is as accurate as or better than knowledge produced from the original data.

Experiments were performed using the learning system C4.5 [13]. The experiments used artificial databases including the MONKs and tic-tac-toe problems, and real world databases including the congressional voting records 84, the iris plants, the wind bracing, the liver cancer, and the contact lenses databases. The experimental results show that attributes relevant to the decision classes may be irrelevant to the learning system.

2. An Overview and Related Work

Most symbolic learning systems use search techniques either to select the most relevant attribute for classification or to determine the set of attributes to be used in generalizing the training examples. Attribute selection criteria can be divided into three categories: logic-based, information-based, and statistics-based. The logic-based criteria for selecting attributes measure relevancy through logical relationships between attribute values and the decision classes. Examples of such criteria include the MAL criterion, Minimizing Added Leaves [8], and the Disjointness criterion [6]. Both criteria were designed to work with decision rules. These criteria use conjunction, disjunction, and other operators to measure the relevancy of an attribute. The information-based criteria are based on the Information Theory. These criteria measure the information conveyed by dividing the training examples into subsets using one attribute. Examples of such criteria include Information Measure IM, entropy reduction measure, and Gain criteria [11], gini index of diversity [2], Gain-ratio measure [12], and others [3, 9].

Statistics-based criteria are usually used to measure the association between decision classes and a given attribute using a statistical distribution. The attribute with the highest association is the best attribute to classify the given decision classes. Examples of statistical criteria include the Chi-square and the G statistic [5, 9, 14].

3. Measuring Attributional Relevancy to Learning Systems

Attributional relevancy is usually determined by a utility function or a statistical test, and it is done before applying the learning system. It estimates the association between one attribute and the decision classes. Evaluating attributes from data before applying the learning system may not convey how attributes influence the learning system. For example, if there are interdependency among attributes, evaluating one attribute at a time is not an effective approach for symbolic learning systems [7].

This section introduces a methodology for measuring the relevancy of an attribute to the learning system. The method evaluates the relevancy of each attribute by running the learning system before and after removing the attribute. Removing an attribute from the data usually increases the complexity of the data. This complexity can be viewed as generating ambiguous and redundant examples. An example is *ambiguous* if it belongs to two or more distinct decision classes. An example is *redundant* of another example if both examples share the same attribute-values set and belong to the same decision class. This complexity can be measured by the change in the error rate before and after removing the attribute. The methodology is based on the assumption that: *"removing an irrelevant attribute should not increase the complexity of the data, however removing a relevant attribute should add both ambiguity and redundancy to the data which increases the error rate of the learned concept"*.

3.1. Description of the Method

Assume that S_i and T_i are samples of training and testing examples, respectively; $DER(X, S_i, T_i, \_)$ denotes the Default Error Rate resulted from testing the knowledge learned by system X, from the set S_i, against the set T_i; and ER(X, S_i, T_i, A) denotes the Error Rate resulted from running system X on sample S_i against the testing set T_i after removing attribute A.

Consider a database contains m attributes, A_1, ..., A_m. The following is a description of the method for determining the Removable Relevancy:

Input: A set of training examples S_i and a set of testing examples T_i.
Output: The Removable Relevancy of all attributes in the data (for system X).

Step 1: Apply system X on the training data S_i, then test the obtained knowledge against the testing data T_i. The resulting error rate is DER(X, S_i, T_i, _).

For each attribute, A_j, repeat step 2 to step 4:

Step 2: Remove only the given attribute, A_j, from the original dataset S_i and T_i to generate two datasets SA_{ij} and TA_{ij}.

Step 3: Apply the learning algorithm on SA_{ij} and test the obtained knowledge against TA_{ij}. The resulting error rate is ER(X, S_i, T_i, A_j).

Step 4: The Removable Relevancy (RR) of A_j to the learning system is determined by:
$$RR(A_j) = ER(X, S_i, T_i, A_j) - DER(X, S_i, T_i, \_)$$
Remove the datasets SA_{ij} and TA_{ij}.

The attribute is relevant if it has a positive Removable Relevancy (e.g., RR(A_j) > 0). The attribute is irrelevant if it has a zero or negative Removable Relevancy (e.g., RR(A_j) ≤ 0). If the default predictive error rate DER(X, S_i, T_i, _) is 100%, then all attributes used for describing the learned concept are relevant and all other attributes are irrelevant. An advantage of such method is that it ranks attributes from most irrelevant to most relevant.

3.2. An Example to Illustrate the Method

The symbolic learning system C4.5 [13] was used to perform this experiment. The experiment is performed on two artificial problems, namely the MONK 1 and 3 problems [15]. The target concept description of both problems and the relevant and irrelevant attributes were given. For each problem, four different sample sizes (10%, 20%, 40%, and 60%) were drawn randomly for training, and the remaining data sets (90%, 80%, 60%, and 40% respectively) were kept for testing. Table 1 shows the relevant and irrelevant attributes for both problems. Attributes have similar domains in each problem.

Table 1: Relevant and Irrelevant attributes of the MONKs 1 & 3 problems.

Problem	x1	x2	x3	x4	x5	x6
MONK-1	Relevant	Relevant	Irrelevant	Irrelevant	Relevant	Irrelevant
MONK-3	Irrelevant	Relevant	Irrelevant	Relevant	Relevant	Irrelevant

The MONK-1 problem contains 3 relevant and 3 irrelevant attributes. The MONK-3 problem has two highly relevant attributes, x2 and x5, one less relevant attribute, x4, and three irrelevant attributes. Figure 1 shows two diagrams illustrating the

Removable Relevancy of attributes of each problem. Negative values mean that the attribute is relevant. Otherwise, the attribute is irrelevant.

These results show that relative changes in the error rate obtained from small sample sizes were not compatible with those obtained from larger sample sizes. For example, in the experiment with the MONK-1, x5 was more relevant than x1 and x2 with small size (e.g., 10%), while it was less relevant with larger sizes (e.g., 20%, 40%, and 60%). In the MONK-3 experiment, x4 was irrelevant with small sizes (e.g., 10%), while it becomes relevant with larger sizes (e.g., 20%, 40%, and 60%).

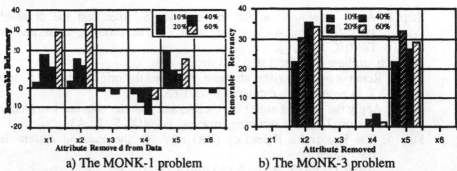

a) The MONK-1 problem   b) The MONK-3 problem

Figure 1: The Removable Relevancy obtained for the MONKs attributes.

4. Experimental Study

4.1. The MONK-1 Problem

The first experiment was performed on the MONK-1 problem [15]. The experiment was performed to determine the relationship between the attributional relevancy determined by both the Gain and the Chi-square criteria and the Removable Relevancy. Table 2 shows the results of evaluating the attributes of the MONK-1 problem using the three criteria. The Removable Relevancy indicates that attributes x1 and x2 are more important for the learning program than attribute x5. However, both the Chi-square and the Gain criteria prefered x5.

Table 2: Results from the MONK-1 database.

Attributes	Chi-Square	Gain Ranking	Removable Relevancy
x5	71.4	1	16.5
x1	1.7	2	39.4
x2	1.3	3	37.8
x4	0.5	4	0
x3	0.6	5	0
x6	0.01	6	0

4.2. The MONK-3 Problem

The same experiments were performed on the MONK-3 problem. Table 3 shows the attributes of the MONK-3 problem and the evaluations given by the three criteria. In this experiment, both the Chi-square and the Removable Relevancy criteria agreed on the most relevant attribute. However, the Gain criterion prefered x5.

Table 3: Results from the MONK-3 database.

Attributes	Chi-Square	Gain Ranking	Removable Relevancy
x5	70.6	1	19.4
x2	94.1	2	22.2
x1	2.9	3	0
x4	2.1	4	2.8
x3	0.9	5	0
x6	0.02	6	0

4.3. The Congressional-Voting-84 Problem

The U.S. Congress Voting Records-1984 contains two decision classes "Democratic" and "Republican". Each voting record of a Democrat or a Republican is described in terms of 16 attributes. The available number of examples was 232. Only 148 examples were selected randomly for training. Table 4 shows the Removable Relevancy, Chi-square, and the Gain ranking of these attribues. The three criteria agreed on the order of relevant attributes, however, the degree of relevancy was not compatible.

Table 4: Results from the Congressional Voting (84) dataset.

Attributes	Chi-Square	Gain Ranking	Removable Relevancy
x4	148	1	4.7
x5	139	2	0
x12	101	3	0
x3	115	4	0
x8	115	5	0
x9	111	6	0
x14	116	7	0
x13	95	8	0
x15	83	9	0
x6	96	10	0
x7	73	11	0
x11	57	12	0
x1	49	13	0
x16	105	14	0
x10	46	15	0
x2	30	16	0

4.4. Classification of Iris Plants

The Iris plants database contains three decision classes describing different kinds of irises, and four attributes describing the length and width of the sepal and petal. All attributes have continuous domains. In this experiment, all attribute domains were quantized into three or four intervals with equal number of examples in each interval. Table 5 shows the estimation of relevancy of each attribute using different criteria. The available number of examples after quantizing the data was 192. Only 117 examples were used for training and 33 examples were used for testing.

When x1 is removed from the data, C4.5 learned a similar decision tree to the one learned from the original data. This result was a bit strange since both the Chi-square and the Gain criteria ranked x1 third.

Table 5: Results from the Iris Plant dataset.

Attributes	Chi-Square	Gain Ranking	Removable Relevancy
x4	104.6	1	6.1
x3	93.9	2	9.1
x1	68.0	3	0
x2	42.4	4	3

4.5. Classification of Wind Bracings for Tall Buildings

The wind bracing problem [1] is concerned with the wind bracing in steel skeleton structures of tall buildings. The data contains four decision classes and seven attributes with nominal domains. The wind bracing data (used in this paper) consists of 338 examples. Only 311 examples were used for training. Table 6 shows the evaluation of all attributes obtained by the three criteria. Again, while x4 was classified as relevant by both the Chi-square and the Gain criteria, it was irrelevant for the learning system. The same decision tree obtained before and after removing x4.

Table 6: Results from the Wind Bracings dataset.

Attributes	Chi-Square	Gain Ranking	Removable Relevancy
x6	223.8	1	5.4
x4	146.2	2	0
x1	115.4	3	10.9
x5	19.9	4	5.4
x7	22.5	5	4.6
x2	3.9	6	2.7
x3	0.7	7	0

4.6. Diagnosing Liver Disorders

The liver database diagnose whether or not there is any disorder in the liver. The decision is made based on six attributes. These attributes represent five blood tests (outcomes presented by values of continuous domains) and the number of drinks per day. The first five attributes were quantized according to a uniform distribution of the number of examples per an intervals. The data contains 345 available examples, only 272 examples were used for learning. Table 7 shows the relevancy of all attributes using the three criteria. One can observe that x1 was classified as highly relevant by both the Chi-square and the Gain criteria, however, it was classified as highly irrelevant by the Removable Relevancy.

4.7. Categorizing Contact Lenses Patients

The contact lenses data classifies patients according to the contact lenses that more suitable for them. The data has three decision classes for soft or hard lenses, and no-fitting. The data contains four attributes describing 24 example. Only 20 examples where selected for training and 4 examples were kept for testing. Table 8 shows that the attribute x4 is classified as the most relevant by the Chi-square and the Gain criteria. However, when x4 was removed from the data a similar concept is learned. Note that, one error represents 25% of the testing data.

Table 7: Results from the Liver Disorders dataset.

Attributes	Chi-Square	Gain Ranking	Removable Relevancy
x5	18.5	1	16.4
x1	12.8	2	1.4
x2	6.8	3	2.7
x4	6.2	4	0
x3	5.5	5	8.2
x6	1.4	6	0

Table 8: Results from the Contact Lenses dataset.

Attributes	Chi-Square	Gain Ranking	Removable Relevancy
x4	9.90	1	0
x3	4.57	2	25
x1	1.30	3	0
x2	1.27	4	0

4.8. The Tic-Tac-Toe Database

The Tic-Tac-Toe database describes a set of all possible board configurations at the end of Tic-Tac-Toe games. The data uses 9 attributes to describe the 9 different cells in the Tic-Tac-Toe board. Each attribute takes 3 values (o, for one player; x, for the other player; and b, for blanck). The available number of examples was 958. Only 763 examples were used for training. Table 9 shows that both the Chi-square and the Gain criteria provided similar ranking for all attributes. However, this ranking is very incompatible with the Removable Relevancy. When attribute x8 was removed from the training data, a decision tree was learned with higher predictive accuracy than the one which obtained from the original training data.

Table 9: Results from the Tic-Tac-Toe dataset.

Attributes	Chi-Square	Gain Ranking	Removable Relevancy
x5	78.7	1	14.1
x9	17.3	2	5.4
x3	15.0	3	6.1
x7	12.5	4	8.1
x1	10.7	5	5.4
x8	9.4	6	0.3
x4	8.6	7	1
x2	7.7	8	1
x6	5.7	9	2.4

4.9. Summary of Results

The results in this section show that measuring relevancy by a utility function is not necessarily measuring the attributional relevancy to the learning system. Figure 2 shows two diagrams summarizing the relationship between the attributional relevancy to the decision classes and to the learning systems over different datasets. The horizontal axis represents the ranking of both the Chi-square and the Gain criteria for the four most relevant attributes. Attributes in these diagrams are descendingly ordered from the most relevant to the least. The vertical axis represents the ranking order of the Removable Relevancy of each attribute. In order to clearly visualize each problem, the ranking of each attribute was subtracted from a constant number. For example, in the Tic-Tac-Toe data, the most relevant attribute was assigned value 14 (e.g. 15 - 1), then 13 for the following, etc. In the lenses data, the most relevant attribute was assigned value 13 (e.g. 14 - 1), etc.

There are linear relationships between the relevancy determined by the Chi-square criterion and by the Removable Relevancy for the MONK-1, MONK-3, and the Congressional datasets. Also, There are linear relationships between the relevancy obtained by the Gain criterion and by the Removable Relevancy only for the MONK-1 and the Congressional datasets. Other datasets show examples of contradiction between the two measurements of relevancy (viewed as a peak).

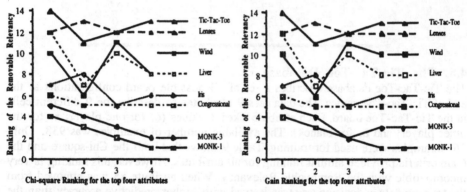

Figure 2: The relationship between relevancy to decision classes (using both the Gain and the Chi-square criteria) and to the learning system (using the Removable Relevancy).

5. Conclusion

This paper investigates the relationship between attributional relevancy to decision classes and to learning systems. Attributional relevancy to decision classes is estimated by two criteria, namely the Chi-square and the Gain. Attributional relevancy to the learning system is estimated by the change in the error rate of concepts learned before and after removing an attribute from the data.

The paper introduces a criterion, called the Removable Relevancy, for measuring the relevancy of an attribute to the learning system. The method is very effective in estimating the relevant and irrelevant attributes. However, a disadvantage of this method is that it requires running the learning system to estimate the attributeional relevancy. The paper includes experiments on 8 different data sets. The experimental results show that some attributes that were characterized as highly relevant by the

Chi-square and the Gain criteria were found irrelevant by the Removable Relevancy criterion.

For future work, it is very important to obtain a utility function that determines the Removable Relevancy from the dataset (without involving the learning system). Finding a global criteria may be more difficult since different learning systems have different biases. However, the next logical step is to find system-dependent criteria.

ACKNOWLEDGMENTS

The author thanks John Doulamis, Ken Kaufman and Mark Maloof for reviewing an earlier draft of the paper. This research was done in the Machine Learning and Inference Laboratory at George Mason University. The Laboratory's activities are supported in part by the Advanced Research Projects Agency under grant No. N00014-91-J-1854 administered by the Office of Naval Research, in part by the Advanced Research Projects Agency under grants F49620-92-J-0549 and F49620-95-1-0462 administered by the Air Force Office of Scientific Research, in part by the Office of Naval Research under grant N00014-91-J-1351, and in part by the National Science Foundation under grants DMI-9496192 and IRI-9020266.

REFERENCES

1. Arciszewski, T, Bloedorn, E., Michalski, R., Mustafa, M., and Wnek, J., "Constructive Induction in Structural Design", Report of the Machine Learning and Inference Labratory, MLI-92-7, Center for AI, George Mason Univerity, 1992.

2. Breiman, L., Friedman, J.H., Olshen, R.A., and Stone, C.J., "Classification and Regression Trees", Belmont, California: Wadsworth Int. Group, 1984.

3. Cestnik, B., and Karalic, A., "The Estimation of Probabilities in Attribute Selection Measures for Decision Tree Induction" Proceedings of the European Summer School on Machine Learning, July 22-31, Priory Corsendonk, Belgium, 1991.

4. Fayyad, U.M., and Irani, K.B., "On the Handling of Continous-Valued Attributes in Decision Tree Generation", Journal of Machine Learning, Vol. 8, No. 1, pp. 87-102, 1992.

5. Hart, A., "Experience in the use of an inductive system in knowledge engineering", Research and Developments in Expert Systems, M. Bramer (Ed.), Cambridge, Cambridge University Press, 1984.

6. Imam, I.F. and Michalski, R.S., "Learning Decision Trees from Decision Rules: A method and initial results from a comparative study", in Journal of Intelligent Information Systems JIIS, Vol. 2, No. 3, pp. 279-304, Kerschberg, L., Ras, Z., & Zemankova, M. (Eds.), Kluwer Academic Pub., MA, 1993.

7. Imam, I.F., and Vafaie, H., "An Empirical Comparison Between Global and Greedy-Like Search for Feature Selection", proceeding of the 7th Florida AI Research Symposium, Florida, 1994.

8. Michalski, R.S., "Designing Extended Entry Decision Tables and Optimal Decision Trees Using Decision Diagrams", Technical Report No.898, Urbana: University of Illinois, March, 1978.

9. **Mingers, J.,** "An Empirical Comparison of selection Measures for Decision-Tree Induction", *Machine Learning*, Vol. 3, No. 3, pp. 319-342, Kluwer Academic Publishers, 1989.

10. **Piatetsky-Shapiro, G., and Matheus, C.J.,** "Measuring Data Dependencies in Large Databases", *Proceedings of the AAAI-93 Workshop on Knowledge Discovery in Databases*, pp. 162-174, Washington D.C., 1993.

11. **Quinlan, J.R.,** "Discovering Rules By Induction from Large Collections of Examples", in D. Michie (Editor), *Expert Systems in the Microelectronic Age*, Edinburgh University Press, 1979.

12. **Quinlan, J.R.,** "Induction of Decision Trees", *Machine Learning* Vol. 1, No. 1, pp. 81-106, Kluwer Academic Publishers, 1986.

13. **Quinlan, J.R.,** "C4.5: Programs for Machine Learning", Morgan Kaufmann, Los Altos, California, 1993.

14. **Sokal, R., and Rohlf, F.,** "Biometry", Freeman Pub., San Francisco, 1981.

15. **Thrun, S.B., Mitchell, T., and Cheng, J.,** (Eds.) "The MONK's Problems: A Performance Comparison of Different Learning Algorithms", *Technical Report*, Carnegie Mellon University, October, 1991.

16. **Ziarko, W.,** "The Discovery, Analysis, and Representation of Data Dependencies in Databases", *Knowledge Discovery In Databases*, Shapiro, G., Frawley, W., (Eds.), AAAI Press, 1991.

Locally Finite, Proper and Complete Operators for Refining Datalog Programs

Floriana Esposito, Angela Laterza, Donato Malerba and Giovanni Semeraro

Dipartimento di Informatica - Università degli Studi di Bari
Via E. Orabona 4 - 70126 Bari, Italy
{esposito, malerbad, semeraro}@vm.csata.it

Abstract. Refinement operators are exploited to change in an automated way incorrect clauses of a logic program. In this paper, we present four refinement operators for Datalog programs and demonstrate that all of them meet the properties of *local finiteness, properness*, and *completeness*. Such operators are based on the quasi-ordering induced upon a set of clauses by the generalization model of *θ-subsumption under object identity*. This model of generalization, as well as the four refinement operators have been implemented in a system for theory revision that proved effective in the area of electronic document classification.

1 Introduction

In inductive synthesis of logic programs, a fundamental problem is the definition of *locally finite, proper*, and *complete* (*ideal*) refinement operators. Indeed, when the aim is to develop incrementally a logic program, that should be *correct* with respect to its *intended model*, it becomes relevant to define operators that allow for a stepwise (incremental) refinement of programs, which turn out to be *too weak* or *too strong*.

The *ideality* of the refinement operators plays a key role when the efficiency and the effectiveness of the design process is an unnegligible requirement [17]. Theoretical studies in Inductive Logic Programming (ILP) have shown that, when a full Horn clause logic is chosen as a representation language and either *θ-subsumption* or *implication* is adopted as a generalization model, there exist no ideal refinement operators [17]. Research efforts in the area of ILP have been directed to improve the efficiency of the search by restricting full first order Horn clause logic by means of suitable language biases. However, these biases are not sufficient to solve the problem of defining ideal refinement operators. Indeed, as Niblett says [10], *"it is an open question as to which restrictions on full first order logic are compatible with complete non-redundant refinement operators."*

In this paper, we define four ideal refinement operators for Datalog programs. These definitions rely on a weaker ordering than θ-subsumption, namely θ_{OI}-subsumption.

In Section 2, we briefly recall the definition of the generalization model based on θ_{OI}-subsumption and give the basic definitions concerning the refinement operators. The non-existence of ideal refinement operators for Datalog clauses under θ-subsumption is investigated in Section 3. Novel refinement operators for Datalog clauses ordered by θ_{OI}-subsumption are defined in Section 4. We formally prove that such operators are ideal.

2 Basic Definitions

We assume the reader to be familiar with the notions of *substitution, literal, fact, Horn clause* and *definite clause* [9]. A clause $C = l_1 \vee l_2 \vee \ldots \vee l_n$, is considered as the set of its literals, that is, $C = \{ l_1, l_2, \ldots, l_n \}$. $| C |$ denotes the number of literals in C - the *length* of C - while *size(C)* denotes the number of symbol occurrences in C (excluding punctuation) minus the number of distinct variables occurring in C [12, 16]. Furthermore, we will denote with $vars(C)$, $consts(C)$, and $terms(C)$ the set of the variables, of the constants and of the terms occurring in C, respectively. Any two clauses will be always assumed to be variable disjoint. This does not limit the expressiveness of the adopted language since any two non-variable disjoint clauses always can be standardized apart.

Henceforth, by clause we mean *Datalog* clause. Datalog is a language for deductive databases. Here, we refer to [7] for what concerns the basic notions about Datalog. A Datalog clause is in the form $Q(x_1, x_2, ..., x_n)$:- $\varphi, n \geq 0$, where Q is an *intensional database symbol* of arity n, $n \geq 0$, and the body φ is a set of literals, which can be equality atoms and relational atoms. Both these kinds of atoms must be positive in Datalog. Negations of such atoms are allowed in *Datalog¬*. If the only negations are inequalities in the bodies, we have a sublanguage of Datalog¬, called *Datalog*.

Let us denote with L a language that consists of all the possible Datalog clauses built from a finite number of predicates. We distinguish two subsets of L, namely L_o and L_h, which are the language of observations and the language of hypotheses, respectively. Shortly, the problem of inductively synthesizing a (correct) logic program can be stated according to the machine learning paradigm, as follows. Given two sets of ground facts E^+ (positive examples) and E^- (negative examples), expressed in the language of observations L_o, and a background knowledge B in the language L (in our setting, B is bound to be a set of ground atoms), the problem consists in finding a logic program P such that $P \cup B \vdash E^+$ (*completeness*) and $P \cup B \not\vdash E^-$ (*consistency*).

In the literature of machine learning, it is possible to find many examples of algorithms for the inductive synthesis of logic programs. For instance, Shapiro's Model Inference System (MIS) [16] is an incremental algorithm based on the Popperian methodology of conjectures and refutations. The importance of this algorithm is not limited to the area of machine learning and inductive synthesis, but extends to algorithmic debugging of logic programs. MIS is able to infer a logic theory from a sequence of examples by modifying incrementally a conjecture (a logic program) whenever a contradiction occurs between the conjectured theory and the given examples, that is to say, whenever the current theory is either not complete (*too weak*) or not consistent (*too strong*). The contradiction backtracing algorithm allows MIS to trace back any contradiction to the false clause that caused it, as well as to construct a counterexample that shows the falsity of that clause. Specifically, MIS starts from a strong conjecture and deletes any over-general (too strong) clause. When the conjecture becomes too weak, specializations of deleted clauses can be added until a complete and consistent conjecture is found.

Computing the specializations of a previously removed clause is the task of a downward refinement operator, which performs a general-to-specific search through the space of the Horn clauses rooted into the deleted clause (*specialization graph*). However, a specialization graph is an infinite search space, since the possible downward refinements of any clause are infinite. Refinement operators take advantage of the structure given to the specialization graph by the definition of a quasi-ordering upon it, in order to control the search and avoid the combinatorial explosion. The most frequently adopted quasi-orderings are those induced by the notions of logical implication and θ-subsumption [11]. Nevertheless, the search remains computationally expensive. Indeed, the algorithm in MIS is exponential.

Here, we recall the notion of object identity given in [13].

Definition 1 (Object Identity) *Within a clause, terms denoted with different symbols must be distinct.*

In Datalog, the adoption of the object identity assumption can be viewed as a method for building an equational theory into the ordering as well as into the inference rules of the calculus. Such a theory is very simple, since it consists of just one further axiom schema, in addition to the set of equality axioms in Clark's Equality Theory [9]:

$$\forall C \in \mathbf{L}, \ \forall t, s \in terms(C) \qquad \neg t = s \in body(C) \qquad \text{(OI)}$$

Henceforth, we will use $t \neq s$ as an abbreviation for $\neg t = s$. Under object identity assumption, the Datalog clause $C = P(x) :- Q(x, x), Q(y, a)$ is an abbreviation for the following Datalog$^{\neq}$ clause $C_{OI} = P(x) :- Q(x, x), Q(y, a) \ \| \ [x \neq y], [x \neq a], [y \neq a]$, where P, Q denote predicate letters, x, y variables, a is a constant and the inequations attached to the clause can be seen as constraints on its terms. These constraints are generated in a systematic way by the (OI) axiom. In addition, they can be dealt with in the same way as the other literals in the clause. Therefore, under object identity, any Datalog clause C generates a new Datalog$^{\neq}$ clause C_{OI} consisting of two components, called $core(C_{OI})$ and $constraints(C_{OI})$, where $core(C_{OI}) = C$ and $constraints(C_{OI})$ is the set of the inequalities generated by the (OI) axiom.

Now, we can formally introduce the ordering relation defined by the notion of θ-subsumption under object identity -θ_{OI}-*subsumption* - upon the set of Datalog clauses. The following definition extends to Datalog the definition given in [5, 13] for constant-free (other than function-free) logic languages.

Definition 2 (θ_{OI}-subsumption ordering) Let C, D be two Datalog clauses. We say that D θ-*subsumes* C *under object identity* (D θ_{OI}-*subsumes* C) if and only if (iff) there exists a substitution σ such that (s.t.) $D_{OI}.\sigma \subseteq C_{OI}$.
In such a case, we say that D *is more general than or equal to* C (D *is an upward refinement* of C and C *is a downward refinement of* D) *under object identity* and we write $C \leq_{OI} D$. We write $C <_{OI} D$ when $C \leq_{OI} D$ and $not(D \leq_{OI} C)$ and we say that D *is more general than* C (D *is a proper upward refinement of* C) or C *is more specific than* D (C *is a proper downward refinement of* D) or D *properly* θ_{OI}-*subsumes* C. We write $C \sim_{OI} D$, and we say that C and D are *equivalent clauses under object identity*, when $C \leq_{OI} D$ and $D \leq_{OI} C$.

Here, we will denote with $\leq_\theta$ the θ-subsumption ordering, with $\leq_{OI}$ the θ_{OI}-subsumption ordering and with $\leq$ indifferently either θ-subsumption or implication ordering. We write $C < D$ when $C \leq D$ and $not(D \leq C)$. We write $C \sim D$ when $C \leq D$ and $D \leq C$.

θ_{OI}-subsumption is a strictly weaker order relation than θ-subsumption. Indeed, the following result holds.

Proposition 1. *Let C, D be two Datalog clauses, $C \leq_{OI} D \Rightarrow C \leq_\theta D$*
Proof. From Def. 2, $C \leq_{OI} D$ means that there exists a substitution σ s.t. $D_{OI}.\sigma \subseteq C_{OI}$. Thus, $core(D_{OI}).\sigma \subseteq core(C_{OI})$, since inequalities cannot occur in a Datalog clause. But, $core(D_{OI}) = D$ and $core(C_{OI}) = C$, therefore it holds also $D.\sigma \subseteq C$. \hfill q.d.e.

The following result provides a practical characterization of the notion of θ_{OI}-subsumption.

Proposition 2. *Let C, D be two Datalog clauses,*
$C \leq_{OI} D \quad \Leftrightarrow \quad \forall \sigma$ s.t. $D_{OI}.\sigma \subseteq C_{OI}$:
$\quad\quad\quad\quad \sigma$ *is injective and* σ: $vars(D) \rightarrow vars(C) \cup (consts(C) - consts(D))$
Proof. ' $\Rightarrow$ ': From Def. 2, $C \leq_{OI} D$ means that $\exists \ \sigma : D_{OI}.\sigma \subseteq C_{OI}$.

In order to prove that σ is injective, ad absurdum, let us suppose there exist $x, y \in vars(D_{ol})$
s.t. $x \neq y$ and $\sigma(x) = \sigma(y) = z$. $x, y \in vars(D_{ol}) \Rightarrow x \neq y \in constraints(D_{ol})$. Since
$constraints(D_{ol}).\sigma \subseteq constraints(C_{ol})$, then $x \neq y.\sigma \in constraints(C_{ol})$.
But $x \neq y.\sigma \in constraints(C_{ol})$ is equivalent to $\sigma(x) \neq \sigma(y) \in constraints(C_{ol})$, that in turn
means $z \neq z \in constraints(C_{ol})$. Absurdum.

Let us prove now that $\sigma : vars(D) \to vars(C) \cup (consts(C) - consts(D))$.
Generally speaking, from Prop. 1, $C \leq_{ol} D \Rightarrow C \leq_{\theta} D \Leftrightarrow \exists \ \sigma : D.\sigma \subseteq C$, where
$\sigma : vars(D) \to terms(C) = vars(C) \cup consts(C)$. Then, we can cast the proof to demonstrate
that there exist no x in $vars(D)$ s.t. $\sigma(x) \in consts(D)$. Ad absurdum, let us suppose there
exists $x \in vars(D)$ s.t. $\sigma(x) = a \in consts(D)$. Then, $x \neq a \in constraints(D_{ol})$ and
$x \neq a.\sigma \in constraints(C_{ol})$. But, $x \neq a.\sigma \equiv \sigma(x) \neq a \equiv a \neq a$. Absurdum.
$' \Leftarrow '$: Trivial.   q.d.e.

Definition 3 (Downward Refinement) Given a quasi-ordered set $(L_h, \leq)$:
1) a *downward refinement operator* ρ is a mapping from L_h to 2^{L_h},
$$\rho : L_h \to 2^{L_h}, \quad \forall C \in L_h : \rho(C) \subseteq \{ D \in L_h \mid D \leq C \}$$
2) let ρ be a downward refinement operator and C a clause in L_h, then
$$\rho^0(C) = \{C\} \quad \rho^n(C) = \{ D \mid \exists E \in \rho^{n-1}(C) \text{ and } D \in \rho(E) \}$$
$$\rho^*(C) = \bigcup_{n \geq 0} \rho^n(C) = \rho^0(C) \cup \rho^1(C) \cup \ldots \cup \rho^n(C) \cup \ldots$$
are the sets of *zero-step downward refinements, n-step downward refinements* and
downward refinements of C, respectively
3) ρ is *locally finite* iff $\forall C \in L_h : \rho(C)$ is finite and computable
ρ is *proper* iff $\forall C \in L_h : \rho(C) \subseteq \{ D \in L_h \mid D < C \}$
ρ is *complete* iff $\forall C, D \in L_h$, if $D < C$ then $\exists E$ s.t. $E \in \rho^*(C)$ and $E \sim D$
ρ is *ideal* iff it is locally finite, proper and complete
4) let C, D, E be clauses in L_h, then C *covers* D if $D < C$ and $\forall E : not(D < E < C)$
if C covers D then we call D a *downward cover* of C
5) let $C, D_1, D_2, D_3, \ldots$, be clauses in L_h,
if $D_1 < D_2 < D_3 < \ldots < D_n < D_{n+1} < \ldots < C$ and C has no downward cover $A \in L_h$ s.t.
$\forall n \geq 1 : D_n \leq A < C$, then $(D_n)_{n \geq 1}$ is an *uncovered infinite strictly ascending chain of* C
6) let $C, D_1, D_2, D_3, \ldots$, be clauses in L_h,
if $D_1 < D_2 < D_3 < \ldots < D_n < D_{n+1} < \ldots < C$ and there is no $A \in L_h$ s.t. $\forall n \geq 1 : D_n \leq A < C$,
then $(D_n)_{n \geq 1}$ is an *unlimited infinite strictly ascending chain* of C.
Similar definitions can be given for *upward refinement operators* δ by properly replacing
ρ with δ, $<$ with $>$, $\leq$ with $\geq$, *downward* with *upward*, and *ascending* with *descending*.

3 Non-existence of Ideal Refinement Operators under θ-subsumption

In the space of Datalog clauses ordered by $\leq$, there exist no ideal refinement operators,
neither downward nor upward ones. This result is a straightforward consequence of
similar results due to van der Laag and Nienhuys-Cheng for unrestricted search spaces
under θ-subsumption [17, Theorem 4.3] and implication [17, Theorem 5.5]. The non-
existence of ideal downward refinement operators follows directly from the existence of
uncovered infinite strictly ascending chains of a clause C in an unrestricted search space.
Dually, the non-existence of ideal upward refinement operators follows from the
existence of uncovered infinite strictly descending chains of a clause C.

Indeed, if we consider the sequence of clauses, reported in [17, p.256]

$$C = q :- P(x_1, x_2), P(x_2, x_1)$$
$$E_n = q :- P(x_1, x_2), P(x_2, x_1), P(y_1, y_2), P(y_2, y_3), ..., P(y_{n-1}, y_n), P(y_n, y_1), n \geq 3$$

an example of uncovered infinite strictly ascending chain of C is $(E_{3n})_{n \geq 1}$. Such a chain is composed of Datalog clauses.

As to the upward refinement operators, examples of uncovered infinite strictly descending chains of a clause C are given by several authors. For instance, in [17, p.255], the following uncovered infinite strictly descending chain of the clause C can be found:

$$G_n = q :- \{ P(x_i, x_j) \mid 1 \leq i, j \leq n, i \neq j \}, \quad n \geq 2 \qquad C = q :- P(x_1, x_1)$$

Most systems that learn Horn clauses from examples adopt the language bias of linkedness [13] in order to restrict the search space and to avoid generating quite insignificant clauses. The uncovered infinite chains $(E_{3n})_{n \geq 1}$ and $(G_n)_{n \geq 2}$ consist of clauses that are not linked, therefore it could be guessed that, if the learning system adopts such a language bias, it is possible to define ideal refinement operators. Unfortunately, even in the space of linked Datalog clauses there exist both uncovered infinite strictly ascending chains of a clause C, such as $(D_{3n})_{n \geq 1}$, where $C = Q(z) :- P(z, x_1, x_2), P(z, x_2, x_1)$

$$D_n = Q(z) :- P(z, x_1, x_2), P(z, x_2, x_1), P(z, y_1, y_2), P(z, y_2, y_3), ..., P(z, y_{n-1}, y_n), P(z, y_n, y_1)$$

and uncovered infinite strictly ascending chains of a clause C, such as $(F_n)_{n \geq 2}$, where

$$F_n = Q(z) :- \{ P(z, x_i, x_j) \mid 1 \leq i, j \leq n, i \neq j \}, \quad n \geq 2 \qquad C = Q(z) :- P(z, x_1, x_1)$$

The linked chains $(D_{3n})_{n \geq 1}$ and $(F_n)_{n \geq 2}$ have been obtained by properly changing the chains $(E_{3n})_{n \geq 1}$ and $(G_n)_{n \geq 2}$, respectively.

In the space of Datalog clauses ordered by θ-subsumption, there exist also infinite strictly ascending/descending chains, which are bounded above/below by a clause C, but are not uncovered. Two examples - the former ascending, the latter descending - are $(H_n)_{n \geq 0}$ and $(I_n)_{n \geq 1}$, (a chain slightly different from $(I_n)_{n \geq 1}$ can be found in [6]), where:

$$C_H = Q(x_1) :-$$
...

$$H_{i+1} = (H_i - \{ \neg P(x_{2^i}, x_1) \}) \cup \bigcup_{j=2^i}^{2^{i+1}-1} (\{ \neg P(x_j, x_{j+1}) \}) \cup \{ \neg P(x_{2^{i+1}}, x_1) \}$$

$$H_3 = Q(x_1) :- P(x_1, x_2), P(x_2, x_3), P(x_3, x_4), P(x_4, x_5), P(x_5, x_6), P(x_6, x_7), P(x_7, x_8), P(x_8, x_1)$$
$$H_2 = Q(x_1) :- P(x_1, x_2), P(x_2, x_3), P(x_3, x_4), P(x_4, x_1)$$
$$H_1 = Q(x_1) :- P(x_1, x_2), P(x_2, x_1)$$
$$H_0 = Q(x_1) :- P(x_1, x_1) \text{ and}$$
$$I_1 = Q(x_1) :- P(x_1, x_2)$$
$$I_2 = Q(x_1) :- P(x_1, x_2), P(x_2, x_3)$$
$$I_3 = Q(x_1) :- P(x_1, x_2), P(x_2, x_3), P(x_3, x_4)$$
$$I_n = I_{n-1} \cup \{ \neg P(x_n, x_{n+1}) \}$$
...
$$C_I = Q(x) :- P(x, x)$$

Both $(H_n)_{n \geq 0}$ and $(I_n)_{n \geq 1}$ are not uncovered chains, since $I_1 = Q(x_1) :- P(x_1, x_2)$ is a downward cover of C_H s.t. $H_n \leq I_1 < C_H$ for any $n \geq 0$, while $H_1 = Q(x_1) :- P(x_1, x_2), P(x_2, x_1)$ is an upward cover of C_I s.t. $C_I \leq H_1 < I_n$ for any $n \geq 1$.

4 Ideal Refinement of Datalog Programs

Before giving the formal definition of the operators for refining Datalog programs and demonstrating that all of them meet the property to be ideal, we need to enunciate (and prove) the result that in the space of Datalog clauses ordered by θ_{OI}-subsumption there exist no uncovered infinite strictly ascending/descending chains of some clause C. To this purpose, we give preliminarily the following proposition.

Proposition 3. *Let C and D be Datalog clauses, $C \sim_{OI} D$ iff $C \approx D$*

($\approx$ denotes the renaming relation, which is usually defined upon atoms, but it can be straightforwardly generalized to clauses)

Proof. '$\Rightarrow$': From Def. 2, the hypothesis $C \sim_{OI} D$ means that $C \leq_{OI} D$ and $D \leq_{OI} C$. From Prop. 2, $C \leq_{OI} D \Rightarrow \exists \; \sigma_1 : D_{OI}.\sigma_1 \subseteq C_{OI}$ and σ_1 is an injection $\Rightarrow$ $\exists \sigma_1 : core(D_{OI}).\sigma_1 \subseteq core(C_{OI})$ and σ_1 is an injection $\Leftrightarrow \exists \sigma_1 : D.\sigma_1 \subseteq C$ and σ_1 is an injection $\Rightarrow \mid D.\sigma_1 \mid \leq \mid C \mid$ (1). Similarly, $D \leq_{OI} C \Rightarrow \exists \sigma_2 : C.\sigma_2 \subseteq D$ and σ_2 is an injection $\Rightarrow \mid C.\sigma_2 \mid \leq \mid D \mid$ (2). Since σ_1 and σ_2 are injections, it holds that $\mid D.\sigma_1 \mid = \mid D \mid$ (3) and $\mid C.\sigma_2 \mid = \mid C \mid$ (4). From (1) and (3) we have $\mid D \mid \leq \mid C \mid$, and from (2) and (4) we have $\mid C \mid \leq \mid D \mid$. Therefore, it holds that $\mid C \mid = \mid D \mid$. As a consequence, σ_1 and σ_2 are variable renamings for D and C respectively, and as a matter of fact (1) and (2) are the equalities $\mid D.\sigma_1 \mid = \mid C \mid$ (1') and $\mid C.\sigma_2 \mid = \mid D \mid$ (2').
But (1') and $D.\sigma_1 \subseteq C$ imply that $D.\sigma_1 = C$. Hence σ_1 maps different variables of D to distinct variables of C, and so C and D are alphabetic variants.
'$\Leftarrow$' : Trivial. q.d.e.

Coming back to the problem of defining ideal refinement operators, the most relevant consequence of Prop. 3 is the absence in the space $(L_h, \leq_{OI})$ of uncovered infinite strictly ascending/descending chains of a clause C, as stated by the following result.

Proposition 4. *Given the space $(L_h, \leq_{OI})$ and a clause C in L_h, there exist no uncovered infinite strictly (a) descending/(b) ascending chains of C.*

Proof. *(a)* Preliminarily, let us denote with $PGEN_{OI}(C)$ the set $\{ [D]_{\sim_{OI}} \in L_h \mid C <_{OI} D \}$ of the proper generalizations under θ_{OI}-subsumption of a clause C in L_h up to renamings ($[D]_{\sim_{OI}}$ denotes the class of clauses in L_h that are equivalent to D under θ_{OI}-subsumption). In order to prove the proposition, we can show that for any clause C of L_h the set $PGEN_{OI}(C)$ is finite. Then, let C be a Datalog clause. From Def. 2 and Prop. 2, for each proper generalization D of C ($[D]_{\sim_{OI}} \in PGEN_{OI}(C)$) there exists at least an injective substitution $\sigma, \sigma : vars(D) \to vars(C) \cup (consts(C) - consts(D))$, s.t. $D_{OI}.\sigma \subseteq C_{OI}$, which implies that $D.\sigma \subseteq C$. Let us denote with D' the clause $D.\sigma$. If C is constant-free, besides being function-free, then the clauses D and D' are alphabetic variants (σ is a renaming). Thus, $D \sim_{OI} D'$ from Prop. 3. We have shown that: $\forall D, C <_{OI} D, \exists D', D' \sim_{OI} D$ and $D' \subseteq C$. Thus, the number of distinct (not equivalent under θ_{OI}-subsumption) D' is finite and bounded above by $2^{\mid C \mid}$, where 2^C denotes the power set of C. If C contains some constants, then $PGEN_{OI}(C)$ is a superset of 2^C, since also the clauses obtained from C by turning some of its constants into variables are proper generalizations of C. Nevertheless, even in this second case $PGEN_{OI}(C)$ has a finite number of elements, since both the length of C and the number of constants in C are finite. More precisely, $\mid PGEN_{OI}(C) \mid \leq 2^{\mid C \mid + \mid consts(C) \mid} - 2^{\mid consts(C) \mid}$.
(b) Reductio ad absurdum. Let us suppose that $(D_n)_{n \geq 1}$ is an uncovered infinite strictly ascending chain of a clause C. Def. 3 yields $D_1 < D_2 < D_3 < ... < D_n < D_{n+1} < ... < C$. Therefore, $PGEN_{OI}(D_n)$ is an infinite set (for any $n \geq 1$). This contradicts point (a). q.d.e.

Corollary 1. *Given the space* $(L_k, \leq_{ol})$ *and a clause* C *in* L_k, *there exist no unlimited infinite strictly (a) descending/(b) ascending chains of* C.
Proof. It follows straightforwardly from the observation that *"every unlimited chain in an ordered set is also an uncovered chain"* [17, p.253]. q.d.e.

Now, we can formally define four refinement operators for Datalog clauses ordered by θ_{ol}-subsumption. Two of them - ρ_{ol} and ρ'_{ol} - are downward, while δ_{ol} and δ'_{ol} are upward ones (the difference between ρ_{ol} and ρ'_{ol} and between δ_{ol} and δ'_{ol} is underlined).

Definition 4 (Downward Refinement : the operator $\rho_{ol}(C)$)
Let C be a Datalog clause. Then, $D \in \rho_{ol}(C)$ when exactly one of the following holds:
(i) $D = C.\theta$, where $\theta = \{ x / a \}$, $a \notin consts(C)$, $x \in vars(C)$, that is, θ is a substitution, a is a constant not occurring in C and x is a variable that occurs in C.
(ii) $D = C \cup \{\neg l\}$, where l is an atom s.t. $\neg l \notin C$.

Definition 5 (Upward Refinement : the operator $\delta_{ol}(C)$)
Let C be a Datalog clause. Then, $D \in \delta_{ol}(C)$ when exactly one of the following holds:
(i) $D = C.\gamma$, where $\gamma = \{ a/x \}$, $a \in consts(C)$, $x \notin vars(C)$, that is, γ is an antisubstitution, a is a constant occurring in C and x is a variable that does not occur in C.
(ii) $D = C - \{\neg l\}$, where l is an atom s.t. $\neg l \in C$.

Definition 6 (Downward Refinement : the operator $\rho'_{ol}(C)$)
Let C be a Datalog clause. Then, $D \in \rho'_{ol}(C)$ when exactly one of the following holds:
(i')   See point (i) of Def. 4.
(ii') $D = C \cup \{\neg l\}$, where l is an atom s.t. $\neg l \notin C$ and $consts(l) \subset consts(C)$.

Definition 7 (Upward Refinement : the operator $\delta'_{ol}(C)$)
Let C be a Datalog clause. Then, $D \in \delta'_{ol}(C)$ when exactly one of the following holds:
(i')   See point (i) of Def. 5.
(ii') $D = C - \{\neg l\}$, where l is an atom s.t. $\neg l \in C$ and $consts(l) \subset consts(C - \{\neg l\})$.

Definition 8 (size$_{ol}(C)$) Let C be a Datalog clause. Then *size of* C *under object identity* ($size_{ol}(C)$) is computed as the number of constants occurring in C ($consts(C)$) plus the number of literals occurring in C ($|C|$). Formally, $size_{ol}(C) = consts(C) + |C|$

Proposition 5. ρ_{ol} *and* ρ'_{ol} (δ_{ol} *and* δ'_{ol}) *are ideal downward (upward) refinement operators for Datalog clauses ordered by* θ_{ol}-*subsumption.*
Proof. A proof of Prop. 5 can be found in [15].

A nice property of the operators ρ_{ol}, ρ'_{ol} and δ_{ol}, δ'_{ol} is that, if a clause C properly θ_{ol}-subsumes a clause D then $size(D) > size(C)$. Indeed, points (i) and (i') of Def. 4 and Def. 6 respectively, increase the size of a clause by 1, while points (ii) and (ii') increase the size of the clause at least by 1 - when all the arguments of the atom l are new variables - and at most by $n + 1$, where n is the arity of the predicate in l - when l does not introduce new variables. Dually, points (i) and (i') of Def. 5 and Def. 7 respectively, decrease the size of a clause by 1, while points (ii) and (ii') decrease the size of the clause at least by 1 - when all the arguments of the dropped atom l are new variables - and at most by $n + 1$ - when all the arguments of l are *old* variables.

Another observation is that the notions of generality (*subsumption*) and refinement unify for spaces of Datalog clauses ordered by θ_{ol}-subsumption, while Shapiro [16] (and Niblett [10]) needs a definition of refinement that does not coincide with that of the quasi-ordering of the clauses (based on logical implication). Furthermore, if C properly

θ_{oi}-subsumes D, then D (C) is in the set of the k-step downward (upward) refinements of C (D), with $k \leq size(D) - size(C)$, as to the operators ρ_{oi} and δ_{oi}. In formulae,

$$D \in \rho^k_{oi}(C), \qquad C \in \delta^k_{oi}(D), \qquad k \leq size(D) - size(C)$$

Practically speaking, this means that the chain of refinements from C to D is guaranteed not to exceed length k. Thus, it is possible to establish syntactically and statically (that is, just by looking at the clauses and computing their sizes) an upper bound to the computational effort required to refine an incorrect clause, if we already have some kind of background information about the structure of the clauses (the *template*) in the Datalog program to be learned, or if we are able to compute the highest complexity of each clause in some way (for instance, from the set $B \cup E^+ \cup E^-$, through the process of *pattern reconstruction* described in [5]). While the size of a clause provides a syntactic criterion to establish an upper bound, the size under object identity allows to determine the exact number of steps needed to refine a clause. Indeed, if C properly θ_{oi}-subsumes D, then

$$D \in \rho'^k_{oi}(C), \qquad C \in \delta'^k_{oi}(D), \qquad k = size_{oi}(D) - size_{oi}(C)$$

Example. Consider the following two clauses (we omit writing the inequations attached to each clause): $C = P(x) :- Q(x, y)$ and $D = P(x) :- Q(x, y), Q(a, b)$. It holds: $size(C) = 5 - 2 = 3$, $size(D) = 8 - 2 = 6$. Fig. 1a and 1b show portions of the space of the Datalog clauses ordered by θ_{oi}-subsumption. Specifically, they are the specialization graphs rooted in C. D can be obtained by C in $size(D) - size(C) = 3$ downward refinement steps, ($D \in \rho^3_{oi}(C)$), through the following sequence of application of the operator ρ_{oi} (the path in bold-face in Fig. 1a):

$$
\begin{array}{lllll}
C' & = & P(x) :- Q(x, y), Q(u, v) & C' \in \rho_{oi}(C), & \text{(ii) of Def. 4} \\
C'' & = & P(x) :- Q(x, y), Q(a, v) & C'' \in \rho_{oi}(C'), & \text{(i)} \\
D & = & P(x) :- Q(x, y), Q(a, b) & D \in \rho_{oi}(C''), & \text{(i)}
\end{array}
$$

In addition, D can be obtained from C in one step by just applying the point (ii) of Def. 4, with $l = Q(a, b)$ (the dashed edge in Fig. 1a). If we consider the operator ρ'_{oi}, it holds $size_{oi}(C) = 0 + 2 = 2$, $size_{oi}(D) = 2 + 3 = 5$, then $D \in \rho'^3_{oi}(C)$, since $size_{oi}(D) - size_{oi}(C) = 3$. Thus, D can be obtained by C in *exactly* 3 downward refinement steps through ρ'_{oi} (the path in bold-face in Fig. 1b), but now this is the only way to obtain D from C. In fact, ρ'_{oi} can be used instead of ρ_{oi} in order to make the refinement graph more sparse. Dually, C can be obtained from D in at most three upward refinement steps, when a specific-to-general search (by means of the operators δ_{oi} and δ'_{oi}) is performed through the generalization hierarchy rooted in D. Fig. 2a and 2b show these search spaces. The path (D, C'', C', C) in bold-face in Fig. 2a mirrors the sequence of application of the operator δ_{oi}:

$$
\begin{array}{lllll}
C'' & = & P(x) :- Q(x, y), Q(a, v) & C'' \in \delta_{oi}(D), & \text{(i) of Def. 5} \\
C' & = & P(x) :- Q(x, y), Q(u, v) & C' \in \delta_{oi}(C''), & \text{(i)} \\
C & = & P(x) :- Q(x, y) & C \in \delta_{oi}(C'), & \text{(ii)}
\end{array}
$$

and $C \in \delta^3_{oi}(D)$. Again, alternatively C can be obtained from D in one step by applying the point (ii) of Def. 5, with $l = Q(a, b)$, that is, it holds $C \in \delta_{oi}(D)$. This case is shown by the dashed edge in Fig. 2a. Moreover, if we consider δ'_{oi} (instead of δ_{oi}), it holds that $C \in \delta'^3_{oi}(D)$. Thus, C can be obtained by D in *exactly* 3 upward refinement steps through δ'_{oi} (the path in bold-face in Fig. 2b), and again this is the only way to obtain C from D.

The notion of ideality can be compared to that of *optimality* [2], defined as follows.

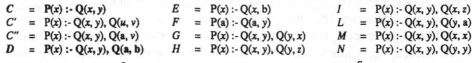

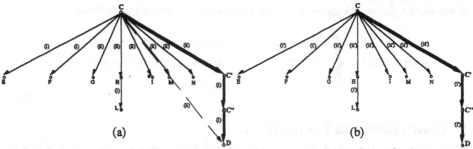

Fig. 1. A portion of the specialization graph rooted in the clause $C = P(x) :\!- Q(x, y)$ for the operators ρ_{oi} (a) and ρ'_{oi} (b). Each node denotes a proper downward refinement of C. An edge from φ to ψ denotes the fact that $\psi \in \rho_{oi}(\varphi)$ (a) and $\psi \in \rho'_{oi}(\varphi)$ (b). Edges are labelled by either (i) or (ii) ((i') or (ii')), according to the corresponding point of Def. 4 (Def. 6) that has been applied.

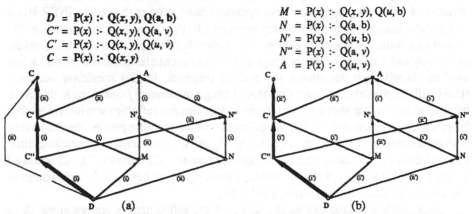

Fig. 2. A portion of the generalization graph rooted in the clause $D = P(x) :\!- Q(x, y), Q(a, b)$ for the operators δ_{oi} (a) and δ'_{oi} (b). Each node denotes a proper upward refinement of D.

Definition 10 (Optimality) A downward refinement operator ρ is *optimal* iff
$$\forall\, C, C_1, C_2 \in \mathbf{L_h}, \text{ if } C \in \rho^*(C_1) \cap \rho^*(C_2) \text{ then } C_1 \in \rho^*(C_2) \text{ or } C_2 \in \rho^*(C_1)$$

Intuitively, an optimal refinement operator generates each candidate clause exactly once, thus any clause in the search space can be derived from the empty clause through exactly one chain of one-step refinement. Because of this property, optimal refinement operators are deemed more efficient than classical ones. As to the relationship between ideality and optimality, the main result we were able to find is the following.

Proposition 6. *Given any partially ordered set* $(P, \leq)$, *and a downward refinement operator* ρ *in* $(P, \leq)$, *then* ρ *complete* $\Rightarrow$ ρ *not optimal* (ρ *ideal* $\Rightarrow$ ρ *not optimal*)

Proof. Let $C_1, C_2 \in \mathbf{P}$ be two uncomparable clauses and C be one of the minimal elements of $\{C_1, C_2\}$ (whose existence is guaranteed by Prop. 1 in [1, p.483]). ρ *complete* $\Rightarrow$ $C \in \rho^*(C_1) \cap \rho^*(C_2)$. Thus, C_1 and C_2 are not uncomparable. Absurdum.   q.d.e.

Corollary 2. *Let* ρ *be a downward refinement operator in* $(L_h, \leq_{oi})$, *then*
$$\rho \text{ complete} \Rightarrow \rho \text{ not optimal} \qquad (\rho \text{ ideal} \Rightarrow \rho \text{ not optimal})$$

Proof. As told above, $(L_h, \leq_{ot})$ is a quasi-ordered set. Then, the quotient set $(L_h/\sim_{ot}, \leq_{ot})$ is a partially ordered set. Thus, the corollary follows straightforwardly from Prop. 6 and from Prop. 3 (the space L_h is equivalent to $L_h/\sim_{ot}$ up to renamings). It is worth noting that in the space $(L_h/\sim_{ot}, \leq_{ot})$, the notion of minimal elements is equivalent to that of *most general downward refinements under object identity* ($mgdr_{ot}$), defined as follows:

$$mgdr_o(C_{ot}, D_{ot}) = \begin{cases} ((C \cup D). \mu)_{ot} & \text{where } \mu = mgu(head(C), head(D)) \\ (C \cup D)_{ot} & \text{when } head(C) = \varnothing \text{ or } head(D) = \varnothing \\ \square & \text{otherwise} \end{cases}$$

q.d.e.

5 Conclusions and Future Work

This paper has presented four operators for refining Datalog clauses ordered by θ_{ot}-subsumption. The weakening of the generalization model from θ-subsumption to θ_{ot}-subsumption allows the refinement operators to satisfy the properties of local finiteness, properness, and completeness, which are deemed fundamental for automated revision of incorrect programs. These operators have been embodied in INCR/H, an incremental learning system for theory revision [3]. Extensive experimentation in the area of electronic document processing has shown that the operators are able to refine effectively and efficiently Datalog programs for document classification. Indeed, when used to classify new documents, the revised programs have a predictive accuracy statistically comparable or better than that of programs learned *from scratch*, that is, in batch mode rather than starting from incorrect programs and refining them incrementally. Nevertheless, as expected, the overall efficiency of the learning process results largely increased when the operators ρ_{ot}, ρ'_{ot} and δ_{ot}, δ'_{ot} are used since the computational time almost halves - it decreases from an average of more than 52 minutes (3153.3 seconds) to less than 31 minutes (1854.3 seconds). A thorough description of the application to document classification can be found in [4, 14].

Future work will also extend the scope of the refinement operators along three dimensions - Datalog programs, introduction of functions in the language, and ambivalent clauses. Furthermore, we planned to investigate the relationship between θ_{ot}-subsumption and Kodratoff and Ganascia's structural matching [8].

References

1. Birkhoff, G., and Mac Lane, S., *Algebra*, The Macmillan Company, New York, 1965.
2. De Raedt, L., and Bruynooghe, M., A theory of clausal discovery, *Proceed. of the 13th Int'l Conf. on Artificial Intelligence, IJCAI'93*, R. Bajcsy (Ed.) ,Morgan Kaufmann, 1058-1063, 1993.
3. Esposito, F., Malerba, D., and Semeraro, G., INCR/H: A System for Revising Logical Theories, *Proceed. of the MLnet Workshop on Theory Revision and Restructuring in Machine Learning*, ECML-94, Arbeitspapiere der GMD N.842, S. Wrobel (Ed.), 13-15, 1994.
4. Esposito, F., Malerba, D., and Semeraro, G., Multistrategy Learning for Document Recognition, *Applied Artificial Intelligence: An International Journal*, 8:33-84, 1994.
5. Esposito, F., Malerba, D., Semeraro, G., Brunk, C., and Pazzani, M., Traps and Pitfalls when Learning Logical Definitions from Relations, in *Methodologies for Intelligent Systems - Proceed. of the 8th Int'l Symp., ISMIS '94*, LNAI 869, Z. W. Ras and M. Zemankova (Eds.), Springer-Verlag, 376-385, 1994.
6. Jung, B., On Inverting Generality Relations, *Proceed. of the 3rd Int'l Workshop on Inductive Logic Programming, ILP'93*, S. Muggleton (Ed.) , J. Stefan Institute TR IJS-DP-6707, 87-101, 1993.

7. Kanellakis, P. C., Elements of Relational Database Theory, in *Handbook of Theoretical Computer Science, Volume B, Formal Models and Semantics*, J. Van Leeuwen (Ed.), Elsevier Science Publ., 1073-1156, 1990.
8. Kodratoff, Y., and Ganascia, J. G., Improving the Generalization Step in Learning, in *Machine Learning: An Artificial Intelligence Approach*, Vol. II, 215-244, Morgan Kaufmann, 1986.
9. Lloyd, J. W., *Foundations of Logic Programming*, Second Edition, Springer-Verlag, New York, 1987.
10. Niblett, T., A note on refinement operators, in *Machine Learning: ECML-93 - Proceed. of the European Conf. on Machine Learning*, LNAI 667, P. B. Brazdil (Ed.), Springer-Verlag, 329-335, 1993.
11. Plotkin, G. D., A Note on Inductive Generalization, in *Machine Intelligence 5*, B. Meltzer and D. Michie (Eds.), Edinburgh University Press, 153 - 163, 1970.
12. Reynolds, J. C., Transformational Systems and the Algebraic Structure of Atomic Formulas, in *Machine Intelligence 5*, B. Meltzer and D. Michie (Eds.), Edinburgh University Press, 135-152, 1970.
13. Semeraro, G., Esposito, F., Malerba, D., Brunk, C., and Pazzani, M., Avoiding Non-Termination when Learning Logic Programs: A Case Study with FOIL and FOCL, in *Logic Program Synthesis and Transformation - Meta-Programming in Logic*, LNCS 883, L. Fribourg and F. Turini (Eds.), Springer-Verlag, 183-198, 1994.
14. Semeraro, G., Esposito, F., Fanizzi, N., and Malerba, D., Revision of Logical Theories, in *Topics in Artificial Intelligence*, LNAI 992, M. Gori and G. Soda (Eds.), Springer-Verlag, 365-376, 1995.
15. Semeraro, G., Esposito, F., and Malerba, D., Ideal Refinement of Datalog Programs, in *Proceed. of LOPSTR '95*, LNCS, M. Proietti (Ed.), Springer-Verlag, 1995 (in press).
16. Shapiro, E. Y., *Inductive Inference of Theories from Facts*, TR 192, Dept. of Comp. Sci., Yale Univ., New Haven, Connecticut, 1981.
17. van der Laag, P. R. J., and Nienhuys-Cheng, S.-H., A Note on Ideal Refinement Operators in Inductive Logic Programming, *Proceed. of the 4th Int'l Workshop on Inductive Logic Programming, ILP-94*, S. Wrobel (Ed.), GMD-Studien Nr. 237, 247-260, 1994.

Forest Fire Management with Negoplan[*]

Sunil J. Noronha[1] and Stan Szpakowicz[2]

[1] School of Business, Carleton University
Ottawa, Ontario, Canada K1S 5B6

[2] Department of Computer Science, University of Ottawa
Ottawa, Ontario, Canada K1N 6N5

Abstract

The control of forest fires is a complex domain that requires a variety of knowledge and skills in decision making and planning under uncertainty. It poses a challenging problem for the design of simulation and support systems, and therefore acts as a good testbed for the application of intelligent system methodologies. One such a methodology is restructurable modelling. It is the theoretical foundation of Negoplan, a software tool based on artificial intelligence technology, which can be used to build simulation, support and training systems for sequential decision making. Comprehensive support for fire management should reflect the different levels of an organizational hierarchy, from efficient resource allocation to policy setting and tradeoffs between goals. We show how the higher levels of fire management can be formulated as a sequential decision making problem and modelled in Negoplan.

1 Introduction

Every year wildland fires burn several million acres of forests in North America. Many fires are considered damaging or disruptive, because they consume timber of commercial value, expose the forest to deterioration or threaten human life and property. On the other hand, the remarkable Yellowstone Park fires of 1988 [3, 12] that devastated nearly half the area of the park brought into wide public attention the fact that forest fires also have an essential and sometimes beneficial role in the ecology of a region. Fires shape the landscape and promote biodiversity. That is why the response to a forest fire must be guided by a balanced strategy that preserves the natural role of fire in a healthy ecosystem while meeting other management goals such as protecting people and commercial interests.

Various policies dictate various fire control actions. A "prescribed fire" is permissible or desirable, and will not be fought so long as it stays within certain geographical limits and does not reach uncontrollable intensity. The only action in this case is to monitor the growth of the fire. A "wildfire" will be actively suppressed or at least limited to certain boundaries. The response is also influenced by the cause of a fire. For example, the Yellowstone Park's policy is to permit all fires started by natural causes, such as lightning, to burn as prescribed fires, unless they threaten human set-tlements in the park or sites of historic value. All other fires, such as those started by careless visitors, would be immediately suppressed in keeping with the Park's policy

---

[*] The paper has considerably benefited from discussions with Gregory Kersten, whose help is gratefully acknowledged. This work has been supported by the Natural Sciences and Engineering Research Council of Canada.

of maintaining an environment as untouched by human hands as possible. Prescribed fires may also be ignited by the forest agency itself to get rid of accumulated natural litter, a dangerous combustible biomass which could fuel an intense fire [10].

When a fire has been classified as a wildfire, suppression is run as an emergency operation, and good organization of firefighting forces is essential [1]. Small fires, however, are not usually associated with a formal organization, and are controlled by small fire crews led by a crew boss. Moderately large fires may require several crews or brigades controlled by the forest fire chief. If a fire grows too large, however, fire command at upper levels may have to be invoked. It may be necessary to borrow firefighting resources from neighbouring forest management organizations or specialized agencies. These agencies may have to coordinate policies among the many competing demands on their resources. It is, therefore, natural to view fire management at the highest level of command at least in part as a negotiation problem.

Thus forest fire management may be characterized as a rich and challenging problem in decision making and planning. There are differences in the support features required for decision makers at different levels of an organizational hierarchy in fire management. Lower levels of the hierarchy deal with efficient resource allocation, for which hard real-time discrete event systems [15], or command, control, communication and intelligence (C^3I) systems would be appropriate models. Decision making agents at these levels are allowed tactical decisions. Higher levels of the hierarchy are more concerned with policy setting and tradeoffs between goals; broad general objectives are difficult to quantify, in contrast with lower levels whose goals are quite specific and readily measurable. As observed in an early study which took a systems approach to modelling fire management [14], the essential characteristics of higher levels of fire management are memory facilities, an ability to achieve goals over a much wider range of environmental stimuli than lower levels, an ability to initiate immediate action based on anticipated needs, and an ability to modify the process whereby the goal is achieved. Even the highest-level goals in fire management may change drastically. That is why a modelling framework for this domain, in addition to ways of representing agents and goals, must include goal restructuring mechanisms.

In particular, from the perspective of a single fire chief, forest fire management can be viewed as a problem of sequential decision making, in which partial decisions open up further possibilities of decisions, and eventually accumulate into a successful final decision. This means that the technology of decision support systems can be brought to bear upon the fire management problem. One approach to decision modelling and support is *restructurable modelling* [4, 9]. It has served, in conjunction with certain AI techniques, as the basis for the development of Negoplan, a software system that can be used to build simulation, support and training systems for sequential decision processes. Negoplan and restructurable modelling are discussed in Section 2. The rest of this paper will describe the modelling of the forest fire control problem within the restructurable modelling framework, and its implementation as a Negoplan case.

Our approach differs in several ways from existing approaches to the modelling of the fire domain, for example, [2, 11]. First, we follow the philosophy of restructurable modelling, placing the emphasis on the decision processes of the primary agents. As a result we do not assume that the sole objective is bringing fires under control; rather, we model fire management from a broader perspective, which includes— besides fire suppression activities—other concerns such as fuel management and ecological concerns, and places lower emphasis on simulating fire behaviour and other physical attributes of the problem. Second, we address decision making by and negotiation between agents at higher levels in the forest management hierarchy, for example, forest supervisors as compared to the crew bosses of [11]. Third, we do not make the artificial assumption of identical agents whose cognitive processes are completely known, as is common in the distributed planning research that has previously addressed this problem [2]. Fourth, our simulation focuses more on the qualitative structure and logical reasoning aspects of the problem.

2 Restructurable Modelling and Negoplan

2.1 The Modelling Methodology

Restructurable modelling is a methodology for the simulation and support of sequential decision problems. Classical decision theory assumes a well defined decision problem with alternatives and value functions specified in advance. On the other hand, restructurable modelling emphasizes the evolving nature of agents' perceptions and preferences: support, at several levels of fineness, for iterative restructuring of formal models of the agents and their situations is an integral part of the decision process.

Restructurable modelling begins with the identification of three key components of a sequential decision making problem:

- the participants in the problem, one of whom is the primary or "supported" agent;
- the relationships between these agents;
- the initial situation.

The participants are not treated symmetrically. The entire model is conceived from the viewpoint of the primary supported agent, and therefore the description of this agent has a significantly greater level of detail than those of the other agents. For example, the goals of the supported agent are always known, though they may change over the course of the simulation. The goals of the other agents, however, can only be conjectured, and it would be unrealistic to require that these agents be completely described. This realism, a characteristic of most decision making interactions between humans, contrasts with the simplifying assumption of identical agents that is often made in distributed AI research. The asymmetry is reflected in Negoplan by providing special knowledge structures for the supported agent.

After the key components of a sequential decision making problem have been identified, restructurable modelling provides representations for them and mechanisms for the simulation of processes. These fall into four main categories, which will be explained momentarily:

- Decompositions for the primary agent.
- Inference rules for processes.
- Agent restructuring mechanisms.
- Process adjustment mechanisms.

In their reasoning and decision making people strongly rely on various forms of decomposition: goal decomposition, situation decomposition, and so on. That is why restructurable modelling places major emphasis on identification and representation of decompositions. In particular, the supported agent is modeled by means of a *problem decomposition graph* (PDG) as described in Section 2.2. Agent restructuring mechanisms model shifts in the agent's perceptions or changes in the situation, whereas process adjustment mechanisms model modifications of or changes in the flows (of information and control) of the decision process. The behaviour of each agent and the last two categories of mechanisms are modeled by several forms of *metarules* (Section 2.2).

The restructurable modelling approach goes beyond the identification of representation schemes and reasoning mechanisms that specially target sequential decision problems. As a framework for the design of simulation systems or decision support systems (DSS) it provides an organized way to invoke external (domain-specific) solution procedures. This may be cast within the generic DSS-as-toolbox paradigm. It views a DSS as a passive system under the control of the user, enhancing the user's capabilities by providing a variety of domain-independent decision tools and methodologies which the user must select to fit a particular problem. Restructurable modelling achieves this by providing a core simulation process (technically, the "Negoplan algorithm" [13, 4]) driven by metarules; these metarules embody qualitative knowledge about when to invoke various quantitative techniques, and thus give support for modelling situation-dependent problem solving knowledge.

Restructurable modelling, treated as a prescription for the design of joint man-machine systems, stresses a highly interactive relationship between the supported agent and the simulation system throughout the simulation. It assumes that the role of the computer is to go in parallel with the decision maker, simulating her decision processes and letting her absorb various possible situations. It relies on the supported agent to interpret situations, make judgments, and guide the simulation of the decision process.

All this shows that restructurable modelling can be directly applied to forest fire management. Restructurable modelling fills the need for interactive support to the fire chief at a cognitive level, during the construction of initial goals and policies, identification of decisions to be made, and continuous modelling of the changes in these representations as the situation in the forest and the fire chief's perceptions evolve. Restructurable modelling, through Negoplan, helps the fire chief develop an understanding of the possible outcomes of negotiation with the other agents, such as neighbouring forest supervisors, and thus helps structure those interactions. Further, it is primarily *qualitative* knowledge that is involved in modelling the fire chief's goals and perceptions and the properties of the forest environment. Restructurable modelling, therefore, offers a more accessible methodology for the simulation of the core fire management problem, from which one can invoke and experiment with additional quantitative models of fire behaviour, logistics and so on.

2.2   The Negoplan System

Many of the mechanisms identified by the restructurable modelling approach have been implemented in the Negoplan system. Negoplan may be viewed at two levels. Conceived as a whole, it is, like an expert system shell, a vehicle for constructing "cases" that follow the restructurable modelling paradigm. Such a construction results in various forms of decision support, training, and interactive problem solving assistance for a possibly non-expert end user. From a case developer's perspective, Negoplan is a logic based programming language for the simulation of sequential decision processes. Apart from the present fire management case, cases developed in Negoplan include medical student training [7], robot planning [6], and softwood lumber negotiations [5].

We will not describe the format of Negoplan code; instead, in the following sections we will present several intuitive examples from our implementation to give a flavour of building simulation cases with the system. Negoplan's rule-based representation language is closely linked to logic programming. Qualitative forms of reasoning figure more prominently in Negoplan than quantitative approaches to problem analysis. Its most important programming constructs are rules, metafacts and metarules. *Rules* are a textual form of a problem decomposition graph (PDG), one of Negoplan's central knowledge structures. (Examples of rules appear in later sections of this paper.) The PDG is a directed acyclic graph, whose each node is associated with a fact—a predicate with its arguments, in the usual Prolog notation. A predicate represent a statement of a goal or issue of interest to the supported agent; a predicate valuated as true in some situation can be viewed as denoting an achieved goal. Branching in the PDG may be disjunctive or conjunctive depending on how subgoals contribute to the achievement of parent goals. The PDG is used to construct a subgraph of facts that together, and in consistency with each other, would make the topmost fact true; each fact in this subgraph, along with its appropriate truth value constitutes a *metafact*. Metafacts are labeled with the name of the agent to which they belong.

Changes in an agent's situation are modeled by *metarules*, if-then rules whose building blocks are metafacts and calls to Prolog procedures (for example, to access externally maintained databases about the forest), and by new decompositions. Of the agent restructuring mechanisms currently available in Negoplan, the most important to us are modification metarules. They change the representation of the agent by modifying the PDG. Process adjustment and changes of strategy are supported through Negoplan's packet mechanism. It is the ability to activate metarules in groups called packets, so that only a specific part of the entire collection of metarules is in effect available at any given moment during the simulation. In other words, this mechanism provides a means for switching the context of the simulation, and therefore can be directly used to implement redirections of the process or strategy elements.

The most advanced implementation of Negoplan is a highly interactive GUI-based system written in AAIS Prolog for Macintosh computers. Its top-level algorithm generates various possible situations, presents these situations to the decision maker, and simulates the evolution of scenarios under the user's partial control. As time passes, the user becomes progressively more familiar with the problem and her own real position with respect to the problem, and can derive insights into the problem.

3 Modelling Fire Management in Negoplan

In this section we present a restructurable modelling formulation of forest fire management as a sequential decision making problem. We describe, with examples, how Negoplan is used to simulate various components of the problem. How these components fit together will be explained in Section 4.

3.1 Multiple Agents, Multiple Perspectives

In order to apply restructurable modelling to fire management, we must determine who are the participants and, in particular, who is the primary agent. If we examine Morrison's account of the Yellowstone fires [12], we find a complex situation with many people influencing each other. The central characters are the forest supervisor who decides on policy, his chief ranger who protects the forest and the people in it, and the scientist who makes several key decisions related to fire behaviour. For our present purposes these three may be considered as one unit, acting as a team without internal conflict. We will refer to this unit in the singular as a *fire chief*. Normally the fire chief deals on his own with a fire within his own forest, but when the fire threatens to spread to a neighbouring forest, or when it becomes necessary to borrow additional firefighting resources, he negotiates with neighbouring fire chiefs. When the blaze becomes too large, overall control passes to the area command, and then to the regional command, requiring complex multi-party negotiations. Finally, during mammoth fires other specialized firefighting organizations can be drawn upon for crews and equipment. Since these organizations often serve demands from all over the country, there are many resource conflicts.

The fire chiefs are the main agents in our simulation. Modelling the perceptions of agents is particularly easy in Negoplan. Negoplan supports direct modelling of two agents other than the primary agent, and one of these represents the fire environment implicitly acting as an agent, Nature. Our examples will refer to fire chiefs A and B as the primary and the other agent, and to the environment. The following declarations illustrate how the three agents are specified in a Negoplan case, and the next section will illustrate how their goals and perceptions are coded.

```
us( fire_chief_a ).
them( fire_chief_b ).
neutral( forest_environment ).
```

3.2   Modelling the Objectives

The many agents, activities and influences that comprise forest fire management imply many, potentially conflicting, objectives. At the level of individual firefighting teams the problem is in essence one of planning under uncertainty and resource conflicts. The basic fire control goals include providing for the safety of firefighters, suppressing fires aggressively, remaining in communication with crew members and commanders, estimating weather and fire conditions and planning suppression activities. At the level of fire chiefs, however, the objectives relate more to fuel management and prescribed fires as described in the introduction. Figure 1 depicts part of the problem decomposition graph that contains the goal hierarchy. To describe this PDG in Negoplan, one writes each decomposition—a node in the PDG—as a Negoplan rule, for example:

```
goals <-
          'promote natural regulation' & 'human safety' &
          'property protection' & 'economic goals' &
          'controlling fires' .
'promote natural regulation' <-
          'preserve biodiversity' & 'protect endangered species' .
```

There are evident conflicts between the basic fire control goals and the fire chiefs' objectives. In fire management practice in real life, however, one often observes a prioritization or policy that helps resolve conflicts quickly. It is a necessity, given the short time frame in which decisions have to be made. Following [12], we have prioritized the major fire management goals:

1.   Allow most naturally caused fires (such as caused by lightning) to burn as "prescribed natural fires".

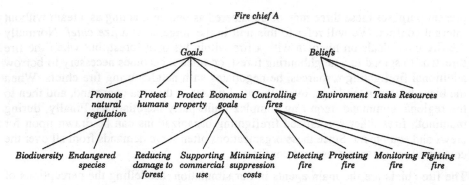

Figure 1. Problem decomposition graph for fire chief A.

2. However, protect human life, property, historic and cultural sites, specific natural features, and endangered species.

3. Suppress wildfire in as safe, cost-effective and environmentally sensitive a way as possible. "Environmentally sensitive" means avoiding bulldozers, trucks and other heavy equipment where possible, to limit the damage to the land.

Different goals appear in different contexts. For example, the second goal is not applicable as long as there is no threat to human life, property and so on; it replaces the first goal when the danger crosses a certain threshold. Similarly, there is a gradation in the strength of the fire suppression techniques that may be used. The PDG that represents the agent should change as the simulation proceeds. Restructurable modelling addresses precisely this issue (Section 3.4), in contrast with traditional static models of an agent's value system. In general, goals are activated by trigger points; for example, a geographic trigger point would be the entry of a fire into a high-priority zone such as a human settlement. Negoplan's metarules are used to represent these trigger points. There are other types of goals, which can be similarly modeled: to ignore all fires except those above a particular size, say 10 acres, or to spread resources over only a certain percentage of fires.

3.3   Modelling Agent and Environmental Behaviour

Metafacts (facts annotated with an agent's name and a truth value) represent the perceptions or situation of an agent in Negoplan. For example, the metafacts

```
fire_chief_b: 'bulldozers available'(time(1), 8) ::= true .
wind( nw ) ::= true .
```

state that fire chief B had 8 free bulldozers at his disposal at the beginning of the simulation, and the wind was blowing from the northwest. When a metafact is not labeled with an agent's name, as is the second example above, it refers to the forest environment.

Changes of situation are modeled by *response metarules*. A response metarule is fired and the metafacts in its right-hand side asserted, when its left-hand side elements are all satisfied. For example, a random change in wind conditions is written as

```
wind( nw ) ::= true &
{ random_uniform(X), X =< 0.1 }
==>
wind( nw ) ::= false & wind( n ) ::= true .
```

where the braces enclose calls to Prolog procedures. Here is a more complex metarule (text from the % sign till the end of the line is a comment):

```
% Enough bulldozers to satisfy full request: agree to share.
fire_chief_a: 'request bulldozers'(BldzRequested, Time) ::= true &
fire_chief_b: 'bulldozers available'(Time, BldzAvail) ::= true &
{ BldzAvail >= BldzRequested }
==>
fire_chief_b: 'offer bulldozers'(Time, BldzRequested) ::= true
--- negotiation_mode.
```

It models the two agents' interaction other during a negotiation: when fire chief A requests a certain number of bulldozers and fire chief B has enough available, he cooperatively agrees to loan the required number of bulldozers. The metarule is placed in a packet designed to simulate negotiation among fire chiefs by the annotation

```
--- negotiation_mode.
```

Here is another example of negotiation. When fire chief A has decided to accept an offer from fire chief B, the transfer of the offered resources requires the update of all the variables associated with their current position—the number of bulldozers available, the recent shortage, and so on. The result is a modification of the representation (the PDG) of fire chief A, and is followed by a switch from negotiation mode to plan generation mode—another packet of metarules which will model how fire chief A will use the new resources:

```
fire_chief_a: 'accept offer and effect transfer' ::= true &
fire_chief_b: 'offer bulldozers'(Time, BldzOfferB ) ::= true &
fire_chief_a: 'bulldozers available'(Time, BldzAvailA ) ::= true &
fire_chief_a: 'bulldozer shortage'(Time, BldzShortA ) ::= true &
fire_chief_a: 'bulldozers borrowed'(Time, BldzBorrowA ) ::= true &
{ BldzAvlA_new is BldzAvailA + BldzOfferB,
  BldzBorrowA_new is BldzBorrowA + BldzOfferB,
  BldzShortA_new is BldzShortA - BldzOfferB }
==>      % Update fire chief A's data.
modify ( 'resources available' <-
              'bulldozers available'(Time, BldzAvailA_new),
            'resources borrowed' <-
              'bulldozers borrowed'(Time, BldzBorrowA_new),
            'resources needed' <-
              'bulldozer shortage'(Time, BldzShortA_new) )
switch_to plan_generation_mode    --- negotiation_mode.
```

3.4   Restructuring the Goals

A critical aspect of our approach to sequential decision making is cyclic restructuring of the goals and perceptions of the primary agent during the simulation, especially at trigger points. The following group of three mutually exclusive metarules implements for a new fire the prescribed natural-fire versus suppressable-wildfire classification policy that we described earlier:

```
fire_chief_a: unclassified(Fire) ::= true &
ignition_cause(Fire, human) ::= true
==>
modify ( burning(Fire) <- suppressing(Fire),
           suppressing(Fire) <- 'plan needed'(Fire) ) .
```

```
fire_chief_a: unclassified(Fire) ::= true &
ignition_cause(Fire, natural) ::= true &
zone_type(Fire, unprotected) ::= true
==>
modify ( burning(Fire) <- 'prescribed fire'(Fire) ).

fire_chief_a: unclassified(Fire) ::= true &
zone_type(Fire, protected) ::= true
==>
modify ( burning(Fire) <- suppressing(Fire),
         suppressing(Fire) <- 'plan needed'(Fire)).
```

After one of these metarules has been applied, its right-hand side modification of the goals in the PDG initiates a suitable management action. For example, metarules for monitoring the fire are triggered by the metafact 'prescribed fire'(Fire), while the metafact suppressing(Fire) triggers metarules to fill out plans for fighting the fire. An example of the latter follows: the need to construct a plan, as asserted by the previous metarule, initializes (to zero) the resources assigned to fight that fire and triggers a change of control to another packet of metarules, where decision will be taken on how to plan in detail for that fire.

```
{ 'current time'(Time) } &
fire_chief_a: 'plan needed'(Fire) ::= true
==>
modify ( suppressing(Fire) <-
         'bulldozers suppressing'(Time, Fire, 0) )
switch_to plan_generation_mode   --- fire_simulation_mode .
```

4   System Overview and Discussion

4.1   System Overview

Figure 2 is a bird's eye view of the knowledge content and information flows that a complete simulation of the forest fire management problem would have to incorporate. Our implementation in Negoplan corresponds to the marked regions of Figure 2 and does not yet incorporate in-depth knowledge requiring specialized expertise (for example, fire behaviour analysis). The implementation works in one of three modes. In the fire simulation mode the germination and growth of a fire and the consequences of firefighting activities are simulated. In the plan generation mode the fire chief determines firefighting activities and allocates resources. In the negotiation mode he lends or borrows resources from another fire chief. Each mode is implemented as a packet of metarules, and Negoplan only examines those metarules which belong to the currently active packet. Figure 3 graphically summarizes the above.

The fire management case in Negoplan starts in fire simulation mode with metafacts constructed from the PDG (as described, for example, in [8]) and with some explicitly stated metafacts. A fire with random characteristics appears and is classified as illustrated by the earlier example, say as a fire to be suppressed and in need of a suppression plan.

This triggers a switch to another group of metarules that implement planning, labeled plan_generation_mode. Part of the planning process is interactive. For example, the user is queried for the levels for resource allocation. Other parts of the planning process are automated: the system allocates resources automatically. A typical metarule from this mode is the following:

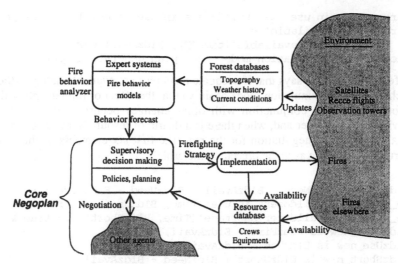

Figure 2. Information flows

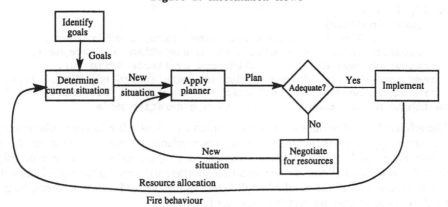

Figure 3. An overview of the implementation.

```
%%% Allocate resources if available resources are adequate.

fire_chief_a: suppressing(Fire) ::= true &
{ 'current time'(Time) } &
fire_chief_a: 'bulldozers available'(time(T), BldzAvail) ::= true &
{ BldzAvail > 0 } &
fire_chief_a:
   'bulldozers needed estimate'(BldzNeed, Time, Fire) ::= true &
fire_chief_a:
   'bulldozers suppressing'(time(T), Fire, BldzFire) ::= true &
{ BldzFire < BldzNeed,  BldzAvail >= BldzNeed - BldzFire } &
fire_chief_a: 'bulldozers in use'(time(T), BldzUse ) ::= true &
{ BldzFire_new is BldzNeed,
  BldzUse_new is BldzUse + BldzNeed - BldzFire,
  BldzAvail_new is BldzAvail - BldzNeed + BldzFire }
==>
modify (
   suppressing(Fire) <-
       'bulldozers suppressing'(time(T), Fire, BldzFire_new),
```

```
    'resources in use' <- 'bulldozers in use'(time(T), BldzUse_new),
    'resources available' <-
        'bulldozers available'(time(T), BldzAvail_new) )
switch_to fire_simulation_mode   --- plan_generation_mode .
```

In effect, the metarule says that if adequate resources are available, allocate them and switch back to fire simulation mode again so that the effect of implementing the plan can be observed in conjunction with other changes occurring due to the fire's behaviour. On the other and, when there is a dearth of resources, allocate whatever is available and begin negotiation for the rest (the first six elements of the following metarule are the same as in the preceding metarule):

```
...
{ BldzFire < BldzNeed,  BldzAvail < BldzNeed - BldzFire } &
fire_chief_a: 'bulldozers in use'(Time, BldzUse) ::= true &
fire_chief_a: 'bulldozer shortage'(Time, BldzShort) ::= true &
{ BldzFire_new is BldzFire + BldzAvail,
  BldzUse_new is BldzUse + BldzAvail,
  BldzShort_new is BldzShort + BldzNeed - BldzAvail }
==>
modify (
  suppressing(Fire) <-
          'bulldozers suppressing'(Time, Fire, BldzFire_new),
    'resources in use' <- 'bulldozers in use'(Time, BldzUse_new),
    'resources available' <- 'bulldozers available'(Time, 0),
    resources <-& 'bulldozers needed estimate'(BldzNeed, Time, Fire),
    'resources needed' <- 'bulldozer shortage'(Time, BldzShort_new) )
switch_to negotiation_mode   --- plan_generation_mode .
```

The left hand side describes a situation in which a particular fire has been classified as one to be suppressed, there are free bulldozers available, an estimate of the number of bulldozers needed to fight that fire is known but happens to be too large to be filled with the available bulldozers. The resulting shortage triggers, on the right hand side, the assignment of all the available bulldozers to the fire and a switch to negotiation mode to try to procure the rest from another fire chief.

Every metarule which is active—that is, which belongs to the current mode (packet)—is considered in turn. Negoplan first cycles through all the metarules that model responses to existing conditions, and then selects a single metarule that performs restructuring of the problem representation. Since fire detection and control is an ongoing process, the simulation works in a loop and can be terminated at any arbitrary point after interesting conditions have been reached.

4.2   Concluding Remarks

We have shown how forest fire management can be formulated as a sequential decision making problem and represented descriptively in a system using logical inference such as Negoplan. Restructurable modelling has aided in this endeavour by identifying the constructs and mechanisms that are appropriate for the simulation of such problems. It places the focus on the agents and their cognitive processes and interactions, and stresses the changing nature of their goals and perceptions of the problem. In so doing, it provides formal tools for representing them and restructuring their representations. Restructurable modelling is therefore a useful and flexible methodology for the design of systems typified by fire management.

The complete fire environment is a dynamic, spatially distributed, ongoing, real-time, multiagent, unpredictable world [2], and our implementation has basically provided a framework that can be fleshed out to invoke detailed domain models. For example, we have used a simple model of negotiation in which the agents are fully cooperative, subject to their individual resource constraints, whereas in real accounts of negotiation between fire chiefs they often display uncooperative behaviour, in anticipation of future negotiations. There is considerable potential for further investigation, for example, by incorporating various planning techniques, models of fire behaviour, and negotiation models into the corresponding parts of our framework.

References

[1] A. A. Brown and K. P. Davis, *Forest Fire Control and Use*, McGraw-Hill 1973.

[2] P. R. Cohen, M. L. Greenberg, D. M. Hart and A. E. Howe, "Trial by fire: Understanding the design requirements for agents in complex environments," *AI Magazine*, **10**, 34–48, Fall 1989.

[3] C. Elfring, "Yellowstone: Fire storm over fire management," *BioScience*, **39**, 667–672, November 1989.

[4] G. E. Kersten, W. Michalowski, S. Szpakowicz and Z. Koperczak, "Restructurable representations of negotiation," *Management Science*, **37**(10), 1269–1290, 1991.

[5] G. E. Kersten, "Simulation and analysis of negotiation processes: The case of softwood lumber negotiations," in *Symposium on Computer Support for Negotiations*, Cambridge, MA: Harvard Law School, May 1994.

[6] G. E. Kersten, P. Lu and S. Szpakowicz, "Indicative and action planning for an intelligent agent," in *Proceedings of the Tenth Canadian Conference on Artificial Intelligence*. R. Elio, ed., 287–294, CSCSI, Banff, May 1994.

[7] G. E. Kersten, S. Rubin and S. Szpakowicz, "Medical decision making in Negoplan," in *Proc Second World Congress on Expert Systems* (J. Liebovitz, ed.), 1130–1137, Macmillan, 1994.

[8] G. E. Kersten and S. Szpakowicz, "Rule-based formalism and preference representation: An extension of Negoplan," *European J. Operations Research*, **45**, 309–323, 1990.

[9] G. E. Kersten and S. Szpakowicz, "Decision making and decision aiding. defining the process, its representations and support," *Group Decision and Negotiation*, **3**(2), 237–261, 1994.

[10] R. E. Martin, "Goals, methods and elements of prescribed burning," in *Natural and prescribed fire in Pacific Northwest forests*, ed. John D. Walstad, Steven R. Radosevich and David V. Sandberg, Oregon University Press, 1990.

[11] T. A. Moehlman, V. R. Lesser and B. L. Buteau, "Decentralized negotiation: An approach to the distributed planning problem,". *Group Decision and Negotiation* (K. Sycara, ed.), **1**, 161–192, 1992.

[12] M. Morrison, *Fire in Paradise*. New York: Harper Collins Publishers, 1993.

[13] S. J. Noronha and S. Szpakowicz, *Negoplan Case Author's Manual*. Ottawa: Decision Analysis Laboratory, School of Business, Carleton University, 1995.

[14] A. J. Simard, *Wildland Fire Management: A Systems Approach,* Forestry Technical Report 17, Canadian Forestry Service, Ottawa, 1977.

[15] J. A. Stankovic and K. Ramamritham, *Hard Real-Time Systems*, Computer Society Press of the IEEE, 1988.

An Architecture for a Deductive Fuzzy Relational Database

Olga Pons, Juan M. Medina, Juan C. Cubero, Amparo Vila

Dept. of Computer Sciences and Artificial Intelligence
University of Granada
18071 Granada, Spain

Abstract. This paper reports on the architecture of a Fuzzy Relational DBMS (FRDBMS) with deduction capabilities, whose main characteristics are: 1) It is built on the basis of a theoretical model for fuzzy relational databases and a theoretical model for logic fuzzy databases; 2) It is implemented entirely on classical RDBMS, using their resources; 3) It conserves all the operations of the host RDBMS and gives them more power, adding new capabilities for dealing with "fuzzy" and "intensive" information; 4) It provides a deductive fuzzy language, DFSQL, and a processor which permits the translation of each DFSQL statement into one or more SQL statements, which can be used by the host RDBMS; 5) It offers a relational representaion of the rules that define an intensive table, in such a way that all necessary information to perform deduction is stored in tables. 6) This system needs to interact with a deduction module which performs the computation of intensive tables.

Keywords: Intelligent Information Systems, Fuzzy relational database, Deductive database.

1 Introduction

Since the appearance of the Relational Data Base model (RDB) proposed by Codd, several approaches have tried to provide a theoretical environment for the representation and handling of fuzzy information. But theoretical models of fuzzy databases require mechanisms to build relational systems (FRDBMS) that operate in accordance with these principles. Most relevant theoretical proposals in this sense are [1, 7, 8, 11]. In [3, 10] we present some ideas on how to represent fuzzy information, and how to implement it on a conventional RDBMS. On the other hand, there exists still a lacking, that is, the possibility of defining information through rules. This could allow us to define even recursive-defined concepts. In [9] we present a logic approach to fuzzy databases which allows to deduce fuzzy (or not) information from a set of fuzzy rules using *"fuzzy facts"*. So, our architecture is based on a suitable theoretical model of Fuzzy Relational Database, a suitable theoretical model of Logic Fuzzy Database and on the use of the resources provided by a conventional RDBMS to implement fuzzy handling and fuzzy data representation and conventional deductive systems to implement fuzzy deduction.

So then, what we pretend is to be able to solve queries involving a deductive process not solvable by a relational system. In this case, our Deductive-Fuzzy Relational DBMS (DFRDBMS) will have to manipulate two types of tables: *Extensive Tables*: Which are physically stored in the database or can be computed by relational methods (p.e. views) and *Intensive Tables*: Whose data must be computed by an independent deduction module.

To illustrate the power of this architecture, let us consider a database with the following scheme:

PARENTS(Name,Father,Mother)
DEAD_PEOPLE(Name,Age,Date)
ALIVE_PEOPLE(Name,Address,)

and a query *"Get person names together with their ancestor names such that the ancestor died young "*. Note that there is not explicit information about *ancestors* in the DB and this information is not computable in relational terms and that there is an attribute value labelled *young*, what implies a fuzzy treatment of information.

The paper is organized as follows: In Sect. 2, the most important characteristics of this architecture are shown. We give its modular description, paying special attention to the Deductive Fuzzy SQL Server. In Sect. 3 we widely explain how imprecise and intensive information is implemented in the DFRDBMS and give an example to illustrate it. Finally, Sect. 4 summarizes the most important contributions of this work and points out the open problems and future avenues for research.

2 Arquitecture of a DFRDBMS

Figure 1 shows the general architecture of the systems; it provides a deductive and fuzzy extension of a conventional RDBMS, adopting a modular structure which permits a Client/Server organization. The main module is the RDBMS, which works as a host; around the RDBMS there are the modules that perform the deductive and fuzzy information handling. Below, we describe the modules in terms of their functional character, structure and implementation.

2.1 Modules Description

- The **Host RDBMS** is the system used as the basis of the implementation of this architecture. The incorporated SQL syntax, is enlarged with a deductive and fuzzy extension.
- **DB** stores all the extensive information, "fuzzy" or not, with a relational scheme.
- **FMB**, the Fuzzy Meta-knowledge Base, is an extension of the host RDBMS catalog, whose mission is to provide FREDDI with the information about all fuzzy structures, data and definitions contained in the DB.
- **RB**, the Rules Base is another extension of the host RDBMS catalog, which contains all information related to intensive tables defined in the DB.

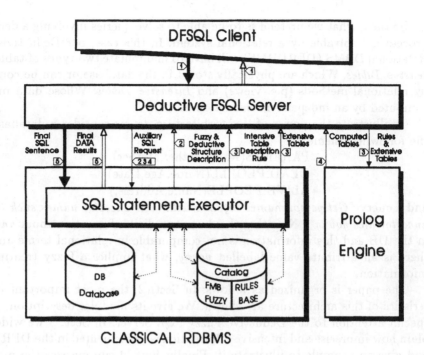

Fig. 1. General architecture

- The **Deductive FSQL Server** module is responsible for processing deductive and fuzzy requests to the system.
- The **Prolog Engine**, which performs the inference processes.

2.2 Deductive Fuzzy SQL Server

This module serves the requests of client applications expressed in DFSQL: analyzes, verifies and processes them to give back the results in a table. In figure 1 we show how this module performs a query. The sequence of steps followed is:

1. It accepts a DFSQL request (black arrow 1) and separates those clauses involving fuzzy treatment or an intensive table. To do this, it must explore the FMB through auxiliary SQL queries (black arrow 2 3 4).
2. It gets from the FMB the structure of the fuzzy clauses, from the Rules Base (RB) the rules that define the intensive tables and, from the DB, the extensive tables involved (white arrows 2 and 3, respectively).
3. It sends all information involved in the deduction process to the Prolog Engine (black arrow 3), gets the results (white arrow 4) and updates the DB with these results (black arrow 2 3 4).
4. It translates fuzzy clauses into SQL clauses and constructs a definitive SQL sentence (black arrow 5).
5. It executes that sentence, obtains the results (white arrow 5) and processes them before sending them to the client application (white arrow 1).

DFSQL Syntax. As we have seen, the system functioning is based on an extended version of SQL syntax provided by the Host RDBMS. Next, we show in YACC format some of the new clauses that DFSQL syntax incorporates.

• Data Definition Language

This sub-language incorporates to SQL new sentences to define tables containing fuzzy attributes and to define intensive tables. The system supports intensive tables with both classical and fuzzy attributes. Among all the sentences needed, we only incide, for the sake of shortness, in the syntax adopted for the definition of these tables.

```
create_table   : CREATE INTENSIVE TABLE table_item
                 '(' column_list ')' RULE rule_descpt ;
table_item     : id_user '.' id_table | id_table ;
column_list    : column_list ',' column_list | column_descpt ;
column_descpt  : column_id datatype ;
data_type      : classical_datatype | fuzzy_datatype ;
fuzzy_datatype : crisp | possibilistic | nearness ;
nearness       : SCALAR '(' NATURAL_NUMBER ')' | SCALAR ;
rule_descpt    : '(' rule_list ')' ;
rule_list      : rule_list ';' rule_list | rule_item ;
rule_item      : rule_item AND rule_item | predicate ;
predicate      : table_descpt | condition ;
table_descpt   : table_item '(' table_arg ')' ;
table_arg      : table_arg ',' table_arg | arg_item ;
arg_item       : '_' | var_id ;
var_id         : 'X'NATURAL_NUMBER ;
condition      : var_id comp var_id ;
comp           : '=' | '<' | '>' | '<=' | '=>' | '<>' ;
```

• Data Manipulation Language

The query is the operation that involves all expressive power of DFSQL. Next, we detail the new clauses attached to SELECT sentence in order to make queries which allow to get intensive and fuzzy information.

```
fcond_simp   : fcond_wtout threshold | fcond_wtout ;
fcond_wtout  : column_item fcomp fuz_constant ;
threshold    : THOLD NUMBER | THOLD '$' ID ;
fuz_constant : '$' ID
             | number
             | '#' NUMBER
             | '[' NUMBER ',' NUMBER ']'
             | '$' '[' NUMBER ',' NUMBER ',' NUMBER ','
               NUMBER ']' ;
fcomp        : FEQ | FGT | FLT | FGEQ | FLEQ ;
comp_deg     : CDEG '(' fuz_arith_op ')' ;
agre_funct   : FMAX '(' column_item ')'
```

```
                | FMIN '(' column_item ')'
                | FSUM '(' column_item ')'
                | FAVG '(' column_item ')' ;
fuz_arith_op    : fuz_arith_op '+' fuz_arith_op
                | fuz_arith_op '-' fuz_arith_op
                | fuz_arith_op '*' fuz_arith_op
                | fuz_arith_op '/' fuz_arith_op
                | '(' fuz_arith_op ')'
                | column_item
                | fuz_constant ;
column_item     : table_id '.' column_id
                | table_alias '.' column_id
                | column_id ;
```

The following sentence is a valid statement of the FSQL syntax adopted, (assuming the existence of the tables and labels noted):

```
CREATE INTENSIVE TABLE ancestor (X char(30), Y char(30)) RULE (
parents(X,Y,_);
parents(X,_,Y);
parents(X,Z,_) and ancestor(Z,Y);
parents(X,_,Z) and ancestor(Z,Y)).
```

3 Implementation of Intensive and Imprecise Information in the DFRDBMS

Implementation of intensive and imprecise information is done considering three levels: the *database level*, the *system catalog level* and the *DFSQL server level*.

3.1 Imprecise Data in the Host Database

The representation used for the imprecise data allows us to distinguish three types of "fuzzy" attributes at the Database level:

Type 1 Attributes with *"crisp data"* having *linguistic hedges* defined on them.
Type 2 Attributes with *"imprecise data on an ordered domain"*.
Type 3 Attributes with *"Discrete Domains with Analogies"*.

3.2 The Fuzzy Meta-Knowledge Base

We use the term **Fuzzy Meta-Knowledge Base** (FMB) to refer to that extension of the System Catalog which captures all necessary information about imprecise data in the Database. Besides, it contains references to the intensive tables of the DB. Accordingly, we will organize all this information in tables or

Table 1. Representation of Type 2 attributes.

Data Type	F_TYPE	F_1	F_2	F_3	F_4
UNKNOWN	0	NULL	NULL	NULL	NULL
UNDEFINED	1	NULL	NULL	NULL	NULL
NULL	2	NULL	NULL	NULL	NULL
CRISP	3	d	NULL	NULL	NULL
LABEL	4	FUZZY_ID	NULL	NULL	NULL
INTERVAL[A,B]	5	A	0	0	B
APPROX(d)	6	d-margin	margin	-margin	d+margin
FUZZY	7	$a - \alpha$	α	β	$b+\beta$

Table 2. Representation of type 3 attributes.

Data Type	F_TYP	F_P1	F_1	F_P2	F_2	F_P3	F_3	...
UNKNOWN	0	NULL	NULL	NULL	NULL	NULL	NULL	...
UNDEFINED	1	NULL	NULL	NULL	NULL	NULL	NULL	...
NULL	2	NULL	NULL	NULL	NULL	NULL	NULL	...
SIMPLE	3	1	d	NULL	NULL	NULL	NULL	...
POS. DISTR.	4	p_1	d_1	p_2	d_2	p_3	d_3	...

relations. The elements stored in the Meta-knowledge Base are the following: 1) The intensive tables present in the Database, 2) the attributes in the Database that will be treated as imprecise, 3) the type of these attributes (see Tab. 3) 4) elements defined in the Database scope, i.e. query fuzzy quantifiers and 5) the fuzzy objects defined on each attribute.

Table 3. Fuzzy_col table: it codifies the nature of an attribute with a value.

Attribute_Type	Column_type Value
Extensive Crisp	0
Extensive Possibilistic	1
Extensive Nearness	2
Intensive Crisp	4
Intensive Possibilistic	5
Intensive Nearness	6

3.3 Rules Representation in the Host Database

To deal with the problem of representing rules in the RDBMS, the creation and manipulation of four tables are necessary. These tables are represented in Fig. 2 and their descriptions are the following:

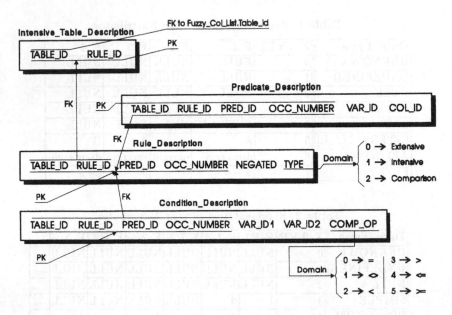

Fig. 2. Relational representation of rules.

- **Intensive_Table_Description**: This table contains the name of the intensive table we are defining and the number of rules it needs to be defined. The attributes are: TABLE_ID: It contains the intensive table name or, what is the same, the head of the rules defining such table and RULE_ID: It contains a different indentifier for each rule defining a concrete intensive table.

- **Rule_Description**: This table contains the description of each rule, that is, the predicates involved. Its attributes are: TABLE_ID, RULE_ID: These two attributes have the same meaning as the ones of the previous table and must coincide with them, that is, both of them constitute a foreign key to the Intensive_Table_Description table, PRED_ID: This column contains the name of the predicates involved in a concrete rule, OCC_NUMBER: In the case that the same predicate name appears more than once in the body of a rule, we need to distinguish different occurrences attaching a number in the column OCC_NUMBER, NEGATED: This column contains value 1 if the corresponding predicate occurrence is negated in the rule and 0, otherwise and TYPE: This column contains a value in the set {0,1,2} standing for extensive, intensive and comparison, respectively.

- **Predicate_Description**: This table contains the description of every predicate occurrence, that is, the variables used, the order in which they appear, etc... Its attributes are: TABLE_ID, RULE_ID, PRED_ID and OCC_NUMBER: They must coincide with the corresponding ones of Rule_Description table, VAR_ID: This column contains the identifiers of the variables that appear in a predicate expression. If the variables are called, p.e. X_i, this column will contain the number i and COL_ID: This column indicates the position of every variable inside a predicate expression (whether X_i is in first, second, ... place in the predicate P expression).

- **Condition_Description**: This table contains the description of comparison expressions appearing in the rules. Its attributes are: TABLE_ID, RULE_ID, PRED_ID and OCC_NUMBER: These columns must coincide with the corresponding ones of table Rule_Description, VAR_ID1 and VAR_ID2: Are the identifiers of the variables involved in a comparison operation and COMP_OP: This column indicates the comparison operator used in the expression. This column can contain one of the values of the set $\{0,1,2,3,4,5\}$ standing for $=$, $<>$, $<$, $>$, $<=$ and $>=$, respectively.

- **Example.**

Let us see with an example how rules are represented in the DFRDBMS. Let us suppose an intensive table (predicate) definition like:

$$P(X_1, X_2, X_3) \ if \ Q_1(X_1, \_) \ and \ not(Q_2(X_2, X_3)) \ and \ (X_1 < X_3).$$
$$P(X_1, X_2, X_3) \ if \ Q_1(X_1, X_4) \ and \ P(X_4, X_2, X_1) \ and \ Q_3(X_3, \_).$$

The representation of the rules defining the intensive table P is shown in Tables 4, 5, 6 and 7.

Table 4. Intensive_Table_Description table.

TABLE_ID	RULE_ID
P	P_1
P	P_2

Table 5. Rule_Description table

TABLE_ID	RULE_ID	PRED_ID	OCC_NUMBER	NEGATED	TYPE
P	P_1	Q_1	1	0	0
P	P_1	Q_2	1	1	0
P	P_1	comp1	1	0	2
P	P_2	Q_1	1	0	0
P	P_2	P	1	0	1
P	P_2	Q_3	1	0	0

4 Conclusions and Future Work

The architecture for DFRDBMS we have presented, satisfies the following general objectives: 1) It provides representation for a wide range of imprecise and

Table 6. Predicate_Description table

TABLE_ID	RULE_ID	PRED_ID	OCC_NUMBER	VAR_ID	COL_ID
P	P_1	Q_1	1	1	1
P	P_1	Q_2	1	2	1
P	P_1	Q_2	1	3	2
P	P_2	Q_1	1	1	1
P	P_2	Q_1	1	4	1
P	P_2	P	1	4	1
P	P_2	P	1	2	2
P	P_2	P	1	1	3
P	P_2	Q_3	1	3	1

Table 7. Condition_Description table

TABLE_ID	RULE_ID	PRED_ID	OCC_NUMBER	VAR_ID1	VAR_ID2	COMP_OP
P	P_1	comp1	1	1	3	2

intensive information. To implement this kind of information, the data structures available in any RDBMS (domains, attributes, relations and system catalogue) are used, 2) it uses standard inference modules to solve the intensive requests, 3) it extends SQL in order to manipulate this type of information, and 4) it establishes an adequate implemention scheme in such a way that the manipulation of fuzzy and intensive information, allows to obtain satisfactory results and reach a high grade of efficiency.

However, further work is needed on the following aspects of the proposed implementation, as 1) to develop a complete DFRDBMS prototype which incorporates all the modules, 2) to increase the variety and applicabiblity of implemented operators, 3) to develop a complete DFSQL extension, including all operations of DDL, DML and DCL sublanguages, and to incorporate tools for the development of applications for Deductive Fuzzy Databases.

References

1. : P. Bosc , M. Galibourg, G. Hamon. Fuzzy Querying with SQL: Extensions and Implementation Aspects, Fuzzy Sets and Systems. v.28 pp. 333-349. (1988)
2. : B.P. Buckles, F.E. Petry. A Fuzzy Representation of Data for Relational Databases, Fuzzy Sets and Systems, 7. 213-226. (1982)
3. : J. M. Medina, M. A. Vila, J. C. Cubero, O. Pons. Towards the Implementation of a Generalized Fuzzy Relational Database Model, To appear in Fuzzy Sets & Systems.
4. : J. M. Medina, O. Pons, M. A. Vila. GEFRED. A Generalized Model of Fuzzy Relational Databases, Information Sciences, 76, 1-2, pp 87-109. (1994)

5. : J. M. Medina , J. C. Cubero, O. Pons, M. A. Vila. Fuzzy Knowledge Representation in Relational Databases, Technical Report #DECSAI-94112. November. (1994)

6. : O. Pons, M. A. Vila, J. M. Medina. Handling Imprecise Medical Information in the Framework of Logic Fuzzy Databases, Fuzzy Systems & A. I. Vol. III. Nr. 1/1994. Ed. Academiei Romane. (1994)

7. : H. Prade, C. Testemale. Generalizing Database Relational Algebra for the Treatment of Incomplete/Uncertain Information and Vague Queries, Information Sciences, 34. 115-143. (1984)

8. : M. Umano. Freedom−0 : A Fuzzy Database System, Fuzzy Information and Decision Processes. Gupta-Sanchez edit. North-Holland Pub. Comp. (1982)

9. : M. A. Vila, J. C. Cubero, J. M. Medina, O. Pons. Logic and Fuzzy Relational Databases: A New Language and a New Definition. In Fuzzy Sets and Possibility Theory in Databases Management Systems. P. Bosc and J. Kacprzyk Eds. Physica-Verlag. (1995)

10. : M. A. Vila, J. C. Cubero, J. M. Medina, O. Pons. Towards the Computer Implementation of a Fuzzy Relational and Deductive Database System, Proceedings of the FUZZ-IEEE/IFES'95 workshop on Fuzzy Relational Systems and Information Retrieval, Yokohama, Japan. March (1995).

11. : M. Zemankova, A. Kandel. Fuzzy Relational Data Bases - A Key to Expert Systems, Verlag TUV Rheinland. (1984)

A Multi-Step Process for Discovering, Managing and Refining Strong Functional Relations Hidden in Databases

Ning Zhong[1] and Setsuo Ohsuga[2]

[1] Department of Computer Science and Systems Engineering, Yamaguchi University
[2] Department of Information and Computer Science, Waseda University, Japan

Abstract. Functional relations are a kind of important regularities hidden in databases. Since erroneous data can be a significant problem in real-world databases and the contents of most databases are ever changing, functional relations that can be discovered from databases are usually *strong* ones which hold qualitatively for the collected data. Moreover, the discovery process is a multi-step process based on incipient hypothesis generation/evaluation and management/refinement. In this process, it is necessary to perform multi-aspect intelligent data analysis and multi-level conceptual abstraction/learning by combining AI techniques with statistical methods in multiple learning phases. This paper describes a multi-step process for discovering, managing and refining strong functional relations hidden in databases.

1 Introduction

Functional relations are a kind of important regularities hidden in databases. Since erroneous data can be a significant problem in real-world databases (i.e., data in databases are generally uncertain and incomplete) and the contents of most databases are ever changing (i.e., data in databases can be often deleted, added or updated), functional relations that can be discovered from databases are usually *strong* ones which hold qualitatively for the collected data [5, 11, 16, 15]. Moreover, the discovery process is a multi-step process based on incipient hypothesis generation/evaluation and management/refinement. In this process, it is necessary to perform multi-aspect intelligent data analysis and multi-level conceptual abstraction/learning in multiple learning phases [14, 17].

This paper describes a multi-step process for discovering, managing and refining *strong* functional relations hidden in databases. In some sense, the discovery process described in this paper can be regarded as an extension for BACON and its several successors for supporting qualitative and quantitative discovery, as well as processing the data with more uncertainty and data change [6, 7, 3]. The key point of this extension is to enhance the capability of processing uncertainty systematically by extending heuristic search and search control, as well as combining AI techniques with statistical methods in the discovery process based on generation/evaluation and management/refinement. In the following sections, we will describe in detail the discovery process. It includes to describe how to generate/evaluate strong functional relations by cooperatively using heuristic search and regression analysis, how to represent the discovered strong functional relations as the deductive rules and the sets of data for showing their errors in a knowledge-base, and how to manage/refine them by using quantitative inheritance and meta reasoning etc. Finally, we give conclusion and future work.

2 Generation and Evaluation

2.1 Generation by Heuristic Search

Heuristics for finding *strong* functional relations are based on heuristics developed by Langley et al. [7, 6], and use Qualitative Mathematics in qualitative reasoning [4, 8]. Here, we first define several concepts and terminology as preparation.

Definition 1. Monotonicity between two attributes.

We say that there is the *monotonicity* between attributes X_I and X_J if X_I increases or decreases as X_J increases.

And let $X_I \propto_Q X_J$ denote that there is the monotonicity between X_I and X_J, and $X_I \overset{not}{\propto}_Q X_J$ denote that there is not the monotonicity between X_I and X_J. $\square$

Definition 2. Qualitative values in an attribute.

Let *qualitative values* in an attribute be ranges of values in this attribute, which are generated by using *landmark*[4], domain knowledge, or other some methods.

And let $[X_I]$ denote the qualitative values in the attribute X_I. $\square$

Definition 3. Sets in an attribute.

Let *sets* in an attribute be groups of data in this attribute corresponding to qualitative values in another attribute.

And let $\{X_J\}_I$ denote the sets, which correspond to the qualitative values $[X_I]$, in the attribute X_J. $\square$

Definition 4. Contradictory values.

We say that *contradictory values* are the ones that destroy the monotonicity between attributes X_I and X_J, or the qualitative values $[X_I]$ and the sets $\{X_J\}_I$. $\square$

Definition 5. Probability of contradictory values.

Let the *probability* of contradictory values be the ratio of the number of contradictory values to the number of total data in an attribute. $\square$

Definition 6. Approximate monotonicity between two attributes.

We say that there is the *approximate* monotonicity between two attributes if the probability of contradictory values is smaller than the threshold value.

And let $X_I \dot{\propto}_Q X_J$ denote that there is the approximate monotonicity between attributes X_I and X_J, and $[X_I] \dot{\propto}_Q \{X_J\}_I$ denote that there is the approximate monotonicity between the qualitative values $[X_I]$ and the sets $\{X_J\}_I$. $\square$

We have developed several heuristics for finding *strong* functional relations [16]. Here, we would like to describe how to execute one of these heuristics,

- If $X_I \overset{not}{\propto_Q} X_J$, but $X_I \dot\propto_Q X_J$ or $[X_I] \dot\propto_Q \{X_J\}_I$, then hypothesize that there is a strong functional relation between X_I and X_J,

as an example. When this heuristic is called, it is executed by the following method:

First, define the qualitative values $[X_I]$ for the attribute X_I, and form the sets $\{X_J\}_I$ for the attribute X_J;
Then, evaluate the uncertainty of contradictory values which destroy the monotonicity between the qualitative values $[X_I]$ and the sets $\{X_J\}_I$;
If the probability of contradictory values is smaller than the threshold value, then hypothesize that there is a strong functional relation between X_I and X_J.

Example 1. By using the heuristic stated above for a sample stars database [12], which consists of several attributes such as the cluster designation of stars, the V magnitude, the color indexes B-V and U-B, effective temperature, luminosity, mass of the stars etc. as shown in Table 1, we can find several strong functional relations between the attribute *effTemp* and other some attributes such as *luminosity*, the color indexes *B-V* and *U-B* in the clusters, and these functional relations can be qualitatively represented as follows:

$effTemp \dot\propto_Q luminosity$, and $effTemp$, $luminosity \in cluster_1$, $cluster_3$, $cluster_4$, $cluster_5$, $cluster_7$, $cluster_8$, $cluster_{10}$, $cluster_{11}$ and $cluster_{12}$;
$effTemp \dot\propto_Q B\text{-}V$, and $effTemp$, $B\text{-}V \in cluster_1$, $cluster_2$, $cluster_3$, $cluster_4$, $cluster_5$, $cluster_7$, and $cluster_{12}$;
$effTemp \dot\propto_Q U\text{-}B$, and $effTemp$, $U\text{-}B \in cluster_1$, $cluster_2$, $cluster_3$, $cluster_4$, $cluster_5$, $cluster_7$, $cluster_8$, $cluster_{10}$, $cluster_{11}$ and $cluster_{12}$.

$\square$

These hypothetical functional relations are first stored in a model-base using qualitative equations [16]. Then they are evaluated by the statistical methods to be stated in Section 2.2.

2.2 Evaluation by Regression Analysis

In general, regression analysis is a statistical method for finding a *structural characteristic* (or call a structural relation, i.e., a kind of approximate functional relation represented by the regression model) hidden in the data, with which the value of the objective variable can be predicted/inferred by the values of descriptive variables. Furthermore, a structural characteristic is a *strong* functional relation if it was qualitatively inferred by the heuristics stated in Section 2.1. Thus, the *strong* functional relations are finally denoted by regression models, so that they can be easily managed and refined [15].

In our application, the main goals of the evaluation by regression analysis are to find the optimal regression model (i.e., the best structural characteristic)

Table 1. DB: stars

id	clusters	v-Magnitude	B-V	U-B	effTemp	luminosity	massStar	...
1	1	13.18	0.30	-0.33	4.19	2.19	3.23	
2	1	14.62	0.34	0.12	4.02	1.32	2.20	...
3	1	14.37	0.67	-0.06	3.87	1.11	1.84	
⋮	⋮	⋮	⋮	⋮	⋮	⋮	⋮	⋮
127	2	12.22	0.83	0.48	4.02	2.41	4.19	
128	2	12.22	0.83	0.48	4.02	2.41	3.53	...
129	2	13.65	0.76	-0.09	4.23	2.12	3.14	
...	...	...	...	...	...	...	...	...

among variables of which there is a hypothetical linear (or quadratic) functional relation and detect its error simultaneously. If it is inferred that there is a linear (or quadratic) functional relation between X_I and X_J by using the heuristics as stated in Section 2.1, then let $Y = X_I$ be an objective variable, X_J be a descriptive variable, and ε be the error (or the residual) which is normally distributed with a mean of zero and a variance of σ^2. The number of descriptive variables can be more than one. In order to evaluate the hypothetical functional relations, three methods of regression analyses, multiple regression (MR), polynomial regression (PR) and auto-regression (AR), are prepared in our system.

However, it usually does not mean that the optimal regression model can be obtained by increasing the number of descriptive variables. Although it may cause a decrease in the variance, it may also decrease the stability of the regression model. Hence, it is very important to select the most effective set of descriptive variables to obtain the optimal model. We need a criterion for the purpose. A criterion called AIC (Akaike Information Criterion) is introduced by Akaike for evaluating the accuracy of prediction, with which we can select the best model [1]. It is defined as follows:

$$AIC = \quad -2 \times (Maximum\ Likelihood\ of\ Model)$$
$$+2 \times (Numbers\ of\ Parameters\ of\ Model). \tag{1}$$

Among all combinations of potential descriptive variables, the model that produces the smallest AIC value is the best one. That is, we select the model with both better stability and smaller variance as the *structural characteristic* discovered by AIC.

Example 2. We can evaluate these hypothesized *strong* functional relations found by using heuristic search as described in Example 1, and select the best ones as *structural characteristics* discovered by using regression analysis and AIC. Table 2 shows a part of the results. In Table 2, Y is *effective temperature*, X_{lum} is *luminosity* and X_{b-v} is *B-V*. □

The process stated this section is a process from qualitative to quantitative discovery by cooperatively using heuristic search and statistical methods. Although regression analysis can both generate and evaluate functional relations, it has also several limits [16]. On the other hand, only use AI techniques such as the heuristic search, the issue of processing the data with more uncertainty cannot be solved satisfactorily. Hence, we try to combine both of them, so that we can (1) use heuristics and domain knowledge etc. for search control. Thus, the search and generation of functional relations are not blind but heuristic; (2) analyse qualitatively if there are strong functional relations. Sometimes, an approximate functional relation with a larger error, which is only generated and evaluated by regression analysis, does not mean that it should be rejected but may be an interesting approximate regularity for some user.

Table 2. The discovered structural characteristics from the DB *stars*

Clusters	Polynomial regression models	σ^2	AIC
1	$Y = 4.83 + 0.08X_{lum} + \varepsilon$	0.0183	-140.303
3	$Y = 5.072 - 0.183X_{lum} + 0.044X_{lum}^2 + \varepsilon$	0.0125	-170.801
...	......	...	...
1	$Y = 4.987 + 0.337X_{b-v} - 0.2X_{b-v}^2 + \varepsilon$	0.0139	-173.207
2	$Y = 4.673 + 0.677X_{b-v} - 0.23X_{b-v}^2 + \varepsilon$	0.0285	-105.978
...	......	...	...

3 Management and Refinement

Since the discovered structural characteristics are finally denoted by regression models as stated in Section 2.2, the management and refinement of the structural characteristics are essentially the ones of regression models which are represented as the deductive rules and the sets of data for showing their errors. This section will describe in detail the management and refinement.

3.1 Inheritance Inference on Regression Models

Inheritance inference on regression models is a central work for managing/refining structural characteristics discovered from databases. Inheritance inference is used to find matches to models for similar situations to those under study, to give a starting model for analysis. A good starting model can save a user much time, and effective inference can also save storage space by eliminating the need to save similar models. Here, we would like to describe two kinds of inheritance inferences, *downward* and *upward* ones [13, 15], which can be mainly used for three purposes:

- Inferring the model for representing the structure of a sample data set when only know/use a sub-set of this data set.
- Inferring the varying degree of a model when the sample data set is partly updated (added/deleted).
- Refining/managing a family of regression models.

It is important that inheritances are quantified for their utility. That is, the strength of the inheritance inference is quantified, or numeric parameters inherited are themselves quantified. These quantizations assume that the data sets in a database are like simple random samples with respect to one another. Although exact-values and bounds derived from inheritance cannot be argued, estimates, which are the most common type of statistical inheritance, can be roughly quantified as to our certainty about the value derived. From a statistical point of view, this means finding standard errors of estimates in using statistics of related sets. If we can approximate the relationship between target and related set as a sampling process in either directions, we can use sampling theory for this [2, 13].

Theorem 1. If the mean of the set is approximately a mean of the superset, then the "approximate" has the standard error of

$$\tau = \sigma\sqrt{\frac{1}{n} - \frac{1}{N}}, \tag{2}$$

where n is the size of the set, N is the size of the superset, and σ is the standard deviation of the set or the superset.

Theorem 1 shows that the strength of inheritance is stronger the closer in size the two sets are. Sample theory also says the standard deviation of the set will be approximately the standard deviation of the superset, when n is not too small. Eq.(2) can be used as a criterion for selecting the best inheritance when there are more regression models that can be selected. That is, among all potential inheritance models, the one that produces the smallest τ value is the best model. However, Eq.(2) is not suitable for evaluating the strength of the inheritance between a set and its superset. This is because it is difficult that the threshold value for distinguishing meaningful inheritance is given in advance. Fortunately, if we know the standard deviations of both a set and its superset, F distribution can be used for quantifying evaluation.

Definition 7. We say there is a stronger inheritance relationship between a set and its superset if

$$F = \frac{\sigma_1^2}{\sigma_2^2} \le F_\alpha(n_1 - 1, n_2 - 1), \tag{3}$$

where σ_1^2 is of the set with larger variance among a set and its superset, n_1 and n_2 are the size of the sets with σ_1^2 and σ_2^2 respectively, and α is either 0.05 or 0.01. □

Eq.(3) is called an F distribution with the degrees of freedom $d.f. = (n_1\text{-}1, n_2\text{-}1)$. This question is whether σ_1^2/σ_2^2 is too far from 1 to be explained by chance. Note that unlike a comparison between two means, which is phrased in terms of the difference $\mu_1 - \mu_2$, a comparison between variances is formulated using the ratio σ_1^2/σ_2^2. This is because a sampling distribution that is instrumental to the present inference situation involves the variances σ_1^2 and σ_2^2 only through the ratio.

Example 3. Inheritance inference can be used for managing/refining the structural characteristic when the sample data in a database are partly updated (deleted/added). In order to describe *downward inheritance*, every cluster of the stars database is divided into *group-1* as a set for fundamental data as shown in Table 1, and *group-1-sub* as a sub-set of *group-1* by deleting some data from *group-1* for its variation. Let the size of *group-1* for $cluster_1$ be 126 and its variance be 0.0183, the size of *group-1-sub* for $cluster_1$ be 116 and its variance be 0.0173. Thus, using Eq.(3), we obtain $F = 1.058 < F_{0.05}(125, 115) \simeq 1.25$.

Example 4. We still use the stars database as an example for describing *upward inheritance*. Every cluster of the stars database is divided into *group-1* as a set for fundamental data, and *group-1-sup* as a superset of *group-1* by adding some data to *group-1* for its variation. Let the size of *group-1* for $cluster_1$ be 126 and its variance be 0.0183, the size of *group-1-sup* be 146 and its variance be 0.0313. Thus, using Eq.(3), we obtain $F = 1.71 > F_{0.05}(145, 125) \simeq 1.25$.

3.2 Knowledge Representation

This section describes a method of the knowledge representation. It is based on the expansion capability of Multi-Layer Logic [9, 10]. That is, when the domain set of a variable is finite, a formula of Multi-Layer Logic can be expanded according to the following equivalent expressions:

$$[\forall X/x]p(X) \cap x = \{x_1, x_2, \ldots, x_n\} \longrightarrow p(x_1) \cap p(x_2) \cap \ldots \cap p(x_n),$$
$$[\exists X/x]p(X) \cap x = \{x_1, x_2, \ldots, x_n\} \longrightarrow p(x_1) \cup p(x_2) \cup \ldots \cup p(x_n).$$

This capability is used for extracting from a set the elements which possess specified properties. It is syntactically defined by appending "#" after the variable to be expanded in the prefix of the Multi-Layer Logic formula. The following *Rule-1* is an example of using the expansion capability:

```
Rule-1: /* the rule for inferring the effective temperature of stars from the luminosity of stars */
!ins_e clusters 1, 3; /* use clusters 1, 3 */
!ins_e variance 0.0183, 0.0125; /* the variances of the regression models belonging to a family */
!ins_e ai-pr-1-0 4.83, 5.072; /* the coefficient A0 */
!ins_e ai-pr-1-1 0.08, -0.183; /* the coefficient A1 */
!ins_e ai-pr-1-2 0, 0.044; /* the coefficient A2 */
[∀ X-luminosity,Y-effTemp/float] [∀ Mode,Check-N/int]
[∀ A0#/ai-pr-1-0] [∀ A1#/ai-pr-1-1] [∀ A2#/ai-pr-1-2] /* declare the domains of variables */
( | (p-stars Mode Check-N Y-effTemp X-luminosity)
    /* infer the effective temperature from the luminosity */
    ~($pr 2 Y-effTemp A0 X-luminosity A1 A2)
    /* infer the effective temperature by the PR model */
    ~($scope_kb rule-set3) /* transfer to the world: rule-set3 */
    ~(storeInfor Mode Check-N pr Y-effTemp X-luminosity)
    /* store the inferred result and the variable */
).
```

Rule-1 is represented as a Multi-Layer Logic formula in the IF-THEN form and the data set called *variance* for showing the errors. Ordinary IF-THEN rules are represented in the form of $A_1 \& A_2 \ldots A_n \to B$, but it writes as $(| (B \sim A_1 \sim A_2 \ldots \sim A_n))$ in our system by using the knowledge-based system KAUS [10]. *Rule-1* reads "The effective temperature of stars can be inferred from the luminosity of stars by the polynomial regression model. As well as the effective temperature inferred will be saved for future use together with the luminosity". On the other hand, "$!ins\_e$ x $x_1 \ldots x_n$;" means $x_1 \ldots x_n$ are elements of x. It is the syntax used for representing the "set-element" relation in KAUS.

In particular, we see that in *Rule-1*, the symbol "#" denoted the expansion capability is used in the prefix of the Multi-Layer Logic formula (i.e., [∀ A0#/ai-pr-1-0] ...) and the regression coefficients are recorded in the sets *ai-pr-1-0* ∼ *ai-pr-1-2*. This is a kind of the model representation. That is, by means of the expansion capability, only the elements of sets are modified, but the Multi-Layer Logic formula (rule) is not generally changed when the refinement (or generalization) is done. For example, if the regression coefficients are changed (added or updated, e.g., the regression coefficients of the model got from *cluster*$_8$ are added), then only the values in the sets *ai-pr-1-0* ∼ *ai-pr-1-2* and *variance* are changed (added or updated).

3.3 Management

In our system, a rule chain and an inheritance graph corresponding to a family of regression models are used for management. By means of them, the following jobs can be done: (1) Regression models discovered from databases are first stored in the rule chain, and then are refined (evaluated/modified) by using the method to be described in Section 3.4; (2) The time and history of regression models are represented and managed. That is, the rule chain of storing regression models is dynamically generated as time goes on for recording the evolution process of regression models; (3) A suitable regression model is selected from a family of regression models by using the method as described in [15]; (4) The inheritance graph of regression models is dynamically generated for describing the relationship among regression models. The rule chain of regression models is defined by the set-elements relations and the Multi-Layer Logic formulae. The rule chain and the inheritance graph are managed by a meta knowledge level.

3.4 Refinement

Based on the preparation stated above, the method of refining the structural characteristics can be roughly described as follows:

> If the structural characteristics (regression models) were discovered, then store them first as the rules such as *Rule-1* shown in Section 3.2 in the dynamic worlds of a knowledge-base in the order of timing of which they were discovered.
>
> If there are more than two regression models, then start meta reasoning to the worlds storing the discovered regression models for finding their inheritance relationship.
>
> If there are two or more *true* in the results of meta reasoning and their answers are nearly same, then evaluate the strength of inheritance among them.
>
>> If there are more than two regression models for several sets and their superset, then first use Eq.(2) for selecting the best model from the ones corresponding to the sets, and use Eq.(3) for evaluating

the strength of inheritance between the selected best model and the model corresponding to its superset.

If there are only regression models corresponding to sibling sets or two models for a set and its superset, then use Eq.(3) for evaluating the strength of inheritance between them.

If Eq.(3) holds and the regression model discovered later has smaller variance, then store the coefficients and the variance value of the regression model discovered later, and delete the coefficients and the variance value of the elder regression model. And then delete the rule discovered later (i.e., delete the Multi-Layer Logic formula and the sets in which the coefficients and the variance value are stored), and create/revise the inheritance graph of a family of regression models.

If there are two or more *true* in the results of meta reasoning but the answers are different, then generalize the rules stored in the dynamic worlds (i.e., merge the Multi-Layer Logic formulae and the sets in which the coefficients and the variance value are recorded), and create/revise the inheritance graph of a family of regression models.

If there are not two or more *true* in the results of meta reasoning, then the rules stored in the dynamic worlds are not modified.

Example 5. After the refinement stated above was done for the cases described in Examples 3 and 4, *Rule-1* is changed into the following *Rule-2*:

Rule-2: /* the rule for inferring the effective temperature of stars from the luminosity of stars */
!ins_e clusters **1-sub, 1-sup**, 3; /* use a subset and superset of cluster-1, and cluster-3 */
!ins_e variance **0.0173, 0.0313**, 0.0125;
     /* the variances of the regression models belonging to a family */
!ins_e ai-pr-1-0 **4.856, 4.673**, 5.072; /* the coefficient A0 */
!ins_e ai-pr-1-1 **0.075, -0.0235**, -0.183; /* the coefficient A1 */
!ins_e ai-pr-1-2 **0, 0.2116**, 0.044; /* the coefficient A2 */
[∀ X-luminosity,Y-effTemp/float] [∀ Mode,Check-N/int]
[∀ A0#/ai-pr-1-0][∀ A1#/ai-pr-1-1] [∀ A2#/ai-pr-1-2]
(| (p-stars Mode Check-N Y-effTemp X-luminosity)
     ~($pr 2 Y-effTemp A0 X-luminosity A1 A2)
     ~($scope_kb rule-set3)
     ~(storeInfor Mode Check-N pr Y-effTemp X-luminosity)
).

Where, the parts denoted in the bold type style are the ones that were revised. That is, we see that the regression model for *group-1* is replaced by the one for *group-1-sub* because there is the stronger inheritance relationship between them and the variance of the regression model for *group-1-sub* is smaller than the one for *group-1*; and the regression model for *group-1-sup* is added because there is not the stronger inheritance relationship between the regression models for *group-1-sup* and *group-1-sub*. In this case, the corresponding inheritance graph for *cluster₁* is as follows:

!ins_e *reg-inheritance-graph-cluster1 r1, r2;
     /* reg-models *r1* and *r2* in the inheritance-graph for cluster1 */
!ins_e r1 reg-model, reg-down; /* r1 is the downward inheritance model of the *reg-model* */
!ins_e r2 reg-model, reg-up; /* r2 is the upward inheritance model of the *reg-model* */.

4 Conclusion

We presented a multi-step process for discovering, managing and refining strong functional relations hidden in databases. That is, we described a more whole discovery process including generation/evaluation and management/refinement. We support qualitative/quantitative discovery, process the data with more uncertainty and data change, and control the discovery process by combining AI techniques with statistical methods in multiple learning phases. This discovery process described in this paper is the basic one that is executed in our GLS discovery system [14, 17].

Several issues remain to be investigated. Currently, the capabilities for management and refinement in our system involve mainly one of two main aspects, i.e., how to manage and refine the discovered strong functional relations when the data in a database were updated (added/deleted). Another important aspect belonging to management and refinement is how to acquire the more high-level knowledge from several strong functional relations discovered from databases. The development of this aspect is a further extension for the discovery process described in this paper. We need to use more domain knowledge for this.

References

1. Akaike, H. A New Look at The Statistical Model Identification. *IEEE Trans. Autom. Contr.*, AC-19 (1974) 716-723.
2. Cochran, W.G. *Sample Techniques*. Wiley, (1977).
3. Falkenhainer, B.C. & Michalski, R.S. Integrating Quantitative and Qualitative Discovery in the ABACUS System. *R.S. Michalski et al. (eds.) Machine Learning - An Artificial Intelligence Approach*, Morgan Kaufmann Publishers (1990) 153-190.
4. Forbus, K.D. Qualitative Process Theory. *Artificial Intelligence*, Vol.24 (1984) 95-168.
5. Hoschka, P. & Klosgen, W. A Support System for Interpreting Statistical Data. *Piatetsky-Shapiro and Frawley (eds.) Knowledge Discovery in Databases* (1991) 325-345.
6. Langley, P., Simon, H.A., Bradshaw, G.L. & Zytkow, J.M. *Scientific Discovery - Computational Explorations of the Creative Processes* (MIT Press, 1987).
7. Langley, P. & Zytkow, J.M. Data-Driven Approaches to Empirical Discovery. *Artificial Intelligence*, Vol.40(No.1-3) (1989) 283-312.
8. Mavrovouniotis, M. & Stephanopoulos, G. Reasoning with Orders of Magnitude and Approximate Relations. *Proc. AAAI-87* (1987) 626-630.
9. Ohsuga, S. & Yamauchi, H. Multi-Layer Logic - A Predicate Logic Including Data Structure as Knowledge Representation Language. *New Generation Computing*, Vol.3(No.4) (1985) 403-439.
10. Ohsuga, S. Framework of Knowledge Based Systems. *Knowl. Based Sys.*, Vol.3(No.4) (1990) 204-214.
11. Piatetsky-Shapiro, G. Discovery, Analysis, and Presentation of Strong Rules. *Piatetsky-Shapiro and Frawley (eds.) Knowledge Discovery in Databases*, AAAI/MIT Press (1991) 229-248.
12. Piskunov A.E. Bull. Inf. CDS, 19, 67, (1980).
13. Rowe, N.C. Managemnet of Regression-model Data. *Data & Knowl. Eng.*, Vol.6(No.4) (1991) 349-363.
14. Zhong, N. & Ohsuga, S. The GLS Discovery System: Its Goal, Architecture and Current Results. *Proc. 8th Inter. Symp. on Methodologies for Intell. Sys. (ISMIS'94)*. LNAI 869 (1994) 233-244.
15. Zhong, N. & Ohsuga, S. Managing/Refining Structural Characteristics Discovered from Databases. *Proc. 28th Hawaii Int. Conf. on Sys. Sciences (HICSS-28)* (1995) Vol.3:283-292.
16. Zhong, N. & Ohsuga, S. KOSI - An Integrated System for Discovering Functional Relations from Databases. *J. of Intell. Infor. Sys.* (KAP, 1995) 5(1).
17. Zhong, N. & Ohsuga, S. Toward A Multi-Strategy and Cooperative Discovery System. *Proc. First Int. Conf. on Knowledge Discovery and Data Mining (KDD-95)* (1995) 337-342.
18. Zytkow, J.M. & Zembowicz, R. Database Exploration in Search of Regularities. *J. of Intell. Infor. Sys.*, Vol.2(No.1) (KAP, 1993) 39-81.

An Architecture and Methodology for the Design and Development of Technical Information Systems*

R. Capobianchi[1] and M. Mautref[1] and M. van Keulen[2] and H. Balsters[2]

[1] Alcatel Alsthom Recherche, Route de Nozay, 91460 Marcoussis, France,
{capobian;mautref}@aar.alcatel-alsthom.fr
[2] University of Twente, Dept. of CS, P.O. Box 217, 7500 AE Enschede, The Netherlands,
{keulen;balsters}@cs.utwente.nl

Abstract. In order to meet demands in the context of Technical Information Systems (TIS) pertaining to reliability, extensibility, maintainability, etc., we have developed an architectural framework with accompanying methodological guidelines for designing such systems. With the framework, we aim at complex multi-application information systems using a repository to share data among applications. The framework proposes to keep a strict separation between Man-Machine-Interface and Model data, and provides design and implementation support to do this effectively.

The framework and methodological guidelines have been developed in the context of the ESPRIT project IMPRESS. The project also provided for "testing grounds" in the form of a TIS for the Spanish Electricity company Iberdrola.

1 Introduction

The software engineering discipline advances both in the direction of better efficiency and effectiveness, as well as in the direction of expanding its application area. A significant part of these advancements can be attributed to the availability of increasingly powerful methodologies and accompanying tools. This has made it possible to build larger and more complex information systems (IS). Examples of these are CASE systems (some even with facilities for cooperative work), GIS's, CIM systems, etc. However, the design and development of these systems demands more from methodologies and tools than they currently often provide. For example, ever more strict requirements for reliability and extensibility emerge.

In the IMPRESS project (ESPRIT 6355), we have focussed on Technical Information Systems (TIS) which is a generalizing term for the aforementioned systems. A TIS can be defined as follows [BCMM94]:

A Technical Information System (TIS) is an active repository of all the information describing a product (e.g. a physical system) or process: design models (structure, functions, behaviour), logistic support data (maintenance plans, operation procedures), documentation of the product and components, experimental knowledge issued from and supporting its operation, repair pieces and so on.

---

* This work has been conducted within the ESPRIT project IMPRESS (Integrated, Multi-Paradigm, Reliable and Extensible Storage System), ESPRIT № 6355

These data are typically produced by the various processes occurring during the product life-cycle: preliminary studies, design, manufacturing, production, deployment and exploitation. Each process retrieves the available information on the product required for its own treatments, and feeds the TIS with results that may be used afterwards by other processes.

In the project, we have built an object-oriented DBMS with special facilities for things that are needed in TIS's like multi-media. To build a TIS, of course, more is required than an OODBMS. We have devised a common architecture for TIS's and special methodological guidelines for the design and development of TIS's for this architecture. The IMPRESS system is accompanied by an extensive array of tools (the IMPRESS support toolkit) supporting this methodology, ranging from general database and user-interface design tools to TIS special purpose tools.

Because TIS's are generally distributed systems, we have paid special attention to this aspect. We have chosen for a repository-based approach meaning that the system is divided into a (possibly distributed) repository containing all shared data, and various independent applications performing specific tasks making use of the shared data in the repository. This architecture is further detailed in section 2. Section 3 gives a brief review of the properties of existing OO methodologies. This section will concentrate on those properties that are especially useful or problematic for the design and development of TIS's. Section 4 will then explain the specific methodological guidelines for IMPRESS. These guidelines work specifically towards the aforementioned architecture. It also describes the accompanying tools.

2 A common architecture for TIS

An IS like a TIS can be functionally decomposed in many parts, however, two major components could be identified: the management of the dialogue between the user and the system, and the management of the real world system. Those elements correspond to the various functions expected by the system end-user.

From the design point of view, we can define the *Model* part of a TIS as the gathering of all the necessary data and functions needed to provide the requested functionality of the application, which is mainly decision-making support based on access to a set of data. Typically, the model is a representation of what is usually called the UoD (Universe of Discourse). Its description should be directly based on the analysis of the real system and should only use terms relevant to the UoD.

One of the interests of designing an extensive model of a real-world system is that it allows the development of many different applications based on the same UoD. In order to make full use of this interest, the Model component may be split into two parts: a shared Model part (reused and shared by all the applications, managed by a database to function as a persistent data repository) and an application-specific Model part (extension of the shared Model to meet the specific demands of a particular application).

In order to distinguish such different Model parts, we have chosen to define the TIS *Database* component as the shared Model part and the TIS *Model View* component as the complete Model needed for a specific application. The Model View will be composed of the relevant subset of the Database, enhanced with specific data needed by the application and not present in the Database, in other words, it defines an enhanced view over the Database [AB90, Ber91].

One of the main functions of the TIS will be to allow the consultation of Model View data by the end-user. Such interaction with the end-user is handled by another TIS component which we call the *Man-Machine Interface* (MMI). The aim of this component is to display the information to the operator in an efficient and useful way. It should also provide ways for the user to act on and modify the displayed information (e.g. actions on buttons or graphical representations of real objects, text editing, ...). More generally, all the multi-media information and the hyper-media navigation could be seen as part of the MMI. In other words, its aim is to translate end-user actions into computer actions by analyzing the requests and triggering the proper functions provided by other software components of the system. Reciprocally, it should interpret display requests, coming from the system, in order to communicate information to the end-user.

In systems designed for novice computer users, the metaphor of direct manipulation of objects by their graphical representations is more and more used [Hud87]. Clearly, this kind of MMI, based on user-driven interaction, seems to be more natural and easier to learn and use for an end-user of the system who is not a computer expert. In terms of computer implementation, this type of interaction needs a relatively complex architecture, mainly due to the huge number of end-user possible actions [Mye89, Hud87].

The main issue encountered while designing and implementing a TIS with Database, Model and MMI parts is the danger to mix together the different parts of the system without taking care of the distribution of responsibilities. This approach always leads to a very tightly-coupled design which raises lots of problems such as software complexity, reusability, evolutivity, maintenance or reliability of the system [HH89].

In the field of MMI design, one of the proposed answers to this problem is to impose a strict separation between the MMI and other parts of the application. Following the Seeheim model [Pfa85], the Model-View-Controller metaphor introduced by Smalltalk [Gol84, PK88] or the multi-agent architecture PAC [Cou90], the MMI and application parts should be separated by a dialog controller responsible for the communication and translation between them. An advantage is the identification of strict responsibilities. Unfortunately, much confusion exists regarding the responsibilities of the Controller.

Ensuring a clear separation between Model part and MMI part and clarifying the position of the Database, we propose to adopt an architectural decomposition of a TIS, that extends the controller approach to multi-application systems like TISs. This decomposition identifies four main parts (see figure 1) :

- *MMI*. This part is composed of objects like windows, buttons, and menus and is in charge of the interaction with the end-user of the application. The provided functionality only deals with the graphical aspect and user event handling. The part only uses "MMI terms"" (e.g. colors, pixels, mouse events, etc.)
- *Model View*. This part describes the functionality of a specific application. The functionality provided by the objects in this part only reflect the ones found in the real system and only use "Model terms" (e.g. substations, voltage, switch state 'on' or 'off'). The data is split in two parts : application-specific objects and shared objects.
- *Translator*. This part synchronizes MMI events with Model View functions to ensure that the Model always faithfully represents the information displayed in the

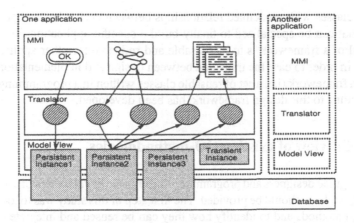

Fig. 1. Example of TIS decomposition

MMI, and the output of the MMI always faithfully represents the Model. To achieve this, the part is responsible for the translation of MMI modifications into Model modifications, and vice versa. (e.g. : if model-object.voltage = 220 KV then MMI-object.color := red).

– *Database*. The objects in this part will be shared among one or more different applications. Such objects will be persistent (i.e. they will survive sessions). The functionality provided by the Database is going to be used to build each specific Model View (common data part).

The expected advantages of this approach are the enhancement of the quality of the design on the following points :

– *Evolutivity* and *maintainability*. Modification of the MMI design (often required to integrate the final user requirements) will have less impact on Model design, and the MMI is be protected against modification of Model object implementation by the Translator.

– *Reusability of Database*. The Model View specializes the Model in the Database allowing some disparity with the fixed database schema and the use of the same database for one or more applications.

– *Modularity*. The separation between the different parts allows the use of different tools (or languages) for Model and MMI development. It also allows to deal with the distribution of the system and the use of communication protocols.

Figure 1 shows an example of TIS decomposition. In this example, two applications have been defined on the same Database. Each Model View is composed of persistent objects, coming from the Database, and transient objects specific to each application. The presentation to the end-user is handled by the MMI component and the coherency management between Model View and MMI is assumed by the Translator part. The arrows represent possible links between objects belonging to different layers.

The decomposition of a TIS in MMI, Translator, Model View and Database objects results in the definition of an *object-oriented framework* [FJ88]. A framework is composed of classes with predefined relationships between each other and predefined behaviour that can be specialized to finally build a specific application. In fact, the primary goal of a framework is to be reusable and refinable for other application developments. In order to ease the transition between design and implementation, an implementation framework (i.e. a set of reusable classes written in a programming language), corresponding to this design framework, has been developed.

3 Brief review of existing OO-methodologies

In order to guide designers and programmers through the development of a TIS, methodological guidelines should be provided. The first step of this study was to look at general OO design methods and to identify how they can be reused and integrated in a proper methodology for TIS development within the IMPRESS environment.

Many methodologies have recently appeared to help a designer of object-oriented (OO) software. Those methodologies adopt more or less different approaches concerning design policies or decomposition in phases. In general, however, they all provide different models for the various views on a system one can have:

- a *static model*, representing the structural aspect of the system, i.e. the attributes and static relationships between objects (e.g. composition, inheritance, instantiation, grouping).
- a *collaboration model*, describing the cooperative side of the system, i.e. the static properties of object interactions (client-server dependencies, the data flow, etc.)
- a *behavioural model*, describing at object level the actions objects can perform, and at system level inter-object behaviour (state transition diagrams, scenarios, etc.)

While studying the different methodologies, we learned that, although these models are general, there are basically two approaches concerning modelling. The first approach, which we have called *data-driven*, focuses on a "natural" data model first, and then enhances the model with, from the UoD's point of view, logical behaviour [CY90, Boo91, RBP+91]. We have called the other approach *responsibility-driven*, because it pays attention to the responsibilities (i.e. behaviour) first and then focuses on the information an object needs to perform the required functionality [Mey88, WBWW90]. Also, not every model seems to be as fruitful or even wanted for the different parts in our architecture. For example, a collaboration model for application objects is perhaps the most interesting and important model, while such a model doesn't clarify much for database objects.

The data-driven approach is an adaptation of ADT (Abstract Data Type) design methods for object-orientation. Firstly, the structure of the "real world" is modelled as closely as possible. Attention is paid to identifying classes, attributes, relationships that exist between those classes (e.g. aggregation, subtyping), and which of the possible states of the objects are valid. Based on this model, one tries to find the operations that the objects must logically be able to perform. We have observed that the resulting model is quite "natural", i.e. it reflects the UoD, and is therefore easily readable. Its high task independence makes the need for change as a consequence of changing demands low. The weak points are, for example, that it may contain more functionality than is actually needed, and the stress on the data results in a model with little large scale functionality.

The responsibility-driven approach is almost an anti-pole. It focuses firstly on structuring the task of an application by dividing responsibilities among the objects. It uses the same modelling primitives (i.e. classes, subtyping, etc.). The attributes of an object follow naturally from the information that is needed for the object to fulfill its responsibility, and, as a result, encapsulation of these attributes is quite natural. An advantage of this approach is that the design is geared towards providing the necessary functionality with the least effort possible. However, as a result, the design is rather specific for the target application and, therefore, changing demands almost always call for changes in the design. On the other hand, changing the design can be done without much effort because of the high data independence.

Although both approaches appear to exclude each other, one need not make an absolute choice. For example, in the responsibility-driven approach, one may decide to refrain from deviating too much from the logical structure of the UoD. It depends on the purpose of the design which of both approaches is likely to work best. We advise to use the data-driven approach for the design of the repository (i.e. database design), because it is often not known what future applications may use it for and, therefore, task independence is a useful property. However, for designing the applications that use this repository, the responsibility-driven approach is likely work well, because the application's task is often clear and the less effort needed is a nice feature. The methodology described in the following section reflects this advise.

4 Methodological guidelines for TIS design

As explained earlier, we have directed our attention concerning methodology towards the specifics of developing TIS's. The common architecture of section 2 forms the basis of our methodological guidelines. We have thought about what guidelines and tools we could give for developing the architectural components. Another issue is a logical order of design and development of these architectural components. In dividing the development of a TIS into phases, we also took notice of the fact that in technical environments, people tend to consider instantiation (i.e. data entry) as part of IS development.

To illustrate the phases in the proposed global development process, the demonstrator application of the IMPRESS project is used as a running example. The demonstrator concerns a TIS for the Spanish electricity company Iberdrola. The users of the system are operators of an electrical network. Their task is to control the flow of electricity inside the system and efficiently and effectively react on malfunctions of electrical components in the network. To be able to do that, the operators need facilities to simulate the effects of possible actions on electricity flow before actually performing these operations in reality. Their tasks also involve retrieving information about the structure of the network, maintenance information, procedures to be followed, and other textual and schematic documentation. Because of the large amounts of information available, advanced querying facilities are required [BCMM94].

Figure 2 shows the proposed global development process. The design phase has been subdivided into the design of each of the four architectural components. Although there

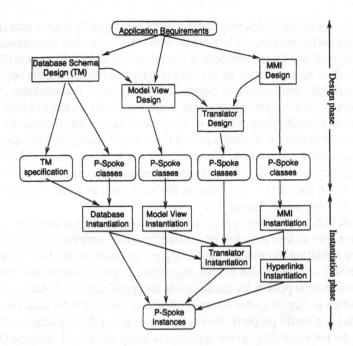

Fig. 2. Global development process

is much freedom to do things in parallel, there are some input/output dependencies between them (see Figure 2). In the sequel, all phases pass the review explaining what each phase is for, which guidelines apply there, and what tool support we provide.

Reliability is in the context of TIS's an important issue. Therefore, we have chosen to base database design on the formal specification language TM [BBZ93, BBdB+95]. The ability to do more advanced kinds of verifications and validations of the schema other than simple syntactical checks is a big advantage. The gentle force imposed on the designer to be more exact also adds to the quality of the resulting schema. By offering a designer high-level OO language constructs and embedding the language in a toolset, he is shielded against the burdens a more formal treatment brings with it [FKS94a, FKS94b]. In the project, we have, together with Iberdrola, specified a database schema, using the data-driven approach, for storing the network configuration and its state.

Based on the database schema of the repository, the *model view*, which is like an external schema in the ANSI/SPARC architecture, can be designed for a particular application. It contains a subset of the classes of the database schema supplemented with application dependent classes for both persistent and transient data. We have decided to do application programming in the programming language PSPOKE, which is a SmallTalk-like "pure" OO language with facilities for persistency (it uses the object server GEODE for this [BHPT]). To achieve a smooth connection between the schema of the repository designed in TM and the model views, we have developed a TM-to-PSPOKE translator, that translates both the structural part of the schema (i.e. the class specifications) as well as the behavioural part (i.e. the constraint and method specifications).

Almost completely parallel to the design of the database and an application's model view, one can design the MMI. For this, the IMPRESS support toolkit provides the Motif GUI design tool CAID which, among other things, takes care of generating almost all PSPOKE code for the GUI. Because a lot of useful results have already been achieved in the area of GUI design, we have not substantial methodological guidelines for GUI design. We did, however, develop a tool (the Synoptic Editor) for designing diagram languages, because in TIS's a lot of schematics is used (e.g. a global view of the network structure, electrical schemas of various levels of detail).

As explained earlier, the greater part of the results of research towards methodology done in IMPRESS, has been in providing a good connection (the Translator) between the MMI and the model view while still leaving them as independent as possible. Because of the way we have defined the translator component, almost all of its design can be taken care of by a tool called POTOMAC. For example, one can define graphically that instances of class Powerplant are represented in the GUI by a specific symbol and that the specific states of a power plant (e.g. operational/nonoperational, hydraulic/nuclear/thermal) are represented by several variations of the symbol (e.g. using color). POTOMAC takes care of generating the code for this including support for automatic propagation of changes in either the GUI or the Model View to the other one.

The result of these design activities is on one hand a TM specification of the database schema and, on the other hand, a PSPOKE program of the application. However, in case of a TIS, this is not considered to be a complete system. Before a TIS can be made operational, it must already contain a significant amount of information. For example, (digital scans of) manuals, detailed schematics of the various electrical circuits, the structure of the electrical network, etc. all being hyperlinked together and supplemented with (cross-)indexes to enable an operator to retrieve all, for his particular situation, relevant information. In the IMPRESS support toolkit, tools for the various kinds of instantiation are provided, for example, a multi-media instance editor for creating multi-media documents, a hyperlinks editor, and many more. Some of the tools aid both in the design and instantiation phases, for example, POTOMAC and the Synoptic Editor. We've also developed an experimental tool for information retrieval called COLORADO, because, as mentioned before, one of the most prominent difficulties for an operator is how to obtain relevant information about a particular crisis situation in the least time possible in order to be able to react to the situation before too much damage has been done.

As a final remark, we note that, of course, database design is not always necessary. Usually, only a new application for an existing repository is required and therefore database design has already been done. Sometimes however, the repository may need some extra functionality which means that some database design has to be performed.

5 Conclusions

Cooperation between end-user companies and research institutions in the context of an ESPRIT project has proven to be fruitful for testing and refining ideas. In the IMPRESS project, this cooperation has led to a well-balanced design and implementation framework for developing Technical Information Systems. The framework proposes an architecture and provides design and implementation support, as well as methodological guidelines to effectively develop TIS's using this framework.

The expected results of maintainability, reusability, and modularity as listed in section 2 have been achieved quite satisfactorily with readily available technology[2]

In the project, we focused on practical usability of the framework and methodological guidelines. There has already been an abundance of research done in the realm of methodology [Boo91, CY90, Mey88, RBP+91, WBWW90], and it has been our incentive to apply this acquired knowledge to the particular application domain of TIS. As a result of this investigation, we came to incorporate database instantiation as part of the global development process, because for a TIS to be useful, it must already contain a lot of information, and because of the crucial nature and the amount of work involved in filling the database, this activity should be addressed during development.

Another issue that was thoroughly investigated for this purpose was the controversy between data- and responsibility-driven design. It turned out that the one is not better than the other, but that both are suitable for different purposes; the data-driven approach is more suitable for the design of the shared Model, while the responsibility-driven approach is more suitable for application-specific design.

To summarize the above, the IMPRESS project offered us the opportunity to bring ideas about methodology into practice in the specific domain of TIS. In the process of developing an architectural framework for building TISs, the subjects of database instantiation and data- vs. responsibility-driven design proved to be major issues. Also, by working towards a common architecture for TISs, it became possible to provide good support for the development process in the form of a design and implementation framework combined with practical methodological guidelines.

Acknowledgements

We would like to thank our partners[3] for a successful project. Concerning the topic of this paper, we'd like to thank in particular Rolf de By (University of Twente), Enrique Burguera (Iberdrola), and Florence Ardorino (Alcatel Alsthom Recherche) for their contributions.

References

[AB90]   S. Abiteboul and A. Bonner. Objects and views. Technical report, INRIA, 1990.

[ACM+94]   F. Ardorino,   R. Capobianchi,   M. Mautref,   R.A. de   By, and M. van Keulen. Methodological guidelines for IMPRESS. Technical Report IMPRESS/AAR-TECH-W4-005-R0, Alcatel Alsthom Recherche, Route de Nozay, 91460 Marcoussis, France, November 1994.

[BBdB+95] R. Bal, H. Balsters, R. A. de By, A. Bosschaart, J. Flokstra, M. van Keulen, J. Skowronek, and B. Termorshuizen. *The TM Manual version 2.0 revision E.* University of Twente, Enschede, The Netherlands, June 1995.

---

[2] We'd also like to mention that the demonstrator application of the project won a prize in the Second Edition of the Prizes to Companies and Institutions in the Basque Country in the field of the application and development of information technologies [BMA95].

[3] Companies and universities participating in the IMPRESS project are: Alcatel ISR (France), EDS (France), Alcatel Alsthom Recherche (France), Iberdrola (Spain), Bureau Van Dijk (Belgium), University of Twente (The Netherlands)

[BBZ93]   H. Balsters, R.A. de By, and R. Zicari. Typed sets as a basis for object-oriented database schemas. In *Proceedings 7th European Conference on Object-Oriented Programming (ECOOP), July 26–30, 1993, Kaiserslautern, Germany*, 1993.

[BCMM94] E. Burguera, R. Capobianchi, F. Marquinez, and M. Mautref. A technical information system for a dispatching control center. In *Proceedings of ISAP'94 (Intelligent System Application to Power systems), Montpellier, France*, September 1994.

[Ber91]   E. Bertino. A view mechanism for object-oriented databases. Technical report, Universita di Genova, 1991.

[BHPT]   J. Besancenot, L. Hammami, P. Pucheral, and J.-M. Thévenin. Geode, a multi-threaded storage object library for advanced transactional applications.

[BMA95]   E. Burguera, F. Marquinez, and I. Angulo. SITED: Systema de informacion tecnica de despacho de maniobras. *PC Week Magazine*, supplement 263, may 1995.

[Boo91]   G. Booch. *Object oriented design with applications*. Benjamin/Cunnings series in Ada and software engineering. Benjamin/Cummings, 1991.

[Cou90]   J. Coutaz. Interface homme-ordinateur - conception et réalisation. Technical report, Dunod, April 1990.

[CY90]   P. Coad and E. Yourdon. *Object-oriented analysis*. Yourdon Press computing series. Yourdon Press, Prentice-Hall, 1990.

[FJ88]   B. Foote and R.E. Johnson. Designing reusable classes. *Journal of Object-Oriented Programming*, June 1988.

[FKS94a]   J. Flokstra, M. van Keulen, and J. Skowronek. IMPRESS database design tool: a high-level design toolset based on formal theory. In *Exhibition and Demonstration program of the 8th european conference on object-oriented programming (ECOOP), Bologna, Italy, July 4–8, 1994*, July 1994.

[FKS94b]   J. Flokstra, M. van Keulen, and J. Skowronek. The IMPRESS DDT: A database design toolbox based on a formal specification language. In R.T. Snodgrass and M. Winslett, editors, *Proceedings of the 1994 ACM SIGMOD International Conference on Management of Data, Minneapolis, Minnesota, May 24-27, 1994*, volume 23, page 506, 1994.

[Gol84]   A. Goldberg. *Smalltalk-80: The Interactive Programming Environment*. Addison-Wesley, 1984.

[HH89]   D. Hix and H.R. Hartson. Human-computer interface development: Concepts and systems for its management. *ACM Computing Surveys*, 21(1), March 1989.

[Hud87]   S.E. Hudson. UIMS support for direct manipulation interfaces. *Computer Graphics*, 21(2), April 1987.

[Mey88]   B. Meyer. *Object-Oriented software construction*. Prentice-Hall international series in computer science. Prentice-Hall, 1988.

[Mye89]   B.A. Myers. User-interface tools: Introduction and survey. *IEEE Software*, January 1989.

[Pfa85]   G.E. Pfaff. *User Interface Management Systems*. Eurographics Seminars. Springer-Verlag, 1985.

[PK88]   S.T. Pope and G.E. Krasner. A cookbook for using the Model-View-Controller user interface paradigm in Smalltalk-80. *Journal of Object-Oriented Programming*, August 1988.

[RBP+91]   J. Rumbaugh, M. Blaha, W. Premeriani, F. Eddy, and W. Lorensen. *Object-Oriented Modeling and Design*. Prentice-Hall, 1991.

[WBWW90] R. Wirfs-Brock, B. Wilkerson, and L. Wiener. *Designing Object Oriented Software*. Prentice-Hall, 1990.

Explaining Explanation Closure

Patrick Doherty[1] and Witold Łukaszewicz[2] and Andrzej Szałas[2]

[1] Department of Computer and Information Science
Linköping University, S-58183 Linköping, Sweden
patdo@ida.liu.se
[2] Institute of Informatics
Warsaw University, 00-913 Warsaw 59, Poland
(witlu,szalas)@mimuw.edu.pl

Abstract. Recently, Haas, Schubert, and Reiter, have developed an alternative approach to the frame problem which is based on the idea of using *explanation closure axioms*. The claim is that there is a monotonic solution for characterizing nonchange in serial worlds with fully specified actions, where one can have both a succinct representation of frame axioms and an effective proof theory for the characterization. In the paper, we propose a circumscriptive version of explanation closure, PMON, that has an effective proof theory and works for both context dependent and nondeterministic actions. The approach retains representational succinctness and a large degree of elaboration tolerance, since the process of generating closure axioms is fully automated and is of no concern to the knowledge engineer. In addition, we argue that the monotonic/nonmonotonic dichotomy proposed by others is not as sharp as previously claimed and is not fully justified.

1 Introduction

Recently, Haas [6], Schubert [16], and Reiter [13], have developed an alternative approach to the frame problem which is based on the idea of using *explanation closure axioms*. The claim is that for characterizing nonchange in serial worlds with fully specified actions, one can have both a succinct representation of frame axioms and an effective proof theory for the characterization. In Schubert's case, the downside is that the explanation closure axioms which are essential to the approach, must be generated manually. In fact, Schubert claims that since the closure axioms are generally domain dependent there is little chance of automating their generation. Reiter fares somewhat better in this respect, because he can generate closure axioms for a restricted class of problems by using a meta theoretic-assumption of completeness together with syntactic transformations applied to action effect axioms. On the other hand, both approaches are limited to deterministic actions and are subject to limitations inherent in the situation calculus.

Briefly, the proposal suggests that rather than generating one frame axiom for each action-fluent pair in a theory, one can generate one (two in the case of Reiter) explanation closure axiom per fluent. Each axiom characterizes the only explanations for a fluent changing value. The explanations are characterized in terms of the actions which potentially effect the fluent. In Schubert [16], an explanation closure axiom is added to an action theory for each fluent. For example, in a robot scenario, given the fluent *Holding* and a number of actions which include *Putdown* and *Drop*, Schubert ([16], p. 27) proposes the following closure axiom,

$$(\forall a, x, s, s')[[Holding(R, x, s) \land \neg Holding(R, x, s') \land s' = Result(a, s)]$$
$$\supset a \in \{Putdown(R, x), Drop(R, x)\}], \quad (1)$$

where $a \in \{a_1, \ldots, a_n\}$ abbreviates $a = a_1 \lor, \ldots, \lor a = a_n$. This states that the only explanations for the robot R ceasing to hold an object x are the actions *Putdown* and *Drop*.

The basic idea is that when given an action theory describing the effects of actions, and possibly including domain constraints, one manually constructs the necessary closure axioms and adds them to the theory. The original theory together with the closure axioms allows one to reason monotonically about the action scenario characterized. The claim is that not only does one avoid the use of nonmonotonic logics, but one also avoids the space complexity associated with the original approach. Throughout the paper, we will focus on Schubert's work, but much of the discussion should apply to any approach using explanation closure that claims to provide a monotonic solution to the frame problem.

Schubert claims to provide "evidence that explanation closure axioms provide a succinct encoding of nonchange in serial worlds with fully specified actions". He also claims that "they also offer advantages over circumscriptive and non-monotonic approaches, in that they relate nonchange to intuitively transparent explanations for change, retain an effective proof theory, and avoid unwarranted persistence inferences".

In this paper, we provide evidence against the claims concerning circumscriptive and nonmonotonic approaches in the following manner. We first present a slightly modified version of PMON ([15], [2]), a logic of action and change, which uses circumscription and is nonmonotonic. PMON can be viewed as a circumscriptive presentation of explanation closure, although the original proposal was made independently of the explanation closure approaches. The implicit non-monotonicity inherent in the "monotonic" solution to the frame problem characterized by explanation closure, is made explicit in the context of PMON. We show that PMON

1. relates nonchange to intuitively transparent explanations for change;
2. retains an effective proof theory;
3. and avoids unwarranted persistence inferences,

unlike a number of other circumscriptive approaches. In addition,

- the equivalent of explanation closure axioms are automatically generated by reducing the circumscription axiom used in PMON to a logically equivalent first-order formula;

- our approach works for a class of problems which includes both non-deterministic and context-dependent actions;
- a smaller number of general axioms may be used due to our use of fluent variables.

Finally, we claim that the distinction between the explanation closure approach as being "monotonic", and circumscriptive approaches as being "non-monotonic" is not fully justified. In this respect, we agree with Lifschitz [10], and also supply evidence "that a circumscriptive presentation of explanation closure may lead to a generalization of this method that will be applicable to nondeterministic actions".[3]

2   Action Scenarios and $\mathcal{L}(FL)$

The formal syntax for specifying scenario descriptions is defined in terms of a surface language $\mathcal{L}(SD)$, consisting of action occurrence statements (ac1,ac2), action (law) schemas (acs1,acs2), and observation statements (obs1). In what follows, all expressions occurring in scenario descriptions will be prefixed. We shall use the symbols "obs", "ac" and "acs" to denote observation statements, action occurrence statements and action schemas, respectively.

Example 1. The following is the Yale shooting scenario (below *al* and *l* are fluent constants standing for *alive* and *loaded*, respectively, while *Load* and *Fire* are action symbols).

> obs1 [0] $al \wedge \neg l$
> ac1 [2,4] $Load$
> ac2 [5,6] $Fire$
> acs1 $[t_1,t_2]$ $Load \rightsquigarrow [t_1,t_2]$ $l := T$
> acs2 $[t_1,t_2]$ $Fire \rightsquigarrow ([t_1]$ $l \rightarrow [t_1,t_2](al \wedge l) := F)$.

Given a scenario description Υ, consisting of statements in the surface language $\mathcal{L}(SD)$, these statements can be translated into formulas in the language $\mathcal{L}(FL)$ via a two-step process. In the first step, action schemas in Υ are instantiated with action occurrence statements, resulting in what are called *schedule statements*. The resulting schedule statements replace the action schemas and action occurrence statements. The result is an *expanded (action) scenario description* Υ', consisting of both schedule and observation statements. In the second step, abbreviation definitions are used to translate statements in Υ' into formulas in $\mathcal{L}(FL)$.

The language $\mathcal{L}(FL)$ is a sorted first-order language with sorts for fluents, actions, and temporal entities. The surface language $\mathcal{L}(SD)$ serves as a convenient set of macros for representing action scenarios. Formal reasoning is done in $\mathcal{L}(FL)$. The notation for an action scenario in $\mathcal{L}(FL)$ is

$$\Gamma_C = \Gamma_{OBS} \cup \Gamma_{SCD} \cup \Gamma_{UNA},$$

---

[3] [10], p. 11.

where Γ_{OBS} and Γ_{SCD} are translations of the observation and schedule statements in the surface language into $\mathcal{L}(FL)$, respectively, while Γ_{UNA} are the unique names axioms for the respective sorts in $\mathcal{L}(FL)$.

The use of $\mathcal{L}(FL)$ and $\mathcal{L}(SD)$ should be clear from the examples in Section 5. See [2] and [1] for detailed definitions of both languages and the translation process.

3 PMON Circumscription

PMON was originally proposed by Sandewall [15], in terms of a model theoretic preferential semantics. It has been assessed correct using the Features and Fluents framework for the $\mathcal{K} - IA$ class of reasoning problems which include nondeterministic actions, actions with duration, partial or complete specification of any state in a scenario, including the first, and incomplete specification of the timing and order of actions. Doherty ([2],[5]) developed PMON by translating Sandewall's representation into a conventional sorted FOPC, providing a circumscription axiom for the PMON logic of preferential entailment and then showing that for the $\mathcal{K} - IA$ class, the circumscription axiom can be reduced to a first-order formula. Consequently, standard classical theorem provers for monotonic FOPC can be used to reason about action scenarios in the $\mathcal{K} - IA$ class. The logic described in this section is a slightly modified version of that in [2]. The main difference is a new sort for actions which allows for their reification.

In the following, $Circ_{SO}(\Gamma;\ldots)$ and $Circ_{PW}(\Gamma;\ldots)$ denote standard 2nd-order and pointwise circumscription as described in [11] and [9], respectively.

3.1 Occlusion

Associated with each action type is a subset of fluents that are influenced by the action. If the action has duration, then during its performance, it is not known in general what value the influenced fluents have. Since the action performance can potentially change the value of these fluents at any time, all that can generally be asserted is that at the end of the duration the fluent is assigned a specific value. To specify such behavior, an *Occlude* predicate is introduced and used in the definition of reassignment expressions. The occlusion predicate is used as part of the definition of a reassignment expression which in turn is used as part of the definition of an action schema.

The predicate *Occlude* takes an action, fluent and timepoint as argument. For example, if the $[t,t']Load$ action is performed then the formula $\forall t''.t < t'' \leq t' \to Occlude(load, t'', loaded)$ represents the fact that *loaded* will be occluded from t to t', the duration of the *Load* action. The definition for a reassignment expression $[s, t]\delta := T$ used in an action occurrence statement with action α is

$$(\exists t.s \leq t < t \land \forall t'.(t < t' \leq t \to Holds(t', \delta)))$$
$$\land (\forall t''.(s < t'' \leq t \to Occlude(\alpha, t'', \delta)))$$

The definition for $[s, t]\delta := F$ is similar, but the *Hold*'s atom is negated. Technically, occlusion is a device which is used to mask fluent changes from influencing choice of preferred models in the minimization process.

3.2 The Nochange Axiom

Let Γ_{NCG} denote the following *nochange axiom set*:

$$\{\forall f, t.Holds(t, f) \oplus Holds(t + 1, f) \supset \exists a.Occlude(a, t + 1, f)\}, \qquad (2)$$

where the connective $\oplus$ is an abbreviation for the exclusive-or connective. This axiom asserts that for any fluent f and time-point t, if the value of f changes from time-point t to $t+1$, then there is an action a which causes f to be occluded from t to $t + 1$. The nochange axiom implicitly asserts a persistence assumption which is observed by taking the contraposition of Γ_{NCG}:

$$\{\forall a, f, t.\neg Occlude(a, t + 1, f) \supset Holds(t, f) \equiv Holds(t + 1, f)\}. \qquad (3)$$

Relation to Explanation Closure It is clear that the nochange axiom

$$\{\forall f, t.Holds(t, f) \oplus Holds(t + 1, f) \supset \exists a.Occlude(a, t + 1, f)\}, \qquad (4)$$

provides an explanation for a fluent f changing value from time t to $t+1$ in terms of actions, provided one has both the necessary and sufficient conditions for a tuple $\langle a, t, f \rangle$ having the property $Occlude$. The schedule axioms provide the sufficient conditions, whereas the minimization of $Occlude$ in Γ_{SCD}, discussed in the next section, provides the necessary conditions.

In PMON, the EC axiom corresponding to (1) would be derived in two stages. First, instantiate formula (4), with the fluent in question:

$$\forall t.H(t, h(R, o)) \oplus H(t + 1, h(R, o)) \supset \exists a.Occlude(a, t + 1, h(R, o)), \qquad (5)$$

where $h(R, o)$ is a fluent constant representing the fact that "Robot R is holding object o" and H is *Holds*. We can of course extend the fluent sort to deal with complex fluents, but will avoid these complications in this paper. Secondly, minimize $Occlude$, but only relative to the schedule axioms. The derived definition of $Occlude$, together with (5), would then be used to show that $a = Putdown(R, o)$ or $a = Drop(R, o)$.

3.3 Filtered Preferential Entailment

Filtered preferential entailment is a technique originally introduced by Sandewall [14] for dealing with postdiction. The filtering technique is based on distinguishing between different types of formulas in a scenario, In this particular case, between schedule and observation axioms. Given a scenario description $\Gamma_C = \Gamma_{OBS} \cup \Gamma_{SCD} \cup \Gamma_{UNA}$, the basic idea is to minimize only the schedule axioms Γ_{SCD} relative to the $Occlude$ predicate and then use the intersection of the $Occlude$ minimal models with the models for the observation axioms and the nochange axiom as the class of preferred models.

3.4 PMON Circumscription

The PMON minimization policy combines the occlusion concept, nochange premises and the filtering technique in the following manner. Given a scenario description Υ, and the corresponding formulas Γ_C in $\mathcal{L}(FL)$, the *Occlude* predicate will be minimized globally relative to Γ_{SCD} and then filtered with Γ_{NCG} and Γ_{OBS}. Let $Circ_{SO}(\Gamma_{SCD}(Occlude); Occlude) =$

$$\Gamma_{SCD}(Occlude) \wedge \forall \Phi. \neg [\Gamma_{SCD}(\Phi) \wedge \Phi < Occlude] \tag{6}$$

denote the PMON circumscription axiom with *Occlude* minimized and *Holds* fixed. PMON circumscription is then defined as

$$\Gamma_{NCG} \wedge \Gamma_C \wedge Circ_{SO}(\Gamma_{SCD}(Occlude); Occlude).$$

Observe that the circumscription policy is surprisingly simple, yet at the same time is assessed correct for the very broad ontological class $\mathcal{K} - IA$.

4 Reduction to the First-Order Case

Although $Circ_{SO}(\Gamma_{SCD}(Occlude); Occlude)$ is a second-order formula, it can be shown that it is equivalent to a first-order formula using two results by Lifschitz [9], and the fact that *Occlude*-atoms only occur positively in Γ_{SCD}. Lifschitz's results allow us to show that for any Γ_C with the required restrictions on *Occlude*-atoms, the PMON circumscription of Γ_C is equivalent to the following first-order formula,

$$\Gamma_{NCG} \wedge \Gamma_C \wedge \forall a, t, f. \neg [Occlude(a, t, f) \wedge$$
$$\Gamma_{SCD}(\lambda a', t', f'.(Occlude(a', t', f') \wedge \langle a', t', f' \rangle \neq \langle a, t, f \rangle))]. \tag{7}$$

More recently, we have shown in Doherty [1] that standard predicate completion can be used to derive a definition of *Occlude*, which is not so surprising considering the form of schedule axioms. More importantly, we have recently proposed an efficient algorithm for reducing a large class of circumscription axioms to logically equivalent 1st-order formulas via quantifier elimination techniques ([3]). The DLS algorithm can be used for the PMON circumscription axiom. Consequently, we have an automatic method for "compiling" away the 2nd-orderness of the circumscription axiom and generating the necessary conditions for a tuple being a member of *Occlude*.

Such reductions are very useful in the sense that one can reason about any scenario description in the $\mathcal{K} - IA$ class using standard theorem provers for monotonic FOL. In addition, since the temporal structure is linear discrete time with $+$, $<$, and $=$, existing logic-based constraint packages could be used to increase efficiency of the implementation. These results provide not only an alternative to, but an explanation for the role of nonmonotonicity in the explanation closure approach.

5 Some Examples

5.1 Yale Shooting Problem

Example 2. This example is due to Hanks and McDermott [7] The YSP scenario description is (below al, l, lo, and fi are fluent constants standing for *alive, loaded, load,* and *fire*, respectively, while *Load* and *Fire* are action symbols),

obs1 $[0]$ $al \land \neg l$

ac1 $[2,4]$ $Load$

ac2 $[5,6]$ $Fire$

acs1 $[t_1, t_2]$ $Load \rightsquigarrow [t_1, t_2]$ $l := T$

acs2 $[t_1, t_2]$ $Fire \rightsquigarrow ([t_1]$ $l \to [t_1, t_2](al := F \land l := F)$.

The corresponding formulas in $\mathcal{L}(FL)$ are,

obs1 $Holds(0, al) \land \neg Holds(0, l)$

scd1 $\exists t. 2 \le t < 4 \land \forall t'(t < t' \le 4 \supset Holds(t', l))$
   $\land \forall t'.(2 < t' \le 4 \supset Occlude(lo, t', l))$

scd2 $Holds(5, l) \supset$
   $([\exists t. 5 \le t < 6 \land \forall t'(t < t' \le 6 \supset \neg Holds(t', al))] \land$
   $\land \forall t'.(5 < t' \le 6 \supset Occlude(fi, t', al)) \land$
   $[\exists t. 5 \le t < 6 \land \forall t'(t < t' \le 6 \supset \neg Holds(t', l))])$
   $\land \forall t'.(5 < t' \le 6 \supset Occlude(fi, t', l))].$

For the YSP scenario, $\Gamma_C = \Gamma_{OBS} \cup \Gamma_{SCD} \cup \Gamma_{UNA}$, where

$$\Gamma_{OBS} = \{obs1\}, \Gamma_{SCD} = \{scd1, scd2\}, \Gamma_{UNA} = \{l \ne al \land lo \ne fi\},$$

$$\Gamma_{NCG} = \{\forall f, t, a. \neg Occlude(a, t+1, f) \supset Holds(t, f) \equiv Holds(t+1, f)\}.$$

After circumscribing *Occlude* in Γ_{SCD}, the following definition for *Occlude* can be derived using predicate completion,

$$\forall a, t, f. \qquad [(2 < t \le 4 \land f = l \land a = lo) \lor \tag{8}$$
$$(Holds(5, l) \land 5 < t \le 6 \land f = al \land a = fi) \lor$$
$$(Holds(5, l) \land 5 < t \le 6 \land f = l \land a = fi)] \equiv Occlude(a, t, f).$$

The derived formula (8) succinctly describes the explanations for a fluent f possibly changing value at a timepoint t. For example, the only actions that can change the value of fluent al are fi. The only actions that can change the value of fluent l are lo, and fi. In order to find the actions a which can change a fluent fl's value, simply look at each disjunct on the left side of (8) where $f = fl$. Each ac in the associated subformula $a = ac$ provides a potential explanation for the fluent changing value. In addition, both the temporal constraints and preconditions can be listed by considering the left side of (8).

Generating Explanations In the following, we will demonstrate the derivation of explanations. Given the scenario above, we can derive that

$$Holds(5, l) \land \neg Holds(6, l). \tag{9}$$

Suppose we would like to explain why this is the case. By (2),

$$\exists a.Occlude(a, 6, l). \tag{10}$$

Which action a occludes l at timepoint 6? Since $f = l$ and $t = 6$, the first two disjuncts on the LHS of (8) are false. Consequently,

$$\forall a.Holds(5, l) \land 5 < 6 \leq 6 \land l = l \land a = fi \equiv Occlude(a, 6, l). \tag{11}$$

It follows that

$$\forall a.Holds(5, l) \land a = fi \equiv Occlude(a, 6, l). \tag{12}$$

This states that if the precondition $Holds(5, l)$ to the action fi is true then $Occlude(fi, 6, l)$. Since $Holds(5, l)$ is true, the action fi provides an explanation for the fluent l changing value from timepoint 5 to 6.

5.2 The Fragile Example

The following example, described in ([16], p. 30), claims to show that one can not automatically generate EC axioms via circumscription or "biconditionalization". The claim is that in the general case, using circumscription together with abnormality theories or causal theories is too strong and would sanction unwarranted inferences. The problem exhibited by the example, is essentially one having to do with context dependent actions. Although we agree that in the general case, where ramification is taken into account, it may not be possible to completely automate generation of EC axioms due to qualification and domain specificity, we do not agree that context dependency is a problem with our particular circumscriptive approach. To be fair to Schubert, his claim of inadequacy is made for particular approaches, (see [12],[8]). On the other hand, PMON has similarities to both approaches. What distinguishes PMON from these approaches, is the ability to fine-tune the application of persistence to particular fluent-timepoint pairs via the use of the $Occlude$ predicate. Consequently, PMON does not suffer from overzealous application of the persistence assumption where disjunction is involved even though circumscription of the $Occlude$ predicate can be interpreted as a form of biconditionalization.

5.3 Fragile Problem

Example 3. The following is a modified version of Schubert's fragile example. (below $br(c)$, $ho(r, c)$, and $fr(c)$ are fluent constants denoting the features $broken(c)$, $holding(r, c)$ and $fragile(c)$, respectively, while $dr(r, c)$ is a fluent constant denoting the action $drop(r, c)$.)

> obs1 [0] $\neg br(c)$
> obs2 [0] $ho(r, c)$
> ac1 [0,1] $Drop(r, c)$
> acs1 [t_1, t_2] $Drop(r, c) \rightsquigarrow$
>   ([t_1] $ho(r, c) \rightarrow$ [t_1, t_2] $ho(r, c) := F$) $\land$
>   ([t_1] $ho(r, c) \land fr(c) \rightarrow$ [t_1, t_2] $br(c) := T$).

The corresponding formulas in $\mathcal{L}(FL)$ are,

obs1 $\neg Holds(0, br(c))$

obs2 $Holds(0, ho(r, c))$

scd1 $(Holds(0, ho(r, c)) \supset$
$[\exists t.0 \leq t < 1 \wedge \forall t'(t < t' \leq 1 \supset \neg Holds(t', ho(r, c)))]$
$\wedge \forall t'.(0 < t' \leq 1 \supset Occlude(dr(r, c), t', ho(r, c)))) \wedge$
$(Holds(0, ho(r, c)) \wedge Holds(0, fr(c)) \supset$
$[\exists t.0 \leq t < 1 \wedge \forall t'(t < t' \leq 1 \supset Holds(t', br(c)))]$
$\wedge \forall t'.(0 < t' \leq 1 \supset Occlude(dr(r, c), t', br(c)))).$

For the fragile scenario, $\Gamma_C = \Gamma_{OBS} \cup \Gamma_{SCD} \cup \Gamma_{UNA}$, where

$$\Gamma_{OBS} = \{obs1, obs2\}, \Gamma_{SCD} = \{scd1\},$$

$$\Gamma_{UNA} = \{ho(r, c) \neq br(c) \wedge ho(r, c) \neq fr(c) \wedge \ldots\},$$

$$\Gamma_{NCG} = \{\forall f, t, a. \neg Occlude(a, t + 1, f) \supset Holds(t, f) \equiv Holds(t + 1, f)\}.$$

After circumscribing $Occlude$ in Γ_{SCD}, the following definition for $Occlude$ can be derived using the output of the DLS algorithm [3]:

$$\forall a, t, f. \quad [(Holds(0, h(r, c)) \wedge 0 < t \leq 1 \wedge f = h(r, c) \wedge a = dr(r, c)) \vee \quad (13)$$
$$(Holds(0, h(r, c)) \wedge Holds(0, fr(c)) \wedge 0 < t \leq 1 \wedge f = br(c) \wedge a = dr(r, c))]$$
$$\equiv Occlude(a, t, f).$$

It follows from Γ_C and (13) that we can neither derive $Holds(x, br(c))$ nor $\neg Holds(x, br(c))$ for $x > 0$.

Note that the explanation closure axiom analogous to (A5,[16]) is derived from the schedule axiom analogous to (A4,[16]) by a systematic and general principle, not dependent on the particular domain. The systematic and general principle is simply the automatic generation of the necessary conditions for a tuple being in $Occlude$ via the circumscription of the schedule axioms.

6   Discussion

Both Schubert and Reiter deal with a class of problems more general than that discussed in this paper. They consider ramification and concurrency and provide evidence that the explanation closure approach generalizes, at least for the situation calculus, to cover this expanded class of problems. PMON is still not equipped to deal with ramification or concurrency, but see [4] for an attempt at extending PMON for ramification. It remains to be investigated just how much one can generalize the reduction results and automatic generation of closure axioms for these expanded classes in the context of PMON.

We have provided a case for a circumscriptive version of explanation closure that has an effective proof theory and is applicable to both context dependent and nondeterministic actions. It also retains a large degree of representational succinctness and elaboration tolerance, since the process of generating closure axioms is fully automated. In addition, we feel some evidence has been provided that the monotonic/nonmonotonic dichotomy is not as clear cut as previously assumed and is not fully justified.

References

1. P. Doherty. Notes on PMON circumscription. Technical Report LITH-IDA-94-43, Department of Computer and Information Science, Linköping University, Linköping, Sweden, December 1994.

2. P. Doherty. Reasoning about action and change using occlusion. In *Proceedings of the 11th European Conference on Artificial Intelligence, Aug. 8-12, Amsterdam*, pages 401–405, 1994.

3. P. Doherty, W. Łukaszewicz, and A. Szałas. Computing circumscription revisited: Preliminary report. In *Proceedings of the 14th Int'l Joint Conference on Artificial Intelligence*, volume 2, pages 1502–1508, 1995. Extended version to appear in Journal of Automated Reasoning.

4. P. Doherty and P. Peppas. A comparison between two approaches to ramification: PMON(R) and $\mathcal{AR}_0$. In *Proceedings of the 8th Australian Joint Conference on Artificial Intelligence*, 1995.

5. P. Doherty and W. Łukaszewicz. Circumscribing features and fluents. In D. Gabbay and H. J. Ohlbach, editors, *Proceedings of the 1st International Conference on Temporal Logic*, volume 827 of *Lecture Notes in Artificial Intelligence*, pages 82–100. Springer, 1994.

6. A. R. Haas. The case for domain-specific frame axioms. In F. M. Brown, editor, *The Frame Problem in Artificial Intelligence*. Morgan Kaufmann, 1987.

7. S. Hanks and D. McDermott. Nonmonotonic logic and temporal projection. *Artificial Intelligence*, 33, 1987.

8. V. Lifschitz. Formal theories of action. In F. M. Brown, editor, *The Frame Problem in Artificial Intelligence*. Morgan Kaufmann, 1987.

9. V. Lifschitz. Pointwise circumscription. In M. Ginsberg, editor, *Readings in Non-monotonic Reasoning*, pages 179–193. Morgan Kaufmann, 1988.

10. V. Lifschitz. Nested abnormality theories. *Artificial Intelligence*, 1995. To appear.

11. W. Łukaszewicz. *Non-Monotonic Reasoning - Formalization of Commonsense Reasoning*. Ellis Horwood Series in Artificial Intelligence. Ellis Horwood, 1990.

12. J. McCarthy. Applications of circumscription to formalizing common-sense knowledge. *Artificial Intelligence*, 28:89–116, 1986.

13. R. Reiter. The frame problem in the situation calculus: A simple solution (sometimes) and a completeness result for goal regression. In V. Lifschitz, editor, *Artificial Intelligence and Mathematical Theory of Computation*, pages 359–380. Academic Press, 1991.

14. E. Sandewall. Filter preferential entailment for the logic of action and change. In *Proc. Int'l Joint Conf. on Artificial Intelligence, (IJCAI-89)*, 1989.

15. E. Sandewall. *Features and Fluents: A Systematic Approach to the Representation of Knowledge about Dynamical Systems*. Oxford University Press, 1994.

16. L. Schubert. Monotonic solution of the frame problem in situation calculus. In H. E. Kyburg, R. P. Loui, and G. N. Carlson, editors, *Knowledge Representation and Defeasible Reasoning*, pages 23–67. Kluwer, 1990.

PAC-Learning Logic Programs under the Closed-World Assumption

Luc De Raedt

Department of Computer Science, Katholieke Universiteit Leuven,
Celestijnenlaan 200A, B-3001 Heverlee, Belgium
email : Luc.DeRaedt@cs.kuleuven.ac.be

Abstract. Positive PAC-learning results are presented for the normal inductive logic programming setting. In our formalisation of this setting, examples are complete models of the target theory, which corresponds to making the closed world assumption. The results obtained here are the first PAC-learning results for ILP in the normal setting, that allow for recursive theories as well as multiple predicates.

1 Introduction

Recently, both inductive logic programming [11], which studies the induction of first order logical formulae from examples and background knowledge, and computational learning theory [15, 13], which is concerned with the convergence and complexity of learning algorithms, have received a lot of attention. It is therefore no surprise that several researchers have started to investigate the computational properties of inductive logic programming [7, 9, 1, 2, 3, 6].

All of these works, with the exception of De Raedt and Džeroski (1994), concentrate on the normal inductive logic programming setting, where the aim is to find a hypothesis H starting from a background theory B and positive and negative examples P and N such that $B \wedge H \models P$ and $B \wedge H \wedge N \not\models \Box$ (cf. [11]), and where examples are ground facts and the background theory is assumed to be extensional, i.e. to be presented as a ground model. Despite that the setting thus studied is severely limited, the results are mostly negative, cf. [9, 3].

De Raedt and Džeroski have recently attempted to extend these learnability results by considering an alternative ILP setting, where examples are logical interpretations. Furthermore, instead of the normal inductive logic programming, they investigated the non-monotonic inductive logic programming, introduced by [8, 5]. De Raedt and Džeroski have argued that using interpretations as examples is more natural for PAC-learning than using facts as examples, as this is also done in PAC-learning approaches to boolean learning, cf. [15, 13].

In this paper, a framework for using models as examples in the normal inductive logic programming setting is presented, which corresponds to learning under the closed world assumption. The PAC-learnability of several classes of logic programs is then investigated and some positive results are proven.

The paper is structured as follows: Section 2 introduces the inductive logic programming setting studied. Section 3 introduces the PAC-learning framework.

In Section 4, we prove our main learnability results. Section 5 discusses problems encountered when learning theories which have infinite intended models, and introduces a novel approach to alleviate these problems.

2 Normal inductive logic programming

We first outline some standard logic programming concepts (see [10]). A first order alphabet is a set of predicate symbols and functor symbols. A definite clause is a formula of the form $A \leftarrow B_1, ..., B_n$, where A and B_i are logical atoms. The atom A is also sometimes called a positive literal, and the B_j negative literals. An atom $p(t_1, ..., t_n)$ is a predicate symbol p followed by a bracketed n-tuple of terms t_i. A term t is a variable V or a functor symbol $f(t_1, ..., t_k)$ immediately followed by a bracketed n-tuple of terms t_i. Constants are functor symbols of arity 0. *Functor free* clauses are clauses that contain only variables.

The above clause can be read as A if B_1 and ... and B_n. All variables in clauses are universally quantified, although this is not explicitly written. We will call A the *head* of the clause and $B_1, ..., B_n$ the *body* of the clause. A *fact* is a definite clause with an empty body, $n = 0$. A definite clause theory, or shortly theory, is a set of definite clauses. The set of variables in a term, atom or clause e, is denoted by $vars(e)$. Throughout the paper, we shall assume that all clauses are *range restricted*, which means that all variables occurring in the head of a clause also occur in its body, i.e. $vars(head(c)) \subset vars(body(c))$.

Following developments in deductive databases, in particular concerning DAT-ALOG, we shall distinguish between the set of extensional predicates EP and the set of intensional ones IP. Extensional predicates will be defined using ground facts only, whereas intensional ones will be defined using definite clauses. It will be the task of the learner to induce the definitions of the intensional predicates.

A substitution $\theta = \{V_1/t_1, ..., V_n/t_n\}$ is an assignment of terms t_i to variables V_n. Applying a substitution θ to a term, atom, or clause e yields the instantiated term, atom, or clause $e\theta$ where all occurences of the variables V_i are simultaneously replaced by the terms t_i. A term, atom or clause e is called ground when there is no variable occurring in e, i.e. $vars(e) = \emptyset$. A *Herbrand interpretation* over a first order alphabet is a set of ground facts constructed with the predicate and functor symbols in the alphabet. A Herbrand interpretation I is a model for a clause c if and only if for all substitutions θ such that $c\theta$ is ground: $body(c)\theta \subset I$ $\rightarrow head(c)\theta \in I$. We also say c is true in I. A Herbrand interpretation I is a model for a clausal theory T if and only if it is a model for all clauses in T. The restricted interpetation I_R with respect to a set of predicates R and an interpretation I, is the set of all facts in I that correspond to predicates in R.

The semantics of a definite clause theory T is given by its least Herbrand model $M(T)$, cf. [10], which is the smallest Herbrand model of T using the same alphabet as T. For our purposes, one can consider $M(T)$ as the set of ground atoms (constructed using the alphabet of T) that are logically entailed by T. Roughly speaking, the truth of a (range-restricted) clause c in a (finite) interpretation I can be determined by running the query $? - body(c), not\ head(c)$

on a database containing I using a PROLOG system. If the query succeeds, the clause is false in I. If the query fails, the clause is true. The *size* of a term, atom, clause, or theory, is the number of symbols in the term, atom, clause or theory.

By now we can formalize the normal inductive logic programming setting with the closed world assumption. In this setting, one starts from a set of definite clauses $\mathcal{L}$ (the language bias), and a set of examples E of an unknown target theory T. The class of concepts considered is thus $2^{\mathcal{L}}$. The examples e in E are interpretations which are consistent with T. As an example is an interpretation, it will be convenient to split it into two parts: e_{IP} contains the facts for the intensional predicates, i.e. for the predicates to be learned, and e_{EP} contains the facts for the extensional predicates. The aim then is to find a hypothesis $H \subset \mathcal{L}$ such that $M(H \cup e_{EP}) = e_{EP} \cup e_{IP}$, i.e. to learn the definitions of the intensional predicates.

Definition 1. An example or interpretation e is consistent with a hypothesis H if and only if $M(H \cup e_{EP}) = e_{EP} \cup e_{IP}$.

An example is thus consistent if the hypothesis correctly predicts the facts for the learned predicates starting from the extensional ones. In this view of learning, the target theory T to be learned can also be considered a function (cf. [13]). Indeed, the target theory T determines a function from the set of all interpretations containing facts for EP to the set of all interpretations containing facts for IP.

Given:

- a set of well-formed definite clauses $\mathcal{L}$ (the bias)
- a set of positive examples E (a set of interpretations $e = e_{EP} \cup e_{IP}$)

Find: $H \subset \mathcal{L}$ such that all examples are consistent with H.

Notice that this setting naturally allows for multiple predicate learning, recursion and functors. Furthermore it is a natural upgrade of the boolean learning paradigm where examples are also interpretations.

Notice also that in this formalization of learning, the background theory that is employed is implicit in e_{EP}. So, our framework also assumes a ground background theory. Working with a non-ground background theory can be realized by replacing e_{EP} with $e \cup B$ where B would be a definite clause background theory. However, as computing $M(e \cup B)$ is not polynomial in the size of B, the use of a non-ground background theory would lead to the intractability of the framework.

Let us now illustrate this rather lengthy definition by adopting Michalski's train examples. The actual notation is due to Muggleton and Page.

Example 1. Let the first example be: *eastbound(east). car(e1). car(e2). car(e3). car(e4). shape(elipse). shape(hexagon). shape(rectangle). shape(u-shaped). train(east). short(e2). closed(e2). long(e1). long(e3). short(e4). open(e1). open(e3). open(e4).*

infront(east, e1). infront(e1, e2). infront(e2, e3). infront(e3, e4). shape(e1, rect-angle). shape(e2, rectangle). shape(e3, rectangle). shape(e4, rectangle). load(e1, rectangle, 3). load(e2, triangle, 1). load(e3, hexagon, 1). load(e3, circle, 1). wheels(e1, 2). wheels(e2, 2). wheels(e3, 3). wheels(e4, 2). hascar(east, e1). has-car(east, e2). hascar(east, e3). hascar(east, e4).

Let the second example be: *westbound(west). car(w1). car(w2). shape(elipse). shape(hexagon). shape(rectangle). shape(u-shaped). train(west). infront(west, w1). infront(w1, w2). long(w1). short(w2). shape(w1, rectangle). shape(w2, rectangle). closed(w1). open(w2). load(w1, circle, 3). load(w2, triangle, 1). wheels(w1, 2). wheels(w2, 2). hascar(west, w1). hascar(west, w2).*

Suppose then that $IP = \{$ westbound, eastbound $\}$ and $EP = \{$ car, train, infront, long, short, shape, closed, open, load, wheels, hascar$\}$, and that $\mathcal{L}$ is the set of definite clauses.

A possible solution in this case would be:
westbound(Train) $\leftarrow$ *infront(Train, Car), closed(Car)*
eastbound(Train) $\leftarrow$ *infront(Train, Car), open(Car)*

The setting corresponds to the classical ILP setting under the closed world assumption. Indeed, we can rewrite the consistency requirement as follows:

1. $M(H \cup e_{EP}) = e_{EP} \cup e_{IP}$
2. let $e_{EP} = \{b_1, ..., b_n\}$ and $e_{IP} = \{p_1, ..., p_m\}$
   and let $HB_{IP}(H \cup e_{EP}) - e_{IP} = \{n_1, ..., n_k\}$ $(HB =$ Herbrand Base$)$
3. if 1. then $H \cup (b_1 \wedge ... \wedge b_n) \models p_1 \wedge ... \wedge p_m$ and $H \cup (b_1 \wedge ... \wedge b_n) \not\models n_1 \vee ... \vee n_k$
4. if 1. then for all i: $H \models b_1 \wedge ... \wedge b_n \rightarrow p_i$ and for all j: $H \not\models b_1 \wedge ... \wedge b_n \rightarrow n_j$

Equation 4 shows that this is exactly the normal setting where the background theory is $b_1, ..., b_n$, the positive examples are the clauses $b_1 \wedge ... \wedge b_n \rightarrow p_i$ (or the facts p_i) and the negatives are the clauses $b_1 \wedge ... \wedge b_n \rightarrow n_j$ (or the facts n_j). As the n_j are obtained as the complement of the p_i, the closed world assumption is made here.

3 PAC-learning

We first formalize the PAC-learning paradigm introduced by [15] (closely follow-ing [13]), and then apply it to our ILP setting.

Definition 2. A concept is a subset of a universal set of objects U. A class of concepts is a set of concepts, i.e. a subset of 2^U, the power set of U. An object e is a positive example for a concept C if $e \in C$ and a negative example otherwise.

Let F be a class of concepts. The target concept f may be any concept in F. A learning algorithm for F is an algorithm that attempts to construct an approximation to the target concept from examples for it. The learning algo-rithm takes as input two parameters: the error parameter $\epsilon \in (0, 1]$ and the confidence parameter $\delta \in (0, 1]$. The error parameter specifies the error allowed in a good approximation and the confidence parameter controls the likelihood of constructing a good approximation.

The learning algorithm has at its disposal a subroutine EXAMPLE, which at each call produces a single example for the target concept f. The probability that a particular example $e \in U$ (positive or negative for f) will be produced at a call of EXAMPLE is $D(e)$, where D is an arbitrary and unknown distribution on U. The choice of the distribution D is independent of the target concept f.

Concept g is a good approximation of concept f if the probability that f and g differ on a randomly chosen example from U is at most ϵ, i.e. $D(f \Delta g) \leq \epsilon$, where $f \Delta g = f - g \cup g - f$. Putting all of the above together, we obtain:

Definition 3. An algorithm A is a *probably approximately correct (PAC)* learning algorithm for a class of concepts F if

1. A takes as input $\epsilon \in (0, 1]$ and $\delta \in (0, 1]$.
2. A calls EXAMPLE, which returns examples for some $f \in F$. The examples are chosen randomly according to an arbitrary and unknown probability distribution D on U.
3. For all concepts $f \in F$ and all probability distributions D on U, A outputs a concept $g \in F$, such that with probability at least $(1 - \delta)$, $D(f \Delta g) \leq \epsilon$.

A class F is *PAC-learnable* if there exists an algorithm A which is a PAC-learning algorithm for F.

Our inductive logic programming problem can now be formulated as:

- The set of objects (examples) U is the set of all finite Herbrand interpretations. An example e is positive if and only if it is consistent with the target theory. Otherwise, it is negative.
- EXAMPLE = MODEL, i.e. each call to the oracle produces an example e of the target theory T such that $M_{IP} = e_{IP}$ where $M = M(T \cup e_{EP})$. This implies that we are learning from positive examples only.
- The language considered will be that of jk-DCT.

Definition 4. jk-DCT, the class of jk definite clause theories, is the class of all theories composed of range-restricted clauses that contain at most k literals per clause, where each literal (atom) is of size at most j.

Without loss of generality, we will assume that the set of predicate symbols P, and the set of functor symbols F, to be used in the theory and its models, are given initially. The size of the problem will be characterized by the sizes of P and F, as well as with m, the size of the largest example model. Thus, m is the largest number of symbols (occurences of predicates, functors and variables) in any single example model.

Definition 5. Let A be a learning algorithm for a class of clausal theories CT over the alphabet over P and F. The *sample complexity* of A is the function $s: \mathbf{R} \times \mathbf{R} \times \mathbf{N} \times \mathbf{N} \to \mathbf{N}$, such that $s(\epsilon, \delta, |P|, |F|)$ is the maximum number of calls of MODEL by A, the maximum being taken over all runs of A on inputs ϵ, δ, with the target concept ranging over all concepts in CT and the probability distribution D ranging over all distributions on U. If no finite maximum exists, $s(\epsilon, \delta, |P|, |F|) = \infty$. A class CT is said to be *polynomial-sample PAC-learnable* if there exists a PAC-learning algorithm A for CT with sample complexity $p(1/\epsilon, 1/\delta, |P|, |F|)$, where p is a polynomial function of its arguments.

Definition 6. Let A be a learning algorithm for a class of clausal theories CT over the alphabet over P' and F. The *time complexity* of A is the function $t{:}\mathbf{R}\times\mathbf{R}\times\mathbf{N}\times\mathbf{N}\times\mathbf{N} \rightarrow\mathbf{N}$, such that $t(\epsilon, \delta, |P|, |F|, m)$ is the maximum number of computational steps consumed by A, the maximum being taken over all runs of A on inputs ϵ, δ, during which m is the size of the largest example seen by A, with the target concept ranging over all concepts in CT, and the probability distribution D ranging over all distributions on U. If no finite maximum exists, $t(\epsilon, \delta, |P|, |F|, m) = \infty$. A class CT is said to be *polynomial-time PAC-learnable* if there exists a PAC-learning algorithm A for CT with time complexity $p(1/\epsilon, 1/\delta, |P|, |F|, m)$, where p is a polynomial function of its arguments.

4 Learnability result

We first present our result for programs where the examples are finite interpretations and then show in the next section how these results can be extended towards handling infinite interpretations.

The **Learn-Theory** algorithm, given in Figure 1, takes as input the language $\mathcal{L}$, the background theory B, and the PAC performance requirements ϵ and δ. It outputs a definite clause theory that is consistent with all examples.

Learn-Theory($\mathcal{L}$, B, ϵ, δ)

1. $H := \mathcal{L}$
2. for $i := 1$ to $max\left(\frac{4}{\epsilon}log\frac{2}{\delta}, \frac{8\times|\mathcal{L}|}{\epsilon}log\frac{13}{\epsilon}\right)$ do
   - $e :=$ EXAMPLE
   - **foreach** $c \in H$ **do**
     if c is false in $e_{BP} \cup e_{IP}$ then delete c from H
3. **return** H

Fig. 1. A PAC-learning algorithm for jk-DCT.

The algorithm attempts to find a good approximation G of a target theory T in $\mathcal{L}$. It has at its disposal a subroutine EXAMPLE mentioned in Section 3. Upon calling, EXAMPLE returns an interpretation which is consistent with the target theory T, i.e. a finite set e of ground facts. An arbitrary probability distribution D is assumed over the set of finite Herbrand models for T.

Theorem 7. *The algorithm* **Learn-Theory** *is a PAC-learning algorithm for jk-DCT and has polynomial sample and time complexity.*

All proofs are omitted due to space restrictions. Both the algorithm and the proof are a natural upgrade of Valiant's [16] algorithm to learn k-DNF.

In contrast to the algorithm for the nonmonotonic setting by [6], this algorithm does not learn with one-sided error.

Whereas the result for jk-DCT assumes a bound j on the arity of all predicates occurring in hypotheses, the usual PAC-learning results in ILP only assume such a bound on the predicates in the background theory, and not on the predicate to be learned.

5 Learning theories with functors

The main complication that arises when learning theories that contain functor symbols, is that they may have only infinite models. Whereas De Raedt and Džeroski (94) handle the problem of infinite models using a procedural way, i.e. using a flattening approach cf. [14], we will attempt to modify the learning setting in a declarative manner. The flattening approach to PAC-learning is procedural in the sense that it requires a change of the notion of consistency, which is unsound, cf. [6]. We will address the problem of infinite models using a notion of h-complex models (cf. [4]).

We first introduce some basic terminology, following [4]:

Definition 8. The depth of a variable is 0, the depth of a constant is 1, and the depth of a term $f(t_1, ..., t_n)$ is $1 + \max_i \text{depth}(t_i)$.

The depth of a fact is defined similarly. Thus the depth of $f(a, f(b, C))$ is 3.

Definition 9. The h-complex model M^h of a model M is defined as follows:
$M^h = \{f \in M \mid depth(f) \leq h\}$.

h-complex Herbrand bases H^h are defined similarly.

Notice that h-complex models are more appealing and declarative than h-easy models as defined by [12]. The reason is h-complex models of a theory only depend on the semantics of a theory and not on the way it is evaluated. In contrast, two logically equivalent theories, may have two different h-easy models.

Instead of working with examples that are infinite models, we shall in the following assume that examples are h-complex models.

Definition 10. A theory T is h-conform if and only if for all atoms $A \in M(T)$ such that $\text{depth}(A) \leq h$, there is a ground SLD refutation proof of A in which all atoms B satisfy $\text{depth}(B) \leq h$.

Many of the standard logic programming examples are h-conform. Consider e.g. the normal definition of append. This program repeatedly decomposes terms in subterms, therefore only simpler terms are constructed and the the proof of a fact of depth h contains only facts of depth h or lower.

The h-complex model $M^h(T)$ of a theory T can be computed by an algorithm $model(T, h)$ suggested in [4]. The algorithm by De Raedt is sound, in the sense that any computed model $model(T, h) \subset M^h(T)$. It is also complete for h-conform theories, i.e. $model(T, h) = M^h(T)$. However, when the theory is not h-conform, the computed h-complex model may be a proper subset of the actual h-complex model. To adapt our learning model towards using h-complex examples or interpretations, we also need a notion of h-consistency.

Definition 11. An h-complex interpretation is h-consistent with a hypothesis H if and only if $M^h(H \cup e_{EP}) = e_{EP} \cup e_{IP}$.

By now we can adopt our learning model as follows:

- The set of objects (examples) U is the set of all finite h-complex Herbrand interpretations.
- This introduces an additional size paramater h into the framework. h will be the maximum depth of the observed examples. This also implies that our complexity results should be polynomial in terms of h.
- An example e is positive if and only if it is h-consistent (cf. Definition 11) with the target theory. Otherwise, it is negative.
- EXAMPLE = MODEL, i.e. each call to the oracle produces an h-complex positive example e of the target theory T.

Given this framework and the above observation that completeness only holds for h-conform theories, we need a way to enforce induced hypotheses to be h-conform. Without guaranteeing h-conformity of induced hypotheses, we might compute hypotheses that are h-consistent with $model(T, h)$ but not with $M^h(T)$. We want the following property to be satisfied by our learning problem:

Definition 12. A language $\mathcal{L}$ is h-conform if and only if $model(T \cup e, h) = M^h(T \cup e)$ for all examples e and all bounds h.

There are various ways to realize this. One syntactic way to guarantee h-conformity was suggested in [4]. Whereas the approach suggested earlier *syntactically* limits the clauses in hypotheses, one can also *semantically* enforce h-conformity. We briefly indicate how this can be realized:

1. replace all clauses $h \leftarrow b_1, ..., b_n$ by $h \leftarrow d(h, T_h), b_1, d(b_1, T_1), ..., b_n, d(b_n, T_n), T_1 \leq T_h, ...T_n \leq T_h,$
2. transform each example $e_{EP} \cup e_{IP}$ of maximum depth h as follows: for each fact $Atom \in e_{EP} \cup e_{IP}$ and for each natural number $g \leq h$ such that $depth(Atom) \leq g$, add $d(Atom, g)$ to $e_{EP} \cup e_{IP}$

It is easy to see that this semantic approach also realizes the desired effect. In the rest of this paper, we will assume h-conform languages but we will ignore how the h-conformity of hypotheses is guaranteed.

The above results can directly be used to obtain a PAC-learning algorithm for h-conform jk-DCT. This is shown in Figure 2.

Theorem 13. *The algorithm* **Learn-Functor-Theory** *is a PAC-learning algorithm for h-conform jk-DCT, and has polynomial sample and time complexity.*

Learn-Functor-Theory($\mathcal{L}$, ϵ, δ)

1. $H := \mathcal{L}$
2. **for** $i := 1$ **to** $max\left(\frac{4}{\epsilon}log\frac{2}{\delta}, \frac{8\times|\mathcal{L}|}{\epsilon}log\frac{13}{\epsilon}\right)$ **do**
   - $e :=$ EXAMPLE
   - **foreach** $c \in H$ **do**
     if $c\theta$ is false in $M^h(e_{BP} \cup e_{IP})$ and $c\theta$ contains only literals of depth less than or equal h **then** delete c from H
3. **return** H

Fig. 2. A PAC-learning algorithm for h-conform jk-DCT.

6 Related Work and Conclusions

To compare our results with PAC-learnability results for the normal ILP setting, let us begin by noting that all of the latter are concerned with learning the definition of a single predicate, i.e. learning a set of definite clauses for a single predicate from a set of true and false facts for that predicate. Several PAC-learnability results exist in the normal ILP setting concerning function-free clauses of bounded length. [7] show that k-literal non-recursive function-free constrained (where all variables in the body of a clause have to appear in the head) predicate definitions (with arbitrarily many clauses) are polynomially PAC-learnable. The results by [1] are closest to ours. Cohen proves that an arbitrary number of function-free non-recursive clauses with at most k literals per clause are PAC-learnable from negative examples only. These can also contain free variables, which appear in the body, but not in the head of a clause). However, adding recursion to the above class of programs makes learning intractable in the normal ILP setting. Namely, Cohen [2] also proves that an arbitrary number of function-free, possibly recursive, clauses with at most k literals per clause are not polynomially predictable, and hence are not PAC-learnable, under cryptographic assumptions. All of the above results use a bound j on the arity of background predicates, which is similar to our bound j on the size of atoms. However, they do not impose a bound on the arity of the predicates to be learned, i.e. the predicates in the head of the clauses. Therefore the two results are not really comparable.

Let us however emphasize that several issues, which are known to be hard or which have as yet not been studied in the "facts as examples" setting, are easy in our setting. This includes learning clauses with more than one literal in the head, learning clauses with different predicates in the head (i.e. multiple predicate learning), dealing with recursion and even mutual recursion, and using functors. This provides hope that the setting presented will allow stronger PAC-learning results.

Acknowledgements

Luc De Raedt is supported by the Belgian National Fund for Scientific Research and in part by the ESPRIT LTR Project no. 20237 on ILP II. He is especially grateful to Maurice Bruynooghe, Stephen Muggleton and Saso Džeroski for interesting and stimulating discussions on this subject.

References

1. W. Cohen. Learnability of restricted logic programs. In *Proceedings of the 3rd International Workshop on Inductive Logic Programming*, 1993.
2. W. Cohen. Pac-learning a restricted class of recursive logic programs. In *Proceedings of the 3rd International Workshop on Inductive Logic Programming*, 1993.
3. W.W. Cohen and D. Page. Polynomial learnability and inductive logic programming: Methods and results. *New Generation Computing*, 13, 1995.
4. L. De Raedt. *Interactive Theory Revision: an Inductive Logic Programming Approach*. Academic Press, 1992.
5. L. De Raedt and M. Bruynooghe. A theory of clausal discovery. In *Proceedings of the 13th International Joint Conference on Artificial Intelligence*, pages 1058–1063. Morgan Kaufmann, 1993.
6. L. De Raedt and S. Džeroski. First order jk-clausal theories are PAC-learnable. *Artificial Intelligence*, 70:375–392, 1994.
7. S. Džeroski, S. Muggleton, and S. Russell. PAC-learnability of determinate logic programs. In *Proceedings of the 5th ACM workshop on Computational Learning Theory*, pages 128–135, 1992.
8. N. Helft. Induction as nonmonotonic inference. In *Proceedings of the 1st International Conference on Principles of Knowledge Representation and Reasoning*, pages 149–156. Morgan Kaufmann, 1989.
9. J.U. Kietz. Some lower bounds for the computational complexity of inductive logic programming. In *Proceedings of the 6th European Conference on Machine Learning*, volume 667, pages 115–124. Lecture Notes in Artificial Intelligence, 1993.
10. J.W. Lloyd. *Foundations of logic programming*. Springer-Verlag, 2nd edition, 1987.
11. S. Muggleton and L. De Raedt. Inductive logic programming : Theory and methods. *Journal of Logic Programming*, 19,20:629–679, 1994.
12. S. Muggleton and C. Feng. Efficient induction of logic programs. In *Proceedings of the 1st conference on algorithmic learning theory*, pages 368–381. Ohmsma, Tokyo, Japan, 1990.
13. B.K Natarajan. *Machine Learning : A Theoretical Approach*. Morgan Kaufmann, 1991.
14. C. Rouveirol. Flattening and saturation: Two representation changes for generalization. *Machine Learning*, 14:219–232, 1994.
15. L. Valiant. A theory of the learnable. *Communications of the ACM*, 27:1134–1142, 1984.
16. L. Valiant. Learning disjunctive dnf concepts. In *Proceedings of the 9th International Joint Conference on Artificial Intelligence*. Morgan Kaufmann, 1985.

Planning, Truth Criteria and the Systematic Approach to Action and Change

Lars Karlsson

Department of Computer and Information Science
Linköping University
S-581 83 Linköping, Sweden

Abstract. This paper presents an analysis of partial-order planning based on Sandewall's systematic approach to reasoning about action and change. The partial-order planner TWEAK is analysed and reconstructed. The main result is a temporal logic-based version of the criterion for necessary truth in TWEAK plans. In a second step, the TWEAK truth criterion is extended to deal with context-dependent and nondeterministic actions. A temporal logic, called the fluent logic, is used for representing plans.

1 Introduction

The topic of this paper is the formalization of the planning problem, the analysis and reconstruction of existing planners and the ways they model a changing world, and the development of new planners, all within Sandewall's *Features and Fluents* framework [14]. The idea behind Sandewall's framework is that problems of reasoning about action and change should not be approached for all possible kinds of worlds (domains) at once. One should instead identify classes of worlds with certain restrictions on their structure, for instance whether actions can occur concurrently and whether actions can be non-deterministic. Specific logics can then be designed for specific classes of worlds. Sandewall presents a number of logics and also proves their soundness and completeness relative to their specific classes.

Observe that in *Features and Fluents*, the systematic approach is applied to logics of action and change. In this paper, the approach is given a wider application. The approach is also relevant for problems that make use of reasoning about action and change, such as planning. The results described in the paper and in [8] provide concrete support for this. Chapman's TWEAK [2] planner is subject to an *analysis and reconstruction* in the paper. The emphasis is on representation and basic operations applied to this representation; the algorithm used by TWEAK need not be changed in any relevant aspects. Then an *extension* of TWEAK to deal with a larger class of worlds is presented. The truth criterion of TWEAK is extended to handle worlds where there are actions with context-dependent and non-deterministic effects.

The first motivation of this work is that making formal analyses and descriptions can contribute to a better understanding of how current planners work, especially concerning how they represent the world. Temporal logics can here provide a plan representation with a formal semantics and furthermore a common basis suitable for comparison and evaluation. The second motivation concerns integration. Planning is but one of the reasoning capabilities required by an agent in a dynamic and complex environment. This puts high demands of expressiveness and flexibility on whatever representation is being used. A third motivation is the implicit assumptions about the structure of the world that underlie classical planners. They might eventually turn out to be too restrictive to scale up to the requirements of modeling a complex changing environment.

2 Classical planning

In the TWEAK formalism and in other classical planners such as STRIPS [6] and SNLP [9], a state is represented syntactically as a set of literals. The aim of planning is to find a sequence of actions (operators) that from a given initial state results in a partially specified goal state. Operators are tuples $\alpha = \langle Pre, Post \rangle$ of sets of precondition and postcondition literals. The preconditions specify when the operator is applicable. The postconditions are said to be *asserted* in the state resulting from applying the operator, and their negations are said to be *denied* there. The result of an applicable operator is the input state of the operator plus the asserted literals minus the denied literals. For instance, if an operator $Fire(gun, turkey) = \langle\{loaded(gun)\}, \{\neg alive(turkey), \neg loaded(gun)\}\rangle$ is applied in the state $\{loaded(gun), alive(turkey), hungry(hunter)\}$ then the resulting state would be $\{\neg loaded(gun), \neg alive(turkey), hungry(hunter)\}$. Applying a sequence of operators is defined as functional composition. Classical partial-order planning assumes complete information about actions, and complete information of the initial state is often implicitly assumed.

Based on the principle of least commitment, a TWEAK plan may be partially instantiated ($Fire(x, turkey)$) and partially ordered (the order between two operators might be unspecified). Further codesignation ($x \approx gun$, $x \not\approx y$) and ordering constraints ($Load(gun) \prec Fire(gun, turkey)$) may be added later during planning. A totally instantiated and totally ordered plan that can be obtained by adding constraints to the plan is called a completion. A partially instantiated and partially ordered plan is interpreted as the set of all its completions.

Some efforts have been made in constructing planners with a greater expressivity; one of the more notable results is Pednault's Action Description Language (ADL) applied to both total-order [11] and partial-order [12] planning. However, Pednault never specified a working partial-order ADL planner. In ADL, context-dependency can be specified like $Fire(gun, turkey) = \{\emptyset, \{\neg loaded(gun), (\neg alive(turkey)|loaded(gun)), (amused(turkey)|\neg loaded(gun))\}\}$. If the gun is loaded when fired, the turkey will die, and if it is not, the turkey will be amused. UCPOP [13] is a provably sound and complete partial-order planner for ADL, using causal links in a manner similar to SNLP [9]. However, UCPOP sacrifices some of the expressivity of ADL for complexity reasons, assuming deterministic actions and completely defined initial state.

3   The Fluent Logic for plan representation

The fundamental tools for representing plans and goals in this paper are scenario descriptions. Generally, a scenario description expresses the agent's more or less correct and complete information about action laws, action occurrences and observations. It is a structure of formal objects such as sets of logical sentences, each one with a specific functionality. The scenarios described here belong to the $\mathcal{K}$-**IA** class in Sandewall's notation. A $\mathcal{K}$-**IA** scenario description can be written as a tuple $\langle \mathcal{O}, \text{LAW}, \text{SCD}, \text{OBS} \rangle$ where $\mathcal{O}$ is a description of the object domain including unique names axioms; LAW is a set of action laws; SCD is a schedule; and OBS is a set of observations. $\mathcal{K}$-**IA** denotes scenarios with correct and complete information about action laws and action occurrences and correct observations ($\mathcal{K}$), inertia, integer time and actions with duration (**I**), alternative effect of actions (**A**) in terms of context-dependency (different initial states may give different results for an action) and non-determinism (same initial state may give different results) but without concurrency and ramification. Properties and relations in the world that may vary over time are called features, and inertia is the principle that features do not change values unless explicitly affected by an action.

The language used for scenario descriptions in this work is the circumscriptive *fluent logic* (FL) [4, 3], also presented in this volume [5]. FL is a reified and typed first-order logic using integer time, based on the PMON logic of Sandewall [14]. The most basic building block in FL is $[t]\delta =_{def} Holds(t, \delta)$, stating that δ holds at time t. The well known Yale shooting scenario is represented in FL as follows.

law1 $[s, t] Load(x) \rightsquigarrow [s, t] loaded(y) := T$
law2 $[s, t] Fire(x, y) \rightsquigarrow [s] loaded(x) \Rightarrow [s, t] alive(y) := F$
obs1 $[0] alive(turkey) \wedge \neg loaded(gun)$ $\qquad\qquad\qquad\qquad\qquad$ (1)
scd1 $[2, 4] Load(gun)$
scd2 $[5, 6] Fire(gun, turkey)$

Lines labeled law belong to the set LAW, and so on. Applying the action laws, which are syntactic expansion rules, to the schedule yields the following result.

obs1 $[0] alive(turkey) \wedge \neg loaded(gun)$
scd1 $[2, 4] loaded(gun) := T$ $\qquad\qquad\qquad\qquad\qquad\qquad\qquad\qquad$ (2)
scd2 $[5] loaded(gun) \Rightarrow [5, 6] alive(turkey) := F$

Context-dependent and non-deterministic actions are possible, like firing the gun $[s, t] Fire(x, y) \rightsquigarrow ([s] loaded(x) \Rightarrow [s, t] loaded(x) := F \wedge [s, t] alive(y) := F) \wedge ([s] \neg loaded(x) \Rightarrow [s, t] amused(y) := T)$ and spinning the chamber of the gun $[s, t] Spin(x) \rightsquigarrow [s, t] loaded(x) := T \vee [s, t] loaded(x) := F$ (the precondition T is implicit). The general form of an action law is:

$$[s, t] A \rightsquigarrow \bigwedge_i ([s] \Phi_i \Rightarrow \bigvee_{j_i} ([s, t] \Delta_{j_i} \wedge [s, t] \gamma_{j_i})) \qquad (3)$$

The conjunction relates preconditions $[s] \Phi_i$ to effects, where in turn each disjunct is a possible non-deterministic outcome (in case of determinism there is only one disjunct). The $[s,t]\Delta_{j_i}$ part of the effects are formulae containing reassignment statements of the form $[s,t]\delta:=\mathcal{B}$, and $[s,t]\gamma_{j_i}$ are (optional) formulae specifying what happens between s and t and constraining the length of the interval $[s,t]$.

Reassignment, $[s,t]\delta:=\mathcal{B}$, plays a key role in the logic. It denotes that somewhere in the interval $(s,t]$ the feature δ will be assigned the value $\mathcal{B}$. The definition is as follows: $[s,t]\delta:=T=_{def}\exists t.(s \leq t < t \wedge \forall t'.(t < t' \leq t \Rightarrow Holds(t',\delta))) \wedge \forall t''.(s < t'' \leq t \Rightarrow Occlude(t'',\delta))$ and similarly for $[s,t]\delta:=F$. The first part describes the result of the reassignment. The $Occlude(t'',\delta)$ expression of the second part denotes that the truth value of feature δ may change at time t''. PMON [14] minimizes $Occlude$ for each timepoint-feature pair in parallel. Then a nochange axiom is applied, stating that features can change from the previous time point only when occluded ($\oplus$ denotes 'exclusive or'): $\forall f,t.Holds(t,f) \oplus Holds(t+1,f) \Rightarrow Occlude(t+1,f)$. Deduction under PMON will be written $\mathrel{\mid\!\sim}$. For YSS, the occluded timepoint-feature pairs after PMON-minimization are $\langle 3, loaded(gun)\rangle$, $\langle 4, loaded(gun)\rangle$, $\langle 6, loaded(gun)\rangle$ and finally $\langle 6, alive(turkey)\rangle$. The conclusions concerning $Holds$ are as follows.

$$\begin{array}{l} [0,2]\,alive(turkey) \wedge \neg loaded(gun) \\ [3]\,alive(turkey) \\ [4,5]\,alive(turkey) \wedge loaded(gun) \\ [6,\infty)\,\neg alive(turkey) \wedge loaded(gun) \end{array} \qquad (4)$$

The object domain may be finite or infinite. There are no object domain functions. PMON has been proved to be correctly applicable for the $\mathcal{K}$-IA class [14].

Scenarios corresponding to classical monotonic theories (denoted $\mathcal{N}$) can be written as a two-tuple, for instance $\langle \mathcal{O}, \text{GOAL} \rangle$ for a set of goals. Finally, the expansion of the schedule according to the action laws is denoted LAW(SCD).

4 Planning with FL

Plan synthesis can be described as the reasoning problem that given the initial state of the world $\langle \mathcal{O}, \text{LAW}, \emptyset, \text{OBS} \rangle$ and a set of goals $\langle \mathcal{O}, \text{GOAL} \rangle$ one is to find a plan $\langle \mathcal{O}, \emptyset, \text{SCD}, \emptyset \rangle$ such that $\langle \mathcal{O}, \text{LAW}, \text{SCD}, \text{OBS} \rangle \mathrel{\mid\!\sim} \langle \mathcal{O}, \text{GOAL} \rangle$ where SCD contains only actions that the agent is allowed to perform. A problem which has to be taken into consideration is the case where the agent is to reason about partial plans where actions are still missing. For instance, assume that an agent has just planned to shoot the turkey but not yet planned to load the gun. Using the YSS (1) with scd2 but without scd1 the agent would not be able to derive anything about the effects and conditions of the shooting action. As $[5]loaded(gun)$ does not hold in the scenario, $[5,6]alive(turkey):=F$ is not a consequence. A plan where some preconditions do not hold is called invalid.

A solution is to split the action laws into two parts. The action qualification[1]

---

[1] The term "qualification" as used here should not be confused with the *qualification problem* [10].

laws state the preconditions of an action. The action effect laws define the result of the action [8]. The separated version of the YSS with a goal added is as follows.

$$
\begin{aligned}
&\text{qlaw1 } [s,t]\, Load(x) \rightsquigarrow T \\
&\text{elaw1 } [s,t]\, Load(x) \rightsquigarrow [s,t]\, loaded(y){:=}T \\
&\text{qlaw2 } [s,t]\, Fire(x,y) \rightsquigarrow [s]\, loaded(x) \\
&\text{elaw2 } [s,t]\, Fire(x,y) \rightsquigarrow [s,t]\, alive(y){:=}F \\
&\text{obs1 } [0]\, alive(turkey) \wedge \neg loaded(gun) \\
&\text{scd1 } [2,4]\, Load(gun) \\
&\text{scd2 } [5,6]\, Fire(gun,turkey) \\
&\text{goal1 } [8]\, \neg alive(turkey)
\end{aligned}
\tag{5}
$$

In the scenario description $\langle \mathcal{O}, \text{ELAW}, \text{SCD}, \text{OBS} \rangle$ above, all actions always have effects as if their preconditions were true. The YSS after expansion is as follows:

$$
\begin{aligned}
&\text{obs1 } [0]\, alive(turkey) \wedge \neg loaded(gun) \\
&\text{scd1 } [2,4]\, loaded(gun){:=}T \\
&\text{scd2 } [5,6]\, alive(turkey){:=}F
\end{aligned}
\tag{6}
$$

and the goal and preconditions $\langle \mathcal{O}, \text{QLAW}(\text{SCD}) \cup \text{GOAL} \rangle$:

$$
\begin{aligned}
&\text{scd1 } T \\
&\text{scd2 } [5]\, loaded(gun) \\
&\text{goal1 } [8]\, \neg alive(turkey)
\end{aligned}
\tag{7}
$$

From $\langle \mathcal{O}, \text{ELAW}, \text{SCD}, \text{OBS} \rangle$ the agent can decide that the turkey will die, and from $\langle \mathcal{O}, \text{QLAW}(\text{SCD}) \cup \text{GOAL} \rangle$ he can tell that the gun should be loaded first. Observe that ELAW does not require $[5]\, loaded(gun)$ to hold. ELAW always produces the intended effects of an action, even if the preconditions do not hold.

When this approach is extended to context-dependent actions, there is a need for relating preconditions to effects. For this purpose, a new type for selecting alternatives is introduced. It will be denoted with d for variables and D_i for constants, and has an integer domain. The type is used as an argument to an action in order to state what alternative outcomes of the action are intended by the planner. The general schema corresponding to (3) is as follows; it can easily be extended to allow multiple arguments.

$$
\begin{aligned}
&\text{qlaw } [s,t]\, A(d) \rightsquigarrow \bigwedge_i (d = i \Rightarrow [s]\Phi_i) \\
&\text{elaw } [s,t]\, A(d) \rightsquigarrow \bigwedge_i (d = i \Rightarrow \bigvee_{j_i} ([s,t]\Delta_{j_i} \wedge [s,t]\gamma_{j_i}))
\end{aligned}
\tag{8}
$$

The context-dependent firing action will thus be:

$$
\begin{aligned}
&\text{qlaw } [s,t]\, Fire(x,y)(d) \rightsquigarrow \\
&\quad (d = 1 \Rightarrow [s]\, loaded(x)) \wedge (d = 2 \Rightarrow [s]\, \neg loaded(x)) \\
&\text{elaw } [s,t]\, Fire(x,y)(d) \rightsquigarrow \\
&\quad (d = 1 \Rightarrow [s,t]\, loaded(x){:=}F \wedge [s,t]\, alive(y){:=}F) \\
&\quad \wedge (d = 2 \Rightarrow [s,t]\, amused(y){:=}T)
\end{aligned}
\tag{9}
$$

If the planner wants to use the action to kill the turkey, it can plan:

$$
\begin{aligned}
&\text{scd1 } [3,4]\, Fire(gun,turkey)(D_1) \\
&\text{scd2 } D_1 = 1
\end{aligned}
\tag{10}
$$

It is now possible to define an FL version of TWEAK. The FL version of a TWEAK plan consists of action effect laws, action occurrences, ordering constraints and codesignation constrains and observations relating to the first time point, following the schemas below.

$$
\begin{aligned}
&\text{elaw} && [t,t']A_j(\overline{x}) \leadsto [t,t']p_1(\overline{x}_1):=\mathcal{B}_1 \wedge \ldots \wedge [t,t']p_n(\overline{x}_n):=\mathcal{B}_n \\
&\text{scd} && [S_i,S_i+1]A_j(\overline{e}_i) \\
&\text{scd} && S_i < S_j \\
&\text{scd} && e_i = e_j \\
&\text{scd} && e_i \neq e_j \\
&\text{obs} && [0][\neg]p(\overline{e})
\end{aligned}
\tag{11}
$$

All e_i, e_j denote atemporal constants, $\overline{e}_i$ is zero or more constants, and $\mathcal{B}_i \in \{T, F\}$. A set of temporal constants $\{S_i\}_i$ represents the time-points of partially ordered actions. Each action occurrence is associated with a unique S_i. As actions are sequential, all these have to be disjoint:

$$\text{scd } S_i \neq S_j \text{ for each } i, j \text{ such that } i \neq j \tag{12}$$

A special set of atemporal constants $\{V_i\}_i$ is introduced to denote arbitrary objects in the domain and are used to represent partial instantiation. The S_i and V_i can be seen as global variables.

The goal and preconditions constitute a scenario description $\langle \mathcal{O}, \text{GOAL} \cup \text{QLAW}(\text{SCD})\rangle$, where GOAL is the goal description, a conjunction of the form:

$$\text{goal } [S_0][\neg]q_1(\overline{e}_1) \wedge \ldots \wedge [S_0][\neg]q_n(\overline{e}_n) \tag{13}$$

where S_0 is a constant representing the unspecified time-point of the goal. QLAW represents the action qualification laws of the form:

$$\text{qlaw } [t,t']A_i(\overline{x}) \leadsto [t][\neg]q_1(\overline{x}_1) \wedge \ldots \wedge [t][\neg]q_n(\overline{x}_n). \tag{14}$$

The next issue is how to synthesize the plan. The central part of TWEAK is the modal truth criterion (MTC), stating necessary and sufficient conditions for necessary and (erroneously, see [8]) possible truth. The former is defined as truth in all completions, the latter in some completion. The MTC can be used to decide whether a literal (Chapman uses the word "proposition") holds in a specific situation in the plan. It can also be used to decide what should be added to the plan in order to make a literal hold in a situation. This is the idea behind Chapman's non-deterministic goal achievement procedure.

Theorem 1 Modal Truth Criterion. [2] A proposition p is necessarily true in a situation s iff two conditions hold: there is a situation t equal or necessarily previous to s in which p is necessarily asserted; and for every step C possibly before s and every proposition q possibly codesignating with p which C denies, there is a step W necessarily between C and s which asserts r, a proposition such that r and p codesignate whenever p and q codesignate. The criterion for possible truth is exactly analogous, with all the modalities switched (read "necessary" for "possible" and vice versa).

The symbols p, q and r denote literals, s and t denote situations and C and W denote steps. The s situation is called an establisher of the proposition. This is the situation, either the initial situation or the output situation of some step, that make the proposition p become true. When planning, each goal and precondition should be given an establisher, either by relating to the initial situation or an existing step, or by adding a new step. Besides establishing goals, a planner also has to resolve conflicts. The C steps are called clobberers, and the W steps are called white knights. A clobberer is a step that might make a precondition or goal become false, and the white knight is used to repair the damage of the clobberer. A second alternative is to add codesignation constraints to separate the clobberer from the goal. For instance, if the goal is $p(x)$ and the clobberer denies $p(y)$ then the two can be separated by constraining $x \not\approx y$. A third alternative is to move the clobberer out of the way. The goal achievement procedure operates by giving a proposition an establisher and resolving conflicts using white knights, separation, and ordering constraints.

Chapman's modal truth criterion can be reconstructed in a fairly straightforward manner. Necessary truth is expressed as logical consequence under PMON circumscription $\mid\sim$. The indexes of the steps are chosen according to the letters in the modal truth criterion above.

Theorem 2 Truth criterion I for partial-order plans (TWEAK).
Let $\Gamma = \langle \mathcal{O}, \text{ELAW}, \text{SCD}, \text{OBS} \rangle$ be a TWEAK plan.

$$\Gamma \mid\sim \ulcorner [S_s] p(\overline{e}_s) \urcorner \text{ iff} \tag{15}$$

$$\exists S_e \: [\Gamma \mid\sim \ulcorner S_e < S_s \urcorner \land \Gamma \mid\sim \ulcorner [S_e, S_e + 1] p(\overline{e}_s) := T \urcorner \lor$$
$$\Gamma \mid\sim \ulcorner [0] p(\overline{e}_s) \urcorner \:] \land$$
$$\forall S_c \: [\Gamma \mid\sim \ulcorner S_s \leq S_c \urcorner \lor$$
$$\forall \overline{e}_c \: [\Gamma \mid\sim \ulcorner [S_c, S_c + 1] p(\overline{e}_c) := F \urcorner \Rightarrow$$
$$\Gamma \mid\sim \ulcorner \lor_i (e_{si} \neq e_{ci}) \urcorner \lor$$
$$\exists S_w, \overline{e}_w \: [\Gamma \mid\sim \ulcorner S_c < S_w \urcorner \land$$
$$\Gamma \mid\sim \ulcorner S_w < S_s \urcorner \land$$
$$\Gamma \mid\sim \ulcorner [S_w, S_w + 1] p(\overline{e}_w) := T \urcorner \land$$
$$\Gamma \mid\sim \ulcorner \land_i (e_{ci} = e_{si}) \Rightarrow \land_i (e_{wi} = e_{si}) \urcorner \:] \:] \:]$$

For negated feature statements, substitute $\ulcorner [..] \neg p(..) \urcorner$ for $\ulcorner [..] p(..) \urcorner$ and F for T (and vice versa) above.

The truth criterion depends on an infinite domain; thus a domain closure assumption is not possible. Observe that the criterion is about plans with ELAW. However, it applies also to complete plans with LAW. A full proof appears in [8]. A few points should be made here. First, the truth criterion is independent of the application, in this case planning. It holds for any scenario that satisfies the restrictions in the previous section. Second, the criterion is applicable to both valid and invalid plans. This is obtained by using ELAW to represent the effects. Third, reassignment plays a key role in the criterion. The nature of the reassignment statement makes it possible to easily identify the points of assertion. As ELAW does not include any conditionals, a sentence such as $\ulcorner[S_e, S_e + 1]p(\overline{e}_s):=T\urcorner$ is either true or false in all models.

The goal achievement procedure retains its structure; only the basic operations need be altered to correspond to the FL representation. These operations consists of adding sentences to the schedule and making derivations. Assume an FL version of TWEAK given the initial state $[0]alive(turkey) \wedge [0]\neg loaded(gun)$ is to achieve the goal $[S_0]\neg alive(turkey)$. The actions from (5) are available. The schedule, representing the actual plan, is initially empty. The planner would first add $[S_1, S_1 + 1]Fire(V_1, turkey)$ and $S_1 < S_0$, as this according to ELAW will yield $[S_1, S_1 + 1]alive(turkey):=F$ (establishment). The $Fire$ action has a precondition $[S_1]loaded(V_1)$. That can in turn be achieved by adding the action $[S_1, S_1 + 1]Load(V_1, turkey)$ and $S_2 < S_1$, as this according to ELAW will yield $[S_2, S_2 + 1]loaded(V_1):=T$. Now no subgoals remains, and the plan can be completed with $V_1 = gun$.

However, there are many planning problems for which TWEAK is too restricted. For instance, assume that $Fire$ is defined as a context-dependent action (9). Here a planner has to be able to select the intended alternative outcome. Likewise, if a firing action is a clobberer, a new possibility is to add further restrictions on the alternatives of the action in question, for instance $D_1 \neq 1$ for $Fire(gun, turkey)(D_1)$ to make sure that the turkey will not die. Context-dependent and non-deterministic actions might not even be detected as potential clobberers, as their effects are not entailed by all models of the plan.

Furthermore, consider the following planning problem with the context-dependent firing action from (9):

obs1 $[0]loaded(gun1) \vee [0]loaded(gun2)$
obs2 $[0]alive(turkey)$ (16)
goal $[S_0]\neg alive(turkey)$

A possible plan is to fire both the guns:

scd1 $[S_1, S_1 + 1]Fire(gun1, turkey)(D_1)$
scd2 $[S_2, S_2 + 1]Fire(gun2, turkey)(D_2)$ (17)
scd3 $(D_1 = 1) \vee (D_2 = 1)$

The preconditions of the two firing actions in QLAW(SCD) can be simplified to $[S_1]loaded(gun1) \vee [S_2]loaded(gun2)$, which in turn can be established by the initial state. The goal holds, as $[S_1, S_1 + 1]alive:=F \vee [S_2, S_2 + 1]alive:=F$ can be derived from ELAW(SCD). The TWEAK truth criterion clearly cannot handle this case, but the following truth criterion can. It has been extended to handle context-dependent and non-deterministic effects and can also take advantage of multiple establishers, as in the last example. The criterion is a generalization of the TWEAK criterion that covers a considerable part of the $\mathcal{K}$-IA class. The TWEAK criterion is the special case when actions are context-independent and deterministic. Actions with duration has not been considered, but can be included by using actions $[S_{i1}, S_{i2}]A$ instead of $[S_i, S_i + 1]A$. Like the previous criterion, this criterion is also based on the use of ELAW. For proofs, see [7].

Theorem 3 Truth criterion II for partial-order plans. ($\mathcal{K}$-IA)

Let $\Gamma = \langle \mathcal{O}, \text{ELAW}, \text{SCD}, \text{OBS} \rangle$ be a plan.

$$\Gamma \vdash \ulcorner [S_s] p(\bar{e}_s) \urcorner \text{ iff} \tag{18}$$

$$\exists S_{e1}, ..., S_{em} \, [\, \Gamma \vdash \ulcorner \bigwedge_{i=1...m} (S_{ei} < S_{si}) \urcorner \wedge$$
$$\Gamma \vdash \ulcorner [0] p(\bar{e}_s) \vee (\bigvee_{i=1...m} [S_{ei}, S_{ei} + 1] p(\bar{e}_s) := T) \urcorner \,] \wedge$$
$$\forall S_c \, [\, \Gamma \vdash \ulcorner S_s \leq S_c \urcorner \vee$$
$$\forall \bar{e}_c \, [\, \Gamma \, |\diamond \ulcorner [S_c, S_c + 1] p(\bar{e}_c) := F \urcorner \Rightarrow$$
$$\Gamma \vdash \ulcorner \bigvee_i (e_{si} \neq e_{ci}) \urcorner \vee$$
$$\exists S_{w1}, ..., S_{wn}, \bar{e}_{w1}, ..., \bar{e}_{wn}$$
$$[\, \Gamma \vdash \ulcorner \bigwedge_{i=1...n} S_c < S_{wi} \urcorner \wedge$$
$$\Gamma \vdash \ulcorner \bigwedge_{i=1...n} S_{wi} < S_s \urcorner \wedge$$
$$\Gamma \vdash \ulcorner [S_c, S_c + 1] p(\bar{e}_c) := F \Rightarrow$$
$$\bigvee_{i=1...n} ([S_{wi}, S_{wi} + 1] p(\bar{e}_{wi}) := T) \urcorner \wedge$$
$$\Gamma \vdash \ulcorner \bigwedge_{i=1...n} \wedge_j (e_{cj} = e_{sj}) \Rightarrow \wedge_j (e_{wij} = e_{sj}) \urcorner \,] \,] \,]$$

For negated feature statements, substitute $\ulcorner [..] \neg p(..) \urcorner$ for $\ulcorner [..] p(..) \urcorner$ and F for T (and vice versa) above.

The establisher part of the criterion corresponds to a set of action occurrences $[S_{e_i}, S_{e_i} + 1] A(D_{e_i})$ such that $(D_{e_0} = 1) \vee \bigwedge_{i=1...n} (D_{e_i} = n_i)$ holds. The initial state can be included with a constraint $(D_{e_0} = 1)$ and a condition $(D_{e_0} = 1) \Leftrightarrow [0] p(\bar{e}_s)$ that is added to the set of goals and preconditions. The white knight part is similar.

In the clobberer part, $|\diamond$ denotes possible entailment under PMON, which is defined as $\Gamma \, |\diamond \alpha =_{def} \Gamma \not\vdash \neg \alpha$. This definition covers context-dependent and non-deterministic actions where one potential outcome can clobber the goal. As mentioned before, in the case of context-dependency there is a possibility to add constraints on the alternatives of the actions to solve the clobbering conflict.

Unfortunately, when using this criterion, the number of possible choices for achieving a goal can be very high. Furthermore, the handling of the resulting subgoals can become complicated. A conclusion is that multiple establishers should be used with economy, if used at all. As far as the author knows, no specification or implementation of a partial-order planner for the multiple establishers case exists. The UCPOP planner totally avoids multiple establishers.

5 Conclusions

This paper argues for the use of temporal logics for plan representation in order to provide a robust formal foundation for the analysis and development of advanced planners. This has been illustrated with a study in partial-order planning. The partial-order planner TWEAK has been the subject of an analysis and reconstruction. An FL representation for TWEAK plans was formulated, and the modal truth criterion was converted to this representation. An extension of

TWEAK plans has also been presented. The resulting plans can represent context-dependency and nondeterminism of action effects. A truth criteria was stated for the new plan representation.

References

1. James Allen, James Hendler, and Austin Tate, editors. *Readings in Planning.* Morgan Kaufmann, 1990.
2. David Chapman. Planning for conjunctive goals. *Artificial Intelligence*, 32:333–377, 1987. Reprinted in [1].
3. Patrick Doherty. Reasoning about action and change using occlusion. In *Proceedings of the Eleventh European Conference on Artificial Intelligence.* John Wiley & Sons, 1994.
4. Patrick Doherty and Witold Lukaszewicz. Circumscribing features and fluents. In *Proceedings of the 1st International Conference on Temporal Reasoning*, pages 82–100. Springer, 1994.
5. Patrick Doherty, Witold Lukaszewicz and Andrzej Szalas. Explaining explanation closure. In *Proceedings of the Ninth International Symposium on Methodologies for Intelligent Systems.* Springer, 1996.
6. Richard E. Fikes and Nils J. Nilsson. STRIPS: A new approach to the application of theorem proving to problem solving. *Artificial Intelligence*, 2:189–208, 1971. Reprinted in [1].
7. Lars Karlsson. Planning, truth criteria and the systematic approach to action and change. Technical report, Department of Computer and Information Science, Linköping University, 1996.
8. Lars Karlsson. Specification and synthesis of plans using the features and fluents framework. Licentiate thesis, Department of Computer and Information Science, Linköping University, 1995.
9. David McAllester and David Rosenblitt. Systematic nonlinear planning. In *Proceedings of the Ninth National Conference on Artificial Intelligence.* AAAI Press, Menlo Park, California, 1991.
10. John McCarthy. Epistemological problems of artificial intelligence. In *Proceedings of the Fifth International Joint Conference on Artificial Intelligence.* Morgan Kaufmann, 1977.
11. Edwin P.D. Pednault. Synthesizing plans that contain actions with context-dependent effects. *Computational Intelligence*, 4:356–372, 1988.
12. Edwin P.D. Pednault. Generalizing nonlinear planning to handle complex goals and actions with context-dependent effects. In *Proceedings of the Twelfth International Joint Conference on Artificial Intelligence.* Morgan Kaufmann, 1991.
13. J. Scott Penberthy and Daniel S. Weld. UCPOP: A sound, complete, partial order planner for ADL. In *Principles of Knowledge Representation and Reasoning: Proceedings of the Third International Conference.* Morgan Kaufmann, 1992.
14. Erik Sandewall. *Features and Fluents.* Oxford Press, 1994.

Automated Inductive Reasoning as a Support of Deductive Reasoning in a User-Independent Automation of Inductive Theorem Proving

Marta Fraňová

CNRS & Université Paris Sud, LRI, Bât. 490, 91405 Orsay, France, mf@lri.lri.fr

Abstract

The terminating recursive programs defined upon a particular kind of inductively defined systems of objects can be divided into two disjoint classes, the usual-recursion and non-usual recursion ones. Non-usual recursion programs make inductive proofs much more complex. Thus, in contrast to usual recursion programs, they are, in a particular sense, inefficient. The paper presents a method that transforms a non-usual recursion program to a computationally equivalent usual-recursion program. For the method presented, the importance of program synthesis examples (PSE) is illustrated and specific requirements on the PSE system to be used in the framework of inductive theorem proving are mentioned. The paper concerns simultaneously at least six (seemingly independent) problems met in automation of inductive theorem proving, namely: (a) logical justification of recursive definitions (read also: proving termination of recursive programs); (b) theoretical characterization of recursive definitions leading a priori to complex proofs; (c) transformation of recursive definitions that lead to complex inductive proofs to recursive definitions that do not increase themselves the complexity of inductive proofs; (d) implementation of a symbolic evaluator suitable for a user-independent automation of inductive theorem proving; (e) elimination of the explicit occurrence of the notion "well-founded relation" from inductive proofs; (f) generation of suitable induction principle schemes.

Introduction

Inductive theorem proving is a way to verify the correctness and/or properties of recursive programs. We shall therefore assume that the reader admits the importance of a *user-independent* automation of inductive theorem proving, i.e., the importance of the research aiming at the construction of a computer system able to provide inductive proofs without any interaction with a user, taking into account that the general undecidability results are put aside and the *constructive feasibility* has to be explored.

Consider the following *toy* problem: Prove

$$\forall x \, \forall y \, \{ mf(x,y) = ap(h(x),y) \}, \tag{1}$$

where mf, h and app are given by the following systems of equations:

$$\{ ap(nil,v) = v; \, ap(cons(u,v),w) = cons(u,ap(v,w)) \}$$

$$\{ mf(unit(a),y) = cons(a,y); \, mf(tree(u,v),y) = mf(u,mf(v,y)) \}$$

$$\{ h(unit(u)) = cons(u,nil); \, h(tree(unit(u),v)) = cons(u,h(v)); \, h(tree(tree(u,v),w)) = h(tree(u,tree(v,w))) \}$$

Here, {nil, cons} and {unit, tree} are primitive operators used to define inductively the sets of lists and binary trees, respectively. These operators are independent in the sense that nil ≠ cons(u,v) and unit(p) ≠ tree(q,r) for arbitrary u, v, p, q, r of the appropriate type. Similarly to a computer system (here, inductive theorem prover) asked to solve this toy problem without no interaction to a user, in order to push a bit the reader to realize the non-trivial character of a formal automated solving this toy problem, the reader is not supplied with the information on what about ap, mf and h are going to compute. Even if it is not specified explicitly, the problem given here consists of two subproblems: (i) prove that ap, mf and h actually are terminating programs, so that, in the second subproblem, these systems of equations can be considered as justified recursive definitions, (ii) prove by induction (1).

The above programs can be represented by a recursive system of conditional equations:

$$f(w) = g(w), \qquad\qquad\qquad \text{if not}(C(w)) \qquad (2)$$
$$f(w) = h(... f(k(w)) ...), \qquad\qquad \text{if } C(w) \qquad (3)$$

If g, h and k are already justified programs not referring to f, it is easy to prove that such a system of equations is a terminating program if neither

$$\forall w \{ C(w) \Rightarrow \text{not}(C(k(w))) \} \qquad (4)$$

nor

$$\forall w \{ C(w) \Rightarrow C(k(w)) \} \qquad (5)$$

hold (i.e., with respect to [Franova&Kodratoff, 92b], (4) and (5) are *partially false formulae*) and if

$$\forall y \{ C(y) \Rightarrow \exists n \, \text{not}(C(\text{appk}(n,y))) \} \qquad (6)$$

is provable. Here, appk is defined by the system

$$\{ \text{appk}(1,y) = k(y), \text{appk}(n+1,y) = \text{appk}(n,k(y)) \}.$$

This shows that proving the termination of ap, mf and h, in the framework of inductive theorem proving is not a difficult task, as it is sufficient to transform the given systems of equations into the form { (2), (3)} and then solve the problems specified by (5) and (6). The termination of ap, mf and h proved in this way, the system may start to consider (1). To see our point, it is desirable that the reader makes at least a short attempt to prove (1) without looking for a further information.

The goal of automation of inductive theorem proving can be compared to that of Aristotle: one tries to handle formulae not taking into account their meaning, but looking at the syntax only. When dealing with a *user-independent* automation, one has to be preoccupied also by the problem of *making possible* to handle formulae syntactically only, i.e., the problem of reformulating a problem that has or seems to have no solution using syntactic means to a problem that can be solved syntactically. In consequence, when developing our *Constructive Matching* methodology ([Franova, 85], [Franova, 95a]) the goal of which is to automate *user-independently* inductive theorem proving, we are concerned by determining the *conceptual switches* allowing to a system such a reformulation of problems without a help of a user. Such conceptual switches enable to bring a flavor of ingeniousness into the behavior of an automated inductive theorem proving system [Franova&Kodratoff&Gross, 93], [Franova, 94]. In this sense, if the termination of programs is treated by a computer system user-independently via (5) and (6), there are no reasons to be impressed by the system. However, we believe that many readers, after trying to prove (1), would be a bit surprised, if the system, having a look at the above definitions would recognize the termination of ap and mf just on the spot and it would say: I shall modify the definition of h, as it leads to complicated inductive proofs. This would mean that the system is able in a sense to *recognize formally* what makes some inductive proofs be characterized as *difficult* (for students) or *non-trivial* (for computer scientists).

This paper (*) summarizes very roughly our theoretical results that enable a formal characterization of the recursive systems of equations the manipulation of which increases the complexity of inductive proofs, (**) illustrates how an inductive reasoning technique, known as, "program synthesis from examples" (PSE), helps an inductive theorem proving system to transform the recursive systems of equations leading to complex inductive proofs to computationally equivalent systems of equations that lead to less complex proofs.

1. Intuitive presentation

Our idea of the formal characterization and modification of recursive systems of equations leading to complex inductive proofs can easily be understood by analogy to something known. Recall, that the system of primitive recursive functions may be defined by an inductive definition, i.e., some basic forms of primitive recursion are specified explicitly and then a function is primitive recursive if and only if it can be obtained by a finite application of the given basic forms. There are several ways to show that a function γ defined recursively is primitive recursive function. One of them is to find a function g defined by a recursive definition that can easily be recognized as primitive recursive and such that $\gamma(x) = g(x)$. For instance, in [Kleene, 80], pg. 271, Kleene shows that the system of equations

$$\{ \varphi(0,z) = z, \varphi(y+1,z) = \varphi(y,\sigma(y,z)) \}$$

can be *reduced* to primitive recursion. To do so, he expresses the value for $\varphi(y,z)$ in terms of an auxiliary ternary function f defined by the system of the equations

$$\{ f(0,y,z) = z, f(n+1,y,z) = \sigma(y-(n+1),f(n,y,z)) \}.$$

This reduction is justified formally by the fact that one can prove (by induction) the formula

$$\forall y \; \forall z \; f(y,y,z) = \varphi(y,z).$$

In order to "discover" the definition of the function f, Kleene considers the sequence

$$z, \sigma(y-1,z), \sigma(y-2,\sigma(y-1,z)), \sigma(y-3,\sigma(y-2,\sigma(y-1,z))), \sigma(y-4,\sigma(y-3,\sigma(y-2,\sigma(y-1,z)))), ... \quad (7)$$

obtained by evaluation of the expression $\varphi(y,z)$. Since in this sequence the variables y and z occur, we can understand (7) as the set of input-output examples

$$\{ ((0,y,z),z), ((1,y,z),\sigma(y-1,z)), ((2,y,z),\sigma(y-2,\sigma(y-1,z))), ((3,y,z),\sigma(y-3,\sigma(y-2,\sigma(y-1,z)))) ... \}.$$

We can thus say that Kleene, by coming from (7) to the definition of f, performs by hand an operation that is nothing but what is called today "program synthesis from examples".

By analogy to this example, we may say that we perform a classification of recursive definitions "suitable" for inductive proofs, or "well-behaving" in inductive proofs. Similarly to the class of primitive recursive functions we introduce a class of recursive definitions "suitable for inductive proofs". Similarly to the inductive definition of primitive recursive functions, we give some basic forms of recursion that represent recursive definitions "suitable for inductive proofs" and we present a constructive method how to transform an "unsuitable form" to a suitable one. Then, we illustrate the place of "program synthesis from examples" in the process of this transformation. Let us note already now that our goal differs from the goal of the program transformation techniques, as we are not preoccupied by the *computational efficiency* of the new programs constructed, but by the behavior of these programs when they are manipulated in inductive proofs, i.e., we are preoccupied by, what we shall call, the *recursion-manipulation efficiency*.

2. On logical justification of recursive definitions

The most "difficult" part of proving that a system of equations E naming a function letter (or hypothetical program) f *defines* recursively a function (or *is* a program) f with the domain of the definition D concerns the equations of the form

$$f(x) = g(x, f(t)), \text{ if } C(x). \quad (8)$$

Any equation that is a part of a system of equations naming an object f and that is of the form (8) will be said *recursive in* f. A system of equations naming a function letter f, noted here Ef, that contains at least one equation recursive in f will be called a *recursive system*. We shall use the notation $f:: \{ t_1//x, t_2//x, ..., t_n//x \}$ to express that an equation naming f is of the form $f(x) = g(x,f(t_1),f(t_2),...,f(t_n))$. $\{ t_i//x \}$, for any i, or $t_i//x$ for short, is called a *recursive call* of f.

The usual (by-hand) way to prove that a system of recursive equations naming a function letter f (i.e., Ef) defines a function -- unless Ef can be recognized as one of the primitive recursion schemes -- is to show that there is a well-founded relation REL on D in which t is "smaller than" x, i.e., that REL(t,x) holds. This usual way can more formally be represented as finding a positive solution for the second-order problem *"among all the binary relations on D there is a relation REL that is well-founded and such that REL(t,x) holds"*, i.e.,

$$\exists \, REL \; \text{well-founded}(REL) \; \& \; REL(t,x). \quad (9)$$

Therefore, if one wants to find a solution for (9) by an inductive theorem prover it is necessary to reformulate in some way this constrained *search* over an infinite system of binary relations over D. In Introduction, we present a very simple example of such a reformulation. However, proving the termination of a program via (4), (5) and (6) *does not* provide an information about the behavior of the considered program in inductive proofs. In the following we present a reformulation that is suitable for a formal characterization of the well-behaving recursive systems of equations. Our results concern domains D that are particular inductively defined systems of objects.

There are several good textbooks [Fejer&Simovici, 90] that present proofs of a well-foundedness of a particular kind of inductively defined systems of objects, we shall call them here *inductive sets* for short. Therefore, it is known that, for an arbitrary inductive set D there is a well-founded relation Rel on D, and thus, the following is a valid inference rule

$$[\ \forall t \ (Rel(t,m) \Rightarrow F(t)) \ ] \Rightarrow F(m) \vdash \forall n \ F(n) \tag{10}$$

called usually the *induction principle*. To specify that it is expressed in terms of Rel, we say that (10) is the *induction principle corresponding to Rel*. Of course, this relation between a well-founded relation and the corresponding induction principle can be specified in a more general way, namely,

if a relation Rel is well-founded
then its corresponding induction principle is justified. (11)

In order to automate user-independently inductive theorem proving, to know that inductive sets are well-founded is *insufficient*. One needs to know the *power* of the well-founded relation found, i.e., one has to be aware that a well-founded relation R specifies a class of formulae that are provable relying on the induction principle corresponding to R. In consequence, one needs to have a possibility to *compare* two well-founded relations, i.e., the power of their corresponding induction principles. Moreover, an inductive theorem prover has to know *when*, *why* and *how* to *replace* an induction principle (i.e., a well-founded relation) by a more powerful or simply a different one. In other words, one has to *formalize* inductive sets so that these concepts specified informally become effectively *manipulable* by a user-independent inductive theorem proving system. This is our goal in [Franova, 95d]. This task is not treated in the literature concerned with the *user-dependent* automation of inductive theorem proving ([Boyer&Moore, 79], [Aubin, 79], [Zhang&al., 88], [Paulson, 95], [Agerholm, 95], [Walther, 93], [Hutter, 94]).

In consequence, as the topic of this paper is closely related to (9), (10) and (11), the theoretical justification as well as the procedural character of the results presented in this paper rely heavily, among others (see section 4 and Conclusion), on our way to *formalize* inductively defined systems of objects for *the purpose of a user-independent implementation* of inductive theorem proving. We call *Theory of Constructible Domains* this particular formalization. Here, we need to resume the most important results of our Theory of Constructible Domains that are relevant to the topic of this paper.

It is known that, when certain conditions are fulfilled, an inductive definition of a system of objects suggests a well-founded relation, namely, the *substructure relation* SBR. Roughly speaking, x is smaller than y in the substructure relation if and only if in the construction of y -- applying the construction rules specified by the inductive definition -- the element x is used. When certain conditions are fulfilled, such an inductive definition suggests also another well-founded relation, called the Peano's relation PEANO. Roughly speaking, x is smaller than y in the Peano's relation if and only if the number of the construction rules applied to construct x is smaller than the number of the construction rules applied to construct y. In other words, the Peano's relation is computed with respect to what is usually called "size" (or "length") of the elements. SBR is weaker than PEANO in the sense that the following formula is valid:

$$\forall x \ \forall y \ \{ \ SBR(x,y) \Rightarrow PEANO(x,y) \ \}. \tag{12}$$

It can be shown that the substructure relation is a *minimal* well-founded relation in the sense that there is no well-founded relation R on D such that

$$\forall x \ \forall y \ \{ \ R(x,y) \Rightarrow SBR(x,y) \ \} \ \& \ \exists a \ \exists b \ \{ \ SBR(a,b) \ \& \ not(R(a,b)) \ \} \tag{13}$$

holds. Similarly, the relation PEANO is a *maximal* well-founded relation, since there is no relation R such that

$$\forall x \{ PEANO(x,y) \Rightarrow R(x,y) \} \ \& \ \exists a \ \exists b \{ R(a,b) \ \& \ not(PEANO(a,b)) \} \tag{14}$$

holds. With respect to (9), we thus have a class of justified recursive definitions, namely the definitions that fall in the scope of SBR or PEANO.

We say that a well-founded relation R is a *usual-recursion relation* if and only if it can be shown that for arbitrary x and y of the considered domain

$$\{ SBR(x,y) \Rightarrow R(x,y) \} \ \& \ \{ R(x,y) \Rightarrow PEANO(x,y) \} \tag{15}$$

holds. If R is a usual-recursion relation, then it justifies recursive definitions with the recursion $\{ t \ // \ x \}$, whenever $R(t,x)$ holds. We say that a unary function is defined by the *standard recursion* if and only if to the recursion of this definition corresponds the substructure relation. A function is defined by *usual recursion* in a constructible domain D if and only if its recursion $\{ t \ // \ x \}$ is justified by a usual-recursion relation, i.e., there is a relation R verifying (15) and such that $R(t,x)$ holds. To check that a recursive equation with the recursion $\{ t \ // \ x \}$ corresponds to a usual recursion, as we prove by the theorems T.4.21 and T.4.23 in [Franova, 95d], it is sufficient to show that $PEANO(t,x)$ holds. In general, this task, i.e., to show that $PEANO(t,x)$ holds may involve inductive theorem proving. Usual recursion well-behaves in inductive proofs.

Note that the intuition behind the results presented so far is straightforward. What is not straightforward is a *logical justification* and *automation* of this intuition, as we point out in [Franova, 95d]. This method of proving user-independently the termination of a usual-recursion program is not only intuitively obvious -- it was used by-hand a long ago --, but it is incomparably simpler than the method presented in [Walther, 89] and that does not go beyond usual-recursion. [Boyer&Moore, 79] requires a user-interaction to justify non-usual recursion, as it is unable to deal user-independently with existential quantifiers, as that occurring in (6), for instance. In our methodology, the basic method enabling us to deal with existential quantifiers is Constructive Matching formula construction presented in [Franova, 85], [Franova, 95a]. This shows that in our methodology, via (4), (5) and (6), it is possible to consider proving a termination of a program given by a recursion that is not recognized as the usual one. However, we are not concerned here only by a termination of a program, but also by its behavior in inductive proofs. Thus, we shall now consider a user-independent justification and modification of programs that do not fall under usual-recursion, such as, for instance, the recursion of h above in Introduction.

3. Inductive theorem proving: a way to justify and modify recursions

In order to prove that a non-usual recursion program f is terminating we shall show that there is computationally equivalent usual-recursion program. Namely, we shall try to find a function φ defined by usual-recursion and such that it verifies the given non-usual recursion system, i.e., if we consider f in Ef as a variable and replace this variable by φ, these equations are provable. More formally: Let f be a *function letter* (i.e., a hypothetical program) specified by Ef. We shall say that Ef represents *pseudo-usual recursion* if and only if there is a system of equations E defining a function φ and such that

$$Ef, E \vdash \forall x \{ f(x) = \varphi(x) \}. \tag{16}$$

In order to find a usual-recursion system of equations E defining a function φ with the property (16), we apply the usual-recursion induction principle scheme(s) to treat the problem

$$Ef \vdash \forall x \ \exists z \{ f(x) = z \}, \tag{17}$$

with the constraint

$z = sf(x)$ is a solution for (17) if and only if

$$sf \text{ is defined by a usual recursion and sf does not refer to f} \tag{18}$$

In other words, we shall use the usual-recursion induction principle to look for an "inductive proof" for (17) taking into account the requirements expressed in (18). A successful "inductive proof" shall provide a usual-recursion system of equations E defining sf $(= \varphi)$ with the property (16). Note that such a successful "inductive proof" for (17) handles the hypothetical program f, and thus this proof is *hypothetical* itself, i.e., it cannot be used as an argument in favor of the termination of f. The proof that Ef actually defines f, (i.e., that f is a terminating program) is implied by other arguments (see [Franova, 96]).

If f does not terminate, solving (17) with respect to the constraint (18) *halts* with the *explanation* that the value f(x) for a particular value x cannot be computed on the basis of the given equations. This means that the only problematic part of our suggested method remains to construct user-independently and in a finite time the usual-recursion system E defining sf.

One of the main tools of an inductive theorem prover is a symbolic evaluator. In the following section we shall illustrate a problem met by a symbolic evaluator when manipulating a non-usual recursion system of equations and we shall show how this particular difficulty can be overcome in the framework of inductive theorem proving.

3.1. On symbolic evaluation in inductive theorem proving

The role of a symbolic evaluator is to *manipulate* in an exact logically expressible way the given definitions, namely, (roughly speaking) to apply the given axioms as far as they are applicable [Franova, 95d]. There are some definitions that may be applied infinitely many times in course of an evaluation of a term. For instance, let EG be the following definition:

$$G(u,v) = 1, \qquad \text{if } u \leq v. \qquad (19)$$
$$G(u,v) = G(u,v+1)*(v+1), \qquad \text{if } v < u. \qquad (20)$$

If an ordinary symbolic evaluator has to compute the value G(a,b) for the parameters a and b, it will, among others obtain

$$G(a,b) = G(a,b+1)*(b+1), \qquad \text{if } b < a. \qquad (21)$$

Here, the evaluator recognizes that the definition for G can be applied to G(a,b+1), thus obtaining, among others,

$$G(a,b) = G(a,(b+1)+1)*((b+1)+1)*(b+1), \text{ if } b < a.$$

Again, the definition of G can be applied to G(a,(b+1)+1), and so on.

This illustrates that an inductive theorem prover cannot rely on a symbolic evaluator the implementation of which corresponds exactly to the logical description of a symbolic evaluator. This means that there is a need to implement an evaluator that always returns a value in a finite time, we shall speak of a *finite evaluator*, but that evaluates enough for the purposes of inductive theorem proving. As we explain in [Franova, 95a], inductive theorem proving is a way to push further (for a human, seemingly insufficient) evaluations of a finite evaluator. On the other hand, our formal introduction of standard, usual and non-usual recursion provides a *formal criterion* by which the behavior of an evaluator is regulated to obtain a finite evaluator. We have no place here to describe the behavior of a symbolic evaluator when it manipulates the standard and the usual-recursion definitions. However, the fact that a definition is given by a non-usual recursion immediately means that a symbolic evaluator, unless it is "told" to do differently, shall fall into an infinite computation. In consequence, exactly one application of non-usual recursive definitions is an answer to the problem met by a symbolic evaluator while manipulating non-usual recursive definitions.

An inductive theorem prover will thus use a finite evaluator when trying to solve the problem (17)-(18) of a justification and a modification of a non-usual recursive system of equations. In course of the attempt to solve this problem, an inductive theorem prover shall generate lemmas, i.e., sufficient conditions under which the given problem is solvable.

3.2. On lemmas generation in inductive theorem proving

Generating lemmas in inductive theorem proving expresses an attempt to overcome *failures* met in course of inductive proofs. In inductive theorem proving the notion of a failure must be understood inter-related to the notion of the *environment* in which this failure is met. Often, a failure can then be overcome by extending this environment. A *failure analysis* and an environment analysis are in charge of expressing formally how such extensions can be built by the inductive theorem prover. In consequence, a user-independent failure analysis reflects exactly an inductive theorem proving methodology [Franova&Galton, 92], [Franova, 95a]. We have no place to speak here of a particular character of lemmas generation in a user-*independent* automation of inductive theorem proving and its enormous difference in comparison with the lemma generation in the user-*dependent* approaches. Neither we can introduce formally our notion of *implicative generalization* [Franova&Kodratoff, 92] that expresses the attempt to replace an infinite sequence of lemmas generated in course of an inductive proof for a theorem Th by a formula that implies each of these lemmas and that is a sufficient condition for provability of Th.

4. Failure analysis for modification of non-usual recursion

Roughly speaking, in this part we are going to *hint at* the following: (i*) non-usual recursion of Ef while solving (17)-(18), leads to a generation of an infinite sequence of lemmas; (ii*) it is meaningful to consider a finite part of this sequence in order to obtain an implicative generation of this sequence; (iii*) it is possible to express formally which part of the infinite sequence of lemmas has to be considered; (iv*) in the framework of inductive theorem proving it is possible to organize this sequence in such a way so that suitable sequences of input-output examples are formed, to which a program synthesis from examples (PSE) can be applied; the final implicative generalization of the sequence of the lemmas is then formed with the help of the results of the PSE system.

To illustrate (i*), consider the task to prove

$$\forall x \, \exists z \, \{ \, G(x,0) = z \, \}. \tag{22}$$

This formula expresses the attempt to find a value of $G(x,y)$ for $y = 0$, i.e., it is one of the problems to be considered in the construction of a definition for G recursive with respect to the second argument (thus, the complementary task would be to express $G(x,n+1)$ in terms of $G(x,n)$ or in terms of a function Γ defined by usual-recursion and such that $G(x,n+1) = \Gamma(x,n)$). For (22), in the induction step, (i.e., for $x \neq 0$), the goal is to prove $\exists z \, G(x,0) = z$ assuming the induction hypothesis $\exists e \, G(x-1,0) = e$. However, a finite symbolic evaluator (as characterized above) returns that $G(x,0) = G(x,1)*1$ and the induction hypothesis shall be impossible to apply to the problem $\exists z \, G(x,1)*1 = z$. In consequence,

$$\forall x \, \exists z \, \{ \, G(x,1)*1 = z \, \} \tag{L1}$$

becomes a lemma for (22). In course of an inductive proof for (L1), again the corresponding induction hypothesis is inapplicable and a new lemma is generated. In this way, a non-forewarned inductive theorem prover is generating an infinite sequence of lemmas

$$\forall x \, \{ \, m-1 < x \Rightarrow \exists z \, G(x,m)*m*(m-1)* \ldots * 2*1 = z \}, \tag{Lm}$$

$m = 1, \ldots$. However, the non-usual recursion of G can be used as the *signal* for vigilance. (Moreover, this non-usual recursion of G is also the signal to non-evaluation of the terms different from G(...). This explains writing 3*2*1 instead of 6, and it concerns (iv*).)

Our goal is now to show how this vigilance can be transformed into a directed control and overcoming the problem met (concerns (ii*) and (iii*) above). For this purpose, let us return to the system

$$f(w) = g(w), \qquad \qquad \text{if not}(C(w)) \tag{2}$$
$$f(w) = h(\ldots f(k(w)) \ldots), \qquad \text{if } C(w) \tag{3}$$

Let us suppose that not (PEANO(k(w),w)) holds (checked by inductive theorem prover). Let us suppose also that $C(w) \Rightarrow C(k(w))$ is a partially false formula (checked by inductive theorem prover). In inductive theorem proving, our predicate synthesis from formal specifications (PreS) [Franova&Kodratoff, 92b] is a general way to obtain a non-trivial precondition under which the partially false formula $C(w) \Rightarrow C(k(w))$ becomes true, i.e., PreS will come out with a formula Cond such that Cond $\Rightarrow \{ \, C(w) \Rightarrow C(k(w)) \, \}$ is true. (In general, PreS can require solving another problem, namely, what we call Synthesis of formal specifications of predicates (SpecS) [Franova&Popelinsky, 93]. Both PreS and Spec rely on Theory of Constructible Domains.) For a concrete value of the parameter w the transition from $C(w)$ to not($C(k(w))$) is important in the analysis of the evaluation sequence f(w), as it renders impossible the application of the recursive equation (3) and makes the last value (via (2)) independent of f. In consequence, with respect to (6), in the generated infinite sequence of lemmas it is interesting to consider the sequence up to the point, in which, for a concrete value of the parameter w, the new lemma generated becomes independent of f.

For EG we have $C(w) = C(u,v) = \{ v < u \}$ and $C(k(w))$ is $C(u,v+1) = \{ v+1 < u \}$. The formula Cond obtained here is $v+1 \neq u$, thus, not(Cond) is $v+1 = u$. Let us denote by $h(x,n)$ the n-th *meaningful* application of (20) to $G(x,0)$, $n \neq 0$. Then, we have

$$G(x,0) =$$

$h(x,1)$	$G(x,1)*1,$	if $0 < x$
$h(x,2)$	$G(x,2)*2*1,$	if $1 < x$
$h(x,3)$	$G(x,3)*3*2*1,$	if $2 < x$
$h(x,4)$	$G(x,4)*4*3*2*1,$	if $3 < x$
...		
$h(x,m)$	$G(x,m)*m*(m-1)*...2*1,$	if $m-1 < x$

Here, inductive theorem proving is already used to separate $G(...)$ in $(G(x,2)*2)*1$. Let us warn the reader that, in the framework of a user-independent inductive theorem proving system) the logical description of this separation corresponds to the second order lemma

$$\forall A\ \forall B\ \forall C\ \exists W\ \exists Z\ \{\ (A*B)*C = W(A,Z)\ \}.$$

for positive A, B and C. First-order inductive theorem proving can nevertheless be applied to this particular type of problems, namely, via some logically-based heuristics [Franova, 95a] or via the notion of the jump-constructor and the jump-constructor representation formula [Franova, 95d]). Thus, here, each $h(x,m)$ is of the form

$$G(x,m) * \text{"something1"}, \text{ if "something2"} < x.$$

where "something1" and "something2" are functional terms that do not depend on x, however, they change with the increasing m. In other words, the inductive theorem prover can be implemented in such a way that it is able to represent the set of couples {(m,something1m)}, analogously for {(m,something2m)}) in the form of the set of input-output examples

$$IOS1 = \{\ (1,1), (2,2*1), (3,3*2*1), (4,4*3*2*1)\ \}.$$

Let us name η the functions the behavior of which conforms IOS1, i.e.,

$$\eta(1) = 1, \eta(2) = 2*1, \eta(3) = 3*2*1, \eta(4) = 4*3*2*1.$$

From IOS1, the PSE algorithm presented in [Le Blanc, 94] constructs the following definition $\{\ \eta(1) = 1\ ;\ \eta(n+1) = (n+1)*\eta(n)\}$. For "something2" this algorithm is able to produce a recursive function, which, via inductive theorem proving, is simplified to m-1. Thus, $G(x,0) = h(x,m)$ for all m such that $m-1 < x$ holds. Let us increase m by 1. Now, if not(Cond(x,m-1)) == $\{\ (m-1)+1 = x\ \}$ holds, i.e., if $x = m$, then the application of (19) to $h(x,m)$ gives $\eta(m) = h(x,m+1)$, i.e., $\eta(x) = h(x,x+1)$. In consequence,

$$\eta(x) = G(x,0).$$

Of course, the previous steps performed do not provide a formal proof for the last equation, but they *suggest* how the value of $G(x,0)$ might be computed. In order to show that it actually can be computed in this way, it is necessary to prove

$$\forall x\ \{\ \eta(x) = G(x,0)\ \}.$$

We have no place to show how such a hypothetical (see section 3) proof can be obtained, but the reader must be aware that the proof shall be a complex one (again requiring implicative generalization), as the non-usual recursion system EG is used in this proof. This illustrates that a transformation of a non-usual recursion system to a usual recursion system requires complex manipulations. However, such complex manipulations *are necessary* whenever a non-usual recursion system is used to prove properties (such as (1)) that refer to usual-recursion systems. This explains the interest of non-usual recursion modification for speeding up the inductive proofs of theorems referring to a function originally defined by non-usual recursion.

The method presented in this paper allows a particular type of modifications, namely it allows to transform a non-usual recursion of a function into a usual one. Complementary are our techniques of Predicate synthesis [Franova&Kodratoff, 92b] and Synthesis of formal specification of predicates [Franova&Popelinsky, 93] that deal with the problems of modifying definitions of predicates, namely coming from a recursive definition of a predicate to a non-recursive one and *vice versa*. Our Theory of Constructible Domains allows also another type of recursion modification (see [Franova, 95c]).

Note that all the other existing approaches to automation of inductive theorem proving do not deal with the problem of definitions modification. They simply assume that the users of their systems either provide definitions in the form suitable for their particular system or that these users are clever enough to solve problems the system runs into when working with unsuitable definitions. In this sense they are user-dependent.

Conclusion

From 1982 we work on a design of a methodology for inductive theorem proving that would enable to automate *user-independently* proving theorems by induction. In our research, we adopt the approach of the *constructive feasibility*. In this sense, our effort consists in a *logical analysis* of the problems *innate* to inductive theorem proving and looking for implementable (in the framework of inductive theorem proving) solutions of these problems. This paper describes a constructive way to transform a non-usual recursive definition of a function to a usual-recursive one. In this construction, program synthesis from examples is shown as a tool that enables to *transform an infinite branch of a well-organized proof to a finite one*. In contrast to available PSE systems, the particularity of this PSE system is that it has to be developed for solving problems generated in the framework of inductive theorem proving and that it (can and) has to be inter-related to inductive theorem proving in the sense that, whenever possible and necessary, in order to "reformulate" or "rearrange" a given set of input-output examples, it must be able to formulate questions to inductive theorem proving.

The example presented in the paper illustrates that a construction of a usual-recursion definition for a function given by a non-usual recursion is a non-trivial task the successful accomplishing of which depends on the power of the whole inductive theorem proving methodology. On the other hand, the concept of modifying a non-usual recursive definition extends the power of an inductive theorem proving methodology. This illustrates the complexity of a design of a user-independent inductive theorem proving system. Once this particular kind of recursion -- in the dependence of the power of an inductive theorem proving methodology on the problems solved and *vice versa* -- is understood, instead of complaining about the difficulty of automation of inductive theorem proving one can understand why we say that a user-independent automation of inductive theorem proving is just a *complex task*. The latter attitude suggests a feasibility. It is in this sense that it is necessary to understood our work on *Constructive Matching* methodology, the goal of which, let us recall again, is to automate user-independently inductive theorem proving. The user-*dependent* approaches in the automation of inductive theorem proving may use the results of this paper, provided they adopt (or develop something formally equivalent to) our results mentioned in the paper, namely, a logically powerful technique to prove atomic formulae that may contain existentially quantified variables [Franova, 85], Predicate Synthesis from Formal Specifications [Franova&Kodratoff, 92b], Synthesis of Formal Specifications of Predicates (SpecS) [Franova&Popelinsky, 93], and Theory of Constructible Domains [Franova, 95d].

This paper presents some of the tools that we deem necessary for achieving a user-independent implementation of inductive theorem proving. Our methodology, as described in [Franova, 95a], gives a complete description of all the tools needed to achieve this purpose. All other tools, developed for other purposes will thus show some unavoidable conceptual weaknesses.

Acknowledgments

The discussions with Yehuda Rav helped me to express the ideas of this paper in a more intelligible form. I thank him very much also for all his encouragements. Thanks to the discussions with Yves Kodratoff, the inter-relation of inductive and deductive tools -- as natural feature of the user-independent automation of inductive theorem proving -- has been captured in the design of Constructive Matching methodology from the start. Thanks to Yves, Laurence Puel and Christiane Weinzaepfel for their encouragements.

References

[Agerholm, 95] S. Agerholm: Non-Primitive Recursive Function Definitions; in: Higher Order Logic Theorem Proving and Its Applications; LNCS 971, 1995, 17-31.

[Aubin, 79] R. Aubin: Mechanizing Structural Induction. Part 1: Formal System; Theoretical Computer Science 9, North-Holland, 1979, 329-345.

[Beth, 59] E. Beth: The Foundations of Mathematics; Amsterdam, 1959.

[Boyer&Moore, 79] R. S. Boyer, J S. Moore: A Computational Logic; Academic Press, 1979.

[Fejer&Simovici, 90] P. A. Fejer, D.A. Simovici: Mathematical Foundations of Computer Science, Volume 1: Sets, Relations, and Induction; Springer-Verlag, 1990.

[Franova&Galton, 92] M. Franova, A. Galton: Failure Analysis in Constructive Matching Methodology: A Step Towards Autonomous Program Synthesizing Systems; in: R. Trappl, (ed): Cybernetics and System Research '92; World Scientific, 1992, 1553-1560.

[Franova&Kodratoff, 92] M. Franova, Y. Kodratoff: Practical Problems in the Automatization of Inductive Theorem Proving; Rapport de Recherche No.752, L.R.I., Université de Paris-Sud, Orsay, France, Mai, 1992.

[Franova&Kodratoff, 92b] M. Franova, Y. Kodratoff: Predicate Synthesis from Formal Specifications; in: B. Neumann, (ed.): ECAI 92, John Wiley & Sons Ltd., 1992, 87-91.

[Franova&Kodratoff&Gross, 93] M. Franova, Y. Kodratoff, M. Gross: Constructive Matching Methodology: Formally Creative or Intelligent Inductive Theorem Proving?; in: proc. of ISMIS'93, L.N.A.I. 689, 1993, 476-485.

[Franova&Popelinsky, 93] M. Franova, L. Popelinsky: Synthesis of Formal Specifications of Predicates; a draft version, Rap. de Recherche No.866, L.R.I., July, 1993.

[Franova, 85] M. Franova: CM-strategy : A Methodology for Inductive Theorem Proving or Constructive Well-Generalized Proofs; in: A. K. Joshi, (ed): Proceedings of the Ninth International Joint Conference on Artificial Intelligence; 1985, 1214-1220.

[Franova, 94] M. Franova: Proving Implications in Inductive Theorem Proving; in: R. Trappl, ed.: Cybernetics and Systems'94; World Scientific, 1994, 1777-1784.

[Franova, 95a] M. Franova: Constructive Matching methodology: a standard way of proving user-independently theorems by induction; Rap.de Recherche No.973, L.R.I., Mai, 1995.

[Franova, 95b] M. Franova: A standard proof by Constructive Matching methodology for a theorem formulated by Skolem; Rapport de Recherche No.972, L.R.I., Mai, 1995.

[Franova, 95c] M. Franova: A synthesis of a definition recursive with respect to the second argument for the Ackermann-Peter's function - a puzzle solved by Constructive Matching methodology; Rapport de Recherche No.971, L.R.I., Mai, 1995.

[Franova, 95d] M. Franova: A Theory of Constructible Domains - a formalization of inductively defined systems of objects for a user-independent automation of inductive theorem proving, Part I; Rapport de Recherche No.970, L.R.I., Mai, 1995.

[Franova, 96] M. Franova: Modifying and Justifying Recursive Programs in Inductive Theorem Proving: Why and How, to appear in proc. of European Meeting on Cybernetics and Systems'96.

[Hutter, 94] D. Hutter: Synthesis of Induction Orderings for Existence Proofs; in: A. Bundy, ed.: Automated Deduction - CADE-12; LNAI 814, Springer-Verlag, 1994, 29-41.

[Kleene, 80] S. C. Kleene: Introduction to Meta-Mathematics, North-Holland, 1980.

[Le Blanc, 94] G. Le Blanc: BMWk Revisited - Generalization and Formalization of an Algorithm for Detecting Recursive Relations in Term Sequences; in: proc. ECML-94; LNAI 784, Springer-Verlag, 1994, 183-197.

[Paulson, 95] L. C. Paulson: Set Theory for Verification ; Journal of Automated Reasoning Vol. 15, No.2, 1995, 167-215.

[Péter, 67] R. Péter: Recursive Functions; Academic Press, New York, 1967.

[Walther, 89] Ch. Walther: Argument-Bounded Algorithms as a Basis for Automated Termination Proofs; in proc. of CADE-10, LNAI 449, 602-621.

[Walther, 93] Ch. Walther: Combining Inductions Axioms by Machine, in proc of IJCAI-93, Morgan Kaufman, 95-101.

[Zhang&al., 88] H. Zhang, D. Kapur, M.S. Krishnamoorthy: A Mechanizable Induction Principle For Equational Specifications; in: E. Lusk, R. Overbeek, (ed): in proc of CADE-9; LNCS 310, 1988, 162-179.

Semantic Query Optimization for Bottom-Up Evaluation

P. Godfrey[1,3], J. Gryz[1], J. Minker[1,2]

{godfrey, jarek, minker}@cs.umd.edu

Department of Computer Science[1] and Institute for Advanced Computer Studies[2]
University of Maryland at College Park

U.S. Army Research Laboratory[3]
Adelphi, Maryland

Abstract

Semantic query optimization uses semantic knowledge in databases (represented in the form of integrity constraints) to rewrite queries and logic programs to achieve efficient query evaluation. Much work has been done to develop various techniques for optimization. Most of it, however, is applicable to top-down query evaluation strategies. Moreover, little attention has been paid to the cost of the optimization. We address the issue of semantic query optimization for bottom-up query evaluation strategies with an emphasis on overall efficiency. We focus on a single optimization technique, join elimination. We discuss factors that influence the cost of semantic optimization, and present two different abstract algorithms for optimization. The first pre-processes a query statically before it is evaluated; the second combines query evaluation with semantic optimization using heuristics to achieve the largest possible savings.

Keywords: Intelligent Information Systems, Databases, Semantic Query Optimization.

1 Introduction

Semantic query optimization (SQO) uses semantic knowledge in the form of integrity constraints to rewrite queries and logic programs to achieve efficient query evaluation. Several methods have been developed for SQO in relational and deductive databases [1, 5, 10]. This work has been extended to programs with recursion [6, 8] and negation [2]. In this paper we accomplish the following. Our SQO method applies to bottom-up query evaluation strategies. Such optimization methods are crucial because bottom-up query evaluation is more efficient, in most cases, than top-down evaluation. To our knowledge only one paper [7] has addressed the issue of SQO for bottom-up evaluation. However, the optimizations they consider are restricted to certain types of integrity constraints, and no general technique for query rewriting is provided. We present a cost analysis of our approach and show how our method exploits this analysis. Our SQO technique allows for the efficient use of integrity constraints (ICs) which contain both EDB and IDB predicates. In most previous work, ICs are restricted to contain only EDB predicates ([6, 8, 10]).

This research was supported by the following grant: NSF IRI-9300691

The paper is organized as follows. Section 2 introduces notation, and discusses the difference between bottom-up and top-down query evaluation. Section 3 describes the focus of our SQO algorithms, the removal of joins of tables, which are known beforehand (via deduction over ICs and rules) not to return answers. The cost of this SQO is discussed in Section 4. An overview of two SQO algorithms is provided in Section 5. A summary and future directions is given in Section 6.

2 Preliminaries

We assume familiarity with the terminology of relational and deductive databases [11]. A database, DB, consists of an extensional database (EDB), an intensional database (IDB), and a set of ICs. We assume DB to be function-free, EDB to consist of ground positive facts and IDB of rules. We also assume that IDB rules are nonrecursive. An IC is a rule with an empty head and whose body contains nonground atoms. EDB predicates are those that appear only in bodies of rules. IDB predicates are the rest.

We also describe the concept of a query tree (an AND/OR tree) of an IDB predicate p to be the "parse tree" of an expression in relational algebra (R.A.) that yields the relation p in terms of the EDB. We are interested in union and join operations, and do not represent selections and projections explicitly in the tree. However, selections and projections are implicitly apparent. Also, whenever an intermediate node of the query tree represents an IDB predicate q, we likewise label that node as q.

The following example shows a query tree.

Example 1 *Let DB contain five base relations:* faculty*(Name, Department, Rank),* staff*(Name, Department, Years_of_Employment),* ta*(Name, Department),* life_ins *(Name, Provider, Monthly_premium) and* health_plan *(Name, Provider, Monthly_premium). Let there be two rules in the DB: the first one defines an* employee *relation (via the union of the* ta *relation and projections from the* faculty *and* staff *relations); the second defines a* benefits *relation (via the union of projections from the* life_ins *and* health_plan *relations).*

$$employee(X,Y) \leftarrow faculty(X,Y,Z). \qquad benefits(X,Z) \leftarrow life\_ins(X,Z,W).$$
$$employee(X,Y) \leftarrow staff(X,Y,Z). \qquad benefits(X,Z) \leftarrow health\_plan(X,Z,W).$$
$$employee(X,Y) \leftarrow ta(X,Y).$$

Let a query ask for the names of all employees of the physical plant, p_p, *whose benefits are provided by* hmo*:*

$$Q(X): \leftarrow employee(X,p\_p), benefits(X,hmo)$$

The query tree representation of this query is given in Figure 1.

A tree representation of a query can be translated to an equivalent R.A. representation. We use the two representations interchangeably. The R.A. representation[1] of the query of Example 1 is:

$$Q = (\pi_X faculty(X,p\_p,Y)) \cup \pi_X staff(X,p\_p,Z) \cup ta(X,p\_p))$$
$$\bowtie (\pi_X life\_ins(X,hmo,W) \cup \pi_X health\_plan(X,hmo,V))$$

---

[1] We ignore for clarity explicit representation of select operations.

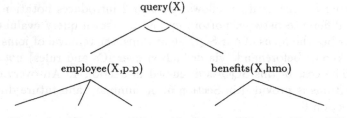

Figure 1: The query tree representation of the query of Example 1

Next we define several concepts which we will use in the paper.

Definition 2.1 *Let Q be a query. U is an* unfolding *of Q in DB iff*
- $U = Q$;
- $U = q_1(v_1), ..., q_{i-1}(v_{i-1}), P\theta, q_{i+1}(v_{i+1}), ..., q_m(v_m)$, *where*
  $U' = q_1(v_1), ..., q_{i-1}(v_{i-1}), q_i(v_i), q_{i+1}(v_{i+1}), ..., q_m(v_m)$
  is an unfolding of Q and there is a rule $< q_i(x_i) \leftarrow P >$ in IDB for which
  $q_i(v_i)\theta = q_i(x_i)\theta$ *and θ is an mgu.*

U is a complete unfolding *of Q if it contains only EDB predicates.*

Example 2 *A set of complete unfoldings of the query of Example 1 is:*
$\leftarrow faculty(X,p\_p,\_), life\_ins(X,hmo,\_).$ $\leftarrow faculty(X,p\_p,\_), health\_plan(X,hmo,\_).$
$\leftarrow ta(X,p\_p), life\_ins(X,hmo,\_).$ $\leftarrow ta(X,p\_p), health\_plan(X,hmo,\_).$
$\leftarrow staff(X,p\_p,\_), life\_ins(X,hmo,\_).$ $\leftarrow staff(X,p\_p,\_), health\_plan(X,hmo,\_).$

Note that atoms in a (complete) unfolding of a query Q represent (leaf) nodes in the respective query tree for Q.

Definition 2.2 *Let U be an unfolding (not necessarily complete) of Q. U is a* null unfolding *of Q in DB iff $IDB \cup IC \models \neg\exists\, U$*

Example 3 *Let an integrity constraint be: $< \leftarrow\ ta(X,Y), life\_ins(X,Z,W) >$. This states that teaching assistants are not entitled to receive life insurance. Then, $ta(X,p\_p), life\_ins(X,hmo,\_)$ is a null unfolding of Q of Example 1.*

Identifying the null unfoldings is a non-trivial task, and is a research topic in its own right. It is not our focus here. For this paper we assume this step, and the set of null unfoldings is an input to our algorithms. For edification of the reader, we briefly sketch an approach to finding null unfoldings.

In the *Carmin* project [4, 3], a project to provide cooperative responses to database queries in addition to their answer sets, we have explored methods to identify the null unfoldings of a query. The general approach that we have developed is as follows.

- Rewrite each *IC* by replacing its empty head with the special predicate *bottom*, '⊥', so it becomes a rule.
- Assume an "answer" to the query, using Skolem constants.
- Employ standard deduction over these facts (the assumed answer), the *IDB*, and the *rule ICs* to determine if '⊥' is derivable.

This basic approach can be extended to reason over the query's unfoldings too. Facts are hypothesized for atoms for all possible unfoldings. A constrained hyper-resolution can then be employed, which only resolves over *compatible* facts—facts which co-exist within some unfolding. All null unfoldings for a query can be determined by running the constrained hyper-resolution to fix-point.

In this paper, we discuss the problem of SQO in the context of bottom-up query evaluation. We assume that query evaluation proceeds bottom-up, as described in the semi-naive algorithm [11]. The problem we address here, albeit informally is: given a query tree and a set of null unfoldings, rewrite the query tree to achieve the largest savings possible. We focus on the elimination of redundant joins. We want to maximize the difference between the savings conferred by join elimination and the cost of computing the optimized form itself. This cost, as shown later, is not always trivial. This approach is different from SQO for top-down evaluation strategies, where the cost of optimization is only the cost of identifying null unfoldings . We share that cost also but we do not consider that issue in this paper.

The difference between top-down and bottom-up query evaluation can be expressed as a difference in query representation. For top-down evaluation, the query is represented as a set of complete unfoldings; for bottom-up evaluation, as a query tree. The two representations differ in their compactness when viewed as formulas in R.A. written over EDB predicates. If this compactness is measured (inversely) by the number of elementary join and union operations that need to be executed to evaluate the query, then the top-down query representation is the least compact of all equivalent query forms (in relational algebra).[2] On the other hand, the query tree *tends* to minimize the number of these operations providing a compact form of query representation.

Unfolding a query distributes one (or more) of the unions of its R.A. representation; *refolding* it factors out one (or more) of its subexpressions from one (or more) of the unions of its R.A. representation. Thus, unfolding a query increases the number of its operations, while refolding decreases the number.

3 General Optimization Strategy

We address first the following problem: given a query tree and a set of null unfoldings of the query, rewrite the tree to guarantee that the joins that these unfoldings represent are not part of the transformed query. By doing this (assuming that the tables to be joined are not empty), we *always* save in terms of query processing time by not having to perform unnecessary join (i.e., a join of tables from the null unfolding) which we know is not going to return any tuples. In the extreme case, when a query itself is a null unfolding, the query does not need to be evaluated at all since the answer set is empty. Redundant join elimination is straightforward for top-down query processing: it consists of simply removing the null unfoldings from the set of all unfoldings of the query. Thus, the first approximation to an optimization algorithm can be stated as follows:

---

[2] We assume non-redundant formulas.

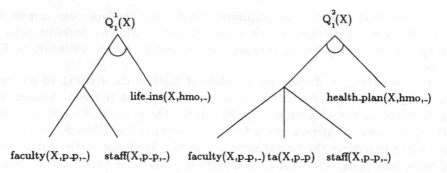

Figure 2: The query tree representation of Q_1^1 and Q_1^2

1. unfold the query in all possible ways;
2. remove null unfoldings; and
3. refold the query resulting from step 2 back as much as possible.

Clearly, we do not need to unfold the query in *all* possible ways. It is enough to unfold the query to the extent that null unfoldings are explicitly represented so that they may be removed, as the following example shows informally.

Example 4 *Consider the DB and the query of Example 1 and the null unfolding of Example 3. The query Q and the null unfolding N expressed in R.A. are:*

$$Q = (\pi_X faculty(X,p\_p,Y)) \cup \pi_X staff(X,p\_p,Z) \cup ta(X,p\_p))$$
$$\bowtie (\pi_X life\_ins(X,hmo,W) \cup \pi_X health\_plan(X,hmo,V))$$
$$N = \pi_X (life\_ins(X,hmo,W) \bowtie ta(X,p\_p))$$

To represent the unfolding explicitly, we may unfold the query (partially) as:

$$Q' = (\pi_X faculty(X,p\_p,Y) \cup \pi_X staff(X,p\_p,Z)) \bowtie \pi_X life\_ins(X,hmo,W)$$
$$\cup ta(X,p\_p) \bowtie \pi_X life\_ins(X,hmo,W)$$
$$\cup (\pi_X faculty(X,p\_p,Y) \cup ta(X,p\_p) \cup \pi_X staff(X,p\_p,Z))$$
$$\bowtie \pi_X health\_plan(X,hmo,V)$$

After the null unfolding is removed we obtain $Q_1 = Q_1^1 \cup Q_1^2$, where:

$$Q_1^1 = (\pi_X faculty(X,p\_p,Y) \cup \pi_X staff(X,p\_p,Z)) \bowtie \pi_X life\_ins(X,hmo,W)$$
$$Q_1^2 = (\pi_X faculty(X,p\_p,Y) \cup ta(X,p\_p) \cup \pi_X staff(X,p\_p,Z))$$
$$\bowtie \pi_X health\_plan(X,hmo,V)$$

Query trees representations of Q_1^1 and Q_1^2 are shown in Figure 2.

Since unfolding a query *always* increases the number of operations in its R.A. representation, it may be viewed as bringing the query form closer to its top-down representation. In the extreme case, when there are many null unfoldings the query may have to be unfolded almost completely and cannot be refolded, this worst case converges on the form of the query's top-down representation.

The last issue addressed is the compactness of the optimized query. As stated above, the difference between top-down and bottom-up query representations can be expressed syntactically as a difference in their number of operations (unions and joins). A top-down approach maximizes that number, while a bottom-up approach tends to minimize it. We assumed above that the query is unfolded *only* to the degree necessary so that the null unfoldings are represented explicitly, and then after removing these null unfoldings, *refolded* back from that form. This does not guarantee, however, that the final form of the query is in the most compact form (i.e., has the least number of operations), as the following example shows.

Example 5 *Let the query be:*

$$Q = G \bowtie (A \bowtie (B \cup C \bowtie D) \cup E \bowtie (F \cup C \bowtie D))$$

and the null unfolding be:

$$U = E \bowtie F$$

By unfolding the query, removing the null unfolding and refolding the query back we get:

$$Q' = G \bowtie (A \bowtie (B \cup C \bowtie D) \cup E \bowtie C \bowtie D)$$

However, the most compact query form is:

$$Q'' = G \bowtie (C \bowtie D \bowtie (A \cup E) \cup A \bowtie B).$$

There are two reasons for not trying to minimize (absolutely) the number of operations in the query. First, it can be shown that the minimization problem is NP-complete. Second, we adopt as a working hypothesis the assumption that the input to the optimization algorithm – the query tree – is close to a minimum representation of the query. We conjecture then that the optimized query is near some *ideal* optimized query. We argue, moreover, that even if a polynomial time algorithm were available for optimality, there are still good reasons for not choosing the number of operations as our sole criterion for designing an algorithm. In the next section, it is shown that other costs of SQO can easily negate the value of an ideal optimal algorithm.

4 Optimization Trade-offs

As stated in the previous section, removing null unfoldings from a query produces a less compact query, taking it closer to the top-down representation. As a consequence, some of the undesirable features of the top-down approach to query evaluation become manifest in the evaluation of the "optimized" query.

1. *Query fragmentation* is an inherent feature of SQO for bottom-up query evaluation. There is only one type of null unfolding, which we call *perfect*, removal of which does not increase the number of operations in the optimized query.[3]

Definition 4.1 *Let* $Q = A_1 \bowtie ... \bowtie A_n$ *be a query expressed in relational algebra and* U *be an unfolding of* Q. U *is perfect iff* $U = A_{i_1} \bowtie ... \bowtie A_{i_{n-1}} \bowtie B$, $i_j \in \{1, ..., n-1\}$, $i_j \neq i_k$ *if* $j \neq k$ *where* B *is a subexpression of* A_{i_n}.

On the other hand, there are cases when the optimized query may have almost twice the number of operation of the original one.

The degree of query fragmentation depends also on the algorithm used. If the optimization algorithm is iterative, i.e., it removes null unfoldings sequentially, independently of one another, query fragmentation can be worse than for a global approach. Consider the following extension of Example 4 where we assume that *health_plan* is not an extensional predicate, but is further defined as:

---

[3]Such integrity constraints (with two atoms) were called *semi-complete join pairs* in [7].

health_plan(X, W, V)← subsidized_health_plan(X, W, V).
health_plan(X, W, V)← unsubsidized_health_plan(X, W, V).

Assume also that there is another null unfolding to consider:

ta(X,p_p),subsidized_health_plan(X,hmo,_).

Removing this unfolding from query Q_1 of Example 4, (where *health_plan (X, hmo, _)* has been rewritten via the above rules fragments the query again. Notice, however, that if the original query were split in a different way, for instance, into $Q_2(X) = Q_2^1(X) \cup Q_2^2(X)$ in which:

$Q_2^1(X) = (faculty(X,p_p,_) \cup staff(X,p_p,_)) \bowtie (subsidized\_health\_plan(X,hmo,_)$
$\cup \ unsubsidized\_health\_plan(X,hmo,_) \cup life\_ins(X,hmo,_))$

$Q_2^2(X) = ta(X,p_p) \bowtie (subsidized\_health\_plan(X,hmo,_)$
$\cup \ unsubsidized\_health\_plan(X,hmo,_))$

then removing the second null unfolding does not increase the number of nodes in the tree (only the second subquery, $Q_2^2(X)$ needs to be rewritten). One of the key differences between the two algorithms presented in the next section is the way they handle the removal of multiple null unfoldings.

2. *Recomputation of joins due to table overlaps.* Materialized tables in bottom-up query evaluation described here do not contain duplicates (we assume duplicates are removed whenever tables are unioned). Consider again the DB and the query of Example 4 and the following condition holds:

health_plan(X,hmo,Y)← life_ins(X,hmo,Z).

Then, all answers to the query Q are computed by Q_1^2 and so Q_1^1 is redundant. This redundant computation would not have occured if the query had not been optimized.

3. *Recomputation of joins due to independent computation of subqueries.* Consider yet another extension of Example 4: assume that *health_plan* is not an extensional predicate, but it is further defined as:

health_plan(X, Y, Z)← personel(SSN, X), insurance(SSN, Y, Z).

Also assume that the query is split as in $Q_3(X) = Q_3^1(X) \cup Q_3^2(X)$ where:

$Q_3^1(X) = (faculty(X,p_p,_) \cup staff(X,p_p,_)) \bowtie$
$(personel(SSN,X) \bowtie insurance(SSN,hmo,_) \cup life\_ins(X,hmo,_))$

$Q_3^2(X) = ta(X,p_p) \bowtie personel(SSN,X) \bowtie insurance(SSN,hmo,_)$

Note that both Q_3^1 and Q_3^2 involve computing the join of *personel(SSN,X)* $\bowtie$ *insurance(SSN,hmo,_)*. However, since the two queries are evaluated independently, the optimal plan for query $Q_2^2(X) = ta(X,p_p) \bowtie personel(SSN,X) \bowtie insurance(SSN,hmo,_)$ may require computing the join *ta(X,p_p)* $\bowtie$ *personel(SSN,X)* first and then joining the result with *insurance (SSN, hmo, _)*. Clearly, considering the fact that the join *personel (SSN,X)* $\bowtie$ *insurance (SSN, hmo, _)* has to be computed as part of Q_3^1, it may be better to compute Q_3^2 in a different order.

4. *Elusive savings.* The savings achieved by join elimination are proportional to the sizes of tables whose join can be eliminated from the query because of the presence of an appropriate null unfolding. These savings may be too small, however, to justify applying semantic optimization, given the overhead costs.

Assume that *ta(X,p_p)* in Example 4 is empty; that is, there is no teaching assistant employed in the physical plant department. Thus, removing the null unfolding $ta(X,p\_p) \bowtie life\_ins(X,hmo,\_)$ saves nothing. In the ideal situation, we should be able to discover such cases to avoid rewriting the query.

The problems discussed in points 2 and 3 can be solved easily. Recomputation of joins due to table overlap can be solved in the following fashion. Let $U_1, ..., U_n$ be a null unfolding, $U_i^1, ..., U_i^k$ be the siblings of U_i, $1 \leq i \leq n$, in the query tree. We state without formal proof that substituting U_i^j, $1 \leq j \leq k$ with $U_i^j - U_i$ does not change the answer set of the evaluated query, while preventing at the same time recomputation of joins due to table overlaps.[4] Note also that this computation does not add an extra cost to query evaluation since it is equivalent to duplicate removal from materialized tables.

The problem of recomputation of joins due to independent evaluation of subqueries is addressed by *multiple query optimization*[9].

If the savings analysis is to be a part of an SQO algorithm, then the sizes of the tables in the query tree must be part of the input to the algorithm. But the only way[5] the sizes of intermediate nodes of a query tree can be learned is by materializing these nodes. Materializing *all* nodes of the tree *before* doing any SQO of course defeats the purpose of optimization (since this is equivalent to evaluating the query). Hence, materialization should be done in stages, interleaving the steps of evaluation and optimization. A consequence, however, is that this type of SQO algorithm must be iterative since we cannot know in advance which null unfoldings should be removed. Thus, there is a trade-off between a global optimization (which produces a potentially more compact query as point 1 of this section showed) and exploiting the savings analysis. The two algorithms in the next section emphasize these different choices.

5 The Algorithms

5.1 A Global Algorithm

We consider a global approach in which all the null unfoldings are removed from the query in parallel, thus ensuring that the rewritten query is minimal.

We wish to avoid "evaluating" any of the known null unfoldings of a query whenever we evaluate the query. Our approach is to rewrite the query as a set of unfoldings that are *independent* of the null unfoldings, but which, when evaluated, result in the same answer set as the query's. This *unfolding set*, call it $\mathcal{S}$, should have the following properties. Let $\mathcal{N}$ be the set of null unfoldings known in advance.

- No unfolding in $\mathcal{S}$ should *overlap* with any unfolding in $\mathcal{N}$; that is, for $U \in \mathcal{S}$ and $V \in \mathcal{N}$, U and V have no unfolding in common. (Call U and V *independent* of one another in this case.)

---

[4]Note that the difference operation makes sense because nodes in the tree represent materialized tables.

[5]Estimating the sizes of intermediate nodes based on the sizes of the tree leaves may be very unreliable.

- $\mathcal{N} \cup \mathcal{S}$ should be a *cover* of the query; that is, any complete unfolding of the query is an unfolding of some unfolding in $\mathcal{N}$ or $\mathcal{S}$.
- Set $\mathcal{S}$ should be *most general*:
  - no unfolding in $\mathcal{S}$ can be refolded at all, and still preserve the above properties; and
  - for any $U \in \mathcal{S}$, $(\mathcal{N} \cup \mathcal{S}) - \{U\}$ is not a cover of the query.

If *Carmin* can find a set of null unfoldings $\mathcal{N}$ for a query which is a *cover* of the query, and each such null unfolding is *provably* null, the query is said to be a *complex misconception*. Detecting that a query is a misconception is the ultimate win in SQO; the query does not need to be evaluated because its answer set is known to be empty. A system like *Carmin* will determine $\mathcal{N}$ while attempting to deduce misconceptions. We are interested in intermediate cases where $\mathcal{N}$ is not a cover, and so we still need to evaluate the query.

Given a query $\mathcal{Q}$ and its set of null unfoldings $\mathcal{N}$, the routine **find_cover** finds the unfolding set $\mathcal{S}$ as defined above.

$$\textbf{find\_cover}\,(\mathcal{Q}, \mathcal{N})$$
$$\mathcal{S} := \{\}$$
$$\text{while } \textbf{new\_unfolding}\,(\mathcal{Q}, \mathcal{N} \cup \mathcal{S}, U)$$
$$V := \textbf{refolding}\,(U, \mathcal{N})$$
$$\mathcal{S} := \mathcal{S} \cup \{V\}$$
$$\text{return } \textbf{parsimonious}\,(\mathcal{S})$$

The routine **new_unfolding** is implemented in *Carmin*. It returns *false* if $\mathcal{N} \cup \mathcal{S}$ is a cover of $\mathcal{Q}$. Otherwise, it evaluates *true*, and returns a new complete unfolding as U which is not a sub-unfolding of any unfolding in $\mathcal{N} \cup \mathcal{S}$. (So U is a witness that $\mathcal{N} \cup \mathcal{S}$ is not a cover.) This routine is the computational bottleneck in this approach. It is NP-hard over the size of $\mathcal{N} \cup \mathcal{S}$. However, for reasonably small input sizes, it runs with good average case performance.

The **refolding** is simple. It refolds the unfolding U as much as possible without *overlapping* with any of the null unfoldings in $\mathcal{N}$. In the end, **parsimonious** ensures that the unfolding set returned (still call it $\mathcal{S}$) is minimal; that is, no member unfolding can be thrown away.

Evaluating each unfolded query in $\mathcal{S}$ and unioning the results is equivalent to evaluating the original query, and obviously does not evaluate any of the join expressions of the null unfoldings. The approach's key advantage is that $\mathcal{S}$ can be guaranteed to be minimal. A disadvantage is that if $\mathcal{N}$ is large, the algorithm will tend towards intractable. This can also happen if the minimal $\mathcal{S}$ deduced is inherently large (although there are reasons to believe that this does not happen, in average case, unless $\mathcal{N}$ is large.)

A second disadvantage is that *every* null unfolding is "removed", whether it truly yields a worthwhile optimization. This does not allow potential savings to be estimated—to decide which null unfoldings to attend and which to ignore—in conjunction with the query rewrite and evaluation. Next, we consider a dynamic approach which integrates estimations, rewriting, and evaluation.

5.2 A Dynamic Iterative Algorithm

We assumed that the null unfoldings of a query are given as input and are to be removed. This is an acceptable strategy if the number of null unfoldings is small (thus the degree of query fragmentation is small). Databases, however, often contain many ICs, resulting in too many null unfoldings for a given query, to make the use of all of them for SQO feasible. We could focus instead on a subset of the null unfoldings for the query. We would like this subset of unfoldings to be *optimal*, in the sense that it contains only unfoldings that yield large savings in the query's evaluation. As demonstrated earlier, the savings can be measured via the sizes of the tables involved in a given null unfolding. Then only those unfoldings that "save" the most in that sense are selected.

We propose a dynamic algorithm to rewrite the query *during* the evaluation, removing null unfoldings iteratively throughout the evaluation. The idea of this approach is to proceed with the evaluation in stages. Each stage proceeds until enough tables have been materialized so that there is enough information to estimate the savings that would be achieved by removing a given null unfolding. If the estimated savings are greater than some fixed threshold, the query is rewritten and the evaluation proceeds until the next checkpoint. Otherwise, that unfolding is not removed, and the query evaluation proceeds as normal.

The downside of this dynamic optimization is a non-optimal query fragmentation. Since we do not know in advance which null unfoldings are to be removed, we cannot predict what the best query rewriting at any given checkpoint will be. Point 1, *Query fragmentation*, of Section 4 illustrates this problem.

We assume for this algorithm that the set of null unfoldings $\mathcal{N}$ for a given query Q with a query tree T is *ordered*.[6] We also assume that we are given some threshold value, say h (for example, determined by experimentation) which indicates how big the tables to be joined ought to be to justify the optimization step. **remove_unfolding**(T,N) is a simple algorithm described informally in Example 4 that given a query tree and a null unfolding unfolds the query, removes that unfolding, and refolds back the query to its compact form.

evaluate_optimize $(T, \mathcal{N})$
    If $\mathcal{N} = \emptyset$
          Materialize all nodes of T, return $Root(T)$ [evaluated query]
    Else
          Let $\mathcal{N} = N_1, ..., N_m$
          Let $N_1 = N_1^1, ..., N_1^n$
          Materialize all subtrees rooted at $N_1^1, ..., N_1^n$
          If $Size(N_1^1) * ... * Size(N_1^n) > h$
                    $T :=$**remove_unfolding**(T, N_1)
          $\mathcal{N} := \mathcal{N} - N_1$
          evaluate_optimize$(T, \mathcal{N})$

---

[6]Informally, N_1 is before N_2 in a sequence of ordered unfoldings if all atoms of N_1 are below atoms of N_2 in the query tree. A formal definition of the ordering and a discussion of a possibility of such ordering is beyond the scope of this paper.

6 Summary and Future Work

We discussed semantic query optimization for bottom-up query evaluation strategies. We presented the goal of such an optimization, analyzed its cost, and proposed two algorithms. Our optimization techniques are general and can be implemented with any particular bottom-up query evaluation method.

We plan to extend this work in two directions. First, algorithms for other types of semantic optimization (such as restriction elimination or restriction introduction) should be developed and tested. Second, the algorithms for join elimination presented here should be generalized to work for databases with resursion and negation (in queries, rules and ICs).

We intend to implement the algorithms on the testbed provided by the *Carmin* system [3]. We plan to experiment with large databases to determine the conditions under which these algorithms perform well, and when to use one method over another.

References

[1] U. Chakravarthy, J. Grant, and J. Minker. Logic-based approach to semantic query optimization. *ACM TODS*, 15(2):162–207, June 1990.

[2] T. Gaasterland and J. Lobo. Processing negation and disjunction in logic programs through integrity constraints. *Journal of Intel. Inf. Sys.*, 2(3), 1993.

[3] P. Godfrey. *An Architecture and Implementation for a Cooperative Database System*. PhD thesis, University of Maryland, Dept. of CS, University of Maryland, College Park, MD 20742, USA, May 1996.

[4] P. Godfrey, J. Minker, and L. Novik. An architecture for a cooperative database system. In W. Litwin and T. Risch, eds., *Proc. of the 1st Int. Conf. on Applications of Databases*, LNCS 819, pages 3–24. Springer Verlag, Vadstena, Sweden, June 1994.

[5] J.J. King. Quist: A system for semantic query optimization in relational databases. *Proc. 7th Int. Conf. on VLDB*, pages 510–517, September 1981.

[6] Laks V.S. Lakshmanan and R. Missaoui. On semantic query optimization in deductive databases. In *Proc. IEEE Int. Conf. on Data Engineering*, pages 368–375, 1992.

[7] S. Lee, L.J.Henschen, and G.Z. Qadah. Semantic query reformulation in deductive databases. In *Proc. IEEE Int. Conf. on Data Eng.*, pages 232–239, Los Amitos, CA, 1991. IEEE CS Press.

[8] A.Y. Levy and Y. Sagiv. Semantic query optimization in datalog programs. In *Proc. PODS*, 1995.

[9] T. Sellis. Global query optimization. *Proc. 1986 ACM-SIGMOD Int. Conf. on Management of Data*, May 1986.

[10] S.T. Shenoy and Z.M. Ozsoyoglu. Design and implementation of a semantic query optimizer. *IEEE TKDE*, 1(3):344–361, Sept. 1989.

[11] J.D. Ullman. *Principles of Database and Knowledge-Base Systems I*. Principles of Computer Science Series. CS Press, Rockville, MD 20850, 1988.

Dynamically Changing Behavior:
An Agent-Oriented View to Modeling
Intelligent Information Systems*

Can Türker   Stefan Conrad   Gunter Saake

Otto-von-Guericke-Universität Magdeburg
Institut für Technische Informationssysteme
Postfach 4120, D–39016 Magdeburg, Germany
E-mail: {tuerker|conrad|saake}@iti.cs.uni-magdeburg.de

Abstract. Although object specification technology is successfully used for modeling information systems, it is not able to get a grasp of dynamically changing behavior. Due to the fact that objects in information systems can have a very long life-span, it often happens that during the life of an object external requirements are changing (e.g. changes of laws or banking rules). Such changes often require the object to adopt another behavior. The main problem for current object specification approaches is that, in general, not all possible changes can be taken into account in advance at specification time. Therefore, a flexible extension is needed to capture this situation. The approach we present and discuss in this paper is an important step towards a specification framework based on the concept of agent by introducing a certain form of knowledge as part of the internal state.

1 Introduction

Nowadays, nearly every organization has to face the situation that in order be competitive the use of modern information systems is indispensable. Considering the frequent and dramatic changes in the international economy and politics, there is a clear demand for advanced information systems which are able to deal with highly dynamic environments, e.g. rapidly changing markets, increasing (world-wide) competition, and new trade agreements as well as (inter)national laws. In the recent years, there are obvious efforts in several computer science communities to build cooperative intelligent information systems which can deal with such aspects (see for example [HPS93]).

Today, object-oriented techniques are in general used for modeling such advanced information systems [Buc90, Bro92]. Most of the existing object-oriented approaches are successful in capturing the properties and behavior of the real-world entities. However, it seems that the concept of "object" (at least in its current understanding) cannot cover all aspects of modern information systems. Whereas structural aspects of such systems can easily be dealt with by current object-oriented approaches, these approaches succeed to cope with *dynamic* behavior only up to a certain degree. Typically, information system objects have

* This research was partially supported by the ESPRIT Basic Research Working Group No. 8319 ModelAge (A Common Formal Model of Cooperating Intelligent Agents).

a longer life-span than application programs, environmental restrictions, etc. Therefore, we need a semantic model where the behavior specification of an object or object system may be modified during its existence, which is not expressible in current formalisms underlying traditional (object-oriented) specification languages until now.

Currently, the concept of *agent* [WJ95, GK94] which can be seen as a further development of "object" is emerging as an important concept in many fields of Information Technology, e.g. Federated Database Systems, Distributed Artificial Intelligence, or Requirements Engineering. Agents differ from conventional objects in several ways. First of all agents are not only reactive, but they are also active in the sense that they are able to act goal-driven without external stimuli. In addition, agents are flexible, e.g. they may change their behavior dynamically during system run-time. Furthermore, they are able to deal with unexpected, unpredictable situations. The properties mentioned above are especially important for modeling human behavior in an appropriate way. In summary, the behavior of an agent is not (or can not be) completely determined at compile or specification time. In order to get a grasp of such properties, we need an agent specification framework which goes beyond the existing object-oriented ones.

The paper is structured as follows. Sect. 2 surveys the current object modeling and specification technology. In Sect. 3, we briefly discuss a concept of agent as a further evolution of the concept of object. Here, we illustrate the properties of agents and point out differences to the traditional concept of object. In Sect. 4, we present a first way of extending object specification towards agent specification. Here, we focus our attention especially on the specification of dynamically changing behavior of agents. Finally, we conclude by pointing out future work.

2 Object-Oriented Modeling and Specification

Recently, object-oriented conceptual modeling of information systems has become a widely accepted approach. Meanwhile, there exists a lot of object-oriented models and specification languages (e.g. Oblog [SSG+91], or TROLL [HSJ+94, JSHS96, SJH93]) proposed for that purposes. In this section, we briefly recall the basic ideas of the concept of object, whereby we base our presentation on the object model as introduced in [SSE87].

Basically, objects are characterized as *coherent units of structure and behavior*. An object has an *internal state* of which certain properties can be observed. The internal state can be manipulated explicitly through a properly defined *event interface*. *Attributes* are the observable properties of objects which may only be changed by event occurrences. The *behavior* of objects are described by *life cycles*, which are built from sequences of (sets of simultaneously occurring) *events*. Thus, each object state is completely characterized by a *life cycle prefix*, which determines the current attribute values. The possible evolution of objects can be restricted by a set of *state constraints* which can be used to define the admissible state transitions for an object.

For textual presentation of object specifications, we use a notation close to the syntactical conventions of the object-oriented specification language TROLL. In Fig. 1 we give a TROLL specification for a class of account objects. For the purposes of this paper, we have only specified a small number of properties an account could have. Here, we assume an account to have an (unique) account number, a bank by which it is managed, a holder, a balance, and a limit for overdrawing. Moreover, we specify some basic events like opening an account, withdrawing money from or depositing money to an account.

```
object class Account
   identification    ByAccountID:  (Bank, No);
   attributes        No:           nat constant;
                     Bank:         |Bank|;
                     Holder:       |Customer|;
                     Balance:      money initialized 0.00;
                     Limit:        money initialized 0.00 restricted >= -5000.00;
                     Counter:      nat initialized 0;
   events  Open(BID:|Bank|, AccNo:nat, AccHolder:|Customer|) birth
                     changing    Bank   := BID,
                                 No     := AccNo,
                                 Holder := AccHolder;
           Withdraw(W:money) enabled    Balance - Limit >= W;
                             changing    Balance := Balance - W;
                             calling     IncreaseCounter;
           Deposit(D:money) changing    Balance := Balance + D;
                            calling     IncreaseCounter;
           IncreaseCounter  changing    Counter := Counter + 1;
           Close death;
end object class Account;
```

Fig. 1. TROLL specification of an Account class.

In TROLL-like languages, an object template specification mainly consists out of two parts: a *signature* section which lists object events and attributes together with parameter and co-domain types, and a behavior section containing the axioms. As axioms we do not have general temporal logic formulas but special syntactic notations for typical specification patterns. For our discussion we restrict the language features to a few basic specification patterns.

In the declaration section for events, we mark some events as *birth* events or as *death* events corresponding to creation and destruction of objects, e.g. Open and Close in our example in Fig. 1. The occurrence of events can be restricted by *enabling conditions* which define explicit preconditions for events, e.g. the event Withdraw may only occur if the the withdrawal amount is less than the balance of the account. Changes of attribute values are caused by event occurrences, e.g. the event Withdraw decreases the balance of an account. These attribute valuation rules can also be restricted using conditions on state attributes, e.g. we may restrict the the credit limit to maximal 5000.00. The *event calling mechanism* is used to model interaction inside (composite) objects, e.g. the event Withdraw enforces the event IncreaseCounter to occur simultaneously. Similar to attribute valuations, we may have conditional event calling, too.

Of course, TROLL-like languages offer additional language features for template description, for example operational process declaration and global behavior constraints. Moreover, further abstraction concepts and associations between objects like relationships, specialization, aggregation are supported, too. Nevertheless, the concepts presented so far have a major drawback: *they succeed in capturing dynamic behavior (of information systems) only up to a certain degree.* Indeed, languages like TROLL or Oblog are expressive enough to model even changing object behavior depending on state changes, *but these modifications have to be fixed during specification time, e.g. before object creation.* But, this is too restrictive for handling object evolution in information systems. Typically, information system objects are characterized by long life-spans. Usually, during that long time-span an object and the environment of object may change in a way that cannot be foreseen. Consequently, dynamic specification changes are needed to overcome the problem that generally not all possible future behaviors of an object can be anticipated in the original system specification.

3   A Concept of Agent

In this section we propose the *concept of agent*, which can be seen as a further evolution of the concept of object, as an adequate means for modeling information systems. We emphasize that the term agent is frequently used in several computer science disciplines, e.g. Federated Database Systems, Distributed Artificial Intelligence, or Requirements Engineering, with slightly different meanings. Basically, agents are interpreted as *dynamic* and *intelligent* objects (cf. [Sho93, GK94, WJ95]), which are assumed to be

- *autonomous* (act without direct (user) intervention),
- *cooperative* (cooperate, coordinate and negotiate with other agents),
- *reactive* (respond flexible to dynamic and unpredictable situations that occur in their environments), and
- *pro-active* (may also exhibit goal-driven behavior by taking the initiative).

In the sequel, we briefly summarize the basic characteristics of agents and point out differences to traditional objects (for a detailed discussion see [SCT95]).

Internal State. Like objects, agents have an *internal state* which is based on their history and influence their behavior. Whereas the internal state of objects is determined by the values of their attributes, agents have a more general notion of internal (mental) state: beside (conventional) attribute values it may contain disjunctive information, partial knowledge, default assumptions, etc. Thus, the state of agents includes an internal, imperfect representation of the world. Essentially, the internal state of an agent reflects the knowledge (belief, intention, obligations, goals, etc.) of that agent at a given time. In contrast to traditional object concepts, this *knowledge is not fixed at specification time, but it is changeable during the lifetime of an agent.* Due to this fact, agents are assumed to have knowledge acquisition and revision capabilities in order to be able to adapt their knowledge to changes in their environments. In order to make use of their knowledge, the states of agents may additionally contain explicit reasoning rules.

Goals. Agents have *goals* which they try to achieve (by cooperation) under given constraints. Each agent is obliged to satisfy its goals. In general, this is done by executing a *sequence of actions*. Since goals are part of the internal state of agents, they may be changed during an agent's lifetime, too. They can be extended, revised or replaced through other goals. Further, they may also be conflicting. Hence, agents must be equipped conflict resolution strategies.

Behavior, Actions and Constraints. Agents are able to (re)act and communicate by executing sequences of *actions*. Thus, agents show an external *behavior* that obeys the given *constraints*. In contrast to traditional objects, agents may

- exhibit reactive behavior as well as goal-driven (or pro-active) behavior;
- perform actions concurrently by asynchronous message passing;
- have varying, non-normative behavior;
- have varying constraints;
- have a preference ordering of alternative "correct" behaviors.

Cooperation. In most cases agents have to cooperate to achieve their goals. Especially in federated information systems, where multiple agents have to interoperate in order to provide a powerful interface for application programs, appropriate structures and protocols for agent communication and cooperation are required [GK94].

Considering all these properties agents can have, it becomes clear that current object specification technology as sketched in Sect. 2 cannot fulfill all these requirements. This is due to the fact that several concepts are not given in current object-oriented approaches. Nevertheless, the existing object specification approaches can be used as a stable basis for extensions which try to get a grasp of those agent-specific properties. By carefully extending the underlying semantic models and logics it should be possible to come closer and closer to the idea of "agents" as sketched before. The best way for allowing such extensions seems to be to consider "states as theories" in contrast to the usual way in object-oriented approaches where the state of an object is described by a simple value map assigning each attribute a corresponding value.

The "states as theories" approach is much more powerful by assuming that a state is described by a set of formulas. Depending on the underlying logic that we apply for formulating such formulas, we can then express different kinds of knowledge, for example knowledge about the future behavior of an agent as part of its own state as well as knowledge about the states of other agents. In this way, simple state changes can become changes of theories by which we can even express the change of knowledge or goals of an agent. Thereby, knowledge revision as well as dynamic knowledge acquisition can be specified. Furthermore, partial knowledge is possible and default knowledge could be integrated. However, for such an agent specification approach we need a logical framework, a *logic of agents*, in which several non-standard logics (e.g. logic of knowledge, default logic, deontic logic [Mey92, Rya93]), can be integrated. First results already show that the composition of different logics can really work [FM91]. In [SSS95] and [CS95] first steps towards the specification of dynamically changeable behavior in an object-oriented setting are presented and discussed.

4 Specifying Information Systems in Terms of Agents

In this section, we sketch the basic frame of an agent-oriented specification language by giving example specifications. We point out that in this first approach only a few, but very important agent-specific concepts like dynamic behavior are respected.

In Fig. 2 the structure of a possible specification of an agent class `Account` is depicted. The specification language used here can be considered as an extension of the object-oriented language TROLL sketched in Sect. 2. Similar to objects, agents have attributes (e.g. `Balance`) and events (e.g. `Withdraw`). The part of the behavior specification which must not be changed is specified in the **rigid axioms** section. In our example the effect of the events `Withdraw` and `Deposit` on the attribute `Balance` is fixed.

```
agent class Account
    identification     ByAccountID: (Bank, No);
    attributes         No:          nat constant;
                       Bank:        |Bank|;
                       Holder:      |Customer|;
                       Balance:     money initialized 0.00;
                       Limit:       money initialized 0.00;
                       Counter:     nat initialized 0;
    events             Open(BID:|Bank|, AccNo:nat, AccHolder:|Customer|) birth;
                       Withdrawal(W:money);
                       Deposit(D:money);
                       IncreaseCounter;
                       Close death;
                       Warning(S:string);
    rigid axioms       Open(BID:|Bank|, AccNo:nat, AccHolder:|Customer|)
                               changing  Bank   := BID,
                                         No     := AccNo,
                                         Holder := AccHolder;
                               calling   ResetAxioms;
                       Withdraw(W)  enabled   Balance - Limit >= W;
                               changing  Balance := Balance - W;
                               calling   IncreaseCounter;
                       Deposit(D)   changing  Balance := Balance + D;
                               calling   IncreaseCounter;
                       IncreaseCounter changing  Counter := Counter + 1;
    axiom attributes   Axioms initialized {};
    mutators           ResetAxioms;
                       AddAxioms(P:setOfAxioms);
                       RemoveAxioms(P:setOfAxioms);
    dynamic specification ResetAxioms     changing Axioms := {};
                       AddAxioms(P)     changing Axioms := Axioms ∪ P;
                       RemoveAxioms(P) changing Axioms := Axioms - P;
end agent class Account;
```

Fig. 2. Specification of an agent class `Account`

In addition to the traditional concept of attributes as used for objects, an agent have **axiom attributes** which contain sets of axioms which are valid under certain circumstances. In our example we have axiom attribute `Axioms` which is initialized by the empty set of axioms. In case we specify several axiom attributes we have to explicitly mark one of them as current axiom set. Each formula which is included in the value of this special axiom attribute at a certain state must be fulfilled in that state. Similar to basic attributes, axiom attributes are changed by

mutators which can be seen as special events. The effect of mutators is described in the **dynamic specification** section. Here, we allow the manipulation of the axiom attribute `Axioms`. We may add further axioms to `Axioms`, remove existing axioms from `Axioms` and reset `Axioms` to the initial state.

Specification of Dynamic Behavior

As already mentioned, one main difference between agents and traditional objects is that agents may change their behavior dynamically during their lifetime. In the sequel, we show different ways how dynamic behavior can be specified.

1. By using only one dynamically changeable axiom attribute. This case is presented in the example in Fig. 2. Here, the axiom attribute must be modifiable during the lifetime of an agent in order to be able to represent changing dynamic behavior of that agent. In our example the axiom attribute `Axioms` can be manipulated by the mutators `AddAxioms`, `RemoveAxioms` and `ResetAxioms`. Whereas `AddAxioms` and `RemoveAxioms` adds further axioms to and removes existing axioms from `Axioms`, respectively, `ResetAxioms` resets `Axioms` to the initial state. Possible values for the parameter P of the mutator `AddAxioms` could be the following ones:

```
{ Withdraw(W) calling {W > 400.00} Warning("Withdrawal limit exceeded!"); }

{ Withdraw(W) enabled (W >= 0.00) and (Balance - W >= Limit); }

{ Withdraw(W) calling {not(occurs(Clock.NextDay)) since last
                       occurs(Withdraw(W))}
                       Warning("Two withdrawals within one day!"); }

{ Close       enabled Balance = 0.00; }
```

The values above are sets of axioms written in the syntax of our specification language. The first value contains an axiom which requires to trigger a warning if the amount of a withdrawal is larger than 400. In the next value there is an additional restriction saying that a `Withdraw` event may only occur with an amount smaller than the current value of the attribute `Balance` minus the current value of the attribute `Limit`. Thereby, overdrawing of an account is ruled out. The third value ensures that a warning is triggered if two withdrawals occur within one day (in this formula we refer to a `Clock` assuming that it is specified elsewhere as a part of the same system). The last value contains a formula which specifies that an account may only be closed if there is no money on this account.

2. By using a set of predefined, unchangeable axiom attributes. Here, a set of axiom attributes, which contain predefined sets of axioms and which can not be modified during the lifetime of an agent, can be defined to model dynamically changing behavior of an agent. One of these axiom attributes must be declared as the current valid set of axioms which determines the current behavior of the agent. By switching between the axiom attributes the behavior of the agent can be changed dynamically.

axiom attributes
  Axioms(N:nat) **initialized**
    N=0: {} **default**,
    N=1: {Withdraw(W) **calling** {W > Balance}
                            Warning("Account has been overdrawn"))},
    N=2: {Withdraw(W) **calling** {not(occurs(Clock.NextDay))
                            since last occurs(Withdraw(W))}
                            Warning("Two withdrawals within one day!");}
    ...;
mutators   SwitchAxioms(N:nat);
dynamic specification SwitchAxioms(N) **changing** Axioms(0) := Axioms(N);

In the example above we define a parameterized attribute Axioms (for details see [HSJ+94]) which contains different sets of axioms. Here, we declare implicitly the attribute term Axioms(0) to be the set with the current valid axioms. By using the mutator SwitchAxioms we are able to change the agent's behavior dynamically. Please notice that this approach restricts the behavior evolution of an agent to various predefined behavior pattern. This is due to the fact that the axioms sets can not be modified during the lifetime of an agent. Furthermore, note that in the rigid axioms part the common behavior of all possible behaviors are specified.

3. By using several dynamically changeable axiom attributes. Here, the ideas of the other cases are combined. We allow to specify several axiom attributes which may be modified during the lifetime of an agent. As in the second case, these attributes may be predefined and one of these attributes is marked as the currently valid one. In the following example we have specified two mutators AddAxioms and RemoveAxioms (in addition to the mutator of the example above) for adding a set of axioms to and for removing a set of axioms from a given axiom attribute, respectively.

mutators   ...
                            AddAxioms(N:nat, P:setOfAxioms);
                            RemoveAxioms(N:nat, P:setOfAxioms);
dynamic specification ...
                            AddAxioms(N,P)   **changing** Axioms(N):= Axioms(N) ∪ P;
                            RemoveAxioms(N,P) **changing** Axioms(N):= Axioms(N) - P;

We emphasize that it might be useful to combine changing as well as predefined, unchangeable axiom attributes. In such cases we have to specify for each changeable axiom attribute own mutators. Further, please note that mutator events may be equipped with enabling conditions as usual events in order to prevent arbitrary manipulations. Moreover, mutator events may also cause the occurrence of other basic as well as mutator events. This fact can be expressed by using the well-known event calling mechanism.

Representation of Goals

In classical object specifications goals are represented implicitly by the behavior specification. In case of agent specifications goals can be expressed in a similar way. Fixed goals can be specified in terms of rigid axioms, whereas changing goals can be represented by axiom attributes.

In order to achieve its goals, an agent can execute different sequences of actions. Suppose, we have a (bank) customer who wants to invest a given amount of money such that his profit is maximal. In general there are several possible strategies to do this. The customer can transfer money from a standard account with a low rate of interest to a saving account with a higher rate of interest, or he can buy stocks or immovables, etc. In order to represent different strategies (which are changeable), we need several axiom attributes.

5 Conclusions

In this paper we have presented a first approach of a framework for modeling information systems in terms of agents. After reviewing the basics of object specification technology (in the context of the object-oriented specification language TROLL), we sketched the concept of an agent as a further evolution of the traditional concept of object. Here, we showed that the concept of agent overcomes the limitations of current object models to describe object behavior evolution. This is due to the fact that the agent paradigm allows agents to have changing goals, behavior, constraints, etc.

Our approach bases on the idea of "states as theories" as described, for instance, in [SSS95]. We proposed a two-level specification framework. The first level contains basic axioms describing usual events and their fixed effects on the specified attributes. In the second level we allow to specify (meta) axioms which describe the possible evolution of the agent specification. Thereby, we are able to consider dynamically changing behavior of agents and agent systems.

We do not want to conceal that there are several properties of agents of which we do not know at the moment how to integrate them into the framework we proposed, for example planning and conflict resolving facilities of agents, or autonomy issues (e.g. which request must be fulfilled by an agent). Besides, we have to investigate how far we can allow dynamic *signature modification*. In order to model evolutionary behavior adequately, it is necessary to allow the dynamic specification of additional events. If we allow arbitrary formulas as parameters for the mutators, it is easy to add new events into the specification during the lifetime of an agent. When defining such events we also may need the specification of additional mutators which describe the evolution of these events. On the other hand, if we do not allow arbitrary formulas as parameters, only the behavior of existing events may be changed and thus we have a restricted evolution of agents. Furthermore, we have to check if we need additionally attributes which may be integrated into the specification during the lifetime of an agent. Further, we have to find out which of the agent-specific concepts presented so far can be assumed to be implicit for each agent specification? Should we assume that a given set of axiom attributes and mutators are implicitly predefined, e.g. an axiom attribute Axioms and the mutators ResetAxioms, AddAxioms and RemoveAxioms as described in Fig. 2 in Sect. 4?

In conclusion, we can state that although there are many open questions, it is obvious that the concept of *agent* can be useful especially for modeling federated information systems in which the single components are assumed to be partially autonomous.

References

[Bro92]   M. L. Brodie. The Promise of Distributed Computing and the Challenges of Legacy Systems. In *Advanced Database Systems: Proc. 10th British National Conf. on Databases*, pp. 1–28. Springer, 1992.

[Buc90]   A. P. Buchmann. Modeling Heterogeneous Systems as an Active Object Space. In *Proc. 4th Int. Workshop on Persistent Object Systems*, pp. 279–290. Morgan Kaufmann, 1990.

[CS95]   S. Conrad and G. Saake. Evolving Temporal Behaviour in Information Systems. In *HOA'95 — Higher-Order Algebra, Logic, and Term Rewriting (2nd Int. Workshop)*, pp. PP7:1–16. Participant's Proceedings, 1995.

[FM91]   J. Fiadeiro and T. Maibaum. Towards Object Calculi. In G. Saake and A. Sernadas, eds., *Information Systems - Correctness and Reusability*, pp. 129–178. TU Braunschweig, Informatik Bericht 91-03, 1991.

[GK94]   M. R. Genesereth and S. P. Ketchpel. Software Agents. *Communications of the ACM*, 37(7):48–53, July 1994.

[HPS93]   M. Huhns, M. P. Papazoglou, and G. Schlageter, eds., *Proc. Int. Conf. Intelligent and Cooperating Information Systems*. IEEE Computer Society, 1993.

[HSJ+94]   T. Hartmann, G. Saake, R. Jungclaus, P. Hartel, and J. Kusch. Revised Version of the Modelling Language TROLL (Version 2.0). Informatik-Bericht 94-03, Technische Universität Braunschweig, 1994.

[JSHS96]   R. Jungclaus, G. Saake, T. Hartmann, and C. Sernadas. TROLL - A Language for Object-Oriented Specification of Information Systems. *ACM Transactions on Information Systems*, 1996. *To appear.*

[Mey92]   J.-J. Ch. Meyer. Modal Logics for Knowledge Representation. In R. P. van de Riet and R. A. Meersman, editors, *Linguistic Instruments in Knowledge Engineering*, pp. 251–275. North-Holland, 1992.

[Rya93]   M. Ryan. Defaults in Specifications. In *Proc. Int. Symposium on Requirements Engineering*, pp. 142–149. IEEE Computer Society, 1993.

[SCT95]   G. Saake, S. Conrad, and C. Türker. From Object Specification towards Agent Design. In *OOER'95 — Proc. 14th Int. Conf. on Object-Oriented and Entity-Relationship Modeling*, pp. 329–340. Springer, 1995.

[Sho93]   Y. Shoham. Agent-Oriented Programming. *Artificial Intelligence*, 60(1):51–92, March 1993.

[SJH93]   G. Saake, R. Jungclaus, and T. Hartmann. Application Modelling in Heterogeneous Environments Using an Object Specification Language. *Int. Journal of Intelligent and Cooperative Information Systems*, 2(4):425–449, 1993.

[SSE87]   A. Sernadas, C. Sernadas, and H.-D. Ehrich. Object-Oriented Specification of Databases: An Algebraic Approach. In *Proc. 13th Int. Conf. on Very Large Data Bases*, pp. 107–116. Morgan Kaufmann Publishers, 1987.

[SSG+91]   A. Sernadas, C. Sernadas, P. Gouveia, P. Resende, and J. Gouveia. OBLOG — Object-Oriented Logic: An Informal Introduction. Technical Report, INESC, Lisbon, 1991.

[SSS95]   G. Saake, A. Sernadas, and C. Sernadas. Evolving Object Specifications. In *Information Systems - Correctness and Reusability*, pp. 84–99. World Scientific Publishing, 1995.

[WJ95]   M. J. Wooldridge and N. R. Jennings. Agents Theories, Architectures, and Languages: A Survey. In *Intelligent Agents — Proc. ECAI'94 Workshop on Agent Theories, Architectures, and Languages*, pp. 1–39. Springer, 1995.

A Multi-Layer Architecture for Knowledge-Based System Synthesis*

Jutta Eusterbrock

GMD, Rheinstr. 75, 64295 Darmstadt, Germany, eusterbr@darmstadt.gmd.de

Abstract. This paper defines a clean multi-layer architecture for the design of knowledge-based synthesis systems within the logic programming paradigm. The intent is to provide an integrated logical framework for modeling the different kinds of knowledge involved during synthesis processes, a workbench of inference-based generic methods for the constructive solution of knowledge acquisition and synthesis tasks. As major advantages, evolutionary synthesis processes, the re-usability of knowledge chunks, and multiple views are facilitated and correctness criteria are provided. The approach depends upon the definition of hierarchically organized abstraction layers: domain, domain abstractions, and finally, distributed knowledge sources. Each layer is partitioned into data type, declarative, and operational specifications. For the interaction between heterogenous representation schemes and abstract representations the concept of *logical viewpoints* is introduced.

1 Motivation

> *"A programming environment suitable for prototyping would support a design methodology that emphasizes creativity, experimentation, learning and evolution."* ([Flo84]), p. 13)

Formal correctness and conformance with user needs are criteria to assess the quality of software. The "proofs-as-programs" paradigm, ie. assuming declarative, first order domain specifications, proving requirement specifications in a constructive manner by (inductive) proofs and elaborating algorithms and programs from proofs, has been proposed in the area of logic programming as a theoretical basis for correct program synthesis. The deductive approach covers only parts of automated development processes due to the inherent complexity (cf. [Low93]) and the incompleteness of uniform proof procedures. One of the major problems is modeling in advance domain and requirements in a non-ambiguous, complete, correct, and adequate way. Thus, specifications are subject to continual changes. Experiences gathered so far from automatically solved complex algorithmic problems[2] suggest that computer-assisted discovery of solutions

---

* This paper is a shortened version of [Eus95].

[2] Eg. the computer-assisted proof of a optimal depth lower bound for nine-input sorting networks [Par91].

for non-trivial problems involves - besides the guidance by abstract principles - comprehensive domain specific and strategic knowledge.

The intent of the SEAMLESS approach is to enhance the derivation of correct, efficiently executable specifications from declarative specifications by providing an integrated knowledge based synthesis environment which supports cyclic phases of "Specification, Experimentation, Abstraction, Modification, Logical validation and Extraction for System Synthesis (SEAMLESS)". Interactive system synthesis is perceived as a non-linear, incremental knowledge acquisition process. Thus, we stress the incremental nature of software development. This contrasts with the traditional approaches, usually based on deductive first order logic or metalogical frameworks. While these are intended to be generally applicable, the domain modeling and the derivation of methods remain ad-hoc processes, which have to be done manually from scratch in each case.

Hence, an architecture is wanted, which allows to apply a coherent notation and a closed concept for knowledge representation as well as for deriving correct and efficient generic synthesis methods. Further - from a practical point of view - it is highly desirable to have synthesis systems which assure the re-usability of components, flexibility and evolution. In the subsequent sections - rather than to propose a new formal language - it will be shown that various useful kinds of knowledge for synthesis tasks, eg. requirements, domain data, strategic knowledge and executable specifications, and knowledge based generic methods, eg. proof tactics, methods for theory formation and software configuration, which support the SEAMLESS approach, can be modeled and organized within a coherent multi-layer logic-based architecture as independent units which are interacting in a well-defined way. The framework bridges the gaps between totally domain driven synthesis, abstract methods devised to support synthesis processes, general theorem proving methods, and some recent work on logic-based software configuration with distributed knowledge bases.

The paper is organized as follows: In the following section, a brief outline of the knowledge representation architecture is given. In the subsequent sections, formal concepts for construction, structuring and generic reasoning about domain data and theories, domain abstractions, and, distributed knowledge bases, are presented. In the last section, this approach is summarized.

2 Design Principles for Knowledge-Based Synthesis

Within the SEAMLESS framework, a synthesis process is seen as a step-by-step construction where in each step knowledge bases are taken and by applying methods, new knowledge bases are being derived. SEAMLESS takes the view - as in ML^2 [vHB92] or SPECWARE [SJ94] - that the whole synthesis knowledge should be organized as an easily extensible family of re-usable encapsulated knowledge units. Synthesis systems are structured as an acyclic directed graph, with nodes being attached to knowledge sources and edges denoting dependency relations. They are interacting by well-defined interfaces. As in SPECWARE

[SJ94] the structuring is independent of the logic inside theories and dependency relations can express abstraction, refinement and importation.

A multiple meta-layer architecture and a comprehensive knowledge representation language seem to be indispensable (cf. [BC93, Kre90, Ohs93, vHB92]) for modeling and integrating different kinds of knowledge and reasoning procedures. The SEAMLESS architecture (cf. Figure 1) to model synthesis knowledge is based upon the definition of three hierarchically organized abstraction layers. The different layers refer to the modeling, structuring, selection, manipulation

Multi−Layer Knowledge Modeling and Interaction

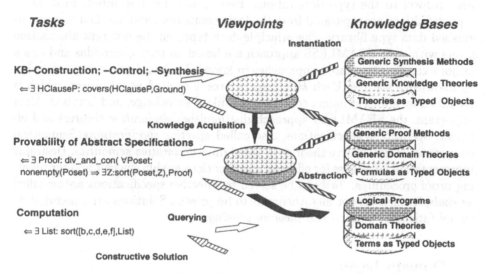

Fig. 1. SEAMLESS Layers

and constructive reasoning on

- domain knowledge;
- generic domain abstractions;
- distributed knowledge sources.

For dialogue purposes, a further knowledge layer, providing a graphical user-interface, has been introduced. However, its representation is not subject of discussion within this paper.

The layers are abstractions from lower layers and may be regarded as separated knowledge bases associated with distinguished specification languages and interpreters for expressions. The communication among layers is realized by *viewpoints*. Two views are possible: a layer may be seen as meta-layer, controlling the behaviour of the lower (object) layers, as well as an object layer which is available to manipulation by higher layers and provides services to them.

For knowledge representation a "Gödel" (cf. [HL94])-like typed logic specification and implementation language is employed, suitably adapted to the specific representation tasks, extended by metalogic features and action operators to specify knowledge source properties and dynamic change. As is well known in logic programming, separating data types within formal specifications is useful for a lot of reasons. Type specifications can be replaced easily by more efficient ones, are easy extensible and can be used in more than one context. It is possible to encode the structure of the domain or additional knowledge directly into the terms, which results in efficient proof procedures. Some of the non-logical constructs in declarative programming can be avoided by employing data types. Type checking procedures ensure that the formulas in the program are correct with respect to the type declarations. Hence, each layer is sub-divided. Data type definitions are separated from the logic component and handled in a distinguished data type library. The principle data types on the different abstraction layers within the SEAMLESS approach are based on terms, formulas and - as a major extension to related approaches in knowledge based reasoning - theories, ie. knowledge sources. Each *knowledge source* is treated as an object, which is identified by a logical name, contains a chunk of knowledge, and is typed. Most important, the SEAMLESS approach distinguishes *declarative theories* and efficient, operational specifications, also called *effective specifications*. Semantical correctness of declarative theories is based on a *declarative semantics*. Desirable representation languages for effective specifications enable efficient and terminating proof procedures. *Tasks* to be solved by effective specifications are specified as *goals*, ie. theorems or metatheorems to be proven. Solutions are generated by computation, ie. *constructive theorem proving*.

3   Domain Layer

Logic based program synthesis or system design in general is conceived as the formal derivation of an efficient operational specification, given a declarative domain model. Both, declarative domain models as target descriptions are theories on the domain layer.

Abstract Data Types   Domain data is given by (real-world) objects, relations among objects, properties of objects and operations defined for the domain. Domain data is specified by means of *first order data types* based on techniques from algebraic specification.

Domain Models   Domain knowledge may be formalized by any representation language, as first-oder, temporal, modal or other non-standard logics, which could be adequate to describe the application domain, re-using already defined data types. The domain theory in Figure 2 defines partial-order sorting problems as a horn clause program, taking for granted that a data type **poset** is implemented.[3] The specification is already executable, however, one might be interested in programs which solve classes of goals efficiently.

Domain Declaration	Partial_Order_Sorting
Uses	Poset

Sorts
poset, domain, bool

Predicates

part_sort :	poset $\times$ poset $\rightarrow$ bool
new_rel :	poset $\times$ (domain $\times$ domain) $\rightarrow$ bool

Axioms

part_sort(P, P) $\Leftarrow$ totally_ordered(P).

part_sort(P, S) $\Leftarrow$ new_rel(P, [X, Y]) $\wedge$ compare(Comp, X, Y)
$\wedge$ add_relation(P, Comp) = PNew
$\wedge$ part_sort(PNew, S).

new_rel([Dom, Rel], [X, Y]) $\Leftarrow$ X $\in$ Dom $\wedge$ Y $\in$ Dom $\wedge$ X $\neq$ Y
$\wedge$ (X < Y) $\notin$ Rel $\wedge$ (X > Y) $\notin$ Rel.

add_relation([Dom, Rel], Comp) = [Dom, New] $\Leftarrow$ New = Rel $\cup$ Comp.

Fig. 2. Specification of Partial-Order Sorting Problems

Logic Programs Programs to be synthesized are described by an extended horn-clause logic. Horn clause logic programs with (canonical) equations is a well-studied theoretical approach. SLD-resolution and term rewriting provide a sound execution mechanism. Commercial interpreters and compilers are available for the programming language PROLOG, which is based on horn clause logic. However, proving can still be untractable. So as a further constraint, synthesized programs have to be efficiently executable.

4 Generic Domain Abstractions

The objective of this section is to provide a framework for constructive proof-oriented synthesis, which is capable to incorporate problem solving principles, strategic knowledge and supplements correctness criteria.

Abstract Types Types on the metalevel provide means for describing object-logic syntax, eg. terms, atoms, formulas, goals, proofs, and functions that manipulate and construct members of these types.

---

[3] The presented examples are taken from our implementation, although some coding details are hidden.

Generic Domain Theories *Generic domain theories* are metatheories which model the syntactic structure and semantical properties of a class of first-order domain theories in an uniform way. They allow to specify relationships among the provability of goals and its solutions. A generic theory is stated by definitions, which are called *soundness axioms*. There is no specific calculus required when defining metatheories, however, each instance of a generic theory should be suitably computational. As a concrete example, *knowledge-based decomposition theories* are introduced below. *Decomposition theories* capture the essence of the class of domain theories, which are amenable to be analyzed by the well known "Divide-and-Conquer"-paradigm. As an enrichment to related approaches, knowledge-based decomposition theories capture strategic and control knowledge.

Sorts
goal $\doteq\Leftarrow \exists Z : \texttt{predicate}(X, Z)$ introduces goals on the domain layer as types on the object layer.

Basic Definitions
$<_{\texttt{goal}}$ is intended to be a well-founded ordering on goals and minimal_goal verifies the minimality condition.

decompose_goal(Goal, X, Goal', Goal") splits Goal into Goal' and Goal", applying a function X, which is computed calling split_goal(Goal, X). Goal is derivable iff Goal' and Goal" are derivable.

Strategic Knowledge
known_case(Goal, Proof, Depth) means that Goal is provable, Proof denotes its proof tree of maximal depth Depth or is an index which refers to the proof tree of Goal.

behav_equiv(Goal, GoalEq, Proof, Depth) is intended to be true, iff GoalEq is a Goal, constructable from Goal with the property provable(GoalEq) iff provable(Goal). In both cases the proof complexity is bounded by Depth. Proof denotes a proof tree or its reference.

Implementing Generic Theories by Viewpoints To analyze concrete specifications, generic theories have to be connected to the object layer. In general, views or viewpoints are used in databases and software engineering to connect heterogenous representation schemes and encapsulate points of interest. A SEAMLESS *viewpoint* is a theory that - at the one side - specifies how a concrete domain theory implements a generic theory and - at the other side - provides an interpretation mechanism for descriptive object-level expressions. Viewpoints are implemented by lifting axioms of the form form left_side $\Leftarrow$ right_side, where left_side, right_side refer to expressions on the meta and domain layer, respectively. All variables on the left hand side have to be defined on the right hand side. As in [Smi92] soundness axioms have to be preserved which ensure *correctness* of the lifting process with respect to the defined generic theory. Implementing generic theories involves more than only theory morphism (cf. [Nov94]), where well defined entities are assigned new ones by translation. A major aspect of generic theories are enriched expressiveness and interpretation of non-computable object-level expressions. Implementing generic theories, additional knowledge as solved cases or behavioural equivalence can be provided optionally. Figure 3 presents a viewpoint which lifts the partial-order sorting theory into the knowledge-based decomposition theory.

Viewpoint   Decompose_Partial_Order_Sorting
Uses   Partial_Order_Sorting
         Data_Type_Formula

Sortinterpretation
def_type(goal, $\Leftarrow \exists S :$ part_sort(P, S)) $\Leftarrow$ poset(P) $\land$ poset(S).

Basic Axioms
minimal_goal(part_sort(P, P)) $\Leftarrow$ totally_ordered(P).
$<_{goal}$ ($\exists S' :$ part_sort(P', S'),
           $\exists S'' :$ part_sort(P'', S'')) $\Leftarrow P' < P''$.
split_goal($\exists S :$ part_sort(P, S), X) $\Leftarrow$ new_rel(P, X).
decompose_goal(G, [X, Y], G', G'') $\Leftarrow G = \exists S :$ part_sort(P, S)
                               $\land$ add_relation(P, Y < X, P')
                               $\land$ add_relation(P, X < Y, P'')
                               $\land$ $G' = \exists S' :$ part_sort(P', S')
                               $\land$ $G'' = \exists S'' :$ part_sort(P'', S'').

Strategic Knowledge
behav_equiv(iso_index, G', G'', _) $\Leftarrow G' = \exists S' :$ part_sort(P', S')
                               $\land$ $G'' = \exists S'' :$ part_sort(P'', S'')
                               $\land$ isomorphic(P', P'').
known_case(G, case_1, 2) $\Leftarrow G = \exists S' :$ part_sort([{a, b, c}, {a < b}], S').

Fig. 3. Implementing Decomposition Theories as Partial-Order Sorting Theories

Verified Knowledge-Based Generic Methods *Generic tasks,* ie. *requirement specifications* state the class of goals which should be solved by the target program and further constraints on the programs to be considered. A *verified generic methods* is a *formally proven metatheorem,* derived from a generic theory, which postulate the provability of a generic tasks for all implementations of the given generic theory. The definitions in Figure 4 give an example of a generic method for solving synthesis tasks. know_div_conq(Goal, Bool, Proof, Depth) declaratively represents the (non-)provability for all admissible interpretations of Goal within at most Depth steps and supplements a constructive explanation Proof while employing SLD-resolution and unification. The method extends the *divide-and-conquer* paradigm by allowing strategic and control knowledge to be employed for guiding constructive proof processes. Correctness is proven by induction on $<_{goal}$. Adding the viewpoint definitions in figure 3 and proving the goal $\Leftarrow$ know_div_conq($\exists S :$ part_sort([{a, b, c, d, e}, {}], S), Proof, 7) causes the variable Proof to be instantiated with an abstract description of the optimal algorithm, which sorts an arbitrary set of 5 elements with at most 7 comparisons.

Generic Proof Method   Knowledge_Based_Divide_and_Conquer
Sorts
goal, bool, proof, nat

Metapredicates
know_div_conq   goal × bool × proof × nat → true
compose_proof   proof × proof × proof → bool

Axioms
know_div_conq(Goal, Proof, Depth) ⇐ known_case(Goal, Proof, Dk) ∧ DK ≤ Depth.
know_div_conq(Goal, Proof, Depth) ⇐ behav_equiv(Goal, GoalBeh, Depth, IndexBeh)
                                                 ∧ <_goal (Goal, GoalBeh)
                                                 ∧ known_case(Goal, ProofK, DK) ∧ DK ≤ Depth
                                                 ∧ compose_proof(IndexBeh, ProofK, Proof).
know_div_conq(Goal, [], Depth)   ⇐ minimal_goal(Goal) ∧ Depth ≥ 0.
know_div_conq(Goal, Proof, Depth) ⇐ split_goal(Goal, X) ∧ DepthNew = Depth − 1
                                                 ∧ decompose_goal(Goal, X, Goal', Goal'')
                                                 ∧ know_div_conq(Goal', Proof', DepthNew)
                                                 ∧ know_div_conq(Goal'', Proof'', DepthNew)
                                                 ∧ compose_proof(Proof', Proof'', Proof).

Fig. 4. Knowledge-based Divide-and-Conquer

5 Structuring, Access, Synthesis of Distributed Knowledge

The ability to deal with knowledge sources as typed data, having facilities for easy definition, addition, deletion, retrieval, refinement and composition of knowledge sources, and reasoning capabilites are prerequisites in order to realize a knowledge-based synthesis workbench. The classical first-order logic approach to knowledge representation is based on the premise that computation is done from a static, flat theory. In this section, some approaches from meta-logic programming (cf. [Cic89]) and logic based software configuration (cf. [SFA90, LA95]) are incorporated in order to propose a solution to the above stated problems.

Theories as Typed and Dynamic Objects Each theory, ie. knowledge source or logic program is treated as an object, which is identified by a logical name, the *theory name* and contains a chunk of knowledge called *value* of the theory object. The value of a *primitive theory* is the set of definitions which are associated with the corresponding theory name. Collections of theories are treated as universes and are represented by abstract types on which one can perform different kinds of operations. Basic types are defined due to syntactical or semantical properties of their entailed formulas, eg. horn clause formulas or positive variable free and negative existence quantified formulas.

Destruction, Construction and Refinement Primitives The notion of "Quantified Dynamic Logic" (QDL) (cf. [vHB92]) is adopted, where a variable may assume different values during the execution of a program and where expressions of the form $\phi \rightarrow \{\texttt{knowledge\_source\_action}\}\psi$ are employed to specify actions on knowledge sources. The expression is to be read as: given certain preconditions ϕ, performing $\texttt{knowledge\_source\_action}$ causes the postcondition ψ to be valid. Let Δ^4 and Θ being finite theories and ϕ be a unary predicate. For example, $\texttt{delete}(\Delta, \phi, \Theta)$ eliminates in the given theory Δ all formulas with property ϕ. Θ is the name of the resulting theory. $\texttt{append}(\Delta_1, \Delta_2, \Theta)$ computes the union (procedural interpretation: Δ_1 followed by Δ_2) of theories. Further complex operations for synthesis tasks are implemented. The formula

$\Delta_s \neq \emptyset \rightarrow \{\texttt{forall\_formula\_trans}(\Delta_s, \Delta_f, \oplus(\texttt{Arguments}))\}$
$\forall \texttt{Formula} \in \Delta_s [\exists \texttt{FormulaNew} \in \Delta_f : \oplus(\texttt{Arguments}, \texttt{Formula}) = \texttt{FormulaNew}]$

specifies an operation $\texttt{forall\_formula\_trans}$ which maps the formulas of a theory into a new one by applying the operation $\oplus$.

Type construction by feature terms The UNIX file system provides a suitable framework for the physical organization of knowledge segments as files and the aggregation of related objects by directories. Several formal specifications using the tree structure have been devised (cf. [Hei95]). We employ yet another formalism, ie. feature terms, in order to be able to access directories and its components in a parametric way. A *feature term* is a tree whose edges are labeled with symbols called features, and whose nodes are labeled with symbols called types. It allows to model *aggregation* relations, such as an "instance of a type τ is composed of instances of types $\tau_1, \tau_2, \ldots, \tau_x$". For example, the feature term

$\tau \doteq \texttt{theo\_f}(\texttt{pos} : \texttt{pos\_atom}, \texttt{neg} : \texttt{neg\_atom},$
$\qquad\qquad \texttt{hyp} : \texttt{maybe\_quant\_formula}, \texttt{neg\_abstract} : \texttt{neg\_existence\_quant})$

may be used to structure collections of theories, whose parts are atomic theories which are separated into sets of positive-ground, negative-ground, maybe-quantified and negative-existential-quantified formulas, respectively, taking for granted that the basic types are defined. Consequently, distributed directories are being considered as aggregated theories typed by feature terms. They are being located by their names or physical adresses. Components are being accessed by path expressions. Eg. let Δ be a theory of type τ. $\Delta.\texttt{hyp}$ accesses a subcomponent of Δ which is intended to entail hypothetic domain knowledge.

Generic Knowledge Theories are logical and parametric descriptions of properties and relationships among theories. For example, the generic predicate $\texttt{subsumption}(\Delta, \texttt{Formula})$ is intended to be true, iff $\texttt{Formula}$ is subsumed by the theory associated with Δ. For restricted types of languages, decidable and efficient decision procedures have been devised.[5] Viewpoints allow to provide the instantiations of these generic predicates as implementations. The lifting of formulas to theories is based on the $\texttt{forall\_formula\_trans}$ operator.

---

[4] Theory names, ie. names of logical programs and theory variables are denoted by Greek letters.

[5] For example, restricting the *subsumption* relation to θ-subsumption provides a decision procedure. [DLNN91] presents conceptual languages which admit tractable subsumption tests.

Synthesis of Knowledge Bases A KB-synthesis (eg. knowledge acquisition, program transformation) method is a higher order logical program that takes knowledge sources as arguments. Expressions of the form $\phi \rightarrow \{\Delta\}\ \psi$ are employed to state synthesis tasks, where ϕ denotes a precondition, ψ postcondition, and Δ a theory variable, refering to the knowledge source to be synthesized. A logical theory is to be synthesized by gradually refining the content of Δ. A *generic KB-synthesis method* which solves a task with respect to a given generic theory Ω is the definition of a metapredicate `method` with the following property. For all implementations of Ω, assuming ϕ, proving $\Leftarrow$ `method(` Δ `)` causes Δ to be transformed into a logical program such that the postcondition ψ is valid. The language for method definition is a horn clause logic, admitting theory variables and augmented by the defined operations on the different abstraction layers.

Example The theory formation task can be stated as follows: Given a set of atoms - labelled as positive or negative - $ex_1, ex_2, \ldots = \Pi^+ \cup \Pi^-$ and a consistent background theory named Θ, which may be empty, construct a minimal set of formulas named Δ, such that
(1) $\forall Ex \in \Pi^+ : \Delta \cup \Theta \models Ex$;   (2) $\forall Ex \in \Pi^- :$ `consistent`$(\Delta \cup Ex)$.
The presented architecture provides some major advantages when deriving and implementing a method `theory_form` $:\tau \rightarrow$ `bool` which solves the stated task. The method definition may be partitioned into a re-usable verified part in terms of generic subtasks as subsumption tests. Efficient implementations can be provided by viewpoints. The location of the concerned data as the positive facts can be treated as argument, due to the typing mechanism for distributed knowledge sources. Basic transformations as appending of theories can be executed re-using already implemented knowledge base actions.

6 Conclusions

Synthesis of realistic software programs using verified data types, formal specifications and provable correct development methods is worthwile. Logic-based synthesis is based upon the unique theory assumption and general purpose procedures. This causes the well-known hard theoretical problems and problems of knowledge maintenance in large knowledge-based systems. The main achievements of the SEAMLESS architecture within logic-based synthesis include

- the definition of a coherent *three-layer abstraction hierarchy* for knowledge structuring, each layer subdivided into unique levels;
- the concepts of *generic theory, generic task, verified knowledge-based generic method* and loosely coupled *viewpoint*.

Using a descriptive logic, tasks on different abstraction levels may be entered as queries and solved constructively by verified proof procedures. Viewpoints allow to analyze problems from multiple perspectives and to employ heuristics and domain specific knowledge in a well-understood way. The presented architecture suggests to develop knowledge based synthesis systems as libraries of encapsulated and easy extensible, re-usable verified knowledge entities.

References

[BC93]   D.A Basin and R.L. Constable. *Logical Environments*, chapter Metalogical Frameworks. Cambridge University Press, 1993.

[Cic89]   I. Cicekli. Design and implementation of an abstract metaprolog engine for metaprolog. In H. Abramson and M. Rogers, editors, *Meta-Programming in Logic Programming*, pages 417–434. MIT Press, 1989.

[DLNN91]   F.M. Donini, M. Lenzerini, D. Nardi, and W. Nutt. Tractable concept languages. In *Proc. Int. Joint Conf. on Artificial Intelligence*, pages 458–463. Morgan Kaufmann Publishers, 1991, 1991.

[Eus95]   J. Eusterbrock. A multi-layer architecture for knowledge-based system synthesis. Technical Report 950, Arbeitspapiere der GMD, 1995.

[Flo84]   C. Floyd. A systematic look at prototyping. In R. Budde, editor, *Approaches to Prototyping*. Springer, 1984.

[Hei95]   M. Heissel. Specification of the Unix File system: A Comparative Case Study. In *Algebraic Methodology and Software Technology*, pages 475–488. Lecture Notes in Computer Science, 1995.

[HL94]   P.M. Hill and J.W. Lloyd. *The Gödel Programming Language*. Logic Programming series. The MIT Press, 1994.

[Kre90]   Chr. Kreitz. The representation of program synthesis in higher order logic. In H. Marburger, editor, *GWAI-90, 14th German Workshop on Artificial Intelligence*, pages 171–180. Springer Verlag, 1990.

[LA95]   C.J.P. Lucena and P.S.C Alencar. A formal description of evolving software systems architectures. *Science of Computer Programming*, 24:41–61, 1995.

[Low93]   M.R. Lowry. Methodologies for knowledge-based software engineering, Proc. 7th International Symposium, ISMIS '93. In J. Komorowski and Z.W. Ràs, editors, *Methodologies for Intelligent Systems*, pages 219–234. Springer Verlag, 1993.

[Nov94]   G.S.Jr. Novak. Composing reusable software components through views. In *Knowledge-Based Software Engineering Conference*, pages 39–47, 1994.

[Ohs93]   S. Ohsuga. How can knowledge-based systems solve large-scale problems: model based decomposition and problem solving. *Knowledge-Based Systems*, 6(1):38–62, 1993.

[Par91]   I. Parberry. A computer-assisted optimal depth lower bound for nine-input sorting networks. *Mathematical Systems Theory*, 24:101–116, 1991.

[SFA90]   C. Sernadas, J. Fiadeiro, and Sernadas A. Modular construction of logic knowledge bases: an algebraic approach. *Information Systems*, 15(1):37–60, 1990.

[SJ94]   Y.V. Srinivas and R. Jüllig. SPECWARE (TM): Formal support for composing software. Technical Report KES.U.94.5, Kestrel Institute, 1994. To appear in Proceedings of the Conference on Mathematics of Program Construction.

[Smi92]   D.R. Smith. Automating the design of algorithms. In B. Möller, H. Partsch, and St. Schuman, editors, *Formal Program Development*, pages 324–354. Springer Verlag, 1992.

[vHB92]   F. van Harmelen and J. Balder. $(ML)^2$: A formal language for KADS models. In *Proc. of the 10th European Conference on Artificial Intelligence*, pages 582–586. John Wiley & Sons, 1992.

MuRaLi: An Architecture for Multiple Reasoning

Mohan Ravindranathan & Roy Leitch
Intelligent Systems Laboratory
Department of Computing and Electrical Engineering
Heriot-Watt University
Edinburgh, EH14 4AS
Scotland, U.K.

Abstract

We propose that to realise a trade-off between the generality of problems that can be solved and efficiency of response, intelligent systems require representations of different 'types' of knowledge, and such heterogeneous knowledge can most effectively be represented through multiple models with heterogeneous representation formats. Three dimensions; generality, precision, and scope of models are suggested here to formulate a frame-work for the structuring of heterogeneous models in intelligent systems. We embed such models within an architecture for intelligent systems that supports adaptive responses to unfamiliar situations by switching between pre-specified models and learning of these for future use.

1 Introduction

It is paradoxical that a shop-floor environment has a number of important messages to convey to architects of *Intelligent systems*. The most important message here is that for problem solving, shop floors employ different 'types' of knowledge and reasoning. Usually, for reasons of efficiency, use of such heterogeneous knowledge is on the basis of *generality*. It is interesting to note that, here even the format of knowledge used also changes; from the highly procedural actions of the operator, through the experience based heuristics of the supervisor to the equations employed by the plant engineer. The operator, supervisor, engineer hierarchy followed in the shop floor therefore trades-off efficiency with generality in problem solving. Also, it is apparent from the common shop floor dialogues like 'high', 'reduce', 'increase' etc., that the format of knowledge can vary in 'precision'[1] from (say) numerical, qualitative or even symbolic values.

The shop-floor certainly reveals the existence of heterogeneous knowledge, and its importance in problem solving. However, this is not unique to shop floor alone. Even in the case of human beings, Neuro-psychology has evidences to suggest that human brain has multiple representations of the same domain in different formalisms, and that during a decision making process humans select suitable, relevant models of the situation on the basis of the current goal[2]. Thus, multiple representations of heterogeneous knowledge appear to be central to both organisational structures and human intelligence.

Building Intelligent systems having the ability to reason with heterogeneous knowledge requires certain options for representing the knowledge, here synonomously termed as '*models*'. Though various techniques are now available for representing such models; what we lack is a clear classification of models and an understanding of how they relate to one another, and crucially which properties are maintained or lost during a change in modelling approach. Here, we first propose a frame-work that structures multiple models for particular purposes, based on the properties of generality, scope and precision of models. The Multiple Reasoning(MR) is then introduced, and based on the concepts of multiple domain representation and reasoning, we then propose an architecture called Multiple Reasoning Architecture with Layered Intelligence -MuRaLi. MuRaLi utilises multiple models of heterogeneous knowledge that are structured based on the properties of generality, precision, and scope to trade-off efficiency of response with generality of knowledge. In operation, the architecture supports model refinement, adaptive and self-learning capabilities within a single conceptual framework.

2 Multiple Models: A Logical Choice for Heterogeneous Knowledge

In general, intelligent systems are expected to operate in a class of real-world environments. Hayes-Roth consider the class of real-world environments, 'niches'[3] and suggest that niches can further be decomposed into objects known as 'problem spaces'. However, we consider the niches of intelligent systems, 'application domains', where it solve a class of problems (e.g. control, start-up, shut-down etc.) and propose such 'problems' as the 'purposes' for representation of heterogeneous knowledge in intelligent systems. This suggests the existence of distinct operating spaces in intelligent systems, and consequently the possible utilisation of different models with distinct representations for solving diverse problems. In other words, the problems of an intelligent system play an important role in the knowledge representation.

In the application domain of physical systems, we identify three primitive choices for representing knowledge about (the problem; controlling, in case the purpose is control) the physical system. We view them with respect to the possible descriptions of physical system behaviours or equivalently, solution of the models. We argue that these dimensions, that we term *precision, generality* and *scope*, as distinct properties and together they describe a frame-work in the *Model Space* for particular purposes, from which models could be selected and utilised for achieving particular goals in prescribed situations.

2.1 Precision

In certain circumstances, more abstract models can be easier to understand, and can be closer to our common-sense understanding of the world. They can also be simpler to represent and, therefore, (potentially) computationally more efficient[4]. The basic operation of *abstraction* modifies the *precision* of the underlying knowledge representation in a model. In terms of physical system modelling this corresponds to modifying the representation of the system variables and the associated primitives (operations) of the language e.g. a quantitative to semi-quantitative or to linguistic transformation. The abstraction operation is usually many-to-one, in the form of a contraction mapping, and therefore many distinctions of the reference system collapse on to one distinction in the more abstract model. However, an important and defining property of abstraction is that the resulting model is still 'faithful' a transformation and therefore it will produce a behaviour that is consistent with an abstraction operation applied to the behaviour of the reference system. In other words, an abstraction is a less precise but still correct a description of the reference model. In the model space, we propose three such precision *planes; precise, less-precise and least-precise* for representing the models.

2.2 Scope

Simpler models can also be obtained from a reference system by modifying the system boundary, thereby affecting *scope* of the model. Hence scope denotes the part of the physical system represented by a model. Such an operation we term as *focusing*, [5] which results in models with various foci of attentions. In the application domain of physical systems, the most natural form of focusing is to segregate the domain into a system, sub-system and component level models in the model space. We suggest them as the three levels of scope; level-one, level-two and level-three.

2.3 Generality

In the application domains like shop floor, the knowledge of control actions is usually distributed between a number of staff on the basis of efficiency and generality. The more frequent operations (less general) are normally undertaken by operators whereas uncommon situations are handled by engineers based on fundamental design knowledge and the underlying principles of operation. We assert that these different 'types' of knowledge are best represented in different formats that maintain the semantic integrity and perspicuity of the knowledge.

- *Procedures* to represent an ordered set of actions representing the skill of the operator in interacting with the physical system. We propose a Procedural Model Layer (PML) consisting of finite sets of procedures organised in a two dimensional space of precision and scope. We have used an extended version of the Fuzzy Petri-Nets[6], for implementing the PML in our candidate architecture MuRaLi.
- *Rules* to represent the set of assumed relations between situations and the possible control actions. In the Rule Model Layer (RML), there exists nine behavioural models of the physical system, representing the relations linking the status of a number of observable system variables (situation), to sets of consequent actions. These essentially are the rules appropriate to particular situations and are again organised based on precision of the situation and scope for which they are applicable.
- *Equations* to represent the value-independent models normally derived from knowledge of the relevant physical laws describing the operation of the physical system. Principle based knowledge of the physical system is represented in the highest layer in generality, since they are basically system dependent rather than state or situation dependent. We have used a component based ontology[7], as system, sub-system and component level for categorising the principles in scope. The applicability of system variable values in principle models is used in deciding the precision of these models, arriving at nine discrete principle models in the Equation Model Layer (EML).

The features of the model layers(PML, EML and EML) are summarised in the table 1.

Based on the primitive choices of precision, scope and generality, we arrive at a cubical frame-work for structuring multiple models for particular purposes in intelligent systems. Figure 1 illustrates the cubical frame-work for multiple models.

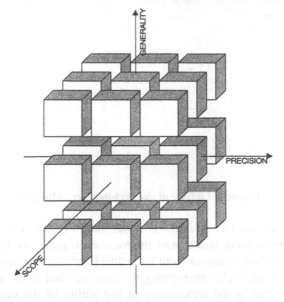

Figure 1. Dimensions of the Model Cube

KNOWLEDGE	REPRESENTATION	BASIS	GENERALITY
Procedures	Petri-Nets	Goal	Least-General
Associations	Rules	Problem	More-General
Principles	Equations	Application Domain	Most-General

Table 1. Features of the layers of models

3 MuRaLi: A Multiple Reasoning Framework

To solve problems in a class of application domains, model space of an intelligent system needs to contain number of instances of the proposed cubical frame-work to structure multiple models corresponding to various problems of respective application domains. While interacting with the application domains, intelligent systems perform three 'functions': *perception* of the environment to determine the *problems* and *goals*, *processing* of the available knowledge suitable to the current goal, and *actuation* of certain primitive actions to produce behaviours to achieve the current goal. Conceptually, perception drives the actions through processing, with or without a reasoning. We consider the 'functions': perception, processing and actuation, as *tasks* of the function domain in intelligent systems[8]. Based on these arguments, an overall structure for MuRaLi can therefore be outlined as shown in the figure 2.

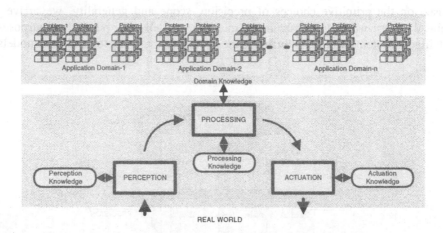

Figure 2. Outline of the architecture: MuRaLi

The basis of the architecture MuRaLi is instanciation of the model cubes based on 'problems', and subsequent selection of the most appropriate models for given goals based on the contextual situations from an instnaciated discrete heterogeneous model space of 3^3 i.e. 27 models [9], representing the cross product of the above dimensions. We define *adaptation* in the architecture as the ability of the system to detect the inappropriateness of a particular model and to select another that is applicable to the current situation. Similarly, the system has the property of *learning* and after a successful adaptation, the results are used to modify the models (knowledge base) such that in future the learned knowledge will be used directly, without the expense of adaptation. Indeed we would define Intelligent Systems, human or artificial, as systems having the capability to adapt and to learn.

3.1 Problem Solving with Heterogeneous Knowledge: Multiple Reasoning

Drawing inspiration from Chandrasekaran's concept of methods [10] we propose that, to achieve a specific goal (g) in a problem, we require a model (m) from the space of available models. This leads to the question about how to organise the processing of such models in order to achieve a particular goal for a particular problem. We term such organisation as Multiple Reasoning (mr). Hence, multiple reasoning can be thought of as a proposal to select a model $m(g, mr)$ from an instance of the model space for a given situation, and to organise the processing of the selected model so as to achieve a prescribed goal for a problem. During the multiple reasoning process, if the selected model $m(g,mr)$ contains the knowledge required to achieve the current goal g, we argue that the knowledge contained in such a model as specific to the current goal. If $m(g, mr)$ does not contain the required knowledge to achieve the current goal g, another model m' from the model space has to be used within an additional reasoning process. In such cases, we believe that the knowledge contained in model m' as more *general* than that contained in model m. Figure 3 illustrates the concept of multiple reasoning.

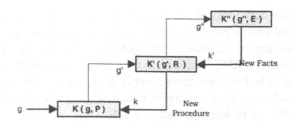

Figure 3. Multiple Reasoning in Intelligent Systems

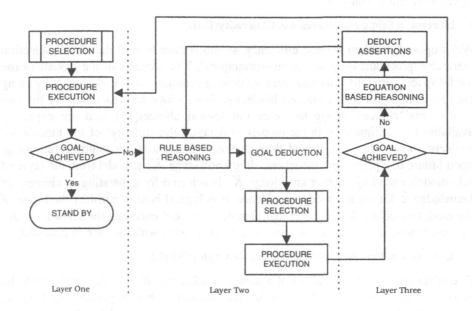

Figure 4. Multiple Reasoning in MuRaLi

In MuRaLi, the selection of procedures from a procedural model layer (PML) is based on the current goal, its precision and scope, and the precision of the required system variables. The execution of procedures is fast and basically reflexive in nature. Figure 4 shows the flow-chart of the multiple reasoning operations in MuRaLi. Consider a case in which a procedure P_1 of lowest scope and the highest precision is selected for execution from the layer of procedural models based on the current goal g. If that procedure is successful in achieving the goal, no further processing will be made. However, in the event of a failure or impasse in procedure P_1, a model R_2 from the RML will be selected by the layer-selection process for a forward reasoning. The forward chaining inference mechanism produces a consequent action, which will be subjected to a goal deduction process to ascertain whether the consequent action is a main-goal or a sub-goal. The deducted goal is then realised through a separate procedure (of different resolution and/or scope) and as a next step, the original procedure from the next plain of precision, P_4 is executed. In case P_4 also fails to achieve the original goal, a principle model, of the highest resolution in that scope E_3 is consulted to enhance the fact-base of the RML model to conduct a reasoning based on A_5, which in fact is a RML model of the next resolution, of the same scope. The forward reasoning of R_5 hence produces another goal and after the execution of which the original procedure at P_4 is one again executed. The present implementation of MuRaLi is capable of performing multiple reasoning up to 18 levels. However, experiments suggest the achievement of a goal generally after two to three levels. The selection of models in the RML and EML of MuRaLi is based on the following two principles determining the precision and scope of the models to be selected in model layers with higher generality;

- **Increase in Scope with Increase in Generality(ISIG)**

We proposed problem solving efficiency as motivation behind the model selection hierarchy 'procedures→ associations→principles'. The property of the models in the model space, generality changes while achieving problem solving efficiency by using the procedure→ rules → equations hierarchy. Since scope and resolution are the two fundamental choices among the other ontological choices[11], that are explicitly available for manipulation in the models in a layer, the 'fidelity' of the models for problem solving can be adjusted through these dimensions. In multiple reasoning, upon failure of a procedural model encoding knowledge K, a model from the layer of rule models encoding another knowledge K' is selected for generating an element of knowledge k for the knowledge K. Hence, it is logical here to consider the scope of the model encoding K' as higher than that of the model encoding the knowledge K. In other words, the scope can be considered as increasing with increase in generality.

- **Reduction in Precision with Increase in Generality(RPIG)**

One of the reasons for the failure of a model in achieving its assigned goal is that the behaviour generated by that model is 'less-accurate' than expected. By keeping uncertainty of the generated behaviour to a constant, accuracy of that behaviour can be varied by varying the precision planes. Reduction in precision does not imply the behaviour as inaccurate, but only less-accurate. Even achievement of less-accurate goals g' and g'' to generate additional knowledge k or k' is sufficient for achieving an original goal g. This could be achieved by execution of the models suitable to generate behaviours of lower precision or in other words using a less-precise knowledge k and k'. In fact in most cases, execution of less-precise models with higher generalities is more than sufficient for fulfilling the requirement of knowledge k or k'. Since less precise models are easier and computationally more efficient, the precision of the models can be reduced with an increase in generality.

4 A Case Study with MuRaLi

We have implemented a prototype of the architecture MuRaLi in Common Lisp in X-Window environment on a DEC Alpha workstation. To demonstrate the adaptively learning, problem solving capability of MuRaLi, we use a scaled model of heat exchanger designed by Bytronic Associates[12]. As depicted in the figure 5, the application domain consists of the physical system with various components, including a tank and a sump storing part of the fluid flowing around the system, a heater that heats the fluid in the tank, a radiator that dissipates the thermal energy of the fluid, and a pump that drives the fluid around. For demonstrating the concepts here, we propose to use a command to 'start the flow-loop'. The pump, driven by a 12V, 6A DC motor has a non-linear characteristic in the form of an initial dead-time of 2.3 volts. For the present case study, we assume a linear characteristic between 2.3 volts to 12 volts for the pump.

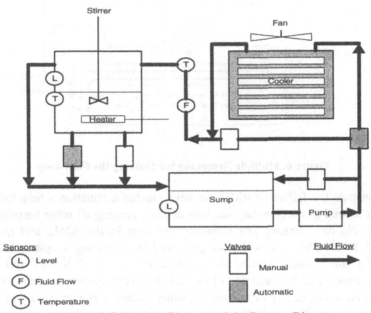

Figure 5. Schematic Diagram of the Process Rig

Figure 6 illustrates the multiple reasoning operations performed by MuRaLi during the starting-up operation of the flow-loop. Here, the perception process selects a procedural model based on the current goal and values of system parameters. While executing the procedural model, the start-up procedure checks the sump-level, status of the valves whether they are in auto or manual, and the flow-rate, and only upon satisfaction of each being equal to a pre-specified value in a quantity space (depending on the model precision, the width of the quantity space increases), the actuation module invokes the executable programs corresponding to the fired places. In a deliberate move, we have induced a fault in the system by considering the pump as requiring a priming operation. The execution of the procedure this time ends up in an impasse due to the inflow to tank being zero. The failure of the procedure switches the control to the RML. A rule based model having a higher scope and precision is then selected from the RML and executed to infer the action to 'prime the pump', which is executed through another procedure.

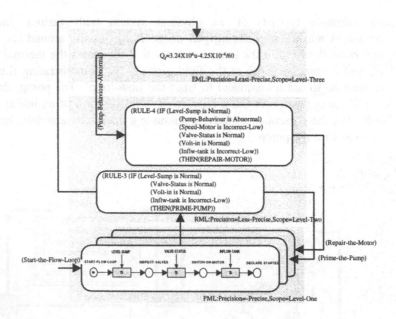

Figure 6. Multiple Reasoning for Starting the Flow-loop

To demonstrate the failure of RML, we have created a situation where the speed of the motor as well as the flow-rate has kept at zero, keeping all other variables in their normalcy. No rules linking this situation was kept in the RML, and the PML is consulted. In the PML a new fact is generated by executing a system level model linking the volt-in and flow-rate $q_f = 3.24 \times 10^{-6}. u - 4.25 \times 10^{-4} /60$ as (pump behaviour-abnormal). The addition of the new fact subsequently enabled the RML to arrive at a reasoning of (repair the motor), which certainly is a procedure of altogether a different scope. This inducts a new rule pertaining to the current encountered situation, illustrating the capability of the architecture to learn from the experience. If a similar situation reoccurred, the system need not have to consult the PML to infer the goal as repair-the-motor, hence demonstrating the adaptation.

5 Conclusion

We have argued that in order to achieve the attributes of intelligent behaviour, systems require multiple representations of heterogeneous knowledge of the application domain as well as multiple reasoning. Multiple reasoning, depicted as equivalent to the division of intelligence is much alike the division of labour, and provides a trade-off between generality and efficiency. In order to structure the multiple models of heterogeneous knowledge to enable multiple reasoning, we have identified three primitive dimensions; precision, scope and generality. These dimensions classify models for particular purposes in a model space from which the most appropriate model for a given situation and control objective can be selected. Based on these concepts, we have then presented an architecture - MuRaLi - for multiple reasoning, outlined the basic operation of the architecture and illustrated the adaptively learning mechanism on a simple case study.

6 References

[1] R. R. Leitch and Q. Shen, *"Qualitativeness does not imply fuzziness"*. Proceedings of third IEEE International Conference on Fuzzy Systems, June 26-29, 1994, Vol.-II, pp. 1257-1262.

[2] J.F. Kihlstrom, " *The Cognitive Unconscious"*, Science, Vol. 237, Sept. 1987, pp. 1445-1452.

[3] Hayes-Roth, B. *"An Architecture for Adaptive Intelligent Systems*: Artificial Intelligence, 72,1-2, 1995, 329-365.

[4] Q. Shen and R. R. Leitch, " *Fuzzy Qualitative Simulation"*, IEEE Transactions on Sys. Man and Cybernetics, Vol. 23, No. 4, pp 1038-1060.

[5] Q. Shen, R.R. Leitch and A.D. Steele, " *A Generic Harness for the Systematic Generation of Multiple Models"* , Working Papers QR'94, Japan, June 7-10, 1994, pp. 234-245.

[6] W. Pedrycz and F. Gomide, " *A Generalised Fuzzy Petri Net Model"*, IEEE Transactions on Fuzzy Systems, Vol. 2, No.4, Nov. 1994, pp 295-301.

[7] G. Tornielli, *"Component Based Language Reference Manual"*, ESPRIT P820 Report, Heriot-Watt University, 1989.

[8] R. R. Leitch and A. Stafanini, " *Task Dependant Tools for Intelligent Automation"*. Int. Journal of Artificial Intelligence in Engineering, Vol. 4, No. 3, 1989, pp. 126-143.

[9] M. Ravindranathan and R.R Leitch " *Multiple Reasoning Architecture for Intelligent Systems"*, Second International Workshop on Architecture for Intelligent Systems, Germany, September 5-9, 1994.

[10] B. Chandrasekaran, *"Models vs. Rules, Deep vs. Compiled, Content vs. Form: Some Distinctions in Knowledge Systems Research"*, IEEE Expert, Vol. 6, No.2, Apr. 1991, pp. 75-79.

[11] R. R. Leitch, M.J. Chantler, Q. Shen and G.M. Coghill, *"A preliminary specification methodology for model-based diagnosis"*. Annals of Mathematics and Artificial Intelligence, Vol. 11, 1994, pp. 11-32.

[12] Bytronic Associates, *"Process Control Unit"* Sutton Coldfield, UK.

Heterogeneous View Integration via Sketches and Equations

Boris Cadish and Zinovy Diskin*

Frame Inform Systems, Riga, Latvia
E-mail: diskin@frame.riga.lv

Abstract. In the paper a new approach to semantic modeling and view integration is proposed. The underlying data model is graph-based yet completely formalized so that graphical schemas themselves are precise specifications suitable for implementation: the approach is an adaptation of a familiar in the mathematical category theory specification framework based on the so called *sketches*. On this ground, a procedure of automated view integration is developed. Its distinctive feature consists in specifying correspondence between different views (on the same universe of discourse) by equations that reduces the integration task to a sequence of formal algebraic procedures.

1 Introduction and preliminary discussion

The term *view* (or, sometimes, *schema) integration* refers to the activity aimed at producing a global conceptual schema of an information domain from a set of locally developed user-oriented schemas (views). Integration is called *heterogeneuos* if local views are specified in different data definition languages. View integration often appears to be a main component of conceptual design which is itself a part of the overall activity of software design. This explains the significant interest in schema integration methodologies: a vast diversity of various approaches, techniques and tools were proposed (see, *eg*, surveys [1, 11, 10]). Moreover, to date the value of the issue has increased greatly due to the tendency of organizing modern (and of the nearest future) information systems into federal environments where schema and data integration are among primary questions.

The main difficulty in view integration consists in managing structural conflicts between view schemas that occur when the same data are modeled differently in different views. Usually, semantic interpretations (extensions) of local schemas are overlapped, and due to possible different perception of the same piece of reality by different users the common part can be modeled by different constructs; the phenomenon is often called *semantic relativism*.[2] As a result, the

---

* Supported by Grant 93.315, and (the second author partly) by Grant 93.254 both from the Latvian Council of Science

[2] Moreover, a good semantic model must be rich enough to support relativism in order to supply each user with modeling constructs suitable to her perception. For

global schema cannot be obtained by simple merging local schemas, and actually there is required a certain additional information (expressed in some language of *correspondence assertions*) about correspondence between local views.Moreover, searching for such a correspondence can reveal the necessity of introducing some new *interschema data* connecting local schemas but not captured by any of them. All this constitutes a heuristic and hard to formalize nature of the subject and leads to an abundance of *ad hoc* solutions and methodologies (see also [9]).

A lot of approaches to classifying and managing structural conflicts were proposed ([3, 1, 8, 12] and others), the most fundamental to date research is that one by Spaccapietra *et al* ([14, 13]) where a taxonomy distinguishing *semantic, descriptional, structural* and *heterogeneity* conflicts was suggested. However, the taxonomy appears to be an informal description rather than a precise specification capable to support automated integration. In general, while the phenomenon of semantic relativism is well known still there is no its formal explication, in other words, there is no a formal definition of what does it mean "the same data structured differently". Thus, semantic relativism is not explained in precise terms, and resolution of structural conflicts within a sufficiently rich data model is still a challenge. The more so is for heterogeneuos conflicts where it seems little was done apart from stating the problem.

Our approach to the problem is based on consistent using two key ideas. The first one is to employ a graphical object-oriented data model possessing precise formal semantics[3]. It is a generalization of the *sketch* model worked out in mathematical category theory (CT) but it needs essential developing the standard sketch machinery (first steps were made in [4, 6]). Following the CT terminology tradition, we also call our graphical specifications *sketches*. The distinctive property of sketches crucial for handling heterogeneity is their provable universality: it can be shown that any formal data specification can be simulated by a sketch[4]. Thus, in our approach, all local views as well as inter-schema data are to be described by sketches so that integration of n views is reduced to integration of $(n + 1)$-sketches $S_1, \ldots, S_n, S_{CI}$ (where CI stands for *correspondence information*).

The second key idea consists in specifying structural conflicts via equations between algebraic terms. To wit, we show (see also [5, 2]) that all the diversity

---

example, in the ER data model the same object of the real world can be presented as an entity, or as an attribute, or as a relationship.

[3] We assert that none of the conventional graphical models has this property

[4] Any formal specification can be expressed in the language of some formal set theory, or in the language of some formal higher-order type theory as well (in fact, this is a definition of *formal specification* adopted in the modern mathematics). Then, there are three well known facts in CT: (1) set theories as well as type theories are interpretable in categorial structures called *toposes*; (2) toposes can be specified by sketches; (3) any topos can be presented as a (kind of nested relational) algebra over the corresponding graph.

The conclusion is that the full power of higher-order logic, including its algebraizability, can be simulated by sketches; or, in other words, *everything that can be specified formally can be specified by sketches.*

of structural conflicts can be uniformly described as follows: data considered as *basic* in one view are considered as *derived* in another view (derived from its own collection of basic data). This is nothing but an instance of the well known in mathematical logic phenomenon when basic operations, relations and even sorts of one many-sorted theory are not basic but derived in another theory. In the database context this means that data intended to be stored in the DB according to one view are considered to be retrieved (if requested) through corresponding queries against another view.

So, specification of structural conflicts is reduced to building augmentations $\overline{S_i}$ of local sketches with new items denoting derived information, $\overline{S_i} \supseteq S_i$, and then setting a set of equations between items of augmented sketches, E_{CI}. Then integration turns into disjoint merging local sketches, $(\overline{S_1} \oplus \ldots \oplus \overline{S_n} \oplus \overline{S_{CI}})$, and factorizing the result by the congruence generated by E_{CI}, that is, gluing together certain items of the merge according to the E_{CI}-equations.

A simple example demonstrating the idea is presented in section 3. In section 2 the machinery of data modeling via sketches developed in [7] is briefly described in the context of view integration.

2   Data modeling via sketches

In the majority of conventional techniques for semantic modeling it is common to specify the intended semantic meaning of some node in a schema by marking the node with a corresponding label. In the context of view integration such a practice can readily lead to conflicts between views. For instance, in the standard of ER diagrams, to specify a node as a relation (say, *Marriage*), *ie*, as a set of relationship objects (marriage couples), one labels it by a diamond. However, if another user perceives the same data objects as entities (*eg*, families), (s)he labels the corresponding node in his schema by a rectangle. How must the node (*Marriage*) of the integrated schema be labeled?

One can observe that structural conflicts like above are caused by determining internal structure of a set via determining the structure of its elements: a relation is a set of tuples, a powerset is a set of subsets etc. In contrast to thinking in terms of elements, the category theory paradigm of arrow thinking suggests to specify internal structure of elements of a given set by characterizing (labeling) the corresponding diagram of functions adjoint to the set. Here is a very simple example: the sketch specification of relations.

We define *a source* to be a set X equipped with a family $\mathcal{F}$ of functions $f_i \colon X \longrightarrow Y_i$, $i = 1, ..., n$. Then one has a function $f = [f_1 \ldots f_n]$ from X into the Cartesian product $Y_1 \times \ldots \times Y_n$ determined in the standard way by setting $fx = [f_1 x, \ldots, f_n x]$. It is easy to see that f is injective, *ie*, X is actually a relation up to isomorphism, iff the family $\mathcal{F}$ satisfies the following *separation* condition: $\forall x, x' \in X$, $x \neq x'$ implies $f_i(x) \neq f_i(x')$ for some f_i. So, to specify a set as a set of tuples one can safely leave the set itself without imposition of any constraints but constrain instead the corresponding source of outgoing functions to be separating. Correspondingly, on the syntax level, to specify a node as a relation one can safely leave the node without any label but mark instead the corresponding source of outgoing arrows by, say, an arc denoting the separation condition (in effect, this is nothing but a well known idea of designating a key of relation).

Similar arrow treatments of other conventional semantic constructs (*eg*, grouping) are presented in the following table in a hopefully self-explained way.

Name	Arity Shape and Designation	Denotational Semantics
Separating Source	X / f_1 ... f_n / Y_1 ... Y_n	$(\forall x, x' \in X)\ x \neq x'$ implies $f_i(x) \neq f_i(x')$ for some f_i
Monic Arrow	$X \xmapsto{\ f\ } Y$	$(\forall x, x' \in X)\ x \neq x'$ implies $f(x) \neq f(x')$
ISA-Arrow or Inclusion	$X \xRightarrow{\ f\ } Y$ or $X \xhookrightarrow{\ f\ } Y$	$X \subset Y$ and $f(x) = x$ for all $x \in X$
Covering Flow	Y / f_1 ... f_n / X_1 ... X_n	$(\forall y \in Y)(\exists i < n) y \in f_i(X_i)$
Cover	$X \xrightarrow{\ f\ } Y$	$Y = f(X)$
Maximal Separating Source	X / f_1 ... f_n / Y_1 ... Y_n	$(\forall x, x' \in X)\ x \neq x'$ implies $f_i(x) \neq f_i(x')$ for some f_i, and $(\forall y_1 \in Y_1, \ldots, \forall y_n \in Y_n)$ $\exists x \in X$ s.t. $f_1(x) = y_1, \ldots, f_n(x) = y_n$.
Disjoint Covering Flow	Y / f_1 ... f_n / X_1 ... X_n	$(\forall y \in Y \exists i < n) y \in f_i(X_i)$ and $i \neq j$ implies $f_i(X_i) \cap f_j(X_j) = \varnothing$
ε-relation	X / f_1 $(\in)$ f_2 / Y_1 Y_2	$(\forall y, y' \in Y_1)\ y \neq y'$ implies $\{f_2 x : x \in f_1^{-1} y\} \neq \{f_2 x : x \in f_1^{-1} y'\}$, *ie*, there is an embedding $Y_1 \longmapsto \mathbf{Powerset} Y_2$.

Following a tradition, we will often omit the marker of commutativity. So, (=) can be considered as the default marker. In contrast, the diagrams not assumed to be commutative are marked with puncture sign $\div$.

3 View integration via sketches and equations

It was demonstrated in the previous section that semantic modeling can be based on imposing conditions on arrow diagrams contrary to imposing conditions on nodes as is often done in current semantic schemas. It is remarkable that even the very replacement of labeling nodes by labeling arrow diagram allows to avoid certain kinds of structural conflicts between views like that one described at the very beginning of the previous section (note, however, these are the conflicts to which a large body of works is devoted, see Spaccapietra *et al* [13]). But what are the real structural conflicts in the arrow approach?

We will expose the idea through considering a very simple example. Let us consider two ER-schemas presented on Fig. 1. It is clear that if the names 'People' in the first schema and 'Person' in the second one refer to the same class of objects in the real world, then the schemas are very much overlapped semantically. The question is how this can be expressed in a formal way.

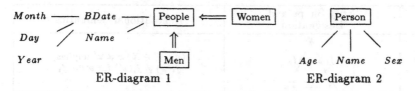

ER-diagram 1   ER-diagram 2

Fig. 1. Two ER-schemas to be integrated

A more thorough analysis of the situation shows that semantic overlapping amounts to the following: a part of the information considered as basic by the first view can be extracted from the second view as derived information (by making the corresponding queries), and vice verse. To specify this observation formally we proceed as follows.

First of all, we convert ER-schemas into sketches, *ie*, directed graphs some of whose diagrams are labeled by special markers - the resulting sketches are depicted on Fig. 2.

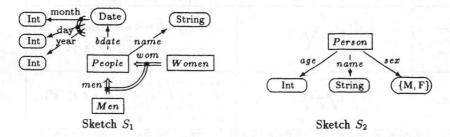

Sketch S_1 Sketch S_2

Fig. 2. Transformation of the ER-schemas into sketches

Note, that all attributes are presented by functions into nodes whose intended semantics is predefined (and supported by the computer system); in fact, these are predefined data types in the sense of programming languages (in particular, the domain of 'sex' consisting of two fixed tags, M and F, is a user-defined data type). In semantic modeling such nodes are usually called *printable* and are specially labeled to distinguish them from *abstract* nodes. We label the former by stadium frames and the latter by rectangles.

REMARK. For us, Int and {M,F} are *markers* (in our precise sense), hung on corresponding nodes, that is, constraints imposed on their intended semantic interpretations. At the same time, 'Person', 'Men' etc. are merely *names* labeling corresponding nodes without imposing any constraints. Generally speaking, we should also give names to the nodes labeled by Int and {M,F}, say, 'Number' and 'Label'. However, since the intended semantics of so marked nodes is fixed and remains the same for all schemas (in any schema the intended semantics of a node labeled by the marker {M,F} is the two-element set consisting of the tag M and the tag F, despite the node's name: 'Label', or 'Tag', or 'Attribute' etc.), we adopt the convention of using such markers also as names; they will be printed in a non-italic font. So, abstract nodes are named, and printable nodes (value domains) are, in addition, labeled by markers expressing their intended semantics (while their names are omitted!).

Distinguishing between names and markers in semantic schemas appears to be a precise formalization of the well known differentiation between abstract and printable classes usually treated less formally.

Thus, semantic schemas are converted into sketches and we turn to specifying correspondence between views in the sketch language.

First of all, we make a default assumption that local sketches are defined over a common system of value domains and their names (markers!). The next step is to extend the original sketches with nodes and arrows denoting derived data so that correspondence between views should become explicit and could be formally described (Fig. 3). Specifically, to get derived elements on Fig. 3 we proceed as follows. [5]

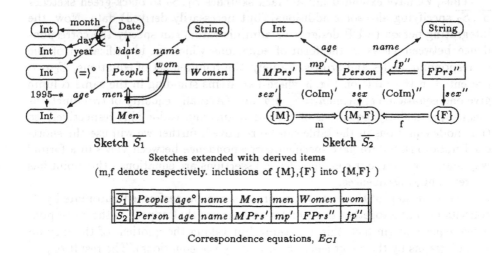

Sketch $\overline{S_1}$ Sketch $\overline{S_2}$

Sketches extended with derived items
(m,f denote respectively. inclusions of {M},{F} into {M,F})

$\overline{S_1}$	People	age°	name	Men	men	Women	wom
$\overline{S_2}$	Person	age	name	$MPrs'$	mp'	$FPrs''$	fp''

Correspondence equations, E_{CI}

Fig. 3. Specifying correspondence information

---

[5] It would be convenient to picture initial sketches by one colour, say, black, and their derived components - by another colour, say, green. For typographical reasons, we replace green-painting derived items by hanging various superscript (like $'$,$''$, $*$, , $^\circ$ etc.) on their names. In addition, derived nodes and arrows obtained simultaneously by applying some operation are marked with the same superscript, and the same superscript labels the very marker of the operation.

To begin with, we extend the first sketch with a predefined function ($1995 - *$) of subtraction, and then compose three arrows, *bdate*, **year**,**1995-*** to get the arrow *age*° (and again, **year** and **1995-*** are markers rather than names). The marker $(=)°$ labeling the corresponding diagram states the fact that *age*° is obtained by the operation of composition. As for the second sketch, we, first of all, enrich it with two inclusions, **m**: $\{M\} \hookrightarrow \{M,F\}$ and **f**: $\{F\} \hookrightarrow \{M,F\}$ whose existence is derivable from the existence of the set $\{M,F\}$. Then we apply twice the operation *CoIm* of taking, for a given function, the coimage of a given subset of the codomain in order to obtain the following derived items:

$$(MPrs', mp', sex') = CoIm(\mathbf{m}, sex), \quad (FPrs'', fp'', sex'') = CoIm(\mathbf{f}, sex).$$

The $\langle\texttt{CoIm}\rangle$-marker labeling the two square diagram states exactly that the corresponding nodes and arrows are obtained by the diagram operation *CoIm* (and hence their extensions can be computed by the corresponding procedure).

The sketch notation for graph-based operations is presented in Table 1. Each operation is specified by its *output sketch*, S_{out}, containing a designated *input* subsketch, S_{in}. Semantics is as follows: if an extension of S_{in} is given, then extensions of the output items belonging to $S_{out} \setminus S_{in}$ can be computed by the corresponding procedure. So, Table 1 presents a (small part of) graph-based query language.

Thus, we have extended initial black sketches S_1, S_2 to black-green sketches $\overline{S_1}, \overline{S_2}$ specifying also some additional (but necessarily derived) data. Now, the integrating person (a DB designer or administrator) can specify the correspondence between views in the form of equations which fix identification of the corresponding nodes and arrows. Namely, the required set of equations, E_{CI}, is presented in the table on Fig. 3 where two items standing in the same column give one equation, eg, $\overline{S_1}.men = \overline{S_2}.mp'$ etc. (Actually equality of two functions means, particularly, equalities of their domains and codomains respectively so that node equations in the table can be removed; further we will use the shortened notation). So, we have specified correspondence between views in a formal way and, moreover, our correspondence assertions are equations - this point has far reaching consequences.

The next step of the integration process can be performed automatedly. It consists in gluing together those nodes and arrows that appear in the correspondence equations (in fact, this is nothing but taking the quotient of the disjoint sum of graphs by the congruence generated by the equations). The result of gluing is presented in Fig. 4; The name *full integrated sketch* refers to the fact that this sketch contains all the necessary information and, in addition, some derived (green) information.

To end the integration one must choose a *generating* subsketch S_I of the full sketch s.t. all items of $\overline{S_I}$ not contained in S_I can be extracted from the latter by means of queries, that is, diagram operations (Fig. 5). (Of course, there are different generating subsketches; the order of preference is determined by psychological reasons like readability, or by readiness for future implementation, or by a combination of both). Together with a generating sketch, S_I, the procedure

Table 1. A collection of diagram operations

Name (marker)	Arity Shape		Denotational Semantics	Linear notation
	Input sketch	Output sketch		
Composition (=)	$Z \xrightarrow{g_2} Y$ $g_1 \uparrow$ X	$Z \xrightarrow{g_2} Y$ $g_1 \uparrow \nearrow_f$ (=) X	$(\forall x \in X) f(x) = g_2(g_1(x))$	$f = g_1 \bowtie g_2$
Graph (Gra)	$X \xrightarrow{f} Y$	G $p \swarrow$ (Gra) $\searrow q$ $X \xrightarrow{f} Y$	$G = \{(x, fx) : x \in X\}$ p, q are projections	$G = Graph(f)$
Push-Out (of ISA-arrows) (PO)	$C \rightrightarrows A$ $g \Downarrow$ B	$C \xrightarrow{f} A$ $g \Downarrow$ (PO) $\Downarrow k$ $B \rightrightarrows S$ l	$S = \{(a,1) : a \in (A \setminus C)\} \cup$ $\{(b,2) : b \in (B \setminus C)\} \cup$ $\{(c,3) : c \in C\}$	$S = PO(f, g)$
Pull-back (PB)	A $\downarrow f$ $B \longrightarrow X$ g	$R \xrightarrow{p} A$ $q \downarrow$ (PB) $\downarrow f$ $B \longrightarrow X$ g	$R = \{(a, b) \in A \times B : fa = gb\}$ p, q are projections	$R = PB(f, g)$
Coimage (CoIm)	B $b \Downarrow$ $X \longrightarrow Y$ f	$B' \xrightarrow{f'} B$ $b' \Downarrow$ (CoIm) $\Downarrow b$ $X \longrightarrow Y$ f	$B' = \{x \in X : fx \in B\}$ $f' = $ restriction of f on B'	$B' = f^{-1}(Y)$ $f' = f \lceil B'$

Following the tradition, we will often omit the marker of composition. So, (=) can be considered as the default marker. In contrast, the diagrams not assumed to be commutative are marked with puncture sign ⊹.

determines mappings $\sigma_i : S_i \to \overline{S_I}$ from local sketches into an expansion of the generating sketch with derived items.

In our example, to fix correspondence between views it was sufficient to state correspondence equations between basic and derived items of the initial schemas because correspondence consisted in *coincidence* of the corresponding items extents. However, in the general case, to specify correspondence equationally it is required to introduce new schema (sketch) fixing more complex correlations between extents than coincidence. For example, if the *People*-set of the first view is a subset of the *Person*-set of the second view, then one must introduce the specification presented by Fig. 6 and proceed with integration of S_1, S_2, S_{CI} along lines described above.

4 Conclusion

The example we have described is very simple yet demonstrates the general strategy for heterogeneuos view integration we suggest. Every particular situation needs elaboration of the appropriate specific signatures of diagram markers

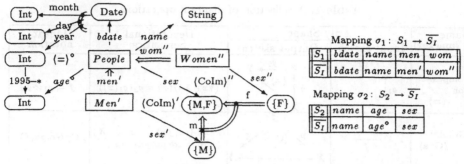

Full integrsated sketch (FIS), $\overline{S_I} = \overline{S_1} \oplus_{E_{CI}} \overline{S_2}$ Mappings of local sketches into FIS

Fig. 4. Integration,I: Merging and Factorizing

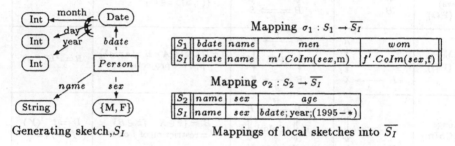

Generating sketch,S_I Mappings of local sketches into $\overline{S_I}$

Fig. 5. Integration,II: Removing redundant items

and operations similar to those described in Tables 1,2. After that is done, integration can be performed along lines we described.

The essence of resolving structural conflicts between view schemas consists in *discovering* suitable augmentations of local schemas (sketches) with derived items so that their correspondence could be described by equations. As a result, several extensive integration steps can be reduced to formal algebraic manipulations with terms and equations that provides their effective computer realization.

Actually the integration procedure is performed in two steps. The first one consists in disjoint merging $(n+1)$ graphs underlying local schemas and then factorizing the merge (this step can be performed in a fully automatic way). The second step consists in converting the integrated graph into a schema by integrating diagram markers from the local sketches. However, here marked diagram conflicts can arise (we avoided them in our very simple example), and these are real conflicts between views which can bring to light their inconsistency (see [4, 6] for details). Interestingly, it seems that just this kind of conflicts were not identified in the DB theory literature.

Clear semantics of sketches makes it possible to distinguish in the general integration procedure the steps which can be fully automated and those that need human assistance. In its turn, the latter can be also made computer-aided and, speaking in general, the sketch framework brings to light limitations and possibilities of automation in schema and data integration(see also [2]). On the other

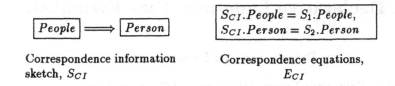

Correspondence information sketch, S_{CI}	Correspondence equations, E_{CI}

Fig. 6. Another example of specifying correspondence information

hand, our experience has shown that sketches turn out to be very handy as a machinery for semantic modeling and integration. In particular, they are convenient for semi-automated phases of integration being performed in a interactive mode.

References

1. C. Batini, M. Lenzerini, and S. Navathe. A comparitive analysis of methodologies for database schema integration. *ACM Computing Surveys*, 18(4):323–364, 1986.
2. B. Cadish and Z. Diskin. Algebraic graph-based approach to management of multibase systems, I: Schema integration via sketches and equations. In *Next Generation of InfoTechnologies and Systems, NGITS'95*, 2nd Int.Workshop (Israel), 1995.
3. U. Dayal and H. Hwang. View definition and generalization for database integration of a multibase system. *IEEE Trans. Software Eng.*, 10(6):628–644, 1984.
4. Z. Diskin. Mathematical aspects of schema integration. TR-9502, Frame Inform Systems, Riga, 1995. (On ftp: //ftp.cs.chalmers.se/pub/users/diskin/tr9502.*).
5. Z. Diskin. Formalizing graphical schemas for conceptual modeling: Sketch-based logic vs. heuristic pictures. TR-9501, Frame Inform Systems, Riga, 1995.
6. Z. Diskin and B. Cadish. Databases as graphical algebras. (On ftp: //ftp.cs.chalmers.se/pub/users/diskin/amast96.*), 1995.
7. Z. Diskin and B. Cadish. Variable sets and functions framework for conceptual modeling: Integrating ER and OO via sketches with dynamic markers. In *Proc. 14th Int.Conf. (OO & ER)'95*, Springer LNCS'1021, 1995.
8. J.A. Larson, S.B. Navathe, and R. Elmasri. A theory of attribute equivalence in databases with application to schema integration. *IEEE Trans. Software Eng.*, 15(4), 1989.
9. S. Navathe. The next ten years of modeling, methodologies and tools. In *ER'92*, number 645 in LNCS, (Karlsrue, Germany), 1992.
10. E. Pitoura, O. Bukhres, and A. Elmagarmid. Object orientation in multidatabase systems. *ACM computing surveys*, 27(2):141–195, 1995.
11. A. Sneth and C. Larson. Federated database systems for managing distributed, heterogeneous, and autonomous databases. *ACM Computing Surveys*, 1990.
12. S. Spaccapietra and C. Parent. Conflicts and correspondence assertions in interoperable databases. *ACM SIGMOD Record*, 20(4):49–54, 1991.
13. S. Spaccapietra, C. Parent, and Y. Dupont. Model-independent assertions for integration of heterogeneous schemas. *Very Large Databases Journal*, 1(1), 1992.
14. S. Spaccapietra, C. Parent, and Y. Dupont. View integration: a step forward in solving structural conflicts. *IEEE Transactions on KDE*, 1992.

$\mathcal{D}$LAB: A Declarative Language Bias Formalism

Luc Dehaspe and Luc De Raedt

Katholieke Universiteit Leuven, Department of Computer Science,
Celestijnenlaan 200A, B-3001 Heverlee, Belgium
email : Luc.Dehaspe,Luc.DeRaedt@cs.kuleuven.ac.be
fax : ++ 32 16 32 79 96; telephone : ++ 32 16 32 75 50

Abstract. We describe the principles and functionalities of $\mathcal{D}$LAB (Declarative LAnguage Bias). $\mathcal{D}$LAB can be used in inductive learning systems to define syntactically and traverse efficiently finite subspaces of first order clausal logic, be it a set of propositional formulae, association rules, Horn clauses, or full clauses. A Prolog implementation of $\mathcal{D}$LAB is available by ftp access.

Keywords: declarative language bias, concept learning, knowledge discovery

1 Introduction

The notion *bias*, generally circumscribed as "a tendency to show prejudice against one group and favouritism towards another" (Collins Cobuild, 1987), has been adapted to the field of computational inductive reasoning to become a generic term for "any basis for choosing one generalization over another, other than strict consistency with the instances" (Mitchell [14]). We borrow a more fine-tuned definition of inductive bias from Utgoff [20].

Definition 1 (inductive bias). Except for the presented examples and counterexamples of the concept being learned, all factors that influence hypothesis selection constitute *bias*. These factors include the following:

1. The language in which hypotheses are described
2. The space of hypotheses that the program can consider
3. The procedures that define in what order hypotheses are to be considered
4. The acceptance criteria that define whether a search procedure may stop with a given hypothesis or should continue searching for a better choice

Utgoff's definition of bias has further developed into a typology which distinguishes three different categories [17]: *language bias* roughly combines Utgoff's factors 1 and 2, and *search bias* and *validation bias* roughly correspond to items 3 and 4 respectively[1]. As the factors that influence hypothesis selection were further charted the idea grew to take them out of the hands of programmers, promote them to parameters in learning systems, and thus make way for the

---

[1] An alternative framework [9] divides bias into *representational* (cf. items 1 and 2) and *procedural* (cf. items 2 and 3) components.

specification and modification of previously unexploited a priori knowledge. For this type of explicit input parameters, Russell and Grosof [18] introduced the concept *declarative bias*.

In this paper, we present a new formalism for the declarative representation of language bias. The formalism is called, somewhat opportunistically, $\mathcal{D}$LAB (Declarative LAnguage Bias). A $\mathcal{D}$LAB grammar intensionally defines the syntax of a finite subspace of first order clausal logic[2], be it a set of propositional formulae, association rules, Horn clauses, or full clauses. With the design of $\mathcal{D}$LAB we have attempted to balance the following conflicting requirements:

1. *Ease of use*: the formalism should be declarative and have a clear semantics
2. *Expressive power*: it should allow the full exploitation of prior syntactic knowledge to maximally reduce the search space
3. *Ease of navigation*: it should suggest a strategy for exploring the search space

The latter concern is inspired by the classical machine learning view on induction as a search process through a partially ordered space induced by the generalization relation, cf. [15]. Machine learning systems typically search the space specific-to-general or general-to-specific. The features of $\mathcal{D}$LAB make it especially compatible with the latter class of systems. We will introduce a so-called refinement operator for $\mathcal{D}$LAB that calculates the maximally general specializations of any clause in the hypothesis space.

We present an overview of $\mathcal{D}$LAB in two stages. First (Section 2), we discuss syntax, semantics, and a refinement operator for $\mathcal{D}$LAB$^\Theta$, a subset of $\mathcal{D}$LAB. We then extend $\mathcal{D}$LAB$^\Theta$ to full $\mathcal{D}$LAB (Section 3). All examples of $\mathcal{D}$LAB at work have been concentrated in Section 4, which we recommend as a reader's refuge. Finally, in Section 5 we relate $\mathcal{D}$LAB to earlier work on declarative language bias.

2 $\mathcal{D}$LAB$^\Theta$

A $\mathcal{D}$LAB$^\Theta$ grammar is a set of templates to which the clauses in the hypothesis space conform. We first give a recursive syntactic definition of the $\mathcal{D}$LAB$^\Theta$ formalism.

---

[2] We assume familiarity with first order logic (see [12, 8] for an introduction), but briefly review the basic relevant concepts.

A first order alphabet is a set of predicate symbols, constant symbols and functor symbols. A clause is a formula of the form $A_1, \ldots, A_m \leftarrow B_1, \ldots, B_n$ where the A_i and B_i are logical atoms. An atom $p(t_1, \ldots, t_n)$ is a predicate symbol p followed by a bracketed n-tuple of terms t_i. A term t is a variable V or a function symbol $f(t_1, \ldots, t_k)$ immediately followed by a bracketed k-tuple of terms t_i. Constants are function symbols of arity 0.

The above clause can be read as A_1 or ... or A_m if B_1 and ... and B_n. All variables in clauses are universally quantified, although this is not explicitly written. Extending the usual convention for *definite clauses* (where $m = 1$), we call $A_1, \ldots, A_m$ the *head* of the clause and $B_1, \ldots, B_n$ the *body* of the clause.

Definition 2 ($\mathcal{D}$LAB$^\Theta$ **syntax**).

1. a $\mathcal{D}$LAB$^\Theta$ atom is either a logical atom, or of the form $Min \cdot\cdot Max : L$, with Min and Max integers such that $0 \leq Min \leq Max \leq length(L)$, and with L a list of $\mathcal{D}$LAB$^\Theta$ atoms;
2. a $\mathcal{D}$LAB$^\Theta$ template is of the form $A \leftarrow B$, where A and B are $\mathcal{D}$LAB$^\Theta$ atoms;
3. a $\mathcal{D}$LAB$^\Theta$ grammar is a set of $\mathcal{D}$LAB$^\Theta$ templates.

The hypothesis space that corresponds to a $\mathcal{D}$LAB$^\Theta$ grammar is then constructed via the (recursive) selection of all subsets of L with length within range $Min \ldots Max$ from each $\mathcal{D}$LAB$^\Theta$ atom $Min \cdot\cdot Max : L$. This idea can be elegantly formalised and implemented using the Definite Clause Grammar (DCG) notation, which is an extension of Prolog (cf. [3, 19])[3].

Definition 3 ($\mathcal{D}$LAB$^\Theta$ **semantics**). Let $\mathcal{G}$ be a $\mathcal{D}$LAB$^\Theta$ grammar, then

$$dlab\_generate(\mathcal{G}) = \{dlab\_dcg(A) \leftarrow dlab\_dcg(B) | (A \leftarrow B) \in \mathcal{G}\}$$

generates all clauses in the corresponding hypothesis space, where $dlab\_dcg(E)$ is a list of logical atoms generated by $dlab\_dcg$:

$$dlab\_dcg(E) \longrightarrow [E], \{E \neq Min \cdot\cdot Max : L\}. \tag{1}$$
$$dlab\_dcg(Min \cdot\cdot Max : []) \longrightarrow \{Min \leq 0\}, []. \tag{2}$$
$$dlab\_dcg(Min \cdot\cdot Max : [\_|L]) \longrightarrow dlab\_dcg(Min \cdot\cdot Max : L). \tag{3}$$
$$dlab\_dcg(Min \cdot\cdot Max : [E|L]) \longrightarrow \{Max > 0\}, dlab\_dcg(E),$$
$$dlab\_dcg((Min - 1) \cdot\cdot (Max - 1) : L). \tag{4}$$

From the semantics of a $\mathcal{D}$LAB$^\Theta$ grammar we derive a formula for calculating the size of its hypothesis space.

Definition 4 (**dlab_size**). Let $\mathcal{G} = \{A_1 \leftarrow B_1, \ldots, A_m \leftarrow B_m\}$ be a $\mathcal{D}$LAB$^\Theta$ grammar.

$dlab\_size(\mathcal{G}) = \sum_{i=1}^{m}(ds(A_i) * ds(B_i))$;

$ds(E) = 1$, where E is a logical atom ;

$ds(Min \cdot\cdot Max : [L_1, \ldots, L_n]) = \sum_{k=Min}^{Max} e_k(ds(L_1), \ldots, ds(L_n))$;

$e_0(L) = 1$;

$e_n(s_1, \ldots, s_n) = \prod_{i=1}^{n} s_i$;

$e_k(s_1, s_2, \ldots, s_n) = e_k(s_2, \ldots, s_n) + s_1 * e_{k-1}(s_2, \ldots, s_n)$, with $k < n$.

Proof. The first rule states that the size of the language defined by a $\mathcal{D}$LAB$^\Theta$ grammar equals the sum of the sizes of the languages defined by its individual $\mathcal{D}$LAB$^\Theta$ templates. The latter size can be found by multiplying the number of

---

[3] To simplify our definition of a generation function we here introduce (and will continue to use) a special list notation in which the head and the body of clauses are written as lists: $[A_1, \ldots, A_m] \leftarrow [B_1, \ldots, B_n]$.

headlists and the number of bodylists covered by the head and body $\mathcal{D}\text{LAB}^\Theta$ atoms.

A $\mathcal{D}\text{LAB}^\Theta$ atom which is not of the form $Min \cdot \cdot Max : L$ has a coverage of exactly one, as is expressed in the second rule.

Some more intricate combinatorics underlies the third rule. Basically, we select k objects from $\{L_1, \ldots, L_n\}$, for each k in range $Min \ldots Max$, hence the summation $\sum_{k=Min}^{Max}$. Inside this summation we would have the standard formula $n!/k! * (n-k)!$ if our case had been an instance of the prototypical problem of finding all combinations, without replacement, of k marbles out of an urn with n marbles. This formula does not apply due to the fact that we rather have n urns ($\{L_1, \ldots, L_n\}$) with one or more marbles ($ds(L_i) \geq 1$), and only combinations that use at most one marble from each urn should be counted. Therefore we need $e_k(s_1, \ldots, s_n)$, where e_k is the elementary symmetric function [13] of degree k and the s_i are the numbers of marbles in each urn. The first base case of this recursive function accounts for the fact that there is only one way to select 0 objects. In the second base case, where $k = n$, one has to take an object from each urn. As for each urn there are s_i choices, the number of combinations equals the product of all s_i. The final recursive case applies if $k < n$. It is an addition of two terms, one for each possible operation on urn 1 (represented by s_1). Either we skip this urn, and then we still have to select k elements from urns 2 to n. The number of such combinations is given by $e_k(s_2, \ldots, s_n)$. Or else we do take a marble from the first urn. We then have to multiply s_1, the choices for the first urn, with $e_{k-1}(s_2, \ldots, s_n)$, the number of $k-1$ order combinations of elements from urns 2 to n. $\qquad\qquad\qquad\qquad\qquad\qquad\qquad\qquad\qquad\qquad\qquad$ □

A *refinement operator* for $\mathcal{D}\text{LAB}^\Theta$ is based on the observation that all clauses c in the hypothesis space are defined by a sequence of subset selections, in casu a string of bits, which we will call the $\mathcal{D}\text{LAB}$ path $dp(c)$, where each 0 and 1 mark the application of *dlab_dcg* Rules 3 and 4 respectively[4].

If we enlarge one of the subsets, then the clause $c' \supseteq c$ defined by the new sequence is a specialization of c under θ-subsumption. Every 0 in the $\mathcal{D}\text{LAB}$ path $dp(c)$ marks an occasion for extending c in the sense that it points at a $\mathcal{D}\text{LAB}$ atom E which has been skipped during generation of c. We only have to switch this bit to 1 to include the corresponding E during generation of supersets of c.

If we somehow enlarge one subset in a minimal way, then c' will be a refinement, i.e. a maximally general specialization of c[5]. In terms of the $\mathcal{D}\text{LAB}$ path: we have to expand exactly one 0 bit, and then only in a minimal way. Additional constraints on the enlargement of subsets, such that each subset is generated at most once, yield a refinement operator that is *optimal*, in the sense that it will

---

[4] The $\mathcal{D}\text{LAB}$ path is not only a basis for the refinement of clauses but also for their storage in a compressed bitstring format. This feature makes $\mathcal{D}\text{LAB}$ especially valuable as an encoding tool in learning systems that manipulate large queues (e.g. doing a best first search) of candidate clauses which in uncompressed format would quickly exhaust memory resources.

[5] Depending on the $\mathcal{D}\text{LAB}^\Theta$ grammar, this refinement (under θ-subsumption) can be proper or not.

generate a node (= clause) in the search space at most once. When using the $\mathcal{D}$LAB path we can achieve optimality for instance if we never expand 0's to the left of already expanded 0's.

As fully described in [6], the $\mathcal{D}$LAB refinement operator sketched above can be implemented in seventeen DCG rules. A more sophisticated Prolog implementation (as well as [6]) is available by anonymous ftp access to *ftp.cs.kuleuven.ac.be.* The relevant directory is *pub/logic − prgm/ilp/dlab.*

3 $\mathcal{D}$LAB$^\Theta$ Extended: $\mathcal{D}$LAB

In an extended version $\mathcal{D}$LAB mainly two features have been added to improve readability of more complex grammars: second order variables, and subsets on the term level.

Definition 5 ($\mathcal{D}$LAB syntax).

1. a $\mathcal{D}$LAB term is either
   (a) a variable symbol, or
   (b) of the form $f(t_1, \ldots, t_n)$, where f is a function symbol followed by a bracketed $n - tuple$ $((0 \leq n))$ of $\mathcal{D}$LAB terms t_i, or
   (c) of the form $Min \cdot\cdot Max : L$, where Min and Max are integers with $0 \leq Min \leq Max \leq length(L)$, and with L a list of $\mathcal{D}$LAB terms;
2. a $\mathcal{D}$LAB atom is either
   (a) of the form $p(t_1, \ldots, t_n)$, where p is a predicate symbol followed by a bracketed $n - tuple$ $((0 \leq n))$ of $\mathcal{D}$LAB terms t_i, or
   (b) of the form $Min \cdot\cdot Max : L$, where Min and Max are integers with $0 \leq Min \leq Max \leq length(L)$, and with L a list of $\mathcal{D}$LAB atoms;
3. a $\mathcal{D}$LAB template is of the form $A \leftarrow B$, where A and B are $\mathcal{D}$LAB atoms;
4. a $\mathcal{D}$LAB variable is of the form $dlab\_var(p_0, Min \cdot\cdot Max, [p_1, \ldots, p_n])$, where Min and Max are integers with $0 \leq Min \leq Max \leq n$, and with p_i a predicate symbol or a function symbol
5. a $\mathcal{D}$LAB$^\Theta$ grammar is a couple $(\mathcal{T}, \mathcal{V})$, where $\mathcal{T}$ is a set of $\mathcal{D}$LAB templates, and $\mathcal{V}$ a set of $\mathcal{D}$LAB variables.

We will now define the conversion of $\mathcal{D}$LAB grammars $(\mathcal{T}, \mathcal{V})$ to the $\mathcal{D}$LAB$^\Theta$ format such that the above definitions of semantics, size, and a refinement operator remain valid for the enriched formalism. First, to remove the second order variables $\mathcal{V}$ we recursively replace all $\mathcal{D}$LAB terms and atoms

$p(t_1, \ldots, t_n)$ in $\mathcal{T}$ such that $dlab\_var(p, Min\text{-}Max, [p_1, \ldots, p_m]) \in \mathcal{V}$, with
$Min \cdot\cdot Max : [p_1(t_1, \ldots, t_n), \ldots, p_m(t_1, \ldots, t_n)]$.

Next we recursively remove subsets on the termlevel by replacing from left to right all $\mathcal{D}$LAB terms

$p(t_1, \ldots, t_i, Min \cdot\cdot Max : [L_1, \ldots, L_n], t_{i+2}, \ldots, t_m)$, with
$Min\text{-}Max : [p(t_1, \ldots, t_i, L_1, t_{i+2}, \ldots, t_m), \ldots, p(t_1, \ldots, t_i, L_n, t_{i+2}, \ldots, t_m)]$.

When applied subsequently, these two algorithms transform a $\mathcal{D}$LAB grammar $\mathcal{G} = (\mathcal{T}, \mathcal{V})$ into $(\mathcal{G}', \emptyset)$, where $\mathcal{G}'$ is an equivalent $\mathcal{D}$LAB$^\Theta$ grammar.

4 $\mathcal{D}$LAB at Work

This section is entirely devoted to the illustration of the expressive power of $\mathcal{D}$LAB. We begin with some elementary grammars and end with a study of $\mathcal{D}$LAB at work in the finite element mesh design domain.

Given a $\mathcal{D}$LAB atom $Min \cdot\cdot Max : L$, four choices of values for Min and Max determine the following cases of special interest:

1. **all subsets:** $Min = 0, Max = len$
   e.g. $\mathcal{G}1 = (\{h \leftarrow 0 \cdot\cdot len : [a, b, c]\}, \emptyset)$
2. **all non-empty subsets:** $Min = 1, Max = 1$
   e.g. $\mathcal{G}2 = (\{h \leftarrow 1 \cdot\cdot len : [a, b, c]\}, \emptyset)$
3. **exclusive or:** $Min = 1, Max = 1$
   e.g. $\mathcal{G}3 = (\{h \leftarrow 1 \cdot\cdot 1 : [a, b, c]\}, \emptyset)$
4. **combined occurence:** $Min = Max = len$
   e.g. $\mathcal{G}4 = (\{h \leftarrow len \cdot\cdot len : [a, b, c]\}, \emptyset)$

These special cases can be nested to construct more complex grammars exemplified below. Table 1 gives the corresponding hypothesis spaces for grammars $\mathcal{G}1 - \mathcal{G}8$. A $\sqrt{}$ in the column of grammar $\mathcal{G}i$ marks the clauses of the first column that are in the corresponding hypothesis space.

$\mathcal{G}5 = (\{h \leftarrow 1 \cdot\cdot len : [a, 1 \cdot\cdot 1 : [b, c]]\}, \emptyset)$
$\mathcal{G}6 = (\{h \leftarrow 1 \cdot\cdot len : [a, len \cdot\cdot len : [b, c]]\}, \emptyset)$
$\mathcal{G}7 = (\{h \leftarrow len \cdot\cdot len : [a, 1 \cdot\cdot 1 : [b, c]]\}, \emptyset)$
$\mathcal{G}8 = (\{h \leftarrow 0 \cdot\cdot len : [len \cdot\cdot len : [a, 0 \cdot\cdot len : [len \cdot\cdot len : [b, 0 - len : [c]]]]]\}, \emptyset)$

Table 1. The semantics of some sample $\mathcal{D}$LAB grammars

	$\mathcal{G}1$	$\mathcal{G}2$	$\mathcal{G}3$	$\mathcal{G}4$	$\mathcal{G}5$	$\mathcal{G}6$	$\mathcal{G}7$	$\mathcal{G}8$
$[h] \leftarrow []$	$\sqrt{}$							$\sqrt{}$
$[h] \leftarrow [a]$	$\sqrt{}$	$\sqrt{}$	$\sqrt{}$		$\sqrt{}$	$\sqrt{}$		$\sqrt{}$
$[h] \leftarrow [b]$	$\sqrt{}$	$\sqrt{}$	$\sqrt{}$		$\sqrt{}$			
$[h] \leftarrow [c]$	$\sqrt{}$	$\sqrt{}$	$\sqrt{}$		$\sqrt{}$			
$[h] \leftarrow [a, b]$	$\sqrt{}$	$\sqrt{}$			$\sqrt{}$		$\sqrt{}$	$\sqrt{}$
$[h] \leftarrow [a, c]$	$\sqrt{}$	$\sqrt{}$			$\sqrt{}$		$\sqrt{}$	
$[h] \leftarrow [b, c]$	$\sqrt{}$	$\sqrt{}$				$\sqrt{}$		
$[h] \leftarrow [a, b, c]$	$\sqrt{}$	$\sqrt{}$		$\sqrt{}$		$\sqrt{}$		$\sqrt{}$

Grammar $\mathcal{G}8$ illustrates how taxonomies can be encoded, such that each atomic formula necessarily co-occurs with all its ancestors and never combines with other nodes. A more elaborate example of how $\mathcal{D}$LAB handles this type of background knowledge is grammar $\mathcal{G}9$, which encodes the taxonomy for suits of playing cards (see Figure 1).

$$\mathcal{G}9 = (T9, \mathcal{V}9)$$
$$T9 = \{ok(C) \leftarrow$$
$$len \cdot\cdot len : [card(C), 0\cdot\cdot 1 : [len \cdot\cdot len : [red(C), p1(C)],$$
$$len \cdot\cdot len : [black(C), p2(C)]$$
$$]$$
$$]\}$$
$$\mathcal{V}9 = \{dlab\_var(p1, 0\cdot\cdot 1, [hearts, diamonds]),$$
$$dlab\_var(p2, 0\cdot\cdot 1, [clubs, spades])\}$$

$$dlab\_generate(\mathcal{G}9) = \begin{cases} [ok(C)] \leftarrow [card(C)] \\ [ok(C)] \leftarrow [card(C), red(C)] \\ [ok(C)] \leftarrow [card(C), red(C), hearts(C)] \\ [ok(C)] \leftarrow [card(C), red(C), diamonds(C)] \\ [ok(C)] \leftarrow [card(C), black(C)] \\ [ok(C)] \leftarrow [card(C), black(C), clubs(C)] \\ [ok(C)] \leftarrow [card(C), black(C), spades(C)] \end{cases}$$

Fig. 1. Encoding taxonomies: $\mathcal{D}$LAB grammar $\mathcal{G}9$

We now step through the development of a $\mathcal{D}$LAB grammar for the finite element mesh design application frequently used to evaluate relational learning algorithms (see e.g. [7, 11]). The training examples in this domain are "hand-constructed" approximations of physical structures. Such an approximation is a set of *finite elements* called a *mesh model*, divided into a collection of edges. The relation to be learned is $mesh(E, N)$, where E identifies the edge and N is the recommended number of finite elements along this edge. The background knowledge contains nineteen unary predicates describing individual edges, and three binary predicates describing topological relations between edges belonging to the same structure.

$\mathcal{G}10$ is a first $\mathcal{D}$LAB grammar for discovering rules in which only the unary descriptions are taken into account (see Figure 2).

$$\mathcal{G}10 = (T10, \mathcal{V}10)$$
$$T10 =$$
$$\{1\cdot\cdot 1 : [mesh(E, 1), mesh(E, 2), mesh(E, 3), mesh(E, 4), mesh(E, 5),$$
$$mesh(E, 6), mesh(E, 7), mesh(E, 8), mesh(E, 9), mesh(E, 10),$$
$$mesh(E, 11), mesh(E, 12), mesh(E, 17)]$$
$$\leftarrow$$
$$0\cdot\cdot len : [long(E), usual(E), short(E), circuit(E), half\_circuit(E),$$
$$quarter\_circuit(E), short\_for\_hole(E), long\_for\_hole(E),$$
$$circuit\_hole(E), half\_circuit\_hole(E), not\_important(E), free(E),$$
$$one\_side\_fixed(E), two\_side\_fixed(E), fixed(E), not\_loaded(E),$$
$$one\_side\_loaded(E), two\_side\_loaded(E), cont\_loaded(E)]\}$$
$$\mathcal{V}10 = \emptyset$$
$$dlab\_size(\mathcal{G}10) = 6.82 * 10^6$$

Fig. 2. Finite element mesh design: $\mathcal{D}$LAB grammar $\mathcal{G}10$

Grammar $\mathcal{G}10$ generates many a priori invalid or uninteresting clauses such as $mesh(E, 1) \leftarrow long(E), short(E)$. In fact three groups of mutually exclusive attributes can be constructed: *edge types*, *boundary conditions*, and *loading*. In $\mathcal{G}11$ we make use of this additional knowledge to reduce the search space significantly. We also use subsets on the termlevel and predicate variables to improve readability (see Figure 3).

```
G11  = (T11, V11)
T11  = {mesh(E, resolution) ← 1··len : [type(E), boundary(E), loading(E)]
V11  = {dlab_var(resolution, 1··1, [1, 2, 3, 4, 5, 6, 7, 8, 9, 10, 11, 12, 17]),
         dlab_var(type, 1··1, [long, usual, short, circuit, half_circuit,
                               quarter_circuit, short_for_hole, long_for_hole,
                               circuit_hole, half_circuit_hole, not_important]),
         dlab_var(boundary, 1··1, [free, one_side_fixed, two_side_fixed, fixed]),
         dlab_var(loading, 1··1, [not_loaded, one_side_loaded, two_side_loaded,
                               cont_loaded])}
dlab_size(G11) = 3887
```

Fig. 3. Finite element mesh design: $\mathcal{D}$LAB grammar $\mathcal{G}11$

With grammar $\mathcal{G}12$ (see Figure 4) the hypothesis space is again extended to include clauses with a second edge in the antecedent. To describe this second edge the former three groups of nineteen attributes can be used, but also the predicate $mesh(E2, N)$, and a binary predicate specifying the topological relation between both edges.

```
G12 = (T12, V12)
T12 = {mesh(E, resolution) ← 1··len : [type(E), boundary(E), loading(E),
                                       type(E2), boundary(E2), loading(E2),
                                       mesh(E2, resolution), topology(E, E2)]}
V12 = V11 ∪ {dlab_var(topology, 1··1, [opposite, neighbour, equal)}
dlab_size(G12) = 4.91 * 10^7
```

Fig. 4. Finite element mesh design: $\mathcal{D}$LAB grammar $\mathcal{G}12$

Finally, domain experts may complain $\mathcal{G}12$ generates rules that are not useful from a practical point of view. Suppose they object to clauses that violate one of the following conditions. Firstly, each antecedent should contain at least one attribute description of the edges that occur in the rule (excludes e. g. $mesh(E, 1) \leftarrow short(E2)$ and $mesh(E, 1) \leftarrow long(E), opposite(E, E2)$). Secondly, if edge $E2$ occurs, then the rule should specify its topological relation with E (excludes e. g. $mesh(E, 1) \leftarrow long(E), short(E2)$) . These constraints can be formulated in the $\mathcal{D}$LAB formalism as shown in our final example grammar $\mathcal{G}13$ (see Figure 5).

$$
\begin{aligned}
\mathcal{G}13 &= (\mathcal{T}13, \mathcal{V}12) \\
\mathcal{T}13 &= \{mesh(E, resolution) \leftarrow \\
&\qquad len \cdot\cdot len : [1 \cdot\cdot len : [type(E), boundary(E), loading(E)], \\
&\qquad\qquad 0 \cdot\cdot len : [len \cdot\cdot len : [topology(E, E2), \\
&\qquad\qquad\qquad\qquad 1 \cdot\cdot len : [mesh(E2, resolution), type(E2), \\
&\qquad\qquad\qquad\qquad\qquad boundary(E2), loading(E2) \\
&\qquad\qquad] \qquad] \qquad\qquad] \qquad]\} \\
dlab\_size(\mathcal{G}13) &= 3.26 * 10^7
\end{aligned}
$$

Fig. 5. Finite element mesh design: $\mathcal{D}$LAB grammar $\mathcal{G}13$

5 Conclusion

We have described and illustrated the principles and functionalities of $\mathcal{D}$LAB a new formalism for the declarative representation of language bias. We conclude with a brief situation of $\mathcal{D}$LAB against some alternative declarative[6] language bias formalisms.

Closest to $\mathcal{D}$LAB are the clausemodels proposed in [1]. Generally speaking, clausemodels are special cases of $\mathcal{D}$LAB templates in which nesting and the choice of *Min* and *Max* is restricted.

As discussed in [1], schemata [10] and predicate sets [2] as used in MOBAL and the FILP system respectively, are special cases of clausemodels, and thus indirectly of $\mathcal{D}$LAB templates.

An antecedent description grammar, as used by Cohen in GRENDEL [4], is in essence a definite clause grammar that generates the antecedents of clauses in the hypothesis space. In general a conversion of antecedent description grammars to $\mathcal{D}$LAB is not always possible[7]. Roughly speaking, $\mathcal{D}$LAB contains a hardwired antecedent description grammar *dlab_dcg* that takes the $\mathcal{D}$LAB grammar as its single argument.

Acknowledgements

This work is part of the Esprit Basic Research projects no. 6020 and 20237 on Inductive Logic Programming. Luc De Raedt is supported by the Belgian National Fund for Scientific Research.

The authors would like to thank Wim Van Laer and Timothy Chow for their elegant solutions of the *dlab_size* combinatorics problem, and Hendrik Blockeel for his helpful comments on this paper.

---

[6] More procedural approaches to syntactic bias specifications use parameters such as the maximal variable depth or term level to control the complexity of the concept language, cf. [5, 16]. Parametrized languages should be considered complementary to $\mathcal{D}$LAB, in the sense that the same parameters trivially define (a series of) $\mathcal{D}$LAB grammars.

[7] A clear case where this conversion is impossible occurs when the antecedent description grammar generates an infinite language.

References

1. H. Adé, L. De Raedt, and M. Bruynooghe. Declarative Bias for Specific-to-General ILP Systems. *Machine Learning*, 20(1/2):119 – 154, 1995.
2. F. Bergadano and D. Gunetti. An interactive system to learn functional logic programs. In *Proceedings of the 13th International Joint Conference on Artificial Intelligence*, pages 1044–1049. Morgan Kaufmann, 1993.
3. W.F. Clocksin and C.S. Mellish. *Programming in Prolog*. Springer-Verlag, Berlin, 1981.
4. W.W. Cohen. Grammatically biased learning: learning logic programs using an explicit antecedent description language. *Artificial Intelligence*, 68:303–366, 1994.
5. L. De Raedt. *Interactive Theory Revision: an Inductive Logic Programming Approach*. Academic Press, 1992.
6. L. Dehaspe and L. De Raedt. DLAB: a declarative language bias for concept learning and knowledge discovery engines. Technical Report CW-214, Department of Computer Science, Katholieke Universiteit Leuven, October 1995.
7. B. Dolsak, I. Bratko, and A. Jezernik. Finite element mesh design: An engineering domain for ilp application. In S. Wrobel, editor, *Proceedings of the 4th International Workshop on Inductive Logic Programming*, volume 237 of *GMD-Studien*, Sankt Augustin, Germany, 1994. Gesellschaft für Mathematik und Datenverarbeitung MBH.
8. M. Genesereth and N. Nilsson. *Logical foundations of artificial intelligence*. Morgan Kaufmann, 1987.
9. D. Gordon and M. desJardins. Evaluation and selection of biases in machine learning. *Machine Learning*, 20(1/2):5–22, 1995.
10. J-U. Kietz and S. Wrobel. Controlling the complexity of learning in logic through syntactic and task-oriented models. In S. Muggleton, editor, *Inductive logic programming*, pages 335–359. Academic Press, 1992.
11. N. Lavrač and S. Džeroski. *Inductive Logic Programming: Techniques and Applications*. Ellis Horwood, 1994.
12. J.W. Lloyd. *Foundations of logic programming*. Springer-Verlag, 2nd edition, 1987.
13. I.G. MacDonald. *Symmetric functions and Hall polynomials*. Clarendon Oxford, 1979.
14. T.M. Mitchell. The need for biases in learning generalizations. Technical Report CBM-TR-117, Department of Computer Science, Rutgers University, 1980.
15. T.M. Mitchell. Generalization as search. *Artificial Intelligence*, 18:203–226, 1982.
16. S. Muggleton and C. Feng. Efficient induction of logic programs. In *Proceedings of the 1st conference on algorithmic learning theory*, pages 368–381. Ohmsma, Tokyo, Japan, 1990.
17. C. Nédellec, H. Adé, and B. Bergadano, F. a nd Tausend. Declarative bias in ILP. In L. De Raedt, editor, *Advances in Inductive Logic Programming*, volume 32 of *Frontiers in Artificial Intelligence and Applica tions*, pages 82–103. IOS Press, 1996.
18. S. Russell and B. Grosof. A Declarative Approach to Bias in Concept Learning. In *Proceedings of the Sixth National Conference on Artificial Intelligence (AAAI87)*, pages 505–510, 1987.
19. Leon Sterling and Ehud Shapiro. *The art of Prolog*. The MIT Press, 1986.
20. P.E. Utgoff. Shift of bias for inductive concept-learning. In R.S Michalski, J.G. Carbonell, and T.M. Mitchell, editors, *Machine Learning: an artificial intelligence approach*, pages 107–148. Morgan Kaufmann, 1986.

Knowledge Discovery in Databases and Data Mining

WILLI KLÖSGEN

kloesgen@gmd.de

GMD-German National Research Center for Information Technology D-53757 St. Augustin

Abstract: This paper gives an overview on some approaches of knowledge discovery in databases (KDD). First, the types of information exploited in a KDD process and the characteristics of this process are summarized. Then we descibe a classification of KDD-patterns. Types of languages to build subgroups of objects and the role of domain knowledge are discussed. Finally, the architecture of modular KDD systems is presented and topics of efficiency are treated.

1. The KDD Pyramid of Information

Rapid advances in data capture, storage, and dissemination technologies (Klösgen et al. 1995) have outrun the common techniques for analysing datasets. Knowledge discovery methods try to overcome the bottleneck of extracting useful information from data caused by the mainly "manual" approaches which are currently still applied by analysts even when facing large amounts of collected data.

Knowledge discovery in databases (KDD) is the search for patterns that exist in large databases, but are "hidden" among the amounts of data, such as relations between patients´ characteristics and their diagnoses, advertisement strategies and market shares of products, or production parameters and faults. These patterns can supply valuable knowledge for decision support, if the database is sufficiently conclusive containing problem relevant attributes for a lot of approximately representative objects of the domain. Provided that these requirements are satisfied, KDD approaches prove particularly useful in comparison to the standard statistical methods, when an analysis problem includes a large number of potentially relevant influence variables.

One of the problems for partially automating data analyses processes is that the number of possible patterns that can be found in datasets is very large, thus prohibiting the search for the significant ones by simply validating each of them. Hence, we need intelligent search and complex evaluation strategies to prevent a flood of significant findings. Another problem is that data are often noisy or missing in some cases. Therefore, statistical techniques should be applied to estimate the reliability of the discovered patterns. Finally, efficient data management and access procedures must deal with large and distributed data. To solve these problems, machine learning, statistical, and advanced database methods are jointly used in the emerging KDD field.

KDD systems support analysts in finding out new knowledge on an application domain with a substantial degree of autonomy of the system. The domain is represented by data which either have been collected directly (e.g. market research data) for decision support purposes, including KDD, or generated during an administrative or transaction process (e.g. a client data base). In addition to data, a knowledge base holding domain knowledge is exploited in KDD.

KDD systems operate on different quality types of information when extracting knowledge from data. The types range from data (lowest level) to knowledge (top level). *Data mining* methods are usually associated to the lower levels, whereas knowledge discovery refers also to the top level aspiring to generate information that can be seen as knowledge (Klösgen & Zytkow 1996, Fayyad & Uthurusamy 1995).

Data

Survey of purchases
male, 62, retired, 72.000, product A, ...
female, 19, secretary, 40.000, product B, ...
...

Fact (aggregation)

	high income	medium income	low income
product A	0.75	0.35	0.08
product B	0.22	0.12	0.48
product C	0.03	0.53	0.44

Statements: Who buys product A?

High income persons (75%)
Employees (71%)
Male employees (76%) ...

Refined Statements (potential knowledge)

71% of employees buy product A	
In particular:	High-income employees (82%)
But less:	Old employees (39%)

Fig. 1: Some examples for the information levels in KDD

The first level deals with *facts* that are derived from data by statistical queries. Facts typically are aggregated information on subgroups of objects. Generally, information derived in KDD refer to a subgroup and not to a single object. Histograms and cross tabulations are examples of aggregated information exploited by datamining techniques. Datamining systems can rely on a *data model* describing the types of facts that can be generated. According to the data model, a *statistical query language* is used within the system to aggregate facts. Examples of such data models are given by Siebes (1995) and Sadreddini et al. (1991).

Elementary datamining systems include only the first level. These so-called OLAP-tools (on-line analytic processing) allow the user to analyse large databases efficiently. However, these tools mainly produce cross-tabulations and thus, they only offer low-level support for the discovery of knowledge. Also, the user applies the statistical query language directly, i.e. he has to specify each individual query.

The next higher level holds information in form of *statements* or findings that describe interesting subgroups. A quality measuring aspects of interestingness is associated to a statement. One aspect relates to the statistical significance of the statement. Typically an index (e.g. mean, share) for the subgroup is statistically evaluated ensuring that the value of the index for an interesting subgroup is statistically significant and no random result. Such a statistical evaluation of quality includes implicitely the strength of the index (e.g. the deviation of the mean in the subgroup from the overall mean) and the size of the subgroup.

Datamining systems rely on a *pattern language* used to construct statements (chapter 2). Typical patterns are rules, mean-, or deviation patterns. Most datamining systems support a single pattern type (e.g. one of various rule types). To compute the quality of a statement, a system must exploit facts that are derived with the statistical query language on the first level.

Constitutive for this second level is the large scale search for interesting statements that is organized and performed by the datamining system according to the directives of the user. That means, that the user does not have to specify each individual statistical query (as in level 1), but the system generates and processes a large search space of hypotheses to identify potentially interesting statements. Effective datamining systems must include autonomous search.

KDD systems evaluate further aspects of interestingness to generate statements that can be regarded as knowledge (level 3). *Simplicity* refers to the syntactical complexity of the presentation of a statement. *Redundancy* amounts to the similarity of a statement with respect to other statements and measures to what degree it follows from another one. *Usefulness* relates a statement to the goals of the user within the task under consideration. *Novelty* includes the deviation from prior knowledge of the user or system. To treat these aspects, a knowledge based process involving selection criteria and refinement procedures (Klösgen 1995) evaluates and elaborates on level 3 the potentially interesting statements identified by mining techniques on level 2.

Datamining and KDD are data analysis processes. Compared to "manual" analysis, a KDD process involves a higher degree of autonomy of the system by processing and evaluating large search spaces of hypotheses. However, a KDD process mostly cannot be specified in advance and automated completely, because it depends on dynamic, result dependent goals and intuitions of the analyst and emerges iteratively. The KDD process and problem types are described in detail in (Klösgen1996).

2. Patterns for KDD

Discovery of relations in data relies on searching for interesting instances of statistical patterns. A database can be seen as a sample drawn from a joint distribution of its variables (attributes). Patterns are typically based on unusual marginal distribution characteristics of some variables. A *pattern* is defined by a schema of a statement (Frawley et al. 1991; Klösgen & Zytkow 1996) and can also be regarded as a generic statement with free variables. The free variables correspond to the arguments of a pattern, i.e. the variable parts in the schema. An *instance* of a pattern is a concrete statement in a high level language that describes an hypothesis on data. For an instance, the variable parts of the pattern schema are substituted by concrete terms. Patterns must be *comprehensible*, i.e. the statements associated to pattern instances shall be understood by the analysts using a discovery system.

The high level *pattern language* is a formalism to communicate new knowledge on a domain. The kind of statements constructed in such a language depends on the pattern type and varies from natural-language-like sentences like rules to more abstract statements like trees or even statements in a graphical language. The main KDD pattern types refer to rules, classification and regression trees, conceptual clustering, and deviation detection. Multipattern systems offer all these types.

Various forms of rules are frequently used pattern types. For most practical applications, *probabilistic rules (1.1.1* in Table 1) are useful. *Exact* or *strong rules (1.1.2)* will often result in institutional relations which usually are already known to the user. Other special forms of rules are *association rules* (Agrawal et al. 1996) and *sequences* (Mannila et al. 1995). Association rules only treat binary variables and sequences introduce a time ordering of events. A typical association rule is the "mustard-example": *95% of sales involving bread and sausages also involve mustard.* An example of a sequence is: *85% of all faults involving types A followed by B also involve type C following B.*

In the KDD system Explora (Klösgen 1996), patterns of a first set offered in the *pattern menu* compare a subgroup of a population (concept) with the whole population. For a second (or third) set of patterns, a concept is unusual when compared in two (or k ($k>2$)) populations. In each set, patterns differ according to the scale of dependent variables. This arrangement resembles method-finding tables of statistics based on problem (one-, two-, k-sample comparison) and variable type. The general form of a pattern available in Explora is:

(1)   Distribution of dependent variables is unusual for a concept.

The primary argument and associated search dimension of a pattern is given by a space of concepts (a concept is a subgroup of objects) built according to the selection of discrete independent variables, their taxonomies, and their combination options. The following definition of "unusual" specializes *(1)* for patterns of the first set:

(1.1)   A concept is unusual within a population, if the distribution of dependent variable(s) in the concept differs significantly from the distribution in the population.

(1.1.1)   Share of a target group is significantly larger in a concept than in a population.
(1.1.2) In population: If object belongs to concept, then object belongs to target group.
(1.1.3) In population: If object belongs to target group, then object belongs to concept.
(1.1.4) Distribution of a dependent variable in a concept differs significantly from
   its distribution in a population.
(1.1.5) Mean of dependent variable is significantly larger in concept than in population.

Table 1: Some pattern types for analysing a single population

Further patterns show *functional dependencies* between a dependent and independent variables. At first, the existence of an exact or approximate dependency can be checked (Zytkow & Zembowicz 1993). Then, for continuous variables, an equation fitting this dependency can be determined within a specified class of curves. Classification or regression *trees* can be seen as a set of rules or mean patterns. By choosing a special search strategy, the Explora user directs the generation of such trees.

For 2-population patterns, the term "unusual" is defined in the following way:
(1.2) A concept is unusual, if the distribution of a dependent variable in the concept in a first population is significantly different from its distribution in this concept in a second population.
The concept is compared in 2 populations. According to the type of the dependent variables, similar specializations are offered as for the one-population patterns $(1.1.i)$. For k-population patterns, the distribution of dependent variables in a concept is compared for k populations. A concept is unusual, if the k distributions are significantly different.

The statistical patterns can be combined with elementary patterns, searching e.g. for regularities in the contingency tables underlying the test of a pattern. For the dependent variable, the independent variable, and the formation of populations, we distinguish the nominal, ordinal, and time-oriented type. Then elementary patterns identify, respectively, ranking, monotonic, and time-series patterns in the tables. These patterns can be defined by heuristic criteria or by further statistical tests. Some examples of ranking patterns are: one value is distinctly the first, there is a leading group of values; monotonic patterns are: monotonic, semi-monotonic (allowing exceptions), edge-centered, convex, concave; simple time-series patterns are: "best value since ...", or "n successive increases".

3. Concept Languages for KDD

An important component of a pattern language is the *concept language* used to build concepts. Concepts are subsets of objects which may have some relevance in the domain. Typical concept languages are attributive (propositional) and first order languages. Restrictions on the allowed terms of a concept language determine which subsets of objects are available for statements.

The number of concepts that can be built in a concept language depends on the type of the language. For languages of strictly conjunctive form of order n with no internal disjunctions, this number is mostly limited enough to prevent severe combinatorial problems. However, the problem of combinatorial explosion is usually present for disjunctive normal forms without any order limitations. A concept lattice is given by the partially ordered space of concept extensions (subset of objects with set inclusion as ordering) and the partially ordered space of concept descriptions (terms in the concept language partially ordered by generality). The ordering of concept descriptions is used in discovery systems to search in concept spaces.

The system Explora relies on strictly conjunctive forms of order n. Concepts are built by conjunctions of selectors, allowing at most n conjunctions. The order n can be specified by the user. A *selector* defines a selection condition with an attribute and one or several values of the attribute domain, for instance *Sex = male*. In case of an ordered attribute domain, one or several intervals may appear in a selector, e.g. *Educational Level > 16*. An internal disjunction includes several values or intervals. The user can select the attributes and for each attribute, the subset of the attribute domain that shall be used in the concept language.

To restrict the number of internal disjunctions of an attribute (e.g., all intervals built with the values of an ordinal variable, or all internal disjunctions with the values of a nominal attribute), the user can define a hierarchical structure (taxonomy) holding only those nodes which correspond to internal disjunctions being of interest in the application domain. Further, the user can generate several interval structures for an ordinal variable like the partially ordered sets of all intervals (e.g.: $c_1 < A < c_2$) or of one sided-intervals (e.g.: $A < c$). For continuous variables, the user can generate several discretizations like quantiles or specified intervals.

Disjunctions of conjunctive concepts are generated for most patterns implicitly in Explora. E.g., a rule set consisting of conjunctive rules can be considered as one rule built as disjunction of the rules of that set. However, this can be regarded only as a heuristic, because only a subset of all disjunctions in disjunctive normal form is treated by the search.

Patterns discovered by most KDD systems are expressed in attributive languages which have the expressive power of propositional logic. These languages are limited and do not allow for representing complex structured objects and relations among objects and their components.

Consider for instance a database of an insurance company with two relations, a client and a claim relation. There is a one to many relation between clients and claims, a client can be involved into several claims. When constructing the target database for an analysis task, the user has to fix the target objects. A first task may consist of describing clients with an overproportional claim amount. Then the accumulated total of claims is associated to the client object by a join operation. Discovery is run in this target relation of clients to identify homogeneous subgroups of clients, using e.g. a mean or regression tree pattern.

If the analysis task has to identify a special subgroup of claims (e.g. claims for stolen cars), the target relation is the claim relation with joint attributes from the client relation, exploited e.g. by a probabilistic rule pattern to describe claims for stolen cars.

Both these examples can be treated with attributive languages. However, if the multiple claims belonging to a client cannot be aggregated and have to be treated as components of the client object existing in a variable number of occurrences, attributive languages are often too restrictive.Consider e.g. the analysis task of describing subgroups of potential fraudulent clients and an example of a first-order rule:

> *has-claim(client,claim1), has-claim(client,claim2), age-client=(20-50), ...,*
> *amount(claim1,high), amount(claim2,high), nearby(claim1,claim2), ...*
>
> ---> *client=fraudulent*

To express this statement in attributive language, it is necessary to join all the associated claims to the client object and to introduce such attributes as amount-claim1, amount-claim2, amount-claim3. Then the descriptions get very clumsy, e.g. "amount-claim1=high, amount-claim2= high or amount-claim1=high, amount-claim3=high or amount-claim2=high, amount-claim3= high". Another example combines relations for persons, regions, branches, companies:

> *lives-in (person,region), labourer (person), small-town (region), exists-in(branch, region), belongs-to (branch, company), aggressive-advertising (company)*
>
> ---> *client-of (person, company)*

This example can more easily be transformed to the propositional approach by joining the relations on persons, regions, branches, companies to an universal relation and including a derived binary attribute corresponding to the conjunction *lives-in (person,region), exists-in (branch, region), belongs-to (branch, company)* on a tupel given by person and company. For all possible conjunctions of relations that result in a binary relation on persons and companies, such a binary attribute must be derived.

To overcome problems that might arise because of unconvenient large universal relations, in case of a dataset with several relations, one can use n-ary predicates ($n=1$ is the attributive case of propositional logic) to represent concepts in some sublanguage of predicate logic (mostly function-free Horn clauses and some extensions to represent numeric quantors). Systems using this approach are e.g. FOIL (Quinlan 1990) or MOBAL (Morik et al. 1993). Then we have sets of object tuples (e.g., pairs of persons and companies) belonging to the premises and conclusions of predicative rules, contrasted to sets of objects for attributive rules. Usually exact and strong criteria (e.g. rule is valid for at least 80% of premise-tuples) are set, but not yet probabilistic criteria. First-order rules can be recursive:

> *married(person,spouse), potential-customer(person)*
> ---> *potential-customer(spouse)*

Another advantage of first-order language is their larger flexibility to include domain (background) knowledge into the discovery process (see chapter 4). However only recently, first-order systems are capable of noise-handling and of exploiting continuous attributes. Also an efficiency problem (chapter 5) may prevent from applying these approaches for large databases.

Other techniques to treat complex structured data rely on object oriented databases. Since the simplicity of the relational data model with its structure of uniform tuples with atomic attributes can lead to problems for multi-component domains, the increase in structural and functional power of object oriented approaches could provide new potentials for discovery in these domains. First approaches simplify the handling of complex object oriented data, but they rely on interfaces to the discovery modules that generate the usual tuples. So this approach can be compared to the join or projection operations of relational databases. Another advantage of object-oriented systems is the uniform environment to integrate data, knowledge and algorithms and to control their relations (e.g., the application of an instantiation of an algorithm to a data instance derives a knowledge instance).

4. Domain Knowledge Used in KDD

One of the main problems for data mining is that the number of possible relations is very large, thus prohibiting the search for the correct ones by simple validating each of them. Hence, we need intelligent search strategies. Domain (or background) knowledge can be used to guide the search and to evaluate and refine the verified statements. The system Explora operates on four types of domain knowledge:

- data dictionary knowledge
- taxonomies
- global statistical characteristics
- specifications for interestingness

Data dictionary knowledge includes labels for variables and their values, their types (nominal, ordinal, continuous), their domains, and "missing data" and "not applicable" specifications. Further metadata, e.g. on the relevance or reliability of a variable, can be included into data dictionary knowledge and exploited by evaluation, where e.g. subgroup descriptions based on more reliable variables can be preferred.

Taxonomies are usually specified by an user and are hierarchies defined on the domains of variables. Often, they are introduced for discrete variables to restrict all possible internal disjunctions of values to meaningful disjunctions , and for ordinal or continuous variables to fix the intervals which are relevant within the application. E.g., for the disjunction of the values "Maine", "Massachusetts", "Connecticut", ... of the discrete variable "State", a node "North-Eastern-Coast-States" is defined. On a next hierarchical level "North-Eastern-Coast-States", "Mid-Eastern-Coast-States", and "South-Eastern-Coast-States" are united in a further node.

A hierarchy of income intervals can e.g. be introduced by the user to specify the relevant intervals within a domain. Therefore, taxonomies usually represent the pre-knowledge of the user about relevant categorizations within the domain.

But additionally, a discovery system can cluster values of variables based on the results of discoveries or of special preprocessing steps. In a preprocessing step, methods to find optimal aggregations of categories in multivariate contingency tables and for the context dependent discretization of continuous variables can be applied (Klösgen et al. 1995). Then the system includes derived taxonomies and concept definitions in its knowledge base and uses these concepts for further discoveries.

A taxonomy can be constructed for a single variable and for a group of variables. In the client and claim example, a hierarchical clustering of clients based on several client variables can be joint as a derived attribute to the associated claim objects and exploited for a classification task on the claim objects.

Explora constructs a search space by utilizing the taxonomical hierarchies and operates on the hierarchies especially during a first brute force process, typically performing a general to specific search (Klösgen 1995).

Various *global statistical characteristics* can be used to enlarge the efficiency of a KDD process. Methods to extract dependency patterns from data could exploit dependency networks that describe the causal structure of variables, e.g. (Spirtes et al. 1993). To capture such dependency information, Explora evaluates the influence of independent variables on a dependent variable. E.g., client attributes which are relevant for the continuous variable *amount-of-claims* (in $) can be different from attributes relevant for the binary variable *submitted-claim* (yes or no). An overview on some methods to determine relevance measures can be found in (Klösgen et al. 1995).

These characteristics can be used in a discovery run to restrict the search process by including only the independent variables with a strong positive evaluation. This and other statistical knowledge about the data can be derived by the discovery system in an exploratory preprocessing step or can be introduced by the user when focusing a discovery process. During discovery focusing, the momentary focal point of interest is directed to a data section.

Some domains differ from others by a high amount of knowledge that an analyst holds already. For these applications, the user will typically introduce much of this knowledge directly when focusing a discovery run. Other applications, however, may need many explorations to derive statistical characteristics and relevant taxonomies using interactive visualization and discovery approaches.

The next category of domain knowledge includes several *specifications related to interestingness of statements*. The user can specify for a domain, what types of statements (patterns) are relevant and which criteria are important for measuring the significance of a statement. Explora offers a general store of patterns which is nearly universally usable for data exploration, but which can be extended, if necessary, by further domain specific patterns or adapted to special requirements of the domain. The adaptation of Explora to a domain has usually to be done but once enabling a user for a sequence of following discovery processes to implicitly select patterns and their verification methods by entering high level analysis goals and subgoals.

Other domain independent, but methodical oriented strategies can be provided by a discovery system as expert system functions that select the appropriate search, evaluation and visualization strategies according to the data and knowledge characteristics of the application.

A second group of specifications refers to all kind of *preferences* that may be relevant for a discovery process. E.g., preferences between independent variables can be specified (prefer Taxable-Income rather than Total-Income, Number-of-taxable-relevant-Children rather than Number-of-Children). When evaluating interestingness of verified findings, Explora uses higher weights for preferred variables (Gebhardt 1994).

Preferences can be specified by users to adapt the discovery processes to their needs. But preferences could also be set by the system after monitoring and analyzing the work of the user. The user emphasizes the findings that are interesting for him and the findings that he expected (then deviations from expected findings are interesting). The system could then apply discovery processes to generalize these indications. In this way, the system could learn from the user and behave adaptively. Adaptive behavior has not yet been implemented in existing discovery systems. Proposals to assess user indications on interesting findings are described in (Gebhardt 1994).

Previously discovered knowledge can be used to direct further discovery processes for similar tasks and for the evaluation of statements, especially when dealing with the aspects novelty and usefulness.

Within the first order approach, one usually refers to background knowledge that is expressed as a set of given first-order rules. These rules introduce new predicates that can be applied in the discovery process to enlarge the hypotheses language used to describe the target predicate. Adapted to the attributive case, this approach consists of introducing new attributes and rules how the values of the new attributes can be derived from the available ones. In attributive based discovery, derived attributes are generated in the preprocessing step when creating the target database.

5. KDD Needs Efficiency: A Modular Architecture

Data mining in very large databases requires massive computer power. In a discovery process, many thousands of simple queries must be scheduled and evaluated to test a large number of nodes in a search space of hypotheses. High performance platforms are then essential to manage data and search activities in interactive mode.

In the KESO project pursued in Esprit framework, we develop a high performance KDD tool which consists of three subsystems. A *data management subsystem*, exploiting a high performance database server, supports the definition of target databases, the statistical query language, and the optimization of data access and caching. In KDD, subsequent database queries are related and considerable speed-ups can be attained by temporary storage of intermediate results. The optimizer translates and sends the statistical queries to the database server. From the answers returned from the database, within the *discovery subsystem*, the quality computation module computes how interesting a group of tuples is with regard to the notion of interestingness the user has decided to use. This information is then passed back to the search modules which execute various search strategies. The search modules get the information on the topology of the search space by a description generator which performs the necessary operations in the concept space to provide e.g. the set of predecessors or successors of a set of descriptions. Before the results are presented to the user, the result refiner elaborates the set of potential results by covering, pruning, clustering, suppression and other redundancy elimination heuristics and algorithms. A strategy composer includes some simple expert system techniques to select and combine the appropriate search and refinement strategies. The third subsystem provides an interactive user interface including a data base composer and a dynamic task editor.

Explora however is limited to data of upto 100.000 records. Its versatility is based on the general search approach (Klösgen 1995) which allows to embed various pattern types. Different alternative verification methods are associated to a pattern type to evaluate a pattern instance. The verification methods rely on a defined interface to access and aggregate data. This partition results in four subcomponents (search, pattern type, verification method, data aggregation) which are highly independent and communicate via some narrow interfaces. A small set of aggregated data structures (e.g. histograms for variables and their conjunctions) is supported by the data interface. A data management subsystem is responsible for the efficient generation of the aggregate structures. Explora relies on a dynamic in-core management of data limiting the number of objects that can be analysed in the system. The search components are independent of the data management subsystem and exploit only the results of the verification method. Search is also modularly implemented with independent subsystems, e.g. for management of the structure of the seach space (partial ordering).

Conclusion

A KDD process consists of the preprocessing steps to join, select, clean, and transform data when constructing the target database, the exploratory steps including data mining, visualization and navigation, and the evaluation and refinement of patterns including consolidating knowledge, resolving conflicts with previous knowledge and converting knowledge to operational form usable by the performance component of the KDD application (usually decision support). KDD iterates many times through the domain, based on search in various hypotheses spaces. KDD methods operate on data and domain knowledge to discover new knowledge. Data dictionary knowledge, taxonomies, global statistical characteristics, and interestingness specifications constitute the domain competence within Explora. Some of this knowledge can be generated also by discovery. Future systems will include discovered knowledge in their domain knowledge to a still higher extent and use these findings for further KDD processes. They will incorporate more learning and adaptive behavior. Discovery methods will be used also to learn from the users by monitoring and analysing their reactions on the discovered and presented findings to assess the novelty facet of interestingness.

References

R.Agrawal, H.Mannila, R.Srikant, H.Toivonen, I.Verkamo 1996. Fast Discovery of Association Rules. In *Advances in Knowledge Discovery and Data Mining*, eds. U.Fayyad, G.Piatetsky-Shapiro, P.Smyth, and R.Uthurusamy, Cambr., MA: MIT Press.

U.Fayyad and R.Uthurusamy 1995. *Proceedings of the First International Conference on Knowledge Discovery and Data Mining (KDDM-95)*, Menlo Park, CA: AAAI Press.

W.Frawley, G.Piatetsky-Shapiro, C.Matheus 1991. Knowledge Discovery in Databases: An Overview. In *KnowledgeDiscovery in Databases*, eds. G.Piatetsky-Shapiro and W.Frawley, Cambridge, MA: MIT Press.

F.Gebhardt 1994. Interessantheit als Kriterium für die Bewertung von Ergebnissen. *Informatik Forschung und Entwicklung*, 9.

W.Klösgen 1995. Efficient Discovery of Interesting Statements. *The Journal of Intelligent Information Systems*, Vol. 4, No 1.

W.Klösgen 1996. Explora: A Multipattern and Multistrategy Discovery Assistant. In *Advances in Knowledge Discovery and Data Mining*, eds. U.Fayyad, G.Piatetsky-Shapiro, P.Smyth, and R.Uthurusamy, Cambridge, MA: MIT Press.

W.Klösgen, P.Nanopoulos, A.Unwin 1995. *New Techniques and Technologies for Statistics*. NTTS-95 Conference Preproceedings, Sankt Augustin: GMD.

W.Klösgen and J.Zytkow 1996. Knowledge Discovery in Databases Terminology. In *Advances in Knowledge Discovery and Data Mining*, eds. U.Fayyad, G.Piatetsky-Shapiro, P.Smyth, and R.Uthurusamy, Cambridge, MA: MIT Press.

H.Mannila, H.Toivonen, I.Verkamo 1995. Discovering Frequent Episodes in Sequences. *Proceedings of First International Conference on Knowledge Discovery and Data Mining (KDD-95)*, eds. U.Fayyad and R. Uthurusamy, Menlo Park: AAAI Press.

K.Morik, S.Wrobel, U.Kietz, W.Emde 1993. *Knowledge Acquisition and Machine Learning: Theory, Methods and Applications*, London, UK: Academic Press.

R.Quinlan 1990. Learning Logical Definitions from Relations. *Machine Learning*, 5(3)

M.Sadreddini, D.Bell, S.McClean 1991. A model for integration of raw data and aggregate views in heterogeneous statistical databases. *Database Technology*, 4, 2.

A.Siebes 1995. Data Surveying: Foundations of an Inductive Query Language. *Proceedings of the First International Conference on Knowledge Discovery and Data Mining (KDDM95)*, eds. U.Fayyad and R.Uthurusamy, Menlo Park, CA: AAAI Press.

P.Spirtes, C.Glymour, R. Scheines 1993. *Causality, Prediction, and Search*. New York: Springer-Verlag.

J.Zytkow, R.Zembowicz 1993. Database Exploration in Search of Regularities. *Journal of Intelligent Information Systems*, 2, 39-81.

Learning with Noise in Engineering Domains

Jerzy W. Bala
Datamat Systems Research, Inc.
8260 Greensboro Dr.
McLean, VA 22102

Peter W. Pachowicz
Systems Engineering Dept.
George Mason University
Fairfax, VA 22030

Harry Wechsler
Computer Science Dept.
George Mason University
Fairfax, VA 22030

Abstract

This paper presents a learning approach which identifies and eliminates noisy examples (outliers) to improve the quality of training on engineering data and the effectiveness of the learned concept descriptions. In this approach, one (1) acquires initial concept descriptions from preclassified attributional training data, (2) optimizes concept descriptions to improve their descriptiveness, (3) applies optimized concept descriptions to filtrate/improve initial training data, and (4) repeats the learning process from improved training data. The implemented algorithm extends the widely used open loop learning approach (divided into concept acquisition phase and concept optimization phase) into a closed loop learning approach. In the closed loop learning approach, learned and optimized concept descriptions are fed back and used to filter training data for the next learning iteration. Thus, the learning program is run at least two times; the first time to acquire concept descriptions for the optimization step, and the second time to acquire the final descriptions. In this approach, noise is detected on the concept description level rather than on the raw data level – where the evaluation of raw data can be impossible since the training data may be composed of numeric, symbolic, relational and structural attributes. This method is successfully applied to different engineering problems, and its effectiveness is illustrated for three qualitatively different problems in computer vision.

1. Introduction

Machine learning algorithms are rapidly finding useful applications in real-world domains. They are joining a family of tools that can help summarize (or synthesize) massive amounts of sensory data to support, for example, intelligent robotics systems. Traditional tools, such as various statistical-based techniques, produce results that are hard to interpret and integrate across several abstraction levels within a system. In addition, machine learning tools used in learning from real-world data can easily introduce qualitative reasoning capabilities in addition to the quantitative models presently in use by statistical methods. New machine learning tools developed for real-world domains find useful applications in engineering domains. They can be used to assist engineers with problems such as design, planning, monitoring, control, diagnosis, and analysis. On the other hand, engineering domains present significant challenges to learning systems. One of the challenges is the presence of systematic and non-systematic noise in data.

Various techniques were developed to handle noise in intelligent systems. They are frequently integrated within operators for feature/attribute extraction. Noise elimination on feature level is handled by statistical methods of feature/attribute filtration or by statistical pattern recognition methods designed to approximate the distribution of training data over the attribute space. These methods, however, operate on numerical data while engineering data includes subsymbolic and symbolic data as well. These methods tend to smooth the distribution of training data rather than identify those training examples which are erroneous (should not be taken into account during the training phase) and draw precise boundaries between classes.

Learning concept description from noisy data sets is a very difficult problem for machine learning. It is particularly important for symbolic learning programs due to their noise sensitivity. Regardless of the source, noise influences the formation and use of classification rules [Quinlan, 1986]. Inductive learning systems perform some form of generalization in order to anticipate unseen examples. A concept description generated by an inductive learning system should cover all examples (including unseen examples) of the concept (completeness criterion) and no examples of the other concepts (consistency criterion). In the case of noisy data, complete and consistent descriptions are problematic since multiple concept descriptions can partially overlap in the attribute space. This is so, because attribute noise skews the distribution of attribute value from the correct value.

There are two basic groups of approaches to learning from data with outliers. One is to allow a certain degree of inconsistent classification of training examples so that the learned descriptions will be general enough to describe basic characteristics of a concept. This approach has been taken by the ID family of algorithms [Quinlan, 1986]. The main outliers-handling mechanism for decision trees is tree pruning. There are two types of tree pruning [Mingers, 1989]: pre-pruning (example removal), performed during the construction of a decision tree, and post-pruning (tree pruning), used after the decision tree is constructed. The second approach, post-pruning, discards some of the unimportant rules/subtrees and retains those covering the largest number of examples. The remaining rules thus provide a general description of the concept. This approach has been taken by the AQ family of programs [Michalski, 1983]. Other approaches to learning from data with outliers are based on the minimum description length principle [Quinlan, 1989], cross validation to control over-fitting during the training phase [Breiman, 1984], and an integrated modification and truncation of disjuncts and conditions [Bergadano, et al., 1992]. Related works for noise tolerant processing of visual data include robust regression methods [Meer, et. al., 1991] and random sample consensus [Fishler, 1981].

This paper contributes to the area of noise tolerant learning by revising the traditional truncation approach (concept optimization) and by presenting a modified approach which performs better for noisy engineering data. In this modified approach, rules are optimized and subsequently they are fed back and used to filtrate the training data set. The filtration process is concept-driven rather than data-driven, where the 'filter' is prepared on the higher abstraction level of the system. The learning process is then run over again but with the filtered training data. This approach differs from the traditional data filtering performed on the input level, because the filter is learned on the higher-level and reflects actual relations between attributes and separations between classes. It also does not require prior knowledge about attribute distribution, and it is applicable to both symbolic and subsymbolic attributes.

2. Learning Approach

Most learning methods share a common problem — they try to remove noise in one step through truncation/pruning of learned concept descriptions. The final concept descriptions are then based on the initial noisy training data. This also causes the complexity of concept descriptions to decrease only by the magnitude of truncated/pruned concept components and does not allow for reorganization of the concept descriptions. In this approach, the resulting descriptions still reflect the influence of erroneous training examples on the formation of larger disjuncts/subtrees. Truncation/pruning processes only partially mitigate this influence by eliminating those components (subtrees/disjuncts) of concept descriptions, for example, which are 'light' (i.e., created by fewer training examples). Such truncation/pruning is supported by higher confidence that the 'light' concept components are generated by a larger proportion of erroneous examples than the 'heavy' concept components. So, some of light concept components can be removed from final descriptions, increasing the confidence that the final descriptions would better represent a concept to be learned. However, such final concept descriptions represent a model of an object which is still learned from the entire erroneous training data set.

The approach we developed for noise-tolerant symbolic learning extends the traditional one step learning into a closed-loop multiple step learning [Pachowicz and Bala, 1994].

Processes of concept acquisition, optimization and data filtration are organized within the loop presented in Figure 1. The learning loop includes:

1) Concept acquisition by a concept learner such as AQ [Miachalski, 1983] learning program,
2) Evaluation of learned class descriptions and detection of these concept components which less likely represent data patterns or which interfere with descriptions of other classes creating confusion in class separability over the attribute space,
3) Optimization of class descriptions according to predefined criteria of class description evaluation,
4) Formulation of a 'filter' from modified concept descriptions, and the filtration of training data.

This learning loop can be run once (i.e., the concept learner is activated twice) or multiple times (i.e., n times, where the concept learner is activated $n+1$ times) with changing learning and/or optimization criteria.

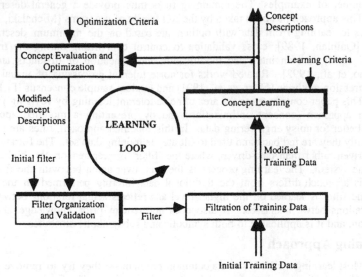

Fig. 1: Architecture of the learning approach

Consequently, those training examples which caused the generation of pruned/truncated concept components are no longer taken into account when concept learning is repeated. In this way, some erroneous training data can be detected and eliminated, so they will not influence the generation of the final concept descriptions.

In the closed-loop learning approach, the intermediate concept descriptions are used to actively improve training data. The acquisition and pruning/truncation of these intermediate descriptions can be guided iteratively by different criteria. Since the detection of erroneous examples is executed on the concept description level rather than on the input data level, data filtration reflects attribute combination in the construction of concept descriptions and inter-class distribution over the attribute space. The final concept descriptions are learned from improved data sets, and they should outperform concept descriptions learned from the initial data set.

Additionally, complexity of final concept descriptions should be decreased because the erroneous training examples which cause split of more general concept components will be eliminated. In order to derive homogenous areas representing concept descriptions and to improve borders between concept descriptions of different classes, one has to merge partitioned concept components. This merging is executed over the space recovered by the removal of less significant concept components of counterclass descriptions.

In summary, the first novel aspect of this approach is that rules/trees optimized through disjunct/subtree removal are used to filter noisy examples, and then the filtered set of training data is used to re-learn improved rules / decision trees. The second novel aspect is that noise detection is done on the higher level evaluating learned object model rather than raw data. The third aspect is that noise removal from training data set is driven by modified object model, it can be run iteratively, and it does not depend on a-priori information about attribute and/or noise distributions. This approach should be particular effective for learning from data sets influenced by non-systematic error.

3. Experiments

3.1 Data characterization

Table 1 depicts the datasets used in our experiments. They represent various types of data that can be encountered in engineering domains – from highly unstructured texture data to structured data representing geometrical information.

3.2 Highly unstructured sensory data: Learning from texture data

The texture domain is extremely complex and texture recognition is very difficult when applied to problems with a large number of texture classes (above 10 classes). For the most methods used in extracting texture information resulting attribute distributions are complex and irregular. In addition, the extraction process introduces some noise and thus the making the texture data highly suitable for evaluating noise-tolerant symbolic learning.

Images of twelve texture classes used in the experiments were selected from the Brodatz album [Brodatz, 1969]. Each texture picture was coded as an image of 256x256 pixels on 256 gray levels and was divided into two separate (non overlapping) large sections, each 180x100 pixels. The first half of an image was used to extract training examples while the second half was used to extract testing examples.

The well known Laws' energy filters method [Laws, 1980] was used to transform raw image data into texture features. This method consists of two steps: (1) the extraction of local micro-characteristics of raw texture data incorporating specially designed energy masks (filters) detecting local pixel variations over a small window, and (2) the computation of local macro-statistics applied to derive statistical measures of filtered images over a larger window. The Chi-square test was run at the 95% level to check distribution normality, and neither of these distributions passed the test. In many cases the distribution was multi-modal. Some attributes had a uniform distribution for a single class but were very distinctive for the remaining classes. The combination of these non-normal 1-D distributions into an 8-D attribute distribution of training data can show the high complexity of vision training data.

The training data set was collected by random selection of examples (attribute vectors) from indicated image sections. The training data set consisted of 200 training examples representing each texture class. The testing data set was extracted from different texture areas than data for the training phase. This set also consisted of 200 testing examples per class.

The introduced learning approach performed very well. The average error rate over twelve classes decreased from 29.3% to 28% level. This decrease was characteristic in the range from 0% to 10% of filtered training data. At the same time, the standard deviation decreased from above 25.5 to 24. Maximum error rate through all twelve texture classes decreased significantly from above 65% to below 59% level. For higher truncation levels the maximum error rate stabilized. Results are presented in Figure 2. White dots represents results for the noise-tolerant approach (learning, rule truncation, data filtration, and learning again) and black dots for the non noise-tolerant learning (learning and data filtration).

Data Sets	Dataset Descriptions	Attribute Descriptions
Highly Unstructured Sensory Data Texture Data	12 classes 200 examples per call 8 attributes per example 55 levels per attribute	Laws' masks [Laws, 1980] were used to transform raw image data into texture features by extracting local micro-characteristics of raw texture data incorporating and computing local macro-statistics applied to derive statistical measures of filtered images over a larger window
Unstructured Hybrid (lines and color) Sensory Data Color Outdoor Images	3 classes 400 examples per class 5 attributes per example 55 levels per attribute	Two Laws' masks that detect horizontal and vertical lines were used as the first two attributes. Additional three attributes were computed as the intensities of RGB composites of color image.
Structured Geometrical Data Geometrical Shapes	2 classes 9 examples per class 5 attributes per example 10 levels per attribute	A shape detection operator is obtained by using morphological processing and genetic algorithms based search. Radii measurements on shapes resulting after applying this operator are used to represent shape data in the attributional form.

Table 1: Data used in experiments

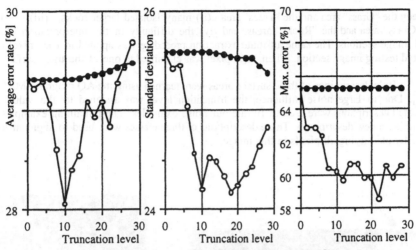

Fig. 2: Experimental results for the texture data

3.3 Unstructured sensory data: Learning from outdoor scene data

The training data set was collected by random selection of examples (attribute vectors) from indicated image sections. The training data set consisted of 200 training examples representing each texture class. The testing data set was extracted from different texture areas than data for the training phase. This set also consisted of 200 testing examples per class.

The introduced learning approach performed very well. The average error rate over twelve classes decreased from 29.3% to 28% level. This decrease was characteristic in the range from 0% to 10% of filtered training data. At the same time, the standard deviation decreased from above 25.5 to 24. Maximum error rate through all twelve texture classes decreased significantly from above 65% to below 59% level. For higher truncation levels the maximum error rate stabilized. Results are presented in Figure 2. White dots represents results for the noise-tolerant approach (learning, rule truncation, data filtration, and learning again) and black dots for the non noise-tolerant learning (learning and data filtration).

Color images of natural scenes in French Alps were used to test the new learning method on real outdoor data (images obtained from the Machine Learning and Inference Lab., GMU). All images contain three classes of surface area: "Trees" area, "Grass" area, and "Rocks" area. Only one image was used for training and the other images were used for testing. All images were taken in different places but in the same mountain area. They are affected by the difference in resolution, lighting, and surface position.

The training image is presented in Figure 3a. A teacher selected three separate windows corresponding to three surface class areas in order to designate image sections to extract attributes and learn class descriptions. "Trees" area was represented by a section of 20x16 pixels, "Grass" area was represented by a section of 19x19 pixels, and "Rocks" area was represented by a section of 17x12 pixels.

Surface area attributes were extracted from designated image sections. There were five attributes computed for each pixel of image section. First two attributes were extracted applying the attribute extraction procedure described in Section 3.2 (Laws' masks). The remaining three attributes represented color intensity of Red, Green and Blue composites of the color information.

A different scene was used in the testing phase; see Figure 3b. This image shows difficulties with the accurate scene segmentation because of (i) the lack of clear border area between the "Grass" area and the "Trees" area, (ii) many isolated larger rocks, (iii) overlap of the "Grass" area and the "Rocks" areas, and (iv) the difficulty in the interpretation of some small image sections. The same attribute extraction procedure was applied to each pixel of the selected testing image section. Then, each pixel was classified to one of the three surface class areas.

Rule descriptions of three surface areas were learned using the AQ program [Michalski, 1983]. Due to large noise influence, the truncation level was assigned to the value 20%. Truncated descriptions were used to filtrate out noise examples. The remaining examples were used to learn new descriptions. These descriptions of three classes were used to segment testing image by classifying all pixels in this image.

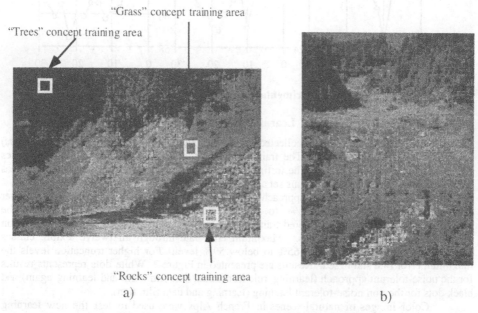

a)   b)

Fig. 3: (a) Learning image (b) Testing image.

The results of pixel classification by surface class descriptions and smoothed classification decisions are presented in Figure 4. The results comparison is presented by (1) applying only truncated rules after the first learning process (Figure 4a), and (2) applying concept descriptions learned after the second learning process using data with filtered out noisy examples (Figure 4b).

There is a significant visual improvement in the classification results when the developed noise-tolerant approach to symbolic learning is applied. First, the distinction between the "Trees" area and the "Grass" area is improved. Second, the false classification of large grass sections (Figure 4a) is eliminated. Moreover, the picture better highlights surface details corresponding to larger rocks and small tree plants.

3.4 Structured geometrical data: Learning from shapes

For our experiments, shape data in the attributional form was acquired by evolving operators that discriminate among image classes comprising different shapes, where the operators are defined as variable morphological structuring elements that can be sequenced as program forms. The optimal operators evolved by Genetic Algorithms derive discriminant feature vectors, which are then used by empirical inductive learning to generate rule-based class description in disjunctive normal form (DNF). Details on the extraction method can be found in [Bala and Wechsler, 1993].

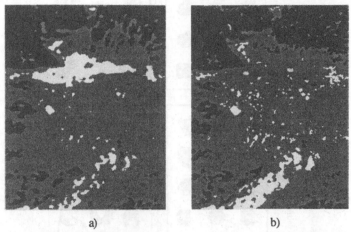

a)　　　　　　　　　　　　b)

Fig. 4:　Classification results for (a) truncated class descriptions learned from the initial data, and (b) learned from the 'noise-filtered-out' data by applying the presented approach

　　　　Two experiment were performed (Figure 5 and 6). The first experiment was concerned with learning to recognize and explain the shape concepts of ellipse, triangle, and rectangle, while the goal for the second experiment was to learn the shape concepts of concavity and convexity. The shape examples used in both experiments were partitioned into training and testing examples. The testing examples were used to evaluate the performance of the learned

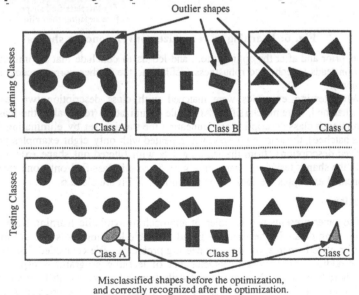

Fig. 5: Learning to recognize three shape classes

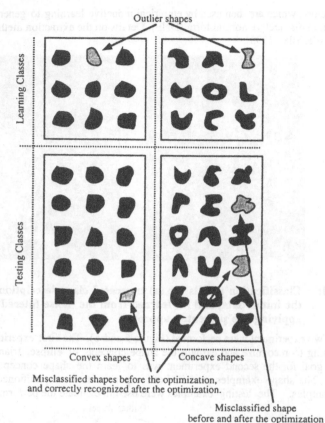

Fig. 6: Learning to recognize convex concave shapes

description, prior and after the optimization, and led us to conclude that optimization followed by truncation leads to enhanced robustness (defined as the higher correct recognition rate for unseen shapes).

When testing examples were matched with class description two testing shapes, depicted as hatched, were misclassified. After rule optimization (removal of the least significant disjunct from each class description and truncating the training set by eliminating those shapes depicted as hatched), the learning process was repeated with only eight examples per class. The newly derived descriptions (from the learning data with filtered out shape examples) correctly matched all the shapes tested for shapes in Figure 5 and misclassified only one shape in Figure 6. The truncated examples are depicted as the outliers in Figure 5 and 6.

4. Conclusions

The paper presents a noise-tolerant approach to symbolic learning from complex and noisy engineering data. In the past, we tested available learning tools and unfortunately they did not perform well when applied to engineering problems. We concluded that more attention is needed to address noise tolerant characteristics of learning programs – especially for these problems where knowledge about attribute distribution and/or noise distribution is not given *a-priori* and where these distributions can be very irregular due to the characteristics of domain data. Real world data, in particular, is very hard and it is an excellent testbed to the development of new learning tools. The vision domain was used in this paper to illustrate the effectiveness of the developed approach.

We extended the widely used open loop learning approach (divided into concept acquisition phase and concept optimization phase) into a closed loop learning approach. In the closed loop learning approach, learned and optimized concept descriptions are fed back and used to filter training data for the next learning iteration. Thus, the learning program is run at least two times; the first time to acquire concept descriptions for the optimization step, and the second time to acquire the final descriptions of visual objects. In this approach, noise is detected on the concept description level rather than on the raw data level – where the evaluation of raw data can be impossible since the training data may be composed of numeric, symbolic, relational and structural attributes.

This closed loop approach was implemented to the rule learning and decision tree learning programs. In both cases, we showed that it performed better than the original program. Substantial improvement in the maximum error calls for special future attention. This effect has been demonstrated for texture recognition problem and then for the image annotation/segmentation problem of natural scenes. The experiments presented did not intend to favor rule based or decision tree based types of learning programs, but they demonstrated the applicability of the developed approach to both learning methods. Additionally, the training data and the testing data were selected from different images to support fair evaluation of the recognition results.

References

Bala J. and H. Wechsler, Shape Analysis Using Genetic Algorithms, *Pattern Recognition Letters*, 14(12), 965-973, 1993.

Bergadano F., S. Matwin, R. Michalski and J. Zhang, Learning Two-tiered Descriptions of Flexible Concepts: The POSEIDON System, *Machine Learning*, 8, 5-43, 1992.

Breiman L., J. Friedman, R. Olshen and C. Stone, Classification and Regression Trees, Wadsworth, Belmont, 1984.

Brodatz, P., Textures: A Photographic Album for Artists and Designers, New York, 1966.

Fishler, M. and Boles, R., Random Sample Consensus: A Paradigm for Model Fitting with Applications to Image Analysis and Automated Cartography," *Communication of the ACM*, 24, November 1981.

Laws, K.I., Textured Image Segmentation, Ph.D. Thesis, Dept. of Electrical Engineering, University of Southern California, Los Angeles, 1980.

Meer, P., Mintz, D., Kim, D., and Rosenfeld, A., Robust Regression Methods for Computer Vision: A Review, *International Journal of Computer Vision*, 6(1), 59-70, 1991.

Michalski R., A Theory and Methodology of Inductive Learning, *Artificial Intelligence*, 20, 111-116, 1983.

Mingers J., An Empirical Comparison of Pruning Methods for Decision-Tree Induction, *Machine Learning*, 3(4), 227-243, Kulwer Academic Publishers, 1989.

Pachowicz, P. W. and J. Bala, A Noise-Tolerant Approach To Symbolic Learning from Sensory Data, *Journal of Intelligent Systems and Fuzzy Systestems*, 2(4), pp.347-361, 1994.

Quinlan J., Learning Relations: Comparison of a Symbolic and a Connectionist Approach, Dept. of Computer Science, University of Sydney, Australia, 1989.

Quinlan J., The Effect of Noise on Concept Learning, *Machine Learning: An Artificial Intelligence Approach*, 2, R. S. Michalski, J. G. Carbonell and T. M. Mitchell (Eds.), Morgan Kaufmann, Los Altos, CA, 1986.

Hierarchical Conceptual Clustering in a First Order Representation

Ch. Vrain

LIFO - Université d'Orléans - BP 6759
45067 Orléans Cedex 2 - France
email : cv@lifo.univ-orleans.fr

Abstract. This paper presents work in progress on unsupervised learning from observations represented in a subset of first order logic. In most systems, observations are described by pairs (attribute, value) and two main approaches can be distinguished: bottom-up methods that consider all the observations and build a hierarchy of concepts starting from the observations and generalizing them / top-down incremental methods that process observations one after the other and incorporate them by a search down the current hierarchy. Our aim is to test how incremental methods could be adapted to representations written in first order logic and we intend to test several similarity measures and generalization methods in order to study their appropriateness.

1 Introduction

Learning concepts from observations is an important field in Machine Learning that can be divided into two sub-domains:

- supervised learning [9, 13, 6, 14]: positive and negative examples of the concepts are provided to the system and it must learn either characteristic descriptions of the concepts, or discriminant descriptions between them.
- unsupervised learning [10, 4, 8, 3, 2]: only observations are given and the system must determine both the underlying concepts and their descriptions. The terms *concept formation* or *conceptual clustering* are often used to denote such kinds of learning.

Learning concepts from positive and negative examples has been widely used to build knowledge bases for Expert Systems: it seems easier for an expert to provide examples and counterexamples of his behavior rather than giving the usually empirical rules that determine his behavior. An application to air traffic control[1] [7] has shown us that truly an expert can quite easily determine the main concepts of his domain and provide a system with positive and negative examples of them. Nevertheless, these concepts are very often too general and should be decomposed into subconcepts. This task can be difficult and therefore,

---

[1] contract PERSPICACE, 86 - 88, C.E.N.A., Athis Mons, France / L.R.I., university of Paris 11, France

even in the case of supervised learning, concept formation can be very useful to help an expert structuring his knowledge.

Most of the approaches in the field of concept formation are based on a attribute-value representation of the observations. This formalism is widely used in Machine Learning because it is much more tractable than first order languages. But, in some applications, as for instance in the field of air traffic control [7], this representation language is not expressive enough and we do need a richer formalism. As far as we know, few systems [2, 6] have been developed in first order representations. In this paper, we intend to study how incremental methods, that enable to reduce the complexity and that are more adapted to real applications and/or to knowledge acquisition, could be adapted to first order representations.

The two incremental systems Cobweb [4] and Adeclu [3] process observations represented by pairs (attribute, value). Although their representations of classes differ, they share the same architecture: they are based on a few operations on hierarchies of classes: creating a new class, inserting an observation into a class, merging two classes, splitting a class into its subclasses, ... and the general algorithm to insert a new observation into a hierarchy can be outlined as follows: (C denotes the current class in which the observation has been inserted):

---

1. insert the observation into the root of the tree;
   the current class C is the root of the tree
2. repeat
      choose one of the operations mentioned above;
      update C
until C contains only this observation.

Algorithm 1

We have developed a hierarchical clustering tool [5] based on the same general algorithm but that handles observations represented in a subset of first order logic. The intensional descriptions of the classes are also described by first order formula. As in the system Adeclu [3], a gain is computed which enables to choose the best operation to perform. The goal of this tool is to test different similarity measures and different ways of computing the intensional description of a class. For the time being, the similarity measure that we have implemented relies on a matching between the objects that compose the two descriptions and the intensional representation of a class is computed by generalization, the generalization process is based on the structural matching principle [6, 14].

2 The classification tool

The tool that we have developed is based on Algorithm 1 given in section 1. But it relies on two functions: a function *gen* that takes as inputs two descriptions and returns a generalization of them and a function *sim* that takes as inputs two descriptions and returns a value representing their similarity. This tool requires that the observations and the classes are described in the same formalism; it enables to use the same function both for generalizing an observation and a class and for generalizing two classes.

Let us call $\mathcal{R}$ the representation language and let us first precise some definitions:

- In the following, we identify an observation and its description in $\mathcal{R}$. It is clear that if the language is not expressive enough, two distinct observations may have the same representation.
- A class is a set of observations; it is described either extensionally by the set of observations that belong to this class or intensionally. In our logical framework, an intensional description of a class satisfies the two following properties: the intensional description of a class restricted to an observation is the observation and every observation of the class satisfies the intensional description of the class.
- A leaf of the hierarchy corresponds to a unique observation and we identify it with the class composed of this unique observation, [2]

As in the systems Fisher [4] and Adeclu [3], our tool is principally based on the following operations:

- Creating a new concept consists in creating a new class C_{n+1} composed only of the observation e.
- Inserting an observation e in the class C_i consists in creating a new class C_i' composed of e and the elements of C_i.
- Merging two classes C_i and C_j, $j \neq i$, consists in deleting the classes C_i and C_j and replacing them by the class C_r composed of e, the observations of C_i and the observations of C_j.
- Splitting a class C_i consists in replacing the class C_i by its subclasses C_{i_1}, ..., C_{i_k} and inserting e in the best subclasses C_{i_j}.
- Inserting e into an empty hierarchy and inserting e into a class C which is a leaf.

Each time a class is modified, a new intensional description of the class is computed.

In the system Adeclu [3], a function $sc(e, C_i, \mathcal{P}_0)$ measures the links between an observation e and a class C_i of a partition $\mathcal{P}_0$ and the adequation of e to the class C_i of the partition $\mathcal{P}_0$ is measured by the formula:
$$ad(e, C_i, \mathcal{P}_0) = sc(e, C_i, \mathcal{P}_0) - \sum_{\{C_j \in \mathcal{P}_0, i \neq j\}} sc(e, C_j, \mathcal{P}_0).$$
The best operation is the operation that maximises the adequation.

Our tool must be provided with a similarity function $sim(D_i, D_j)$ that measures the similarity between two descriptions and a generalization function $gen(D_i, D_j)$ that computes a generalization of two descriptions. If e is an observation and if D_i is the intensional description of the class C_i, then in our tool

---

[2] We shall see that this assumption is not always desirable and a further improvement of our classification tool will be to relax it.

we take $sc(e, C_i, P_0) = sim(e, D_i)$. Moreover, the intensional description of the class composed of e and the observations of C_i is $gen(e, C_i)$. In next section, we present the first order representation that we have adopted and we propose two generalization functions and a similarity measure.

3 Application to first order logic

3.1 Representation

Logical representation. The observations and the descriptions of the classes are represented in a subset of first order logic.

Example 1. Let us consider for instance the observations $\mathcal{E}_1$ and $\mathcal{E}_2$, where the first one is composed of a small square put on a large rectangle whereas the second one is composed of a small rectangle put on a large square. The first example may be expressed by the following formulae:

$$(rectangle\ x_1) \wedge (large\ x_1) \wedge (on\ y_1\ x_1) \wedge (small\ y_1) \wedge (square\ y_1) \quad (1)$$

in which *rectangle*, *square*, *large* and *on* are predicate symbols whereas x_1 and y_1 are variables. It means that there exist two objects, represented by the variables x_1 and y_1, x_1 is a large rectangle and y_1 is a square put on x_1. The information that x_1 is a rectangle and y_1 is a square could also have been expressed by *(shape x_1 (rectangle))* and *(shape y_1 (square))*.

The sets of predicate symbols and of constants needed to express the observations must be chosen according to the application. Let us call P the set of predicate symbols, C the set of constant symbols and V the set of variables used to describe the observations and the intensional descriptions of the classes.

Definition 1. *An atom is an expression $(p\ t_1 \ldots t_n)$ where $p \in P$ and for all i, either $t_i \in V$ or $t_i = (a_i)$ with $a_i \in C$. An atom $(p\ t_1 \ldots t_n)$ is ground if for all i, $t_i \notin V$, i.e., $t_i = (a_i)$ and $a_i \in C$. An atom $(p\ t_1 \ldots t_n)$ is relational if it contains at least two distinct variables, otherwise the atom $(p\ t_1 \ldots t_n)$ is unary. If A is an atom, we note $Var(A)$ the set of distinct variables of A and if D is a conjunction of atoms, we note $Var(D)$ the set of distinct variables that occur in D*

In this work, observations and intensional descriptions are expressed in the same way and the description of a class composed of a single element is equal to the description of this element. The intensional descriptions are computed by generalizing either two observations or an observation and an intensional description of a class. Different ways of generalizing can be considered depending on whether we stress on the relations or on the objects that compose the descriptions. In this latter case, we transform the initial representation into a more "object-oriented" representation, which is equivalent to the first one.

Object representation. For this purpose, we introduce two special symbols $\$x$ and $?y$, where $\$x$ denotes the object under consideration and $?y$ denotes another object.

Definition 2. *A characteristic is an atom $(p\, t_1 \ldots t_n)$ where $t_i = \$x$ or $t_i =?y$ or $t_i = (a_i)$, $a_i \in C$. A characteristic is unary if no occurrences of $?y$ appears. An object representation, $\mathcal{D}^{obj}$, is composed of:*
– a set, called $\mathcal{R}el(\mathcal{D}^{obj})$, of relational atoms,
– a set, called $\mathcal{O}bj(\mathcal{D}^{obj})$, of pairs $(x_i, set\_char(x_i, \mathcal{D}^{obj}))$, $i = 1 \ldots n$, where x_i is a variable, $set\_char(x_i, \mathcal{D}^{obj})$ is a set of characteristics and $i \neq j \Rightarrow x_i \neq x_j$.

Example 2. The characteristic $(rectangle\ \$x)$ means that the object under consideration and referred to as $\$x$ is a rectangle; the characteristic $(on\ \$x\ ?y)$ means that it is put on an object referred to as $?y$.

We can associate to a logical representation an object-oriented one, as follows:

Definition 3. *Let x be a variable and $\mathcal{A}$ an atom in which x occurs. The characteristic of x linked to $\mathcal{A}$, written $char(x, \mathcal{A})$ is the formula obtained by replacing in $\mathcal{A}$ all the occurrences of x by the special symbol $\$x$ and all the occurrences of variables different from x by the special symbol $?y$. If $\mathcal{D}^{log}$ is a conjunction of atoms and x a variable, we note $set\_char(x, \mathcal{D}^{log}) = \{char(x, \mathcal{A})|$ $\mathcal{A}$ belongs to $\mathcal{D}^{log}$ and x occurs in $\mathcal{A}\}$.*

The set of characteristics linked to an object is important to evaluate the similarities it shares with other objects. This notion was already used in [14].

Example 3. If we consider the representation of observation 1, given by formula 1, then:
$$set\_char(x_1, \mathcal{E}) = \{(rectangle\ \$x)\ (large\ \$x)\ (on\ ?y\ \$x)\}.$$

Definition 4. *Let $\mathcal{D}^{log}$ be a conjunction of atoms. The object-representation linked to $\mathcal{D}^{log}$ is defined by:*
– $\mathcal{R}el(\mathcal{D}^{obj}) = \{\mathcal{A}|\mathcal{A}$ is an element of $\mathcal{D}^{log}$ and $\mathcal{A}$ is relational$\}$,
– $\mathcal{O}bj(\mathcal{D}^{obj}) = \{(x, set\_char(x, \mathcal{D}^{log}))|x \in Var(\mathcal{D}^{log})\}$.
It is written $TR_{log \rightarrow obj}(\mathcal{D}^{log})$.

For sake of understandability, $\mathcal{D}^{obj}$ represents an object representation of a concept whereas $\mathcal{D}^{log}$ represents a logical representation.

Example 4. The object representation of the example given in formula 1 is translated into:

$$\mathcal{R}el(\mathcal{D}^{obj}) = \{\ (on\ y_1\ x_1)\}$$
$$\mathcal{O}bj(\mathcal{D}^{obj}) = \{\ (x_1\ \{(rectangle\ \$x)\ (large\ \$x)\ (on\ ?y\ \$x)\}\ )$$
$$(y_1\ \{(square\ \$x)\quad (small\ \$x)\quad (on\ \$x\ ?y)\}\ )\ \}\qquad (2)$$

3.2 Generalization

As has already been mentioned, we can distinguish different ways of generalizing depending on whether we stress on the relations that compose the descriptions or on the objects. We intend to test both kinds of generalization. For the time being, we have implemented a generalization function based on the structural matching principle [6] that gives more importance to the objects (represented by variables) that compose the descriptions than to the relations (expressed by predicate symbols). On the other hand, we are currently implemented a generalization function that computes the least general generalization defined in [12] but we have to solve complexity problems. Let us illustrate both by the following example:

Example 5. Let us suppose that $\mathcal{E}_1$ and $\mathcal{E}_2$ are expressed by:

$$(rectangle\ x_1) \wedge (large\ x_1) \wedge (on\ y_1\ x_1) \wedge (small\ y_1) \wedge (square\ y_1) \quad and \quad (3)$$

$$(square\ x_2) \wedge (large\ x_2) \wedge (on\ y_2\ x_2) \wedge (small\ y_2) \wedge (rectangle\ y_2) \quad (4)$$

(For sake of understandability, in this paper, the variables that appear in a description differ from those that appear in another one. It is not necessary in the current implementation.)

The least general generalization of $\mathcal{E}_1$ and $\mathcal{E}_2$, as defined by Plotkin [12], would be:

$$(large\ x_4) \wedge (on\ y_4\ x_4) \wedge (small\ y_4) \wedge (rectangle\ x_5) \wedge (square\ y_5) \quad (5)$$

In such a generalization, no information is lost, but this formula is quite difficult to understand for an expert, since different variables must be instantiated by the same object to get back the observations. For instance, to prove that the formula 5 is a generalization of $\mathcal{E}_1$, the variables x_5 and x_4 must be instantiated by the same variable x_1 and the variables y_4 and y_5 must be instantiated by the same variable y_1, so that we get back $\mathcal{E}_1$.

In the structural matching principle, generalizations are computed by matching objects that compose the descriptions. For instance $\mathcal{E}_1$ and $\mathcal{E}_2$ can be generalized into:

$$(large\ x_3) \wedge (on\ y_3\ x_3) \wedge (small\ y_3) \quad (6)$$

which means that in both observations, there is a small object put on a large one, or

$$(square\ x_3) \wedge (rectangle\ y_3) \quad (7)$$

which means that in both observations there are a square and a rectangle.

The generalization given by formula 6 is obtained by matching the object represented by the variable x_1 with the object represented by x_2 and the object represented by y_1 with the object represented by y_2, while the generalization represented by the formula 7 is obtained by matching the object represented by the variable x_1 with the object represented by y_2 and the object represented by y_1 with the object represented by x_2.

These two generalizations are not comparable from the point of view of generality. In our system, we choose the generalization that maximizes the similarity between the objects that we match. In the previous example, we choose the generalization given in 6, since it conveys more information. Weights can be put on some predicates; they enable to give information on the predicates that seem the most relevant to the problem to solve. For instance, higher weights on the predicates *rectangle* and *square* that represent the form of the objects would enable to choose the generalization 7.

In the structural matching principle, it is also possible to duplicate objects and then to get generalizations more specific than 6 and 7, but then, we have to deal with the same problems as the problems encountered with the least general generalization approach, that is to say complexity and comprehensibility problems.

The generalization function that we have implemented differs from the system OGUST [14] previously developed: It is simpler than the first one, since no background knowledge is used to detect hidden similarities between observations and when background knowledge has been used, it has been applied to the observations before the learning process. It is also more expressive than it, since constants and numeric values have been introduced and knowledge can be expressed in different ways. Moreover, it is based on the transformation of the logical representation into the more "object-oriented" one.

3.3 Similarity measure

The similarity between two logical representations is based upon the similarities of the objects that compose it. The characteristics of the objects are well expressed in the object-oriented representation. It explains why we use this representation to compute the similarity.

In order to handle numeric values, numeric predicates of arity 2 can be defined. They enable to link an object with its corresponding value for this predicate, as for instance (*age John* (30)). The specification of a numeric predicate must include its name and the length of its definition intervals, this length must be finite.

In most applications, some predicates are more relevant than other ones. In order to take this into account, weights are put on predicates. By default, they are equal to 1.

In the following, if p is a predicate, we note $weight(p)$ the weight of p and if p is a numeric predicate, we note $length(p)$ the length of its definition interval.

Definition 5. *Let C_1 and C_2 be two characteristics. We define*

– $sim(C_1, C_2) = 0$, if $C_1 = (p\ t_1 \ldots t_n)$, $C_2 = (q\ s_1 \ldots s_l)$ and $p \neq q$

- $sim(C_1, C_2) = weight(p) * \frac{length(p) - |l_1 - l_2|}{length(p)}$, if p is a numeric predicate, $C_1 = (p \, \$x \, (l_1))$ and $C_2 = (p \, \$x \, (l_2))$
- $sim(C_1, C_2) = weight(p)$, if $C_1 = C_2 = (p \, t_1 \ldots t_n)$.

Definition 6. Let $\mathcal{D}_1^{obj}$ and $\mathcal{D}_2^{obj}$ be two object-oriented representations. Let $(x_1, set\_char(x_1, \mathcal{D}^{obj})) \in Obj(\mathcal{D}_1^{obj})$ and $(x_2, set\_char(x_2, \mathcal{D}^{obj})) \in Obj(\mathcal{D}_2^{obj})$. We define

$$sim(x_1, x_2) = \Sigma_{C_1 \in set\_char(x_1, \mathcal{D}^{obj}), C_2 \in set\_char(x_1, \mathcal{D}^{obj})} sim(C_1, C_2)$$

We give here one of the similarity measures that we have implemented:

Definition 7. Let $\mathcal{D}_1^{obj}$ and $\mathcal{D}_2^{obj}$ be two object-oriented representations. Let $x_1^1, \ldots, x_{n_1}^1$ (resp. $x_1^2, \ldots, x_{n_2}^2$) be the objects that appear in $\mathcal{D}_1^{obj}$ (resp. $\mathcal{D}_2^{obj}$) and let us suppose that $n_1 \leq n_2$. A matching from $\mathcal{D}_1^{obj}$ to $\mathcal{D}_2^{obj}$ is an application M from $\{x_1^1, \ldots, x_{n_1}^1\}$ to $\{x_1^2, \ldots, x_{n_2}^2\}$.
The score of a matching M is: $sc(M) = \sum_{x_i^1 \in \{x_1^1, \ldots, x_{n_1}^1\}} sim(x_i^1, M(x_i^1))$.

The similarity between $\mathcal{D}_1^{obj}$ and $\mathcal{D}_2^{obj}$ is the score of the best matching from $\mathcal{D}_1^{obj}$ to $\mathcal{D}_2^{obj}$.

3.4 Example

We are currently testing this tool. To illustrate it, we give a few examples about chemical formulae. We have chosen six molecules, namely $CH3COOH$, $CH3CHO$, $CH4$, $CH2O$, $CHOOH$, $CH3OH$.

To represent the observations, we have chosen four predicates: the unary predicates *carbon*, *oxygen* and *hydrogen* describe the nature of an atom and the binary predicate *link* expresses a link between two atoms. We could have been more precise, for instance, by distinguishing simple links between two atoms from double links.

For instance, the molecule $CH4$ is represented by the list of properties[3]:
((carbon c) (link c h1) (hydrogen h1) (link c h2) (hydrogen h2) (link c h3) (hydrogen h3) (link c h4) (hydrogen h4))

No weights on the predicates: We have first run the system on two sequences of observations. In the first experiment, predicates are not weighted. The results are not very relevant, because in fact all the predicates have the same weights and all the molecules share some common properties: same kind of atoms and links. Nevertheless, it shows how the order observations are given to the system influences the result of the learning process. The only operations that have been applied are *creation* and *insertion*. The operations that enable to recover from a bad choice, that is to say *merging* and *split* have not been applied, presumably because the number of observations that have been processed is too low.

---

[3] The tool is implemented in a version of Scheme, therefore a conjunction of logical atoms is represented by a list.

Background knowledge: We have then introduced background knowledge that expresses functional properties of the molecule: *alcohol, aldehyd* and *acid* that can be expressed by theorems like:

$$\forall x \forall y \forall z \forall t \; (carbon \; x) \wedge (link \; x \; y) \wedge (hydrogen \; y) \wedge (link \; x \; z) \wedge (oxygen \; z)$$
$$\Rightarrow (fn\_aldehyd \; x \; y \; z \; t)$$

We have applied the knowledge base to the observations before processing them and we have put weights only on the predicates *fn_aldehyd, fn_acid* and *fn_alcohol.* We obtained the following results (figure 1):

▷ Hierarchy obtained with sequence 1: $CH3COOH, CH4, CH3CH0, CHOOH, CH3OH, CH2O$

▷ Hierarchy obtained with sequence 1 + $CH3CHO$

```
+{CO}
|-----+{ch4}
|-----+{ch3cho}
|-----+{C3}
|     |-----+{ch3cooh}
|     +-----+{chooh}
|-----+{ch3oh}
+-----+{ch2o}
```

```
+{CO}
|-----+{ch4}
|-----+{C2}
|     |-----+{ch3cooh}
|     +-----+{chooh}
|-----+{ch3oh}
+-----+{C6}
      |-----+{ch2o}
      +-----+{C8}
            |-----+{ch3cho}
            +-----+{ch3cho}
```

Figure 1: The functions *alcohol, acid* and *aldehyde* have been added.
Their weights are 100.

In the first column of figure 1, we can notice that the observations $CH3COOH$ and $CHOOH$ have been clustered according to their common function *acid.* $CH3OH$ which is an alcohol and $CH4$ which has no particular function remain alone. If we had to this sequence a molecule which is an aldehyde, as for instance $CH3CHO$, the molecules $CH2O$ and $CH3CHO$ are clustered according to their function *aldehyde,* as shown in the second column of figure 1.

4 Discussion and further improvements

We have presented in this paper ongoing research. We are currently experimenting it in the following directions:

Testing different similarity measures and studying their properties.

Testing other generalization functions. For the time being, we have implemented an "object-oriented" generalization that chooses the best matching between the objects that compose the descriptions. The solution that consists in considering all the possible matching has the same drawback as the least general generalization approach, that is to say, the exponential growing of the size of formulae. Syntactic biases have been introduced in [11] for clauses and we must study how they could be adapted.

Influence of the order observations are processed. The experiments that we have processed confirm a problem that is inherent in this kind of approach: the order observations are presented to the system influences the result. Therefore, we would like to study on one hand, how the operations of splitting and merging enable to recover from initial misclassifications and on the other hand, the number of observations that must be given to the system before obtaining, if possible, a stable hierarchy in terms of the intensional descriptions that are learnt.

A new control strategy. Different classes that are not linked in the hierarchy may have the same intensional description. Therefore, we would like to study new operations based on the intensional descriptions of the classes and their relations of generality. Moreover, it would enable to prune the hierarchy tree.

References

1. Allen J., Thompson K. : Probabilistic Concept Formation in Relational Domains. Unknown reference.
2. Bisson G., 1992. Conceptual Clustering in a First Order Logic Representation. Proceedings of the tenth ECAI, Vienna, Austria.
3. Decaestecker C., 1991. Apprentissage en Classification Conceptuelle Incrémentale. Thèse de Docteur en Sciences, université libre de Bruxelles, 1991.
4. Fisher D.H., 1987. Knowledge Acquisition via Incremental Conceptual Clustering. Machine Learning 2, pp. 139-172.
5. Issert C., 1993. Classification Conceptuelle Incrémentale et application à la Logique d'ordre 1. Internal report, university of Orléans.
6. Kodratoff Y., Ganascia Y. 1986. Improving the generalization step in Learning, *Machine Learning: An Artificial Intelligence Approach*, Vol. 2, Michalski R.S., Carbonell J.G., Mitchell T.M. (Eds.), Morgan Kaufmann Publishers, pp. 215-244.
7. Kodratoff Y., Vrain C., 1993. Acquiring first-order knowledge about air traffic control. Knowledge Acquisition 5, Academic Press Limited, pp. 1-36.
8. Langley P., Thompson K., 1989. Incremental Concept Formation with Composite Objects. Proceedings of the Sixth International Workshop on Machine Learning, pp. 371-374.
9. Michalski R.S., 1983. A Theory and Methodology of Inductive Learning, *Artificial Intelligence*, Vol.20, $N°$ 2.
10. Michalski R.S., Stepp R.E. 1986. Conceptual Clustering: Inventing Goal-Oriented classifications of structured objects, Artificial Intelligence 28, pp. 43-69.
11. Muggleton S., Feng C., 1992. Efficient Induction of Logic Programs. Inductive Logic programming. The A.P.I.C. Series $N°$ 38, S. Muggleton (Ed.), Academic Press. pp. 281-298.
12. Plotkin G.D., 1970. A note on Inductive Generalization. Machine Intelligence 5, pp. 153-163. Meltzer, Michie (Eds.), Edinburgh University Press.
13. Quinlan J.R., 1983. Learning Efficient Classification Procedures and their Application to Chess End Games. Machine Learning, an Artificial Intelligence Approach, Michalski R.S., Carbonell J.G., Mitchell T.M., eds. Tioga Publishing Company 1983, chap. 15, p. 463-482.
14. Vrain C., OGUST, a system that learns using domain properties expressed as theorems, *Machine Learning: an Artificial Intelligence Approach*, Vol. 3, pp.360-381, Morgan Kaufmann, 1990.

Rule Discovery from Databases with Decision Matrices*

Wojciech Ziarko, Nick Cercone

Department of Computer Science, University of Regina

Regina, Sask., Canada S4S 0A2

Xiaohua Hu

DMS Data Management, Bell-Northern Research Ltd.

Ottawa, Ontario, Canada K1Y 4H7

Abstract

In this paper, we propose a new method which can compute all maximal general rules in relational databases. The method is based on the idea of a decision matrix and Boolean decision function. The problem of finding the maximal general rules is reduced to the problem of simplifying a group of associated boolean expression. The novel feature of our algorithm is its generation and use of explicit redundant knowledge rules instead of a set of minimum cover rules. Our algorithm generates all potential interesting and useful rules even though there is some overlapping between the examples covered by the rules. The test on some data sets demonstrates the effectiveness and high classification accuracy of a decision system based on redundant rules.

1 Introduction

Knowledge discovery from databases is a procedure to find interesting and useful pattern hidden in the databases. Different kinds of knowledge rules can be learned from databases. No matter what kinds of rules the algorithm generates, the discovered rules usually are expression of propositional logic built of symbols corresponding to attribute names and some relational operators such as $=$, $\leq$, $\geq$ etc.. A number of algorithms for finding knowledge rules from databases have been reported [4]. Although some of them, in particular ID3 [7], have been implemented in commercial software systems, they fail to satisfactory address the following two problems:

(1) The description typically is a disjunction of conjunctions of some conditions each of which is called an induced rule. The conjuncts, or the rules in general,

---

*The authors are members of the Institute for Robotics and Intelligent Systems (IRIS) and wish to acknowledge the support of the Networks of Centres of Excellence Program of the Government of Canada, the Natural Sciences and Engineering Research Council, and the participation of PRECARN Associates Inc.

are not minimal, meaning that there is a possibility that some redundant conditions are included in the rules.

(2) Moreover, many existing algorithms for rule discovery are concerned with finding a set of minimum cover rules. This approach is satisfactory for typical machine learning application, where the computation of a set of minimum rules is the objective. In knowledge discovery applications, however, one of the objectives is to find all potentially interesting rules which can be extracted from the data being checked. The computation of maximally general rules is of particular importance for knowledge discovery or data mining application which seek the maximally general patterns existing in the data.

Developing a systematic method for computing all maximally general rules is the main goal of this paper. The maximally general rules are, in a sense, optimal because their conditions are non-redundant. In what follows we present a methodology for computing all maximal and deterministic (i.e., with unique, non-probabilistic outcomes) rules based on the information encoded in information system. The methodologies stem from the theory of rough sets introduced by Pawlak [6], and is related to earlier research results on properties of information system [6]. In particular, Skowron and Rauszer introduced the concept of a discernibility matrix [8] underlying the idea of a decision matrix described here.

2 Rules and Maximal General Rules

2.1 Rules in Information System

By an information system S, we mean that $S = \{U, A, V, f\}$, where U is a finite set of object, $U = \{e_1, e_2, ..., e_n\}$, A is a finite set of attributes, the attributes in A are further classified into disjoint *condition* attributes C and *decision* attributes D, $A = C \cup D$, $V = \bigcup_{p \in A} V_p$, and V_p is a *domain* of attribute p, we use V_{ij} to denote the value of attribute j of the ith object in U. f is an information function such that $f(e_i, a) \in VAL_a$ for every $a \in A$ and $e_i \in U$.

Let $P \subset A$, $e_i, e_j \in U$, we define a binary relation $\tilde{P}$, called an *indiscernibility relation*, as $\tilde{P} = \{(e_i, e_j) \in U \times U : for\ every\ p \in P\ p(e_i) = p(e_j)\}$

Suppose one of the attributes, say $d \in A$, is considered to be the learning target, or decision attributes representing the "concept" or "concepts" to be learned. The concept is simply a particular value V_d of the attribute d. The object of learning is to find a discriminating description of the subset $|V_d|$ of objects with the value of the attribute d equal to V_d that is as simple as possible, i.e., to learn the description of the set

$$|V_d| = \{e \in U : d(e) = V_d\}$$

For a value V_d of the decision attribute d (which is the "concept" we intend to learn), a rule r for V_d is defined as a set of attribute-value pair

$$r : (a_{i1} = V_{i1}) \wedge (a_{i2} = V_{i2}) \wedge ... \wedge (a_{in} = V_{in}) \rightarrow (d = V_d)$$

Make_Model	compress	power	trans	mileage
USA	HIGH	HIGH	AUTO	MEDIUM
USA	MEDIUM	MEDIUM	MANUAL	MEDIUM
USA	HIGH	LOW	MANUAL	MEDIUM
USA	HIGH	MEDIUM	AUTO	MEDIUM
USA	MEDIUM	HIGH	MANUAL	MEDIUM
USA	MEDIUM	HIGH	AUTO	MEDIUM
USA	HIGH	HIGH	MANUAL	HIGH
JAPAN	HIGH	LOW	MANUAL	HIGH
JAPAN	MEDIUM	MEDIUM	MANUAL	HIGH
JAPAN	HIGH	HIGH	MANUAL	HIGH
JAPAN	MEDIUM	LOW	MANUAL	HIGH
JAPAN	HIGH	MEDIUM	MANUAL	HIGH
USA	HIGH	MEDIUM	MANUAL	HIGH

Table 1: A Generalized Car Relation

2.2 Maximal General Rules & Decision Matrix

We say two rules r_1, r_2 with respect to the same concept V_d are comparable if either $cond(r_1) \subseteq cond(r_2)$ or $cond(r_1) \supseteq cond(r_2)$ ($cond(r)$ denotes the rule condition part). In fact, the set of rules is partially ordered with regard to the relation of inclusion.

Definition 2.1 A maximal general rule is a minimal element of the partially ordered rule set.

The maximal general rules minimize the number of rule conditions and are in a sense optimal because their conditions are non-redundant. We use RUL to denote the collection of all maximal general rules for the decision V_d.

For the selected decision attribute $d \in A$ and its particular value V_d, we will focus on the collection of objects e (the concept), for which $d(e) = V_d$, i.e., the set $|V_d|$. Before attempting to find discriminating rules for $|V_d|$ in terms of other attributes belonging to $A - \{d\}$, we will summarize all the attribute-value pairs distinguishing objects belonging to $|V_d|$ and $U - |V_d|$ in the matrix format defined as follows.

Definition 2.2 Let e_i denotes any object belonging to $|V_d|$, i.e., $i = 1, 2, ...,$ $card(|V_d|) = \rho$ and let $e_j \in U - |V_d|$, $j = 1, 2, ..., card(U - |V_d|) = \gamma$. the decision matrix $DM = (DM_{ij})_{\rho \times \gamma}$ is defined as $DM_{i,j} = \{(a, a(e_i)) : a(e_i) \neq a(e_j)\}$ The set $DM_{i,j}$ contains all pairs whose values are not identical on both e_i and e_j. The distinguishing attributes for different combination of i and j can be represented in the form of a matrix $DM = [DM_{ij}]_{\rho \times \gamma}$.

Example 2.1: Suppose we have a car information system in Table 1. Table 2 is a decision matrix derived for the decision class $mileage = MEDIUM$.

Let $e_i \in |V_d|$, we will use the symbol RUL_i to denote the set of all maximal general rules whose conditions match the features of object e_i, that is

$$RUL_i = \{r \in RUL : A_r(e_i) = V_r\}$$

Clearly, if the collection of rules RUL_i is known for each $e_i \in |V_d|$ then all the maximal general rules for target decision $|V_d|$ can be obtained by taking

	1	2	3	4	5	6	7
1	(T,0)	(M,0),(P,0) (T,0)	(M,0),(C,0) (P,0),(T,0)	(M,0),(T,0)	(M,0),(C,0) (P,0),(T,0)	(M,0),(P,0) (T,0)	(P,0),(T,0)
2	(C,1),(P,1)	(M,0),(C,1) (P,1)	(M,0)	(M,0),(C,1) (P,1)	(M,0), (P,1)	(M,0),(C,1)	(C,1)
3	(P,2)	(M,0)	(M,0),(C,0) (P,2)	(M,0)	(M,0), (C,0)	(M,0), (P,2)	(P,2)
4	(P,1),(T,0)	(M,0),(P,1)	(M,0),(C,0) (T,0)	(M,0),(P,1) (T,0)	(M,0),(C,0) (P,1),(T,0)	(M,0),(T,0)	(T,0)
5	(C,1)	(M,0),(C,1) (P,0)	(M,0),(P,0)	(M,0),(C,1)	(M,0),(P,0)	(M,0),(C,1) (P,0)	(C,1),(P,0)
6	(C,1),(T,0)	(M,0),(C,1)	(M,0),(P,0) (P,0),(T,0)	(M,0),(C,1)	(M,0), (P,0) (T,0)	(M,0),(C,1) (P,0), (T,0)	(C,1),(P,0) (T,0)

Table 2: Decision matrix for the class mileage=MEDIUM

M:Make-model T:trans P:Power C: Compress
M:0—USA 1—Japan T:0—Auto 1—Manual
P:0—High 1—Medium 2—Low C:0—High 1—Medium

the union

$$RUL = \bigcup_i RUL_i$$

Consequently, in what follows we focus on the method to compute the maximal general rules matching an arbitrary objects $e_i \in |V_d|$.

For the given decision matrix DM and fixed decision value V_d, let us consider the Cartesian product $F_i = DM_{i1} \times DM_{i2} \times ... \times DM_{ir}$ of sets of attribute-value pairs constituting the components of the decision matrix DM contained in the row i. Since some components of the vectors belonging to F_i may be identical, we will consider the associated set

$$\tilde{F}_i = \{\{t\} : t \in F_i\}$$

where $\{t\}$ is a set of all distinct components contained in the vector t.

The elements of $\tilde{F}_i$ are all rules for $|V_d|$ since they match at least one object from $|V_d|$ (i.e., object e_i) and do not match any of the objects belong to the complement of $|V_d|$, $(U - |V_d|)$. The rules in $\tilde{F}_i$ are partially ordered by inclusion relation with the set of minimal elements in this denoted as MIN_i.

Theorem 1. *Each maximal general rule in $\tilde{F}_i$ computed from the decision matrix DM is also minimal in the set of all rules for $|V_d|$ and each maximal general rule for $|V_d|$ is minimal in a certain set $\tilde{F}_i$.*

The above theorem states that, in essence, $RUL_i = MIN_i$ which in practice means that decision matrix can be used to find all maximal general rules for the target concept $|V_d|$. A simple, systematic procedure described later can be used to produce maximal general rules in the set $\tilde{F}_i$. (For the proof, please refer to [11]). The maximal general rules in the set MIN_i can be computed by simplifying an associated Boolean function called decision function which is inspired by the idea of discernibility function introduced in [8].

The decision function B_i is constructed out of the row i of the decision matrix, that is, $(DM_{i1}, DM_{i2}, ..., DM_{ir})$ by formally treating each attribute-value pair occurring in component DM_{ij} as a Boolean variable and then forming Boolean conjunction of disjunctions of components belonging to each set DM_{ij} $(j = 1, 2, ..., \gamma)$. That is,

$$B_i = \bigcap_j \bigcup DM_{ij}$$

where $\bigcap$ and $\bigcup$ are respectively general conjunction and disjunction operators.

3   Principles and Algorithm for Computing Maximal General Rules in Relational Databases

In this section, a new algorithm DBMaxi is presented which is feasible to be used in large database to compute all the maximal general rules for the decision attribute. The method integrates attribute-oriented generalization [1, 3] and rough set theory and provides a simple, efficient and effective way for learning in large databases. Our method performs as follows: first generalize the data by performing attribute-oriented concept tree ascension, then the decision matrixes for the decision values of the decision attribute are constructed from the generalized form and the maximal general rules are inferred from the decision matrixes. In order to generalize the primitive data in the databases, it is necessary to incorporate the conceptual hierarchy information for learning. Each attribute in a data relation may contain a large set of distinct values. Without generalizing data to a higher level concepts, learned results can not be represented in a clear and concise manner. Similar to other learning algorithms [1], it is necessary to provide information about higher level concepts for the learning process. We restrict our candidate rules to formulas with a particular vocabulary, that is, a basis set which we call the *conceptual basis*, permitting the learned rules to be represented in a simple and explicit form. A detailed discussion of the attribute-oriented generalization can be found in [1, 3].

3.1   DBMaxi

We use Example 3.1 to demonstrate our algorithm DBMaxi.

Example 3.1: Suppose we have a collection of Japanese and America cars with the attributes as plate number (**plate#**), **Make_model**, **colour**, compression ratio (**compress**), **power**, type of transmission (**trans**), and **mileage** depicted in Table 3 and the concept hierarchy tree for the attribute "Make_model" depicted in Figure 1:

Plate#	Make_Model	colour	compress	power	trans	mileage
BCT89U	Ford escort	silver	High	high	auto	medium
UYT342	Chervolet corvette	green	High	medium	manu	high
LKIPO8	Chevrolrt corvette	brown	High	medium	auto	medium
IUTY56	Dodge stealth	green	Medium	medium	manual	medium
DSA321	Toyota paseo	black	Medium	low	manual	high
ERTW34	Ford probe	yellow	Medium	medium	manual	medium
9876T	chrysler Le B	blue	Medium	high	auto	medium
UYTHG7	Dodge sprite	light blue	Medium	high	auto	medium
RST45W	Dodge Stealth	red	Medium	high	auto	medium
RGW45W	Dodge daytona	light green	Medium	high	auto	medium
78YUTE	Ford escort	black	High	high	manual	high
7HGY65	Chervot corvette	black	High	high	manual	high
....	....	...	...	....	....	..
Ot76SAD	Mazda 323	red	High	low	manual	high
UI89P0	Dodge shadow	red	Medium	medium	manual	medium
P0967H	Ford festival	brown	High	medium	auto	medium
WEQ546	Toyota corolla	navy	Medium	medium	manua	high
PLMNH7	Mazda 323	yellow	High	low	manual	high
QAS453	Dodge Dayton	green	Medium	medium	manual	medium
PLMJH9	Honda accord	brown	High	high	manu	high
PLMJH9	Honda prelude	yellow	High	high	manu	high
KNM876	Chevrolet beretta	green	High	high	auto	medium
IKLO90	Chevrolet cavalier	black	Medium	high	auto	medium
OPL876	Mazda 626	purple	High	medium	manual	high
TYUR45	Ford mustang	black	Medium	medium	manual	medium
0987UO	Dodge dayton	orange	Medium	medium	manual	medium
UYT789	Chervote Corvette	black	High	Low	manual	medium

Table 3: Car Relation.

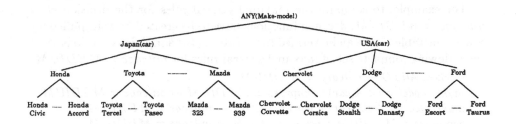

Figure 1: Concept Hierarchy Tree for Make_model

Strategy 1 (Attribute-Oriented Induction)

For the car relation in Table 3, if the class threshold is set to 3, then the generalized relation in Table 1 is obtained by applying attribute-oriented concept hierarchy ascension. (with redundant tuples eliminated and the tuples with the same mileage value are grouped together). After the generalization process, rough set method is performed on the general relation. Taking "mileage" as the decision attribute, we examine how to apply the decision matrix to compute the maximal general rules.

Strategy 2 (Construct the decision matrix for the current decision category in the general relation)

In the general relation as shown in Table 1, "mileage" has two distinct values "mileage=Medium" and "mileage=High". The decision matrix for "mileage=Medium" is shown in Table 2.

Strategy 3 (For each positive case e_i, $(i = 1, 2, ..., \rho)$ compute the set of all maximal general rules MIN_i matching this case by evaluating and simplifying (using the absorption law) the associated decision function B_i.)

For each row in the decision matrix, we con construct a decision function, which corresponds to a maximal general rule. For example, based on the decision matrix given in Table 2, we can construct the following decision function for row 1

$B_1 = ((T, 0)) \wedge ((M, 0) \vee (P, 0) \vee (T, 0)) \wedge ((M, 0) \vee (C, 0) \vee (P, 0) \vee (T, 0)) \wedge ((M, 0) \vee (T, 0)) \wedge$
$((M, 0) \vee (C, 0) \vee (P, 0) \vee (T, 0)) \wedge ((M, 0) \vee (P, 0) \vee (T, 0)) \wedge ((P, 0) \vee (T, 0))$

By applying the distributivity and absorption laws of Boolean algebra, each decision function can be expressed in a simplified form of a disjunction of minimal conjunctive expressions. It can be demonstrated based on [8] that such conjunctive expressions correspond to the minimal elements occurring in the set MIN_i.

The decision function B_1 can be easily simplified to $B_1 = (T, 0)$,

This corresponds to the rule:

$trans = AUTO \rightarrow mileage = MEDIUM$

Strategy 4 (Compute the union $\cup MIN_i$ of maximal general rule sets to find all maximal general rules for the current decision category.)

For example, to compute the maximal general rules for the decision class $mileage = MEDIUM$, decision functions have to be created and simplified for row 1-6 in Table 2. As can be verified from Table 2, the simplified functions yield the following complete set of maximal general rules for $mileage = MEDIUM$:

$trans = AUTO \rightarrow mileage = MEDIUM$
$make\_model = USA(car) \wedge compress = MEDIUM \rightarrow mileage = MEDIUM$
$make\_model = USA(car) \wedge power = LOW \rightarrow mileage = MEDIUM$
$compress = MEDIUM \wedge power = HIGH \rightarrow mileage = MEDIUM.$

In summary, the algorithm (DBMaxi) for computing all maximal general rules is presented as below:

Algorithm 1 *Compute the maximal general rules (DBMaxi)*

Input: a relational system R
Output. all the maximal general rules for the decision attribute of R
Step 1. Attribute-oriented induction.
Step 2: Construct decision matrix for the current decision category in R
Step 3: For each positive case e_i, $(i = 1, 2, ..., \rho)$ compute the set of all maximal general rules MIN_i matching this case by evaluating and simplifying (using the absorption law) the associated decision function B_i.
Step 4: Compute the union $\cup MIN_i$ of maximal general rule sets to find all maximal general rules for the current decision category.

3.2 Complexity of Computing the Potential Rules

Suppose after data generalization, there are N' tuples with K attributes left. For a particular learning task, the number of positive tuples is n and so the number of negative tuples is $N' - n$. Then we can construct a $n \times (N' - n)$ decision matrix, for each entry of the decision matrix, there are maximal K terms because that is the maximal number of different attributes values between the positive and negative tuples. Each row of the decision matrix corresponds a set of maximal general rules, so the maximal number of maximal general rules from each row is $K^{N'-n}$, there are total n row in the decision matrix, so the total number of possible maximal general rules are $n \times K^{N'-n}$. As a example, if we have 30 tuples with 5 attributes and 10 positive tuples, then the possible maximal general rules are 9.536E+14. From a practical point of view, we are not able to compute all these possible maximal general rules even using the fastest computer. Hence in order to define a tractable algorithm, we will need to "prune" the set of possible maximal general candidate rules considerably. We believe that using a good rule measure can help considerably when we are trying to learn rules from data. A feasible algorithm should learn the best set of rules rather than exhaustive learning all the possible rules. In our experimental test, we use $J_{measure}$ [9] to evaluate the generated rules and find the best K rules based on the $J_{measure}$.

4 Experimental Results

To demonstrate the effectiveness of our algorithm, we performed some tests on four data sets: Iris data, Appendicitis data, Thyroid data and Cancer data and compared our results with the results reported in [10]. For the detailed explanations of these data sets, please refer to [10]. Table 4 shows the results of decision matrix method and the comparison results reported by Weiss [10]

One of the novel features of our algorithm is its use of redundant knowledge rules. Recently, in order to enhance the accuracy of expert system, the concept of redundant knowledge or multiple knowledge bases emerged. Typically one object is classified with several rules in the multiple knowledge bases system, and the decisions are then combined to obtain the final conclusion. Many research results illustrated that such multiple rules, if appropriately combined during classification, can improve the classification accuracy [2]. The phenomenon of importance of redundant knowledge in real life is empirically shown in [2]. Our algorithm, like GINSYS [2] generate some amount of redundant rules which is probably one of the reasons for the successful behaviour. Most algorithms tested in [10] and some most popular learning algorithms such as AQ-family algorithm [5], use a covering strategy during learning. That means these algorithms are concerned to find a set of minimum cover rules, in which objects of the databases covered by a rule are not subsumed by another rule. These systems would consider a rule useless if it covered examples that are already covered by other rules. AQ-algorithm uses a set of weights (t-weight and

Methods	Iris	Appendicitis	Thyroid	Cancer	Average
Decision Matrix	96.33	91.05	98.86	98.30	96.14
Linear	98.00	86.80	93.85	97.06	93.92
Quadratic	97.3	73.60	88.39	96.56	88.96
Nearest Neighbour	96.00	82.10	95.27	96.53	92.48
Bayes Independence	93.3	83.00	96.06	97.18	92.39
Bayes 2nd Order	84.00	81.10	92.44	96.56	88.53
Neural Net (BP)	96.67	85.80	98.54	97.15	94.54
PVM Rule	96.00	89.60	99.33	97.71	95.66
CART Tree	95.33	84.90	99.36	97.71	94.32

Table 4: The Comparative Performance

u-weight) to remove this type of rules. Our method does not follow this way. In our system all potential interesting and useful rules are generated even though there are some overlapping of the examples covered by rules and there are negative effects on simplicity and comprehensibility. We believe that system that strives to eliminate redundant rules becomes more sensitive to noise because a small number of rules means that few alternatives existed when classify unseen objects. In our test we adopt the Voting method to combine decisions of multiple knowledge rules. A detailed discussion on different strategy of combing redundant knowledge rules can be found in [4],

5 Conclusion

In this paper, an approach for constructing maximal general rules based on decision matrix is presented. There are several advantages of using decision matrix method: (1) the decision matrix method has the ability of multiple learning to concurrently generate multiple knowledge bases. It can compute all maximal general decision rules and the reducts of a knowledge representation system, (2) the decision matrix method has the ability to incremental learning new knowledge in a dynamic environment. Incremental learning system has the significant capability to change the knowledge base in a dynamic environment. The decision matrix method has the multiple learning and incremental learning capability. The new information (objects) can be processed by modifying the current knowledge bases instead of regenerating new knowledge bases. Most of known incremental learning algorithms based on generating a single knowledge base and can not concurrently generate multiple knowledge bases. (3) the main computation of rules and reducts is reduced to the problem of simplifying a group of associated boolean expressions.

References

[1] Y. Cai, N. Cercone and J. Han, Attribute-Oriented Induction in Relational Databases, *Knowledge Discovery in Database, AAAI/MIT Press*, G.Piatetsky-Shapiro and W.J. Frawley (eds) pp. 213-228, 1991.

[2] M. Gams, New Measurements Highlight the Importance of Redundant Knowledge, in *Proc. 4th Europe Working Session on Learning*, Momtpellier, pp71-80, 1989

[3] X. Hu, N. Cercone, J. Han, A Concept-Based Knowledge Discovery Approach in Databases, *The 10th Canadian AI Conf.*, Banff, Canada, May 1994.

[4] X. Hu, Knowledge Discovery in Databases: An Attribute-Oriented Rough Set Approach, Ph.D Thesis, Dept. of Computer Science, University of Regina, Canada, June 1995

[5] R. S. Michalski, L. Mozetic, J. Hong and N. Lavrac, The Multi-purpose Incremental Learning System AQ15 and Its Testing Application to Three Medical Domains, in *Proceedings of 1986 AAAI Conference*, Philadelphia, PA, 1041-1045, 1986

[6] Z. Pawlak, Rough sets, *International Journal of Information and Computer Science* (1982) 11(5), 341-356

[7] J. R. Quinlan, Generating Production Rules from Decision Trees, *Proceedings of the 10th IJCAI*, pp304-307

[8] A. Skowron, C. Rauszer, The discernibility matrices and functions in information systems. *ICS Research Report 1/91*, Wawsaw University of Technology, Nowowiejska 15/19, 00-665, Warsaw, Poland

[9] P. Smyth and R.M. Goodman, An Information Approach to Rule Induction from Databases, *IEEE Trans. on Knowledge and Data Engineering*, Vol. 4, 301-316, 1992

[10] S.M. Weiss and I. Kapouleas, An Empirical Comparison of Pattern Recognition Neural Nets, and Machine Learning Classification Methods, *Proc. of the 11th International Joint Conf. on AI*, pp781-787, 1989

[11] W. Ziarko, N Shan, A Rough Set-Based Method for Computing All Minimal Deterministic Rules on Attribute-Value Systems, *Computational Intelligence: An International Journal* (to appear).

INDEX

Springer-Verlag
and the Environment

We at Springer-Verlag firmly believe that an international science publisher has a special obligation to the environment, and our corporate policies consistently reflect this conviction.

We also expect our business partners – paper mills, printers, packaging manufacturers, etc. – to commit themselves to using environmentally friendly materials and production processes.

The paper in this book is made from low- or no-chlorine pulp and is acid free, in conformance with international standards for paper permanency.

Lecture Notes in Artificial Intelligence (LNAI)

Lecture Notes in Computer Science